D0204301

STUDIES IN MANUSCRIPT ILLUMINATION

Number 9

KURT WEITZMANN
Editor 1947–73

HERBERT L. KESSLER
Editor

STUDIES IN MANUSCRIPT ILLUMINATION

———

PUBLISHED FOR
THE DEPARTMENT OF ART AND ARCHAEOLOGY
PRINCETON UNIVERSITY

THE
BENEDICTIONAL
OF ÆTHELWOLD

BY

Robert Deshman

PRINCETON UNIVERSITY PRESS

Copyright © 1995 by Princeton University Press
Published by Princeton University Press, 41 William Street, Princeton, New Jersey 08540
In the United Kingdom: Princeton University Press, Chichester, West Sussex

All Rights Reserved

Library of Congress Cataloging-in-Publication Data
Deshman, Robert.
The benedictional of Æthelwold / by Robert Deshman.
p.   cm. — (Studies in manuscript illumination: 9)
Includes bibliographical references (p.   –   ) and index.
ISBN 0-691-04386-8 (CL : alk. paper)
1. Benedictionals—Illustrations.   2. Catholic Church—Liturgy—Texts—
Illustrations.   3. Illumination of books and manuscripts, Anglo-Saxon—England—
Winchester.   4. Illumination of books and manuscripts, Romanesque—England—
Winchester.   5. Benedictional of Aethelwold—Illustrations.   6. British Library.
7. Aethelwold, Saint, Bishop of Winchester, ca. 908–984.   I. Title.   II. Series.
ND3362.5.D47   1995
745.6'7'09422735—dc20   94-36661

Publication of this book was supported by a grant from the Publication Fund of the
Department of Art and Archaeology, Princeton University

This book has been composed in Palatino by The Composing Room of Michigan, Inc.

Princeton University Press books are printed on acid-free paper and meet the guidelines
for permanence and durability of the Committee on Production Guidelines for Book
Longevity of the Council on Library Resources

Printed in the United States of America

10 9 8 7 6 5 4 3 2 1

DESIGNED BY LAURY A. EGAN

ND
3362.5
.D47
1995

For Linda, Abigail, Elizabeth, and Jonathan

Contents

List of Plates

The plates reproduce all the miniatures and a selection of initial pages of the Benedictional in their original scale and in the sequence they follow in the manuscript: MS Add. 49598, British Library, London. All plates are reproduced by permission of the British Library.

List of Figures

The source of the photograph is indicated in parentheses.

Preface

I AM GRATEFUL to many institutions and individuals for their support of my work on this book. The Social Sciences and Humanities Research Council of Canada (formerly the Canada Council) and the University of Toronto generously provided numerous leave and research fellowships. I was honored to spend a stimulating year as a Kress Fellow and temporary member of the Institute for Advanced Study in Princeton. I began my research at the Marquand Library and the Index of Christian art at Princeton University, and later the marvelous library resources and staff of the British Library, the Warburg Institute, the University of Toronto, and the Pontifical Institute of Medieval Studies proved indispensable. The Department of Art and Archaeology of Princeton University has generously under-written the costs of publication.

It would be difficult to overestimate my indebtedness to Kurt Weitzmann. When I was a fledgling graduate student, his seminars introduced me to the serious study of medieval art in general and the Benedictional of Æthelwold in particular. He patiently guided my initial dissertation research with constructive criticism and countless fruitful suggestions, and over the years he continually offered friendly support. I have been fortunate to benefit from both the knowledge and the friendship of Herbert Kessler, whose generous committment of time and energy as editor of the Princeton Manuscript series has speeded the book's publication. Michael Lapidge has liberally contributed his time and his inestimable erudition. He has freely provided me with the results of much of his work in advance of publication, often stimulating new directions in my own research. Preliminary drafts of the book were read by Michael Lapidge, Elizabeth Leesti, Jens Wollesen, Kathleen Openshaw, and Herbert Kessler, and their comments have proved invaluable. My thanks to Sharon Herson for her careful and thoughtful copyediting and to Giles Knox for proofreading and preparation of the index.

Finally, I am eternally grateful to Murray Wilson and to my wife Linda for their continuous encouragement and concern.

ROBERT DESHMAN
The University of Toronto
New Year, 1994

List of Abbreviations

AB *Art Bulletin.*

Ælfric, *Hom.* Ælfric. *Homilies.* In *Homilies of the Anglo-Saxon Church*, ed. and tr. B. Thorpe. 2 vols. London, 1844–46.

Alexander, "Ben." Alexander, J. J. G. "The Benedictional of St. Aethelwold and Anglo-Saxon Art of the Reform Period." In *Tenth-Century Studies.*

Alexander, *Manuscripts* Alexander, J. J. G. *Insular Manuscripts: 6th to the 9th Century.* A Survey of Manuscripts Illuminated in the British Isles, 1. London, 1978.

Amalarius, *Lib. Ant.* Amalarius. *Liber de Ordine Antiphonarii.* In *Amalarii Episcopi Opera Liturgica Omnia*, 3, ed. J. M. Hanssens. Vatican City, 1950.

Amalarius, *Lib. Off.* Amalarius. *Liber Officialis.* In *Amalarii Episcopi Opera Liturgica Omnia*, 2, ed. J. M. Hanssens. Vatican City, 1948.

ASE *Anglo-Saxon England.*

Beckwith, *Ivory Carvings* Beckwith, J. *Ivory Carvings in Early Medieval England.* London, 1972.

Bede, *Hom.* Bede the Venerable. *Homilies on the Gospels.* Tr. L. T. Martin and D. Hurst. Cistercian Studies, 110–111, 2 vols. Kalamazoo, 1991.

Bede, *In Lucam* Bede. *In Lucae Evangelium Expositio.* Ed. D. Hurst. CC, 120.

Ben. Rob. *The Benedictional of Archbishop Robert.* Ed. H. A. Wilson. Henry Bradshaw Society, 24. London, 1903.

Bishop, *Minuscule* Bishop, T. A. M. *English Caroline Minuscule.* Oxford, 1971.

Bishop Æthelwold *Bishop Æthelwold: His Career and Influence.* Ed. B. Yorke. Woodbridge, 1988.

Blickling *The Blickling Homilies of the Tenth Century.* Ed. and tr. R. Morris. Early English Text Society, o.s., 58, 63, 73. London, 1880.

Burlin, *Advent* Burlin, R. E. *The Old English Advent.* Yale Studies in English, 168. New Haven, 1968.

Byrhtferth, *VO* Byrhtferth. *Vita Sancti Oswaldi.* In *Byrhtferth of Ramsey: The Lives of Oswald and Ecgwine*, ed. and tr. M. Lapidge. Forthcoming.

CAO *Corpus Antiphonalium Officii.* Ed. R.-J. Hesbert. 6 vols. Rome, 1963–79.

CBP *Corpus Benedictionum Pontificalium.* Ed. E. Moeller. CC, 162,162A–162C. 4 vols. Turnhout, 1961–69.

CC Corpus Christianorum, Series Latina. Turnhout, 1953–.

CCCM Corpus Christianorum, Continuatio Mediaevalis. Turnhout, 1966–.

CCM Corpus Consuetudinum Monasticarum. Siegburg, 1963–.

Clayton, *Cult* Clayton, M. *The Cult of the Virgin in Anglo-Saxon England.* Cambridge Studies in Anglo-Saxon England, 2. Cambridge, 1990.

CSEL Corpus Scriptorum Ecclesiasticorum Latinorum. Vienna, 1866–.

Deshman, "Anglo-Saxon Art after Alfred" Deshman, R. "Anglo-Saxon Art after Alfred." *AB* 56 (1974): 176–200.

Deshman, "Benedictus" Deshman, R. "*Benedictus Monarcha et Monachus*: Early Medieval Ruler Theology and the Anglo-Saxon Reform." *Frühmittelalterliche Studien* 22 (1988): 204–40.

Deshman, "Exalted Servant" Deshman, R. "The Exalted Servant: The Ruler Theology of the Prayerbook of Charles the Bald." *Viator* 11 (1980): 385–417.

Deshman, "Kingship" Deshman, R. "*Christus Rex et Magi Reges*: Kingship and Christology in Ottonian and Anglo-Saxon Art." *Frühmittelalterliche Studien* 10 (1976): 367–405.

Deshman, "Leofric" Deshman, R. "The Leofric Missal and Tenth-Century English Art." *ASE* 6 (1977): 145–73.

Deshman, "Living Ecclesia" Deshman, R. "The Imagery of the Living Ecclesia and the English Monastic Reform." In *Sources of Anglo-Saxon Culture*, ed. P. E. Szarmach. Studies in Medieval Culture, 20. Kalamazoo, 1986.

Deshman, "Servants" Deshman, R. "Servants of the Mother of God in Byzantine and Medieval Art." *Word and Image* 5 (1989): 33–70.

Deshman, "Warmund Sacramentary" Deshman, R. "Otto III and the Warmund Sacramentary." *Zeitschrift für Kunstgeschichte* 34 (1971): 1–20.

DOP *Dumbarton Oaks Papers.*

Drogo-Sak. Koehler, W. and F. Mütherich. *Drogo-Sakramentar.* Codices Selecti, 49. Graz, 1974.

Dunstan *St. Dunstan: His Life, Times and Cult.*

Ed. N. Ramsay, M. Sparks, and T. Tatton-Brown. Woodbridge, 1992.

Gage, "Ben." Gage, J. "A Dissertation on St. Æthelwold's Benedictional." *Archaeologia* 24 (1832): 1–117.

Gneuss, "List" Gneuss, H. "A Preliminary List of Manuscripts Written or Owned in England up to 1100." *ASE* 9 (1981): 1–60.

Golden Age *The Golden Age of Anglo-Saxon Art: 966–1066.* Ed. J. Backhouse, D. H. Turner, and L. Webster. London, 1984.

Goldschmidt, *Elf.* Goldschmidt, A. *Die Elfenbeinskulturen.* 4 vols. 1918–26. Rpt. Berlin, 1969–70.

Goldschmidt and Weitzmann, *Byz. Elf.* Goldschmidt, A. and K. Weitzmann. *Die byzantinischen Elfenbeinskulpturen.* 2nd ed. 2 vols. Berlin, 1979.

Homburger, *Anf.* Homburger, O. *Die Anfänge der Malschule von Winchester im X. Jahrhundert.* Studien über christliche Denkmäler, n. s., 13. Leipzig, 1912.

Jumièges *The Missal of Robert of Jumièges.* Ed. H. A. Wilson. Henry Bradshaw Society, 11. London, 1896.

Kantorowicz, "Quinity" Kantorowicz, E. H. "The Quinity of Winchester." *AB* 29 (1947): 73–85. Rpt. idem, in *Selected Studies.* Locust Valley, N. Y., 1965 (citations are to the reprint).

Keynes, "Athelstan's Books" Keynes, S. "King Athelstan's Books." In *Learning and Literature in Anglo-Saxon England,* ed. idem and H. Gneuss. Cambridge, 1985.

Klauser, *Capitulare* Klauser, T. *Das römische Capitulare Evangeliorum.* Liturgiegeschichtliche Quellen und Forschungen, 28. Münster in Westfalen, 1935.

Koehler, *Kar. Min.* Koehler, W. *Die karolingischen Miniaturen.* 4 vols. Berlin, 1930–71.

Koehler and Mütherich, *Kar. Min.* Koehler, W. and F. Mütherich. *Die karolingischen Miniaturen.* Vol. 5. Berlin, 1982.

Lantfred, *Translatio* Lantfred. *Translatio et Miracula S. Swithuni.* Ed. and tr. M. Lapidge. In *The Cult of Saint Swithun,* ed. Lapidge.

Lapidge, "Æthelwold as Scholar" Lapidge, M. "Æthelwold as Scholar and Teacher." In *Bishop Æthelwold.*

Lapidge, "Booklists" Lapidge, M. "Surviving Booklists from Anglo-Saxon England." In *Learning and Literature in Anglo-Saxon England,* ed. idem and H. Gneuss. Cambridge, 1985.

Lapidge, *Cult of Saint Swithun* Lapidge, M., ed. *The Cult of Saint Swithun.* Winchester Studies, 4, 2. Oxford, forthcoming.

LCI *Lexikon der christlichen Ikonographie.* 8 vols. Rome, 1968–76.

Magnani, *Sacramentario* Magnani, L. *Le miniature del sacramentario d'Ivrea.* Vatican City, 1934.

MGH Monumenta Germaniae Historica

Missal *The Missal of the New Minster.* Ed. D. H. Turner. Henry Bradshaw Society, 93. Leighton Buzzard, Bedfordshire, 1962.

Ohlgren, *Illustration* Ohlgren, T. *Anglo-Saxon Textual Illustration.* Kalamazoo, 1992.

PL Patrologia Latina Cursus Completus. Ed. J.-P. Migne. 221 vols. Paris, 1844–64.

Portiforium *The Portiforium of Saint Wulstan.* Ed. A. Hughes. Henry Bradshaw Society, vols. 89, 90. Leighton Buzzard, Bedfordshire, 1958–60.

Prescott, "Text" Prescott, A. "The Text of the Benedictional of St. Æthelwold." In *Bishop Æthelwold.*

RAC *Reallexikon für Antike und Christentum.* Stuttgart, 1950–.

Raw, *Crucifixion.* Raw, B. *Anglo-Saxon Crucifixion Iconography and the Art of the Monastic Revival.* Cambridge Studies in Anglo-Saxon England, 1. Cambridge, 1990.

RBK *Reallexikon zur byzantinischen Kunst.* Stuttgart, 1966–.

RC *Regularis Concordia Anglicae Nationis.* Ed. T. Symons, S. Spath, M. Wegener, and K. Hallinger. CCM, 7, 3. Siegburg, 1984.

Sac. Fuld. *Sacramentarium Fuldense Saeculi 10.* Ed. G. Richter and A. Schönfelder. 1912. Rpt. Henry Bradshaw Society, 101. Farnborough, Hampshire, 1977.

Schapiro, "Dis. Christ" Schapiro, M. "The Image of the Disappearing Christ: The Ascension in English Art around the Year 1000." *Gazette des Beaux-Arts,* ser. 6, 23 (1943): 135–52. Rpt. idem. *Late Antique, Early Christian, and Mediaeval Art, Selected Papers,* 3. New York, 1979 (citations are to the reprint).

Schiller, *Icon.* Schiller, G. *Iconography of Christian Art.* Tr. J. Seligman. 2 vols. Greenwich, Conn., 1971–72.

Schiller, *Ikon.* Schiller, G. *Ikonographie der christlichen Kunst.* 5 vols. Gütersloh, 1969–90.

Sources *Sources of Anglo-Saxon Literary Culture: A Trial Version,* ed. F. M. Biggs, T. D. Hill, and P. E. Szarmach. Medieval and Renaissance Texts and Studies, 74. Binghamton, 1990.

Stuttgarter Bilderpsalter Der Stuttgarter Bilderpsalter. 2 vols. Stuttgart, 1968.

Temple, *Manuscripts* Temple, E. *Anglo-Saxon Manuscripts: 900–1066. A Survey of Manuscripts Illuminated in the British Isles*, 2. London, 1976.

Tenth-Century Studies Tenth-Century Studies. Essays in Commemoration of the Millennium of the Council of Winchester and Regularis Concordia. Ed. D. Parsons. London, 1975.

Utrecht Van der Horst, K. and J. H. A. Engelbrecht. *Utrecht Psalter*. Codices Selecti, 75. Graz, 1982–84.

Volbach, *Elf.* Volbach, W. F. *Elfenbeinarbeiten der Spätantike und des frühen Mittelalters*. 3rd ed. Mainz am Rhein, 1976.

Warner and Wilson, *Ben.* Warner, G. F. and H. A. Wilson. *The Benedictional of Saint Aethelwold*. Oxford, 1910.

Weitzmann, *Studies* Weitzmann, K. *Studies in Classical and Byzantine Manuscript Illumination*. Ed. H. L. Kessler. Chicago, 1971.

Wormald, *Ben.* Wormald, F. *The Benedictional of St. Ethelwold*. London, 1959.

Wormald, "Psalter" Wormald, F. "An English Eleventh-Century Psalter with Pictures, British Library, Cotton MS Tiberius C. VI." *Walpole Society* 38 (1962): 1–13. Rpt. idem. *Writings* (citations are to the reprint).

Wormald, "'Winchester School'" Wormald, F. "The 'Winchester School' before St. Æthelwold." In *England before the Conquest: Studies in Primary Sources Presented to Dorothy Whitelock*, ed. P. Clemoes and K. Hughes. Cambridge, 1971. Rpt. Wormald. *Writings* (citations are to the reprint).

Wormald, *Writings* Wormald, F. *Collected Writings*, 1. London, 1984.

Wulfstan, *Life* Wulfstan of Winchester. *The Life of St. Æthelwold*. Ed. and tr. M. Lapidge and M. Winterbottom. Oxford, 1991.

English translations from the Bible are based on the Douay-Reims version (Baltimore, 1899). Latin passages are translated in the text; when the translation is my own, an accompanying footnote gives the original Latin text.

THE BENEDICTIONAL OF ÆTHELWOLD

INTRODUCTION

"THIS BOOK of the advent of the Son of the loving Father"—this description of the richly illuminated Benedictional commissioned by Bishop Æthelwold of Winchester (963–984) is found in a couplet written in gold over the first blessing in the manuscript (pl. 9).[1] The Benedictional of Æthelwold (London, British Lib., MS Add. 49598) is one of a number of deluxe liturgical books produced in England and Germany in the late tenth and eleventh centuries.[2] Stimulated by monastic reform and royal support, the Anglo-Saxon and German churches experienced a period of strong growth and relative security, and these conditions fostered a demand for service books. Since the celebration of the Eucharist was the central rite of the Christian Church, books containing the various texts used in the mass were among the most elaborately decorated of medieval manuscripts. Bishop Æthelwold's Benedictional, however, stands out as an unusual and exceptionally interesting mass book.

The most common types of illuminated early medieval Latin liturgical manuscripts were the sacramentary and the Gospel lectionary.[3] The sacramentary comprised only the mass prayers recited by the celebrating priest or bishop, and

the lectionary contained the excerpts or lections from the Gospels read by the deacon in the mass. The text of a benedictional was limited to the solemn blessings that were pronounced just before communion, and usually only a bishop could give this kind of benediction. Unlike sacramentaries and lectionaries, benedictionals were rarely decorated in the Middle Ages.[4] Æthelwold's is the first extant benedictional with a comprehensive cycle of illustrations and initial pages. Not only does it far surpass all others in the abundance and opulence of its illumination, it is among the most lavishly produced of all medieval liturgical manuscripts.

Originally the book began with a magnificent prefatory cycle of approximately nineteen full-page miniatures depicting Christ, the choirs of the saints—each choir occupying a pair of facing pages—and the twelve apostles (pls. 1–7).[5] The texts of major feasts begin with a sumptuous double-page display of shimmering gold and rich color: within matching frames a full-page picture preface on the verso and an initial page on the recto (pls. 8–13, 16–17, 22–23, 28–29). In one instance the initial page is even replaced by a second full-page miniature (pls. 18–19). No fewer than twenty-one of these feast pictures

---

[1] See below, chap. 1, n. 43.

[2] For Anglo-Saxon manuscripts, see Temple, *Manuscripts*, nos. 23–26, 53, 69, 72, 91, 92, 96, 97, 104; also H. Gneuss, "Liturgical Books in Anglo-Saxon England and their Old English Terminology," *Learning and Literature in Anglo-Saxon England*, ed. idem and M. Lapidge (Cambridge, 1985), pp. 91–141; D. N. Dumville, *Liturgy and the Ecclesiastical History of Late Anglo-Saxon England*, Studies in Anglo-Saxon History, 5 (1992), pp. 66ff. et passim. There is no specific survey of German illuminated liturgical books, but most are included in the comprehensive catalogue by H. Hoffmann, *Buchkunst und Königtum im ottonischen und frühsalischen Reich*, Schriften der MGH, 30, 1 (Stuttgart, 1986), textband, pp. 127ff.

[3] See chap. 4 for a more detailed discussion. Regarding

the classification of liturgical books, see K. Gamber, *Codices Liturgici Latini Antiquiores*, 2nd ed. (Freiburg, 1968); V. Fiala and W. Irtenkauf, "Versuch einer liturgischen Nomenklatur," *Zur Katalogisierung mittelalterlicher und neuerer Handschriften*, Zeitschrift für Bibliothekswesen und Bibliographie, Sonderheft 1 (Frankfurt am Main, 1963), pp. 105–37; Gneuss, "Liturgical Books," pp. 91ff.

[4] See below, chap. 4.

[5] The first twelve pictures are lost, and the manuscript now opens with half of the choir of confessors, the choir of the virgins, and the apostles (pls. 1–7). For a reconstruction and a more detailed description of the manuscript, as well as a consideration of provenance and dating, see Appendix One.

are extant, and they have a wide thematic range: the infancy and later life of Christ, apocryphal scenes of the Virgin and the saints, hagiographic portraits, and even a liturgical rite.

Since the Benedictional was ordered by one of the great figures of Anglo-Saxon history and culture for his own personal use, the manuscript would be important if for no other reason than its direct connection to Æthelwold. The principal leader of the Anglo-Saxon Benedictine reform, he introduced monks into both the cathedral (the Old Minster) and the New Minster at Winchester, as well as into other foundations.[6] In conjunction with his translation of the relics of Saint Swithun, he rebuilt the Old Minster into one of the grandest churches of the tenth century.[7] As the chief adviser of King Edgar (959–975), a strong backer of the reform, he was deeply involved in the relations between the court and the Church.[8] Well read in patristic authors and skilled in Latin, Old English, and metrics, Æthelwold was a renowned scholar and teacher and a significant liturgical innovator.[9] Under his tutelage Winchester became the leading literary and intellectual center of the day. He established what became the standard form of Old English language in Anglo-Saxon England.[10] His intellectual stature was reflected in two of his pupils at Winchester who went on to become luminaries of late Anglo-Saxon literature: Wulfstan, the precentor of Winchester and an accomplished Latin poet, hagiographer, and liturgist, and Ælfric, the abbot of Cerne and Eynsham and the learned author of numerous Old English homilies and other writings.[11] The patron and owner of the Benedictional was a prime mover in late tenth-century Anglo-Saxon religious, political, and cultural life.

Earlier Scholarship on the Benedictional

As early as 1832, John Gage[12] published a study of the manuscript with an edition of its text and engravings of its miniatures. As an antiquarian, Gage was mainly interested in the liturgical text and the costumes, though he also appreciated the paintings. In 1910 George Frederic Warner and Henry Austin Wilson[13] reproduced the Benedictional completely in a black-and-white facsimile along with another textual edition and a lengthy introduction. In addition to describing the pictures thoroughly, Warner identified Carolingian art as a significant stylistic and ornamental source, though he cited only a spotty selection of comparative material. He also saw the Benedictional as a prominent example of the "Winchester style," which he believed originated there during Æthelwold's tenure and soon spread to other centers.

Two years later Otto Homburger[14] in his doctoral dissertation on the beginning of the Winchester school brought a broader art historical perspective to the Benedictional. Although he did not dwell on the comparative material, he overlooked few relevant Carolingian parallels. He conclusively demonstrated the close connection of the Benedictional's iconography and ornament to the Carolingian Metz school and of its style to the court school of Charlemagne.

---

[6] See the introduction in Wulfstan, *Life*, pp. li–lx; *Bishop Æthelwold*.

[7] M. Biddle, *"Felix Urbs Winthonia*: Winchester in the Age of Monastic Reform," *Tenth-Century Studies*, pp. 123ff., 233ff.; idem, "Archaeology, Architecture, and the Cult of the Saints in Anglo-Saxon England," *The Anglo-Saxon Church*, ed. L. A. S. Butler and R. K. Morris (London, 1986), pp. 22–25.

[8] Wulfstan, *Life*, pp. xlv, lx, 42f.; E. John, "The King and the Monks in the Tenth-Century Reformation," *Orbis Britanniae*, Studies in Early English History, 4 (Leicester, 1966), pp. 154ff.; B. Yorke, "Æthelwold and the Politics of the Tenth Century," *Bishop Æthelwold*, pp. 65ff.; Deshman, "*Benedictus*," pp. 219ff.

[9] For the following, see Lapidge, "Æthelwold as Scholar";

idem, "Schools, Learning and Literature in Tenth-Century England," *Settimane di studio del centro italiano di studi sull'alto medioevo* 38 (1990): 977–89; Wulfstan, *Life*, pp. lx–ci.

[10] H. Gneuss, "The Origin of Standard Old English and Æthelwold's School at Winchester," *ASE* 1 (1972): 63–83; W. Hofstetter, *Winchester und der spätaltenglische Sprachgebrauch*, Texte und Untersuchungen zur englischen Philologie, 14 (Munich, 1987); idem, "Winchester and the Standardization of Old English Vocabulary," *ASE* 17 (1988): 139–61.

[11] Regarding Æthelwold's relation to Wulfstan and Ælfric, see Lapidge, "Æthelwold as Scholar," pp. 107ff.; Wulfstan, *Life*, pp. xciii–ci.

[12] Gage, "Ben."

[13] Warner and Wilson, *Ben.*

[14] Homburger, *Anf.*

Nonetheless, he postulated that the Benedictional did not depend directly on these ninth-century sources but on an Eastern early Christian archetype that supposedly also influenced Carolingian art. He did not adduce any evidence from early Christian art to support this hypothesis, and in an article written shortly before his death, he discarded this youthful conclusion in favor of the view that the Benedictional directly copied a Carolingian Metz miniature cycle.[15] Homburger's final verdict that Carolingian art was a major direct source of the Benedictional prevailed in Francis Wormald's short, popularizing monograph[16] and Elżbieta Temple's survey of Anglo-Saxon illumination.[17]

While acknowledging the predominance of Carolingian influence, recent scholarship has raised the possibility that indigenous English traditions might also have been influential. Robert Freyhan[18] and the present author[19] traced some ornamental and compositional features back to early tenth-century Winchester art, and Albert Boeckler[20] and Jonathan J. G. Alexander[21] suggested that the same might be done for a few stylistic motives. Francis Wormald[22] drew attention to several previously unknown Anglo-Saxon drawings, and we[23] have stressed their significance as stylistic antecedents for the Benedictional, at the same time affirming the manuscript's importance in the genesis of the influential "Winchester style."

Despite this long history of study, many essential questions about Bishop Æthelwold's book have remained unanswered and even unasked. There has not been a detailed assessment of the debt that each of the miniatures owes to Carolingian iconography, nor has there been a clarification of the sources of several pictures that seem independent of Carolingian iconography. Homburger was always aware of the possibility of Eastern influence on the Benedictional, but the problem has hitherto not been investigated. Notwithstanding the acknowledged role of Carolingian and earlier Anglo-Saxon styles, the feeling persists that they are not entirely adequate to explain the origins of the Benedictional's figural style. Were there still other sources? Although many have recognized that the ornament from the Carolingian Franco-Saxon school was a major ingredient of the Benedictional, the extent of this influence awaits full assessment. These issues all flow from the major preoccupation of earlier scholarship, the discovery of pictorial sources, and this concern has tended to overshadow other questions of equal or perhaps greater significance.

The Benedictional's iconography includes many extraordinary, original features that remain unexplained, indeed features that have often not been noticed. The interpretation of the iconography raises fundamental issues of the relationship between pictures and texts. Although originally the Benedictional's scenic iconography was invented to illustrate New Testament and apocryphal narratives, in the manuscript the scenes preface liturgical benedictions for feasts. It is an axiom of the study of book illumination that the text accompanying a miniature is often essential for its interpretation. Nonetheless, the Benedictional's text has never been a factor in the analysis of its images. According to Barbara Raw,[24] the miniatures represent the events commemorated in the blessings for the feasts, but do not illustrate the liturgical texts they accompany. She goes even further in the case of the Benedictional's portraits of saints: in addition to having no illustrative function, they "convey no message." In fact, exactly the opposite is true: that many significant and innovative features in the iconography were responses to the manuscript's own text.

[15] O. Homburger, "L'Art carolingien de Metz et l'`école de Winchester,'" *Gazette des Beaux-Arts*, 6th ser., 62 (1963): 42.

[16] Wormald, *Ben.*

[17] Temple, *Manuscripts*, pp. 49ff., no. 23, with a relatively complete bibliography to 1976. A monograph on the Benedictional by A. Prescott is forthcoming.

[18] R. Freyhan, "The Stole and Maniples: (c) the Place of the Stole and Maniples in Anglo-Saxon Art of the Tenth Century," *The Relics of St. Cuthbert*, ed. C. F. Battiscombe (Oxford, 1956), pp. 409–32. The germ of the idea was already in Homburger, *Anf.*, pp. 46f.

[19] Deshman, "Anglo-Saxon Art after Alfred," 195–200.

[20] *Abendländische Miniaturen bis zum Ausgang der romanischen Zeit*, Tabulae in Usum Scholarum, 10 (Berlin, 1930), pp. 53f.

[21] Alexander, "Ben.," pp. 169–83, 241–45.

[22] F. Wormald, *English Drawings of the Tenth and Eleventh Centuries* (London, 1952); Wormald, "'Winchester School.'"

[23] Deshman, "Leofric."

[24] Raw, *Crucifixion*, pp. 23f., 28–30.

The Relationship between Miniatures and Texts in the Benedictional

It is not difficult to understand why the relationship between the images and their texts has been overlooked. Since relatively few of the benedictions are original to the Benedictional, their study has fallen to liturgists chiefly concerned with their textual history.[25] The conventional nature of these blessings has made their meaning of little interest to modern scholars, but we would go seriously astray if we assumed an equal disinterest on the part of the medieval creators of the Benedictional. The conservativeness of these texts, as part of the liturgy of the mass, endowed them with the authority of a venerable and sacred tradition, enhancing rather than detracting from their value. We know that Æthelwold took a special interest in them. One of his most important and influential liturgical innovations was to combine in the Benedictional two different textual traditions of blessings in an exceptionally comprehensive and systematic arrangement;[26] he also included in the manuscript several new benedictions that were composed under his supervision, if not by him personally.[27] If Æthelwold also took the unusual step of having his benedictional illuminated, it stands to reason that the pictures in "this book of the advent of the Son" would have more than a casual relationship to the texts he so thoughtfully selected and organized.

The benedictions invariably ask for divine blessings on the members of the congregation, but they change according to the feast. The general theme of celestial benediction is perceived through the lens of the specific person or event celebrated in the liturgy of the day. Densely written with an abundance of parenthetical phrases, these texts mix hackneyed Christian expressions with brief allusions to abstruse theological concepts. Nonetheless, they are highly sophisticated literary constructs that, like poetry, use language precisely to express complex symbolic ideas in condensed, minimal form. They distill the essence of long traditions of theological and exegetic writing, and their content comes to life when they are read against the background of these writings, which expound similar concepts at greater length and in much more detail. Though it is no easy task for a modern reader to fathom these texts, it goes without saying that Æthelwold, with his learning and his acute literary sensibility, as well as the Winchester community educated by him, would have possessed the background necessary for an immediate and profound understanding of the benedictions. The influence of the blessings on the iconography can be discerned only when they are appreciated on this level; therefore, we shall often have to undertake a detailed literary analysis of them.

The argument that the Benedictional's text influenced its pictures rests squarely on the foundation of their direct physical connection with each other in the manuscript, but there are also many instances when the pictures seem influenced by ideas occurring in texts outside the Benedictional. The case for such an influence is strongest if there is a likelihood that one way or another the ideas would have been familiar to the manuscript's makers. Several of Æthelwold's own writings have come down to us, and these in turn permit us to determine some of what he read.[28] Also extant is a list of the books he donated to Peterborough.[29] Even so, we have only a very incomplete knowledge of the specific texts he knew. We can safely assume, however, that he and his illuminators, who undoubtedly were brethren of Winchester Cathedral, would have been well acquainted with not only the Benedictional's prayers but also the other texts of the mass and the Divine Office. The latter was another liturgical field in which Æthelwold was an active innovator. He drafted the *Regularis Concordia*, a monastic customary with detailed instructions for the Office, and several private devotions for his monks.[30] It is also likely that his erudition and influence are

---

[25] For the Benedictional's text, see Prescott, "Text," pp. 119ff.; idem, "The Structure of English Pre-Conquest Benedictionals," *British Library Journal* 13 (1987): 118–58.

[26] See the preceding note.

[27] Wulfstan, *Life*, pp. lxxxi–lxxxiii.

[28] Lapidge, "Æthelwold as Scholar," pp. 89ff.

[29] Lapidge, "Booklists."

[30] Wulfstan, *Life*, pp. lix–lxxviii; *RC*.

reflected in the writings of his Winchester students.[31] The homilies of Ælfric[32] are especially valuable, since, like the pictures and prayers of the Benedictional, they were composed for the feasts of the liturgical calendar. There are also several collections of anonymous Old English homilies from the late tenth century.[33] The Anglo-Saxon homilists borrowed liberally from earlier homiliaries that circulated freely in England, for example, those of Bede (d. 735) and the Carolingians Haymo of Auxerre (d. ca. 875), Smaragdus (d. ca. 840), and Paul the Deacon (d. ca. 800).[34] All these homiliaries give us some insight into the exegesis and theology that Æthelwold's contemporaries associated with various feast days. Old English poetry offers another avenue to approach Anglo-Saxon religious thought, especially since Æthelwold was interested in verse. Although frequently composed by authors of unknown date, the extant poems were collected in late–tenth– and early–eleventh-century manuscripts[35] and so belong to the culture of the period.

The pictures often relate to a liturgical or exegetic idea that was reiterated in one form or another from the patristic period onwards in many different sources. The more widespread the idea, the more probable its influence on the imagery. For this reason we shall often cite multiple textual sources when positing a relation to the iconography, though of course we shall emphasize, whenever possible, those sources that are the most likely to have been known to the makers of the Benedictional.

It has been commonplace to acknowledge that

the monastic reform and the stable political climate reinvigorated Anglo-Saxon art, fostering the creation of masterpieces such as the Benedictional. Despite Æthelwold's prominence in the affairs of the cloister and the court, there has been little study of how his specific political and religious concerns might have informed the art he sponsored.[36] It is symptomatic of this state of affairs that a recent book of essays honoring the millennium of his death treats his political, scholastic, and teaching accomplishments while omitting entirely his artistic patronage.[37] Historians tend to value the evidence of texts over that of images, but this bias is methodologically unjustified. Pictures can provide as much historical insight as texts—sometimes more—and can also reveal aspects of an historical context that texts pass over in silence. Æthelwold's art can be no less important than his writings for our understanding of his role in the religion and the politics of his time.

CENTRAL to this book is the thesis that many of the miniatures are iconographically interrelated on various levels. Certain pictorial motifs and themes recur intermittently in various guises throughout the cycle, a technique that might be termed cyclic symbolism. One picture often colors the interpretation of others. As one advances through the investigation of the Benedictional's large cycle, each successive miniature opens fresh vistas into those previously considered. As a result, some repetition and recapitulation has been deemed necessary, so that the reader will not be constantly forced to reread

[31] Lapidge, "Æthelwold as Scholar," pp. 104ff.; Wulfstan, *Life*, pp. xcii–ci.

[32] Ælfric, *Hom.*; *Ælfric's Catholic Homilies: the Second Series, Text*, ed. M. Godden, Early English Text Society, s. s. 5 (London, 1979); *Homilies of Ælfric. A Supplementary Collection*, ed. J. C. Pope, Early English Text Society, o. s. 259–60, 2 vols. (London, 1967–68).

[33] *Blickling*; *Die Vercelli-Homilien, I. Hälfte*, ed. M. Förster, Bibliothek der angelsächsischen Prosa, 12 (Hamburg, 1932); *Vercelli Homilies IX-XXIII*, ed. P. E. Szarmach (Toronto, 1981); *The Vercelli Book Homilies*, ed. L. E. Nicholson (Lanham, Maryland, 1991).

[34] Bede, *Hom.*; Haymo, *Homiliae de Tempore*, PL, 118, cols. 11–746; Smaragdus, *Collectiones in Epistolas et Evangelia*, PL, 102, cols. 15–552; for Paul the Deacon, see C. L. Smetana, "Paul the Deacon's Patristic Anthology," *The Old English Homily and its Backgrounds*, ed. P. E. Szarmach and B. E. Huppé (Albany, 1978), pp. 75ff. Among the innumerable

publications on the sources of Anglo-Saxon homilies, see C. L. Smetana, "Ælfric and the Early Medieval Homiliary," *Traditio* 15 (1959): 163ff.; idem, "Ælfric and the Homiliary of Halberstadt," *Traditio* 17 (1961): 457ff.; J. E. Cross, *Cambridge Pembroke College MS 25: A Carolingian Sermonary Used by Anglo-Saxon Preachers*, King's College London Medieval Studies, 1 (London, 1987); J. Hill, "Ælfric and Smaragdus," *ASE* 21 (1992): 203–37.

[35] N. R. Ker, *Catalogue of Manuscripts Containing Anglo-Saxon* (Oxford, 1957) pp. 542f.

[36] I have made several preliminary studies of these issues: Deshman, "*Benedictus*," "Living Ecclesia," and "Kingship."

[37] *Bishop Æthelwold*. Cf. also M. Gretsch, "The Benedictine Rule in Old English: A Document of Bishop Æthelwold's Reform Politics," *Words, Text and Manuscripts*, ed. M. Korhammer (Woodbridge, 1992), p. 158, who omits art history from the long list of different disciplines required to assess Æthelwold.

preceding sections of the book. The chapters should be read in order, since each partially depends on and reinforces the antecedent ones.

The first three chapters consider the miniatures devoted respectively to Christ's infancy and baptism, his later life, and the saints. In these three analytic chapters the pictures will be considered in an order that best suits the understanding of their content and not necessarily in their narrative or physical sequence in the manuscript. The analysis of the iconographic sources of each miniature leads to the investigation of more original features that were apparently absent from the model. The fourth chapter treats issues involving the pictorial sources and structure of the cycle as a whole. The impact of Æthelwold's religious and political policies on the iconography is the subject of chapters five and six. The seventh deals with the stylistic and ornamental sources and their synthesis into a new Anglo-Saxon style. Following the concluding chapter, three appendixes consider special topics: a description of the manuscript, its date, and provenance; the Benedictional's copy relationship to the ninth-century Metz ivory casket in Brunswick; and the copy relationship to the Benedictional of Archbishop Robert in Rouen.

Chapter One

THE MINIATURES OF THE INFANCY AND BAPTISM OF CHRIST

FIVE PICTURES in the Benedictional portray Christ's infancy: the Annunciation, the Nativity, the Adoration of the Magi, the Naming of Christ, and the Presentation in the Temple.[1] The liturgical calendar groups the latter four events together, commemorating them in their chronological order in a little more than the span of a month. The feast of the Annunciation fell on 25 March, almost two months after the day commemorating the Presentation (2 February), but in the Benedictional the representation of the Annunciation prefaces the text for an alternative celebration of the event, the first Sunday in Advent, which came four or five weeks before Christmas. This placement allowed all five infancy miniatures in the manuscript to occur in narrative sequence and in close physical proximity to each other: the Annunciation on folio 5v (first Sunday in Advent), the Nativity on folio 15v (Christmas, 25 December), the Naming on folio 22v (Octave of Christmas, 1 January), the Adoration on folio 24v (Epiphany, 6 January), and the Presentation on folio 34v (Purification of the Virgin, 2 February). Though the picture of the Birth and Naming of John the Baptist (24 June) is located later in the manuscript (fol. 92v), it will also be treated in this chapter since the infancies of John and Christ are chronologically and thematically interwoven in the Gospels. The Baptism, of course, belongs to Christ's public life rather than his infancy, but that event on folio 25 is coupled with the Adoration of the Magi on the facing verso—the only instance in the manuscript where more than one full-page picture prefaces a feast (Epiphany, 6 January)—and therefore can appropriately be treated here.

The Annunciation (First Sunday in Advent)

The Annunciation (pl. 8) is one of three miniatures in the Benedictional (the other two are the Nativity and the Baptism) that bear a striking iconographic likeness to the scenes on the Carolingian ivory casket in Brunswick, carved in Metz about 870 (figs. 1, 2).[2] A detailed analysis of the relationship between the two works (see Appendix Two) establishes that the miniatures did not copy the casket, but another, very similar contemporary work from the same Carolin-

---

[1] A picture of the Massacre of the Innocents has been lost; see Appendix One.

[2] For the casket, see Goldschmidt, *Elf.*, 1, pp. 52f., no. 96, pls. 44, 45; V. H. Elbern, "Vier karolingische Elfenbein-

gian atelier. In the case of the Annunciation, the Anglo-Saxon illuminators followed their Metz model closely for the most part; one notable difference in the miniature is the cloud that slopes downward, as if dropping from heaven, to surround Gabriel and the Virgin and to fill her baldachin.[3] The radial pattern it forms around her head creates a special kind of cloud nimbus markedly different from the ordinary gold one of Gabriel. There is no trace of a comparable cloud on the Brunswick casket, where the Virgin has a conventional halo like the angel's. Unparalleled in other medieval Annunciation scenes, the cloud is a remarkably original Anglo-Saxon invention.

A Carolingian Antecedent

There is at least one non-narrative Carolingian depiction of Christ's advent in a cloud. In the lunette of a canon table of the Soissons Gospels (Paris, Bibl. Nat., MS lat. 8850; fig. 3),[4] made in the court school of Charlemagne about 800, the youthful figure of Christ stands on billowing clouds in a starry medallion carried by angels. This iconography refers to the parallel passages of Matthew 1:18 and Luke 1:35 listed below in the canon.[5] Since both recount the Incarnation, the image is a non-narrative representation of the incarnational advent of Christ Emmanuel, which in Hebrew means "God with us." The Anglo-Saxon scene also associates the cloud with the coming of the Emmanuel because the Virgin is shown reading from a book on a lectern, a motif illustrating the legend that at the Annunciation she was reading Isaiah's famous prophecy of the Incarnation: "Behold a virgin

shall conceive, and bear a son, and his name shall be called Emmanuel" (7:14).[6] This prediction of the Emmanuel's birth was quoted in Matthew 1:23, and like the Soissons Gospels, the Benedictional links the cloud to Luke 1:35, Gabriel's Annunciation speech to Mary. Despite the great iconographic differences, these common features suggest that some such Carolingian imagery might have influenced the inclusion of a cloud in the Benedictional's scene.

Yet this influence does not explain the significance of the cloud in the Anglo-Saxon composition. Since the cloud is associated with the Virgin, the archangel, and the baldachin, we shall have to examine its relationship to each of these features in succession to comprehend its meaning. Both exegesis and liturgy assist in fathoming the cloud motif's multilayered symbolism.

The Cloud and the Virgin

According to Luke 1:35, Gabriel said to Mary: "The Holy Ghost shall come upon thee, and the power of the Highest shall overshadow (obumbrabit) thee." In the Vulgate the verb "overshadow" describes the action not only of the power of the Highest, usually interpreted as Christ, but also of the bright cloud that had covered Christ, Moses, and Elijah at the Transfiguration (Matt. 17:5, Mark 9:7, Luke 9:34). This led Ambrose and later commentators on the Transfiguration to maintain that the power of the Highest that overshadowed the Virgin was also a cloud.[7]

The idea, however, rests on much more than this linguistic resemblance. In the Old Testament God had often manifested his awesome

kästen," *Zeitschrift des deutschen Vereins für Kunstwissenschaft* 20 (1966): 11–16; also R. Melzak, "The Carolingian Ivory Carvings of the Later Metz Group,"(Ph.D. diss., Columbia University, 1983); *Bernward von Hildesheim und das Zeitalter der Ottonen*, ed. M. Brandt and A. Eggebrecht (Hildesheim, 1993), 2, pp. 400ff., no. VI–63. The connection to the casket was first observed by Homburger, *Anf.*, pp. 8–13.

[3] Rubbing has obscured the cloud beneath the curtain.

[4] Koehler, *Kar. Min.*, 2, p. 73, pl. 76.

[5] P. A. Underwood, "The Fountain of Life in Manuscripts of the Gospels," *DOP* 5 (1950): 69f.

[6] O. Pächt, F. Wormald, and C. R. Dodwell, *The St. Albans Psalter (Albani Psalter)*, Studies of the Warburg Institute, 25 (London, 1960), pp. 63ff. A variant of the legend in the Carolingian vernacular paraphrase of the Gospels by Otfrid of

Weissenburg said that she was reading a Psalter; see M. E. Gössmann, *Die Verkündigung an Maria im dogmatischen Verständnis des Mittelalters* (Munich, 1957), pp. 94, 119f. Also K. Schreiner, "Marienverehrung, Lesekultur, Schriftlichkeit," *Frühmittelalterliche Studien* 24 (1990): 314ff.

[7] Ambrose, *Expositio Evangelii secundum Lucam*, 7, 19, ed. M. Adriaen, CC, 14, p. 221; Paschasius Radbertus, *Expositio in Evangelium Matthaei*, 8, 17, PL, 120, col. 587B–C. W. C. Loerke, "Observations on the Representation of *Doxa* in the Mosaics of S. Maria Maggiore, Rome, and St. Catherine's, Sinai," *Gesta* 20 (1981): 19, argues that the Annunciation and Transfiguration scenes in SS. Nereo ed Achilleo in Rome illustrate this exegetical concept, but the clouds are only in the latter scene; it is also difficult to accept that the clouds over several infancy scenes in S. Maria Maggiore have any

presence in a stormy cloud flashing lightning or in a less threatening light-filled cloud, a phenomenon that the Septuagint termed the *doxa*.[8] Christ appeared in the *doxa* at three New Testament events: the Transfiguration, the Ascension, and the Second Coming; thus the representations of these events, including the Benedictional's depictions of the latter two (pls. 10, 25), portrayed him in clouds. The notion that the power of the Highest appeared in clouds at the Incarnation is an extension of the pervasive biblical phenomenon of the *doxa* to this fourth New Testament event, when two divinities, Christ and the Holy Spirit, came to mankind.

Medieval commentators regarded many of the Old Testament manifestations of God in the *doxa* of clouds as prefigurations of the advent of the power of the Highest. Jerome, for instance, interpreted Isaiah's prophecy that "Behold the Lord will ascend upon a light cloud (nubem leuem) and will enter into Egypt" (19:1) as a prediction that

> the Lord ascends upon a light cloud, the body of the Virgin Mary, which was not burdened with the weight of any human seed. Or certainly [the light cloud is] his own body, which was conceived by the Holy Spirit. And he entered into the Egypt of this world.[9]

This explanation of Isaiah's "light cloud" as the pure "unburdened" flesh of both the Virgin and the incarnate Christ also occurred in the writings of Ambrose[10] and many Carolingians.[11] Bede[12]

combined this interpretation with a thoughtful scientific analysis of the "overshadowing" by the power of the Highest. Reasoning that this phenomenon must have been a shadowing produced by light striking some interposing body such as a "light little cloud," Bede proposed that the light cloud was Christ's unburdened, sinless human nature, which tempered or shaded the intolerable incorporeal light of his divinity so that he could be physically received by the human Virgin to go forth into the world.

God's appearance in a column of clouds to lead the Israelites out of Egypt (Ex. 13:21, 14:19–20) was interpreted in the same vein, often in conjunction with Isaiah 19:1. Æthelwold's student Ælfric followed the well-worn path of Ambrose, Isidore, and Hrabanus Maurus when he wrote in a homily that "the cloud [leading the Israelites] betokened Christ, . . . gentle in his humanity, as in a semblance of a cloud."[13]

It is of the utmost importance that this broad exegetical tradition also penetrated the liturgy, for the Benedictional's Annunciation picture prefaces the liturgical blessings for the first Sunday in Advent. By the Carolingian period clouds were a recurrent theme in the Office for this day. The first two responses in the first nocturn were: "Looking from afar, behold I see the power of God coming, and a cloud covering the whole earth," and "I beheld therefore in a vision of the night, and behold, the Son of man came in the clouds of heaven" (Dan. 7:13–14).[14] The Carolingian liturgical commentator Amalarius of Metz said the latter response manifested Christ's hu-

---

special symbolic reference to the Annunciation. Gössmann, *Verkündigung*, p. 122, believes that the Annunciation miniatures in two Ottonian manuscripts, the Sacramentary of St. Gereon in Paris and the Hitda Codex in Darmstadt, have symbolic cloudy backgrounds, but these have also been interpreted as hills by P. Bloch and H. Schnitzler, *Die ottonische Kölner Malerschule* (Düsseldorf, 1967–70), 1, pp. 38, 47, pls. 85, 125; 2, pp. 93f.

[8] Loerke, "*Doxa*," 15ff.

[9] Jerome, *Commentaria in Esaiam*, 7, 19, 2–4, ed. M. Adriaen, CC, 73, p. 278: "Ascendit Dominus super nubem leuem, corpus sanctae uirginis Mariae, quod nullo humani seminis pondere praegrauatum est. Vel certe suum corpus, quod de Spiritu sancto conceptum est. Et ingressus est in Aegyptum huius mundi." See also ibid., 5, 19, 1, p. 192, and his *Tractus de Psalmo 77*, 14, ed. G. Morin, CC, 78, p. 72. English translations of Isaiah usually render "leuem" as "swift," but it is apparent from the exegesis that medieval commentators understood it to mean "light."

[10] Ambrose, *Expositio Psalmi 118*, 3, 19, and 5, 3, ed.

M. Petschenig, CSEL, 62, pp. 51, 83f.; *Secundum Lucam*, 10, 42, CC, 14, p. 357.

[11] E.g., Hrabanus Maurus, *Commentaria in Ecclesiasticum*, 5, 13, PL, 109, cols. 925f.; *De Universo*, 22, 9, 18, PL, 111, col. 276A–B. Remi of Auxerre, *Commentariorum in Isaiam Libri Tres*, 2, 19, PL, 116, col. 807D.

[12] Bede, *In Lucam*, 1, pp. 33f.; Bede, *Hom.*, 1, 3, p. 25, and 2, 15, p. 143.

[13] Ælfric, *Hom.*, 2, p. 201. Cf. Ambrose, *Secundum Lucam*, 10, 42, CC, 14, p. 357; *Expositio Psalmi 118*, 5, 3, CSEL, 62, pp. 83f. Isidore of Seville, *Mysticorum Expositiones Sacramentorum*, 18, 1, PL, 83, col. 296B. Hrabanus Maurus, *De Universo*, 22, 9, 18, PL, 111, col. 276B; *Enarrationes in Librum Numerorum*, 2, 3, PL, 108, cols. 648–49A. Pseudo-Jerome, *Breviarium in Psalmos*, PL, 26, col. 1112B.

[14] CAO, 4, p. 32, nos. 6129, 6128: "Aspiciens a longe, ecce uideo Dei potentiam uenientem, et nebulam totam terram tegentem." "Aspiciebam in uisu noctis, et ecce in nubibus coeli Filius hominis uenit."

man birth.[15] Moreover, the vespers service on this and every day during Advent included Isaiah 45:8: "Drop down dew, ye heavens, from above, and let the clouds rain the just: let the earth be opened, and bud forth a savior."[16] These liturgical texts, as well as the exegesis associating clouds with Christ at the Annunciation, must have inspired the cloud in the Benedictional's feast picture.[17]

The liturgy helps to elucidate one particularly intriguing iconographic detail, Mary's cloud nimbus. The literal meaning of *nimbus* is a storm or rain cloud, as is evident in its etymological derivation from the combination of *imber* (rain) and *nubis* (cloud).[18] *Nimbus* was often used in its literal sense in classical literature, but it was also the term for the bright cloud that surrounded the bodies and particularly the heads of ancient gods and heroes. Since rain clouds could thunder and lighten majestically, they were associated with the shining clouds about divinities who radiated supernatural light, fire, or lightning. Thus Servius, writing about 400, defined *nimbus* as "a divine cloud" or "a flashing light" painted around the heads of gods.[19] Late antique art depicted the nimbus as an abstract geometric disk, a convention adopted by early Christian and medieval artists. By the time it entered early Christian art, the nimbus had lost much of its original meaning as a specific attribute of a deity and had become instead a sign that the wearer was raised in some way above ordinary mankind. Not only such divinities as Christ and angels, but also such exceptional mortals as saints and rulers could be haloed. Nonetheless, Isidore of Seville ensured that the Middle Ages did not forget the original, classical meaning of the nimbus. In his *Etymologiae* he wrote that "the light which is painted around the heads of angels is called a nimbus, yet a nimbus may also be a mass of cloud," and in

another chapter he added that "the nimbus is a stormy and dark mass of cloud; whence *nimbus* is from *nubis*. Nimbi are unexpected and sudden rains."[20]

In the Benedictional, the substitution of a radial pattern of clouds for the conventional disk portrayed the original, literal sense of the nimbus —a bright cloud. Numerous Anglo-Saxon copies of Isidore's *Etymologiae* survive,[21] and this standard medieval encyclopedic text was surely known at Winchester, which under Æthelwold was the preeminent Anglo-Saxon educational center. The illuminators must have learned the exact nature of the nimbus from this text, but they also probably had a visual source. Although the Benedictional's naturalistic form of nimbus is unique, the related iconographic attribute of the mandorla, which also depicted a supernaturally illuminated aura around a figure, was sometimes portrayed as cloud-filled. The motif occurs in the Benedictional itself in the historiated initial of Christ, illustrating the Octave of Pentecost (pl. 27). Thus the painters fashioned the Virgin's cloud-nimbus on Christ's cloud-mandorla.[22]

This form of nimbus illustrated some of the literary explanations of the Incarnation. As a cloud illuminated by the light of a divinity, the Virgin's special nimbus visualized Bede's idea that the power of the Highest overshadowing her was the supernatural light of the divine Christ entering the tempering cloud of his human nature. The account of the Incarnation in the Gospel of John (1:4–5, 7–9) stressed that the Word was "the light of men" and "the true light, which enlighteneth every man"; thus her halo also represented the illumination that Christ's advent brought to Mary and mankind. Moreover, the nimbus, according to its original definition, was not simply a supernaturally radiant cloud: it was also a rain cloud. The text of Isaiah

---

[15] Amalarius, *Lib. Ant.*, 8, 7, p. 38.

[16] *CAO*, 4, p. 499, no. 8188; *Portiforium*, 1, pp. 1–6.

[17] Cf. the clouds in the iconography and titulus of the depiction of Christ's advent illustrating the first Sunday in Advent in the north Italian Warmundus Sacramentary (ca. 1001); Magnani, *Sacramentario*, p. 34, pl. 30.

[18] K. Keyssner, "Nimbus," *Paulys Realencyclopädie der classischen Altertumswissenschaft*, 17, 1 (Stuttgart, 1936), cols. 591ff.; also A. Krücke, *Der Nimbus und verwandte Attribute in der frühchristliche Kunst* (Strassburg, 1905); M. Collinet-Guérin, *Histoire du nimbe* (Paris, 1961).

[19] *Servianorum in Vergilii Carmina Commentariorum*, ed.

E. K. Rand et al., 2 (Lancaster, Pa., 1946), p. 471; see Keyssner, "Nimbus," cols. 598f.

[20] Isidore, *Etymologiae*, 19, 31, 2 and 13, 10, 3, ed. M. W. Lindsay (Oxford, 1911), 2: "Nam et lumen quod circa angelorum capita pingitur nimbus uocatur, licet et nimbus sit densitas nubis." "Nimbus est densitas nubis intempesta et obscura; et inde nimbus a nube. Sunt autem nimbi repentinae et praecipites pluuiae." See Keyssner, "Nimbus," cols. 594, 598f.

[21] Gneuss, "List," nos. 176 (Winchester?), 469, 821, 885, 889.

[22] For further discussion of the relationship, see chap. 2.

45:8, recited daily in the Advent Office, called on heavenly clouds to rain dew upon the earth so that it might open and bring forth a savior. Medieval commentators had long given typological incarnational interpretations to this and also to other Old Testament passages that employed the simile of life-giving rain or dew falling to earth to describe the descent of God's heavenly blessings upon mankind.[23] Carolingian art had already linked the Annunciation to one of these biblical texts, Psalm 71:6: "He shall come down like rain upon the fleece; and as showers falling gently upon the earth." The Annunciation miniature illustrating this verse in the Psalter in Stuttgart (Württembergische Landesbibl., MS Bibl. Fol. 23; fig. 5) has an inscription which explains that the "rain in the fleece" is "God in the womb of holy Mary."[24] Nothing in the iconography itself portrays this symbolism; only the picture's placement in the text and its explanatory titulus convey its deeper typological sense. The imaginative illuminators of the Benedictional, who might have known such psalter illustration, found an essentially visual means, the Virgin's nimbus of rain cloud, to express the literary concept that Christ came down to her like rain from a cloud. This unique nimbus is an especially profound symbol because it represents both the mysterious means of Christ's advent to the Virgin and the consequences of this event for her, namely, sanctification, glorification, and illumination. In addition to the prominence of Isaiah 45:8 in the Advent Office, the Metz iconography of the Virgin reading Isaiah 7:14 must have contributed to the depiction of the symbolic rain cloud. Isaiah's two incarnational prophecies were associated in exegesis[25] and in the mass for the feast of the Annunciation.[26] The cloud complemented the typological motif of Mary reading.

THE CLOUD AND GABRIEL

Although the Virgin's special nimbus emphasizes her unique relation to the cloud, the cloud also surrounds Gabriel. To understand the angel's connection to the cloud, two preliminary matters must be addressed: the exegetical significance of the angel's speech to Mary and the interpretation of clouds as a symbol of prophets and other holy men who voiced God's words.

An association between Gabriel's words and the divine Word Christ led to the medieval conviction that the Virgin had literally conceived the Word Christ through her ear when she heard the angel's message. So a response in the Office of the third Sunday in Advent says: "Receive the Word, Virgin Mary, which was sent to you by the Lord through the angel: you will conceive through the ear; you will bear God and man at the same time, so that you may be called blessed among all women."[27] At Æthelwold's Winchester a hymn for the feast of the Annunciation proclaimed "that the angel bore the seed, . . . the Virgin conceived through her ear, and believing in her heart, became pregnant. . . . She was blessed by the messenger of heaven."[28] Mary's acquiescence (Luke 1:38) to Gabriel's announcement was taken as an indication of her faith in the mystery of the Incarnation, and her belief made her spiritually worthy to conceive the Word and to be blessed among all women.[29]

The basis of medieval belief that clouds symbolized prophets, apostles, and preachers was the Old Testament usage (e.g., Deut. 32:1–2) of the image of the skies dropping rain upon the earth as a simile for a prophet voicing the heavenly words of God to mankind. Patristic and medieval commentators extended this simile to most, if not all, of the biblical passages that mentioned clouds and rain. Augustine, for ex-

---

[23] Gen. 27:28; Deut. 32:2; 2 Kings 1:21; 3 Kings 8:35; Ps. 71:6; Prov. 19:12; Is. 26:19, 27:3, 30:23, 35:7, 41:18, 44:3, 55:10; Jer. 3:3, 14:22, 17:8; Hos. 6:3, 14:6; Joel 2:23; also Acts 14:16. See Y. Hirn, *The Sacred Shrine*, 2nd ed. (London, 1958), pp. 215ff.; also below, nn. 31, 35

[24] *Stuttgarter Bilderpsalter*, 1, fol. 83v below; 2, pp. 107, 178. See also E. Kitzinger, "The Descent of the Dove. Observations on the Mosaic of the Annunciation in the Cappella Palatina in Palermo," *Byzanz und der Westen*, ed. I. Hutter (Vienna, 1984), pp. 106ff.

[25] See below, n. 31.

[26] *Missal*, pp. 83f.

[27] *CAO*, 4, p. 427, no. 7744: "Suscipe Verbum, Virgo

Maria, quod tibi a Domino per angelum transmissum est: concipies per aurem, Deum paries pariter et hominem, ut benedicta dicaris inter omnes mulieres." See Hirn, *Sacred Shrine*, pp. 211ff.

[28] H. Gneuss, *Hymnar und Hymnen im englischen Mittelalter* (Tübingen, 1968), p. 347, no. 65: "quod fert angelus semina, . . . quod uirgo concepit aure et quod parturit credens corde. . . . Est benedicta nuntio celi."

[29] A. Müller, *Ecclesia-Maria*, 2nd ed., Paradosis, 5 (Freiburg, 1955), pp. 200ff.; L. Scheffczyk, *Das Mariengeheimnis in Frömmigkeit und Lehre der Karolingerzeit*, Erfurter theologische Studien, 5 (Leipzig, 1959), pp. 246, 361ff.

ample, regarded the clouds in Psalm 35:6 as the preachers of the word of God.[30]

The concepts of Gabriel as the "preacher" of the Word to the believing Virgin and the cloud as a symbol of the preacher became linked to each other as well as to the notion that Christ came in a cloud of rain or dew at the Incarnation. The Carolingian author Remi of Auxerre (d. 908), for example, fused all three themes in his comments on Isaiah 45:8:

> By dew [is meant] angelic words. . . . Let the archangel Gabriel come, and emit dew to us, that is, announce the Nativity of the Lord the Savior, and let the clouds rain the just. What should we understand by clouds, if not prophets who gave us the saving rain which irrigates our hearts by announcing the Nativity of our Lord, his Passion, his Resurrection, and his Ascension. . . . Let us cite one cloud from many, the prophet Isaiah: "Behold (he said) a virgin shall conceive and shall bear a son, and his name shall be called Emmanuel." . . . Behold the rain of salvation, by which our hearts are irrigated for the understanding of the Nativity of our Redeemer. There follows: "Let the earth be opened and bring forth a savior." The most blessed Virgin Mary, who brought forth the Lord, the Savior, the prophet calls the earth. Let the earth be opened, that is, let the heart of the Virgin be opened to believing. For when she heard [the words] from the angel . . . her heart was opened to believing. . . . And she brought forth the Savior.[31]

For Remi, Gabriel is a cloudlike preacher voicing the "dew" of the Word of God to the Virgin, who listened faithfully and therefore conceived the incarnate Logos.

The same ideas underlie a Winchester introit trope for Annunciation day, perhaps composed by Wulfstan, a student of Æthelwold:

> Splendid Gabriel announces the happy advent,
> and shining Isaiah echoes in truthful voice:
>> *Drop down dew ye heavens*
> Pouring forth the renowned seed of the heavenly Christ:
>> *and let the clouds rain*[32]

In this Winchester liturgical text the voices of Isaiah and Gabriel echo one another—both heavenly clouds raining down Christ at the Annunciation. The nearly contemporary Benedictional showed rain clouds around Gabriel as well as the Virgin to visualize this notion of the angel as the cloudlike preacher pouring the heavenly dew of the Word upon Mary.

Both the trope and Remi's comments have yet another level of meaning relevant to the iconography. The present tense of the trope's verbs makes the Annunciation seem a current event, and Remi says that Gabriel should come and emit dew to us and that he and other prophetic "clouds" "irrigate" our hearts to understand the Incarnation and other events in Christ's life. The faithful of the present are thus identified with the faithful Annunciate, and they both receive the angel's words in their believing hearts.

Their identification with each other was based

---

[30] Augustine, *Enarrationes in Psalmos*, 35, 8, ed. E. Dekkers and J. Fraipont, CC, 38, p. 327; also Ambrose, *Secundum Lucam*, 10, 42, CC, 14, p. 357; Gregory, *Moralia in Job*, 27, 8–12, PL, 76, cols. 405–410; Alcuin, *Commentaria super Ecclesiasten*, PL, 100, col. 713A–B; Hrabanus Maurus, *De Universo*, 22, 90, 18, PL, 111, col. 276D; Pseudo-Jerome, *Breviarium in Psalmos*, PL, 26, col. 1113B.

[31] Remi of Auxerre, *Commentaria in Isaiam*, 2, 45, PL, 116, 944B-D:

> Per rorem uerba angelica. . . . Veniat Gabriel archangelus, et emittat nobis rorem, id est annuntiet natiuitatem Domini saluatoris, et nubes pluant justum. Quid per nubes intelligere debemus, nisi prophetas qui nobis pluuiam salutarem dederunt unde irrigantur corda nostra, annuntiando natiuitatem Domini, passionem, resurrectionem, ascensionemque ejus. . . ? Ponamus unam nubem ex multis Isaiam prophetam, et

> consideremus quid nobis protulerit: Ecce (inquit) uirgo concipiet et pariet filium, et uocabitur nomen ejus Emmanuel. . . . Ecce pluuia salutaris, qua irrigantur corda nostra ad intelligendam natiuitatem nostri Redemptoris. Sequitur: Aperiatur terra et germinet Saluatorem. Terram appellat beatissimam uirginem Mariam, quae germinauit Dominum Saluatorem. Aperiatur terra, hoc est cor Virginis ad credendum. Nam cum ab angelo audisset [uerba] . . . , apertum est cor ejus ad credendum. . . .Et germinet Saluator.

See also Quodvultdeus, *Adversus Quinque Haereses*, 5, 7, ed. R. Braun, CC, 60, p. 277.

[32] A. E. Planchart, *The Repertory of Tropes at Winchester* (Princeton, 1977), 2, p. 156, no. 150: "Splendidus aduentum Gabriel denuntiat almum, ueridicaque nitens Esaias uoce resultat: / *Rorate caeli* / Inclita celsithroni fundentes germina Christi: / *et nubes pluant*"

on the traditional sacramental theology that the grace of baptism caused a spiritual advent and indwelling of Christ in the hearts of the individual believers and the Church, a reenactment of the Virgin's reception and bearing of Christ.[33] As Christ had daily developed in the Virgin's womb, so in an individual's soul after baptism Christ daily came anew and grew through the continual moral striving for a virtuous life of prayer and good works. The believing Virgin's reception of Christ the "Word" was repeated in the coming of the Logos to the heart of the individual, not only through his acceptance of the "word of faith" in baptism but also through his faith in the "word of God" he heard preached in church.[34]

Because our miniature is a liturgical illustration, it is essential to underscore once more that these concepts had become firmly entrenched in the liturgy of Advent and the Annunciation. Commenting on the singing of Isaiah 45:8 in the Advent vespers, the Carolingian liturgist Amalarius of Metz interpreted the prophet and the preachers voicing him as "clouds" raining their godly words upon their listeners, who, like Mary hearing Gabriel, believe and therefore conceive the Word, Christ.[35] Amalarius' remarks occur in his treatise on the Office, a work well known to the Anglo-Saxons and probably to Æthelwold.[36]

Similar ideas occur in the Benedictional's own texts. The blessing for the feast of the Annunciation[37] asks that Gabriel, who came and announced the Son to Mary, conceiving through faith, should come now to the Church as a guardian. The same "blessing" of the Holy Spirit that formed Christ in the Virgin is also called down upon the Church; and just as Mary

was glorified because of Christ, the "fruit" of her womb (Luke 1:42), so the Church exults because of its progeny, "the congregated people." The prayer for Annunciation day applies the concept of the Church or the believer mystically conceiving and bearing Christ, to the liturgical rite of episcopal benediction: the Church mystically plays the role of Mary in the Incarnation, enabling all the congregation to share the blessings Christ's advent bestowed.

This relationship between the Incarnation and liturgical benediction is also expressed, in different terms, in the two blessings for the first Sunday in Advent, the texts the Annunciation picture illustrates. The first of these says:

> May almighty God, the advent of whose only begotten Son you believe to have happened in the past . . . , sanctify you by the illumination of the same [Son's] advent, and enrich you with his blessing.[38]

Christ's original advent to the Virgin is typologically equated to his advent to the congregation in episcopal benediction. The antitype of the "illumination" and sanctification that Christ's liturgical advent bestows on the faithful is shown in the miniature on the facing page, where the Virgin's cloud nimbus is a symbol of the sanctifying light of Christ's divinity encompassing her humanity.

No less relevant to the iconography is the second benediction:

> Open, O Lord, the gates of heaven, and visit your people in peace, and send your Spirit from above, and irrigate our earth, so that it might bring forth spiritual fruit for us.[39]

---

[33] See H. Rahner, "Die Lehre der Kirchenväter von der Geburt Christi aus dem Herzen der Kirche und der Gläubigen," *Symbole der Kirche* (Salzburg, 1964), pp. 13–80.

[34] Rahner, "Geburt Christi," pp. 32f., 43.

[35] Amalarius, *Lib. Off.*, 4, 30, 9–10, p. 503.

[36] For Anglo-Saxon copies, see Gneuss, "List," nos. 61, 174, 394, 741, 803, 804, 814; also Wulfstan, *Life*, pp. lxi, cxlix; D. N. Dumville, *Liturgy and the Ecclesiastical History of Late Anglo-Saxon England*, Studies in Anglo-Saxon History, 5 (Woodbridge, 1992), pp. 135f.

[37] *CBP*, no. 874; Warner and Wilson, *Ben.*, p. 12.
> Deus qui cum te non capiant celi dignatus es in templo uteri uirginalis includi, da aecclesiae tuae custodem angelum, qui filium mariae fide concipiente praedixit. Amen.

Sanctificetque gregem tuum illa benedictio, quae sine semine humano, redemptorem nostrum uirginis formauit in utero. Amen.

Ut te protegente exultet ecclesia de congregato populo, sicut maria meruit gloriari de fructu pretioso. Amen.

[38] *CBP*, no. 1544; Warner and Wilson, *Ben.*, p. 2: "Omnipotens deus, cuius unigeniti aduentum et praeteritum creditis . . . , eiusdemque aduentus uos illustratione sua sanctificet, et sua benedictione locupletet."

[39] *CBP*, no. 37; Warner and Wilson, *Ben.*, p. 2: "Aperi domine ianuas caeli, et uisita plebem tuam in pace, et mitte spiritum tuum de alto, et irriga terram nostram, ut germinet nobis spiritualem fructum."

The heavenly blessings that the bishop calls down upon the congregation are both the Lord Christ and the Holy Ghost whose advent causes the people to bear "spiritual fruit." This prayer mystically reenacts the object of the day's celebration, when the same two deities had come down to the Virgin who had conceived Christ, the fruit of her womb, and thus become "full of grace" and "blessed . . . among women" (Luke l:28, 42, 48). The prayer also applies the original biblical metaphor of life-giving rain falling upon earth to the liturgical bestowal of these celestial blessings on the members of the Church; indeed, this metaphor is used once again in one of the prayers for the following Sunday in Advent which asks Christ "to pour out through the dew of blessings."[40] These benedictions could hardly have failed to call to mind the similar metaphor of Isaiah's incarnational prophecy in the Advent Office and the associated exegetical concept of the spiritual advent of Christ to the hearts of the believers. The bishop reciting this prayer would have been understood as an example of the cloudlike ecclesiastic preacher pouring out the blessed dew of God's word upon the faithful who spiritually conceived Christ in themselves.

This was not lost upon the painters. In gold capitals above the figures and the cloud are two hexameters:

> The messenger from heaven stands here
>   announcing (praedicando) to Mary.
> Behold you, blessed, shall bear God and
>   man and at the same time.[41]

Ultimately this poem derived from Gabriel's salutation to Mary (Luke l:28) as well as the other Gospel passages (Luke l:42, 45, 48) which called Mary blessed because of her bearing of Christ. The more immediate sources, however, were the previously quoted Advent respond and Annunciation hymn, both liturgical texts that associated Mary's blessedness with her conceiving

through the ear and the angel's agency. The same associations are probably implicit in the mention of her blessedness in the miniature's poem. The word *praedicando* in the verse can mean "preaching" as well as "announcing," an ambiguity that strengthened the analogy between the angel and an ecclesiastical preacher (the bishop).[42] Gabriel's gesture in the scene can signify blessing as well as speech; indeed, the angel bears some resemblance to the bishop blessing the congregation in the Benedictional's final miniature (pl. 35), especially since both figures extend the blessing arm over an open gold book.

One final piece of evidence dispels any doubts about the illuminators' intentions. The miniature's couplet has a counterpart on the facing text page (pl. 9), another two hexameters written in gold rustic capitals over the large decorated initial beginning the benedictions:

> You, O bishop, whoever you are who looks
>   upon this heading, a blessing
> of this book of the advent of the Son of the
>   loving Father is at hand for you.[43]

The characterization of the manuscript as the "book of the advent of the Son" distills the concept of liturgical benediction implicit in the prayers themselves: the heavenly blessing that the bishop calls down on the congregation is Christ himself. Moreover, this and the matching verse of the miniature together imply that the "blessing" that Mary received when Christ came to her is the "blessing" that humanity in general receives when Christ comes anew in the liturgical reenactment of his first advent.

The Benedictional's prayers and related liturgical texts inspired the illuminators to endow the miniature with profound ecclesiastic symbolism. On its deepest level the picture's rain cloud symbolized both Gabriel, the heavenly agent preaching the dew of the Word to Mary,

---

[40] *CBP*, no. 1352g; Warner and Wilson, *Ben.*, p. 3: "Tu ergo omnipotens domine iesu christe benedictionum rore perfunde." See also the blessing for Pentecost 23, *CBP*, no. 1871c; Warner and Wilson, *Ben.*, p. 37. Raw, *Crucifixion*, pp. 29ff., simplifies the contents of the Benedictional's texts and their relation to the iconography, and she sets up a false dichotomy between images expressing theology and typology and those stimulating the viewer's vicarious participation.

[41] "Nuntius e caelo hic stat pr(a)edicando mariae. / Ecce d(eu)m paries homine(m)q(ue) simul benedicta." Warner and Wilson, *Ben.*, p. xix, dropped a word from their transcription.

[42] The source of this word play was the Benedictional's blessing for Annunciation day; see above, n. 37.

[43] Warner and Wilson, *Ben.*, p. 2: "Quisq(ue) caput cernis presto est benedictio p(re)s(u)l / Libri huius nati aduentus tibi nam patris almi."

and the bishop who rained the words of godly blessing upon the members of the Church so that they too could receive Christ. The cloud represents the typological counterpart of the liturgical "dew of blessings" written on the opposite page. The matching format of the facing picture and initial pages expressed their fundamentally related content: the Virgin's reception of Christ portrayed on the verso recurs liturgically for those who hear the words written on the recto.

THE CLOUD AND THE BALDACHIN

The final feature of the miniature associated with the cloud is the Virgin's baldachin. In antiquity the baldachin[44] was a symbol of the heavens placed over thrones to indicate the cosmic significance and dominion of rulers. Eventually this architectural symbol was absorbed into Christian usage where it became a general symbol of the sanctity and importance of the person or place beneath it. The baldachin covered the Christian altar, which was considered the abode or throne of Christ because it held the Eucharist.[45] So in the Benedictional's miniature of the Bishop Blessing the Congregation (pl. 35) an archlike baldachin surmounts an altar with the Eucharist, and in Carolingian art an altar with its ciborium sometimes served as an abbreviated representation of a church or temple (fig. 23).[46]

The baldachin over the enthroned Virgin signified her unique eminence as the mother of God on the occasion of the Incarnation, but it also complemented the ecclesiastic symbolism of the Virgin and the cloud. Medieval texts often applied architectural terms synonymous with the Church to the Virgin's womb, which was Christ's dwelling. The Benedictional's own blessing for the feast of the Annunciation says that Christ was "enclosed in the temple of the virginal womb."[47] A poem of Paulinus of Nola (d. 431) even relates this architectural theme to Christ's advent in rain clouds: "In this consecrated virgin God built himself a pleasing temple with a hidden roof-aperture (impluvio). Silently he glided down like the rain that falls as noiseless dew from a high cloud upon fleece."[48] In the Benedictional the entire baldachin is filled with clouds to show that Christ filled the "temple" of Mary's womb.

The baldachin can also be viewed as an altar covering.[49] Since the Incarnation had made the Eucharist possible, the Annunciation was intrinsically related to this sacrament. Thus the Secret of the mass for Annunciation day compared the Holy Ghost investing the altar (with the Eucharist on it) to the Spirit filling the womb of the Virgin.[50] In the Annunciation scene in the late eleventh-century Bohemian Coronation Gospels in Prague (Univ. Lib., MS XIV. A. 13; fig. 6),[51] an altar—complete with crosses, candles, and a pyxis containing the Eucharistic host—appears next to the Virgin to manifest that both are symbolically equivalent abodes of Christ. Although the Benedictional's picture did not go so far as to interpolate an entire altar into the composition, the ciborium over the Virgin implies she is a symbolic altar.[52]

---

[44] O. Treitinger, "Baldachin," *RAC*, 1, cols. 1150–53; T. Klauser, "Ciborium," *RAC*, 3, cols. 67–86.

[45] J. Braun, *Der christliche Altar*, 2 vols. (Munich, 1924), 2, pp. 185ff., 275; Klauser, "Ciborium," cols. 79f.

[46] *Drogo-Sak.*, fol. 38; also *Utrecht*, fol. 76.

[47] See above, n. 37; also *Blickling*, pp. 4, 6.

[48] Paulinus of Nola, *Poem* 25, 153, tr. P. G. Walsh, *The Poems of St. Paulinus*, Ancient Christian Writers, 40 (New York, 1975), p. 250. Regarding Paulinus' poems in Anglo-Saxon England, see *Sources*, pp. 144f.

[49] C. Feckes, "Altar als Maria," *Lexikon der Marienkunde*, 1 (Regensburg, 1957), cols. 153f.

[50] *Missal*, p. 84.

[51] J. Mašín, *Codex Vyšehradensis*, Edito Cimelia Bohemica, 13 (Prague, 1970), p. 21, fol. 20v.

[52] For a similar interpretation of the motif in Byzantine art, see J. Fournée, "Architectures symboliques dans le thème iconographique de l'Annonciation," *Synthronon*, Bibliothèque des Cahiers Archéologiques, 2 (Paris, 1968), pp. 229ff. This liturgical symbolism might shed some light on the problematic elliptical gold object the Virgin holds in her left hand in the Benedictional's miniature. This object is quite unlike the spindles she holds in the casket's scene (fig. 1), and what it represents is unclear. Warner and Wilson, *Ben.*, p. xviii, called it a shuttle. It strikingly resembles the gold paten on the altar under the ciborium in the picture of the Bishop Blessing the Congregation (pl. 35). Were the object not tilted steeply, one might be tempted to identify it as a paten.

The Nativity (Christmas, 25 December)

In the Nativity miniature (pl. 12) the Winchester illuminators made more numerous changes in their rendition of their Metz model, which resembled the scene on the Brunswick casket in many respects (figs. 7, 8). The most obvious of these are the drastic rearrangement of the composition and the introduction of another cloud, but the midwife behind Mary and Christ's crib also have unusual features that deserve attention.

THE MIDWIFE AND THE CLOUD

The servant's identity is crucial for an understanding of the iconography. Although unmentioned in the canonical accounts of Christ's Birth, various types of midwives often appear in Nativity scenes.[53] Some of these attendants, such as the ones bathing the baby (e.g., figs. 10, 18), derived from the anonymous servants in ancient representations of the birth of gods and heroes, while others illustrated the specific midwives who figure prominently in the apocryphal infancy gospels, the Protevangelium and the Pseudo-Matthew. The servant on the casket and in the Benedictional has sometimes been identified as Salome, the midwife in the Protevangelium (chaps. 19–20),[54] whose hand withered when she doubted the virgin birth and then healed after she touched the Christ child. Though the casket's midwife gestures toward Christ, her hand appears perfectly healthy. Usually Salome was represented with a visibly limp and withered hand supported by her sound hand, and she customarily appeared either directly before the crib or facing the Virgin, not behind her as on the casket.[55]

The modifications introduced in the Benedic-

tional make it even more implausible that the servant is Salome. No longer empty-handed, as on the casket, she now adjusts the Virgin's pillows;[56] there can be no question of her seeking to restore her hand. She still looks to the right side of the composition; but because of Christ's new position, the objects of her attention can only be the cloud and Joseph. That some relationship with Joseph was intended is confirmed by a derivative of the Benedictional's scene in the Romanesque Winchester Psalter (London, British Lib., MS Cotton Nero C. IV; fig. 9).[57] The servant actually gestures and speaks with open mouth to Joseph, who reacts with surprise as he looks down at Mary and perhaps also Christ. The Gospels and other sources related that Joseph harbored doubts about his wife's virginity,[58] and apparently what the midwife tells Joseph causes him to recognize the miraculous birth of Christ.

The servant in these scenes cannot be the doubting Salome, who in the Protevangelium does not even speak to Joseph. Is she the other midwife, whom the Pseudo-Matthew names Zelomi, who attended Mary? Ashamed of Mary's mysterious pregnancy, Joseph hid his wife in a cave and went out to seek a Hebrew midwife. Finding Zelomi, he conversed with her about Mary's miraculous conception. Upon their return they saw that

> a bright cloud overshadowed the cave. And the midwife said: "My soul is magnified today, for my eyes have seen wonderful things; for salvation is born to Israel." And immediately the cloud disappeared from the cave, and a great light appeared. . . . A short time afterwards that light withdrew

---

[53] Deshman, "Servants," pp. 33ff.

[54] The Protevangelium of James, tr. A. J. B. Higgins, *New Testament Apocrypha*, ed. E. Hennecke, W. Schneemelcher, and R. McL. Wilson (Philadelphia, 1963), 1, pp. 384f. Cf. Goldschmidt, *Elf.*, 1, p. 53; Homburger, *Anf.*, p. 12.

[55] Regarding the iconography of Salome, see K. Weitzmann, *The Fresco Cycle of S. Maria di Castelseprio* (Princeton, 1951), pp. 55f.

[56] Carolingian and Ottonian Nativity scenes dependent on the same archetype and free of Anglo-Saxon influence also show the midwife without a pillow. Cf. especially the Cranenburg ivory situla (fig. 209), a lower Rhenish work (ca.

1000) closely affiliated with the prototype of the casket and the Benedictional; see Appendix Two. See also Goldschmidt, *Elf.*, 1, nos. 67a, 109; 2, nos. 71, 102b, 103b; *Utrecht*, fol. 88v; R. Stettiner, *Die illustrierten Prudentiushandschriften*, 2 (Berlin 1905), pl. 27.

[57] K. E. Haney, *The Winchester Psalter* (Leicester, 1986), pp. 21, 96f., fig. 9. See, however, R. Green, "The Missing Midwife," *Romanesque and Gothic: Essays for George Zarnecki* (Woodbridge, 1987), 1, p. 104.

[58] Matt. 1:19f.; Protevangelium, 13–18, pp. 381ff. See also the seventh Old English Advent lyric; Burlin, *Advent*, pp. 112ff.

until the child appeared. . . . And the midwife cried: "How great is this day to me, that I have seen this new sight."[59]

The servant is thus surely Zelomi, the believing Hebrew midwife who speaks to the incredulous husband, witnesses the birth, and affirms its miraculousness.

Her identity accounts for the cloud added in the miniature. As in the Annunciation picture, it is not conventional atmosphere, but is confined to the area between the midwife and Joseph, who both turn toward it. It is another narrative feature illustrating the Protevangelium: the "bright cloud" that Zelomi and Joseph witnessed overshadowing the site of Christ's birth. Its introduction strengthened the connection to the text.[60] The boldness and originality of this innovation can be gauged from the fact that almost all later derivatives of our miniature omit the cloud,[61] evidently because this particular apocryphal element was deemed too eccentric.

Neither the Protevangelium nor any other Nativity account explains the midwife's new action of arranging Mary's pillows. Schapiro[62] considered this an instance of the distinctive and precocious tendency of Anglo-Saxon illuminators to invest traditional religious themes with fresh naturalistic details drawn from their personal experience of the real world. The midwife's new activity does inject a note of familiar domesticity into the iconography, and the painters' personal concern for Mary's comfort might well have been a factor in the innovation. They also took care to make the Christ child more comfortable, as well as the infant John the Baptist in the miniature of his birth (pl. 30), for both babes rest on pillows, a novelty in the iconography of both scenes.

Nonetheless, the midwife's action cannot be a mere projection of the Anglo-Saxon painters' personal emotions and empirical observations, for Carolingian and Ottonian infancy scenes of-ten included servants engaged in menial domestic chores such as adjusting Mary's blankets or her bed curtains.[63] Hence the motif of the midwife arranging pillows in our manuscript did not result from a distinctively Anglo-Saxon mentality but was a new variation on an older iconographic theme that was well established on the continent. Since the motif of the maid adjusting Mary's cushions was repeated in the Benedictional's miniature of her Death and Coronation (pl. 34), further consideration of this feature must be delayed until we can bring the Death and Coronation miniature more fully into the discussion.[64]

THE COMPOSITION AND THE CRIB

One motivation for the Benedictional's rearrangement of the Metz model's composition, which probably had a horizontal or square picture field similar to the one on the Brunswick casket, must have been to adjust it to the vertical format of the full page. Shifting Christ and the animals to the area beneath the bed allowed the midwife and Joseph to be moved toward the vacated center of the composition. The tilting of the bed fitted it into a narrower space and also filled some of the upper part of the picture field. The addition of the cloud filled the remainder. All this resulted in a horizonal contraction and vertical expansion of the composition.

This extensive rearrangement, however, was more than a matter of an adjustment to a new format. Since Joseph and the midwife illustrated the Protevangelium, their new position closer to each other tightened their narrative relationship, especially since Christ and the animals no longer separated them; and the midwife's location near the center of the composition gave her greater prominence as an important witness of the miraculous event. The composition also sub-

---

[59] Protevangelium, 19, pp. 384f. In some manuscripts "dark cloud" is an alternate reading for "light cloud."

[60] Regarding Anglo-Saxon knowledge of a Latin translation of the Protevangelium, see *Sources*, pp. 37f.; Clayton, *Cult*, pp. 23, 245; also D. N. Dumville, "Biblical Apocrypha and the Early Irish," *Proceedings of the Royal Irish Academy* 73C (1973): 303, 328f., for other early Insular evidence of the Protevangelium.

[61] See fig. 9, and below, n. 65. The scene in the Missal of Robert of Jumièges (fig. 204) is an exception, but the cloud here completely fills the upper half of the composition and lacks any particular relationship to the servant, who turns her back to it. It seems to have lost any narrative significance and reverted to a conventional atmospheric background.

[62] Schapiro, "Dis. Christ," pp. 281ff.

[63] Deshman, "Servants," pp. 54ff., figs. 29, 35; also M. Ribbert, *Untersuchungen zu den Elfenbeinarbeiten der Älteren Metzer Gruppe*, Beiträge zur Kunstgeschichte, 7 (Bonn, 1992), pp. 33ff.

[64] See below, chap. 3.

tly called attention to the narrative connection between the supernatural cloud and the crib with the newborn Christ, for both are divided into multicolored bands in a rectangle.

All the same, the composition seems odd, even eccentric. The enhancement of the narrative linkage of the midwife and Joseph was at the expense of Christ, the most important figure. Incongruously placed beneath the bed, he has become a footnote to the other figures. While this did narrow the composition, the shifting of Joseph rather than Christ to this position would have achieved the same result. Despite the anomalous placement of Christ, the Benedictional's scene influenced many later Nativities (e.g., figs. 9, 204).[65] Could it have won such popularity if it demeaned Christ?

The explanation of the strange placement of Christ in the Benedictional lies in the new form of his crib.[66] On the evidence of the Brunswick casket, the crib in the Metz model was a simple if misshapen box, like the one in the Benedictional's miniature of the Birth of the Baptist (pl. 30). Christ's crib has been transformed into an elaborate architectural affair. Since the Baptist was not accorded this new form of crib, its meaning must pertain only to Christ.

Christ's crib resembles the architectural types of altar sometimes represented in such Carolingian works as the Drogo Sacramentary (fig. 23) and the Turonian Raganaldus Sacramentary (Autun, Bibl. Mun., MS 19 bis; fig. 119).[67] The infant lies more on than in his crib, and this too suggests the equation of Christ on the crib with the Eucharist on the altar.

Although apparently not in the Benedictional's Metz model, this symbolic motif was not uncommon.[68] The early-tenth-century Anglo-Saxon miniature of the Nativity from the Galba Psalter, now a detached leaf inserted in an unrelated manuscript (Oxford, Bodl. Lib., MS Rawl. B. 484; fig. 10), portrays Christ on an altarlike architectural crib.[69] Since the Galba Psalter was at Winchester during the Middle Ages, its picture probably prompted the form of the crib in the Benedictional.[70] The Psalter's placement of Christ in a basin beneath the Virgin also seems to have influenced the Benedictional's location of the crib. Indeed, the chiastic arrangement of Christ's parents and the midwives in the Psalter must have been a factor in the general rearrangement of the Benedictional's composition.

What really makes the crib in the Benedictional so unusual, however, is the degree to which it is architectural. With its two stories, windows, doorlike openings, and towers, it has

---

[65] See also Temple, *Manuscripts*, text figs. 44–46, fig. 146. W. Dale, "Ivory and Miniature: A Matter of Comparison," *British Museum Yearbook* 1 (1976): 228–36, argues that the Anglo-Saxon ivory in Liverpool predates the Benedictional, but the plaque's style is close to the Boulogne Gospels dated ca. 1000; see Temple, *Manuscripts*, no. 44, fig. 148.

[66] I have made a preliminary study of this problem in Deshman, "Living Ecclesia," pp. 261–82.

[67] Koehler, *Kar. Min.*, 1, 1, p. 396, pl. 68b; 3, pls. 82d, 89b, 90a. The top of the crib also resembles the framed slab of a portable altar; see E. Okasha and J. O'Reilly, "An Anglo-Saxon Portable Altar: Inscription and Iconography," *Journal of the Warburg and Courtauld Institutes* 47 (1984): 32ff., pl. 15b.

[68] For Carolingian examples, see Goldschmidt, *Elf.*, 1, nos. 14, 18, 26, 53, pls. 8, 18, 13, 23. Regarding the motif, see K. Weitzmann, "*Loca Sancta* and the Representational Arts of Palestine," *DOP* 28 (1974): 36ff; A. Katzenellenbogen, *The Sculptural Programs of Chartres Cathedral* (New York, 1959), pp. 12f.; A. A. Barb, "Krippe, Tisch und Grab," *Mullus. Festschrift Theodor Klauser*, Jahrbuch für Antike und Christentum, Ergänzungsband, 1 (Münster, 1964), pp. 17–27; U. Nilgen, "The Epiphany and the Eucharist: On the Interpretation of Eucharistic Motifs in the Medieval Epiphany Scenes," *AB* 49 (1967): 311ff.

[69] O. Pächt and J. J. G. Alexander, *Illuminated Manuscripts in the Bodleian Library Oxford*, 3 (Oxford, 1973), p. 3, no. 19, pl. 2. Regarding the Psalter, see Deshman, "Anglo-Saxon

Art after Alfred," pp. 177ff., figs. 1, 2; E. Parker McLachlan, "The Athelstan Psalter and the Gallican Connection," *Transactions of the Third Canadian Conference of Medieval Art Historians*, ed. W. Dale (London, Ont., 1985), pp. 21–27; Temple, *Manuscripts*, pp. 36f., no. 5, figs. 32, 33; Ohlgren, *Illustration*, p. 1, no. 1, pl. 1.18. The manuscript was formerly named the "Athelstan Psalter" because of its supposed association with King Athelstan (924–939), but recent palaeographic studies have dated the initial Anglo-Saxon additions (which include the miniatures) before his reign; see D. N. Dumville, "English Square Minuscule Script: The Background and Earliest Phases," *ASE* 16 (1987): 161, 176; Keynes, "Athelstan's Books," pp. 193–96. See also the next note.

[70] The long accepted connection between the Psalter and Winchester has recently been questioned by D. N. Dumville, *Wessex and England*, Studies in Anglo-Saxon History, 3 (Woodbridge, 1992), pp. 73–77, 87f. However, its Winchester provenance is assured by its influence on later Winchester illuminated manuscripts, e.g., the Tiberius Psalter (ca. 1050) and the Nero Psalter (ca. 1150); see Haney, *Winchester Psalter*, pp. 126f., figs. 33, 36, 150. Regarding further influence of the Galba Psalter on the Benedictional, see the discussion of the Second Coming and Entry into Jerusalem in chap. 2 and the choirs of the saints in chap. 3. For a thorough consideration of the Galba pictures, see R. Deshman, *Studies in Anglo-Saxon Manuscript Illumination*, Cambridge Studies in Anglo-Saxon England, chap. 1, in preparation.

a pronounced resemblance to the buildings in other miniatures (e.g., pls. 4, 5, 8, 21). The crib is portrayed as a miniature building as well as an altar.[71]

This extraordinary multivalent crib was inspired in part by one of the Christmas blessings following the picture. The benediction, which described Christ as "the bread of the angels, . . . the food of the faithful animals in the crib of the church,"[72] gave the newborn Christ a Eucharistic significance, implicitly identifying the manger with the altar. The "faithful animals," namely the ox and the ass who normally feed from the manger, are the symbols of the faithful of the Church who partake of Christ as the Eucharist at the altar. This liturgical symbolism originated in the Gospel of John, where Christ compared himself to the manna which fell upon the Israelites in the desert and declared himself the "living bread which came down from heaven" (6:51). Many commentators related this passage to the folk etymological interpretation of Bethlehem as the "house of bread" and explained that the newborn infant lay in the manger to feed the "grain" of his flesh to the faithful, represented by the animals.[73] Often exegesis drew an explicit parallel between the crib and the altar.[74]

The Benedictional's characterization of Christ as "the food of the faithful animals in the crib of the church" also accounts for the depiction of the crib as a building. The phrase "crib of the church" (*in praesepi ecclesiae cibum*) can be understood in two slightly different senses: either the crib is *in* the church or the crib *is* the Church itself. The ambiguity was deliberate, since the altar was generally thought to symbolize the universal Ecclesia.[75] The blessing intentionally implied that Christ's crib symbolized the altar *and* the Church; the representation of the crib as both an altar and an ecclesiastic building illustrated this nuance of the text.

[71] For a related crib-building in the Bury Psalter, see Deshman, "Living Ecclesia," pp. 267, 280, n. 27, fig. 6; Ohlgren, *Illustration*, pl. 3.37.

[72] *CBP*, nos. 321, 339; Warner and Wilson, *Ben.*, p. 5: "Benedicat uos omnipotens dominus . . . qui eum qui panis est angelorum, in praesepi ecclesiae cibum fecit esse fidelium animalium."

[73] E.g., Ambrose, *Epistola* 18 (70), 13, ed. O. Faller, CSEL, 82, pt. 10, pp. 134f.; Gregory, *40 Homiliarum in Evangelia Libri Duo*, 8, PL, 76, col. 1104A–B. This passage was incorporated into the Office for Christmas. Also Ælfric, *Hom.*, 1, pp. 34f.; and below, n. 97.

The building was a traditional iconographic symbol of Ecclesia that also occurs in the two complementary miniatures of Christ and the saints in the Galba Psalter.[76] In the first picture on folio 2v (fig. 11) two small buildings representing *ecclesia ex circumcisione* (Jerusalem) and *ecclesia ex gentibus* (Bethlehem)[77] are beneath Christ's mandorla. The choirs of the angels, patriarchs (mislabeled prophets), prophets, and apostles adoring Christ in this picture comprise the congregation of the Church of the believing Jews, while the choirs of the martyrs, confessors, and virgins in the second picture on folio 21 (fig. 12) are the Gentiles, the other people of the Church. In the latter composition Christ rests his feet on another small building, which is also a symbol of Ecclesia, but in this case it is the unitary Church, whose head, Christ, gathers the two peoples into his one body. The crib in the Benedictional fused two separate motifs from the Psalter's iconography: the Church as a building from the choir miniatures and the crib as an altar from the Nativity scene.

We have previously noted that the Psalter's picture of the Nativity influenced the curious location of Christ and the crib in the Benedictional's composition, but it is the second of the Psalter's choir pictures that holds the key to this feature. In the Psalter the building of Ecclesia was placed, if not at the foot of the composition, then beneath the feet of Christ. In medieval iconography the attribute of a building as a footrest characterized Christ as the cornerstone and foundation of the spiritual edifice of the Church.[78] One major New Testament source for this Christological architectural metaphor was Ephesians 2:11–22, which concerned the controversy about

[74] E.g., Augustine, *Sermo* 194, PL, 38, col. 1016; Ambrose, *Secundum Lucam*, 2, 41, PL, 15, col. 1649B.

[75] Braun, *Altar*, 1, pp. 751f. See also the rubric "altare uel eclesia" in the Winchester rite for the dedication of the church, *Ben. Rob.*, p. 89.

[76] Deshman, "Anglo-Saxon Art after Alfred," pp. 176f. See Greisenegger, "Ecclesia," *LCI*, 1, col. 568.

[77] This motif was common in early Christian art; see B. Brenk, *Die frühchristlichen Mosaiken in S. Maria Maggiore zu Rom* (Wiesbaden, 1975), pp. 33f., 46f.

[78] Deshman, "Living Ecclesia," p. 268. See also U. Maiburg, "Christus der Eckstein," *Vivarium. Festschrift Theodor*

whether the Gentiles had to submit to the Jewish initiation rite of circumcision before they could join the Church. In this passage Christ is the cornerstone that removed the barrier of the Old Law for the estranged Gentiles and peacefully bonded the two walls, the Gentiles and the Jews, into the one living edifice of the Church. Because of him, both peoples are now

> fellow citizens with the saints, . . . built upon the foundation of the apostles and the prophets, Jesus Christ himself being the chief cornerstone: In whom all the building, being framed together, groweth up into an holy temple in the Lord. In whom you also are built together into an habitation of God in the Spirit (Eph. 2:19–22).

The reference here to the "saints" and "the apostles and the prophets" who are also part of the structure explains the association of the Christological cornerstone with the choirs of the saints in the Psalter. The building beneath Christ in the second picture symbolized not only the ecclesiastic cornerstone and foundation of Christ,[79] but also the Jewish and Gentile saints. They are built with him into the one Church that unifies their two churches, represented by celestial Jerusalem and Bethlehem in the first picture.

Influenced by the Psalter's iconography, the Benedictional's illuminators found an imaginative new way to introduce this architectural symbolism into their miniature of the Nativity: not only did they once more represent Christ resting on the building of Ecclesia, they even located this symbol in a lower corner of the composition. Far from being a demotion for Christ, this position literally illustrated the metaphorical concept of Christ as the foundation and cornerstone of Ecclesia.

Since the Benedictional's Christmas text does not mention the cornerstone, we might ask why this architectural symbol was incorporated into the crib-altar in the Nativity? One reason is that the cornerstone and sacramental sacrifice were closely associated themes. The passage from Ephesians (2:13, 16) says the two peoples were reconciled "by the blood of Christ" and "by the cross"; thus in the Psalter's second miniature Christ on the cornerstone holds a cross-staff as blood trickles from his exposed chest wound.[80] A second New Testament text, 1 Peter 2:4–10, also emphasized the cornerstone's sacramental significance. Christ first came as a "living stone" which men rejected, but later "chosen and made honorable by God," he became the "head of the corner;" now believers can be "also as living stones built up, a spiritual house, a holy priesthood, to offer up spiritual sacrifices, acceptable to God by Jesus Christ." In the light of these passages, it is not difficult to see why the Winchester liturgy of church dedication symbolically equated the altar to the cornerstone and foundation of the Church, as well as to the Church itself.[81] The relationship between the cornerstone and sacramental Christological sacrifice in the New Testament, the liturgy, and the Psalter's iconography facilitated the depiction of the crib-altar as the cornerstone in the Benedictional.

Two texts from the Office probably also influenced the incorporation of this architectural symbolism into the picture for Christmas. Just before Christmas, Psalm 117:22–23 was recited: "The stone which the builders rejected, this was made the head of the corner; this was done by the Lord, and it is wonderful in our eyes."[82] An antiphon from a few days earlier said: "O King of the peoples and their desire and the cornerstone, you who have made the two one; come, save man."[83] This text, which is partly based on the passage from Ephesians (2:14) illustrated in the Galba Psalter, seems to have especially interested the Anglo-Saxons, since it inspired one of the Old English Advent lyrics in the late tenth-century Exeter Book.[84]

Klauser zum 90. Geburtstag (Münster, 1984), pp. 247–56; G. B. Ladner, "The Symbolism of the Biblical Corner Stone in the Mediaeval West," *Mediaeval Studies* 4 (1942): 43–60.

[79] For a rather different Hiberno-Saxon instance of cornerstone symbolism, see R. Deshman, "Anglo-Saxon Art: So What's New?" forthcoming.

[80] J. O'Reilly, "Early Medieval Text and Image: The Wounded and Exalted Christ," *Peritia* 6–7 (1987–88): 92, suggests that Christ is seated on an actual altar, but an altar would not have finials like those on the throne.

[81] See below, chap. 3, nn. 221, 222.

[82] *CAO*, 4, p. 63, no. 6251A: "Lapidem quem reprobauerunt aedificantes, hic factus est in caput anguli; a Domino factum est istud, et est mirabile in oculis nostris."

[83] *CAO*, 3, p. 376, no. 4078: "O Rex gentium et desideratus earum, lapisque angularis, qui facis utraque unum; ueni, salua hominem."

[84] Burlin, *Advent*, pp. 56ff.; S. Rankin, "The Liturgical Background of the Old English Advent Lyrics: A Reappraisal," *Learning and Literature in Anglo-Saxon England*, ed.

The central theme of these texts and the Psalter's imagery is that Christ was the cornerstone that united the faithful Jews and Gentiles into the Church. This brings us to one of the most important reasons for the application of this architectural metaphor to the Benedictional's miniature. According to the Benedictional's own Christmas blessing, the animals adoring Christ in the Nativity miniature are symbols of the faithful. Although this benediction does not stipulate that the animals are the believing Jews and Gentiles, this was well established in exegesis.[85] In the miniature the animals at Christ's crib and the crib as the altar, cornerstone, and building of Ecclesia were complementary symbolic motifs illustrating one rich phrase of the manuscript's text. With great visual economy Christ was shown as the very foundation and cornerstone of the Church, whose advent at the Nativity cemented the Jews and the Gentiles peacefully together into the one living Ecclesia and provided them with the spiritual sustenance of "living bread."

There is still a second blessing in the Benedictional that this symbolic iconography illustrates, but its relevance will emerge only after we return to the exegesis of the cornerstone. The second chapter of Ephesians stated that all believers are built into the same ecclesiastic habitation with Christ and the saints. This notion of a universal Church comprising all humanity from Abel to the believers of today engendered an alternative exegetical interpretation: the cornerstone Christ, "our peace, who made the two one" (Eph. 2:14), was taken to refer to the peaceful union of the angels and mankind as well as that of the Jews and the Gentiles. Ælfric, for example, wrote that Christ came as "the living stone that . . . holds together all the buildings of the faithful church. . . . All angels and all righteous men are his temple."[86] Ælfric also interpreted the angels' hymn of peace and goodwill to the shepherds (Luke 2:13–14) at the Nativity as a sign that the Incarnation of Christ the cornerstone had restored peace and unity between men and angels, enabling mankind to replace the fallen angels in heaven.[87]

The association between the angelic Nativity hymn and the Christological cornerstone was traditional;[88] it is in this light that one must read the Benedictional's blessing for the vigil of Christmas, one of the texts preceding the Nativity miniature:

> May almighty God, who by the incarnation of his only begotten Son put to flight the darkness of the world, and by his glorious nativity irradiated this most sacred night, put to flight the darkness of sins from us, and irradiate your hearts with the light of virtues. Amen.
>
> And may he, who wished the great joy of his most sacred Nativity to be announced to the shepherds by the angel, pour over you the most graceful dew of his blessing. . . . Amen.
>
> And may he, *who by his Incarnation joined earthly to heavenly inhabitants, fill you with the nectar of inner peace and good will, and make you colleagues of the heavenly troop.* Amen.[89]

This prayer would have reminded the painters of the familiar iconography of the Galba Psalter, which represents sainted humanity united with the angels in heavenly homage to the cornerstone Christ. Their union is evident in both the first miniature, which includes a choir of the angels, and the second one, which shows angels in the corners of the composition.

M. Lapidge and H. Gneuss (Cambridge, 1985), pp. 317ff.

[85] Pseudo-Jerome, *Expositio Quatuor Evangelia*, PL, 30, col. 569B, repeated in a commentary on Matthew doubtfully attributed to Walafrid Strabo, *Expositio in Quatuor Evangelia*, PL, 114, col. 896C; Gregory, *Moralia in Job*, 38, 8, PL, 76, cols. 458f.; Jerome, *Commentaria in Esaiam*, 1, 1, 3, CC, 73, pp. 8ff.

[86] Ælfric, *Hom.*, 2, pp. 577, 579. For this passage and the exegetic background, see Burlin, *Advent*, pp. 60f.

[87] Ælfric, *Hom.*, 1, pp. 33, 39.

[88] E.g., Gregory, *Moralia in Job*, 38, 8, PL, 76, cols. 458D–459A. Here Gregory also gave the historical interpretation.

[89] Emphasis added. *CBP*, no. 1643; Warner and Wilson, *Ben.*, p. 4:

Omnipotens deus qui incarnatione unigeniti sui mundi tenebras effugauit, et eius gloriosa natiuitate hanc sacratissimam noctem inradiauit, effuget a uobis tenebras uitiorum, et inradiet corda uestra luce uirtutum. Amen.

Quique eius sacratissimae natiuitatis gaudium magnum pastoribus ab angelo uoluit nuntiari, ipse super uos benedictionis suae gratissimum imbrem infundat. . . . Amen.

Et qui per eius incarnationem terrena caelestibus sociauit, internae pacis et bone uoluntatis uos nectare repleat, et caelestis militiae consortes efficiat. Amen.

Thus the cornerstone symbolism of the Nativity miniature illustrates two of the manuscript's own texts, implying both the historical and the eschatological interpretation. The depiction of Christ as the cornerstone at the Nativity symbolized the establishment of the Church on earth that unified the Jews with the Gentiles, who include the believers of today. Their present edification with Christ in a terrestrial ecclesiastic house on earth prefigured and promised their future edification with him, as well as the "heavenly troop," in the celestial *domus Dei*, which was represented in the Psalter's choir miniatures. The transmigration of the cornerstone from the celestial realm in the Psalter to the terrestrial one in the Benedictional expressed the idea that even now the faithful below are joined to the angels and the saints above, since the cornerstone and foundation of Christ joins all churches—terrestrial and celestial—into one church or congregation.

The cornerstone symbolism is not isolated from the midwife and the cloud illustrating the Protevangelium, for each of the features complements the others and adds to meaning of the whole. Although the Protevangelium's narrative does not allude to the theme of the cornerstone, the inclusion of both this architectural symbol and the Hebrew midwife in the same scene was not fortuitous. At Christ's birth Zelomi had exclaimed, "my eyes have seen wonderful things; for salvation is born to Israel. . . . I have seen this new sight." Her declaration is reminiscent of the verses in the Office that influenced the miniature's cornerstone iconography: "The stone which the builders rejected, the same is become the head of the corner. . . . And *it is wonderful in our eyes*" (Ps. 117:22–23). It seems that the midwife in the picture was to be an eyewitness to the coming of the Christ as the cornerstone.

The cloud is another apocryphal feature that reinforced the symbolism of Christ on the crib, although the latter's Eucharistic significance derived from a Christmas blessing rather than from the Protevangelium. The characterization of Christ as the "bread of the angels" in this benediction alluded to the association between the "living bread" of Christ and the manna of the Israelites in John (6:41, 48–52), but the actual scriptural source of the phrase "bread of angels" was the description of the miracle of the manna in Psalm 77(23–25): "And he [God] commanded the clouds from above, and opened the doors of heaven. And rained down manna upon them to eat, and gave them the bread of heaven. Man ate the bread of angels." Thus the cloud in the picture could be regarded equally well as the one that overshadowed Christ's birth place, according to the Protevangelium, and the one that rained down the Eucharistic "bread of angels," according to Psalm 77, John 6, and the Christmas benediction. In ways quite unforseen by the author of the Protevangelium, the miniature unified the apocryphal narrative with the liturgical symbolism of the Benedictional's text. The creator of this iconography possessed a highly refined literary as well as visual intelligence; he was acutely sensitive to the nuances of the episcopal benedictions as well as to their resonances in other liturgical and scriptural texts.

THE RELATIONSHIP TO THE ANNUNCIATION

If we now review the complex symbolism of both the Nativity and the Annunciation (pl. 8), some common patterns of meaning can be discerned. In both a bright cloud accompanies Christ's advent into the world. This similarity between the two events was already implied in the Protevangelium, whose description of the cloud that "overshadowed" the site of the Nativity echoed the canonical account (Luke 1:35) of the power of the Highest "overshadowing" Mary at the Annunciation.[90] The likelihood is strong that the motif in the Nativity possessed the same, deeper levels of symbolism as in the Annunciation, namely, the cloud as a bearer of Christ in the symbolic form of rain or dew at the Incarnation and in preaching, and the cloud as a source of divine illumination.[91]

The liturgy associated with the Nativity miniature and its feast would have suggested that a rain cloud brought the "bread of angels." The

---

[90] Cf. also the overshadowing bright cloud of the Transfiguration (Matt. 17:5, Mark 9:6, Luke 9:34), which exegesis connected to the cloud at the Annunciation.

[91] A later English variant of the Protevangelium replaced the cloud at the Nativity with a miraculous light born like dew from heaven and also described the newborn Christ as "shining as in the dew of the most high God." M. R. James, tr., *Latin Infancy Gospels* (Cambridge, 1927), pp. xx, xxi.

biblical source of this all-important phrase from the Benedictional's Christmas blessing, Psalm 77:23–25, said that the cloud *rained* down . . . the bread of angels" (emphasis added). The notion that Christ came like rain is explicit in an antiphon sung in the Office on the Saturday before Christmas and the vigil of Christmas: "Let the eloquence of the Lord be expected like the rain, and let our God come down like dew over us."[92]

This antiphon likens the rain to godly words as well as to God himself, the same dual simile underlying the ecclesiological symbolism of the cloud in the Annunciation. The rain cloud in the miracle of the manna was also interpreted as a symbol of both Christ and the preaching of him. Isidore of Seville, for example, wrote that "the manna . . . is Christ, who descended as living bread from heaven, who is rained by evangelical clouds to the whole world . . . [and] is given to the Church."[93]

The Benedictional's own texts would also have encouraged analogous symbolic interpretations of the cloud in both scenes. The previously quoted blessing for the vigil of Christmas[94] likened the annunciation to the shepherds of Christ's birth to the pouring out of the "most gracious dew of his [God's] benediction" on the congregation. At the same time it drew an analogy between the radiance Christ's Nativity shed on the world (Luke 2:9) and the divine light that shines on the congregation receiving the blessing. This was one of the benedictions that inspired the cornerstone iconography of the Nativity; hence the miniature's "bright cloud" was also viewed symbolically in the light of the text's association of dew, supernatural illumination, and blessing.

We should also take into account the Advent benediction that influenced the cloud symbolism in the Annunciation miniature: "Open, O Lord, the gates of heaven, and visit your people . . . and irrigate our earth."[95] This paraphrased

the beginning of the account of the miracle of the manna in Psalm 77: "And he commanded the clouds from above, and opened the doors of heaven". The next verse of this psalm provided the phrase "bread of the angels" in the Christmas blessing. This parallelism between two benedictions that helped to inspire the cloud in the two miniatures confirms that in each scene the cloud symbolized both the advent of Christ, when he first came to the world like dew from a cloud, and the reenactment of his coming, when preachers rained down divinely illuminating words on the Church.

Both pictures coupled the cloud with a symbol of the Church and its congregation: the crib was the spiritual altar and edifice of Ecclesia, constructed from Christ and the faithful, while the Virgin under the baldachin also represented the living altar and the Church of the believers.[96] Central to both miniatures was the liturgical renewal of Christ's advent to mankind in communion and episcopal benediction. In the Annunciation, Christ indwelled in the faithful of the Church, just as he inhabited the "temple" of the Virgin's womb. In the Nativity, too, Christ inhabited the believers. Coming as the cornerstone, he literally edified mankind and the angels into "a holy temple in the Lord" and "a habitation of God in the Spirit" (Eph. 2:22). In addition, his representation as the Eucharistic "bread of angels" implied that those receiving him became his "house." Thus Bede explained that the birth of the "living bread" of Christ in Bethlehem, the "house of bread," continually recurred in the believers:

> But to this day today and until the end of the world the Lord does not cease to be conceived in Nazareth [and] to be born in Bethlehem when any one of the hearers, having received the flower of the word, is himself effected into the house of eternal bread. Daily in the virginal womb, that is,

[92] *Portiforium*, p. 7, no. 130; *CAO*, 3, p. 220, no. 2806: "Expectetur sicut pluuia eloquium Domini, et descendat super nos sicut ros Deus noster."

[93] Isidore of Seville, *Mysticorum Expositiones Sacramentorum*, 23, 3, PL, 83, col. 298B: "Manna . . . est Christus, qui tanquam panis uiuus de coelo descendit, qui per nubes euangelicas uniuerso orbi pluitur, . . . datur Ecclesiae." This is repeated in the ninth century by Hrabanus Maurus, *Commentaria in Exodum*, 2, 6, PL, 108, cols. 80D–81B. See also Cassiodorus, *Expositio Psalmorum*, ed. M. Adriaen, CC,

98, pp. 717f.; Pseudo-Jerome, *Breviarium in Psalmos*, PL, 26, col. 1113B–C. A tenth-century copy of the Pseudo-Jerome might have belonged to Winchester; Gneuss, "List," p. 30, no. 455, also 453.

[94] See above, n. 89.

[95] See above, n. 39.

[96] If the object she holds is a paten, she would be even more analogous to the the crib-altar on which the "bread of the angels" rests.

in the soul of the believers he is conceived by faith [and] born by baptism.[97]

Bede connected the believer's edification into a *domus Dei* not only to Christ's birth, but also to his advent to the Virgin at the Annunciation and to those who hear "the flower of the word." The two pictures visualized similar themes by means of the interrelated motifs of the cloud and a symbol of the living altar: the advent of the Word at the Annunciation and the Nativity was reenacted in the Church when the congregation partook of the Eucharist and heard the bishop raining down Christ's benediction—the very words the pictures illustrated.

The Adoration of the Magi (Epiphany, 6 January)

THE MODEL

The Magi march in a rhythmic procession, offering their gifts with veiled hands to the Christ child on the Virgin's lap (pl. 18).[98] Related Carolingian compositions of the Wise Men in identical striding poses occur in a later Metz ivory in the Victoria and Albert Museum (fig. 13)[99] and in the Stuttgart Psalter (fig. 14).[100] The scenes in the Psalter and the Benedictional are also comparable in the figures of Christ, wearing a tunic and mantle, holding a book (or an iconographically equivalent scroll), and blessing. In both miniatures the Virgin is enthroned beneath an arch, though the structure in the Anglo-Saxon picture is actually an abbreviated baldachin that adjoins a foreshortened building (cf. pl. 35). A similar Carolingian scene must have been the source of the Anglo-Saxon miniature. Since the figures spill over the lateral borders but do not fill the upper and lower zones of the picture field, this model must have had a horizontal composition like the ones in the Psalter and on the Metz ivory.

MAGI REGES

In earlier images the Magi are bareheaded or wear Phrygian bonnets, but in the Benedictional gold crowns have replaced their traditional headgear. This is evidently their earliest representation as crowned kings, though this new Anglo-Saxon iconography soon spread to Ottonian art and thereafter became commonplace on the continent and eventually in England.[101]

The account of the Magi in Matthew (2:1–13) makes no reference to their kingship, but by the sixth century commentators had declared that they were kings and this became widely accepted.[102] Their royalty was influenced by Isaiah 60:1–6 and Psalm 71:10, which both spoke of kings paying homage to the Lord.

What motivated the Benedictional's innovative portrayal of the Magi as crowned kings, centuries after the comparable exegetic development? Psalm 71:10 was incorporated in the Office of Epiphany,[103] the feast the miniature illustrates; hence the Office must have influenced the new iconography. Carolingian Psalters were another stimulus. The miniature of the Adoration in the Stuttgart Psalter (fig. 14) illustrates Psalm 71:10 typologically. The Magi, however, still wear their traditional Phrygian bonnets rather than crowns; thus they are likened to but not actually transformed into kings. In the Utrecht Psalter (fig. 15)[104] three crowned kings presenting gifts also illustrate the verse, but nothing indicates that they were intended to be the Magi. The drawing is a literal rather than typological illustration of the text. Such Psalter illustrations might have reminded the illuminators of the typological justification for the Magi's kingship and helped to prepare for their depiction as crowned rulers.

---

[97] Bede, *In Lucam*, 1, p. 48: "Sed usque hodie et usque ad consummationem saeculi dominus in Nazareth concipi nasci in Bethleem non desinit cum quilibet audientium uerbi flore suscepto domum se aeterni panis efficit. Cotidie in utero uirginali, hoc est in animo credentium per fidem concipitur per baptisma gignitur."

[98] Homburger, *Anf.*, pp. 16f.; Warner and Wilson, *Ben.*, pp. xxif., fol. 24v.

[99] Goldschmidt, *Elf.*, 1, p. 59, no. 118, pl. 51.

[100] *Stuttgarter Bilderpsalter*, 2, pp. 108, 178f.

[101] Deshman, "Kingship," pp. 377ff.; also V. Ortenberg, *The English Church and the Continent in the Tenth and Eleventh Centuries* (Oxford, 1992), pp. 85, 91f.

[102] G. Vezin, *L'Adoration et le cycle des Mages dans l'art chrétien primitif* (Paris, 1950), pp. 31f.; H. Kehrer, *Die heiligen drei Könige in Literatur und Kunst* (Leipzig, 1908–9), 1, pp. 13, 36, 51ff.

[103] *CAO*, 4, nos. 7522, 7523; *Portiforium*, pp. 12f.

[104] *Utrecht*, fol. 40v.

A second unusual feature in the Benedictional's miniature affords a deeper insight into the innovation. While two of the Magi offer bowls, the first one, who is singled out by gold tassels on his legs, presents three vertically held gold diadems.[105] Early Christian representations of the Adoration often showed the first Magus giving Christ a diadem or wreath, a motif that characterized the event as an *aurum coronarium*. In this ancient Roman ceremony the citizens of the empire and the provinces presented a gold diadem and other tributes to the emperor to acknowledge his imperial supremacy. Early Christian artists transferred this imperial iconography to the Christological theme to show that the Magi's Adoration was an acknowledgment of Christ's imperial sovereignty.[106]

Despite its initial popularity, the iconography of a Magus presenting a diadem died out after the early Christian period.[107] The Anglo-Saxon miniature seems to be the first representation after the early Christian period to portray the Adoration as an *aurum coronarium*. It was no accident that the Benedictional revived a long-dead Christian imperial tradition and at the same time introduced the new motif of crowned Magi. There was a close connection between these two novel features: the Magi's kingship and their adoration as an *aurum coronarium* were both founded on the typological association with Psalm 71:10. The presentation of gifts to the messiah-king by the kings of Tarshish and the isles in this Psalm was an Old Testament version of the imperial ceremony of *aurum coronarium*.[108]

Later Christian artists were well aware of the intrinsic imperial significance of the verse. Although the illustration in the Utrecht Psalter does not show the kings of Tarshish presenting a diadem to Christ, the imperial significance of their offerings is manifested by the triumphal wreath above the head of the messiah-king. The Psalter's makers must have understood the scene as an *aurum coronarium*.

Since the Magi in the Benedictional have now become crowned kings themselves, the imperial significance of their presentation of diadems to Christ is underlined. This explains why the first Magus presents three diadems rather than the one that had been customary in early Christian art: the number of diadems was increased to correspond to the number of crowns on the heads of the Magi. In the clearest possible terms the painters sought to show that it is *Christus Rex regum*, Christ the King of kings, who receives the tribute of the Magi-kings. The revival of the iconography of the *aurum coronarium* and the introduction of crowned Magi were complementary means to express the imperial rulership of Christ.

One reason why the Anglo-Saxon illuminators decided to give new life to the old iconographic concept of the Adoration as an act of imperial homage to Christ is found in the miniature's text. The second Epiphany benediction mentions that the star, which shines prominently above Christ and the Virgin in the miniature, has revealed Christ to be the "king of salvation."[109]

The Birth and Naming of John the Baptist
(Nativity of John the Baptist, 24 June)

THE RELATION TO
THE TEXT AND THE MODEL

The miniature (pl. 30) illustrates the narrative of Luke 1:58–63. In the upper register, Elizabeth

prone on a mattress and John in a cradle depict the birth, while the lower register represents the child's naming eight days later. On the latter occasion a dispute arose between Elizabeth, who wished to name him John, and some relatives

---

[105] See the detail reproduced in Deshman, "Kingship," fig. 32.

[106] T. Klauser, "Aurum coronarium," *Mitteilungen des deutschen archaeologischen Instituts*, Roem. Abt. 59 (1944): 129–53; also J. G. Deckers, "Die Huldigung der Magier in der Kunst der Spätantike," *Die heiligen drei Könige—Darstellung und Verehrung* (Cologne, 1982), pp. 25f.

[107] A reminiscence of the association between the Adoration and the *aurum coronarium* survived in the exegetic interpretation of the Magi's gift of gold (Matt. 2:11) as a symbol of Christ's kingship; see, e.g., Ælfric, *Hom.*, 1, p. 117.

[108] Klauser, "Aurum coronarium," pp. 132f.

[109] See below, n. 224.

and neighbors who wanted to call him Zachariah after his father. The relatives appealed to Zachariah, who indicated his choice by writing down the name John. Thus in the lower half of the composition four seated relatives address Zachariah writing on a diptych inscribed "Iohannes e[st] nom[en eius]" (John is his name) (Luke 1:63).[110]

Earlier in Carolingian art the history of the Baptist's infancy was illustrated in several episodes. The Metz Drogo Sacramentary (fig. 16)[111] allotted individual scenes to his birth, his naming, and the subsequent prophecy of Zachariah (Luke 1:64–79). In the Benedictional, however, neither register is complete in itself. The upper one lacks the neighbors and relatives who, according to Luke, went to Elizabeth at the birth, and the lower one lacks Elizabeth and John, who should be at the naming. The miniature seems to have resulted from the conflation of a model with distinct scenes of the birth and naming; in the process of conflation some figures from each were omitted. Even so, the Jews had to be crowded together to fit into the lower register.

Whether the Anglo-Saxon painters were responsible for this conflation is uncertain. The telescoping of John's birth and naming into a single composite scene was relatively common. For instance, in a mid-eleventh-century Reichenau lectionary in Berlin (Staatl. Museen, Kupferstichkabinett, MS 78 A 2; fig. 17)[112] Elizabeth is in bed as at the nativity, but she also converses with the relatives about the name her husband is writing. Had the immediate model of the Benedictional already conflated several scenes from an archetype in this manner, it would have been an easy matter for the Winchester painters to divide the broad composition, superimposing one half over the other.[113]

The source of the model is difficult to ascertain. The only two earlier representations of John's infancy, in the Drogo sacramentary and a related Metz manuscript,[114] have little in common with our miniature. Most later scenes of the Naming also differ because they show the relatives standing.[115] The Reichenau lectionary, however, does depict them seated, and its figures of Zachariah and Elizabeth also correspond well to their counterparts in the Anglo-Saxon miniature. John is held by the Jews in the lectionary rather than being in a crib, but this difference could have resulted from independent adaptations of a common cyclic archetype. The German miniature might have retained the figure of the Baptist from a model's scene of the Naming and omitted the infant from a model's picture of the Birth, while the Anglo-Saxon one might have kept the babe from the Nativity but left out the infant from the Naming. One detail of the Benedictional that might indicate that the common source of the iconography was Carolingian is the cradle of the same curious shape as the one on the Brunswick casket (fig. 7).

The Innovations

Although the two registers of the Anglo-Saxon miniature ultimately derived from separate scenes of the Birth and Naming, the illuminators sought to give them narrative and compositional unity. The speaking gesture of Elizabeth's right hand, which would have been inappropriate at the birth, was probably introduced when the conflation was made. Elizabeth can only be addressing the figures in the bottom register, and so she has been made to participate with them in the argument about the child's name, as required by the Gospel account. The two levels

---

[110] Warner and Wilson, *Ben.*, pp. xxviif.; Homburger, *Anf.*, pp. 23f.

[111] *Drogo-Sak.*, p. 26, fol. 84.

[112] P. Bloch, *Reichenauer Evangelistar*, Codices Selecti, 31 (Graz, 1972), p. 82.

[113] Regarding such adjustments of format, see K. Weitzmann, *Illustrations in Roll and Codex*, 2nd ed., Studies in Manuscript Illumination, 2 (Princeton, 1970), pp. 106f.

[114] Koehler, *Kar. Min.*, 3, p. 141, pl. 74a. Regarding infancy iconography of John, see E. Weis, "Johannes der Täufer, der Vorläufer (Prodromos)," *LCI*, 7, cols. 164–90; K. Wessel, "Johannes Baptistes (Prodromos)," *RBK*, 3, cols. 631ff.

[115] E.g., the late-tenth-century Fulda sacramentary in Göttingen (*Sac. Fuld.*, pl. 30, our fig. 21); the north Italian Warmundus sacramentary (ca. 1001) in Ivrea (Magnani, *Sacramentario*, pl. 22); the early-eleventh-century Bernward Gospels in Hildesheim and the pericopes of Henry II in Munich (*Das Kostbare Evangeliar des Heiligen Bernward*, ed. M. Brandt [Munich, 1993], pp. 40f., pl. 21 and fig. 23); the eleventh-century Escorial Codex Aureus of Henry III (A. Boeckler, *Das goldene Evangelienbuch Heinrichs III.* [Berlin, 1933], pl. 111); the late-eleventh-century Florentine Byzantine Gospels (T. Velmans, *Le Tétraévangile de la Laurentienne*, Bibliothèque des Cahiers Archéologiques, 6 [Paris, 1971], fig. 183).

are also connected by the vertical alignment of her right hand with the similarly gesturing hand of one of her opponents, which is framed and emphasized by a curious dip in the ground line. Luke wrote that a relative "made signs to his (John's) father, how he would be called" (1:62). The hands of Elizabeth and the relation, aligned but pointing in opposite directions, stress their disagreement.[116] Besides helping to unify the two registers, the sharp dip in the ground line serves several other functions. It creates a curious cloud-filled pocket that effectively isolates the protesting right hand of the foremost Jew from the remainder of the bottom register, diminishing the force of his gesture against Zachariah. The cloudy heavens in the upper register seem to have dropped down to encompass and enervate the argument of those who opposed the name of John. In doing so the clouds also call attention to the name's divine origin. At the annunciation of the child's conception to Zachariah, an event mentioned in one of the benedictions the miniature prefaces,[117] the archangel Gabriel had commanded the father to "call his name John" (Luke 1:13). Ælfric and other commentators[118] also believed that Elizabeth miraculously learned the name when the Holy Ghost had infused her at the Visitation (Luke 1:41). The clouds around the speaking hand of the opponent of the parents show celestial powers continuing their role in the naming.

The prominent clouds around the child and his mother are unusual in the iconography of the Baptist's Birth and Naming. We have found that such clouds in the miniatures of the Annunciation and Christ's Nativity (pls. 8, 12) symbolized Christ's advent and the prophets and preachers who rained heavenly words of his coming. One of the Advent blessings that inspired the symbolic cloud in these Christological infancy scenes mentions that before Christ's advent "the holy prophet John" had foretold the time of salvation,[119] and this raises the possibility of a related significance for the clouds in John's infancy scene.

Augustine[120] had applied such cloud symbolism specifically to John the Baptist in his character as preacher. John's role as a prophet of Christ's advent was closely associated with the events of his infancy and their liturgical commemoration. After naming the child, Zachariah proclaimed that his son was the "prophet of the Highest" (Luke 1:76). In a homily for the feast of the Nativity of the Baptist, the feast our miniature illustrates, Ælfric explained that John's name meant "God's grace" and that he was called this because he preached the grace-giving advent of Christ.[121] John's prophecy also pervades the two episcopal blessings that the miniature illustrates. The first one mentions that John had pointed out the Lamb of God (John 1:29, 36) and that "even before his birth, [he] had recognized the advent of the Redeemer."[122] John was believed to have performed this prenatal prophecy when he had leaped for joy in his mother's womb when she met the pregnant Mary (Luke 1:41, 44). The second blessing once again mentions this precocious act of prophecy and also refers to Christ's own declaration that John was the greatest prophet (Matt. 11:7–13).[123]

While the cloud symbolized the newborn John's prophecy of Christ, it also signaled a deeper typological relationship between their infancies. When Mary had asked at the Annunciation how she could conceive and give birth to a child without having known man, Gabriel replied:

"the power of the most High shall overshadow thee. . . . And behold, thy cousin Elizabeth, she also hath conceived a son in her old age; and this is the sixth month

---

[116] In the scene in the Caligula troper, Zachariah is caught between the opposing gestures of Elizabeth and a relative; E. C. Teviotdale, "The Cotton Troper (London, British Library, Cotton MS Caligula A. XIV, ff. 1–36): A Study of an Illustrated English Troper of the Eleventh Century," (Ph.D. diss., University of North Carolina, Chapel Hill, 1991), pp. 159ff., fig. 34.

[117] *CBP*, no. 835; Warner and Wilson, *Ben.*, p. 38.

[118] Ælfric, *Hom.*, 1, pp. 354ff.; Haymo of Auxerre, *Homiliae de Sanctis*, 2, PL, 118, cols. 756D–57A; Hrabanus Maurus,

Homilia 114, PL, 110, col. 342B.

[119] *CBP*, no. 37; Warner and Wilson, *Ben.*, p. 2; see above, n. 39.

[120] Augustine, *Enarrationes in Psalmos*, 88, 1, 7, ed. E. Dekkers and J. Fraipont, CC, 39, p. 1225.

[121] Ælfric, *Hom.*, 1, pp. 354ff.

[122] *CBP*, nos. 179, 275; Warner and Wilson, *Ben.*, p. 38: "aduentum redemptoris mundi, necdum natus cognouit."

[123] See above, n. 117.

with her that is called barren: because no word shall be impossible with God" (Luke 1:35–36).

The aged Elizabeth's unexpected and mysterious conception of John was a precedent for the Virgin's miraculous conception of Christ. This typology was often a subject of exegesis. An Old English homily on the Nativity of the Baptist[124] in the late-tenth-century Blickling manuscript explained that the old and barren Elizabeth had been purified of "every human fault" before the conception and birth of the saintly John. She had become "a house of holiness" for Christ's messenger, "an abode of the Holy Spirit, a temple altogether fit for God." These characterizations of Elizabeth echo those of the Virgin in order to emphasize the typological connection between the two miraculous mothers. The homily also claimed that John himself "in his birth overcame . . . all the laws of natural birth." While in the womb he recognized Christ, "who himself again was not conceived after the manner of men," and immediately upon his birth John restored the voice of his father, who had previously been struck mute because he had not believed his wife pregnant (Luke 1:20, 64). The conception and birth of John were a kind "proto-Incarnation" that prefigured and heralded the true Incarnation of Christ.

In the Benedictional the first blessing prefaced by the miniature of John's Nativity and Naming[125] mentions his pre-natal acknowledgment of Christ, his removal of his mother's sterility, and his freeing of his father's tongue. The painters would have recognized that these were the very miraculous features that commentators such as the Blickling homilist cited to demonstrate John's typological relationship to Christ. Since the cloud in the Annunciation depicted the Virgin's overshadowing, which the Gospel of Luke specifically associated with John's conception, this motif was repeated in the scene of the Precursor's Birth and Naming to connect it symbolically with the pictures of Christ's infancy.

The typological association of the births of Christ and John was widespread in art. In middle Byzantine depictions, for example, the motif of washing the child was transferred from Christ's Nativity to John's.[126] In the birth scenes of John and Christ in the Drogo Sacramentary (figs. 16, 18) servants are similarly positioned behind the beds of the mothers, who recline in identical but reversed contrapposto poses.[127] The Benedictional, part of this broader tradition, employed a new motif, the cloud, to visualize the typological relationship between the two events. This enabled the additional Christological theme of the Annunciation to be drawn into a symbolic association with John's Birth, establishing a direct connection to the primary scriptural source of the typology, the Gospel account of the overshadowing of the Virgin. Finally, the novel use of the cloud brought out John's role as a prophet of Christ's coming and reinforced the prophetic symbolism of the motif in the miniatures of the Annunciation and the Nativity.

The Naming of Christ
(Octave of Christmas, 1 January)

THE SUBJECT MATTER AND
THE SOURCES

The miniature that illustrates the blessings for the Octave of Christmas (pl. 16) is one of the most enigmatic in the entire manuscript. In the cloud-filled upper register Mary lies in bed with the Christ child on her lap, while below three seated men engage in animated conversation. The identity of these men and the exact subject

[124] *Blickling*, pp. 160–67. See also Ælfric, *Hom.*, 1, pp. 356–59; Augustine, *Sermones*, 287, 289, 290, 291, 293, PL, 38, cols. 1301f., 1308, 1313f., 1317f., 1327f.; Caesarius of Arles, *Sermo* 217, 2, ed. G. Morin, CC, 104, pp. 862f.; Haymo of Auxerre, *Homiliae de Sanctis*, 2, PL, 118, cols. 755D, 757C; and the mass Preface for John's feast, *Jumièges*, p. 182.

[125] See above, n. 122.

[126] Cf. two Mt. Athos lectionaries, Dionysiu, MS 587, fol.

154v, and Panteleimon, MS 2, fol. 243v; S. M. Pelekanidis et al., *The Treasures of Mt. Athos*, 2 vols. (Athens, 1973–74), 1, fig. 268; 2, fig. 293. For the relation between the two mothers, see also Deshman, "Servants," pp. 51ff.; G. Kaster, "Drei Mütter," *LCI*, 6, cols. 98f.; Hirn, *Sacred Shrine*, pp. 157ff.

[127] *Drogo-Sak.*, p. 22, fol. 24v.

of the image are two interrelated problems that have never been conclusively solved.[128]

It is a reasonable assumption that the content of this miniature, like the other feast pictures in the book, must be related to the feast it prefaces. The Octave, eight days after Christmas, primarily celebrated Christ's Circumcision and Naming. Both incidents are mentioned in the pericope for the day, Luke 2:21: "And after eight days were accomplished, that the child should be circumcised, his name was called Jesus, which was called by the angel, before he was conceived in the womb."[129] The only earlier illustration of this feast is a rather oblique representation of the Circumcision in the Metz Drogo Sacramentary (fig. 19),[130] a composition that we shall return to later. For now we need only remark that the Anglo-Saxon iconography has no obvious resemblance to this or any other depiction of the Circumcision,[131] and nothing in our miniature suggests this event. Both Warner and Homburger[132] preferred to relate the picture to the Naming of Christ. Noting a resemblance to the composition of the Birth and Naming of John (pl. 30), they proposed that the Christological picture might depict the analogous event in Christ's life.

There is much to be said in favor of this idea. A strong resemblance undoubtedly exists between the two miniatures. Both show a recumbent mother and child in a cloudy upper register, and both mothers lean on two pillows and gesture to seated figures conversing in a lower register. Since Luke's Gospel provided almost no narrative details about Christ's Naming, an artist wishing to depict the event might well have sought guidance from a representation of the corresponding occasion in John's life, which

Luke described much more fully. This procedure was followed in a late-tenth-century Fulda sacramentary in Göttingen (Niedersächsische Staats– und Universitätsbibl., MS theol. Fol. 231).[133] Its illustration for the Octave of Christmas (fig. 20) depicts Mary holding Christ and Joseph conversing with a group of men identified by a titulus as relatives ("parentes"). This scene was modeled after the sacramentary's own composition of the Naming of John (fig. 21), and it must represent the Naming of Christ. In the Benedictional, too, the resemblances between the miniatures of Christ and John imply an analogous content. The three men in the lower register are most probably Christ's relatives discussing his name.[134] The more prominent central figure, who discourses with his companions, might be Joseph.[135] This is the first known representation of the Naming of Christ, which was rarely depicted in medieval art.

While John's birth scene was a major source of the miniature, it was not the only one. Mary in a golden bed, her head on pillows and her left hand on her left knee, is less like Elizabeth than the Virgin in the Nativity a few folios earlier (pl. 12). The Virgin in the Naming was copied from the one in the Nativity, but with one significant difference—the Christ child is on her lap rather than in the crib. This modification greatly increased the physical intimacy between the mother and her newborn son, departing notably from the more impersonal relationship between them that was customary in early medieval Nativity images. It is a remarkably precocious and original feature that anticipated humanizing Gothic depictions of the event that also showed the Virgin in bed with her infant.[136]

Except that the Virgin is in bed rather than on

---

[128] Gage, "Ben.," p. 25, suggested the men are the Magi, but they are quite different from the figures in the Adoration (pl. 18). Wormald, *Ben.*, p. 11, connected it to Luke 2:52, but this text, which was not part of the day's pericope, refers to the Christ's adolescence rather than his infancy.

[129] F. Bünger, *Geschichte der Neujahrsfeier in der Kirche* (Göttingen, 1911), pp. 52f., 58f.; Klauser, *Capitulare*, p. 189.

[130] *Drogo-Sak.*, fol. 32v.

[131] F. Aurenhammer, "Beschneidung Christi," *Lexikon der christlichen Ikonographie* (Vienna, 1959–62), pp. 351–56; Schiller, *Icon.*, 1, pp. 88–90; C. A. Isermeyer, "Beschneidung Christi," *LCI*, 1, cols. 271–73.

[132] Warner and Wilson, *Ben.*, p. xxi; Homburger, *Anf.*, p. 16.

[133] *Sac. Fuld.*, pls. 15, 30.

[134] The New Testament mentions Christ's brothers but not in conjunction with his infancy; see A. Meyer and W. Bauer, "The Relatives of Jesus," in E. Hennecke, *The New Testament Apocrypha*, ed. W. Schneemelcher (Philadelphia, 1963), 1, pp. 418–32; J. Blinzler, *Die Brüder und Schwestern Jesu*, 2nd ed., Stuttgarter Bibelstudien, 21 (Stuttgart, 1967). Joseph's sons figure in some apocryphal infancy accounts (cf. James, *Latin Infancy Gospels*), but none of these satisfactorily explains the iconography. There remains the possibility that the miniature illustrates a text that has not survived.

[135] He wears a chlamys and two tunics rather than the mantle and tunic of Joseph in the Nativity (pl. 12), but this variation in costume also occurs in the same two scenes in the Göttingen sacramentary; *Sac. Fuld.*, pls. 11, 15.

[136] E.g., Schiller, *Icon.*, 1, figs. 179, 180, 183. Besides the

a throne, her physical relationship to her son is much the same as in the traditional iconography of the Adoration of the Magi. A comparison between the groups of the Virgin and child in the Naming and the Adoration (pl. 18), the very next picture, two folios later, discloses numerous similarities: the mother's outstretched right hand; the child seated on her lap in a hieratic, enthroned pose; and his mantle, gold tunic, crossnimbus, and gold book (scarcely visible in reproductions). It seems that the painters combined these features from the Adoration with the motif of the recumbent Virgin from the Nativity to create the unusually intimate group of mother and child in the Naming. This novel Christological infancy scene is a fusion of elements from three other pictures in the manuscript: the Birth and Naming of John, the Nativity, and the Adoration.

The Symbolic Relationship to Other Miniatures

The illuminators almost certainly lacked a model depicting the extremely unusual subject matter of Christ's Naming, but they had a deeper purpose for combining motives from these other, more common scenes. This eclectic procedure associated these pictures with each other and visually expressed underlying symbolic themes common to them all.

The resemblances between the Naming of Christ and the Birth and Naming of John called attention to their typological relationship, which was also conveyed by the association of the Johannine miniature with two other Christological infancy scenes, the Annunciation and the Nativity. This additional parallel between John and Christ is based on the Gospel of Luke (1:13,

31), which states that each child had been named before birth by the archangel Gabriel when he announced the miraculous conception to an apprehensive parent.

The explanation of the iconographic association of Christ's Naming with his Nativity and his Adoration lies in the liturgy of the Octave of Christmas, the feast the Naming illustrates. The Preface of the mass for the day indicates that this feast commemorated other events in Christ's infancy besides his Naming and Circumcision:

> It is truly fitting, O eternal God, whose day of Circumcision and Octave of the Nativity we celebrate today, that we, Lord, should venerate your miracles, because she who gave birth is mother and virgin, [and] he who was born is infant and god. Justly the heavens have declared, the angels celebrated, the shepherds rejoiced, [and] the Magi have been moved.[137]

This prayer recalls both the Nativity, celebrated on Christmas eight days earlier (25 December), and the Adoration of the Magi, celebrated on Epiphany five days later (6 January); the visual allusions to both these events in the picture for the Octave illustrates this feast's connection to them. At the same time the miniature represents the essence of the day's celebration, the "miracles" of the Incarnation, in which Mary was both "virgin and mother" and Christ both "infant and god." The intimate physical contact between Mary and Christ on the birth bed itself established with unmistakable clarity their human kinship as mother and son. Yet Christ is not entirely a child. He is not dressed in a babe's swaddling clothes (cf. pl. 12). Instead, his tunic, gold mantle, and gold book characterize him as a teacher or philosopher, and his hieratic pose makes him appear a tiny adult. These features

---

Benedictional, the only other instance of the motif before the late twelfth century seems to be a Nativity miniature in an eleventh-century St. Gall sacramentary; see A. Merton, *Die Buchmalerei in St. Gallen von neunten bis zum elften Jahrhundert* (Leipzig, 1912), pp. 76ff., pl. 77, 1. A few other early medieval Nativity scenes portray some degree of physical intimacy between the mother and child at the Nativity, though they are not on a bed. An unusual later Metz ivory in Paris represents the enthroned Virgin suckling Christ between a midwife and Joseph; Goldschmidt, *Elf.*, 1, p. 44, no. 79, pl. 32; 2, p. 7; *Bernward von Hildesheim und das Zeitalter der Ottonen*, 2, pp. 202ff., no. IV–41; Deshman, "Servants," p. 55, fig. 34. Middle Byzantine and Ottonian scenes occasionally

show the seated Mary taking Christ from his crib; see Goldschmidt and Weitzmann, *Byz. Elf.*, 2, nos. 25, 199, pls. 8, 66; H. Schiel, *Codex Egberti* (Basel, 1960), pp. 115f.; J. M. Plotzek, *Das Perikopenbuch Heinrichs III. in Bremen und seine Stellung innerhalb der Echternacher Buchmalerei* (Cologne, 1970), pp. 116ff.

[137] *Jumièges*, p. 52: "Uere dignum aeterne deus, cuius hodie circumcisionis diem et natiuitatis octauum caelebrantes tua domine mirabilia ueneramur, quia quae peperit et mater et uirgo est, qui natus est, et infans et deus est. Merito caeli locuti sunt, angeli gratulati, pastores laetati, magi mutati."

portray him as a god and not merely the human infant of Mary. This theme of the two natures of Christ was already present in the iconography of the Adoration, where the same hieratic type of Christ sits intimately on his mother's lap. Commentators such as Ælfric[138] made the point that the three Magi worshipped Christ's three-fold character of king, god, and man.

In the miniatures of the Nativity and the Adoration, the miraculous Incarnation is revealed to representatives of mankind, the Hebrew midwife and the Magi; and in the associated picture of the Naming, the three male figures in animated discussion should probably also be understood as witnesses of the Incarnation, revealed by the group of the Virgin and Christ above them. The revelational aspect of the Octave is apparent not only in the feast's mass Preface, which stresses the reaction of the shepherds, Magi, and even the heavens to the "miracles," but also the day's epistle: "For the grace of God the Savior hath appeared to all men" (Titus 2:11).[139] The interpretation of the men as witnesses is entirely consistent with the assumption that they are discussing the child's name, Jesus, which meant "savior" in Hebrew. At the Annunciation Gabriel had given him this name and also said that he would be called the "Son of God" (Luke 1:31, 35). Hence several homilies for the Octave that were well known in late-tenth-century England saw incarnational significance in Christ's Naming. Haymo of Auxerre, for instance, wrote that "because the Son of God was made man, he was called by name Jesus, because Jesus in Hebrew means our savior or salvation in our own tongue."[140]

Still another feature that links the Naming to the other infancy scenes of Christ and also John the Baptist is the cloud, which in three of the four miniatures surrounds the recumbent new mother. In view of the elaborate symbolism of the cloud in the other miniatures, the same motif in Christ's Naming is not likely to be merely a conventional atmospheric background. Although no literary source, to my knowledge, connects clouds to this particular event in Christ's life, there was an exegetic tradition that could indirectly explain their presence on this occasion.

In his comments on Psalm 88:7–8 Augustine[141] expounded the familiar notion that Christ received the "clouds" of his flesh from the Virgin and that all prophets and preachers are clouds raining heavenly words on the earth. But Augustine went on to relate these two concepts to Christ's entire life on earth, where he was born, suffered, and was resurrected: "In that place you [Christ] thundered out of your own cloud, but to scatter rain upon the Gentiles round about you have sent other clouds."[142] Augustine considered the incarnate Christ during his entire terrestrial mission to be a cloudlike preacher raining his truth upon men, a mission continued by "other clouds," that is, other prophets and preachers. These ideas were developed in a homily by Bede, who connected them to themes that we have previously encountered in his exegesis of the power of the Highest overshadowing the Virgin at the Annunciation.[143] Bede once more asserted that in the Incarnation Christ had made the light of his divinity tolerable to mankind by shading it in the cloud of his humanity, and that in fulfillment of the prophecy of Isaiah (19:1) Christ had entered the world on the "light" cloud of his sinless, unburdened human flesh. Moreover, he revealed the tempered radiance of his divinity to the Gentiles throughout his terrestrial life:

---

[138] Ælfric, *Hom.*, 1, pp. 116f. See also J. E. Rosenthal, "Three Drawings in an Anglo-Saxon Pontifical: Anthropomorphic Trinity or Threefold Christ?" *AB* 63 (1981): 548ff., esp. 557, n. 54.

[139] Bünger, *Neujahrsfeier*, p. 59.

[140] Haymo of Auxerre, *Homilia* 14, PL, 118, col. 93C: "quod Filius Dei homo factus, hoc nomine uocaretur uidelicet Jesus: quia Jesus Hebraea lingua, in nostra saluator siue salutaris dicitur." Also Paul the Deacon (= Ambrose, *Expositio Euangelii secundum Lucam*, 2, 56, ed. M. Adriaen, CC, 14, p. 55); R. Grégoire, *Homéliaires liturgiques médiévaux* (Spoleto, 1980), p. 437, no. 39.

[141] Augustine, *Enarrationes*, 88, 1, 7–8, ed. Dekkers and

Fraipont, pp. 1224ff.

[142] Augustine, *Enarrationes*, 88, 1, 9, ed. Dekkers and Fraipont, pp. 1226f.:
Si enim ibi solum praedicareris, ubi nasci, ubi pati, ubi resurgere, unde adscendere uoluisti, impleta esset illa ueritas promissi Dei, ad confirmandas promissiones patrum; sed non impleretur: Gentes autem super misericordia glorificare Deum, nisi illa ueritas expanderetur, et ab illo loco ubi apparere uoluisti, in circuitu diffunderetur. Tu quidem illo loco de nube propria intonuisti, sed ad rigandum in circuitu gentium alias nubes misisti.

[143] See above, n. 12.

He who is not confined in a place willed to go from place to place by means of this cloud, his human nature; in it he who always remains invisible in divinity willed to endure mockery, scourging and death; by means of it he who fills heaven in the power of his divinity ascended into heaven.[144]

On the basis of this exegetic tradition clouds could be present at Christ's Naming or at any other event in his life as the symbol of the humanity that he had received from the Virgin when the power of the Highest had overshadowed her.

The Virgin's overshadowing was intrinsically related to Christ's name, for Gabriel had announced to her that "the power of the most High shall overshadow thee. And therefore also the Holy which shall be born of thee shall be called the Son of God" (Luke 1:35). Thus Christ's name as well as his human nature derived from this action of the power of the Highest. In the iconographic context of the Naming, the cloud signified Christ's human nature—also vividly manifested by his intimate physical contact with his mother—and at the same time it alluded to the event that gave him both his humanity and his name: the most High overshadowing the Virgin. The clouds in the Naming change their regular wavy pattern to flow around Mary's head in a rather distinct fashion. Without actually assuming the radial configuration of a nimbus, which in the Annunciation is the symbol of the unique moment when the Highest came over her, the clouds nonetheless clearly evoke their special relationship to her on that earlier occasion.

The realization that this picture is not a simple narrative representation of the Naming but a complex symbolic liturgical illustration for the Octave of Christmas requires a reappraisal of its relationship to the only earlier extant illustration for this feast, the historiated initial representing the Circumcision in the Drogo Sacramentary (fig. 19).

The Carolingian Octave illustration is also visually linked to other Christological infancy scenes. The figure of Joseph is virtually identical to the one in the Sacramentary's initial of the Nativity illustrating Christmas (fig. 18), and the group of the enthroned Virgin and child has a close counterpart in the initial of the Adoration of the Magi illustrating Epiphany (fig. 22).[145] The Preface for the Octave mass in the Sacramentary[146] is the same one used in the Anglo-Saxon liturgy, and as in the Benedictional, the Preface seems to have inspired the iconographic association of the illustrations for the Octave, Christmas, and Epiphany. In the Sacramentary, too, the purpose of this was to underscore the common incarnational significance of all these depictions. The relegation of Joseph and the servants to the initial's periphery deemphasized the narrative content and allowed the Virgin and child, who are larger in scale, to be isolated like a devotional image in the center. The Christ child's physical intimacy with his mother establishes his humanity while his hieratic pose and philosopher's costume manifest his divinity. Placed before the final letter S within the initial D, the group of Christ and his mother almost appears to be part of the abbreviated word *Deus*, and this too subtly expressed that "he who was born is infant and god."

Despite their different narrative content, the Octave illustrations of the Sacramentary and the Benedictional used a similar technique of visual association and even one of the same motifs, the intimate group of the mother and child, to express the feast's incarnational theme and its relation to the liturgical celebrations of other events in Christ's infancy. Clearly the Anglo-Saxons must have known something of the Carolingian tradition of liturgical illustration, but at the same time they improved on this earlier tradition, in so far as it can be glimpsed in the rather isolated evidence of the Drogo Sacramentary.

In the Carolingian manuscript the repetition of the figure of Joseph, a secondary participant in the Incarnation, established the relationship between the illustrations for Christmas and its Octave, but in the Benedictional one of the primary figures, the Virgin (and her bed), became the means of visual association. This modification also increased the unity of these two scenes

---

144 Bede, *Hom.*, 2, 15, p. 143.

145 *Drogo-Sak.*, fol. 34v.

146 F. Unterkircher, *Zur Ikonographie und Liturgie des Drogo-Sakramentars*, Interpretationes ad Codices, 1 (Graz, 1977),

p. 35, no. 104. The Preface on fol. 33 falls between the Octave initial on the opposite folio (32v) and the Epiphany initial on fol. 34v.

with that of the Adoration, for now the figure of the Virgin linked all three. In the Benedictional the change in the narrative content of the Octave illustration from the Circumcision to the Naming and the use of the new unifying motif of the cloud extended the network of associated infancy scenes beyond the Nativity and the Adoration to include the Baptist's Birth and Naming, and the Annunciation. To a certain extent the Sacramentary does offer a precedent for the typological linkage between the infancies of Christ and John, since there the scenes of their birth, if not their naming, are related (figs. 16, 18).

The Presentation in the Temple (Purification of the Virgin, 2 February)

THE PRIMARY MODEL

Several features of the miniature of the Presentation (pl. 20) recall Carolingian iconography.[147] At the far left of the composition is a female servant whose presence is not explained by the biblical account of the event. Luke (2:22–32) describes only Mary and Joseph presenting Christ to the priest Simeon in the presence of the prophetess Anna in the temple in Jerusalem. In the ninth-century Metz representations in the Drogo Sacramentary (fig. 23) and on the ivory casket in the Louvre Museum in Paris (fig. 24), a maid, who carries the doves, also appears behind one or both of the parents.[148] Neither Metz scene includes Anna, but in the Utrecht Psalter (fig. 25, above)[149] she stands behind Simeon, as in the Benedictional. These Carolingian scenes also show Christ held over an altar, which is sometimes turned at an angle to the picture plane, and in both the Drogo Sacramentary and the Benedictional Christ wears a tunic and mantle and blesses. While no single Carolingian image includes every feature of the Benedictional, the resemblances are numerous enough to suggest that the Anglo-Saxon scene depends on a Carolingian source.

The Benedictional's composition is a crowded one. Both Anna and the servant are partially obscured by the frame, and only Joseph's head and his covered hands holding the doves are visible above Mary and her attendant. Homburger[150] recognized that this crowding indicated that the model had a horizontal format, like several of the Carolingian scenes. To fill the upper portion of the page, the Winchester illuminators raised the groundline well above the bottom of the frame and also added the hand of God in the clouds, a very rare motif unknown in all earlier and most later Presentation scenes.[151] The additions, however, were not merely expedients to adjust the composition, for they endowed the scene with a wealth of new meaning.

THE INNOVATIONS

On the simplest level the Bible itself explains the presence of the *manus Dei*. Luke 2:22 specified that Christ's parents "carried him to Jerusalem, to present him *to the Lord*" (emphasis added), in accordance with the Old Testament law (Ex. 13:1–2, 11–16) that every first-born male child should be brought to the temple to be conse-

---

[147] The only earlier Anglo-Saxon representation, on the Wirksworth slab (ca. 800; fig. 52), is unrelated; see B. Kurth, "The Iconography of the Wirksworth Slab," *Burlington Magazine* 86 (1945): 117, pl. 1c; also R. W. P. Cockerton, "The Wirksworth Slab," *Derbyshire Archaeological and Natural History Society Journal* 82 (1962): 14f.; P. Harbison, "Two Panels on the Wirksworth Slab," *Derbyshire Archaeological Journal* 107 (1987): 38ff. For the iconography of the Presentation, see D. C. Shorr, "The Iconographic Development of the Presentation in the Temple," *AB* 28 (1946): 17–32; E. Lucchesi Palli and L. Hoffscholte, "Darbringung Jesu im Tempel," *LCI*, 1, cols. 473–77; Schiller, *Icon.*, 1, pp. 90–94.

[148] *Drogo-Sak.*, p. 23, fol. 38; Goldschmidt, *Elf.*, 1, p. 52,

no. 95c, pl. 41; cf. also no. 118, pl. 52. For a Turonian example, see Deshman, "Servants," pp. 59ff., fig. 39.

[149] *Utrecht*, fol. 89v.

[150] Homburger, *Anf.*, p. 17.

[151] The hand appears in only two other depictions, both of the eleventh century: the Chronicles of St. Germain-des-Pres in Paris (Y. Deslandres, "Les Manuscrits décorés au XIᵉ siècle à Saint-Germain-des-Pres par Ingelard," *Scriptorium* 9 [1955]: 9ff., pl. 5a) and the Bohemian evangeliary in Gnesen (S. Sawicka, "La Bibliothèque du chapitre de Gniezno," *Bulletin de la Société Française de Reproductions de Manuscrits à Peintures* 19 [1935]: 256ff., pl. 38). There is evidence of Anglo-Saxon influence on the scriptorium of the Chronicles.

crated to God. In the miniature the axiality of the hand of God and Christ relates them to each other. The hand, however, points to the doves, and for this too there is a biblical explanation. Old Testament law required a woman to purify herself after childbirth by presenting doves or pigeons to the temple priest "who shall offer them before the Lord" (Lev. 12:7). The hand in the scene signified God's acceptance of the offering of the birds as well as of Christ.

While these biblical texts must have been an important factor in the illuminators' decision to depict the divine hand, the same texts would also have been known to other artists who, for the most part, did not include the motif in their versions of the Presentation. Additional influences were probably at work in the Benedictional. To discover what these were we must look more closely at the unusual position of Joseph's offering.

Joseph holds the doves directly over the Virgin, almost seeming to rest his veiled hands on her head. In representations of the Presentation this placement of the birds seems to be unique, but in another and very different context there was an established tradition for the depiction of a dove over or on the Virgin's head. In the ninth-century Byzantine Chludov Psalter[152] the coming of the Holy Spirit over the Virgin at the Annunciation (Luke 1:35) is illustrated by a dove perching on her nimbus. A related incarnational iconography was in vogue in Anglo-Saxon England. In the late-tenth-century Arenberg Gospels from Canterbury or Glastonbury (New York, Pierpont Morgan Lib., MS M. 869; fig. 26), the Virgin with the dove on her head is one of a group of figures atop a canon table. This motif refers in part to the first pair of parallel Gospel passages listed below in the fifth canon, Matthew 1:18 and Luke 1:35, which both mention the Spirit coming to the Virgin at the Incarna-

tion.[153] The so-called Quinity drawing in the New Minster Prayerbook (London, British Lib., MS Cotton Titus D. XXVII; fig. 27),[154] made at Winchester ca. 1020–1029, also represents the Virgin with the dove on her head and her child in her arms, standing next to the enthroned Father and Son.

The imagery of both these Anglo-Saxon drawings derived from the Utrecht Psalter, which was in England by the end of the tenth century at the latest. The Arenberg drawing was modeled after the illustration of the *Gloria* on folio 89v of the Psalter (figs. 25, 28) where Mary, with the dove on her head and the Christ child in her arms, stands to the left of the enthroned Christ and the Lamb of God.[155] The Winchester "Quinity" combined features from the illustrations of the *Gloria* and the Apostles' Creed (figs. 29, 30). In the latter picture the Virgin with the dove on her head places the Christ child on a throne next to the enthroned Father.[156] The influence of the Psalter's incarnational iconography of the Virgin on this early eleventh-century book from Winchester raises the question of whether the Psalter might have been known there earlier and have influenced the placement of the doves in the Benedictional.

The correspondence between the Benedictional and the Psalter is not limited to the location of the birds. In both the Virgin also holds the Christ child in her arms. Moreover, the Psalter's illustration of the *Gloria* occurs on folio 89v, beneath a drawing of the Presentation in the Temple illustrating the canticle of Simeon (figs. 25, 28). On folio 90, directly opposite this picture of the Presentation, is the illustration of the Apostles' Creed. On folio 89, the recto of the leaf with the pictures of the Presentation and the *Gloria*, is an illustration of the *Magnificat* depicting the Virgin offering the Christ child to the hand of God emerging from clouds (fig. 31).[157]

[152] M. V. Ščepkina, *Miniatiury Khludovskoi Psaltiri* (Moscow, 1977), fol. 45, also fol. 44.

[153] Ohlgren, *Illustration*, p. 57, pl. 6.5; Temple, *Manuscripts*, pp. 74f., no. 56, fig. 167; J. Rosenthal, "The Historiated Canon Tables of the Arenberg Gospels,"(Ph.D. diss., Columbia University, 1974), pp. 219ff., 238ff., overlooks the connection to the canon texts.

[154] Kantorowicz, "Quinity"; J. O'Reilly, "St. John as a Figure of the Contemplative Life: Text and Image in the Art of the Anglo-Saxon Benedictine Reform," *Dunstan*, pp. 175–77; *Ælfwine's Prayerbook*, ed. B. Günzel, Henry Bradshaw Soci-

ety, 108 (London, 1993), pp. 12ff., pl. 2; B. Raw, "What Do We Mean by the Source of a Picture?" *England in the Eleventh Century*, ed. C. Hickes, Harlaxton Medieval Studies, 2 (Stamford, 1992), pp. 292–97; also J. A. Kidd, "*The Quinity of Winchester* Reconsidered," *Studies in Iconography* 7–8 (1981–82): 21–33; Temple, *Manuscripts*, pp. 94f., no. 77, fig. 245.

[155] *Utrecht*, fol. 89v; Rosenthal, "Arenberg Gospels," pp. 219ff.

[156] Kantorowicz, "Quinity," pp. 109f., pl. 28, figs. 1, 13, 14.

[157] *Utrecht*, fols. 89–90.

This group of the mother and child was obviously excerpted from a Presentation. On these three successive pages of the Utrecht Psalter are a scene of the Presentation and other images of the Virgin holding the child with features that correspond to the innovations of the Benedictional's Presentation miniature—the dove upon her head and the hand of God emerging from clouds to accept her offering. The Benedictional's illuminators must have had the Utrecht Psalter (or a copy of it) before them,[158] and they imaginatively combined different motifs from its sequence of images to create their own unusual iconography of the Presentation. The particular Anglo-Saxon fascination with the Psalter's drawings for the *Gloria* and *Credo* originated in the Benedictional.

The explanation of why these motifs from the Psalter were incorporated into the miniature of the Presentation lies in the text of the blessing for the feast of Purification, which the picture prefaces and illustrates:

> May almighty God, who on this day wanted his only begotten [Son] to be presented in the temple in the flesh that he had assumed, make you, supported by the gift of his blessing, to be adorned with good works. Amen.
>
> And may he, who wanted him [Christ] to be made a servant of the law in order to fulfill it, instruct your minds in the spiritual teachings of his law. Amen.
>
> So that you might be able to offer him gifts of chastity in place of turtle doves and that you may be enriched with the gifts of the Holy Spirit in place of young doves. Amen.[159]

The basic themes of this tripartite prayer are the relationship of the Presentation to the Old Law and the consequences of this relationship for mankind. The first paragraph establishes that the Christ who was presented in the temple

is God's divine Son in assumed human flesh. The second and central paragraph succinctly expresses the concept (cf. Matt. 5:17, Gal. 4:4–7) that because of his godhood the incarnate Christ was exempt from the Old Law that had hitherto bound other men, who were purely human. Nonetheless, at his Circumcision and Presentation in the Temple, Christ had willingly submitted to the rites of the Old Law, becoming a voluntary "servant of the law" to redeem ordinary men from literal obligation to it. Hence mankind is instructed in the "spiritual" rather than the literal "teachings of the law." The flanking first and third paragraphs of the benediction give specific examples of the reinterpretation of the Old Law that Christ's deed had made possible: the material offerings of the first-born child and the birds, both mandated by the law, are replaced respectively by the believers' spiritual offerings of good works and virtues such as chastity.

Although the blessing does not mention the Virgin, its themes also concern her. Commentators[160] pointed out that the Incarnation had relieved Mary as well as Christ of any obligation to the Old Law. Since the grace of the Holy Ghost had purified her of any sin and allowed her to remain unblemished after conceiving Christ, she had no need of the ritual purification other new mothers required. Like Christ, she was thought to have submitted to the Old Law at the Presentation as a voluntary act of condescension for the salvation of ordinary humanity.

In the light of these ideas we can now begin to see some connection between the Benedictional's text and its unusual iconography. The close physical association between the birds and Mary emphasized that the birds are the purificatory offerings that Mosaic law required of her. According to the Benedictional's prayer, however, the turtle doves symbolized chastity; and although the meaning of the young doves is unstated, exegesis and the liturgy commonly

---

[158] For the question of how the Psalter might have been known at Æthelwold's Winchester, see chap. 4.

[159] *CBP*, no. 1674; Warner and Wilson, *Ben.*, p. 11:

Omnipotens deus qui unigenitum suum hodierna die in assumpta carne in templo uoluit praesentari, benedictionis suae uos munere fultos bonis operibus faciat exornari. Amen.

Quique eum ut legem adimpleret ministrum uoluit effici legis, mentes uestras instruat legis suae spiritalibus documentis. Amen.

Quo ei et pro turturibus castitatis munera offerre ualeatis, et pro pullis columbarum spiritus sancti donis exuberetis. Amen.

[160] E.g., Bede, *In Lucam*, 1, p. 62, and *Hom.* 1, 18, p. 180; Vercelli Homily 17, ed. P. E. Szarmach, *The Vercelli Homilies 9–23*, Toronto Old English Series, 5 (Toronto, 1981), pp. 51f.; Hrabanus Maurus, *Homilia* 8, PL, 110, col. 19D; Haymo of Auxerre, *Homilia* 14, PL, 118, col. 99B. See Clayton, *Cult*, pp. 218ff.

equated them with simplicity or innocence.[161] Hence the birds' physical relationship to Mary stressed her purity after the birth of the child she holds. Moreover, the location of the sacrificial birds over her head visually alluded to the dove of the Holy Spirit coming over her at the Incarnation. This incarnational allusion illustrated the blessing's first paragraph, reminding viewers of just how the only begotten Son of God presented in the temple had assumed his human flesh, and at the same time it indicated that the Virgin's pure conception of Christ had transformed the Old Law's obligatory material sacrifice for impurity into the New Law's voluntary spiritual gift of chastity and innocence.

The blessing's third paragraph states that the believers' offerings of moral virtues are directed to God, who will in turn reward the offerers with the "gifts of the Holy Spirit." This reward is in fact one of the godly blessings that the liturgical benediction calls down upon the believers, a point underlined by the parallelism between the "gifts of the Holy Spirit" in the last paragraph and the "gift of his [God's] blessing" in the first.[162] The benediction envisions an exchange of gifts: for the believers' moral offerings or sacrifices, symbolized by the birds, God gives the believers his benediction, the gifts of the Holy Spirit. Of course the Spirit of God had appeared at the Baptism "descending as a dove [Spiritum Dei descendentem sicut columbam]" (Matt. 3:16) (cf. pl. 19); thus the sacred gifts exchanged in the prayer are really birds of a feather. The wording of the Latin benediction makes inescapable the idea that the offertory doves are traded for the dove of the Holy Spirit, for *columbarum* is directly followed by *spiritus sancti*: "pro pullis columbarum spiritus sancti donis."

The Benedictional's makers were clearly sensitive to all the text's subtleties and imaginatively visualized them. The birds, because of the incarnational connotations of their position over Mary, symbolized both the offering and the

reward—the Holy Spirit. Furthermore, the text's emphasis on these offerings to God and his return "gift" led the painters to include the *dextera Dei* in the composition. Like the birds, this was a multivalent motif. It signified the Lord's acceptance of the offering of the birds and the moral virtues they represented, but the hand's gesture was also one of speech and benediction (cf. pls. 8, 35). Hence it also signified that God, as recompense for the moral sacrifices represented by the doves, would bestow his benediction upon the donors, the believers who took the events of the Presentation as "spiritual teachings." The birds and the hand are perfectly complementary, for each simultaneously represents both the giving and the receiving of a gift.

Unlike earlier representations of the Presentation that show the bearer of the doves waiting his or her turn behind the Virgin, (figs. 13, 23–25), the Winchester composition emphasizes the offering of the birds as an event simultaneous with and parallel to the presentation of the Christ child. Some later depictions also imply a correspondence between the two offerings. In the eleventh-century Echternach lectionary of Henry III (Bremen, Staatsbibl., MS b. 21; fig. 32),[163] for instance, the position of the doves held by the Virgin on one side of the altar mirrors the placement of Christ held by Simeon on the other side. What did this parallelism between the birds and Christ signify?

Though biblical law specified that the birds were to have been sacrificed on behalf of the mother, commentators also referred them to Christ. In a Purification homily Ambrosius Autpertus (d. 778),[164] for example, said the offering of the birds to God prefigured the sacrifice of Christ in the Passion and in the sacraments of the Church as well as diurnal virtuous offerings of the elect, the members of Christ, who present their mortified "bodies a living sacrifice, holy, pleasing unto God" (Rom. 12:1). Some of these same typological themes also underlie the structural symmetry of the Benedictional's Presenta-

---

[161] E.g., *Vercelli*, 17, p. 52; Ælfric, *Hom.*, 1, pp. 142f.; Bede, *Hom.*, 1, 18, pp. 129f.; Hrabanus Maurus, *Homilia* 8, PL, 110, col. 20C. See also below, chap. 3, n. 217.

[162] For other benedictions equating the blessing of God and the bestowal of the Holy Spirit, see Warner and Wilson, *Ben.*, pp. 2 (*CBP*, no. 37), 6 (1566), 11 (1956), 12 (874), 24 (381), 25 (948).

[163] Plotzek, *Perikopenbuch Heinrichs III.*, pp. 130ff.; also

Boeckler, *Evangelienbuch Heinrichs III.*, pp. 24, 50, fig. 113. See also H. Maguire, "The Iconography of Symeon with the Christ Child in Byzantine Art," *DOP* 34–35 (1980–81): 262f.

[164] Ambrosius Autpertus, *In Purificatione Sanctae Mariae*, 5, ed. R. Weber, CCCM, 27B, p. 989; for Anglo-Saxon manuscripts with this homily, see Clayton, *Cult*, pp. 24, also 218f. See also Bede, *Hom.*, 1, 18, pp. 181f.

tion text: the presentation of Christ in the first paragraph balances the offering of the birds, which symbolize the chaste virtue of the believers, in the last one.

Traditionally artists had portrayed the sacrificial typology of Christ's presentation by positioning him over or on the altar (figs. 13, 23–25). The Anglo-Saxon illuminators adopted this device, but influenced by the accompanying blessing and related exegesis, they went further and illustrated the relation of the birds to this typology. The iconographic parallelism between the offerings of the doves and Christ signified that both prefigured the sacrifice of Christ on the cross and the altar of the church, as well as the believers' participation in Christ's sacrifice through the Eucharist and the daily self-offerings of chastity and other virtues.

The issue of sacramental symbolism brings us to what is surely the miniature's most unusual, if not eccentric, feature, the covered altar (fig. 33). Homburger[165] noticed that the altar cloth resembles two human arms covered in drapery! A comparison with the draped arms of the angel standing behind John in the scene of the Baptism (pl. 19) confirms this. The hollow between the arms, the flex at the elbow, and the gathering of the drapery at the clenched hands can all be recognized in the altar cloth.

Homburger assumed that the illuminators mistakenly confused the altar's draped top with Simeon's veiled arms. The arms of the altar do seem to emerge from between the arms of the high priest, but this was not necessarily the result of an error. In a manuscript of the highest quality like the Benedictional, such a gross mistake is unlikely. Despite the association between the altar and Simeon, there is no actual confusion between them: the blue cloth over the prophet's arms is clearly distinguished by both line and color from the gold one over the altar. The underdrawing, which flaking has exposed in many places, also raises doubts that this feature is a mistake. For the most part, the finished painting seems to have followed the preliminary drawing, but it did deviate at one place. In the large flaked patch within the foremost arm of the altar is a straight line of red underdrawing that slants slightly upward toward the Virgin.

This cannot have corresponded to any part of the completed painting, which must have shown a smooth oval of drapery in this area. This underdrawing evidently depicted a diagonally receding side of a rectangular altar top turned at an angle to the picture plane, like the altar in the miniature of the Bishop Blessing the Congregation (pl. 35). The painters seem to have originally designed a conventional geometric altar, but had second thoughts and redrew it in the form of veiled human arms. Far from being an error, the anthropomorphic altar resulted from deliberation, and it must have meaning.

The likeness between the altar and Simeon's arms strengthened the sacramental typology of Christ's presentation to the prophet. In earlier images, the symbolic placement of Christ above or on the altar as Simeon received him implied an analogy between the altar and the prophet's arms. Just as Simeon's arms were veiled so that their direct physical contact did not defile the sacred person of Christ, so the altar was covered because it too received Christ—in the form of the Eucharist.[166] Thus one reason the altar was represented as veiled arms was to indicate that the reception of Christ in the prophet's arms prefigured the placement of the Eucharist on the church altar.

Our interpretation of the altar should also take into account its other features. If its upper half has assumed an animate, living form, its lower half has remained decidedly inanimate, almost architectural in character. The altar is on axis with the frame's inner column, and both the altar and the column's capital are similarly constructed of multicolored architectural moldings. The omission of the lower part of the column creates the illusion that the base of the altar is the base of the column. One motivation for this must have been aesthetic. Throughout the manuscript, frame and picture are fused into a unified decorative design. In this miniature, however, the column is not simply ornamental, for it characterized the setting of the Presentation as the interior of the temple of Jerusalem. The altar takes the place of the column base of the Jewish temple. Finally, the altar is turned at an angle to the picture plane so that its corner is prominently displayed. In sum, this altar is "liv-

---

[165] Homburger, *Anf.*, p. 18; also Alexander, "Ben.," p. 177.

[166] Braun, *Altar*, 2, p. 22.

ing" architecture, built as a base into the temple and turned on its corner.

We have previously encountered another "altar" with similar conceptual, though not visual, characteristics—the crib in the Nativity miniature (pl. 12), which represents the cornerstone and foundation of Ecclesia constructed from the "living stones" of Christ and the faithful. The same symbolic concept seems to have been depicted in very different pictorial terms in the altar in the Presentation.

The cornerstone theme is prominent in two Carolingian homilies for the feast of the Purification known to the Anglo-Saxons. Both Ambrosius Autpertus and Haymo of Auxerre associated the location of the Presentation in the temple in Jerusalem, which was etymologically interpreted as the "vision of peace," with the cornerstone and the foundation as metaphors for the peaceable union of Christ and the faithful in the Church under the New Law. For Ambrosius[167] the coming of Christ, the "humble stone," to be offered in the temple symbolized the spread of his dispensation from the Jews to the Gentiles, the two peoples who constituted the Church, which the temple and Jerusalem foreshadowed. Haymo[168] suggested that Christ's voluntary submission to Old Testament purification rites and his entrance into the temple in Jerusalem signified that Christians must be baptismally cleansed before entering the temporal Church to partake of Christ in the Eucharist, and must purify themselves anew through a life of penance and good works to enter after death the celestial Church of heavenly Jerusalem, built with the pure "living stones" of the faithful.

These interpretations cast more light on the iconography. Since the altar is a living cornerstone and foundation built into the temple of Jerusalem, it portrays this building as the prefiguration of the terrestrial Church and its celestial counterpart, the heavenly Jerusalem. The motif also expresses that Christ's fulfillment of the Old Law at the Presentation—a theme central to the miniature's own liturgical text—had removed this legal barrier for both Jews and Gentiles, enabling them through the sacramental and moral purification of the New Law to be joined peacefully with Christ into the one living spiritual edifice of the Church, first on earth and finally in heaven.

This typology makes it evident that the Presentation, like the Nativity, was influenced by the iconography of the Galba Psalter (figs. 11, 12), for there the Christological cornerstone of Ecclesia is associated with the heavenly Jerusalem as well as the heavenly Bethlehem. The Benedictional's makers once again transposed cornerstone iconography from the heavenly realm in the Psalter to the earthly one in the Benedictional, to indicate here that the Jewish temple in Jerusalem prefigured the celestial Church and city.

In the Presentation the cornerstone is associated with Simeon's arms as well as the temple architecture, and Ambrosius' homily also helps to explain this additional feature. Upon taking Christ in his arms, Simeon said:

> Now thou dost dismiss thy servant, O Lord, according to thy word in peace; because my eyes have seen thy salvation, which thou hast prepared before the face of all peoples: a light to the revelation of the Gentiles, and the glory of thy people Israel (Luke 2:29–32).

Three features of Simeon's speech prompted Ambrosius to link it to the *topos* of the cornerstone: Christ's bringing peace, his revelation to the two peoples of Ecclesia, and his revelation to the *eyes* of Simeon. Psalm 117 (22–23), it will be recalled, had declared that the cornerstone is "wonderful in our eyes." Paraphrasing Simeon, Ambrosius wrote:

> You dismiss in peace, because according to your promise through the mystery of the incarnate Word, enmities having been cancelled, I merited to be reconciled to you. You dismiss in peace, because I see peace. For he himself is our peace, who made the two one (Eph. 2:14). Indeed, all the elect say this, they who take Christ in their arms, who perceive through eyes of faith the salvation of God. For what is it to receive Christ in the arms, but to embrace him by pious works in his members? For by arms . . . the capacity of work is expressed. . . .

---

[167] Ambrosius, *In Purificatione*, 3–4, ed. Weber, pp. 987f.

[168] Haymo, *Homilia* 14, PL 118, col. 98.

By devout actions as if by arms they daily embrace the same boy himself. . . . With the eyes of faith we have deserved to regard your salvation, that is, the Lord Jesus in his members, and with pious works we have merited to embrace him.[169]

Ambrosius equated Simeon with all the faithful who see the incarnate Christ spiritually through faith and who daily "embrace" him through good works, thereby becoming mystically one with him. A word play upon "members" (*membri*) also expressed their spiritual union. The members were simultaneously the arms of the faithful which embrace Christ and the faithful themselves who are the limbs of the corporate body of Christ. The New Testament (1 Cor. 6:15–20, 12:12–27; Rom. 12:4–5) had already used "members" in a double sense to mean both the participants in the spiritual fellowship of Christ and the Church, and the anatomical parts of the corporate body of Christ, which is the Church. Thus Ambrosius expounded Simeon's reception of Christ in terms of two different metaphors for the joining of Christ and the believers: the embracing or carrying of Christ and membership in his corporate body.

Ambrosius' quotation of part of the cornerstone passage from Ephesians alluded to still a third metaphor for the union of Christ and the faithful—their construction together into "an habitation of God in the Spirit" (Eph. 2:22). Earlier in his homily Ambrosius had explained Simeon's relation to this concept of the living edifice. Simeon, who "came by the Spirit into the temple" (Luke 2:27) to receive Christ in his arms, stood for all virtuous Christians whose

"bodies are a temple of the Holy Spirit" (cf. 1 Cor. 6:19). . . . Those ones in fact dwell in Jerusalem, and they also come into the tem-

ple in the Spirit. For they themselves . . . are Jerusalem . . . and the temple, . . . in whom and by whom Christ is received.[170]

Simeon symbolized the temple and Jerusalem, where he physically received both the Holy Spirit and Christ, and the spiritual edifice of the believers themselves, who receive the Spirit and Christ in their souls. Ambrosius quoted from a passage in Corinthians that is at the heart of his interpretation: "Know you not that your bodies are members of Christ. . . [and] that your members are the temple of the Holy Ghost? . . . Glorify and bear God in your body" (1 Cor. 6:15–20).

In visual terms the miniature's creators interpreted Simeon's reception of Christ in a comparable way. The altar, the symbol of Simeon's arms bearing the Christ child, is the cornerstone that unites Christ with all the believers—Jews and Gentiles—in the single living building of Ecclesia; the altar is also the single corporate ecclesiastic body of Christ literally animated by its arms or "members." Since the members of Christ's body—in the form of the anthropomorphic altar—are architecturally incorporated into the temple of Jerusalem, which Christ himself had likened to "the temple of his body" (John 2:21), the image literally shows that the "members are the temple."

Although the themes of the cornerstone and corporate membership were established in the exegesis of the Presentation, the commentaries on this event did not specifically identify the temple altar with either the cornerstone or the corporate body of Christ. What caused this symbolism to be focused on the altar?

The Utrecht Psalter might once again have been influential. In its drawing of the Presentation (fig. 25), thin rays emanate from the altar to a crowd of men in the lower left corner. This

[169] Ambrosius Autpertus, *In Purificatione*, 8, ed. Weber, pp. 992f.:

Dimittis in pace, quia secundum promissionem tuam per incarnati Uerbi mysterium, solutis inimicitiis, tibi merui reconciliari. Dimittis in pace, quia uideo pacem. "Ipse enim est pax nostra, qui fecit utraque unum." Hoc denique et omnes electi dicunt qui Christum in ulnas suscipiunt, qui fidei oculis salutare Dei conspiciunt. Quid enim est Christum in ulnas suscipere, nisi piis hunc operibus in membris suis amplectere? Per ulnas . . . uirtus operationis exprimitur. . . . Deuotis ac-

tionibus tamquam brachiis cotidie eundem ipsum puerum amplectuntur. . . . Fidei oculis salutare tuum, id est Dominum Iesum Christum in membris eius intueri, eumque piis operibus amplectere meruimus.

[170] Ambrosius Autpertus, *In Purificatione*, 6, ed. Weber, pp. 990f.: "'Corpora . . . templum sunt Spiritus Sancti.' . . . Habitant etiam isti in Hierusalem, atque in Spiritu in templum, quo Christus introducitur, ueniunt. Ipsi enim sunt Hierusalem. . . et templum, . . . in quibus et a quibus Christus exciptur." See also Origen, *Homilia in Lucam* 15, ed. M. Rauer, *Origenes Werke*, 9, 2nd ed. (Berlin, 1959), p. 93.

detail illustrates a verse of the accompanying text of the canticle of Simeon: "my eyes have seen your salvation, which you have prepared before the face of all peoples: a light to the revelation of the Gentiles, and the glory of your people Israel" (Luke 2:29). The rays are the light of Christ's revelation illuminating the Gentiles, who are balanced on the right by a group of Jews holding palms. The radiation from the altar rather than from Christ suggests that his revelation and offering to Simeon at the altar of the temple prefigured his revelation to the faithful at the altar of the Church and that the Gentiles have gained admission to the altar of Ecclesia because Christ had fulfilled the Old Law at the Presentation. Although they did so in entirely different ways, both the Psalter and the Benedictional identified the altar with Christ to convey the typological and ecclesiological meaning of the Presentation.[171]

More important than the Psalter, however, were the various symbolic values generally assigned to the Christian altar and its covering. Since the altar was thought to symbolize the body[172] as well as the cornerstone and foundation of Christ, the Jewish altar, as the prefiguration of the Christian one, was also associated with all these meanings. The altar in the miniature is covered with a gold cloth, the corporale, which commentators interpreted as the believers or the members of Christ who received his body in themselves and "clothed" him through their good works and chastity.[173] This symbolism bears directly on the relationship between the draped anthropomorphic altar and the covered arms of Simeon, for Simeon's reception of Christ in his arms also signified the "members" embracing and vesting Christ through virtuous acts. Haymo of Auxerre, for instance, commented that

> Ecclesia carries spiritually in good works him whom Simeon carried physically in his hands: because by the hand and the arms are understood works, as the apostle Paul advised and said: "Glorify and carry the Lord in your body" (1 Cor. 6:20). . . . Figuratively, however, when the old man carried [the Christ child], this signifies to us that we, putting off the old man with his deeds, should carry and put on the new one, that is Christ (cf. Col. 3:9–10).[174]

Haymo's remarks, part of the same homily that associated Christ in the temple with the "living stones" of Ecclesia, disclose still another reason for the assimilation of the draped altar to Simeon's arms: both symbolized the "members" whom good works make worthy to embrace and clothe Christ, thereby becoming a limb of his corporate body. Interest in this vesting symbolism might well have been aroused by the miniature's own text which asks God, who presented his Son in the temple, to make the faithful "to be adorned with good works."

One other idea that contributed to this iconography is the symbolic concept of the altar as the heart of the believer.[175] Elaborating on the theme that God dwells in the hearts of the faithful who are holy temples of God (cf. 1 Cor. 3:17), Augustine[176] explained that the altar within this corporeal temple was the heart on which the believer offered self-sacrifices of pure body, mind, and deeds to God. The purpose of these sacrifices was to enable the offerer to "cling to" (*in-*

---

[171] The altar in the Psalter is turned at an angle, like the one in the Benedictional, and the Psalter illustrates the cornerstone metaphor of Psalm 117:22 with the motif of men placing a stone in the corner of a foreshortened building (*Utrecht*, fol. 67v). Since such foreshortenings are no rarity in the manuscript (cf. *Utrecht*, fols. 2v, 8, 11, 13, etc.), it would be unwarranted to assume any intent to assimilate the altar to the cornerstone in the Psalter.

[172] Braun, *Altar*, 1, p. 751; also Sicard of Cremona, *Mitrale*, 1, 3, PL, 213, cols. 18D–19B.

[173] L. Eisenhofer, *Handbuch der katholischen Liturgik* (Freiburg im Breisgau, 1932), 1, pp. 357f. Cf. Durandus, *Pontificale*, 11, 11, ed. M. Andrieu, *Le Pontifical romain au Moyen-Age* (Vatican City, 1940), 3, pp. 355f.

[174] Haymo, *Homilia* 14, PL, 118, col. 105C:
Portat autem spiritualiter Ecclesia in bonis operibus,

quem Simeon portauit corporaliter in manibus: quia per manus et brachia opera intelliguntur, monente Paulo Apostolo ac dicente: "Glorificate et portate Dominum in corde [*sic* corpore] uestro." . . . Figurate autem cum senex portat, innuit nobis ut ueterem hominem cum actibus suis exuentes, portemus et induamus nouum, id est Christum.
Also Bede, *In Lucam*, 1, p. 66, repeated by Smaragdus, *In Octaua Natiuitas Domini*, PL, 102, col. 62A.

[175] J. Sauer, *Symbolik des Kirchengebäudes und seiner Ausstattung in der Auffassung des Mittelalters*, 2nd ed. (Freiburg im Breisgau, 1924), pp. 162f.; Braun, *Altar*, 1, p. 753.

[176] Augustine, *De Civitate Dei*, 10, 3–6, ed. and tr. D. S. Wiesen, Loeb Classical Library (Cambridge, Mass., 1968), 3, pp. 261–77.

haerere) or "embrace" (*amplecteri*) God. Bede[177] adopted this interpretation to expound the typological significance of the altars of the Jewish tabernacle and temple. From here it was but a short step to apply it to Christ's Presentation, which concerned both sacrifice in the temple and the relationship between the Old and the New Law. Thus in his homily on the Presentation, Bede compared the chaste birds sacrificed on the temple altars to the innocence, chastity, and compunction by which the faithful offer themselves to the Lord on the "altar of the heart."[178]

This interpretation of the birds is essentially the same as that of the Benedictional miniature's text, which asked God to instruct the believers in the "spiritual teachings" of his law so they might offer him "gifts of chastity in place of turtle doves" and be enriched with the "gifts of the Holy Spirit in place of young doves." Though no altar is mentioned, the painters would have known that under the Old Law the birds were offered on the temple altar, and they would have recognized that spiritual counterparts of these birds under the New Law—the believer's self-offerings of chastity and other virtues—were to be sacrificed on an equivalent spiritual altar. The anthropomorphic form of the temple altar indicated that the material Jewish altar foreshadowed the spiritual Christian one within the believer himself. At the same time this animate altar is the cornerstone and foundation of the living edifice of Christ and his members; therefore, it also expressed that the altar of the heart was within the spiritual temple of the member's body, equivalent to the temple of Christ's body. The members were portrayed "as living stones built up, a spiritual house, a holy priesthood, to offer up spiritual sacrifices, acceptable to God by Jesus Christ," who is "the chief cornerstone" (1 Peter 2:5, 6). In the final analysis, the miniature's own text was the prime literary inspiration for its extraordinary altar.

The Symbolic Relationship to Other Scenes

The Presentation shares with the Nativity (pl. 12) the theme of the faithful servant who witnesses and proclaims the advent of Christ as the saving ecclesiastic cornerstone, which is "wonderful in our eyes" (Ps. 117:23). The altar (or crib-altar) in each picture symbolizes the Christological cornerstone whose arrival has bonded together all men as "living stones" in the spiritual edifice of the Church. In the Presentation the female servant, who looks with rapt attention at Christ, and Simeon, the self-declared "servant" of the Lord (Luke 2:29), are the counterparts of the believing Hebrew midwife, who waits on Mary in the Nativity. The servants at the two events are connected by the Protevangelium, which modeled the midwife's acclamation of Christ's birth ("my eyes have seen wonderful things; for salvation is born to Israel")[179] after Simeon's acknowledgment of Christ's coming ("my eyes have seen your salvation, . . . the glory of your people Israel" [Luke 2:29–30]). Like Simeon, the female servants in both scenes represent "all the elect . . . who . . . perceive the salvation of God [i.e., Christ] through eyes of faith."[180]

Altar symbolism also associates the Presentation with the Annunciation (pl. 8), where Mary beneath the baldachin is another symbol of the living church and its spiritual altar, the hearts of the believers, which receive Christ.[181] The symbolic position of the doves over the Virgin in the Presentation reinforces the allusion to the Annunciation, though this scene does not actually portray the Holy Spirit upon her. The two miniatures do share, however, the motif of a blessing hand in clouds. The hand of God in the Presentation and of Gabriel in the Annunciation both symbolize on the deepest level the divine blessings bestowed through the episcopal benediction on the individual and the Church as a whole, both prefigured by the Virgin.

---

[177] *De Tabernaculo*, 2 and 3, and *De Templo*, 2, ed. D. Hurst, CC, 119A, pp. 76f., 125, 224f.; repeated by Amalarius, *Lib. Off.*, 3, 19, 17; 3, 26, 15, pp. 316, 318.

[178] Bede, *Hom.*, 1, 18, pp. 132f.; repeated in the homiliary of Paul the Deacon, ed. Grégoire, *Homéliaires*, p. 442, no. 67.

[179] Protevangelium, 19, 2, ed. Hennecke, p. 384.

[180] See above, n. 169.

[181] In the late-eleventh-century Bohemian Coronation Gospels in Prague, the repetition of the motif of a Christian altar, with crosses, candles, and the Eucharist, associates scenes of the Annunciation (fig. 6) and the Presentation; Mašín, *Codex Vyšehradensis*, p. 21, fols. 19b, 20b.

The Presentation is also tied to other infancy scenes by the lack of a nimbus for the Virgin. It seems a strange contradiction that the illuminators omitted this prominent and obvious attribute of her sanctity even as they exercised so much ingenuity and subtlety portraying her purity and holiness symbolically with the doves. That Christ and even Simeon are haloed makes the omission all the more curious. It is true that in two other miniatures, the Naming of Christ and the Adoration of the Magi (pls. 16, 18), she is also unnimbed, but in three more—the Nativity, the Ascension, and the Dormition (pls. 12, 25, 34)—she has a gold halo. The omission of her nimbus in the three infancy scenes could be attributed to carelessness. While this explanation might be acceptable in the case of a lesser personage such as Joseph[182] or in other manuscripts in which the pictures in the cycle are not interrelated, it is not entirely satisfactory for the Virgin in the Benedictional. If anything, her unique nimbus of clouds in the Annunciation seems to suggest that the manuscript's makers had a particular interest in her relationship to the halo.

In the trio of infancy miniatures in which she is unnimbed she holds the Christ child, while in those in which she is nimbed there is no physical contact, even when he is present. The three scenes also share the same Christ type: the small human child who is at the same time the hieratically posed divine teacher holding a gold book and wearing a mantle and gold tunic. As we have seen, this figural type expressed the dogma of Christ's two natures, while his physical contact with his human mother further emphasized his humanity. There is a correlation between the Virgin's lack of a nimbus and her inclusion in an incarnational grouping with her child.

The significance of this becomes apparent if the meaning of the physical intimacy between Christ and the Virgin is considered from her point of view as well as his. Their contact showed not only that he, a divinity, shared his mother's humanity, but also that she, a human, was the mother of God. Because she had been uniquely honored to bear a divinity, she was also privileged to come into physical contact with the godhood on subsequent occasions. For any human it was a mark of special distinction to touch or even see a god. So Haymo wrote that "blessed indeed [was] Simeon, who merited not only to see but to carry Christ in the flesh."[183] The sacredness of the Lord's person is evident in the miniature of the Presentation, where Simeon, despite the fact that he is "just and devout" and filled with the Holy Ghost (Luke 2:25), must hold the divine child with covered hands, so that direct contact with his ordinary, impure human flesh will not defile the immaculate incarnate Lord.[184] In marked contrast, the Virgin holds Christ in her bare hands. The mother of God and a virgin before and after his birth, she still shares the same uniquely pure human flesh with him—her bare hands do not debase his divinity. The doves above her, which symbolize her chastity and her incarnational sanctification by the Holy Spirit, leave the viewer in no doubt about why she has this singular honor of direct physical contact with the divinity.

The Annunciation scene showed that the Virgin was entitled to wear the nimbus, the external sign of her eminence and sanctity, because of her physical conception of the divine Christ. The illuminators seem to have regarded the halo in her case to be a specifically incarnational symbol. They apparently reasoned that the Virgin did not require this attribute in images where her renewed physical intimacy with her divine son proclaimed her privileged and sanctified status as the pure mother of God: her direct corporeal contact with his sacred person was the best sign of her singular sanctity. Paradoxically, the absence of her halo heightened the viewer's awareness of both the incarnational import of the group of the Virgin and child and the symbolic, dogmatic relationship of this group to her representation in the Annunciation, where her special cloud nimbus demonstrated the incarnational origin of her holiness.

We have already seen that in the Drogo Sacra-

---

[182] He is nimbed in the Nativity but not in the Presentation.

[183] Haymo of Auxerre, *Homilia* 14, PL, 118, col. 105B: "Felix quidem Simeon, qui non solum uidere, sed etiam Christum portare meruit in carne."

[184] A few Byzantine images show Simeon's hands bare to illustrate the liturgical theme that Christ blessed them; J. T. Cummings, "The Hands of Simeon: The Presentation Scene at Ligurio and in Manuscripts from Mt. Athos," *Manuscripta* 21 (1971): 49–51.

mentary the scenes of the Circumcision (for the Octave of Christmas) and the Adoration were also linked by the repetition of the figural group of the Virgin and child (figs. 19, 22). Mary does not rest the child directly on her lap, as might be expected, but holds him in her cupped hands, much the same way as in the Sacramentary's depiction of the Presentation (fig. 23). The three scenes also correspond in the pose and costume of the Christ child.[185] Moreover, the Presentation and the Circumcision include similar attendants holding ritual paraphernalia, and still other servants interrelate the birth scenes of the Baptist and Christ (figs. 16, 18). As in the Benedictional, the group of the Virgin and child as well as the servant are leitmotifs relating the Presentation to a variety of other infancy scenes.

The midwife in the Benedictional's Nativity was certainly copied from a model made by the Metz workshop that produced the Drogo Sacramentary; hence there can be little doubt that this Metz model was the source of the idea of using the motifs of the servant and the group of the Virgin and child to link infancy pictures. Characteristically, the Benedictional's illuminators improved upon their exemplar. The omission of the Virgin's nimbus reinforced the resemblances between the groups of the mother and child and at the same time related them to the incarnational imagery of the Annunciation. Moreover, the addition of cornerstone symbolism to both the Presentation and the Nativity strengthened and deepened the association between witnessing servants in these scenes.

The Baptism of Christ (Epiphany, 6 January)

The many similarities to the Baptism on the Brunswick casket (figs. 34, 35) make obvious the heavy dependence of the Benedictional's miniature (pl. 19) on a model from the later Metz school.[186] Yet this dependence did not prevent the Anglo-Saxon painters from introducing some significant changes. Besides adjusting a horizontal composition to the vertical format of a full page,[187] they added the diadems and scepters the flying angels bestow on Christ[188] and the knotted girdle of John the Baptist.

THE DIADEMS AND SCEPTERS

The angels investing Christ with the regalia characterize his Baptism as a coronation. The regal significance of the occasion was already implicit in the Gospels, which applied technical terminology of royal consecration and enthronement to the event.[189] In many Eastern baptismal rites the initiate after his immersion was crowned and hailed in a manner recalling the acclamations at a royal coronation.[190] Early Christian

---

[185] See also the silver casket of Paschal I (817–824) from the Sancta Sanctorum, where the unusual enthroned Virgin with the child in the Presentation was patterned after the similar group in the adjacent Adoration scene; H. Grisar, *Die Römische Kapelle Sancta Sanctorum und ihr Schatz* (Freiburg im Breisgau, 1908), p. 81, fig. 38.

[186] Regarding the copy relation to the casket, see Appendix Two.

[187] See Appendix Two.

[188] While the angels on the casket lid over the Baptism are empty-handed, the angel above the Nativity (figs. 37, 7) holds a short scepter in its right hand. Pächt, *St. Albans Psalter*, pp. 54f., associated this angel with the Nativity, but it flies from the Virgin toward the Baptism on the front. Nonetheless, this angel should not be taken as evidence that angels investing Christ with royal attributes at the Baptism were already in the Metz archetype of the casket and the Benedictional. The manuscript's angels properly offer Christ the scepters, but the casket's figure inexplicably brandishes the scepter wrong-end first—inexplicably, that is, if the scepter is meant for Christ. In Carolingian art angels with scepters appear in a variety of narrative themes, such as the

Annunciation, the Women at the Tomb, the Annunciation to the Shepherds, and the Crucifixion; see Goldschmidt, *Elf.*, 1, nos. 9, 13, 14, 31, 41, 75, 95g, 138. For an Ottonian scene of the Baptism with a sceptered angel, see W. Milde, *Mittelalterliche Handschriften der Herzog August Bibliothek*, Kataloge der Herzog August Bibliothek Wolfenbüttel, Sonderband 1 (Frankfurt am Main, 1972), p. 54, pl. 27. In all these the scepter is clearly the angel's own attribute, and this must also be the case on the casket. The angel here might have been an *ad hoc* addition by the carver to adapt the model's composition to the casket's format; thus it is by no means certain whether a comparable sceptered angel was in the Benedictional's Metz model. If one was, then the Anglo-Saxon painters fundamentally altered the meaning by transferring ownership of the scepter to Christ and by adding the complementary royal insigne of a diadem.

[189] E. Klostermann, *Das Markus Evangelium*, Handbuch zum Neuen Testament, 3 (Tübingen, 1926), p. 9 (Mark 1:9–11); T. Averdson, *Das Mysterium Christi* (Upsala, 1937), pp. 123ff.

[190] E. H. Kantorowicz, *The King's Two Bodies* (Princeton, 1957), p. 490. The concept but not the practice of baptismal

art had occasionally depicted the crowning of Christ at his Baptism. On a sixth-century Eastern ivory in the British Museum (fig. 38), for instance, the dove of the Holy Spirit descends with a diadem in its beak.[191] Although this old iconography might have been known to the Winchester illuminators, it must be borne in mind that they innovated within the framework of much more recent Carolingian iconography. Their innovation should not be isolated from two other significant iconographic features that were taken over from the Metz model (cf. figs. 34, 35): the two vials of chrism in the dove's beak and the mandorla of Christ.

From the earliest times of Christianity the descent of the Holy Spirit on Christ at his Baptism was interpreted as the spiritual anointment of the incarnate Messiah.[192] To illustrate this idea, a Carolingian plaque in Antwerp (fig. 39) depicted the dove pouring over Christ a stream of holy oil from a chrismatory, the liturgical vessel for chrism. The dove bears this chrismatory to emphasize that Christ's divine unction in the Jordan was the New Testament model for the sacramental anointing that was an essential part of liturgical baptism.[193]

The representation of the dove with *two* vessels of chrism on the casket and in the Benedictional visualized the relation of baptismal anointing to Christ's dual role as *rex et sacerdos*.[194] In the Old Testament, kings and priests had received an unction, a *chrisma*, which transmitted the Holy Spirit and consecrated them to their royal or priestly offices. They were the forerunners of the Messiah Christ whose very name, *Christos*, meant "Anointed One." Unlike the anointments of most of the Old Testament predecessors, the salving of Christ by the Holy Spirit at his Baptism conferred the roles of both *rex et sacerdos* on him. Through the sacramental baptismal anointing, the ordinary individual became a new *Christos*, that is, a *Christianos* or Christian, for in baptism the catechumen was reborn as a member of the corporate body of Christ, which was also the Church. Anointing enabled one to participate mystically in Christ and in Christ's dual messianic offices, becoming a "member of a kingly priesthood" (1 Peter 2:9). Thus the Carolingian commentator Theodulf of Orléans gave this explanation of the baptismal unction:

> It is most fitting that his [Christ's] holy Church, which is indeed his body, should be a kingdom and a priesthood, and that we, who are his members, regenerated in the Church, should be both kings and priests. . . . We are priests so that we, erecting altars of faith in the holy temple of God, which we are, might offer peacemaking sacrifices of good works to him.[195]

The iconographic motif of the two vials of chrism symbolized the two messianic roles of king and priest that baptismal anointing conferred upon Christ and upon all those baptized into his ecclesiastic body.[196]

Complementing the meaning of the double chrismatory is Christ's mandorla, a rare baptis-

---

coronation was well known in the Latin West. See below, nn. 203, 205.

[191] Volbach, *Elf.*, p. 94, no. 141, pl. 74; for other examples, see M. Ross, *Catalogue of the Byzantine and Early Medieval Antiquities of the Migration Period*, 2 (Washington, 1965), pp. 35ff., no. 37.

[192] L. Koch, "Die Geistsalbung Christi bei der Taufe im Jordan in der Theologie der alten Kirche," *Benediktinische Monatsschrift* 20 (1938): 15f.

[193] Deshman, "Warmund Sacramentary," pp. 2ff.; also L. Kötzsche-Breitenbruch, "Das Elfenbeinrelief mit Taufszene aus der Sammlung Maskell im British Museum," *Jahrbuch für Antike und Christentum* 22 (1979): 200, 204f., fig. 18c.

[194] F. Oppenheimer, *The Legend of the Ste. Ampoule* (London, 1953), pp. 134ff. For the theme of *rex et sacerdos*, see J. Daniélou, *The Bible and the Liturgy* (London, 1956), pp. 114ff.; P. Dabin, *Le Sacerdoce royal des fidèles dans la tradition ancienne et moderne* (Paris, 1950); F. Kern, "Der Rex et Sacerdos in bildlicher Darstellung," *Festschrift für Dietrich Schäfer* (Jena, 1915), pp. 1ff.;

1915), pp. 1ff.; also U. Schubert, "Christus, Priester und König. Eine politisch-theologische Darstellungsweise in der frühchristlichen Kunst," *Kairos* n.s. 15 (1973): 201–36.

[195] Theodulf of Orléans, *Liber de Ordine Baptismi ad Magnum Senonensem*, 16, PL, 105, col. 235A:

> Decentissimum est ut sancta ejus Ecclesia, quae utique corpus ejus est, et regnum sit et sacerdotium, et nos in ea regenerati, qui ejus membra sumus, reges simus et sacerdotes. . . . [Sumus] sacerdotes, ut in templo Dei sancto quod sumus nos, altare fidei aedificantes, bonorum operum ei hostias pacificas offeramus.

See also Alcuin, *Epistola 134*, ed. E. Dümmler, MGH, *Epistolae* (Berlin, 1895), 4, p. 203; Jesse of Amiens, *Epistola de Baptismo*, PL, 105, col. 792B; Hrabanus Maurus, *De Clericorum Institutione*, 1, 29, PL, 107, col. 313D.

[196] The motif might also reflect the Carolingian baptismal practice of administering two unctions of chrism, both conveying the Spirit; see J. D. C. Fisher, *Christian Initiation: Baptism in the Medieval West* (London, 1965), pp. 12ff.

mal feature.[197] As a symbol of the supernatural light radiating from Christ, the mandorla stressed that Christ's Baptism was an epiphany, a manifestation of his divinity to mankind. One of the Epiphany benedictions prefaced by the miniature asks: "[O God,] allow your people to recognize the full brightness of the Redeemer himself, so that . . . they might attain perpetual splendor. . . . [May Christ] grant that your people . . . are always illumined in the brilliance of your brightness."[198] In this textual context the mandorla was also a symbol of divine Christological grace. In fact, it must have already possessed this significance in the Carolingian model, for, like the two ampullae of chrism, it illustrated 1 Peter 2:9–10: "But you are a chosen generation, a kingly priesthood, . . . a purchased people: that you may declare his virtues, who hath called you out of darkness into his marvelous light." The mandorla represented Christ's "marvelous light," the grace that his baptismal anointing poured upon mankind, enabling them to share his royal priesthood.[199]

The double chrismatory and the mandorla were not the only features of the Benedictional's Metz model that conveyed the regal and priestly significance of the Baptism. Elbern[200] demonstrated that the Baptism on the Brunswick casket is part of a comprehensive iconographic program that embraced its three other scenes. The Baptism and the Crucifixion (figs. 34–37) pictorialized the fundamental relation between baptism and Crucifixion set forth in Romans 6:3–6. This conceived baptism, which washed the believer of his sins and initiated him into a pure new Christian life, as a mystic typological, liturgical participation in Christ's death and resurrection. The alignment of the baptized Christ on the casket's front panel with the crucified

Christ on the back panel illustrated that in the cleansing baptismal water the old sinful man was "crucified" (Romans 6:6) with Christ to be reborn a pure new man with the resurrected Savior.[201]

Particularly important for our study is a previously unnoticed point: the symbolic parallelism between the casket's two scenes also encompasses their lid panels. Opposite the dove descending with the ampullae to anoint Christ king and priest in the Jordan is the hand of God (assisted by an angel), descending with a wreath to crown him on the cross. The wreath symbolized Christ's victory over death, personified by the serpent subjugated beneath his feet, and also Christ's subsequent royal exaltation on the heavenly throne beside the Father.[202] That Christ is crowned with the wreath even as he acts as priest, sacrificing himself on the cross, reinforces the theme of his dual consecration as king *and* priest at his Baptism.

The casket's emphasis on Christ's royal priesthood at his Baptism and his Crucifixion is elucidated by Carolingian baptismal commentaries. Theodulf of Orléans, for example, offered the following explanation of why the covering placed upon the initiate's head after his baptismal anointing symbolized the "diadem of kingship" and the priestly veil:

> Since our same Redeemer [was] a king, . . . who triumphed marvelously over the devil, death and the world, and a priest, . . . who offered himself to God the Father in sacrifice, it is most fitting that his holy Church, which indeed is his body, should be the kingdom and the priesthood, and we, regenerated in it, who are his members, should be kings and priests.[203]

---

[197] Besides the Benedictional, the casket, and the Cranenburg situla (fig. 210; see Appendix Two), only an eleventh-century ivory in Agram from the region of Cologne includes this detail; see Goldschmidt, *Elf.*, 2, no. 62, pl. 21.

[198] *CBP*, no. 1087; Warner and Wilson, *Ben.*, p. 8: "Da plebi tuae redemptoris sui plenum cognoscere fulgorem, ut . . . ad perpetuam claritatem perueniat. . . . [Christus] tribue populis tuis . . . splendore gratiae tuae semper accendae [accende]."

[199] The inclusion of a chrismatory as well as a mandorla in the Baptism scene on the Agram plaque (see n. 197) also demonstrates the connection to the two motifs. The mandorla might also illustrate one of the legends that light or fire appeared during the Baptism; J. Squilbeck, "Le Jourdain

dans l'iconographie médiévale du baptême du Christ," *Bulletin des Musées Royaux d'Art et d'Histoire*, ser. 4, 38–39 (1966–67): 74.

[200] Elbern, "Elfenbeinkästen," pp. 14ff.

[201] See also the Cranenburg situla (cf. Appendix Two), where the Crucifixion is directly above the Baptism (fig. 210).

[202] Deshman, "Kingship," pp. 375ff.; idem, "Exalted Servant," pp. 392ff.; J. Reil, *Christus am Kreuz in der Bildkunst der Karolingerzeit* (Leipzig, 1930), pp. 82f., 85ff., 92f.

[203] Theodulf of Orléans, *Liber de Ordine Baptismi*, 16, PL, 105, cols. 234D–235A:

Quia igitur idem Redemptor noster [erat] rex, . . . qui diabolum, mortem, et mundum mirifice triumphauit: et

The parallelism between the casket's two scenes signified that Christ's baptismal hallowing as king and priest was appropriate because of his sacrificial victory on the cross, and that through the sacramental baptismal anointing, the members of his body—the Church—shared his dual consecration.

Tenth-century Anglo-Saxons were doubtless familiar with the basic theological and liturgical tenets embodied in this Metz imagery. Theodulf's popular baptismal treatise was known to them,[204] and Wulfstan, bishop of London (996–1002) and archbishop of York (1002–1023), repeated the common Carolingian interpretation of the covering placed on the head after the baptismal anointing as a "diadem of kingship" and a priestly insigne.[205]

The immediate inspiration of the Benedictional's innovation was the Metz model's stress on the anointing of Christ and his members as *rex et sacerdos*. The painters interpolated the regal attributes of the diadem and scepter to reinforce the royal significance of the double containers of chrism. In the Metz workshop the double chrismatory and the wreath, the equivalent of the diadem, were already considered analogous and complementary emblems of royal consecration, as their juxtaposition on the casket's lid demonstrates. Of course, the casket itself was not the Benedictional's model, nor does the Winchester manuscript portray the Crucifixion. However, the picture cycle of the common Metz archetype of the ivory and the Benedictional might well have included the Crucifixion as well as the other three New Testament themes found on the casket. If so, then an image of the coronation of the crucified Christ in the Metz model[206] stimulated the Benedictional's illuminators to transfer the crowning motif to the symbolically associated iconography of the Baptism.

THE GIRDLE OF JOHN THE BAPTIST

A second novel feature of the Benedictional's iconography is the knotted form of blue girdle around John's waist. Although the Gospels (Matt. 3:4; Mark 1:6) said he wore a camel's hair garment with a leather girdle about his loins, earlier representations usually did not show him girded. A significant exception, however, is the Baptism scene on the Metz ivory cover of the Drogo Sacramentary[207] (fig. 40), where a broad band cinches a long tunic of skins rather than an exomis. The Metz prototype of the Benedictional might already have combined a girdle with an exomis. Even if this were so, the girdle in the Benedictional would still differ because of its prominent knot, a small but significant detail probably added by the Winchester painters.[208]

This knot is identical to the type that often ties Christ's loincloth in Crucifixion images such as the one on a Rhenish enamel cross of ca. 1000 in Essen (fig. 41).[209] The loincloth here has two parts, a darker girdle knotted about the lighter loincloth. The Benedictional's makers probably intended to liken the Baptist's girded costume to the crucified Christ's loincloth. A similar motif occurs in a miniature in a mid-eleventh-century Salzburg Gospels (New York, Morgan Lib., MS 781; fig. 42),[210] where both the knot in John's girdle and the slits in his garment clearly give the impression of a loincloth.

This curious iconography finds an explanation in a homily by Bede that interpreted the Baptist's rough garments in penitential and Christological terms. Bede suggested that the camel-hair vestment represented those who remove sins through penitence, and that the

> leather girdle signifies those who "have crucified their flesh with vices and concupiscences" (Gal. 5:24). And because it is

---

[erat] sacerdos, . . . qui se Deo Patri in sacrificium obtulit: decentissimum est ut sancta ejus Ecclesia, quae utique corpus ejus est, et regnum sit et sacerdotium, et nos in ea regenerati, qui ejus membra sumus, reges simus et sacerdotes.

[204] It is found in a late-tenth-century Canterbury manuscript, London, British Lib., MS Royal 8. C. III, fols. 26v–50; Gneuss, "List," p. 31, no. 475.

[205] *The Homilies of Wulfstan*, ed. D. Bethurum (Oxford, 1957), p. 171, line 59. See also the Carolingian commentators Magnus of Sens (PL, 102, col. 983); Jesse of Amiens (PL, 105, col. 792); Alcuin (MGH, Ep., 4, p. 203); also above, n. 203.

[206] The crowning of the Christ at the Crucifixion by angels

or a dove occurs in two eleventh-century Anglo-Saxon works: an ivory in Brussels and the so-called Sherborne Missal, which originated in Winchester; Raw, *Crucifixion*, pp. 195f., 197f., pls. 3a, 12b.

[207] Goldschmidt, *Elf.*, 1, pp. 41f., no. 74a, pl. 30.

[208] One other unusual, unexplained feature is the division of the exomis into two parts, clipped above the girdle and shaggy below.

[209] H. Schnitzler, *Rheinische Schatzkammer* (Düsseldorf, 1957), pp. 32f., no. 44, fig. 149.

[210] G. Swarzenski, *Die Salzburger Malerei von den ersten Anfängen bis zur Blütezeit des romanischen Stils*, 2nd ed. (Stuttgart, 1969), pp. 33f., pl. 15, fig. 46.

written, "Therefore as many of you as have been baptized in Christ have put on Christ" (Gal. 3:27), when such people cling to Christ with the concentration of zealous love, they are, as it were, clothed with camel's hair, and they gird their loins with a leather girdle.[211]

Bede has applied to John's costume the Pauline concept of liturgical baptism as a mystic death and resurrection with Christ. In the baptismal rite the "old man is crucified with him, that the body of sin may be destroyed" (Rom. 6:6); stripped of the old man and his sinful deeds, the believer clothes himself with the new man, the pure resurrected Christ (Col. 3:9–10; Gal. 3:27). The Baptist's symbolic garments identified him with both Christ crucified in the flesh and the purified faithful who through their baptism with Christ have "crucified" or mortified their flesh. Bede also implied an inversion of the Pauline metaphor of baptismal vesting: when the believers "put on Christ," they also "cling" to him.[212]

The Benedictional's illuminators concisely visualized this exegesis. The specially knotted girdle indicated that the ascetic John the Baptist was a figure of the crucified Christ in a loincloth and of those who had baptismally shared Christ's death and resurrection, thereby clothing themselves in his garment of purity.

One of the Benedictional's own texts might have been a factor in the iconography's creation. The first benediction for the feast of John the Baptist called down God's blessing through the intercession of the Baptist, who had pointed out the Lamb, so that you "might be able to be clothed in the wool of virtues, and to emulate the innocence of the very Lamb . . . by whose immolation you have been redeemed."[213] This prayer links the Lamb's Passion to concepts intrinsically baptismal. John had announced the Lamb of God while bearing witness to Christ's Baptism (John 1:29, 36), and it was through baptism that the Christian clothed himself in Christ's own garment of virtue and innocence or, in the prayer's terms, in the innocent Lamb's fleece.[214] Since the benediction uses the baptismal metaphor of the faithful vesting Christ and emphasizes that the Baptist mediates between the faithful and Christ, this prayer could easily have brought to mind the related exegesis of John's own clothing.

Another influence might have been the angels holding Christ's clothing and the chrismatory in the Metz iconography. The angels, a common baptismal motif,[215] reflected liturgical practice. The catechumen shed his old clothing before immersion and after donned a clean white garment.[216] This signified taking off the sinful old man and putting on the pure Christ—essentially symbolizing the same thing as the Baptist's girdle-loincloth. Indeed, in the Coptic baptismal liturgy the initiate leaving the font was vested about the loins with a girdle in the form of a cross.[217] The Baptist's girdle complemented the angels, a more traditional symbol of sacramental vesting.

As a mystic figure of the crucified Christ and those who with Christ "crucify" their flesh through asceticism, the girded Baptist signified the shared priesthood of Christ and baptized Christians. This sacerdotal theme was already present in the Metz model in the form of the double chrismatory that represented the priestly as well as the royal office of Christ and the believers. As the chrismatory was also symbolically associated with the Crucifixion, the Baptist's girdle-loincloth reinforced the priestly symbolism of the double chrismatory.

---

[211] Bede, *Hom.*, 1, 1, p. 5. A related passage appears in Bede, *In Marci Evangelium Expositio*, ed. D. Hurst, CC, 120, p. 441. Æthelwold owned this text; see Lapidge, "Booklists," pp. 53f., no. 2.

[212] See also Hrabanus Maurus, *Commentaria in Matthaeum*, 1, 3, PL, 107, cols. 768B, 769B–C; Paschasius Radbertus, PL, 120, col. 154B–C; and Pseudo-Bede, PL, 92, cols. 15D–16A.

[213] *CBP*, nos. 179, 275; Warner and Wilson, *Ben.*, p. 38: "Benedicat uos omnipotens deus beati iohannis baptistae intercessione. . . . Quatinus ipsius agni quem ille digito ostendit, cuius immolatione estis redempti, ita uirtutum lanis uestiri, et innocentiam ualeatis imitari."

[214] Theodulf of Orléans, *Liber de Ordine Baptismi*, 16, PL, 105, col. 234B, relates baptismal vesting to the saints who, "sicut lana alba," are Christ's clothing.

[215] J. Strzygowski, *Iconographie der Taufe Christi* (Munich, 1885), pp. 16f.; T. Klauser, "Engel," *RAC*, 5, col. 300. G. de Jerphanion, *La Voix des monuments* (Paris, 1930), p. 182, argued that the angels are simply covering their hands in reverence, but in some early medieval Latin representations they hold clearly recognizable tunics; cf. H. Belting, *Studien zur Beneventanischen Malerei* (Wiesbaden, 1968), fig. 192.

[216] Daniélou, *Bible and the Liturgy*, pp. 37ff., 49ff.

[217] H. Denzinger, *Ritus Orientalium* (1863; rpt. Graz, 1961), 1, p. 210.

The Anglo-Saxon innovations were responses to the sophisticated Metz sacramental iconography. The Baptist's costume developed the liturgical symbolism of Christ's vesting and sacerdotal anointing, while the diadems and scepters highlighted the regal aspect of the unction. The Carolingian imagery had interpreted baptism as the liturgical reenactment of Christ's death and Resurrection, and the Winchester painters reinforced this interpretation by transferring into the Baptism two features of Crucifixion iconography, the crowning of Christ and the girdle of his loincloth.[218] Stimulated by their model's rich symbolism, the illuminators made thoughtful and creative enhancements even as they copied.

The Baptism and the Infancy Miniatures

Although the Baptism depicts the inauguration of Christ's public mission, its placement opposite the Adoration of the Magi (pl. 18) suggests a relationship to this and possibly the other infancy miniatures.

The early Latin Church associated Epiphany with the Baptism and the Miracle at Cana, as well as the Adoration, but by the tenth century the Adoration had gained ascendancy over the other two themes. Nevertheless, the early connection between Epiphany and the other two events lingered in the liturgy. In the Benedictional itself the day's blessings mention all three events,[219] and undoubtedly this must have induced the illustration of the feast with both the Baptism and the Adoration.[220]

In several ways the two miniatures empha-sized their common relationship to the main theme of Epiphany, the revelation of the Christ's divinity to mankind. On both occasions heaven acknowledged Christ's theophany: at the Baptism the dove descended from the skies and the voice of God declared Christ his son; and at the Adoration a new star led the Magi to Christ. This similarity is visually expressed by the thick bands of heavenly clouds in both scenes and by the placement of the gold star and the gold dove directly over Christ. Commentators frequently interpreted the star as the Holy Spirit that had appeared as a dove at the Baptism.[221]

Matthew's Gospel (2:9) stipulates that the star "stood over where the child was," but the Benedictional's two prayers for Epiphany invested the location of the star in the miniature with additional symbolism. The first prayer says that God, "the true light," wished the guiding star to reveal his only begotten son to the people, and the second asks that the people recognize the "full light of the Redeemer," the "lux itineris."[222] The star above Christ is a symbol of Christ himself and the divine light he shed on mankind.[223] The second benediction goes on to request Christ, whose baptism had sanctified the water, to kindle the congregation with the "splendor" of his grace;[224] thus the blessing parallels the supernatural spiritual illumination that Christ bestowed on men at the Adoration and the Baptism. There is a corresponding parallelism in the images, where Christ's gold mandorla in the Baptism, a symbol of his "marvelous light" (1 Peter 2:9), is the counterpart of the gold star in the Adoration.

Subtle compositional adjustments unified the two miniatures. In the Baptism the main vertical axis with Christ and the dove was shifted to the

---

[218] Christ was sometimes depicted in a loincloth or a long tunic at his Baptism; see Goldschmidt, *Elf.*, 1, no. 27a, pl. 14; J. Baum, "Karolingische geschnittene Bergkristalle," *Frühmittelalterliche Kunst in den Alpenländern*, Akten zum III. internationalen Kongress für Frühmittelalterforschung (Olten, 1954), figs. 61, 62.

[219] Warner and Wilson, *Ben.*, pp. 7f.; *CBP*, nos. 732, 1087.

[220] Two late-tenth– or early-eleventh-century German and Italian sacramentaries illustrate Epiphany with all three themes; see *Sac. Fuld.*, pl. 16; Magnani, *Sacramentario*, pls. 9, 10.

[221] R. E. McNally, "The Three Holy Kings in Early Irish Writing," *Kyriakon. Festschrift Johannes Quasten*, ed. P. Grenfield and J. A. Jungmann (Münster, 1970), 2, pp. 672, 674, 676, 681; A. von Euw, "Darstellungen der hl. drei Könige in

Kölner Dom und ihre ikonographische Herleitung," *Kölner Domblatt* 23–24 (1964): 293ff.

[222] See above, n. 219.

[223] See also F. W. Deichmann, "Zur Erscheinung des Sternes von Bethlehem," *Vivarium. Festschrift Theodor Klauser zum 90. Geburtstag* (Münster, 1984), pp. 98–106.

[224] *CBP*, no. 1087; Warner and Wilson, *Ben.*, p. 8:

Deus . . . esto quaesumus tuae familiae, ipse lux itineris, qui stella indice clarificatus es rex salutis. Amen.

Da plebi tuae redemptoris sui plenum cognoscere fulgorem.

Et qui dignatus es hodie ad iordanis fontem fons aquae uiuae descendere, et tuo baptismate sanctificare, tribue populis tuis perpetua pace gaudere, et splendore gratiae tuae semper accendae [for accende].

left of center so that the composition mirrored as much as possible the facing one of the Adoration. The almost identical poses of the Magi and the angel to the right of John the Baptist reinforced the symmetry. With his stooped pose and covered hands, the attending angel pays homage to the Christ just as the Magi do. In the two miniatures the inhabitants of both heaven and earth acknowledge the lord and king of all creation.

These resemblances in form also had a deeper symbolic and liturgical significance. A matins antiphon in the Epiphany Office said that "today the Church is united with the heavenly bridegroom, since Christ washes her faults in the Jordan; the Magi hasten to the royal wedding with gifts."[225] The Baptism of Christ is thus the wedding of a king whose vassals bring presents. Because of the unusual pairing of the pictures, these very dependents, the Magi, could be interpreted as hurrying with their gifts toward Christ in the Jordan as well as on his mother's lap. The gold regalia given to Christ by the Magi in one picture and the hovering angels in the other illustrate the description of him as "the king of salvation" in the second Epiphany benediction, but these gifts also underscore that his wedding is royal. Indeed, the parallel gifts of multiple diadems in both scenes (and also scepters in the Baptism) characterize the nuptials as imperial.[226]

The marriage of Christ and the Church was seldom visualized in narrative form,[227] but one of the few other Baptism scenes to portray the mystic wedding does bear some relationship to the Benedictional's iconography. An Ottonian metal plaque in Baltimore once portrayed Christ in the Jordan flanked by John the Baptist and a nimbed female personification of the Church (fig. 43); Verdier plausibly suggested that the unusual presence of this figure of Ecclesia next to Christ alludes to their betrothal at the Baptism.[228] In her hand Ecclesia holds a chrismatory, the type of liturgical vessel the dove carries in the Benedictional; in both scenes matrimonial symbolism occurs in conjunction with this sacramental motif.

This dual emphasis on the matrimonial and liturgical significance of the Baptism reflects the intrinsic bond between these two aspects of the event.[229] Every time liturgical baptism sacramentally reenacted Christ's Baptism, the wedding of Christ and the Church was renewed. The baptismal waters cleansed Christ's bride anew (cf. Eph. 5:23–28), her womb—the font—was fertilized by the Holy Ghost, and she conceived and gave birth to a new child of God, the new Christian, who was incorporated into Ecclesia, the body of the celestial bridegroom. The Benedictional's iconography of the Baptism probably possessed intrinsic matrimonial connotations simply by virtue of the presence of the chrismatory, which so forcefully emphasized the scene's sacramental meaning.

These nuptial associations were very likely present in the Benedictional's Metz model, which included the motif of the chrismatory. Indeed, the Brunswick casket, which was closely connected to this model, also pictorialized this marital theme through the programmatic association of the Baptism with the Annunciation and the Nativity (figs. 1, 2, 7, 8, 34, 35). As Elbern[230] has demonstrated, the casket's two infancy scenes (as well as its Crucifixion scene) reinforced the sacramental symbolism of the Baptism: Mary symbolized Ecclesia conceiving and bearing a

---

[225] *Portiforium*, p. 12; *CAO*, 3, p. 255, no. 3095: "Hodie coelesti Sponso iuncta est Ecclesia, quoniam in Jordane lauit Christus eius crimina; currunt cum muneribus Magi ad regales nuptias." P. H. Frank, "Hodie Caelesti Sponso Iuncta est Ecclesia," *Vom christlichen Mysterium. Gesammelte Arbeiten zum Gedächtnis von Odo Casel OSB*, ed. A. Mayer, J. Quasten, and B. Neunheuser (Düsseldorf, 1951), pp. 192–226. The nuptial theme also occurred in an Epiphany introit trope in the tenth-century Winchester liturgy; see Planchart, *Repertory of Tropes at Winchester*, 2, p. 70, no. 47.

[226] The duplication of insignia also balanced the composition of the Baptism.

[227] O. Gillen, "Christus und die Sponsa," *Die christliche Kunst* 33 (1936–37): 202–24; idem, "Bräutigam u. Braut," *LCI*,

1, cols. 318–24; Schiller, *Ikon.*, 4, 1, pp. 94ff.

[228] When the plaque was later split and remounted on a portable altar, the figure of John the Baptist was severed from the Baptism. P. Verdier, "Plaques d'un *antependium* ottonien et iconographie mariale du Baptême," *Mélanges offerts à René Crozet*, ed. P. Gallais and Y.-J. Riou (Poitiers, 1966), 1, pp. 185–95; see also Gillen, "Christus und die Sponsa," p. 204.

[229] O. Casel, "Die Taufe als Brautbad der Kirche," *Jahrbuch für Liturgiewissenschaft* 5 (1925): 144ff.; idem, "Die Kirche als Braut Christi nach Schrift, Väterlehre und Liturgie," *Mysterium der Ekklesia* (Mainz, 1961), pp. 59–86.

[230] Elbern, "Elfenbeinkästen," pp. 14ff., esp. n. 33.)

new Christian in baptism. This equation between Mary and the Church was based on the belief that they both were the bride and virginal mother of Christ.[231] There was probably a similar sacramental, nuptial association among the scenes of the Baptism, Annunciation, and Nativity in the Benedictional's Metz model.

These symbolic themes also occurred in other works we have related to the Benedictional. The washing of the Christ child in a fontlike basin in the Nativity miniature of the Galba Psalter (fig. 10) had a baptismal significance.[232] In the canon table lunette facing the figure of Christ Emmanuel in the Carolingian Soissons Gospels is a depiction of the *fons vitae* which Underwood[233] showed to be a symbol of both the Virgin's womb and the baptismal font (figs. 3, 4). These juxtaposed images illustrated the analogy between the Incarnation and baptism, typologically associating the Emmanuel's incarnational advent in clouds and his sacramental coming in baptism.

The Benedictional's creators would certainly have perceived the nuptial, ecclesiological connotations of their iconographic sources, for the underlying concept of the mystic baptismal and bridal relationship between Christ and Mary as a figure of the Church was well known in late-tenth-century England.[234] Is there reason to think that these sources might have influenced the Benedictional's illuminators themselves to link the Baptism with the Annunciation and the Nativity (pls. 8,12)?

Of course we have already discovered that the two infancy scenes are associated with each other in their own right, and one of the central themes linking them is intrisically baptismal. The baptismal grace that had first enabled Christ to indwell in the believer, literally incorporating him into Christ's ecclesiastic body, also enabled Christ continually to come anew into him when he listened to godly words in the liturgy, partook of the Eucharist, and performed other virtuous acts. Thus Bede in the homily quoted above compared Christ's daily conception and

birth in the "womb" of the believer's soul by baptism to Christ's diurnal conception and nativity in Bethlehem, when the believer hearing the word is effected into the house of eternal bread.[235]

It is of some import that the cloud, which was added to the compositions of the Annunciation and Nativity to signify the coming of the Emmanuel, also was added to the Baptism and is present as well in the other Epiphany illustration, the Adoration of the Magi. In the two Epiphany pictures the cloud once again depicts the abode of divine grace that is bestowed on humanity, namely the Holy Spirit in the Baptism and the star in the Adoration. In the case of the latter miniature an association with the two other infancy scenes was clearly intended: the cloud lit by the star symbolizing Christ's divine light is the counterpart of the cloud illuminated by his godhood in the Annunciation and Nativity. Reinforcing the Adoration's connection to the Annunciation are similarities in the rendering of the Virgin. In both she is turned to the left, her left arm extended, her right arm encompassing Christ or a gold object (a paten?), and enthroned in an arched baldachin attached to a foreshortened building and surmounted by walls and towers. The allusions in the Adoration to the two incarnational scenes show that the God whom the Magi adore had assumed humanity from the Virgin.

In the Baptism the cloud once more occurs in conjunction with a symbol of Christ's supernatural light, his golden mandorla. There are two reasons to think that the painters intended the cloud and the mandorla in this image to be cognate symbols of the illuminated cloud in the three infancy miniatures. First, the cloud nimbus of the Virgin in the Annunciation was patterned after a mandorla of Christ (pl. 27). Second, the passage in the first epistle of Peter that inspired the mandorla, Christ's "marvelous light" (1 Peter 2:9), and other ecclesiological symbols in the Baptism, also relates closely to the Annunciation and the Nativity as well as to

---

[231] A. Müller, *Ecclesia-Maria*, 2nd ed., Paradosis, 5 (Freiburg, l955), pp. 196ff.; H. Coathalem, *Le Parallelisme entre la Sainte Vierge et l'église dans la tradition latine jusqu'à la fin du XIIᵉ siècle*, Analecta Gregoriana, 74 (Rome, 1954), pp. 33ff., 60ff.; L. Scheffczyk, *Das Mariengeheimnis in Frömmigkeit und Lehre der Karolingerzeit*, Erfurter theologische Studien, 5 (Leipzig, 1955), pp. 402ff., 414ff.

[232] Deshman, "Servants," pp. 33f., figs. 6, 7.

[233] Underwood, "Fountain of Life," pp. 68ff.

[234] E.g., Ælfric, *Hom.*, 2, pp. 11, 13; see also Bede, *In Lucam*, 1, p. 48.

[235] See above, n. 97. Regarding this typology, see Rahner, "Geburt Christi," passim.

a third infancy scene, the Presentation in the Temple (pl. 20).

The epistle (2:1–11) urges the believers, who "as newborn babes . . . have tasted that the Lord is sweet," to lead a pure, virtuous life because they have become God's people, sharing Christ's royal priesthood. Like Christ, who came "as to a living stone," they are also to be "as living stones built up, a spiritual house, and a holy priesthood, to offer up spiritual sacrifices, acceptable to God by Jesus Christ." Christ is "a stone of stumbling, and a rock of scandal" for disbelievers. But he is the "chief cornerstone, elect and precious" (cf. Isaiah 28:16) and "the head of the corner" (cf. Psalm 117:22) for the faithful, a "kingly priesthood . . . [and] a purchased people . . . called . . . into his marvelous light."

The strange coincidence that the baptismal iconography of the Metz prototype and the choir miniatures of the Galba Psalter (figs. 11, 12) both illustrate this passage must have set the Benedictional's creators thinking about its themes of Christ's radiance,[236] the cornerstone, and self-offering. The epistle's quotation of Psalm 117:22 probably triggered a recollection of the occurrence of the same Psalm verse in the Christmas Office, and its reference to the believers as "newborn babes" who have "tasted" the Lord likely brought to mind the Eucharistic symbolism of the Benedictional's Nativity blessing. This train of thought could easily have led to the association of the epistle and baptism with the Nativity and also other infancy events.

The addition of cognate symbols of the living spiritual altar and edifice of Ecclesia to the Annunciation, Nativity, and Presentation linked these three miniatures to the Baptism as well as to each other, especially since another symbol of the priesthood of Christ and the faithful—the girded John the Baptist—was introduced into the Baptism. The connection is particularly evident in the Nativity and Presentation, for there animate altar-buildings in one form or another visually reified the epistle's metaphor of the priesthood of Christ and his members making their spiritual self-sacrifices in a spiritual house constructed from the cornerstone of Christ and the living stones of the believers.

In assessing the relationship of the Baptism to the Presentation in the Temple, which is the very next picture in the manuscript, we should keep in mind that the Baptist with his Christological girdle and the angel with Christ's garments were allied symbols: both stood for the catechumen who after his immersion dons a glittering white garment to signify that he has stripped off the sinful old man and put on the pure Christ. In the Presentation the gold cloth covering the limbs of the altar, which not coincidentally resembles the gold garment over the arms of the angel, had a very similar meaning. The draped altar represented the veiled arms of Simeon carrying Christ, and Simeon's action symbolized, in the words of one Carolingian homilist, "that we, putting off the old man with his deeds, should carry and put on the new one, that is Christ."[237] Like the Baptist in his girdle-loin cloth, the anthropomorphic altar signified the crucified Christ and the believers who have "crucified" their sinful body (cf. Gal. 5:24) through baptism and a virtuous life and become worthy to gird the loins of their Lord.[238] Bede, for instance, equated the Jewish altar not only with the hearts of the believers but also with "the life of the righteous who daily join together to crucify their own flesh with sins and concupiscences and to offer [their bodies] a living sacrifice to God."[239]

We have found that the unusual position of doves over the Virgin in the Presentation alluded to the Incarnation, but this feature could also refer to the dove of the Holy Spirit over Christ at the Baptism. The dove's descent is mentioned in one of the texts of the Baptism miniature, the first blessing for Epiphany day:

---

[236] In the Psalter's second choir miniature the enclosure of the saints in a large mandorla surrounding Christ's smaller one illustrates the idea that his people are "in his marvelous light."

[237] See above, n. 174. Even without any association with the Presentation, the corporale of the altar was compared to the garment of purity clothing Christ and the catechumen; see Theodulf of Orléans, *De Ordine Baptismi*, 13, PL, 105, col. 233C-D.

[238] See above, pp. 48f.

[239] Bede, *De Tabernaculo*, 3, ed. Hurst, p. 125: "altare holocausti de quo supra dictum est generaliter uitam designat iustorum qui carnem suam cotidie crucifigere cum uitiis et concupiscentiis atque in hostiam uiuentem Deo offerre consuerunt." In the earlier passage to which he refers, Bede had written that the altar signified the heart of the elect (2, p. 76); thus he considered these equivalent meanings of the altar. Cf. also Amalarius (after Bede), *Lib. Off.*, 3, 19, 17, p. 316.

"And may he [God], who wished the Holy Spirit to be indicated by the dove over his only begotten [Son], give you true innocence of minds."[240] In this prayer, God sending the Spirit in the form of the dove over Christ at the Baptism is the paradigm for God bestowing his blessing, presumably also the Spirit, on the faithful who, like Christ, are endowed with innocence.[241] It seems to have occurred to the painters that the relationship of Christ to the dove of the Holy Spirit and the believers in this blessing is analogous to that of the Virgin in the Presentation prayer, where her reception of the blessings of God and her innocence also prefigure the believers' endowment with the heavenly gifts of the Spirit and virtue. There was a long-standing exegetic association between the birds at the Presentation and the dove of the Holy Spirit at the Baptism. Origen's fourteenth homily on Luke, known to the Anglo-Saxons through Paul the Deacon's homiliary, related Mary's unique virginal conception of Christ to an extraordinary new kind of offering at the Presentation: the birds were "such as the Holy Spirit, which in the form of the dove descended and came over the Savior, when he was baptized in the Jordan."[242] Origen viewed this new type of divine offering as an indication of Christ's new dispensation.

Origen's exegesis and the Benedictional's images both associated the Presentation offerings with the Baptism on the one hand and the Incarnation on the other. Underlying this twofold association is the same baptismal typology that we have already encountered in the miniatures of the Annunciation and the Nativity: the Holy Spirit's fertilization of the Virgin, allowing her to bring forth and present Christ, was mystically reenacted in liturgical baptism when the fructifying Spirit enabled Mater Ecclesia to conceive and present the Christlike believer to God. This typology was often connected to Luke's statement that Christ was presented to the Lord in the temple in accordance with the law that "every male opening the womb shall be called holy to the Lord" (Luke 2:22; Ex. 13:2). Bede, for instance, took this to mean that "none but the Lord is able to open the womb of the virgin Church to generate the sons of God by water and the Holy Spirit and therefore this male by [this] incomparable honor is able to be called holy to the Lord."[243] The dual incarnational and baptismal meaning of the doves over the Virgin suggested that her presentation of her new child Christ symbolized the Church presenting the newborn Christian to God in baptism.

On reflection, the congruent symbolism of the miniatures of the Presentation and the Baptism should not be too surprising. At the Presentation the Virgin and Christ's fulfillment of the Old Law's lustral rites for admission to the Jewish temple had permitted the institution of baptism, the New Law's equivalent purificatory ceremony for entrance into the Church. So in exegesis the pure Christ's entrance into the material building of the temple of Jerusalem foreshadowed the believers' baptismal purification, which allowed admittance to the spiritual edifice of the earthly Ecclesia and ultimately to the celestial one of the heavenly Jerusalem.[244] The prayer accompanying the Presentation miniature asks that the minds of the congregation be instructed "in the spiritual teachings" of the law, and through its dual allusions to the Incarnation and the Baptism the picture does just that.

---

[240] *CBP*, no. 732; Warner and Wilson, *Ben.*, p. 7: "Detque (Deus) uobis ueram mentium innocentiam, qui super unigenitum suum spiritum sanctum demonstrari uoluit per columbam."

[241] Ælfric, *Hom.*, 2, pp. 45–47, explained that the Spirit appeared as a dove over Christ at the Baptism to signify his innocent humanity and the innocence all men should emulate.

[242] Origen, *In Lucam* 14, ed. Rauer, p. 91:

Sicut noua fuit generatio Saluatoris non ex uiro et muliere, sed ex sola tantum uirgine, sic et par turturum et duo pulli isti columbarum non fuerunt tales, quales oculis carnis adspicimus, sed qualis Spiritus sanctus est, qui in specie columbae descendit et uenit super Saluatorem, quando in Iordane baptizatus est.

Paul the Deacon, ed. Grégoire, *Homéliaires*, p. 436, no. 38. Cf. Bede (*Hom.*, 1, 12 and 1, 18, pp. 117f., 181; *In Lucam*, 1, p. 64), who interpreted the birds at both events similarly.

[243] Bede, *In Lucam*, 1, p. 63: "Quamuis possit etiam mystice designari nullum praeter dominum ecclesiae uirginis uterum per aquam et spiritum sanctum ad generandos Deo filios posse reserare ideoque hunc masculum incomparabili dignitate domino sanctum uocari." See also Smaragdus (after Bede), *In Octaua Natiuitas*, PL, 102, col. 60C–D; Ambrose, *Secundam Lucam*, 2, 57, ed. Adriaen, p. 55, repeated in the homiliary of Paul the Deacon, ed. Grégoire, *Homéliaires*, p. 442, no. 66.

[244] Bede, *Hom.* 1, 18, p. 182; Haymo, *Homilia* 14, PL, 118, col. 98.

Conclusions

Carolingian art seems to have been the primary source for most of the infancy miniatures. The Naming of Christ is an exception, since it is an eclectic combination of motifs from more common infancy scenes. Yet even here Carolingian influence is evident in the symbolism of the Virgin and child. The use of this group and the servant as linking motifs suggests that a Carolingian work from Metz furnished the models for all the infancy pictures, not just the three scenes with counterparts on the Brunswick casket. In the case of the Presentation the Utrecht Psalter was also a significant influence.

Commentators maintained that many of the incidents in the childhoods of Christ and John the Baptist manifested the miraculous coming of the incarnate Savior to mankind. The specter of Simeon, who had long expected Christ, led Ambrose, for instance, to recall other testimonies to the Incarnation:

> The generation of the Lord receives attestation not only from angels and prophets, from shepherds and relatives, but even from elders and the just. All ages, each sex, and the miracles of events furnish faith: a virgin conceives, a sterile woman gives birth, a mute speaks, Elizabeth prophesies, a Magus adores, one who is yet in the womb exults, a widow [Anna] acknowledges [and] a just man [Simeon] waits.[245]

Ambrose wove together in a purposeful pattern of testimony almost all the infancy events that the Benedictional interrelated: the Birth and Naming of the Baptist, the Annunciation, the Nativity, the Adoration of the Magi, and the Presentation. Only the Naming of Christ is absent, though Ambrose did mention the witness of Christ's relatives. In Carolingian homiliaries well known in tenth-century England, this text was a reading for either the Purification or the Octave of the Nativity;[246] hence, this passage might have been a factor in the cyclic symbolism of the illustrations of these and other infancy

feasts in both the Drogo Sacramentary and the Benedictional.

Ambrose focused on the recognition of the incarnate Christ's advent, but this is only one of the major themes unifying the images. The Benedictional combined the complex sacramental typology that links the Annunciation, the Nativity, and the Baptism on the Brunswick casket with the incarnational theme of the group of the Virgin and child that runs through the infancy scenes of the Drogo Sacramentary. Although the Baptism is absent from the Sacramentary's picture cycle, such sacramental and incarnational themes might already have been combined in the Benedictional's Metz source. In any event, the Anglo-Saxons refined and enriched the programmatic symbolism of their Carolingian model in many ways.

The inclusion of the Baptism as a second Epiphany illustration made the liturgical symbolism of Christ's infancy much more evident. Its placement opposite the Adoration of the Magi and before the Presentation in the Temple allowed these two additional infancy scenes, with their linking motif of the Virgin and child, to be drawn into typological association with baptism. To tighten and deepen the visual and thematic bonds among the pictures, the illuminators introduced a variety of new motifs: the doves over the Virgin, the nimbus (or its absence), the birth bed, and especially the cloud, which had already been associated with the coming of the Emmanuel and baptism in the Carolingian Soissons Gospels. Under the influence of the Benedictional's text, the ecclesiological and liturgical consequences of Christ's miraculous advent and assumption of humanity were given new emphasis. Recurrent architectural and altar symbolism, influenced in part by the imagery in the Galba Psalter, emphasized that his unique conception allowed the fulfillment of the Old Law, freeing all mankind to accept the new dispensation of spiritual baptismal grace. The events in Christ's life were depicted

---

[245] Ambrose, *Secundum Lucam*, 2, 58, ed. Adriaen, pp. 56f.: Non solum ab angelis et prophetis, a pastoribus et parentibus, sed etiam a senioribus et iustis generatio domini accipit testimonium. Omnis aetas et uterque sexus euentorumque miracula fidem adstruunt: uirgo generat, sterilis parit, mutus loquitur, Elisabet prophe-

tat, magus adorat, utero clausus exsultat, uidua confitetur, iustus exspectat.

[246] Paul the Deacon, ed. Grégoire, *Homéliaires*, p. 442, no. 66; Smaragdus, *In Octaua Natiuitatis Domini*, PL, 102, col. 61C.

as both the cause and the prefiguration of this new dispensation. His past advent to individuals such as the Virgin, servants, the Magi, and Simeon foreshadowed his present coming to the congregation through the liturgical rites of baptism, the Eucharist, and episcopal benediction, and also through a daily life of virtuous self-sacrifice. The places where he was revealed, such as the manger in Bethlehem and the temple in Jerusalem, prefigured his dwelling in the living edifice of the Church. Previous actions such as the animals adoring Christ on the crib, the offering of Christ and the birds at the Presentation, and the baptismal anointing and vesting of Christ symbolized the spiritual service that the royal priesthood of his members carried out in his name in the temple of the New Law. To reify these highly abstruse, metaphorical concepts within the limitations of narrative imagery was a creative and intellectual achievement of the first order.

Chapter Two

THE MINIATURES OF
THE LATER LIFE
OF CHRIST

THIS CHAPTER examines the six miniatures representing New Testament events before and after the Passion— the Entry into Jerusalem, the Women at the Tomb, the Doubting of Thomas, the Ascension, Pentecost, and the Second Coming —as well as the figured initial of Christ enthroned that illustrates the blessings for the Octave of Pentecost.

The Women at the Tomb (Easter)

Many features relate the miniature of the Women at the Tomb (pl. 22) to Carolingian Metz iconography.[1] Christ's sepulcher is a basilican type that occurs almost exclusively in later Metz ivories, such as two plaques in Paris.[2] Both panels differ in some respects from the Benedictional, but the differences can be attributed to the Metz carvers adjusting a broad composition to a narrower space: on one panel (fig. 44) the tomb and the guards are placed on a separate register above the angel and the three women;[3] on the other (fig. 45) the tomb remains on the same register as the angel, as in the Benedictional, but the guards are omitted. There was more room in the Drogo Sacramentary (fig. 46),[4] which has a broad frieze composition like the one in the Benedictional; in both manuscripts the guards, sleeping with their shields and spears to the left of the tomb, are very similar. Though the initial retained an older type of domed tomb, both scenes frame similar angels against the architecture. There are also resemblances between the women in the two scenes: the first holds a censer and the last raises her right arm to her neck in a gesture of bewilderment and wonder.

No one work contains every feature of the Anglo-Saxon picture, but the numerous and precise resemblances to Metz iconography make it certain that the model was from this Carolingian center and was probably contemporary with the later Metz ivories of about 860–870.

Not all the differences between the Anglo-

---

[1] Homburger, *Anf.*, pp. 18f.; also Warner and Wilson, *Ben.*, pp. xxivf.; Alexander, "Ben.," p. 178.

[2] Goldschmidt, *Elf.*, 1, pp. 47f., nos. 84, 86, pls. 35, 36; see also no. 89, pl. 38, and idem, *Elf.*, 4, p. 60, no. 309, pl. 79. Homburger, *Anf.*, pp. 18f.; see also Warner and Wilson, *Ben.*, pp. xxivf.; Alexander, "Ben.," p. 178.

[3] For another explanation, see H. Schnitzler, "Eine Metzer Emmaustafel," *Wallraf-Richartz-Jahrbuch* 20 (1958): 50f.; V. H. Elbern, "Vier karolingische Elfenbeinkästen," *Zeitschrift des deutschen Vereins für Kunstwissenschaft* 20 (1966): 8f.

[4] *Drogo-Sak.*, fol. 58.

Saxon and Metz iconography are due to compositional adjustments. Following an established convention of Latin Western iconography,[5] the Metz ivories portray the linen wrapping from Christ's body in a sarcophagus deep inside the tomb. The Benedictional, however, shows the wrapping prominently suspended in mid-air in the tomb door without a sarcophagus. In the Gospels (Luke 24:11–12, John 20:5–9) the discarded wrapping is an important proof of the Resurrection, and the more conspicuous display stresses its significance. The *Regularis Concordia*,[6] Æthelwold's monastic rule, described a dramatic reenactment of the Resurrection on Easter Sunday, when a napkin symbolizing the grave windings of the risen Lord was shown to a monastic audience. Æthelwold's personal interests must have influenced the prominent representation of the wrappings, but his illuminators did not invent the motif. Byzantine scenes such as the one in a thirteenth-century Gospel book in Paris (Bibl. Nat., MS gr. 54; fig. 47)[7] usually depict the linen in the same way. How Winchester painters knew this Byzantine iconographic element is difficult to determine. Since Eastern art sometimes influenced the later Metz workshop, this motif might already have been incorporated into the Benedictional's lost Metz model. However, as extant Metz works do not include this particular Byzantine detail,[8] it is also possible that the Anglo-Saxons might have independently known Byzantine imagery.

One other feature of the Benedictional relevant to this problem is the form of the stone on which the angel sits. The molding projecting around its lower edge transforms this block into a throne,[9] increasing the angel's majesty. This extremely rare feature is paralleled in the scene in the Byzantine Gospels in Paris.[10] It must have been the Anglo-Saxons who incorporated this, along with the other Byzantine motif of the windings, into their copy of the Metz model.

The Ascension (Ascension Day)

THE MODELS

The miniature of Christ's Ascension (pl. 25) displays a blend of Western and Eastern features reminiscent of Carolingian iconography.[11] The actively striding Christ with the cross-staff symbolizing his triumph over death was a purely Western figural type frequently found in such Carolingian works as the Drogo Sacramentary (fig. 48), an ivory plaque in Minden (fig. 49), and the San Paolo Bible in Rome (fig. 50).[12] In sharp contrast, such Byzantine works as the twelfth-century Gospel book in the British Library (MS Harley 1810; fig. 51)[13] always portray Christ passively seated or standing without a cross-staff.

Other details of the Benedictional's iconogra-

---

[5] Cf. Volbach, *Elf.*, pp. 82f., no. 116, pl. 61; also Goldschmidt, *Elf.*, 1, no. 41, pl. 20.

[6] *RC*, 78–79, pp. 424ff. P. Weber, *Geistliches Schauspiel und kirchliche Kunst* (Stuttgart, 1894), pp. 32f., associated the windings in the Metz scenes with liturgical drama.

[7] H. Omont, *Miniatures des plus anciens manuscrits grecs de la Bibliothèque nationale du VIe au XIVe siècle* (Paris, 1929), pl. 94, 12; cf. also Goldschmidt and Weitzmann, *Byz. Elf.*, 2, nos. 122, 198; L. Kötzsche-Breitenbruch, "Windel und Grablinnen," *Jahrbuch für Antike und Christentum* 29 (1986): 181ff., pl. 31b.

[8] Some ivories from other Carolingian centers do include this motif; Goldschmidt, *Elf.*, 1, nos. 126, 147d, 165.

[9] For similar Carolingian thrones, see Koehler, *Kar. Min.*, 2, pls. 41a, 87, 94, etc.

[10] Cf. also the closely related Gospels on Mt. Athos, Ivron 5; S. M. Pelekanidis et al., *The Treasures of Mount Athos*, 2 (Athens, 1975), pp. 37, 299, fig. 17. Although both manuscripts are thirteenth century, Byzantine art of this period often closely copied tenth-century models. See K. Weitzmann, "The Character and Intellectual Origins of the Mace-donian Renaissance," *Studies*, pp. 212ff.; H. Buchthal and H. Belting, *Patronage in Thirteenth-Century Constantinople*, Dumbarton Oaks Studies, 16 (Washington, 1978), pp. 17ff. The only other Western examples of the motif are a later copy of the Benedictional (fig. 211, see Appendix Three) and a scene in a Byzantine-influenced Reichenau lectionary (ca. 1030) in Augsburg; *Suevia Sacra*, 3rd ed. (Augsburg, 1973), pp. 175f., no. 167.

[11] Homburger, *Anf.*, pp. 19ff.; Alexander, "Ben.," pp. 177f.; Warner and Wilson, *Ben.*, p. xxvf. Regarding the Ascension, see S. H. Gutberlet, *Die Himmelfahrt Christi in der bildenden Kunst*, 2nd ed. (Strassburg, 1935); H. Schrade, "Zur Ikonographie der Himmelfahrt Christi," *Vorträge der Bibliothek Warburg* (1928–29): 66–190; Schiller, *Ikon.*, 3, pp. 141ff.

[12] *Drogo-Sak.*, p. 26, pl. fol. 71v; Goldschmidt, *Elf.*, 1, pp. 34f., no. 65, pl. 27; H. Schade, "Studien zu der karolingischen Bilderbibel aus St. Paul vor den Mauern in Rom, 2. Teil," *Wallraf-Richartz-Jahrbuch* 22 (1960): 24ff., fig. 5.

[13] A. W. Carr, *Byzantine Illumination, 1150–1250* (Chicago, 1987), pp. 50ff., 251f., no. 70, fiche 6F9.

phy were originally Eastern but were probably transmitted indirectly through a Byzantine-influenced Carolingian model. Christ's mandorla is an Eastern motif (fig. 51)[14] that had already been adopted by the Minden ivory and other Carolingian works. In Byzantine scenes the Virgin frequently stands in a strictly frontal, orant pose in the center of two groups of apostles. A modified version of this scheme appears in the Benedictional. No longer frontal, she looks dramatically over her shoulder at Christ and stands off-center, giving greater emphasis to Peter at the head of the right group of apostles. Similar modifications of the Byzantine iconography had occurred in the Drogo Sacramentary and the San Paolo Bible and must have already been present in the Benedictional's model. Since many of these Greek motifs entered the Latin tradition during the ninth century, the primary source of the Anglo-Saxon image was surely Carolingian.[15]

One detail, however, does seem to relate to the Byzantine-inspired miniature that an Anglo-Saxon illuminator added to the Galba Psalter in the early tenth century (fig. 53). In the Benedictional the gestures of the lower pair of half-length angels, who reassure the disciples that Christ will return (Acts 1:11), conform to Carolingian iconography (figs. 48, 50), but the corresponding angels in Carolingian as well as Byzantine art are usually full-length. Half-length angels do occur, however, in the Galba Psalter, and the upper angels here also compare well with their counterparts in the Benedictional. These figures in the Psalter apparently influenced the Benedictional.

Also without parallel in Carolingian art are the red rays emanating from Christ's body. Originally these filled his mandorla, but rubbing has obscured them except around his left hand and foot and along his mantle. Like the mandorla, these rays represent the supernatural light radiating from Christ during his theophany. It was a common ancient and medieval idea that a god emanated supernatural light at his theophany. Though the New Testament did not apply this *topos* to the Ascension, Anglo-Saxon authors often did. Cynewulf in his Old English poem on the Ascension (*Christ II*) described the ascending Christ as "shining resplendently,"[16] and Bede in an Ascension homily termed him the "sun of righteousness" (Malachi 4:2) and "the light of the world" (John 8:12).[17] In the miniature the rays, in addition to emphasizing the theophanic nature of the event, probably had symbolic significance, characterizing Christ as the illuminating spiritual "light" of salvation.

Despite the popularity of the *topos* in Anglo-Saxon literature, the Anglo-Saxons were not the first to illustrate it. The earliest example occurs on a ninth– or tenth-century Eastern icon on Mount Sinai (fig. 54),[18] and the motif reappears in such later Byzantine works as the Harley Gospels (fig. 51), where the uniform emanation of the rays from the perimeter of Christ's body is especially close to the English iconography. The motif undoubtedly originated in Eastern art and first appeared in the West in the Benedictional. The proposal of a Byzantine source as the most likely inspiration for the rays of light in the Benedictional[19] is strengthened by the Galba Psalter, which shows a knowledge of Eastern Ascension iconography at Winchester in the early tenth century.

---

[14] Gutberlet, *Himmelfahrt*, pp. 180ff.

[15] Conceivably an earlier Anglo-Saxon scene influenced by Carolingian iconography, such as the one on the Wirksworth slab (fig. 52; see above, chap. 1, n. 147) or the Reculver cross (R. Kozodoy, "The Reculver Cross," *Archaeologia* 108 [1986]: 71ff., pl. 32) could have been the Benedictional's source; but the specific features of the Benedictional are closer to Carolingian art, and the Western iconography was by no means dominant in earlier Insular art; cf. fig. 53 as well as the adulterated Byzantine iconography on the Rothbury cross (ca. 800) and in the Turin Gospels (8th–9th c.); Deshman, "Anglo-Saxon Art after Alfred," pp. 186ff., figs. 25, 26.

[16] I. Gollancz, *The Exeter Book*, Early English Text Society, original ser., 104 (London, 1895), 1, p. 35, line 522.

[17] Bede, *Hom.*, 2, 15, p. 144.

[18] K. Weitzmann, *The Monastery of Saint Catherine at Mount Sinai, the Icons*, 1 (Princeton, 1976), pp. 73ff., no. B45, pls. 30, 100B.

[19] Homburger, *Anf.*, p. 20, n. 6, noted an instance of the motif on a late-tenth-century Fulda metal plaque in Essen. H. Schnitzler, "Nachträge zur spätkarolingischen und frühottonischen Goldschmiedekunst," *Festschrift für Peter Metz*, ed. U. Schlegel and C. Zoege von Manteuffel (Berlin, 1965), pp. 105f., fig. 4, speculated that the scenes on the plaque and in the Benedictional derived from similar Carolingian models, but they differ from each other in most respects and Schnitzler seemed unaware of the motif's Eastern origin.

THE INNOVATIONS

Christ's mandorla in the Ascension and also in the Second Coming (pl. 10) has a very unusual form: its thick gold border is omitted along the leading edge. This seems to be paralleled only in the Utrecht Psalter which several times depicts the mandorla foreshortened (fig. 55).[20] Another instance of the Psalter's influence on the Benedictional, the motif in Anglo-Saxon hands served not to create depth but to heighten the sense of Christ's rapid forward movement.

Throughout most of the picture cycle Christ's hair and beard are reddish blond, but in the Ascension and the Second Coming, as well as in the Doubting of Thomas (pl. 24), they are gold. These three scenes portray theophanies of Christ after his Resurrection; thus his gilded hair and beard must be a special attribute of divinity in his post-Resurrection state. The use of gold rather than ordinary pigment symbolized supernatural light radiating from his godhead on these theophanic occasions. Ancient literature abounds with examples of shining golden hair as an attribute of divinity. One Roman emperor even sprinkled gold dust on his hair to characterize himself as divine.[21] Centuries later Cynewulf in his Old English poem on the Ascension wrote that "light . . . glistened from the Saviour's head" as he rose into the heavens.[22] Much as the rays of light reinforced the meaning of the mandorla, Christ's golden hair and beard emphasized the significance of his golden nimbus, the more conventional symbol of the supernatural light radiating from his head. The Benedictional, to my knowledge, is unparalleled in its representation of Christ with gilded hair. The Byzantine motif of the rayed mandorla might very well have set the illuminators thinking about a connection between the radiance of Christ after the Resurrection and the Anglo-Saxon literary *topos* of shining hair.

Christ's relation to earth is also very unusual. His right foot barely touches the hill as he strenuously strides forth into the cloud-filled sky. Some Carolingian scenes (figs. 48, 50) perpetuated the Western early Christian type of Christ treading up the Mount of Olives with both feet firmly on the ground,[23] but others (figs. 49, 56) showed him suspended in mid-air. The figure in the Benedictional—one foot on the earth and the other in heaven—is midway between these two Carolingian types. This novel position seems to have been an afterthought. Originally Christ was to have been suspended high in the air, as in the Carolingian ivory in Minden; this is clear from traces of an underpainting of wavy lines of clouds[24] showing beneath the green hills between the Virgin and the apostles. Having taken the trouble to make this change, the painters must have had a good reason.

Both Gregory the Great in his popular Ascension homily and Cynewulf in his Ascension poem had interpreted the events of Christ's life as a series of divine "leaps," beginning with his descent from heaven to the Virgin and ending with his ascent to heaven at his Ascension.[25] The latter "leap" fulfilled the text of the Song of Songs 2:8: "Behold he cometh leaping upon the mountains, springing over the hills." The Benedictional's illuminators modified Carolingian iconography to illustrate this exegesis, for Christ appears literally leaping from one hill over another to the right.[26]

The two upper angels flanking the mandorla clasp their hands in a gesture of homage, a modification of their model in the Galba Psalter (fig. 53), which depicts them delicately carrying the mandorla, their normal function in Byzantine art. Even in other miniatures of the Benedictional angels adjacent to Christ's mandorla usually support it (pls. 14, 19). Why were the angels at the Ascension relieved of this task?

The role of the angels at the Ascension was

---

[20] *Utrecht*, fols. 44, 48v, 53, 54v, 56.

[21] Regarding golden hair, see K. Keyssner, "Nimbus," *Paulys Realencyclopädie der classischen Altertumswissenschaft*, 17, 1 (Stuttgart, 1936), cols. 594–96.

[22] Gollancz, *Exeter Book*, p. 33, lines 504f. T. D. Hill, " 'Byrht Word' and 'Haelendes Heafod': Christological Allusion in the Old English *Christ and Satan*," *English Language Notes* 8 (1970): 8, n. 6, and P. Clemoes, "Cynewulf's Image of the Ascension," *England before the Conquest. Studies in Primary Sources Presented to Dorothy Whitelock*, ed. P. Clemoes and K. Hughes (Cambridge, 1971), p. 229, suggest that Cynewulf was influenced by depictions of nimbed figures, but

the *topos* of a shining head had a long history in non-Christian literature. Cf. A. S. Cook, *The Christ of Cynewulf* (Boston, 1900), p. 124, n. line 505, who cited a passage from Homer as a parallel.

[23] See Volbach, *Elf.*, no. 110, pl. 59.

[24] Cf. the engraved reproduction in Gage, "Ben.," pl. 22.

[25] Gregory, *Homilia* 29, PL, 76, col. 1219B; Cynewulf, *Christ II*, lines 712–46; Gollancz, *Exeter Book*, pp. 46–49; A. Breeze, "The 'Leaps' that Christ Made," *Ériu* 40 (1989): 190–93.

[26] Some Ottonian works also independently illustrated this idea; see Gutberlet, *Himmelfahrt*, pp. 197f.

often treated in homilies. Following Gregory the Great, Carolingian and Anglo-Saxon homilists[27] maintained that Christ had risen entirely by his own power, unaided by angels. Bede[28] claimed that the angels had done nothing but pay him homage. Thus the angels' passive gestures of worship in the Benedictional show that Christ did not require their assistance to ascend. A ninth-century ivory in Weimar from the court school of Charles the Bald (fig. 56)[29] depicts Christ in a mandorla ascending independent of throngs of adoring angels; such Carolingian iconography might have influenced the Benedictional's illuminators to modify the traditional carrying function of the angels.

Still one other feature of the iconography visualized Christ's unassisted ascent. In contrast to the earliest Western iconography, reflected in the Drogo Sacramentary (fig. 48), the hands of Christ and the Father are not yet joined in the *dextrarum iunctio*. This change negated any impression that the Son required the Father's helping hand to rise. As some Carolingian scenes such as the one on the Minden ivory (fig. 49) had already loosened or separated the gripping hands, this modification seems to be another motif taken over from the Carolingian model.

The interest in the mode of Christ's Ascension was less a matter of mechanics than a question of deep dogmatic significance. To the commentators Christ's independent ascent demonstrated not only his divine omnipotence but also his unstained human nature. Haymo,[30] for example, explained that Christ had been able to penetrate heaven entirely on his own because his human body, which had been conceived in unique purity from the Virgin, was not weighted down with mortal sin. Christ's independent ascent affirmed the fundamental dogmatic tenet that the divine Christ had exalted human nature to heaven, opening it to all mankind. This incarnational significance was traditionally visualized by including the Virgin, his human mother,

among the spectators at his Ascension, although the New Testament does not mention her presence.[31] The portrayal of Christ ascending unassisted complemented this older incarnational iconography.

The miniature's emphasis on the relation of the Ascension to the Incarnation poses a question about the meaning of the thick cloud surrounding Christ. This motif illustrates the statement in Acts 1:9 that "a cloud received him out of their sight." But in the pictures of the Annunciation and Nativity (pls. 8, 12), as well as in some other infancy scenes, the cloud was a symbol of the divine Christ's presence in the flesh in the world. Did the cloud in the Ascension also have this symbolic connotation?

Commentators certainly regarded the cloud at the Ascension in this light. Citing Psalm 103:3 ("Who makest the clouds thy chariot"), Gregory interpreted the cloud as the "chariot" of human flesh that Christ took to heaven.[32] Expanding on this idea, Bede[33] explained that the cloud at this event symbolized the humanity in which Christ, the "sun of righteousness," had dressed himself at the Incarnation so that mankind could tolerate the light of his divinity and receive its illumination. Christ had entered the world on the supernaturally illuminated "light cloud" (Isaiah 19:1) of his unburdened human nature which he carried with him in his subsequent earthly life and in his ascent to heaven. Bede interpreted the cloud at the Ascension in reference to the very same incarnational concepts represented in the illuminated cloud in the Annunciation and the "bright cloud" in the Nativity.

The unusually heavy emphasis on Christ's supernatural radiance at the Ascension suggests that the cloud in this scene had a similar symbolic significance. The rays in his mandorla and the glistening gold of his hair and nimbus were included to pictorialize the notion that the light of the ascending Christ's divinity was "shaded"

[27] Gregory, *Homilia* 29, PL, 76, cols. 1216C–17C; Haymo of Auxerre, *Homilia* 96, PL, 118, col. 547B–D; Ælfric, *Hom.*, 1, pp. 306ff. See O. Brendel, "Origin and Meaning of the Mandorla," *Gazette des Beaux-Arts*, 6th ser., 25 (1944): 12.

[28] Bede, *Hom.*, 2, 15, p. 146.

[29] Goldschmidt, *Elf.*, 1, p. 28, no. 45, pl. 21. Also Schrade, "Himmelfahrt," pp. 129ff.; Gutberlet, *Himmelfahrt*, pp. 168ff., 193.

[30] Haymo, *Homilia* 96, PL, 118, col. 547B–D; see also Gregory, *Homilia* 29, 5, PL, 76, col. 1216D; Ælfric, *Hom.*, 1, pp. 308, 309.

[31] K. Weitzmann, "*Loca Sancta* and the Representational Arts of Palestine," *DOP* 28 (1974): 43f.; rpt. idem, *Studies in the Arts at Sinai* (Princeton, 1982), pp. 29f. Cf. the titulus of the scene in the Ottonian Codex Aureus in Nuremberg: "Hunc deus assumpsit hominem, quem uirgine sumpsit;" R. Kahsnitz, U. Mende, and E. Rücker, *Das Goldene Evangelienbuch von Echternach* (Frankfurt am Main, 1982), p. 93.

[32] See below, n. 219; also Hrabanus Maurus, *Commentaria in Ezechielem*, 2, PL, 110, cols. 547f.

[33] Bede, *Hom.*, 2, 15, pp. 142f.; see also the text by Augustine quoted above, chap. 1, n. 142.

by the surrounding clouds symbolizing his assumed humanity. The repetition of the illuminated cloud in one form or another in the Annunciation, the Nativity, and the Ascension symbolically linked these scenes to show that Christ entered and exited the world in the same divinely lit cloud of human nature.

In Anglo-Saxon exegesis and iconography the themes of Christ's supernaturally bright cloud and his unassisted ascent were complementary. The cloud symbolizing his humanity was "light," according to the interpretations of Isaiah 19:1, because his flesh had not been "weighed down" by any sin,[34] and for the very same reason—because his human body had escaped the heavy burden of ordinary mortal corruption—he was able to ascend unaided. Thus Bede considered the two topics successively in his Ascension homily,[35] and in the late tenth century Ælfric and the Blickling homilist went a step further and actually fused them. Both these vernacular authors gave a new twist to the traditional explanation of Christ's independent ascent by insisting that the cloud did not support Christ but went before or with him to heaven.[36]

Although the Benedictional's Ascension image clearly illustrated the concept of the divinely illuminated cloud, it was less successful in showing that Christ carried this "cloud" of his humanity up to heaven. Whereas in the Annunciation the slope of the cloud visualized its movement down to earth, in the Ascension his cloud merely surrounds his mandorla and thus does not suggest a directional movement up to heaven. A

generation after the Benedictional, Anglo-Saxon artists invented a new type of ascending Christ, the so-called disappearing Christ, that dispelled the ambiguous relationship between the images and the exegesis.[37] From the Benedictional they took over the motif of the angels refraining from assisting Christ;[38] but they now portrayed Christ with the upper part of his body hidden in the cloud, so that he appears to take it up with him. In one of the earliest instances of the new iconography in the English-influenced Odbert Gospels (New York, Morgan Lib., MS 333; fig. 57),[39] made at St. Bertin about the year 1000, the cloud is even confined within Christ's mandorla, precisely illustrating Bede's notion that Christ carried to heaven the cloud of his humanity illuminated by the light of his divinity. In improving on the Benedictional, later artists sought to turn the Ascension into a more perfect mirror image of the Annunciation: they adapted the Benedictional's iconography of Christ's descent with the cloud to portray his later ascent with the same cloud.

The hindsight afforded by the subsequent iconographic development confirms the symbolic linkage of the Benedictional's pictures of the Annunciation, Nativity, and Ascension. Christ himself had affirmed that "no man hath ascended into heaven, but he that descended from heaven, the Son of Man who is in heaven" (John 3:13). Accordingly, the Benedictional represented the divine man who ascends with the symbolic illuminated cloud as the same one who had descended with it.

The Second Coming (Third Sunday in Advent)

THE MODELS

Images of the Second Coming[40] most often depicted Christ enthroned or standing frontally.

A few isolated Continental examples portrayed him in profile and actively striding as in the Benedictional (pl. 10),[41] but the Anglo-Saxon illuminators did not have to look so far afield for a

---

[34] See Bede, *In Lucam*, 1, pp. 33f.; also chap. 1, nn. 9–11.

[35] Bede, *Hom.*, 2, 15, pp. 142ff.

[36] Ælfric, *Hom.*, 1, p. 299; *Blickling*, pp. 120, 121.

[37] Schapiro, "Dis. Christ," pp. 267ff. I shall consider this in more detail elsewhere.

[38] Schapiro, "Dis. Christ," pls. 3, 4, 7; cf. also our fig. 57 where the angels are omitted altogether.

[39] Schapiro, "Dis. Christ," fig. 8.

[40] Y. Christe, *La Vision de Matthieu (Matth. XXIV–XXV)*, Bibliothèque des Cahiers Archéologiques, 10 (Paris, 1973); B. Brenk, *Tradition und Neuerung in der christlichen Kunst des er-*

sten Jahrtausends, Wiener byzantinistische Studien, 3 (Vienna, 1966); S. Dufrenne, "Une Image de la Seconde Venue dans un Évangile byzantin," *Studien zur mittelalterlichen Kunst 800–1250. Festschrift für Florentine Mütherich zum 70. Geburtstag*, ed. K. Bierbrauer, P. K. Klein, and W. Sauerländer (Munich, 1985), pp. 175–80.

[41] E.g., the Carolingian fresco in Müstair (Brenk, *Tradition*, pp. 57f., 112f., text fig. 10, fig. 34) and the Cappadocian one in Ayvali Kilise, dated 913–920 (N. Thierry and M. Thierry, "Ayvali Kilise ou Pigeonnier de Gülli Dere, église inédite de Cappadoce," *Cahiers Archéologiques* 15 [1965]: 131,

model. Homburger[42] suggested that they were inspired by the Benedictional's own miniature of the Ascension (pl. 25), and there can be no doubt that he was right. Not only are the poses of the two figures of Christ striding in a field of cloud virtually identical, but their specific attributes also correspond. Each has gold hair and beard, shoulders a cross-staff, and radiates red rays of divine light which fill a yellow mandorla open on the right side. The adaption of the descending figure of Christ from the ascending one resulted in a certain ambiguity in the former: despite the downward tilt of his mandorla and his upper body, he still seems to step upward.

The Ascension could not have been the source, however, of the throng of angels emerging from the cloud above Christ in the Second Coming. The angels carry one of the books of life (Apoc. 5:8, 20:12)[43] and the instruments of the Passion —the cross, the nails, the sponge, and the spear. In both the East and the West the Passion implements began to appear in various contexts during the ninth century.[44] One of the earliest depictions of the motif in a Second Coming or Last Judgment is in the first miniature in the Galba Psalter, which shows the cross, the lance, and the sponge propped against the back of Christ's throne (fig. 11).[45] Although the Psalter strongly influenced other miniatures in the Benedictional and must also have been a factor in the latter's inclusion of the Passion implements, the Psalter does not provide a complete explanation because the Benedictional represents the instruments in a very different manner.

Angels carrying the instruments of the Passion occurred first in the Benedictional and then some fifty years later in Byzantine art. In the scene of the Anastasis on the gold cover of a Greek lectionary of the first quarter of the eleventh century on Mount Athos (fig. 58),[46] half-figures of angels holding the lance and the sponge hover above the descending Christ, who carries the cross, another implement of the Passion. The angels are not the only aspect of Eastern Anastasis iconography comparable to the Anglo-Saxon image. The poses and attributes of the figures of Christ are also similar. Though on the book cover Christ is not in a mandorla, he often has this attribute in other Byzantine Anastasis scenes, for instance, the one in a mid-tenth-century lectionary in St. Petersburg (Public Lib., MS gr. 21; fig. 59).[47] Many other Eastern representations of the Anastasis show rays of light radiating from his body and filling his mandorla,[48] another detail paralleled in the Anglo-Saxon iconography. Since all these aspects of Anastasis iconography corresponded to the Benedictional's Ascension imagery, it was a simple matter to combine elements from Eastern Anastasis and Latin Ascen-

fig. 24; M. Restle, *Die byzantinische Wandmalerei in Kleinasien* [Recklinghausen, 1967], 1, pp. 139f., no. 29). Both are probably independent *ad hoc* adaptions of an Ascension or Anastasis. W. E. Kleinbauer, "The Iconography and the Date of the Mosaics of the Rotunda of Hagios Georgios, Thessaloniki," *Viator* 3 (1972): 43f., figs. 3, 7, proposed that the Benedictional was indirectly related to the underdrawing of this early Christian mosaic, but the figures are too dissimilar to allow this conclusion. Some Mozarabic Beatus manuscripts illustrate Apoc. 1:17 with Christ striding in clouds, but the differences in pose cast doubt on any connection to the Anglo-Saxon iconography; see M. Mentré, "Les Théophanies de l'Apocalypse dans les manuscrits hispaniques du haut Moyen Âge et les traditions méditerranéennes," *Les Cahiers de Saint-Michel de Cuxa* 6 (1975): 207ff., fig. 2.

[42] Homburger, *Anf.*, p. 14; also Brenk, *Tradition*, pp. 57f.; Christe, *Vision*, p. 53.

[43] As does Christ.

[44] E.g., the Homilies of Gregory of Nazianzus (L. Brubaker, "Politics, Patronage, and Art in Ninth-Century Byzantium [B.N. Gr. 510]," *DOP* 39 [1985]: 10, fig. 7); the Utrecht Psalter (*Utrecht*, fol. 12); the Turonian Arnaldus Gospels and Bamberg Bible (Koehler, *Kar. Min.*, 1, 1, pp. 384, 391, pls. 35c, 56b); cf. also the ninth-century Rothbury cross head, though here one figure holds two circlets, calling into question an identification as the crown of thorns (R. Cramp,

Corpus of Anglo-Saxon Stone Sculpture, 1, 1 [Oxford, 1984], pp. 219f.; 1, 2, figs. 1207, 1210). The instruments in the sixth-century mosaic from S. Michele in Affricisco from Ravenna are a modern restoration; A. Effenberger, "Eine frühe Kopie des Mosaiks aus San Michele in Affricisco," *Studien zur spätantiken und byzantinischen Kunst*, ed. O. Feld and U. Peschlow (Bonn, 1986), 2, pp. 167, 169, pls. 36, 37/1.

[45] Deshman, "Anglo-Saxon Art after Alfred," pp. 179ff.; also J. O'Reilly, "Early Medieval Text and Image: The Wounded and Exalted Christ," *Peritia* 6–7 (1987–88): 84ff. The first example of the instruments in a Byzantine Last Judgment also dates to the tenth century; Brenk, *Tradition*, p. 99, fig. 23.

[46] N. Kondakov, *Monuments of Christian Art on Mt. Athos* (in Russian) (Petrograd, 1902), pl. 27; K. Weitzmann, "Das Evangelion im Skevophylakion zu Lawra," *Seminarium Kondakovianum* 8 (1936): 83f. For later examples, see G. Galavaris, *The Illustrations of the Liturgical Homilies of Gregory Nazianzenus*, Studies in Manuscript Illumination, 6 (Princeton, 1969), pp. 73f., 75, n. 150.

[47] K. Weitzmann, *Die byzantinische Buchmalerei des 9. und 10. Jahrhunderts* (Berlin, 1935), pp. 59f.; A. D. Kartsonis, *Anastasis: The Making of an Image* (Princeton, 1986), p. 165, fig. 62.

[48] E.g., the early-eleventh-century fresco in St. Barbe at Soganli, Cappadocia; Kartsonis, *Anastasis*, pp. 167f., fig. 67; also figs. 15, 23, 26e, 44b.

sion images to create the new scene of the Second Coming.[49]

Byzantine Anastasis imagery was well known in late Anglo-Saxon England. It appears—though without the angels with the instruments of the Passion—on the eleventh-century stone slab in Bristol cathedral (fig. 60)[50] and in the English-influenced Odbert Gospels (ca. 1000) from St. Bertin (fig. 61).[51]

Thus the primary model for the Benedictional's scene of the Second Coming was its picture of the Ascension, but the Galba Psalter and a Byzantine Anastasis image were the sources of the angels with the instruments of the Passion. Since the instruments and Christ's attribute of the cross-staff seem to have been introduced into the iconography of the Anastasis in the middle Byzantine period,[52] the Eastern model must have been comparatively recent in date.

The Symbolic Content

The angels on the Byzantine book cover hover on either side above Christ, but in the Benedictional they are asymmetric and are led by an angel shouldering a cross prominently projecting over the frame—a figure without a counterpart in Anastasis iconography. This rearrangement must have been prompted by a desire for heightened dynamism and drama—characteristic Anglo-Saxon qualities—but the alteration also had iconographic significance.

Christe related the angels in the Anglo-Saxon composition to a passage in a homily by the Pseudo-Chrysostom that compared the Second Coming to an imperial advent.[53] Just as a ruler was preceded into a city by his army shoulder-

ing his *vexillum* and other regalia, so the returning heavenly King will be preceded by his army of angels shouldering his triumphal *vexillum* of the cross, "the sign of the Son of man in heaven" (Matt. 24:30) that will announce his advent to earth. The miniature appears to illustrate this passage by representing the leader of an "army" of angels bearing the cross over his shoulder as he flies before Christ's mandorla. Although the homily does not say that the angels also will bring the other instruments of the Passion, it does mention that the ruler's army bears several regal insignia. This could have easily served to justify the expansion of the number of Christ's own insignia in the image, especially since the homily subsequently linked the display of Christ's cross at the Last Judgment to the display of his wounds. This Greek homily was the basis of a Latin one by the Pseudo-Augustine,[54] and the passage about the Second Coming was also translated into Latin in the *Prognosticum Futuri Saecula* by Julian of Toledo (d.690).[55] Æthelwold owned a copy of Julian's treatise,[56] and this text must have induced Æthelwold to order his painters to depict the angels carrying the instruments like triumphal imperial insignia.

The characterization of the scene as an imperial advent is evident in still other features that lack a source in the *Prognosticum* and related texts. On Christ's mantle is the gold inscription "Rex regum et Do(mi)n(u)s dominatiu(m)," a literal illustration of Apocalypse 19:16: "And he hath on his garment, and on his thigh written: 'King of kings, and Lord of lords.'" The occurrence of this apocalyptic text as a response in the Office for the third Sunday in Advent, the feast the picture prefaces, must have inspired this very unusual motif.[57] The pose of Christ

---

[49] So also P. Verdier, "Dominus Potens in Praelio," *Wallraf-Richartz-Jahrbuch* 43 (1982): 68. Others have accepted a relation to the Anastasis but excluded one to the Ascension; see W. Paeseler, "Die Römische Weltgerichtstafel im Vatikan," *Kunstgeschichtliches Jahrbuch der Bibliotheca Hertziana* 2 (1938): 337f.; K. Weitzmann, "Various Aspects of Byzantine Influence on the Latin Countries from the Sixth to the Twelfth Century," *DOP* 20 (1966): 18f.; rpt. idem, *Art in the Medieval West and its Contacts with Byzantium* (London, 1982), no. 1, pp. 18f.

[50] *English Romanesque Art 1066–1200*, ed. G. Zarnecki, J. Holt, and T. Holland (London, 1984), p. 150, no. 96; M. Q. Smith, "The Harrowing of Hell Relief in Bristol Cathedral," *Transactions of the Bristol and Gloucestershire Archaeological Society* 94 (1976): 101–106.

[51] Schapiro, "Dis. Christ," pp. 277f., fig. 8.

[52] Kartsonis, *Anastasis*, pp. 83, 85, 205ff.

[53] Christe, *Vision*, pp. 47ff. See Pseudo-Chrysostom, *Homilia in Crucem et in Latronem*, 1, 4; 2, 4, ed. J.-P. Migne, Patrologia Graeca, 49 (Paris, 1862), cols. 404, 414.

[54] *Sermo* 155, PL, 39, col. 2051.

[55] *Prognosticum Futuri Saeculi*, 3, 5, ed. J. N. Hillgarth, CC, 115, pp. 85f.; see also Dungal (d. after 827), *Liber Adversus Claudium Taurinensem*, PL, 105, cols. 490f.

[56] Lapidge, "Booklists," pp. 53f., no. 5. Ælfric excerpted passages of the *Prognosticum*, including the one about the Second Coming; M. McC. Gatch, *Preaching and Theology in Anglo-Saxon England* (Toronto, 1977), p. 140, lines 202–204.

[57] *CAO*, 4, p. 149, no. 6578. The only other instance of the motif is a later Canterbury drawing (fig. 90) influenced directly or indirectly by the Benedictional; see below, n. 226.

with his cross-staff also subtly expressed the imperial nature of the event. Although the immediate source of this was the Ascension, the ultimate origin was the ancient imperial figural type of the victor shouldering his trophy.[58]

Symbolism also played a part in the choice of models. The features derived from the Ascension were equally appropriate for the Second Coming. The cloud and the symbols of Christ's divine light—the ray-filled mandorla, the nimbus, and gold hair and beard—all illustrate the description of the Second Coming in Matthew 24:27–31: "For as lightning cometh out of the east, and appeareth even into the west: so shall also the coming of the Son of man be. . . . And they shall see the Son of man coming in the clouds of heaven with much power and majesty." On a deeper level, however, the modeling of the Second Coming after the Ascension expressed the typological relationship between the two events. Two men in white had informed the disciples at the Ascension that "this Jesus who is taken up from you (in a cloud) into heaven, shall so come, as you have seen him going into heaven" (Acts 1:11). To illustrate this typology the Benedictional's illuminators showed Christ ascending and descending in cloud in the same manner.[59]

Similar typological relationships had long been a feature of Insular art. Eighth- or ninth-century Irish pictures of the Ascension and the Second Coming face each other in a Gospel book in Turin (Bibl. Naz., MS O. IV. 20).[60] In the Galba Psalter the Last Judgment on folio 2v and the Ascension (figs. 11, 53) both depict Christ enthroned in a mandorla flanked by angels, holding a book, and displaying his open hand, and in the bottom register of each composition are two symmetrical groups of apostles flanking a raised group of the Virgin and two other figures. Not only certain details but also the typological relationship between the Psalter's two pictures influenced the Benedictional.

If typological considerations governed the selection of the Ascension as one model for the Second Coming, they also guided the choice of the Anastasis as a second source. Christ's descent to hell to resurrect Adam was thought to be an act of judgment and salvation that prefigured his future descent to earth to judge resurrected mankind at the Last Judgment. In the East the typological affiliation between the Anastasis and the Last Judgment led to an exchange of iconographic features between the two themes;[61] the incorporation of the instruments of the Passion, a staple motif in middle Byzantine Last Judgments, into the Anastasis (fig. 58) is an example of this practice. The Benedictional's creators would certainly have recognized the typological connotations of the motif in Eastern Anastasis iconography. The typology of the Harrowing of Hell and the Last Judgment was also a well-established theme of Old English literature,[62] and this *topos* even occurred in the Anglo-Saxon mass for the third Sunday in Advent, the feast illustrated by the Benedictional's miniature.[63] The painters chose the Anastasis as a secondary model for the Second Coming to remind viewers that the one event foreshadowed the other.

That this picture of the Second Coming combined elements of the Anastasis and the Ascension is worthy of closer scrutiny, for all three themes were associated with each other. Ephesians 4:9–10 related the Harrowing and the Ascension: "Now that he ascended, what is it, but because he also descended first into the lower parts of the earth? He that descended is the same also that ascended above all the heavens." In the Winchester liturgy of Ascension day, Ephesians 4:10 was used as an antiphon after the epistle of Acts 1:11, which typologically associated the Ascension and the Second Coming.[64] Most important, the three events are linked in the Benedictional's own text for the Sunday after Ascension day:

> O God, you who rising again have broken hell, you who ascending have opened the heavens, so that those people by faith will

[58] Christe, *Vision*, pp. 50ff., figs. 73, 74.

[59] Brenk, *Tradition*, pp. 57f.; Christe, *Vision*, p. 53; O'Reilly, "Text and Image," p. 86.

[60] Christe, *Vision*, p. 54; Alexander, *Manuscripts*, no. 61, figs. 279, 280. For this typology in Byzantine and Ottonian iconography, see Brenk, *Tradition*, pp. 58f.

[61] Kartsonis, *Anastasis*, pp. 155ff.

[62] J. J. Campbell, "To Hell and Back: Latin Tradition and Literary Use of the 'Descensus ad Inferos' in Old English," *Viator* 13 (1982): 123ff., 127f., 135ff., 156; M. A. Dalbey, "Patterns of Preaching in the Blickling Easter Homily," *American Benedictine Review* 24 (1973): 487–92.

[63] See below, n. 75.

[64] *Missal*, p. 9.

approach where the apostles saw you enter with glory; as you ascend into heaven, regard [them] for the very reason that you deigned to descend to hell, . . . so that on the day of judgment they might not be among those on the left.[65]

In this prayer, which was also used on Ascension day itself,[66] the opening of hell at the Harrowing and of heaven at the Ascension mirror one another as cognate deeds of salvation that prefigured the redemption of worthy mankind after the Second Coming. The presence of this benediction among those prefaced by the miniature of the Ascension leaves no doubt that fusion of Ascension and Anastasis iconography to create the image of the Second Coming was intended to visualize the typological parallelism of these three acts of redemption.

In the Second Coming the Benedictional's makers once again represented a cloud illuminated by Christ's divinity; this raises the issue of whether the motif here possessed symbolic significance similar to that in the other miniatures discussed. For exegetes the meaning of the supernaturally irradiated cloud was bound up with the vexing question of how Christ would appear to mankind at the Second Coming.[67] Both the righteous and the sinful would see him, for Apocalypse 1:7 said that "he comes with the clouds, and every eye shall see him, and they also that pierced him." Yet the New Testament also stated that the beatific vision of God "face to face" (1 Cor. 13:12) was to be the supreme and exclusive reward of the blessed, "the pure of heart" (Matt. 5:8). This apparent contradiction was resolved by Augustine and later commenta-

tors who maintained that the sinners would be able to see only Christ's humanity—the body they had pierced in the Passion—while the just would behold his radiant divinity as well as his humanity.[68]

In his comments on Apocalypse 1:7, Ambrosius Autpertus[69] (d. 784) related this idea to God's previous manifestations in a cloud in the Old and New Testaments. He noted that the column of cloud in which God led the Israelites by day from Egypt became fiery at night, illuminating them but blinding the pursuing Egyptians (Ex. 14:19–20). Ambrosius Autpertus also recalled that, according to Isaiah 19:1, Christ came into the world in the cloud of the "light" or sinless human flesh he assumed from the Virgin. God's earlier appearances prefigured his final one in a cloud at the Second Coming:

> He will truly come with a cloud both illuminating and blinding, because he will flood the elect with the light of his divinity, . . . and he will deliver the damned into exterior darkness, concerning which . . . it is said: "Let the impious one be taken away so that he does not see the glory of God" (Is. 26:10, Septuagint version). . . . He will come both with the cloud and also in the cloud of his body, so that both the elect and the damned, beholding him in judgment, shall recognize him. . . . "And every eye shall see him, and they also who pierced him." . . . The vision of the Son of man, not humble as before, but very exalted, will appear to all.[70]

Such interpretations of the cloud of the Second Coming were widely diffused in Anglo-Saxon England and elsewhere.[71] In his commentary on

---

[65] *CBP*, no. 1152; Warner and Wilson, *Ben.*, p. 25: "Deus qui tartara fregisti resurgens, aperuisti caelos ascendens, ut populi illuc per fidem accederent, ubi te apostoli cum gloria uiderunt intrare, respice ascendens in caelum, propter quod dignatus es descendere ad infernum. . . . Ut in die iudicii non sint sinistro numero."

[66] Warner and Wilson, *Ben.*, p. 25, n. 2.

[67] For the following, see T. D. Hill, "Vision and Judgement in the Old English *Christ III*," *Studies in Philology* 70 (1973): 233–42.

[68] Augustine, *De Trinitate*, 1, 12, PL, 42, cols. 840f.; Hill, "Vision and Judgement," pp. 236ff.

[69] Ambrosius Autpertus, *Expositionis in Apocalypsin Libri I–IV*, 1, ed. R. Weber, CCCM, 27, pp. 50–53.

[70] Ambrosius Autpertus, *In Apocalypsin*, 1, 7a–b, pp. 52f.: Veniet uero cum nube inluminationis simul et obcaeca-

tionis, quia et electos diuinitatis suae luce perfundet, . . . et reprobos mancipabit in tenebras exteriores, de quibus . . . dicitur: "Tollatur impius ne uideat gloriam Dei." . . . Veniet etiam cum nube atque in nube corporis sui, ut simul eum et electi et reprobi in iudicio aspicientes cognoscant. . . . "Et uidebit eum omnis oculus, et qui eum pupugerunt." . . . Viso Filii hominis, non ut prius humilis, sed ualde excelsa cunctis apparebit.

[71] Echoing Ambrosius are Haymo of Auxerre, *Expositio in Apocalypsin*, 1, PL, 117, cols. 947B–48A, and Pseudo-Alcuin, *Commentariorum in Apocalypsin Libri Quinque*, 1, PL, 100, col. 1094B–D. See also Isidore of Seville, *Quaestiones in Vetus Testamentum*, 18, PL, 83, col. 296B; Hrabanus Maurus, *De Universo*, 9, 18, PL, 111, col. 276B–C; Remi of Auxerre, *Enarrationes in Psalmos*, PL, 131, col. 550D.

the Apocalypse Bede wrote that Christ "coming in judgment, overshadows the glory of [his] divinity with the cloud of [his] flesh, so that the impious might see him whom they pierced."[72] Æthelwold's own student, Ælfric, claimed that the pillar of cloud that had led and protected the Israelites

> betokened Christ, who is our guide in ghostly things; and he was gentle in his humanity, as in the semblance of a cloud [during his first visit to earth], and he will be very awful, in likeness of fire, at the great doom, when he will shine to the righteous and burn to the unrighteous. . . . The Lord will be gentle to the righteous, and awful to the unrighteous.[73]

This exegesis suggests that the repetition of the symbols of the cloud and divine light in the Ascension and the Second Coming was a means to depict the necessary relation between Christ's prior heavenly elevation of his human nature and his subsequent return with it.[74] In the Second Coming, however, the cloud is far denser and more turbulent than in the Ascension, the Annunciation, the Nativity, and the other pictures (pls. 8, 12, 14, 15, 16, 18, 19, 20, etc.), and only in the Second Coming is it tinged with red representing fire. These differences expressed the contrasting nature of Christ's two visits to earth in his human body. The stormy fire-cloud of the Second Coming manifested the awesome, wrathful character of his return in his body to judge and punish sinners. The fiery character of his "cloud" of humanity implied that it no longer tempered his divinity, allowing the blessed to bask in the full, illuminating light of his godhood, but burning and blinding the sinners who could see only the human being they had crucified. The combination of this punishing cloud with the instruments of the Passion illustrated Apocalypse 1:7 and indicated that Christ would come back in the very flesh that had been pierced on the cross. The less threatening "bright clouds" that appear in one guise or another in other scenes showed that in his First Advent Christ

had come in gentleness and humility rather than wrath, and that then he had mercifully tempered the light of his divinity with his humanity so that he could be the "the true light, which enlighteneth every man" (John 1:9). This is particularly evident in the Annunciation (pl. 8), where the cloud nimbus, the symbol of his divine light overshadowed by his moderating cloud of humanity, literally illuminates the Virgin. In the Nativity (pl. 12) there is another "bright cloud" illuminating the eyes of another member of mankind, the midwife, with the truth of the incarnate Christ. Christ's placement as the cornerstone at the bottom of this composition literally depicted the humility of his initial journey into the world. In the New Testament the characterizations of Christ as the stone "rejected" but "become the head of the corner" and as "a stone of stumbling" and a grindstone (Matt. 21:42; Luke 20:17; 1 Peter 2:8) are metaphors of his rebuff in his First Advent and his glorification in his Second Coming. The illuminators were certainly aware of this eschatological dimension of the cornerstone, since they had taken over the motif from the second picture in the Galba Psalter which portrayed Christ as the judge triumphant on the cornerstone (fig. 12). In the Nativity the cornerstone as well as the cloud alluded to the contrast between his merciful first visit and his terrifying final one.

The placement of the miniatures in the manuscript reinforced these dogmatic and typological relationships between Christ's two advents. The Annunciation does not preface Annunciation day (fols. 37v–38), as might be expected, but the first Sunday in Advent. This scene on folio 5v is the first feast picture in the book. The very next one in the cycle is the Second Coming on folio 9v illustrating the third Sunday in Advent, and the one after that is the Nativity on folio 15v, prefacing Christmas. Thus the feast cycle begins with a kind of typological triptych—the Second Coming flanked by the Annunciation and the Nativity, the two critical initial events of the First Coming—and binding this sequence of pictures together is the recurrent motif of the

---

[72] Bede, *Explanatio Apocalypsis*, 2 (Apoc. 14:14), PL, 93, col. 176A: "[Christus] qui ad judicium ueniens, gloriam diuinitatis nube carnis obumbrat, ut uideant impii quem compunxerunt."

[73] Ælfric, *Hom.*, 2, p. 201; also p. 197. See also *Blickling*, p. 122, for the idea that Christ first came and ascended in a

meek human body but would return in the same body "with all terror."

[74] Cf. *Blickling*, p. 122: "So our Lord shall hereafter come on Doomsday, in a cloud and in the same body with which he has now ascended into heaven."

bright cloud symbolizing Christ's divine and human natures. These first three feast miniatures establish the chronological and typological framework that encompasses all the events and personages in the following images in the book.

The illustration of Advent feasts with the Annunciation and Second Coming respectively reflects the essentially typological character of the Advent season. Although it precedes Christmas, Advent celebrates *all* the comings of the Lord to mankind. The Preface of the mass for the third Sunday, for instance, asked that "he who has redeemed us from the darkness of hell might lead us to eternal reward, and that he who has redeemed us in the First Advent, might vindicate us in the Second Advent."[75] In this text Christ's past advents at the Incarnation and the Harrowing of Hell are typologically aligned with his future one at the Last Judgment, and the mercy he showed to mankind on these prior occasions provides hope for another and final act of salvation. This prayer from the feast that the picture of the Second Coming illustrates would have been known to the painters, and it helps us to see that the allusions to the Harrowing of Hell in this picture belong to a broader pattern of typological relationships between the various events of the First Advent and the Second Coming.[76]

In the prayer the two advents of Christ are related to the believer in the present who, it must be remembered, is participating in the mass, the rite which brings Christ liturgically to the members of the Church. Christ's past advents revolve around his present one in the liturgy. Since we have discovered that the bright cloud in the Annunciation and Nativity scenes symbolized not only Christ's prior advent in the Incarnation but also his present one in the Church, where cloudlike prophets and preach-

ers rain down the heavenly "dew" of the Word on the congregation, there is a strong implication that the illuminated cloud in the Second Coming is likewise related to Christ's liturgical advent.

Many of the commentators who saw the cloud of the Second Coming as the humanity that Christ had assumed in the Incarnation also viewed it on another level as the prophets and preachers whose words continue to bring him spiritually to the faithful.[77] Augustine, interpreting Psalm 105:14 ("he comes to judge the world"), explained that Christ "first came in his Church in clouds. . . . [that is,] in his own preachers, and he filled the whole orb of the earth. Let us not resist his first coming, that we may not tremble at his second."[78]

The notion that Christ's prior advents prefigure and prepare for his final one pervades the Benedictional's own Advent texts, including the first blessing for the first Sunday in Advent, which we have seen to be a major literary inspiration of the typological cloud symbolism in the prefacing Annunciation miniature:

May omnipotent God, the advent of whose only begotten Son you believe to have happened in the past and expect to occur in the future, sanctify you by the illumination of the same [Son's] advent, and enrich you with his blessing. Amen.

May he protect you from all adversity in the contest of the present life and show himself mild to you in judgment. Amen.

So that you, freed by him from all contagions of sins, might await the day of that terrible examination unafraid. Amen.[79]

Once again Christ's First and Second Comings typologically frame his current advent, which is equated to the heavenly blessing the bishop

[75] *Jumièges*, p. 140: "Ipse nos quesumus ad aeternum perducat praemium, qui redemit de tenebris infernorum. Iustificetque in aduentu secundo, qui nos redemit in primo."

[76] The typological association of the Incarnation and the Harrowing of Hell was common in Latin and Old English literature; see Campbell, "Hell and Back," pp. 119, 124f., 147ff.; T. D. Hill, "Cosmic Stasis and the Birth of Christ: The Old English *Descent into Hell*, Lines 99–106," *Journal of English and Germanic Philology* 71 (1972): 386f.

[77] E.g., Ambrose, *Expositio Evangelii secundum Lucam*, 10, 39–42, ed. M. Adriaen, pp. 356f.; Paschasius Radbertus, *Expositio in Evangelium Matthaei*, 11, 24, PL, 120, cols. 819f.; Ambrosius Autpertus, *In Apocalypsin*, 1, pp. 50ff., esp. 51,

lines 74–76; Pseudo-Alcuin, *In Apocalypsin*, 1, 7, PL, 100, col. 1095C; Haymo, *In Apocalypsin*, 1, PL, 117, cols. 947D, 818B–21D.

[78] Augustine, *Enarrationes in Psalmos*, 95, 14, CC, 39, p. 1351: "Primo uenit in ecclesia sua in nubibus . . . in praedicatoribus suis, et impleuit totum orbem terrarum. Non resistamus primo aduentui, ut non expauescamus secundum."

[79] *CBP*, no. 1544; Warner and Wilson, *Ben.*, p. 2:

Omnipotens deus, cuius unigeniti aduentum et praeteritum creditis et futurum expectatis, eiusdemque aduentus uos illustratione sua sanctificet, sua benedictione locupletet. Amen.

In presentis uitae stadio uos ab omni aduersitate de-

calls down on the congregation in the mass. The grace stemming from Christ's liturgical advent continues that flowing from his earlier one in the Incarnation and prepares the believer to receive ultimate grace at his final coming. Virtually all of the manuscript's other Advent blessings—including those for the third Sunday, which are illustrated by the Second Coming —are in a similar vein, emphasizing the threefold coming of the grace of Christ in the past, present, and future.[80]

The consecutive pictures of the Annunciation and the Second Coming stressed the common theme of these blessings: the divine enlightenment that mankind receives from Christ's past and present advents foreshadows and makes possible the supernatural illumination that humanity hopes to receive from his final coming. The Virgin nimbed with the Christological cloud represented the necessary prototype of those liturgically blessed in their current life "by the illumination of the same [Son's] coming," while Christ lighting the fiery cloud portrayed the ultimate reward promised them in their future life —the unveiled sight of the radiant godhead.[81]

The idea of Christ's multiple advents seems to have fascinated the Anglo-Saxons about the time of the Benedictional. A recurrent theme of the Old English Advent lyrics (*Christ I*) in the late-tenth-century Exeter Book is that the coming of Christ has rescued or will rescue imprisoned mankind.[82] The poems are often deliberately ambiguous about exactly which coming of Christ is meant, so that the identity and time of the prisoners can be interpreted on different typological levels. They are simultaneously: mankind expecting the Incarnation, the forefathers in hell before the Harrowing, the contemporary congregation awaiting Christ's coming in the Advent and Christmas liturgy and at the Last Judgment. These are, of course, the same multiple advents of Christ that are typologically associated in the miniatures of the Annunciation, Nativity, and Second Coming (with its allusions to the Harrowing).[83] Since the first of the extant lyrics is based on one of the antiphons that inspired the cornerstone iconography of the Nativity, the relationship to the Benedictional is all the more striking. Clearly, the pictures and the poems emanate from the same Anglo-Saxon thought world.[84]

The Doubting of Thomas (Octave of Easter)

THE MODEL

The composition of the Doubting of Thomas (pl. 24) is unusual. Thomas, Peter, and a crowd of other apostles are to the left of Christ, but only a single disciple stands to the right. Two symmetrical groups of apostles invariably flank Christ in Byzantine works such as a tenth-century ivory in Washington (fig. 62)[85] and often in such Western ones as two ninth-century Carolingian ivo-

---

fendat, et se uobis in iudicio placabilem ostendat. Amen.

Quo a cunctis peccatorum contagiis liberati, illius tremendi examinis diem expectetis interriti. Amen.

[80] *CBP*, nos. 37, 663, 1200, 1307, 1352, 1722; Warner and Wilson, *Ben.*, pp. 2f.

[81] Raw, *Crucifixion*, pp. 29f., believed that the pictures did not illustrate the benedictions, but she did not treat either the texts or the iconography in depth.

[82] Burlin, *Advent*, pp. 65, 76f., 137, 176ff.; R. Lass, "Poem as Sacrament: Transcendence of Time in the *Advent Sequence* from the Exeter Book," *Annuale Mediaevale* 7 (1966): 3–15.

[83] There are also other similarities to the Exeter Book. C. Chase, "God's Presence through Grace as the Theme of Cynewulf's *Christ II* and the Relationship of this Theme to *Christ I* and *Christ III*," *ASE* 3 (1974): 87ff., suggested that the theme of Christ's threefold coming prompted the book's sequential arrangement of poems dealing with Advent,

Ascension, and Last Judgment, and as corroborating evidence he cited the very Advent blessings that are in the Benedictional.

[84] The theme of the threefold coming of Christ also occurred in Continental art. It has been previously mentioned that the depictions of Christ Emmanuel and the fountain of life in the Soissons Gospels (figs. 3, 4) represent Christ's advents in the Incarnation and the liturgy, but it has escaped attention that the Emmanuel also illustrates a reference to the Last Judgment in the canon table below. See also the early-tenth-century ivory diptych in Darmstadt; Goldschmidt, *Elf.*, 2, pp. 79f., no. 162, pl. 74; R. B. Green, "A Tenth-Century Ivory with the Response 'Aspiciens a Longe,'" *AB* 28 (1946): 112ff.; A. von Euw, *Elfenbeinarbeiten von der Spätantike bis zum hohen Mittelalter* (Frankfurt am Main, 1976), no. 6.

[85] K. Weitzmann, *Ivories and Steatites*, Catalogue of the By-

ries in Aachen and Narbonne (figs. 63, 64).[86] An alternative Western iconography that bunches all the apostles together on one side occurs on the silver reliquary casket of Pope Paschal I (817–824) in the Vatican (fig. 65).[87] The Anglo-Saxon scene seems to be a unique fusion of these two traditions: the disciples flank Christ but the composition is nonetheless strongly asymmetrical. The arrangement frames Christ hieratically and at the same time emphasizes Thomas's dramatic thrust by weighting his side of the composition.

The manner in which the upper right quarter of Christ's tunic is completely omitted to display the wound in his side also helps to trace the source of the iconography. Byzantine art showed the wound either through a hole in Christ's tunic, as in the ivory in Washington, or with his drawn-back sleeve.[88] In the Drogo Sacramentary (fig. 66), however, the wound is revealed just as in the Benedictional.[89] This is the first appearance of the motif, and it confirms that Carolingian art, perhaps even a work from Metz, was the major source of the Benedictional's iconography.

The Typological and Incarnational Symbolism

In addition to the composition, several other features of the image are highly original. Christ's gold hair and beard and his gold mandorla are apparently unparalleled in any other scene of the Doubting. His cross-staff is also unprecedented in this context and very precocious; only in the twelfth century did this become a relatively common Christological attribute in depic-

tions of the theme.[90] Finally, few if any other depictions set the scene in a cloud.

In representations of other events in Christ's life these motifs were not so unusual. The mandorla was his traditional attribute in theophanies such as the Transfiguration, the Harrowing of Hell, the Ascension, the Stoning of Stephen, and the Second Coming, and in the Benedictional's renderings of the latter three events as well as the Baptism he appears in one (pls. 10, 14, 19, 25). Christ often carries the cross-staff symbolizing his victory over death in such triumphal post-Resurrection events as the Ascension (pl. 25, figs. 48, 49, 52) and the Second Coming (pl. 10, fig. 12), the only other themes represented in the Benedictional where he has this attribute, as well as gold hair and beard, another theophanic feature. Finally, in accordance with the New Testament, Christ at the Ascension and the Second Coming appears in a *doxa* of cloud, a motif the Benedictional's illuminators extended to other of his epiphanies.

This brief survey makes it clear that not only the cloud but the other Christological attributes were transferred from these more traditional theophanic events to the Doubting. This appearance of Christ, which is described in John 20:24–31, was an obvious manifestation of his divinity. He appeared suddenly and miraculously to his disciples in a room with closed doors, and Thomas's sceptical probing of his wounds proved his Resurrection. The transference of the theophanic and triumphal attributes emphasized that the Doubting was one of the epiphanies of the resurrected man-God.

At the same time the depiction of Christ with the same set of attributes (mandorla, gold hair, cross-staff, and cloud) in the Doubting, the As-

zantine and Early Mediaeval Antiquities in the Dumbarton Oaks Collection, 3 (Washington, 1972), pp. 43–48, no. 21, pls. 22, 23, color pl. 4.

[86] Goldschmidt, *Elf.*, 1, pp. 17, 20, nos. 22a, 31, pls. 12, 15; H. Fillitz, "Elfenbeinreliefs vom Hofe Kaiser Karls des Kahlen," *Beiträge zur Kunst des Mittelalters. Festschrift für Hans Wentzel zum 60. Geburtstag* (Berlin, 1975), pp. 46–51, fig. 2; A. Bonnery, "L'Ivoire de la crucifixion de cathédrale de Narbonne," *Les Cahiers de Saint-Michel de Cuxa* 23 (1992): 121–27.

[87] *Ornamenta Ecclesiae*, 3 (Cologne, 1985), pp. 85f.; H. Grisar, *Die Römische Kapelle Sancta Sanctorum und ihr Schatz* (Freiburg im Breisgau, 1908), p. 100, fig. 45. This iconography originated in Western early Christian art and is common in Ottonian works; see Schiller, *Ikon.*, 3, p. 109, figs. 341,

268; F. J. Ronig, *Codex Egberti* (Trier, 1977), pp. 116f.

[88] T. Velmans, *Le Tétraévangile de la Laurentienne*, Bibliothèque des Cahiers Archéologiques, 6 (Paris, 1971), fig. 300.

[89] *Drogo-Sak.*, p. 23, fol. 43; Schiller, *Ikon.*, 3, p. 111. The slight asymmetry of this Carolingian scene is probably an *ad hoc* adjustment to the shape of the letter; hence it is not a true parallel to the Anglo-Saxon composition.

[90] There are only two instances of the motif in the eleventh century: a copy of the Benedictional's scene in the Tiberius Psalter (Wormald, "Psalter," p. 133, fig. 140) and a Rhenish portable ivory altar in Osnabrück (Goldschmidt, *Elf.*, 2, no. 102d, pl. 31; W. Borchers, *Der Osnabrücker Domschatz*, Osnabrücker Geschichtsquellen und Forschungen, 19 [Osnabrück, 1974], pp. 42–45, fig. 25).

cension, and the Second Coming differentiates them from all other miniatures in the manuscript, drawing the trio of post-Resurrection scenes into a special narrative and symbolic relationship with each other. The fact that the Ascension follows the Doubting in the picture cycle helps to connect them. The Ascension, however, has an even closer visual relation to the Second Coming, since only these two pictures include the additional similarities of Christ's pose, the rays of light, and the unusual form of his mandorla.

The Doubting of Thomas was typologically associated with the two other events in the very homily of the Pseudo-Chrysostom[91] that, directly or indirectly, influenced the Benedictional's iconography of the Second Coming. The homilist first noted that Christ ascending had taken the cross up to heaven and that returning in judgment he would bring it back to earth. In the text as in the miniatures, the Ascension and the Second Coming are typological mirror images. After comparing the angels bringing Christ's cross at the Second Coming to the troops bearing an emperor's insignia, the author explained that Christ would display the cross and also his wounds at the Last Judgment so that mankind would see whom they had pierced on the cross. These are ideas the Benedictional illustrated by the angels carrying the instruments of the Passion. The Pseudo-Chrysostom went on to say that Christ's exhibition of his wounds and his cross on the Last Day had been prefigured by his manifestation of his wounds to Thomas, which then too had allayed men's misgivings

about the Resurrection. The same comparison was made by Bede, Haymo of Auxerre, and Smaragdus[92] in their homilies for the Octave of Easter, the feast illustrated by the miniature of the Doubting. These Anglo-Saxon and Carolingian homilists also observed that Christ's earlier manifestation of his Resurrection in a palpable yet incorruptible human body prefigured and vouched for the future resurrection of mankind at the Last Judgment.[93] The symbolic association of the Doubting with the Ascension and the Last Judgment even occurs in the Benedictional's own text, a point to which we shall return. All this assures us that the theophanic and triumphal attributes were transferred into the Doubting to bring out its typological resemblance to the two later manifestations of the risen Christ.

Bede and the Carolingian homilists also likened Christ displaying his wounds on these occasions to a soldier proudly exhibiting his battle scars as tokens of his triumph,[94] and this analogy probably prompted the use of a figural type that had imperial overtones for the Christ in the Doubting. Christ bears a strong similarity—even in a detail like the way the cross-staff is held—to the portrait of the Carolingian emperor Louis the Pious that often illustrates Hrabanus Maurus' treatise *De Laudibus Sanctae Crucis*, as in a ninth-century copy in Vienna (Österr. Nationalbibl., MS Vindobonensis 652; fig. 67).[95] Two illustrated Anglo-Saxon manuscripts of this popular Carolingian text are extant from the tenth and eleventh centuries,[96] and one was also available at Glastonbury during the abbacy

---

[91] *Homilia in Crucem et in Latronem*, 2, 5, Patrologi Graeca, 49, cols. 413f.; also 1, 4, cols. 404f. See also Pseudo-Augustine, *Sermo* 155, 10–11, PL, 39, cols. 2051f.

[92] Bede, *Hom.*, 2, 9, pp. 82ff.; also *In Lucam*, 6, pp. 419f., repeated by Smaragdus, *Dominica in Octava Paschae*, PL, 102, col. 282D; Haymo, *Homilia* 81, PL, 118, cols. 496D–97A.

[93] Bede, *In Lucam*, 6, pp. 418; Haymo, *Homilia* 81, PL, 118, col. 495C–D; Smaragdus, *In Octava Paschae*, PL, 102, col. 281A. Ælfric (ed. Gatch, *Preaching*, p. 141) inserts this typology into a description of the Second Coming derived from Julian of Toledo and ultimately the Pseudo-Chrysostom. Ælfric's homily for the Octave of Easter (*Hom.*, 1, pp. 230ff.) concludes an exposition of the Doubting with a refutation of the doubts about mankind's future resurrection. Regarding this typology, see also O'Reilly, "Text and Image," pp. 100ff., who briefly noted the resemblances among the Benedictional's three scenes.

[94] Bede, *In Lucam*, 6, p. 420, repeated by Haymo, *Homilia*

81, PL, 118, col. 497A–B, and Smaragdus, *In Octava Paschae*, PL, 102, col. 283C.

[95] P. E. Schramm, *Die deutschen Kaiser und Könige in Bildern ihrer Zeit 751–1190*, 2nd ed., ed. F. Mütherich (Munich, 1983), pp. 158f., 294; E. Sears, "Louis the Pious as *Miles Christi*: The Dedicatory Image in Hrabanus Maurus's *De Laudibus Sanctae Crucis*," *Charlemagne's Heir: New Perspectives on the Reign of Louis the Pious*, ed. P. Godman and R. Collins (Oxford, 1990), pp. 605ff. For the imperial character of Anglo-Saxon images of Christ with a cross-staff, see J. E. Rosenthal, "Three Drawings in an Anglo-Saxon Pontifical: Anthropomorphic Trinity or Threefold Christ?" *AB* 63 (1981): 551ff.

[96] Cambridge, Trinity Coll., MS B. 16. 3 (Temple, *Manuscripts*, pp. 42f., no. 14; S. Keynes, *Anglo-Saxon Manuscripts in Trinity College* [Binghamton, 1992], no. 4) and Cambridge, Univ. Lib., MS Gg. 5. 35 (T. Ohlgren, *Insular and Anglo-Saxon Illuminated Manuscripts. An Iconographic Catalogue c. A.D.*

of Dunstan (ca. 940–956), while Æthelwold was there.[97] The influence of this Carolingian ruler image can be detected elsewhere in the Benedictional, as well as in the copies of Æthelwold's lost frontispiece for his Old English translation of the Benedictine *Rule*;[98] it is highly likely that a portrait of Louis the Pious was the source of the imperialized pose of Christ in the Doubting. This influence reinforced the scene's typological relationship to the Second Coming, where Christ has a pronounced imperial character because of the inscription on his garments ("King of kings and Lord of lords"), his pose, and his angelic cohort bearing the insignia of his Passion.

Although in the Second Coming Christ does not actually expose his wounds as in the Doubting, viewers would still have perceived the bared wounds in the Doubting as a typological allusion to Doomsday. In the Last Judgment on a damaged early-eleventh-century Anglo-Saxon ivory in Cambridge (fig. 68),[99] Christ displays the stigmata in his palms and the wound in his side through the omission of his tunic over his right shoulder. Since this manner of revealing the lance mark had first occurred in the Carolingian iconography of the Doubting of Thomas (fig. 66), the adoption of this feature for the Judge on the ivory visually referred to his display of the wounds before the Ascension. Underscoring this allusion is the inscription in the border of Christ's mandorla: "O uos om(ne)s, ui(det)e manus et p(edes)" (O you all, see [my] hands and feet).[100] This paraphrases Christ's words when he had appeared to the disciples after the Resurrection (Luke 24:39, John 20:27). This particular iconographic type of Christ the

Judge was known to the Benedictional's makers, for it appears in the second picture in the Galba Psalter (fig. 12). The relationship between the Psalter and the Benedictional's picture of the Doubting is especially close because both show Christ exhibiting only his side wound with his right arm raised and holding a cross-staff in his other hand.

In the Psalter, as in the later ivory, the figure of the Judge alluded typologically to the iconography of the Doubting. This same figure in the Psalter is also typologically related to the manuscript's Ascension (fig. 53), a feature that, as we have noted, influenced the Benedictional's typological linkage of these two themes. In the last analysis the Psalter's iconography presaged and influenced the Benedictional's more explicit symbolic association of these two themes with the Doubting of Thomas.

Nonetheless, the best antecedent for the Benedictional's linkage of the Doubting and the Ascension is not Anglo-Saxon but Carolingian. Both events are depicted on a ninth-century ivory in Weimar (fig. 56). There was, of course, a narrative basis for the plaque's coupling of these themes, since Christ ascended soon after he had appeared to Thomas and the disciples. At the same time, however, there is a calculated similarity between the two scenes that visualized a deeper relationship as analogous manifestations of the resurrected man-God to the apostles. In the upper register the ascending Christ, looking and gesturing to his right, mirrors his figure on the same axis below in the Doubting. The Virgin is among the spectators in both scenes. As she was customarily represented at the Ascension but not at the Doubting,[101] her incorporation

---

625–1100 [New York, 1986], pp. 301ff., no. 224). Neither includes the ruler portrait. Another Anglo-Saxon copy has been lost from London, British Lib., MS Cotton Tib. B. V, pt. 1; N. R. Ker, *Catalogue of Manuscripts containing Anglo-Saxon* (Oxford, 1957), p. 256, no. 139.

[97] H. Gneuss, "Dunstan und Hrabanus Maurus. Zur HS. Bodleian Auctarium F. 4. 32," *Anglia* 96 (1978): 136–48; J. Higgitt, "Glastonbury, Dunstan, Monasticism and Manuscripts," *Art History* 2 (1979): 278f.; M. Budny, "'St. Dunstan's Classbook' and its Frontispiece: Dunstan's Portrait and Autograph," *Dunstan*, pp. 117f., 133f.

[98] See the discussion of the initial for the Octave of Pentecost (pl. 27) later in this chapter. For the frontispiece, see Deshman, "*Benedictus*," pp. 236ff.

[99] Goldschmidt, *Elf.*, 4, p. 9, no. 2, pl. 1; Beckwith, *Ivory Carvings*, p. 121, no. 18, fig. 41.

[100] E. Okasha, *Handlist of Anglo-Saxon Non-Runic Inscriptions* (Cambridge, 1971), p. 104, no. 97. O'Reilly, "Text and Image," pp. 72ff., has recently treated the ivory and its relation to other themes in great detail. She very properly emphasizes the multivalence of the iconography, but her attempt to distance it from the Last Judgment is less convincing. Absent from her discussion is the earliest example of an enthroned Christ displaying the stigmata, the Last Judgment in the ninth-century Byzantine Sacra Parallel; K. Weitzmann, *The Miniatures of the Sacra Parallela*, Studies in Manuscript Illumination, 8 (Princeton, 1979), pp. 169f., fig. 441.

[101] She does appear in the scene in an eleventh-century Regensburg manuscript; G. Swarzenski, *Die Regensburger Buchmalerei* (Leipzig, 1901), pl. 26, no. 70. See also the depiction of Christ's Appearance to the Apostles on the cruciform

into the Doubting strengthens the analogy between the two events. In the imagery of the Ascension she was a reminder of the divine Christ's assumed human body, and in the new context of the Doubting she served the same function. Ælfric and other commentators frequently compared Christ's miraculous entrance in a palpable body through closed doors to the apostles to his birth in that same human body from the closed womb of the Virgin.[102]

The ivory's transference of an iconographic feature of the Ascension to the Doubting to draw attention to their typological and dogmatic relationship anticipated in principle the similar phenomenon in the Benedictional a century or so later, though the specific motives associating the scenes are very different in the two works. It should also be remembered that both the plaque and the Benedictional linked the Doubting with an Ascension scene that stressed Christ's two natures by portraying his miraculous self-elevation. Clearly the Anglo-Saxons must have known something of the Carolingian association of the two themes, but they put this knowledge into practice in a rather independent fashion.

While the Benedictional's illuminators did not go so far as to include the Virgin in the Doubting, they did transfer other motifs from the Ascension and the Second Coming that portrayed Christ's two natures: the mandorla and golden hair symbolizing the supernatural light of his divinity and the cloud symbolizing his assumed human flesh. Bede did not expressly mention the Doubting in his Ascension homily, but he did say that Christ, having received "his cloud of human nature" in the Incarnation, went through "mockery, scourging, and death" before ascending with it.[103] The illuminated cloud is an iconographic symbol that links the Doubting to Christ's later manifestations, when he would ascend and return in his human body, and to his initial entrance into the world in the

flesh at the Annunciation and the Nativity (pls. 8, 12).

One final innovative feature of the Doubting still to be considered is the enormous key held by Peter, who stands behind Thomas. While Peter was often included in scenes of the Doubting, he surprisingly seldom appears there with the key, his customary attribute.[104] Elsewhere in the Benedictional he also has his key (pls. 7, 26), but the key's unusual prominence in the Doubting gives it special importance in this scene.

Christ himself gave the key to Peter: "And I will give unto thee the keys of the kingdom of heaven: and whatsoever thou shalt bind on earth shall be bound in heaven; and whatsoever thou shalt loose on earth shall be loosed in heaven" (Matt. 16:19). It symbolized the power that the Lord delegated to the apostle to condemn or forgive sins, to designate who should be excluded from or included in the heavenly kingdom. Only Peter received such authority in this passage, but commentators[105] maintained that the other apostles received the same authority later when Christ told them during his first manifestation after the Resurrection that they could forgive or retain the sins of others (John 20:22–23). Thomas had been absent on this occasion (John 20:24, 26), and it was at Christ's second manifestation to the disciples eight days later that he had probed Christ's wounds. These two appearances of Christ were closely associated with each other, however. Both times the resurrected Lord miraculously appeared in a room with a shut door, blessing the apostles with the same words and showing his wounds to quell their doubts. On a Carolingian ivory in Aachen (fig. 63) the Doubting in the upper register is placed over a very similar representation of the first appearance, and English Romanesque art sometimes conflated these two events into one scene.[106] The liturgy celebrated the two manifestations on successive days: the

silver casket of Paschal I; Grisar, *Sancta Sanctorum*, pp. 97ff., fig. 43.

[102] Ælfric, *Hom.*, 1, p. 231; also Jerome (*Epistola* 49, 21, ed. I. Hilberg, CSEL, 54 [Vienna, 1910], pp. 386f.), Augustine (PL, 38, col. 1157), Gregory (PL, 76, cols. 1197D, 1201D), and Smaragdus (PL, 102, col. 280C).

[103] See above, chap. 1, n. 144.

[104] The only other examples before the thirteenth century known to me are a relief in S. Domingo de Silos and a miniature in the Glasgow Psalter (Glasgow, Hunterian Lib., MS U. 3. 2); Schiller, *Ikon.*, 3, figs. 353, 360. Regarding the key, see

J. Poeschke, "Schlüssel," *LCI*, 4, cols. 81f.; F. P. Pickering, *Literatur und darstellende Kunst im Mittelalter* (Berlin, 1966), pp. 87–89.

[105] E.g., Augustine, *Sermo* 295, PL, 38, col. 1349; Bede, *Hom.*, 1, 20, pp. 201f.; Hrabanus Maurus, *In Matthaeum*, 5, 16, PL, 107, col. 992B–C.

[106] See the twelfth-century Winchester Psalter (K. E. Haney, *The Winchester Psalter* [Leicester, 1986], pp. 122f., fig. 25) and the St. Albans Psalter (O. Pächt et al., *The St. Albans Psalter* [*Albani Psalter*] [London, 1960], pp. 78, 94, pl. 32a).

first on the Saturday after Easter and the second on the Octave of Easter.[107] In his homily for the latter feast Haymo of Auxerre[108] treated not only the Doubting of Thomas but also the delegation of the power of the key to Peter and the other apostles. In the Benedictional's miniature the prominent key symbolized the authority to bind and loose that Christ granted Peter and the other disciples after his Resurrection.

The text the picture prefaces, the benediction for the Octave, does not refer to the key, but it does mention the opening of doors:

> May God whose only begotten [Son] on this day deigned to appear to his disciples with the doors closed, deign to enrich you with the gift of his blessing, and to open for you the doors of the celestial kingdom. Amen.
>
> And may he, who removed the wound of doubt from their breasts by the touching of his body, grant that through the faith by which you have believed him to be resurrected, you may be freed of the stain of all transgressions. Amen.
>
> And may you, who with Thomas believe him to be God and Lord and call him with suppliant voices, be able to be protected by him from all evils in this age and to stand with the ranks of the saints in the future. Amen.[109]

Here is the idea that the same divine power that previously allowed Christ to appear miraculously through closed doors to bless the apostles should bless mankind in the Church in the present and yet again in the future by opening the gates of heaven for them. The benediction aligns Christ's post-Resurrection appearances to the apostles behind closed doors, his present advent to the faithful through the liturgical blessing, and his final manifestation at the Last Judgment in a threefold typological relationship, and the apostles at the Doubting prefigure the saints in heaven whom the believers hope to join. The prayer's play on divine power over closed and open doors is highly relevant for the meaning of Peter's key in the accompanying miniature.

The Apocalypse used the key that locks or unlocks doors as a metaphor for Christ's power to damn or save at the Last Judgment: "He hath the key of David, he that openeth, and no man shutteth; and shutteth, and no man openeth; I know thy works: behold, I have set before thee an open door, and no man can shut it" (3:7–8).[110] Because Christ had delegated the power of the key to Peter, the prince of the apostles was traditionally accorded the role of the gate keeper of heaven. The Benedictional's text for the feast of the *Cathedra Sancti Petri* celebrated him as the "ianitor caeli" who admits whomever he wishes to heaven,[111] and a Winchester poem addressed to Æthelwold expressed the wish that the righteous "may be compatriots of Peter in the summit of heaven, Peter who unlocks the threshold of Olympus with huge keys, to whom God the thunderer entrusted his snowy-white flocks."[112] One of the first representations of the Last Judgment with Peter as the heavenly gate keeper comes from early-eleventh-century Winchester. In the upper register of the recto of a two-page composition in the Liber Vitae of New Minster (London, British Lib., MS Stowe 944; fig. 69) Peter, key in hand, opens the door of the heavenly city and beckons the choirs of the blessed to enter,[113] his action contrasting with that of the an-

---

[107] The pericopes for the Saturday and Sunday after Easter are John 20:19–31 and 20:24–31, respectively; Klauser, *Capitulare*, pp. 193, 194.

[108] *Homilia* 81, PL, 118, col. 493C.

[109] *CBP*, no. 679; Warner and Wilson, *Ben.*, p. 21:

Deus cuius unigenitus hodierna die discipulis suis ianuis clausis dignatus est apparere, suae uos benedictionis dono locupletare, et caelestis uobis regni ianuas dignetur aperire. Amen.

Et qui ab eorum pectoribus ad tactum sui corporis uulnus amputauit dubietatis, concedat ut per fidem qua eum resurrexisse creditis omnium delictorum maculis careatis. Amen.

Et qui eum cum thoma deum et dominum creditis, et cernuis uocibus inuocatis, ab eo et in hoc saeculo a malis omnibus tueri, et in futuro sanctorum coetibus adstare ualeatis. Amen.

[110] See also Apoc. 1:18, 9:1, 20:1–3.

[111] *CBP*, no. 851; Warner and Wilson, *Ben.*, p. 12. Regarding the culting of Peter in England, see V. Ortenberg, *The English Church and the Continent in the Tenth and Eleventh Centuries* (Oxford, 1992), pp. 163ff.

[112] *Carmen de Libero Arbitrio*, lines 162–63, ed. and tr. M. Lapidge, "Three Latin Poems from Æthelwold's School at Winchester," *ASE* 1 (1972): 136, 137.

[113] Temple, *Manuscripts*, pp. 95f., no. 78. Peter also appears as the heavenly gate keeper in middle Byzantine Last Judgments; see Brenk, *Tradition*, p. 86, fig. 24.

gel in the lower register who uses a key to lock the door of hell (cf. Apoc. 20:1–3, Matt. 16: 18–19).

In the Benedictional's miniature of the Doubting, which the draftsman of the Liber Vitae surely knew, Peter's attribute simultaneously alluded to Christ's power over doors in his past manifestations after the Resurrection and his coming one at the Last Judgment; the key symbolized both the initial delegation of this authority to Peter and his future eschatological exercise of this power.

Our interpretation of the miniature's benediction has thus far regarded the mention of Christ's power "to open the doors of heaven for you" as a reference to the Last Judgment, but there is a meaningful lack of temporal specificity in the prayer. It might also refer to the Ascension when Christ opened the gates of heaven to human nature, preparing the way for mankind's future admission at the Last Judgment.

This is borne out by other benedictions in the manuscript, such as one for Ascension day, which faces the picture of the event:

> May omnipotent God, whose only begotten [Son] today entered the height of the heavens, bless you and open for you the gate of the Ascension where he is. Amen.
>
> And may he graciously grant that as [Christ was made] manifest to the apostles after his Resurrection, so he coming in judgment may appear peaceful to you. Amen.[114]

In this benediction Christ's appearances to the disciples after the Resurrection, when he had repeatedly blessed them with peace (e.g., John 20:19–20, 26), again prefigure his manifestation

and bestowal of grace on the righteous in the present through the liturgical benediction and in the future at the Second Coming. The Ascension, however, is explicitly included in the typology: then too Christ had manifested himself to the apostles and blessed them (Luke 24:51), and his entrance into heaven on that occasion made possible and prefigured his future opening of the same "gate of the Ascension" to the blessed at the Last Judgment.

This theme is echoed and amplified in the very next blessing, the prayer for the Sunday after Ascension day: "O God, you who rising again have broken hell, you ascending have opened the heavens . . . so that on the day of judgment they [the people] might not be among those on the left."[115] This benediction, which helped to motivate the typological association of the iconography of the Ascension, the Second Coming, and the Harrowing of Hell, introduces yet another typological dimension, for Christ's breaking open the gate of hell to rescue mankind foreshadows his merciful opening of the heavenly gates at the Ascension and, by implication, the Last Judgment. The Harrowing is also included in the blessing for the Wednesday after Easter, a few days before the Octave: "May our Lord God, who rescued you from the pit of misery, lead you to the tree of life, [and] may he, who broke the gates of hell, open for you the gate of paradise."[116]

In the benedictions associated with the miniatures of the Doubting and Ascension the recurrent typological theme of Christ's power over doors leading to blessing or damnation connects the Harrowing, the Doubting, and the Ascension as cognate prefigurations of the Second Coming.[117] Peter's key in the Doubting was the

---

[114] *CBP*, nos. 280, 281; Warner and Wilson, *Ben.*, p. 25:
Benedicat uos omnipotens deus, cuius hodierna die unigenitus caelorum alta penetrauit, et uobis ubi ille est ascendendi aditum patefecit. Amen.
Concedat propitius, ut sicut post resurrectionem suam discipulis [uisus est] manifestus, ita uobis in iudicium ueniens uideatur placatus. Amen.

[115] See above, n. 65.

[116] *CBP*, no. 1268; Warner and Wilson, *Ben.*, p. 20: "Dominus deus noster, uos perducat ad arborem uitae, qui eruit de lacu miseriae, ipse uobis aperiat ianuam paradysi, qui confregit portas inferni."

[117] The doors of the room where Christ appeared after the Resurrection and the gates of hell at the Harrowing had long been associated in exegesis; see the sermon of Basil of Seleucia (d. ca. 459), tr. A. Hamman and F. Quéré-Jaulmes, *La*

Mystère de Pâcques (Paris, 1965), p. 156. It might not be entirely coincidental that middle Byzantine art represented the interrelated motifs of Christ at the Anastasis trampling the gates of hell, sometimes amid shattered fragments of locks and keys, and Christ ascending to the open heavenly gates; S. G. Tsuji, "Destruction des portes de l'Enfer et ouverture des portes du Paradise à propos des illustrations du Psaume 23, 7–10 et du Psaume 117, 19–20," *Cahiers Archéologique* 31 (1983): 5–23; Kartsonis, *Anastasis*, figs. 54, 60, 80, 81, etc. This Eastern Ascension motif was imitated in Ottonian art; cf. Goldschmidt, *Elf.*, 2, nos. 53–55, 58; also Schiller, *Ikon.*, 3, pp. 155f. In the eleventh-century Anglo-Saxon versions of the Harrowing on the Bristol slab (fig. 60) and in the Winchester Tiberius Psalter (Wormald, *Studies*, fig. 139) the open door of hell is behind Christ.

artists' response to this textual theme—an additional feature that interrelated these events.[118]

The key is another architectural theme—besides that of the cornerstone—that associates the Benedictional with the contemporary Old English Advent lyrics. In the second poem, which is based on the Advent antiphon *O clavis David*, mankind, imprisoned in darkness and awaiting "the sun," pleads for deliverance to the "Ruler and rightful King, who guards the lock, who opens the blessed way to heaven, yet withholds from another that bright, longed-for journey."[119] Typological plays on various celestial, terrestrial, and infernal doors and locks also occur in other lyrics. While the doors of the room where Christ appeared to the apostles are not specifically mentioned, the key in the poetry, as in the picture, is a multivalent emblem of Christ's power to save (or condemn) mankind at a series of typologically related advents in the past, present, and future.

In the miniature Peter holds up his gold key almost as if to juxtapose it to Christ's gold cross-staff. The key itself terminates in a cross,[120] confirming that it was to be viewed as a kind of cross, analogous to Christ's. Key and cross are also closely associated in the miniature on folio 4 (pl. 7), where Peter's cross almost seems to be another key on his key ring. On a Carolingian ivory in Paris (fig. 70) Christ simultaneously bestows both attributes upon the apostle.[121] The Benedictional's artists must have known of the prior linkage of the key and the cross. What was the meaning of their association in the context of the Doubting?

Like the key, the cross was a traditional attribute of Peter. He had been martyred on it, as the Benedictional itself illustrates (pl. 31). The juxtaposition of his key-cross and the resurrected Christ's triumphal cross-staff alluded to the apostle's crucifixion in Christ's image and to his future resurrection by means of Christ's own victory over death. The association of the attributes subtly established a meaningful connection between the miniatures of the Doubting and the Crucifixion of Peter.

Yet this interpretation does not suffice to explain the literal fusion of the key and the cross into a single hybrid attribute. Exegesis equated the key and the cross on the authority of Isaiah 22:22: "And the key of the house of David will I lay upon his shoulder: so he shall open, and none shall shut; and he shall shut, and none shall open." A commentary on Isaiah ascribed to Remi of Auxerre (ca. 841–908), for example, interpreted this key as Christ's "power of the kingdom, and the insigne of victory, that is, the cross which he carried on his own shoulder."[122] As we have mentioned, the "key of David" also became a metaphor for the Last Judgment in the Apocalypse (3:7–8). The key's passional and eschatological meanings were tied together by such exegetes as Jerome, who wrote that "the cross of Christ is the key to paradise, the cross of Christ opened paradise."[123]

The combination and juxtaposition of the key and the cross in the miniature signified that the power to open and shut the gates of heaven which Christ had delegated to the disciples came from his own victory over death. Previous works had visualized this idea in various ways, but the Benedictional gave this symbolism added force by introducing it into the theme of the Doubting of Thomas. Here the resurrected Christ's triumphal display of his wounds and of his *vexillum* of the cross vividly manifests to the apostles his

[118] In the Ascension miniature Peter, though prominently positioned, does not hold the key, but in later Anglo-Saxon or Anglo-Saxon influenced scenes (fig. 57) he often shoulders a large key, a visible sign that Christ—even as he opens heaven—leaves this power to his apostles on earth; cf. also the Caligula troper, reproduced by Schapiro, "Dis. Christ," fig. 7.

[119] Burlin, *Advent*, p. 69, also pp. 70ff., 134f., 143ff.

[120] Already noted by Warner and Wilson, *Ben.*, p. xxv, and C. Fox, "Anglo-Saxon Monumental Sculpture in the Cambridge District," *Proceedings of the Cambridge Antiquarian Society* 23 (1920–21): 32f., who found another example of the motif on a tenth- or eleventh-century grave slab in Cambridge castle.

[121] Goldschmidt, *Elf.*, 1, p. 37, no. 71a, pl. 28; A. L. Vandersall, "Two Carolingian Ivories from the Morgan Collec-

tion in The Metropolitan Museum of Art," *Metropolitan Museum Journal* 6 (1972): 17ff.; see also *Stuttgarter Bilderpsalter*, 1, fol. 103v; Weitzmann, *Mt. Sinai, Icons*, no. B. 5, pl. 8.

[122] Remi of Auxerre, *Commentaria in Isaiam*, 2, 22, PL, 116, col. 823C: "Per clauem . . . possumus intelligere imperium regni, et signum uictoriae, id est, crucem quam ipse proprio humero portauit." Also Jerome, *Commentaria in Isaiam Prophetarum*, 7, 22, PL, 24, col. 283B.

[123] Jerome, *Homilia in Lucam Euangelistam [16, 19–31]*, ed. G. Morin, *Anecdota Maredsolana*, 3, pt. 2 (Maredsoli, 1897), p. 385: "Crux Christi clauis paradisi est, crux Christi aperuit paradisum." Also Augustine, *Enarrationes*, 45, 1, p. 518. Some late medieval representations of the Crucifixion show the upper arm of the cross terminating in a hand with a key unlocking the gate of the heavenly city; R. L. Füglister, *Das lebende Kreuz* (Einsiedeln, 1964), pp. 180ff., pls. 1–29.

victory in the Passion, thereby showing with utmost clarity the source and character of the power he bestows on them at his manifestations.

As the emblem of the disciples' judgmental authority, the key might also be related to the symbolic clouds in the scene. In Gregory's *Moralia in Job*, a well-known text, no fewer than five chapters treat the cloudlike apostles and their successors, the preachers, who carried out Christ's dispensation of judgment. Empowered to bind and loose sin at Christ's first manifestation after the Resurrection, these apostolic "clouds" enacted judgment through their preaching, which watered the parched hearts of mankind with fear of damnation and hope of heavenly joy.[124] The cloud in the Doubting, as in many of the other typologically related miniatures, very likely symbolized not only Christ himself but also those whose words continued to reveal him to men,

preparing them for the ordeal of his last manifestation in clouds.

Although built on Carolingian foundations, the Anglo-Saxon iconography of the Doubting greatly expanded the symbolism of the theme. Carolingian art had typologically linked the Doubting to the Ascension, another theophany to the apostles that manifested Christ's two natures; but under the influence of the Galba Psalter and various texts, above all those of the Benedictional itself, the network of typologically associated themes was extended to include the incarnate Christ's first and final appearances in the world. The novel incorporation of key symbolism stressed Christ's empowerment of the apostles and their ecclesiastic successors, and this in turn reinforced the typological meaning of the Doubting as yet another prefiguration of Christ's present and final advents to mankind.

The Entry into Jerusalem (Palm Sunday)

THE MODELS

Before considering the sources of the Entry miniature, we must clarify the identity of the figures following Christ (pl. 21). Warner[125] believed they were the apostles, but many obstacles stand in the way of this identification. One of the figures is a veiled woman who must be a citizen of Jerusalem, and typically the citizens and the disciples remain separated (e.g., figs. 71–75). Moreover, the figures hold palm branches, which were usually, though not always, an attribute of the city residents (cf. Matt. 21:8; Mark 11:7; John 12:12–13). Elsewhere in the manuscript the apostles are invariably nimbed and dressed in loose-sleeved tunics and mantles (pls. 4–7, 24–26, 31, 34), but the men in the Entry lack haloes and wear tight-sleeved tunics and chlamides fastened by fibulae —a costume appropriate only for secular personages. Their attributes and costumes indicate that these figures must be citizens,[126] who seem to have displaced the apostles from their custom-

ary place. The explanation of this anomaly will be considered in due course.

Of more immediate concern are the implications for the reconstruction of the model. The source probably showed the disciples behind Christ and two different groups of inhabitants before him next to the city: adults in long tunics and youths in short ones spreading garments. A search through Carolingian art for the source of this iconography turns up little. Two later-ninth-century Metz ivories in the Victoria and Albert Museum (fig. 71)[127] and the British Museum (fig. 72)[128] depict the apostles behind or next to Christ and citizens in front of him. The inhabitants, however, are not clearly differentiated by function and costume into age groups, and neither the city nor its inhabitants chopping and strewing branches is represented. In the Stuttgart Psalter (fig. 73)[129] the citizens are divided by function into two age groups: a child spreading his chlamys and older figures holding palms. The latter, however, are unbearded youths in short

[124] Gregory, *Moralia in Job*, 27, 7–12, PL, 76, cols. 405ff., esp. 411.

[125] Warner and Wilson, *Ben.*, p. xxiv; also Homburger, *Anf.*, p. 18.

[126] A copy of this miniature in the twelfth-century Winchester Psalter shows one of these men wearing a Jewish hat

and another a secular short tunic and chlamys; see Haney, *Winchester Psalter*, p. 110, fig. 18.

[127] Goldschmidt, *Elf.*, 1, p. 56, no. 107, pl. 49.

[128] Goldschmidt, *Elf.*, 1, p. 55, no. 103, pl. 48.

[129] *Stuttgarter Bilderpsalter*, 1, fol. 8v; 2, pp. 64, 183.

tunics, very different from the type of mature, bearded men in long tunics in our manuscript. The Psalter also does not show female inhabitants, figures strewing branches, and Jerusalem itself. On the whole, its relationship to the Anglo-Saxon iconography is slight.[130] Carolingian art does not seem to have been a primary source, but there is some evidence that it was a secondary one.

The Benedictional does conform to the Latin tradition of depicting Christ riding astride rather than sidesaddle as in Byzantine art (cf. figs. 74–76). Some unusual foliage in the scene also points to a Western source. While the citizens behind Christ hold palm branches, blossoming foliage appears elsewhere in the composition. The seed of the idea came from Carolingian art. On one of the Metz ivories (fig. 71) a citizen grasps a palm branch, but another holds a branch with trefoil terminations which might be flowers. In the Stuttgart Psalter the foremost Jerusalemite holds a sprig of unmistakable flower buds in his left hand as well a palm branch in his right. Thus a few details of the Benedictional's scene came from a Carolingian model, but for the most part it derived from another source.

This other source was very likely Byzantine. In the sixth-century Syrian Rossano Gospels (fig. 74)[131] the citizens are also differentiated by age, costume, and function, and the city is similarly represented with some spectators holding branches in the windows and others emerging from an arched gate. This comparison also suggests that the figures were rearranged in the Benedictional to change a horizontal composition into a vertical one. To save space the apostles were simply omitted, the adult citizens before Christ were shifted into their place, and the youths spreading garments were moved back into the vacated space in the gate. The Eastern model was not necessarily early in date, for virtually all the features of the scene in the Rossano Gospels survived Iconoclasm.

The tenth-century Byzantine ivory in Berlin (fig. 75)[132] differentiates the populace in the same way, and the adults even include a woman, as in the Benedictional. The abbreviated city on the plaque lacks the spectators, but this detail occurs in another, contemporary Byzantine scene.[133] On a tenth-century Byzantine triptych in the Louvre (fig. 76)[134] a citizen throwing branches from a tree is so close to the city that he seems almost to be in it, and a similar figure probably inspired the citizen in the Benedictional who leans out rather precariously from the top of the city to toss flowers. He is not so convincingly integrated into the city as the other spectators. The two boys on the hill at the left side of the Anglo-Saxon composition who chop and strew foliage can also be traced to Byzantine iconography, although here too there were changes. Both youths are in extremely awkward positions. One unaccountably rests his knee on a tree stump dangling his foot in mid-air behind his other leg. Though reversed, the upper boy in the tree next to the city on the Berlin ivory is very similar, especially if one mentally restores the palm branches that he once held in his right hand.[135] The English illuminators evidently shifted this figure from his original position in a tree beside the city to the left side of the composition. He had to be reversed to make sense of his new position behind Christ, but the adjustment to his new, solid footing on the mountain was not entirely successful. The other youth with a hatchet seems almost to brace his feet against the trunk of the tree, and this was probably his position in the model.[136]

It thus seems that the primary source of the miniature was comparatively recent middle Byzantine art, which all but supplanted the Carolingian tradition. Extensive modifications adjusted

---

[130] The scenes in the Drogo Sacramentary (*Drogo-Sak.*, fol. 43), the Antwerp Sedulius manuscript (Alexander, *Manuscripts*, p. 83, no. 65, fig. 297), and the Gospels of Otfried of Weissenburg (H. Butzmann, *Otfrid von Weissenburg Evangelienharmonie*, Codices Selecti, 30 [Graz, 1972], pp. 25f., fol. 112) all represent Jerusalem, but this is a generic feature that could have been independently inspired by the Gospel narrative. More specific similarities are absent.

[131] G. Cavallo, J. Gribomont, and W. C. Loerke, *Codex Purpureus Rossanenses* (Rome, 1985), fol. 1v.

[132] Goldschmidt and Weitzmann, *Byz. Elf.*, 2, p. 25, no. 3, pl. 1.

[133] Goldschmidt and Weitzmann, *Byz. Elf.*, 2, p. 60, no. 122, pl. 45.

[134] Goldschmidt and Weitzmann, *Byz. Elf.*, 2, pp. 25f., no. 4, pl. 2; A. Cutler, "Un Triptyque byzantin en ivoire: *La Nativité* du Louvre," *Revue du Louvre et des Musées de France* 38 (1988): 21–28, figs. 1–4.

[135] Cf. the related figure in the scene on the Pala d'Oro in Venice; H. R. Hannloser, *La Pala d'Oro. Il tesoro di San Marco* (Florence, 1965), pl. 43.

[136] Cf. the figure with a hatchet in a tree represented in chapel 23 in Göreme, dated about 1200 by Restle, *Byzantinsche Wandmalerei*, 1, pp. 128f., no. 22; 2, figs. 233, 234.

the composition to the narrower format of the manuscript page and at the same time integrated it with the surrounding frame. This is not the whole story, however, for as in other miniatures (pls. 12, 20), symbolism played a part in the compositional rearrangement.

THE ECCLESIOLOGICAL AND ESCHATOLOGICAL SYMBOLISM

Flowers, which were an inconspicuous and minor detail in Carolingian iconography, are strikingly prominent in the Benedictional. The Vulgate says only that the inhabitants of Jerusalem carried palm fronds (John 12:13) and strewed branches from unspecified trees (Matt. 21:8; Mark 11:8), but the Old Latin version of the Gospel of John (12:13) states that they had the "flowers of palms" (flores palmarum).[137] Moreover, in the Anglo-Saxon liturgy for Palm Sunday, the feast the picture illustrates, an antiphon said that the crowds greeted Christ with both palms and flowers.[138] The antiphon was sung during a procession into the church, and in this liturgical reenactment of the Entry into Jerusalem the congregation, playing the part of the citizens, carried flowers as well as palms in the procession into the church.[139] On the simplest level the iconography illustrated the liturgy's descriptions of the Entry.

At an early date, however, commentators interpreted the flowers symbolically. According to Ambrose, the welcoming citizens represented mankind. Christ's advent caused them to renew themselves spiritually like old trees sprouting new shoots. They

> took upon themselves the hearts (medullas) of palms; for "the righteous shall flower like the palm" (Ps. 91:13). And therefore when Christ came, the vexilla of righteousness and the insignia of triumphs were raised over the shoulders of men.[140]

Later the Pseudo-Jerome, who perhaps was the seventh-century Irishman Cumain, also related Psalm 91:13 to the Jerusalemites who were "broad in [their] flowers and fruits since they are the good fragrance of Christ and they strew the way of the commandments of God with good character."[141] Thus in exegesis the flowering, fruitful foliage symbolized the blossoming of virtue and the bearing of spiritual fruit within those who have received Christ. This concept is a Christianized version of a *topos* often applied to the *adventus* of ancient and medieval rulers: nature herself joyously celebrated the salutary royal arrival with the unseasonable return of spring, suddenly adorning the barren earth with verdancy and flowers.[142]

The blossoms in the miniature undoubtedly had symbolic meaning. Many of the Benedictional's blessings use flowers as a metaphor for virtue or paradise: the first blessing for All Saints day says that God "adorns the church with the flower of the [saint's] virtues" and that by following their example the faithful, "with the fruit of good work," might be able to join them;[143] the benediction for the Saturday after Easter expresses the hope that God's flock might

[137] *Itala. Das Neue Testament in altlateinischer Überlieferung*, ed. A. Jülicher, 4 (Berlin, 1963), pp. 136f.: "uenit Iesus in Hierosolyma, acceperunt flores palmarum."

[138] *The Canterbury Benedictional*, ed. R. M. Wooley, Henry Bradshaw Society, 51 (London, 1917), p. 26.

[139] The *ordo* for the procession includes an "Exorcismus siue adiuratio florum" and a blessing upon "palmarum ac florum ramos"; *Canterbury*, ed. Wooley, pp. 23, 24. Palm Sunday was also sometimes called "dominica florum" or "pascha floridum"; A. Franz, *Die kirchlichen Benediktionen im Mittelalter* (Freiburg im Breisgau, 1909), 1, p. 475.

[140] Ambrose, *Secundam Lucam*, 9, 12–13, CC, 14, p. 336: "Quod ad figuram hominum pertinere sanctus Iohannes euidentius declarauit addendo quia acceperunt sibi medullas palmarum; 'iustus' enim 'ut palma floriet.' Et ideo aduentante Christo erigebantur iam supra humeros hominum uexilla iustitiae et insignia triumphorum."

[141] Pseudo-Jerome, *Commentarius in Evangelium secundum Marcum*, 11, PL, 30, col. 621D: "Justi ut palma florebunt: an-

gusti in radicibus, lati in floribus et fructibus: quoniam bonus odor Christi sunt: et sternunt uiam mandatorum Dei bona fama." Regarding the author, see E. Dekkers, *Clavis Patrum Latinorum* (Steenbrugis, 1961), no. 632. See also the mention of "blooming palm-twigs" (blowende palmtwigu) in the Old English Blickling Palm Sunday homily; *Blickling*, pp. 68, 69.

[142] E. H. Kantorowicz, "The 'King's Advent' and the Enigmatic Panels in the Doors of Santa Sabina," *Selected Studies* (Locust Valley, N. Y., 1965), p. 41; idem, "Kaiser Friederich II. und das Königsbild des Hellenismus," *Selected Studies*, p. 278, n. 69; also S. G. MacCormack, "Change and Continuity in Late Antiquity," *Historia* 21 (1972): 728, 733.

[143] *CBP*, no. 1743; Warner and Wilson, *Ben.*, p. 42: "[Dominus] sanctam ecclesiam flore uirtutum perornat, corda uestra ad eorum [sanctorum] exempla uigilanter accendat. . . . Ut . . . cum fructu boni operis perpetualiter eorum societati ualeatis adiungi."

be entitled "to feast among the flowers of paradise."[144] The painters were certainly aware of such floral symbolism, for they represented Saint Æthelthryth (pl. 28) holding the symbol of her virtue, a sprig of flowers identical to the ones in the Entry.

The Palm Sunday benediction illustrated by the Entry does not specifically mention flowers, but it does use a metaphor of botanical fecundity for virtue:

> May omnipotent God whom you endeavor to please by the mortification of fasts and the observances of the present days bless you. Amen.
>
> And may he grant you that, as you endeavored to be presented to him with the branches of palms and other foliage, so you might be able to appear to him after death with the palm of victory and the fruit of good works. Amen.[145]

Like many blessings in the manuscript, this links the present with the past and the future in a threefold typology. The Palm Sunday procession of the congregation imitates the welcoming of Christ by the citizens and also anticipates the Second Coming when he will again meet mankind, who will then present their past deeds for judgment. Because the congregation's participation in the observances of the feast and the preceding Lenten mortifications is itself a virtuous deed pleasing to God, the "branches of palms and other foliage" they carry before Christ in this world will become "the palm of victory" and bear "the fruit of good works" in the next one, ensuring salvation at the Last Judgment.

Since the Anglo-Saxons carried flowers as well as palm branches in the Palm Sunday procession, the illuminators probably took the "other foliage" in the prayer to refer to flowers. The mention of "the fruit of good works" must also have been a factor, since a plant must flower to bear fruit. In the benediction for All Saints day and the comments of Pseudo-Jerome mentioned above, the flowering of virtue and yielding of spiritual fruit are related metaphors.

The floral symbolism implicit in the miniature's text is more expressly stated in other parts of the Anglo-Saxon liturgy for Palm Sunday, for example, this blessing over the faithful holding flowers and palm branches:

> May omnipotent God, source of good and origin of virtue, who by his only begotten [Son] showed to you examples of suffering and also humility, help you to blossom with an increase of good works. Amen.
>
> And may he who . . . on the present day wished to be made the rider upon an ass and, coming to Jerusalem, wished to be called king by the multitudes, grant that you be so ornamented with flowers of virtues that you may be pleasing to him in the end with the blessed. Amen.
>
> So that when the severe Judge comes at the end of time to make an examination of the world, you, adorned by the ornaments of moral character, might be able to meet him undaunted, and to be planted in peace in celestial pastures. Amen.[146]

This blessing expresses in liturgical form some of the exegesis we have already encountered. The "examples" of divine virtue and goodness provided by Christ's original advent to man, an advent liturgically reenacted in the present, help the believers to "blossom" with virtuous good works and make it likely that Christ at his future advent will "plant" them, blossoming with virtue, in "celestial pastures."

On the basis of this and the Benedictional's re-

---

[144] *CBP*, no. 995; Warner and Wilson, *Ben.*, p. 21: "paradysi mereantur floribus epulari." See also the blessings for Agnes, Easter 2 alia 2, Pentecost 16 alia, Swithun, and virgins not martyrs. *CBP*, nos. 149, 877, 1088, 1920, 1956; Warner and Wilson, *Ben.*, pp. 11, 23, 34, 39, 46.

[145] *CBP*, nos. 180, 278; Warner and Wilson, *Ben.*, p. 17:
Benedicat uos omnipotens deus cui ieiuniorum maceratione et praesentium dierum obseruantia placere studetis. Amen.
Concedatque uobis ut sicut ei cum ramis palmarum ceterarumue frondium presentari studuistis, ita cum palma uictoriae, et fructu bonorum operum ei post obitum apparere ualeatis. Amen.

[146] *Canterbury*, ed. Wooley, p. 26:
Deus omnipotens fons bonitatis, et origo uirtutis, qui per unigenitum suum uobis patientiae ac humilitatis exempla monstrauit, uos bonorum operum adiuuet florere incrementis. Amen.
Quique . . . hodierna die sessor aselli fieri, et hierusalem ueniens a turbis rex uoluit appellari, concedat uobis uirtutum floribus sic exornari, ut ei placere ualeatis in fine cum beatis. Amen.
Ut cum uenerit districtus iudex in fine seculi, discussionem facere mundi, uos morum ornamentis decorati, ei obuiare possitis intrepidi, et celestibus pascuis inseri pacifici. Amen.

lated blessing we can conclude that the flowers in the scene were symbols of the divine inner goodness and virtue which originated in God and which the advent of Christ caused to "blossom" in the hearts of men who receive and acknowledge him. The citizens in the picture symbolically prefigured both the congregation in the present, who again virtuously acknowledge Christ's advent in the mystical liturgical celebrations of Palm Sunday, and the righteous in the future, who will welcome his final advent when he will "plant" them in paradise.[147] Traditionally paradise was portrayed as verdant and flowering.[148] The composition was purposely rearranged to create a more luxuriant, flower-filled landscape, the symbol of the celestial pastures where the elect will flourish and flower in virtue after the Second Coming.

It is of some significance that the only figures holding palm branches rather than flowers are the Jews following Christ, for there was a long-standing pictorial tradition for the representation of palm-bearing figures—apostles rather than the citizens—behind Christ. One of several early Christian examples of this motif occurs on the sixth-century Eastern ivory diptych from Echmiadzin (fig. 77).[149]

Kantorowicz[150] noted two features that lent a messianic air to the ivory's scene of the Entry, associating it with the eschatological advent of Christ at the Second Coming: the personification of Jerusalem welcoming Christ and the pro-

cessional quick march of the apostles. The latter detail was influenced by the iconography of imperial *adventus* that showed the emperor-god entering a city followed by a procession of his subordinates shouldering his triumphal insignia. It has been overlooked that this "eschatalogical" influence also explains why the apostles, in contradiction to the Gospel narrative, have palms: they too carry the triumphal insigne of *their* ruler Christ. Commentators on the Entry equated the palms to Christ's imperial insigne, the tropaeum of the cross, which symbolized his triumph over sin and death in the Passion and the Harrowing of Hell.[151] In the scene the apostles' bearing of Christ's palm signified their participation in the victory of their Savior, who not coincidentally holds his tropaeum of the cross: through the triumph of the king of heaven they too would overcome death. The file of apostles with imperial insignia of martyrdom in this terrestrial scene has its counterpart in the celestial scene on a fifth-century sarcophagus in the cathedral of Ferrara (fig. 78).[152] Two heavenly processions of apostles march to present crowns of tribute to the enthroned Cosmocrator, and Peter and Paul shoulder crosses symbolizing triumphal martyrdom in the same way as the apostles on the ivory bear the palm branches. The ivory's scene of the Entry of Christ into Jerusalem was carefully crafted to prefigure and symbolize the eschatological advent of the Savior and his followers at the Second Coming.

---

[147] Haymo of Auxerre (*Homilia* 2, PL, 118, col. 23) compared the righteous mortifying themselves in their earthly lives to a tree which is barren in winter, but they will flower and bear fruit in the "summer" of the Last Judgment when the *sol iustitiae* will shine on them. For the long-standing association between the renewals of nature in spring and Christ in the Easter celebration, see T. Michels, "Das Frühjahrssymbol in österlicher Liturgie, Rede und Dichtung des christlichen Altertums," *Jahrbuch für Liturgiewissenschaft* 6 (1926): 1–15. This association and the Benedictional's floral imagery explains the reference to "floribus Paschae" in the inscriptions of the drawings of God revealing the calculation of Easter in the Leofric Missal and the Tiberius Psalter; Deshman, "Leofric," pp. 168ff., pls. 4, 7c, fig. 4.

[148] Cf. the early Christian apse mosaic of San Vitale in Ravenna; F. W. Deichmann, *Frühchristliche Bauten und Mosaiken von Ravenna*, 2nd ed. (Wiesbaden, 1958), pls. 352, 353.

[149] Volbach, *Elf.*, pp. 94f., no. 142, pl. 75; cf. also nos. 119, 145, pls. 63, 77.

[150] "'King's Advent,'" pp. 37ff., esp. 50, 56. For advent iconography, see also MacCormack, "Change and Continu-

ity," pp. 721ff.; idem, *Art and Ceremony in Late Antiquity*, The Transformation of the Classical Heritage, 1 (Berkeley, 1981), pp. 17–89; D. Stutzinger, "Der Adventus des Kaisers und der Einzug Christi in Jerusalem," *Spätantike und frühes Christentum* (Frankfurt am Main, 1984), pp. 284–307.

[151] Augustine, *In Iohannes Euangelium Tractatus 124*, 51, 2, CC, 36, p. 440; idem, PL, 35, col. 1764; Paschasius Radbertus, *Expositio in Euangelium Matthaei*, 9, 21, PL, 120, col. 707C–D; Pseudo-Alcuin, *Liber de Divinis Officiis*, 14, PL, 101, cols. 1200D–1201A; see also above, n. 140. The late-tenth-century Anglo-Saxon Sherborne Pontifical represents Christ holding the palm frond in one drawing and the cross-staff in two others; Rosenthal, "Three Drawings," pp. 555ff., figs. 1, 2, 4; idem, "The Pontifical of St. Dunstan," *Dunstan*, pp. 154ff., pls. 1–3.

[152] J. Kollwitz and H. Herdejürgen, *Die Ravennatischen Sarkophage*, Die antiken Sarkophagreliefs, 8, 2 (Berlin, 1979), pp. 68f., 138, no. B 17, pl. 53, 3; also nos. B 14, B 15. Heavenly triumphal processions of apostles and other saints are common in Ravenna mosaics; see Deichmann, *Frühchristliche Bauten*, pls. 40, 98–107, 251.

Reminiscences of this early Christian iconography of the Entry survived on the Carolingian Metz ivory in the Victoria and Albert Museum (fig. 71) and in the Bernward Gospels (ca. 1015) from Hildesheim (Dom- und Diözesanmuseum, MS 18; fig. 79),[153] both of which depict one or more of the palm-bearing apostles following Christ. Later artists were well aware of the motif's traditional eschatological significance. In the Hildesheim miniature Jerusalem is a walled square with twelve gates inscribed with the Greek initials of the apostles. These are features of the heavenly Jerusalem as described in the eschatological vision of the Apocalypse that culminates with the blessed walking in glory and honor into the celestial city (21: 10–12, 24–27).

The Benedictional's Carolingian model probably also represented apostles carrying palms behind Christ, and this feature seems to have inspired the manuscript's illuminators to replace them with citizens having the same attribute. The fact that they alone retain the traditional palm branches (rather than flowers) suggests that the illuminators wished to preserve the traditional eschatological symbolism of palm-bearing followers of Christ. Certainly the painters would have been aware of the ancient triumphal and eschatological symbolism of palm fronds. The miniature's own text draws a parallel between the palms and other foliage carried in the Palm Sunday procession and the future "palm of victory" carried in heaven. Moreover, Ælfric reveals that contemporary Anglo-Saxons perceived the carrying of palms on Palm Sunday as a triumphal event, simultaneously reenacting the historical past and anticipating the eschatological future:

> Everywhere in God's congregation the priest should bless [and distribute] palm-twigs . . . to the people; and God's servants should then sing the hymn which the Jewish people sang before Christ, when he was approaching

to his passion. We imitate the faithful of that people with this deed, for they bare palm-twigs with hymn before Jesus. Now we should hold our palm until the singer begins the offering-song, and then offer to God the palm for its betokening . . . [of] victory. Victorious was Christ when he overcame the great devil and rescued us [at the Harrowing of Hell]: and we should also be victorious through God's might, so that we overcome our evil practices . . . and the devil, and adorn ourselves with good works, and at the end of our life deliver the palm to God, that is, our victory, and thank him fervently, that we, through his succour, have overcome the devil.[154]

In Ælfric's vision the past and present terrestrial processions of singing palm-bearers march in step with the future celestial one, much as the inhabitants of earth and heaven had marched in parallel files in early Christian art.

Ælfric here twice mentioned only Jews marching and singing *before* Christ, but the Gospels (Matt. 21:9; Mark 11:9–10) said that some had also *followed* him singing the same hymn. Elsewhere in his homily Ælfric interpreted the two groups of escorting populace:

> Those who walked before Christ, are the patriarchs and prophets, who were before Christ's incarnation; and those who went after him, are those who inclined to Christ after his birth, and daily incline to him: and all these sing one hymn; because we and they all hold one faith, as Peter the apostle said, when he spake of the patriarchs: "We believe that we shall be saved by Christ's grace, as well as they."[155]

In accordance with a long tradition,[156] Ælfric viewed the populace as an allegory of the two peoples of the Church. The populace going be-

---

[153] R. Kahsnitz, "Inhalt und Aufbau der Handschrift," *Das Kostbare Evangeliar des Heiligen Bernward*, ed. M. Brandt (Munich, 1993), pp. 47f., pl. 28; *Bernward von Hildesheim und das Zeitalter der Ottonen*, ed. M. Brandt and A. Eggebrecht (Hildesheim, 1993), 2, pp. 570ff., no. VIII–30; H. H. Josten, *Neue Studien zur Evangelienhandschrift Nr. 18* (Strassburg, 1909), pp. 22–24, 65, 71ff.; S. Beissel, *Des hl. Bernward Evangelienbuch im Dom zu Hildesheim* (Hildesheim, 1891), p. 13; F. J. Tschan, *Saint Bernward of Hildesheim* (Notre Dame, 1942–52), 2, pp. 38, 51f.; 3, fig. 75; M. Stähli and H. Härtel, *Die Handschriften im Domschatz zu Hildesheim* (Wiesbaden, 1984),

pp. 17–20, 46. See also Goldschmidt, *Elf.*, 1, p. 73, no. 151, pl. 63.

[154] Ælfric, *Hom.*, 1, p. 219. It is noteworthy that immediately after this passage Ælfric turns to the Last Judgment.

[155] Ælfric, *Hom.*, 1, p. 215.

[156] E.g., *Blickling*, pp. 80–83; Paschasius Radbertus, *Expositio Euangelium in Matthaei*, 9, 21, PL, 120, col. 704C; Bede, *Hom.*, 2, 3, pp. 203f.; idem, *In Marci Evangelium Expositio*, 3, ed. D. Hurst, CC, 120, pp. 573f. Æthelwold owned a copy of the latter; Lapidge, "Booklists," pp. 53f.

fore Christ symbolized the righteous Jews of the Old Testament who temporally preceded him, while those following represented the Gentiles —including the present-day believers—who temporally came after him. The common song of the two groups, one already in heaven and the other still on earth, signified their shared belief in Christ and their hope that the Gentiles would achieve the same salvation that the Jewish patriarchs and prophets had won. The eschatological implications for these contemporaries who "follow" Christ emerge more clearly in Ælfric's exposition of the relationship between the Entry and the prophecy (Matt. 21:4–5) that the daughter of Sion would see her king riding upon an ass:

> Sion is a hill, and it is interpreted, "A place of contemplation;" and Jerusalem, "Sight of peace." The daughter of Sion is the congregation of believing men, who belong to the heavenly Jerusalem, in which is ever "a sight of peace,". . . to which Jesus will bring us, if we follow him.[157]

This eschatological symbolism was intrinsic to the Palm Sunday reenactment of the populace's procession at Christ's Entry. Æthelwold himself specified in the *Regularis Concordia* that the blessing and distribution of the palm fronds was to be prefaced by the reading of John's account of the Entry (12:12–27) "as far as the words 'Behold the whole world is gone after him.'"[158] A blessing of the palms in the Benedictional of Archbishop Robert in Rouen, a later Winchester copy of our manuscript, cited Moses exiting from Egypt and Noah from the ark as Old Testament figures of Christ leading the Church to salvation and asked that, like these patriarchs, "we, carrying palms or branches of trees, with good deeds might come to meet Christ, and through him we might enter into eternal joy."[159]

The Benedictional modified the older iconography of apostles bearing palms after Christ to configure it to the eschatological symbolism of the Palm Sunday procession. The substitution of palm-bearing citizens for the traditional apostles

showed that not just the apostles but all the present-day believers who receive Christ in the Palm Sunday liturgy and in daily life can hope to carry his insigne of victory over sin and death and to follow him triumphantly through the gate of the celestial city into perpetual beatitude. The Jerusalemites with palms behind Christ complemented and reinforced the liturgical and eschatological symbolism of the flowering paradisiacal landscape. Christ's historical Entry into Jerusalem was represented as the symbolic prefiguration of both the Palm Sunday procession into the church[160] and the Second Coming, when the Messiah will arrive to the acclamations of the saints inhabiting heavenly Jerusalem and lead in the remainder of the righteous mankind.

According to our interpretation, the figures inside Jerusalem should symbolize the believing patriarchs and prophets already blissfully dwelling in the celestial city. To evaluate this possibility, we should pay particular attention to the youth holding flowers in a window, for unlike the other inhabitants he does not seem to throw the foliage in the Lord's path, as the Gospels specified. Instead he appears to present the flowers in a bouquet to Christ. Furthermore his blossoms are gilded, in contrast to the others in the scene which are cream-colored; this mark of distinction shows that this particular bunch of flowers is being given directly to Christ.

This remarkable iconographic motif might have expressed the illuminators' own intense religious emotion, the same lyrical piety that induces worshippers of many religions to make votive floral offerings to a beloved deity. But this feature also had a much more profound and objective significance based on liturgy, exegesis, and art.

Both Ælfric[161] and Æthelwold[162] inform us that on Palm Sunday the congregation carried palms and presumably flowers into the church to present them later to the priest in the offertory procession of the mass. The offertory was a presentation of the bread and wine for the Eucharistic sacrifice along with other gifts such as fruit and grain. The offering of these gifts of the

---

[157] Ælfric, *Hom.*, 1, p. 211; also *Blickling*, p. 80.

[158] *RC*, 60, p. 106. See also the Palm Sunday *ordo* in *Canterbury*, ed. Wooley, p. 23.

[159] *Ben. Rob.*, p. 12: "nos portantes palmas aut ramos arborum, cum bonis actibus occurramus obuiam christo, et per ipsum introeamus in gaudium aeternum."

[160] The eleventh-century copy of the Benedictional's miniature in the Tiberius Psalter is inscribed: "Hic aequitauit Iesus Christus in Palma Dominica"; Wormald, "Psalter," p. 132, fig. 133.

[161] See above, n. 154.

[162] *RC*, 60, p. 107.

earth, symbols of the firstlings of creation,[163] was the initial step in the offering that would eventually culminate in the Eucharistic offering of Christ, "the first-born of all creation" (Col. 1:15) and "the first fruits of them that sleep" (1 Cor. 15:20), to God in heaven. Hence Ælfric could say that the palms (and flowers) were offered "to God." Even on other feast days when there was no Palm Sunday procession, the offertory procession was customarily compared by commentators[164] to the parade of the Jerusalemites who met and accompanied Christ into the city to the temple with its altar. On one level the bouquet presented to Christ in the scene refers to the donation "to God" of palms and flowers in the Palm Sunday offertory procession.

The motif also had an eschatological dimension. Ælfric indicated that this liturgical offering to God, the goal of the Palm Sunday procession, prefigured the final presentation of the "palm of victory" and the righteous themselves, adorned with the good works which had resulted from their victory over sin, to Christ after death. The same eschatological typology occurs in the miniature's text, which says that the "branches of palms and other foliage" carried in this world prefigure the "palm of victory and the fruit of good works" that the righteous will bear to Christ in the next one. Since the flowers in the scene signify the triumphant blossoming of virtue and good works in the believers, the giving of the bouquet must also symbolize the righteous presenting the virtuous deeds of their past life, "the fruit of good works," to Christ on Doomsday.

It was especially appropriate that this motif also symbolized the faithful's presentation to the priest of the flowers carried in the Palm Sunday offertory procession, for, as the Benedictional's prayer makes clear, these liturgical acts are good works that will please God now and in the future at the Second Coming. In the scene Christ's raised right forearm and his fingers extended in benediction direct the eye to the figure presenting the bouquet, suggesting that the Lord rewards this offering with the gift of his

blessing—a prefiguration of his liturgical benediction on Palm Sunday and his perpetual blessing on Judgment Day.

This iconography should also be viewed as an inventive adaption of the earlier pictorial tradition of a celestial procession of the elect thankfully offering tokens of tribute or triumph to their Savior Christ (cf. fig. 78). The paradisiacal imagery had begun early on to influence scenes of the terrestrial Entry into Jerusalem in the placement of palm-bearers behind Christ (figs. 71, 77, 79), and the motif of the presentation of the flowers in the Anglo-Saxon scene signals a renewal of this influence.

The source of this influence on the Benedictional was the pictures of *ecclesia ex synagogia* and *ecclesia ex gentibus* in the Galba Psalter. Amid the patriarchs (mislabeled prophets) in the second register of the former (fig. 11) Abel offers a lamb and another patriarch a vessel of foliage to Christ. In the Old Testament God had frequently enjoined the Israelites, beginning with Cain and Abel, to offer him the first fruits of the land and the first-born of the flock.[165] In the miniature's context the offering patriarchs have both a liturgical and an eschatological dimension. On the one hand, they refer to the Canon of the mass which recalls God's acceptance of the past offerings of Abel and other patriarchs when imploring him to accept through Christ the Eucharistic offering an angel carried up from the earthly to the heavenly altar.[166] On the other hand, the patriarchs allude to the eschatological connotations that the theme of the offering of fruit assumed in the Gospels. Addressing the Jewish priests and Pharisees after he had entered Jerusalem, Christ quoted Psalm 117:22, comparing himself to the stone "rejected" and then "become the head of the corner," as well as to a grindstone of those who had failed to render fruit in due season. The kingdom of God would be taken from these people and "given to a nation yielding the fruits thereof" (Matt. 21:41–45; also Luke 20:17–19). In the Psalter the patriarchs are emblematic of the entire nation of believing Jews whose past offering of fruit to the

---

[163] J. A. Jungmann, *The Mass of the Roman Rite: Its Origins and Development* (New York, 1951–55), 1, pp. 26f.; 2, p. 2.

[164] Amalarius, *Lib. Off.*, 3, 19, pp. 314f. For other authors, see Jungmann, *Mass*, 2, p. 9, n. 38.

[165] Gen. 4:3–4; Ex. 22:29–30, 23:16, 19, 34:22, 26; Lev. 2:12,

14, 23:10–20; Num. 15:19–21, 18:12–30; Deut. 12:17, 26:2, 10.

[166] One of the angels above the patriarchs makes a similar offering of foliage, and the instruments of the Passion also allude to Christ's sacrifice. See also O'Reilly, "Text and Image," p. 93.

Lord has earned them, as Christ promised, a place in the heavenly kingdom of the Church, which is symbolized by the two celestial cities between them. They are joined by the other nation of the Church, the Gentiles, who in the complementary picture (fig. 12) pay homage to Christ, portrayed simultaneously as the unifying cornerstone and punishing grindstone.

In a brilliant stroke of imagination the Benedictional's makers transposed the motif of a patriarch offering foliage to Christ from the eschatological realm in the Psalter to the historical one in the Benedictional. In this way they indicated that the Jewish populace that preceded Christ into the terrestrial Jerusalem at the Entry symbolized the same Old Testament citizens of the heavenly Jerusalem (and Bethlehem) portrayed in the Psalter. This iconographic transposition also emphasized the relationship between the offering of the "patriarch" in the city and the present-day "followers" of Christ, symbolized by the palm-bearing figures behind him. The patriarch's offering prefigured those the congregation would make after they had proceeded into the church and eventually into its celestial counterpart, the heavenly Jerusalem. And as the righteous Jews' past presentations of fruit to the Lord on earth had earned them the honor of perpetually rendering him his due in heaven, so the contemporary believers' propitious offerings of palms and flowers in the Palm Sunday mass foreshadowed and facilitated their future presentation of the "fruit of good works" to him at the Second Coming.

To get to the bottom of the Psalter's influence, however, we must pause briefly to take a closer look at the hymn sung by both those preceding and following Christ into Jerusalem: "Hosanna to the son of David: Blessed is he that cometh in the name of the Lord: Hosanna in the highest" (Matt. 21:9, also Mark 11:9–10, Luke 19:38, John 12:13). In part this quotes Psalm 117:26. As we have already mentioned, soon after the Entry Christ had reproved the Jews for failing to offer due fruit by quoting the twenty-fourth verse of this same Psalm: "The stone which the builders rejected, the same has become the head of the corner. . . . And it is wonderful in our eyes."

Thus for commentators such as Bede[167] the common hymn of the populace before and after Christ signified the song of praise that the believing Jews and the Gentiles sang together in recognition that Christ had come as the cornerstone which had redeemed and united them. The phrase "hosanna in the highest" in the hymn also engendered a complementary interpretation: that both the angels in heaven and mankind on earth sang this hymn together because Christ's advent in the flesh had saved and reunited the inhabitants of the two realms; the dispensation of his Incarnation and Passion was the means through which redeemed humanity could be restored to an angelic heavenly existence, replenishing the ranks of the angels depleted by the fallen angels.[168] These two interpretations are largely congruent, for the believing Jews—the patriarchs and prophets—have already attained a beatific existence with the angels in heaven while all the present members of the Church on earth are Gentiles. It must have struck the Benedictional's creators that many of these very themes are present in the Psalter's two complementary miniatures.

The first one depicts the believing Jews already with the angels in the celestial cities, (fig. 11) and the second the Gentile saints, the first of the many "followers" of Christ to join the patriarchs and prophets there (fig. 12). All pay homage to Christ who is characterized in the second picture as the cornerstone that has brought the two peoples and the angels together. Moreover, the tituli indicate that these inhabitants of heaven are organized into "choirs." The blessed saints leading an angelic heavenly life were believed to join the angels in their continuous hymn of thanksgiving and praise to God (cf. Isaiah 6:3, Apoc. 4 and 5). The "choirs" of saints and angels in the Psalter were meant to be viewed as literally singing an eternal song to the Lord, and they are not the only ones to give voice.

The idea that the inhabitants of heaven and earth united in a common song of praise to God, already found in the Old Testament (e.g., Ps. 95:11, 148:2ff., Isaiah 49:13), was familiar to every Christian. In the hymn Te Deum, which was part of the Benedictine Office, all the earth and

---

[167] Bede, *Hom.*, 2, 3, pp. 28f.; also Paschasius Radbertus, *Expositio in Evangelium Matthaei*, 9, 21, PL, 120, col. 704C–D; Jerome, *Commentariorum in Matheum Libri 4*, 3, ed. D. Hurst

and M. Adriaen, CC, 77, pp. 184f.

[168] See the preceding note; also Bede, *In Marci Evangelium Expositio*, 3, CC, 120, p. 574; Ælfric, *Hom.*, 1, pp. 214f.

and the celestial choirs of angels and saints laud the Father and the Son,[169] and in the Preface of the mass the terrestrial voices of the faithful join the celestial ones of the angels and the other heavenly hosts in the Sanctus, the angelic song of adoration and thanksgiving to God through Christ. Both texts were pictured in Carolingian art. In the illustration of the Te Deum in the Utrecht Psalter (fig. 80), two groups of people on earth join the choirs of the angels, the palm-bearing martyrs, the apostles, and the prophets in heaven in homage to the Trinity.[170] The Carolingian Metz Sacramentary (Paris, Bibl. Nat., MS lat. 1141; figs. 81, 82)[171] illustrates the Sanctus with a two-page composition of the heavenly choirs of saints and angels adoring Christ. Below him are personifications of the earth and ocean, the symbols of the terrestrial realm of humanity which sings along with the celestial hosts. The association of this idea with the Entry into Jerusalem caused the Benedictus, a version of the hymn of the city's populace, to be appended to the Sanctus, and commentators transferred the explanations of the Entry hymn to its liturgical derivative.[172]

The choirs of the saints in the Galba Psalter do not literally illustrate either the Te Deum or the Sanctus, but the offering patriarchs, the instruments of the Passion, and other features did have eucharistic associations. The Benedictional's illuminators very likely knew the Utrecht Psalter with its Te Deum drawing, and they might also have been aware that in Carolingian art the choirs of the saints illustrated the Sanctus, with its relation to the hymn of the Entry. The Galba Psalter's representations of the choirs of the angels, Jews, and Gentiles in the celestial cities united in an eternal song of praise to Christ would have carried the intrinsic connotation that the remaining Gentiles in the terrestrial Church below also participated in this hymn of thanksgiving to the Redeemer, who would eventually enable them, too, to proceed from earth to heaven. The Benedictional's borrowing of the motif of the offering patriarch from the Psalter is symptomatic of a much deeper bor-

rowing from the same source: the theme of the universal Ecclesia in heaven and earth unified in a hymn of praise to the Christ, the bonding cornerstone.

THE RELATIONSHIP TO OTHER MINIATURES

Many of the symbolic chords sounded in the Entry resonate in other pictures in the cycle. The thematically related miniatures fall into two distinct but not entirely separate groups—the Nativity and the Presentation in the Temple, and the Doubting of Thomas and the Second Coming.

The Entry and the two infancy scenes (pls. 12, 20) share the theme that the incarnate Christ's first advent to the world united all mankind—Jews and Gentiles—in the one terrestrial and celestial Church. The influence of the Galba Psalter on all three pictures confirms that the Benedictional's illuminators thought of them in related terms. The motif of the cornerstone, associated with the heavenly Bethlehem and Jerusalem in the first miniature in the Psalter, was transposed to the Nativity and the Presentation, events which had taken place in the terrestrial, historical counterparts of the two celestial cities. In the Entry the cornerstone theme is only implied, but in this case another of the Psalter's motifs, the offering patriarch, was shifted from the heavenly to the earthly Jerusalem. These transferences configured the terrestrial locales of Christ's first advents to mankind to the likeness of the celestial cities and the Church they foreshadowed and mirrored. In their new iconographic contexts the cornerstone and the offering patriarch retained their ecclesiological and eschatological connotations and reinforced the significance of these events in Christ's life as typological figures of his subsequent advents to humanity in ecclesiastic rites, daily life, and finally the Second Coming.

The typological themes that associate the miniatures of the Presentation and the Entry are clear

---

[169] *RC*, 46, 78, pp. 98, 126. E. Kähler, *Studien zum Te Deum* (Göttingen, 1958).

[170] *Utrecht*, fol. 88.

[171] F. Mütherich, *Das Sakramentar von Metz*, Codices Selecti Phototypice Impressi, 28 (Graz 1972), pp. 28ff., fols.

5v–6.

[172] E.g., Remi of Auxerre, *De Celebratione Missae* (=Pseudo-Alcuin, *De Divinis Officiis*, 40), PL, 101, col. 1256B–C, following Bede, *Hom.*, 2, 3, pp. 28f.

in Bede's homily on the Presentation. Christ's advent to the temple of Jerusalem to make an offering is aligned with a whole series of subsequent entries—Christological and ecclesiological, terrestrial and celestial:

> It is good that the boy Jesus was first circumcised, and then after some intervening days he was brought to Jerusalem with sacrificial offerings. Because when still a young man, he first trampled upon all the corruption of the flesh by dying and rising, and then, after some intervening days, he ascended to the joys of the heavenly city, with the very flesh, now immortal, which he had offered to God for our salvation. Each one of us is also first purged by the water of baptism from all sins, as though by a true circumcision, and thus advancing . . . to the holy altar, we go in to be consecrated by the saving sacrificial offering of the Lord's body and blood. Now also since the humanity of our Savior itself is uniquely simple and chaste, and since it is offered to the Father for us, it can fittingly be represented by the immolation of a pigeon or a dove. But the entire Church too will, at the end of the world, first put off all blemish of earthly mortality and corruption in the general resurrection, and then be transferred into the kingdom of the heavenly Jerusalem, commended to the Lord by the offerings of good works.[173]

Bede's remarks shine a bright light on the typological and ecclesiological association of the two miniatures, confirming their correspondence not only in the themes of terrestrial and celestial advent but also in the interrelated themes of earthly and heavenly offering.

Since the Entry follows the Presentation in the picture cycle, the miniatures' placement in the manuscript helped to bring out the thematic parallels between them. Visually, however, the two scenes stressed different aspects of the events: in the Entry, the procession into Jerusalem which led to the sacrifice of Christ in the Passion; and in the Presentation, the offering of him after his entrance into the city. Nonetheless, the crowding of the holy family and the servant on the left side of the Presentation could be taken as a faint reminiscence of the old iconographic tradition that portrayed the event as an advent in which Christ and his parents proceed to Simeon waiting before the city or the temple.[174] There are also other indications that the scene was meant to be perceived as symbolically parallel to the Entry.

The liturgical commemorations of both events featured processions dramatically reenacting Christ's entrance into the city. Just as on Palm Sunday the faithful carried into the church symbolic palm fronds and flowers and then donated them in the offertory, so on the feast of the Purification they carried into the church blessed candles, symbolizing Christ and his supernatural light, and later presented them in the offertory. On both occasions the procession into the church foreshadowed the final march into the celestial Jerusalem.[175] In the *Regularis Concordia* Æthelwold's instructions for the Palm Sunday procession repeated some of his preceding directions for the Candlemas one; indeed, he even referred his readers back to them.[176] The Benedictional itself includes one text used for this Candlemas ceremony, a long blessing of the candles that immediately precedes the miniature of the Presentation.[177] This prayer stands out as the only one in the entire manuscript that is not an episcopal mass benediction. There must have been a very special reason why Æthelwold in this single instance loosened the strict definition of the book's contents to allow the inclusion of this different type of text. In addition to asking Christ's blessing on the candles, the prayer implores him, through the prayers of all the saints, to hear as he sits in heaven the pleading voices of his people singing his praises and carrying candles. Æthelwold must have included this prayer

[173] Bede, *Hom.*, 1, 18, pp. 182f.; idem, *Homilia*, 1, 8, ed. D. Hurst, CC, 122, pp. 130f. This text was incorporated into the homiliary of Paul the Deacon; see C. L. Smetana, "Aelfric and the Early Medieval Homiliary," *Traditio* 15 (1959): 169, no. 67.

[174] Cf. Schiller, *Icon.*, 1, figs. 226, 230–33. *Hypapante* and *Occursus*, alternative names of the feast of the Purification, stressed the concept of a meeting or advent.

[175] L. Eisenhofer, *Handbuch der katholischen Liturgik* (Freiburg im Breisgau, 1932), pp. 585f.; cf. also Ælfric, *Hom.*, 1, p. 151.

[176] *RC*, 54, 60, pp. 101f., 105f.

[177] Warner and Wilson, *Ben.*, p. 11: "Domine iesu christe creator caeli et terrae." See also *Missal*, p. 70.

because it placed the Candlemas procession in the same eschatological perspective as the Palm Sunday one: the singing voices of the faithful reenacting Christ's first entrance into Jerusalem join those of the saints in heaven in praise and prayer to Christ. Placed before the representation of the Presentation, this text served as a subtle reminder that the event portrayed was the culmination of a procession into Jerusalem, symbolically analogous to the one represented in the Entry.[178]

The typological theme of the final *adventus* to the heavenly city relates the Entry to the Doubting of Thomas (pl. 24). In the former the golden arch and columns of the entrance of Jerusalem emphasize its symbolic significance as the terrestrial counterpart of the gate of the celestial city, and in the latter Peter holds the large golden key-cross that will open this gate to Christ's followers. Later Winchester art brought out the tacit association between these two motifs. The Last Judgment in the Liber Vitae of New Minster (fig. 69) shows Peter, key in hand, at the open arched gate of the celestial Jerusalem. He beckons the choirs of saints to follow those already inside (the patriarchs and prophets?). These inhabitants, like their terrestrial counterparts in the Benedictional, acclaim Christ, who has already arrived. Two of the elect (martyrs?) about to enter shoulder the triumphal insigne of palm branches terminating in a trefoil blossom, an indication that these righteous souls "flower like a palm" on the last day.[179] This later Winchester drawing combined the eschatological motifs that link the Entry and the Doubting in the Benedictional.

Peter's golden key-cross in the latter can also be related to the populace's golden palm branches in the former: both symbolized the cross, Christ's own imperial insigne of victory over death which he has given to his followers to enable them to share his triumph. In this instance, too, another Winchester miniature, the dedication picture of the New Minster charter of 966 (fig. 135), confirms the relationship of these motifs, for in this composition the gold key of Peter is juxtaposed to both the gold cross and palm frond of the Virgin.[180]

Finally, the theme of Christ's imperial *adventus* on Doomsday binds the Entry not only to the Doubting but also to the Second Coming (pl. 10). In the symbolic imagery of the Entry Christ is an emperor in triumphant procession to the heavenly city accompanied by his troop carrying his *vexilla*, palms of victory. He is once again an emperor, the King of kings and Lord of lords, in the Second Coming where his angelic entourage carry the cross and the other instruments of the Passion in the likeness of the *milites* bearing the emperor's triumphal insignia into a city. Moreover, through its typological reference to the Harrowing of Hell, when Christ rescued the patriarchs and prophets from death and brought them with him to heaven, the Second Coming makes the very same point as the Entry into Jerusalem: Christ's redemption of his righteous predecessors prefigures his salvation of his worthy successors at the Last Judgment. Contemporary Anglo-Saxons were familiar with this idea. To explain the significance of the populace who had preceded and followed Christ at the Entry, the Palm Sunday homily in the late-tenth-century Blickling manuscript cited Christ's past redemption of the patriarchs and prophets from "hell-torment" to reassure "we . . . who come after . . . that he will come to judge and put an end to this world."[181]

The relationship between the Entry and these other pictures is purely conceptual: only an intellectual grasp of the analogous symbolic values in the images allows the viewer to detect the connections among them. Elsewhere the illuminators repeated specific motifs in associated miniatures to express their symbolic affinity in concrete visual terms, and they seem to have contemplated doing the same for the Entry. The sky in the scene is a uniform pale purple, but traces of an underpainting of wavy clouds are visible between the youths throwing flowers.[182] Initially the sky was cloud-filled. Of course the

---

[178] The Presentation and the Entry are associated advents in the later mosaics of the Cappella Palatina; see E. Kitzinger, "The Mosaics of the Cappella Palatina in Palermo," *The Art of Byzantium and the Medieval West: Selected Studies*, ed. W. E. Kleinbauer (Bloomington, 1976), pp. 279ff., figs. 12, 18.

[179] Cf. the similar attribute of St. Stephen in the Caligula Troper, which mentions his "florigera uita"; T. D. Kendrick,

Late Saxon and Viking Art (1949, rpt. London, 1974), pl. 22. The flowering palm, the key, and celestial gate also occur together in the Creation of Eve in the Junius manuscript; Ohlgren, *Illustration*, pl. 16.6.

[180] For more detailed discussion, see below, chap. 6, pp. 196f.

[181] *Blickling*, pp. 80, 82.

[182] See Gage, "Ben.," pl. 19.

cloud was a prominent symbol of Christ's advent and his blessing in the picture cycle, symbolically and visually associating, among others, the Nativity, the Second Coming, the Presentation, and the Doubting of Thomas—all the scenes related to the Entry. Here too it would have been symbolically appropriate.[183] This makes it all the more surprising and puzzling that the final version of the scene omitted the clouds.

In its symbolic association of the Entry with other events in Christ's life the Benedictional followed an old iconographic tradition. The Entry and the Adoration of the Magi, Christ's epiphanies to the Jews and the Gentiles respectively, are juxtaposed on the bottom panels of the left and right halves of the Echmiadzin diptych (fig. 77).[184] Above the Adoration are other infancy scenes such as the Nativity that glorify the Virgin and her role in the Incarnation. On a

closely related diptych in Paris[185] the Entry supplanted the Adoration on the bottom panel of the leaf with the infancy scenes. These early Christian ivories represent the Entry as the symbolic triumph of Christ's mission of salvation that had begun with the events of his Incarnation. The Entry on the Echmiadzin diptych also alludes to the future as well as the past. The palm-bearing apostles behind him refer to their triumph with him at the Second Coming, and in the central panel two of them stand with their Savior who is enthroned as the universal ruler in a timeless, heavenly realm.[186] In the final analysis it is not just the motif of the followers with palms that relates the Benedictional to the iconographic tradition exemplied by the Echmiadzin diptych; it is also the association of the Entry with a larger cycle of Christological incarnational and eschatological themes.

Pentecost (Pentecost Sunday)

THE SOURCES

The Pentecost miniature (pl. 26) closely resembles the Byzantine iconography found in the ninth-century manuscript of the homilies of Gregory Nazianzus in Paris (Bibl. Nat., MS gr. 510; fig. 83) and the mid-tenth-century lectionary fragment in St. Petersburg (Public Library, MS gr. 21; fig. 84),[187] though the composition of the Anglo-Saxon version has been flattened and compressed. Seated in an arc, the apostles share a common footstool. The similarities extend to such small details as the rendering of the lower edge of the footstool in the lectionary and the overlapping seating arrangement of the right-hand group of apostles in the homilies. Though

the Benedictional does not include the groups of people in the lower corners, many Byzantine representations also omit this feature.[188]

None of the four earlier Western representations of Pentecost follows this Byzantine scheme. The abbreviated scene in an initial of the Frankish Gellone Sacramentary (ca. 800)[189] shows only the hand of God outstretched above the busts of several figures. The Carolingian ivory in Narbonne (fig. 85) depicts the disciples seated but not in an arched arrangement. In the Metz Drogo Sacramentary (fig. 86)[190] the initial's loop acts as curved bench for them, but the manner in which the apostles sit with their backs to the viewer differentiates it from the Eastern imagery. Finally, in the San Paolo Bible (fig. 50)[191] the

[183] Cf. Augustine, *Enarrationes*, 88, 6, p. 1223, who likened prophetic and apostolic preachers to clouds showering the "dew" of Christ's word on the parched soil of the Church, so that it might bring forth good fruit which would escape the withering fire of the Last Judgment (cf. Matt. 3:10, 12); see also Gregory, *Moralia in Job*, 27, 10, 18, PL, 76, col. 409B–C.

[184] Kantorowicz, "'King's Advent,'" p. 50.

[185] Volbach, *Elf.*, p. 97, no. 145, pl. 77.

[186] See also the depiction of Christ enthroned in heaven directly above Christ entering Jerusalem on the sarcophagus of Junius Bassus; Stutzinger, "Adventus des Kaisers," pp. 295f., fig. 296.

[187] Omont, *Miniatures*, pl. 44; N. Ozoline, "La Pentecôte

du Paris. Grec. 510: un témoignage sur l'église de Constantinople au IXᵉ siècle," *Rivista di archeologia cristiana* 63 (1987): 245–55; Weitzmann, *Byzantinische Buchmalerei*, pp. 59ff. The similarity was noted by Warner and Wilson, *Ben.*, pp. xxvif., and Homburger, *Anf.*, p. 12.

[188] E.g., Goldschmidt and Weitzmann, *Byz. Elf.*, 2, no. 221b, pl. 71.

[189] Schiller, *Ikon.*, 4, 1, p. 20, fig. 16.

[190] *Drogo-Sak.*, p. 26, pl. fol. 78; E. Leesti, "The Pentecost Illustration in the Drogo Sacramentary," *Gesta* 28 (1989): 205ff.

[191] Schrade, "Studien," pp. 24ff., fig. 5; Leesti, "Pentecost Illustration," pp. 208f., fig. 7.

Virgin is surrounded by a circle of seated apostles within city walls, also a conception far removed from the Byzantine iconography.

The Benedictional's scene seems to have derived directly from an Eastern source rather than from a Byzantine-influenced Western intermediary.[192] Since this scheme of the Pentecost evidently originated soon after the end of Iconoclasm in 843,[193] the Byzantine model must have been comparatively recent in date. This conclusion corroborates the evidence of middle Byzantine influence in the miniatures of the Second Coming and the Entry (pls. 10, 21).

There are also many features of the Pentecost scene that differ from the Byzantine iconography. Eastern art gave equal prominence to Peter and Paul who share the center of the bench, but in various ways the Anglo-Saxon miniature emphasizes Peter as the founder of the Latin papacy.[194] The first figure on the right side, Peter has a gold tunic and a key which single him out from the other apostles. Moreover, only he is identifiable, for none of the others has Paul's facial features. The descending dove spewing undulating streams of fire and flanked by angels is also not usually found in the post-iconoclastic scheme of Pentecost. The Eastern iconography showed rays with small jets of fire emanating from either a simple arc of heaven or the Etiomasia, and angels are never present. If the dove is included at all, it usually sits quietly on the empty throne. The ninth- or tenth-century Eastern icon on Mt. Sinai (fig. 54)[195] does show it hovering above the disciples, but this is still rather different from the Benedictional where it dives steeply downward. Finally, the rather staid demeanor of the disciples in Byzantine scenes contrasts with their agitation in the Benedictional, where they throw up their hands excitedly and look up eagerly.

The probable source of some of these divergent features is Carolingian art. The agitation of the apostles has a precedent in the San Paolo Bible (fig. 50). The descending dove appears in the Drogo Sacramentary (fig. 86), though here conjoined with the hands of God and Christ to form a Trinity. Nevertheless, the fact that in both the Sacramentary and the Benedictional the dove is in a mandorla confirms a relationship to Carolingian art, perhaps even to a Metz work, since this feature first appeared in the Metz initial. The Benedictional is a blend of Carolingian and Byzantine traditions.

Neither Carolingian nor Byzantine art accounts for the undulating tongues of fire. The Drogo Sacramentary and the Narbonne ivory (fig. 85) show rays emanating from either the dove or God's hand. The divine fire is present in the Sacramentary as well as the San Paolo Bible but in the form of small jets of flame atop each apostle's head, as in Byzantine art. The streams of fire are most likely an Anglo-Saxon innovation, one which lends drama and vivacity to the scene and complements the excitement of the disciples. The tongues of flame touch the disciples' mouths,[196] illustrating the idea (Acts 2:4) that the heavenly fire gave them the gift of diverse tongues. The only precedent for this rare feature, to my knowledge, is the Sinai icon (fig. 54) which shows a small jet of fire at the mouth of each disciple. The Anglo-Saxon painters must have incorporated this feature of their recent Byzantine model[197] into their own, more dynamic form of heavenly fire.

---

[192] Ottonian art also did not usually imitate the Byzantine scheme; see J. M. Plotzek, *Das Perikopenbuch Heinrichs III. in Bremen und seine Stellung innerhalb der Echternacher Buchmalerei* (Cologne, 1970), pp. 236–41. Two exceptions are the scenes on the late-tenth-century ivory in Manchester (Goldschmidt, *Elf.*, 1, pp. 18f., no. 27b, pl. 14) and in the early-eleventh-century Montecassino copy of Hrabanus Maurus' encyclopedia (M. Reuter, *Text und Bild im Codex 132 der Bibliothek von Montecassino "Liber Rabani de originibus rerum"* [Munich, 1984], pp. 49ff., fig. 19). The middle Byzantine features of the latter might be an Italian interpolation. In any event both are less faithful to the Eastern iconography than the Benedictional.

[193] O. Demus, *Byzantine Mosaic Decoration* (London, 1948), pp. 83f.; K. Weitzmann, "A 10th Century Lectionary. A Lost Masterpiece of the Macedonian Renaissance," *Revue d'Études*

Sud-est Européenes 9 (1971) 624; rpt. idem, *Byzantine Liturgical Psalters and Gospels* (London, 1980), no. 20, p. 624.

[194] Peter is beardless and tonsured, an "Anglo-Saxon" facial type that might also emphasize his papal character; see J. Higgitt, "The Iconography of St. Peter in Anglo-Saxon England," *St. Cuthbert, his Cult and his Community to AD 1200*, ed. G. Bonner, D. Rollason, and C. Stancliffe (Woodbridge, 1989), pp. 267ff., 282.

[195] See above, n. 18.

[196] J. J. G. Alexander, *Norman Illumination at Mont St. Michel 966–1100* (Oxford, 1970), pp. 132, 152f. Flaking has obscured this detail, but it is more apparent in the copy in the Benedictional of Archbishop Robert (fig. 212).

[197] Weitzmann, *Mt. Sinai, Icons*, p. 75, notes the icon's relation to middle Byzantine iconography.

THE BAPTISMAL SYMBOLISM

No earlier representation of Pentecost shows angels escorting the dove.[198] Conceivably the lost Carolingian model already included this feature, but more likely the Winchester illuminators added this motif under the influence of the baptismal iconography of the Metz model (cf. figs. 34, 35). In earlier Pentecost scenes even the presence of the dove alone can be regarded as an interpolation from baptismal imagery.[199] Acts 2:3 says only that the Holy Spirit came at Pentecost in the form of fire; the idea that it appeared as a dove originated in the narratives of Christ's Baptism.[200] The addition of angels in the Benedictional strengthened the traditional iconographic association between Pentecost and Baptism.[201]

The New Testament established an inner affinity between these two events.[202] Shortly before his Ascension Christ predicted the future descent of the Paraclete at Pentecost, saying that "John indeed baptized with water, but you shall be baptized with the Holy Ghost, not many days hence" (Acts 1:5). He echoed the words of John the Baptist before the Spirit descended on Christ at the Baptism (Matt. 3:11, Mark 1:8, Luke 3:16; cf. also Acts 11:15–16). On both occasions the gift of the Spirit had a similar purpose. As it inaugurated Christ for his public mission of spreading the Word, so it inaugurated the apostles for their mission of preaching and baptism. Thus Christ shared the gift of the Spirit he had received in his Baptism, first with the disci-

ples at Pentecost and then with all mankind through the Church, which dispensed the Pentecostal Spirit in the sacrament of baptism. In recognition of this connection to Pentecost, baptism was administered on the vigil of Pentecost as well as Easter.

Baptismal themes suffuse many of the Benedictional's Pentecostal blessings, for example, the one for the Saturday after Pentecost:

> May omnipotent God, who . . . granted you remission of all sins in baptism by the Holy Spirit, bless you. Amen.
>
> And may he, who gave the same Holy Spirit in tongues of fire to his disciples, completely purify your hearts by its illumination. . . . Amen.
>
> So that, having been cleansed of all sins by his gift, you might be worthy to be protected from all adversities by its help, [and] to be effected its temple. Amen.[203]

The descent of the Spirit on the apostles at Pentecost prefigures its bestowal on the individual not only in baptism but also in the episcopal benediction, which renews the purifying baptismal grace and renders the person a fit dwelling for the Holy Spirit.

Influenced by such benedictions, the illuminators added the angels to visualize more clearly the typological and liturgical relationship to the descent of the Spirit in the miniatures of Pentecost and Baptism. This borrowing was all the easier because the dove in the latter was already endowed with sacramental meaning. Its vials of

---

[198] This motif with the undulating tongues of fire reappears in the early-eleventh-century Missal of Robert of Jumièges in Rouen; Temple, *Manuscripts*, frontispiece fig. These and other iconographic resemblances between the two manuscripts (pl. 12, fig. 204) more likely result from the influence of the Benedictional than from the common Carolingian model proposed by O. Homburger, "L'Art carolingien de Metz et l'école de Winchester,'" *Gazette des Beaux-Arts*, ser. 6, 62 (1963): 35ff. Angels flanking the dove also appear in a Fulda sacramentary ca. 1000 in Munich, a related contemporary Gospel book from the Weser area in Kassel, and an eleventh-century Reichenau lectionary in Wolfenbüttel; see A. Goldschmidt, *German Book Illumination* (1928, rpt. New York, 1970), 1, pl. 83b; A. Ludorff, *Die Bau- und Kunstdenkmäler von Westfalen, Kreis Paderborn* (Münster in Westfalen, 1899), pp. 107f.; *Kunst und Kultur im Weserraum 800–1600* (Münster in Westfalen, 1966), 2, pp. 484f., no. 173; O. Lerche, *Das Reichenauer Lektionar der Herzog-August-Bibliothek zu Wolfenbüttel* (Leipzig, 1928), pl. 13.

[199] Leesti, "Pentecost Illustration," p. 209.

[200] Matt. 3:16; Mark 1:10; Luke 3:22; John 1:32.

[201] The Ottonian plaques in Manchester pair the two events; Goldschmidt, *Elf.*, 1, no. 27, pl. 14.

[202] L. Koch, "Die Geistesalbung Christi bei der Taufe im Jordan im der Theologie der alten Kirche," *Benediktinische Monatsschrift* 20 (1938): 18ff.; I. de la Potterie, "L'Onction du Christ," *Nouvelle Revue Théologique* 80 (1958): 238.

[203] *CBP*, nos. 187, 301; Warner and Wilson, *Ben.*, p. 26:

> Benedicat uos omnipotens deus, qui . . . uobis in baptismate per spiritum sanctum remissionem omnium peccatorum tribuit. Amen.
>
> Quique eundem spiritum sanctum in igneis linguis discipulis suis dedit ipsius illustratione corda uestra perlustret. . . . Amen.
>
> Quatinus eius dono a cunctis uitiis emundati, ipsius opitulatione ab omnibus aduersitatibus defensi, templum ipsius effici mereamini. Amen.

See also the blessings for the vigil of Pentecost and the Octave of Pentecost alia; *CBP*, nos. 186, 294,; Warner and Wilson, *Ben.*, p. 25; below, n. 222.

chrism signified that its anointing of Christ in the Jordan was the prototype of liturgical baptismal unction that enabled the initiate to become "a spiritual house" and to share Christ's royal priesthood (1 Peter 2:5, 9).

Although the dove's mandorla in the Pentecost miniature was probably taken over from a Carolingian source, the Benedictional's texts gave the motif particular meaning. The prayer for the Saturday after Pentecost refers to the Spirit's "illumination" of the hearts of the believers, and in a similar vein the first blessing for Pentecost Sunday speaks of the fire of the Spirit purifying their hearts "by the infusion of its light."[204] Hence the mandorla was not simply a sign of supernatural light. Together with the tongues of flame, it symbolized the Spirit's powers of spiritual illumination and purification. This contributed subtly to the symbolic relationship to the Baptism miniature in which a mandorla —Christ's in this case—represents "the marvelous light" (1 Peter 2:9) that the baptismal anointing with the Spirit conferred on the believers.

One last detail of the Pentecost picture that merits attention is the seat of the apostles, clearly visible above the column bases and consisting of concentric gold, yellow, and green bands. Lacking the architectural perforations and thin articulating moldings found in the communal benches in other miniatures of the cycle (pls. 16, 30) and

also in the Gregory manuscript (fig. 83), these flat, multicolored, sharply arced bands resemble not so much a plastically articulated piece of furniture as a rainbow.

The rainbow was often represented as the throne of Christ. To find an example one needs only to turn a few pages to the very next image in the manuscript, the historiated initial on folio 70 illustrating the Octave of Pentecost (pl. 27). Arcing over the globe on which Christ sits are colored bands of a rainbow like the one in the Pentecost miniature. The latter seems to be the very first instance of the transference of the specifically Christological attribute of the rainbow throne to another personage. This innovation of the Benedictional was soon imitated, though not in Pentecost iconography. In the New Minster Prayerbook (ca. 1020–1029) Peter is enthroned on a rainbow and also a globe (fig. 87).[205] The draftsman of this later Winchester manuscript must have been influenced by the Benedictional's Pentecost picture in which Peter as well as the other apostles sit on a rainbow throne.

The repetition of the rainbow forges a strong bond between the consecutive illustrations of Pentecost and its Octave; thus the investigation of the rainbow in the new context of Pentecost will be delayed until after the consideration of the motif in the more traditional Christological setting of the initial.

Christ or the Triune Deity (Octave of Pentecost)

THE SOURCES

The pose of the enthroned and blessing Christ (pl. 27) is too conventional to offer any insight into the initial's iconographic sources, but his attributes are more distinctive and therefore more useful for tracing the origins of the iconography. Christ wears a broad gold diadem tooled with markings indicating settings of precious stones. This seems to be the earliest representation of Christ wearing a diadem or crown directly on

his head,[206] though this innovation soon influenced other Anglo-Saxon and Continental works. The problem of the sources of this motif has been treated in detail elsewhere[207] and needs only to be summarized here.

Carolingian scenes of the Ascension (fig. 56) and Crucifixion (figs. 36, 37) often represented the hand of God in the process of crowning Christ with a triumphal royal wreath or diadem. This Crucifixion iconography in a Metz model probably influenced angelic investiture of Christ

---

[204] *CBP*, no. 948; Warner and Wilson, *Ben.*, p. 25.

[205] *Ælfwine's Prayerbook*, ed. B. Günzel, Henry Bradshaw Society, 108 (London, 1993), p. 15, pl.3; Temple, *Manuscripts*, pp. 94f., no. 77, fig. 243, also 218. Perhaps the earliest Continental examples are the famous evangelist portraits of the Gospels of Otto III in Munich (ca. 1000); F. Mütherich, "Ausstattung und Schmuck der Handschrift," *Das Evangeliar*

Ottos III., Textband (Frankfurt am Main, 1978), pp. 84–89, also fig. 44.

[206] Regarding a supposed Carolingian example of the motif, see Deshman, "*Benedictus*," p. 219, n. 70.

[207] Deshman, "Kingship," pp. 368–405; see also Raw, *Crucifixion*, pp. 139ff.

in the Benedictional's miniature of the Baptism (pl. 19) and might also have influenced the crowned Christ in the initial. Non-narrative Carolingian images of Christ enthroned in majesty should also be taken into account. Even if they did not actually include a crown, their tituli often described Christ as the celestial ruler. The ninth-century Turonian Gospels in Stuttgart (Würtembergische Landesbibl., MS H. B. II, 40), for instance, labels Christ, seated on a globe as in the Benedictional, "the supreme king and creator of heaven and earth" (fig. 88).[208] The Utrecht Psalter shows the enthroned Christ being crowned with a wreath by the hand of God in the illustration of the Te Deum (fig. 80) and with a wreath suspended over his head in the drawing for Psalm 71 (fig. 15).[209] Since the Benedictional's makers knew the Psalter, its drawings probably influenced the initial's representation of Christ as a crowned monarch. The placement of the diadem on rather than over his head, however, portrayed his kingship with a new directness and emphasis.

Another feature of the initial that points to Carolingian sources is the cloud-filled globe mandorla. Christ sits on the orb of heaven (cf. Isaiah 66:1, Matt. 5:34, Acts 7:49), which intersects at waist level with a mandorla to form a figure eight. The globe mandorla in various forms first occurred in Carolingian art.[210] The figure-eight type, for instance, appears in a miniature of Christ and the twenty-four Elders (fig. 89) in the ninth-century Apocalypse in Trier (Stadtbibl., MS 31).[211] The mandorla here lacks clouds, but this detail can be paralleled in other Carolingian forms of the globe mandorla such as the one in the Maiestas of the Stuttgart Gospels.[212]

What distinguishes the Anglo-Saxon iconography from its Carolingian antecedents is the rainbow surmounting the orb throne. Caro-

lingian art almost never depicted Christ on a rainbow, but this was a traditional Byzantine motif.[213] In Eastern iconography, however, the rainbow was not combined with either the globe or cloud, which were both Western, Latin motifs.[214] The initial in the Benedictional thus united the Greek motif of the rainbow throne with the Latin one of the cloud-filled globe mandorla.

A similar combination of motifs is found in the slightly earlier dedication miniature of the New Minster charter of 966 (fig. 135). The charter's illuminator added the rainbow to another type of globe mandorla but did not include clouds. The Winchester atelier knew both the Eastern and Western iconography of Christ enthroned and experimented with blending the two traditions.

"THE RAINBOW WHEN
IT IS IN A CLOUD
ON A RAINY DAY"

The depiction of Christ on a rainbow illustrates the visions of God in Ezekiel and the Apocalypse:

I saw as it were the resemblance of amber as the appearance of fire within it round about: from his loins upward, and from his loins downward, I saw as it were the resemblance of fire shining round about. As the appearance of the rainbow when it is in a cloud on a rainy day: this was the appearance of the brightness round about (Ez. 1:27–28).

And behold there was a throne set in heaven, and upon the throne one sitting. . . . And there was a rainbow round about the throne, in sight like unto an emerald (Apoc. 4:2–3).

---

[208] "Hic mundi caelique sedet rex summus et auctor." Koehler, *Kar. Min.*, 1, 1, pp. 376f., pl. 20a; H. Boese, *Die Handschriften der ehemaligen Hofbibliothek Stuttgart*, Die Handschriften der Württembergischen Landesbibliothek Stuttgart, ser. 2 (Wiesbaden, 1975), 2, 1, pp. 44ff. For other Turonian tituli, see H. L. Kessler, *The Illustrated Bibles from Tours*, Studies in Manuscript Illumination, 7 (Princeton, 1977), p. 55.

[209] *Utrecht*, fols. 40v, 88.

[210] W. W. S. Cook, "The Earliest Painted Panels of Catalonia (II)," *AB* 6 (1923–24): 38ff.; Kessler, *Bibles*, pp. 39ff.; H. B. Meyer, "Zur Symbolik frühmittelalterlicher Majestasbilder," *Das Münster* 14 (1961): 82ff.

[211] P. K. Klein and R. Laufner, *Trierer Apocalypse* (Graz, 1975), pp. 121f., fol. 14v.

[212] See also Kessler, *Bibles*, fig. 52.

[213] E.g., Goldschmidt and Weitzmann, *Byz. Elf.*, 2, nos. 115, 123. Cook, "Panels," p. 44; U. Nilgen, *Der Codex Douce 292 der Bodleian Library zu Oxford. Ein ottonisches Evangeliar* (Bonn, 1967), pp. 76ff., 101ff. The only Carolingian instance of the motif is the Byzantine-inspired fresco of the Ascension in the lower church of San Clemente in Rome.

[214] The sole exception known to me is a tenth-century Byzantine ivory in Florence that shows the ascending Christ seated on an orb; Goldschmidt and Weitzmann, *Byz. Elf.*, 2, no. 58, pl. 23.

Since these texts also described God either explicitly or implicitly in a cloud, the initial's combination of the previously separate motifs of the rainbow and the cloud illustrated these biblical visions with a new accuracy. The most obvious reason why the Benedictional's painters chose this subject matter for the initial beginning the blessings for the Octave of Pentecost is that the epistle of the day was Apocalypse 4:1–10.[215]

One detail of the iconography suggests that the exegesis of this and the related vision of Ezekiel also influenced them. The rainbow's outer band is gold, representing light, and the inner ones are green and red.[216] Many commentators maintained that these were the rainbow's two principal hues, representing water and fire respectively. After the flood the rainbow had appeared in the clouds as a sign of God's peace covenant with mankind that water would never again destroy earth (Gen. 9:11–17). The New Testament had interpreted the flood as a prefiguration of the destruction of earth by fire at the Last Judgment (Matt. 24:37–39; 2 Peter 3:3–9). On the basis of this, the commentators reasoned that the green and red colors of Christ's rainbow signified respectively his past condemnation of humanity by water and his future one by fire.[217]

The flood, however, was also interpreted in the New Testament (1 Peter 3:18–21) as a prefiguration of baptism. Noah's salvation from the judgment by water foreshadowed the deliverance of those who would escape the judgment by fire because the baptismal water had purged their sins.[218] This typology led many of the exegetes who had proposed an eschatological, judgmental interpretation of the green and red rainbow to suggest additional and related levels of meaning. Gregory the Great, for example, after giving the first explanation, continued with a series of others that embraced not only the rainbow but the cloud in which it appeared:

By the fire is designated the ardor of . . . the Holy Spirit. . . . In the rainbow . . . water and fire appear. And after the advent of the Mediator, the power of the Holy Spirit began to shine in mankind in such a way that the water of baptism washes the elect of God and the fire of divine love kindles them. For as if by the admixed color of water and fire together a certain rainbow was put in the cloud for propitiation, when the Truth says: "Unless one is reborn of water and the Holy Spirit, he cannot enter the kingdom of God" (John 3:5). Which rainbow is in a cloud on a day of rain, because it is manifest in the lordly Incarnation and in the effusion of preaching, so that through the mercy of the Lord the hearts of the believers may be called back to grace. We accept, indeed, that the cloud not inappropriately is the flesh of the Redeemer, about which it is said by the psalmist: "Who makest the clouds his chariot" (Ps. 103:3). He made the cloud his chariot, because he who by divinity is everywhere ascended to heaven in the flesh.[219]

If the green and red of the rainbow could represent God's past and future condemnations of humanity, then these two colors of the rainbow —the sign of his peaceful reconciliation with mankind—could also symbolize respectively the water and the fire of the Holy Spirit in baptism, the means of humanity's salvation from the coming judgment by fire. The fiery red of the rainbow also stood for another bestowal of the illuminating Spirit on mankind, in the Incarnation, which prefigured the gift of the Spirit

---

[215] *Missal*, p. 22.

[216] A thin white glaze covers part of the red.

[217] E.g., Bede, *Explanatio Apocalypsis*, 1, 4, PL, 93, col. 113B; Haymo of Auxerre, *Expositio in Apocalypsin*, 2, 4, PL, 117, col. 1006B. For other authors, see below, nn. 219, 220.

[218] J. Daniélou, *From Shadows to Reality* (London, 1960), pp. 69–97.

[219] Gregory, *Homilia in Ezechielem Prophetam*, 1, 8, 29, PL, 76, cols. 867f.:

Per ignem . . . ardor sancti Spiritus designatur. . . . In arcu . . . aqua et ignis apparent. Et post Mediatoris aduentum, eo uirtus Spiritus sancti in humano genere claruit, quo electos Dei et aqua baptismatis lauit, et igne diuini amoris incendit. Quasi enim admisto colore aquae simul et ignis quidam arcus in nube ad propitiationem ponitur, cum Veritas dicit: "Nisi quis renatus fuerit ex aqua et Spiritu sancto, non potest introire in regnum Dei." Qui arcus in nube est in die pluuiae, quia in dominica incarnatione, et in effusione praedicationis ostenditur, ut ad ueniam corda credentium, Domino parcente, reuocentur. Nubem enim Redemptoris carnem non inconuenienter accipimus, de qua per Psalmistam dicitur: "Qui ponit nubem ascensum suum." Nubem quippe ascensum suum posuit, quia is qui diuinitate ubique est, carne ad coelestia ascendit.

in baptism. The rain cloud in which the rainbow appeared complemented the latter's propitiatory meaning, for the rain cloud symbolized both the human flesh that Christ assumed in his mission of mercy to earth and the preachers whose rain of words manifested Christ and his grace to mankind. Gregory's elaborate symbolic explanation is by no means unique. Variations frequently occur in Carolingian exegesis of the visions of God on a rainbow in a cloud.[220]

Although the colors of the rainbow in the initial indicate the illuminators were aware of this broad exegetic tradition, this alone does not prove that they intended the iconography to express these complex symbolic concepts. To determine the extent of its symbolism, we shall examine the iconography in the light of each of the interrelated exegetic themes—baptism, the Last Judgment, the Incarnation, and preaching —and also consider its Trinitarian connotations, a theme not mentioned in the exegesis.

The Baptismal Symbolism

Gregory supported the association of the colors of the rainbow with the fire of the Spirit and the water of baptism with the citation of John 3:5. This very text was included in the Gospel lection (John 3:1–15) for the Octave of Pentecost,[221] the feast the initial illustrates. Moreover, John's text is paraphrased in the second of the two Octave benedictions the initial prefaces:

O Lord Jesus Christ, you who have bestowed your Spirit on your disciples, grant gifts to your catholic church. Amen.

So that *whoever has been reborn by water and the Holy Spirit*, might always be enriched by his protection. Amen.

May he pour into them the love diffused by the Holy Spirit, which might work and overcome all the multitude of sins. Amen.

May he, who full of glory formerly reposed on the apostles, graciously repose on them. Amen.[222]

Like many of the other benedictions for the Pentecostal season,[223] this treats Pentecost as a baptismal type. The gift of the Holy Spirit that removed all sin from the apostles at Pentecost prefigured the bestowal of the purifying Spirit on the members of the Church in baptism and also in the episcopal benediction. The blessing mentions only "water and the Holy Spirit," but at Pentecost the Spirit had come down in the form of fire. The tongues of flame in the preceding picture of Pentecost (pl. 26) are the same color as the red arc of the rainbow in the initial (pl. 27). Hence the depiction of fire and water in Christ's rainbow must be understood as a symbol of the Spirit and baptismal water mentioned in the accompanying benediction. The repetition of the Spirit's fire in the two pictures indicated that the redeeming bestowal of the Spirit in baptism had been manifested to mankind in God's rainbow and at Pentecost.

Christ's gold diadem in the initial is also related to its baptismal symbolism. In the Baptism miniature (pl. 19) Christ receives this regal attribute as well as scepters from angels. In conjunction with the ampullae of chrism, these royal insignia portray the baptismal investiture of Christ as the messianic king and priest and also the investiture of the faithful who, baptized in him, join in his sacerdotal rulership of his kingdom. According to John 3:3–5, part of the Octave pericope, baptism was essential for those who wanted to see and enter "the kingdom of God," and commentators regarded God's rainbow as a sign of his future mercy for those who, after penance and purging of sins (in baptism), "would merit to see God ruling."[224] In the initial

---

[220] Repeating Gregory is Hrabanus Maurus, *Commentaria in Ezechielem*, 2, PL, 110, cols. 547f. See also Ambrosius Autpertus, *In Apocalypsin*, 3, 4, ed. Weber, CCCM, 27, pp. 209f.; Haymo, *Expositio in Apocalypsin*, 2, 4, PL, 117, cols. 1005f.; Pseudo-Alcuin, *Commentaria in Apocalypsin*, 3, 4, PL, 100, cols. 1116f.

[221] *Missal*, p. 22; Klauser, *Capitulare*, p. 191.

[222] Emphasis added. *CBP*, no. 1832; Warner and Wilson, *Ben.*, p. 26:

Domine iesu christe qui discipulis tuis tuum spiritum tribuisti, aecclesiae tuae catholicae dona largire. Amen.

Ut quicumque sunt ex aqua et spiritu sancto renati, semper sint eius protectione muniti. Amen.

Redundet in eis caritas diffusa per spiritum sanctum, quae operiat ac superet omnem multitudinem peccatorum. Amen.

Requiescat in istis propitius, qui quondam requieuit in apostolis gloriosus. Amen.

[223] See above, n. 203.

[224] Hrabanus Maurus (after Jerome, *Commentaria in Hiezechielem*, 1, 2, 1a, ed. F. Glorie, CC, 75, p. 25), *Commentaria in Ezechielem*, 2, PL, 110, col. 545D: "Ex quo [arcu in nube] os-

Christ's diadem and rainbow are complementary attributes. They signify that God provided the means of salvation in the water and the fire of the Spirit in baptism, so that mankind can hope to enter the heavenly kingdom to behold its king.

Quite apart from their mutual connection with the initial, the Pentecost and Baptism miniatures are symbolically associated with each other by the motifs of the mandorla and the angels flanking the dove. Cyclic symbolism, the deliberate repetition of significant features, connects all three images in a triangular relationship that visualizes the typology of baptism and Pentecost.

THE VISION OF THE JUDGE

The initial illustrates Old and New Testament *visions* of God, and the visionary theme is echoed by the first of the two blessings that the initial illustrates:

> May the omnipotent Trinity, the one and true God, the Father, the Son, and the Holy Spirit, allow you to desire him faithfully, to recognize him truly, and to love him sincerely. Amen.
> May he so impress in your minds the equality and immutability of his essence, that he may never permit you to wander from him through any phantasms. Amen.
> And may he allow you to continue so steadfastly in his faith and love, that afterward because of them he might lead you to his endless manifestation and appearance. Amen.[225]

This benediction was another inspiration for the diadem of the figure of Christ that historiates the initial of "omnipotens." The crown visualizes his almighty power by characterizing him as the ruler of heaven. The text also gives particular meaning to his conventional gesture of blessing.

It shows that in this life the crowned, omnipotent God blesses the congregation with the faith and love that permit them to recognize and believe in his triune nature and eternal existence, and it also indicates that, if they persevere in this true belief, he will allow them the blessing of the eternal contemplation of his "manifestation and vision" in the next life.

We have already mentioned that the beatific vision of God face to face, the perpetual apprehension of his unveiled radiant divinity as well as his humanity, was considered the ultimate reward of the elect at the Last Judgment. As a symbol of the past and future judgments, Christ's rainbow illustrated the eschatological content of the initial's text. The diadem and the cloud could also be taken in this sense. Matthew's account of the Second Coming and Last Judgment described how mankind would "see the Son of man coming in the clouds of heaven with much power and majesty" (24:30) and twice termed Christ "king" (25:34, 40). Taking their cue from the liturgical benediction and the exegesis of the feast's Apocalyptic lection, the painters portrayed Christ as the omnipotent royal Judge whom the blessed will behold in all his glory.

Later representations influenced by the initial confirm its eschatological import. The frontispiece of an eleventh-century Canterbury book of homilies (Cambridge, Trinity Coll., MS B. 15. 34; fig. 90)[226] depicts Christ wearing a narrow diadem. Inscribed on his mantle over his knees is "Rex regum" (King of kings), an abbreviation of the apocalyptic text (Apoc. 19:16) written on the garment of the returning Judge in the Benedictional's scene of the Second Coming (pl. 10).[227] A somewhat different selection of motifs from the Benedictional occurs in the miniature of Christ the Judge in the Gospel book in Boulogne (Bibl. Mun., MS 11; fig. 91), painted about the end of the tenth century by an Anglo-Saxon visitor at St. Bertin.[228] Christ wears a gold diadem and sits on a rainbow within a globe man-

---

tenditur post poenas . . . et purgationem peccatorum, futuram misericordiam: duntaxat in his qui Deum meruerint uidere regnantem." Cf. John 3:3.

[225] *CBP*, no. 1804; Warner and Wilson, *Ben.*, p. 26:
Omnipotens trinitas unus et uerus deus, pater, et filius, et spiritus sanctus det uobis eum desiderare fideliter, agnoscere ueraciter, diligere sinceriter. Amen.
Aequalitatem atque incommutabilitatem suae essentiae, ita uestris mentibus infigat, ut ab eo numquam uos quibuscumque fantasiis oberrare permittat. Amen.

Sicque uos in sua fide et caritate perseuerare concedat, ut per ea postmodum ad sui manifestationem uisionemque interminabilem introducat. Amen.

[226] Deshman, *"Benedictus,"* p. 214; Keynes, *Anglo-Saxon Manuscripts*, pp. 34f., no. 22; Temple, *Manuscripts*, no. 74.
[227] Cf. also the inscriptions on his breast ("iust[us] Iudex") and on his book (in part) ("Ego uenio in die iudicii").
[228] Ohlgren, *Illustration*, p. 54, pl. 5.7; Temple, *Manuscripts*, pp. 66f., no. 44.

dorla. He blesses with his right hand and with his left one holds on his knee a gold book inscribed "liber uitae" (Apoc. 5:8, 20:12). All these details relate to the Benedictional's initial, but the yellow interior of the mandorla (now badly rubbed) filled with thin red rays emanating from Christ recalls the mandorla—even in the colors—in the Second Coming in the Benedictional. As there, cloud surrounds the mandorla.

These two later images of the enthroned Judge permit some hindsight into their source, the Benedictional. In the initial, Christ's unlabeled book was probably already a book of life.[229] That the creators of the homiliary and the Gospels both independently conflated different motifs from the initial and the miniature of the Second Coming suggests that these two images of the Benedictional were associated with each other from the very beginning.

Both pictures emphasize the *vision* of the Judge and its consequences. In the Second Coming Christ's gold hair and rayed mandorla, lighting the fiery, turbulent cloud of his humanity, portray the radiance of divinity that illuminates the just and blinds the sinners. The instruments of the Passion emphasize that "every eye will see" him who had been pierced (Apoc. 1:7). In the initial Christ has neither gold hair nor rayed mandorla. Nonetheless, the cloud is manifestly illuminated by the light of his divinity since it is actually enclosed within the mandorla symbolizing his supernatural radiance. Moreover, Christ's diadem is an iconographic variation on the theme of regality that the Second Coming portrays through the inscription on his mantle and the "army" of angels bearing his vexilla of the Passion. These overlapping iconographic themes draw the two images into a complementary relationship to each other.

This interpretation is supported by a homily on the Last Judgment that Ælfric wrote for the Octave of Pentecost. His text—including his account of the contrasting visions of the radiant Christ that awaits the saved and the damned—

is a reworking of Julian of Toledo's *Prognosticum Futuri Saeculi*,[230] the very treatise that inspired the angels with the Passion implements in the picture of the Second Coming. The fact that this shared textual source influenced both Ælfric and the Benedictional's illuminators shows how closely those in Æthelwold's circle linked the themes of the miniature of the Second Coming with the feast day of the initial. If Ælfric associated these ideas from the *Prognosticum* with the Octave of Pentecost, it is because he learned to do so from his mentor Æthelwold, who owned a copy of this treatise.

"Omnipotens Trinitas Unus et Uerus Deus"

The initial historiates the first benediction's address to "the omnipotent Trinity, the one and true God, the Father, the Son, and the Holy Ghost," and the word "Trinitas" is placed like a titulus directly below the image. Panofsky[231] suggested that this was a Trinitarian figure portraying the indivisible unity of the three persons of the triune Godhead, and there is much to recommend his interpretation.

In the later Middle Ages the Octave of Pentecost was dedicated to the Trinity, but in late-tenth-century Anglo-Saxon England the feast's Trinitarian character was not yet fully established.[232] Nonetheless, the fact that one of the Benedictional's two blessings for the day addressed the Trinity indicates that the feast had already acquired some Trinitarian connotations. In the *Regularis Concordia* Æthelwold wrote that during the week of the Octave of Pentecost, mass "should be of the Holy Trinity."[233] Ælfric in the introduction to his Octave homily remarked that the day's service praised the Trinity "because they three are one all-ruling God, in one godhead, ever ruling, in one nature, all similarly mighty. But the Son alone, to be sure, undertook humanity of us with which he re-

[229] A book inscribed "uita" is held by the crowned figure of God in the English-influenced Bernward Gospels; Deshman, "Kingship," p. 373, fig. 23; Kahsnitz, "Inhalt und Aufbau," pp. 43f., pl. 26.

[230] Ælfric, *Sermo ad Populum in Octauis Pentecosten [Dicendus]*, ed. J. C. Pope, *Homilies of Ælfric. A Supplementary Collection*, Early English Text Society, 259 (London, 1967), 1, pp. 415ff., esp. 430f., 443–46, with references to the *Prog-*

nosticum. See also Gatch, *Preaching*, pp. 95ff.

[231] E. Panofsky, "Once More 'the Friedsam Annunciation and the Problem of the Ghent Altarpiece,'" *AB* 20 (1938): 433, fig. 12; also W. Braunfels, *Die Heilige Dreifaltigkeit* (Düsseldorf, 1954), p. xliv, n. 9.

[232] P. Browe, "Zur Geschichte des Dreifaltigkeitsfestes," *Archiv für Liturgiewissenschaft* 1 (1950): 65ff.

[233] *RC*, 90, pp. 135f.; cf. also *RC*, 59, p. 58.

deemed us."[234] Ælfric then turned to the Last Judgment, his main subject, but in the conclusion he reintroduced the Trinitarian theme, this time in an eschatological context. Christ presents the saved to his Father in his kingdom where they are rewarded with the true sight of God "face to face" (1 Cor. 13:12). Endlessly praising Christ, the blessed in heaven "ever shine as bright as the sun in their Father's kingdom (Matt. 13:43). He loves and rules with his beloved Son and the Holy Spirit, in one divinity, the one almighty God, ever without end, amen."[235]

Ælfric's repeated emphasis on the rulership and omnipotence of the Trinity, though with a distinct partiality toward the Son, is analogous to the initial's iconography which shows the crowned Deity historiating "omnipotens Trinitas." Ælfric's comments also suggest that the eschatological, visionary theme of the initial and its text is compatible with Trinitarian content. Already Augustine[236] had proposed that the blessed at the Last Judgment would finally see Christ in the divine form in which he is equal to God the Father, unlike the damned who would apprehend only his human nature. Haymo of Auxerre[237] connected this idea to a verse from the Apocalypse, which was included in the epistle for the Octave of Pentecost. The Carolingian commentator proposed that the angels' triple chant of *sanctus* to the "Lord God Almighty, who was, and who is, and who is to come" (Apoc. 4:8) expressed their devotion to the three persons who are perennially and immutably one. All three members of the Trinity would be equally present at the Last Judgment, but only Christ in his assumed flesh would be visible to the wicked.

Closely related to the initial's melding of Trinitarian, apocalyptic, and eschatological themes is an unusual evangelist portrait of John in the Grimbald Gospels (London, British Lib., MS Add. 34890; fig. 92), probably made at Canterbury in the early eleventh century.[238] John gazes up at the three, virtually identical members of the Trinity in the upper border. Enthroned in a mandorla on a gold rainbow circumscribing a blue globe, they each bear a strong likeness to the Deity in the Benedictional's initial. The later painter brought out the Trinitarian significance of the original iconography by the simple expedient of repeating the figure three times. John's vision is shared by choirs of the saints in the other borders on this and the facing initial page (fig. 93). Among them are crowned male figures who are most likely the apocalyptic Elders.[239] Thus John, the author of the Apocalypse as well as his Gospel, is inspired by his celestial apprehension of the threefold Deity on "a rainbow round about the throne" (Apoc. 4:3–4). John's vision also has connotations of the Last Judgment. The choirs of the saints are a feature of Anglo-Saxon images of the Last Judgment (figs. 11, 12, 69), and the border medallion beneath the evangelist depicts angels taking souls up "in the clouds to meet Christ" (1 Thes. 4:16). In many respects the Grimbald Gospels developed the themes of the Benedictional's initial: the apocalyptic vision of the glorious triune Godhead that all righteous would behold at the Last Judgment and forever after.[240]

The Trinitarian and Christological interpretations of the initial need not be mutually exclusive. Since the three persons of the Trinity were held to be indivisible, the ahistorical representation of the Deity in human form could imply, at

---

[234] Ælfric, *Sermo ad Populum*, ed. Pope, p. 418: "for ðan ðe hi ðrý sind án þrymwealdend God on anre Godcundnysse æfre rixiende, on anum gecynde, ealle gelíce mihtige; ac sé sunu ána soðlice underfeng ða menniscnysse of us, þe hé us mid alysde."

[235] Ælfric, *Sermo ad Populum*, ed. Pope, pp. 445–47: "and hí scínað æfre swa beorhte swa sunne on heora Fæder ríce. Se ðe leofað and rixað mid his leofan Suna and ðam Halgan Gáste, on ánre godcundnysse, án ælmihtig God, á butan ende, AMEN."

[236] *De Trinitate*, 1, 13, PL, 42, cols. 840–44.

[237] *Expositio in Apocalypsin*, 2, PL, 117, cols. 1011D–12A. Commentators traditionally gave a Trinitarian interpretation of Apoc. 4:5, 7; cf. Bede, *Explanatio Apocalypsis*, 1, PL, 93, col. 144D; Ambrosius Autpertus, *In Apocalypsin*, CC, 27, p. 227.

[238] *Golden Age*, p. 72, no. 55, color pl. 16; Rosenthal,

"Three Drawings," p. 548, fig. 3; J. O'Reilly, "St. John as a Figure of the Contemplative Life: Text and Image in the Art of the Anglo-Saxon Benedictine Reform," *Dunstan*, pp. 179f.; Temple, *Manuscripts*, pp. 86f., no. 68.

[239] So F. Wormald, "Late Anglo-Saxon Art: Some Questions and Suggestions," *Studies in Western Art*, 1: Romanesque and Gothic Art, Acts of the Twentieth International Congress of the History of Art, 1 (Princeton, 1963), p. 22, rpt. idem, *Writings*, p. 107. Schiller, *Icon.*, 1, p. 8, proposed that the kings were Christ's ancestors.

[240] The Trinity and the Adoration of the Elders were also included in the twelfth-century portal sculpture of the Last Judgment at St. Denis; P. L. Klein, "Programmes eschatologiques, fonction, et réception historiques des portails du XIIᵉ s.: Moissac—Beaulieu—Saint Denis," *Cahiers de Civilisation Médiévale* 33 (1990): 338, fig. 38.

least in theory, the presence of the other two.[241] Images made this doctrine intelligible through the accompanying texts. In the sixth-century mosaic of San Michele in Affricisco from Ravenna, now in Berlin, the book of the enthroned Christ is inscribed "Qui uidit me uidit et patrem. Ego et pater unum sumus" (He that seeth me seeth the Father. I and the Father are one [John 14:9; 10:30]).[242] Christ adored by two angels illustrates a votive feast to the Trinity in the late-tenth-century Fulda sacramentary in Göttingen (Univ. Lib., MS theol. Fol. 231; fig. 94).[243] The inscription "missa de s(an)c(t)a Trinitate" beneath his mandorla expresses his Trinitarian significance. A similar group of Christ and two seraphs appears above Boethius in a late-tenth-century miniature in a manuscript from Fleury (Paris, Bibl. Nat., MS lat. 6401; fig. 95).[244] This composition was intended to be the author portrait for *De Trinitate* by Boethius (which was never written out). Following the formula of an evangelist inspired by his symbol, Boethius is moved to write by a vision of the indivisible triune Godhead in the guise of Christ.[245] The enthroned Deity in this picture, which is under strong Anglo-Saxon influence, has a marked resemblance to the Trinitarian figure in the Benedictional's initial.[246] The painter of the Boethius portrait transformed the letter "O" into a second mandorla and omitted only the diadem and the clouds in the globe mandorla. He also added the

seraphim, the alpha and omega, and the sealed scroll to emphasize the visionary, apocalyptic aspect of the initial's iconography (cf. Is. 6:2–3; Apoc. 1:8, 4:8, 5:5).

The related Trinitarian imagery in the Boethius manuscript and the Grimbald Gospels confirm that contemporaries would have interpreted the Benedictional's initial as a multivalent apocalyptic vision of both Christ the Judge and the Christlike triune God.

The Incarnational Symbolism

Gregory interpreted the cloud in the biblical visions of God as a symbol of Christ's assumed humanity, but Gregory did not elaborate on the relationship between the cloud's incarnational significance and the rainbow. Others, however, explained that the rainbow must have been caused by sunlight refracted from the rain in clouds, and they interpreted this phenomenon as an allegory of Christ's two natures. Thus Haymo said that Christ was

> the sun by [his] divinity. . . . The ray of this same sun, that is, the splendor of the Eternal Light, entered the cloud when he received flesh in the womb of the Virgin. Concerning this cloud it is said by the prophet: "Behold the Lord ascends over a light cloud

[241] Cf. Panofsky, "'Friedsam Annunciation,'" p. 433: "It is therefore an error to assume that every image of the Deity in human form is either Christ, or God the Father. On the contrary, from a dogmatic point of view one Person of the Trinity, unless specifically identified as the First, the Second or the Third Person, *ipso facto* implies the two others."

[242] F. W. Deichmann, *Ravenna. Hauptstadt des spätantiken Abendlandes*, 2, 2 (Wiesbaden, 1976), pp. 39f.; Braunfels, *Dreifaltigkeit*, pp. viii–ix. For the iconography of the Trinity, see idem, "Heilige Dreifaltigkeit," *LCI*, 1, cols. 527–37.

[243] *Sac. Fuld.*, pl. 38; A. Krücke, "Zwei Beiträge zur Ikonographie des frühen Mittelalters," *Marburger Jahrbuch für Kunstwissenschaft* 10 (1937): 11ff.; V. H. Elbern, "Das Engerer Bursenreliquiar und die Zierkunst des frühen Mittelalters. Zweiter Teil," *Niederdeutsche Beiträge zur Kunstgeschichte* 13 (1974): 43, fig. 67. In the related sacramentary in Udine an historiated initial of Christ enthroned illustrates the votive feast of the Trinity; A. Comoretto, *Le miniature del sacramentario fuldense di Udine* (Udine, 1988), pp. 81ff., fig. 37. See also Magnani, *Sacramentario*, p. 36, pl. 34.

[244] F. Avril and P. D. Stirnemann, *Manuscrits enluminés d'origine insulaire VIIe–XXe siècle* (Paris, 1987), pp. 15f., no. 19, with additional bibliography. Temple, *Manuscripts*, p. 59,

no. 32.

[245] While the miniature emphasizes the unity of the Trinity, the complementary initial on the facing page, which was to historiate the first word of the text, stresses its threefold nature by showing Boethius again viewing the Trinity, but this in the form of its three individual persons; Temple, *Manuscripts*, fig. 95.

[246] So Temple, *Manuscripts*, p. 59, no. 32; *Golden Age*, p. 65, no. 44. The book seems to have been begun in England but taken unfinished to Fleury by the late tenth century. The miniature and initial have usually been ascribed to an Anglo-Saxon hand, but the dotted background, the garbled throne and ornament, and the heaviness of the drawing and coloring seem more characteristic of a Continental imitator. Cf. the miniature of David in the Odbert Psalter; A. Boeckler, *Abendländische Miniaturen* (Berlin, 1930), p. 58, pl. 52. The picture and initial might well have been based on a preliminary Anglo-Saxon drypoint sketch later completed by a French artist. Elements of the miniature's iconography are drawn in drypoint on the preceding page. A preliminary drypoint sketch was used for the earlier unfinished Anglo-Saxon drawing on fol. 5v (fig. 145).

and will enter Egypt" (Is. 19:1). Which cloud, that is the flesh of the Lord, is rightly called rainy because of the multitude of teachings. The rainbow is a sign of propitiation, because manifestly all our welfare and propitiation exists in Christ.[247]

The initial illustrates these exegetical concepts with great precision. The innovative combination of the cloud and the rainbow shows that Christ does indeed appear "on a rainy day" (Ez. 1:28), and this rain cloud is manifestly suffused with the supernatural radiance of his divinity since it is enclosed within his mandorla of light. The incarnational implications of this iconography are apparent from the fact that Christ's mandorla of rain cloud inspired the Virgin's nimbus of rain cloud in the Annunciation (pl. 8). To proceed any further in our investigation of the initial, we must pause to reconsider the related cloud symbolism of the Annunciation.

The passage in Isidore of Seville's *Etymologiae* that informed the illuminators that the *nimbus* was literally a rain cloud also explained how the sun's irradiation of such a cloud produced the rainbow.[248] Thus the Benedictional's painters would have been well aware that the sunlit rain cloud, the rainbow, and the nimbus were interrelated natural phenomena. The transference of the illuminated rain cloud from Christ's mandorla to Mary's nimbus ingeniously illustrated the exegetic connection between his appearances in his *doxa* in heavenly visions and at the Incarnation. In each picture the bright rain cloud

symbolized the light of Christ's divinity permeating the rainy cloud of his humanity. We should also not forget that many commentators regarded the cloud as a symbol of Mary's flesh as well as his, since he had received his humanity from her.[249] Thus the appearance of both of them in an aura of bright cloud could also signify that they shared a common, uniquely pure humanity that had been illuminated by his divinity.

This transfer of the illuminated cloud from Christ's mandorla to the Virgin's nimbus was a highly original variation of the old practice of encompassing her in a Christological mandorla. Originating in pre-iconoclastic Byzantium, the motif of the Virgin sharing the mandorla of the Christ child[250] appears in the illustration of the Apostles' Creed in the Utrecht Psalter (figs. 29, 30).[251] A mandorla (difficult to see in reproductions) circumscribes the upper half of Mary and the Christ child, whom she places on a throne on the right side of the Christ-like Father. The Virgin could share the mandorla, the symbol of Christ's *doxa*, because she had come within its compass at the Incarnation.[252] In the Psalter the incarnational import of the motif is especially evident because she is also overshadowed by the dove of the Spirit and holds her child in her arms.

This iconography in the Psalter, which we have already found to have influenced the Benedictional's miniature of the Presentation (pl. 20), seems also to have inspired the use of the cloud nimbus to associate the Virgin with Christ's

---

[247] Haymo, *Expositio in Apocalypsin*, 2, 4, PL, 117, cols. 1005D–1006A:

> Ipse est enim sol per diuinitatem. . . . Radius istius solis, id est claritas lucis aeternae ingressa est nubem, quando in utero uirginis accepit carnem. De hac quippe nube per prophetam dicitur: "Ecce Dominus ascendit super nubem leuem et ingredietur Aegyptum." Quae nubes, id est, caro Domini, recte imbrifera dicitur, propter multitudinem scilicet doctrinarum. Est autem arcus signum propitiationis, quia uidelicet in Christo omnis nostra salus et propitiatio consistit.

See also Ambrosius Autpertus, *In Apocalypsin*, 3, 4, 3b, CCCM, 27, p. 209; Pseudo-Alcuin, *In Apocalypsin*, 3, 4, PL, 100, col. 1116D.

[248] Isidore, *Etymologiae*, 13, 10 ("De Arcu et Nubium Effectibus"), 1–2, ed. W. M. Lindsay (Oxford, 1911), 2, unpaginated.

[249] See chap. 1, nn. 9–11.

[250] M. Sacopoulo, *La Theotokos à la mandorle de Lythrankomi*

(Paris, 1973), figs. 4–6, also 35; N. Mezoughi, rev. of Sacopoulo, *Theotokos*, in *Bulletin Monumental* 134 (1976): 360–62; A. Grabar, "The Virgin in a Mandorla of Light," *Late Classical and Mediaeval Studies in Honor of Albert Mathias Friend, Jr.*, ed. K. Weitzmann (Princeton, 1955), pp. 305–11, fig. 4.

[251] *Utrecht*, fol. 90 below; Sacopoulo, *Theotokos*, pp. 100ff., fig. 64; also S. Dufrenne, *Les Illustrations du Psautier d'Utrecht*, Association des Publications près les Universités de Strasbourg, 161 (Paris, n. d.), pp. 62f., 136. The Virgin also appears in a mandorla, both with the child and alone, in the ninth-century frescoes in the crypt of San Vincenzo al Volturno; Deshman, "Servants," figs. 18, 19.

[252] Grabar, "Virgin in a Mandorla," pp. 310f.; Sacopoulo, *Theotokos*, pp. 100ff., mistakenly assumes that a mandorla around Mary implied her divinity, and so she is forced to the conclusion that the Virgin in this context is only a symbol of Christ's humanity.

mandorla.[253] This innovative motif was a device to show that she had been encompassed by the *doxa* of Christ at the Incarnation, even though they were not literally together in a mandorla. Moreover, the replacement of a conventional aureole and nimbus with a cloud-filled mandorla and halo added a new level of symbolism. No longer simply signs of the light and the presence of divinity, these attributes became symbols of the union of the Eternal Light and the cloud of human flesh.

The Utrecht Psalter includes a second representation of a purely human figure in a mandorla that might also have been influential. Psalm 18:14 ("from those [sins] of others spare thy servant") is illustrated with the Lord's crowned servant enthroned in a mandorla which protects him from the adjacent sinners (fig. 96).[254] The mandorla was closely associated with the *imago clipeata*,[255] and so it could sometimes encompass human beings as a sign of their protection by the "shield" of God's *doxa*.[256] There is good reason to believe that in the Benedictional too the enclosing *doxa* indicated the protection as well as the presence of divinity.

Like the Psalter's crowned figure, the Virgin was the Lord's servant divinely shielded from sin. She had consented to the Incarnation because she was the "ancilla Dei," the maid servant of God (Luke 1:38, also 48), and her overshadowing by the Godhead was thought to have sanctified and protected her. Ælfric, for instance, remarked that in the Incarnation she "was so overshadowed that she was purified from, and shielded against all sins."[257] The theme of the Lord protecting his servants from sin is even present in one of the texts the Annunciation miniature prefaces, the second blessing for the second Sunday of Advent:

> May the strength of your right hand protect your servant, for whom you deigned in this time to put on virginal flesh. Amen.
>
> As long as your mercy does not disregard our weakness, protect all this your Church with the shield of your divinity, so that you might free us from the temptation of that fierce ancient enemy. . . . Amen.
>
> O Lord Jesus Christ, pour out the dew of blessings, so that now in the present life they [the people] might have you as a deliverer from all enemies, and here and in eternity they might always feel that you are with them as a protector. Amen.[258]

This blessing makes an analogy between the Incarnation, when the Spirit and Christ overshadowed and protected the weak human nature of the Virgin, and the liturgical benediction, through which divine power again comes and guards mankind. The "dew of blessings" and the "shield of your divinity" ("tuae diuinitatis clypeo") are equivalent metaphors for the divine succor lent to humanity. Since the Virgin's nimbus of rain cloud visualized the first of these metaphors, it probably also pictorialized the second one.

This is all the more likely because the nimbus, like the mandorla, could be considered the protective "shield" of God. On the authority of Psalm 5:13 ("O Lord, thou hast crowned us as with a shield of thy good will)", commentators explained that saints were depicted nimbed with "crowns" of divine protection in the form of round shields ("in formam scuti rotundi").[259]

---

[253] Christ's mandorla in the Second Coming and Ascension (pls. 10, 25) also indicates their special interest in the Psalter's representations of this attribute (cf. fig. 55).

[254] *Utrecht*, fol. 10v; Sacopoulo, *Theotokos*, p. 33, fig. 33.

[255] G. W. Elderkin, "Shield and Mandorla," *American Journal of Archaeology* 42 (1938): 227–36; A. Krücke, *Die Nimbus und verwandte Attribute in der frühchristlichen Kunst* (Strassburg, 1905), pp. 95ff.

[256] For other examples of shielding mandorlas, see C.-O. Nordström, "Rabbinica in frühchristlichen und byzantinischen Illustrationen zum 4. Buch Mose," *Idea und Form*, Figura, n. s., 1 (Stockholm, 1959), pp. 28ff.; Sacopoulo, *Theotokos*, pp. 28ff., figs. 30, 31; also the illustration of Psalm 90:5–6 in the Stuttgart Psalter; A. Heimann, "Three Illustrations from the Bury St. Edmunds Psalter and their Prototypes," *Journal of the Warburg and Courtauld Institutes* 29 (1966): 44, pl. 8d.

[257] Ælfric, *Hom.*, 1, pp. 199, 202.

[258] *CBP*, no. 1352; Warner and Wilson, *Ben.*, p. 3:

Sit fortitudo dextere tuae ad protectionem huius familiae tuae, pro qua dignatus es hoc tempore carnem induere uirginalem. Amen.

Ut dum infirmitatem nostram tua clementia non ignorat, ita omnem hanc ecclesiam tuam tuae diuinitatis clypeo protege, ut de saeui illius antiqui hostis temptatione nos liberes. . . . Amen.

Tu ergo omnipotens domine iesu christe benedictionum rore perfunde, ut et in presenti uita positi, de omnibus inimicis te habeant ereptorem, et hic et in aeternum semper sentiant protectorem. Amen.

[259] E.g., Sicard of Cremona (1160–1215), *Mitrale*, 1, 12, PL, 213, col. 43C–D; Gulielmus Durandus, *Rationale Divinorum Officiorum*, 1, 3, 20 (Lyon, 1612), p. 15. See G. B. Ladner,

This interpretation of the nimbus is prominent in the illustrations of the popular Carolingian treatise *De Laudibus Sanctae Crucis* by Hrabanus Maurus. The explanatory text of the *carmen figuratum* miniature of the crucified Christ in the Vienna copy describes Christ's halo as the crown around his head, a point also emphasized by the inscription of "King of kings and Lord of lords" in the border of the nimbus.[260] In the next illustration of the treatise, the dedication portrait of Emperor Louis the Pious (fig. 67), the nimbus is inscribed "You, O Christ, crown Louis," and the text explains that the emperor in military costume is the soldier of Christ clothed in "the armor of God" (Ephesians 6:11–17).[261] Thus in accordance with Psalm 5:13, the triumphant crucified Christ has "crowned" Louis with another piece of his (Christ's) own armor, the protective nimbus or "shield" of his good will.[262]

This transference of Christ's protective nimbus to the emperor anticipates the Anglo-Saxon imagery in which Christ's cloud mandorla, the equivalent of his *clipeus*, was shifted in the form of a cloud nimbus to the Virgin. The influence of Louis's portrait on the miniature of the Doubting (pl. 24) has already been remarked, and the Hrabanus illustrations seem also to have influenced the symbolism of the Virgin's protective nimbus.[263] The transposition of this symbolism from the crucified Christ and a Carolingian ruler to Christ on the rainbow and the Virgin was not as great an imaginative leap as it might seem, for the idea of the bestowal of godly protection and a crown on the righteous occurred in the exegesis of the apocalyptic vision of God on a rainbow in the cloud. So Haymo, after his previously quoted incarnational interpretation of the vision, added that "the rainbow . . . was round about the throne, because he [Christ] himself is the crown and the protection of his saints."[264]

It is important to bear in mind that the figure in the Benedictional's initial could be perceived as the Trinitarian Godhead as well as Christ. This is another link to the Creed illustration of the Utrecht Psalter, for the Virgin there shares Christ's mandorla in the presence of the other persons of the Trinity. This is not the place for thorough study of this Carolingian image, but some analysis is essential to elucidate the Benedictional's own association of Trinity and Incarnation.

The celestial group in the drawing (fig. 30) refers simultaneously to different parts of the Apostles' Creed.[265] Christ's inclusion in a Trinity illustrates the text's first article which was regarded as an affirmation of the existence of the divine Son from the beginning, co-equal, co-eternal, and consubstantial with his Father,[266] but Christ's depiction as a child in the arms of his mother who is overshadowed by the dove also illustrates the beginning of the second article which states that he was conceived by the Spirit and born to the Virgin. Her pairing with the Trinity alludes to the participation of all three persons of the Trinity in the Incarnation, a concept long associated with this section of the Creed.[267] Since she places Christ on a throne next to the Father, this group also depicts the statement in the second article that Christ now sits at the right of his Father in heaven after his

---

"The so-called Square Nimbus," *Mediaeval Studies* 3 (1941): 35, n. 131.

[260] K. Holter, *Hrabanus Maurus, Liber de Laudibus Sanctae Crucis,* Codices Selecti, 33 (Graz, 1973), pp. 14f., fols. 3v, 6v, also figs. 3, 7; for the text, see PL, 107, col. 154C–D.

[261] See above, n. 95; for the text, see PL, 107, cols. 141–46.

[262] See also the *carmen figuratum* dedication portrait of Judith, the second wife of Louis, in the ninth-century copy of Hrabanus' commentary on the books of Judith, Esther, and the Maccabees in Geneva, Bibl. de la Ville, MS 22; Schramm and Mütherich, *Kaiser und Könige in Bildern,* pp. 159f., 295, no. 17. The inscription within the divine hand and the empress invokes Christ and says that the right hand of God protects her, while the inscription in the rim of her *clipeus* states that God has given her gifts and a crown. As in her husband's portrait, the *clipeus* itself represents the protective shield or crown God gives her.

[263] They also influenced the symbolism of Benedict's Christological halo in the frontispiece for Æthelwold's translation of the Benedictine Rule, which survives in later copies

(figs. 136, 137); see Deshman, *"Benedictus,"* pp. 236ff., figs. 51, 54.

[264] Haymo, *Expositio in Apocalypsin,* 2, 4, PL, 117, col. 1006B: "Iris . . . erat in circuitu sedis, quia ipse est corona et protectio sanctorum suorum." See above, n. 247.

[265] E. T. DeWald, *The Illustrations of the Utrecht Psalter* (Princeton, 1932), p. 71; Schiller, *Ikon.,* 4, 1, p. 137; for the text of the Creed, see J. N. D. Kelly, *Early Christian Creeds* (London, 1952), p. 369.

[266] Kelly, *Creeds,* p. 372.

[267] E.g., Rufinus, *Commentary on the Apostles' Creed,* 9, tr. J. N. D. Kelly, Ancient Christian Writers, 20 (London, 1955), pp. 43f. See also M. E. Gössmann, *Die Verkundigung an Maria* (Munich, 1957), pp. 20ff., 186ff. For related Byzantine imagery, see E. Kitzinger, "The Descent of the Dove. Observations on the Mosaic of the Annunciation in the Cappella Palatina in Palermo," *Byzanz und der Westen,* ed. I. Hutter, Österreichische Akademie der Wissenschaften, phil.-hist. Kl., Sitzungsberichte, 432 (Vienna, 1984), pp. 114f., figs. 7, 9, 11.

earthly life, which is represented beneath the Trinity in a series of scenes ranging from the Passion to the Ascension (fig. 29). The article concludes with the assertion that Christ will come from heaven to judge mankind, and the judgment over which he and the rest of the Trinity will preside appears in the lower right corner of the composition. Essentially the drawing shows that the Virgin's human child was also the eternally ruling heavenly divinity who in his assumed flesh will return to earth in judgment.

The Benedictional's imaginative painters incorporated the complex content of the Psalter's Creed iconography into their own imagery. Like Christ in the Psalter, the figure in the initial is multivalent, simultaneously relating to the entire temporal scheme of Christianity. In conjunction with the first of the accompanying benedictions for the Octave, the Christological figure could be viewed as the immutable and eternal triune Godhead that would fully manifest itself at the Last Judgment, but at the same time the "sharing" of the Godhead's *doxa* with the Virgin at the Annunciation showed that all three of its persons had cooperated in Christ's Incarnation. The Deity on a rainbow in cloud could also be interpreted as the apocalyptic vision of the ascended Christ, now enthroned in heaven in his assumed humanity as well as his divinity. As a symbol of his two natures, the luminescent rain cloud about him served the same purpose as the Psalter's characterization of the second person of the celestial Trinity as the child of a human mother. In the Psalter the Trinity was linked not only to the Incarnation but also to the subsequent events in Christ's earthly life, culminating in his Ascension, and this is also true of the initial. We have already discovered that the initial is iconographically associated with the Second Coming, Pentecost, and the Baptism (pls. 10, 26, 19). The motif of the illuminated rain cloud that connects

it to both the Annunciation and the Second Coming also associates it with many others in the Christological cycle. This recurrent symbol visualized the exegetic *topos* that Christ came into the world in the cloud of his human nature, which he elevated to heaven in his Ascension and which he would bring back to earth at the Second Coming. Gregory, it will be recalled, had applied this *topos* to Christ's enthronement on a rainbow in a rain cloud.[268]

The Benedictional's creators were attracted to the Psalter's drawing of the Creed because this text had much in common with the liturgy of the Octave of Pentecost. Both of the feast's mass lections included passages that said in so many words that Christ was the alpha and the omega. In Apocalypse 4:8 the four winged beasts hail the Deity on the rainbow throne as "Lord God almighty, who was, who is, and who is to come," and John 3:13 states that "no man hath ascended into heaven, but he that descended from heaven, the Son of man who is in heaven." The Gospel reading was followed in the mass by the Niceno-Constantinopolitan Creed, which is similar in content to the Apostolic Creed.[269] This combination of liturgical texts must have reminded the illuminators of the temporally multivalent group of the Trinity and the Virgin in the Creed illustration.

The baptismal, Trinitarian, and eschatological themes of the initial's liturgical benedictions also related to the Creed. Catechumens professed their belief in the Trinity by reciting or affirming the Creed before their baptism in the name of the Trinity (cf. Matt. 28:19).[270] Belief in the tenets of the Creed was an essential precondition for the baptismal grace that the initial's second prayer renews through liturgical blessing. When the first prayer asks that the congregation continue to recognize the true nature of the Trinity, it seeks the continuation of the belief in the Creed that had first been professed in

---

[268] The Benedictional's interpretation of the Psalter's Creed iconography influenced the two-page illustration of John's prologue in the Grimbald Gospels which juxtaposes the Trinity on the verso with the Virgin and child in a shared mandorla on the recto (figs. 92, 93). Like the Psalter and the Benedictional, the Grimbald Gospels illustrated the role of the Trinity in the scheme of Christianity from before the Incarnation to the Last Judgment. Related images of the enthroned Virgin and child in a mandorla occur on two eleventh-century English ivories in the Ashmolean Museum in Oxford and the Victoria and Albert Museum in London;

Beckwith, *Ivory Carvings*, nos. 15, 40, figs. 36, 75; *Golden Age*, p. 120, no. 122; *English Romanesque Art 1066–1200*, p. 212, no. 178. The Virgin alone in a mandorla appears in a canon table of the early-eleventh-century Pembroke Gospels; Ohlgren, *Illustration*, p. 65, pl. 9.3.

[269] Kelly, *Creeds*, pp. 351ff.; cf. Ælfric, *Hom.*, 2, pp. 596–99.

[270] Kelly, *Creeds*, pp. 30ff. and passim. For the Anglo-Saxon rite, see *Jumièges*, p. 99. Ælfric's homily on the Creed (*Hom.*, 1, pp. 274–95; also 2, pp. 604ff.) is a long Trinitarian discourse.

baptism. And so ultimately this belief, as part of the baptism which is necessary for all who hope to "see the kingdom of God" (John 3:5), will give them perpetual grace, allowing them to behold the triune God's "endless manifestation and appearance." In borrowing from the Psalter's drawing, the Benedictional's creators acknowledged the central importance of the Creed to the themes of the initial's feast day.

The Preaching Symbolism

The Psalter's influence is also germane to the issue of preaching symbolism in the initial. The apostles were believed to have written their Creed soon after Pentecost.[271] Supposedly they composed it as a common version of the doctrine the Spirit had bestowed on them, so that after they separated speaking different tongues they could nonetheless all preach the same dogma. This popular legend would surely have come to the mind of anyone reading part of the Benedictional's first blessing for Pentecost:

> And may he who deigned to unify the diversity of tongues in the confession of one faith, cause you to persevere in the same faith, and by this to come from the hope to the vision [of God].[272]

The unifying "confession of one faith" would have been understood as the Apostles' Creed, and according to the blessing, continued faith in it offered the prospect of the ultimate beatitude of the saved, the vision of God. The initial of the associated feast of the Octave illustrates this very vision and also, in conjunction with other pictures in the cycle, the creedal doctrine that the disciples received at Pentecost to preach to mankind.

Exegetes related the biblical propitiatory visions of God on a rainbow in a cloud to preach-

ing. Gregory associated the rainy cloud with not only the flesh of the Savior but also the "effusions of preachers" which call back the hearts of believers to grace. Haymo went into more detail. He explained how the combination of sun and rain cloud, the respective symbols of Christ's divinity and humanity, caused the propitiatory sign of the rainbow, and then interpreted these natural phenomena in terms of preaching:

> Or else by the rainy cloud we are able to understand the saints, who rain words, flash miracles, and irradiated by the brightness of heavenly light and illuminated with the most pious supplications for us, they bend the justice of the Creator to mercy.[273]

The rainy cloud once more symbolizes humanity, but now the humanity of the saints who rain words of preaching and intercession. When the divine light illuminates this symbolic rain cloud, it again produces the rainbow whose curvature now symbolizes the tempering effects of the saint's intercessions on the judgment of the Sun of Righteousness. This was a long-standing interpretation of the rain cloud and the rainbow.[274] Often, as in Gregory and Haymo, the explanation occurred together with the incarnational, baptismal, and eschatological ones; for preaching, like the Incarnation and baptism, was a means to bring Christ and his mercy to humanity, holding out to them the possibility of escape from the second, fiery judgment.

Two later images related to the Benedictional's initial associate the Deity directly with propitiating saints. The Grimbald Gospels (figs. 92, 93) combined the Trinitarian figural type of the initial with choirs of the saints who in part function as intercessors for the souls held by the angels. The feast of All Saints in the eleventh-century Norman sacramentary of Mont Saint Michel (New York, Morgan Lib., MS M. 641), a manuscript deeply influenced by English art, is illus-

---

[271] Regarding the legend, see Kelly, *Creeds*, pp. 1–6; cf. Ælfric, *Hom.*, 2, pp. 292, 293.

[272] *CBP*, no. 948; Warner and Wilson, *Ben.*, p. 25: "Quique dignatus est diuersitatem linguarum in unius fidei confessione adunare, in eadem uos faciat fide perseuerare, et per hanc ab spe ad speciem peruenire."

[273] Haymo, *Expositio in Apocalypsin*, 2, 4, PL, 117, col. 1006B–C: "Sive per nubem imbriferam possumus intelligere sanctos, qui pluunt uerbis, coruscant miraculis, et claritate superni luminis irradiati et illustrati piissimis supplica-

tionibus pro nobis justitiam conditoris ad pietatem inflectunt." For Haymo's antecedent incarnational, eschatalogical, and baptismal interpretations, see above, nn. 220, 247.

[274] E.g., Ambrosius Autpertus, *In Apocalypsin*, 3, 4, 4, ed. Weber, p. 210; Pseudo-Alcuin, *In Apocalypsin*, 3, 4, PL, 100, col. 1116D; Bede, *Explanatio Apocalypsis*, 1, 4, PL, 93, col. 143B; Primasius, *Commentarius in Apocalypsin*, 1, 4, ed. A. W. Adams, CC, 92, p. 47; also Isidore, *De Natura Rerum*, 31, 1–2, ed. J. Fontaine, *Isidore de Seville: Traité de la nature* (Bordeaux, 1960), pp. 284, 285.

trated by a figure of Christ (fig. 98) very like the one in the Benedictional in pose, attributes, and placement within the initial "O" of "omnipotens."[275] The later initial, however, adds two groups of eleven saints emerging from clouds in the interstices of the rainbow and the mandorla of the letter. In this location the saints illustrate the initial's text[276] which asks for God's propitiation through their intercession: the rainy clouds of the saints are within Christ's mandorla and are therefore illuminated by his divine light, producing the rainbow that symbolizes the mercy resulting from their supplications to him.

In addition to the figure of Christ, the saints within his mandorla reflect the innovations of the Benedictional, for there too Christ had conferred his attributes on humanity. He shares the cloudy substance of his mandorla with the Virgin and his rainbow throne with the apostles in the Pentecost miniature. As we shall see, this repetition of the rainbow signified the co-enthronement of Christ and the disciples. The influence of this Pentecost iconography on the Norman initial can hardly be mistaken since it too shows a similar number of male saints in two nearly symmetrical groups above Christ's rainbow.[277]

The interpolation of the saints into the sacramentary's initial gave more literal expression to concepts already present in the Benedictional's two associated images. Though the Christological Deity is alone in the initial, the rainbow in the mandorla of rain cloud symbolized the presence of the sainted apostles who reflected his divine illumination in their mercy-giving preaching. In the Pentecost miniature the Christological attribute of the rainbow signified that not only the Spirit but also Christ, indeed the triune Godhead, was symbolically present with the disciples when they received the gift of tongues and the creedal doctrine for their future preaching. The New Testament (John 14:14–28, 15:26; Acts

2:30, 33–35) stressed that Christ would send the Paraclete from the Father, with whom he was one, after he had ascended to sit beside him in heaven. Byzantine images of Pentecost sometimes represented the figure of Christ with the Spirit (fig. 54), or the Trinity in the symbolic form of the dove on the Etiomasia (fig. 83), and the Drogo Sacramentary (fig. 86) depicted all three persons of the Trinity.[278] Some antecedent version of Christ or the Trinity participating in Pentecost may well have influenced the Benedictional.

The preaching symbolism of the Octave initial reinforced its association with other miniatures in the cycle in which the cloud also had connotations of preaching. The repetition of this motif as well as the fire of the rainbow and the diadem of Christ created a series of interlocking symbolic relationships between the initial and other scenes, investing the deceptively simple imagery of the initial with virtually all the levels of symbolism that Gregory and other commentators attached to the visions of God.

In the iconography as in the exegesis these various strata of significance were congruent. The rainbow in the cloud mandorla signified God's past and future judgments of mankind. Yet as a sign of God's peace covenant after the flood, these motifs also manifested the various means of divine propitiation that might enable humanity to escape condemnation at the Last Judgment: the illuminating advent of Christ and the Spirit to mankind in the Incarnation, baptism, and preaching. The liturgy, especially the Benedictional's own texts, led the illuminators to incorporate Pentecost and episcopal benediction into this scheme of divine dispensation. For several reasons this was a logical extension. Pentecost was yet another occasion when mankind had received divine light, and this foreshadowed the bestowal of heavenly illumination in baptism and episcopal blessings. Moreover, benedictions, like all the words of

[275] Alexander, *Norman Illumination*, pp. 159–61, pl. 45d, noted the resemblance.

[276] For an edition of the prayer (*Omnipotens sempiterne deus qui nos*), see *Jumièges*, p. 221.

[277] Alexander, *Norman Illumination*, p. 160, fig. 45e (our fig. 12) also connects the Norman initial to the composition of the Galba Psalter representing saints in the outer compartments of Christ's mandorla. Here too the motif had an intercessory meaning since on one level the picture illustrates the litany of the saints; Deshman, "Anglo-Saxon Art after Al-

fred," pp. 176ff.

[278] Leesti, "Pentecost Illustration," pp. 205ff., figs. 1, 3, 4; S. Seeliger, "Das Pfingstbild mit Christus, 6.–13. Jahrhundert," *Das Munster* 9 (1956): 146–52; R. Kahsnitz, "Der christologische Zyklus im Odbert-Psalter," *Zeitschrift für Kunstgeschichte* 51 (1988): 118ff.; N. Ozoline, "Les Représentations de la Trinité dans l'iconographie byzantine de la Pentecôte," *Trinité et Liturgie*, ed. A. M. Triacca and A. Pistoia (Rome, 1984), pp. 195ff.

the liturgy, could be construed as ecclesiastic "preaching."

THE APOSTLES ON THE RAINBOW

We can now finally return to the question of why the Christological attribute of the rainbow throne was transferred to the apostles in the Pentecost miniature. According to the Apocalypse (4:3–4), twenty-four Elders sat on twenty-four seats adoring the Deity on its throne with a rainbow. Commentators identified half the Elders as the patriarchs and prophets who had preached Christ's coming and the other half as the twelve apostles and also righteous individuals who had followed the example of the apostles.[279] The Elders are termed "apostolic company" ("coetus apostolicus") in the inscription of the picture of the Adoration in the Codex Aureus of the Carolingian king Charles the Bald (Munich, Staatsbibl. Clm. 14000; fig. 134).[280] The exegetes believed that the Elders were enthroned to exercise judgment with Christ, who had promised the apostles and those who followed him that "when the Son of man shall sit on the seat of his majesty, you also shall sit on twelve seats judging the twelve tribes of Israel" (Matt. 19:28; also Luke 22:30). The New Testament statements that Christ and his co-judges would have separate thrones were not taken literally, however. The preceding chapter of the Apocalypse (3:21) said that "to him that shall overcome, I will give to sit with me in my throne: as I also have overcome, and am set down with my Father in his throne." Hence commentators held that Christ and the Elders of the two Testaments would all be seated together on one throne exercising one judicial power. In the Carolingian Apocalypse manuscript in Trier the Elders are in two groups of twelve, each group on a long single throne, although Christ is separately seated on a globe mandorla (fig. 89). To illustrate

the exegesis the Benedictional's illuminators went futher than the Trier miniature. They evidently reasoned that since the Apocalypse implied that Christ's throne was a rainbow, the apostles who, as Elders, were co-enthroned with him should also have a rainbow instead of an ordinary throne. Since the initial depicted the three persons of the Trinity enthroned as one on a rainbow, the implication is that the apostles have fulfilled the promise of Apocalypse 3:21: they have imitated Christ and won a place beside him and the Father on the heavenly throne.

The related drawing of Peter on a rainbow and globe in the New Minster Prayerbook (fig. 87) substantiates that at Winchester the apostolic rainbow symbolized the power of judgment.[281] This combination of Christological attributes depends on the Benedictional's initial, while the motif of Peter on a rainbow derived from its Pentecost picture. In fusing features from these two images in the Benedictional, the Prayerbook's draftsman reveals an awareness of their relationship to each other. In the drawing Peter's pose, like his attributes, is Christological. Rigidly frontal with a book on his knee, he resembles the figure of Christ in the initial and even more the one in the dedication miniature of the New Minster Liber Vitae (fig. 97). The latter, which is probably by same hand as the Prayerbook, depicts Christ as the heavenly judge with the book of life receiving the intercessions of Peter and Mary and the monks below for the royal couple.[282] Thus in the Prayerbook Peter has been cast in the vicarious role of Christ the Judge. In imitating Christ, the apostle has won the reward that Christ promised (Apoc. 3:21) to all who overcome as he did: heavenly co-enthronement with the Father and Son. This theme of *imitatio Christi* could scarcely be overlooked since the Prayerbook also contains the Quinity drawing which shows Christ and his Father *synthroni* on the rainbow as they judge the devil and his accomplices (fig. 27). The link-

---

[279] E.g., Primasius, *Commentarius in Apocalypsin*, 1, 4, CC, 92, p. 48; Bede, *Explanatio Apocalypsis*, 1, 4, PL, 93, col. 143C; Ambrosius Autpertus, *In Apocalypsin*, 3, 3, 21; 4, 4, ed. Weber, pp. 200f., 210ff.; Haymo, *Expositio in Apocalypsin*, 2, 3–4, PL, 117, cols. 1001C–D, 1006D; Pseudo-Alcuin, *In Apocalypsin*, 3–4, PL, 100, cols. 1115C, 1117B.

[280] Koehler and Mütherich, *Kar. Min.*, 5, p. 181, pl. 47; O. K. Werckmeister, *Der Deckel des Codex Aureus von St. Emmeram*, Studien zur deutschen Kunstgeschichte, 332 (Baden-

Baden, 1963), p. 76; also H. L. Kessler, "Pictures as Scripture in Fifth-Century Churches," *Studia Artium Orientalis et Occidentalis* 2 (1985): 24, 28.

[281] See also the apostles on rainbows in the Last Judgment in the twelfth-century Winchester Psalter; Haney, *Winchester Psalter*, figs. 31, 35.

[282] Deshman, "*Benedictus*," pp. 223f., fig. 65; also below, chap. 6.

age between the Prayerbook's two drawings reflects the association between the Benedictional's Pentecost picture and initial which also depicted the apostles imitating the enthronement of the Trinity on the rainbow.

Although the Prayerbook confirms the Christological, judicial import of the rainbow-throne of the apostles in the Benedictional, it does not explain the motif's relation to Pentecost. No commentator seems to have connected the apostolic Elders sharing Christ's judgment throne to this event. The idea was apparently originated by the Benedictional's creators who must have been influenced by the use of Apocalypse 4:1–10 as a lection for the Octave of Pentecost. As a symbol of judicial throne-sharing, the rainbow throne could be appropriately transferred from an apocalyptic to a historical context because Pentecost was intrinsically associated with the apostles' participation in Christ's powers of judgment.

Pentecost itself prefigured the Last Judgment.[283] The account of Pentecost in Acts endowed the event with eschatological overtones; after Pentecost Peter quoted Joel's prophecy of the coming of the Spirit and the Lord, changing it to refer to "the last days" (Acts 2:17–21; cf. Joel 2:28–32). Pentecost's occurrence fifty days after Easter led commentators to provide various arcane numerological explanations of its typological relation to the Final Day.[284] Romanesque and Gothic art sometimes amalgamated the two events. The thirteenth-century remodeling of the monastic church of Grottaferrata, for example, added figures of the Trinity with angels and prophets to a preexisting mosaic of Pentecost, reconstituting it to resemble contemporary Last Judgment iconography.[285] Employing a Byzantine miniature illustrating the Nicene Creed[286] as the model for their Trinitarian group, the Grottaferrata painters followed a procedure akin to that of the Benedictional's illuminators, who several centuries before had also used a Trinity associated with creedal iconography to invest Pentecost with connotations of the Last Judgment.

The rainbow throne at Pentecost implied that the apostles were able to exercise Christ's judicial authority in this as well as the next world. Before the Ascension, Christ had explicitly shared this authority with them by giving them the power of the keys to the heavenly kingdom (John 19:19–23) and at the same time the Holy Spirit. Pentecost, when another bestowal of the Spirit confirmed and completed the earlier one,[287] inaugurated them for Christ's mission, which entailed the exercise of his power of the key. In the Pentecost miniature the gold key that Peter holds is a cognate of the rainbow throne: both symbolize the judgmental power that Christ had entrusted to the disciples. In the Prayerbook's related drawing Peter on a rainbow once again grasps the key, but its enormous size and prominent display also recall the Benedictional's miniature of the Doubting of Thomas (pl. 24) where it again alludes to Christ's bestowal of its power on Peter and his colleagues. The disciples' terrestrial authority to forgive or condemn sin foreshadowed their future celestial power when co-enthroned with Christ they would join him in deciding who would or would not pass through the heavenly gate.[288] In the Benedictional the conflation of their earthly confirmation of the power of the key at Pentecost with their future exercise of this power on the heavenly judgment throne of Christ expressed this typology.

Their throne, like the one of the triune Deity in the initial, also held out to viewers the hope of escape from condemnation. This is because the apostolic Elders, by imitating Christ—whose triumph over death led to his heavenly co-enthronement with the other members of the Trinity—became models for all who hope to win this promised celestial throne-sharing (cf. Apoc. 3:21). Haymo said that the throne-sharing Elders represented not only the apostles but also "all the righteous, who in the present life have followed the examples of the apostles, just as through Peter the other apostles and preachers received the key of the kingdom of heaven."[289]

[283] For the following, see Kitzinger, "Mosaics of the Cappella Palatina," p. 278, rpt. in idem, *Art of Byzantium*, p. 299.

[284] E. g., Isidore, *De Ecclesiasticis Officiis*, 1, 34, PL, 83, col. 769. Cf. Kitzinger, "Capella Palatina," p. 278, nn. 53, 54, rpt. p. 299.

[285] H. L. Kessler, "'Caput et Speculum Omnium Ecclesiarum': Old St. Peter's and Church Decoration in Medieval Latium," *Italian Church Decoration of the Middle Ages and Early Renaissance*, ed. W. Tronzo, Villa Spelman Colloquia, 1 (Bologna, 1989), pp. 137ff., figs. 21, 22, with further bibliography. See also Kitzinger, "Cappella Palatina," pp. 278f., n. 55, rpt. pp. 299f., for this and other amalgamated examples.

[286] Kessler, "'Caput et Speculum,'" pp. 138f., fig. 23.

[287] Cf. Ælfric, *Hom.*, 1, pp. 232–35, 324–27.

[288] Speaking of the judgment seat to which Christ ascended, Ælfric, *Hom.*, 1, p. 311, said that he judged now and in the future on the last day.

[289] Haymo, *Expositio in Apocalypsin*, 2, 4, PL, 117, cols.

The theme of the imitation of the apostles' achievement of heavenly grace was also prominent in the exegesis and liturgy of Pentecost. According to an Old English Blickling homily,

> the Holy Ghost came upon the disciples . . . and thereby were they set free from all sins, and brought to everlasting life, and that they might also, through that gift blot out other men's sins. . . . Not alone to the apostles was this gift [of the Spirit] bestowed, but also, indeed to all mankind was given forgiveness of all sins. . . . To us also is permitted a way of return to everlasting life, and to occupy heaven's kingdom along with all saints and with the Lord himself.[290]

The homily, like the Benedictional's picture, telescoped the apostles' Pentecostal reception of the Spirit with the event's consequence, their "everlasting life" with Christ. The grace they had received at Pentecost they subsequently bestowed on others by preaching and baptism (cf. Acts 2:38). Hence all mankind, receiving grace like the apostles, could aspire to the same final reward—heavenly dwelling with Christ and the saints. The Benedictional's own texts for the vigil of Pentecost stress that the apostles' Pentecostal grace could be conferred on the faithful in baptism and the episcopal blessing, enabling them to enter the heavenly kingdom after death.[291]

The similar representations of the dove and angels in the pictures of Pentecost and Baptism (pls. 26, 19) illustrated this typological relation between the descent of the Spirit at Pentecost and in baptism. Since the Octave initial also showed in no uncertain terms that the Pentecostal gift of the Spirit had given the apostles the final reward of heavenly co-enthronement with the triune Godhead, those contemplating these pictures were led to hope that in this respect too they might imitate the disciples. In the Pentecost miniature no less than the initial the rainbow throne symbolized both the judgment and the propitiation of the Lord.

Conclusions

Although the miniatures of Christ's later life and Pentecost derived from disparate Carolingian, Anglo-Saxon, and Byzantine sources, cyclic symbolism unified them with each other and with many of the pictures of his earlier life.

The Doubting of Thomas and the Ascension both prefigured the Second Coming, and the interrelated themes of Christ's advent and his assumption of human nature related all three to the associated pictures of the Annunciation and the Nativity. The Second Coming was also linked typologically to the Entry into Jerusalem, which led back once more to the Nativity with its cornerstone symbolism. The Doubting, moreover, was tied to Pentecost and its Octave initial through the themes of the apostolic succession and preaching. The Pentecostal imagery was symbolically associated with the scenes of the Incarnation, the Baptism, and the Second Coming, strengthening the typological and dogmatic relationships among these latter pictures. In many of these images the advents of Christ to mankind in the past and the future related typologically to his coming to the believers in the present through the preaching and liturgy, especially the rite of episcopal benediction. The post-Resurrection cycle stresses the crucial role of the apostles and their ecclesiastic successors in bringing Christ and his dispensation to the faithful.

1006D: "In duodecim apostolis omnes perfecti, qui exemplum apostolorum in praesenti uita sunt secuti, sicut in Petro caeteri apostoli et praedicatores acceperunt claves regni coelorum." Haymo repeated Ambrosius Autpertus, *In Apoc-alypsin*, 4, 4, ed. Weber, p. 211.

[290] *Blickling*, pp. 134, 136.

[291] *CBP*, nos. 186, 294; Warner and Wilson, *Ben.*, p. 25.

Chapter Three

THE MINIATURES OF
THE SAINTS

MORE THAN HALF of the Benedictional's pictures represent saints. Apart from the Birth and Naming of John the Baptist, discussed already, there are narrative scenes of the Stoning of Stephen, the Martyrdoms of Peter and Paul, and the Death and Coronation of the Virgin, as well as portraits of John the evangelist, Benedict, Æthel-thryth, and Swithun. A partially preserved sequence of the choirs of the saints and the apostles opens the manuscript. In this chapter we shall consider these hagiographic pictures and also the miniature of the Bishop Blessing the Congregation.

John the Evangelist
(John the Evangelist, 27 December)

The figure of John, seated in profile with his right hand extended over the book he holds on a lectern (pl. 15), is an example of a widespread type of author portrait that was also used for Matthew in the ninth-century Turonian Gospels in Stuttgart (fig. 99),[1] for Paul in a Carolingian New Testament manuscript also in Stuttgart (Württembergische Landesbibl., MS H. B. II 54; fig. 100)[2] and for Luke in a tenth-century Anglo-Saxon miniature added to an Irish pocket Gospels in London (Brit. Lib., MS Add. 40618; fig. 101).[3] All these figures ultimately derive from a common archetype, even though the evangelist symbols, when present, are quite different. The Benedictional's iconographic relationship to the Carolingian portraits is not close enough to indicate anything more than a remote common ancestor, but the resemblance to Luke in the Irish Gospel book is very strong, even in details such as the feet on the floating footstool.

The Benedictional cannot have copied the Irish manuscript. John's draped lectern is correctly rendered, but the base of Luke's has been omitted, leaving its cloth oddly suspended from the book; in any case, the miniatures added to the Gospel book are probably slightly later than the Benedictional.[4] Conversely, the composition in the Gospel book does not seem to de-

---

[1] See above, chap. 2, n. 208.

[2] H. Boese, *Die Handschriften der ehemaligen Hofbibliothek Stuttgart*, Die Handschriften der Württembergischen Landesbibliothek Stuttgart, ser. 2 (Wiesbaden, 1975) 2, 1, pp. 56f.

[3] Temple, *Manuscripts*, pp. 43f., no. 15, fig. 49; F. Henry, "An Irish Manuscript in the British Museum (Add. 40.618)," *Journal of the Royal Society of Antiquaries of Ireland* 87 (1957): 147ff.

[4] Concerning the date, see R. Deshman, "Anglo-Saxon Art: So What's New?" forthcoming. The sketchy, highly ornamentalized drapery in the Gospel book should be compared to the mantle of the center apostle on fol. 2v of the Benedictional (pl. 4). Cf. also the acanthus in the rosettes of the evangelist portraits in the two manuscripts. Regarding the draped lectern, see C. Nordenfalk, "The Draped Lectern," *Intuition und Kunstwissenschaft. Festschrift für Hanns*

rive directly from the one in the Benedictional. The evangelist in the former writes with a pen in his open book, a feature which agrees with the related Carolingian images and which therefore probably accurately reflects an early prototype. In the Benedictional John looks at first glance as if he too were writing, but his book is closed and he simply makes a speaking gesture. These features are more unusual and are probably modifications of a conventional writing evangelist. The two Anglo-Saxon evangelist portraits must derive independently from a common model.

If this is so, then one of the two must have changed its evangelist symbol.[5] Symbols were interpolations introduced when classical figures of poets and philosophers were transformed into evangelists;[6] medieval artists often freely rearranged or replaced them. This makes it difficult to decide which of the two Anglo-Saxon evangelist portraits modified the common model, but the probability is that in regard to the symbol the one of Luke is less faithful. The twisting mass of drapery interlacing the frame is a highly ornamentalized feature that is difficult to imagine in a common prototype, which must have antedated the Benedictional. If the illuminator of the Gospel book did introduce the decorative curtain, then he might also have changed the symbol above it.

The type and placement of the Benedictional's evangelist symbol are relatively traditional. The eagle blows a horn, and the trumpeting symbol is a specifically Insular type first seen in the portrait of Matthew in the Lindisfarne Gospels (ca. 698),[7] where the symbol is balanced, like the eagle in the Benedictional, by a curtain carefully attached to the frame (fig. 102). A better comparison for the compositional relationship between symbol and evangelist, which is quite different in the two pictures, is found in the Matthew portrait of a fragmentary eighth-century Insular Gospels in St. Gall (Stiftsbibl., MS 1395; fig. 103).[8] In both miniatures the symbol and the evangelist are facing and level with each other, and the symbol touches the evangelist's book to manifest the scripture's divine inspiration. There is every indication that the Benedictional's evangelist portrait ultimately goes back to a Hiberno-Saxon archetype,[9] though the close relationship to the miniature in the Irish Gospel book suggests that an earlier tenth-century Anglo-Saxon intermediary might have transmitted the early Insular iconography.

THE SYMBOLIC CONTENT

Various explanations for the trumpeting symbol have been proposed. Underwood[10] thought it visualized the idea that the evangelists and their symbols literally expressed the musical harmony of the universe. If this were the case, one would expect that in a set of evangelist portraits all four symbols would blow horns. Usually, however, only some of the symbols trumpet.[11] More likely is Weisbach's suggestion that the horn repre-

---

Swarzenski zum 70. Geburtstag am 30. August 1973, ed. P. Bloch et al. (Berlin, 1973), pp. 81–100; J. Rosenthal, "The Unique Architectural Settings of the Arenberg Evangelists," *Studien zur mittelalterlichen Kunst 800–1250: Festschrift für Florentine Mütherich zum 70. Geburtstag*, ed. K. Bierbrauer, P. K. Klein, and W. Sauerländer (Munich, 1985), pp. 146f.

[5] It is also possible that the common model did not include a symbol (cf. fig. 105). This alternative seems less likely, however, since, as we shall see below, the relation between the author and symbol in the Benedictional reflects established iconographic practice.

[6] A. M. Friend, Jr., "The Portraits of the Evangelists in Greek and Latin Manuscripts," *Art Studies* 5 (1927): 115ff.

[7] Warner and Wilson, *Ben.*, pp. xxf.; Homburger, *Anf.*, p. 15; R. L. S. Bruce-Mitford et al., *Evangeliorum Quattuor Codex Lindisfarnensis* (Olten, 1960), 2, pp. 159f., n. 9. There are no Carolingian trumpeting evangelist symbols, but in some Carolingian Bibles the Apocalypse frontispieces represent the apocalyptic "beast" of the man with horn; see H. L. Kessler, *The Illustrated Bibles from Tours*, Studies in Manuscript Illumination, 7 (Princeton, 1977), p. 78, figs. 107–109.

[8] Alexander, *Manuscripts*, p. 79, no. 57, fig. 281. The manuscript might have originated in an Insular monastery on the Continent; see N. Netzer, "Observations on the Influence of Northumbrian Art on Continental Manuscripts of the 8th Century," *The Age of Migrating Ideas*, ed. R. M. Spearman and J. Higgitt (Edinburgh, 1993), p. 48, fig. 5.6; L. Nees, "The Irish Manuscripts at St. Gall and their Continental Affiliations," *Sangallensia in Washington*, ed. J. C. King (New York, 1993), pp. 113ff., fig. 14. This relationship between an author and his symbol is rare, though not unknown, in Carolingian art; cf. A. Goldschmidt, *German Illumination* (1928; rpt. New York, 1970), 1, pl. 52.

[9] Cf. the Anglo-Saxon Copenhagen Gospel book which copies the evangelists of the Lindisfarne Gospels or a related manuscript; Temple, *Manuscripts*, p. 69, no. 47, figs. 153, 154.

[10] P. Underwood, "The Fountain of Life in Manuscripts of the Gospels," *DOP* 5 (1950): 124f.

[11] Cf. the Lindisfarne Gospels where only the man and the lion trumpet; Alexander, *Manuscripts*, figs. 28–31.

sented the divine inspirational voice of the celestial symbol "trumpeting" the Word to the terrestrial evangelist who transcribed it.[12] Aldhelm (d. ca. 709), an Anglo-Saxon contemporary of the Lindisfarne illuminator, described a passage from Matthew as "the evangelic trumpet,"[13] and this metaphor of the "trumpeting" of the Gospels was current in Æthelwold's circle when the Hiberno-Saxon iconography was revived.[14]

Other features of the Benedictional's portrait of John assume symbolic significance when they are seen in the context of the text it illustrates, the benediction for the evangelist's feast:

> May almighty God deign to bless you through the intercession of the blessed apostle and evangelist John, through whom he wished to reveal the secrets of his Word to the Church. Amen.
>
> May he grant to you that what he [John], inspired by the gift of the Holy Spirit, poured into your ears, you might be able to receive in your mind through the gift of that same Spirit. Amen.
>
> So that, having been instructed by his lesson of the divinity of our Redeemer, and by loving what he has related, and by preaching what he has taught, and by carrying out what he has commanded, you might be found worthy to attain the rewards which the same Jesus Christ, our Lord, promised. Amen.[15]

This prayer celebrates John as the preacher and teacher of the sacred mysteries of the divinity of

Christ the Word to the faithful of the Church, and to illustrate this the illuminators transformed John from a writer into a speaker. Though they retained from the model (cf. fig. 101) the close physical association between John's right hand and his Gospel book, the change from a writing to a speaking gesture altered the meaning of the hand's association with the book: it now indicated that the evangelist preaches rather than writes the contents of his Gospel, thereby teaching and blessing the Church.

The alteration in the evangelist's action also subtly transformed his relationship to the symbol. No longer simply transcribing the eagle's divine message, he and the symbol together now orally expound the content of the Gospel that joins them. Their relationship has become more one of equals, especially since they are almost level with each other in the composition. The similarity between John and his symbol was, in fact, a common theme in exegesis and art.

Commentators believed that John's superior mind had been able to soar into hidden celestial realms like the eagle, the only living creature able to fly high enough to behold the rays of the sun.[16] This was because in his Gospel prologue the evangelist had written about the Word Christ pre-existing in heaven in equal divinity with the Father before the Incarnation—celestial mysteries that were hidden from the other, "terrestrial" evangelists who had mostly written about Christ from the time of his Incarnation.

Schapiro[17] traced the influence of this concep-

---

[12] W. Weisbach, "Die Darstellung der Inspiration auf mittelalterlichen Evangelistenbildern," *Rivista di archeologia cristiana* 16 (1939): 119f.; idem, "Les Images des évangélistes dans 'l'évangéliaire d'Othon III,' " *Gazette des Beaux-Arts*, ser. 6, 21 (1939): 136. See also C. Nordenfalk, "Der inspirierte Evangelist," *Weiner Jahrbuch für Kunstgeschichte* 36 (1983): 175–90.

[13] Aldhelm, *De Virginitate*, 21, tr. M. Lapidge and M. Herren, *Aldhelm: The Prose Works* (Ipswich, 1979), p. 77, also pp. 81, 126.

[14] See below, chap. 5, n. 56.

[15] *CBP*, no. 1566; Warner and Wilson, *Ben.*, p. 6:

Omnipotens deus dignetur uobis per intercessionem beati iohannis apostoli et euangelistae benedicere, qui per eum archana uerbi sui uoluit ecclesiae reuelare. Amen.

Concedat uobis ut quod ille spiritus sancti munere afflatus uestris auribus infudit, eiusdem spiritus dona [dono] capere mente ualeatis. Amen.

Quo eius documento de diuinitate nostri redemptoris

edocti, et amando quod tradidit, et praedicando quod docuit, et exequendo quod iussit, ad dona peruenire mereamini, quae idem iesus christus dominus noster repromisit. Amen.

[16] Augustine, *De Consensu Evangelistarum*, 1, 4–5, ed. F. Weihrich, CSEL, 43, pp. 6–8; Gregory, *Homiliarum in Ezechielem Prophetam Libri Duo*, 1, 4, 10, PL, 76, col. 815B–C; Bede, *Hom.*, 1, 8, pp. 73f.; idem, *In Lucam*, prologue, pp. 9–10; Alcuin, *Commentaria in S. Joannis Evangelium*, PL, 100, cols. 742B, 744D; Haymo of Auxerre, *Homilia 9*, PL, 118, col. 55C; John the Scot, *Homilia in Prologum S. Evangelii secundum Joannem*, PL, 122, cols. 283–85. See R. E. McNally, "The Evangelists in the Hiberno-Latin Tradition," *Festschrift Bernhard Bischoff* (Stuttgart, 1971), pp. 13f.

[17] M. Schapiro, "Two Romanesque Drawings in Auxerre and Some Iconographic Problems," *Studies in Art and Literature for Belle da Costa Greene*, ed. D. Miner (Princeton, 1954), pp. 335ff.; rpt. idem, *Romanesque Art*, Selected Papers, 1 (New York, 1977), pp. 308ff.

tion of John on Carolingian art. Ninth-century portraits of John, such the one in the Turonian Gospels in Stuttgart (fig. 104), sometimes include a titulus that likens his words aspiring to heaven to the flying eagle,[18] and at least one late tenth-century Anglo-Saxon portrait of him has the same inscription.[19] The Turonian miniature also shows John and his symbol amid the clouds of heaven, and the evangelist's frontal teaching pose and orb throne liken him to the celestial Christ, indicating John's quasi-divine, celestial character. It has been overlooked that John is assimilated to the manuscript's own *Maiestas* miniature (fig. 88), which represents Christ in clouds, frontally seated on the celestial globe with an open book on his knee. Christ is even directly below the eagle, like the evangelist. John, who was likened to the ascending Christ as well as to the eagle,[20] is here identified with the object of his sublime, superhuman vision—the mysterious divine Christ in heaven. The evangelist embodies what he sees and teaches.

The Benedictional did not invest John with Christological attributes, but like the Turonian evangelist portrait, it did show him with his symbol against a celestial backdrop of cloud. Although the breast of the eagle touches the book, the bird is perched on neither the lectern nor any other terrestrial object: wings spread in flight, it emerges from a green cloudy arc of heaven cut off by the vertical border of the frame. The top of John's head is actually above the level of this arc which symbolizes the highest, hidden zone of heaven.[21] In its own way the Anglo-Saxon picture also portrayed John as the celestial evangelist, his mind soaring into the clouds like his symbol to comprehend the secret heavenly mysteries of the divine Word.

Another feature of the Benedictional that the Turonian portrait of John anticipates is an emphasis on John's preaching the sacred secrets in

his Gospel. His preaching differentiates him from the three other evangelists in the Carolingian manuscript who are all writing their Gospels (cf. fig. 99).[22] This distinguishing feature of John illustrates another aspect of the medieval lore about him.[23] John supposedly spent most of his life preaching in Asia without the aid of any writing. Heretics began to disrupt the Church with denials of Christ's pre-existent divinity and equality with the Father before the Incarnation, and the Gospels of the other three evangelists, at the time the only written ones, could not dispel these falsities since they said little about Christ's divinity. Hence when John finally returned from exile, the orthodox bishops of the Church asked him to combat the heretics by preaching his special celestial knowledge of Christ's godhood and his eternal membership in the Trinity and to preserve his teachings in permanent written form in his Gospel for the enlightenment of future generations. The opening verses of the prologue of his Gospel were the core of his heavenly wisdom on the divine Christ's co-eternity with the Father.

The Benedictional's own prayer alludes to this lore when it says that God wished the evangelist "to reveal the secrets of his Word to the Church" and that the members of the Church are to be instructed "by his lesson of the divinity of our Redeemer" and to love and preach "what he [John] has taught, and . . . commanded." It is in light of this prayer that one must understand the inscription on John's book in the miniature, the beginning of his Gospel's prologue: "In the beginning was the Word and the Word [was with God]" (John 1:1).[24] In addition to identifying the book as his Gospel, this verse contained the essence of his preaching on "the secrets of his [God's] Word" and "his [John's] lesson of the divinity of our Redeemer."[25]

Anglo-Saxon illuminators were well aware of

[18] "More volans aquile verbu(m) petit astra Iohannes." Koehler, *Kar. Min.*, 1, 2, pp. 251f., pl. 22b; see also pls. 25b, 37d, 95b. Concerning this text, which derives from the *Carmen Paschale* of Sedulius, see C. T. Little, "A New Ivory of the Court School of Charlemagne," *Studien zur mittelalterlichen Kunst*, pp. 13–16.

[19] See John in the Arenberg Gospels; Rosenthal, "Arenberg Evangelists," pp. 151f., fig. 4.

[20] E.g., Bede, *Hom.*, 1, 8, p. 74; Alcuin, *In S. Joannem*, 1, PL, 100, col. 741D.

[21] Regarding the highest zone of heaven, see A. Grabar, "L'Iconographie du ciel dans l'art chrétien de l'antiquité du haut moyen âge," *Cahiers Archéologiques* 30 (1982): 5ff.

[22] The evangelists are also differentiated in this way in the Lindisfarne Gospels and on an ivory in Paris from the court school of Charlemagne; see Little, "New Ivory," fig. 5

[23] Jerome, *Liber de Viris Inlustribus*, 9, ed. E. C. Richardson (Leipzig, 1896), pp. 12f.; Bede, *Hom.*, 1, 8; 1, 9, pp. 52f., 66f.; Alcuin, *In S. Joannem*, PL, 100, col. 741; Haymo of Auxerre, *Homiliae*, 9 and 11, PL, 118, cols. 54ff., 74f.; Ælfric, *Hom.*, 1, pp. 70ff. See Schapiro, "Romanesque Drawings in Auxerre," p. 338; rpt. *Romanesque Art*, p. 310.

[24] "In principio erat Verbum et Verbu[m erat apud deum]."

[25] The Preface of the mass for his feast celebrates John as the transcendent celestial evangelist proclaiming the first verse of his Gospel prologue; *Jumièges*, p. 148.

the special significance of this verse of the pro-logue. In a Canterbury Gospel book of about 1020 in Hanover (Kestner Mus., MS W. M. XXI[a], 36; fig. 105)[26] John uses a long scroll inscribed with the first two verses of his prologue to strike the heretic Arius who is trampled in defeat be-neath him. Arius has his own scroll inscribed with his discredited denial of Christ's pre-existent divinity: "There was a time when he was not."[27] This battle of words literally illustrates the com-mentators' assertion that the evangelist used the opening of his prologue to "destroy" those who uttered this heretical slogan.[28] Though much more subtle in tone, the earlier character portrait of the evangelist in the Benedictional strikes a similar chord: John appears as the defender and the teacher to the Church of the orthodox dog-matic secrets of the eternal divinity of the Word.

In addition to the evangelist portrait, one other picture in the Benedictional was designed to in-still in the beholder the proper orthodox belief in the co-eternity and divinity of Christ—the historiated initial of Christ or the triune Deity (pl. 27). This depiction of the eternal omnipo-tent Trinity enthroned in perfect unity in the clouds of heaven illustrated its liturgical text which asked that the triune God "so impress in your minds the equality and immutability of his essence, that he may never permit you to wan-der from him through any phantasms."[29] One of these misleading "phantasms" would have been the heresies denying the pre-existent di-vinity of Christ that John's teachings combated. The initial illustrated another of John's visions of the Godhead (Apocalypse 4), which Jerome in his *Plures fuisse*, one of the standard Gospel prefaces, associated with John in his role as the celestial evangelist contesting heresies.[30] Two later works that we have already related to the Benedictional confirm that the connection be-tween the evangelist and the Trinity was very much on the minds of the Anglo-Saxons.

In the Grimbald Gospels (figs. 92, 93) John looks up at the three persons of a Trinity, which is essentially an expanded version of the single triune God in the Benedictional. The evangelist is portrayed in the very act of beholding the heavenly vision that he recorded in the first verse of the prologue of his Gospel, which be-gins on the facing initial page.[31] The initial il-lustrating All Saints in the Mont St. Michel sacramentary (fig. 98) is related not only to the Benedictional's initial and Pentecost miniature but also to the sacramentary's own depiction of John the evangelist (fig. 106).[32] With his hieratic frontal pose and his nominally Christological at-tribute of an orb-footrest (cf. Isaiah 66:1), the dis-ciple was patterned on Christ in the All Saints initial. Like the saints in Christ's mandorla, John was assimilated to Christ because the evan-gelist's heavenly words brought Christ to his listeners. The text of the Norman evangelist por-trait, like the one in the Benedictional, empha-sizes John's role as the transcendent heavenly teacher of the Church.[33]

The common denominator of the Grimbald Gospels and the Norman sacramentary is the Benedictional, in which the images of the evan-gelist and the Trinitarian Christ must already have been intended as associated visual state-ments of orthodox dogma.[34] The linkage between these two iconographic themes goes further back, however, for it is found in the Turonian Gospel book (figs. 88, 104). Indeed, one of the motifs that relates the two Carolingian minia-tures to each other—heavenly clouds—also oc-curs in the two Anglo-Saxon pictures. The cloud as celestial backdrop, one of the favorite iconog-raphic leitmotifs of the Benedictional's makers, assimilated John to the object of his heavenly vi-sion, the immutable Word ruling in perfect one-ness with the Father and the Holy Spirit.

On a deeper allegorical level the luminous clouds in the mandorla of the initial's Trinitarian

---

[26] J. O'Reilly, "St. John as a Figure of the Contemplative Life: Text and Image in the Art of the Anglo-Saxon Benedic-tine Reform," *Dunstan*, pp. 178f.; W. Cahn, "Heresy and the Interpretation of Romanesque Art," *Romanesque and Gothic Art: Essays for George Zarnecki* (Woodbridge, 1987), 1, p. 32, fig. 5; Ohlgren, *Illustration*, p. 64, pl. 8.20.

[27] "Erat tempus quando non erat."

[28] E.g., Haymo, *Homilia 9*, PL, 118, cols. 55D, 57B.

[29] See chap. 2, n. 225.

[30] Jerome, *Commentariorum in Matheum Libri 4, praefatio*, ed. D. Hurst and M. Adriaen, CC, 77, pp. 2–4.

[31] O'Reilly, "St. John," p. 179.

[32] J. J. G. Alexander, *Norman Illumination at Mont St. Michel 966–1100* (Oxford, 1970), p. 161.

[33] *Ecclesiam tuam domine benignus*, and *Beati apostoli tui*. For an edition, see *Jumièges*, pp. 147f.

[34] The fact that the defeated Arius appears beneath John in the Hanover Gospels and below the "Quinity" in the ap-proximately contemporary New Minster prayer book (figs. 105, 27) is additional evidence of the thematic linkage. See O'Reilly, "St. John," pp. 174ff.

figure stood for the divinely illuminated members of humanity such as the apostles whose preaching rained heavenly words on the members of the Church. Similar symbolism was applied to the celestial evangelist John. Alcuin, for example, equated him with "the heavens that narrate the glory of God" (Ps. 118:1) "because . . . from heavenly light he thundered forth the prologue saying: 'In the beginning was the Word.' "[35] Elsewhere in the Benedictional's cycle John was linked to the preaching symbolism of the cloud. In the Pentecost miniature (pl. 26) he must be one of the apostles celestially enthroned on the rainbow that resulted from the apostolic "rain clouds" reflecting heavenly light in the related initial of the Trinitarian Christ, and he must also be among the crowd of disciples in the Doubting of Thomas (pl. 24) where

the cloud symbolizes their preaching mission. The portrait of John specifically illustrates him preaching the heavenly secrets of the Word to the Church; hence in this instance, too, the clouds must symbolize the cloudlike nature of the evangelist raining celestial words on mankind. The cloud associates the evangelist portrait with the many other miniatures in the cycle that include the motif as a sign of preaching.

The illuminators subtly but profoundly modified the relatively conventional iconography of a writing evangelist ultimately inherited from a Hiberno-Saxon model. Under the influence of the manuscript's liturgical text and Carolingian iconography, they transformed John into the celestially inspired teacher of Trinitarian orthodoxy to the Church and linked him to other pictures in the cycle.

The Martyrdom of Saint Stephen
(Saint Stephen, 26 December)

The Benedictional's scene (pl. 14) can be compared with one of the historiated initials of the Drogo Sacramentary (fig. 107),[36] although the adjustment of the latter's composition to the letter makes the comparison less than ideal. Both agree in the representation of a standing full-length figure of Christ with angels. These illustrate the saint's vision: "the heavens opened and the Son of man standing on the right hand of God" (Acts 7:55–56). Our picture includes neither the figure nor the hand of the Father, but such omissions were far from unusual in Western iconography. Christ appears in a mandorla without the Father in a miniature in the late-tenth-century Fulda sacramentary in Göttingen (fig. 108).[37] These Western formulations of the vision differ from the Byzantine iconography,

which almost always showed only God's hand projecting from the arc of heaven, as in the ninth-century manuscript of Cosmas Indicopleustes in the Vatican (Biblioteca Apostolica, MS gr. 699; fig. 109).[38]

Another point of comparison between the Benedictional and the Drogo Sacramentary is the location of the executioners in a single group before Stephen. This is also the case in some other Western depictions such as the miniatures in a Carolingian copy of the Pauline Epistles in Munich (Staatsbibl., MS lat. 14345; fig. 110)[39] and the Göttingen sacramentary. This feature too contrasts with the Byzantine iconography in which the executioners stand either in a semicircle around Stephen or in a group behind him.[40] The Benedictional's relation to an earlier and dis-

[35] Alcuin, *In S. Joannem*, PL, 100, col. 743B–C: "Iste est unus de illis de quibus Propheta praedixit: 'Caeli enarrant gloriam Dei.' Unde filius tonitrui ab ipso Domino appellatur, quia . . . ex coelesti claritate intonuit proemium dicens: 'In principio erat Verbum.' "

[36] *Drogo-Sak.*, fol. 27; Homburger, *Anf.*, p. 15.

[37] *Sac. Fuld.*, p. xxxv, pl. 12. For a possible early Christian example, see the drawing of the destroyed fresco in San Paolo fuori le mura in Rome; S. Waetzoldt, *Die Kopien des 17. Jahrhunderts nach Mosaiken und Wandmalereien in Rom* (Vienna, 1964), pp. 59f., no. 630, fig. 368. The murals, however, were repainted later.

[38] C. Stornajolo, *Le miniature della topografia cristiana di*

Cosma Indicopleuste (Milan, 1908), pp. 44f., pl. 47. The only exception, to my knowledge, is the ninth-century Sacra Parallela which depicts both the Father and the Son; K. Weitzmann, *The Miniatures of the Sacra Parallela: Parisinus Graecus 923*, Studies in Manuscript Illumination, 8 (Princeton, 1979), p. 190, fig. 490.

[39] Goldschmidt, *German Illumination*, 1, p. 17, pl. 53; *Karl der Grosse, Werk und Wirkung* (Aachen, 1965), p. 291, no. 472.

[40] E.g., in the menologion of Basil II (*Il menologio di Basilio II*, Codices e Vaticanis Selecti, 8 [Turin, 1907], pl. 275) and the Rockefeller McCormack New Testament (H. R. Willoughby, E. J. Goodspeed, and D. W. Riddle, *The Rockefeller McCormack New Testament* [Chicago, 1932], 1, fol. 114v).

tinctively Western iconographic tradition suggests that Carolingian art was a source, though not necessarily the only source.

Stephen's pose differs from that in the Drogo Sacramentary, but another figural type, closer to the Anglo-Saxon iconography, occurs in the Munich Epistles, a Carolingian mural in the cathedral crypt in Auxerre (fig. 111),[41] and the Göttingen sacramentary. Byzantine art probably originated this alternative figural type; indeed, the best comparison to Stephen's position in the Benedictional is found in the Cosmas manuscript. In other details such as the saint's orant gesture and his costume of a tunic and mantle (in contrast to the deacon's garments he wears in Carolingian art), the Benedictional goes beyond its Carolingian antecedents in the adoption of Eastern features; thus Byzantine as well as Carolingian art might have influenced its iconography.

An unusual aspect of the scene is the way the clouds dip down between Stephen and his enemies. Carolingian and Ottonian scenes (figs. 107, 108) often included parted clouds to illustrate his vision of "the heavens opened," but in these the clouds usually stay above the figures —even in the Drogo Sacramentary where they fill the awkward space of the initial's stem.

The explanation for the exceptional position of the clouds in the Benedictional's scene lies in the texts it prefaces. The second blessing for Stephen's feast begins: "Open, we ask, Lord, your heavens and open our eyes; may your gifts descend to us from thence, and may our hearts look upon you from this side."[42] God opens heaven to send down his heavenly gifts to the worshipper who in response opens his eyes and heart to the Lord and his blessings. The model for this relationship to God was the saint who in his hour of need had beheld Christ in the opened heavens and had received the reward of the blessed martyrdom that the Church celebrated on this day.[43] It was to create a visible symbol of the heavenly gifts that will descend upon those who keep their eyes steadfastly on the Savior that the celestial clouds were shown literally descending to separate Stephen from his terrestrial enemies. Clouds were used in a similar manner to separate Zachariah from his opponents at the Birth and Naming of John the Baptist (pl. 30).

In itself the idea of depicting the descent of divine favor on Stephen was not unusual. In the Cosmas miniature, for example, the hand of God reaches down from the heavenly arc to crown the martyr with a diadem, and in the Drogo Sacramentary rays emanate from the divine hand toward him. The originality of the Anglo-Saxon image was to replace these more conventional signs of heavenly reward with the clouds of heaven itself. Once more the painters employed their favorite leitmotif of the cloud to symbolize the divine blessings bestowed on mankind in the past and the present.

The Martyrdoms of Peter and Paul
(Peter and Paul, 29 June)

The Decapitation of Paul

There are Carolingian representations of the Martyrdom of Paul in both the Drogo Sacramentary[44] and the Utrecht Psalter,[45] but neither resembles the version in the lower part of the Benedictional's miniature (pl. 31). In the Metz initial the swordsman, instead of holding a scabbard, grabs the apostle by the hair. The poses of the apostle are also dissimilar, and there are no accessory figures in the Anglo-Saxon scene. In the Psalter the executioner does hold an empty scabbard, but otherwise the iconography is very different.

A much better comparison occurs in the late-tenth-century antiphonary made in Prüm (Paris, Bibl. Nat., MS lat. 9448; fig. 112).[46] The ultimate origin of this iconography, however, was most

[41] A. Grabar and C. Nordenfalk, *Early Medieval Painting* (n. p., 1957), p. 72; E. S. King, "The Carolingian Frescoes of the Abbey of Saint Germain d'Auxerre," *AB* 11 (1929): 359–75.

[42] *CBP*, no. 38; Warner and Wilson, *Ben.*, p. 6: "Aperi quesumus domine caelos tuos, aperi oculos nostros, inde nobis tua dona descendant, hinc te corda nostra respiciant."

[43] The model of Stephen's martyrdom is explicitly invoked in the first benediction; *CBP*, no. 854; Warner and Wilson, *Ben.*, p. 6.

[44] *Drogo-Sak*, fol. 86.

[45] *Utrecht*, fol. 19.

[46] S. Beissel, "Miniaturen aus Prüm," *Zeitschift für christliche Kunst* 19 (1906): 11ff.; Goldschmidt, *German Illu-*

likely Byzantine art, which is known to have influenced the antiphonary.[47] The poses of Paul and the swordsman in a twelfth-century menologion in Jerusalem (Greek Patriarchal Lib., MS Saba 208; fig. 113)[48] closely resemble those in the two Western books, though the grouping of the figures is different.[49] Possibly the variant grouping already existed in Byzantine art. Alternatively, the Benedictional's illuminators might have reversed Paul to create the series of crisscrossing diagonals that decoratively unite the figures in both scenes with the frame. The chiastic composition recalls that of the Nativity (pl. 12) which also resulted from the rearrangement of a model (cf. fig. 7).

THE CRUCIFIXION OF PETER

The iconography of Peter's Martyrdom in the upper part of the miniature also differs from the versions found in the Drogo Sacramentary and the Utrecht Psalter. While the executioners tie the apostle's feet in the Benedictional, they nail him to the cross in both Carolingian scenes. Since the apocryphal accounts of his martyrdom specify that he was crucified upside down, this feature of the scenes is no indication of an iconographic relationship. Closer to the Benedictional are the representations in some later Western manuscripts: the Prüm antiphonary, the sacramentary commissioned about the millennium by Bishop

Warmund of Ivrea (Bibl. Cap., MS 86; fig. 114),[50] and the lectionary of Custos Perhtolt illuminated at Salzburg about 1070 (New York, Pierpont Morgan Lib., M. MS 780; fig. 115).[51] Though there are differences of detail in costume and pose, all these share with the Benedictional the motif of a pair of executioners roping Peter's feet to the cross. What was the source of this iconographic type appearing in widely separated regions of the Latin West in the late tenth and eleventh centuries?

Some miniatures in all three Continental manuscripts display patently Byzantine features,[52] and this raises the possibility of an Eastern origin. Byzantine art most often showed Peter nailed to the cross and without executioners present (fig. 113),[53] but a variant iconography occurs on a panel from the bronze doors cast in Constantinople in 1070 for the Roman basilica of San Paolo fuori le mura (fig. 116).[54] One executioner ropes the apostle's ankles as another is about to club him. In the Anglo-Saxon scene both executioners pull the rope and it does not pass over the suppedaneum. All the same, Byzantine art remains the most likely source of the iconography of the Benedictional and the other Western manuscripts, especially since Eastern art seems to have inspired the lower part of the Winchester picture.[55]

The martyrdom scenes of Peter and Paul were probably already combined in a single Byzantine miniature illustrating their common feast day.

mination, 2, p. 17; M. R. Lagerlöf, "A Book of Songs Placed upon the Altar of the Saviour Giving Praise to the Emperor," *Research on Tropes*, ed. G. Iversen (Stockholm, 1983), p. 140, fig. 16.

[47] Cf. the miniature of the Death of the Virgin; R. Kahsnitz, "Koimesis—Dormitio—Assumptio," *Florilegium in Honorem Carl Nordenfalk Octogenarii Contextum* (Stockholm, 1987), p. 99, fig. 12.

[48] A. Baumstark, "Ein illustriertes griechisches Menaion des Komnenenzeitalters," *Oriens Christianus*, ser. 3, 1 (1926): 71, pl. 2, 2.

[49] Homburger, *Anf.*, p. 24.

[50] Magnani, *Sacramentario*, p. 31, pl. 23.

[51] M. Harrsen, *Central European Manuscripts in the Pierpont Morgan Library* (New York, 1958), pp. 19f., no. 10; G. Swarzenski, *Die Salzburger Malerei* (Leipzig, 1913), pp. 48ff. See also the twelfth-century fresco at Vicq; M. Kupfer, "Spiritual Passage and Pictorial Strategy in the Romanesque Frescoes at Vicq," *AB* 68 (1986): 35–53; O. Demus, *Romanesque Mural Painting* (London, 1970), p. 242.

[52] E.g., the sacramentary's miniatures of the Baptism and the Annunciation; Magnani, *Sacramentario*, pls. 10, 12. For

the lectionary, see G. Swarzenski, *Die Regensburger Buchmalerei* (Leipzig, 1901), p. 166. For the antiphonary, see above, n. 47.

[53] Cf. also the depiction in the ninth-century homilies of Gregory Nazianzus in Paris; H. Omont, *Miniatures des plus anciens manuscrits grec de la Bibliothèque Nationale du VIe au XIVe siècle* (Paris, 1929), pl. 22. This iconography also appears on the Aycliffe cross (ca. 1000); R. Cramp, *Corpus of Anglo-Saxon Stone Sculpture in England*, 1 (Oxford, 1984), p. 42, pl. 8/28.

[54] E. Josi, V. Federici, and E. Ercadi, *La porta bizantina di San Paolo* (Rome, 1967), pp. 19f.; G. Matthiae, *Le porte bronzee bizantina in Italia* (Rome, 1971), pp. 73–82, figs. 16, 33.

[55] The Romanesque scenes of the Martyrdoms of Peter and Paul in the murals of the north apse of the church in Müstair (G. Lorenzoni, *Monumenti di età carolingia* [Padua, 1974], fig. 36) are related to Byzantine iconography. If these Romanesque frescos followed the design of the Carolingian paintings they overpainted, then it would become more likely that the Byzantine iconography was known to the Anglo-Saxon illuminators through a Carolingian intermediary.

The pictures in the Jerusalem menologion and the Prüm antiphonary both illustrate the texts for the feast of the two apostles. The Anglo-Saxon painters, however, unified the two scenes in a decorative composition.

In the Benedictional and other works Peter, nailed alive and erect on the cross and often in a loincloth, resembles the crucified Christ (cf. fig. 36).[56] It is only to be expected that the Christo-logical iconography, one of the most popular themes in Christian art, would have influenced the conception of the apostle's Crucifixion, but the resemblance also manifested Peter's willingness to follow the example of his crucified Lord.[57] The juxtaposition of Peter's key-cross and Christ's cross in the miniature of the Doubting of Thomas made the same point (pl. 24).

Saint Benedict
(Translation of Saint Benedict, 11 July)

The portrait of Benedict, enthroned beneath an archlike baldachin adjoined by a building on either side (pl. 33), is the earliest extant representation of the saint from north of the Alps. It resembles neither earlier Italian nor later Ottonian depictions.[58] While it might reflect some lost and otherwise unknown tradition, it is more likely an Anglo-Saxon invention, especially since its symbolism is so innovative.

BENEDICTUS MONARCHA ET MONACHUS

Benedict wears a broad gold diadem on his head. Since he was not martyred, this must be a crown of life symbolizing his blessed co-rule with Christ in the kingdom of heaven. This is confirmed by another depiction of the saint in the center of the choir of confessors (pl. 1), where he and his companions all wear crowns of eternal life, though here trefoiled crowns rather than simple diadems. Only two other representations of Benedict diademed (or crowned) are known to me: a miniature in a Psalter (London, British Lib., MS Arundel 155; fig. 136) illuminated at Christ Church, Canterbury between 1012 and 1023 and a related frontispiece to the *Rule of St. Benedict* in a manuscript (London, British Lib., MS Cotton Tib. A. III; fig. 137) made there several decades later.[59] Both ultimately derived from a lost frontispiece that Æthelwold devised for his Old English translation of the *Rule*.

Since Benedict in the Benedictional wears a diadem on his head, it is curious that he also holds a trefoiled crown in his left hand, a feature unique in the iconography of the saint. The miniature's text, a blessing for the feast of his translation, helps to account for the two crowns:

> May the omnipotent Lord, who called to himself the holy blessed abbot in the time of his youthful grace, and also chose him for ruling the monastic throng through the ardor of the Holy Spirit, sanctify you by the gift of his benediction. Amen.
>
> And may he illumine your heart so that you might be able to understand inwardly those things that are read in the house of God from the life of this father and by understanding you might be able to imitate him as often as possible. Amen.

[56] Homburger, *Anf.*, p. 24; T. Sauvel, "Le Crucifiement de Saint Pierre," *Bulletin Monumental* 97 (1938): 343f., claimed that the Benedictional adapted a scene of Christ's Crucifixion, but the widespread occurrence of this particular iconography of Peter's Crucifixion rules out this possibility.

[57] This is a prominent theme in the apocryphal accounts of Peter's martyrdom. See M. R. James, *The Apocryphal New Testament*, 2nd ed. (Oxford, 1966), pp. 333ff.; *Acta Apostolorum Apocrypha*, ed. R. A. Lipsius and M. Bonnet (Hilde-sheim, 1959), 1, pp. 7f., 171, 233.

[58] See H. Aurenhammer, "Benedikt," *Lexikon der christlichen Ikonographie* (Vienna, 1959–67), pp. 319ff.; E. Dubler, *Das Bild des heiligen Benedikt* (Munich, 1966), pp. 1ff., 17ff., figs. 1, 2, 4, 6, 10, 18, 19, 21, 23; V. Mayr, "Benedikt von Nursia," *LCI*, 5, cols. 354ff.

[59] Deshman, "*Benedictus*," pp. 204ff., figs. 51, 54; J. Higgitt, "Glastonbury, Dunstan, Monasticism and Manuscripts," *Art History* 2 (1979): 283ff., figs. 8, 9.

So that instructed by his examples and not to mention strengthened by his prayers, you might pass unharmed [through] the moment of this life of laboring and might be worthy to be joined to him with the palm of glory in eternal peace. Amen.[60]

The prayer says that Benedict was rewarded with heavenly bliss because of his virtuous life and that by imitating his virtue the faithful can hope to obtain a comparable celestial reward after death. Hence the miniaturists portrayed him in a state of heavenly grace symbolized, if not by the "palm of glory," then by crown of life, the gold diadem on his head.[61] The crown that he holds is also a crown of life, but in this instance the reward that awaits those who heed the admonition of the benediction to imitate the saint's holy life. One reason why the crowns were substituted for the "palm of glory" must have been the offertory antiphon in the mass for the day: "Lord, you have put on his head a crown of precious stone. He asked for life from you, and you gave it to him" (Ps. 20:4).[62] Another factor must have been 2 Timothy 4:7–8:

I have fought the good fight, I have finished my course, I have kept the faith: henceforth there is laid up for me a crown of righteousness, which the Lord, the righteous judge, shall give me at that day: and not to me only, but unto all them also that love his appearing.

This passage and the miniature's text have a similar message, and recognizing this, the illuminators cast Benedict in the role of the successful contestant who has won his crown and thereby set an example for others.

If this interpretation is correct, then one might have expected the saint to wear and hold identical crowns. This would have clearly illustrated the concept that the faithful by emulating Benedict could win the same celestial prize as he had. Instead he has a jewelled diadem on his head and a trefoiled, proper crown in his hand. Among the confessors (pl. 1) he wears a crown just like the one he holds in his feast picture. Was it merely a caprice to portray him crowned with a diadem in his feast portrait? A survey of the types and uses of crowns in the cycle sheds some light on the problem.

The gold diadem occurs in three other pictures besides the one of Benedict: in the initial for the Octave of Pentecost Christ or the Trinity wears one (pl. 27), in the Baptism angels crown Christ with diadems (pl. 19), and finally in the Adoration the first Magus offers Christ three diadems (pl. 18). The Wise Men themselves, however, wear trefoiled crowns. The Virgin is also crowned with a trefoil crown in the scene of her death (pl. 34), as are the saints in the heavenly choirs (pls. 1–3). Thus the diadem, with the exception of the feast picture of Benedict, is a royal attribute belonging only to Christ, while the crown belongs to lesser sacred personages. This implies that Benedict wears the diadem to assimilate him to Christ. Other signs point in the same direction.

Benedict is depicted not only as the paradigm of those seeking the crown of life but also as the *coronator* who bestows the crown on them. Usually this is the function of Christ himself, "the righteous judge . . . at that day" (2 Timothy 4:8). The iconographic precedents for a hieratically enthroned figure holding a crown of life for the righteous are primarily Christological rather than hagiographic.[63] Benedict has usurped the traditional role of Christ as the heavenly king and

---

[60] *CBP*, no. 1770; Warner and Wilson, *Ben.*, p. 39:

Omnipotens dominus uos suae benedictionis dono sanctificet, qui beatum benedictum abbatem primaeue [? primaeui] decoris aetate sibi asciuit, atque spiritus sancti ardore ad regendam monachicam praeelegit cateruam. Amen.

Sicque cor uestrum irradiet, ut ea quae in domo dei ex huius uita patroni recitantur, uisceraliter intelligatis, et intelligendo quantotius imitari possitis. Amen.

Quatinus eius exemplis eruditi, necnon et suffragiis muniti, momentum labentis aeui transeatis illesi, atque in aeterna requiae [requie] illi cum palma gloriae ualeatis adiungi. Amen.

[61] In light of the text the architecture surrounding the saint more likely represents the celestial city than his monas-

tery at Montecassino (Warner and Wilson, *Ben.*, p. xxviii).

[62] *Missal*, p. 124, also p. 82: "Posuiste domine in capite eius coronam de lapide pretioso uitam petiit a te et tribuisti ei."

[63] E. g., the early Christian apse mosaic of San Vitale in Ravenna; F. W. Deichmann, *Ravenna: Hauptstadt des spätantiken Abendlandes*, 2, 2 (Wiesbaden, 1976), pp. 178ff. An apparent exception is the representation of St. Ambrose crowning the artist Wolvinus on the Carolingian antependium in Milan. V. H. Elbern, "Neue Studien zum Goldaltar von S. Ambrogio," *Christliche Kunstblätter*, 4 (1961): 134, 137, has noted that the antependium typologically equates the saint with Christ; this work anticipates the Christological hagiographic iconography of the Benedictional.

judge. In the choir of confessors the saint wears a trefoil crown rather than a diadem because here he does not act in a Christological capacity. In his feast picture, however, Benedict's diadem indicates that he functions as an *imago Christi*, and the different type of crown he holds directs attention to his Christological office of *coronator*, an office which distinguishes him from those he crowns.

There is a particularly strong resemblance between the diadems of Benedict and Christ in the initial for the Octave of Pentecost, and the way in which both these enthroned figures rest an oddly shaped book on the left knee increases the similarity between them. In the initial Christ's diadem was an attribute that characterized him as the royal judge who will reward the blessed with the perpetual vision of his full glory at the Last Judgment. Benedict's special relationship to this figure of Christ emphasizes that the saint has been cast in the Christological role of the righteous judge.

This interpretation is confirmed by the miniature in the Arundel Psalter (fig. 136) which adopted the iconography of the diademed Benedict from a Winchester prototype related to the Benedictional.[64] The saint's rectangular breastplate or rationale, which is inscribed "iustus" (just or righteous), refers to Ephesians 6:11–17, which exhorts believers to don the "breastplate of justice" and the other "armor of God." In his *Rule* Benedict applied this Pauline concept of the soldier of Christ to monks.[65] The Christological connotations of Benedict's breastplate and diadem would have been obvious to viewers, because both these attributes also appear in contemporary imagery of Christ. At about the same time the Christ Church scriptorium produced the picture of Benedict, it probably also made the drawing of the enthroned Christ in the Cambridge homiliary (fig. 90).[66] On Christ's head is a narrow royal diadem; and though he does not actually have a breastplate, the tunic over his breast is inscribed "iust(us) iudex" (just judge).[67] In the Arundel Psalter the attributes of Christ the king and just judge have been transferred to Benedict. The divine hand with a scroll above Bene-

dict expressly sanctions his Christlike role, for the half directed to him is inscribed "He that heareth you, heareth me" (Luke 10:16).[68] This text is twice cited in the fifth chapter of Benedict's *Rule* to support the admonition that monks must obey their abbot because he rules them as the representative of Christ in the monastery, relaying, as it were, divine commands to them.[69] The crowned Benedict is unmistakably portrayed as the ideal Benedictine abbot whom God himself manifestly confirms to be an *imago Christi* governing the monks with the Lord's own authority.

The meaning of the diademed Benedict in the Psalter and the Benedictional is much the same. The later manuscript is related to the Benedictional not only by the motif of Benedict's diadem but also by the technique of assimilating the saint to a figure of Christ enthroned as the royal judge. The Winchester roots of this later Canterbury iconography are also apparent in the Cambridge drawing of Christ, for Christ's diadem and the inscription "Rex regum" on his mantle derived respectively from the Benedictional's initial of Christ and its miniature of the Second Coming (pls. 27, 10).

In the Benedictional the saint's assimilation to Christ was based on Benedict's office of abbot. The titulus "S(an)c(tu)s Benedictus abba" designates him abbot. His monastic office is also mentioned in the accompanying benediction which says that "the Lord . . . chose him for the ruling (*regiandam*) of the monastic throng." This regal term for his governance links his abbatial office to the insigne of rulership on his head. Moreover, the prayer declares his abbacy one of the virtuous activities in his life that led the Lord to reward him with heavenly blessings. In other words, because Benedict was a worthy "ruler" of the monks, he is entitled to wear the diadem, the eternal crown of heavenly life. His virtuous rulership as abbot both prefigured and caused his celestial co-rulership with Christ.

Such concepts are intrinsically Christological. For if Benedict was a virtuous abbot, it must have been because he had lived up to the Christlike ideal for the holders of the abbatial office that the saint himself had set forth in his

---

[64] For a detailed treatment, see Deshman, *"Benedictus,"* pp. 211ff.

[65] *Benedicti Regula*, prolog. 3, ed. R. Hanslik, CSEL, 75, pp. 1f.

[66] See above, chap. 2, n. 226.

[67] Cf. Is. 59:17–18 for the association of the breastplate of justice and the vestments of the judge.

[68] "Qui uos audit me audit."

[69] *Benedicti Regula*, 5, pp. 36, 37.

Rule.[70] There he said that the worthiness of an abbot depended on his rulership of the monastery as an *imago Christi* who applied only the just laws of the Lord to his charges, and that the abbot's virtue, that is, his conformity to the model of the heavenly ruler and judge Christ, would determine the abbot's fate at the Last Judgment. In the Benedictional (and the Psalter) Benedict was depicted as the crowned image of Christ in heaven to remind the viewer that this blessed state was the reward for the saintly abbot's righteous Christlike governance of the monks during his life on earth.

The monastic, Christological significance of the diademed Benedict has ramifications for the meaning of the crown he holds, the crown of life destined for those who follow the exhortations of the manuscript's blessing to "imitate him" and to be "instructed by his examples." Because Benedict is shown as the ideal abbot and because many of those receiving this blessing would have been the monks of Winchester, these admonitions would have been taken as an exhortation to lead Benedict's own monastic mode of life, the way of life laid down in Benedict's *Rule* and administered by his successors in the abbatial office. In this representation of Benedict the monks were meant to perceive not only the heavenly archetype of all good abbots, Christ the ruler and just judge, but also the earthly prototype for their own present abbot who ruled them according to the precepts of both Christ and Benedict in the *Rule.*[71]

In his portrait Benedict holds a large book as well as the crown. The book was the attribute of a teacher and contained his teachings, and so Benedict's book must surely be his *Rule.* The parallelism between his and Christ's books in the initial visualized the concept that the teachings of the *Rule* were those of Christ. The *Rule* itself recommended the Gospels as an additional source of precepts for the monastic way of life.[72] Benedict's juxtaposition of the codex and the

crown suggested that the way for the monastic brethren to earn their own crown of life was to adhere to the teachings of Benedict in the *Rule* as well as to the instructions of their own abbot who ruled them in the place of Benedict and Christ. The miniature almost guaranteed them that such monastic obedience in this life would win the crown of life from the heavenly king Christ, because Benedict himself, by virtue of his monastic Christological office of abbot, has assumed Christ's role as their heavenly judge and *coronator.*

The notion that obedience to the *Rule* and the abbot would lead monks to the kingdom of heaven permeates the *Rule* itself, and one passage specifically mentions the crown, the symbol of blessed heavenly existence, as the reward for the monks' humble obedience to God's (and thus their abbot's) will.[73] The crown of life also figured prominently in the writings of Smaragdus (d. ca. 840), the abbot of Saint-Mihiel and an associate of the great Carolingian monastic reformer Benedict of Aniane. In his commentary on the *Rule* Smaragdus frequently evoked the crown of life as the celestial prize awaiting monks who successfully completed the arduous course of monastic life. For instance, he compared the testing of gold by heating in a furnace to the trial of a good monk by monastic discipline:

> As proven gold is made into the diadem of a king, so the proven monk is made into the diadem of the true king Christ. . . . The crown of Christ is all the elect, among whom are reckoned well tested monks.[74]

This text harmonizes particularly well with the iconography because Benedict, the prototypical good monk, does in fact wear Christ's diadem. Smaragdus also entitled another of his monastic writings the *Diadema Monachorum.* He did not explain this title, but he must have meant the diadem of monks to be synonymous with the crowns he several times mentioned as the celes-

---

[70] *Benedicti Regula,* 2 and 3, pp. 19ff., 27ff.

[71] Benedict's dual meaning as an *imago Christi* and the prototypical abbot is evident in the Arundel Psalter, where the inscription on his half of the divine scroll confirms that he acts as Christ's vicar while the inscription on other half orders the monks to obey their superior; Deshman, "Benedictus," p. 211.

[72] *Benedicti Regula,* 73, p. 164.

[73] *Benedicti Reguli,* 7, p. 45.

[74] *Smaragdi Abbatis Expositio in Regulam S. Benedicti,* 1, 3, ed. A. Spannagel and P. Engelbert, CCM, 8, pp. 56f.: "sicut in diademate regis probatum fabricatur aurum, ita in diademate ueri regis Christi bene probatus fabricetur monachus. . . . Corona enim Christi sunt omnes electi, inter quos bene probati computati sunt monachi." See also pp. 27, 50, 166, 169.

tial reward for the monks' difficult life of monastic obedience and virtue.[75]

The Anglo-Saxon reformers of the tenth century took over this close association between the crown of life and monastic life. In his late-tenth-century *Life of St. Oswald* the Ramsey monk Byrhtferth described the monks at Fleury as "the most perfect servants of God, adorned before others with the diadem of religion."[76] Here monastic life, which was understood to be an earthly anticipation of the heavenly existence of the elect,[77] has become virtually synonymous with the heavenly prize it will win, the *diadema monachorum*. Byrhtferth was surely influenced by the writings of Smaragdus which were well known to the Anglo-Saxon reformers. Two Anglo-Saxon manuscripts of the *Diadema Monachorum* survive from the late tenth century,[78] and about the middle of the tenth century a copy of Smaragdus' commentary on the *Rule* was written at Glastonbury and glossed apparently by Dunstan, a leader of the monastic reform.[79] Æthelwold used the latter commentary when he translated the *Rule* into Old English.[80] The emphatic connection between monasticism

and the crown of life in Benedict's portrait undoubtedly reflects the impact of Smaragdus' writing on the Winchester bishop.

Drawing on the texts of Smaragdus, the *Rule*, and the Benedictional itself, the illuminators created an unusual image of Benedict that transcends the boundaries of traditional hagiographic portraiture to become a complex didactic exposition of the theology, duties, and rewards of Benedictine monasticism. Portrayed as the paradigmatic abbot of the order, Benedict, on the one hand, demonstrates to his abbatial successors that they must conform in their monastic governance to the model of the heavenly ruler and judge Christ if they hope to wear Christ's diadem of eternal life. Benedict, on the other hand, shows ordinary monks that the divine authority of Christ is vested in their abbot, Christ's vicar. Since their obedience to the abbot and the *Rule* is obedience to Christ, the monks are assured that their observance of monastic discipline will ultimately result in the abbot's heavenly model, Christ, crowning them with the *diadema monachorum* at the Last Judgment.

Saint Æthelthryth and Christ
(Saint Æthelthryth, 23 June)

Facing the portrait of Saint Æthelthryth (d. 679) is the historiated initial O of Christ, which begins the text for her feast (pls. 28, 29). This image of Æthelthryth and the one in the choir of the Virgins at the beginning of the manuscript (pl. 3, left) are the only extant representations of her before the thirteenth century.[81] The lack of comparative material makes it pointless to spec-

[75] Smaragdus, *Diadema Monachorum*, 6, 7, 86, PL, 102, cols. 602, 604, 679; F. Rädle, *Studien zu Smaragd von Saint-Mihiel* (Munich, 1974), pp. 68–77.

[76] Byrhtferth, *VO*, 2, 5.

[77] J. Leclercq, *La Vie parfaite*, Tradition Monastique, 1 (Paris, 1948), passim.

[78] Cambridge, Corpus Christi Coll., MS 57 (Abingdon), and Cambridge, Univ. Lib., MS Ff. 4. 43 (Christ Church, Canterbury). See Gneuss, "List," nos. 8, 41, also 31, 37; R. Grégoire, "La tradizione manoscritta del 'diadema monachorum' di Smaragdo," *Inter Fratres* 34 (1984): 6, nos. 10, 11; W. Witters, "Smaragde au moyen âge. La Diffusion de ses écrits d'après la tradition manuscrite," *Études ligériennes d'histoire et d'archéologie médiévales*, ed. R. Louis (Auxerre, 1975), p. 367.

[79] Cambridge, Univ. Lib., MS Ee. 2. 4; Bishop, *Minuscule*, p. 2, no. 3.

[80] M. Gretsch, "Æthelwold's Translation of the *Regula Sancti Benedicti* and its Latin Exemplar," *ASE* 3 (1974): 144ff.; idem, *Die Regula Sancti Benedicti in England und ihre altenglische Übersetzung*, Texte und Üntersuchungen zur englischen Philologie, 2 (Munich, 1973), pp. 257ff.

[81] The *Liber Eliensis*, 2, 6, ed. E. O. Blake, Camden Third Series, 92 (London, 1962), p. 79, mentions that Abbot Brihtnoth (970–ca. 999) of Ely flanked the high altar with four images of saints, probably Æthelthryth and her sisters. Regarding the saint and her cult, see P. A. Newton, "Etheldreda (Ediltrudis, Aeldrith, Aetheldreda, Audry) von Ely," *LCI*, 6, cols. 170f.; P. A. Thompson and E. Stevens, "Gregory of Ely's Verse Life of St. Æthelthryth," *Analecta Bollandiana* 106 (1988): 334ff.; S. J. Ridyard, *The Royal Saints of Anglo-Saxon England* (Cambridge, 1988), pp. 176ff; S. Hollis, *Anglo-Saxon Women and the Church* (Woodbridge, 1992), pp. 67ff., 247f., 258–61.

ulate whether or not there was an earlier iconographic tradition for the saint. Her figural type is conventional, but the juxtaposition of her portrait and the initial with Christ calls for some comment. No other feast in the book has both a full-page frontispiece miniature and a historiated initial; almost all the other text pages facing miniatures have only an undecorated initial and a frame.[82] The figured initial singles out Æthelthryth's feast as an especially important one. Why this was so will concern us later,[83] but now we shall concentrate on the relationship between the miniature and the initial.

The poses of the figures connects them. Æthelthryth turns toward Christ on the facing page, and he, though frontal, responds with the blessing of his right hand.[84] Raw[85] believed that the saint's portrait conveyed "no message" and was not intended as an illustration of the accompanying text. In actual fact, the benediction for Æthelthryth's feast, possibly written by Æthelwold himself, is fundamental for an understanding of the two images:

> May the one omnipotent and eternal God, the Father and the Son and the Holy Spirit, who made the will of blessed Æthelthryth steadfast and so ablaze with the bounty of seven-fold grace that, summoned to the marriage beds of two husbands, she avoided them, remaining intact, and was taken as a chaste bride in perpetuity by the most just one, remove you from the burning desire of lust by protecting you, and kindle the fire of his own love. Amen.

And may he, who displayed her purity manifestly through her incorruptible body after death, and revealed her ineffably by signs of miracles, allow you to persevere faithfully in holy works, chaste to the end of your life. Amen.

So that remote from the desire for this vain world, [and] adorned with the lamps of all virtues, you may merit to have in heaven the company of her who on account of her love, rejected the marriage bed of an earthly king and, having spurned the broad path of earthly desire, wished to adopt the narrow life of monasticism and on this day, obtaining her wish (uoti), deserved to enter the heavenly palace of the eternal king. Amen.[86]

The daughter of King Anna of East Anglia, Æthelthryth married King Ecgfrith of Northumbria after the death of her first husband. She remained celibate in both marriages and eventually donned the nun's veil, becoming the foundress and abbess of Ely. The prayer contrasts her rejection of the bedroom of her terrestrial royal husband to her selection of monastic life and her perpetual marriage to the celestial king Christ, her "chaste spouse." Through her vows a nun became betrothed to Christ, and the association of the images of Æthelthryth and Christ showed that the virtuous monastic bride had been united to him in celestial marriage.[87]

The inscription and attributes of Æthelthryth reinforce this meaning. The surrounding titulus expressly identifies her as "abbess and perpet-

---

[82] The exception is the undecorated text page facing the miniature of a Bishop Blessing; Warner and Wilson, *Ben.*, pls. fols. 118v–119. An initial enclosing Christ begins the blessings for the Octave of Pentecost (pl. 27), but there is no prefacing full-page miniature.

[83] See below, chaps. 5 and 6.

[84] It was not uncommon to represent Christ frontally with lesser figures; e.g., Temple, *Manuscripts*, figs. 144, 232.

[85] Raw, *Crucifixion*, p. 24.

[86] *CBP*, no. 1805; Warner and Wilson, *Ben.*, p. 37:

Omnipotens unus et aeternus deus pater et filius et spiritus sanctus, qui beatae aeðeldryðe animum septiformis gratiae ubertate ita succensum solidauit, ut duorum coniugum thalamis asscita immunis euaderet, castamque sibi piissimus sponsam perpetim adoptaret, uos ab incentiua libidinum concupiscentia muniendo submoueat, et sui amoris igne succendat. Amen.

Et qui eius integritatem per imputribile corpus post obitum manifeste designauit, signisque miraculorum

ineffabiliter ostendit, uos in sanctis operibus castos fideliter usque ad uitae terminum perseuerare concedat. Amen.

Quatinus ab huius recidiui saeculi cupiditate remoti, uirtutum omnium lampadibus adornati, eius in caelis mereamini habere consortium, quae terreni regis caritatiue contempsit thalamum, spretaque lata terrenae cupiditatis uia, artam monasticae conuersationis eligere uoluit uitam, ac hodierna die uoti compos, caelestem aeterni regis intrare promeruit aulam. Amen.

Regarding Æthelwold's possible authorship, see Wulfstan, *Life*, pp. lxxxif.

[87] J. van der Meuelen, *The West Portals of of Chartres Cathedral*, 1 (Washington, D.C., 1981), pp. 27f., suggests that the initial represents the triune Deity rather than Christ because it illustrates the address "omnipotens unus et aeternus deus pater et filius et spirtus sanctus." However, as in the case of the similar initial for the Octave of Pentecost (pl. 27), such figures can represent Christ as well as the Trinity. Despite

ual virgin."[88] Her golden book probably represents her vows, which the prayer mentions were fulfilled in her heavenly marriage. Since Christ also holds the same attribute, the unity of the two images is enhanced. A similar device associates another monastic superior, Benedict, with Christ (pls. 33, 27). The sprig of golden blossoms Æthelthryth holds has a meaning analogous to that of the flowers in the scene of the Entry into Jerusalem (pl. 21), where they symbolize the virtues that cause the faithful to "flower" in paradise. The benediction for the feast of All Saints mentioned that God "adorned his holy Church with the flower of virtues," one of which is "the virgin's love of chastity."[89] Although this floral symbolism is not in the benediction for Æthelthryth's feast, it does occur in the major early medieval source for her life, Bede's *Ecclesiastical History*.

In a hymn to her, Bede compared Æthelthryth to Mary, the paradigm of all virgins:

The devoted Virgin maid [Mary] bore the parent of the world. . . . / The company of virgins (amica cohors) rejoices because of the Virgin, the mother of the Thunderer; the shining company of virgins rejoice because of [her] virginity. / Her worthiness bears many from the chaste shoot. Her worthiness bore virgin flowers: [there follows a list of female virgin saints ending with Æthelthryth]. . . . / Why seek a mate, dear maid [Æthelthryth], when you have been given the highest spouse? Christ the Spouse is here. . . . / Even as you follow now the mother of the heavenly king, I believe, so you too might be the mother of the heavenly king. / . . . In the cloister the bride was pledged to God, where she, wholly devoted to heaven flowered in lofty deeds.[90]

On the basis of Isaiah's incarnational prophecy (11:1) that the tree of Jesse would flower, Bede likened the Virgin Mary to a "chaste shoot" producing "virgin flowers." Christ was the first of the many "virgin flowers" which sprang from Mary. Æthelthryth and the other virgins in the heavenly choir are other pure "flowers" from the same shoot since they emulated Mary's chastity. Accordingly Æthelthryth, who already began to "flower" with virtuous deeds while leading the heavenly life on earth in her nunnery, also mystically shared Mary's dual roles as the chaste mother and spouse of Christ.

Bede's poem and the blessing for All Saints day[91] were the impetus for the representation of Æthelthryth with flowers. The attribute symbolized her virtue of chastity and her paradisiacal state, achieved through emulation of her paradigm, the Virgin Mary. Bede's poem also confirms that Æthelthryth and Christ appear together in the manuscript as the heavenly bride and bridegroom.[92]

In the Benedictional's prayer the saint is the model for the faithful who, by emulating her virtuousness, much as she had imitated that of the Virgin Mary, might hope to join her in heaven. Christ's gesture of blessing in the initial represents not only the grace that he bestowed on the saint in both this and the next world but also an analogous blessing that her imitators hope to receive in the present, through the episcopal benediction, and in the future. Æthelthryth's virginity, which resulted from this divine grace, was thus associated with mankind's future resurrection. The blessing mentions that God "displayed her integrity manifestly through her incorruptible body after death," a reference to Bede's story that her corpse was perfectly preserved after sixteen years in the grave.[93] In his life of the saint, Ælfric considered this miracle as proof of

---

its opening address, the prayer is decidedly Christological, and Bede's related hymn (see below, n. 90) uses *Deus* and *Christus* synonomously.

[88] "Imago s(an)cte aeþeldryþe abb(atisse) ac perpetue uirgin(is)."

[89] *CBP*, no. 1743; Warner and Wilson, *Ben.*, p. 42: "Omnipotens dominus . . . quique apostolorum fidei dogmate, martyrum sanguinis effusione, . . . ac uirginum castitatis amore, sanctam ecclesiam flore uirtutum perornat."

[90] *Bede's Ecclesiastical History of the English People*, 4, 20, ed. and tr. B. Colgrave and R. A. B. Mynors (Oxford, 1969), p. 398.

[91] Wulfstan of Winchester, a student of Æthelwold, modeled his poem on All Saints and other hagiographic verses on Bede's poem on Æthelthryth; see P. Dronke, M. Lapidge, and P. Stotz, "Die unveröffentlichten Gedichte der Cambridger Liederhandschrift (CUL Gg. 5.35)," *Mittellateinisches Jahrbuch* 17 (1982): 60f.

[92] See also S. Morrison, "The Figure of *Christus Sponsus* in Old English Prose," *Liebe—Ehe—Ehebruch in der Literatur des Mittelalters*, ed. X. von Ertzdorff and M. Wynn, Beiträge zur deutschen Philologie, 58 (Giessen, 1984), pp. 9ff.

[93] *Ecclesiastical History*, 4, 19, p. 393.

her innocence and a manifestation of God's power "to raise up corruptible bodies."[94] Hence the image of Æthelthryth united in heaven with the blessing celestial bridegroom held out the hope for the beholder that after the general resurrection he too would stand physically and morally pure before the Savior with her and the other saints.

The Death and Coronation of the Virgin
(Assumption of the Virgin, 15 August)

THE TEXTUAL SOURCES

The miniature (pl. 34) illustrates two episodes from the Transitus, the apocryphal account of the Virgin's death, which was the basis for some Old English homilies for Assumption day.[95] The lower register with Peter leading an animated discussion among the disciples represents the Reunion of the Apostles. Most versions of the Transitus[96] relate that a few days before the Virgin's death the disciples were suddenly and mysteriously reunited outside her house where Peter led them in a prayer asking for an explanation of this miraculous gathering. In the cloud-filled upper register the Virgin, her eyes open, lies on her bed gesturing to two weeping women, one of whom replies with a speaking gesture of her left hand. A third woman adjusts the Virgin's pillow. Above them the hand of God descends with a crown and one of the flying angels brings a scepter. Some recensions of the Transitus include a dialogue between the Virgin and several women.[97] Before the apostles' arrival Mary informed friends and neighbors of her impending death in three days. Some virgins present began to weep and to express their apprehension to Mary, who reassured them. Later the narrative mentions that the virgins attending her were three in number.[98] The upper register surely depicts this exchange between Mary and her weeping maids,[99] though why one of them adjusts her cushions rather than weeps remains to be clarified.

The Transitus narrative does not directly account for the royal crown and scepter that Mary is about to receive as the queen of heaven.[100] Al-

[94] *Ælfric's Lives of Saints*, ed. W. W. Skeat, Early English Text Society, 76 (Oxford, 1881), 1, p. 439.

[95] O. Sinding, *Mariae Tod und Himmelfahrt* (Christiania, 1903), pp. 66f.; Homburger, *Anf.*, p. 25. Regarding the Transitus and the homilies, see M. Jugie, *La Mort et l'assomption de la Sainte Vierge*, Studi e Testi, 114 (Vatican City, 1944); A. Wenger, *L'Assomption de la T.S. Vierge dans la tradition byzantine du VIe au Xe siècle*, Archives de l'Orient Chrétien, 5 (Paris, 1955); Clayton, *Cult*, pp. 8ff., 23f., 232ff., 249 n. 145.

[96] E.g., James, *Apocryphal New Testament*, pp. 202ff., 211f.

[97] See the next two notes.

[98] E.g., Transitus A, 21, ed. Wenger, *Assomption*, pp. 251, 252f., 254.

[99] So also M.-L. Thérel, *A l'origine du décor du portail occidental de Notre-Dame de Senlis: le triomphe de la Vierge-Église* (Paris, 1984), pp. 53f.; Clayton, *Cult*, pp. 162f., disputes the miniature's relation to the incident in Transitus A on two grounds: Transitus C, which was popular in England, adequately explains the iconography, and there is no evidence of Transitus A, which is preserved in a ninth-century Reichenau manuscript, in England. In Transitus A weeping "virgines," "mulieres," and "puelle" address Mary, but Transitus C (chaps. 5 and 6, ed. A. Wilmart, *Analecta Reginensia*, Studi e testi, 59 [Vatican City, 1933], p. 329) adulterated the incident, omitting any reference to the virgins; instead the conversation is with an anonymous group. The first mention of Mary's maids occurs much later (chap. 21, p. 339), and nowhere do they converse with her. Hence Transitus C cannot explain the scene's restriction of the weeping figures to the Virgin's three maids. Given early medieval manuscript losses, not much weight can be placed on the *ex silentio* argument that evidence of Transitus A is lacking in England. In any event, the scene need not illustrate Transitus A since the conversation between the Virgin and the weeping women also occurs in other Transitus versions: the Greek one of John of Thessalonica (610–649) (chap. 5, ed. M. Jugie, *Patrologia Orientalis*, 19 [1926], pp. 382f.), and the Gaelic one thought to have been circulating in Ireland by the middle of the eighth century (C. Donahue, *The Testament of Mary*, Fordham University Studies, Language Series, 1 [New York, 1942], pp. 1ff., 26f., 35; R. Willard, "The Testament of Mary. The Irish Account of the Death of the Virgin," *Recherches de Théologie Ancienne et Médiévale* 9 [1937]: 341ff., esp. 351f.). As Wenger (*Assomption*, pp. 21ff., 72f.) makes clear, Transitus A with its dialogue between Mary and her maids derived from a more complete version that was widely disseminated at an early date in Greek, Syriac, and Latin. Gregory of Tours (d. 593), for instance, knew the Latin text.

[100] Schiller, *Ikon.*, 4, 2, p. 102; P. Verdier, *Le Couronnement de la Vierge*, Conférence Albert-le-Grand, 1972 (Paris, 1980), pp. 19f.; and apparently also Thérel, *Vierge-Église*, p. 237, interpret the crown as a symbol of triumph over death and a crown of life rather than as an insigne of Mary's celestial royalty. The scepter she receives, however, confirms that the crown is part of her regalia as queen of heaven, though this by no means excludes the other meanings.

though many Transitus versions relate that she was glorified in heaven, most do not describe or even mention her Coronation. The concept of the Coronation of the Virgin developed outside these narratives. In the East her queenship[101] was a popular literary *topos* from the fifth century, but in the Latin West she was seldom accorded the title *regina* before the ninth century. The Carolingians, however, enthusiastically championed her royalty and the Anglo-Saxons were not slow to follow. In England as well as on the Continent the homilies written for the feast of her Assumption often celebrated her queenship.[102] This was because coronation and enthronement beside Christ were the greatest honors she received when she entered heaven after her Death and Assumption. Though not actually part of the Transitus, her Coronation complemented this apocryphal narrative, providing a fitting finale to her life. By linking the Transitus events with the Coronation the Benedictional portrayed a condensed, selective history of the final events in Mary's life.

The Iconographic Sources

With the exception of an abbreviated direct copy of the Benedictional in a late-tenth- or early-eleventh-century Winchester manuscript (fig. 213),[103] there are no other extant illustrations of either Mary's Dialogue with her Servants or the Miraculous Reunion of the Apostles. Represen-

tations of other episodes of the Transitus do survive, however.[104]

The Koimesis of the Virgin,[105] a popular theme of Byzantine post-iconoclastic art, illustrated this apocryphal text and probably originated as part of a more extensive narrative cycle. In middle Byzantine manuscripts and frescoes the Koimesis appears with an earlier Transitus episode, the Miraculous Transportation of the Apostles to the Virgin's House,[106] and comprehensive Transitus cycles survive in Serbian murals of the thirteenth and fourteenth centuries.[107] In Rome Transitus illustrations seem to have enjoyed a certain popularity. The *Liber Pontificalis*[108] records several Carolingian papal donations of altar cloths representing the story of either the Transitus or the Assumption of the Virgin. The ninth-century frescoes in Santa Maria Secundicerii (Santa Maria Egiziaca) in Rome originally included an extensive narrative cycle of Transitus pictures.[109] Separating the three surviving scenes—the transportation of three apostles to Mary's house, John greeting them there, and Christ announcing the Virgin's Death—are large areas of blank wall that must originally have been filled with the intervening events of the Transitus. The two extant scenes involving the apostles bracket the portion of the narrative that recounts their reunion, and so quite possibly the frescoes might have included the incident portrayed in the lower register of the Anglo-Saxon miniature. Finally, narrative illustration of the Transitus occurred in England

[101] G. Steigerwald, "Das Königtum Mariens in der Literatur der ersten sechs Jahrhunderte," *Marianum* 37 (1975): 1–52; L. Scheffczyk, *Das Mariengeheimnis in Frömmigkeit und Lehre der Karolingerzeit*, Erfurter theologische Studien, 5 (Leipzig, 1959), pp. 461–96; H. Barré, "La Royauté de Marie pendant les neuf premiers siècles," *Recherches de Science Religieuse* 29 (1939): 129–62, 303–34.

[102] For Carolingian homilies, see Scheffczyk, *Mariengeheimnis*, pp. 461ff.; for Anglo-Saxon ones, Ælfric, *Hom.*, 1, pp. 444ff., and *Old English Homilies of the Twelfth Century*, R. Morris, ed. and tr., Early English Text Society, 53 (London, 1873), pp. 158–60; also Burlin, *Advent*, pp. 140f.; Clayton, *Cult*, pp. 164f. et passim.

[103] See Appendix Three.

[104] Concerning the iconography of the Virgin's Death and Assumption, see Sinding, *Mariae*, pp. 29ff.; E. Staedel, *Ikonographie der Himmelfahrt Mariens* (Strassburg, 1935); Kahsnitz, "Koimesis—Dormitio—Assumptio," pp. 92–122; J. Hecht, "Die frühesten Darstellungen der Himmelfahrt Mariens," *Das Münster* 4 (1951): 1–12; J. Myslivec, "Tod Mariens," *LCI*, 4, cols. 333–38; J. Fournée, "Himmelfahrt Mariens," *LCI*, 2, cols. 276–83; Schiller, *Ikon.*, 4, 2, pp. 83ff.; C. Schaffer, *Koimesis*.

Der Heimgang Mariens, Studia Patristica et Liturgica, 15 (Regensburg, 1985); Verdier, *Couronnement*, pp. 53ff.; Thérel, *Vierge-Église*, pp. 39ff.

[105] L. Wratislaw-Mitrovic and N. Okunev, "La Dormition de la Sainte Vierge dans la peinture médiévale orthodoxe," *Byzantinoslavica* 3 (1931): 134–80; also J. L. Schrader, "An Ivory Koimesis Plaque of the Macedonian Renaissance," *The Museum of Fine Arts, Houston, Bulletin*, n.s. 3 (1972): 75ff.

[106] Wratislaw-Mitrovic and Okunev, "Dormition," pp. 140f., pl. 5, 2; A. Grabar, "Un Rouleau liturgique constantinopolitain et ses peintures," *DOP* 8 (1954): 176, 185, 192, fig. 20.

[107] Wratislaw-Mitrovic and Okunev, "Dormition," pp. 148ff.; J. Lafontaine, *Peintures médiévales dans le temple dit la Fortune Virile à Rome* (Brussels, 1959), p. 34, n. 2.

[108] L. Duchesne, *Le Liber Pontificalis* (Paris, 1955), 2, pp. 14, 61, 145; also 1, p. 500.

[109] Lafontaine, *Peintures*, pp. 29ff., pls. 8–10; M. Trimarchi, "Per una revisione iconografica del ciclo di affreschi nel Tempio della 'Fortuna Virile,'" *Studi Medievali*, ser. 3, 19 (1978): 653–77; also J. Osborne, "A Note on the Medieval Name of the so-called 'Temple of Fortuna Virilis' at Rome," *Papers of the British School at Rome* 56 (1988): 210–12.

some two centuries before the Benedictional. One of the scenes on the Wirksworth stone slab (fig. 52)[110] illustrates the Transitus account of the disbelieving Jew attacking the Virgin's funeral procession.

This scattered and fragmentary evidence suggests that developed cycles of Transitus illustration existed at a comparatively early date in several regions of the medieval world in a variety of media—textile, stone carving, fresco, and book illumination. Lafontaine has posited the existence of an extensively illustrated Transitus manuscript as a model for the Roman fresco cycle,[111] a particularly interesting hypothesis since such a manuscript would have belonged to a textual recension of the Transitus near the one illustrated in the Benedictional. The Wirksworth slab establishes that Transitus iconography existed in Anglo-Saxon England long before the tenth century. Although it cannot be proved, an illustrated Transitus manuscript might have provided models for the Benedictional's unusual iconography.

Another possibility suggested by Alexander[112] is that the miniaturists had no pictorial Transitus model but illustrated the text themselves with a pastiche of motifs borrowed from more conventional iconographic themes. The apostles in the lower register resemble their counterparts in scenes of the Ascension (cf. pl. 25, figs. 48, 53) and the weeping maids are similar to the Virgin and other female mourners in depictions of the Crucifixion (cf. fig. 36). The midwife adjusting

the cushions of the recumbent Virgin in the upper register is also found in the Benedictional's own miniature of the Nativity (pl. 12). The presence of this figural group in the Nativity scene on the Brunswick casket (fig. 7) confirms that the influence went from the Nativity to the Transitus rather than vice versa, though in both the Anglo-Saxon miniatures the action of the servant was modified. The larger scale of these two figures might reflect the difficulty of interpolating them into the composition, but equally it could be a means to give them special prominence.

The problem of the visual sources of the hand of God with the crown and the angels with the scepter raises the broader issue of the depiction of the Virgin as queen.[113] In Byzantium the iconography of Mary crowned or being crowned was unknown,[114] but from the sixth century representations of the Virgin wearing an imperial crown and often other regalia, an iconographic type known as *Maria regina*, frequently appeared in Italian art. The donor panel of mosaic in the oratory of John VII (705–707) in St. Peter's in Rome, for example, showed the crowned Virgin receiving the chapel from the pope (fig. 117).[115]

The Benedictional's iconography differs from this Italian tradition in that Mary is receiving rather than wearing the crown. In other words, the Benedictional depicts the Coronation of the Virgin, the very first instance of a theme that would not become popular until the twelfth century.[116] The Italian imagery of *Maria regina*

[110] B. Kurth, "The Iconography of the Wirksworth Slab," *Burlington Magazine* 86 (1945): 118f., pls. 1a, 3c; Clayton, *Cult*, pp. 154f., pl. 3.

[111] Lafontaine, *Peintures*, pp. 34f.; also Schrader, "Koimesis," pp. 76ff. See, however, Trimachi, "Revisione," pp. 664ff. Regarding the illustration of other popular apocrypha, see K. Weitzmann, "The Selection of Texts for Cyclic Illustration in Byzantine Manuscripts," *Byzantine Books and Bookmen* (Washington, 1975), pp. 77ff.

[112] Alexander, "Ben.," p. 178; also Clayton, *Cult*, p. 162.

[113] M. Lawrence, "Maria Regina," *AB* 7 (1924–25): 150–61; C. Bertelli, *La Madonna di Santa Maria in Trastevere* (Rome, 1961), pp. 47–59; U. Nilgen, "Maria Regina—ein politischer Kultbildtypus?" *Römisches Jahrbuch für Kunstgeschichte* 19 (1981): 1ff.; Thérel, *Vierge-Église*, pp. 231ff.; R. L. Freytag, *Die autonome Theotokosdarstellung der frühen Jahrhunderte*, Beiträge zur Kunstwissenschaft, 5 (Munich, 1985), pp. 404ff., 640ff.

[114] It is far from certain that the imperial figure in the mosaic in Durrigo, Albania, is a woman, much less the Virgin, as proposed by M. Andaloro, "I mosaici parietali di Durazzo o dell'origine constantinopolitana del tema iconografico di Maria Regina," *Studien zur spätantiken und byzantinischen*

Kunst, ed. O. Feld and U. Peschlow (Bonn, 1986), 3, pp. 103–112, pl. 36.

[115] M. Andaloro, "I mosaici dell'Oratorio di Giovanni VII," *Fragmenta picta* (Rome, 1989), pp. 169–77; P. J. Nordhagen, "The Mosaics of John VII (705–707 A. D.)," *Acta ad Archaeologiam et Artium Historiam Pertinentia* 2 (1965): 124ff., pl. 18.

[116] G. Zarnecki, "The Coronation of the Virgin on a Capital from Reading Abbey," *Journal of the Warburg and Courtauld Institutes* 13 (1950): 1–12; P. Wilhelm, *Die Marienkrönung am Westportal der Kathedrale von Senlis* (Hamburg, 1941); Verdier, *Couronnement*; Schiller, *Ikon.*, 4, 2, pp. 83ff.; Thérel, *Vierge-Église*. Several other representations of the theme occurred soon after the one in the Benedictional. The miniature in the Winchester Benedictional of the Archbishop Robert (fig. 213) copied our manuscript (see Appendix Three), and two Continental representations in the Bernward Gospels and the Prüm antiphonary might owe something to Anglo-Saxon art, though their renderings are very different. Regarding English influence on Hildesheim, see Deshman, "Kingship," pp. 396ff.; also W. Tronzo, "The Hildesheim Doors: An Iconographic Source and its Implications," *Zeitschrift für*

does not seem to have inspired any of the specific motifs of the Anglo-Saxon iconography, though later we shall have to reopen the question of Italian influence.

Since there does not seem to have been any earlier iconographic tradition for the Coronation of the Virgin, the upper part of the English miniature was most likely an ad hoc invention based on motifs eclectically drawn from different sources. Once again the illuminators seem to have turned to other miniatures in the manuscript for inspiration. In the Baptism of Christ (pl. 19) the angels flying down from heaven with diadems and scepters for Christ resemble the angels in the Coronation of the Virgin in form and function. In the latter the hand of God rather than the angels brings the crown, but this difference should not disguise the relationship between the two scenes. The dove with the ampullae of chrism for Christ's baptismal consecration is a royal feature analogous to the hand of God with a crown, as is apparent from the deliberate juxtaposition of the two motifs on the lid of the Brunswick casket (figs. 35, 37). On the ivory the *manus Dei* with the wreath belongs to a Crucifixion scene.[117] The Benedictional's Metz model might have included a comparable Crucifixion, and this or a similar Carolingian Crucifixion scene could have been the source for the divine hand crowning the Virgin. An alternative or perhaps additional source might have been a representation of the Ascension of Christ. On a Carolingian ivory in Weimar, for instance, the *manus Dei* flanked by hovering angels crowns the ascending Lord (fig. 56).[118] Since the bottom register of the English miniature also resembles Ascension iconography, the influence of this Christological theme seems assured.

It appears undeniable that the miniature combines features from the manuscript's own pictures of the Nativity and the Baptism as well as from the iconography of the Ascension and perhaps also the Crucifixion. All the same, the possibility of an influence from an older tradition of narrative Transitus illustration should not be completely discounted. The Benedictional's creators would certainly have been capable of reworking such Transitus imagery with new features borrowed from the more familiar realm of New Testament iconography.

Although we have clarified the textual and pictorial sources, the miniature remains an enigma in some essential respects. Mary's Coronation was believed to have taken place after her Death when she had been raised to heaven, but the miniature depicts her Coronation while she converses with her servants three days before her death. When faced with the task of depicting a sequence of events in a limited space, medieval artists often conflated or telescoped successive incidents into one composite scene.[119] The iconographic convention of the triumphal crowning of Christ or a saint dying on earth (figs. 36, 37, 109) seems to have influenced the Anglo-Saxon illuminators. Yet this influence raises as many questions as it answers, for on the basis of this precedent one would have expected a depiction of the significant moment of the Virgin's Death rather than what seems to be a trivial earlier incident. Moreover, in their illustration of this apparently minor event the painters took another liberty with the narrative by showing one of the servants arranging Mary's pillows rather than weeping. Although influenced by the iconography of the Nativity, they could have easily modified the servant's action to accord with the Transitus. The decision to illustrate the Reunion of the Apostles is also puzzling. One of the later incidents in the narrative involving a more direct interaction between the apostles and Mary would seem to have been a more suitable subject for a Mariological feast picture. A more detailed reading of the Transitus will help to clear up some of these enigmatic features.

Kunstgeschichte 46 (1983): 357ff.; U. Kuder, "Ottonische Buchmalerei und Bernwardinische Handschriftenproduktion," *Bernward von Hildesheim und das Zeitalter der Ottonen*, ed. M. Brandt and A. Eggebrecht (Hildesheim, 1993), 1, p. 198. Another Prüm manuscript includes a Nativity scene related to the one in the Benedictional; see R. Schilling, "Das Ruotpertus-Evangelistar aus Prüm, MS 7 der John Rylands Library in Manchester," *Studien zur Buchmalerei und Goldschmiedekunst des Mittelalters. Festschrift für Karl Hermann Usener zum 60. Geburtstag*, ed. F. Dettweiler (Marburg, 1967), pp. 145f., 152, figs. 7–9.

[117] For this motif, see Deshman, "Exalted Servant," pp. 385–417.

[118] Goldschmidt, *Elf.*, 1, p. 28, no. 45, pl. 21. These Carolingian Christological scenes are more likely to have been known in tenth-century England than the early Christian triumphal iconography suggested by Thérel, *Vierge-Église*, p. 237.

[119] K. Weitzmann, *Illustrations in Roll and Codex*, 2nd ed., Studies in Manuscript Illumination, 2 (Princeton, 1970), pp. 24ff., 162f., 190f.

The Moralizing and Eschatological Symbolism

Just before the account of the incident illustrated in the upper register, the Transitus relates that Mary urged the virgins and the others gathered at her house to do good works and to have faith. She also requested them to remain with her and to light lamps which were to be kept burning until her death. After the lamps were lit, she said to them, "Let us be watchful since we do not know at what hour the thief will come,"[120] and then she delivered a little sermon about how the soul's fate after death depends on whether one has done good or bad works. Mary's maid servants, however, misunderstood her, and becoming upset, tearfully reproached her:

> "If we all have cried, we fear rightly; you, however, who is the mother of the Lord, the Savior, what is it that you fear. Therefore, we who are humble and poor, what will we do or where will we flee? And if the shepherd fears the wolf, where will the sheep flee?" And Mary said to them: "Silence, daughters, and do not cry but magnify him who is in our midst. Do not cry, O virgins of God, but recite a psalm instead of crying, so that he might be named in all generations of the earth."[121]

These incidents are heavily laced with moralizing, eschatological symbolism. Mary's attendants weep less from grief about their mistress than from selfish fear about their own salvation, and their lack of faith causes them to impugn hers. Mary replies that they should praise God, an act which is both a reassertion of faith and a good deed, and so she urges them to practice what she had earlier preached, namely, faith and good works. Since the soul's fate depends upon good works and presumably also faith, Mary herself shows the way to the salvation after death that her doubting maids desire.

Eschatological symbolism explains why Mary had asked the people and her maids to keep a vigil with burning lamps as they await the unknown hour of the coming of the "thief." This alluded to a New Testament parable for the Second Coming:

> But this know ye, that if the householder did know at what hour the thief would come, he would surely be awake and would not suffer his house to be broken open. But you then also be ready; for at what hour you think not, the Son of man will come (Luke 12:39–40; also Matt. 24:42–45; 1 Thess. 5:2; Apoc. 3:3, 16:15).

The burning lamps are a symbol of moral vigilance referring to other related eschatological parables. In Matthew 25:1–13 Christ likened the kingdom of heaven to the wise and foolish virgins who took their lamps and went to meet the bridegroom. When he comes, he admits only the virgins who had the foresight to keep their lamps burning. Also relevant is the parable immediately preceding the one of the "thief" in Luke:

> Let your loins be girt, and lamps burning in your hands. And you yourselves like to men who wait for their lord when he shall return from the wedding; that when he cometh and knocketh, they may open to him immediately. Blessed are those servants whom the Lord when he cometh, shall find watching (Luke 12: 35–37).

Underlying these eschatological allusions in the Transitus is the idea that the virtuous Mary, confidently awaiting death and the heavenly reward which will follow from Christ's return to earth for her worthy soul, is a model prefiguring righteous mankind awaiting the Second Coming. Mary's three women servants are also symbols of mankind who must serve the Lord through vigilant faith and good works, if, like the exemplary Mary before them, they are to be rewarded after death.

The subsequent narrative of the Transitus[122] drives home this eschatological symbolism. As the three maids and the people later continue their vigil, Peter consoles them with the thought

---

[120] Chap. 5, ed. Wenger, *Assomption*, pp. 246f.: "Uigilemus quia nescimus qua hora fur ueniet."

[121] Chaps. 5–6, ed. Wenger, *Assomption*, p. 247:
"Si omnes nos fleuimus, iuste timenus; tu autem, quid est quod times, que es mater domini saluatoris. Nos ergo que exigue sumus et misere quid faciemus aut ubi fugiemus? Et si pastor timuerit lupum, ubi fugient oues?" Et dixit illis maria: "Silete, filie, et nolite flere sed magnificate eum qui in medio nostrum est. Nolite flere, o uirgines dei, sed psalmum dicite pro fletu, [ut] nominetur in omnes generationes terrae."

[122] Chaps. 19–21, ed. Wenger, *Assomption*, pp. 251f.

that the Virgin's death is not death but eternal life. The virgins then ask how they too might be worthy of "the great miracles of Christ." In a long reply that deliberately echoes the Virgin's earlier sermon on the soul, Peter cites the parable of the wise and foolish virgins and assures the maids that their virginity is a good deed which will result in their souls being led "with praise to the bridegroom unto the place which was promised to all who keep his commandments, that is, the seventh heaven."[123] Soon afterwards Christ finally comes for Mary's soul, and significantly everyone is sleeping at the time "except the three virgins whom he made vigilant so that they might testify concerning the glory in which the blessed Mary was taken up."[124] The implication is that the virgins have learned from their model mistress, the queen of all virgins, and their vigilance makes them worthy not only to witness but also eventually to imitate and follow her Assumption to the heavenly bridegroom.

This moralizing, eschatological symbolism attracted the illuminators to the episode of the Transitus illustrated in the upper register. The anachronistic conflation of this scene with the subsequent Coronation of the Virgin highlights the narrative's underlying symbolic content. At the very moment when Mary reassures her faithless attendants not to "cry but magnify him who is in our midst," the painters showed the hand of God reaching down to crown Mary. The truth of her words, the continuing presence of Christ or God with the faithful (cf. Matt. 28:20), is manifested, as is the heavenly reward for her faith. The divine hand and the angels in the clouds also illustrate the Transitus' account of the subsequent advent of Christ when before the wakeful eyes of the maids he "came on clouds with a multitude of angels without number" to take the Virgin's soul.[125] The crown and scepter that God and the angels bestow can be taken to refer to still a later time, the moment after the Assumption when Mary receives her final reward of co-rule with the Bridegroom Christ

in heaven. The anachronistic inclusion of the crowning divine hand in the earlier scene between Mary and her weeping attendants makes it patently obvious just how groundless are the maids' doubts about the fates of the Virgin and themselves after death.

The other liberty the miniaturists took with the Transitus narrative, the modification of the action of one of the maids, also brought out the story's meaning. Mary's attendants are symbols of mankind who, in accordance with the New Testament parables, must at all times be the faithful servants of the Lord; when he returns unexpectedly at the Second Coming, he will reward them for their faithful service. The two weeping virgins who lack faith and reproach Mary are, at this particular juncture in the story, anything but good servants, and the thoughtful painters made this all the more apparent by contrasting them with their colleague who now obeys Mary's command not to weep and faithfully continues to serve her. Because this maid actively fixes her mistress's pillows, we are left in no doubt about her service. The anachronistic manifestation of God in the middle of this scene illustrates the deeper meaning of the Virgin's admonition to be vigilant because "we do not know at what hour the thief will come." As in the eschatological parables, the master returns unexpectedly to discover which of his servants are good and which are bad, and the fact that none of them yet notices the divine hand emphasizes the element of surprise. Significantly neither the crown nor the scepter is directly over the Virgin's head; they could just as easily relate to the servants as to her. This visual ambiguity was deliberate and meaningful, for the regalia symbolized the reward not only for Mary but also for the good servants of Mary and the Lord—the faithful whose loyalty will also be suitably recompensed at the Second Coming. Though at this particular moment two of the servants in the scene do not deserve this reward, the Transitus implied that they eventually learned from the Virgin the lesson of

---

[123] Chap. 21, ed. Wenger, *Assumption*, p. 252: "Tunc egredietur anima de corpore et ducitur ad sponsum cum laudibus usque ad locum qui est promissus omnibus qui custodiunt mandata eius, hoc est in septimum celum."

[124] Chap. 23–24, ed. Wenger, *Assumption*, pp. 252f.: "Somnum occuparet omnes qui stabant circa mariam, exceptis tribus uirginibus quas fecit uigilare ut testificarent de gloria

qua suscepta est beata maria. Tunc dominus ihesus christus aduenit super nubes cum multitudine angelorum quorum non erat numerus."

[125] See the previous note; also *Blickling*, pp. 144ff. The Byzantine iconography of the Koimesis and its Western derivatives often show similar flying angels; cf. Kahsnitz, "Koimesis—Dormitio—Assumptio," figs. 4, 5, 7–12.

good service that would win them too the crown of life.

The Anglo-Saxons' awareness of the symbolic nuances of the Transitus must have been heightened by the writings for the feast of the Assumption which often voiced similar concepts more directly. The entry for this day in the martyrology of Notker of St. Gall (d. 912),[126] for example, said that the Virgin's privileged assumption to heaven was a precedent for and evidence of the future general resurrection and ascension of mankind. Paschasius Radbertus (d. ca. 860) in one of his influential Assumption homilies urged the faithful to

> imitate the Lord's mother, who bore the immortal bridegroom for you. . . . Follow the bridegroom and speedily enter that place where today the blessed Virgin entered into eternal nuptials. Prepare your lamps, so that when the bridegroom comes and knocks, he will find you vigilant; because blessed are those servants whom, when the Lord comes, he will find prepared and vigilant.[127]

The symbolism in the scene reflected a broad current of early medieval thought that flowed through both narrative and non-narrative literature.

In the Transitus miniature God's manifestation amid clouds and flying angels, one of whom bears a royal insigne, is analogous to Christ's appearance in clouds at the Second Coming with angels carrying the instruments of the Passion like imperial insignia (pl. 10).[128] This analogy, which is a precocious anticipation of

the frequent association of the Coronation of the Virgin and the Last Judgment in Gothic art,[129] brought out the symbolic, typological relationship between the two events: the Virgin's resurrection and celestial co-rulership with Christ are the prototype of the reward that awaits the remainder of the righteous who will follow her to heaven after the Last Judgment.[130]

Transitus and Incarnation

The interpolation of the maid adjusting pillows into the Transitus scene associated it closely with the Nativity miniature. There are obvious analogies between the roles of the servants in the two scenes. The maid at Mary's Death and Coronation is the proverbial good servant because she does not share her companions' doubts about Christ and the Virgin, but continues unwaveringly in loyal service. The maid at the Nativity, the believing Hebrew midwife of the Protevangelium, also affirms her faith in Christ and his virgin mother and is contrasted in the apocryphal gospel to the scepticism of a companion servant, the midwife Salome.[131] Though Salome is absent from the miniature, Joseph is present in a pose that traditionally expressed his doubts about the miraculous conception and birth, and he even occupies a place analogous to that of the doubting servants in the Transitus miniature. An additional similarity between the two pictures is that both the Hebrew midwife and the faithful maid witness Christ or God coming in clouds to the Virgin. The servants behind Mary in the two

---

[126] *Martyrologium*, PL, 131, col. 1142A–B.

[127] Paschasius Radbertus (Ps.-Ildefonse), *Sermo 1*, PL, 96, col. 244C:

> Imitamini matrem Domini, quae uobis sponsum genuit immortalem. . . . Sequimini sponsum, et festinate ingredi, quo hodie ingressa est beata Uirgo ad aeternas nuptias. Praeparate lampades uestras, ut cum uenerit sponsus, et pulsauerit, uos uigilantes inueniat, quia beati sunt serui illi quos, cum uenerit Dominus, inuenerit praeparatos ac peruigiles.

See also cols. 241B, 245B–D, 253B–54C, 255C–56D; idem (Ps.-Jerome), *Cogitis me*, PL, 30, cols. 139D–40. See W. Cole, "Theology in Paschasius Radbertus' Liturgy-Oriented Marian Works," *De Cultu Mariano Saeculis VI–XI*, Acta Congressus Mariologici-Mariana Internationalis in Croatia Anno 1971 Celebrati, 3 (Rome, 1972), pp. 249ff. For Ælfric's knowledge of *Cogitis me* and possibly the Ps.-Ildefonsian sermons, see Clayton, *Cult*, pp. 235ff., 243.

[128] See above, p. 64.

[129] Verdier, *Couronnement*, pp. 9ff., 135f., figs. 27, 88; Schiller, *Ikon.*, 4, 2, pp. 107ff. See especially a French Gothic ivory diptych in the Metropolitan Museum of Art in New York which juxtaposes an angel crowning Mary and angels with the instruments of the Passion above Christ wearing the crown of thorns at the Last Judgment; C. T. Little, "Ivoires et art gothique," *Revue de l'Art* 46 (1979): 64, fig. 20; H. Schnitzler, F. Volbach, P. Bloch, *Skulpturen. Sammlung E. und M. Kofler-Truniger, Luzern* (Lucerne, 1964), 1, p. 21, no. S 57.

[130] Late medieval art illustrated this concept by depicting Christ crowning a small figure on a common throne between himself and the Virgin; see Verdier, *Couronnement*, p. 111, fig. 749.

[131] Protevangelium, 19–20, tr. A. J. B. Higgins, *New Testament Apocrypha*, ed. E. Hennecke and W. Schneemelcher (Philadelphia, 1963), 1, pp. 384f.

scenes had a comparable meaning: both represented believing humanity whose devoted service to God is symbolized by diligent attendance upon the Mother of God.

The idea of the good servant of God was no doubt already present in the Nativity of the Metz model (cf. fig. 7), but in the two Anglo-Saxon scenes the modification of the servant to show her arranging her mistress's pillows dramatized the idea that this midwife was engaged deeply symbolic service to Christ's mother. In making this change the Anglo-Saxons followed the example of other Carolingian depictions of the Nativity in which a midwife undertook a domestic duty to emphasize her good service to God.[132] They also might have been influenced by the Nativity picture of the Galba Psalter (fig. 10) which portrayed two female servants, who were identified with the two midwives of the Protevangelium, washing the Christ child.[133]

On a deeper level the pictorial association of the Nativity and the Transitus reflected the causal relation between the Virgin's role in the Incarnation and her exceptional privileges after death. The thought that Mary's pure, inviolate body—the body which had borne Christ—would decay after her death was naturally abhorrent and helped to stimulate the Transitus apocrypha which claimed that her uncorrupted body as well as her soul were raised to heaven.[134] In various ways these narratives emphasized that Mary was granted this honor because of her earlier part in the Incarnation. In the Old English Blickling Transitus homily, for example, Christ's speech as he resurrects his mother's body clearly reveals his motives: "Arise my kinswoman, my dove, and my habitation of glory; for thou art the vessel of life, and thou art the heavenly temple, and no vices were committed in thy heart; and thou shalt suffer no pain in thy body."[135] Moreover, in the Transitus the events of her death often deliberately mirrored those of the Incarnation. Just as Gabriel had previously descended to earth to announce Christ's advent to

Mary in the Incarnation, so an angel returned to announce to her that Christ would again come to her to receive her soul after death.[136] In the Blickling homily,[137] after the angel departed, Mary paraphrased part of the Magnificat (Luke 2:42–55), her incarnational hymn of thanksgiving after the angel's first visit, and the account of Christ's elevation of her body to heaven concluded with a recitation of the Magnificat "in Mary's name"—an obvious indication that the blessedness she had received from Christ's first advent was the cause of the renewed grace she would receive when he returned to her at her death. Carolingian Assumption homilies also repeatedly stressed that the Virgin's role as mother of God was why she had merited immediate entry into heaven, exaltation above all the saints and angels, and coronation and enthronement as queen of heaven beside her son and husband Christ.[138]

The similarity between the two miniatures expressed that Mary becomes the queen of heaven because she has been the mother of Christ. To make the point the illuminators even used a pictorial technique analogous to the literary one of the Transitus: an event at the end of the Virgin's life was assimilated to an earlier one from the Incarnation. Related practices can be found in other works of art.

On the Wirksworth slab (fig. 52) the Annunciation is represented beneath the Transitus scene of the Virgin's funeral procession assaulted by a disbelieving Jew whose hands withered and cleaved to her bier when he touched it. Like the doubting Salome in the Protevangelium, his limbs were restored when he professed belief in Mary's virginity and Christ.[139] The placement of the two scenes emphasized the reason for his punishment and healing, and affirmed that her motherhood of God was the cause of her future resurrection, which is symbolized by the triumphal palm an apostle carries before the bier.

Maguire[140] has recognized that Byzantine programs of church decoration juxtaposed repre-

[132] Deshman, "Servants," pp. 54ff., figs. 29, 35.

[133] Deshman, "Servants," pp. 33, 39f.

[134] Y. Hirn, *The Sacred Shrine* (London, 1958), pp. 287–93.

[135] *Blickling*, p. 156.

[136] Wenger, *Assumption*, pp. 245f.; James, *Apocryphal New Testament*, pp. 201, 210f.; *Blickling*, pp. 136ff.

[137] *Blickling*, pp. 138, 139, 156–59. See also Wenger, *Assomption*, p. 250; James, *Apocryphal New Testament*, pp. 201,

210ff.

[138] E.g., Paschasius Radbertus (Ps.-Ildefonse), *Sermo* 2, PL, 96, col. 251B–C. See Scheffczyk, *Mariengeheimnis*, pp. 467ff.

[139] *Blickling*, pp. 150ff.; James, *Apocryphal New Testament*, pp. 214ff.; Wenger, pp. 255f.

[140] H. Maguire, *Art and Eloquence in Byzantium* (Princeton, 1981), pp. 59ff.

sentations of the Nativity and the Koimesis, modifying them to heighten their resemblance to each other. Whether this Byzantine phenomenon was a factor in the Benedictional is difficult to say. The specific iconographic features that associate the two themes in Byzantine art and in the Benedictional are quite different from one another. In the East this practice evidently began in the eleventh century and was limited to monumental art, which the Anglo-Saxons were unlikely to have known. Perhaps the literary technique of the Transitus inspired parallel but independent visual responses in both the East and the West. The Benedictional also once again anticipated much later Western developments, for Gothic art frequently linked the Virgin's Death and Coronation with her maternity.[141]

SERVUS MARIAE GENETRICIS DEI AND MARIA REGINA

The use of the servant to associate the Benedictional's miniatures was especially meaningful because service was fundamental to the Virgin's related roles as the mother of God and the queen of heaven and to medieval devotion to her. In his treatise *De Virginitate Beatae Mariae* Ildefonse of Toledo (d. 667) formulated the influential devotional concept of *servus Mariae genetricis Dei*.[142] Mary had declared herself the humble "maid servant of the Lord" (*ancilla Domini*) when she assented to the Incarnation (Luke 1:38). Ildefonse pledged himself to be her servant because she had been the servant and mother of his Lord Christ; and he also acknowledged that she had been made the exalted queen of heaven because of her humble incarnational service. Ildefonse imitated the humility of the maid servant of Christ and in doing so Ilde-

fonse indirectly served him: "the honor which is brought in servitude to the queen passes over to the king."[143] Ildefonse thus placed himself at the bottom of a hierarchy in which the Virgin acts as an intermediary between himself and Christ. By becoming a servant of the queen of heaven, the bishop obtained her services as an intercessor with her son, Christ the king. Indeed, the theme of the Virgin's intercession runs through Ildefonse's treatise. The association between her royalty and her intercession is a basic one, for the pious desire for her intercession was a major motivation for declaring her *regina* in the Latin West.[144] When Ildefonse and later authors elevated her to rulership next to Christ in heaven, they literally and figuratively put her in the position where she could be the most effective intercessor for mankind. Implicit in Ildefonse's imitation of the Virgin's role as servant is the hope that his earthly service would be rewarded as hers was—with heavenly exaltation.

These devotional concepts were adopted in Carolingian Assumption homilies. Paschasius Radbertus, for example, singled out Mary's humility in the Incarnation as her chief virtue and a primary cause of her later reward of celestial queenship, and in his first Assumption homily he exhorted:

> She is the maid servant of the Lord. . . . Wherefore, dearest ones, learn to be humble, . . . so that you might be able to exult on account of this same humility; for she is said to be queen of our world. Do as she, so that you might be worthy to rule where the humble are exalted.[145]

When in the same sermon Paschasius had urged his audience to be vigilant and wakeful servants of the Lord so that they might emulate Mary

[141] Verdier, *Couronnement*, pp. 13f., 23ff., figs. 29, 69; Schiller, *Ikon.*, 4, 2, p. 124. See also E. Valdez del Alamo, "Triumphal Visions and Monastic Devotion: The Annunciation Relief of Santo Domingo de Silos," *Gesta* 29 (1990): 167ff.

[142] Chap. 12, *Textos latinos de la edad medina española*, ed. V. B. García (Madrid, 1937), pp. 163ff. Regarding Ildefonse's Marian theology and service to Mary, see H. M. Köster, "Ildefons von Toledo als Theologe der Marienverehrung," *De Cultu Mariano Saeculis VI–XI*, Acta Congressus Mariologici-Mariani Internationalis in Croatia Anno 1971 Celebrati, 3 (Rome, 1972), pp. 197–222; J. M. Cascante Dávila, "La devoción y el culto a María en los escritos de S. Ildefonso de Toledo

(s. VII)," *De Cultu Mariano*, pp. 223–48; Barré, "Royauté," pp. 305ff.; Scheffczyk, *Mariengeheimnis*, pp. 362ff.

[143] *De Virginitate*, 12, p. 176: "transit honor in regem qui defertur in famulatum reginae."

[144] Scheffczyk, *Mariengeheimnis*, pp. 433, 491ff.

[145] Paschasius Radbertus (Ps.-Ildefonse), *Sermo* 1, PL, 96, col. 241B: "Ipsa est ancilla Domini. . . . Quapropter discite, charissimae, humiliari, . . . ut et uos ex eadem humilitate gloriari possitis; nam et ipsa regina nostri orbis dicitur. Agite cum ea, ut regnare ualeatis, ubi exaltantur humiles." See also Ambrosius Autpertus, *De Adsumptione*, 12, ed. R. Weber, CCCM, 27B, p. 1036.

and follow her to a heavenly union with the bridegroom,[146] he was telling them in effect to imitate the Virgin's related roles as the *ancilla Domini* and *regina coeli*.

The twin themes of the Virgin's divine maternity and her intercession pervade the liturgy for the Assumption feast.[147] The Assumption benediction following the picture of her Coronation asks for her protection even while mentioning her motherhood of the "author of life."[148] While there is no mention of service to the Virgin in the blessing, there can be little doubt that Æthelwold was aware of the concept. Winchester's place as the most prominent and innovative center of Mariological devotion seems to stem from the bishop's personal veneration of the Virgin, who was one of his favorite intercessors.[149] Æthelwold devised and instituted a supplementary office in her honor, probably devotions preserved in the New Minster Prayerbook. In one of these prayers the supplicant terms himself her "servant" and asks for the intercession of the "virgin of virgins, Mary, mother of God, mother of our Lord Jesus Christ, queen of the angels and of all the world."[150] A hymn in the Winchester Assumption liturgy strikes a similar note:

> Mary, queen of heaven because of your
> glorious sanctity,
> hear the prayers of your servants and
> intercede with the Lord.
> He who founded the whole world took form
> in you;
> he whom the whole world adores and
> cannot confine lay in your womb.[151]

Mary's sanctity as the mother of Christ has caused her elevation to the rank of queen of heaven where she intercedes for her servants, mankind.[152]

The theme of service to the mother of God in the exegesis and liturgy of the Assumption reveals another level of meaning for the leitmotif of the servant in the two miniatures. In the Nativity Mary herself appears as the servant of God who has humbly conceived and borne Christ, and the associated Transitus scene illustrates the reward for her service at the Incarnation, her celestial queenship after her death. The maids adjusting her pillows in the two pictures are symbols of believing mankind—a meaning already implicit in the Protevangelium and the Transitus—who render her devoted service because she is the *ancilla Dei* and *regina coeli*; in doing so they visually admonished beholders to emulate Mary's service, through faith and humility, if they hoped to win her intercession and be rewarded as she was, with celestial co-rule with her son.[153]

The concept of *servus genetricis Dei* stimulated an enormous proliferation of servants in a wide variety of Carolingian infancy scenes (figs. 13, 19, 23, 207),[154] and through Metz Nativity iconography this Carolingian tradition influenced the Benedictional. The Anglo-Saxon manuscript progressed further than antecedent northern European art by infusing this devotional concept into the iconography of her royalty, but precedents for this step can be found in the Italian iconography of *Maria regina*. The early eighth-century mosaic in the Roman oratory of John VII[155] showed the crowned orant figure of the Virgin receiving a model of the chapel from the pope (fig. 117). Called "the servant of the blessed mother of God" in the panel's inscription, he gave the chapel as an act of humble service to his

---

[146] See above, n. 127.

[147] *Jumièges*, pp. 200f.

[148] Warner and Wilson, *Ben.*, p. 40; *CBP*, no. 105.

[149] Clayton, *Cult*, pp. 110–21. For Mary as one of his favorite intercessors, see the Thorney foundation charter (ca. 973–975), *The Early Charters of Eastern England*, ed. C. R. Hart, Studies in Early English History, 5 (Leicester, 1966), no. 7, p. 167.

[150] *O uirgo uirginum*, ed. and tr. M. Lapidge and M. Winterbottom, in Wulfstan, *Life*, pp. lxxiif.; Clayton, *Cult*, pp. 112f.

[151] H. Gneuss, *Hymnar und Hymnen in englischen Mittelalter* (Tübingen, 1968), p. 377, no. 92: "Maria celi regina / sanctitate gloriosa / audi preces famulorum / et deprecare dominum. / Qui totum mundum condidit / in te formatus extitit / quem totus mundus adorat non capit / in tuo uentre iaciut."

See also the Latin poem "Assumpta est Maria" dedicated to Abbot Siweard of Abingdon (1030–1044), ed. Clayton, *Cult*, pp. 107f.

[152] Old English literature also associated Christmas with Mary's rulership and intercession; see Burlin, *Advent*, pp. 141ff., and Ælfric, *Hom.*, 2, pp. 22, 23.

[153] The intercession was emphasized in the copy in the Benedictional of Archbishop Robert which modified the Virgin to show her orant, the traditional gesture of prayer and intercession (fig. 213). Regarding this gesture, see Verdier, *Couronnement*, pp. 68, 78; Schiller, *Ikon.*, 4, 2, pp. 97f.; Thérel, *Vierge-Église*, pp. 40ff., 49ff.

[154] Deshman, "Servants," pp. 33ff., 50ff.

[155] For the following, see Deshman, "Servants," pp. 35ff.

sovereign, the Virgin. The Virgin in the Nativity scene above this donor panel was vertically aligned with the figure *Maria regina*, indicating that her heavenly queenship resulted from her earthly incarnational service. The theme of *servus genetricis Dei* was also present in the Nativity scene. The two midwives washing her divine child should be understood as good, faithful servants, who are contrasted to the bad servant, Salome, kneeling before Christ's crib and displaying her withered hand, the punishment for her lack of faith in and service to Mary. The devoted midwives in the Nativity as well as the exalted *ancilla Dei* are models of exemplary service and reward for the pope whose own servitude to the orant *Maria regina* wins him her intercession with Christ.

Like the oratory,[156] the Benedictional symbolically associated Mary's humble service as the *ancilla Dei* in the Incarnation with her consequent exaltation as queen of heaven. Here too Mary's dual roles as the *genetrix Dei* and *regina* had a paradigmatic and eschatological significance for the believers, who became her servant by emulating her faith and humility. Indeed, in each case her attendant(s) at the Nativity became symbols of the good (or bad) servants of the Lord who are linked to other symbolic servants in an image of her as queen.

There were many contacts between England and Rome[157] that might have allowed the Anglo-Saxons to become familiar with the Italian imagery of *Maria regina*. Anglo-Saxons in the Roman militia occupied one section of the city. Tenth-century English kings often sent a yearly donation known as Peter's pence to Rome. Anglo-Saxon archbishops customarily traveled to Rome to receive their pallia from the pope. The itinerary of Archbishop Sigeric's journey in 990 mentions his visit to the basilica of St. Peter's.[158] John the VII's oratory must have been famous in Anglo-Saxon England, for Bede's *De Temporum*

Ratione[159] singled out its decoration for special praise. There is a distinct possibility that the Benedictional's iconography was influenced by these very Roman mosaics. The Anglo-Saxons, however, might not have had to travel to Rome to see examples of *Maria regina*, as it occurred in portable as well as fixed monumental media. The iconography of *Maria regina* is found in a Roman icon, perhaps another commission of John VII,[160] and in a miniature in the late-tenth-century Ottonian Petershausen sacramentary.[161] Since this Italian iconography had spread to one area of northern Europe toward the end of the tenth century, it might also have been known in England either directly through an Italian work or indirectly through an early Ottonian intermediary.[162]

Guided by the exegesis and the liturgy of the Assumption, the creators of the Benedictional selected a symbolic incident from the Transitus that allowed them to express devotional concepts akin to those embodied in the traditional Italian iconography of *Maria regina*. The transposition of devotional imagery of the Virgin wearing a crown into narrative imagery of her being crowned was not really a very large step. In the Roman mosaic the coupling of a nominally atemporal image of *Maria regina* with narrative scenes of the Incarnation and later events in Christ's life imbued the regal Virgin with a temporal dimension, implying that she became celestial queen only after her earthly service in the Incarnation and her death and exaltation. The change to narrative imagery in the Benedictional allowed a greater emphasis on the conditional nature of the heavenly reward that even the Virgin had to earn. In the Anglo-Saxon picture Mary receives her crown and scepter not simply for her past service in the Incarnation but for her continued faith as she awaits death. The presence of doubtful as well as faithful servants in the scene underscored the concept that only

---

[156] See also the related program of the Carolingian frescoes of San Vincenzo al Volturno; Deshman, "Servants," pp. 44ff., figs. 15–20.

[157] For the following, see V. Ortenberg, "Archbishop Sigeric's Journey to Rome in 990," *ASE* 19 (1990): 197ff.; also idem, *The English Church and the Continent in the Tenth and Eleventh Centuries* (Oxford, 1992), pp. 127ff., 194.

[158] Ortenberg, "Archbishop Sigeric's Journey," pp. 199, 210–12.

[159] Ed. C. W. Jones, CC, 123B, p. 530.

[160] Bertelli, *Madonna*; M. Andaloro, "La datazione della tavola di S. Maria in Trastevere," *Rivista dell'istituto nazionale d'archeologia e storia dell'arte*, n.s. 19–20 (1972–73): 139–215.

[161] A. von Oechelhäuser, *Die Miniaturen der Universitäts-Bibliothek zu Heidelberg* (Heidelberg, 1887), 1, pp. 4ff., pls. 1, 2; Wilhelm, *Marienkrönung*, p. 28; Bertelli, *Madonna*, pp. 50f., fig. 39.

[162] Anglo-Saxon images of the Virgin wearing a crown began to appear after the millennium, e.g., figs. 27, 68.

the deserving will receive the heavenly prize. The use of a narrative image of the Virgin's Death and Coronation also permitted the miniaturists to tighten the symbolic visual correspondences to the Second Coming and, above all, the Nativity, where the theme of *servus genetricis Dei* had long been established. In a highly sophisticated and original fashion the Anglo-Saxon imagery fused this devotional theme with the moralizing eschatology of the Transitus.

ASSUMPTION AND ASCENSION

Since so much thought went into the choice of an episode from the Transitus for the picture's upper register, there must have been a good reason for selecting the Miraculous Reunion of the Apostles for its lower one. Yet a close reading of the Transitus fails to turn up any special underlying symbolic significance for their Reunion. Probably the illuminators chose it less for of its intrinsic content than because it could be readily assimilated to the iconography of the apostles at the Ascension of Christ (cf. pl. 25, figs. 53, 56). We have seen that there are also reminiscences of the Ascension in the crowning hand of God and angels in the upper register. The background of the miniature should also be taken into consideration.

An irregular wavy border separates the green background behind the apostles from the cloud-filled upper register with the Virgin and the divine hand. This kind of backdrop is ambiguous. It can indicate two quite separate settings for distinct scenes such as the Martyrdoms of Peter and Paul (pl. 31), or it can represent a single unified space of a hilly landscape under the cloudy heavens as in the Ascension (pl. 25).

If both registers of the Transitus miniature are viewed together as a single composition representing a continuous space,[163] then the resemblance to Christ's Ascension becomes even more evident. The hand of God in the Benedictional's Ascension picture does not hold a

crown, but it is surrounded by flying angels. The one immediately to the right of the *dextera Dei* in both miniatures presses his hands together in homage, a very specific gesture that does not occur elsewhere in the cycle. It must not be forgotten that the upper scene of the Transitus composition is actually a conflation in which the single figure of the Virgin has been made to serve two different narrative functions: she is reassuring her maids on earth three days before her demise, but she is also receiving her regalia and angelic homage in heavenly clouds at her Death and Assumption. In this latter narrative context she is analogous to Christ at his Ascension. Like the Virgin, the apostles below her simultaneously serve two distinct narrative purposes. Separated from the upper register they illustrate the Miraculous Reunion, but joined to it they become the witnesses of Mary's heavenly Coronation at her Assumption, just as they had earlier witnessed Christ's glorification at his Ascension.

The assimilation of the iconography of the Virgin's Assumption to imagery of Christ's Ascension was not a new practice. The earliest known depiction of the Assumption, an eighth-century textile in Sens, was obviously modeled after a scene of Christ's Ascension, as are some later representations of the Assumption.[164] The Anglo-Saxons might have known something of this earlier iconographic tradition, which has been all but lost.

The pictorial relationship between the two events was rooted in the Transitus narratives. In the Blickling Assumption homily,[165] for example, the Virgin's resurrection and bodily assumption virtually reenact the corresponding events from Christ's life. An angel rolls a stone from the door of her tomb (cf. Matt. 28:2) and Christ's speech to the apostles as he is about to ascend with her is a pastiche of his earlier words to the disciples before his own Ascension (cf. Matt. 28:20; John 20:19–22). Before Christ resurrects Mary's body, Peter says to him, "And thou didst overcome death and thou art ruling in thy glory,

---

[163] Both Sinding, *Mariae Tod*, p. 67, and Wilhelm, *Marienkrönung*, p. 50, thought the two registers were part of a single scene, but they saw this arrangement as the negative result of a lack of artistic skill.

[164] E. Chartraire, "Une Représentation de l'assomption de la Très Sainte Vierge au VIIIᵉ siècle," *Revue de l'Art Chrétien*,

ser. 4, 8 (1897): 227–29; Hecht, "Himmelfahrt," p. 10; Verdier, *Couronnement*, pp. 65ff.; M. Menz-von der Mühll, "Die St. Galler Elfenbeine um 900," *Frühmittelalterliche Studien* 15 (1981): 403ff.; Kahsnitz, "Koimesis—Dormitio—Assumptio," pp. 110f.

[165] *Blickling*, pp. 154ff.

so art thou now able to raise again thy mother's body from the dead."[166] In other words, Christ's own Resurrection and Ascension prefigured and made possible the Virgin's.[167] The resemblance between the miniatures of the Transitus and Ascension in the Benedictional made the same point.

CORONATION AND BAPTISM

To represent Mary's Coronation the illuminators borrowed from iconography of yet another Christological theme, the Baptism, in which angels invest Christ with diadems and scepters (pl. 19). This adaptation of a Christological motive to Mary also had various levels of meaning.

Commentators recognized that the Virgin had become queen only by virtue of the fact that Christ was king,[168] and artists conveyed this relationship in various ways. In the earliest extant depiction of *Maria regina* in Santa Maria Antiqua in Rome, angels present the Christ child with diadems as tokens of his supreme rulership as he sits on the lap of his crowned mother.[169] Images of the enthroned, crowned Virgin and Christ in majesty were juxtaposed in the Carolingian frescoes in the crypt of San Vincenzo[170] and the Ottonian Petershausen sacramentary. Although the Virgin is uncrowned in the Assumption on the Tuotilo ivory (ca. 900) from St. Gall she was paired with Christ in majesty on a matching book cover.[171] It is no coincidence that the earliest depictions of the Virgin being crowned and Christ wearing a crown (pl. 27) occur together in the Benedictional.[172]

The close connection between Mary's regality and Christ's also led Carolingian authors to transfer Christological traits and titles of majesty to the Virgin.[173] An analogous process of assimilation to Christ occurred in early medieval art which gave some of the trappings of Christ in majesty to the Virgin.[174] At San Vincenzo, for example, figures of *Maria regina* were enclosed in a mandorla, usually Christ's attribute.[175] In its own way the Benedictional also assimilated Mary to Christ. Even though the miniatures of his Baptism and her Coronation are not physically juxtaposed, the transference of a royal motif from the former to the latter created a meaningful connection between them. Mary's royal investiture was modeled after Christ's to show that his made hers possible.

This parallelism also drew attention to the fact that Christ's Baptism and the Virgin's Coronation were both occasions when he had married the Church. We have already seen that the technique of association with other miniatures endowed the Baptism with matrimonial significance.[176] Its pairing with the Adoration (pl. 18) referred to the wedding of Christ and the Church at the Baptism on Epiphany day, and the liturgy's characterization of the nuptials as a *royal* ceremony gave the angels with the regalia at the Baptism a specifically nuptial connotation. The association of the Baptism with the Annunciation and the Nativity (pls. 8, 12) also had intrinsic matrimonial overtones, since Mary, the virgin mother of Christ, symbolized Ecclesia, the virgin bride of Christ who conceived and bore new children of God in the womb of the baptismal font. In the Coronation of the Virgin, the third Mariological theme associated with the Baptism, she once more symbolized Christ's bride, Ecclesia.

Her bridal relationship to him is already implicit in the Transitus narrative illustrated by the miniature. The apocryphon associated Christ's coming to the Virgin and her servants with New Testament parables in which he is the bride-

---

[166] *Blickling*, p. 156.

[167] For this idea in Carolingian Assumption homilies, see Scheffczyk, *Mariengeheimnis*, p. 474.

[168] E.g., Walafrid Strabo, *In Initium Evangelii S. Matthaei*, PL, 114, col. 859C. See Barré, "Royauté," pp. 328ff.; Scheffczyk, *Mariengeheimnis*, pp. 483ff.

[169] P. J. Nordhagen, "The Earliest Decorations in Santa Maria Antiqua and their Date," *Acta ad Archaeologiam et Artium Historiam Pertinentia* 1 (1962): 56f., pl. 1.

[170] Deshman, "Servants," p. 48, figs. 15, 18.

[171] J. Duft and R. Schnyder, *Die Elfenbein-Einbände der Stiftsbibliothek St. Gallen*, Kult und Kunst, 7 (Beuron, 1984), pp. 62ff., pls. 5–8.

[172] For the coupling of these themes in the Bernward Gospels, see Deshman, "Kingship," pp. 398f., figs. 23, 39.

[173] E.g., Paschasius Radbertus (Ps.-Jerome), *Cogitis me*, PL, 30, col. 128D; Ps.-Ildefonse, *Sermo* 4, PL, 96, col. 258B. See Scheffczyk, *Mariengeheimnis*, pp. 452, 480.

[174] F. Rademacher, *Die Regina Angelorum in der Kunst des frühen Mittelalters* (Düsseldorf, 1972), pp. 22ff.

[175] For other examples of the Virgin in a mandorla during or following her Assumption, see Schiller, *Ikon.*, 4, 2, figs. 595, 605, 609, 612, 625. Implicit in this iconography is a relation to Mary's role in the Incarnation, since the motif also occurs in this context, e.g., fig. 30.

[176] See above, chap. 1.

groom, and Peter tells the three maids awaiting Christ's arrival that the souls of the righteous after death "are led to the bridegroom . . . in seventh heaven."[177]

The connection between the Virgin's Coronation and her marriage to Christ resulted from her assimilation to the Church.[178] In patristic theology Mary was merely the bridal chamber of the mystical marriage of Christ and Ecclesia at the Incarnation, but eventually Mary assumed an ecclesiological role at the Annunciation and became identified with the bride herself. Carolingian Assumption sermons lauded the Virgin's Coronation as the celestial fulfillment of the royal nuptials between Christ and the Church that had begun on earth,[179] and the Old English Advent lyrics indicate that Anglo-Saxons in the late tenth century also sometimes regarded the Virgin as both the heavenly queen and the ecclesiastic bride of Christ.[180]

It had long been customary to represent the coronation of a bridal couple. Early Christian and Byzantine works such as a gold glass in Paris (fig. 118) often showed Christ or the hand of God crowning the newlyweds.[181] This iconography reflected the practice of crowning the bridal couple in ancient and early Christian wedding ceremonies, a custom which has survived in the Eastern rite to the present day, and it also symbolically portrayed the bridal couple's triumph over carnal desire. Since early Christian regal imagery (cf. fig. 38) seems to have influenced the Benedictional's pictures of the Baptism and the

Adoration of the Magi, both themes with matrimonial connotations, the possibility that the iconographic tradition of nuptial coronation influenced the Benedictional's parallel crownings of Christ and the Virgin-Ecclesia should not be dismissed.

The symbolic relationship between the two miniatures foreshadows the interweaving of the themes of the Coronation of the Virgin and the marriage of Christ and Ecclesia in later medieval art.[182] Matrimonial baptismal symbolism led to the representation of the Virgin's Coronation, sometimes with the Baptism, on Romanesque and Gothic fonts.[183]

The bridal symbolism of the Virgin's Coronation is related to another pair of images in the manuscript, the facing portraits of Saint Æthelthryth and Christ (pls. 28, 29). Æthelthryth and Christ are juxtaposed as bride and bridegroom, another instance of the associative technique that expressed the matrimonial relationship of Mary and Christ. The Benedictional's text stressed that Æthelthryth, who was a queen on earth, entered "the heavenly palace of the eternal king" as a chaste bride.[184] Like Mary, she was the royal bride of Christ the king. The painters were certainly aware of these analogies between Æthelthryth and Mary, for Bede's hymn explicitly characterized her as an imitator of Mary, the archetypal virgin bride of Christ. Indeed, a major theme of the Transitus miniature is that the Virgin is the ideal model for the three attending virgins who hope that their imitation of her will

[177] See above, n. 123.

[178] H. Coathalem, "Le Parallelisme entre la sainte Vierge et l'église dans la tradition latine jusqu'à la fin du XIIᵉ siècle," *Analecta Gregoriana* 74 (1954): 38ff.; Scheffczyk, *Mariengeheimnis*, pp. 414ff. For the concept and iconography of the marriage of Christ and the Church, see O. Casel, "Die Kirche als Braut Christi nach Schrift, Väterlehre und Liturgie," *Mysterium der Ekklesia* (Mainz, 1961), pp. 59–86; J. Schmid, "Brautschaft, heilige," *RAC*, 2, cols. 546ff.; O. Gillen, "Christus und die Sponsa," *Die christliche Kunst* 33 (1936–37): 202–24; idem, "Bräutigam u. Braut," *LCI*, 1, cols. 318–24; Schiller, *Ikon.*, 4, 1, pp. 94ff.

[179] Scheffczyk, *Mariengeheimnis*, pp. 414ff.

[180] Burlin, *Advent*, pp. 140ff., no. 9; Morrison, "*Christus Sponsus*," pp. 8f.

[181] C. R. Morey, *The Gold-Glass Collection of the Vatican Library*, Catalogo del Museo Sacro, 4 (Vatican City, 1959), p. 65, no. 397, pl. 33. For the hand of God with the crown, see J. Wilpert, *I sarcophagi cristiani antichi* (Rome, 1929), 1, p. 90, pl. 94, 1. Concerning marriage crownings, which later Byzantine art also depicted, see C. Walter, "Marriage Crowns in Byzantine Iconography," *Zographe* 10 (1979): 83–91; L. Reekmans, "La 'Dextrarum iunctio' dans l'iconographie romaine

et paléochrétienne," *Bulletin de l'Institut Historique Belge de Rome* 31 (1958): 69ff.; G. Vikan, "Art and Marriage in Early Byzantium," *DOP* 44 (1990): 152f.

[182] Verdier, *Couronnement*; Schiller, *Ikon.*, 4, 2, pp. 103ff., 114ff.; Thérel, *Vierge-Église*. Even the early examples of *Maria regina* were probably ecclesiological symbols; Nilgen, "Maria Regina," pp. 22ff., 30. For matrimonial and ecclesiologic symbolism in the Coronation of the Virgin in the Ottonian Bernward Gospels, see E. Guldan, *Eva und Maria* (Graz, 1966), pp. 13ff.

[183] Verdier, *Couronnement*, p. 18. The twelfth-century Sélincourt font in Amiens (Verdier, *Couronnement*, p. 35; Thérel, *Vierge-Église*, p. 220, fig. 98) depicts adjacent scenes of the Baptism and Christ Crowning Ecclesia. Ecclesia shares Christ's throne, a formula also used for the Coronation of the Virgin. The two adjacent sides of the font represent angels descending with wreaths from clouds, a feature recalling the Anglo-Saxon baptismal iconography. In both works the crowns signify that those born from the baptismal union of Christ and the Church have been incorporated into his ecclesiastic body and share his royalty.

[184] See above, n. 86.

eventually also lead them to the heavenly bridegroom. Though very different in appearance, the pictures of Mary and Æthelthryth carried similar messages.

To sum up, the miniature of the Death and Coronation of the Virgin is a complex fusion of the interrelated iconographic traditions of *servus Mariae genetricis Dei* and *Maria regina*, the symbolic narrative of the Transitus, and the liturgy. Through a wide range of visual and thematic associations with other pictures in the cycle, it visualized the relation of her Death and Coronation to her life and to her son's life, as well as to the future life of all mankind. On the one hand, she is exalted as queen of heaven, rewarded

for her humble service in the Incarnation in a way that mirrored Christ's elevation as king of heaven, and on the other hand, she is the virtuous model for the rest of humanity, particularly virgins, who hope to follow her to eternal union with the heavenly royal bridegroom after the Last Judgment. Her heavenly Coronation completes the terrestrial nuptials between Christ and the Church that began at the Incarnation and at the Baptism on Epiphany day; in her ecclesiastic role as the virgin bride and heavenly queen, Mary intercedes with her royal son and spouse on behalf of all those who serve her as faithfully as she served him.

Saint Swithun
(Deposition of Saint Swithun, 2 July)

Wearing episcopal vestments, Saint Swithun, the bishop of Winchester (852–862), cradles a golden book in his left arm and blesses with his right hand (pl. 32). This is the first known depiction of him and the only one extant before the twelfth century.[185] Whether there were earlier representations of the saint is uncertain. Æthelwold himself seems to have been responsible for the propagation of Swithun's cult,[186] and, as a rule, devotional popularity was an important factor in the creation of hagiographic imagery.

The saint's pose is conventional, but his relation to the architecture is notable. Beneath a gold, free-standing baldachin indicating his sanctity, he stands on the base of a central column whose shaft and capital are hidden behind him. The hard, vertical contours of his golden tunic have been assimilated to the geometric shape of a column, and two small arches which

presumably rest upon the hidden capital almost seem to spring from his nimbed head. This assimilation of his body to architecture created a decorative unity between the figure and the framework, but symbolism as well as aesthetics motivated the saint's architectonic character.

The mass commemorating Swithun's translation in 971 described him as an "Olympic column of shining glory, illustrious with miraculous splendor" and compared him to "one of the apostles."[187] Galatians 2:9 described several of the apostles as "columns," and on the basis of this and other biblical texts commentators often likened the disciples and their successors, the doctors and preachers of the faith, to symbolic columns supporting and strengthening the spiritual edifice of the Church with their firm belief, upright deeds, and illustrious preaching.[188] Influenced by the liturgy, the miniature character-

[185] As we shall see below, the Benedictional's lost miniature of the Choir of the Confessors almost certainly portrayed him. For later images of Swithun, see R. Deshman, "St. Swithun in Medieval Art," in Lapidge, *Cult of Saint Swithun*, forthcoming.

[186] Deshman, "Swithun"; D. J. Sheerin, "The Dedication of the Old Minster, Winchester, in 980," *Revue Bénédictine* 88 (1978): 261ff.; see also below, chap. 5.

[187] *Missal*, pp. 125, xxiv, n. 6: "Tu [Deus] idem quoque columnam rutile claritatis olimpicam sanctum pontificem suuithunum . . . contulisti; O felicem anglorum gentem cui dominus rerum talem concessit patronum: ut merito ad predictarum populis gentium colatur quasi unus apostolorum."

Swithun is also termed a "columna praeclua Christi" in a hymn attributed to Æthelwold's student Wulfstan; *Analecta Hymnica Medii Aevi*, ed. C. Blume and G. M. Dreves, 40 (1902; rpt. New York, 1961), p. 289, no. 337. The column is a symbol of Swithun in two Winchester accounts of his translation and miracles: Lantfred, *Translatio*, 3, and Wulfstan, *Narratio Metrica de S. Swithuno*, 3, both ed. and tr. Lapidge, *Cult of Saint Swithun*, forthcoming.

[188] B. Reudenbach, "Säule und Apostel. Überlegungen zum Verhältnis von Architektur und architekturexegetischer Literatur im Mittelalter," *Frühmittelalterliche Studien* 14 (1980): 310–51.

ized Saint Swithun as a successor of the apostles and a symbolic column of Ecclesia. The liturgy also mentioned his supernatural radiance, and this was visualized by the liberal use of gold for his nimbus and all his vestments except his blue chasuble.[189]

In devising this iconography the miniaturists might well have been influenced by the architectural symbolism of earlier images. In a canon table in a late-eighth-century Gospels from Flavigny (Autun, Bibl. Mun., MS 4),[190] John the Baptist and the evangelists are assimilated to the bases and Christ and the evangelist symbols to the capitals of the columns. The Benedictional, however, used a different manner of associating the human body with the column, one that anticipated the symbolic form of Gothic column statues.[191]

The Bishop Blessing the Congregation of the Church (Dedication of the Church)

The last miniature in the manuscript represents a bishop, presumably Æthelwold, pronouncing a blessing from a gold book which an assistant helps to support (pl. 35). The bishop stands under a baldachin and in front of an altar. Receiving his benediction are clerics and monks standing before him and the laity in a separate compartment above, which might represent a balcony. The scene is set in a church building, complete with towers, a belfry, and two weathercocks.

This miniature is anomalous in several respects. It is executed in two different techniques, pigment and line drawing, although all the others in the manuscript are completely painted.[192] This scene and the facing text page lack foliate frames, deviating from the standard treatment of the other feasts with full-page picture prefaces. Instead the framelike architecture of the church encloses the figures in the dedication picture. Above it are the last three lines of text of the preceding benediction, and nowhere else in the book does the antecedent text spill over onto a page with a picture. Finally, it is unclear why a depiction of the episcopal benediction prefaces the blessing for the dedication of the church.

These oddities cannot be explained by the assumption that the miniature is a later addition to the manuscript. Its style is consistent with the other miniatures, and the writing at the top of the page is spaced around the belfry, proving that the picture preceded the text.[193] The picture is undoubtedly an original and integral part of the manuscript.

Warner raised the possibility that the scene was unfinished. The red ink used in the outlined parts of the composition is the type used elsewhere in the manuscript for the underdrawing of painted miniatures,[194] and conceivably one could also attribute the absence of a frame to the incomplete state of the scene. However, the size of the composition and the three lines of text above it rule out the possibility that any ornamented frame was ever planned. It is also improbable that the mixed technique resulted from an interruption in work. So far as we know, Anglo-Saxon painters first did an underdrawing and then blocked out the basic ground colors of the entire composition. Only then did they add the finishing internal details of drapery folds, highlights, and facial features.[195] In an unfinished miniature one would not expect to find, as in the Benedictional, one part complete in all its details while the other lacks entirely the prelimi-

---

[189] Swithun also often appears "with shining garments" or with supernatural light in Lantfred's *Translatio*.

[190] *Karl der Grosse*, p. 268, no. 439, fig. 67; F. Carlsson, *The Iconology of Tectonics in Romanesque Art* (Hässleholm, 1976), pp. 62ff., fig. 25. For the iconography of column figures in general, see Reudenbach, "Säule und Apostel," pp. 337ff.

[191] Cf. W. Sauerländer, *Gothic Sculpture in France 1140–1270* (London, 1972), fig. 120.

[192] For a color reproduction, see Wormald, *Ben.*, pl. 8.

[193] Warner and Wilson, *Ben.*, p. xxx.

[194] The underdrawing is visible in the flaked portions of the miniature of the Presentation in the Temple (fig. 33).

[195] C. R. Dodwell, "Techniques of Manuscript Painting in Anglo-Saxon Manuscripts," *Settimane di studio del centro italiano di studi sull'alto medioevo* 18, 2 (1971): 649ff.; also idem and P. Clemoes, *The Old English Illustrated Hexateuch*, Early English Manuscripts in Facsimile, 18 (Copenhagen, 1974), pp. 61ff.

nary application of ground color. In all probability we see the miniature today in its intended, finished state.

Wormald[196] has more convincingly explained the mixed technique as a deliberate device to single out the more important elements of the composition. The bishop and the liturgical furnishings of the altar, the baldachin, and the book are all painted, but the subsidiary figures and the architecture are left in outline. The same device was used in a miniature in the later Arundel Psalter (fig. 136),[197] where gouache emphasizes St. Benedict and the patron in contrast to the outline used for the less important crowd of monks. The Benedictional's miniature is the first known example of mixed technique, which might have been invented by Æthelwold's scriptorium. The fact that the Psalter's picture derived from an approximately contemporary Winchester model supports this hypothesis.

The absence of a decorative frame for the miniature and the facing text might have been a means to establish a hierarchy of subject matter within the picture cycle. All the other full-page miniatures depict sacred historical persons or events and are fully painted and elaborately framed. Since the miniature of the Bishop Blessing represents contemporary individuals performing a liturgical rite, perhaps the illuminators thought its content less sacred and therefore deserving of a simpler treatment. Because there was no frame, the top of the page could be used for the end of the preceding text.

There might be some truth to this explanation, but it is not entirely satisfactory. In such a deluxe manuscript it is unlikely that either the illuminators or Æthelwold would have been so concerned about saving space that they would have carried over a few lines of text onto the top of what was clearly intended to be a full-page miniature. Even without an ornamental frame this large format still singles out the dedication

of the church as an important feast. In the case of the Octave of Pentecost a historiated initial (pl. 27) rather than a full-page miniature—framed or unframed—indicated the feast's lower status. If the dedication of the church was really considered a less significant feast, then here too we might have expected less than a full-page composition. The solution to the problem lies elsewhere, but first we must consider the related issue of why the painters chose in the first place to illustrate this feast with apparently unrelated subject matter.

Warner[198] suggested that the picture might illustrate the bestowal of the episcopal benediction at the consecration of the remodeled Winchester cathedral in 980. The *Narratio Metrica de S. Swithuno*, composed by the Winchester precentor Wulfstan probably between 992 and 994, described this dedication and extolled a golden weathercock crowning a tower of the church,[199] and Warner tentatively connected the weather vane of the renovated cathedral to the one on the belfry in the miniature. Both Homburger and Wormald[200] shared his caution about this hypothesis.

Their caution was thoroughly justified. Even before its reconstruction Winchester cathedral might have possessed a tower with a weathercock. The presence of *two* weathercocks in the picture calls into question any connection with the new tower and its weather vane and suggests that the weathercock was a motif freely used to characterize an ecclesiastic building.[201] A careful reading of Wulfstan's poem[202] reveals that the new tower with its weathercock was begun only after Æthelwold's death by his successor Bishop Ælfheah (984–1005). Since the miniature in its present state is complete, there is no reason to doubt that the entire manuscript was finished in the Æthelwold's lifetime; indeed, stylistic and historical evidence suggest that it originated some years before the dedica-

[196] Wormald, *Ben.*, p. 30.

[197] See above, n. 59; also Dodwell, "Techniques," pp. 649ff.

[198] Warner and Wilson, *Ben.*, p. xxx.

[199] Wulfstan, *Narratio*, ed. and tr. Lapidge, *Cult of St. Swithun*, forthcoming. For the date, see Wulfstan, *Life*, p. xxii.

[200] Homburger, *Anf.*, p. 25; Wormald, *Ben.*, p. 30.

[201] In later Anglo-Saxon art the motif frequently appeared in a variety of contexts: buildings in the Harley Psalter (Ohlgren, *Illustration*, pls. 2.7, 2.63), Noah's ark in the Junius manuscript (Ohlgren, pl. 16.38), the church in the Lanalet

Pontifical (J. E. Rosenthal, "Three Drawings in an Anglo-Saxon Pontifical: Anthropomorphic Trinity or Threefold Christ?" *AB* 63 [1981]: fig. 14); Westminster Abbey in the Bayeux tapestry (*The Bayeux Tapestry*, 2nd ed., ed. F. Stenton [London, 1965], fig. 32). See also L. Kretzenbacher, "Real-Bildwerke und Symbol-Auslegungen zum 'Hahn auf dem Kirchturm' zwischen Frühmittelalter und Reformation," *Archiv für Kulturgeschichte* 63–64 (1980–81): 29–47.

[202] R. N. Quirk, "Winchester Cathedral in the Tenth Century," *The Archaeological Journal* 114 (1957): 61–63.

tion ceremony in 980.[203] The theory that the miniature relates to this event can be safely set aside.

The picture's anomalous placement is highlighted by the fact that other early medieval pictures of the episcopal benediction, such as the one in the ninth-century Turonian Raganaldus sacramentary (Autun, Bibl. Mun., MS 19 bis; fig. 119),[204] preface a series of pontifical blessings. This and other representations of pontifical benediction bear only a generic likeness to the one in the Benedictional; the few points of similarity such as the presence of an assistant with the book can be explained as independent reflections of common liturgical practice. Nonetheless, it is clear that earlier depictions of the benediction were no rarity. The Anglo-Saxon composition very likely derived from a tradition of frontispiece illustrations for liturgical blessings. In the Benedictional, however, the iconography was given a new and unique function as the preface of the blessing for the dedication of the church.

THE SYMBOLIC CONTENT

To explain the miniature's anomalies we must discard the prevailing assumptions that it is simply a realistic depiction of a liturgical ceremony

and that it has "no necessary reference"[205] to the dedication blessing on the facing recto. In fact, this text is critical for the interpretation of the picture:

> May the omnipotent God bless and keep you and this house [and] may he deign to illuminate you and this house by the presence of his gift, and deign to open the eyes of his kindness over it day and night. Amen.
>
> And may he beneficently grant that all you who devoutly gather at the dedication of this basilica might be worthy, through the blessed intercession of N. and his other saints, whose relics here are devoutly venerated with love, to obtain the forgiveness of your sins. Amen.
>
> Since with their intervention, you yourselves might be made the temple of the Holy Spirit, in which God, the Holy Trinity, might deign to dwell continuously, and after the running out of the excursion of this life of laboring, you might merit to come successfully to eternal joy. Amen.[206]

The dedication rite removed the church from the secular to the sacred realm.[207] Like baptism, which first purified and consecrated an individual for the indwelling of Christ, the dedication of the church had two fundamental parts: a lus-

---

[203] See below, chaps. 6 and 7.

[204] Koehler, *Kar. Min.*, 1, 1, pp. 393f.; J. Décréaux, *Le Sacramentaire de Marmoutier*, Studi di antichità cristiana, 38 (Vatican City, 1985), 1, p. 162; *La Neustrie: les pays au nord de la Loire*, ed. P. Périn and L.-C. Feffer (Créteil, France, 1985), no. 19. An unfinished stylus sketch in a St. Gall benedictional in Cambridge, made for Adalbero of Augsburg (877–909), shows the bishop with a crouching assistant blessing the lay congregation, which includes a kneeling woman; see F. Wormald and P. M. Giles, *Illuminated Manuscripts in the Fitzwilliam Museum* (Cambridge, 1966), p. 7., no. 9 (with an incomplete description); W. Berschin, "Das Benedictionale Salomons III. für Adalbero von Augsburg (Cambridge, Fitzwilliam Museum MS 27)," *Churrätisches und St. Gallisches Mittelalter: Festschrift für Otto P. Clavadetscher zu seinem fünfundsechzigsten Geburtstag*, ed. H. Maurer (Sigmaringen, 1984), pp. 227–36. A Regensburg benedictional (Malibu, J. Paul Getty Mus., MS Ludwig VII 1) made ca. 1025–1050 for Bishop Engilmar of Parenzo depicts him blessing the congregation on the other side of the altar; see *Regensburger Buchmalerei*, ed. F. Mütherich and K. Dachs (Munich, 1987), p. 36, no. 22, pl. 15; A. von Euw and J. M. Plotzek, *Die Handschriften der Sammlung Ludwig* (Cologne, 1979), 1, pp. 292ff., fig. 186. Rosenthal, "Three Drawings," p. 558, has tentatively reinterpreted the donor portrait in the Lanalet Pon-

tifical as a depiction of the episcopal blessing, but the bishop makes no gesture of benediction.

[205] Warner and Wilson, *Ben.*, p. xxix.

[206] *CBP*, no. 123; Warner and Wilson, *Ben.*, p. 47:

> Benedicat et custodiat uos omnipotens deus domumque hanc sui muneris praesentia illustrare, atque suae pietatis oculos super eam die ac nocte dignetur aperire. Amen.
>
> Concedatque propitius ut omnes qui ad de[di]cationem huius basilicae deuote conuenistis, intercedente beato, illo, et ceteris sanctis suis, quorum reliquiae hic pio uenerantur amore, uobiscum hinc ueniam peccatorum uestrorum, reportare ualeatis. Amen.
>
> Quatinus eorum interuentu, ipsi templum sancti spiritus, in quo sancta deus trinitas iugiter habitare dignetur efficiamini, et post huius uitae labentis excursum, ad gaudia aeterna feliciter peruenire mereamini. [Amen.]

[207] For the following, see D. Stiefenhofer, *Die Geschichte der Kirchweihe vom 1.–7. Jahrhundert*, Veröffentlichungen aus dem kirchenhistorischen Seminar München, ser. 3, 8 (Munich, 1909), pp. 11ff., 126ff.; L. Eisenhofer, *Handbuch der katholischen Liturgik* (Freiburg im Breisgau, 1933), 2, pp. 448ff.; L. Bowen, "The Tropology of Mediaeval Dedication Rites," *Speculum* 16 (1941): 469–79.

tration or exorcism, which drove out evil, and a hallowing, which called down divine grace upon the church, enabling it to become a *domus Dei*, a worthy dwelling for God. From an early date commentators repeatedly interpreted the construction and dedication of the material church as symbolic of the edification and consecration of a spiritual Ecclesia in souls of the believers, and this symbolism underlies the Benedictional's blessing.

The prayer calls down a divine blessing simultaneously upon both the newly dedicated church building and the congregation within it, effectively equating them. With the intercession of the saints, whose relics have just been translated into the newly purified church as part of its dedication, God also cleanses the believers of evil. Therefore, they themselves can become the spiritual equivalent of the consecrated physical church—a holy spiritual temple worthy for the habitation of the Holy Spirit and the other members of the Trinity (cf. 1 Cor. 3:16–17, 6:19). This in turn allows them to hope for salvation after death.

In the miniature the Eucharistic chalice and paten are prominently represented in gold on the purple-draped altar. This depicts actual liturgical practice since the bishop pronounced his benediction between the consecration of the Eucharist and the communion.[208] The facing text, however, endows this detail with added significance: it clearly showed that Christ now dwells in the newly consecrated and divinely blessed church. The text also would have suggested to the viewers that the members of the congregation who receive from the bishop the very same purifying divine blessing as the church building and who are about to partake of the Eucharist have also become houses of God, each a spiritual temple in which the Trinity dwells. Through the simple but ingenious expedient of placing the picture before the dedication text, the painters represented not only the external appearance but also the inner spiritual meaning of the rite of episcopal benediction.

This symbolism is also visualized by one unusual feature that has hitherto gone unnoticed. The altar was customarily located directly beneath its ciborium, but in the picture the bishop has displaced the altar which was shifted back before the rear column of the ciborium. The bishop seems to have been assimilated to the altar itself.

This becomes comprehensible in light of the symbolism of the altar in the contemporary Winchester dedication liturgy.[209] Like the church building, the altar underwent a "baptism" which included lustration and consecration. In preparation for its hallowing with chrism, it was washed with the remainder of the water that had been used to asperse and purify the church. The antiphon sung during the altar's cleansing was: "Behold the tabernacle of God with men, and the spirit of God shall dwell in them (Apoc. 21:3); for the temple of God is holy, which you are (1 Cor. 3:17)."[210] The altar symbolized both the material church building and the spiritual temple of the faithful, both a pure and fitting habitation for God.

This antiphon quotes 1 Corinthians 3:17, which was paraphrased in the miniature's text, and the painters must have recognized that both the dedication benediction and the antiphon espoused much the same symbolic interpretation of the physical fabric of the church. The miniature's assimilation of the bishop to the altar with the Eucharist was another means to visualize the concept that through an infusion of divine blessings and the subsequent partaking of the Eucharist each individual in the church became its spiritual counterpart, a holy house in which God comes and dwells. Constrained by the limits of a "realistic" depiction of the benediction ceremony, the miniaturists had to apply this altar symbolism to the officiant rather than to the recipients of the blessing. This does not really alter the significance, however, since in pronouncing his benediction on the congregation the bishop acted as an intermediary, passing on the divine grace and power that he himself had

---

[208] Warner and Wilson, *Ben.*, pp. liii–lv; Prescott, "Text," pp. 120ff. Cf. also the depiction of episcopal benediction in the Engilmar benedictional; see above, n. 204.

[209] *Ben. Rob.*, pp. 73ff. See also J. Gage, "The Anglo-Saxon Ceremonial of the Dedication and Consecration of Churches," *Archaeologia* 35 (1834): 235–74; D. H. Turner, *The Claudius*

Pontificals, Henry Bradshaw Society, 97 (Chichester, 1971), pp. xx–xxiv.

[210] *Ben. Rob.*, p. 83: "Ecce tabernaculum dei cum hominibus et spiritus dei habitat in illis, templum enim dei sanctum est quod uos."

first received from God.[211] The bishop no less than the congregation was a member of Ecclesia who strived to become a temple of God.

The miniature's profound symbolism reduces the likelihood that it lacks an ordinary frame because it was regarded as less important than others in the manuscript. A more probable reason is that this omission allowed the concluding lines of the preceding blessing to be carried over onto the same page as the miniature. Because of this the picture can be viewed as an illustration of the preceding as well as the following text. Indeed, the forceful penetration of upper parts of the church into the text above physically integrates them.

This text is the blessing for the feast of several virgins:

> May the almighty Lord, who wished to triumph over the ancient enemy not only through men, but even through women, deign by the intercessions of his holy virgins, to bless you. Amen.
>
> And may he who wished to bestow on them . . . the honor of virginity, . . . deign to purify you of the foulness of sins, and to adorn you with the lamps of virtues. Amen.
>
> May the lamps of your hearts *be so filled* with the oil of virtues, *that you may be able to enter with them into the marriage chamber of the heavenly bridegroom.*[212]

This prayer likens the believers to both the saintly virgins celebrated in the feast and the wise virgins in the Gospel parable (Matt. 25:1–13) who conserved the oil in their lamps and were admitted into the kingdom of heaven by the bridegroom. Just as God gave the saints the "honor of virginity" which allowed them to wed Christ, he gives the faithful his blessing that purifies them so that they too, with their spiritual lamps filled with virtue, can hope for the same happy

end. The isolation of the last part of this prayer (italicized in the quote) over the picture effectively turns these few lines into a titulus explaining what is represented beneath: the bishop bestows God's blessing on the members of the church so that they "might be able to enter with them (the virgins) into the marriage chamber of the heavenly bridegroom."

This matrimonial explanation of the iconography also bears on its function as an illustration for the dedication of the church, for traditionally this rite, in which Christ possessed and united with the church, was understood as the wedding of Christ and Ecclesia, his virgin bride.[213] One of the lections for the consecration mass began with Apocalypse 21:2–3[214]:

> And I saw the holy city, the new Jerusalem, coming down out of heaven from God, prepared as a bride adorned for her husband. And I heard a great voice from the throne, saying: Behold the tabernacle of God with men, and he will dwell with them.

In the context of the dedication ceremony this lection equated the newly consecrated church both with the heavenly Jerusalem as the bride of Christ and with the members of the congregation as the "tabernacle" in which he will dwell.[215]

It is only by virtue of membership in the Church, the body of Christ, that any individual —be he a virgin saint or an ordinary Christian— can marry Christ, the head of the Church (cf. Eph. 5:22–30). Thus the text above the miniature reinforced its relationship to the text opposite it. The divine power and presence that the bishop calls down on the members of the congregation makes them, individually and collectively, the spiritual counterparts of the newly consecrated church building—the temple and bride of Christ and the terrestrial reflection of the celestial Jerusalem.

---

[211] See Ælfric, *Hom.*, 1, p. 37, and the related blessing for the vigil of Christmas; *CBP*, no. 1643; Warner and Wilson, *Ben.*, p. 4.

[212] Emphasis added. *CBP*, no. 1742; Warner and Wilson, *Ben.*, p. 46:

> Omnipotens dominus, intercedentibus sanctis uirginibus suis, uos dignetur benedicere, qui de antiquo hoste, non solum per uiros, uerum etiam per feminas uoluit triumphare. Amen.
>
> Et qui illis uoluit . . . decoremque uirginitatis, . . .

conferre, uos dignetur et uitiorum squaloribus expurgare, et uirtutum lampadibus exornare. Amen.

> Quatinus uirtutum oleo ita peccatorum [pectorum] uestrorum lampades possint repleri, ut cum eis caelestis sponsi thalamum ualeatis ingredi.

[213] Casel, "Kirche als Braut Christi," *Mysterium der Ekklesia*, p. 81, also pp. 244, 355–60.

[214] *Ben. Rob.*, pp. 97f.

[215] Cf. also the combination of Apoc. 21:3 and 1 Cor. 3:17 in the antiphon for the cleansing of the altar (above, n. 210).

THE RELATIONSHIP TO
OTHER MINIATURES

These symbolic themes recur in various guises elsewhere in the picture cycle. The concept of the believers as the living Ecclesia with particular reference to the altar is found in both the Nativity (pl. 12) and the Presentation of Christ in the Temple (pl. 20, fig. 33) which portrayed the altar symbolically as the spiritual edifice of the Church that bonds Christ and all believers together. It is the Presentation, however, that relates particularly closely to the dedication miniature.

We have seen that in this infancy scene Christ's coming to the Jewish temple in Jerusalem prefigures the Christian's entrance into the terrestrial Church in this life and its celestial counterpart, the heavenly Jerusalem, after death. The altar of the Old Law foreshadows the altar of the New Law, which is both the cornerstone Christ and the members of his mystic body, the Church. Since the members themselves are the "temple of God" (1 Cor. 3:16f.; 6:19; 2 Cor. 6:16), the anthropomorphic altar symbolizes the inner altar of the heart on which they make spiritual sacrifices under the New Law. These had been prefigured by the material offerings of the doves which Christ had made at the Presentation according to the Old Law.

This typology of the altar penetrated the exegesis and the liturgy of the dedication of the church. In a dedication homily Cæsarius of Arles (d. 542)[216] explained that the two altars of the temple of Solomon in Jerusalem prefigured the newly consecrated altar of the church and the two altars in the spiritual temple of the believers. Every Christian has within himself the twin altars of the heart and the body, on which God expected the offerings of pure thoughts and a chaste body respectively. Similar symbolism occurred in the Winchester dedication liturgy. After citing a long series of antetypes of sacrifice under the Old Law, the prayer over the newly consecrated altar concluded with a declaration of the new type of offerings that were to be made on the altar of the temple of the New

Law: "In this altar . . . may a sacrifice of chastity be offered in place of turtle doves, [and] a sacrifice of innocence in place of the young of doves, through the Lord."[217] This recalls the wording of the text of the Presentation miniature, the blessing for the feast of the Purification of the Virgin, which asks that the believer, instructed in the "spiritual teachings" of God's law, "might be able to offer him gifts of chastity in place of turtle doves and that you may be enriched with the gifts of the Holy Spirit in place of young doves."[218]

The illuminators seem to have perceived the relationship between these texts, for the miniatures of the Presentation and the Bishop Blessing the Congregation have similar symbolic content: the coming of Christ and divine blessings into the material church (or its prefiguration, the temple of Jerusalem) symbolizes the advent and indwelling of God and his sanctifying power in the spiritual temple of the believer who makes moral offerings to him on the altar within the living Ecclesia of himself.

Visual similarities subtly called attention to these conceptual ones. Corresponding to the partially anthropomorphized altar in the Presentation is the bishop whose location beneath the baldachin implies that he has become a kind of human altar. The displacement of the actual altar to the left so that it is on axis with a column mirrors the placement of the altar in the Presentation where it is assimilated to the base of a column of the temple, and both altars are turned at a 45 degree angle to the picture plane. In the Presentation these features represented the altar as the Christological cornerstone and foundation of Ecclesia, and in the other miniature they probably conveyed a comparable symbolism.

The theme of the cornerstone runs through the liturgy and exegesis of the dedication of the church. The famous dedication hymn, *Urbs Beata Jerusalem*,[219] for example, described the newly consecrated church as Christ's bride and the descending celestial city resting on the foundation and cornerstone of Christ and constructed from the living stones of the believers. Ælfric's

---

216 *Sermo 228, De Templo vel Consecratione Altaris*, ed. G. Morin, CC, 104, pp. 901–904.

217 *Ben. Rob.*, p. 87: "In hoc . . . altare . . . offeratur pro turturibus sacrificium castitatis, pro pullis columbarum innocentiae sacrificium, per dominum nostrum."

218 See above, chap. 1, n. 159.

219 C. Blume, *Analecta Hymnica Medii Aevi*, 51 (Leipzig, 1908; rpt. New York, 1961), p. 110, no. 102. For the hymn in eleventh-century Anglo-Saxon dedication liturgy, see Gneuss, *Hymnar und Hymnen*, p. 78.

144

homily for the consecration ceremony[220] also applied the cornerstone *topos* to the material church and its prefiguration, the temple of Solomon, which was portrayed in the Presentation picture. Finally, in the Winchester dedication rite the prayer after the anointing of the walls of the new church stated that God constructs his eternal dwelling "from living and precious stones,"[221] and two other prayers applied cornerstone symbolism to the newly anointed altar.[222] Hence it is not surprising that the altar in the picture for the dedication of the church should possess connotations of the cornerstone.

Marriage to Christ is another theme that relates this miniature to others in the manuscript. The concept that the believer should imitate a holy virgin and achieve union with the heavenly bridegroom is central to the preceding miniature in the cycle, the Death and Coronation of the Virgin (pl. 34), and the representations of Saint Æthelthryth and Christ (pls. 28, 29). Matrimonial symbolism is also found in the Baptism (pl. 19), the illustration for Epiphany when Christ wed the Church, which, like Mary at the Annunciation and Nativity (pls. 8, 12), conceived and bore a new child of God. There are other themes in addition to marriage that are shared by the images of the Baptism and the Bishop Blessing the Church.

According to the latter's text, the pontifical benediction makes the members of the church themselves "the temple of the Holy Spirit, in which God, the Holy Trinity, might dwell continuously," and in the Baptism the Spirit literally descends on Christ who symbolizes his members baptized into his ecclesiastic body. The dove's vials of chrism represent the baptismal anointment that consecrates the believers into Christ's royal priesthood, making them "as living stones built up, a spiritual house, a holy priesthood, to offer up spiritual sacrifices" (1 Peter 2:5). In other words, the theme of the edification of the faithful into a *domus Dei* is at the heart of the Baptism as well as the dedication miniature. Moreover, in the latter the bishop beneath

the baldachin, a symbol of the human altar, is the conceptual counterpart of the girded Christological figure of John the Baptist, who exemplifies the priesthood of the believers making spiritual self-sacrifices. Since the dedication rite was perceived as the "baptism" of the church,[223] there can be little doubt about the conceptual association of the two miniatures.

Finally, there are close parallels between the ecclesiastic and nuptial symbolism of the dedication miniature and the Annunciation picture. Not only did the Virgin in the latter represent both the ecclesiastic temple and bride of Christ, but this symbolism was once more associated with the inner meaning of the episcopal benediction. The matching tituli of the miniature and its text, the blessing for the first Sunday in Advent, implied a typological analogy between the blessings that Christ's advent brought to the Virgin in the Incarnation and the blessings that his renewed advent brought to the members of the Church through the liturgical benediction. Pictorial resemblances between the two miniatures underlined their symbolic parallelism. The poses of Gabriel blessing the Virgin and the bishop blessing the congregation are quite similar, especially since both stand before an open gold book. Moreover, in each picture a baldachin covers the figure who is a symbol of the living spiritual Ecclesia in which Christ dwells. Indeed, the Virgin holds a golden object strikingly similar to the paten on the altar in the other picture, perhaps a device to relate her symbolically, like the bishop, to the church altar. In the dedication ritual the prayer accompanying the anointing of the altar compared the transubstantiation of the eucharistic offerings to the Incarnation when the Word was made flesh.[224] These two compositions balance each other not only symbolically but physically, marking the first and the last of the blessing texts in the book. At the beginning of these the Annunciation establishes that Christ's first advent was the historical and dogmatic origin of all subsequent blessings bestowed on mankind, and at the end

---

[220] Ælfric, *Hom.*, 2, pp. 580ff.

[221] *Ben. Rob.*, p. 86: "Deus qui de uiuis et electis lapidibus aeternum maiestati tuae condis habitaculum."

[222] *Ben. Rob.*, p. 84.

[223] In the later Winchester Benedictional of Archbishop Robert, a homily of Caesarius of Arles (no. 229) prefacing the dedication *ordo* specifically mentions that it was through baptism that the faithful first became the "temple of Christ,"

analogous to the dedicated church; *Ben. Rob.*, p. 69. A book cover of the Drogo Sacramentary (Goldschmidt, *Elf.*, p. 41, no. 74A, pl. 30) depicts the Baptism (fig. 40), Christ blessing the apostles, and the liturgical rites of baptism and the dedication of the church, thus anticipating the Benedictional's symbolic association of divine consecration through blessing, baptism, and church dedication.

[224] *Ben. Rob.*, p. 85.

the Bishop Blessing the Congregation illustrates more directly how God in the present continues

to come into the material and spiritual Ecclesia through liturgical benediction.

The Choirs of the Saints and the Apostles

Originally the Benedictional probably began with a miniature of Christ, two-page compositions of each choir of the saints (angels, patriarchs, prophets, apostles, martyrs, confessors, and virgins) and finally four pictures of the apostles.[225] All that remains of this series are half of the confessors (pl. 1), the virgins (pls. 2, 3), and the twelve apostles (pls. 4–7).

THE ICONOGRAPHIC SOURCES

The idea for this prefatory cycle came from the Galba Psalter. Opening the Psalter on folio 2v is a picture of Christ and the choirs of the angels, patriarchs, prophets, and apostles (fig. 11), and a complementary picture of Christ and the remaining choirs—the martyrs, confessors, and virgins—follows on folio 21 (fig. 12). The first miniature is opposite the beginning of a liturgical calendar on folio 3, and this very likely gave the Benedictional's creators the idea of prefacing their own book, whose liturgical texts follow the order of the ecclesiastic calendar, with images of the heavenly hierarchy. Although not the actual models for the Benedictional's stately full-length figures, the Psalter's pictures did influence the division of each choir and its titulus into two facing halves. Our manuscript projected this arrangement onto facing pages for each choir, omitting *omnis* from the inscription for greater balance.

In part the process of creating the double-page compositions can still be followed. A comparison

of the two pages of the virgins discloses that both derived from a single model. The three foremost figures in each correspond closely. The painters introduced some variations in the gestures and the form of book of the virgin on the left, and this resulted in the anomaly that the figure on the verso blesses with her left hand. On the recto the central and left figures are identified by inscriptions on their books as Mary Magdalene and Æthelthryth respectively, the only named saints on either page.[226] To single them out they were raised slightly, the anonymous full-length virgin on the right was shifted back, and the head of the figure behind Æthelthryth's right shoulder was omitted. Thus the model depicted only one group of virgins which was copied twice to make a more impressive double-page composition. No doubt the same procedure was followed for the other, lost pairs of choirs.

This technique of elaborating a model seems to have been an established practice of the atelier. To create the series of standing prophets embroidered on the stole of Bishop Frithestan in Durham, made between 909 and 916, the Winchester workshop often repeated the same standing figure, sometimes reversing it for the sake of variety.[227] This precedent is particularly relevant since the Benedictional originally also included the prophets.

The procedure does not seem to have been used for the apostles, however, since no one is like any other. The model must have included all twelve. As the disciples are not tightly grouped like the confessors and the virgins, they did not

---

[225] For a reconstruction, see below, Appendix One.

[226] "S(an)c(t)a Æþeldrid(a)" and "S(anct)a Ma(r)ia Ma(gdale)-n(a)." Without explanation J. O. Westwood, *Facsimiles of the Miniatures and Ornaments of Anglo-Saxon and Irish Manuscripts* (London, 1868), p. 134, first identified the central figure as the Magdalene. Because she does not have a feast in the manuscript, Warner and Wilson, *Ben.*, p. xvi, reidentified her as the Virgin Mary, reconstructing the flaked inscription as "S(an)c(t)a Maria Ma(ter Christi)." This argument does not stand scrutiny, however, since the lack of a feast for Saint Cuthbert did not prevent his inclusion as one of the three labeled confessors (pl. 1). Westwood probably based

his identification on the inscription which must have been less damaged in the nineteenth century. The scrupulously accurate engraving published by Gage, "Ben.," pl. 5, shows the inscription as "S(an)c(t) a Maria Magdalen." See also Ortenberg, *English Church*, pp. 252f.

[227] *The Relics of St. Cuthbert*, ed. C. F. Battiscombe (Oxford, 1956), pls. 33, 34; D. H. Wright, rev. of *Relics, AB* 43 (1961): 156. The same technique seems to have been used for the series of angels and apostles on the coffin of St. Cuthbert; E. Kitzinger, "The Coffin Reliquary," in *Relics*, ed. Battiscombe, pp. 267, 273, pls. 4–6, 8, 9.

necessarily come from the same source as the choirs of the saints.

The origin of the model for the disciples is highly problematic. There is no close iconographic resemblance to the standing apostles on two related Carolingian Fulda ivory caskets.[228] In Byzantine art non-narrative figures of the standing apostles must have been relatively common, though few complete sets of all twelve have come down to us. One of what must have originally been a pair of eleventh-century miniatures portraying the twelve apostles is preserved in Baltimore (Walters Art Gallery, MS W 530C; fig. 120).[229] A similar arrangement of six apostles in two registers occurs in an approximately contemporary book of Old English homilies in Cambridge (Corpus Christi Coll., MS 198; fig. 121).[230] The Benedictional's illuminators could easily have split such a composition horizontally, rearranging the figures three to a page. However this may be, the Benedictional's apostles bear only a generic resemblance to the later ones; thus their source remains uncertain.

The model for the choirs of saints is also difficult to ascertain. Several depictions of the celestial hierarchy can be found in Carolingian and Ottonian art. The earliest is the illustration of the Te Deum in the Utrecht Psalter (fig. 80).[231] Standing celestial choirs of martyrs, apostles, and prophets turn to adore the enthroned Christ, the dove of the Spirit on his book, and the crowning hand of the Father. Seraphs and angels flank this Trinity. The double-page Sanctus composi-

tion in the Metz Sacramentary of Charles the Bald[232] (figs. 81, 82) shows half-length choirs of the angels, apostles, martyrs, confessors, and virgins in clouds adoring Christ in majesty. The All Saints picture in the late-tenth-century Fulda sacramentary in Udine (Archivio Capitolare, MS 1; fig. 122)[233] also depicts half-length celestial choirs which adore the Lamb. None of these Carolingian and Ottonian representations is very similar to the Benedictional's depiction of full-length frontal choirs.

In the Byzantine iconography of the Last Judgment, choirs of the saints petition Christ. On a late-eleventh-century icon on Mount Sinai (fig. 123)[234] the apostles, the prophets, and the martyrs are in the upper row, and the monks and ascetics, and the holy women in the lower one. The saints in this and most other Byzantine Last Judgments stand in three-quarter profile, but frontal choirs like the Anglo-Saxon ones also exist in Byzantine art. The twelfth-century manuscript of the homilies of the monk James in the Vatican (Biblioteca Apostolica, MS gr. 1162; fig. 124)[235] illustrated the feast of the Conception of the Virgin with a miniature of the Virgin presiding over groups of frontally standing choirs of saints. In the upper level from left to right are the bishops, and the monks and ascetics, while below are the emperors and kings, the soldier saints and martyrs, and the empresses and other holy women. The archetype of this miniature might very well have been adapted from a Last Judgment. Possibly such a Byzantine compo-

[228] Goldschmidt, *Elf.*, 1, pp. 32ff., nos. 58–62, pls. 24, 25; K. Weitzmann, "Eine Fuldaer Elfenbeingruppe," *Adolph Goldschmidt zu seinem siebenzigsten Geburtstag* (Berlin, 1933), pp. 15ff.; rpt., idem, *Art in the Medieval West and its Contacts with Byzantium* (London, 1982), no. II, pp. 15ff. The relationship posited on stylistic grounds by Homburger, *Anf.*, pp. 13f., is unconvincing.

[229] *Illuminated Greek Manuscripts from American Collections*, ed. G. Vikan (Princeton, 1973), pp. 106f., no. 22, fig. 37. This leaf originially prefaced the text of Acts in Mt. Athos, Vatopedi, MS 762.

[230] Temple, *Manuscripts*, p. 105, no. 88, p. 240, text fig. 58; M. Budny, "Worcester Manuscripts at Corpus Christi College, Cambridge: A Report on Recent Research," *Old English Newsletter* 26 (1993): 29f., pl. 5. The twelve apostles also appear in the canon tables of the Pembroke Gospels; Ohlgren, *Illustration*, pls. 9.6–9.9.

[231] See above, chap. 2, n. 170. For the iconography of the choirs, see H. Aurenhammer, "Allerheiligenbild," *Lexikon der christlichen Ikonographie*, fasc. 1 (Vienna, 1960), pp. 89–94;

anon., "Allerheiligenbild," *LCI*, 1, cols. 101–104.

[232] See above, chap. 2, n. 171.

[233] A. Comoretto, *Le miniature del sacramentario fuldense di Udine* (Udine, 1988), pp. 75f., fig. 33. See also the similar pictures in the Fulda sacramentaries in Göttingen (*Sac. Fuld.*, pl. 33) and Bamberg, Staatl. Bibl., MS lit. 1.

[234] G. Sortiriou and M. Sortiriou, *Icones du Mont Sinaï* (Athens, 1958), p. 130, fig. 151; K. Weitzmann, "Byzantine Miniature and Icon Painting in the Eleventh Century," *Proceedings of the XIIIth International Congress of Byzantine Studies*, ed. J. M. Hussey et al. (London, 1967), pp. 22f., pl. 43, rpt. Weitzmann, *Studies*, pp. 304f., fig. 304.

[235] C. Stornajolo, *Miniature della omilie di Giacomo monaco e dell'evangeliario greco urbinate* (Rome, 1910), pp. 8f., pl. 3; see also H. Omont, "Miniatures des homélies sur la Vierge du moine Jacques," *Bulletin de la Société Française de Reproductions de Manuscrits à Peintures* 11 (1927): pl. 2, 1; J. Anderson, "The Illustrated Sermons of James the Monk: Their Date, Order, and Place in the History of Byzantine Art," *Viator* 22 (1991): 69–120.

sition of the Last Judgment was the model for the Benedictional, but this must remain only a hypothesis.

The Meaning of Christ and the Choirs of Saints

This elaborate opening picture cycle undoubtedly reflects Æthelwold's own special devotion to the saints. He is known to have composed a special supplementary private office to All Saints to be recited at matins and vespers.[236] It would be a mistake, however, to regard the miniatures as only an expression of his personal veneration, for this would ignore their specific manuscript context.[237] When the miniaturists took over the idea of prefatory miniatures of the heavenly hierarchy from the Galba Psalter, they also appropriated some of the many different layers of meaning from the rich iconography of the earlier manuscript, adapting them to a benedictional.

On one level the Psalter's pictures represented a Last Judgment,[238] and the Benedictional's miniatures can also be seen in the same light. The later Anglo-Saxon representations of Christ and the heavenly choirs in the New Minster Liber Vitae (fig. 69) and the Grimbald Gospels (figs. 92, 93)[239] are both connected to the Last Judgment. That the Benedictional's iconography also had connotations of this eschatological event becomes evident if we take into consideration the manuscript's hexameter dedication poem, which fills the two pages immediately after the miniatures of choirs and apostles and before the cycle of feast pictures. Written entirely in gold and in the unusual display script of Roman rustic capitals, this text is given special prominence in the book:

> A bishop, the great Æthelwold, whom the Lord made patron of Winchester, ordered a certain monk subject to him to write the present book—truly knowing well how to

preserve Christ's fleecy lambs from the malignant art of the devil; illustrious, venerable and benign, he desires also to render, as a steward, full fruit to God, when the Judge who sifts the acts of the whole world, what each has done, shall come and shall give such reward as they deserve, to the just eternal life, and punishment to the unjust. He commanded also to be made in this book many arches well adorned and filled with various figures decorated with numerous beautiful colors and with gold. This book the Boanerges aforesaid caused to be indited for himself and in order that he might be able to sanctify the people of the Saviour by means of it and pour forth holy prayers to God for the flock committed to him, and that he may lose no lambkin of the fold, but may be able to say with joy, "Lo, I present to Thee myself and the children whom Thou didst give me to keep; by Thy aid not one of them has the fierce ravening wolf snatched away, but we stand together and desire to receive abiding life and to enjoy it in the heavens with the supreme sovereign whose members we are, who by right is the head and salvation of those baptized in the clear-sounding name of the Father and of the Son and of the Holy Ghost, so that, if they wander not astray but hold the faith, and by their deeds also perform the commands of salvation and repel all heresy from their hearts, ever striving to overcome the evil of sin, they may be joined to the Lord in heaven without end." May Christ the Saviour, who is the good King of the world, mercifully grant this to all who are sprinkled with holy baptism; and to the great father who ordered this book to be written may he grant an eternal kingdom above. Let all who look upon this book pray always that after the term of the flesh I may abide in heaven—Godeman the writer, as a supplicant, earnestly asks this.[240]

---

[236] Wulfstan, *Life*, pp. lxviii–lxxvii.

[237] Cf. Raw, *Crucifixion*, pp. 23f., who claims the cycle "conveyed no message" and has no relation to the manuscript's texts.

[238] Deshman, "Anglo-Saxon Art after Alfred," pp. 179ff.; J. O'Reilly, "Early Medieval Text and Image: The Wounded

and Exalted Christ," *Peritia* 6–7 (1987–88): 84ff., 91ff.

[239] See above, n. 31.

[240] Tr. Wormald, *Ben.*, pp. 7f.; see also Warner and Wilson, *Ben.*, pp. xii–xiii, 1, fols. 4v–5; Lapidge, "Æthelwold as Scholar," pp. 106f.

The poem says that Æthelwold commissioned the book so that through its prayers he could sanctify his flock, preparing them as well as himself for the day of judgment. The bishop is even envisaged shepherding his flock before Christ at the Last Judgment and pleading for his and their salvation.

The prefacing picture cycle can be understood as an illustration of the poem, showing Christ and the saints in a kind of Last Judgment. As in the Galba Psalter, it is not a conventional Last Judgment. Although Christ might well have been characterized as the heavenly Judge in the lost opening miniature, there is no depiction of those who will be damned or saved. Instead we see the saints—those who have already been saved. Almost all of them wear golden crowns, the imperishable crowns of eternal life (1 Cor. 9:25; 2 Tim. 4:8; James 1:12; 1 Peter 5:4). This is a feature of neither Byzantine iconography, where only imperial saints wear crowns signifying their former station in life (figs. 123, 124), nor earlier Latin representations (figs. 80, 81).[241] The manner in which the crowns seem to float insecurely on the heads of the virgins on folio 1v suggests that these regal insignia were Anglo-Saxon interpolations. The dedication poem calls Christ "the supreme sovereign" and "the good King of the world" and describes the reward of the righteous as "an eternal kingdom above"; the crowns were added to show that the saints have become co-rulers of the heavenly kingdom with Christ the king. In other words, the saints are represented in the beatific celestial life that Æthelwold and his congregation hope to share after the Last Judgment. In the poem Æthelwold imagines that he and his flock "stand together" before Christ, seeming to have already succeeded in joining the saints who are portrayed standing together in heavenly choirs, originally before Christ.

The dedication does not mention the saints,

but many of the benedictions ask God to bless and sanctify the members of the congregation so that after death they might receive the ultimate reward of joining the saints in their blissful heavenly life with Christ. The blessing for the Octave of Easter, for example, concludes with the wish that "you [the congregation] might be worthy to stand with the ranks of the saints in the future."[242] Sometimes the goal of community with the saints is even linked to the crown of life, as in the benediction for the feast of Saint Cecilia: "And may he who allowed her . . . to ascend in triumph to heavenly glory, allow you . . . to be clothed in an imperishable crown of glory with all the elect."[243] Placed at the beginning of the manuscript, the sequence of Christ and the crowned saints reminded the reader of the eschatological event and the heavenly goal that gave purpose to all the following liturgical texts.

The Psalter's two pictures illustrated not only the Last Judgment but also the litany of the saints,[244] a type of intercessory prayer that was used in private devotions, processions, and liturgical rites such as baptism and the dedication of the church.[245] After imploring the mercy of Christ or the Trinity, the litany asked the aid of the Virgin Mary and the various heavenly choirs, usually beginning with the angels, then the saints of both Covenants, ending with the virgins. The leading members of each choir were first petitioned individually by name and then collectively, often by the formula that labels the saints in the Psalter, *omnis chorus angelorum* (*patriarchum*, etc.). Many litanies added a list of the trials and evils that the supplicant hoped to escape, and these often included the Lord's "future wrath" and the Last Judgment.[246] The Psalter's iconographic fusion of the litany and the Last Judgment alluded to the ultimate reason for the intercessory prayer.

The Benedictional's prefatory cycle would also

---

[241] Crowned saints do appear, however, in the late-tenth-century Fulda sacramentaries (fig. 122); see above, n. 233.

[242] See above, chap. 2, n. 109. See also, e.g., the prayers for Advent 1 alia (Warner and Wilson, *Ben.*, p. 2; *CBP*, no. 37), Epiphany 3 (Warner and Wilson, *Ben.*, p. 8; *CBP*, no. 1711), Lent 1 (Warner and Wilson, *Ben.*, p. 15; *CBP*, no. 192), Tibertius and Valerian (Warner and Wilson, *Ben.*, p. 23; *CBP*, no. 153), Æthelthryth (see above, n. 86), Swithun (Warner and Wilson, *Ben.*, p. 39; *CBP*, no. 1088); All Saints (Warner and Wilson, *Ben.*, p. 42; *CBP*, no. 1743), etc.

[243] *CBP*, no. 1948; Warner and Wilson, *Ben.*, p. 43: "Et qui

eam . . . caelestem ad gloriam fecit cum triumpho scandere, ipse uos concedat . . . cum electis omnibus indui inmarcescibilis corona gloriae." See also the prayers for Stephen (*CBP*, no. 1948; Warner and Wilson, *Ben.*, pp. 5f.), Lawrence (*CBP*, no. 1948; Warner and Wilson, *Ben.*, p. 39), and Lent 1 (*CBP*, no. 192; Warner and Wilson, *Ben.*, p. 15).

[244] Deshman, "Anglo-Saxon Art after Alfred," pp. 178ff.

[245] M. Lapidge, *Anglo-Saxon Litanies of the Saints*, Henry Bradshaw Society, 106 (London, 1991).

[246] For a Winchester example, see Lapidge, *Litanies*, no. 21; also nos. 1, 4, 6, 7ii, 13, 15, 18, etc.

have been associated with the litany of the saints, if only because this was the most common form of devotion to the heavenly choirs. There is a close correlation between the saints singled out by name in the miniatures and the ones featured in litanies. The inscriptions on the pallia of the three foremost confessors identify them from left to right as Gregory, Benedict, and Cuthbert. In most Anglo-Saxon litanies Benedict heads the list of confessors, and Gregory and Cuthbert are seldom far down.[247] Although it might seem surprising to find Mary Magdalene given the greatest prominence in the choir of the virgins, she was in fact often featured in the list of virgins in litanies from Winchester and other English houses;[248] and Saint Æthelthryth, who occupies the second place of honor in the Benedictional, also ranked high in litanies.[249]

The central theme of the litany, the supplication of Christ and the saints, is also implicit in the depictions of Christ and the choirs and the dedication poem. The latter imagines Æthelwold with his flock pleading to the heavenly judge to spare them. It also says that the manuscript's benedictions were to sanctify and prepare him and his charges for the Judgment. Many of these benedictions commemorated a saint's feast day, and most of these hagiographic prayers requested the saint's aid and intercession, so that the believer might win God's blessing in this and/or the next world. The blessing for the translation of Saint Benedict, for instance, asks that the believer, "instructed by his [Benedict's] examples and . . . strengthened by his prayers," might pass unharmed through this life to join him in the next one.[250] Every saint celebrated in the feasts would have been understood to belong to one of the celestial choirs at the beginning of the manuscript, since these systematically encompassed all hagiographic categories. This is especially obvious in the case of Benedict, Gregory, and Æthelthryth who have feasts in the manuscript and are identified by

name in the choirs. Thus the prefatory cycle of the saints—at once the blessed crowned with eternal life and holy intercessors—portrays not only the final reward that the manuscript's benedictions held out to Æthelwold and his flock but also a means of achieving that blessed end.

This relation between the choirs and the liturgical feasts they preface once more reflects the influence of the Galba Psalter. The hagiographic entries in the metrical calendar that the first miniature (fig. 11) precedes and the second one (fig. 12) follows often laud in one way or another the saint's presence in heaven. The text for Saint Cyriacus (16 June), for instance, says that the martyr "reposes with his companions in eternity."[251] The pictures of the companies of saints in heaven can therefore be regarded as illustrations of the calendar of feasts they bracket. Indeed, the calendar itself is illustrated on the lower left corner of each verso with a figure of a saint (fig. 125),[252] an anonymous representative of the saints commemorated individually in the feast entries and collectively in the choir pictures. The Psalter gave the Benedictional's creators the idea of iconographically relating the feast pictures—some portraying an individual saint like the Psalter's calendar—to the prefatory choirs.

In the depictions of the Death and Coronation of the Virgin (pl. 34) and of Benedict (pl. 33) the saint winning or having won the crown of life is at once the intercessor and the model for those seeking the same prize. The link to the choirs is especially clear in the case of Benedict. In the choir he wears a crown like the one he holds in his feast picture—the reward awaiting those who supplicate and emulate him. Mary at her Coronation is the exemplar for female virgins. Thus it is highly meaningful that one of the heavenly choirs consists of female virgins and that most of them wear crowns similar to the one over Mary and her maids. As we shall see below, there is a possibility that Mary, whom the lit-

---

[247] For Winchester litanies, see Lapidge, *Litanies*, nos. 3i, 3ii, 8i, 8ii, 12, 42i. In the litany-like sequence in Æthelwold's office for All Saints, Benedict and Cuthbert respectively are the second and third of six confessors; Wulfstan, *Life*, p. lxxvi.

[248] For Winchester examples, see Lapidge, *Litanies*, nos. 8i, 8ii, 12, 21, 27, 46; also nos. 1, 7ii, 9i, 13, 18, 19, etc.

[249] For Winchester examples, see Lapidge, *Litanies*, nos. 8i, 8ii, 12, 21, 24, 27, 42i; also nos. 1, 2i, 13, 40. Æthelthryth

is the only virgin (other than the Virgin Mary) in the litanic sequence in Æthelwold's office for All Saints; Wulfstan, *Life*, p. lxxvi.

[250] See above, n. 60.

[251] Ed. P. McGurk, "The Metrical Calendar of Hampson. A New Edition," *Analecta Bollandiana* 104 (1986): 100: "Cum sociis martyr pausat Cyriacus in aeuum."

[252] Ohlgren, *Illustration*, pls. 1.2–1.13.

anies often addressed as the *virgo virginum*,[253] appeared crowned in the lost opening miniature of the manuscript. If this was so, then the theme of Mary as the exemplary queen of all virgins would have been visualized in the introductory cycle as well as in the feast picture.

The presence of Æthelthryth among the choir of virgins (pl. 3, left) reinforced this theme of Mariological emulation since in her feast picture the saint (pl. 28) imitates Mary's role as the virginal bride of Christ in heaven. In Bede's hymn,[254] which was an important source for the feast portrait, the saint is one of the choir of virgins ("amica cohors") who rejoice in Mary's part in the Incarnation and emulate her role as the royal virgin bride of Christ in heaven. The intertwined themes of Æthelthryth's participation in this celestial choir, which had the function of singing God's praises, and her Mariological role as Christ's bride are emphasized again in the poem's conclusion which envisions Æthelthryth in heaven playing a harp and singing to her spouse, the Lamb. In both the choir of virgins and the feast picture Æthelthryth holds an open gold book in her right arm and turns slightly to the right. The similarity called attention to the relation between the pictures, implying that she and the other virgins had attained their blessed celestial marriage to Christ through the imitation of the queen of all virgins.

If Æthelthryth's presence in the choir emphasized her emulation of the Virgin, then one might have expected that the saint would wear a crown, the attribute of eternal life associated with Mary and her imitators in the picture of Mary's Coronation. Curiously, however, Æthelthryth as well as Mary Magdalene, the most prominent and the only other named saint in the choir, are the only uncrowned virgins. Instead they have large and elaborately ornamented gold nimbi, an attribute that again contrasts them with the other figures on folio 2 who are unnimbed. The virgins in the other half of the choir on folio 1v (pl. 2) have both a crown and nimbus, but their haloes are blue and therefore less prestigious than the ornamented gold ones of Æthelthryth and the Magdalene.[255]

The most likely explanation is that the haloes of Æthelthryth and Mary Magdalene symbolize crowns of life, as in the All Saints illustration in the Fulda sacramentary (fig. 122), which shows only the saints holding or wearing a gold crown without a gold nimbus. It will be remembered that on the basis of Psalm 5:13 ("For thou wilt bless the just. Lord, thou hast crowned us, as with the shield of thy good will.") the haloes of divinely protected saints were interpreted as a form of "crown."[256] This symbolic concept also influenced the iconography of the Annunciation (pl. 8) in which the cloud nimbus of the Virgin Mary (=Ecclesia) represented the protective "shield" of Christ's divinity, deriving from his cloud mandorla (pl. 27). The application of this symbolism of the nimbus to Æthelthryth and the Magdalene placed them in a special relation to the Virgin Mary at the Incarnation and suggested that their preeminence among the virgins resulted from their particularly faithful emulation of the *virgo virginum*.[257]

Like Benedict, Æthelthryth and her companions in the choir were themselves models for salvation. The blessing for her feast sets the saint and the believers as parallel. As her steadfast chastity allowed her to join the "eternal king," so the believers with divine protection from lustful desire might also be allowed "to have in heaven the company of her."[258] Standing crowned with the protective "shield" of God's favor in the heavenly choir, the saint manifestly exemplifies the happy fate awaiting those whom God shields from sin in this life.

Although Æthelthryth and Benedict are named in choirs, this is not true in the case of the confessor Swithun, who is also honored with a feast portrait (pl. 32). Another group of confessors, however, would also have been portrayed in the lost miniature that once faced folio 1. This missing composition would have had a framework matching the one of the surviving half of the choir: a pair of arches supported by two

[253] For Winchester examples, see Lapidge, *Litanies*, nos. 8, 12, 15, 21, 46.

[254] See above, n. 90.

[255] Regarding the use of color to establish a hierarchy of nimbi, see C. Davis-Weyer and I. J. Emerick, "The Early Sixth-Century Frescoes at S. Martino ai Monti in Rome," *Römisches Jahrbuch für Kunstgeschichte* 21 (1984): 43.

[256] See above, chap. 2, n. 259.

[257] Regarding the association of the Magdalene and the Virgin, see D. Iogna-Prat, "Le Culte de la Vierge sous le règne de Charles le Chauve," *Les Cahiers de Saint-Michel de Cuxa* 23 (1992): 112f.

[258] See above, n. 86.

large flanking columns and a smaller central column like the one behind Benedict. The paired arches intersect a free-standing archlike baldachin raised on two slender columns—the architectural symbol of the dome of heaven, marking the sanctity of the saints beneath it. A similar baldachin appears over Swithun in his feast picture, and here also it intersects a pair of arches supported by the central and outer columns of the frame. Since this exact combination of ciborium and frame appears no where else in the manuscript, it is all but certain that Swithun appeared in both his feast picture and the lost choir miniature. The resemblance between the two pictures would have been a calculated means to show that the saint individually celebrated in the feast belonged to the celestial choir of confessors. Swithun's presence among this group of heavenly intercessors would have underlined the sentiment of his feast benediction: that through his support and intercession the believer "might be found worthy to be joined to him in the heavenly realm."[259]

Swithun's feast portrait and the confessors' miniature share one additional architectural feature, a central column behind the figure(s). In Swithun's case this symbolically portrayed him as a spiritual "column" of the Church. Like him, the confessors are assimilated to the form of the column behind them. The trefoil terminations of their crowns mirror the acanthus of the capitals, and the rigid straight lines of their pallia and gold hems are architectonic. Since Swithun was undoubtedly included in the missing half of the choir, the column of the confessors must have had the same symbolic meaning as the one in his feast picture.[260]

The miniatures of the choir of the virgins also include central columns which are all but replaced by their bodies. If the confessors are represented as "columns" of the Ecclesia, which included all the saints and Christ, then one would expect the same of the other choirs of saints who are also part of this spiritual living edifice. The absence of columns behind the apostles (pls. 4–7), whom Christ specifically called "columns" (Gal. 2:9), does not undermine

the case for the ecclesiastic architectural symbolism in the preceding pictures. We have previously noted that these four miniatures of the apostles also differ in other ways from the antecedent choirs, and we have argued that there was another set of apostles among the missing miniatures of the choirs. Possibly this two-page composition of the *chorus apostolorum* as well as all the other lost pictures of the choirs included the symbolic central column.

The source of this architectural symbolism was the Galba Psalter, which used a building to symbolize the heavenly cities of Bethlehem and Jerusalem (fig. 11) and the Christological cornerstone and foundation of Ecclesia (fig. 12). In the Benedictional the column replaced the building, but the underlying meaning remained the same: the architecture is equivalent to the choirs of the saints, symbolizing their union with Christ in the spiritual edifice of the heavenly Church and the celestial Jerusalem (cf. Eph. 2:14–22). The kinship between the column and the cornerstone is evident in the Benedictional's scenes of the Presentation in the Temple and the Bishop Blessing (pls. 20, 35). These combined the two architectural motifs to create another type of living column that was animated by the base rather than the shaft.[261]

Were other narrative Christological feast pictures besides the Presentation iconographically associated with the choirs? Before addressing this question, it is important to realize that for this too the Galba Psalter offered a precedent.

In addition to the choir pictures, the Psalter included narrative miniatures of the Nativity and the Ascension (figs. 10, 53). It will be recalled that the figures of Christ, Mary, and the apostles in the latter are mirrored in the choir miniatures. These resemblances characterized the Ascension not only as a prefiguration of the Last Judgment (cf. Acts 1:11) but also as a precondition of the establishment of the Church in heaven. The elevation of Christ's human nature to heaven opened the way for humanity to join him and the angels in the celestial Jerusalem (cf. 1 Cor. 15:20–24; Hebrews 12:22–24). The Nativity with its crib-altar depicts the Incarnation

---

[259] *CBP*, no. 1088; Wulfstan, *Life*, pp. lxxxif.; Warner and Wilson, *Ben.*, p. 39: "illi in caelesti regione mereamini adiungi."

[260] One obvious difference, the angel over the confessors, will be discussed below.

[261] The alignment of the Christ child with the column might also be significant, however, since he could also be associated symbolically with the column. See Deshman, "Living Ecclesia," p. 262, pl. 2.

when Christ began his mission on earth and established his Church there, and its sacrificial, eucharistic theme resonates in the miniature of the choirs, the celestial counterpart of the terrestrial Church. Christ's exposed wounds and the instruments of the Passion recall his death, and the offerings of angels and the patriarchs allude to the Eucharist sacrifice carried up from earth to be offered to him in heaven. Together the Psalter's four miniatures encapsulate the economy of salvation: the earthly mission of the incarnate Christ that founded the terrestrial and celestial Ecclesia, the institution which joined all the saints to him in heaven. The other members of the Church on earth could achieve union with him now through the Eucharist; and with the intercession of the Church—that is, the choirs of the saints whom they petitioned in the litany—they might join him in heaven after the Last Judgment.

The Benedictional advanced beyond the Psalter by extending the architectural symbolism from the heavenly choirs to Christological narrative scenes. The column associated the choirs not only directly with the miniatures of Swithun and the Presentation but also indirectly with other feast pictures that used different means to visualize the underlying theme of the living spiritual Church. In the case of three of these—the Nativity, the Presentation, and the Entry into Jerusalem (pls. 12, 20, 21)—we have previously discovered that their architectural symbolism derived, like that of the prefatory cycle, from the Galba Psalter, and this makes it plain that all these images in the Benedictional are programmatically interrelated.

These three narrative Christological miniatures figuratively or literally depicted the Church, the temple, or Jerusalem as symbols of both the terrestrial and the celestial Church and the heavenly city. This symbolism draws them into an allegorical relationship with the prefatory cycle of saints who literally embody the columnar fabric of the celestial Jerusalem and the heavenly Church. The relationship reveals how these events of Christ's life established the universal Church, which encompassed heaven and earth and joined him to all believing Jews and Gentiles, past and present. At the same time the architectural symbolism emphasized that membership in the heavenly choirs and edification in the celestial city and Church were the rewards awaiting those who had already become a *domus Dei* in their earthly existence through their virtuous daily life and their participation in sanctifying liturgical rites.

As in the Galba Psalter, the choirs of both Jewish and Christian saints that in all probability originally began the Benedictional comprised the celestial *ecclesia ex synagogia et gentibus*, and both the Nativity and the Presentation included terrestrial counterparts, symbols of animate ecclesiastic architecture representing the union of the two peoples in a spiritual house of God. The Entry into Jerusalem, however, visualized the relation to the choirs somewhat differently: the figures before Christ in Jerusalem and following after him correspond respectively to the believing Jews and Gentiles.

In the prefatory cycle the organization of the citizens of the celestial city into choirs was intrinsically bound up with the idea that they joined the inhabitants of earth in a continuous song of universal praise and thanksgiving to the Deity, and all three feast pictures had similar connotations. In the case of the Nativity one of the prefacing benedictions[262] evoked the traditional exegesis that the angels' hymn of peace and goodwill to the shepherds (Luke 2:13–14) signified that Christ's incarnational advent as the cornerstone had restored the harmony and the unity between men and angels. In the Entry the groups before and after Christ singing the same hymn were also taken to indicate that his coming as the cornerstone reunited inhabitants of heaven and earth in a common hymn of faith to him. Most striking of all, however, is the Presentation miniature which is preceded by a blessing of the candles.[263] This text, the only liturgical one in the manuscript that is not a pontifical mass benediction, entreats Christ in heaven to listen beneficently—through the invocation of his name and the intercession of the Virgin and all the saints—to the pleas and the songs of praise of the congregation in the Candlemas procession, the liturgical reenactment of the entrance of Christ and the Virgin into the temple of Jerusalem. Readers of this text would have been reminded of the beginning of the manuscript, which originally depicted Christ,

---

[262] See above, chap. 1, n. 89.

[263] See above, chap. 2, n. 177.

the Virgin (as we shall see below), and all the choirs of saints singing his accolades and, as a pictorial litany,[264] interceding for humanity. In various ways these three feast pictures portrayed Christ's advents as the events that united the members of Ecclesia in heaven and earth, eventually enabling those below to join those above.

The prefatory cycle is also related to the feast picture for the Dedication of the Church (pl. 35), yet another miniature which equated the consecrated building and altar of the church with the members of the congregation who individually and collectively are temples of God. Here too there were strong overtones of the allegorical relationship of the church and its congregation to the heavenly Jerusalem. The lection of Apocalypse 21:2–5 in the dedication ceremony implied that on this occasion the new bride of Jerusalem descended from heaven and virtually merged with its earthly counterpart, the newly consecrated church.

The saints played a large role in this rite. The Benedictional's blessing for the day says that the intercession of the dedication saint and the other saints, whose relics were venerated in the church, helps to purify the believers and make them the "temple" and dwelling place of God, so that they merit "eternal joy."[265] The prayer recalled in this way the earlier parts of the ceremony when the intercessory litany of the saints had twice been chanted and the relics of the dedication saint had been translated into the new church.[266] Thus the saints in the pictorial litany at the beginning of the manuscript assisted in the edification of the believers represented at the end of the book. Depicted as the living embodiment of the heavenly Jerusalem and Church, the saints intercede so that the faithful below might become their terrestrial reflection, an earthly *domus Dei*, and might attain "eternal joy."

This "eternal joy" would have been understood as admission to the ranks of the saints in heaven. This is spelled out in an alternate episcopal benediction for the dedication of the church in the Winchester Benedictional of Archbishop Robert:

> [O Lord,] bless the bodies and souls of them [the congregation], so that in the company of the saints they might receive heavenly benediction. . . .
>
> And as you blessed the patriarchs and prophets, the apostles, the martyrs, and confessors, virgins and priests, so bless, O Lord, this flock of yours.[267]

In the Dedication miniature the liturgical blessing that the members of the congregation receive in the terrestrial church foreshadows and facilitates the future blessing of eternal life that they will receive with the saints in heaven. In relation to the miniature of the Dedication of the Church, the saints of the prefatory cycle, literally edified into the new Jerusalem, once more assume the dual role of heavenly intercessors and archetypes for the earthly members of the congregation who similarly embody Ecclesia.

The thematic relations between the choirs and the Dedication miniature are visually expressed in various ways. We have mentioned above that the column overlapped by the altar in the latter alludes to the columnar symbolism of the saints. It should not be overlooked, however, that the symbolic central columns in the choir miniatures and also in the Presentation and Saint Swithun are intregral parts of the arched columnar frames of the pictures. This implies that the entire frame and not just the central column symbolized the Church. The symbolic placement of Christ as the ecclesiastic cornerstone in the corner of the frame of the Nativity suggests that this rectangular framework too had ecclesiological significance, even though it is less like architecture than the arched columnar frames. The Dedication miniature made the ecclesiastic symbolism of the frames explicit, for here the figures are framed by the architecture of the

---

[264] The litany of the saints was commonly chanted during processions, though evidently not in Palm Sunday and Candelmas processions; see Lapidge, *Litanies*, pp. 8ff., 46ff.

[265] See above, n. 206.

[266] *Ben. Rob.*, pp. 73–76, 96–97; also Lapidge, *Litanies*, p. 83, no. 42.

[267] *CBP*, no. 1429; *Ben. Rob.*, p. 99: "bendic corpora et animas eorum, ut in consortio sanctorum accipiant benedictionem caelestem. . . . Et sicut benedixisti patriarchas et prophetas, apostolos, martyres, et confessores, uirgines et sacerdotes, sic benedic domine gregem istum." Preceding this prayer is the one found in our manuscript. See also the dedication hymn *Urbs Beata Hierusalem*, 8, ed. Blume, *Analecta Hymnica*, 51, p. 111.

church itself rather than by the usual foliate borders.[268] Another linking motif is the archlike baldachin over the blessing bishop, and the choir of the confessors as well as Saint Swithun in the related feast picture. In the Dedication scene this architectural motif referred to the spiritual altar of the heart within the living temple of the bishop's body, and the baldachin probably also had similar connotations for the confessors and Swithun, who are also symbolically identified with another architectural component of Ecclesia, the column. It was particularly appropriate for the blessing bishop to be likened to Swithun and the other confessors, for it was this category of saint that the bishop (Æthelwold) sought to join in heaven.[269]

The baldachin, in fact, was one of the most common leitmotifs in the cycle. A ciborium over the Virgin in both the Annunciation and the Adoration of the Magi (pls. 8, 18) emphasized her ecclesiological significance. The one over Saint Benedict in his feast picture (pl. 33) must have had connotations of the heavenly Jerusalem and Church, for he is portrayed as the winner of eternal heavenly life. Since he is also centered beneath a baldachin in the choir of the confessors, the architecture (as well as the crown) associates the two pictures, much as it must have linked Swithun's portrait with the other, missing page of confessors.

The ciborium of the confessors also covers the angel above them. Moreover, the angels over the apostles on folios 2v and 3 (pls. 4, 5) all have their own truncated baldachin, and perhaps the double arches above the flying angels on folios 3v and 4 (pls. 6, 7) should also be understood as ciboria. The relation between the angels and this architecture brings us to the broader issue of the function of these celestial beings in the introductory cycle.[270]

Hovering above the saints and apostles, the angels indicated that these elect members of humanity had won the joyful heavenly existence that only the angels had been privileged to enjoy before Christ's Incarnation (cf. Luke 20:36). The same idea later inspired the interspersing of angels among the crowned saints in heaven in the Romanesque *Hortus Deliciarum* (fig. 126).[271] As in the Galba Psalter, a choir of angels must originally have begun the sequence of choirs in the Benedictional, and these and the other angels over the saints would have been viewed in relation to several of the manuscript's prayers that express the wish that the faithful after death might join the angels or even the "singing choirs of angels."[272] At the same time, the representation of angels reinforced the symbolism of the Nativity and the Entry into Jerusalem (pls. 12, 21) which implied that Christ's advent made peace between men on earth and the angels, enabling them to sing in harmony to Christ and providing humanity the means to replenish the depleted ranks of the angels in heaven. The depiction of angels, saints, the Virgin, Christ, and the blessing bishop beneath baldachins visualized their common membership in the Church encompassing heaven and earth. As Ælfric said in his homily on the dedication of the church, "all angels and all righteous men are his [God's] temple."[273]

In the prefatory miniatures the saints, the apostles, and the angels all appear in clouds. In addition to indicating the heavenly setting, the clouds probably also possessed some of the same symbolic values they did in the feast pictures. Most of the figures hold books or scrolls, and some gesture in speech and benediction; their attributes and gestures suggest that the surrounding clouds are symbols of the figures themselves, whose divinely illuminated, heav-

---

[268] Confirmation that the frames and the church were meant as cognate symbolic forms is provided by the evangelist portraits of the late-tenth-century Arenberg Gospels. J. Rosenthal, "Arenberg Evangelists," pp. 150ff., figs. 1–4, 12, has observed that their columnar frames incorporate architectural features similar to those of the Benedictional's church in order to invest them with ecclesiolgical meaning.

[269] After his death, Æthelwold was often among the confessors petitioned in litanies; see Lapidge, *Litanies*, nos. 6, 8ii, 9i, etc.

[270] Angels were often represented in the arches and pedi-

ments of canon tables; cf. Ohlgren, *Illustration*, pls. 5.1, 5.4, 5.8, 5.10, 6.2, etc.

[271] R. Green et al., *Hortus Deliciarum*, Studies of the Warburg Institute, 36 (London, 1979), 1, pp. 214f.; 2, pl. 137 (fol. 244). The text explained that the saints in heaven will receive crowns and be equal to the angels.

[272] Michael 1 and 2 (*CBP*, nos. 1501, 342; Warner and Wilson, *Ben.*, p. 42), and the Invention of the Cross (*CBP*, no. 310; Warner and Wilson, *Ben.*, p. 23) Pentecost 10/1 (*CBP*, no. 921; Warner and Wilson, *Ben.*, p. 31).

[273] Ælfric, *Hom.*, 2, p. 581.

enly words of preaching and intercession rain celestial blessings on humanity below on earth. The clouds are another leitmotif relating the preliminary cycle to the feast pictures, which often portray a cloud-filled terrestrial scene.

Our comprehension of the choirs and their relationship to the feast pictures would have been much more complete had the first miniature in the manuscript survived. This must have been a representation of Christ which would have been the focus of the following pictures of the saints. We can never know for certain what it looked like, but certain surmises are possible.

Christ was very likely not alone in the composition. Since the Virgin is absent from the choir of the virgins,[274] she must have been represented elsewhere in the opening miniatures. As the queen of heaven, she ranked above all the saints and angels.[275] She was occasionally portrayed as the *regina angelorum* leading the choir of the angels, as in the Fulda sacramentary in Udine (fig. 122). While it is conceivable that in our manuscript she might have been included in one of the missing miniatures of the choir of angels, abundant evidence suggests that she was with Christ himself in the very first miniature.

Because she was such an important intercessor, the litanies almost always placed her immediately after Christ, ahead of all the angels and saints.[276] She also occupies this place in the sequence of saints in the poem on All Saints written by Æthelwold's student Wulfstan.[277] In Byzantine images of the Last Judgment (fig. 123), which might have influenced the choir miniatures, the Virgin has a comparable position: along with John the Baptist she invariably flanks Christ in the intercessory group of the

Deesis. A variant of this iconography occurs in Anglo-Saxon art. In the Last Judgment on the eleventh-century ivory in Cambridge (fig. 68)[278] the crowned Virgin stands to the left of Christ while Peter with his key substitutes for the Baptist on the right, and the same intercessory group appears in the dedication miniature of the Liber Vitae of New Minster (fig. 97).[279] Several Old English homilies singled out Mary and Peter (together with Michael) as special intercessors at the Last Judgment.[280] Æthelwold himself seems to have had a particular regard for them. The foundation charter of Thorney (ca. 973–975) recorded that he dedicated the church to the Trinity and his favorite intercessory saints, Mary, Peter, and Benedict;[281] and in Æthelwold's *Regularis Concordia*[282] the prayer on the occasion of a monk's death requests the intercession of the same trio and also all saints. The Virgin and Peter could have quite appropriately flanked Christ in the first miniature.

More likely, however, Mary appeared with the entire Trinity. This group would have been just as suitable as the Insular Deesis as the focal point of the sequence of heavenly choirs. Many Anglo-Saxon litanies began with the supplication of the Trinity followed by the Virgin.[283] Already in the illustration of the Te Deum in the Utrecht Psalter (fig. 80) the choirs of saints adore the Trinity, and in the Psalter's drawing of the Apostolic Creed (figs. 29, 30) the Trinity and the Virgin preside over a kind of Last Judgment. As we have seen, the latter composition influenced the Benedictional's symbolic association of the Virgin in the Annunciation (pl. 8) with the multivalent Octave initial (pl. 27), which represented both the triune Godhead and Christ the Judge.

---

[274] Wormald, *Ben.*, p. 16, proposed that one of the anonymous virgins on fol. 1v is the Virgin Mary. Unlike the Magdalene and Æthelthryth on fol. 2, none of these figures has an inscribed book, a gold tunic, or a gold halo, and it is unthinkable that the Virgin would not have been singled out like the two lesser virgins. See also above, n. 226.

[275] Scheffczyk, *Mariengeheimnis*, pp. 466ff.; F. Rademacher, *Die Regina Angelorum in der Kunst des frühen Mittelalters*, Die Kunstdenkmäler des Rheinlandes, 17 (Düsseldorf, 1972).

[276] For Winchester examples, see Lapidge, *Litanies*, nos. 3i, 3ii, 8i, 12, 15, etc.

[277] F. Dolbeau, "Le *Breviloquium de omnibus sanctis*: un poème inconnu de Wulfstan, chantre de Winchester," *Analecta Bollandiana* 106 (1988): 66–68. See also Clayton, *Cult*, p. 120.

[278] See above, chap. 2, nn. 99, 100.

[279] Regarding these examples of the "Insular Deesis," see

Deshman, "*Benedictus*," pp. 223f.; E. H. Kantorowicz, "Ivories and Litanies," *Journal of the Warburg and Courtauld Institutes* 5 (1942): 78. O'Reilly, "Text and Image," pp. 78ff., questions whether Mary and Peter need be considered as a variant of the Deesis, but offers no clear alternative function for them on the ivory. Peter's intercessory role in the Liber Vitae is evident from the donor portrait's close association with the Last Judgment (fig. 69) where he, again with his key, plays a dominant role.

[280] M. Clayton, "Delivering the Damned: A Motif in Old English Homiletic Prose," *Medium Ævum* 55 (1986): 92ff.; Clayton, *Cult*, pp. 254ff.

[281] See above, n. 149.

[282] *RC*, 102, p. 145.

[283] For Winchester examples, see Lapidge, *Litanies*, nos. 8i, 8ii, 12, 15, 21, 27, 40, 46.

Later, the Quinity drawing in the New Minster Prayerbook (fig. 27) as well as the Grimbald Gospels depicted the Trinity and the incarnational Virgin (figs. 92, 93). In the latter manuscript they are even enthroned above choirs of saints in the frame of the initial page of the prologue of the Gospel of John. The form of the Trinity there owes more to the Benedictional's Trinitarian initial than to the Carolingian Psalter, and we may well ask whether the Benedictional's prefatory cycle also originally combined the Trinity and Mary with the choirs of the saints.

Another look at the dedication poem provides some corroboration. In his imagined address to the "Judge who sifts the actions of the whole world," Æthelwold asks that his flock might enjoy heavenly life

> "with the supreme sovereign whose members we are, who by right is the head and salvation of those baptized in the clear-sounding name of the Father and of the Son and of the Holy Ghost, so that, if they wander not astray but hold the faith, and . . . repel all heresy from their hearts, . . . they may be joined to the Lord in heaven without end." May Christ the Saviour, who is good King of the world, mercifully grant this to all who are sprinkled with holy baptism.[284]

The repeated coupling of the kingship of Christ and baptism would have alluded to the miniature of the Baptism (pl. 19) where Christ is invested with royal insignia. The poem also intertwined these two themes with those of the Trinity and non-heretical belief, evoking the baptismally related iconography of the Octave initial: the crowned Trinitarian figure of Christ, the perpetual vision of the heavenly ruler and judge who will reward those who do not stray from the orthodox Trinitarian beliefs of the Creed professed in baptism and the mass.[285]

We have discovered that the deliberate repetition of similar iconographic motifs in the extant miniatures of the prefatory cycle and the feast pictures visualized the relationship between them. Although it can never be conclusively proven, the dedication poem and the Grimbald Gospels provide circumstantial evidence that this practice might also have been followed in the lost opening miniature by representing the Virgin with some version of the initial's Trinitarian iconography. It cannot be determined whether the three persons of the Trinity were portrayed collectively, as in the initial, or individually, as in the Grimbald Gospels or the Winchester "Quinity." The emphasis on kingship in the dedication and the extant miniatures might lead one to speculate that the Virgin and perhaps the Trinity were crowned.[286] Finally, however, all that can be safely said is that there were any number of ways in which the opening miniature could have incorporated iconographic features of Christ and the Virgin found elsewhere in the manuscript.

Conclusions

Derived from the Galba Psalter and possibly a Byzantine Last Judgment, the sequence of the choirs and the apostles probably began with an image of the Trinity and the Virgin. These prefatory miniatures, like those in the Galba Psalter, portrayed the Last Judgment, the litany of the saints, and the celestial Church and Jerusalem. In the Benedictional, however, this complex subject matter was adapted to illustrate the dedication poem, representing the final reward that the manuscript's liturgical benedictions promised to the members of the terrestrial Church: celestial union with Christ, the angels, and all the saints. The principle of relating this heavenly imagery to hagiographic feast portraits and historical scenes of Christ's life also originated in the Galba Psalter, but the Benedictional vastly extended the scope and complexity of the

---

[284] See above, n. 240.

[285] The dedication's description of Æthelwold "as the steward" desiring "to render full fruit to God, when the Judge . . . shall come" also alluded to the themes of the related pictures of the Second Coming (pl. 10) and the Entry

(pl. 21) with its eschatologically symbolic offering of flowers to Christ.

[286] The Virgin is crowned in both the Quinity drawing and the Cambridge ivory.

related subject matter to include additional New Testament themes, hagiographic scenes, and liturgical rites—virtually the entire cycle of feast pictures.

Yet the illustration of the manuscript was structured to emphasize the essentials of the program. Marking the beginning and end of the feast cycle are the typologically related miniatures of the Annunciation, which first brought Christ and his blessings to mankind, and the Bishop Blessing the Congregation, which continues to bring him to the Church. These past and present unions between Christ and humanity prefigured and prepared for the final union between Christ and the choirs of the elect in the heavenly Church and city. The prefatory cycle ensured that this celestial goal first met the eye of whoever opened "this book of the coming of the Son of the loving Father."[287]

[287] It remains an unsolved mystery why the apostles appear after the choir of virgins, evidently for the second time in the series.

Chapter Four

THE SOURCES

AND STRUCTURE OF

THE CYCLE

IN THIS CHAPTER we shall consider what types of works contained the models for the pictures and how these works influenced the selection and arrangement of the miniatures.

The Metz Model

One basic source was a later Metz work closely related to and contemporary with the prototype of the Brunswick casket. Thanks to the casket, we know that this lost Metz exemplar included the models for the Annunciation, the Nativity, and the Baptism. The Metz cycle, however, must have been more extensive. The Benedictional's Women at the Tomb certainly copied a later Metz scene, and still other miniatures are related to Metz iconography: the manner of revealing the wound in Christ's side at the Doubting of Thomas first occurred in the Drogo Sacramentary; this Metz manuscript is also an important precedent for the Benedictional's use of the servant and the group of the Virgin and child to associate the illustrations for the Octave of Christmas, Epiphany, and the Purification of the Virgin; the motif of palm-bearing figures behind Christ at the Entry is found in a later Metz ivory, as is the rhythmic procession of the Magi. All these depictions of subjects from the Gos-

pels, as well as the miniature of the Ascension, which also had a Carolingian source, must have derived to a greater or lesser extent from the Metz model.

Carolingian art also influenced three other pictures, not based on the Gospels: the Stoning of Stephen, Pentecost, and the Bishop Blessing the Congregation. Both narrative scenes illustrate the Acts of the Apostles, but this does not necessarily imply that these and the Gospel scenes stemmed from different Carolingian works. Any type of liturgical book organized according to the ecclesiastic year—a sacramentary, lectionary, or benedictional, for instance—could have been illustrated with "polycylic" miniatures, that is, with a cycle that brought together pictures originally based on different texts such as the Gospels and Acts.[1] Indeed, the picture cycle of the Drogo Sacramentary includes the two themes from Acts as well as most of the others depicted in the Benedictional.[2] The Acts illustrations in the two

[1] Regarding this type of mixed picture cycle, see K. Weitzmann, *Illustrations in Roll and Codex*, 2nd ed., Studies in Manuscript Illumination, 2 (Princeton, 1970), pp. 139ff.

[2] The illustrated feasts common to the two manuscripts are: Christmas, Stephen, John the evangelist, the Saturday after Christmas (the miniature of the Massacre of the Inno-

manuscripts have some specific resemblances: the dove descending in a mandorla at Pentecost, a motif which first appeared in the Sacramentary, and the full-length Christ with angels at the Stoning of Stephen. The heterogeneous textual sources of the Anglo-Saxon scenes with Carolingian, often Metz, features support the conclusions of both Homburger and Wormald[3] that the Benedictional copied an illustrated Metz liturgical book.

The picture of the Bishop Blessing the Congregation must have had a model associated with a collection of episcopal benedictions, probably as a frontispiece. Yet the Metz exemplar need not have been a benedictional extensively illustrated with New Testament scenes as well as with a picture of the episcopal blessing. This type of illustrated benedictional is a great rarity. Æthelwold's manuscript is the very first surviving example. Only three others with a cycle of feast pictures dated before the fourteenth century are known to me, and two of these were inspired directly or indirectly by our manuscript. The first, a reduced cycle of full-page miniatures illustrating the blessings in the eleventh-century Winchester Benedictional of Archbishop Robert (figs. 211, 212, 213), is a direct copy.[4] The second, a benedictional (Ivrea, Biblioteca Capitolare, MS XVIII [8]) with a cycle of eight New Testament and hagiographic miniatures, was made in the late tenth century in the scriptorium of Bishop Warmund of Ivrea (963–ca. 1001).[5] Its Nativity

composition with the crib and animals in the left corner beneath the slanting bed (fig. 127) obviously reflects an Anglo-Saxon model related to the Benedictional (pl. 12). Ivrea in northern Italy was on the pilgrimage route between England and Rome. Archbishop Sigeric of Canterbury stopped there on his return from Rome where he had received his pallium from the pope in 990,[6] about the time the Italian benedictional was made. Sigeric or another Anglo-Saxon traveler must have brought along an illustrated English benedictional which influenced the Italian scriptorium. The third benedictional, now in Malibu (J. Paul Getty Mus., MS Ludwig VII 1), was made in Regensburg ca. 1025–1050 for Bishop Engilmar of Parenzo.[7] This book exhibits no trace of Anglo-Saxon influence, and its cycle of seven full-page New Testament feast pictures seems to have been independently patterned on those in Ottonian lectionaries and sacramentaries.

Even unillustrated benedictionals were not all that common before the tenth century. In the Carolingian period pontifical benedictions were not normally isolated in a separate book, that is, in a benedictional, but were included in a sacramentary or a pontifical.[8] This is the case in the ninth-century Turonian Raganaldus sacramentary in which the section with the episcopal benedictions is prefaced by an illustration of the blessing rite (fig. 119).[9] The Drogo Sacramentary, which also contains episcopal benedictions, does not happen to depict this particular

cents has been lost from the Benedictional), the Octave of Christmas, Epiphany, the Purification of the Virgin, Palm Sunday, Easter, the first Sunday after Easter, Ascension day, Pentecost Sunday, the Birth of John the Baptist, and Peter and Paul. The Baptism and the Annunciation, which were assuredly in the Metz cycle, are not in the Sacramentary, but the former is represented on one of its covers (fig. 40) and the latter in an initial of another Metz manuscript. See Koehler, *Kar. Min.*, 3, pl. 71a.

[3] O. Homburger, "L'Art carolingien de Metz et 'l'école de Winchester,'" *Gazette des Beaux-Arts* 105, 2 (1963): 42; F. Wormald, "Continental Influence on English Medieval Illumination," *Transactions of the Fourth International Congress of Bibliophiles, 1965* (London, 1967), p. 8.

[4] See Appendix Three.

[5] F. dell' Ordo, "Le benedictiones episcopales del codice warmondiano (Ivrea, bibl. capit., cod. 10 [XX])," *Archiv für Liturgiewissenschaft* 12 (1970): 154ff.; M. A. Mazzoli Casagrande, "I codici warmondiana e la cultura a Ivrea fra IX e XI secolo," *Richerche medievali* 6–9 (1971–74): 94–96.

[6] V. Ortenberg, "Archbishop Sigeric's Journey to Rome in 990," *ASE* 19 (1990): 199, 230f., 238, no. 45; idem, *The English*

Church and the Continent in the Tenth and Eleventh Centuries (Oxford, 1992), pp. 103–105.

[7] See above, chap. 3, n. 204. An eleventh-century Lorsch benedictional in Paris (Bibl. Sainte-Geneviève, MS 2657) opens with three full-page miniatures of Christ enthroned, two standing saints, and Christ standing. See H. Hoffmann, *Buchkunst und Königtum im ottonischen und frühsalischen Reich* (Stuttgart, 1986), Textband, pp. 214f.; A. Boinet, "Les Manuscrits à peintures de la Bibliothèque Sainte-Geneviève de Paris," *Bulletin de la Société Française de Reproductions des Manuscrits à Peintures* 5 (1921): 18f., pl. 2.

[8] See K. Gamber, *Codices Liturgici Latini Antiquiores*, 2nd ed. (Freiburg, 1968), 1, pp. 183–86; *CBP*, 3, pp. 37–102; also J. Baudot, "Bénédictionnaire," *Dictionnaire de Archéologie Chrétienne et de Liturgie*, 2, 1, cols. 727ff.; J. Brückmann, "Latin Manuscript Pontificals and Benedictionals in England and Wales," *Traditio* 29 (1973): 391ff.; also H. Gneuss, "Liturgical Books in Anglo-Saxon England and their Old English Terminology," *Learning and Literature in Anglo-Saxon England*, ed. M. Lapidge and H. Gneuss (Cambridge, 1985), pp. 133f.

[9] See above, chap. 3, n. 204.

ceremony, but it does portray a number of other liturgical rites.[10] It is quite possible that the Benedictional's Metz exemplar was a sacramentary with a picture of episcopal blessing as well as New Testament scenes. Alternatively, the source of the Bishop Blessing could have been an otherwise unillustrated Carolingian benedictional, while the source of the New Testament scenes was a different type of Metz liturgical manuscript. Given the existence of the extensively illustrated Drogo Sacramentary, the Metz manuscript exemplar of the Benedictional was in all probability a sacramentary—with or without a picture of the blessing ceremony.

The conclusion that the Benedictional copied a Metz illuminated manuscript is not inconsistent with the fact that ivory carvings offer the closest comparisons to the Anglo-Saxon paintings. In the Metz school there was an extremely close relationship between the two media. Many illuminated Metz manuscripts had ivory covers[11] and the same artisans might well have worked in both media. The sketchy style of some of the earlier Metz ivories, such as the covers of the Drogo Sacramentary (fig. 40), betrays a dependence on painted models.[12] A later Metz carver with a style very similar indeed to that of the Brunswick casket used the Utrecht Psalter and other illuminated manuscripts as models for the reliefs on the throne of Charles the Bald in St. Peter's.[13] On the casket itself the illusionistic treatment of the partially submerged bodies

of Christ and John (fig. 34) is a pictorial effect more at home in painting than in sculpture. The casket and many other later Metz ivories very probably copied contemporary manuscripts illuminated in the same workshop.[14]

Many of the Benedictional's miniatures reveal that the scenes in its Metz prototype were wide, striplike compositions which had to be adjusted to a new, full-page format. The horizontal format was a traditional one for narrative pictures[15] and was sometimes used for New Testament cycles in Carolingian manuscripts (figs. 5, 14, 73).[16] The New Testament illustrations in extant Metz manuscripts are all in the format of historiated initials,[17] but an astrological manuscript in Madrid,[18] probably done in Metz, is illustrated with horizontal compositions. This format is common in the Gospel scenes on the workshop's ivories (figs. 13, 24, 71, 205, 207); thus, it appears to be a chance of preservation that Metz manuscripts with New Testament pictures in this format have not come down to us.

If the Metz exemplar was a sacramentary, how might such horizontal pictures have been arranged in the text? In the Drogo Sacramentary the illustration for a feast is usually located in the first word of the day's text; hence, a strip picture would probably have been placed at the head of the text for the principal mass of a feast day, as in late-tenth-century Fulda sacramentaries (figs. 20, 21, 94, 108).[19]

The Byzantine Model

The second basic source of the Benedictional was Byzantine art. This was a major influence on the Entry into Jerusalem, the Second Com-

ing, Pentecost, the Martyrdoms of Peter and Paul, and possibly the choirs of the saints, and a minor one on the Ascension, the Stoning of Ste-

[10] *Drogo-Sak.*, fols. 46v, 48v, 51v, 54. See also its ivory covers; Goldschmidt, *Elf.*, 1, no. 74, pl. 30.

[11] Goldschmidt, *Elf.*, 1, pp. 38f.

[12] Goldschmidt, *Elf.*, 1, p. 38.

[13] K. Weitzmann, "The Iconography of the Carolingian Ivories of the Throne," *La Cattedra lignea di S. Pietro in Vaticano*, Atti della Pontificia Accademia Romana di Archeologia, ser. 3, Memorie 10 (Vatican City, 1971), pp. 217ff.

[14] Koehler, *Kar. Min.*, 3, p. 106, believed that Metz for the most part ceased producing illuminated books after Drogo's death in 855, but Koehler did not take into account the many late Metz ivories that must have covered lost luxury Metz manuscripts.

[15] Weitzmann, *Roll and Codex*, pp. 47ff.

[16] W. Koehler, "An Illustrated Evangelistary of the Ada School and its Model," *Journal of the Warburg and Courtauld Institutes* 15 (1952): 48–66; idem, *Kar. Min.*, 2, pp. 47f., pl. 32c.

[17] Koehler, *Kar. Min.*, 3, pls. 71, 74, 80–91. Because of this discrepancy, Alexander, "Ben.," p. 181, has questioned the idea that the Benedictional's model was a Metz sacramentary.

[18] Koehler, *Kar. Min.*, 3, pp. 119ff., pls. 53–60.

[19] A. Comoretto, *Le miniature del sacramentario fuldense di Udine* (Udine, 1988), figs. 20–29, 43, 46, 48, 49, 51–53.

phen, and the Women at the Tomb. These pictures are based on a variety of texts. The Entry, the Women at the Tomb, and the Ascension illustrated the Gospels; Pentecost and the Stoning of Stephen depended on Acts; and the Martyrdoms of Peter and Paul and the Anastasis (a source of the Second Coming) derived from apocrypha. Obviously Winchester illuminators did not have illustrated Byzantine copies of all these texts. Much more plausible is Weitzmann's suggestion that a Greek Gospel lectionary influenced them.[20]

The lectionary divided the Gospels into liturgical readings arranged according to the feast calendar. As the most important middle Byzantine liturgical book, the lectionary was often lavishly decorated with a series of full-page pictures prefacing the great feasts.[21] Among the standard feast pictures were the Entry into Jerusalem, the Ascension, the Anastasis, and Pentecost. It is no accident that the miniatures of the latter two themes in the tenth-century Byzantine lectionary fragment in St. Petersburg offer excellent comparisons for the Anglo-Saxon miniatures of the Second Coming and Pentecost (pls. 10, 26, figs. 59, 84). The picture cycle of lectionaries often included more than illustrations of the great feasts. The St. Petersburg manuscript prefaced the lection for the Sunday before Easter with a picture of the Women at the Tomb,[22] another of the Byzantine-influenced themes in the Benedictional. A Greek lectionary could also have supplied the models for the miniatures of the Stoning of Stephen and the Martyrdoms of Peter and Paul. The second part

of the lectionary contained the pericopes for the feasts of saints, which were often illustrated with miniatures of their martyrdom.[23] That no extant lectionary includes a fully developed scene of the Last Judgment—the possible source of the choirs of the saints—might be an accident of survival.[24] In any event, the heterogeneous picture cycle of a Byzantine lectionary best accounts for the broad thematic range of Eastern influences on the Benedictional.

What might have been the date of this Byzantine source? The type of Pentecost in the Benedictional first appeared in Byzantium in the late ninth century. The motif of angels carrying the instruments of the Passion at the Anastasis, which influenced the Second Coming, was evidently a middle Byzantine innovation. Finally, the Benedictional's iconography of the Entry into Jerusalem is closely related to tenth-century Byzantine art. There is every indication that the Byzantine model was comparatively recent.

The selection of themes illustrated in the Benedictional was influenced by both its sources. Like the historiated initials of the Drogo Sacramentary and the major feast pictures of a Byzantine lectionary, the Benedictional completely omitted scenes of Christ's miracles, concentrating instead on the beginning and the end of his life.[25] A most unusual feature of the Benedictional is its emphasis on the apocryphal scenes of the life of the Virgin. While the Drogo Sacramentary has only an ornamental initial for the Assumption of the Virgin,[26] the Benedictional illustrates the feast with a miniature of the Death of the Virgin, the earliest surviving representation of the theme in

[20] K. Weitzmann, "Various Aspects of Byzantine Influence on the Latin Countries from the Sixth to the Twelfth Century," *DOP* 20 (1966): 18f.; rpt. idem, *Art in the Medieval West and its Contacts with Byzantium* (London, 1982), no. I, pp. 18f.

[21] K. Weitzmann, "The Narrative and Liturgical Gospel Illustrations," *New Testament Studies*, ed. M. M. Parvis and A. Wikgren (Chicago 1950), pp. 151ff.; and idem, "Byzantine Miniature and Icon Painting in the Eleventh Century," *Proceedings of the XIIIth International Congress of Byzantine Studies* (London 1967), pp. 215ff.; both articles rpt. idem, *Studies*, pp. 247ff., 289ff. (subsequent citations are to the reprint); idem, "A 10th Century Lectionary. A Lost Masterpiece of the Macedonian Renaissance," *Revue des Études Sud-Est Européennes* 9 (1971): 617–40; rpt. idem, *Byzantine Liturgical Psalters and Gospels* (London, 1980), no. X; see also nos. IX, XI, XIV; E. Kitzinger, "Reflections on the Feast Cycle in Byzantine Art," *Cahiers Archéologique* 36 (1988): 51ff.

[22] C. R. Morey, "Notes on East Christian Miniatures," *AB* 11 (1929): fig. 100; K. Weitzmann, "Das Evangelion im

Skevophylakion zu Lawra," *Seminarium Kondakovianum* 8 (1936): 95; rpt. idem, *Liturgical Psalters*, no. XI.

[23] Weitzmann, "Gospel Illustration," pp. 258ff.; idem, "Miniature and Icon Painting," pp. 295f. This type of lectionary picture was taken over from menologia, but few of this rather specialized type of Byzantine manuscript would have been exported to the Latin West.

[24] The developed iconography of the Last Judgment penetrated into Gospel books influenced by lectionaries, e.g., Paris, Bibl. Nat., MS gr. 74 (H. Omont, *Évangiles avec peintures byzantines du XIᵉ siècle* [Paris, n. d.], pls. 41, 81), and the liturgical programs of icons with the Last Judgment are intimately related to lectionaries. See Weitzmann, "Gospel Illustration," pp. 264f.; idem, "Miniature and Icon Painting," pp. 290ff., 296ff.

[25] The Transfiguration was an important lectionary picture illustrating Metamorphosis (August 6th), but this feast was prominent only in the East.

[26] *Drogo-Sak.*, fol. 90.

the Latin West. The manuscript has also lost a miniature prefacing the feast of the Birth of the Virgin, probably a depiction of the event.[27] If this were the case, it would have been among the earliest Western representations of that event. Indeed, before the twelfth century there seems to be only one existing Latin depiction.[28] Both apocryphal subjects were far more popular in the East. In Greek lectionaries the Death of the Virgin frequently illustrated the Koimesis, one of the great feasts,[29] and the Birth of the Virgin was also sometimes represented in a supplementary feast cycle.[30] It must have been the picture cycle of a Byzantine lectionary that gave Æthelwold, with his personal devotion to the Virgin, the novel idea of including feast pictures of her Birth and Death in his own manuscript. It is revealing that all the other early Latin representations of these two themes are patently Byzantine-inspired.[31] The Eastern influence is much less obvious in the Benedictional because its rendering of the Dormition bears no likeness to Byzantine iconography. Although stimulated by the lectionary's unusual subject matter, Æthelwold and his painters were independent enough to devise their own novel version of the theme. Whether they followed a similar procedure for the lost miniature of the Birth of the Virgin can only be a matter for speculation.

They also seem to have learned from a Byzantine lectionary how to select illustrations according to liturgical rather than narrative principles.

In the Benedictional, as in many Greek lectionaries, the illustration of a feast is usually limited to the single most important event commemorated in the day's liturgy.[32] This might not have been the case in the Benedictional's Metz model. In the Drogo Sacramentary, for example, Epiphany is illustrated with a sequence of three equally prominent scenes: the Magi before Herod, the Journey of the Magi, and the Adoration of the Magi (fig. 22). Only the last is liturgically significant for Epiphany; the Carolingian miniaturist seems to have been interested in the narrative flow of events as much as in the liturgy. The Benedictional's treatment of this feast is an instructive contrast. Prefacing Epiphany are pictures of the Adoration and the Baptism (pls. 18, 19), a combination inspired by liturgy rather than narrative.[33] The adherence to a strict system of liturgical illustration probably explains the absence of the Crucifixion from the cycle. This was commemorated on Good Friday, a day for which the Benedictional has no text. Evidently the painters preferred to omit a miniature of this important theme rather than associate it with another, less appropriate feast day.[34]

The Byzantine lectionary also influenced how the Benedictional illustrated the feasts of saints. Swithun and Æthelthryth are represented standing in static, hieratic poses (pls. 28, 32). Similar portraits do not occur in the Drogo Sacramentary or in the Ottonian Fulda sacramentaries; their illustrations for saints' days usually depict narra-

[27] It is conceivable, however, that the lost picture portrayed another incident from Mary's infancy. The Caligula Troper (ca. 1050) illustrated this feast with the Annunciation to Joachim and the infant Mary with her parents; Temple, *Manuscripts*, no. 97, fig. 294; E. C. Teviotdale, "The Cotton Troper (London, British Library, Cotton MS Caligula A.xiv, ff.1–36): A Study of an Illustrated English Troper of the Eleventh Century," (Ph.D. diss., University of North Carolina, Chapel Hill, 1991), pp. 185–99.

[28] In the Warmund sacramentary (ca. 1001) in Ivrea; Magnani, *Sacramentario*, p. 32, pl. 25. See also J. Lafontaine-Dosogne, *Iconographie de l'enfance de la Vierge dans l'empire byzantin et en occident* (Brussels, 1964–65), 1, pp. 89ff.; 2, p. 23. The "Italo-Byzantine" representation she mentions (2, p. 85, fig. 1) on an eleventh- or twelfth-century steatite plaque in Berlin is quite possibly purely Byzantine.

[29] E.g., the eleventh-century Lavra lectionary; Weitzmann, "Evangelion," pp. 83ff., pl. 3, 1; also idem, "A 10th Century Lectionary," pp. 638ff.

[30] Lafontaine-Dosogne, *Enfance*, 1, p. 92, fig. 56; Weitzmann, "Evangelion," pp. 83ff., pl. 3, 1; idem, "A 10th Century Lectionary," pp. 630f.; Kitzinger, "Reflections on the Feast Cycle," p. 53.

[31] Weitzmann, "Various Aspects," pp. 15ff.; also R. Kahsnitz, "Koimesis—Dormitio—Assumptio," *Florilegium in Honorem Carl Nordenfalk Octogenarii Contextum* (Stockholm, 1987), pp. 91ff., figs. 1–9, 12.

[32] The Assumption illustration (pl. 34) is not really an exception since symbolism motivated its combination of events. For the principle of liturgical illustration in Byzantine lectionaries, see Weitzmann, "Gospel Illustration," pp. 254f.

[33] The illustration of Epiphany with the Baptism as well as the Adoration might also be due to the fact that the former was the customary Byzantine feast picture. Even among Anglo-Saxon liturgical manuscripts, the Benedictional is exceptionally rigorous in its adherence to a liturgical cycle. Cf. the early–eleventh-century Anglo-Saxon Missal of Robert of Jumièges, which illustrates Epiphany with a narrative sequence of four Magi scenes. See *Jumièges*, pls. 3, 5; Raw, *Crucifixion*, p. 30.

[34] Raw, *Crucifixion*, p. 94. Cf. the Drogo Sacramentary where the absence of a text for Good Friday led to the Crucifixion scene illustrating a Palm Sunday collect; *Drogo-Sak.*, fol. 43v.

tive events from their lives (figs. 16, 21, 107, 203).[35] Byzantine lectionaries also employed this kind of narrative hagiographic scene, but alternatively, the text for a saint's feast could be prefaced with an iconic portrait like the one of Gregory the theologian in an eleventh-century lectionary on Mount Athos (Dionysiu, MS 587; fig. 128).[36] Once again the Benedictional's departure from a Western narrative tradition to a more strictly liturgical, hieratic type of illustration followed the lead of a Byzantine lectionary. The single saints standing in the corners of the calendar of the Galba Psalter (fig. 125) were also a contributing factor, though of course these anonymous figures illustrate the calendar in general rather than specific feasts.

The pictures prefacing major feasts in Greek lectionaries were frequently full page, and this feature may well have inspired the expansion from the relatively modest horizontal compositions in the Metz model to the luxurious full-page pictures in the Benedictional. The earlier Latin tradition also played a part. In England full-page New Testament miniatures occur in the Galba Psalter (figs. 10, 53) as well as in Hiberno-Saxon Gospel books,[37] and they are also found in Carolingian manuscripts. A Franco-Saxon Gospels in Prague prefaced each Gospel with a full-page narrative scene in addition to the usual evangelist portrait.[38] On both sides of the last of five folios of an unfinished ninth-century Reims lectionary in Düsseldorf[39] are full-page drawings of Christ Healing the Leper and another, unidentified Christological subject. It is not clear whether these drawings were placed near the appropriate Gospel text in the book, nor is it known how extensive the picture cycle of the completed manuscript would have been. In any case, although some earlier Latin manuscripts had several full-page narrative miniatures, books with extensive liturgical cycles of New Testament

miniatures in this format do not seem to have been common in the West before the end of the tenth century. Even comparatively early Ottonian manuscripts like the Fulda sacramentaries and the Codex Egberti[40] continued to employ the traditional format of horizontal pictures. About the turn of the millennium, however, Byzantine lectionaries inspired Ottonian illuminators to adopt the more deluxe full-page format for their miniature cycles.[41] Several decades earlier in Anglo-Saxon England the same type of Byzantine liturgical book sparked a similar development in the Benedictional.

The lay-out of the Benedictional and a typical Byzantine lectionary differed in some essential respects. In the latter the portraits of the saints are seldom full-page as in our book. Greek painters evidently did not believe it proper to give the illustration for a saint's day the same grand format as the pictures for the Christological and Mariological feasts. The Anglo-Saxon illuminators did not possess such a finely tuned sense of hierarchy; indeed, the decoration for Saint Æthelthryth's feast is among the most sumptuous in the book. Another difference is that picture and text are much more coordinated in the Benedictional than in any Byzantine lectionary. The Anglo-Saxon feast pictures are usually placed on a verso facing an identically framed initial page with the beginning of the day's text (pls. 8, 9, 28, 29). In the Greek books, however, a full-page picture prefacing the text was not always on a verso,[42] and even when it was, the opposite text page was seldom ornamented with anything more than a headpiece and small initial. There was no counterpart in Byzantine lectionaries or any other kind of Greek manuscript to the elaborate Anglo-Saxon initial pages. What was the source of the Benedictional's impressive orchestration of picture and text?

[35] E.g., *Drogo-Sak.*, fols. 86, 89, 91, 98v; Comoretto, *Sacramentario fuldense*, figs. 29–32, 35, 36, 51–54; *Sac. Fuld.*, figs. 12, 13, 27–29, 31, 32, etc.

[36] S. M. Pelekanidis et al., *The Treasures of Mount Athos*, 1 (Athens, 1974), figs. 258, also 216, 241, 245. This type of hagiographic miniature was taken over from menologia.

[37] Alexander, *Manuscripts*, nos. 10, 32, 44, 52, 61, figs. 202, 203, 206, 255, 279, 280.

[38] A. Podlaha, *Die Bibliothek des Metropolitankapitels*, Topographie der historischen und Kunst-Denkmale, 2, 2 (Prague, 1904), pp. 3ff., no. 1.

[39] E. Galley, "Das karolingische Evangelistarfragment aus der Landes- und Stadtbibliothek Düsseldorf," *Düsseldorfer*

Jahrbuch 52 (1966): 120ff.; V. H. Elbern, "Das Essener Evangelistarfragment aus dem Umkreis des Utrechtpsalter," *Das erste Jahrtausend* (Düsseldorf, 1964), 2, pp. 992ff.

[40] H. Schiel, *Codex Egberti* (Basel, 1960).

[41] Weitzmann, "Various Aspects," pp. 35ff. An Ottonian manuscript might have influenced an early–eleventh-century fragment of an Anglo-Saxon lectionary or Gospels with full-page miniatures now in the Getty Museum, Malibu; see J. J. G. Alexander, "Some Aesthetic Principles in the Use of Colour in Anglo-Saxon Art," *ASE* 4 (1975): 150ff.; Temple, *Manuscripts*, pp. 53ff., no. 53, figs. 173–76.

[42] E.g., the lectionary on Mt. Athos, Iviron, MS 2; Pelekanidis et al., *Treasures*, pp. 259ff., figs. 3, 4, 6.

The Franco-Saxon Model

The frames derive from manuscripts of the Carolingian Franco-Saxon school, which flourished during the last half of the ninth century at Saint-Amand and other centers in northwestern France.[43] This ninth-century school specialized in the production of Gospels and liturgical manuscripts that were often elaborately ornamented, though seldom with figural compositions. The liturgical books are most like the Benedictional since their texts were also organized into a series of feasts. A number of Franco-Saxon sacramentaries are preserved, but their major decoration is usually limited to the opening section of the manuscript, where the facing versos and rectos of several folios have matching frames enclosing the directions, the title, the Preface, and the Canon of the mass.[44] For the most part, the texts of the feasts themselves are unframed, thus the decorative layout of Franco-Saxon sacramentaries is not comparable to that of the Benedictional.

Another kind of liturgical book produced by this Carolingian school was the Gospel lectionary. Only one example remains, a manuscript in Arras (Bibl. Mun., MS 1045) that was made at Saint-Vaast, not far from Saint-Amand.[45] Every page of its text is framed, with facing pages matching. Often the first pair of framed pages for a particular lection is especially elaborate (figs. 130, 131). On the verso in capitals is the title of the feast and/or the name of the Gospel from which the following pericope was excerpted, and on the matching recto opposite is an initial marking the beginning of the lection. This extraordinarily luxurious format cannot have been employed very often for Franco-Saxon lectionaries, which probably were also sometimes less elaborately decorated.

This supposition is supported by a tenth-century English copy of a Franco-Saxon lectionary. Only a single bifolium of this Anglo-Saxon manuscript survives, bound as folios 84–85 in an unrelated book in the College of Arms in London (MS Arundel 22).[46] This bifolium seems to have been the outer one of a gathering since its two folios are conjoint but not textually consecutive. On the first recto (fol. 84) is a splendid Franco-Saxon type of frame enclosing an initial "I" which begins the pericope for the vigil of Christmas (fig. 129). On the analogy of the St. Vaast lectionary, we can safely reconstruct a lost facing verso with a matching frame enclosing either the title of the feast or the name of the Gospel. Since the three other extant pages of this fragment are unframed, only the first pair of facing pages for a reading were framed. Not every lection, however, began with such decoration. On folios 85 and 85v are the readings for the Wednesday and the Friday after Epiphany respectively, and only a minor initial in the page margin marks the beginning of these pericopes. Only the beginnings of major feasts, such as Christmas, were singled out for decoration with a pair of matching frames and a large initial on the recto.

This system of decoration is very similar to the Benedictional's, the main difference being that in the latter the framed page on the verso contained a miniature rather than a display text. The resemblance between the two Anglo-Saxon manuscripts is not confined to layout. The same man, presumably Godeman, the scribe of the Benedictional, wrote both books,[47] and detailed examination of the ornament confirms that both are contemporary products of the Winchester scriptorium.[48] This makes it a virtual certainty that these two Winchester manuscripts were both influenced by the same Franco-Saxon lectionary.

The Anglo-Saxon illuminator of the Winchester lectionary fragment applied the decorative scheme from the Carolingian lectionary exemplar to the same type of liturgical book with relatively few changes, but the Benedictional's makers transposed the decorative format to a different kind of liturgical manuscript, a bene-

[43] See below, chap. 7. For the Franco-Saxon school, see C. M. Niver, "A Study of the More Important Manuscripts of the Franco-Saxon School," (Ph.D. diss., Harvard University, 1941); A. Boutemy, "Le Style franco-saxon, style deSaint-Amand," *Scriptorium* 3 (1949): 260ff.

[44] Niver, "Franco-Saxon School," pp. 85ff.; V. Leroquais, *Les Sacramentaires et les missels manuscrits des bibliothèques publiques de France* (Paris, 1924), 1, nos. 7, 8.

[45] L. Delisle, *L'Évangélaire de Saint-Vaast d'Arras* (Paris,

1888).

[46] F. Wormald, "A Fragment of a Tenth-Century English Gospel Lectionary," *Calligraphy and Palaeography. Essays Presented to Alfred Fairbank*, ed. A. S. Osley (London, 1965), pp. 43ff.; rpt. Wormald, *Writings*, pp. 101–104, color frontispiece pl.; Temple, *Manuscripts*, pp. 54f., no. 26.

[47] Bishop, *Minuscule*, p. 10.

[48] See below, chap. 7.

dictional. The transposition was not difficult since both types of book were similarly organized into feasts. The artists also introduced another significant modification: they substituted full-page miniatures for the display texts in the framed versos opposite the initial pages. This substitution was probably influenced by the arrangement of Hiberno-Saxon and Carolingian Gospel books where full-page framed portraits of evangelists often faced similarly framed initial pages.[49] Basically, however, the decorative format of the Benedictional resulted from the fusion of the systems of decoration of two quite distinct types of Gospel lectionary, Franco-Saxon and Byzantine. The artists drew upon still a third liturgical manuscript, a Carolingian Metz sacramentary, though the decorative structure of this book was less influential than its iconography.

An analogous systematic fusion of different Continental liturgical traditions is evident in the Benedictional's text. Prescott[50] has shown that it resulted from a skillful synthesis of two distinct textual recensions. Major feasts were provided with a Gallican benediction followed by a Gregorian one as an alternative. Extraneous texts

that were commonly included in other collections of episcopal blessings were eliminated, so that Æthelwold's manuscript included only those used before communion in the mass.[51] The result was a rigorously organized and comprehensive benedictional clearly distinguished from other types of service-book. Æthelwold was a major liturgical innovator,[52] and he undoubtedly stands behind the carefully arranged and comprehensive text in his personal book. The same systematic and creative mind was at work in its decoration.

Before the Benedictional there was little in Western manuscript illumination that could compare to the liturgical system of illustration in the middle Byzantine lectionary, with its highly selective cycle of hieratic, full-page feast pictures. But the Benedictional was also heir to an indigenous Latin tradition of opulently ornamented text pages that was far richer than the limited store of ornament in classically oriented Greek art. Creatively drawing on both the Eastern and Western traditions of liturgical book illumination, Æthelwold and his artists combined the best of both worlds.

Other Sources

While liturgical manuscripts from Metz, Byzantium, and the Franco-Saxon school were the Benedictional's principal sources, they were not its only ones. The Utrecht Psalter's representations of the Trinity, the Virgin, and mandorlas were also influential. The Benedictional also revived the early Christian iconography of the Magi offering diadems, the baptismal crowning of Christ, and perhaps bridal coronation. How Anglo-Saxon artists became familiar with these old imperial motifs is unknown, but early Christian works were certainly imported into Anglo-Saxon England in the seventh and eighth centuries. The preservation of the late-sixth-century Italian St. Augustine Gospels at Canter-

bury during the Middle Ages[53] is proof that some of these must have survived the ninth-century Viking invasions.

Earlier English art was a significant influence on the Benedictional. The portrait of John derived from a Hiberno-Saxon evangelist portrait, and indigenous and ultimately Hiberno-Saxon traditions can also be detected in the Second Coming with its typological relation to the Passion and the Ascension. A particularly important intermediary between Hiberno-Saxon art and the Benedictional was the group of early-tenth-century Winchester miniatures in the Galba Psalter, which exercised a broad influence on the iconography and general program of the

[49] E.g., Alexander, *Manuscripts*, figs. 262, 263, 265, 267–69; Koehler, *Kar. Min.*, 2, pls. 58, 61, 83, 84; R. G. Calkins, *Programs of Medieval Illumination*, The Franklin D. Murphy Lectures, 5 (Lawrence, Kansas, 1984), pp. 23ff.

[50] Prescott, "Text," pp. 127ff.; idem, "The Structure of English Pre-Conquest Benedictionals," *British Library Journal* 13 (1987): 118ff.

[51] For the one significant exception, see above, chap. 2, n. 177.

[52] Wulfstan, *Life*, pp. lx–lxxxvi.

[53] F. Wormald, *The Miniatures in the Gospels of St. Augustine, Corpus Christi College, Cambridge, MS 286* (Cambridge, 1954); rpt. idem, *Writings*, pp. 13–35.

Benedictional's cycle. Had more early Anglo-Saxon New Testament iconography survived, the Benedictional's debt to indigenous tradition might appear far larger than it now does.

Nonetheless, the predominance of Carolingian and Byzantine iconographic influence is not in question. The Benedictional's ornament offers an analogy. There too foreign sources predominated, and there is no lack of information about earlier Anglo-Saxon ornament. The Benedictional's illuminators seem to have deliberately sought fresh inspiration abroad.

The Transmission of the Models

We can never determine just how the Winchester scriptorium obtained the models for the Benedictional, but there are some clues that make speculation worthwhile.

A member of the West Saxon royal family is known to have owned at least one Carolingian Metz illuminated manuscript. The Metz Gospel book (ca. 860) in Coburg (Landesbibl. 1) was inscribed by a tenth-century Anglo-Saxon hand with the names of King Athelstan (924–939) and Queen Eadgifu, presumably the king's half-sister.[54] The most likely explanation is that Eadgifu brought the book to England after her husband, the West Frankish king Charles the Simple, was deposed in 932.[55] Charles the Simple was the grandson of Charles the Bald (840–877), who was crowned at Metz in 869 and patronized Metz artists.[56]

Charles the Bald's artists also had access to the Utrecht Psalter, which was in Canterbury by the year 1000. How and when this Reims book reached England is uncertain, but Charles the Bald had close ties to the West Saxon royal house. His daughter Judith married King Æthelwulf of Wessex in 856.[57] Judith was probably not the one who brought the Psalter to England, however, since about 870 it was copied on the throne of Charles the Bald.[58] Perhaps the Psalter was inherited by his grandson Charles the Simple, who then gave it to his Anglo-Saxon consort Eadgifu. However this may be, the contacts between the Carolingian and West Saxon courts were one means by which the Utrecht Psalter and the Metz manuscript model might have come to England.

Carolingian manuscripts also passed into the hands of the tenth-century Ottonian rulers, who had many close links to the West Saxon royal family as the result of the marriage in 929–930 of Otto I to Edith, half-sister of King Athelstan.[59] The late-ninth-century illuminated Gospels from the region of Lobbes (London, British Lib., MS Cotton Tib. A. II) that Athelstan owned was probably a gift from the Ottonian court.[60] Relations between the Germans and the Anglo-Saxons continued after Edith's death in 946. King Edgar, for example, shortly before his coronation in 973, concluded a peace pact and exchanged gifts with Otto I, and Edgar also called an Ottonian artist to his court.[61] Such exchanges opened another avenue by which illuminated Carolingian manuscripts might have come to England. That the Anglo-Saxon monarchs often donated precious books and other works of art to English religious houses is well known. One of Athelstan's many donations, for instance, was the Carolingian Gospels from Lobbes which went to Canterbury.[62] As an important Wessex royal residence, Winchester also enjoyed generous regal patronage,[63] and at some stage the West Saxon rulers might have given both a Metz manuscript and the Utrecht Psalter to Winchester.

---

[54] Koehler, *Kar. Min.*, 3, p. 163. The manuscript contains no narrative illustration.

[55] Keynes, "Athelstan's Books," pp. 189–93; also Ortenberg, *English Church*, pp. 61f.

[56] F. Mütherich, "Der Elfenbeinschmuck des Thrones," in *Cattedra*, pp. 26ff.

[57] P. Stafford, "Charles the Bald, Judith and England," *Charles the Bald: Court and Kingdom*, ed. M. Gibson and J. Nelson, 2nd ed. (Aldershot, 1981), pp. 139ff.

[58] See above, n. 13.

[59] K. Leyser, "Die Ottonen und Wessex," *Frühmittelalterliche Studien* 17 (1983): 73–97. For Ottonian and Anglo-Saxon relations, see also Ortenberg, *English Church*, pp. 41ff.

[60] Keynes, "Athelstan's Books," pp. 147–53.

[61] Deshman, "Kingship," pp. 390ff.; Leyser, "Ottonen," pp. 89ff.; also M. Lapidge, "Aethelwold and the *Vita S. Eustachii*," *Scire Litteras*, ed. S. Krämer and M. Bernhard (Munich, 1988), pp. 264f.

[62] Keynes, "Athelstan's Books," pp. 143ff.

[63] Deshman, "Anglo-Saxon Art after Alfred," pp. 193ff.

The many contacts between English and Continental churches could also have provided the opportunity for the export of these Carolingian manuscripts to England. Archbishop Fulk of Reims, for instance, sent his assistant Grimbald to Winchester in ca. 886–887.[64] If the Utrecht Psalter had only been loaned temporarily to Charles the Bald, then Grimbald might have been the one who brought this Reims book to Winchester long before it passed to Canterbury.[65] As a leader of the Anglo-Saxon monastic renewal, Æthelwold himself had strong associations with reformed Continental houses such as St. Peter's in Ghent.[66] This Flemish monastery had been reformed by Gorze, which was at the center of the Lotharingian monastic movement and closely linked to neighboring Metz.[67]

One late-ninth-century ornamented Franco-Saxon manuscript, the Leofric Missal in Oxford (Bodl. Lib., MS Bodley 579) was in England, perhaps at Glastonbury or Canterbury, by the second quarter of the tenth century, but how it arrived is not known.[68] Once again contacts between courts could have been a factor; Charles the Bald also patronized the Franco-Saxon school.[69] Moreover, this Carolingian style was centered in northwestern France, England's gateway to the Continent.[70] In any number of ways the Franco-Saxon model of the Benedictional might have come to Winchester.

To account for the presence there of a relatively recent tenth-century Byzantine lectionary is much more difficult. Post-iconoclastic Byzantine art influenced Winchester as early as the first quarter of the tenth century.[71] Tenth- and eleventh-century Anglo-Saxon rulers seem to have possessed Byzantine works of art. Athelstan gave a Greek paten to the shrine of St. Cuthbert in Chester-le-Street about 934, and his successor Edmund gave two Byzantine robes to this shrine.[72] Queen Emma donated a Byzantine shrine ("grecysscan scrine") to the New Minster, Winchester, in 1041.[73] Possibly these had been gifts to the royal family from the Byzantine court. During the tenth century Anglo-Saxon kings adopted Byzantine-style titles that are thought to have stemmed from diplomacy with the East, although there is no hard evidence of such activity.[74] Greeks were undoubtedly in England at this time. A Greek bishop named Sigewoldus was a magnate of King Edgar (959–975), who was particularly close to Æthelwold,[75] and among the early-eleventh-century brethren of the New Minster was a certain "Andreas grecus."[76] Since Byzantine liturgical illustration was a probable factor in the Benedictional's representations of the Birth and Death of the Virgin, it is especially interesting that about fifty years later (ca. 1030) Winchester introduced the Eastern feasts of the Conception of the Virgin (8 December) and the Presentation of the Virgin in the Temple (21 November) into the Latin West, most likely as the result of direct Eastern influence.[77] There is a possibility, too,

---

[64] P. Grierson, "Grimbald of St. Bertin's," *English Historical Review* 55 (1940): 529–61.

[65] There were many opportunities for the transfer of books from Winchester to Canterbury about the millennium; see Deshman, *"Benedictus,"* p. 219. Alternatively, the Psalter might have been in Canterbury from the outset and have been known at Winchester through a lost copy. See also D. Tselos, "English Manuscript Illustration and the Utrecht Psalter," *AB* 40 (1959): 137ff.

[66] See below, chap. 5, n. 120.

[67] P. Wormald, "Æthelwold and his Continental Counterparts: Contact, Comparison, Contrast," *Bishop Æthelwold*, pp. 26ff.; E. Boshof, "Kloster und Bischof in Lotharingien," *Monastische Reformen im 9. und 10. Jahrhundert*, Vorträge und Forschungen, 38 (Sigmaringen, 1989), pp. 219ff.

[68] Deshman, "Leofric," pp. 145ff., pl. Ia; D. N. Dumville, *Liturgy and Ecclesiastical History*, Studies in Anglo-Saxon History, 5 (Woodbridge, 1992), pp. 39ff.

[69] See above, n. 43.

[70] See Ortenberg, *English Church*, pp. 34ff.

[71] Deshman, "Anglo-Saxon Art after Alfred," pp. 183ff. Regarding Byzantine and Anglo-Saxon relations, see Ortenberg, *English Church*, pp. 197ff.

[72] C. F. Battiscombe, "Historical Introduction," *The Relics of St. Cuthbert*, ed. idem (Oxford, 1956), pp. 33, 34. See also C. R. Dodwell, *Anglo-Saxon Painting: A New Perspective* (Ithaca, 1982), pp. 154ff.

[73] W. de G. Birch, *Liber Vitae: Register and Martyrology of New Minster and Hyde Abbey* (London, 1892), pp. xxxii, lxv, 161f.

[74] R. S. Lopez, "Le Problème des relations anglo-byzantines du septième au dixième siècle," *Byzantion* 18 (1948): 139ff.

[75] *Liber Eliensis*, ed. E. O. Blake, Camden Third Series, 92 (London, 1952), pp. xvii, 73, 396.

[76] Birch, *Liber Vitae*, p. 33; J. Gerchow, *Die Gedenküberlieferung der Angelsachsen* (Berlin, 1988), p. 324, no. 75. Also a Greek monk named Constantine came to Malmesbury ca. 1030 and stayed until his death; William of Malmesbury, *Gesta Pontificum Anglorum*, ed. N. E. S. A. Hamilton, Rolls Series, 52 (London, 1870), pp. 415f.

[77] M. Clayton, "Feasts of the Virgin in the Liturgy of the Anglo-Saxon Church," *ASE* 13 (1984): 209–33; idem, *Cult*, pp. 43ff.

that an intermediary such as the Ottonian rulers, whose contacts with the East are well known, might have presented a Byzantine manuscript to a member of the Anglo-Saxon royal family. The evidence is certainly fragmentary and circumstantial, but it does not deny that there were ways for a tenth-century Greek manuscript to have reached England.

Chapter Five

THE MONASTIC PROGRAM

ÆTHELWOLD commissioned the Benedictional while vigorously leading a movement to reform Anglo-Saxon monasteries and churches.[1] The beginnings of the reform dated back to Dunstan's abbacy of Glastonbury (ca. 940–957), where Æthelwold was consecrated a monk. About 954 Æthelwold became abbot of the derelict monastery of Abingdon, which he revitalized with monks from Glastonbury. In November 963 King Edgar (959–975) promoted him to the bishopric of Winchester, and early the following year Æthelwold gave the reform new impetus by expelling the secular canons from the Old Minster and replacing them with regular Benedictine monks from Abingdon. Later that year he also ejected the clerks from the New Minster and substituted monks. The establishment of monks at Winchester was a turning point in the monastic movement. Subsequently Æthelwold and the other leaders of the reform, Dunstan and Oswald, founded and renewed many other monasteries. These events must have loomed large in the minds of Æthelwold and his illuminators, who were surely some of the monks recently introduced into the Old Minster. In this chapter we shall consider the reform's influence on the imagery they created.

Vita Angelica

As a portrayal of the elect enjoying beatific heavenly existence, the choirs of the saints and the apostles (pls. 1–7) represented the celestial goal that all Christians sought to reach after their earthly life. For monks, however, the prefatory cycle would have been especially meaningful.

Turning from ordinary worldly affairs, monks devoted themselves more completely than other men to the pursuit of a perfect spiritual life.[2] This led them more quickly and surely along the path to salvation in heaven where the angels lived blissfully with God. Monks sought to transcend the world and to realize while still on earth the heavenly existence to which they aspired. They modeled their manner of living on the ideal celestial life of the angels; hence, monasticism was considered the heavenly, angelic life. Monks such as Dunstan were often described as "angelic."[3] Since the saints in their celestial choirs had already attained blissful equality with the angels, the promise of membership in their ranks was an important theme of monastic spirituality. Smaragdus in the *Diadema Monachorum*,[4] the Carolingian monastic treatise which influenced the miniature of St. Benedict (pl. 33), equated incorporation into the

---

[1] Wulfstan, *Life*, pp. xxxixff.; *Tenth-Century Studies*; *Bishop Æthelwold*; D. Knowles, *The Monastic Order in England*, 2nd ed. (Cambridge, 1966), pp. 57ff.; E. John, "The King and the Monks in the Tenth-Century Reformation," *Orbis Britanniae*, Studies in Early English History, 4 (Leicester, 1966), pp. 154–80.

[2] J. Leclercq, *La Vie parfaite*, Tradition Monastique, 1 (Paris, 1948); K. Hallinger, "The Spiritual Life of Cluny in the Early Days," *Cluniac Monasticism in the Central Middle Ages*, ed. N. Hunt (London, 1971), pp. 29–55.

[3] See Wulfstan, *Life*, 14 and 38, pp. 27, 57.

[4] Chaps. 6, 47, PL, 102, cols. 603B, 644C.

choirs of the saints with the heavenly reward for virtuous monks. According to Adelard,[5] Dunstan's early-eleventh-century biographer, the "angelic" reformer was welcomed after death into the heavenly Jerusalem by each of the celestial choirs—beginning with the angels and ending with the virgins—who acclaimed and accepted him as one of themselves. For monks the pictures of the choirs of the saints leading the heavenly *vita angelica* before God would have vividly represented the joyous existence they were striving to attain.

The saints in these miniatures would also have been considered monastic figures. The prophets, who were probably represented among the lost miniatures, were thought to have followed a monastic form of life even before the coming of Christ and the formal establishment of monasticism. The Benedictine *Rule* urged monks to follow the example of the "forefathers," and Smaragdus in his commentary on the *Rule*, which Æthelwold knew well, interpreted this as a reference to Old as well as New Testament saints.[6] Æthelwold in the prologue to his Old English translation of the Benedictine *Rule*[7] expressed the common notion that the disciples had founded monasticism after Pentecost when they lived in unanimity without private possessions (Acts 4:32). This belief might help to account for emphasis on the apostles in the prefatory pictures, where they originally seem to have been represented twice.

The monastic character of the choirs is particularly evident in the choice of saints specially honored by being singled out by name. The Anglo-Saxons associated Mary Magdalene (pl. 3, center) with the anchorite Saint Mary of Egypt; this connection is seen in the ninth-century Old English martyrology that related how, after Christ's Resurrection, the Magdalene retreated to the desert and lived there thirty years unknown to men and without human food.[8] Already in the eighth century her reputation as a biblical prototype of the nun had led to her inclusion in the eremitic program of the Ruthwell cross.[9] Saint Æthelthryth, to the left of the Magdalene in the choir, was the founder and abbess of the double monastery at Ely. Among the confessors (pl. 1), the founder of Benedictine monasticism, Saint Benedict, occupies the central position of honor, and he is flanked on the left and right respectively by two other monks, Pope Gregory and Saint Cuthbert.

The choirs also taught a lesson in monastic history. In addition to including the Old Testament precursors and the apostolic founders of monasticism, the choir miniatures featured people who had been instrumental in the establishment of the movement in England. The juxtaposition of Saint Benedict and Pope Gregory emphasized that the latter had ordered the mission that introduced Benedictine monasticism to the Anglo-Saxons, and Saints Cuthbert and Æthelthryth represented the first fruits of that endeavor, the flowering of Anglo-Saxon monasticism in the seventh and eighth centuries.

For Æthelwold this monastic history had a bearing on the events of his own time. In the preface of his translation of the *Rule*[10] he told how Pope Gregory had sent the Augustinian

[5] *Epistola Adelardi ad Elfegum Archiepiscopum de Vita Sancti Dunstani*, 12, ed. W. Stubbs, *Memorials of Saint Dunstan*, Rolls Series, 63 (London, 1874), pp. 66–68.

[6] *Benedicti Regula*, 7, ed. R. Hanslik, 2nd ed., CSEL, 75 (Vienna, 1977), p. 54; Smaragdus, *Expositio in Regulam S. Benedicti*, 1, 7, 55, ed. A. Spannagel and P. Engelbert, CCM, 8, p. 187. Regarding Æthelwold's knowledge of this text, see above, chap. 3, n. 80. For the prophets as monastic paradigms, see Leclercq, *Vie parfaite*, pp. 57ff.

[7] *An Account of King Edgar's Establishment of Monasteries*, ed. and tr. D. Whitelock, M. Brett, and C. N. L. Brooke, *Councils & Synods with other Documents relating to the English Church*, 1, 1 (Oxford, 1981), p. 145. See also D. Whitelock, "The Authorship of the Account of King Edgar's Establishment of the Monasteries," *Philological Essays: Studies in Old and Middle English Language and Literature in Honour of Herbert Dean Meritt*, ed. J. L. Rosier (The Hague, 1970), pp. 125–36; Lapidge, "Æthelwold as Scholar," pp. 102ff.; M. Gretsch, "The Benedictine Rule in Old English: A Document of Bishop Æthelwold's Reform Politics," *Words, Text and Manuscripts*, ed. M. Korhammer (Woodbridge, 1992), pp. 134ff.; also *Ælfric's First Old English Pastoral Letter for Wulfstan, Archbishop of York (Past. L. II)*, 42, Whitelock et al., *Councils*, p. 271; Leclercq, *Vie parfaite*, pp. 82ff.

[8] *Das altenglische Martyrologium*, 133, ed. G. Kotzor, Bayerische Akademie der Wissenschaften, Phil.-hist. Kl., Abh. n. s., 88/2 (Munich, 1981), 2, pp. 156f.; J. E. Cross, "Mary Magdalen in the *Old English Martyrology*: The Earliest Extant 'Narrat Josephus' Variant of her Legend," *Speculum* 53 (1978): 16–25; V. Ortenberg, *The English Church and the Continent in the Tenth and Eleventh Centuries* (Oxford, 1992), pp. 250ff.

[9] M. Schapiro, "The Religious Meaning of the Ruthwell Cross," *AB* 26 (1944): 237f.

[10] Whitelock et al., *Councils*, pp. 143–54. Wulfstan, *Life*, preface, pp. 2, 3, characterized Æthelwold as one of a series of apostolic teachers continuing Christ's mission. For the reformers' sense of continuity with earlier Anglo-Saxon monas-

mission to teach the Anglo-Saxons the apostles' monastic way of life. The missing portion of the text that followed must have recounted the decline of monasticism in the ninth century,[11] and the preface then concluded with the contemporary restoration of monasticism during Edgar's reign. Æthelwold viewed his reform as the continuation of a monastic mission that had originated with Christ and the apostles, and he seems to have regarded the first age of Anglo-Saxon monasticism as a precedent and a justification for his own efforts to renew the monasteries.

Æthelthryth's prominence in the choir of virgins and the special opulence of her feast picture, the only one coupled with a historiated initial (pls. 28, 29), undoubtedly reflects Æthelwold's restoration of the monastery of Ely in 970. Wulfstan's late-tenth-century *Life of Æthelwold* emphasized that the bishop's love for Æthelthryth had induced him to renew Ely, which "is made glorious by the relics and miracles of Saint Æthelthryth."[12] Pious regard for the saint, however, was not Æthelwold's only motive. Wulfstan preceded his description of the refoundation of Ely with an account of Æthelwold's appointment of a certain Æthelthryth, a namesake of the original Ely abbess, as the abbess of the newly reformed Winchester nunnery of Nunnaminster.[13] The bishop sought to place his pious restoration of the famed old monastery with its relics of the illustrious sainted abbess in the same light as his renewal of the Nunnaminster. For the new Winchester abbess and her charges the Benedictional's emphasis on Saint Æthelthryth held a special message. When the manuscript's blessing for her feast admonished them to imitate the saint's virtue in "the narrow life

of monasticism" so that they could have her company in heaven,[14] it implicitly lent some of the saint's prestige and authority to her namesake. The representations of Saint Æthelthryth in the heavenly choir of the virgins and in matrimonial union with Christ in her feast picture manifested the goal of their own monastic life at Winchester.

Another feature of the iconography that should also be understood in the context of the reform is the anomalous costume of Saint Benedict. In the choir of confessors he wears pontifical vestments, including the pallium, the insigne of metropolitan rank,[15] and in his feast picture (pl. 33) he is also clothed in mass garments (a purple chasuble, gold dalmatic, and white alb), though here he has no pallium. As Benedictine monks, Æthelwold and his illuminators would certainly have known that the founder of their order had not been a priest, much less an archbishop; they must have had a purpose in depicting the abbot saint as a member of the episcopacy. There is no authority in the Benedictine *Rule* for the dual office of abbot and bishop, but the Anglo-Saxon reform had the unusual policy of regularizing or monasticizing cathedrals. As Wulfstan[16] carefully noted, Æthelwold became both abbot and bishop of the monks he installed in the Old Minster, and Æthelwold stipulated in the *Regularis Concordia* that bishops appointed in sees with monks should be monks themselves and should continue to live communally according to the *Rule*.[17] In one of his pastoral letters Ælfric justified this practice as a traditional one, arguing that "Gregory was a monk and a famous bishop; and Cuthbert was a monk and a famous bishop."[18] These very saints flank Benedict in

---

ticism, see also P. Wormald, "Æthelwold and his Continental Counterparts," *Bishop Æthelwold*, pp. 38ff., and A. Gransden, "Traditionalism and Continuity during the Last Century of Anglo-Saxon Monasticism," *Journal of Ecclesiastical History* 40 (1989): 159ff.

[11] Whitelock, "Authorship," p. 126.

[12] Wulfstan, *Life*, 23, p. 39. The *Liber Eliensis*, 2, 52, ed. E. O. Blake, Camden ser. 3, 92 (London, 1962), p. 120, reports that Æthelwold discovered her remains next to the high altar of the abbey church. For his use of relics to symbolize continuity with the monastic past and to bolster the proprietary rights of Ely and other foundations, see S. J. Ridyard, *The Royal Saints of Anglo-Saxon England* (Cambridge, 1988), pp. 181ff.; D. Rollason, *Saints and Relics in Anglo-Saxon England* (Oxford, 1989), pp. 197ff.

[13] Wulfstan, *Life*, 22, pp. 37–39.

[14] See above, chap. 3, n. 86.

[15] As a pope, Gregory on the left was entitled to wear the pallium. Cuthbert on the right was just a bishop, but bishops were sometimes accorded the honorary privilege of wearing a pallium. See J. Braun, *Die liturgische Gewandung* (Freiburg im Breisgau, 1907).

[16] Wulfstan, *Life*, 16, pp. 30, 31.

[17] *RC*, 9, pp. 74f. As a result, most late-tenth-century Anglo-Saxon bishops were monks; see G. Lanoë, "Approche de quelques évêques moines en Angleterre au Xᵉ siècle," *Cahiers de Civilisation Médiévale* 19 (1976): 135–50; Wormald, "Æthelwold and his Continental Counterparts," pp. 37ff.

[18] *Ælfric's First Old English Pastoral Letter for Wulfstan*, ed. Whitelock et al., *Councils*, p. 287. Regarding the culting of Gregory in England, see Ortenberg, *English Church*, pp. 180ff.

the choir of the confessors. By depicting Benedict himself as a bishop, Æthelwold pushed the argument for monastic bishops a step further than his more cautious pupil Ælfric, who must have been echoing some of his teacher's ideas.

The prefatory cycle represented the leading members of the heavenly Ecclesia as the monastic saints who had helped to establish the Church in Anglo-Saxon England, and in doing so it showed both the historical precedent and the celestial model for the monasticized English Church that was the goal of the tenth-century reform.

The complementary relationship between the choirs and many of the feast pictures strengthened the monastic overtones of the iconography. We have already found this to be the case for the feast portrait of Saint Æthelthryth. Another obvious example is the feast miniature of Benedict. This illustrates a benediction that urges believers to follow his monastic way of life so that they can win a heavenly prize, which is portrayed as the *diadema monachorum*. The monastic significance of the diadem and crown in his portrait implies that the crowns that he and the other, largely monastic saints wear in the choirs represent the final reward that is assured for all those who have led the monastic life. As the representations of the saintly abbess Æthelthryth strengthened the authority of her namesake, the mother superior of Nunnaminster, so the feast picture of Benedict, which urged obedience to the abbot and the *Rule*, bolstered Æthelwold's power as abbot of the Old Minster.

Though there are no overt monastic references in the miniature of the Death and Coronation of the Virgin (pl. 34), a case can be made that this picture also had monastic connotations. It will be recalled that Mary and Æthelthryth in their feast pictures were related models of virtuous chastity for other virgins to imitate.[19] Bede's hymn, which influenced Æthelthryth's portrait, said

that the abbess in her chaste monastic marriage to Christ emulated the Virgin Mary in her matrimonial relation to him. Bede also described Mary as the mother of Christ and many "virgin flowers" such as the saint herself,[20] a characterization that deliberately echoed his previous description of Æthelthryth as abbess of Ely where she "began to be, by the examples of her heavenly life and teaching, the virgin mother of many virgins dedicated to God."[21] Thus Mary's exemplary virginal maternity made her the paradigm for Æthelthryth in her role as the mother superior of the Ely nuns. The relationship between the overtly monastic feast picture of Æthelthryth, who is labeled "abbess," and the miniature of the Virgin, where she is the model for her three virgin servants who hope also to become brides of Christ, suggests that Mary was portrayed there as the ideal of the abbess.

Traditionally the Virgin Mary was considered the supreme model for consecrated virgins or nuns. One of the blessings in the Winchester rite for the consecration of a nun declared that God had selected the novice, "according to the likeness of holy Mary, the mother of our Lord Jesus Christ," to preserve her virginity, so that she might be worthy to receive the crown of her virginity.[22] The nun imitated the life of Mary whose chastity was rewarded with celestial queenship. The customary medieval designation of the nun as an *ancilla Dei* or maid servant of God recalled the description of Mary at the Incarnation as the "ancilla Domini" (Luke 1:38, 48).[23]

This brings us back to the Benedictional's Transitus illustration; for here the Virgin is rewarded with the regalia of celestial queenship because she had been the *ancilla Domini*, and the devoted maid behind her emulates her humble incarnational service according to the devotional concept of *servus Genetricis Dei*, which was particularly popular in monastic circles.[24]

It has been suggested that the original author

---

[19] See the discussions of these two miniatures above, chap. 3.

[20] See above, chap. 3, n. 90.

[21] *Bede's Ecclesiastical History of the English People*, 4, 19, ed. and tr. B. Colgrave and R. A. B. Mynors (Oxford, 1969), p. 392.

[22] *Ben. Rob.*, p. 135: "deus pater omnipotens qui te eligere dignatus est, ad instar sanctae mariae matris domini nostri ihesu christi, ad conseruandum integram et inmaculatam uirginitatem . . . ut coronam uirginitatis tuae accipere digna sis." For Mary as the nun's model, see M. Byrne, *The Tradi-*

tion of the Nun in Medieval England (Washington, 1932), pp. 35f., 53f.; M. Bernards, *Speculum Virginum. Geistigkeit und Seelenleben der Frau im Hochmittelalter*, Forschungen zur Volkskunde, 36/38 (Cologne, 1955), pp. 59f.

[23] E.g., *The "Constitutions" of Archbishop Oda*, 7, ed. Whitelock et al., *Councils*, no. 20, p. 72: "monacham, quam Dei ancillam appellant." Also R. Metz, *La Consécration des vierges dans l'église romaine* (Strasbourg, 1954), pp. 91f., 173.

[24] H. Barré, "La Royauté de Marie pendant les neuf premiers siècles," *Recherches de science religieuse* 29 (1939): 307; J. Leclercq, "Dévotion et théologie mariales dans le mon-

of the Transitus included the episodes involving Mary and her virgin maids to imply that communal female monastic life originated with the Virgin Mary, who plays the part of a kind of monastic superior in the narrative.[25] Whatever the original intent, to a tenth-century monastic audience these events in the Transitus would almost certainly have evoked the life of the cloister.

In the narrative Mary, awaiting death, urged her maid servants to keep continuously vigilant with burning lamps because they did not know the hour of the coming of the "thief." When Christ finally came for their mistress, they were indeed awake.[26] Hoping to follow her into a bridal relationship with the celestial spouse, they were taught the parable of the Wise and Foolish Virgins by Peter.

The necessity of vigilant good service to the Lord was a fundamental theme of the Benedictine *Rule*. The prologue[27] described the monastery as "a school for service of the Lord" and admonished monks to serve Christ well, so they will not be condemned as wicked servants. Monks were to be roused by the Scripture which says: "Now is the hour for us to rise from sleep" (Rom. 13:11). Smaragdus' commentary on the *Rule* interpreted Benedict's warning to "keep death daily before one's eyes" as an admonition to serve God alertly:

> Therefore, being vigilant, we ought to fear death lest we are suddenly carried off by it. For it is written, "Blessed is that servant, whom when his lord shall come he shall find vigilant" (Matt. 24:46; Luke 12:37). . . . Blessed, therefore, is that monk . . . [who,] because of the fear of his death, is always vigilant and prepared, so that when at midnight a cry was made, "Behold the bride-

groom cometh, go ye forth to meet him" (Matt. 25:6), he might go to meet him without delay [and] furnished with lamps, and with him he might enter the eternal marriage chamber as a joyous dweller.[28]

Smaragdus also devoted an entire chapter of his treatise *Diadema Monachorum* to the proposition that monks must be good, vigilant servants of the Lord so that they are prepared for his advent, and once again he cited as scriptural authority some of the parables of the good servant (Mark 13:35–36; Luke 12:37) that underlie the eschatalogical symbolism of the Virgin and her servants in the Transitus.[29] Both of Smaragdus' monastic treatises were well known to Æthelwold,[30] and similar ideas were also in Anglo-Saxon sources.

The legatine council of 786, for example, ordered that monks should be "always prepared, with girded loins and lamps burning, expecting the master of the house, so that when he finds them vigilant, he might make them partakers of the eternal feast."[31] Dunstan's biographer Adelard[32] stressed that his subject's diligent monastic chanting fulfilled the Lord's command to "take ye heed, watch and pray, for ye know not when the time is" (Mark 13:33). This application of the *topos* of vigilance to the monks' chanting of the Divine Office, which in large part consisted of Psalms, strengthens the analogy with the Transitus, for Mary had admonished her maids to sing a Psalm and magnify the Lord while awaiting him.

Adelard goes on to say that when Dunstan's time came, the Lord did find him vigilant and so, as we have already mentioned, presented him to each of the heavenly choirs of angels. His introduction to the company of virgins is partic-

achisme bénédictin," *Maria. Études sur la sainte Vierge*, ed. H. du Manoir (Paris, 1952), 2, p. 554.

[25] C. Schaffer, *Koimesis: der Heimgang Mariens*, Studia Patristica et Liturgica, 15 (Regensburg, 1985), p. 71.

[26] See above, chap. 3, nn. 120–124.

[27] *Benedicti Regula*, prologue, p. 9: "dominici scola seruitii."

[28] *Benedicti Regula*, 4, p. 34; Smaragdus, *Expositio*, 4, 47, p. 128:

> Propterea debemus sollicite mortem ne ab illa subito rapiamur uigilantes timere. Scriptum est enim "Beatus seruus ille quem cum uenerit dominus inuenerit uigilantem." . . . Beatus est ergo ille monachus . . . [qui] semper est uigilans et paratus, ut cum media nocte clamor factus fuerit "Ecce sponsus uenit exite obuiam ei," sine mora cum ornatis lampadibus obuiam illi egre-

diatur et cum illo ad aeternum laetus habitator ingrediatur thalamum.

[29] Smaragdus, *Diadema Monachorum*, 75: *Ut uigilantes sint monachi*, PL, 102, cols. 670C–671B.

[30] See above, chap. 3, nn. 78–80.

[31] *Legatine Council*, 5, ed. E. Dümmler, MGH, *Epistolae Karolini Aevi*, 2 (Berlin, 1895), no. 3, p. 22: "parati semper precinctis lumbis ardentibusque lucernis patremfamilias expectantes, ut dum uigilantes inuenerit, faciat eos aeterni conuiuii esse participes." Also the *"Constitutions"* of Archbishop Oda, 6, ed. Whitelock et al., *Councils*, p. 72.

[32] *Vita S. Dunstani*, 9–12, pp. 62–68. See also B., *Vita S. Dunstani*, 16 and 17, ed. and tr. M. Lapidge and M. Winterbottom, forthcoming; Lantfred, *Translatio*, 3.

ularly noteworthy: "The virgins received the virgin (Dunstan) and they presented him crowned by the Son and his Lord to their queen, namely the mistress of the angels, Mary."[33] As the mother of the "Son" and the "mistress" (*dominatrix*) next to the "Lord" (*Dominus*), the Virgin has a unique relationship to Christ that has raised her above the angels and made her the queen of the choir of virgins which Dunstan joins. Her coronation as their queen foreshadowed Dunstan's own crowning as a virgin by her Son. Christ, the Virgin Mary, and Dunstan are in a descending hierarchy in which the royal exaltation of Mary is the precedent for that of her virginal follower Dunstan. Once more there is a parallel to the Benedictional's miniature which suggests that the Lord, when he comes, will reward the three servants with heavenly crowns like that of their mistress, his mother, if they imitate her life of virginity. If, as we have suggested, the Benedictional also depicted the Virgin crowned with the Trinity at the head of the choir of saints, then the analogy to Adelard's text becomes even more pronounced.

These analogies between the themes of the iconography and monastic spirituality are too numerous and too specific to be entirely fortuitous. Like the miniatures of the choirs of the saints, the Transitus picture must have had a topical monastic meaning as well as a universal Christian one. Portrayed as a paragon of the monastic life, the Virgin, no less than Æthelthryth and Benedict, showed both nuns and monks the path to the celestial choirs.

Songs to God

One of the themes that links the miniatures of the Nativity, the Presentation in the Temple, and the Entry into Jerusalem (pls. 12, 20, 21) to the opening cycle of the Trinity and the celestial choirs is the idea that the inhabitants of heaven and earth sing a common hymn of praise to God. This was another concept that had special relevance to monasticism.

Leading the *vita angelica* on earth, monks continually chanted the Divine Office so that they could imitate and join the angels' celestial song. In fact, the angels were supposed to have helped compose the Office.[34] This conception of monastic chanting is very prominent in the *vitae* of Dunstan. Adelard related that when Dunstan was introduced to the choirs of saints, the angels greeted him with celestial music and invited him "to sing without end the Sanctus like some angel or archangel."[35] They received him in this manner because during his previous earthly life as a monk he had already learned and joined spiritually in their celestial hymns. By their chanting on earth, monks anticipated their future induction into the choirs of angels and saints in heaven.

Æthelwold had a special interest in monastic chant. He invited monks from Corbie to instruct his *familia* at Abingdon in plain chant.[36] He and the monks of Winchester might very well have perceived the iconography in terms of monastic chanting. In the Entry the populace behind Christ symbolized the present-day believers of this world who will temporally and spiritually follow him into the heavenly Jerusalem; as they tread in his path they sing in unanimity with those who preceded him—the angels, patriarchs, and prophets in heaven—symbolized by the figures already within the city. The inhabitants of earth already participate in the heavenly life they hope to enjoy eternally in the company of the saints.

The hymn everyone sang at the Entry was the Benedictus (Matt. 21:9). Aldhelm (d. ca. 709) in his prose treatise *De Virginitate*, a text dedicated to the nuns of Barking and well known to Æthelwold, related this hymn to Benedict, who shared

the blessed privilege of the appellation [i.e., *benedictus* = blessed] with our . . . Redeemer, of whom the evangelizing babes, hymn-

---

[33] Adelard, *Vita S. Dunstani*, 12, p. 67: "Uirginem uirgines suscipiunt et reginae suae, angelorum uidelicet dominatrici, Mariae a Filio et Domino suo coronatum offerunt."

[34] Leclercq, *Vie parfaite*, pp. 24ff.

[35] Adelard, *Vita S. Dunstani*, 12, p. 66: "Maxime autem

dum per sancta cherubin et seraphin, uelut quidam angelus aut archangelus ad concinendum sine fine Sanctus, gloriose per testem idoneum inuitari sit uisus."

[36] *Chronicon Monasterii de Abingdon*, ed. J. Stevenson, Rolls Series (London, 1858), 1, p. 129; Wulfstan, *Life*, pp. lxxxiiif.

ing with a melodious harmony of voice, had sung euphoniously: "Blessed is he that cometh in the name of the Lord." My mediocre talent too . . . celebrates . . . with harmonious voice in the holy celebration of the Psalms . . . reverberating "Osanna."[37]

This association of the Entry hymn with Benedict and the chanting of the Benedictine Office strongly suggests that the symbolism of singing in the related miniatures of the Entry and the heavenly choirs had similar monastic connotations.

Also relevant to the monastic interpretation of the miniatures are two dreams of Dunstan recounted by his biographers. According to Adelard,[38] the saint once dreamed he was transported to heaven where he listened to the angels singing in praise of the Trinity and chanting "Kyrie eleyson, Christe eleyson, Kyrie eleyson." Originally some form of the Trinity seems to have headed the choirs of the angels and saints in the Benedictional, and these miniatures also illustrated the litany of the saints which frequently began and ended with the Kyrie.[39] This makes it all the more likely that the choirs in the Benedictional visualized the celestial music in which monks participated through their chanting.

A related dream is found in the late-tenth-century *Life of Saint Dunstan* by the anonymous author B.[40] The saint had dreamed of a marriage between his mother and a great king, who was constantly praised by the psalms and hymns of his knights. One of them taught Dunstan their unfamiliar song so that he could join in their chorus of rejoicing. After waking, Dunstan taught it to monks and clerks so that they too could sing it. The biographer interpreted this to mean that Dunstan had spiritually ascended to heaven, the true home of the monk (cf. Phil. 3:20), to witness the marriage of "King Christ" and the Church. The knights lauding their ruler were the angels of heaven, who taught Dunstan supernatural hymns suitable for praising Christ in the Divine Office. The angels

once were enemies of men because of the jarring sins that separated them, but now, because they see earth-dwellers and heaven-dwellers joined in one family under one father, they do not cease day or night to sing songs like this to God, the true king: "Praise our God, all ye his saints. . . ." This same honor in the highest the multitude of the heavenly host sang on the day of the birth of the Lord, announcing peace on earth to men of good will (Luke 2:13–14), the same peace that the blessed apostle [Paul] explained in these words: "He is our peace, who hath made both one" (Eph. 2:14) and what follows.[41]

It is striking that here there is a monastic interpretation of themes that also occur in the iconography. In the Nativity, the Presentation, and the Entry into Jerusalem Christ is characterized as the ecclesiastic cornerstone according to the passage from Ephesians. His advent restored peace and unity between men on earth and the angels in heaven, and the saints and angels in the choirs portray the consequence of Christ's reconciliation: righteous mankind replenishing the depleted ranks of the angels singing in heaven. By representing how these events in Christ's life had reestablished a literally musical harmony between men and angels, the three feast pictures showed how monastic life on earth anticipated the future *vita angelica* in heaven with the choirs of the saints.

---

[37] Aldhelm, *De Virginitate*, 30, tr. and ed. M. Lapidge and M. Herren, *Aldhelm: The Prose Works* (Ipswich, 1979), pp. 89f. For Æthelwold's familiarity with this text, see Lapidge, "Æthelwold as Scholar," pp. 99f., 103.

[38] Adelard, *Vita S. Dunstani*, 9, p. 63.

[39] M. Lapidge, *Anglo-Saxon Litanies of the Saints*, Henry Bradshaw Society, 106 (London, 1991), nos. 1, 3, 4, etc.

[40] B., *Vita S. Dunstani*, 29. See also Leclercq, *Vie parfaite*,

pp. 28f.; S. P. Millinger, "Liturgical Devotion in the Vita Oswaldi," *Saints, Scholars, and Heroes: Studies in Medieval Culture in Honour of Charles W. Jones*, ed. M. H. King and W. M. Stevens (Collegeville, Minn., 1979), 2, p. 247; M. Lapidge, "B. and the *Vita S. Dunstani*," *Dunstan*, pp. 247–59.

[41] B., *Vita S. Dunstani*, 30. Cf. John of Salerno, *Vita Sancti Odonis*, 1, 5, PL, 133, col. 63C, which compared Abbot Odo of Cluny, both angelic and human, to the cornerstone.

Vita Contemplativa

The biographers' tales of Dunstan's transports to heaven touch on another facet of monastic spirituality relevant to the imagery. Through their ascetic life monks sought to transcend the encumbrances of the world and to ascend spiritually to their true home, the heavenly Jerusalem, where they could contemplate the face of God, an essential activity of the angels (cf. Matt. 18:10).[42] The Ramsey monk Byrhtferth[43] in his late-tenth-century life of Oswald wrote that the saint and his monks fervently desired to behold the celestial city promised by the "supreme king Christ," and that their monastic exertions caused them to appear continually before the face of the Savior. Noteworthy is the emphasis on Christ as king both here and in Dunstan's dream, for the Benedictional illustrates the Octave of Pentecost with the crowned Trinitarian Christ (pl. 27). This initial portrayed the "endless manifestation and appearance"[44] of God that all blessed men would see at the Last Judgment, but it also represented what monks struggled to behold in their daily devotions. The connection between the initial's visionary image of the Deity and the contemplative monastic *vita angelica* would have been much more apparent if, as is likely, the lost opening miniature of the manuscript showed a related Trinitarian figure(s) as the object of veneration for the choirs of saints enjoying heavenly life.

The initial's monastic significance is reinforced by its association with the Christological portrait of Abbot Benedict. Monks were meant to see in the figure of the royal judge Christ the heavenly archetype of the righteous Benedictine abbot, who as Christ's representative in the monastery exemplified the way they could win their special crown of life, the *diadema monachorum*. Smaragdus wrote that "the proven monk is made into the diadem of the true king Christ;"[45] thus the diademed Christ portrayed the ultimate reward of the arduous monastic life.

The portrait of John (pl. 15) is also related to the initial, which illustrates the evangelist's apocalyptic vision (Apoc. 4). His depiction as the celestial evangelist, mentally soaring to heaven like his eagle to behold and teach the hidden secrets of the divine Word, was very likely associated with monastic transcendence and contemplation.

Augustine[46] had argued that John, because of his heavenly character, represented the contemplative life through which one began the ascent from the world to see heavenly truth. Anglo-Saxon and Carolingian commentators[47] also maintained that the evangelist had fasted for three days so that he might be worthy to begin writing his Gospel, and this fast so filled him with the Holy Spirit that he experienced the heavenly vision recorded in the prologue of his Gospel. His virginity was deemed another reason for his exceptional worthiness to perceive and disclose celestial secrets.[48] These qualities made John a paragon of the ascetic, contemplative monastic life. Aldhelm in his prose *De Virginitate* urged monks and nuns to imitate the evangelist's virginity so that they too could experience his ecstatic vision of a multitude of virgins singing a new canticle before the Lamb (Apoc. 14:1–5), a vision of the heavenly life awaiting them.[49] The anonymous life of Dunstan twice likened his chastity to John's.[50] Adelard[51] compared Dunstan, whose vigilance and prayers took him along the road to heaven, to one of the heavenly beasts around Christ en-

---

[42] Leclercq, *Vie parfaite*, pp. 30, 34f., 48; Hallinger, "Spiritual Life of Cluny," pp. 34f.

[43] Byrhtferth, *VO*, 3, 8; see also the similar passage in B., *Vita S. Dunstani*, 37.

[44] See above, chap. 2, n. 225.

[45] See above, chap. 3, n. 74.

[46] *De Consensu Evangelistarum*, 1, 5, 8; 4, 10, 20, ed. F. Weihrich, CSEL, 43, pp. 7–9, 415–18; Augustine, *In Iohannis Evangelium Tractus 124*, 5–8, ed. R. Willems, CC, 36, pp. 685–88. For Augustine's influence on monasticism, see G. B. Ladner, *The Idea of Reform* (Cambridge, Mass., 1959), pp. 334ff. Bede, *Hom.*, 1, 9, p. 92f., and Haymo, *Homilia 11*,

PL, 118, col. 74B–C, specifically equated John's contemplative life with monasticism.

[47] Bede, *Hom.*, 1, 9, p. 94; Alcuin, *Commentaria in S. Joannis Evangelium, Epistola Albini*, PL, 100, col. 741C; Haymo of Auxerre, *Homilia 9*, PL, 118, col. 55A–B; Ælfric, *Hom.*, 1, pp. 70, 71.

[48] Bede, *Hom.*, 1, 8; 1, 9, pp. 73, 94; Alcuin, *Comm. in S. Joannis, Epis. Alb.*, PL, 100, col. 743A–B.

[49] Aldhelm, *De Virginitate*, 7 and 22, pp. 64, 79.

[50] B., *Vita S. Dunstani*, 8, 30.

[51] Adelard, *Vita S. Dunstani*, 9, p. 63.

throned on a rainbow in John's vision (Apoc. 4:6–8). This is the manifestation of God the Benedictional's initial illustrates. Of course the beasts are not included in the initial, but the apocalyptic creature symbolizing John, the eagle, is prominent in his portrait.

The eagle was a common *topos* in monastic literature. Several times Smaragdus[52] used the sharp-eyed eagle, which could soar to sublime heights to behold the light of the sun, as a metaphor for monks whose fasting and other monastic exercises enable them to penetrate the mysteries of heaven. Wulfstan's life of Æthelwold[53] related that the bishop's pregnant mother had dreamed of a large golden eagle that flew from her mouth and shielded the town of Winchester with its wings before climbing out of sight. This gold eagle symbolized

> Æthelwold, who thought on divine things with a mind whose acute sight could not be averted, [and who] always flew in contemplation to the heavenly. He spread far and wide the shade of his fatherly protection of the church, "the city of the great king," which was under attack from hostile powers. And when he completed the race of his good struggle, he came to the sight of God in the company of the saints.[54]

A subsequent chapter described Æthelwold as "the eagle of Christ, [who] spread his golden wings" when he drove the canons from New Minster and replaced them with monks.[55] This metaphorical characterization of the bishop introducing monasticism as the result of his monastic celestial contemplation, which foreshadows his ultimate vision of God with the saints after his death, is analogous to the depiction of John as the contemplative heavenly evangelist ascending mentally to comprehend divinity, especially since the bishop and the evangelist are both likened to a gilded eagle spreading its wings in flight.

The miniature stressed not only the heavenly inspiration of John and the eagle but also their preaching of their revelations. The evangelist's

speaking gesture corresponds to the symbol's horn literally "trumpeting" its Gospel. This aspect of the iconography also finds a parallel in Wulfstan's account of Æthelwold's activities in the monastic reform:

> He was splendidly strong in word and deed, dedicating churches in many places and everywhere preaching the gospel of Christ in accordance with the instruction of the prophet Isaiah (58:1): "Cry aloud, spare not, lift up thy voice like a trumpet."[56]

In this passage Æthelwold's preaching of the Gospel must be taken as the propagation of monasticism. Benedict considered his *Rule* to be an abridged version of the Gospels, which he recommended as the principal rule for monks,[57] and monasticism was considered the evangelical life par excellence.[58] Wulfstan went on to say that Æthelwold's preaching was aided by the miracles of Saint Swithun, whose relics had been recently translated into the cathedral:

> So it was that at one and the same time two lamps blazed in the house of God, placed on golden candlesticks; for what Æthelwold preached by the saving encouragement of his words, Swithun wonderfully ornamented by display of miracles. . . . So it came about . . . that . . . monasteries were established everywhere in England.[59]

Wulfstan's metaphors for the partnership of Æthelwold and Swithun in the reform recalls a formula used in an alternate episcopal benediction for the feast of John the evangelist that was almost certainly on a leaf now missing from the Benedictional:

> O God, you who prepared your apostles [to be] precious lamps of the peoples, and you who placed James and John among the vessels of the Church as candlesticks of the faith for the enlightenment of souls, bring it to pass that your people imitate what the one directed by exhorting, [and] the other uttered by preaching.[60]

---

[52] *Diadema Monachorum*, 24; 93, PL, 102, cols. 619D, 684A–C.

[53] Wulfstan, *Life*, 2, pp. 4, 5.

[54] Wulfstan, *Life*, 3, p. 7.

[55] Wulfstan, *Life*, 20, p. 37. See also Byrhtferth, *VO*, 2, 8.

[56] Wulfstan, *Life*, 25, p. 43.

[57] *Benedicti Regula*, 73, p. 180; Leclercq, *Vie parfaite*, pp. 112ff.

[58] Leclercq, *Vie parfaite*, pp. 109–13.

[59] Wulfstan, *Life*, 26–27, p. 43.

[60] *CBP*, no. 1161; Warner and Wilson, *Ben.*, pp. 49f. (with a reconstruction of the missing leaf): "Deus qui tuos apos-

The characterizations of Æthelwold in the *vita* and John in the miniature and text of the Benedictional are closely analogous. Indeed, the first benediction for the evangelist's feast characterized him as a model for the members of the Church: as he was inspired by the Holy Spirit to perceive and teach the heavenly secrets of the Word, so they should be inspired by same Spirit to understand and preach his "lesson" of Christ's divinity.[61] Æthelwold must have viewed the image of the celestial evangelist as a model for his own divinely inspired preaching of the "gospel" of monastic reform.[62]

A Living Sacrifice

The asceticism that enabled monks to cast off the world and contemplate heaven was in its own right an essential aspect of monasticism.[63] Heeding Christ's admonition to take up the cross and follow him (Matt. 16:24), monks imitated his martyrdom on the cross through their asceticism, becoming living martyrs through their daily life of rigorous self-sacrifice. This has some bearing on the recurrent theme of self-offering in the miniatures.

In the Baptism (pl. 19) John the Baptist's leather girdle was assimilated to Christ's loincloth to signify that the ascetic Baptist symbolized those who have "crucified" or mortified their flesh and clothed themselves in the pure "new man," that is, those who through baptism and penitential observances have participated in Christ's Crucifixion and Resurrection, sharing his priestly office.

Because he was a prophet and a martyr who had led an isolated, penitential life, John the Baptist was considered a founder of monasticism, and his rough, ascetic clothing was regarded as a prototype of the monk's habit, which included a girdle.[64] Smaragdus[65] in his commentary on the Benedictine *Rule* said that monks girded themselves with a leather girdle like John to signify their abstinence from deeds of the flesh. Although Smaragdus in his influential *Diadema Monachorum* did not mention the Baptist's girdle, he did include a long and revealing discourse on monastic girding.[66] He devoted a whole chapter (78) to the notion that monks should gird the "loins of the mind" by refraining from concupiscences and preserving physical and mental purity. The next chapter continued the theme of the mortification of the flesh and urged monks to crucify with Christ their sinful "old man," according to Galatians 5:24: "And they that are Christ's, have crucified their flesh, with vices and concupiscences."[67] This was the very biblical text cited in exegesis to relate the Baptist's girdle symbolically to those who have baptismally "put on Christ" (Gal. 5:27).

Smaragdus' application of these Pauline baptismal metaphors to monks reflects the belief that monastic profession was a second baptism which initiated monks into an ascetic existence of living martyrdom.[68] Like the catechumen, the novitiate was assimilated to the dying and res-

---

tolos pretiosa gentium lumina praeparasti, quique iacobum et iohannem ad illustrandas animas inter uasa ecclesiae candelabra fidei praetulisti, fac plebem tuam imitari quod unus exor[ta]ndo formauit, alter euangelizando eruct[uauit]." See also Prescott, "Text," pp. 127f. This formula (cf. Matt. 5:15) was also used for other apostles; cf. *CBP*, 981a, 988, also 906.

[61] See above, chap. 3, n. 15.

[62] For some related themes in later Anglo-Saxon portraits of John, see J. O'Reilly, "St. John as a Figure of the Contemplative Life: Text and Image in the Art of the Anglo-Saxon Benedictine Reform," *Dunstan*, pp. 165ff.

[63] Leclercq, *Vie parfaite*, pp. 125ff.; J. Wollasch, "Das Mönchsgelübde als Opfer," *Frühmittelalterliche Studien* 18 (1984): 529–45.

[64] P. Oppenheim, *Das Mönchskleid im christlichen Altertum* (Freiburg im Breisgau, 1931), pp. 175f., 182, 240ff.; idem, *Symbolik und religiöse Wertung des Mönchskleides im christlichen Altertum*, Theologie des christlichen Ostens, 2 (Münster in

Westf., 1932), pp. 83, 86; Leclercq, *Vie Parfaite*, pp. 59ff., 66ff., 77ff.

[65] *Expositio in Regulam*, 4, 4, pp. 89f. See also Benedict of Aniane, *Concordia Regularum*, 62, 4 (from the *Rule of St. Basil*); 62, 21 (from the *Rule of Cassian*), PL 103, cols. 1240D, 1250D. Æthelwold also knew this Carolingian compilation since he adapted its title for his own customary, *RC*, p. 69, n. 1.

[66] PL, 102, cols. 673f.

[67] PL, 102, col. 674B–C.

[68] G. Constable, "The Ceremonies and Symbolism of Entering Religious Life and Taking the Monastic Habit, from the Fourth to the Twelfth Century," *Settimane di studio del centro italiano di studi sull'alto medioevo* 33 (1985): 799ff.; O. Casel, "Die Mönchweihe," *Jahrbuch für Liturgiewissenschaft* 5 (1925): 1–47; E. E. Malone, "Martyrdom and Monastic Profession as a Second Baptism," *Vom christlichen Mysterium. Gesammelte Arbeiten zum Gedächtnis von Odo Casel OSB*, ed. A. Mayer et al. (Düsseldorf, 1951), pp. 115–34.

urrected Lord, crucified to the world and regenerated into the pure new monastic life. The vesting of the new monk in his habit had the same significance as the changing of garments in baptism: the putting off of the old sinful man and the donning of the new pure one. After Smaragdus applied Pauline baptismal metaphors to monks, he continued that "the power which I see standing over baptism, the same I see also over the vestments of the monk, when he receives the spiritual habit."[69] Since this habit signified that henceforth the monk would live in the image of the crucified Christ, monastic garments were sometimes interpreted as symbols of the Crucifixion.[70] Urging monks to configure themselves to Christ on the cross, Smaragdus related how an elder had set an example:

> Removing his own garments from himself, and girding his own loins and extending his hands, [he] said: "So ought monks to be stripped of all matter of the world, and to crucify themselves with the adversities, temptations, and struggles of the world."[71]

Reenacting his consecration, the old monk's extended hands and girdle reflect his monastic assumption of the image of the crucified Christ in the loincloth.

Æthelwold, who was familiar with Smaragdus' writings, would probably have paid close attention to these discussions of monastic girding, for this subject seems to have held a particular fascination for the bishop and his painters. The lost frontispiece for his Old English translation of the *Rule*, best preserved in a copy in the Arundel Psalter from Canterbury (fig. 136), portrayed a girded monk, probably Æthelwold himself, humbly kneeling and kissing Benedict's feet. The girdle's inscription, "zona humilitatis" (girdle of humility), emphasizes its meaning as a symbol of monastic mortifica-

tion.[72] Another lost creation of Æthelwold's scriptorium, the frontispiece of the *Regularis Concordia*, copied in another Canterbury manuscript (fig. 138), depicted a monk girding himself with a scroll, a symbolic gesture indicating his acceptance of the consuetudinary and its rigorous discipline.[73] In the light of this preoccupation with the iconography of the monastic girdle and Smaragdus' discussions, the figure of the Baptist in the Benedictional should also be understood as a symbol of the ascetic monk girded as a living martyr in the image of the crucified Christ.

Balancing this symbol of self-offering in the miniature are the attributes of kingship, the diadems and scepters the angels bring to Christ. As we know from the interrelated representations of Benedict and Christ enthroned, the diadem of Christ in the Benedictional could symbolize the *diadema monachorum*. Since the initial's iconography had a level of baptismal as well as monastic symbolism, the diadems in the Baptism miniature probably also had monastic connotations. Just as Christ's sacrifice on the cross had won him the triumphant crown of kingship (cf. figs. 36, 37), so monks, imitating his self-offering, could also win the comparable reward of the *diadema monachorum*.

Another symbol of self-offering in the Benedictional was the animate altar. The miniatures of the Annunciation, the Nativity, the Presentation in the Temple, and the Bishop Blessing the Congregation (pls. 8, 12, 20, 35) all expressed the concept that the material altar was the outward symbol of the altar within the believer, who makes spiritual sacrifices to God in the temple of the body. This theme, too, had monastic connotations.

Smaragdus[74] devoted the final chapter of the *Diadema Monachorum* to the idea that every man possessed two altars, the body and the heart. Only those who exhibited to God sacrifices of good works and chastity on the altar of their

---

[69] Smaragdus, *Diadema Monachorum*, 79, PL, 102, col. 674C: "uirtutem quam uidi stantem super baptisma, eamdem uidi etiam super uestimentum monachi, quando accipit habitum spiritualem."

[70] See the consecration rite in the early-eleventh-century Anglo-Saxon pontifical (Cambridge, Corpus Christi Coll., MS 44), quoted by Constable, "Ceremonies and Symbolism," pp. 813f., 817; also Leclercq, *Vie parfaite*, pp. 128ff.; Casel, "Mönchweihe," pp. 8f., 31.

[71] Smaragdus, *Diadema Monachorum*, 83, PL, 102, col.

677B–C: "ille exspolians se uestimento suo, et cingens lumbos suos, atque extendens manus suas, dixit: 'Sic debet monachus nudus esse ab omni materia saeculi, et crucifigere se aduersus tentationes atque certamina mundi.'" See Oppenheim, *Mönchskleid*, p. 176.

[72] Deshman, "Benedictus," p. 215, fig. 54.

[73] Deshman, "Benedictus," p. 205, fig. 50, also fig. 51.

[74] *Diadema Monachorum*, 100: "De duobus altaribus in homine, quorum alterum in corpore est, et alterum in corde," PL, 102, cols. 689f.

body and pure thoughts on the altar of their heart were worthy to celebrate the "double feast" of the consecration of the church altar: "Even as we visibly celebrate the consecration of the altar of the temple, so invisibly may we merit to rejoice in chastity of body and spiritual purity of soul."[75]

Æthelwold would likely have been familiar with this last chapter of the *Diadema Monachorum*, and anyone reading it cannot fail to note that it bore some relationship to the "double feast" of the dedication of the church. In fact, Smaragdus excerpted it virtually unchanged from a sermon of Caesarius of Arles, *De Templo vel Consecratione Altaris*.[76] The theme of the living altar is also associated with this feast in the Benedictional since the illustration for the dedication of the church assimilated the officiating bishop, probably Æthelwold, to the altar beneath its ciborium. Like Smaragdus' text, the picture conveyed the idea that the hallowing of the physical church and altar must be matched by the consecration of the believer as a spiritual house and altar of God. Since in Smaragdus the altar became a specifically monastic symbol of the monk's pure life of self-sacrifice, the same was probably also the case in this, as well as in the other miniatures representing a living altar.

In the case of the Presentation the anthropomorphic altar probably possessed still another dimension of monastic symbolism. In the Benedictine rite of oblation[77] the parents brought their young son as well as offerings to the altar in the offertory procession of the mass. They placed the child's hand and his articles of monastic profession on the altar, wrapping them in the altar cloth. This act, which was patterned on the covering of the Eucharist with a corner of the altar cloth, signified that the oblate's profession was a self-offering to God, analogous to Christ's sacrifice.[78] To justify the practice Carolingian authors such as Hrabanus Maurus cited Christ's Presentation in the Temple as a precedent:

> For if Jesus wanted to be brought by his parents to the temple, and there to be offered as a sacrifice himself to God, who is it who should presume to reproach parents' oblation of their own children, and to defend that they should not exhibit them a living sacrifice to God?[79]

The association with oblation influenced the Romanesque fresco of the Presentation near the altar of the formerly monastic upper church of St. Clemens in Schwartzrheindorf (fig. 132).[80] Like the father in the monastic rite, Joseph brings the clasped hands of the Christ child into contact with the altar. In the Benedictional's version of the Presentation, monastic viewers would inevitably have perceived the altar draped in the form of human hands and arms as an allusion to the covering of the oblate's hand (and vows) with the altar cloth, and the motif's connotations of the baptismal vesting of Christ would have reinforced its connotations of monastic profession.

The Living Ecclesia

The animate altar is but one part of a broader iconographic pattern in the cycle: the column and the baldachin are other architectural elements that also symbolize the living spiritual

---

[75] Smaragdus, *Diadema Monachorum*, 100, PL, 102, col. 690: "Et quomodo uisibiliter de templi altaris consecratione gaudemus, sic inuisibiliter de corporis castitate uel animi puritate spirituale gaudium habere mereamur."

[76] *Sermo* 228, 2, ed. G. Morin, CC, p. 902. Conceivably Æthelwold might have known this text. Another of Caesarius' dedication sermons (no. 229, pp. 905ff.) prefaces the *ordo* for church consecration in the eleventh-century Winchester Benedictional of Archbishop Robert; see *Ben. Rob.*, pp. 69–72.

[77] *Benedicti Regula*, 59, pp. 151f. The Winchester rite of profession began with the novice offering God his articles of profession "propria manu" on the altar; see *Ben. Rob.*, p. 131.

[78] Wollasch, "Mönchsgelübde," pp. 531ff. M. Lahaye-Geusen, *Das Opfer der Kinder*, Münsteraner theologische Abhandlungen, 13 (Altenberge, 1991), pp. 45, 69f.

[79] Hrabanus Maurus, *Liber de Oblatione Pueroum*, PL, 107, col. 428D: "Si enim Jesus a parentibus ad templum deferri uoluit, ibique offerri pro se hostiam Deo, quis est qui parentum oblationem in filiis suis reprehendere praesumat, et prohibere quod non exhibeant eos hostiam uiuentem Deo?" For other sources see I. Herwegen, "Der Gemäldezyklus in der Oberkirche zu Schwarzrheindorf," *Das Buch Ezechiel in Theologie und Kunst bis zum Ende des XII. Jahrhunderts*, ed. W. Neuss (Münster in Westf., 1912), pp. 309ff.

[80] Herwegen, "Gemäldezyklus," pp. 308ff., fig. 84; O. Demus, *Romanesque Mural Painting* (London, 1970), pp. 604–606.

Church of Christ and the believers. The monastic features of this pervasive theme of the living Ecclesia stand out most clearly against the background of Æthelwold's veneration of Swithun, the Winchester saint so prominently identified with the column (pl. 32).

On 15 July 971 Æthelwold translated Swithun's relics into the Old Minster from a tomb outside the west entrance; soon after he began to rebuild and extend the western part of the church to house them in a more fitting architectural setting. In a second translation, probably in 974, the relics were placed in a splendid new reliquary. In 980 the addition to the cathedral was dedicated, though work continued later.[81] The reference to Swithun's numerous miracles in the Benedictional's text for his feast indicates that the manuscript postdates the first translation; Swithun's equation with a column in the miniature and the liturgy for the feast of his translation commemorated his literal incorporation into the Old Minster.

Contemporary Winchester sources emphasized that Swithun was virtually unknown until the time of Æthelwold. The bishop deliberately propagated the saint's cult through the translations, the portrait in the Benedictional, and the *Translatio et Miracula S. Swithuni*, written between 972 and 974 by Lantfred, a Fleury monk at Winchester.[82] The above-quoted passage from Wulfstan's *Life of St. Æthelwold*[83] indicates that Swithun became the bishop's partner in the mission of monastic reform. Lantfred's contemporary narrative reveals that Æthelwold manipulated the saint's cult so that his unexpected rise from obscurity and his sudden spate of miracles became signs of celestial approval for Æthelwold's actions, particularly his controversial expulsion of the secular canons from the Winchester monasteries.[84] Lantfred said that the saint revealed himself and asked to be moved

into the Old Minster only after the wicked impurity of the non-monastic canons had been expunged from it. Cleansed of these defiling canons and now housing pure monks, the church was once more fit to become a dwelling for God and his saint. Lantfred paralleled the entrances into the church of the saint's holy relics and the reforming monks. The translation and the ensuing miracles inside the cathedral demonstrated that monasticism had literally sanctified Ecclesia once more and that the rebuilding of the Old Minster to house the relics was an external sign of the internal moral renewal brought by monasticism to the Church. In Winchester art and liturgy the emphatic association of the saint with the column, part of the material church, was another way to propagandize the view that the monks and their saintly ally were the only rightful possessors, indeed the very embodiment, of Ecclesia.

The late–tenth- and early– eleventh-century *vitae* of the leaders of the reform leave no doubt that the column and also the related motif of the cornerstone were monastic as well as ecclesiological symbols. Byrhtferth, for example, wrote that Oswald's monastic devotions and virtues were spiritual columns that edified him into an unshakable spiritual house of wisdom.[85] The imagery derived from the description of wisdom's house of seven columns in Proverbs 9:1 and of the wise man's house founded on the rock of belief in Matthew 7:24–25. Benedict himself had given this Gospel passage monastic significance by quoting it in his *Rule*.[86] Since Matthew twice mentioned that this spiritual house is built on rock, it comes as no surprise that Byrhtferth also applied the cornerstone metaphor to Oswald. Oswald's chanting and prayers at Fleury earned him "the forgiveness and the grace . . . of Jesus. They were the precious stones placed in the corners of his own

[81] M. Biddle, "Excavations at Winchester, 1969: Eighth Interim Report," *Antiquaries Journal* 50 (1970): 317–21; idem, "*Felix Urbs Winthonia*: Winchester in the Age of Monastic Reform," *Tenth-Century Studies*, pp. 132–39; idem, "Archaeology, Architecture, and the Cult of Saints in Anglo-Saxon England," *The Anglo-Saxon Church*, ed. L. A. S. Butler and R. K. Morris, Council for British Archaeology, Research Report, 60 (London, 1986), pp. 22ff.; D. J. Sheerin, "Dedication of the Old Minster, Winchester, in 980," *Revue Bénédictine* 88 (1978): 266–77; R. Deshman, "St. Swithun in Medieval Art," in Lapidge, *Cult of Saint Swithun*, forthcoming, and the other

studies in this volume.
[82] Lantfred, *Translatio*.
[83] See above, n. 59.
[84] For the following, see Deshman, "Living Ecclesia," pp. 273ff.; idem, "St. Swithun in Medieval Art"; Sheerin, "Dedication of the Old Minster," pp. 266–77. For Æthelwold's culting of relics to enhance other foundations, see A. Thacker, "Æthelwold and Abingdon," *Bishop Æthelwold*, pp. 59ff.; also Rollason, *Saints and Relics*, pp. 177ff.
[85] Byrhtferth, *VO*, 2, 7.
[86] *Benedicti Regula*, prologue, p. 7.

holy house, which [stones] supported it firmly."[87] Already in Smaragdus' *Diadema Monachorum*,[88] which Æthelwold knew, an entire chapter exhorted monks to become living stones built upon Christ into a spiritual temple, and the abbot Anthony was termed a "columna lucis."

These related architectural symbols were also repeatedly used to characterize Dunstan in Adelard's *Vita*.[89] Particularly illuminating is the account of Dunstan's foundation of the first reformed monastery at Glastonbury:

> First, eliminating whatever offended the eyes of the heavenly Inspector, he, having been made monk and abbot, the first one, began firstly to establish a school of monks. By his zeal in that place holy religion so increased in such a short time, just as I said that the lamps of others throughout the entire church were kindled from a lamp. . . so through him the column of monastic religion spread from this place throughout the whole land of the English.[90]

This account of the reform at Glastonbury has analogies with Lantfred's description of events at Winchester. After being cleansed of impurity displeasing to God (presumably non-monks), the house of God (the church) is occupied by fittingly pure monks and also, in the case of Winchester, by a saintly supporter of the monks. The holy monastic way of life of these new occupants allows them to become, like Dunstan or Swithun, "the column of monastic religion," that is, to build themselves into the living spiritual edifice of the monastic Ecclesia.

From these literary sources it is clear that the Benedictional's cornerstone and column imagery—and also the associated monastic symbol of the living altar—belonged to a widely diffused propaganda campaign to identify monasticism spiritually and materially with Ecclesia itself. Æthelwold himself must have conceived this monastic propaganda, for it first appeared in the Benedictional some two decades before the lives of the other reformers were written.[91] Of course, Æthelwold did not invent the idea that monasticism was a means of constructing a sound spiritual house in Christ—this derived from earlier monastic writings. But in Æthelwold's hands the traditional metaphors for the inner moral effects of monasticism assumed a new level of polemical and even practical political significance: they became a religious rationale legitimatizing the monks' wresting physical, economic, and spiritual control of the churches and the monasteries from the secular canons and their powerful lay allies.

The presence of the symbolic motifs of the living altar, the cornerstone, and the column in the Benedictional's illustration for the dedication of the church implies that the miniature as a whole was related to the monastic reform. Æthelwold would have known from Smaragdus' *Diadema Monachorum* that this ceremony could symbolize the continuous consecration of the monk through his ascetic monastic life as a spiritual dwelling of the Deity. In the context of the reform, however, the rite won a more general monastic significance. Byrhtferth wrote that King Edgar had "restored all the ruined monasteries, building thus a new Jerusalem, expelling through his royal authority the trifles of the secular clerics."[92] The consecration ceremony, which assimilated the new church to the new Jerusalem descending as a heavenly bride to earth (cf. Apoc. 22:2), symbolized the hallowing not only of the individual, purified by monastic life to become a spiritual house of God, but also of the entire Church, cleansed by the monastic reform to become once more a suitable habitation for the Lord. The Benedictional's picture for the ceremony must be taken as a symbolic portrayal of the advent of God and his blessings to the monks and the monastically renewed Church.

---

[87] Byrhtferth, *VO*, 3, 2.

[88] Chaps. 44, 60, PL, 102, cols. 641D, 656D–57.

[89] Adelard, *Vita S. Dunstani*, 6, 8, 11, 12, pp. 59, 62, 66, 67; see Deshman, "Living Ecclesia," p. 276.

[90] Adelard, *Vita S. Dunstani*, 3, p. 56:
Unde primum eliminato quicquid oculis superni Inspectoris offendebat, monachus et abbas effectus, monachorum ibi scholam primo primus instituere coepit.

Cujus ibi studio sic in breui sancta excreuit religio, ut sicut dixi de lampade . . . caeterorum per omnem ecclesiam lampades accensas, ita per eum ex hoc loco columen religionis monasticae toto Anglorum orbe diffusum sit.

[91] Winchester hagiography also designated Dunstan a "column." See Wulfstan, *Life*, 14, p. 26.

[92] Byrhtferth, *Vita S. Ecgwini*, 4, 11; also idem, *VO*, 5, 9.

Paradise on Earth

In her feast picture Saint Æthelthryth holds a sprig of golden flowers symbolizing the virtue that entitled her to "blossom" in heaven (pl. 28, fig. 154). Although the flower could signify the moral righteousness of any Christian, in her case it had a specifically monastic value. Bede's hymn, which inspired her attribute, said that "in the monastery the bride [Æthelthryth] was pledged to God, where she, wholly devoted to heaven, flowered in lofty deeds."[93] Blossoming is here a metaphor for the virtuous monastic life that anticipates life in heaven.[94]

Underlying this metaphor was the medieval conception of the cloister as a paradisiacal garden, a heaven on earth where monks and nuns blossomed in their virtuous angelic life.[95] That Æthelwold himself saw the reformed monastery in these terms is evident from one of his own writings, the New Minster charter of 966.[96] The charter is nothing less than his view of the place of the monastic reform in the scheme of divine salvation. He equated the evil, "proud cast-down canons"[97] who had been expelled from the monastery of New Minster to the sinful, arrogant angels whom God had thrown out of heaven. The monks, who are "adorned with the flower of all virtues"[98] in the monastery, corresponded to innocent, prelapsarian mankind, who had been "flowering with all good fortune" and had "flowered in the strong hope of spiritual joy,"[99] as they enjoyed the fellowship of the angels in paradise.

Of course Æthelthryth is not actually portrayed in her paradisiacal monastic habitation, but the picture of the Entry (pl. 21) represents Jerusalem in a floriferous landscape as a symbol of the heavenly city and church in celestial fields. Byrhtferth had called the reformed monasteries a terrestrial "new Jerusalem." Should the iconography be interpreted as an allegorical image of the flowering paradise of the renewed monastery?

It is important to recall that one scriptural source of the miniature's bucolic symbolism was Psalm 91:13 ("The righteous shall flower like the palm tree: he shall grow up like the cedar of Lebanon"),[100] for this very text was given a monastic significance. Dunstan's first biographer claimed that Dunstan righteously "flowered like the cedar of Lebanon in the energy of his virtues" when he entered the monastery of Glastonbury.[101] Byrhtferth continually painted the monasteries of Ramsey and Fleury in the colors of the *paradisus claustri*:

> The lover of righteousness [Oswald] spent a good many years in the monastery at Fleury, where the sons of that Floriac monastery flower . . . more gloriously than lilies, more splendidly than roses. These [sons] know how to offer to God flowers and fruits which abide and can flourish (florere) unwitheringly with God into perpetual eternities.[102]

The metaphor of the monks offering God the flowers and fruits of their virtuous monastic life which make them worthy to flourish eternally with him in heaven[103] has its counterpart in the miniature's figure of an inhabitant of Jerusalem presenting a gold bouquet to Christ. On the one hand, this figure symbolized the righteous patriarchs who are worthy to pay perpetual tribute to God in heavenly Jerusalem because of their offerings to him in their former life on earth. On the other hand, the figure represented the present-day participants in the Palm Sunday procession whose meritorious donation of palms and flowers "to God" at the altar anticipated their future presentation of the good fruits of their earthly life to God at the Second Coming. The commentators on the floral symbolism of the Entry into Jerusalem did not, to my knowledge, mention any offering to Christ, and apparently the analogous monastic exegesis influenced the interpolation of the motif into the narrative

---

[93] See above, chap. 3, n. 90.
[94] This was a common monastic metaphor; cf. Aldhelm, *De Virginitate* (prose), 28, 29, 57, 60, pp. 87, 88, 131.
[95] Leclercq, *Vie parfaite*, pp. 164ff.
[96] Ed. Whitelock et al., *Councils*, pp. 119–33; W. de G. Birch, *Cartularium Saxonum*, 3 vols. (London, 1885–93), no. 1190; P. H. Sawyer, *Anglo-Saxon Charters* (London, 1968), no. 745.
[97] Chap. 8, p. 126: "superbientes . . . deiecti canonici."

[98] Chap. 13, p. 128: "omniumque uirtutum flore decorati."
[99] Chap. 2, p. 122: "omnibus florens prosperis;" "gaudii spiritalis spe pollente florebat."
[100] See above, chap. 2, nn. 140, 141.
[101] B., *Vita S. Dunstani*, 5.
[102] Byrhtferth, *VO*, 2, 9; also 3, 7 and 19; 4, 16; 5, 8.
[103] For another example of this votive floral metaphor, see Byrhtferth, *VO*, 3, 19.

Christological context. This depiction of Jerusalem in floriferous fields must have symbolized the paradisiacal monastery as well as the terrestrial church. Both were reflections of the celestial Jerusalem.

To progress any further in our assessment of the monastic symbolism of the Entry, we must pause for an excursis into some aspects of monasticism on the Continent that strongly influenced the Anglo-Saxon reformers.

The Continental Background
and the Translations of Saint Swithun

The *Vita S. Oswaldi* associated the portrait of Fleury as a *paradisus claustri* with the etymological relationship between *flos* and Fleury, but another passage discloses that Fleury's possession of Benedict's relics was no less a factor:

> Benedict . . . flourished (florere), became renowned and shone brilliantly. After a lengthy space of time his bones were taken . . . to the Frankish kingdom, and were housed in . . . Fleury. How gloriously that shining jewel rejoices in heaven with Christ his dead bones reveal on earth: not only do diseased bodies receive . . . the remedy of health from him, but even souls . . . receive at his instigation the whiteness and purity which they previously possessed [when] baptized in the river Jordan. Rightly is that sacred place called Fleury, because . . . the jewels and flowers of Paradise flourish in it with rosy hue and snow-white brightness; and not only are they the flowers of that exquisite place, but they are also the flowers of the land of heavenly bliss. . . . The indefatigable monk Oswald flourished mightily alongside these other flowers.[104]

Benedict's migration to heaven where he flowers in paradisiacal pastures is mirrored in his relics' translation into Fleury.[105] His presence causes the monastery to become a terrestrial heaven where the monks blossom like him and the sick of body and soul are restored, like monks in their consecration, to a paradisiacal state of baptismal purity.

Similar ideas occurred in the early–eleventh-century *Illatio Sancti Benedicti* by Thierry (Theoderich) of Fleury,[106] a narrative of the return of the relics to Fleury on 4 December 883 after their temporary removal during the Viking invasions. In wintry weather the saint's remains were festively greeted by a great throng of monks, bishops, and laymen singing "Blessed is he who cometh in the name of the Lord" (Matt. 21:9). When the procession bearing the relics reached the *porta Paschalis*, suddenly, "as if in the middle of April," the surrounding trees and foliage burst into flowers, causing everyone to recognize Benedict's great glory with Christ and the magnitude of the Lord's gift to them.

As often in medieval translation accounts, Benedict's translation was treated as an *adventus* in which God reveals his power and presence through the saint.[107] Benedict's entrance into the monastery was carefully patterned on Christ's Entry into Jerusalem. The crowds greeting his relics sang the same chant as the populace who had welcomed Christ. As in Aldhelm, this was a play on the saint's name (*Benedictus* = blessed), suggesting that Benedict, the archetypal Benedictine abbot, came to them as Christ's blessed representative in the monastery. The miraculous flowering is another *topos* of the Entry, as we see in the Benedictional. The miracle occurred when the relics reached the "porta Paschalis," a symbolic allusion to Easter the week after Palm Sunday. Thierry[108] also mentioned that the *Illatio*, the feast on 4 December commemorating the translation, occurred during the Advent season, when

---

[104] Byrhtferth, *VO*, 3, 6.

[105] Cf. the eleventh-century poem on Benedict, ed. R. B. C. Huygens, "Poèmes inédits de Geraldus, moine de Saint-Benoît-sur-Loire," *Latomus* 18 (1959): 452, lines 45f.: "Flos, paradise, tuus caelestem migrat ad aulam, / Ad Gallos transit flos, paradise, tuus."

[106] Chap. 9, ed. J. Mabillion, *Acta Sanctorum Ordinis S. Benedicti*, 2nd ed. (Venice, 1738), 4, 2, p. 366.

[107] For the *topos* of translation as *adventus*, see N.

Gussone, "Adventus-Zeremoniell und Translation von Reliquien. Victrinus von Rouen, De Laude Sanctorum," *Frühmittelalterliche Studien* 10 (1976): 124–33; N.-N. Huyghebaert, *Une Translation de reliques à Gand en 944* (Brussels, 1978), pp. xxiv–xxvi; M. Heinzelmann, *Translationsberichte und andere Quellen des Reliquienkultes*, Typologie des Sources du Moyen Âge Occidental, 33 (Turnhout, 1979), pp. 66ff.

[108] *Illatio*, p. 362.

Eastern monks, "as in Lent," customarily practiced the greatest monastic austerity in expectation of Christ's Birth. Benedict's translation into the monastery and its commemorative feast were typologically aligned with Christ's advent into Jerusalem and its Palm Sunday reenactment; as in the Benedictional, the blossoming of nature symbolized the virtue of both the saint (or Christ) and those who have made themselves worthy to welcome him. For Thierry the disciplined monastic life prepared the Fleury monks to receive the honor of Benedict's advent just as the Lenten mortifications prepared all Christians for Christ's advent on Palm Sunday.

The association between the Entry into Jerusalem and Benedict's presence in Fleury is also found in John of Salerno's near-contemporary account of the reform of the monastery by Abbot Odo of Cluny (d. 942).[109] John reported that the unruliness of the unreformed monks had caused Benedict's spirit, though not his bones, to leave the monastery, not to return until accompanied by a man of his own persuasion from Aquitaine. The distraught Fleury monks sought in vain to find and to bring back Benedict. Even so, when the Aquitanian Abbot Odo came to reform them, they violently resisted his entrance into the monastery for three days. Only when Odo imitated Christ at the Entry into Jerusalem by riding to the monastery on an ass did they relent and receive him. Subsequently Benedict appeared to a Fleury monk, telling him that he had been in England rescuing the soul of a former Fleury monk and that he would soon return to the reformed monastery. On the morrow Benedict made a dramatic miraculous advent to the church as his protégé Odo celebrated the mass on the saint's feast day.

Although in John's account there is an analogy between Christ's Entry into Jerusalem and Odo and Benedict's advents to Fleury, the earliest Continental source to connect Benedict's advent to an unseasonable blossoming is the *Illatio*, which Thierry wrote a decade or so after he left Fleury in 1002.[110] Very likely, however, the legend of the saint's miraculous translation originated earlier. Thierry mentioned that the feast of the *Illatio* was well established at Fleury, where he seems to have resided for some years before his departure.[111] An account of Fleury's rituals that he also wrote after leaving is known to reflect the life at the monastery several decades earlier, for its contents correspond to many of the Fleury observances that Æthelwold incorporated into the *Regularis Concordia*.[112] The previously quoted passage from the *Vita S. Oswaldi*, which Byrhtferth wrote by 1005, indicates that the legend of the miraculous flowering at Benedict's translation into Fleury was known in England no later than the early eleventh century.

If the tale was already current at Fleury in Æthelwold's day, then he would have known it. His disciple Osgar had studied at Fleury before succeeding Æthelwold as abbot of Abingdon in 963 or 964.[113] In the *Regularis Concordia*[114] Æthelwold stated that monks from Fleury as well as Ghent had been invited to Winchester to advise on monastic customs. Lapidge[115] has identified the Fleury adviser as Lantfred, who wrote the account of Swithun's translations and miracles after he came to Winchester. He certainly would have told Æthelwold about Benedict's translation and Fleury's reform, especially since Benedict was supposedly in England while awaiting Odo's arrival at Fleury. Fleury, however, need not have been the only source from which Æthelwold could have learned of the association of the reformed paradisiacal monastery with the Entry into Jerusalem and the translation of relics.

[109] John of Salerno, *Vita S. Odonis*, 3, 8 and 11, PL, 133, cols. 80–83.

[110] A. Davril, "Un Moine de Fleury aux environs de l'an mil: Thierry, dit d'Amorbach," *Études ligériennes d'histoire et d'archéologie médiévales*, ed. R. Louis (Auxerre, 1975), pp. 97–104; A. Vidier, *L'Historiographie à Saint-Benoît-sur-Loire et les miracles de Saint Benoît* (Paris, 1965), pp. 170ff.

[111] Thierry, *Illatio*, p. 362.

[112] K. Hallinger and A. Davril, CCM, 7, 1, pp. 149ff., 331ff., 351ff.; L. Donnat, "Recherches sur l'influence de Fleury au Xe siècle," *Études ligériennes*, ed. Louis, pp. 165ff. For Thierry's text, see *Consuetudines Floriacenses Antiquiores*, ed. A. Davril and L. Donnat, CCM, 7, 3, pp. 4–60.

[113] Wulfstan, *Life*, 14, p. 26. A number of other Anglo-Saxons also resided there during the late tenth century; see J. Vezin, "Leofnoth. Un Scribe anglais à Saint-Benoît-sur-Loire," *Codices Manuscripti* 3 (1977): 109–20; D. Gremont and L. Donnat, "Fleury, le Mont Saint-Michel et l'Angleterre à la fin du Xe et au début du XIe siècle," *Millénaire monastique du Mont Saint-Michel*, ed. J. Laporte et al. (Paris, 1967), 1, pp. 751–93; L. Gougaud, "Les Relations de l'abbaye de Fleury-sur-Loire avec les Iles Britanniques (Xe et XIe siècles)," *Mémoires de la Société d'Histoire et d'Archéologie de Bretagne* 4 (1923): 4–30.

[114] *RC*, prohemium, 5, p. 72.

[115] Lapidge, *Cult of Saint Swithun*.

In the autumn of 944 Gérard of Brogne had translated the relics of Wandrille and other saints into the recently reformed abby of St. Peter's in Ghent. According to a twelfth-century account,[116] Saint Wandrille himself had earlier caused the secular canons to be expelled from the abbey and replaced with monks, so that he could be received by suitably religious individuals worthy of the honor. Upon the advent of the relics at the monastery the surrounding vegetation blossomed unseasonably.[117] This miracle, which recurred annually on the feast of the translation, reminded an Eastern prelate of the Palm Sunday commemoration of the Entry into Jerusalem when Christ had been met by children holding palms and flowers. Supposedly the Lord had also ordered nature to blossom at the saints' advent as a sign that the saints flowered in heaven because they had adorned themselves with the imperishable flowers of virtue in their earthly life. This miracle also set an example for the monks who were to flower like the palms of the Lord (Ps. 91:13), spiritually germinating perennial, fragrant blossoms and good fruit, so that with the saints they might also make fragrant self-offerings to the Lamb.

This text's linkage of the *topos* of the *paradisus claustri* with the Entry into Jerusalem and Palm Sunday offers an especially compelling analogy to the Benedictional's miniature, for both refer to the floral imagery of Psalm 91:13 and an eschatological offering of blossoms. This account of the translation used tenth-century sources contemporary with the event. Evidently the particular section with the miraculous flowering was composed in the first half of the twelfth century,[118] but the tale in some form might have originated much earlier, perhaps already in the lifetime of Æthelwold.

If this was the case, then he would likely have known of story. His mentor Dunstan spent sev-

eral years in exile at St. Peter's in Ghent after King Eadwig's accession in 955, and Dunstan's biographer Adelard,[119] himself a Ghent monk, implied that one reason Dunstan had gone there was because it housed the recently translated relics of Wandrille and other saints. The Ghent advisor whom Æthelwold called to Winchester was the monk Womar, who was listed among the *familia* of the Old Minster in the New Minster *Liber Vitae*.[120] Womar established a confraternity between the monastic communities of the Old Minster and Ghent, and at the time of his death in 981 he was the abbot of St. Peter's as well as St. Bavo's in Ghent.

These Ghent and Fleury sources seem to reflect monastic themes that apparently originated on the Continent and circulated among the tenth-century monastic reformers on both sides of the Channel. Not only do these texts corroborate that the miniature of the Entry is an allegorical portrait of the earthly paradise of the cloisters, but also they raise the possibility that the iconography is related to another Continental concept that influenced Æthelwold: the parallel advents of reform and relics into the monastery.

At Fleury and Ghent, as at Winchester, the absence of a saint's relics or spirit from the church was taken as a token of heavenly disapproval of the lack of proper monastic observance, and conversely the introduction or return of the saint in one form or another placed a celestial seal of approval on the reform of the monastery. Æthelwold's manipulation of the cult of Saint Swithun in the interests of the reform at Winchester was very probably influenced by what he learned from Lantfred and Womar, if not from other sources, about the role that saints had played in the earlier, precedent-setting Continental reforms.[121] Indeed, it was Lantfred's own account of Swithun's transla-

---

[116] *Sermo de Adventu Sanctorum Wandregisili, Ansberti et Vulframni in Blandinium*, 22–23, ed. Huyghebaert, *Translation*, pp. 24f.

[117] *Sermo*, 48–51, ed. Huyghebaert, pp. 53–56.

[118] Huyghebaert, *Translation*, pp. xliii–liv.

[119] Adelard, *Vita S. Dunstani*, 6, pp. 59f.

[120] For Womar, see W. de G. Birch, *Liber Vitae: Register and Martyrology of New Minster and Hyde Abbey* (Winchester, 1892), p. 24; J. Gerchow, *Die Gedenküberlieferung der Angelsachsen* (Berlin, 1988), p. 323; Wulfstan, *Life*, p. lix. See also Ortenberg, *English Church*, pp. 241ff.

[121] A. Thacker, "Cults at Canterbury: Relics and Reform under Dunstan and his Successors," *Dunstan*, pp. 226ff., has also recently highlighted the importance of Continental precedents for the culting of Swithun. The use of relics in the interest of reform was quite widespread on the Continent; see B. Töpfer, "Reliquienkult und Pilgerbewegung zur Zeit der Klosterreform im burgundisch-aquitanischen Gebiet," *Vom Mittlelalter zur Neuzeit. Zum 65. Geburtstag von Heinrich Sproemberg*, ed. H. Kretzschmar (Berlin, 1956), pp. 420–39. J. Leclercq, "La Réforme bénédictine anglaise du Xᵉ siècle vue du continent," *Studia Monastica* 24 (1982): 105–25, mis-

tions and miracles that cast the saint in the role of the celestial counterpart of the monks who had reformed Winchester.

We have already seen that Æthelwold in the New Minster charter associated the monks he introduced into the reformed monasteries with paradisiacal blossoms, and it is no coincidence that this was also the case for their ally Swithun. In a late-tenth-century metrical reworking of Lantfred's text, Wulfstan[122] described the preparations for the first translation, which he had personally witnessed as a young oblate. Æthelwold asked the cathedral congregation to fast for three days and to implore God to cleanse them of sin and adorn them with "the flowers of the virtues so pleasing to him," so that they might be found worthy to translate the saint into the church where his glorious presence would confer heavenly favors on them. Though there is no miraculous blossoming of nature, the underlying theme is the same as in the iconography of the Entry and the accounts of the Continental translations: the flowering of heaven-sent virtue and purity in those who have made themselves worthy to receive the advent of a celestial personage and the divine blessings his presence brings. Both Lantfred and Wulfstan related that after the translation a nobleman seeking to cure an illness dreamed of Swithun appearing in a golden, bejeweled church set in a verdant, flowering celestial field.[123] The presence of the relics in the Old Minster caused the church to assume the likeness of the heavenly Ecclesia in the pastures of paradise, just as Benedict's relics had transformed Fleury.

The Winchester authors did not liken Swithun's translations directly to Christ's Entry, but it is clear from Wulfstan that the translations were regarded as the saint's festive *adventus* to the cathedral. The second translation included many of the standard features of the advent *topos*.[124] The retinue escorting the relics to the city (they had previously been moved to the king's palace to be placed in a new shrine) was met by a vast, rejoicing throng of citizens of all ages and classes. When the procession reached the gates of Winchester, a miracle manifested the saint's divinely bestowed *virtus*, revealing that God's power and presence came in the person of the saint.[125]

Special attention must be paid to the singing that, as Wulfstan repeatedly mentioned, accompanied the two translations, for the chanting at Christ's Entry is at the heart of the miniature's symbolism. At the second translation King Edgar ordered that "every tongue might magnify God in unison," and during the first one, just before the procession with the relics went through the open doors of the church, all present, "young and old alike," joined Æthelwold in singing the Te Deum in hexameters:

> All the earth venerates you as the eternal Father. The angelic chorus and every power in heaven . . . cry out to you: "Holy, over all things Holy, Holy in the highest, Lord God of Sabaoth, heaven and earth are filled with your majesty." The apostolic throng . . . adores you; the praiseworthy number of prophets with harmonious voice, the noble army of martyrs too praises you. . . . The Church's faith spread through the whole world . . . acknowledges you alone as Lord. . . ; your Son too, to be adored in like deity, and the Holy Paraclete. . . . You, Christ rule as King of kings . . . [and] are also held to be future judge of the world. And so, we pray, come to the aid of your miserable servants . . . and make them blessed with your saints without end. Save your people, . . . [and] raise it up kindly above the heavens forever.[126]

As in the miniature of Christ's Entry, the advent of a sacred personage caused all faithful on earth to sing the praises of God in unison with the choirs of the angels and saints in heaven. The crowd at the translation sang a paraphrase of the Sanctus,[127] which in the mass preceded the Benedictus, the people's hymn at the Entry. Since the participants in the translation hoped

---

takenly believed that the close relationship between relics and the Anglo-Saxon reform was largely an English phenomenon.

[122] Wulfstan, *Narratio Metrica de S. Swithuno*, 1, 873, ed. and tr. Lapidge, *Cult of Swithun*.

[123] Lantfred, *Translatio*, 35; Wulfstan, *Narratio*, 2, 952–1020.

[124] Wulfstan, *Narratio*, 2, 1–77; for the *topos*, see above, n. 107.

[125] Hence Wulfstan (*Narratio*, 2, 61–63) says that the populace sang the praises not of Swithun but of the Trinity "who produce such mighty miracles through our patron saint."

[126] Wulfstan, *Narratio*, 1, 984–1012.

[127] Cf. also Isaiah 6:3, Apoc. 4:8, and the Te Deum.

to be blessed like the saints (i.e., Swithun and his companions) and to join them in heaven, they are again analogous to the populace following Christ in the miniature who symbolized the believers on earth who also sought to join the saints in heaven. These saints were represented not only symbolically in the terrestrial Jerusalem in the scene but also literally in the associated opening cycle of the heavenly choirs, which originally almost certainly included Swithun. The lost opening miniature must have depicted the object of the choirs' hymns of praise, very likely some form of crowned Trinity with connotations of the heavenly Judge, and at the translation both the people and the celestial hosts addressed their hymn to the Trinity and the heavenly king and judge Christ.

Christ's Entrance into Jerusalem was portrayed as a prefiguration of the believers' procession into the church on Palm Sunday and into heaven at the Second Coming, and the translation had a related symbolism. Since Æthelwold and the congregation sang their hymn as they were about to pass through the doors of the Old Minster where the saint's relics were to be housed, the cathedral was implicitly likened to the heavenly city where they hoped to dwell with Swithun and the other saints. Their procession into the cathedral foreshadowed their final march into the heavenly Ecclesia, with the saint representing Christ.[128]

This eschatological symbolism is especially pronounced in another hymn that Æthelwold and the monks had previously sung as they marched to Swithun's old tomb to dig up his relics:

> The Lord conducted the just man along the way of righteousness and revealed to him the lofty kingdom of the Almighty, and bestowed on him the learned teaching of the saints, and mercifully made him righteous in his work and completed his labors in the bright heaven.[129]

The monks in procession to the tomb and eventually the church were indeed moving down the path of righteousness toward the "lofty kingdom of the Almighty," which the church represented and revealed to them. Saint Swithun was a model of the "just man" who, like Christ himself, had already taken the way of righteousness to heaven. The monks benefited from the saint's "learned teaching," for his glorious translation into the monastic cathedral reenacted his advent to the celestial kingdom and prefigured their own arrival there.

The eschatology of these translations deliberately recalled the symbolism of the earlier occasion when the reformers had first entered Old Minster to oust the secular canons. Wulfstan[130] related that the monks outside the church door heard the secular clerics inside chanting "Serve ye the Lord with fear, and . . . embrace discipline, lest ye perish from the just way" (Ps. 2:11–12). The monks interpreted this as a heavenly sign speeding their "journey" into the cathedral and admonishing them to maintain monastic discipline lest, like the negligent canons, they "perish from the way which opens the kingdom of heaven to those who preserve justice." Æthelwold's disciple Osgar, who had returned from Fleury, then urged the monks to go in and "follow the way of justice," so that at the Last Judgment they would share the fate of the blessed (cf. Ps. 2:13). As when they later accompanied Swithun's relics, the monks' passage through the door of the Old Minster was a significant step along the path of righteousness that eventually led through the gate of heaven to the saints.

Underlying this eschatological symbolism is the basic concept of the life of a monk as a spiritual *peregrinatio* through the world, following Christ and the saints to the heavenly Jerusalem.[131] In the *Regularis Concordia* Æthelwold himself termed the reformed monks as those "who walk humbly in the royal way of the Lord's commandments"[132] and "eagerly strived with great joyousness to follow the footsteps of the saints."[133] The symbolism of the monastic *peregrinatio* suffuses the advents to the Old Min-

---

[128] For the Second Coming as a prototype for translations, see Heinzelmann, *Translationsberichte*, pp. 67f.

[129] Wulfstan, *Narratio*, 1, 5.

[130] Wulfstan, *Life*, 17, pp. 30–33.

[131] A. Angenendt, Monachi Peregrini. *Studien zu Pirmin und den monastischen Vorstellungen des frühen Mittelalters*, Münstersche Mittelalter-Schriften, 6 (Munich, 1972), pp. 124ff., 145ff.; G. Constable, "Monachisme et pèlerinage au Moyen Âge," *Revue Historique* 258 (1977): 4ff., 14ff.

[132] *RC*, prohemium, 5, pp. 72: "qui uiam regiam mandatorum domini . . . humiliter incedunt."

[133] *RC*, prohemium, 4, p. 70: "sanctorum sequi uestigia . . . certatim cum magna studuerunt hilaritate." See also the similar metaphor in the last prayer of the Winchester ordination rite for an abbot; *Ben. Rob.*, p. 131.

ster of the reforming monks and their saintly ally Swithum—related events that foreshadowed for Æthelwold and his contemporaries their final triumphant advent to heaven after the Last Judgment.

Although there is no absolute proof, the many different points of contact between the symbolism of these events and the Benedictional's iconography argue forcefully for a close relationship between them. The miniature allegorically portrayed Christ's Entry as a prefiguration of the Winchester community following the footsteps of Christ and his saint, Swithun, into the cathedral. Restored by the monks, who blossom in the virtuous heavenly life, it becomes a terrestrial image of their final destination, the celestial Jerusalem in the flowering fields of paradise.

Benedictus *and* Benedictional

In the iconography of the Entry there are distinct monastic overtones to the theme of benediction: Christ blesses the young citizen of Jerusalem presenting him a golden bouquet that symbolized the monk's offering of the imperishable blossoms of virtue; and the populace's hymn of the Benedictus was taken as a punning reference to the name that Benedict shared with Christ because the saint was blessed (= *benedictus*) and served as Christ's abbatial vicar in the monastery. Many other miniatures in the manuscript also typologically related the blessings that Christ bestowed on men when he came into the world to the benedictions that they receive in the liturgy. Was this theme more generally related to Benedictine monasticism?

This was certainly the view of the fifteenth-century Winchester monk Thomas Rudborne. In his history of Winchester he explained how Christ himself had instituted Benedictine monasticism, which had supposedly existed in essence under different names before Saint Benedict. As Christ had founded and given his name to Christianity, so he had established and lent his name to Benedictine monasticism:

> Thus, the monastic religion had been founded by the first act of *Blessing*, Christ who,

coming into the world, progressing through the world, and returning from the world to the Father, is always our salvation in acts of benedictions . . . , and in substance it [monasticism] has always remained the same since it was first instituted. Although it appears in various observances as a result of differences in persons, origins, times, and places, just as the Christian religion, it took the name of benediction anew from the most holy father Benedict, blessed in substance and name. He was like a specially designated minister, most suited to the first act of *Blessing*, which is Christ, so that *Benedict*, passive in name [i.e., *benedictus* = blessed], would descend directly from the highest active *Blessing* itself, and so that he would compile a monastic rule . . . and would give it a special name from his own name of perpetual benediction . . . Blessed Benedict, as if succeeding the first act of *Blessing* . . . , gave to the monastic life the everlasting name of benediction, so that the religion of eternal benediction might be named truly.[134]

Rudborne used some authentic tenth-century Winchester sources such as Lantfred. His Bene-

---

[134] T. Rudborne, *Historia Major de Fundatione et Successione Ecclesiae Wintoniensis*, 3, 12, ed. H. Wharton, *Anglia Sacra*, 1 (1691, rpt. Farnborough, Hants., 1969), p. 222:
Unde a primo *Benedicere* Christo, qui mundum ingrediendo, in mundo progrediendo, de mundo ad patrem regrediendo semper in benedictionibus operatus est salutem nostram . . . religio Monastica instituta, et quantum ad rem eadem ab institutionis initio semper manens; licet in aliis et aliis observantiis propter diversitatem personarum, causarum, temporum, et locorum sicut Christiana religio nomen benedictionis de novo sumpsit a

Patre sanctissimo re et nomine Benedicto, et specialiter ideo praeelecto tanquam ministro aptissimo ipsius primi *Benedicere*, qui est Christus; quatenus ab ipso summo activo *Benedicere* passive immediate descenderet *Benedictus*; ut regulam monasticam declararet . . . et ei a suo nomine perpetuae benedictionis nomen imponeret speciale. . . . Beatus . . . Benedictus quasi primo *Benedicere* subordinatus, . . . vitae monasticae nomen benedictionis attulit perpetuo duraturum; ut sempiternae benedictionis religio veraciter nominetur.

dictine interpretation of Christ, "the first act of *Blessing*," might well go back to a local tenth-century source since it prefaces the account of Æthelwold's reform. Some substantiation is found in Byrhtferth's account of the greetings that Oswald conveyed from his uncle Oda to the Fleury brethren:

> That agent of heavenly gifts, Bishop Oda, sends to you . . . the inexpressible blessings of Christ (Christi benedictiones), . . . pouring over you the very name of the excellent order whose devotees you are on earth.[135]

As in Rudborne, the *benedictiones* of Christ are the source of the name of the "blessed" monastic religion of Benedict.

These concepts are of paramount importance for our interpretation of the Benedictional. The notion in Rudborne that Christ's advent to and passage through the world were acts of blessing that continue to be bestowed on mankind in the present is a central theme of many of the Benedictional's texts and illustrations. Indeed, the matching couplets over the picture and benedictions for the first Sunday in Advent (pls. 8, 9), the first feast, suggest that this is *the* theme of the entire manuscript: as the Virgin was blessed by Christ's coming to her, so the congregation is blessed when he comes to them liturgically through the benedictions written in "this book

of the advent of the Son."[136] This theme must have been emphasized because of the equation of Christological benediction with Benedictine monasticism, "the religion of eternal benediction" that Æthelwold sought to institute.

Indeed, the special monastic significance of blessing must have been a critical factor in Æthelwold's decision to commission the manuscript in the first place. Until then the sacramentary and the Gospel lectionary had been the two principal types of illuminated Latin books with liturgically arranged texts. Æthelwold, however, broke with this tradition and chose instead to make a benedictional, hitherto a relatively uncommon and modest type of liturgical book, the object of lavish decoration and illustration—in all probability for the very first time. Episcopal benedictions had long been part of the Latin mass, and there are no changes in liturgical usage that account for Æthelwold's elevation of the benedictional to the aristocratic class of decorated liturgical manuscripts. The explanation lies not in liturgy but in the reformers' symbolic association of benediction with Benedictine monasticism.[137] Every time Æthelwold pronounced a benediction from his luxurious book, he reaffirmed to the congregation, both monks and laymen, that Benedictine monasticism had been founded by Christ himself and that it continued to bestow on them the first and greatest blessing of all—Christ.

---

[135] Byrhtferth, *VO*, 2, 5.

[136] See chap. 1, n. 43.

[137] This also explains the large number of later Anglo-Saxon benedictionals (sometimes combined with a pontifical). See H. Gneuss, "Liturgical Books in Anglo-Saxon En-

gland and their Old English Terminology," *Learning and Literature in Anglo-Saxon England*, ed. M. Lapidge and H. Gneuss (Cambridge, 1985), pp. 133f.; J. Brückmann, "Latin Manuscript Pontificals and Benedictionals in England and Wales," *Traditio* 29 (1973): 391–458.

THE ROYAL PROGRAM

A STRONG ROYAL CURRENT runs through the Benedictional. No fewer than eight of its thirty images include crowns and/or diadems, and four others have regal connotations. Though some of these royal elements derived from earlier sources, the presence of so many makes it improbable that they were simply inherited by chance. That the miniaturists employed royal motifs deliberately is confirmed by frequent innovations in their efforts to emphasize the regality of Christ, the Virgin, and the saints. All these royal motifs have been interpreted individually in liturgical or theological terms. Yet such religious interpretations are not sufficient to explain the cycle's systemic stress on regality, nor do they exclude the possibility that these motifs had other, more topical levels of meaning related to the particular historical milieu of the illuminators and their patron.

Æthelwold had long enjoyed close relations to the monarchy. Of aristocratic descent, he was raised at the court of King Athelstan (925–939), who personally commanded his ordination.[1] When Æthelwold later wished to study at a foreign monastery, the queen mother Eadgifu (d. ca. 966–967) prevailed upon King Eadred (946–955) to keep this valuable man in the kingdom. Eadred installed him as abbot of Abingdon in ca. 955, and the king and his mother both generously supported the new foundation.[2] Eadred visited the monastery to direct its layout and construction; one reflection of his personal interest might be the central plan of the church, which seems to have resembled the Carolingian royal chapel at Aachen.[3]

The church was completed during the reign of Edgar (959–975), who had an especially strong personal relationship with Æthelwold. Æthelwold might have tutored the young Edgar at Abingdon. The prince promised to aid the monastery, a vow he later honored when he gained the throne. In two writings, the prologue of the Old English translation of the *Rule*[4] and the *Regularis Concordia*,[5] Æthelwold stressed the critical importance of this childhood promise for the king's subsequent support of the monastic reform. The reform was very much a court movement that depended heavily on the good will and authority of the monarchy. Only with royal (and papal) backing were Æthelwold and the other reformers able to wrest control of the monasteries from the secular clerks who had been accustomed to using religious endowments for their own personal support rather than communally, as the Benedictine *Rule* required.[6] Once Edgar became king, the reform accelerated and gained momentum. His fervent promotion of the monastic cause cannot be separated from his continuing personal relationship with Æthelwold. In 963 Edgar promoted him to the bishopric of Winchester, a strategic post close to himself. Winchester was an important royal cen-

---

[1] Wulfstan, *Life*, 1, 7, pp. 3f., 10f.; B. Yorke, "Æthelwold and the Politics of the Tenth Century," *Bishop Æthelwold*, pp. 68f.

[2] Wulfstan, *Life*, 10–11, pp. 16–22; A. Thacker, "Æthelwold and Abingdon," *Bishop Æthelwold*, pp. 43–64.

[3] Wulfstan, *Life*, 12–13, pp. 22–24; R. Gem, "Towards an Iconography of Anglo-Saxon Architecture," *Journal of the Warburg and Courtauld Institutes* 46 (1983): 8f.

[4] *An Account of King Edgar's Establishment of Monasteries*, ed. and tr. D. Whitelock, M. Brett, C. N. L. Brooke, *Councils & Synods with other Documents Relating to the English Church* (Oxford, 1981), 1, 1, pp. 147–49; see above, chap. 5, n. 7.

[5] *RC*, 1, prohemium, p. 69.

[6] E. John, "The King and the Monks in the Tenth-Century Reformation," *Orbis Britanniae*, Studies in Early English History, 4 (Leicester, 1966), pp. 154–80.

ter.[7] All three of its religious houses had been regal foundations, and both the Old and the New Minster sometimes served as royal burial churches. A regal residence might have been in the vicinity of the Old Minster. Already in the late ninth and the early tenth century the royal family had been great patrons of Winchester artists and churches.[8] As bishop of this regal center with privileged access to the king, Æthelwold was Edgar's principal counsellor and the driving force of the reform during his reign.[9]

Æthelwold commissioned the Benedictional as his own personal liturgical book rather than as a gift for the king, but political concerns could still have been a factor in its emphasis on regality. Politics and religion were tightly interwoven during the monastic reform. Because Æthelwold

and the other reformers relied heavily on royal support and protection, they allowed the king and queen to intervene substantially in religious affairs. In a medieval Christian society, pragmatic considerations—no matter how compelling—were not in themselves sufficient reason for the involvement of the secular sphere in the spiritual one. Such intervention also had to be justified in terms of a divinely ordained transcendental order that governed all human institutions and activities. On one level the multivalent regalized imagery of the Benedictional can be interpreted as the visual statement of the celestially sanctioned concept of rulership that Æthelwold believed to be the theological rationale for the partnership of the court and the Church during the reform.

The Baptism and the Adoration of the Magi

The facing miniatures of the Baptism and the Adoration of the Magi (pls. 19, 18) must loom large in any consideration of the political connotations of the iconography, for they contain one of the heaviest concentrations of royal features in the book.

In the Baptism angels invest Christ with diadems and scepters while the Spirit anoints him king as well as priest. There are precedents for the diadems in earlier representations (fig. 38), but the scepters were a notable innovation. Few, if any, other representations show Christ in any context receiving a scepter,[10] and the English iconography is contemporary with or perhaps earlier than the first depictions of him holding this insigne.[11] The Benedictional's imagery must

therefore be understood as a bold assimilation of the Baptism of Christ to the coronation ritual of a temporal ruler which invested him with a crown and a scepter as well as with other regalia.

The association with temporal coronation would have been all the more apparent because of the relationship between the crowns of Christ and the king in the *ordo* used for Edgar's consecration in 973. The rite stated that the Lord himself crowned the king "with the crown of glory and . . . honor" so that he might attain "the crown of the perpetual kingdom, by the bounty of him whose kingdom and power last forever."[12] This paraphrased Hebrews 2:9 which said that Christ had been "crowned with glory

---

[7] M. Biddle, *"Felix Urbs Winthonia*: Winchester in the Age of Monastic Reform," *Tenth-Century Studies*, pp. 123ff.; idem, "Winchester: The Development of an Early Capital," *Vor- und Frühformen der europäischen Stadt im Mittelalter*, Abhandlungen der Akademie der Wissenschaften in Göttingen, phil.-hist. Kl., ser. 3, 83 (Göttingen, 1973), 1, pp. 246ff.; B. A. E. Yorke, "The Bishops of Winchester, the Kings of Wessex and the Development of Winchester in the Ninth and Early Tenth Centuries," *Proceedings of the Hampshire Field Club and Archaeological Society* 40 (1984): 61–70; idem, "The Foundation of the Old Minster and the Status of Winchester in the Seventh and Eighth Centuries," *Proceedings of the Hampshire Field Club and Archaeological Society* 38 (1982): 75–83.

[8] Deshman, "Anglo-Saxon Art after Alfred," pp. 192–95; Wulfstan, *Life*, 10, pp. 17–19.

[9] Wulfstan, *Life*, 25, pp. 42f.; Byrhtferth, *VO*, 3.11.

[10] In the eleventh-century Bury Psalter the hand of God holds a scepter over Christ on the cross, but it is unclear whether it is an attribute of the Father or is intended for the Son. See Raw, *Crucifixion*, pp. 147f., fig. 12a.

[11] P. E. Schramm, *Sphaira, Globus Reichsapfel* (Stuttgart, 1958), pp. 67f., figs. 53b, 55d. J. Higgitt, "Glastonbury, Dunstan, Monasticism, and Manuscripts," *Art History* 2 (1979): 280, pl. 2, suggested connections between coronation liturgy and Christ's staff in the earlier Glastonbury or Canterbury drawing in Dunstan's "classbook" (fig. 139).

[12] P. E. Schramm, *Kaiser, Könige und Päpste*, 4 vols. (Stuttgart, 1968–71), 2, p. 237 (219), par. 14: "Coronet te Dominus corona gloriae atque . . . honore . . . ut . . . ad coronam pervenias regni perpetui. Ipso largiente, cuius regnum et

and honor." Hence Christ's coronation and heavenly rule were reflected in the king's crowning and reign.

The two vessels of chrism that the dove brings to anoint Christ *rex et sacerdos* would also have had resonances in the coronation *ordo*, which expressly stated that the ruler's unction, the most important step in his ritual transformation from an ordinary man into a sacred king, followed the examples of the anointment of Christ as well as the unctions of Old Testament kings and priests.[13]

On the Continent the double chrismatory was sometimes associated with the cult of the ruler. In the Warmund sacramentary,[14] made in Ivrea about the turn of the millennium, the inclusion of this motif in the miniatures of the Baptism of Christ and the coronation of a ruler, perhaps Otto III, implied that the latter's royal unction was modeled on Christ's baptismal anointment as *rex et sacerdos*. Since the sacramentary's north Italian scriptorium was influenced by iconography derived indirectly from the Benedictional (cf. fig. 127, pl. 12),[15] the source of the double ampullae might well have been Anglo-Saxon rather than Carolingian.

Christ's baptismal investiture with multiple diadems and scepters sounded an imperial note echoed in the facing miniature of the Adoration of the Magi. Enacting an *aurum coronarium*, the first Magus presents Christ with three gold diadems as tokens of their submission to his supreme rulership. The innovative crowns on the heads of the Magi reinforced the idea that Christ received their homage because he was the King of kings. This theme was reiterated in the miniature of the Second Coming (pl. 10), where Christ's mantle is inscribed "King of kings and Lord of lords" (Apoc. 19:16).

The Benedictional revived a long-dormant, early Christian association between the *aurum coronarium* and the Adoration of the Magi. In the ninth and tenth centuries, however, the iconography of this imperial ceremony survived as a living tradition in its original context—ruler portraits. The Codex Aureus of Charles the Bald (Munich, Staatsbibl., MS Clm. 14000), made in 870 at his court school, represents crowned personifications of the provinces presenting offerings to the Carolingian king (fig. 133).[16] This depiction of a secular *aurum coronarium* took on Christological connotations by virtue of the facing miniature of the Adoration of the Elders (fig. 134). Casting their crowns before the Lamb of God (Apoc. 4:10), the Elders are heavenly courtiers enacting an *aurum coronarium* in tribute to the celestial ruler.[17] The paired miniatures parallel the earthly and the heavenly courts, so that the Carolingian ruler reigns as Christ's terrestrial counterpart.[18] The Codex Aureus demonstrates that the analogy between the terrestrial and celestial rulers that had initially induced the transfer of the *aurum coronarium* from late antique ruler portraits to early Christian depictions of the Adoration of the Magi was still operative in the ninth century. A century later the same analogy fostered an association in Ottonian court circles between ruler portraits depicting the *aurum coronarium* and images of the crowned Magi. The latter motif, a recent invention in the Benedictional, seems to have rapidly spread to the Continent through the travels of the Trier artist Benna; this German master, whom Æthelwold almost certainly knew personally, had been summoned to England by King Edgar.[19] Thus in England, too, the newly regalized iconography of the Adoration likely had court associations.

Although there are no extant portraits of an

---

imperium permanent in secula seculorum." See also H. Kleinschmidt, *Untersuchungen über das englische Königtum im 10. Jahrhundert*, Göttinger Bausteine zur Geschichtswissenschaft, 49 (Göttingen, 1979), pp. 129ff.

[13] Schramm, *Kaiser, Könige und Päpste*, 3, pars. 6, 7, 18, pp. 236 (218, 228), 238; also Kleinschmidt, *Englische Königtum*, pp. 151ff.

[14] Deshman, "Warmund Sacramentary," pp. 1–20, figs. 3, 4; P. E. Schramm, *Die deutschen Kaiser und Könige in Bildern ihrer Zeit 751–1190*, 2nd ed., ed. F. Mütherich (Munich, 1983), pp. 205, 360, no. 108.

[15] See above, chap. 4, p. 160.

[16] Schramm, *Kaiser und Könige*, pp. 170, 312, no. 40.

[17] For the Adoration of the Elders as an *aurum coronarium*, see T. Klauser, "Aurum coronarium," *Mitteilungen des deutschen archaeologischen Instituts*, Roem. Abt. 59 (1944): 149f.

[18] A. von Euw, "Darstellungen der Hl. Drei Könige in Kölner Dom und ihre ikonographische Herleitung," *Kölner Domblatt* 23–24 (1964): 310; K. Hoffmann, *Taufsymbolik im mittelalterlichen Herrscherbild*, Bonner Beiträge zur Kunstwissenschaft, 9 (Düsseldorf, 1968), pp. 51ff.

[19] See Deshman, "Kingship," pp. 367ff.; also H. Hoffmann, *Buchkunst und Königtum im ottonischen und frühsalischen Reich*, Schriften der MGH, 30, 1 (Stuttgart, 1986), pp. 123–26.

Anglo-Saxon king in an *aurum coronarium*, the characterization of King Edgar in contemporary literary sources reveals some correspondences to the imperialized Christological iconography.

Anglo-Saxon kings did not claim to be the successors of the Roman emperors, but their rulership was nonetheless considered imperial. The hegemony of a powerful Anglo-Saxon king over weaker rulers gave rise to an imperial style of address which was well established by the tenth century.[20] Edgar, for example, was hailed in a contemporary charter as "the basileus of the English and the ruler and leader of the other peoples existing in the vicinity."[21] The Benedictional's depiction of multiple diadems and scepters to characterize Christ as the King of kings has a counterpart in the sources' metaphorical expressions of Edgar's imperial rulership of lesser kings and peoples. The *ordo* used to crown him in 973 described his kingdom as "the scepters of the Angles and the Saxons" and "the scepters of the Saxons, Mercians, and Northumbrians,"[22] and Byrhtferth in the *Vita Sancti Oswaldi* lauded "King Edgar [as] powerful in arms, mighty with scepters and diadems, whom not only the princes and tyrants of the isles but even the kings of very many peoples feared."[23]

Byrhtferth also indicated that Christ was both the source and the model for Edgar's imperial authority. According to the Ramsey hagiographer, "the most powerful emperor" Edgar, honoring Christ in the kingdom which Christ had bestowed on him, gave orders, which none dared disobey, to establish monks and nuns in the monasteries: "The king submitted to the King of kings; he began more solicitously to submit all glory to God, since as long as the supreme head is mercifully ruled by him (God), the other members are ruled gloriously and virtuously." Byrhtferth then went on to say that at this time King Edgar had concluded a peace pact and exchanged gifts with the German emperor (Otto I), and that the Anglo-Saxon king was praised and feared by neighboring princes and the kings of other peoples.[24]

Byrhtferth presented Edgar's "imperial" might as the reason why his order for monastic reform was unopposed.[25] As King Edgar ruled other kings, so Christ ruled him. Christ is the head of the Church governing the members of his body, the chief of whom is the Anglo-Saxon king, and Edgar's virtuous governance of the lesser members of Christ's ecclesiastic body mirrors the supreme rulership of Christ, the King of kings. In view of the Ottonian political ramifications of the Benedictional's imperial Christological iconography, it is also noteworthy that Edgar in this text gained imperial stature through his association with the Ottonian emperor as well as with Christ.[26] The sources paint a literary portrait of King Edgar that bears a marked likeness to the Benedictional's representation of Christ as the King of kings.

Christ the Royal Judge

The picture cycle often depicts Christ as both king and judge. In the Second Coming the inscription on Christ's garment and the assimilation of the angels carrying the instruments of the Passion to the *militia* bearing a ruler's insignia express the regality of the returning heavenly judge. The Entry into Jerusalem (pl. 21) symbolically represented Christ's imperial *adventus* at the Second Coming when he will lead the blessed bearing his triumphal insignia into the heavenly city. In the Doubting of Thomas (pl. 24) Christ is an imperial figure (cf. fig. 67) whose manifestation to the apostles foreshadowed his triumphal appearance at the Last

---

[20] C. Erdmann, *Forschungen zur politischen Ideenwelt des Frühmittelalters* (Berlin, 1951), pp. 1–16, 38–43; E. John, "'Orbis Britanniae' and the Anglo-Saxon Kings," *Orbis Britanniae*, pp. 1ff.

[21] "Basileus Anglorum ceterarumque gentium in circuitu persistentium gubernator et rector." W. de G. Birch, *Cartularium Saxonicum*, 3 vols. (London, 1888–93), no. 1068; P. H. Sawyer, *Anglo-Saxon Charters* (London, 1968), no. 699; H. Kleinschmidt, "Die Titulaturen englischer Könige im 10.

und 11. Jahrhundert," *Intitulatio*, 3, ed. H. Wolfram and A. Scharer (Vienna, 1988), p. 95, n. 68.

[22] J. L. Nelson, "The Second English *Ordo*," *Politics and Ritual in Early Medieval Europe* (London, 1986), pp. 363ff.

[23] Byrhtferth, *VO*, 3.10.

[24] Byrhtferth, *VO*, 4.3–4.

[25] See also Kleinschmidt, *Englische Königtum*, pp. 95ff.

[26] K. Leyser, "Die Ottonen und Wessex," *Frühmittelalterliche Studien* 17 (1983): 89ff.

Judgment when, like a proud battle-scarred soldier, he will display his wounds from the Passion and his vexillum of the cross. The initial for the Octave of Pentecost (pl. 27) portrays him for the first time as a crowned king, as well as the eternal celestial judge. Finally, the missing opening miniature of the book probably also showed Christ crowned to illustrate the dedication poem's description of him as the "supreme sovereign," "king of the world," and the heavenly judge. Why was there such an emphasis on these two aspects of Christ?

One of Æthelwold's own writings, the New Minster charter of 966, suggests that the bishop saw a relation between these two roles of Christ and the actions of King Edgar in the reform. The charter[27] narrates how Edgar, seeking heavenly co-rule with Christ and the angels, refrained from evil and pursued good deeds, so that he could become a model of virtue for his subjects. Edgar then moved to bring about a similar moral reform in his subjects by punishing wickedness and rewarding goodness. Acting as Christ's vicar, the king emulated the Creator, the "supreme judge," who had evicted the rebel angels and disobedient man from paradise. Edgar expelled the sinful canons from the monastery because they had opposed divine will and because their intercessory prayers were of no benefit to him; and in their stead he established monks pleasing to God who could intercede for him.

Thus Edgar reformed himself by conforming to the heavenly model of the righteous judge Christ who ruled him. As Christ was his model, so Edgar himself became the model of justice for his own subjects. As the heavenly Judge had expelled the rebel angels from heaven, so his terrestrial imitator King Edgar evicted from the monastery the canons, who opposed God.[28] And as the Creator had established sinless man in paradise to replace eventually the wicked angels expelled from heaven, so the king established pure monks in the angelic life in the terrestrial paradise of the monastery to replace the ejected canons. In doing so he helped the monks toward their goal of everlasting heavenly life with the angels, while their intercession in turn helped him toward the same end.

Complementing the text's characterization of King Edgar as the Christological judge is its dedication portrait (fig. 135).[29] In the center of the lower register the king offers the charter to Christ above him. Flanking the ruler are the Virgin and Peter, the patron saints of the New Minster, who intercede for him. In symbolic terms the miniature illustrates the charter's intercessory theme: the king's donation of the charter to Christ signifies his establishment of the monks in the monastery, a virtuous act that earns him their intercession, represented by the flanking patron saints. In Anglo-Saxon England Peter and the Virgin were also the chief human intercessors at the Last Judgment, and as such they flank Christ in the Last Judgment on an English ivory in Cambridge (fig. 68).[30] In the miniature these celestial intercessors have migrated to earth where they flank King Edgar in a way that resembles their grouping around Christ at the Last Judgment. The king is noticeably larger in scale than the interceding saints, and this inversion of the usual hierarchy emphasized his role in the composition as the terrestrial image of Christ, who is directly above him in heaven. The charter's miniature as well as its text portrayed King Edgar undertaking the monastic reform as the vicar of Christ, the celestial ruler and judge who had punished evil and rewarded virtue in the past and who would do so again at the Last Judgment. Conforming to this Christological paradigm of righteous rulership, the king acts to win heavenly crowns for himself and his subjects.

The attributes of the Virgin and Peter—the palm branch, the cross, and the key—relate the donor portrait to the Benedictional's images of Christ as the royal judge. The same three attri-

---

[27] *King Edgar's Privilege for New Minster, Winchester*, 1–5, ed. Whitelock et al., *Councils*, pp. 121–24. I am grateful to Dr. A. R. Rumble who kindly made available to me the edition and translation he is preparing for *Winchester Studies*, 4, 3.

[28] The charter's characterization of Edgar, purging the monastery as "a keen investigator" ("avidus inquisitor"), foreshadows the description of God as the "heavenly In-

spector" of the newly reformed monastery of Glastonbury in Adelard's *Vita S. Dunstani*; see above, chap. 5, n. 90. See also M. J. Silverman, "Aelfric's Designation of the King as Cristes Sylfes Speligend,'" *Review of English Studies*, n. s. 35 (1984): 332ff.

[29] Deshman, "*Benedictus*," pp. 223ff.

[30] See above, chap. 3, n. 279.

butes are associated with each other in the Entry and the Doubting where the palm branch and the key are analogous symbols of the tropaeum of the cross that Christ bestowed on followers who shared his victory over death.[31] In the charter too these attributes were triumphal symbols: they manifested that the Virgin and Peter had achieved salvation through Christ and therefore could intercede with him for the king. Mary's cross and palm branch both betokened the victory over death that Christ had awarded her.[32] The Virgin and Peter display these attributes in a like manner, implying their symbolic equivalency. The similar juxtaposition of the key and the cross-staff in the Doubting of Thomas betrays the direct influence of the charter's iconography.[33] In fact, in both compositions Peter displays his key, the symbol of Christ's judicial power, next to a royal judge: in the Benedictional Christ himself and in the charter King Edgar, the imitator of Christ. This direct relationship between the two compositions, both in Winchester manuscripts personally associated with Æthelwold, suggests that one reason the Benedictional represented Christ as the royal judge was to emphasize that he was the celestial model for King Edgar in monastic reform.

The pictorial allusion to the charter was not the only feature that imbued the Doubting with political overtones. Peter's key-cross and Christ's cross-staff are cognate symbols of the Christological *clavis David*. This signified Christ's power to open or close the gates of heaven, earth, and

hell at a series of typologically related advents— the Doubting, the Harrowing of Hell, the Ascension, and the Last Judgment. Similar themes occur in the prayer for the king's investiture with the staff in the second Anglo-Saxon coronation *ordo*. According to this rite, this insigne was "the staff of virtue and equity" that symbolized the king's duty to rule justly: he is to destroy the wicked and extend his hand to raise up the humble. By reigning righteously he imitates Christ. The prayer says expressly that the ruler is anointed after the example of Christ, and it describes Christ as "the key of David and the scepter of the house of Israel," who opens and shuts doors and who has delivered captive man from the prison of death. This last deed referred to the Harrowing of Hell, when Christ destroyed Satan and lifted up imprisoned humanity with his hand (cf. figs. 58–60). Thus the king's righteous actions are to mirror Christ's own just acts; becoming virtuous in this way, the king can hope that Christ, "who is the door" (John 10:9), will open the gate of heaven to him.[34] This prayer, which was used for Edgar's coronation, must certainly have been known to Æthelwold.[35] The marked resemblances between Christ in the prayer and in the Doubting add weight to the conclusion that the imperialized judicial figure of Christ with the cross-staff symbolizing the triumphal *clavis David* was designed to represent the celestial archetype for King Edgar, establishing righteousness through the monastic reform.

---

[31] See above, pp. 76f., 81f., 88.

[32] Cf. the Grimbald Gospels (fig. 93) where the Virgin holds the palm of victory as she is enthroned in heavenly glory with Christ. Mary's association with the palm branch stems from apocryphal narratives. The Pseudo-Matthew (20–21, tr. M. R. James, *The Apocryphal New Testament*, 2nd ed. [Oxford, 1963], p. 75) related that on the flight into Egypt Christ ordered a palm to bow and give fruit to her, and thereafter one of its branches was planted in heaven as a "palm of victory." In the Transitus (e.g., the Pseudo-Melito, 3, ed. James, *New Testament*, p. 210) an angel brings Mary a palm branch as a token of "the paradise of the Lord" that awaits her. The Assumption scene in the English-influenced sacramentary of Mont St. Michel shows Mary holding a palm branch; J. J. G. Alexander, *Norman Illumination at Mont St. Michel 966–1100* (Oxford, 1970), pl. 42a. For the Virgin's cross, see E. Weigand, "Zum Denkmälerkreis des Christogrammnimbus," *Byzantinische Zeitschrift* 32 (1932): 70f.; S. Lewis, "A Byzantine 'Virgo Militans' at Charlemagne's Court," *Viator* 11 (1980): 71ff.

[33] For the charter's earlier date, see below, chap. 7.

[34] Schramm, *Kaiser, Könige und Papste*, 2, pp. 237f., par. 18: Accipe uirgam uirtutis atque aequitatis, qua intellegas mulcere pios et terrere reprobos; errantes uiam doce, lapsis que manum porrige, disperdasque superbos et releues humiles; et aperiat tibi hostium Ihesus Christus dominus noster, qui de se ipso ait: "Ego sum hostium; per me, si quis introierit, saluabitur"; et ipse, qui est clauis David et sceptrum domus Israel, qui aperit et nemo claudit, claudit et nemo aperit, sit tibi adiutor, qui educit uinctum de domo carceris sedentem in tenebris et umbra mortis, ut in omnibus sequi merearis eum. . . ; propterea uncxit te Deus . . . oleo laetitiae ad exemplum illius, quem ante secula uncxerat . . . : Ihesum Christum, dominum nostrum (Ps. 44:7–8). See also Kleinschmidt, *Englische Königtum*, pp. 138ff.

[35] The *ordo* occurs in the Winchester Benedictional of Archbishop Robert; See *Ben. Rob.*, pp. 145f.; Nelson, "Second English *Ordo*," pp. 369ff.; also below, Appendix Three.

The Entry into Jerusalem

The Entry into Jerusalem (pl. 21) also presented Christ in a context that would have prompted comparison to King Edgar. The motif of Jerusalem in a paradisiacal floriferous landscape has previously been linked to the theme of the reformed monastery as a *paradisus claustri* in the New Minster charter. This text likened King Edgar establishing the pure monks in the monastery to the heavenly judge Christ who had introduced innocent mankind into paradise before the Fall and who now seeks to reintroduce humanity there after the Last Judgment. If the related iconography is seen in terms of this analogy, then the imperial figure of Christ leading the way into Jerusalem, the counterpart of the celestial city, would correspond to the king instituting the monks in the reformed paradisiacal Church. There is, in fact, evidence that Æthelwold and his contemporaries did view Edgar's leadership in such terms.

Accounting for the king's support of monasticism, Æthelwold wrote in the prologue of the *Regularis Concordia* that "a certain abbot" (Æthelwold) had explained to Edgar at an early age "the royal road of the catholic faith."[36] This "road" was monastic as well as regal, for later in the prologue Æthelwold stated that the customs of the *Regularis Concordia* are for those "who walk humbly in the royal road of the commandments of the Lord."[37] These references to the *via regia* were influenced by the writings of Smaragdus, who was deeply involved in the Carolingian monastic reform. In the mirror of princes entitled *Via Regia*,[38] which he most likely composed for King Louis the Pious, the *via regia*[39] is the path of virtuous life and rulership. Only by following it will the king retain his royal office in this world and reach the King of kings in the next one. Imitating Christ as the head of the Church, the king is to correct any of his own subjects who stray from this royal road of virtue and to lead them along it to the celestial kingdom. In the *Diadema Monachorum* and the commentary on the Benedictine *Rule*, two treatises by Smaragdus which influenced the iconography of the crowned Saint Benedict (pl. 33),[40] the *via regia* is a metaphor for the virtuous monastic life of the *Rule* that leads monks to the heavenly kingdom.[41] Following Smaragdus, Æthelwold in the *Regularis Concordia* deliberately played on both senses of the term: the monks follow a monastic road that is "royal" not only because it takes them to the celestial king Christ and his kingdom, but also because they are led down this path by King Edgar who, acting as Christ's vicar, has reformed both himself and his subjects.

Although Edgar was not personally present when the reforming monks first entered the Old Minster, the idea that the king "led" them into the church and toward its counterpart in heaven was not merely a metaphorical abstraction. Only with the king's permission and help did Æthelwold undertake the expulsion of the canons. Edgar commanded his thegn Wulfstan of Dalham to be present, and Wulfstan used the king's authority to order the canons to yield the cathedral to Æthelwold and his monks.[42] They entered when they heard the clerks inside chanting Psalm 2:11–12: "Serve the Lord with fear . . . so that you do not depart from the just way." The monks took this as a divine sanction for their entrance, which they believed would take them further along "the path of justice" toward blessed habitation in heaven.[43] In the *Via Regia* Smaragdus cited Psalm 2:11 to explain that fear of the Lord is the third "step" in the royal road that leads the king (and his subjects) to the celestial companionship of the choirs of saints.[44] Because King Edgar imitated the just judge Christ when he gave the monks their marching orders,

[36] *RC*, prohemium, 1, p. 69: "Edgar . . . ab ineunte suae pueritiae aetate, licet uti ipsa solet aetas diuersis uteretur moribus, attamen respectu diuino attactus abbate quodam assiduo monente ac regiam catholicae fidei uiam demonstrante cepit magnopere deum timere, diligere ac uenerari."

[37] *RC*, prohemium, 5, p. 72: "qui uiam regiam mandatorum domini . . . humiliter incedunt."

[38] Smaragdus, *Via Regia*, PL, 102, cols. 931–70; cf. *RC*, p. 69 n. 8, 72 n. 6.

[39] O. Eberhardt, *Via Regia. Der Fürstenspiegel Smaragds*

von St. Mihiel und seine literarische Gattung, Münstersche Mittelalter-Schriften, 28 (Munich, 1977), pp. 501ff., 517ff.; also Deshman, "Benedictus," pp. 230ff.

[40] For Æthelwold's use of the commentary for his Old English translation of the *Rule*, see above, chap. 3, n. 80.

[41] Eberhardt, *Via Regia*, pp. 513ff.

[42] Wulfstan, *Life*, 16–18, pp. 30–33.

[43] Wulfstan, *Life*, 17, pp. 30–33.

[44] Smaragdus, *Via Regia*, 3, PL 102, cols. 939C–D, 940B–C.

the path of justice they traveled was very much the *via regia* of both King Edgar and Christ.

The king's involvement meant that he stood to gain as much as Æthelwold from the seal of divine approval that Saint Swithun stamped on the monks' reform of the cathedral. Wulfstan[45] stressed that the Lord revealed Swithun to the king's subjects at the time when Edgar, "by the gift of Christ," ruled in exceptional peace and prosperity, implying that the Lord rewarded the king for his sponsorship of the monks with both a felicitous reign and the saint's unexpected manifestation.[46] Wulfstan[47] also gave King Edgar much of the credit for Swithun's two translations. It was the king, at Æthelwold's instigation, who actually commanded that the relics be brought into the cathedral the first time, and the second translation is described as the king's completion of this pious work. Edgar commissioned the fabrication of the saint's reliquary at his own residence ten miles north of Winchester, donating three hundred pounds of silver for the purpose. Depicted on the reliquary were the Passion, the Resurrection, the Ascension, and "many other scenes," and the Entry into Jerusalem might well have been one of these. The king also ordered the elaborate *adventus* ceremonial that accompanied the translation. Since the procession with the relics set out from the king's residence and was escorted by his own retinue, which he had placed in the saint's service, the advent to the church manifested the *virtus* of Edgar no less than of Christ and Swithun.

The sources stressed that the advents of the reforming monks and Swithun to the church were steps along the path of justice and righteousness to the heavenly kingdom,[48] and in the scene of the Entry the blossoms symbolized the righteousness and virtue that flourish (cf. Ps. 91:13) in the paradisiacal church when the purging advent of monasticism renders it fit to re-

ceive God and his saint. Beneath this veneer of Christian symbolism, the theme of an advent accompanied by the unseasonable display of spring was an ancient *topos* of the ruler cult that still retained its original secular meaning in the early Middle Ages.

Carolingian panegyrics sometimes described how nature celebrated the king's ceremonial entrance into a city or even a monastery with a miraculous manifestation of flowers and foliage,[49] and a version of this *topos* was applied to King Edgar. Byrhtferth in his early-eleventh-century *Life of Saint Ecgwine* said that Christ reigning in heaven had bestowed earthly rule on King Edgar, who had subjected all surrounding kings and kingdoms to his authority, and

> in his time the English race flowered like a lily, blossomed like a rose. . . . In praise of the King of kings he restored all the ruined monasteries, building thus a new Jerusalem, expelling through his royal authority the trifles of secular clerics. . . . The king . . . ordered . . . many churches in his realm to be restored, desiring thus to flourish (*florere*) through God's indescribable power, "like an olive tree in the house of the Lord" (Ps. 51:10).[50]

This text attributed the building of an Anglo-Saxon *paradisus claustri*, indeed a *paradisus regni*,[51] reflecting the heavenly Jerusalem, to King Edgar acting with terrestrial imperial power derived from and mirroring the celestial authority of the King of kings. The parallels to the symbolic themes of the iconography are striking.

Æthelwold had used a related metaphor in his New Minster charter to describe how King Edgar, mindful of God's charge to Jeremiah (1:10) "to root up, and to pull down, . . . and to build, and to plant," had replaced canons with monks:

[45] *Narratio Metrica de S. Swithuno*, praef. 168–89, ed. and tr. Lapidge, *Cult of Saint Swithun*, forthcoming.

[46] See also D. W. Rollason, "Relic-Cults as an Instrument of Royal Policy *c.* 900–*c.* 1050," *ASE* 15 (1986): 91ff.; idem, *Saints and Relics in Anglo-Saxon England* (Oxford, 1989), pp. 134ff.

[47] For the following, see Wulfstan, *Narratio*, 2.1–77, esp. 5–15; also J. Crook, "King Edgar's Reliquary of St Swithun," *ASE* 21 (1992): 177–202; idem, "St. Swithun of Winchester," *Winchester Cathedral. Nine Hundred Years 1093–1993*, ed. idem (Winchester, 1993), pp. 57–68.

[48] See above, chap. 5, nn. 126, 129.

[49] See above, chap. 2, n. 142; also P. Willmes, *Der Herrscher-"Adventus" im Kloster des Frühmittelalters*, Münstersche Mittelalter-Schriften, 22 (Munich, 1976), p. 104.

[50] Byrhtferth, *Vita S. Ecgwini*, 4, 11, ed. and tr. M. Lapidge, *Byrhtferth of Ramsey: The Lives of Oswald and Ecgwine*, forthcoming.

[51] For related bucolic themes in Carolingian regal literature and the second Anglo-Saxon coronation *ordo*, see Kleinschmidt, *Englische Königtum*, pp. 165ff.

acting on earth through Christ's operation as he himself has justly acted in heaven, namely clearing the filth of evil deeds from the Lord's field, as a diligent farmer, I (Edgar), have planted the seeds of virtues.[52]

Later in the text Æthelwold extended the metaphor when he said that the monks whom Edgar had introduced into the monastery were "adorned with the flower of all virtues."[53] Hence for Æthelwold it was the Christ-like king who "planted"

the monks in the *claustrus paradisi*, edifying them in the counterpart of the new Jerusalem, where they blossom in the virtue of the heavenly monastic life. The Benedictional depicted a paradigm for this Christological role of the king: the Entry in which Jerusalem blooms with righteousness in recognition of the imperial advent of Christ, the cornerstone, and those who follow his path of justice.

The Deity and the Choirs of the Saints

Despite the loss of the miniature of the Deity that headed the choirs of the saints (pls. 1–3), some inferences regarding the political connotations of this introductory cycle are possible. In conjunction with the texts of the related hagiographic feast pictures, the opening sequence of miniatures pictorially admonished beholders to emulate the saints to earn their intercession and their company in heaven. Related themes occur in the political context of Æthelwold's New Minster charter.

There King Edgar says he undertook the reform of the monasteries to win a heavenly crown and a place "in the heaven of Christ and his saints."[54] This goal of the king is what, in essence, the introductory cycle (and the Entry into Jerusalem) depicts, and in both the Benedictional and the charter the achievement of this goal entailed imitation and intercession.

In the text Edgar explains that he replaced the canons with monks for two reasons: he wished to emulate the heavenly rulership and justice of Christ, and the monks' prayers for him pleased God, unlike the ineffectual intercessions of the canons, who had lost divine favor.[55] Efficacious intercession was one of the king's most important rewards for supporting the reform. There was a mutually beneficial trade-off between the king and the monks which is also evident in the charter's stipulation that the king had the duty

to protect the abbot and the monks from the enemies of the reform while the abbot and the monks had the obligation to defend the king from devils and invisible enemies—in other words, to pray for him. Æthelwold also ensured that Edgar received his due in the *Regularis Concordia*, which stipulated an unusually large number of prayers for the royal family in the Office and the mass. The bishop even warned against reciting these too quickly.[56]

The charter's donor portrait (fig. 135) represented the monks' intercession symbolically by showing King Edgar between Peter and the Virgin, the monastery's patron saints. Since at the same time this grouping assimilated Edgar to Christ in an Anglo-Saxon variant of the Deesis (cf. figs. 68, 97), the iconography also showed that it was the king's imitation of the righteous rulership of his heavenly exemplar, Christ, the just judge, that made him worthy of the monks' suffrages.

If the missing miniature at the head of the choirs of the saints did represent a Trinitarian Christ, possibly crowned, in an insular Deesis, then this composition, like the miniature of the Doubting, would have recalled the grouping of the king and his intercessors in the charter. Even if Christ were not in a Deesis group, he would nonetheless have been analogous to the Anglo-Saxon king. In the Benedictional Christ

---

[52] *Edgar's Privilege*, 6, ed. Whitelock et al., p. 124: "agens Christo faciente in terris quod ipse iuste egit in celis, extricans videlicet Domini cultura criminum spurcitias, virtutum semina sedulus agricola inserui."

[53] See above, chap. 5, n. 98.

[54] *Edgar's Privilege*, 6, ed. Whitelock et al., p. 124.

[55] See above, n. 27. Edgar's foundation charter for Ely,

which probably incorporates some authentic material, also stressed the ability of the monks and nuns to intercede for him. See *Anglo-Saxon Charters*, ed. and tr. A. J. Robertson, (Cambridge, 1939), no. 48, p. 99.

[56] *RC*, 8, 19, pp. 74, 83; see T. Symons, "Sources of the Regularis Concordia," *Downside Review* 54 (1941): 147f.

—in whatever form—was depicted as the just ruler of the choirs of the saints, the members of the celestial church who were shown as the models and the intercessors for the members of the monasticized Anglo-Saxon church.[57] In the charter Edgar plays this Christological part when he reforms his subjects so that they conform to the angelic heavenly life of the elect.

By the Carolingian period the conviction that terrestrial and celestial society paralleled and mirrored one another made Christ and the choirs of saints a model for a ruler and his subjects. In Smaragdus' *Via Regia*, which Æthelwold used for the prologue of the *Regularis Concordia*, the choirs of the saints await the king at the end of his road of righteousness, and his place in this heavenly society is anticipated by his present felicitous terrestrial station among "troops of peoples" and "multitudes of men." As the son of an earthly ruler and the heir to an earthly realm, the king will eventually receive a portion of the heavenly kingdom and be confirmed the son of the celestial king, a position that assimilates him to Christ, the son and heir of the Father.[58]

The Carolingians also associated the litany of the saints, the intercessory prayer illustrated in the Benedictional's introductory cycle, with the ruler cult. They inserted the *laudes regiae*, liturgical acclamations to Christ as the triumphant heavenly emperor, into the framework of the litany.[59] The *laudes* emphasized the parallelism of heavenly and earthly society by assigning saints from each rank of the celestial hierarchy as intercessors to a corresponding grade of terrestrial society. The earliest *laudes*, which originated in Charlemagne's court, likened the king to Christ by designating as his intercessors the Virgin and John the Baptist, the saints of the Deesis;[60] thus the praise and acclamation directed at the heavenly emperor Christ also served to glorify his terrestrial imperial counterpart. This propagandistic association of the ruler with the intercessors of the Deesis to assimilate him to Christ foreshadows the iconography of the New Minster Charter. The *laudes* were not used in England until after the Conquest,[61] though the Anglo-Saxons might have known of them long before then. In any event, the idea that the earthly king benefited from the accolades directed to the heavenly ruler was not limited to the *laudes*, but was widespread.

In the Codex Aureus, for example, Charles the Bald is acclaimed in an *aurum coronarium* in his own court as he turns toward the Lamb reigning over the celestial court on the opposite page (figs. 133, 134). The text of the latter says that the king looks praying to the Lamb,[62] and so he joins with the Elders, who represent the heavenly hosts of the Old and New Testament,[63] in their adoration of the Lamb. The personifications of earth and ocean at the bottom of the composition emphasize that the inhabitants of the terrestrial realm join the citizens of the heavenly one in the hymn of homage (cf. Apocalypse 5:13). In these facing pictures the glorification of the celestial and terrestrial monarchs virtually merges.

Similar themes underlie the two-page composition of the choirs of the saints paying homage to Christ in majesty in the Metz sacramentary, also made for Charles the Bald by his court scriptorium (figs. 81, 82). Once again personifications of earth and ocean are present, stressing that heaven and earth join in the Sanctus, the liturgical chorus of praise. Like the Elders in the Codex Aureus, the angels and the virgins offer Christ crowns in an *aurum coronarium*. Although in this instance Charles the Bald is not included in the composition, this imperial Christological iconography was surely designed to remind viewers of the portraits of the Carolingian king in this same ceremony.[64] Thus in Carolingian art and liturgy the choirs of the saints sometimes possessed overtones of royal propaganda.

The Anglo-Saxons also associated liturgical

---

[57] The connection between the choirs and intercession for the king is also apparent in the New Minster Liber Vitae (figs. 69, 97); see Deshman, "*Benedictus*," pp. 23ff., figs. 65, 66.

[58] Smaragdus, *Via Regia*, 3, 9, PL 102, cols. 940C, 949C–50A.

[59] E. H. Kantorowicz, "Ivories and Litanies," *Journal of the Warburg and Courtauld Institutes* 5 (1942): 56ff.; idem, *Laudes Regiae. A Study in Liturgical Acclamations and Mediaeval Ruler Worship* (Berkeley, 1946). The *laudes* were eventually emancipated from their original context in the litanies.

[60] Kantorowicz, "Ivories and Litanies," pp. 67ff.; idem, *Laudes Regiae*, pp. 49ff., 61f.

[61] H. E. J. Cowdrey, "The Anglo-Norman Laudes Regiae," *Viator* 12 (1981): 37–78.

[62] For the text, see Koehler and Mütherich, *Kar. Min.*, 5, p. 176.

[63] See above, chap. 2, n. 280.

[64] R. Deshman, "Antiquity and Empire in the Throne of Charles the Bald," *Byzantine East, Latin West: Art Historical Studies in Honor of Kurt Weitzmann*, forthcoming.

and devotional praise of God with ruler worship. Byrhtferth's *Life of Saint Oswald*[65] relates that one Easter the bishops, abbots, and abbesses assembled with their charges "to sing vespers together before the eyes of the celestial king and the terrestrial king." Looking at this gathering of the entire Church around him, King Edgar exclaimed:

> "I thank you, O Jesus Christ, great king, you who rule whom you love, who has appointed me over your people. May there be perpetual praise and undiminished glory to you, who has granted to be gathered to me so many male and female servants who can render your praises with due honors."

The king then ordered

> more than forty monasteries to be constituted with monks, loving in everything Christ the Lord, . . . the king having been instructed in the knowledge of the true king [Christ] by Æthelwold. . . . In fact, it was Æthelwold who urged this very king [Edgar] to expel the clerics from the monasteries and to bestow them on our order, because he [Æthelwold] had been his chief adviser.

Retiring from this Easter celebration "with the terrestrial king," "the army of the Lord" prayed for his welfare.

Because of his subservience and similarity to the King of kings, Edgar basks in the glory that Christ receives in this service. The passage plays on the notion that the chants and prayers brought the participants into Christ's presence, an idea we have found to be prominent in the Benedictional's iconography; thus Edgar's presence at the celebration proclaims his status as an *imago Christi*. Christ's supreme rulership over all the ranks of heaven and earth is reflected in Edgar's reign over all the grades of the earthly Church. Since Christ has appointed Edgar as his intermediary to rule over Christ's people, Christ's servants become Edgar's, and their homage to their heavenly lord and master passes to his earthly vicar. As in the New Minster charter, Edgar's *imitatio Christi* leads his subjects in the Church to intercede for him, not only as they depart but also in the prayers for the king that were part of the vespers Office they had just celebrated.[66] No wonder Edgar thanks the "great king" Christ for this gathering. At the very moment when Edgar enjoys this Christological limelight, he commands the establishment of monks in numerous monasteries. The timing is explained by Æthelwold's New Minster charter which explictly stated that the king imitated the rulership of Christ when he replaced the canons with monks. Byrhtferth acknowledges Æthelwold's role in the formulation of this Christological ruler theology when he credits the Winchester bishop with instructing "the king in the knowledge of the true king" and inspiring him to reform the monasteries.

Although the passage does not mention the choirs of the saints, it does connect the Church's praise of and intercession for Edgar with its singing the perpetual praises of Christ, a theme intrinsic to the choirs of the saints in the Benedictional. If we also take into account the iconography's relation to the New Minster charter and the Carolingian association of the celestial choirs and the litany with the ruler cult, then the political connotations of the Benedictional's imagery emerge. Viewed from many different angles, this prefatory cycle of the Deity and the saints could represent the heavenly ideal of Christological governance that Æthelwold and King Edgar sought to emulate in the reform.

Benedictus Monarchas et Monachus

The theme of Christ as the royal Judge also permeates the portrait of the crowned Saint Benedict (pl. 33). Benedict is the exemplary abbot whose monastic governance imitates the heavenly righteousness of the just Judge (pl. 27), so that after the Last Judgment the abbot can wear

---

[65] Byrhtferth, *VO*, 3.11. See also H. Vollrath, "König Edgar und die Klosterreform in England: die 'Ostersynode' der 'Vita S. Oswaldi auctore anonymo,'" *Annuarium Histo-riae Conciliorum* 10 (1978): 67ff.

[66] See above, n. 56.

the monastic crown of eternal life, the Christological *diadema monachorum*. He holds another "crown of righteousness" (2 Tim. 4:7) for those of his charges who imitate his holy life and who therefore can hope for his intercession, which will help them win the same celestial prize as he had. This ideal of abbatial office has much in common with Æthelwold's conception of Edgar's royal office.[67]

In the New Minster charter the king's governance of his subjects, which include the monks, is also to imitate Christ's heavenly justice, so that he becomes a righteous personal "model for the flock," converting his charges and enabling them as well as himself to secure the crown of life. The monastic tenor of this ruler ideology is unmistakable in the prologue of Æthelwold's translation of the Benedictine *Rule*, which King Edgar himself commissioned. Æthelwold says that to prepare for the good work of establishing monasticism throughout the kingdom, the king made "a beginning with himself" by amending his own life with "true piety." To achieve this moral perfection and avoid damnation, Edgar ordered Æthelwold to translate the *Rule*, so that the king and other laymen might "abandon this wretched life . . . and choose the holy service of this *Rule*; lest any unconverted layman should in ignorance and stupidity break the precepts of the *Rule* and employ the excuse that he erred on that day because he knew no better."[68] King Edgar seems to have deliberately emulated the abbot whose rulership of his charges was guided by the *Rule* as well as by the heavenly exemplar of the just judge Christ. Like a monastic superior, the king became a personal model of rectitude for his subordinates, and his fate at the Last Judgment would depend on how well he had instilled the *Rule*'s spiritual precepts in his charges.

The ideal of monasticized monarchy that Æthelwold propounded for King Edgar was intimately related to the imagery of the monarchic Benedict. Copies of a version of the diademed abbot closely related to the one in the Benedictional survive in two eleventh-century Canterbury manuscripts in the British Library, the Arundel Psalter (fig. 136) and Cotton Tiberius A. III (fig. 137).[69] The

painter of the latter introduced a revealing modification into his rendering of the model. Influenced by the drawing prefacing the *Regularis Concordia* in the same manuscript (fig. 138),[70] he interpolated the figure of the monk dramatically girding himself with a scroll to signify acceptance of the *Rule*'s discipline. This addition forged an analogy between Saint Benedict expounding his *Rule* and Æthelwold, King Edgar, and Dunstan issuing the monastic ordinances of the *Regularis Concordia*. The relationship between Benedict and Edgar is especially close: the abbot is crowned like the king, while the king is wearing a chlamys fastened in the center of the chest like the abbot's cope rather than in the customary position at the left shoulder (cf. figs. 97, 135). The abbot and the ruler are mutually assimilated to each other: the one mirrors the role and to a certain extent the attributes of the other.

It seems to have been the idea of the illuminator of the Tiberius manuscript to link these two frontispieces directly; in doing so he drew on a long-standing association of the iconography of Benedict with King Edgar. The archetype of the two Canterbury pictures was almost certainly invented by Æthelwold to serve as the frontispiece for his translation of the *Rule* for the king.[71] In Edgar's personal copy, this frontispiece would have illustrated the ideal of monasticized kingship that Æthelwold set forth in his prologue: simultaneously assimilated by his diadem to a temporal king and Christ, Benedict was the paradigm of both the abbot and the king, each of whom governed his realm in imitation of the righteous heavenly rulership of Christ.

The association between *Benedictus monarcha* and King Edgar is corroborated by the prayer accompanying the notice of Edgar's death in Byrhtferth's *Life of Saint Oswald*:

Rightly the faithful monks and particularly the shepherds of the people pray for him, since he was not only the lord but father of them. O Benedict the monarch (*Benedicte monarches*), grant aid through your kindly prayers to this defender of your servants,

---

[67] For a fuller treatment, see Deshman, "*Benedictus*," pp. 204ff.

[68] *Edgar's Establishment*, ed. Whitelock et al., pp. 149ff.

[69] Deshman, "*Benedictus*," pp. 211ff., figs. 51, 54.

[70] Deshman, "*Benedictus*," pp. 205ff., fig. 50; Temple, *Manuscripts*, pp. 118f., no. 100, fig. 314.

[71] Deshman, "*Benedictus*," pp. 219ff.

and bring it to pass that he who was your holy friend might be crowned on the right side![72]

By calling King Edgar the "father" of the monks, Byrhtferth gave him a customary appellation of an abbot; this very term is inscribed around the nimbus of the diademed Benedict in the Arundel Psalter.[73] Byrhtferth implied that Edgar in his terrestrial kingdom had previously mirrored *Benedictus monarcha*. Thus it is a foregone conclusion that the abbot would intercede so that the king might continue to imitate him in the celestial kingdom, eternally crowned with the saint and Christ, the archetype of all righteous kings and abbots. Similarly, the regal Saint Benedict in the Benedictional could be regarded as the model and the intercessor for both the king and the abbot.

The Coronation of the Virgin

If the images of Christ as king were understood on one level as representations of a celestial Christological model for King Edgar, did the Virgin as queen in the Assumption miniature (pl. 34) and perhaps also in the lost opening miniature portray a Mariological paradigm for Edgar's queen, Ælfthryth?

There was an archetypal correspondence between the queens of heaven and earth that was rooted in the medieval belief in the parallelism of celestial and terrestrial society. In this instance heaven was made in the image of earth. The prominence of Frankish queens helped to elevate the Virgin to the rank of *regina* in the Carolingian period.[74] The anointing and crowning of Carolingian queens gave them an important, hallowed position in the royal hierarchy. The link between their sacred regality and family was projected into the maternal, bridal relationship between Mary and Christ. The queen's intimacy with the king often enabled her to intercede with him on behalf of his subjects, and this strengthened the analogy to the Virgin, who had a similar intercessory role with Christ. Having formed the ideal of *Maria regina*, the Carolingians cited her as a sacred model for their queens.[75]

The Anglo-Saxons also seem to have connected the earthly and heavenly queens. At about the same time as the first depiction of the Coronation of the Virgin in the Benedictional, Ælfthryth's political status was raised. Unlike their Continental counterparts, West Saxon royal consorts had traditionally been denied the authority and title of a queen; nor had they been anointed like their husbands.[76] Ælfthryth, however, was titled *regina* during her husband's lifetime and was anointed and crowned with him in 973.[77]

The *ordo* for Ælfthryth's hallowing did not invoke the Virgin as a sacred precedent for her.[78] However, Byrhtferth in his *Vita Sancti Oswaldi*

[72] Byrhtferth, *VO*, 4.11. Unavailable to me was H. Hoffmann, *Mönchskönig und Rex Idiota. Studien zur Kirchenpolitik Heinrichs II. und Konrads II.*, MGH, Studien und Texte, 8 (Hannover, 1993).

[73] "S(an)c(tu)s Benedictus, pater monachor(um)."

[74] L. Scheffczyk, *Das Mariengeheimnis in Frömmigkeit und Lehre der Karolingerzeit*, Erfurter theologische Studien, 5 (Leipzig, 1959), pp. 486ff.; T. Vogelsang, *Die Frau als Herrscherin im hohen Mittelalter* (Göttingen, 1954), pp. 38f. Regarding the coronation of queens, see also G. Wolf, "Königinnen-Krönungen des frühen Mittelalters bis zum Beginn des Investiturstreits," *Zeitschrift der Savigny-Stiftung für Rechtsgeschichte*, Kanonistische Abt., 76 (1990): 62–88.

[75] J. Hyam, "Ermentrude and Richildis," *Charles the Bald: Court and Kingdom*, 2nd ed., ed. J. L. Nelson and M. Gibson (Aldershot, 1990), p. 159; D. Iogna-Prat, "Le Culte de la Vierge sous le règne de Charles le Chauve," *Les Cahiers de Saint-Michel de Cuxa* 23 (1992): 113–16.

[76] P. Stafford, "The King's Wife in Wessex 800–1066," *Past and Present* 91 (1981): 3ff.

[77] Stafford, "King's Wife," p. 17, esp. nn. 42, 44. There is some later evidence that the use of *regina* possibly began about the middle of the century. J. Nelson, "Second English Ordo," pp. 366f., 372ff., emphasizes the exceptional nature of Ælfthryth's consecration in 973 but argues that the *ordo* used for this was composed for the consecration of Edward the Elder and his consort Ælfflaed in 900. There is, however, not the slightest evidence that Ælfflaed was inaugurated or entitled queen. Prescott, "Text," pp. 35ff., has cast doubt on textual evidence supporting such an early date for the *ordo*.

[78] Schramm, *Kaiser, Könige und Päpste*, 2, pp. 239f. The Virgin was invoked in the blessing of the queen in the Ottonian Mainz coronation *ordo* (ca. 960). This Mariological aspect of the German rite might have some relevance to England since the consecrations of Ottonian queens and empresses likely influenced the decision to depart from West Saxon custom and inaugurate Ælfthryth. Leyser, "Ottonen und Wessex," pp. 95f.; Nelson, "Second English Ordo," pp. 373f.

borrowed phrases from Psalm 44 (verses 10, 14, 16) to describe the queen at the coronation banquet.[79] The tenth verse was used in the Office for the feast of the Assumption and was associated in exegesis with the Coronation of the Virgin and Ecclesia.[80] Moreover, the *ordo* that Byrhtferth consulted for his account of the coronation quoted two preceding verses (7–8) of Psalm 44 in connection with the statement that the king was anointed after the example of Christ.[81] Byrhtferth's application of the following verses to Ælfthryth completed the parallel between the Anglo-Saxon royal couple and their celestial counterparts, Christ and the Virgin.

Since the Benedictional's iconography associated the Virgin's coronation and her wedding to Christ, it is noteworthy that Ælfthyrth's crowning also had nuptial connotations. After mentioning that Ælfthryth had promised to enter the king's "bridal chamber," Byrhtferth characterized the coronation as "the distinguished nuptials of the royal bridal bed."[82] Ælfthryth had married Edgar nine years before their crowning; but even when not part of a wedding, the anointing and coronation of a queen had overtones of a fertility rite that conferred God's blessings upon her, thereby increasing the likelihood that she would produce royal heirs.[83] Byrhtferth was echoing the rubric that prefaced the queen's coronation *ordo*. The rubric said that the queen is to be "consecrated in the church . . . to the consortship of the royal bed . . . and [to] be adorned with a ring . . . and a crown for the glory of eternity."[84] The crown that the queen received in the ceremony[85] symbolized her meritorious

rulership, for which she would receive the future reward of the crown of perpetual life. The rubric, however, is deliberately ambiguous: it almost seems as if the coronation invests the queen with an eternal rather than a temporal crown.

There is an analogous blending of coronation and wedding, of present and future, in the iconography. The Virgin in bed on earth receives an eternal crown that rewards her for her virtuous life, but also signifies her perpetual marital co-rule with her royal spouse. Since the miniature specifically presents the Virgin as a model for other women who also strive to win the crown of life, she could be taken as a paradigm for the Anglo-Saxon queen as well as for monastic women.

That Mary and her three maids enact roles that are analogous to an abbess and her nuns might also have some political resonances, for the reform placed Queen Ælfthryth in a special relationship to religious women.[86] In both the *Regularis Concordia* and the preface of the Old English *Rule*[87] Æthelwold stated that Edgar made his queen the protectress of the nuns he had established in reformed convents. Since both documents stressed that the queen's responsibility for the nuns paralleled and imitated the king's for the monks, the nature of her office must be assessed in the context of his.

The *Regularis Concordia* said that Edgar performed his royal office like the "Shepherd of shepherds" (*pastorum pastor*), defending the "sheep" he had gathered in the monasteries from the savage jaws of the wicked "wolves" (the

[79] Byrhtferth, *VO*, 4.7.

[80] *CAO*, 4, p. 334, no. 7340; cf. also 3, no. 3707. For exegesis, see Ælfric, *Hom.*, 2, pp. 586, 587; M.-L. Thérel, *A l'origine du décor du portail occidental de Notre-Dame de Senlis: le triomphe de la Vierge-Église* (Paris, 1984), pp. 133ff., 228f.

[81] See above, n. 34.

[82] Byrhtferth, *VO*, 4.7: "egregiis nuptiis regalis thori."

[83] C. A. Bouman, *Sacring and Crowning* (Groningen, 1957), p. 151. That Byrhtferth alluded to the marriage between a bishop and his diocese is less likely; see E. John, "King Edgar's Coronation," *Orbis Britanniae*, pp. 276ff., 288f. See also Hyam, "Ermentrude and Richildis," *Charles the Bald*, p. 159; P. Stafford, "Charles the Bald, Judith and England," *Charles the Bald*, pp. 146f.; idem, *Queens, Concubines and Dowagers. The King's Wife in the Early Middle Ages* (London, 1983), pp. 87, 130ff.

[84] L. G. W. Legg, ed. and tr., *English Coronation Records* (Whitehall, 1901), pp. 21, 27.; Nelson, "Second English

Ordo," pp. 372f.

[85] Schramm, *Kaiser, Könige und Päpste*, 2, p. 240 (221), par. 28 (25).

[86] Regarding Ælfthryth's monastic patronage and her close relations to Æthelwold, see C. Hart, "Two Queens of England," *The Ampleforth Journal* 82 (1977): 13ff.; Stafford, "King's Wife," pp. 23f.; idem, *Queens, Concubines and Dowagers*, pp. 125ff.; M. A. Meyer, "Women and the Tenth Century English Benedictine Reform," *Revue Bénédictine* 87 (1977): 51ff.; idem, "Patronage of the West Saxon Royal Nunneries in Late Anglo-Saxon England," *Revue Bénédictine* 91 (1981): 342ff.; B. Yorke, "Æthelwold and the Politics of the Tenth Century," pp. 81ff.; M. Gretsch, "The Benedictine Rule in Old English: A Document of Bishop Æthelwold's Reform Politics," *Words, Text and Manuscripts*, ed. M. Korhammer (Woodbridge, 1992), pp. 143ff.

[87] *RC*, prohemium, 3 and 10, pp. 70, 76; *Edgar's Establishment*, ed. Whitelock et al., p. 150.

enemies of the reform). This likened the king to Christ, the "Prince of shepherds" (*princeps pastorum*) who at the Last Judgment will bestow the crown of life on bishops that have properly cared for and been "a model for the flock" (1 Peter 5:2–4). The Benedictine *Rule* also applied this pastoral metaphor to the abbot who, as the vicar of Christ in the "sheep-fold" of the monastery, is also a "shepherd" who must account for his governance of his flock as well as himself to the "Shepherd" Christ after the Second Coming.[88] Thus in this passage of the *Regularis Concordia*, Æthelwold once again characterized Edgar's rulership as Christological and abbatial. In assuming pastoral responsibility for the monks, Edgar was to function as a Christ-like abbot of abbots;[89] presumably his queen Ælfthryth in her parallel office would have acted as a supreme abbess of the nuns.

Preoccupied with the king's role, the sources are less informative about the queen's. In the preface of the Old English *Rule*, however, the statement of king and queen's responsibilities in the reform immediately precedes the explanation of how the king ordered the translation of the *Rule* so that it could guide him and his subjects. Another reliable source reported that Queen Ælfthryth as well as King Edgar commissioned and paid Æthelwold for the translation.[90] Her involvement suggests that the spiritual precepts of the *Rule* were to govern her duties as well as his, and that she too was to function like a monastic superior. To strengthen her effectiveness in this religious role, the reformers ritually elevated her to the new sacred status of a queen and implicitly likened her to the queen of heaven.[91]

There was a long-standing relationship between women of royal blood and nunneries that helped to sanction the queen's office as the superior of the nuns.[92] Six Wessex convents (Nunnaminster at Winchester, Shaftesbury, Wilton, Romsey, Amesbury, and Wherwell) were established by the West Saxon royal family, often as refuges for royal princessess and retired queens. In the late ninth century, for example, King Alfred appointed his daughter Æthelgifu as abbess of his foundation at Shaftesbury. One daughter of King Edward the Elder, Eadburg, entered Nunnaminster, and another, Æthelflaed, became abbess of Romsey. King Edgar installed his repudiated first wife Wulfthryth as abbess of Wilton, where she brought up their illegitimate daughter Edith. Queen Ælfthryth herself founded Amesbury and Wherwell, the latter probably in cooperation with Æthelwold. Eventually she retired to Wherwell. She remained the titular head of at least three convents until shortly before her death in 1002.[93] Though she did not actually become an abbess, other retired queens did. The most famous example of this practice is Queen Æthelthryth, the seventh-century foundress and abbess of Ely.[94] Ely received exceptionally lavish endowments from Queen Ælfthryth as well as the dowager queen Eadgifu,[95] and their particular concern

[88] *Benedicti Regula*, 1, 8; 2, 7–9, 37–40; 27, 8–9, ed. R. Hanslik, CSEL, 75, pp. 20, 22, 28f., 91.

[89] With the same intention Æthelwold also applied related Christological, pastoral metaphors to Edgar and the royal office in the New Minster Charter; see Deshman, "Benedictus," pp. 222–25.

[90] *Libellus Æthelwoldi*, 49, ed. and tr. A. Kennedy and S. Keynes, *Anglo-Saxon Ely*, forthcoming; also *Liber Eliensis*, 2, 37, ed. E. O. Blake, Camden ser. 3, 92 (London, 1962), p. 111.

[91] D. A. Bullough, "The Continental Background of the Reform," *Carolingian Renewal: Sources and Heritage* (Manchester, 1991), pp. 287f.; also Stafford, *Queens, Concubines and Dowagers*, pp. 126ff.; idem, "King's Wife," pp. 16f; S. Hollis, *Anglo-Saxon Women and the Church* (Woodbridge, 1992), pp. 177ff., 208ff.

[92] B. Yorke, " 'Sisters under the Skin?' Anglo-Saxon Nuns and Nunneries in Southern England," *Reading Medieval Studies* 15 (1989): 97ff.; Meyer, "Patronage of the West Saxon Royal Nunneries," pp. 334ff.; Stafford, *Queens, Concubines and Dowagers*, pp. 120, 145f., 178ff.; S. J. Ridyard, *The Royal Saints of Anglo-Saxon England* (Cambridge, 1988), pp. 96ff., 140ff.; Hollis, *Anglo-Saxon Women*, pp. 212ff.

[93] Meyer, "Patronage of the West Saxon Royal Nunneries," pp. 342ff.

[94] She was succeeded by her sister Sexburga, who had been a queen in Kent, and then by Sexburga's daughter Eormenilda, who had been married to King Wulfhere of Mercia; Ridyard, *Royal Saints*, pp. 176ff. The seventh-century dowager queen Eanfled retired to Whitby and became abbess; Stafford, *Queens, Concubines and Dowagers*, p. 120.

[95] Hart, "Two Queens," pp. 14f. The Old Minster also benefited from Ælfthryth's help. She intervened with Edgar for the renewal of the freedom of an Old Minster estate, and the grateful Æthelwold thanked her with fifty mancuses of gold. *Anglo-Saxon Charters*, ed. Robertson, p. 95, no. 45; also Stafford, "King's Wife," p. 23; Hart, "Two Queens," p. 15. The queen's intercessory role is also relevant to the political interpretation of the iconography, since the Virgin's intercession was an important theme of the Assumption miniature and probably also of the lost opening picture.

for this house must have been due in no small part to the fact that its foundress and abbess had been a queen herself.[96]

The prominence of Saint Æthelthryth in the Benedictional (pls. 3, 28) can be interpreted in this light. She could allude to Ælfthryth's special support of Ely as well as Æthelwold's refoundation of the abbey, and, as a queen who became an abbess, Æthelthryth could serve as an illustrious and venerable precedent for Queen Ælfthryth's official position as patroness and supervisor of the nunneries. Ælfthryth's relation to Saint Æthelthryth indirectly reinforced her association with the Coronation of the Virgin, for we have seen that the Virgin Mary was the role model for Æthelthryth as abbess and royal bride of the eternal king. Queen Ælfthryth's emulation of the saintly royal abbess was also an emulation of the heavenly queen, just as King Edgar's imitation of the regal abbot Benedict was an imitation of the celestial king.

Regnum Ecclesiae

The Benedictional offered a series of overlapping models of sacred royalty for Edgar and his queen, but at the same time it also regalized the ecclesiastic hierarchy. Benedict and Æthelthryth represented ideals of sacred authority for the bishops, abbots, and abbesses of the Anglo-Saxon Church as well as for the king and queen. The choirs of the saints wearing crowns signifying their co-rulership of the heavenly kingdom with Christ and the Virgin were the celestial archetype of the Anglo-Saxon Church, which assumed the likeness of a terrestrial *regnum ecclesiae*.

The concept of a regal Church was integral to the ideology that Æthelwold devised to explain the monarchy's relation to the reformed Church. In his preface to the Old English *Rule* Æthelwold explained the felicity of Edgar's reign as a divine reward for the king's backing of monasticism. The bishop imagined God, "the righteous . . . rewarder," addressing the king:

> "Now that you zealously protect and advance my name and dominion—that is, my church which I rightly have in my special dominion—as a recompense to you I will glorify your name and advance in prosperity your kingdom which you hold under my dominion." What man is there dwelling in England who does not know how he advanced and protected God's kingdom, that is, God's church (*Godes rice, þæt is Godes cyricean*), with benefits both spiritual and worldly, with all his strength?[97]

Edgar had a kind of divine contract regarding God's two terrestrial dominions, the secular kingdom and the Church. Edgar supported the latter and in return God supported him in the former. Although God established the king as his intermediary to rule the secular realm, God seems to exercise direct rule over the Church, his own "special dominion." This helps to create a strong analogy between Edgar and God: ruling the worldly sphere as the vicar of God, Edgar parallels God ruling the spiritual one. The advance of God's "name" in the ecclesiastical realm is mirrored in the advance of the king's "name" in the secular one. Nonetheless, the separation and balance between the secular and spiritual dominions are more apparent than real. Æthelwold omitted any mention of the king's spiritual counterparts, the ecclesiastics who in the traditional Gelasian theory of the two powers were to rule the Church as God's intermediaries. Their absence caused a vacuum of terrestrial power in the ecclesiastic domain which was filled by the king acting in God's name[98] and as his vicar. Hence in the final sentence Æthelwold said that Edgar advanced and protected the Church with "spiritual" as well as worldly benefits. Since "God's church" is here

---

[96] For the political motives behind the court's promotion of the cult of Æthelthryth and other saints, see Ridyard, *Royal Saints*.

[97] *Edgar's Establishment*, ed. Whitelock et al., p. 147.

[98] "God" in the prologue is a generic term for the Deity rather than the appellation of the Father. Earlier the text used "the Lord Christ" as a synonym for "God." The relation between the names of God and king might refer to the fact that the king ruled as a *christus Domini*. See Deshman, "Kingship," p. 401.

explicitly equated with "God's kingdom," an equation reinforced by the word play between *cyrice* and *rice*, it seems entirely appropriate that the king should rule both the spiritual and the secular "kingdom" on God's behalf.

Æthelwold employed a related iconographic device in the Benedictional's opening cycle. The choirs depicted not only the heavenly *regnum ecclesiae* ruled by Christ, but also the transcendental archetype of the earthly ecclesiastic "kingdom" governed by King Edgar who represented and reflected the celestial just Judge.

Nonetheless, our evaluation of the relationship of the iconography to Æthelwold's political theology should not assume that the prologue fully states his views. Since he wrote for the king and queen, he might well have slanted his text in their favor. The regalization of the Church was actually a double-edged sword: if it enabled the king, as the spiritualized royal head of the Church, to participate in sacred affairs, it also allowed ecclesiastics, as the leaders of the spiritual "kingdom," to join in the affairs of the secular kingdom.

The Benedictional's images frequently stress that Christ, as the head of the Church, shares his royal power with its members, especially the ecclesiastical hierarchy. Peter's key-cross (pl. 24) represents the judicial power that the imperial victor Christ delegated to the apostles and their ecclesiastic successors; the crowns of the saints symbolize their celestial co-rulership; and the enthronement of the apostles on a Christological rainbow indicates that they are symbolically *synthronoi* with the heavenly monarch (pls. 26, 27), jointly exercising power with him.

Co-enthronement was a prominent political theme among the monastic reformers. Byrhtferth's *Vita Sancti Oswaldi* characterized the inaugurations of Oswald as archbishop in 972 and Edgar as king in the following year as analogous "regal" ceremonies that consecrated them to co-rule *synthronoi* the Church and the state.[99] Byrhtferth wrote that King Edgar crowned Oswald with the "two diadems" of the episcopacy of the Mercians and Northumbrians. Since the *Vita* elsewhere used the same metaphor of multiple crowns (and scepters) to describe Edgar's rulership of several peoples and kings,[100] Oswald's archiepiscopal office assumed an impe-

rial character analogous to Edgar's own royal office. Byrhtferth went on to say that after Oswald returned from Rome, where he received the pallium from the pope, King Edgar commanded the new archbishop to join him on the royal throne. This co-enthronement consolidated the regal character of his archiepiscopal consecration. The reason given for his throne-sharing with the king is Oswald's spiritual authority, his occupation of an episcopal *cathedra* descended from the papal "apostolic throne." Byrhtferth also mentioned parenthetically that Christ had appointed the archangel Raphael to be the minister of Christ's own throne for Christ himself, subtly likening the king and the archbishop to Christ and the archangel. The ensuing account of Edgar's coronation related that the officiating archbishops, Oswald and Dunstan, consecrated the king on Christ's authority rather than their own. Oswald is termed "the minister of Christ," reinforcing the previous analogy between himself and Christ's angelic minister. Although Byrhtferth described most of the royal rite in minute detail, he omitted entirely the concluding enthronement of the king. This was replaced with the "elevation to the high throne" of both the king and the archbishops, a symbolically charged description of their common seating at the high table during the subsequent coronation banquet.

If the king, acting like Christ, had installed his minister Oswald as a regal archbishop, the archbishop, acting as the minister of both Christ and Edgar, returned the favor and installed Edgar as king. The two parallel co-enthronements of the monarch and the archbishops mirror the heavenly ideal of Christ's own power-sharing with his angelic minister. Conforming to this celestial model of concord and cooperation, King Edgar and the archbishops are *synthronoi*, jointly ruling the secular and ecclesiastic kingdoms which have virtually become one. They could share the same throne, each participating in the office and prerogatives of the other, because all the worldly and spiritual powers they exercise derived from and reflected the same single heavenly source, Christ, the model of both kings and bishops.

In the Tiberius manuscript the picture prefacing Æthelwold's *Regularis Concordia Anglicae*

---

[99] Byrhtferth, *VO*, pp. 4.5-7. For a fuller treatment of the following, see Deshman, *"Benedictus,"* pp. 208ff.

[100] See above, n. 23, also n. 22.

Nationis, a text whose very title emphasizes harmony, shows King Edgar co-enthroned with Dunstan and Æthelwold (fig. 138). The composition expressed both the king's preeminence in the monastic reform and his co-rule with the ecclesiastics. The king had convened the Winchester council that drafted the *Regularis Concordia*. The common seating of the trio and the single scroll they hold stressed their joint authorship of the consuetudinary. No less than the two prelates, the figure of Edgar conveys its monastic precepts to the monk in the lower register, who girds himself with another scroll of the text to signify his acceptance of it. In the dominant central position with all the other figures turned deferentially toward him, King Edgar appears in the role he is given in the text: a regal superior who governs the monasteries like Christ, the monastic "pastorum pastor." The king, however, is not the only one to gain authority in this composition. Since Edgar appears as a crowned king on his throne, an insigne of his royal office, his co-enthronement with the two monastic prelates implies they shared power with him.

We have mentioned that the redactor of the Tiberius manuscript underscored the interrelated roles of the king and the clerics by associating them with the figure of Saint Benedict in the same book (fig. 137). In both compositions the author(s) of a consuetudinary expounds it to monk(s), so that the ideal Christ-like abbot Benedict, assimilated by his diadem to a king, became the model for King Edgar's Christological, abbatial office and for Dunstan and Æthelwold's monarchic authority. Moreover, the association between the crowned abbot and the crowned just judge Christ illustrated a point also made in the *Vita Sancti Oswaldi*: secular and spiritual rulers could share their powers because all terrestrial authority, whether temporal or spiritual, ultimately derived from the single celestial source of Christ.

Although the Tiberius manuscript and the *Vita Sancti Oswaldi* postdate Æthelwold's death, their religious and royal ideology can be traced back to him. In all probability, both pictures in the Tiberius manuscript reflect lost archetypes that Æthelwold conceived at Winchester, and the associated iconography of Christ the just judge is related to his Benedictional (pls. 10, 27, fig. 90).[101] Indeed, there the crowned Christ was already linked not only to the diademed abbot Benedict, but also to a group of co-enthroned figures, the apostles at Pentecost (pl. 26) Like the throne-sharing of Christ and his archangel minister in the *Vita Sancti Oswaldi*, the symbolic co-enthronement of the righteous judge Christ and the apostles in the Pentecostal illustrations portrayed a heavenly model of power-sharing for King Edgar and the monastic and episcopal princes of the Anglo-Saxon Church.[102] In fact, the *Vita* hints at the political connotations of the type of co-enthronement in the Benedictional when it says that Edgar invited Oswald to join him on the royal throne because the prelate had been invested in Rome with the spiritual authority of the papal "apostolic throne."

It is the miniature of the Baptism (pl. 19), however, that most explicitly represents the essential unity of *regnum et sacerdotium* that was the core of Æthelwold's political theology: simultaneously anointed king and priest, Christ unites in himself the royal and ecclesiastic authority jointly wielded on his behalf by King Edgar and the ecclesiastic hierarchy. Christ was the model for the rulers of both of God's terrestrial "kingdoms"; hence multiple diadems (and scepters), the emblems of his imperial power in the miniature, could also be used in the *Vita Oswaldi* as a metaphor for both the imperial rulership of Edgar over other kings and peoples and archiepiscopal sovereignty of Oswald over the peoples of the two dioceses.

The Carolingian Background and the Coronation of King Edgar

During the Middle Ages there was a widespread tendency for monarchy and Church to encroach on each other.[103] Kings sought to expand their authority at the expense of ecclesiastics by appro-

---

[101] Deshman, "*Benedictus*," pp. 210f., 218f.

[102] For the designation of the reform leaders as *princeps* in the *Vita Oswaldi*, see Deshman, "*Benedictus*," p. 228.

[103] P. E. Schramm, "Sacerdotium und Regnum im Austausch ihrer Vorrechte: 'Imitatio Imperii' und 'Imitatio Sacerdotii,'" *Kaiser, Könige und Päpste*, 4, 1, pp. 57–102.

priating their rights and insignia and vice versa. Rivalry between secular and spiritual leaders most often fueled this development, but during the Anglo-Saxon reform cooperation rather than competition induced the mutual assimilation of *regnum* and *sacerdotium*. Although the broader tradition lies beyond our horizon, we should realize that the Anglo-Saxons quite deliberately erected their ideology of cooperation on the foundations of the Carolingian monastic reform of Emperor Louis the Pious and his monastic adviser Benedict of Aniane.[104]

The redactor of the Tiberius manuscript emphasized the relation by placing several texts associated with Louis the Pious and his reform before the prefatory drawing of the *Regularis Concordia*.[105] Among them are the *Memoriale Qualiter*, a short supplement to the Benedictine *Rule* which the Anglo-Saxons erroneously ascribed to Louis the Pious himself,[106] and the Aachen capitulary of 818–819, one of the pieces of legislation issued by the great series of councils that Louis convened at his palace to impose uniform monastic and ecclesiastic reform on his realm.[107] The manuscript's arrangement of texts and picture implied that the Carolingian national monastic reform was the precedent and model for the Anglo-Saxon one. Corresponding to the councils of Louis and Benedict at the capital of Aachen was the assembly of Edgar, Æthelwold, and Dunstan at the royal center of Winchester. King Edgar, promulgating the monastic observances of the *Regularis Concordia*, is cast in the role of Emperor Louis the Pious, the instigator of the Aachen reforms and the supposed author of the monastic regulations of the

Memoriale, and Æthelwold and Dunstan take the part of Benedict of Aniane.

Æthelwold himself had signaled the relationship between the two monastic movements in the *Regularis Concordia*. Its title echoed that of the *Concordia Regularum*, a compendium of monastic ordinances that Benedict of Aniane had compiled for the earlier reform.[108] Æthelwold also borrowed titles and whole passages from the *Memoriale*, featuring them in his own text to remind readers of the source.[109] His description of the Winchester synod's reception of a message from King Edgar was modeled on the account of an Aachen council's response to a speech of Emperor Louis the Pious.[110] Moreover, in the very first sentence of the customary Æthelwold alluded to the Carolingian source of King Edgar's monastic political theology.

Explaining the king's concern for the monasteries, the *Regularis Concordia* began with the statement that "a certain abbot" (Æthelwold) had shown the king at an early age "the royal road of the catholic faith."[111] As we have mentioned, this referred not only to Edgar's childhood promise to foster monasticism but also to the *Via Regia*, the prince's mirror Smaragdus composed for Louis the Pious. According to Smaragdus' preface, God had proclaimed and confirmed the recipient as king "from infancy," and the treatise was intended to guide the king down the *via regia*, the path of virtuous rulership and life leading to the King of kings in the heavenly kingdom.[112] Thus King Edgar, setting out at an early age on the *via regia*, followed the path of Emperor Louis the Pious. Even in the

---

[104] For the following, see Deshman, "*Benedictus*," pp. 228ff.; also P. Wormald, "Æthelwold and his Continental Counterparts: Contact, Comparisons, Contrast," *Bishop Æthelwold*, pp. 31ff.; J. Semmler, "Le Souverain occidental et les communautés religieuses du IXᵉ au début du XIᵉ siècle," *Byzantion* 61 (1991): 63ff.; idem, "Das Erbe der karolingischen Klosterreform im 9. und 10. Jahrhundert," *Monastische Reform im 9. und 10. Jahrhundert*, Vorträge und Forschungen, 38 (Sigmaringen, 1989), pp. 44ff., 73f.

[105] For the original order of the texts in the manuscript, see N. R. Ker, *Catalogue of Manuscripts Containing Anglo-Saxon* (Oxford, 1957), pp. 240–49, no. 186. Lapidge and Winterbottom, in Wulfstan, *Life*, pp. lvi–lviii, suggest that Æthelwold played a part in propagating these Carolingian texts.

[106] C. Morgand, ed., CCM, 1, pp. 177–282. The incipit in an Abingdon copy ascribes the text to "Emperor Louis"; see

Ker, *Catalogue*, pp. 46f.; Deshman, "*Benedictus*," pp. 228f., n. 106.

[107] J. Semmler, ed., CCM, 1, pp. 501–36.

[108] PL, 103, cols. 713–1380.

[109] Deshman, "*Benedictus*," pp. 229ff.

[110] *RC*, prohemium, 4, p. 71, nn. 7–11; T. Symons, "*Regularis Concordia*: History and Derivation," *Tenth-Century Studies*, p. 47. Also, like Edgar in the New Minster charter (see above, n. 27), Louis the Pious as well as Charles the Bald had cited Jeremiah 1:10 to justify their religious reforms; Semmler, "Souverain occidental," pp. 46, 53, 64f.

[111] See above, n. 36.

[112] PL, 102, cols. 933f. Eberhardt, *Via Regia*, pp. 227ff. attempts to interpret the recipient's kingship *ab infantia* as a reference to his spiritual humility rather than his age, but neither this nor the related passage in chap. 1 (col. 935C) mentions humility.

Carolingian period this path was monastic as well as royal.

The concepts of morality and abbatial office in the Benedictine *Rule* deeply influenced the personal and public conduct of Louis the Pious.[113] Called "monkish" and the "rule of the monks" by his contemporaries, Louis considered himself to be the abbot of the monastery of Inde as well as the emperor.[114] As King Edgar would later do, the Carolingian ruler undertook his reforms because he knew that one day he would have to account to the heavenly Judge for his words, his deeds, and his governance of his subjects—a concept of royal office probably modeled on the Rule's precepts for the abbot.[115]

The life of moral perfection that Smaragdus urged on the king in the *Via Regia* had much in common with monasticism. Smaragdus very likely intended to apply appropriate aspects of the monastic ethos to the king, so that he became, as Wallace-Hadrill has remarked, "an anointed vicar of Christ, almost a crowned abbot."[116] Indeed, Smaragdus subsequently reused large sections of the *Via Regia* in two monastic treatises he wrote for Louis' reform movement, the *Diadema Monachorum* and the commentary on the Benedictine *Rule*,[117] and in both Smaragdus equated the *via regia* with monasticism.[118] Even if Smaragdus had not originally intended to assimilate kingship to monasticism in the *Via Regia*, this assimilation became inevitable, if only retroactively, once he had reworked the royal treatise for the monastic ones. Indeed, the converse also occurred: monasticism became assimilated to kingship. The title *Diadema Monachorum* speaks for itself, and

his commentary on the *Rule* compared the arduous discipline of the monk to the refining of gold for a king's diadem.[119] Both king and monk were identified with and shared Christ's diadem. The *via regia* of the monks was "royal" not only because it led to the heavenly king and kingdom, but also because it was the path of his vicar, the earthly king, who led the way with his own life and his monastic and ecclesiastic reforms. This role for the king was envisaged in the *Via Regia*. As the "pillar and model of the Church" who imitates Christ as the head of the Church, the king was to correct anyone in the Church (which includes monks) who strayed from the path of virtue.[120] When Smaragdus later composed the two monastic treatises in the milieu of Louis' Aachen reforms, he must certainly have sought to endow monasticism with regal overtones. Even in the time of Louis the Pious the *Via Regia* and the *Diadema Monachorum* must have been viewed as the opposite sides of the same coin—monasticized royalty and regalized monasticism.

Æthelwold seems to have been fully cognizant of this. In addition to the *Via Regia*, he also knew the two related monastic treatises, the *Diadema Monarchorum* and the commentary on the *Rule*. In fact, the latter's comparison of monks to the diadems of a king and the true king Christ very likely influenced the representation of the diademed Benedict and Christ as interrelated monastic and royal paradigms. In the prologue of the *Regularis Concordia* Æthelwold also used the term *via regia* in much the same dual regal and monastic sense as Smaragdus had. Smaragdus' concept of the king as the vicar of Christ

[113] See T. F. X. Noble, "The Monastic Ideal as a Model for Empire: The Case of Louis the Pious," *Revue Bénédictine* 86 (1976): 235–50; idem, "Louis the Pious and his Piety Reconsidered," *Revue Belge de Philologie et d'Histoire* 58 (1980): 297–316. For other aspects of his reign, see *Charlemagne's Heir. New Perspectives on the Reign of Louis the Pious (814–840)*, ed. P. Godman and R. Collins (Oxford, 1990).

[114] Ermoldus Nigellus, *In Honorem Hludowici*, v. 1248; *Ad Pippinum Regem*, 2, v. 193; *Poème sur Louis le Pieux*, ed. E. Faral (Paris 1932), pp. 96, 230; Ardo, *Vita Benedicti Abbatis Anianensis et Indensis*, 42, ed. MGH, Scriptorum, 15, 1 (Hannover, 1887), p. 219. The designation of the king as *pater monachorum*, which was applied to Edgar (see above, n. 72), already occurred in Carolingian sources. See N. Staubach, *Das Herrscherbild Karls des Kahlen: Formen und Funktionen monarchischer Repräsentation im früheren Mittelalter*, 1 (Ph.D. diss., Münster, 1981), p. 86.

[115] Noble, "Monastic Ideal," pp. 243ff.

[116] J. M. Wallace-Hadrill, *The Frankish Church* (Oxford 1983), p. 239. Also H. M. Klinkenberg, "Über karolingische Fürstenspiegel," *Geschichte in Wissenschaft und Unterricht* 7 (1956): 91ff.; H. H. Anton, *Fürstenspiegel und Herrscherethos in der Karolingerzeit*, Bonner historische Forschungen, 32 (Bonn, 1968), pp. 176, 355, 426. For a different view, see Eberhardt, *Via Regia*, pp. 583ff., 623ff.

[117] Eberhardt, *Via Regia*, pp. 199ff., 583ff.; F. Rädel, *Studien zu Smaragd von Saint-Mihiel*, Medium Aevum, Philologische Studien, 29 (Munich, 1974), pp. 68ff.; Anton, *Fürstenspiegel*, pp. 136ff.

[118] See above, n. 41.

[119] See above, chap. 3, n. 74.

[120] PL, 102, col. 958B, also 938B–C; Eberhardt, *Via Regia*, pp. 105, 527ff., 561f., 671f.; Anton, *Fürstenspiegel*, pp. 178, 376f.

and head of the Church who leads the monks and other members of the Church along the *via regia* to the heavenly kingdom may well have contributed to the political overtones of the miniature of the Entry of Christ into Jerusalem (pl. 21). On one level this scene represented a Christological model for King Edgar leading the monastic reformers and his other subjects toward the celestial city. The *Via Regia* also left its mark on the iconography of Christ's Baptism (pl. 19).

In the prologue Smaragdus[121] explained that the king wears his diadem because God had led him to the baptismal font and anointed him with chrism. The unction was one of the signs that declared him king "from infancy."[122] The association between the baptismal and royal unctions was premised on Christ's baptismal anointment as king and priest,[123] a dual office that all Christians shared with him through their own baptismal unction (cf. 1 Peter 2:9). When the anointing of Frankish kings for royal office was introduced in the eighth century, one of its models was the baptismal unction.[124] In the *Via Regia* the ruler's baptismal anointing was a stated cause of his temporal kingship; baptismal unction into spiritual kingship with Christ assumed the character of a coronation unction, assimilating the king in his terrestrial office to the heavenly ruler Christ.[125]

This relationship between the ruler's baptism and his coronation in the *Via Regia* probably influenced the assimilation of Christ's Baptism to temporal coronation in the Benedictional.[126] The bestowal of scepters, a motif from coronation ritual rather than religious iconography, is

chiefly responsible for the pronounced overtones of temporal regal investiture, but even the crowning with diadems, an old feature of baptismal iconography (fig. 38), had acquired temporal political connotations by the tenth century. The association of regal anointing with the ruler insigne of the crown in Carolingian coronation liturgy soon stimulated a retroactive interpretation of the baptismal unction: ninth-century treatises started to interpret the covering placed on the head after the baptismal anointing as a "diadem of kingship," even though the Latin West did not actually practice baptismal crowning.[127] These very commentaries on baptism contributed to the addition of diadems to the Benedictional's Baptism miniature.[128] Political content was built into this iconography.

The explanation of why the association of Louis the Pious' baptism and coronation in the *Via Regia* should have influenced the imagery in Æthelwold's personal book must be sought in the problematic circumstances of Edgar's coronation in 973, fourteen years after he had become ruler of England in 959. Since such a long delay would be most unusual, it has been argued that there must have been a previous inauguration at the time of his accession and that in 973 he was anointed and crowned again in an imperial rite which celebrated his rulership over all England.[129] This is certainly not impossible. The Benedictional itself reflects the imperial style of rulership of Edgar and earlier Anglo-Saxon kings, and the ceremony in 973 had strong imperial overtones.[130] Yet no other Anglo-Saxon king had a second coronation, imperial or otherwise. Even granting the possibility that Edgar was

---

[121] PL, 102, col. 933B–C.

[122] This linkage of baptismal anointment and temporal kingship reflects the actual circumstances of Louis' childhood coronation as king of Aquitaine by the pope, who probably also baptized him a few days previously. See P. Classen, "Karl der Grosse und die Thronfolge im Frankenreich," *Festschrift für Hermann Heimpel*, Veröffentlichungen des Max-Planck-Instituts für Geschichte, 36 (Göttingen, 1972), 3, pp. 114–21; A. Angenendt, "Das geistliche Bündnis der Päpste mit den Karolingern (754–796)," *Historisches Jahrbuch* 100 (1980): 70–90.

[123] See above, chap. 1, n. 194.

[124] Hoffmann, *Taufsymbolik*, pp. 1ff.; Deshman, "Warmund Sacramentary," pp. 1ff.; A. Angenendt, "Rex et Sacerdos. Zur Genese der Königssalbung," *Tradition als historische Kraft*, ed. N. Kamp and J. Wollasch (Berlin, 1982), pp. 100–118; A. Angenendt, *Kaiserherrschaft und Königstaufe*, Arbeiten zur Frühmittelalterforschung, 15 (Berlin, 1984), pp. 42f., 64,

157ff.; also M. J. Enright, *Iona, Tara and Soissons: The Origins of the Royal Anointing Ritual* (Berlin, 1985), pp. 125ff., 138f.

[125] Regarding the preface of the *Via Regia*, see Angenendt, "Rex et Sacerdos," pp. 215f. For a different interpretation, see Eberhardt, *Via Regia*, pp. 232ff., 536ff.

[126] For other evidence of the impact of the Carolingian "baptismal" coronations and the *Via Regia* on the Anglo-Saxons, see Deshman, "*Benedictus*," pp. 233f., nn. 138, 143.

[127] Angenendt, "Rex et Sacerdos," pp. 113f.

[128] See above, chap. 1, n. 205.

[129] J. L. Nelson, "Inauguration Rituals," *Early Medieval Kingship*, ed. P. H. Sawyer and I. N. Wood (Leeds, 1977), pp. 63ff.; Kleinschmidt, *Englishe Königtum*, pp. 173ff.

[130] Deshman, "Kingship," pp. 399ff.; also N. Banton, "Monastic Reform and the Unification of Tenth-Century England," *Religion and National Identity*, ed. S. Mews (Oxford 1982), pp. 71–85.

crowned a second time as "emperor," it remains to be explained why the ceremony was scheduled in 973. At his accession in 959 Edgar already ruled over the united kingdom, and there was no subsequent material expansion of his power and territory. There must have been more to his coronation in 973 than a celebration of his imperial authority.

Some historians have proposed that Edgar was crowned for the first and only time in 973 in a deliberately delayed ceremony. The entry for this year in the contemporary Anglo-Saxon chronicle stressed that Edgar was anointed in his thirtieth year when he was 29.[131] Stenton and others have noted that this was the normal minimum canonical age for the inaugural anointing of a priest or bishop and have suggested that Edgar's royal anointing was delayed to draw a deliberate parallel to episcopal consecration.[132]

This may well be, but it still does not go to the heart of the problem. This age was prescribed for ecclesiastic ordination because Christ was "about the age of thirty years" (Luke 3:23) when his baptism inaugurated him for his mission. The chronicle with its emphasis on Edgar's regal anointing in his thirtieth year clearly alluded to Christ's Baptism. The chronicle also mentions that the consecration occurred on Pentecost, when baptism was administered. Whether or not there was an earlier consecration, Edgar evidently scheduled his coronation on Whitsun in 973 to liken it to the baptismal investiture of Christ as *rex et sacerdos* and the "baptismal" coronation of Louis the Pious alluded to in the *Via Regia*. The ceremony might also have been timed to liken Edgar's inauguration to a monk's profession, for this monastic rite was considered a second baptism.[133] The relationship between baptism and monastic profession might already have been a factor in the emphasis on the king's baptism and royal consecration in the preface of the *Via Regia*. Even if this was not Smaragdus' intention, Æthelwold could very well have interpreted the text in this way.[134] In any case, when Edgar was

anointed and crowned in his thirtieth year, like Christ at the Baptism, he manifested that he had earned a royal diadem like the *diadema monachorum* because he had faithfully followed the Christological and monastic *via regia* that Louis the Pious had previously traveled.

Many indicators point to a close connection between Edgar's coronation and the Benedictional's iconography. The miniature of the Baptism was regalized in a manner calculated to present the event as a model for the king's consecration and crowning. The miniature's political significance must have been a factor in its inclusion as a supernumerary illustration for Epiphany, even though this entailed a departure from the usual format of one picture per feast. The miniature's typological association with the picture of Pentecost and the initial for the Octave of Pentecost strengthened the bond to Edgar's crowning on Pentecost, and the further association of the initial, the earliest image of Christ as a crowned king, with the portrait of the diademed abbot Benedict reflected the monastic as well as the Christological significance of the coronation ceremony. The depiction of the Christological ideal of royal justice in the Doubting of Thomas subtly called attention to Edgar's dual relationship to Christ and Louis the Pious. Influenced by a portrait of Louis the Pious ruling as the just King of kings, the figure of Christ in the Doubting alluded to the precedent that Louis set for Edgar's own imitation of Christ.[135] The dual coronation of Edgar and Ælfthryth in 973 had its iconographic counterpart in the Benedictional's pairing of the regal investitures of Christ at the Baptism and the Virgin at her Death and Assumption. Indeed, much of the evidence suggesting that Mary in this picture was conceived as a royal and monastic model for Queen Ælfthryth comes from the description of the coronation in the *Vita Sancti Oswaldi*. This account of the ceremony also furnishes some evidence that the symbolic co-enthronement of Christ and the apostles in

[131] *The Anglo-Saxon Chronicle*, C (A, B) 973, tr. D. Whitelock (London, 1962), p. 77.

[132] F. Stenton, *Anglo-Saxon England*, 3rd ed., Oxford History of England, 2 (Oxford, 1971), p. 368; John, "Edgar's Coronation," pp. 276–89; A. Jones, "The Significance of the Regal Consecration of Edgar in 973," *Journal of Ecclesiastical History* 33 (1982): 375–90.

[133] See above, chap. 5, n. 68.

[134] Regarding the relationship between monastic and royal inauguration and its possible influence on Æthelwold, see Deshman, "*Benedictus*," p. 226.

[135] Æthelwold had used a similar device when he transposed Christological features from this Carolingian ruler portrait to another role model for Edgar, the regalized figure of Benedict (cf. figs. 136, 137, 90). See Deshman, "*Benedictus*," pp. 236ff.

the two Pentecostal illustrations could be perceived as a transcendental archetype for the co-rule of King Edgar and the monastic reformers.

All this suggests that Æthelwold commissioned the Benedictional about the time of the coronation in 973.

Conclusions

In his book Æthelwold seems to have gone to great lengths to represent the religious and political ideals that underpinned the coronation, the culmination of his long-laid plans to solemnize King Edgar's leadership of the reforming partnership of the monarchy and the Church. Following the venerable precedent of the Carolingians, Æthelwold justified the king's role in ecclesiastic and monastic affairs by wrapping his secular power in the spiritual mantles of Christ and Saint Benedict. Both were regalized to represent interrelated heavenly exemplars for King Edgar who, like a Christ-like abbot, could legitimately exercise his authority over the monasticized Church. A parallel process portrayed the Virgin and Saint Æthelthryth as associated royal models for Queen Ælfthryth in her capacity as the superior of the nunneries. Other saints and the apostles were also given a royal character to indicate that they shared the rulership of the heavenly *regnum ecclesiae* with their king Christ. The Benedictional celebrated the ideal of celestial harmony that Æthelwold sought to realize in the terrestrial union of the Anglo-Saxon *regnum et sacerdotium*.

Chapter Seven

THE BENEDICTIONAL AND THE WINCHESTER STYLE

THE BENEDICTIONAL is one of the earliest and most magnificent examples of the Winchester style, which dominated England until the early twelfth century. Both Warner[1] and Homburger[2] believed that this style originated at Winchester in the Benedictional and the New Minster charter and then rapidly diffused throughout southeast England. Wormald,[3] however, disputed Winchester's special role, arguing that the style was common to many reformed Anglo-Saxon monasteries. No doubt the "Winchester style" has become a rather elastic term that has been stretched to cover much of later Anglo-Saxon art, but no one has ever seriously maintained that Winchester had a monopoly on the style in the late tenth and eleventh centuries. The real question is whether Winchester created the style before it spread to other centers.

The answer depends on exactly what we mean by the "Winchester style." If it is simply a matter of figures, then Winchester certainly did not originate it: the earliest examples of a new figural style that departed from older ones of the first half of the century occurred in non-Winchester books. More often, however, the "Winchester style" is understood to include foliate borders as well as figures, and rightly so, for the unity of figures and ornament is one of its most notable characteristics. If this is how we define it, then there is good reason to credit Winchester with the creation of the style that bears its name. It was there during Æthelwold's tenure that the characteristic combination of figures and lush ornamental frames first appeared, and one of the first instances of the style from another locale is clearly under the sway of the Benedictional or a very similar Winchester manuscript.[4]

To know where the style originated is one thing; to know how it originated is quite another. Our chief goal in this chapter is to reach an understanding of the Benedictional's role in the genesis of the Winchester style. The style seems to appear quite suddenly in the Benedictional in a highly finished and elaborate form, with few antecedents. Was it really invented in one fell swoop in the Benedictional, or was it the product of an older development?

Our inquiry begins with an analysis of the Benedictional's style, which expresses an exceptionally profound and subtle aesthetic vision.

[1] Warner and Wilson, *Ben.*, p. xxxix.

[2] Homburger, *Anf.*, passim.

[3] F. Wormald, "Decorated Initials in English MSS. from A.D. 900 to 1100," *Archaeologia* 91 (1945): 131–33; rpt. Wormald, *Writings*, pp. 69–72. More recently Wormald (*Ben.*, p. 15; "'Winchester School,'" pp. 76ff.) confused matters even more by extending the term to works from the first half of the century which are quite distinct in style and ornament from those of the second half.

[4] Deshman, "Leofric," pp. 145ff., esp. 171ff. See also below, Appendix One, n. 15.

Then we turn to the historical problem of the style's origins. This involves establishing the chronology of the Benedictional and related Winchester manuscripts, determinating their sources, and investigating the transformation of these sources into an essentially new and original Anglo-Saxon idiom. For study purposes we shall have to make, at least initially, a somewhat artificial separation between figural style and ornament. This method is not entirely without justification, however, since the illuminators did not necessarily derive their figural style and ornament from the same source; the creative combination of elements from disparate models is a feature of all periods of medieval art. We close with a consideration of the origins of the Benedictional's distinctive synthesis of figures and decoration.

The Winchester Style in the Benedictional

An intense expressive energy suffuses the figures in the Benedictional, whether or not they are in motion. Animating the edges of their clothing are nervous bunches of folds winding in torturous paths across and along the body. Drapery frequently blows out unnaturalistically, gathering into extraordinarily intricate and convoluted linear patterns splayed out on the picture plane (pls. 21, 24, 25). The expressiveness of the irregular, broken drapery folds is heightened by juxtaposition with contrasting regular, geometrized ones. The jagged ends of Zachariah's chlamys (pl. 30), for example, flare out before and behind him to frame the taut abstract curve of his back and thigh, which intersects the arcs of his halo and lower leg. The smooth, curving contours of Saint Æthelthryth's halo and left shoulder descend into a rippling cascade of folds, which in turn serve as an agitated foil for her straight, boardlike tunic (pl. 28, fig. 154). The concentric curved and oval patterns of the enthroned Christ's mantle (pl. 27, fig. 150) contrast sharply with its ruffled hems.

Some graphic indicators of the underlying anatomy are preserved. Ovals or circles delineate the protuberances of the knees, elbows, and stomach; nested loops or v-folds signify the recessions of the abdomen and lower legs as well as the hollow between the legs; and smooth areas, sometimes highlighted with broader glazes, mark where the garment is drawn tightly over the body (pl. 27, figs. 147, 150, 158, 163). The organic integrity of the human body is not entirely lost amid the drapery, but the overwhelming impression is of highly charged, ornamentalized figures.

Adding to this impression are the poses of the figures, which often have powerfully hunched head and shoulders. When combined with flexed knees, this creates a tense, dynamic zigzag pose (pls. 10, 18, 19, 24, 25). Frequently the figures gesture dramatically with open palms or elongated fingers. Yet even in the midst of the most violent movement, the figures appear stiff and rigid. For example, Thomas (pl. 24) and Paul (pl. 31), for all the frantic excitement of their draperies and poses, are in suspended animation, as if frozen in a snapshot.

Kinetic energy is not confined to the figures but pervades the entire composition. Cloths with the same excited rhythms as the figures' garments drape the architectonic forms of furniture such as beds, thrones, and lecterns (pls. 8, 12, 15, 16, 30, 34),[5] and pleated and knotted curtains are also employed to activate the picture plane (pls. 8, 15, 33). On one level the omnipresent clouds are a continuation of the antique tradition of atmospheric illusionism that had survived in Carolingian and Byzantine art, but on a deeper level they function to fill the surface of the compositions with areas of swirling or convulsively undulating linear pattern (pls. 10, 15, 24). Similar dynamic linear rhythms animate hills (pls. 21, 25), ground lines (pls. 4–7, 24), and water (pl. 19).

Color adds enormously to the restless activity rippling over the surfaces of the pictures, which lose far more in black-and-white reproduction than do most other manuscripts.[6] Although the palette of the Benedictional includes gray, dark blue, gray-blue, and brown, the miniatures ap-

---

[5] The Brunswick casket (figs. 1, 7) lacks the drapery over the Virgin's bed and lectern.

[6] For color and technique, see Homburger, *Anf.*, pp. 35–38; H. Roosen-Runge, *Farbgebung und Technik frühmit-*

pear as scintillating mosaics of bright colors, such as salmon pink, pale peach, white, mustard yellow, lilac purple, and emerald green. An elaborate technique gave the figures rich coloration. After an underdrawing of red ink was filled in with solid ground colors, pairs of thin parallel light and dark lines were added to indicate the highlights and shadows of the drapery folds (figs. 147, 150, 154, 158). The hues of these paired lines vary according to the ground color: yellow and black on blue-gray; wine red and aquamarine on white; black and white on blue or green, etc. This "double line" technique covers the figures with flickering, multicolored light and dark striations. Broad glazes of translucent milky white or yellow highlights as well as patterns of rosettes also relieve the uniformity of ground colors.

Care was taken to distribute a great variety of color throughout a composition. Furniture and architecture, for example, are fragmented into a multitude of small, diversely colored and patterned parts (pls. 8, 12, 15, 33). The ground on which the figures stand changes color from one knurl to the next (pls. 1, 2, 4–8, 14, 18). The backgrounds of the pictures are often abstractly divided into different color fields. The interior of Saint Swithun's baldachin (pl. 32), for instance, is dark purple, the area between its columns and the frame is lilac, and the zone between the interior arches and the exterior one of the frame is blue-green. Many times the coloristic partitioning of the picture surface is reinforced and enriched by banks of clouds which, like the modeling on drapery, vary in color according to the hue of the underlying ground. The clouds consist of thin lines snaking within the boundaries of undulating ribbons of darker colored, translucent paint. The washlike glazes in the clouds and on the drapery continually modulate the tone of the underlying ground. The fiery storm cloud in the miniature of the Second Coming (pl. 10) provided an oppor-

tunity to exploit this technique to the hilt. Swirling in ever-changing permutations of red, blue, gray, and white and highlighted by convulsively undulating white lines, the thick clouds are a coloristic tour de force. Constantly shifting colors spotted throughout the compositions as well as vibrant linear patterns cause the eye to transcend the limits of individual forms and to roam in ceaseless movement over the painted surfaces.

The visual effect of the miniatures depends on the frames as much as the pictures. The relationship between frame and image is fundamentally nonclassical.[7] Ancient foliated frames were usually narrow and filled with unobtrusive leafwork, so that the borders remained subordinate to the image.[8] The frame was inconspicuous and inert in contrast to the prominence and mobility of the enclosed image. How different is the Benedictional! The borders are very broad in relation to the picture field, and the foliage has assumed a life of its own. The fringed acanthus leaves of the friezes curl sideways and forward in vigorous organic movement, expressively contrasting with the static geometric gold borders that contain their rippling energy. In the rosettes at the cardinal points of the frame, tongues of foliage burst through and entwine the trellis of the framework to form dynamically swirling patterns of centrifugally curling leaves. In a completely nonclassical way the frame has attained visual parity with the image. This is implicitly acknowledged in the dedication poem, which says that Æthelwold commanded that there "be made in this book many frames (circos) well adorned and filled with various figures."[9] The author, Godeman, even mentions the frames before the figures.

In ancient works the frame usually delimited and isolated the picture field from its surroundings. Picture and frame remained independent of each other. When a picture had perspective, the frame enhanced its illusion of three-

---

telalterlicher Buchmalerei, Kunstwissenschaftliche Studien, 38 (Munich, 1967), 1, pp. 34ff.; also J. J. G. Alexander, "Some Aesthetic Principles in the Use of Colour in Anglo-Saxon Art," *ASE* 4 (1975): 145ff.

[7] Regarding frames, see H. R. Broderick, "Some Attitudes toward the Frame in Anglo-Saxon Manuscripts of the Tenth and Eleventh Centuries," *Artibus et Historiae* 5 (1982): 31–42; M. Schapiro, "On Some Problems in the Semiotics of Visual Art: Field and Vehicle in Image-Signs," *Semiotica* 1 (1969):

223ff.; H. Zaloscer, "Versuch einer Phänomenologie des Rahmes," *Zeitschrift für Ästhetik und allgemeine Kunstwissenshaft* 19 (1974): 189–224; W. Ehlich, *Bilderrahmen von der Antike bis zur Romantik* (Dresden, 1979); idem, *Bild und Rahmen in Altertum* (Leipzig, 1955); J. Hurwit, "Image and Frame in Greek Art," *The American Journal of Archaeology* 81 (1977): 1ff.

[8] E.g., Volbach, *Elf.*, nos. 2, 3, 5, 6, 55, 57, 59, 119, etc.

[9] Wormald, *Ben.*, p. 7; Warner and Wilson, *Ben.*, pp. xiii, 1.

dimensionality, moving the image's surface into depth. The frame belonged to the viewer's real space rather than to the picture's imaginary one. Like a window, the frame opened a vista into a fictive receding space. If it overlapped the composition, the frame gave the impression that the field of the image extended in all directions beyond and behind the borders. This classical concept of the frame is totally overturned in the Benedictional. There the frame loses its independence as well as its inertia and becomes an active part of the picture, negating rather than fostering the illusion of depth.

The overlapping of the borders by the image was instrumental in this radical redefinition of the frame. In most of the miniatures parts of the picture cross over the border, sometimes covering large sections of it (pls. 12, 18, 19, 21, 22, 24, 25). Since the image usually does not extend beyond the outer edge of the frame, the frame still sets the absolute limits of the representational field.[10] Now, however, it serves as a kind of anchorage or background rather than as an enclosure for a picture. The representation seems to exist on or before the plane of the frame rather than to recede behind it.

Though almost all the frames also overlay some part of the image,[11] no depth is created because other parts of the picture overlap the borders. In the Presentation scene (pl. 20), for example, the frame's outer columns cut boldly over the figures on either side, but the inner column, which presumably is on the same plane as the others, disappears behind the central trio of figures which also overlap the other figures at the sides. The composition weaves over the frame in the center and under it at the sides. Even at the sides the figures and the frame interweave. The left column covers much of the servant's body, but a fold of her headdress just overlaps the tip of a capital molding and the lower hem of her hanging tunic flares ever so slightly over the column's edge. Though Anna's torso is behind the right column, her head is interwoven with the foliage of the capital. In the Ascension scene (pl. 25) the lower bodies of the apostles overlay the rosettes while their upper bodies emerge from beneath the outer borders,

and the lateral boundaries of the Mount of Olives and the clouds also undulate over and under the borders. In this and other miniatures (pls. 18, 21, 24), the picture passes over the frame's inner gold border and acanthus frieze and under its outer border, behaving like the foliage interlacing the geometric framework of the rosettes. Woven into a two-dimensional entity, picture and frame become interdependent.

The lateral attraction of figures to the rosettes and the borders often seems stronger than the force of gravity. Figures appear to be suspended from the side and sometimes also from the top borders, especially when the ground line is omitted (pls. 12, 15, 21, 25, 26, 31, 32, 34). Even when it is included, its supporting function is often enervated. In the Doubting (pl. 24), for instance, Christ and the disciples are not anchored to earth, but float before or above it. While the figures in the Adoration of the Magi and the Presentation (pls. 18, 20) do step on a strip of ground, the solid green background field continues below · as well as above it. Consequently, the ground becomes a horizontal member of a flat trellis strung from the side borders across the impenetrable background surface.

The painted background field of the picture sometimes stops abruptly short of the bottom of the bases of the columnar frame (pls. 20, 24, 30), severing any connection between the bottom of the frame and the illusionistic space of the image. In the Presentation the unpainted surface of the parchment extends halfway up the column bases and reappears between the figures and the two interior arches, heightening the impression that the figures, the colored background field, and the frame are fused into a single thin openwork pattern pasted onto the neutral surface of the parchment. The miniatures of Pentecost and Saint Æthelthryth (pls. 26, 28) completely dispense with a painted background, so that the trellis of colored figures and frame is even more starkly silhouetted against the blank vellum.

The repetition of forms and colors in frame and picture field creates a decorative fusion of the two. The rhythmic and coloristic contrast between the rippling, colored acanthus leaves

---

[10] In a few instances the foot of a figure does extend slightly into the outer margin (pls. 4–6, 14, 25).

[11] The only exceptions are the miniatures of Saint Æthel-

thryth and the Martyrdoms of Peter and Paul (pls. 28 , 31), and even in the latter a leaf tip curls slightly over a corner of the left arm of the cross.

and their geometric gold trellis constantly recurs in various guises in the compositions. Juxtapositions of agitated and geometrized drapery are frequent, as in the miniatures of Saints Swithun and Æthelthryth (pls. 28, 32, fig. 154). In the latter the hems of the pink paenula rippling along the straight edges of her gold tunic mirror the pink and blue serrated acanthus leaves playing about the adjacent geometric gold borders. The similar widths of her tunic and the border underscore their relationship. Not only drapery but virtually every other representational object was visually assimilated to the forms of the frames. Furniture (pls. 12, 15, 16), architecture (pls. 8, 18, 21, 22, 32, 33), mandorlas, and haloes (pls. 3, 10, 26, 28) reflect the geometric shapes and often the gold color of the border trellis, while the undulations and swirls of clouds and ground lines pick up the rise and fall of the curling acanthus lobes (pls. 19, 24). The arrangement of ground lines and clouds in horizontal bands strengthens their resemblance to the bordering leaf friezes.

Often the compositions subtly combine the overlapping of the borders with the repetition of their forms. The architectural forms above the arched baldachin in the Adoration (pl. 18) are confined to the area over the architectonic border. In the Doubting of Thomas (pl. 24) Peter's gold key on the left and the silhouette of the disciple's body on the right are vertically aligned with invisible edges of the gold frame. Not only do the bodies of the three Women at the Tomb echo the verticals of the border (pl. 22, fig. 147), but the abstractly curved patterns of the paenula of the woman on the far right and the guards' shields on the left correspond to the radiating forms of the foliage in the half-hidden rosette next to Christ's tomb.

The frame sometimes substitutes for a representational object. The border above John the evangelist serves as a rod for a curtain carefully fastened to it by rings (pl. 15). A column base acts like a pillowed throne for Zachariah (pl. 30). Figures often stand on the frame as if it were the ground (pls. 24, 28, 31, fig. 147), and in the Entry into Jerusalem gold borders metamorphose into the columns of the city gate (pl. 21).

The frame is not only integral to the composition, it often determines it. The design of the whole page frequently takes its cue from the borders with their rosettes. In the miniature of the Nativity (pl. 12), for example, the four ma-

jor corner rosettes anchor the chiastic arrangement of the Virgin's bed, on the one hand, and Joseph and the crib, on the other, while the center of the composition is stabilized by a vertical formed by the joints of the horizontal border panels and the edges of the midwife and the crib. Square fields of equal dimension contain the crib in the lower left and the clouds (and part of Joseph) in the upper right, and the diagonal symmetry of these squares is emphasized by the subdivision of both the clouds and the crib into multicolored bands as well as by the black and white outlining of parts of the squares. Other diagonals spring from the minor rosettes with their oblique foliage in the vertical borders. The upper edge of the mattress and the lower edge of the bed frame each link a major corner rosette with the opposite minor one. The heads of the Virgin and the midwife connect the rosette on the left side to the joint of the upper border panels, while the footrest of the bed ties the right side rosette to the joint of the lower border panels and the rosette in the lower left corner.

The diagonals in the pictures often align important points and parts of the borders. In the Nativity (text fig. 1) the corner of the square with the crib and the knobs of two bed posts, which deliberately resemble the centers of rosettes, are on a line stretching between the center of the lower left rosette and the edge of the one in the right border. The mirror image of this diagonal runs along the lower edge of the bed to join the rosettes in the lower right corner and the middle of the left side. The line between the center of the upper left rosette and the lower right corner of the crib passes through the knobs of a bedpost and a crib tower.

The picture's layout also depends, at least in part, on the length of a side of the square framework of a corner rosette. This determined the radius of the circles that circumscribe not only the foliage of both the corner and side rosettes but also the square fields enclosing the crib and the clouds. The height of the crib equals the length of this radius, as does the diagonal interval between the two lower bed posts. Encircling the square with the clouds are the curves of the left arms of Joseph and the Virgin, the stripes of the pillow, and the nodding head of the midwife, subtly reflecting the combination of square and circle in the corner rosettes and at

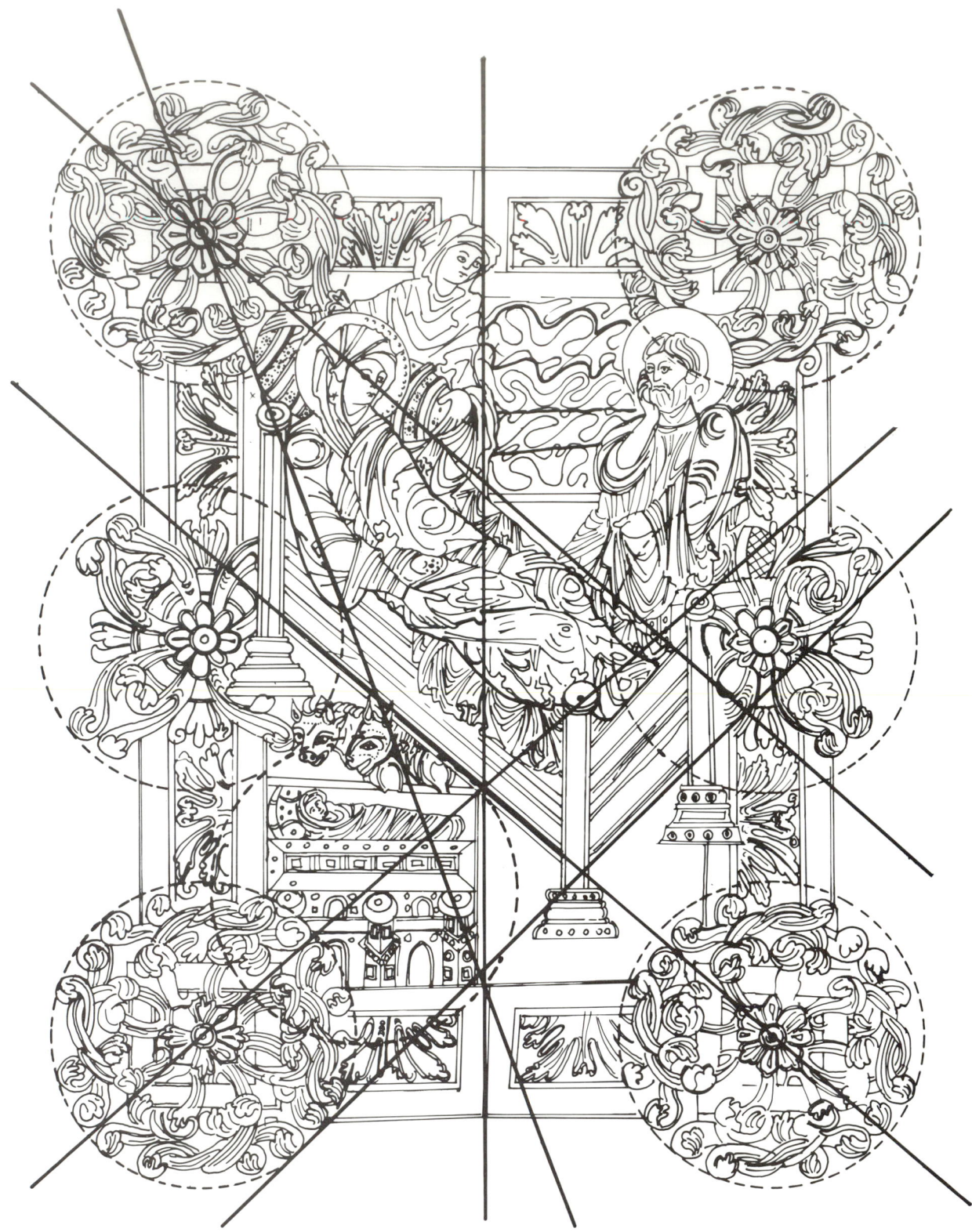

Text fig. 1. London. British Library, MS Add. 49598, folio 15v: Nativity (Giuliana Bianco).

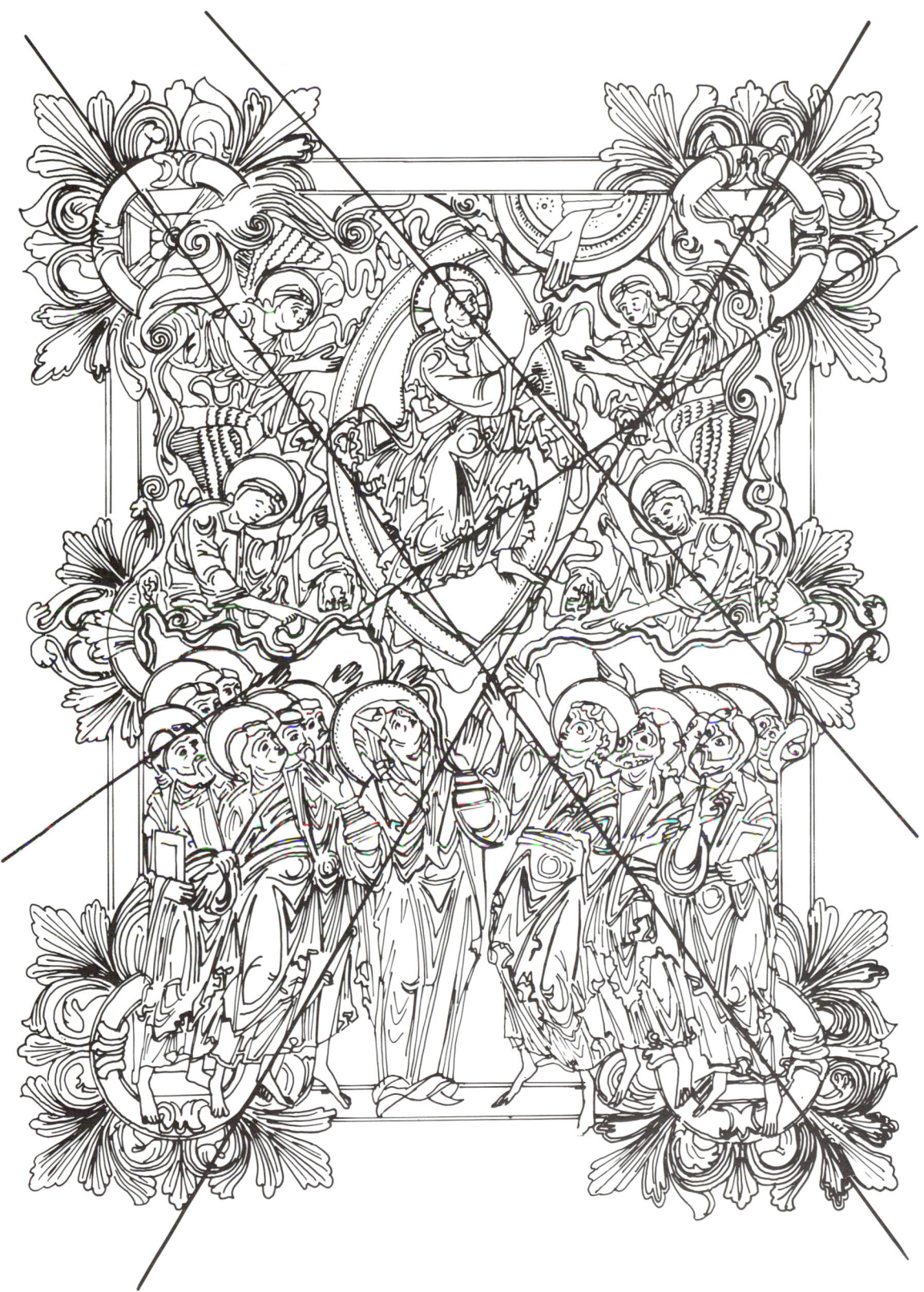

Text fig. 2. London, British Library, MS Add. 49598, folio 64v: Ascension (Giuliana Bianco).

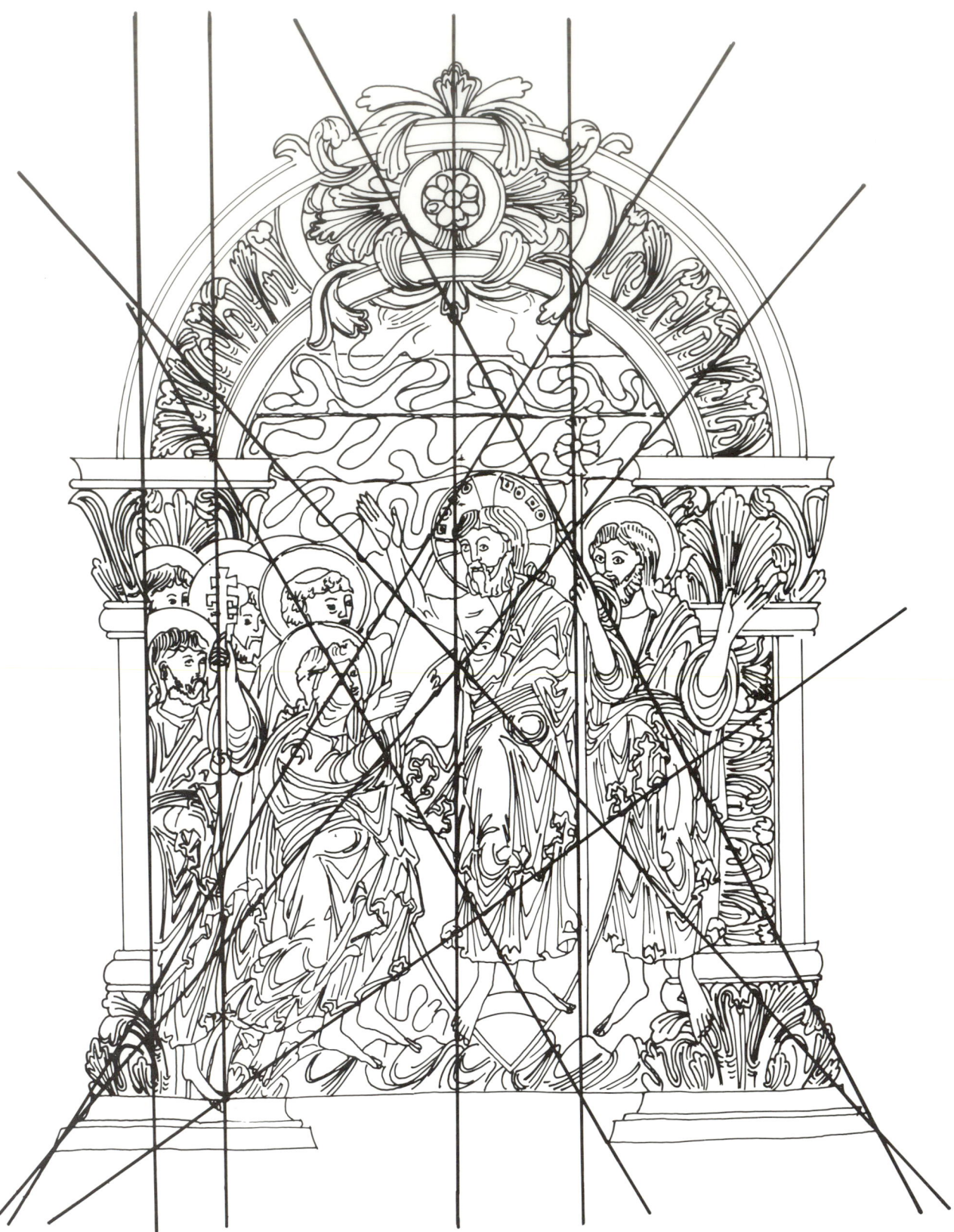

Text fig. 3. London, British Library, MS. Add. 49598, folio 56v: Doubting of Thomas (Giuliana Bianco).

the same time tightening the figures' dramatic interaction.[12]

In the scene of the Ascension (text fig. 2) the hems of Christ's tunic, which at first glance seem to flutter randomly, align on two diagonals crossing at approximately 90 degrees. One of these diagonals intersects the centers of the upper left and the lower right rosettes, and the other is tangent to the upper right rosette and an apostle's nimbus. Christ's cross-staff is on a line with the obscured center of the rosette in the right border. The diagonal tangent to the circle of the lower left rosette passes through a hem of an apostle's mantle, the hand of the Virgin, the tips of Christ's foot and an angel's finger, and finally the center of the upper right rosette. In a similar fashion many of the other miniatures with rectangular frames systematically integrate the picture and the rosettes in an abstract diagonal or chiastic composition (e.g., pls. 8, 15, 21, 31, 33).

Column capitals and bases often served the same compositional function in arched frames as the rosettes in rectangular ones. The extremities of the abaci and the bases in the Doubting of Thomas miniature (text fig. 3), for instance, are carefully aligned in various diagonals with the figures as well as the rosette. The scene's dramatic center—Thomas's outstretched finger and Christ's wound—are located at the intersection of the major diagonal vertical axes. Even so small a detail as the crisscrossed feet of Thomas and another disciple extending over a molding of a column base was calculated to emphasize the intersection of important compositional lines.

The patterns and colors of the border acanthus help to unify frame and picture into an abstract design. In the Annunciation (pl. 8), for instance, the chiasmic correspondences between the form and color of the lower left and upper right vertical panels, on the one hand, and the upper left and lower right panels, on the other, reinforce the crisscrossing diagonals of the sloping cloud, and the angel's arm and wing and the building's roof. The upper and lower halves of the frame of the miniature of the Martyrdoms of Peter and Paul (pl. 31) each have their own chi-

astic color rhythm, so that they coordinate with the diagonals within each half of the picture field. The frame could even be subtly adjusted to the narrative content of the scene within it. In the Nativity (pl. 12) there are chiastic color agreements between the blue acanthus panels above the cloud and below the crib, and among the salmon-colored acanthus in the panels behind the midwife, Joseph, and the crib. These correspondences reinforce the main compositional diagonals and the dramatic interaction among the midwife, the cloud, Joseph, and the crib. Yet there is no color coordination between other parts of the frame where one might expect it, namely, the upper left and lower right horizontal panels, and the upper left and lower right vertical ones. As a result, the diagonal between the upper left and lower right corners was deemphasized. This must have been because this diagonal did not contribute to the narrative: the lower right corner of the composition is an iconographic void.

We should keep in mind that in the original manuscript the feast miniatures are seen together with facing initial pages (pls. 8–13, 16, 17, 22, 23, 28, 29). The image is treated like the text of the matching initial page where both the letters and the surrounding frame float on the surface of the page. This effect is especially evident in the decoration for the feast of Saint Æthelthryth (pls. 28, 29). The saint herself coexists on a two-dimensional plane with the titulus around her, and on the opposite folio the figure of Christ historiates an initial, making it even plainer that picture and text are equivalent. The analogous treatment of image and word was probably motivated by more than the aesthetics of the book. In the Annunciation miniature the inclusion of text on blank parchment within the framed field asserts the planarity of word and image; here the text, in conjunction with the matching verse on the facing initial page, implies that the picture and the liturgical benediction match in content. The placement of the tops of the initial and the painted scene on the same level also stresses the parity of word and image.

The Winchester style is often characterized

---

[12] A straight edge and compass were used in the layout of the geometric scheme of many of the miniatures. Close examination of the original miniatures (e.g., the Nativity) reveals the circles of faint red underdrawing that determined the circumferences of the rosettes. Compass pricks are also occasionally visible; in the Presentation (pl. 20), for instance, they mark the centers of the circles used to design the border arches and also the arc of the arms of the Virgin, the altar, and Simeon.

mainly in terms of its dynamism and expressiveness, as an undisciplined "whirlwind of feeling" that is a projection of the artist's own inner excitement.[13] This is an oversimplification, however, at least in regard to the Benedictional's miniatures, which were certainly not spontaneous effusions of heated emotions. The style may be intensely expressive and emotive, but it is also carefully structured and disciplined. Although suffused with energy, the pictures are nonetheless organized in abstract geometric designs that could only have resulted from very

deliberate thought and planning. Everywhere a conscious balance is struck between exuberance and restraint. Color creates effervescent, constantly shifting pictorial surfaces and yet reinforces compositional geometry. Clouds snake and swirl, but often within defined geometric areas which are building blocks of a larger compositional structure. There is no denying that the style of the Benedictional is filled with emotion, but it is—to borrow a phrase from Wordsworth —emotion recollected in tranquility.

Figural Style

Carolingian art has been considered the chief source of the Benedictional's figural style. The manuscript's relationship to the later Metz group is not as apparent in style as in iconography, and Homburger found better stylistic comparisons among the works of the "Ada" or court school of Charlemagne, located in Aachen during the late eighth and early ninth centuries.[14] Although Homburger was reluctant to see a direct connection,[15] later scholars[15] have accepted that this early Carolingian atelier did influence the Benedictional and also other Anglo-Saxon manuscripts in the "first" style, the name Wormald[16] gave to the style that predominated in southern England during the second half of the tenth century. The same scholars, however, acknowledge that Charlemagne's court school does not completely account for the Anglo-Saxon style, and they suggest that other Carolingian styles might also have been involved. Most have agreed with Wormald that the "ultimate origin [of the Anglo-Saxon style] remains unsolved."[17]

In an effort to solve this old problem, we shall take a relatively familiar path to chart Anglo-

Saxon and Carolingian stylistic influences on the Benedictional, before venturing into the hitherto unexplored territory of Byzantine influence. Our starting point will be the earlier developments at Glastonbury and Winchester that set the stage for the Benedictional.

ANGLO-SAXON ANTECEDENTS

When the Benedictional's illuminators began work in the early 970s, they adopted a figural style that had been introduced into England a decade or two before. The earliest example of the "first" style is the drawing of Dunstan kneeling before Christ on the flyleaf of the so-called Classbook of St. Dunstan (Oxford, Bodleian Lib., MS Auct. F. 4. 32; fig. 139).[18] Dunstan's autograph over his figure, the paleography of this inscription, and the book's Glastonbury provenance have usually been taken as grounds for ascribing the drawing to an artist working at Glastonbury during Dunstan's tenure as abbot (940–956). Recently, however, Dumville[19] has

[13] E.g., Schapiro, "Dis. Christ," p. 280.

[14] Homburger, *Anf.*, pp. 33f.

[15] A. Boeckler, *Abendländische Miniaturen*, Tabulae in Usum Scholarum, 10 (Berlin, 1930), p. 54; Wormald, *Ben.*, pp. 14f.; Alexander, "Ben.," pp. 180ff.; Temple, *Manuscripts*, p. 51.

[16] F. Wormald, *English Drawings of the Tenth and Eleventh Centuries* (London, 1952), p. 26.

[17] Wormald, *Ben.*, p. 14.

[18] Deshman, "Leofric," pp. 148ff., pl. 3a; M. Budny, "St. Dunstan's 'Classbook' and its Frontispiece: Dunstan's Portrait and Autograph," *Dunstan*, pp. 103ff., pl. I, fig. 4; Tem-

ple, *Manuscripts*, p. 41, no. 11; Wormald, *Drawings*, pp. 24f., 74, no. 46, pl. 1; Bishop, *Minuscule*, no. 1.

[19] D. N. Dumville, *English Caroline Script and Monastic History*, Studies in Anglo-Saxon History, 6 (Woodbridge, 1993), pp. 3, 50f., 86f., 96–98, 142ff. Related drawings in later, apparently Canterbury books strengthen the case for Canterbury; see fig. 140 and the next note, as well as the so-called Dunstan or Sherborne pontifical (J. Rosenthal, "The Pontifical of Dunstan," *Dunstan*, pp. 143ff., pl. I, fig. 1). Nonetheless, a Glastonbury origin for the Classbook drawing remains a strong possibility. Since there were Continental manuscripts and scribes in England, Dunstan could have

proposed that it was done between 957 and 959, when Dunstan was a Mercian bishop, or soon after he became archbishop of Canterbury in 959. Wherever it was made, it seems prudent to date the drawing to the 950s or early 960s.

Another early example of the style is the drawing of Christ on a flyleaf of a manuscript of Gregory's *Pastoral Care* in Oxford (St. John's College, MS 28; fig. 140), tentatively assigned on paleographic evidence to St. Augustine's in Canterbury, where Dunstan became archbishop in 959.[20] The close stylistic relation of the two drawings is evident in the similarities in face and drapery as well as in the firmly drawn lines sensitively varied in value to suggest plasticity. However, the more summary execution of the figure in the Gregory manuscript and its more decorative surface patterns, particularly apparent in the multiplication of nervous zig zag folds along the hems, suggest that it should be placed after the Glastonbury drawing, perhaps later in the 960s.

The figure of St. Peter on folio 4 of the Benedictional (pl. 7) is a stylistic descendant of these two drawings. Strongly resembling each other, the apostle and Christ in the Gregory manuscript both exhibit similar stocky proportions, high waist, narrow sloping shoulders, and drapery patterns. Yet there are also significant differences. In the Benedictional's figure, the linear pattern of loops over the lower legs is denser, the flare of the tunic at the ankles more pronounced, and the folds more sharply broken. The figure's mass and volume are diminished by the dangling feet and the flattening of the body against the foil of the flared mantle. The tendency toward a more decorative, two-dimensional treatment, already apparent in the Gregory manuscript, is still more evident in the Benedictional.

The progress of this stylistic development can be followed even within the Benedictional itself. The rendering of the drapery subtly changes, for example, in the four consecutive pictures of the apostles at the beginning of the manuscript. The flaring of the ends of the mantle and the tunic at the ankles is much more pronounced in the second pair of miniatures (pls. 6, 7) than in the first pair (pls. 4, 5), rendering the figures less isolated from each other. An evolution is also apparent in the comparison between the confessors on folio 1 and Saint Swithun on folio 97v (pls. 1, 32), or the virgins on folio 1v and Saint Æthelthryth on folio 90v (pls. 2, 28, fig. 154). The contours of the figures, relatively calm and continuous at the beginning of the manuscript, become much more nervous and irregular by the end because of increasingly numerous and contorted zigzag folds.[21] These stylistic differences are the first of many indications that the miniatures were executed in approximately the same order as they occur in the manuscript.

The stylistic relationship between Æthelwold's manuscript and earlier ones associated with Dunstan's houses requires little historical explanation. Æthelwold had begun his monastic career at Glastonbury under Dunstan, and several Glastonbury monks followed him to Abingdon when he became abbot there.[22] Even if the drawing in the Classbook were done after Dunstan or Æthelwold had left Glastonbury, Dunstan's involvement with the "first" style is significant since he and Æthelwold continued to maintain close contact.

It would be an oversimplification, however, to regard the Benedictional's style merely as the product of a simple linear development progressing from the earlier drawings. Two other works by Winchester artists, the New Minster charter and a drawing in a Boethius manuscript

---

begun experimenting with Caroline minuscule before his Ghent exile; there is apparently no particular relationship between the scripts of the drawing and this Continental center. That another manuscript written at Glastonbury during Dunstan's tenure is written in square minuscule rather than the new Anglo-Caroline script carries no weight, since, as Dumville (pp. 53f., 153) emphasizes, both scripts were also used for Latin manuscripts at Worcester and Canterbury, the locales of Dunstan's later career.

[20] J. J. G. Alexander and E. Temple, *Illuminated Manuscripts in Oxford College Libraries, the University Archives, and the Taylor Institution* (Oxford, 1985), p. 3, nos. 4 and 5. The collation contradicts their hypothesis that the first four folios were added from a different manuscript. Fols. 1–6 belong to a single quire, and fol. 2 with the drawing is the conjugate of fol. 5 with titles for the *Pastoral Care*. The original scribe seems to have left the first four folios blank. The drawing was probably added soon after. Bishop, *Minuscule*, p. 3, no. 5, assigns the original script to the third quarter of the tenth century (a later hand added the text around the figure). For the picture's date, see Deshman, "Leofric," pp. 152ff., pl. 3b; also Rosenthal, "Pontifical of St. Dunstan," p. 157; Temple, *Manuscripts*, no. 13, fig. 42; Wormald, *Drawings*, pp. 25, 77, no. 51, pl. 2.

[21] Already Homburger, *Anf.*, p. 32, noted that the later miniatures emphasized ornamental surface movement at the expense of plasticity.

[22] Wulfstan, *Life*, 11, pp. 20f.

in Paris, reveal a more complex situation in the Winchester workshop in the years immediately preceding the Benedictional.

The dating clause of the New Minster charter states that it was written in 966;[23] if this date is accepted, then the charter with its dedication miniature (fig. 135) is at least five years older than the Benedictional, which certainly dates after the translation of Saint Swithun in 971 and probably about 973. Wormald,[24] however, questioned the charter's authenticity. The codex is unusual in both its format and its content, which defends the introduction of monks into the New Minster in 964 rather than confirming properties. Wormald therefore concluded that it is not really a charter but a special concoction by Æthelwold to propagandize the reform and to commemorate the installation of the monks, and that it is not necessarily dated 966.

Stylistic analysis of the charter's text has confirmed Æthelwold's authorship,[25] and our own study of its text and iconography supports the view that it was intended to propagate the monastic reform. It does not follow, however, that the charter is later than 966. Wormald himself acknowledged that it does not seem to copy an earlier charter, and its witness lists, factual contents, and paleography are all consistent with the date of 966.[26] Had Æthelwold falsified its date, he would more likely have dated it to 964, when he ejected the canons from New Minster, than to 966. It is difficult to see why he would have delayed any longer than two years the production of a document that provided crucial political and ideological justification for this contentious event. Despite the charter's unusual form and content, there is no compelling reason why we should not accept at face value its statement that it was written in 966.

The charter's figural style is in keeping with this date. Homburger[27] tentatively suggested that its facial types continued an earlier Anglo-Saxon tradition. Indeed, Peter's round head flattened on the averted side, his rectangular hair line, and his curved and straight eyebrows (fig. 141) compare favorably with the features of Saint Cuthbert in the dedication miniature of the manuscript of the saint's life (Cambridge, Corpus Christi Coll., MS 183; fig. 142) which King Athelstan commissioned in Wessex between 934 and 939.[28] Since the charter still retains an element of the style of the first half of the tenth century, its date is probably not too far removed from this time.

In other respects the charter miniature is more up-to-date. Despite the differences in scale and medium, Peter's drapery resembles Christ's in the Gregory manuscript (fig. 140) in details such as the fluttering hems, the flared mantle end, and the nested loops over the lower legs. There are also strong similarities between the angels in the charter (fig. 143) and those hovering over the apostles in the Benedictional (pl. 6). Yet in the latter the modeling is more linear, and the bodies are not as organically articulated but rather curve abstractly in response to the frame. The style of the charter is less decorative than that of the Benedictional and consequently is nearer to the two drawings of Christ, which we have dated to the 950s or 960s. Moreover, the older facial type that persists in the charter is replaced in the Benedictional by a new type unrelated to earlier Anglo-Saxon images. The style of the charter clearly indicates a date before the Benedictional, no doubt in 966. The charter is a transitional work falling into the chronological gap between the illumination of the first half of the century and the Benedictional, which is completely under the sway of newer stylistic influences.

[23] *Councils & Synods with other Documents Relating to the English Church*, ed. D. Whitelock, M. Brett, and C. N. L. Brooke, 1, 1 (Oxford, 1981), no. 31, p. 130.

[24] F. Wormald, "Late Anglo-Saxon Art: Some Questions and Suggestions," *Studies in Western Art*, ed. M. Meiss, Acts of the Twentieth International Congress of the History of Art, 1 (Princeton, 1963), pp. 23–26; rpt. Wormald, *Writings*, pp. 108–10.

[25] Lapidge, "Æthelwold as Scholar," pp. 95f.; Wulfstan, *Life*, pp. lxxxixf.

[26] E. John, "The Newminster Charter," *Orbis Britanniae*, Studies in Early English History, 4 (Leicester, 1966), pp. 271–75; Bishop, *Minuscule*, p. xxi; and Dumville, *English Caroline Script*, p. 53, n. 236, accept this date. The argument of H. Kleinschmidt, *Untersuchungen über das englische Königtum im*

10. Jahrhundert, Göttinger Bausteine zur Geschichtswissenschaft, 49 (Göttingen, 1979), p. 99, n. 245, that the omission of Æthelred from the witness list indicates a date before his birth in 968 does not enter into the problem, since, as Simon Keynes has kindly informed me, æthelings did not attest Edgar's charters after 966.

[27] Homburger, *Anf.*, p. 45.

[28] D. Rollason, "St. Cuthert [sic] and Wessex: The Evidence of Cambridge, Corpus Christi College MS 183," *St. Cuthbert, his Cult and his Community to AD 1200*, ed. idem, G. Bonner, and C. Stancliffe (Woodbridge, 1989), pp. 413–24; Keynes, "Athelstan's Books," pp. 180ff., pl. 9; Deshman, "Anglo-Saxon Art after Alfred," p. 195; Temple, *Manuscripts*, pp. 37f., no. 6, fig. 29.

The second work that can be ascribed to a Winchester artist active in the period before the Benedictional is an incomplete drawing in a Boethius manuscript (Paris, Bibl. Nat., MS lat. 6401; figs. 145, 146) that seems to have been begun in England and taken unfinished to Fleury by the late tenth or early eleventh century.[29] The picture of Boethius in Prison between Philosophy and the Muses was intended to introduce the prefaces to Boethius's text *De Consolatione Philosophiae*.[30] There is a general consensus that an Anglo-Saxon did the drawing but no agreement about its date, which has been set anywhere between the middle and the end of the tenth century.[31]

The stocky proportions and swelling plasticity of the figures and the relative lack of fluttering drapery are generally comparable to the style of the two drawings (figs. 139, 140), especially the one in the Gregory manuscript, but there is a hardness of line and stiffness of pose in the Boethius composition that are absent in these. Much better comparisons occur in the Benedictional's picture of the Women at the Tomb (fig. 147). The first Muse and the foremost Woman are similar in proportion and stance, even in such details as hunched shoulders and slightly protruding feet, and the lower halves of their bodies are virtually identical. The parallel thick and thin lines on the drapery in the drawing derived from the painted "double line" modeling technique used in the Benedictional: linear patterns of parallel light and dark colors indicating highlights and shadows.[32] The intimate relation to the Benedictional's style and technique argues strongly that the artist of the Boethius drawing was trained at Winchester and was a contemporary of the Benedictional's illuminators.[33]

There are nevertheless some stylistic divergences between the drawing and the Benedictional that help to determine their chronology. The paenulae of Philosophy and the second Muse are more plastic and less abstractly patterned than that of the last of the Women. Moreover, Boethius shows none of the fluttering hems that Elizabeth displays in the Benedictional (pl. 30). The less animated and decorative drapery style of the drawing is closer in character and presumably date to the earlier drawings of Christ and the New Minster charter. Differences in the rendering of faces point in the same direction. The profile type in the drawing does not occur in the Benedictional, nor are the three-quarter facial types in the two manuscripts similar. The ones in the Benedictional are rounded and broader, while those in the Boethius drawing recall the more traditional types of the New Minster charter and the Cuthbert miniature. The Boethius drawing, then, retains a trace of the earlier figural style that still lingers in the charter but has largely disappeared in the Benedictional. The drawing certainly antedates the Benedictional.

The charter and the Boethius drawing indicate that after the "first" style made its debut at a center(s) associated with Dunstan, it spread to Winchester soon after Æthelwold became bishop in 963. Winchester, however, was a long-established, major artistic center,[34] and the older Anglo-Saxon style that had reigned there for half a century was not immediately or entirely displaced. In the decade prior to the Benedictional, Winchester artists were experimenting with the new style—and with considerable variety in their experiments. The monumental, rigid figures in the Boethius drawing are very different from the delicate, animated ones in the charter. One would hesitate to ascribe both works to

[29] M. Mostert, *The Library of Fleury* (Hilversum, 1989), p. 212, no. BF1083; F. Avril and P. D. Stirnemann, *Manuscrits enluminés d'origine insulaire VIIe–XXe siècle* (Paris, 1987), pp. 15f., no. 19, with further bibliography. Their assertion that a later hand has redrawn the drapery is mistaken, with the possible exception of the faintly drawn lower part of the third Muse. Nor is the inscription "LAN" on fol. 15 proof of a Canterbury origin.

[30] The prefaces were never written, and a later hand added an unrelated text below the drawing and on the blank pages.

[31] C. Nordenfalk and A. Grabar, *Early Medieval Painting* (n. p., 1957), p. 179 (950–975); Wormald, *Drawings*, p. 10 (after 950); Wormald, "'Winchester School,'" pp. 82ff. (975–1000); so also Temple, *Manuscripts*, p. 59, no. 32; *Golden Age*, no. 44; Avril and Stirnemann, *Manuscrits*, pp. 15f. Wormald

inexplicably attributed the drawing to the same hand as the miniature and historiated initial on fols. 158v and 159 (fig. 95), which are obviously by a very different and later artist (ca. 1000).

[32] See also Deshman, "Leofric," pp. 158ff. The Anglo-Saxon technique is not to be confused with the ninth-century Eastern "double-line" fold style discussed by K. Weitzmann, "The Classical Mode in the Period of the Macedonian Emperors: Continuity or Revival?" *The "Past" in Medieval and Modern Greek Culture*, ed. S. Vryonis, Byzantina Kai Metabyzantina, 1 (Malibu, 1978), pp. 75ff.

[33] The equally strong similarities in framing and composition between the drawing and the Benedictional will be treated below.

[34] Deshman, "Anglo-Saxon Art after Alfred," pp. 192ff.

the same center were it not for the similarities in facial type and their common relation to the Benedictional, which includes close comparisons for both kinds of figures.

THE BENEDICTIONAL AND CAROLINGIAN STYLES

While the Benedictional certainly drew on earlier Anglo-Saxon versions of the "first" style, it also looked anew to Carolingian art. We open our investigation of Carolingian stylistic influence with a reconsideration of the role of the later Metz school. Did the Metz model that provided so much of the Benedictional's iconography really have little or no effect on its style?

There is, in fact, some stylistic relation to later Metz ivories, as is evident in the figures of Simeon in the Presentation (pl. 20) and the Virgin in the Visitation on the Louvre casket[35] (fig. 148). Both stand in an unsteady, slightly swaying stance with heads and shoulders hunched, their mantles tightly pulled about their torsos in even, gently curving folds that converge below their extended arms. The Benedictional's primary Carolingian iconographic model was also a stylistic source.

Even before the Benedictional, this Metz work had influenced Winchester artists. Homburger observed that the hovering angels in the New Minster charter (fig. 143) and on later Metz ivories such as the Crucifixion plaque in Paris (fig. 149)[36] share some common features: large hands with open palms, drawn-back sleeves, and tightly wrapped drapery. Moreover, both the Virgin in the charter and Ecclesia in the Crucifixion on the Brunswick casket (fig. 36) are framed between the long, thin dangling ends of the paenula, and the chlamys of King Edgar and of the soldiers on the ivory frames the tunic and hangs in a wedge from the shoulder.[37]

While there are these traces of Metz influence in Winchester illumination, nowhere in this Carolingian style are there the fluttering hems that are the most striking feature of the Anglo-Saxon style. There must also have been other influences that predominated over that of Metz. The current consensus is that the most important of these was Charlemagne's court school.

A comparison between Christ in the Benedictional and John the evangelist on recently discovered court school ivory (figs. 150, 151)[38] reveals the relationship. In both, horizontal folds atop the knees mask the upper legs. The smooth circular and oval areas marking the knees contrast with the mantle's jagged edges, and trumpet folds sometimes animate the hem of the richly gathered tunic. Also the evangelists in the Benedictional and on the Harrach ivory diptych in Cologne[39] (pl. 15, fig. 152) are both modeled by bundles of dynamically curving folds relieving areas of drapery pressed flat to their bodies.

Since comparisons between different media render stylistic judgments more difficult, it might be expected that the Benedictional would resemble the court school's illuminations even more than its ivories. In fact, the opposite is true. The evangelist Matthew in the Harley Gospels (London, British Lib., MS Harley 2788; fig. 153),[40] for instance, differs from the figures in the Benedictional (cf. pls. 15, 22) not only in drapery patterns but also in technique. The pervasive Anglo-Saxon technique of paired light and dark lines occurs only occasionally in this and other court school miniatures.[41] Nor does one see there the broad glazes that the Benedictional uses for highlights. Instead the court school usually rendered highlights by a hatching or comb of thin, light-colored lines on a darker background, a technique not found in our manuscript.

It is quite possible that the ivory carvings rather than the miniatures of Charlemagne's court school influenced Winchester illuminators. Yet even granting that the translation from a plastic to a painted technique would have in-

---

[35] Goldschmidt, *Elf.*, 1, no. 95i, pl. 43.

[36] Homburger, *Anf.*, p. 44; Goldschmidt, *Elf.*, 1, no. 86, pl. 36.

[37] There might also be a slight Metz influence on the style of the Boethius drawing in details such as the wedge shape and drapery bands of Philosophy's paenula.

[38] C. T. Little, "A New Ivory of the Court School of Charlemagne," *Studien zur mittelalterlichen Kunst 800–1250. Fest-*

schrift für Florentine Mütherich zum 70. Geburtstag, ed. K. Bierbrauer, P. K. Klein, and W. Sauerländer (Munich, 1985), pp. 11–28, figs. 1, 4.

[39] Goldschmidt, *Elf.*, 1, no. 18, pl. 10; Homburger, *Anf.*, p. 33.

[40] Koehler, *Kar. Min.*, 2, pl. 54.

[41] Cf. the lower hems of Matthew's mantle and tunic.

evitably introduced significant changes, many elements of the Anglo-Saxon style remain unexplained. Nothing, for example, in the style of either the ivories or the miniatures of the court school could have inspired the rigidly geometrized, boardlike lower bodies of Simeon, the Women, and Saint Æthelthryth (pl. 20, figs. 147, 154). Such differences make it easy to understand why this Carolingian style has never been regarded as the exclusive source of the Anglo-Saxon one.

It has often been suggested that the Benedictional's illuminators must have also drawn eclectically on still other, unspecified Carolingian styles. This supposition receives some support from the reminiscences of the later Metz style in the Benedictional. Yet taken together, the Metz and court school styles do not add up to the Anglo-Saxon style. Although the Utrecht Psalter did influence the Benedictional's iconography, its style had no discernable impact on Anglo-Saxon art until the introduction of the "second" or "Utrecht" style at the end of the tenth century.[42] Nor do the styles of the other Carolingian schools exhibit much relationship to the Benedictional, and the same can be said of early Ottonian styles.[43]

THE BENEDICTIONAL
AND BYZANTINE STYLES

The way around this impasse lies in Byzantine rather than Western art. The hieratic figural type of Saint Æthelthryth (fig. 154), for instance, compares well to that of Saint Alexios on a tenth-century Byzantine ivory in Verona (fig. 155).[44] The tunic of each saint presses smoothly against the slightly flexed legs, which are framed between stiff vertical folds, and their outer garments hang down in straight lines, terminating

in a series of angular zigzags. In both works the linearity of the drapery tends to flatten the body. The weightlessness of Alexios is emphasized by the masking of his feet with an undulating, turned hem, a convention found elsewhere in the Benedictional (pls. 2, 3, fig. 147).

There are contemporary Byzantine paintings in a related style that can also be compared to the Benedictional. On an icon panel of the first half of the tenth century on Mt. Sinai, for example, the flat, dematerialized figure of Saint Damian[45] (fig. 156), with his hard contours and striated tunic, resembles the rigid, geometrized figures in the Choir of Virgins, the Presentation in the Temple, and the Women at the Tomb (pls. 2, 3, 20, fig. 147).

The less hieratic Anglo-Saxon figural types can be compared to Byzantine representations of prophets and evangelists. In the portrait of Luke in an early-tenth-century lectionary from Constantinople, now in the Vatican (Biblioteca Apostolica, MS gr. 1522; fig. 157),[46] the delicate network of thin, parallel lines with ball-like highlights on knee and elbow as well as broader patches resembles the linear patterns of highlights that abound in the Benedictional (fig. 158). Another similar technical feature is the pairs of parallel light and dark lines modeling the mantle on Luke's right arm and calf. Covering his upper leg is a thin layer of white paint which allows the darker, green ground to show through, and over the glaze are smaller patches of opaque white highlights. Similar translucent glazes, sometimes combined with more opaque highlights, are common in the Benedictional (figs. 147, 150).

Some of the best Byzantine comparisons to the Benedictional are in a prophet manuscript in the Vatican Library (MS Chisianus R. VIII. 54), made in Constantinople about the middle of the tenth century.[47] The figures of Isaiah and the left-hand

---

[42] Wormald, *Drawings*, pp. 29ff.; Wormald, *Ben.*, p. 15; E. Kitzinger, *Early Medieval Art* (1940, rpt. Bloomington, 1974), pp. 64ff.; R. Gameson, "Manuscript Art at Christ Church, Canterbury, in the Generation after St. Dunstan," *Dunstan*, pp. 203ff. A comparison with the Ebbo Gospels reveals at a glance the vast differences between the painting styles of the Benedictional and Reims; cf. J. Hubert, J. Porcher, and W. F. Volbach, *The Carolingian Renaissance* (New York, 1970), figs. 92, 93.

[43] Wormald, "'Winchester School,'" pp. 81f., suggested there was influence from the Ottonian Fulda school, which derived its style from the court school of Charlemagne. Any resemblance to Anglo-Saxon art was more likely due to this

common Carolingian source than to direct contact between Fulda and England.

[44] Goldschmidt and Weitzmann, *Byz. Elf.*, 2, no. 8a, pl. 2; K. Weitzmann, "Ivory Sculpture of the Macedonian Renaissance," *Kolloquium über spätantike und frühmittelalterliche Skulptur*, 2 (Mainz, 1970), pp. 3ff., pl. 5, 1.

[45] K. Weitzmann, *The Monastery of Saint Catherine at Mount Sinai, the Icons*, 1 (Princeton, 1976), pp. 88ff., no. B.55, pls. 34b, 110b.

[46] K. Weitzmann, *Die byzantinische Buchmalerei des 9. und 10. Jahrhunderts* (Berlin, 1935), p. 6, fig. 22.

[47] J. Lowden, *Illuminated Prophet Books* (University Park, Pa., 1988), pp. 9ff., 109ff., pls. 1, 3, figs. 1–13.

apostle on folio 2v (fig. 159, pl. 4) resemble each other in the way the mantle falls from the waist in a series of parallel diagonal folds. Both Haggai and the right-hand apostle on folio 3v (figs. 160, 158) are schematically modeled with a combination of thin parallel lines and patches of highlights. The treatments of their right arms, slung in the opening of the mantle abstractly formed from parallel elliptical lines and with a broader highlight on the forearm, are particularly close. Though a coat of shellac has considerably darkened the Byzantine miniature, it is still possible to detect in the sling and lower part of the mantle the technique of paired light and dark lines that is so prominent in the Benedictional. This feature is more apparent in the unvarnished picture of Jonah (fig. 161).[48] The alternation of light and dark lines creates a bold striated effect very much like that of V-folds on the stomach of Paul (pl. 6, fig. 158) or, for that matter, the thick vertical stripes on Philosophy in the Boethius drawing (figs. 145, 146).

Middle Byzantine art was also the source of the new facial type that appeared in the Benedictional. Thomas in the Doubting (pl. 24) and a figure in the tenth-century Byzantine Leo Bible (Vatican, Biblioteca Apostolica, MS Regina gr. 1 B; fig. 162)[49] both have a straight nose and a mouth set well forward of a broad curving cheek, small eyes with prominent dots for pupils, and a tiny ear half-covered by a diagonal hairline. The face in the Bible is modeled impressionistically in loose red and white brush strokes, a classicizing technique that inspired the thick impasto mixture of the same two colors in the Benedictional's faces. The modeling of Thomas and many of the other figures in the manuscript is not entirely successful, with the result that the faces appear somewhat pasty or smudged; but the classicizing spirit of the Byzantine style was more fully captured in the miniature of St. Æthelthryth and its initial of Christ where the lively brushwork creates the impression of vividly modeled, plastic faces (figs. 154, 163).

Though Carolingian and antecedent Anglo-Saxon art were the major sources of the fluttering hems in the Benedictional, Byzantine art might also been a factor. We have already remarked the similar handling of the drapery hanging from the left arms of Saint Æthelthryth and the figure on the Byzantine ivory in Verona (fig. 155). The contrast between irregular zigzag and even continuous drapery folds of the Byzantine saint is particularly noteworthy, because this is a feature that constantly appears in the Benedictional, albeit in a more exaggerated form. The rippling hems of the figures in the scene of the Doubting of Thomas on a mid-tenth-century Byzantine ivory in Dumbarton Oaks (fig. 62)[50] also compare well to those in the Anglo-Saxon work (pl. 31, fig. 150). Another contemporary Byzantine ivory, the Veroli casket in London (fig. 164),[51] offers a comparison for one of the most extreme Anglo-Saxon drapery mannerisms, the dense gatherings of material that flare from the body with masses of trumpet folds splayed in convoluted, circular configurations on the picture plane (pls. 21, 24).

Painting technique, drapery patterns, and facial type all indicate that Byzantine art, in addition to Carolingian and earlier Anglo-Saxon art, was a major source of the Benedictional's style. The best comparisons are from the tenth century, and this supports the iconographic evidence that a relatively recent tenth-century Byzantine manuscript directly influenced the Benedictional. That the miniatures reflect several different Byzantine stylistic modes does not necessarily mean that Winchester illuminators had access to more than one Greek manuscript. It was not unusual for a single Byzantine manuscript to contain miniatures in different styles, as in a Greek lectionary of about the year 1000 on Mt. Sinai.[52] If the Byzantine model of the Benedictional was a liturgical manuscript of this type, as we have argued,[53] then its miniatures would probably also have been painted in several styles. The evangelist

---

[48] For a color detail, see Lowden, *Prophet Books*, pl. 1.

[49] *Die Bibel des Patricius Leo. Codex Reginensis graecus I B*, ed. S. Dufrenne and P. Canart (Zurich, 1988).

[50] Goldschmidt and Weitzmann, *Byz. Elf.*, 2, p. 28, no. 15, pl. 4; K. Weitzmann, *Ivories and Steatites*, Catalogue of the Byzantine and Early Mediaeval Antiquities in the Dumbarton Oaks Collection, 3 (Washington, 1972), pp. 43–48, no. 21, pls. 22, 23, color pl. 4.

[51] Goldschmidt and Weitzmann, *Byz. Elf.*, 1, pp. 30ff., no.

21, pls. 9, 10.

[52] Mt. Sinai MS 204. K. Weitzmann and G. Galavaris, *The Monastery of Saint Catherine at Mount Sinai: The Illuminated Greek Manuscripts*, 1 (Princeton, 1990), pp. 45–47, no. 18, figs. 93–97, color pls. 3–7; K. Weitzmann, "The Classical in Byzantine Art as a Mode of Individual Expression," *Studies*, pp. 164–66, figs. 143, 144.

[53] See above, chap. 4.

portraits and scenic feast pictures would have had a relatively classicizing style like that of the Chisianus manuscript (figs. 159–161) or the Dumbarton Oaks plaque (fig. 62), which probably copied a lectionary miniature,[54] and the pictures of saints, which customarily illustrated the calendar part of a Greek lectionary, would have been rendered more abstractly, like the saints on the Verona plaque or the Sinai icon (figs. 155, 156). Byzantine artists usually represented hagiographic portraits in a less classicizing mode than narrative scenes, and in the Benedictional it is among the portraits of saints that a non-naturalistic, hieratic style predominates.

To place this Eastern influence in context, one has to realize that it played a prominent role in the "first" style from its inception. The earliest example of the style, the drawing of Christ and Dunstan (fig. 139), presents a stylistic problem analogous to the one encountered in the Benedictional. Wormald accepted some relation to the Carolingian style of the court school of Charlemagne but only with the reservation that "in the Dunstan drawing the lines are much softer and more flowing."[55] Its superb economy of line also contrasts with the multiplicity of folds that create denser, more nervous surface patterns in court school works.

Once again the Chisianus book, the Byzantine manuscript closest in style to the Benedictional, helps to fill the gap between the Carolingian and Anglo-Saxon styles. Despite the flaking along the right side of Jeremiah (fig. 165), it is still possible to see that his proportions—narrow shoulders, high waist, broad thighs, and long tapering legs—were like those of Christ in the Dunstan drawing. In the Byzantine miniature one also finds the gracefully flowing folds, which emphasize smooth expanses of drapery, that Wormald missed in court school manuscripts. In both figures a bundle of parallel folds (badly flaked in the prophet) sweeps down from the right hip, framing the swelling volume of the leg and curving

across the body. The better preserved figure of Isaiah in the same Greek manuscript (fig. 159) also resembles the Anglo-Saxon one in the nested V-folds, smooth areas, and large zigzag hems of the mantle and the flat, wedge-shaped segmentation of the tunic over the lower legs. Classicizing tenth-century Byzantine art was as much a factor in the genesis of the "first" style as the Carolingian court school.

The earliest Winchester painting in the new Anglo-Saxon style, the dedication portrait of the New Minster charter (figs. 135, 141, 143), likewise blends Carolingian and Byzantine sources. The angels, which have been compared to those on Metz ivories, also resemble the angels on a tenth-century Byzantine casket in Stuttgart (fig. 144) in details such as the outlined upper leg, the hard V-folds over the midriff, and the fluttering trumpet folds of the hems.[56]

Byzantine style had already influenced early-tenth-century works such as the Galba Psalter (figs. 10, 53) and the Cuthbert embroideries (909–916) from Winchester.[57] Indeed, the embroideries in their adoption of two different Byzantine stylistic modes presage the Benedictional. These earlier Anglo-Saxon works, however, had drawn on Byzantine models of the second half of the ninth century, while the illuminated manuscripts of the reform period all seem to reflect the more recent tenth-century Byzantine styles. Anglo-Saxon artists seem to have kept abreast of the latest Byzantine developments, a situation analogous to that of the twelfth century in England.

After the ninth-century Viking invasions Anglo-Saxon artists had probably turned to Carolingian and Byzantine styles because they were more naturalistic than Hiberno-Saxon styles. The classicizing aspects of Byzantine art, which came to the fore in the tenth century during the Macedonian renaissance, might explain why the newer Byzantine style was readily adopted when it reached England about 950. The monumentality, plasticity, and foreshortening of the Dun-

---

[54] See above, n. 50.

[55] Wormald, *Drawings*, p. 25.

[56] Goldschmidt and Weitzmann, *Byz. Elf.*, 2, pp. 30f., no. 24, pl. 7; K. Weitzmann, "A Tenth Century Lectionary. A Lost Masterpiece of the Macedonian Renaissance," *Revue des Études Sud-est Européennes* 9 (1971): 623; rpt. idem, *Byzantine Liturgical Psalters and Gospels* (London, 1980), X, p. 623; C. Nordenfalk, "Karolingisch oder Ottonisch," *Kolloquium über spätantike und frühmittelalterliche Skulptur* 4 (1972): 49ff. Hom-

burger, *Anf.*, p. 43, also noted an iconographic relation to the Byzantine scheme of the Ascension, which was adopted in the Galba Psalter (fig. 53).

[57] Deshman, "Anglo-Saxon Art after Alfred," pp. 190ff. Boeckler, *Abendländische Miniaturen*, p. 54, observed a few similarities between the Galba Psalter and the Benedictional, which are best explained as a reflection of the common middle Byzantine influence on the two works.

stan drawing—features unparalleled in earlier Anglo-Saxon art—reveal the impression that tenth-century Byzantine naturalism had on the Anglo-Saxons. This Eastern style was all the more appealing because it also contained abstract features that facilitated its adaption to the traditional Insular taste for line, pattern, and movement. The earliest extant work of the reform period, the Dunstan drawing, adhered most closely to Byzantine plastic values, but its technique of line drawing is already a concession to the Anglo-Saxon predilection for linearity. Later Anglo-Saxon miniaturists gave an increasingly free rein to their native fondness for dynamic two-dimensional pattern. They did not totally reject Byzantine style but elaborated and exaggerated certain of its more abstract elements to suit their own ends, while making greater use of the agitated drapery mannerisms from the Carolingian court school of Charlemagne. Though the Benedictional's style was still firmly based on relatively naturalistic Continental models, these foreign styles were more completely transformed in the Benedictional than in any previous Anglo-Saxon work into an indigenous, ornamentalized idiom. It was the dynamism and expressiveness of the Benedictional's miniatures that held the seeds of the future, while the naturalistic Byzantine style ceased, for the most part, to be of any further interest to the Anglo-Saxons.

Ornament

Homburger[58] contributed valuable insights into the later Metz sources and internal development of the Benedictional's ornament, but several factors prevented him from making a comprehensive analysis. He was unaware of two important Winchester works, the Boethius manuscript in Paris and the lectionary fragment in the College of Arms in London. He also did not consider the Franco-Saxon influence,[59] which is as significant as the Metz. We shall attempt to rectify these omissions. The Benedictional's ornament will first be placed in a broader workshop context. We shall then focus not only on the Benedictional's Carolingian sources but also on their recasting into an original Anglo-Saxon style of ornament. Although our analysis often involves lengthy examinations of decorative details, such study does eventually yield significant insights into the cultural milieu that produced the Benedictional.

THE NEW MINSTER CHARTER

The borders of the charter's donor portrait (figs. 135, 143) are filled with pairs of stems or "trees" growing in opposite directions from the center to the corners. The stems are often obscured by sessile leaves and acorns, and elongated acanthus lobes frequently branch symmetrically outward to curl around the gold bands of the frame. Growing into the margins of the page is a fringe of leaf blossoms and grape clusters.

This ornament resembles the rosettes in the Annunciation frames on folios 5v and 6 of the Benedictional (pls. 8, 9), where pairs of stems with calices and symmetrically branching leaves also grow out from a central knob toward the corners.[60] The foliage almost completely hides the stems, but they are visible at the ends of the rosettes in the horizontal borders. Both manuscripts also have similar twining leaves that split into voluted and lobed parts.

Nowhere else in the Benedictional are there such close resemblances to the charter's ornament, and this supports the stylistic evidence that the charter is the earlier work. The development in the Benedictional's figural style suggested that its miniatures were executed in the sequence in which they occur in the manuscript; thus we might also expect to find an analogous development in the ornament from the beginning to the end of the book. The miniatures on folios 5v and 6 would have been among the earlier ones completed; indeed, the rosettes here

[58] Homburger, *Anf.*, pp. 26ff.

[59] Homburger, *Anf.*, pp. 18, 31, n. 1, briefly noted several Franco-Saxon features. For Franco-Saxon influence on Anglo-Saxon art, see G. Micheli, *L'Enluminure du moyen âge et les influences irlandaises* (Brussels, 1939), pp. 157ff.; A. Boutemy,

"L'Enluminure anglaise de l'époque saxonne (Xe et XIe siècles) et la Flandre française," *Bulletin de la Société Nationale des Antiquaires de France* (1956): 42–50.

[60] Homburger, *Anf.*, p. 46.

are the first in the manuscript. The Benedictional's illuminators seem to have begun conservatively, clinging to the earlier type of stem ornament used in the charter before venturing into new forms in the later folios.[61]

In many respects the charter's ornament looked back to Anglo-Saxon traditions of the first half of the century. Freyhan pointed out that the motif of a stem or "tree" with symmetrically branching acanthus leaves and acorns at the dividing points occurs in the Cuthbert embroideries.[62] An even better comparison is the dedication miniature of the Cuthbert manuscript (fig. 142). In the lower vertical borders a stem with symmetrically sprouting leaves grows between the two thin bands of the frame, and here also are calices on the stems and leaf blossoms like the ones in the charter.[63] The charter's long elastic leaves with their voluted and lobed subdivisions have antecedents in the lower corners of a miniature in the Galba Psalter (fig. 12) and an initial in the early-tenth-century Junius Psalter (Oxford, Bodl. Lib., MS Junius 27; fig. 166).[64]

Yet the charter's ornament also departs significantly from the earlier tradition. The zone between the fillets of the frame is no longer an impenetrable surface containing two-dimensional foliage, as in the Cuthbert miniature. The purple ground of the page now shows between the bands, creating the illusion of depth behind them.[65] Furthermore, the leaves extend over and under the frame, sometimes curling forward. In earlier tenth-century Anglo-Saxon art the foliage usually curled parallel to the picture plane. These innovations turned the charter's frame into an open trellis for plastically entwining leaves.

The new features can be attributed to the influence of the Carolingian Metz school.[66] In the initials of the Drogo sacramentary, for example, tendrils of vegetation often twine around the framing letter, sometimes forming a fringe around the initial like the one around the charter's borders (figs. 22, 23, 46, 48, 86). The charter's leaf blossoms resemble the ones in the upper border of a later Metz ivory in London (fig. 13).[67] The three-dimensional curl of the charter's leaf tips was also inspired by the Metz acanthus (figs. 7, 36). The Metz work that influenced the ornament and style of the charter was very likely the same manuscript that influenced the Benedictional a few years later.

The Carolingian influence on the charter is further apparent in its complete lack of zoomorphic or interlace initials, the most common type of ornamentation in earlier tenth-century Anglo-Saxon manuscripts (fig. 166). Instead there are framed decorative pages, which had not been used in Insular manuscripts since the Hiberno-Saxon period. The charter's heading and opening words face each other in matching frames on folios 3v and 4 (figs. 167, 168). Their chaste frames and lettering, however, are devoid of "barbaric" embellishments such as interlace or zoomorphic motifs; they resemble classicizing Carolingian display pages much more than Hiberno-Saxon types. Nowhere is this more evident than in the restrained monogram of the opening, which turns its back on the long and splendid tradition of Chi Rho initial pages in pre-Carolingian Insular Gospel books.[68] The charter was clearly intended as an exercise in the Carolingian manner.

THE WINCHESTER LECTIONARY

The fragmentary lectionary in the College of Arms in London (fig. 129) reveals another Carolingian influence on Winchester. We have previously argued that its initial page copied a Franco-Saxon lectionary, probably the very one that influenced the Benedictional.[69] That Godeman wrote both

[61] D. M. Wilson, *Anglo-Saxon Art* (Woodstock, N. Y., 1984), p. 174, tried to date the charter after the Benedictional, but he overlooked the charter's ornamental relationship to prior tenth-century art and the early decoration in the Benedictional.

[62] R. Freyhan, "The Place of the Stole and Maniples in Anglo-Saxon Art of the Tenth Century," *The Relics of St. Cuthbert*, ed. C. F. Battiscombe (Oxford, 1956), pp. 426f., pls. 31, 3; 32, 34.

[63] Homburger, *Anf.*, p. 47.

[64] Temple, *Manuscripts*, pp. 38f., no. 7, fig. 1.

[65] In the Cuthbert miniature the orange background of the borders differs from the unpainted background of the scene. For color reproductions of both donor miniatures, see Wilson, *Anglo-Saxon Art*, figs. 203, 261.

[66] Warner and Wilson, *Ben.*, p. xxxix; also Homburger, *Anf.*, pp. 46f.

[67] Goldschmidt, *Elf.*, 1, no. 118, pl. 51.

[68] Cf. C. Nordenfalk, *Celtic and Anglo-Saxon Painting* (New York, 1977), pls. 18, 23, 38, 44.

[69] See above, pp. 165f.

manuscripts might indicate that they are near in date. Their ornament casts more light on their relationship.

In the lectionary the foliage of the rosettes is confined within their geometric borders, in conformity with Franco-Saxon practice (cf. figs. 182, 186), but in the Benedictional the leaves climb around them. As we shall see, this seems to have been an innovation of the Benedictional, one that was widely copied in later Anglo-Saxon manuscripts. The leaf friezes provide additional chronological clues. The pattern of lotuses alternating with groups of three flat trilobed leaves in the lower left vertical border of the lectionary (fig. 169) can be matched in the upper arch on folio 1v of the Benedictional (fig. 170). The variant of this pattern in the lectionary's upper right vertical border (fig. 171), where short unlobed leaves replace the two outer trilobed leaves in a group, also appears in the Benedictional in the lower right side of the arch on folio 2 (fig. 172). Finally, near relatives of the foliage in the upper panel of the lectionary's initial (fig. 173) occur in the top right and bottom left vertical borders of folios 5v and 6 (fig. 174). These close parallels to the lectionary are found only in the Benedictional's first six folios, which must have been among the earliest completed in the manuscript. This implies that the Winchester scriptorium produced the lectionary at about the same time it began the Benedictional, which in its later pages moved away from these leaf patterns.

The Boethius Manuscript

The impact of Franco-Saxon illumination on Winchester miniaturists is also evident in the Boethius drawing (fig. 145). Although its frame is unfinished, guide marks and faint stylus lines (difficult to see in a reproduction) allow us to reconstruct it with some assurance (text fig. 4).[70] The frame with rectangles in the corners and circles in the sides obviously derived from a ninth-century Franco-Saxon model such as an initial page in the Gospels of Francis II (Paris, Bibl. Nat.,

MS, lat. 257; fig. 177).[71] The Boethius manuscript also contains an initial C with a central roundel, cusped panels, and interlaced ends (fig. 178), which imitated a Franco-Saxon exemplar (fig. 131).[72] The initial's foliage, however, depended on earlier Anglo-Saxon ornament. The acorn between symmetrically branching voluted leaves in the roundel and the heavily veined, voluted leaves in the panels are motifs recalling the foliage in the initial in the Junius Psalter (fig. 166). The leaf forms in the Boethius initial have been naturalized with plastically projecting tips, but they are still less naturalistic than the foliage in the lectionary and the Benedictional. Hence the Boethius initial probably originated sometime between the charter and these two manuscripts, a chronology that also suits the figural style of the drawing.[73]

The Benedictional

Like the lectionary, the Benedictional was deeply influenced by Franco-Saxon ornament. Almost all its frames derived from Franco-Saxon prototypes. One of the commonest frames in the Benedictional, closely related to the one in the lectionary, is a rectangle with rosettes in circles, squares, or parallelograms in the corners and often smaller rosettes in the center of two or all four sides (e.g., pls. 12, 13, 15–19, 22, 23, 33). Such frames occur in numerous Franco-Saxon manuscripts (fig. 177). More unusual are the frames on folios 5v and 6 (pls. 8, 9), which have unarticulated, beveled corners and rosettes in each side; however, this type is found in the Franco-Saxon lectionary from St. Vaast in Arras (fig. 179).[74] Many other frames in the Benedictional are columnar types which ultimately derived from canon tables. The simplest consist of two columns supporting a single arch, sometimes with a square or roundel at the apex (e.g., pls. 14, 30). The St. Vaast lectionary includes this kind of frame, both with and without the articulated arch,[75] as well as other columnar types with triangular pediments[76] or three segmented arches (fig. 180) that

---

[70] For details of the reconstruction, see R. Deshman, "Anglo-Saxon Art: So What's New?" forthcoming.

[71] *Les Manuscrits à peintures en France du VIIᵉ au XIIᵉ siècle*, 2nd ed. (Paris, 1954), p. 30, no. 59.

[72] Cf. also H. Omont, *Peintures et initiales de la seconde bible de Charles le Chauve* (Paris, n. d.), pl. 7.

[73] Resembances between the foliage in the initial and the column base and capital in the drawing confirm their contemporaneity.

[74] See above, chap. 4, n. 45.

[75] E.g., fols. 39v, 40, 44v, 45, unpublished.

[76] E.g., fols. 22v, 23.

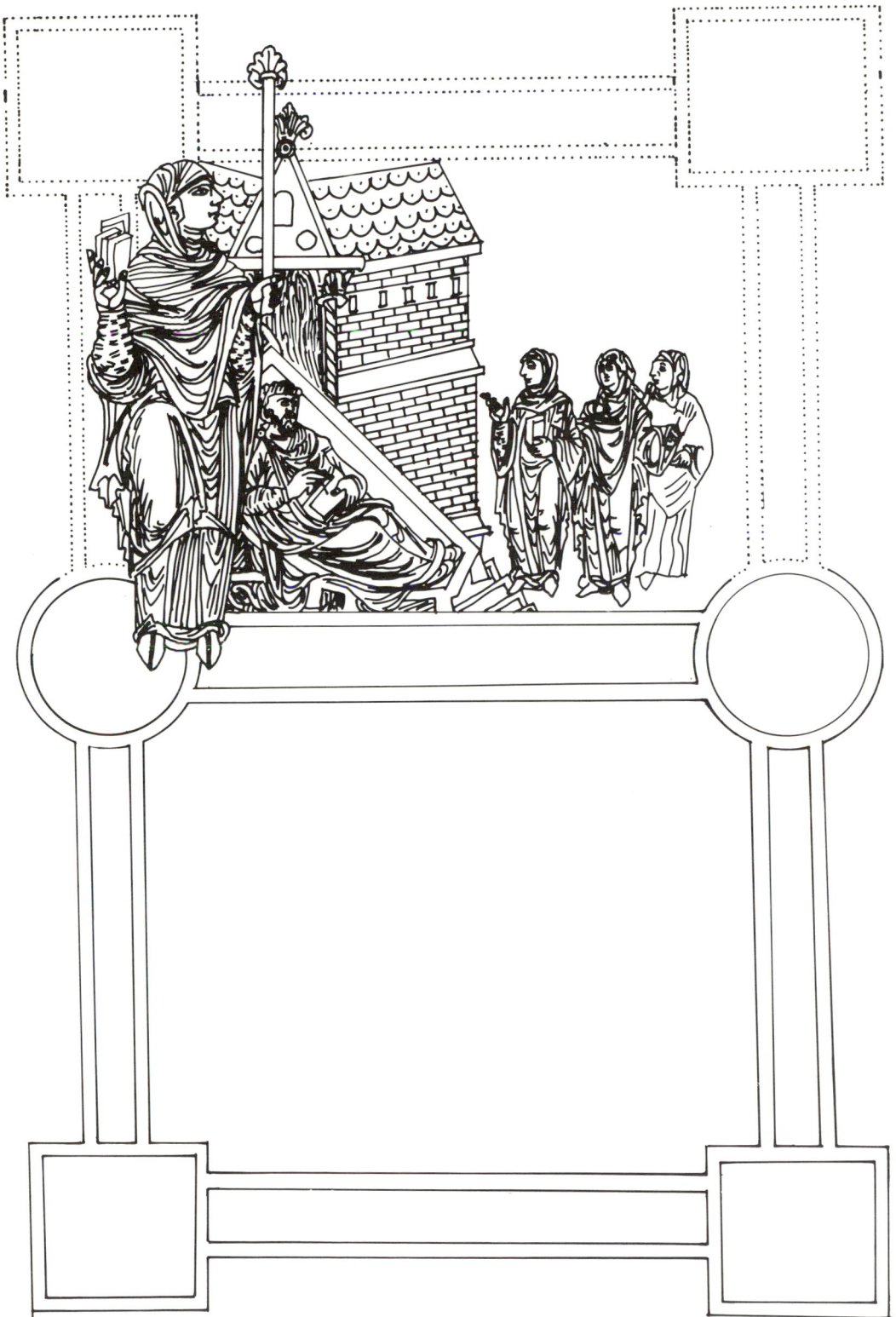

Text fig. 4. Paris, Bibliothèque Nationale, MS lat. 6401, folio 5v: reconstruction of the intended finished state (Giuliana Bianco).

occur in the Benedictional (pl. 4, fig. 181).[77] There are no parallels, however, for the frames of the miniature of the Second Coming and its initial page (pls. 10, 11), which combine two common Franco-Saxon varieties: the rectangle with circular corner rosettes and the arch on columns. The Anglo-Saxon frame could be either a reflection of a lost Franco-Saxon type or an invention.

Despite the heavy debt to Franco-Saxon decoration, the Benedictional's frames could never be mistaken for Franco-Saxon; the Anglo-Saxons were discriminating in their use of Carolingian ornament, discarding or transforming features that were not to their liking. Framed Franco-Saxon initial pages always have a large, elaborate initial decorated with interlace, zoomorphic, or foliate motifs (figs. 131, 177, 180). This type of initial was copied in the Winchester lectionary and on the very first framed text page (fol. 6) of the Benedictional (pl. 9).[78] The subsequent framed text pages of the Benedictional also have large initials (pls. 11, 13, 17, 23, figs. 181, 200), but contrary to Franco-Saxon custom, these are devoid of ornament. They are nothing more than enlarged versions of the plain minor initials that mark the lesser text divisions in the manuscript. After succumbing to the ornate charms of elaborate Franco-Saxon initials in the opening initial page, the Benedictional's painters spurned them for a much more austere, less decorative type. The stark simplicity of this kind of initial is essentially classicizing, for late antique and early Christian Mediterranean manuscripts avoided obscuring the form of the letter with elaborate ornamentation.[79] The only concession to "barbaric" northern European taste in the Benedictional's later initials was the historiation of two of them with figures of Christ (pls. 27, 29, fig. 163).

As staples in the repertoire of Franco-Saxon ornament, linear and zoomorphic interlace must have been included in the Benedictional's Franco-Saxon model. This is confirmed by the presence of such ornament in the Winchester lectionary (fig. 129), which copied the same Franco-Saxon manuscript. In the Benedictional, however, linear and zoomorphic interlacing are conspicuous by their absence,[80] which can have resulted only from a conscious decision to omit these blatantly non-naturalistic northern European motifs from the manuscript.

In many of the first frames in the book the illuminators seem merely to have left blank any border panels derived from models containing interlace (pls. 1, 4–7).[81] After folio 4, however, they abandoned this practice, perhaps because it left static areas in the frames, and settled on a filling of foliate friezes.[82]

Some of these were derived from the Franco-Saxon model. The frieze of alternating palmettes and lotus blossoms in the lower border on folio 9v, for instance, has a close relative in the St. Vaast lectionary (pl. 10, fig. 175). The related pattern in the arches on folios 1v and 2 (figs. 170, 172) as well as in the lower left and upper right vertical borders of the Winchester lectionary (figs. 169, 171) also occurs in this Franco-Saxon manuscript (fig. 176).

Other friezes in both the lectionary and the Benedictional have much more naturalistic acanthus with three-dimensionally curling tips. In the Benedictional one need compare only the lower border on folio 9v to the others on the page or to those of the next pair of frames on folios 15v and 16 to see the difference (pls. 10, 12, 13). The source of this acanthus was the later Metz school.[83] The seven-lobed leaves in the borders of the Nativity (pl. 12), for instance, have their counterparts in the lower borders of a later Metz ivory in Berlin (fig. 183),[84] and the more complex arrangement of alternating large and small acanthus leaves in the vertical borders of folio 92v (pl. 30) matches the friezes of the Brunswick

---

[77] For the pedimented type, see also the Franco-Saxon Gospels in Cambrai, Bibl. de la Ville, MS 327; A. Boinet, *La Miniature carolingienne* (Paris, 1913), pl. 109d.

[78] A good comparison for the latter is found in the Franco-Saxon Bible of Charles the Bald in Paris; Omont, *Peintures et initiales*, pl. 36; J. Guilmain, "The Illuminations of the Second Bible of Charles the Bald," *Speculum* 41 (1966): 246ff.

[79] C. Nordenfalk, *Die spätantiken Zierbuchstaben* (Stockholm, 1970).

[80] Only in the roundels on fols. 34v (pl. 20) and 35 does line interlace occur. Homburger, *Anf.*, p. 18, recognized the

motif's Franco-Saxon origin (cf. fig. 177).

[81] Franco-Saxon borders invariably have some kind of ornamental fill.

[82] The panels of the columns on fol. 67v are an exception (pl. 26), but these were left blank so that the columns could mirror the tripartite division of the rainbow, unifying the frame with the composition. It is revealing that acanthus fills the columns of the matching initial page on fol. 68; see Warner and Wilson, *Ben.*, fol. 68.

[83] Homburger, *Anf.*, pp. 26ff.

[84] Goldschmidt, *Elf.*, 1, p. 46, no. 81, pl. 34.

casket (fig. 34). Since Metz did not influence the Franco-Saxon school, it must have been an Anglo-Saxon initiative to insert Metz-style acanthus into frames from a completely different, Franco-Saxon source.

The most literal copies of the flat Franco-Saxon foliage occur among the first eleven frames of the Benedictional, the earliest work in the manuscript, and in the contemporary Winchester lectionary. In the lectionary and initially in the Benedictional, the illuminators tended to stick to their Franco-Saxon model for many of the friezes as well as the frames, but by the time they had progressed to folio 9v of the Benedictional (pl. 10) they had become bolder and were more willing to deviate. Here only one of the four borders has the Franco-Saxon style of foliage. In the frame of the next miniature on folio 15v (pl. 12) the Metz type of acanthus has completely supplanted it, and thereafter the classicizing foliage predominated.[85]

The painters were carrying on an established workshop practice. In the New Minster charter (figs. 135, 143) and the Boethius manuscript (fig. 178) two-dimensional Anglo-Saxon foliage had already been revamped with the Metz motif of spatially projecting leaf tips, and in the case of the latter manuscript this was done within the framework of a Franco-Saxon type of initial. The painters of the lectionary and the Benedictional seem to have found the Franco-Saxon leaves too flat and abstract; hence they infused Metz acanthus motifs into the border panels to naturalize them.

The changes in the design of the rosettes were more complex and far reaching. Like the Franco-Saxon lectionary in Arras (fig. 179), the model for the frames on folios 5v and 6 (pls. 8, 9) must have had an interlace motif in the center of each border; for a replacement the miniaturists fell back upon the type of Anglo-Saxon tree-stem ornament that had been used in the New Minster charter. These are the first rosettes in the Bene-

dictional, and in subsequent ones the illuminators were not content to repeat timidly earlier Anglo-Saxon forms. They synthesized elements from different sources to invent an astonishing variety of new patterns.

Though Franco-Saxon rosettes were never copied literally, they nonetheless exercised a vast influence. The interlacing design of the rosettes in the corners of the Nativity miniature (fig. 184), for example, resemble the pattern in a rosette of a Franco-Saxon sacramentary in Reims (Bibl. Mun., MS 213; fig. 185).[86] Here the eight pairs of lines springing (between leaves) from the center are analogous to the eight pairs of leaves in the Benedictional. The pairs are grouped in twos—in the diagonal axes of the Franco-Saxon rosette and in the horizontal and vertical axes of the Anglo-Saxon one. Each twosome is linked by its outer strands: the lines are fused into a continuous loop while the leaves are entwined. Both inner strands of each twosome bend symmetrically outward from each other, crossing over or under the two outer strands and ending opposite one of the inner strands of an adjacent twosome. The Franco-Saxon and Anglo-Saxon patterns are essentially the same, even though one consists of lines and the other of acanthus.

While there are Franco-Saxon leaf rosettes, they are always much simpler in design (figs. 182, 186), like the ones in the Winchester lectionary.[87] The Benedictional's painters apparently translated the linear interlace of a Franco-Saxon rosette into acanthus.[88] The metamorphosis of interlace into foliage was common in Carolingian and earlier Anglo-Saxon art,[89] and certain features of the Franco-Saxon design might have stimulated this metamorphosis in the Benedictional. In the Franco-Saxon rosette, leaves are interspersed with the interlace, which itself shows some foliate characteristics. The bases of the lines are modeled with the sort of linear highlights that are often used on the leaves in Franco-Saxon ornament (fig. 176) and the Benedictional, and

---

[85] Franco-Saxon leaf forms were sometimes interspersed with Metz types, e.g., the left column frieze on fol. 97v (fig. 32) alternates lotus and acanthus leaves.

[86] *Manuscrits à peintures*, p. 32, no. 67.

[87] Simple acanthus rosettes also occur in earlier Anglo-Saxon art (fig. 142) and in other late Carolingian schools; see *La cattedra lignea di S. Pietro in Vaticano*, Atti della Pontificia Accademia Romana de Archeologia, ser. 3, Memorie 10 (Vatican City, 1971), pls. 20, 1; 21, 1; 22, 2.

[88] The same process probably resulted in the systematically interlaced foliage in the capitals on fols. 17v and 34v (pls. 14, 20). Franco-Saxon capitals sometimes consist of linear interlace (Arras, fol. 54, unpublished), but the foliate ones (cf. figs. 180, 199) are never so abstractly interwoven.

[89] Cf. F. Mütherich and J. E. Gaehde, *Carolingian Painting* (New York, 1976), pls. 3, 34, 42, 48; our fig. 166, and Temple, *Manuscripts*, figs. 1, 20–24.

the ends of the lines thicken and curl like voluted foliage. The Benedictional's miniaturists completed a process of naturalization that had already begun to a limited extent in their Franco-Saxon model.

In Anglo-Saxon hands, however, the design became much more intricate. Each of the leaves in the Benedictional splits as it sprouts from the center of the rosette, so that the pattern has twice as many interlacing elements as the Franco-Saxon one. In addition, the foliage interlaces the gold geometric borders, while the Carolingian design stays within them.

This last feature of the Benedictional reflects several different influences. Although the leaves in Franco-Saxon rosettes are invariably confined within the framework, the St. Vaast lectionary includes some rosettes that combine leaves with a simple radial pattern of lines which interlace the surrounding borders (figs. 130, 131).[90] There is no indication that more complex Franco-Saxon line patterns like the one in the Reims sacramentary ever interlaced the rosette framework. In all likelihood the Benedictional's rosette derived from the creative combination of features from two distinct kinds of Franco-Saxon interlace rosettes.

Another influence was earlier Winchester manuscripts such as the New Minster charter (figs. 135, 143) where acanthus also divides to entwine geometric gold borders. The impact of this type of ornament is most evident in the Benedictional's first set of rosettes (pls. 8, 9), which retained the traditional stem format, but the concept of twining foliage was also adapted to the rosettes without stems. The charter had derived the motif of climbing foliage from a Metz work, and this Carolingian source also directly influenced the Benedictional's rosettes. The figures in the *Te igitur* initial in the Drogo Sacramentary[91] (fig. 187) are framed by two entwined strands of the vinelike acanthus that are quite similar to the elongated twining leaves in the rosettes of the Nativity miniature.

Other rosettes in the Benedictional took as their point of departure a type of Franco-Saxon rosette consisting of a simple radial design of conventional leaves. The rosettes in the vertical borders of folio 52 (fig. 188), for instance, can be compared to one in a Franco-Saxon Gospels in Boulogne (Bibl. Mun., MS 12; fig. 182).[92] In each case eight stiff, straight leaves radiate from the center, the four diagonal ones subdividing so that their outer lobes bend symmetrically to either side toward the adjacent horizontal and vertical leaves. In characteristic fashion the English illuminators replaced the abstract Franco-Saxon leaf forms with classicizing Metz-style acanthus, multiplying the subdivisions of the leaves and interweaving them with the geometric borders. Another innovation was to change the rosette's gold framework from a simple roundel to a circle circumscribing a square.

The earliest frames in the Benedictional (pls. 10–17) had followed the Franco-Saxon practice of framing a rosette with a single geometric border. Beginning on folio 24v (pl. 18) a second border was included in each corner rosette, and in the last pair of rectangular frames on folios 99v and 100 (pl. 33) even a third one. In their desire for a more elaborate geometric trellis for the climbing leaves, the Winchester illuminators gradually distanced themselves from simple Carolingian frameworks.

Nonetheless, this development might not have been entirely independent of Franco-Saxon rosettes, for these are sometimes filled with an interlaced circle or square. The square frame of a rosette in a Franco-Saxon Gospels in New York (Morgan Lib., MS 862; fig. 189),[93] for instance, circumscribes a circle interlaced by four pairs of lines radiating from the center. This design is not unlike the corner rosettes on folios 51v and 52 (pl. 22, 23, fig. 190), where eight radiating arms of foliage interlace a double framework of a circle in a square. The Benedictional's illuminators have simply changed the circle of the filling into part of the frame.

They also made use of Franco-Saxon motifs that were originally quite independent of rosettes. At the corners of a frame in the Arras lectionary (fig. 191) a large leaf subdivides symmetrically into one pair of short leaves extending out into the margin and a second pair of longer ones curling back into a gap in the corner of the border. This motif was reworked for the rosettes

---

[90] See also fols. 42v and 43; unpublished.
[91] *Drogo-Sak.*, fol. 15v.
[92] Boinet, *Miniature*, pl. 96b.
[93] J. Guilmain, "On the Classicism of the 'Classic' Phase of Franco-Saxon Illumination," *AB* 49 (1967): 243, fig. 7. For an example of an interlaced square in a round frame, see Omont, *Peintures et initiales*, pl. 32.

of the Benedictional's portrait of John (fig. 192). The Franco-Saxon foliage was repeated at the four corners to form a radial pattern. Some of these leaves do not quite align with their bases in the rosette frame, indicating that these bases were interpolated to create the illusion that the leaves sprang organically from the inside. Paradoxically, their addition also gave the foliage a more abstract rhythm of interlace. The Franco-Saxon leaves bend gently without intersecting each other, but the Anglo-Saxon ones curve in tense, crisscrossing arcs. Still another form of Franco-Saxon corner foliage found in the Arras lectionary (fig. 193) was recast into the complex rosettes of the frame of the Entry into Jerusalem (fig. 194). Naturalized versions of the Franco-Saxon leaf were repeated at the corners of the rosette's square framework, while a tall leaf flanked by two short ones, a Metz motif derived from the Benedictional's border friezes, was grafted onto each side of the square. Using such ingenious techniques the miniaturists fabricated all the rosettes in the Benedictional from the repertoire of Carolingian Franco-Saxon and Metz ornament.

It is a measure of the painters' inventiveness that in no two pairs of frames are the rosette designs exactly duplicated. Just as variations of an iconographic motif or theme were developed in a series of miniatures, so the ramifications of an ornamental design were explored from one set of frames to the next. The minor rosettes on folio 52 (fig. 188), for example, were slightly reworked for the major ones on folio 64v (fig. 195): the diagonal leaves that had curled back over the circular border curl beneath it and through it. The same basic pattern also appears on folio 95v (fig. 196), but the shapes of the geometric frames have been reversed and the divided leaves on the diagonal axes interlace the outer frame instead of merely crossing under it. In the corner rosettes on folio 99v (fig. 197) a second square frame, rotated 90 degrees, was added. The bases of the leaves now pass under both rather than only one of the inner frames, and the foliage on the horizontal and vertical axes has been omitted, an idea that had been introduced on folio 95v. Like a musical composer, the painters stated their basic theme and then delighted in creating a series of variations.

The illuminators' imaginative processes are also evident in their reinterpretation of the Anglo-Saxon motif of the tree-stem.[94] After using it once in a relatively traditional form in the first set of rosettes on folios 5v and 6, they gradually elaborated it later in the manuscript. The revamped design seems to have developed from the simple rosette on folio 17v (pl. 14), which is tightly hemmed in by flanking acanthus friezes. In most of the later arched frames, however, the rosettes push back the adjacent friezes (pls. 24, 26). On folios 90v and 91 (pls. 28, 29) the extensions of the rosettes completely displaced the usual acanthus friezes, becoming a type of double stem. One has only to compare these borders with those of the New Minster charter (figs. 135, 143) to see how a traditional Anglo-Saxon motif has been totally transformed and fused with Carolingian ornament.

As the Benedictional's painters synthesized previously unrelated Metz and Franco-Saxon ornamental forms, they also gradually imposed a stricter decorative unity on all parts of the frames, without sacrificing structural integrity. The first three miniatures (pls. 1–3) sometimes copied the heavy architectonic capitals and bases that appear in Franco-Saxon manuscripts like the Second Bible of Charles the Bald (fig. 198).[95] Subsequent columnar frames, however, employed only foliate capitals and bases, which were also Franco-Saxon in inspiration (figs. 181, 199; pl. 24, fig. 180). As usual, the Anglo-Saxon painters translated the conventional Franco-Saxon leaves into Metz-style acanthus. This not only classicized the capitals and bases, it also unified them decoratively with the other parts of the frame. In the manuscript's final frame (fig. 200), for example, the lack of overlapping and the alternation of long and short leaves cause the capitals and bases to look like excerpts from the friezes in the arch. Architectonic capitals and bases did not lend themselves to such decorative unification, and this must have been why they were discarded after the beginning folios. The first miniature in the book (pl. 1), however, reveals that even at this early stage of their work the miniaturists had begun to think about the relation between the different members of the frame, for here the foliage in the capitals is simply an enlarged

---

[94] Homburger, *Anf.*, p. 30; Freyhan, "Stole and Maniples," pp. 427f.

[95] Omont, *Peintures et initiales*, pl. 4.

fragment of a Metz-type acanthus frieze.[96] The monolithic leaves of these capitals are disproportionately large in relation to the foliage of the arch frieze as well as to the figures; thus beginning on folio 2v (pl. 4) the painters switched to the Franco-Saxon type of capital and base with smaller leaves, a type that also allowed more opportunity for the lively movement and multicolored pattern the Anglo-Saxons loved.

In other frames the illuminators preferred to unify the capitals and bases with the rosette in the arch rather than the border panels. On folio 56v (pl. 24) the group of three flat leaves in the center of the capitals is echoed in the horizontal arms of the rosette, and in each case the foliage grows approximately at a right angle to the acanthus in the adjacent friezes. The omission of this triadic leaf pattern from the friezes tightens the visual link between the capitals and the rosette.

The architectural moldings as well as the foliage of the capitals and bases are carefully calculated to enhance the unity of the design. The forms of the moldings of the capital and base of a column frequently differ from each other in the earlier frames (pls. 1, 7, 20), but were made uniform from folio 56v (pl. 24): the foliage is always sandwiched between a pair of thick gold moldings (flanked by one or two very thin ones). Thus the profiles of a capital and base began to mirror each other (though the base often has a plinth for structural clarity) and to reflect the arrangement of acanthus between the framing gold bands of the column panels and the rosettes.

Toward the end of the cycle two innovations, which first appear on folio 97v (pl. 32), brought the structural forms of the capitals and bases even closer to the ornamental design of the rosettes. The leaves of the columns and bases are no longer confined to their architectural boundaries but now curl decoratively over the abaci and tori, and a gold bar is suspended amid the foliage of each base. The bars are without structural function and seem to have been

added for no other reason than to create a more complicated framework for the climbing leaves. In the next pair of columnar frames on folios 102v and 103 (pl. 34), a segmental arch rather than a bar was added to the bases and now to the capitals as well. These innovations were influenced by the twining foliage of the rosettes, an influence that is particularly obvious on folio 102v where the rosette also has segmental arches. These modifications in the capitals and bases enhanced decorative unity since the friezes with their comparatively regular, tightly confined rows of acanthus are now flanked at the bottom, middle, and top of the frame by varied masses of foliage climbing freely over the borders.

This assimilation of capitals and bases to rosettes might have been inspired by certain Franco-Saxon columnar frames that substituted conventional rosettes, like those used in the corners of rectangular frames, for capitals and bases (fig. 198).[97] Indeed, this is the case in the arched frame of the Second Coming (pl. 10). That the Benedictional's illuminators found a different means to unify the capitals and bases with the rosettes—one that did not completely sacrifice the illusion of foliate architectural members—is another indication of their classicizing mentality.[98]

The design of the friezes was also refined to increase decorative homogeneity. The borders were gradually widened, so that in the last miniatures they have become almost a third wider than in the first group (pls. 1, 33, 34).[99] Consequently, the obvious disparity in height between the long leaves in the capitals and bases and the shorter ones in the friezes in the earlier frames (pl. 14) has diminished in the later ones. On folio 92v (pl. 30) the frieze at the apex of the arch has exactly the same height as the capitals. Because there is also more space between the leaves in the Anglo-Saxon friezes than in their densely packed Metz counterparts (figs. 7, 183), the leaves could be more like the highly individualized, mobile ones in the capitals, bases, and

---

[96] The same pattern occurs in the upper left and lower right vertical borders in the Winchester lectionary (fig. 129).

[97] Cf. also P. Lauer, *L'Évangéliaire carolingien de Lyon*, Documents, paleographiques, typographiques, iconographiques, 7 (Lyon, 1928), p. 11, pl. 7; Micheli, *Enluminure*, fig. 212.

[98] In a derivative of one of the Benedictional's frames in the Benedictional of Archbishop Robert (fig. 213) the development comes full circle. Any pretense of structural capitals has been given up. The profiles have been combined with the type of quatrefoil that frames some Franco-Saxon ro-

settes, and the foliage is arranged in the radial fashion of a rosette.

[99] Homburger, *Anf.*, p. 31. This feature also corroborates the chronology of the Boethius drawing, the Winchester lectionary, and the Benedictional (figs. 145, 129, pls. 8, 31). The width of a border in relation to a rosette shows a clear progression from the narrow borders of the Boethius drawing, which is closest to Franco-Saxon proportions (fig. 177), to the broad ones of the Benedictional.

rosettes. The rhythms in the friezes sometimes varied in response to the other parts of the frame. On folio 19v (pl. 15), for instance, many of the leaves bend, echoing the powerfully curving forms of the rosette; but on folio 95v (pl. 31) the curvature of the acanthus in the friezes is reduced to conform to the relatively straight foliage in the rosettes.

CONCLUSIONS

The Benedictional and the three other related Winchester manuscripts all reveal a heightened desire to infuse Anglo-Saxon ornament with a new spirit of classicizing naturalism drawn from Carolingian Metz and Franco-Saxon models. As early as the first half of the tenth century Anglo-Saxon artists were gradually enriching such traditional Insular decorative forms as the zoomorphic interlace initial and the tree-stem with less abstract Carolingian-style foliage,[100] but they usually eschewed the clear, logical structures of Continental ornament. This was not for want of opportunity. An ornamented Franco-Saxon sacramentary, now part of the so-called Leofric Missal (Oxford, Bodl. Lib., MS Bodley 579), was in southern England by the second quarter of the century when a typical English zoomorphic interlace initial was added to it.[101] The artist was completely uninfluenced by the Carolingian manuscript's elaborate Franco-Saxon frames and initials, which were apparently too lucid and balanced to suit his native taste for nonclassical complexity and irregularity. This taste began to change at Winchester under Æthelwold. Three stages can be discerned in the development of the scriptorium's ornament.

The New Minster charter belongs to the first phase. It is a transitional work in which Carolingian features were absorbed from Metz but in which older Anglo-Saxon ones were not completely discarded. The Metz scrolled and twining foliage must have been particularly attractive because its forms were not unlike traditional Anglo-Saxon interlace and scroll work. Nonetheless, the charter pointedly refrained from in-

cluding any of the older types of Anglo-Saxon zoomorphic and interlace initials, and no prior Anglo-Saxon work so wholeheartedly embraced the three-dimensionality of Carolingian ornament.

The Boethius manuscript and the Winchester lectionary marked the next phase of the development. The former adopted for the first time in Anglo-Saxon art the clear structure of Carolingian Franco-Saxon frames and initials, which were combined with traditional Anglo-Saxon forms of foliage. The latter, however, relied so heavily on Carolingian models that indigenous Anglo-Saxon ornament was largely excluded. The lectionary not only imitated the structure of a framed Franco-Saxon initial page, it also adopted the leaf frieze from its Franco-Saxon and Metz sources. This Carolingian motif is almost never found in earlier Anglo-Saxon art,[102] which preferred the rinceau because it was better suited to the English fondness for dynamic, freely varied ornament. The adoption of the foliage frieze in the lectionary is a token of the determination of Winchester miniaturists to impose the more ordered, naturalistic forms of Carolingian ornament on their own traditions.

The Winchester lectionary, however, did not stand completely outside indigenous tradition. Since Franco-Saxon manuscripts perpetuated the ornament of pre-Carolingian Insular art, the lectionary's copying of a zoomorphic, interlace initial and heavy rectangular frame with corner pieces from a Franco-Saxon model was essentially an act of repatriation. In Franco-Saxon decoration Anglo-Saxon illuminators must have recognized a Continental descendent of their own ancestral ornament. Yet it was not solely the Hiberno-Saxon component of this Carolingian school that attracted the Anglo-Saxons. Franco-Saxon painters had recast Insular, abstract forms into clear, balanced, symmetrical arrangements that reflected the classicism of the Carolingian age. Franco-Saxon art offered Winchester miniaturists a "prepackaged" solution to a major aesthetic problem of the tenth century: the synthesis of the abstract Insular ornamental tradition with the more naturalistic Carolingian one.

The Benedictional ushered in the third and fi-

---

[100] Wormald, "Decorated Initials"; Deshman, "Anglo-Saxon Art after Alfred," pp. 195ff.

[101] Deshman, "Leofric," pp. 146f., pls. 1a, b.

[102] The only exception to my knowledge is one panel in an

initial in the Cambridge Cuthbert manuscript; Wormald, "Decorated Initials," p. 116, pl. 4a; rpt. Wormald, *Writings*, p. 55.

nal stage of the development. Here too, Franco-Saxon ornament exercised a profound influence because of its reconciliation of "barbaric" Northern and naturalistic Mediterranean traditions. Whereas the painter of the lectionary for the most part passively accepted the Franco-Saxon solution to the problem, the illuminators of the Benedictional sought to improve upon it.

During a long and deliberate process of selection and experimentation, various features and combinations of Franco-Saxon, Metz, and Anglo-Saxon ornament were tried out. On the one hand, openly "barbaric" northern motifs, such as zoomorphic and linear interlace and decorated initials in the Franco-Saxon model, were almost completely eliminated, and the conventional type of Franco-Saxon foliage was transformed or replaced with the classicizing forms of Metz acanthus. On the other hand, the comparatively simple, lucid rhythms of Franco-Saxon interlace and vegetation were made much more complex and dynamic. By adopting the patterns of linear interlace, the acanthus in the Benedictional often became more abstractly organized than Franco-Saxon or Metz foliage. Indeed, some of the Benedictional's foliate interlace was made more complex than the Franco-Saxon linear interlace that inspired it. Even in the border friezes the Anglo-Saxon illuminators suffused the leafwork with an abstract, dynamic power that is absent from the Franco-Saxon school. Finally, ornament in the Benedictional was given a new decorative unity and consistency. The different parts of the frame were assimilated to each other in contrast to the relatively distinct appearance they had in Franco-Saxon art. The paradoxical result of these changes is that the ornament of the Benedictional became both more and less naturalistic than that of Franco-Saxon manuscripts. The Winchester illuminators succeeded in creating a synthesis of Mediterranean and northern ornamental traditions that was still more profound than the Franco-Saxon one.

Although Byzantine art strongly influenced tenth-century Anglo-Saxon figural style, it had virtually no effect on ornament. The Latin West, with its mixture of northern European and Mediterranean ornament, had a much more extensive and varied ornamental tradition than the Greek East; the Anglo-Saxons understandably preferred their own rich Western decorative heritage. There is, however, one rather special instance of Byzantine ornamental influence, namely, the wavy clouds that are ubiquitous in the manuscript (pls. 8, 10, 18, 19, 24). Cloudy backgrounds are no rarity in Carolingian art (figs. 50, 88, 89, 110), which has been cited as the source of the Anglo-Saxon motif.[103] Yet neither in Carolingian art nor anywhere else are clouds formed as in the Benedictional. The inspiration for these came from a rather different and unexpected source. Some of the borders of the miniatures in the Vatican lectionary (fig. 201) and the Chisianus codex,[104] two of the tenth-century Byzantine manuscripts closest in figural style to the Benedictional, are filled with an illusionistically undulating ribbon alternately revealing its two sides. The similarities of this motif to the peculiar clouds in the Benedictional could not be greater. What had been a perspectival ornamental motif in a Byzantine model became ribbonlike clouds in the Benedictional.

Such a bold and unorthodox transformation becomes less surprising when we recall that the Benedictional's makers were fascinated with all varieties of fanciful and imaginative visual transformation. In iconography this manifests itself in the different guises in which a symbolic theme such as the cornerstone appears throughout the cycle and also in the propensity to invest a single object like the altar in the Presentation with several different levels of physical and symbolic significance. In ornament the predilection for transformation is apparent in the metamorphosis of a decorative motif from one set of frames to the next. Even so, the transmutation of an ornamental motif in a border into a representational object in the picture field is explicable only in the context of a manuscript in which a deliberate fusion of frames and figural compositions was sought by the use of similar forms in both.

---

[103] Wormald, *Ben.*, p. 14; Alexander, "Ben.," p. 180.

[104] Lowden, *Prophet Books*, fig. 13; also A. Cutler, *The Aristocratic Psalters in Byzantium*, Bibliothèque des Cahiers Archéologiques, 13 (Paris, 1984), fig. 255. For a late antique example, see C. H. Kraeling, *The Synagogue*, 2nd ed., The Excavations at Dura Europas, Final Report, 8, 1 (n. p., 1979), pls. 54–74. A debased version of the motif appears in Car-

olingian art (Koehler, *Kar. Min.*, 2, pls. 11g, 84), but the Benedictional's clouds are much closer to the unadulterated Byzantine ribbon-form. A distant derivative of the motif was employed in its original function as border ornament in a later Anglo-Saxon manuscript; see *The York Gospels*, ed. N. Barker (London, 1986), fol. 85v.

Frames, Figures, and Compositions

More than any preceding work, the Benedictional achieved the systematic synthesis of picture and frame into a single composition. As this achievement rested on the foundation of earlier Insular and Carolingian art, we must now consider the influence of prior concepts of decorative integration.

Both the New Minster charter and the Boethius drawing reveal some preliminary experimentation with the unification of picture and frame. The treatment of the figures and borders as a single, flat openwork trellis, which is so prominent in the Benedictional (pls. 12, 18, 31), is already evident in the charter (fig. 135) and the drawing (fig. 145, text fig. 4). In the latter the manner in which the building would have touched the upper border and is adjacent to the three Muses floating in space clearly presages the Benedictional's handling of Christ's tomb and the three Holy Women (pl. 22). The drawing also introduced many innovations that would play a major role in the Benedictional.

The most notable of these was the combination of figures in the new Anglo-Saxon style with a Franco-Saxon type of frame. Moreover, in the charter the figures had only touched the frame,[105] but in the completed drawing Philosophy would have boldly overlapped the left border, much like the Holy Women in the Benedictional. Indeed, in both works the figure(s) was carefully placed to harmonize with the covered border. The pupil of Philosophy's eye would have coincided with the hidden corner of the rectangular rosette, and her right side and arm would have aligned with a vertical bar of the border. The borders were probably to have been filled with foliage, as in the manuscript's initial (fig. 178), the Winchester lectionary (fig. 129), and the Benedictional. Hence the jagged trumpet fold along the right thigh of Philosophy and also the prison's acroterium would have blended with the overlapped foliage. This is the germ of an idea that would grow to major proportions in the Benedictional. Another forward-looking feature of the drawing is the mirroring of the geometric forms of the border within the picture. The aisle roof and founda-

tion of the building, for instance, reiterate the tripartite articulation of the border. The base of the gable and the shaft of Philosophy's scepter intersecting at a right angle were to have reflected the rectangles at the corners of the frame, and the bedframe, like the ones in the Benedictional (pls. 12, 16, 30, 34), resembles the border fillets. Finally, both the drawing and the Benedictional exhibit a predilection for compositional diagonals that intersect the frame at critical points. The rear side of Boethius's bed, for instance, is aligned with the guidemark to the upper left of Philosophy's head that indicated the position of the corner rectangle and the upper horizontal border. The diagonal extending from the foot of the bed passes through the intersection of the lower left vertical border and corner rectangle,[106] while the corresponding intersection on the right side of the frame is aligned with the right side of the triangular gable of the building. The similar alignment of pediment to picture frame in the Benedictional's miniature of the Holy Women (pl. 22) underscores the extent to which its illuminators used decorative compositional techniques that were already in vogue at Winchester.

Some of these methods of ornamentally unifying pictures and frames had roots deep in Hiberno-Saxon soil. The transformation of organic forms into two-dimensional pattern in pre-Carolingian Insular art was accompanied by the transformation of the surrounding frame, which now negated rather than enhanced pictorial depth. Symptomatic of this fundamental change in purpose is the Hiberno-Saxon innovation of framing pages of decorated initials and abstract ornament like pictures. This is the ultimate source of the concept in the Benedictional of treating a picture like an initial and vice versa.

To assert their planarity, Hiberno-Saxon pictures and frames actively interacted with each other, presaging similar features in the later Winchester miniatures. The fusion of the picture and frame into a two-dimensional espalier was already common in Insular miniatures (cf. figs. 102, 103, pls. 26, 28, 31),[107] where one also finds many antecedents for the utilization of

---

[105] Edgar's foot and the wing tip of the upper right angel slightly overlap the border.

[106] Erasures around the two lower corner rectangles indicate that the artist struggled to find their proper size and

placement.

[107] See also Nordenfalk, *Painting*, pls. 9, 11, 14, 21, 24, 25, 27, etc.

similar forms and colors in both the picture and the borders. Long before the tenth century, for example, Hiberno-Saxon art mirrored or even continued the fillets of the borders in the picture.[108] The joining of the picture and its frame in a chiastic composition is yet another feature of the Benedictional paralleled in early Insular art. The miniature of the Doubting Thomas in the Benedictional (text fig. 3, pl. 24) and a composition in the Book of Kells[109] (fig. 202), though vastly different in style, both align the figures with the capitals and bases of the frame in a series of crisscrossing diagonals. Moreover, in each Christ is framed in a chiastic color rhythm. In the Winchester picture Thomas on Christ's right wears a blue tunic and gray mantle, while these colors are reversed in the tunic and mantle of the apostle on the other side of Christ. In the Kells miniature the tunics and mantles of the two men flanking Christ alternate in the same way. *Horror vacui*, which rules many of the Benedictional's compositions (pls. 7, 10, 24, 33), was a common Hiberno-Saxon trait.[110] One might also compare Insular carpet pages with the Benedictional's miniatures in the manner in which the composition is subdivided into abstract geometric zones tightly packed with a variety of kinetic colors and forms (pls. 12, 18, 19, 33). The undulating clouds and contorted drapery that activate the surfaces of the Anglo-Saxon miniatures are the spiritual descendants of the ribbon and zoomorphic interlace in Hiberno-Saxon ornamental pages.

There is nothing improbable about the conclusion that the decorative compositional principles of early Insular manuscripts might have influenced Winchester illuminators. Later tenth-century Anglo-Saxon miniaturists were undoubtedly familiar with Hiberno-Saxon illuminated books; indeed, the Benedictional's portrait of the evangelist John copied an Hiberno-Saxon exemplar.[111] Some pre-Carolingian traditions, however, must have been transmitted indirectly through the

intermediary of earlier tenth-century Anglo-Saxon art.[112]

The trellised compositions of the Galba Psalter and the Cambridge Cuthbert manuscript (figs. 10, 53, 142), for example, look back to the Lindisfarne Gospels (fig. 102) and forward to the Winchester manuscripts (figs. 135, 145, text fig. 4, pl. 31). Both these earlier tenth-century books also continue the older Insular practice of decoratively segmenting the picture field. This is evident not only in the Psalter's two non-narrative pictures (figs. 11, 12), but also in its Nativity scene, which is partitioned by the band-like ground line and the arcade. Architecture also segments the Cuthbert dedication miniature into geometric compartments, some of which are further ornamentally subdivided by nominal architectural detail such as tiles, bricks, and steps. The king and the saint are decoratively framed by their compartments, as are the midwives in the Nativity scene. These features anticipate the Benedictional where architecture and other features such as cloudy or monochromatic backgrounds partition the picture field, frequently framing the figures (pls. 6, 8, 12, 19). Other Hiberno-Saxon traditions that early-tenth-century art revived were chiastic composition and an *horror vacui*. It is of particular interest that both appear in the Galba Psalter, because it in turn directly influenced the Benedictional. The chiasmus of the Psalter's Nativity miniature was taken up in the Benedictional's version of the scene,[113] and the crowded ranks of heads in the Psalter's choir miniatures, which hark back to Hiberno-Saxon compositions, reappear in the guise of the serried angels in the picture of the Second Coming (pl. 10).[114] The Psalter provides a concrete example of how early-tenth-century English works mediated between Hiberno-Saxon and later Anglo-Saxon art.

To a certain extent Carolingian art also transmitted Hiberno-Saxon decorative values to later Anglo-Saxon artists. The attraction that the classi-

---

[108] E.g., Nordenfalk, *Painting*, pls. 9, 14, 24, 27, 30, 32, 41.

[109] Nordenfalk, *Painting*, pl. 47; J. O'Reilly, "The Book of Kells, Folio 114r: A Mystery Revealed yet Concealed," *The Age of Migrating Ideas*, ed. R. M. Spearman and J. Higgitt (Edinburgh, 1993), pp. 106–14, fig. 12.1. For other examples of chiastic composition, see pls. 8, 10, 18, 23, 25, figs. 43, 44, 46.

[110] Alexander, *Manuscripts*, figs. 75, 207–13, 241, 262–64.

[111] For other Anglo-Saxon evangelist portraits copied from

or added to Hiberno-Saxon books, see Temple, *Manuscripts*, nos. 15, 47, 55, figs. 49 (our fig. 101), 51, 52, 153, 154, 172.

[112] Deshman, "Anglo-Saxon Art after Alfred," pp. 197ff.

[113] Broderick, "Attitudes toward the Frame," pp. 31f., has also observed a chiastic color rhythm in the four lions at the corners of the Psalter's first picture (fig. 11).

[114] For the iconographic relationship between the two scenes, see above, p. 63.

cized version of Insular ornament in Franco-Saxon manuscripts held for Winchester illuminators has already been mentioned. Since this Carolingian school usually preferred abstract ornament to the human figure, it was almost certainly a Winchester initiative to combine frames from a Franco-Saxon manuscript with representational subject matter from Metz and other sources.[115] Nonetheless, at least one feature of Franco-Saxon initial pages did influence the integration of frames and pictures in the Benedictional. Following a Hiberno-Saxon practice,[116] the panels of Franco-Saxon frames are often articulated in a chiastic rhythm. In the Arras lectionary, for example, variations in the interlace and/or foliage patterns establish diagonal correspondences between the two vertical borders or the horizontal ones (figs. 130, 131).[117] The Benedictional adopted this principle of Franco-Saxon border design, but extended it by coordinating the chiasmus of the frame with the picture in highly original ways.[118]

An undercurrent of pre-Carolingian decorative values also flowed through the Metz school, the second major Carolingian contributor to the Winchester scriptorium. This is most clearly seen in the Metz fondness for historiated initials, an Hiberno-Saxon invention that decoratively combined a picture with an initial. The integration of figural compositions, ornament, and frames in these Metz initials and Winchester miniatures is closely related.

In the *Te igitur* initial of the Drogo Sacramentary (fig. 187), for example, the figure of Melchizedek in the crossing of the initial is unified with the border and the ornament in several ways. He overlaps the initial's framework, so that his rear profile conforms to the hidden border. Melchizedek's feet and flared mantle mirror the forms of the twining acanthus rinceau on the other side of the initial. Much the same techniques were used in the Boethius drawing (fig. 145, text fig. 4), where the figure of Philosophy

was designed to overlap and align with the border and the flaring trumpet fold of her garment was to pick up the rhythm of border foliage.[119]

The visual equation of the geometric border forms with the architectonic elements of the picture is another shared feature of Metz initials and Winchester illuminations. Thin gold bands are employed for the borders of the letters and also for furniture (figs. 16, 18, 19) and parts of buildings such as columns, architraves, pediments, and foundations (figs. 22, 46).[120] In the Sacramentary's scenes of the Naming of John the Baptist and Pentecost[121] (figs. 16, 86) the frame of the letter becomes a throne for the figures, a device that is the same in principle as the Benedictional's substitution of a column base for the throne of Zachariah (pl. 30). In fact, in both manuscripts one of the same narrative themes is involved.

Finally, the Sacramentary's initial for the feast of Saint Arnulf[122] (fig. 203) provides a parallel for the Benedictional's interweaving of picture and frame. The crowd in the initial's upper left corner overlaps both the inner and outer gold borders of the letter stem, but another group below emerges from behind the outer gold border, much like the apostles in the Doubting of Thomas (pl. 24). The way in which the head and legs of the apostles at the rear of this group both overlap and are overlapped by the solid moldings of the capital and base of the column is reminiscent of the treatment of Saint Arnulf as he bends over the font. His back overlaps and then disappears into the inner border of the letter, which finally overlays his lower body.

Although the pictures in the Benedictional's Metz model must have had pictures in rectangular frames, it might also have included some historiated initials. After all, both formats occur in the Benedictional. If Winchester illuminators were familiar with Metz historiated initials, they would not have found it difficult to adapt some

---

[115] For Franco-Saxon figural compositions, see A. von Euw, *Das Buch der vier Evangelien: Kölns karolingische Evangelienbüchen* (Cologne, 1989), p. 39, and Mütherich and Gaehde, *Carolingian Painting*, pls. 30, 31, 39, 40. The subject matter and format of the Boethius drawing (fig. 145) indicate that the picture and the frame came from separate models. Franco-Saxon representations were usually limited to evangelist portraits and symbols and occasionally New Testament themes, and Franco-Saxon frames do not divide the page horizontally.

[116] Cf. Alexander, *Manuscripts*, figs. 208, 262–64, 266–69.

[117] See also fols. 16, 38, 42v, unpublished.

[118] This coordination is entirely lacking in Franco-Saxon figural compositions.

[119] The acroterium of the prison was also to blend with border foliage, a device similar to the assimilation of the acroteria of Christ's tomb to the surrounding ornamental acanthus in the Easter initial of the Sacrmentary (fig. 46).

[120] *Drogo-Sak.*, fols. 24v, 27, 29, 32v, 34v, 38, 58v, 78, 83, 84.

[121] *Drogo-Sak.*, fols. 78, 84.

[122] *Drogo-Sak.*, fol. 91.

of the techniques for the decorative integration of scenes and letters to pictures in a rectangular frame.

It was not necessarily the Anglo-Saxons, however, who extrapolated from one format to the other. Metz artists themselves had already moved in this direction. Like Metz initials, many later Metz ivories boldly overlay the frame with a scene, deliberately merging the borders with the picture. On the Brunswick casket the wings of the angels at the Baptism (fig. 34) align with the inner boundary of the borders, and the feathers continue the rhythm of the border's egg-and-dart motif. The notched edges of Christ's mandorla in this scene, and the bed, throne, and arcade in the Nativity (fig. 7) restate the serration of the border acanthus. In the image of the Adoration of the Magi on a Metz plaque in the Victoria and Albert Museum[123] (fig. 13) a door frame assumes the form of the border fillet it covers. Drapery folds are also assimilated to leaf forms. In the Visitation on the Louvre casket[124] (fig. 148) Mary's paenula projects out stiffly over the left border, ending in trumpet folds that merge with the overlapped acanthus curl, and the lower bodies of the two embracing women reflect the wedge shape of the long acanthus leaves. In this and many other later Metz ivories there is a subtle resonance between the parallel curving lines of the drapery folds and the veined foliage.

The carvings also reveal that the Metz school inspired the abstract suspension of a strip of ground line from the vertical borders of a picture (cf. pls. 18, 20, fig. 44).[125] The complete omission of the ground line so that the figures

seem suspended from the borders they overlap was also a Metz idea (pl. 12, fig. 7).

These Carolingian compositional devices initially seem to have made little impression on Æthelwold's miniaturists. Despite the influence of Metz style and ornament on the New Minster charter, the earliest of the Winchester manuscripts, its trellised composition stood squarely in the earlier Anglo-Saxon tradition. The draftsman of the Boethius drawing also relied to some extent on this indigenous tradition, but he was much more open to Continental ideas. From a Franco-Saxon manuscript he took a new type of frame and from a Metz book he learned new methods for the decorative fusion of frame and picture: the overlapping of the borders and the repetition of its forms in the picture. It was the achievement of this Winchester artist to bring elements eclectically gathered from disparate sources into an essentially new and systematic relationship to each other.

The Benedictional inherited and refined this Winchester compound of domestic and foreign sources, realizing for the first time its full expressive and decorative potential. In the drawing the restless, fluttering folds of the prevailing Anglo-Saxon style had been stilled in the interests of establishing an architectonic bond between the figures and the frames. The Benedictional, however, retained this geometric unity while reintroducing, indeed, intensifying, agitated drapery and a host of other kinetic forms. The expressive tension between organic and architectonic forms of the borders was extended to the entire composition.

Conclusions

Carolingian, Byzantine, and Anglo-Saxon art all contributed to the formation of the Benedictional and the Winchester style. In the initial years of the reform, houses under Dunstan had turned to the styles of the court school of Charlemagne and recent Eastern art to create a new Anglo-Saxon figural style. This seems to have arrived at Winchester with Æthelwold, who would have been personally familiar with ar-

tistic developments in Dunstan's houses. In fostering the new art Æthelwold must have been to Winchester what Dunstan had been to his centers.

When Winchester adopted the new figural style, it looked to the same foreign sources as well as to another Carolingian one, the later Metz school. Metz art, however, had less influence on figural style than on ornament and

[123] Goldschmidt, *Elf.*, 1, no. 118, pl. 51.
[124] Goldschmidt, *Elf.*, 1, no. 95i, pl. 43.

[125] Goldschmidt, *Elf.*, 1, nos. 81–86.

framing, and of course iconography. A long-established artistic center, Winchester did not entirely reject the old when accepting the new. Some reminiscences of early-tenth-century Anglo-Saxon figural style and ornament persisted in the New Minster charter and to a lesser extent in the Boethius manuscript. Winchester illuminators were apparently the first to frame figures in the new style, adopting older Insular and newer Carolingian methods for the combination of figures and ornament. In doing so the Winchester scriptorium invented the Winchester style. This was the corporate creation of the workshop during the first decade of Æthelwold's episcopacy. Winchester manuscripts before the Benedictional had already made essential contributions to the style's development. Although the Benedictional did not invent the style, it did bring it to a peak of refinement and perfection.

The framing of figural compositions also led Winchester illuminators to confront anew what has rightly been termed "the outstanding aesthetic problem of English pre-Conquest art, that of combining the glittering abstract patterns of insular 'barbaric' illumination with . . . the classical tradition."[126]

In the wake of the classicizing Carolingian revival, Anglo-Saxon illuminators could no longer accept the Hiberno-Saxon solution to the problem, which had been to turn the human figure itself into a form of abstract ornament. Moreover, by the tenth century the issue was no longer a strictly Insular one, for the different Carolingian schools had also sought in various ways to reconcile Mediterranean naturalism with Northern abstraction. If anything, Carolingian art had raised the stakes by introducing new levels of naturalism in figures and ornament into northern Europe. The full dimensions of the problem were recognized at Winchester where Æthelwold's painters set themselves the formidable challenge of finding a new solution that bettered the best of both worlds, the Insular and the Continental.

The style of Charlemagne's court school had managed to retain a measure of the organic integrity of the human body while suffusing it with Northern dynamic decorative rhythms. This combination could hardly fail to appeal to the

Anglo-Saxons' traditional fondness for kinetic linear pattern. Nonetheless, they seem to have found this Carolingian style wanting in some respects. Initially they seem to have desired a greater degree of naturalism than it had to offer, and they found this in recent Byzantine art. At Winchester the illuminators must have felt the absence of an integral relation between the figures and the ornament of the court school. Sumptuous ornament often framed these Carolingian images, but there was little compositional or decorative coordination between the borders and the picture. As in classical art, a clear distinction was maintained between them. To be sure, this and other Carolingian ateliers had addressed the issue of how to strike a compromise between Northern and Mediterranean ornament. The Franco-Saxon school was the culmination of a hundred years of Carolingian experimentation in the imposition of a classicizing spirit on the unruly, abstract forms of Hiberno-Saxon initial pages, and this must be why Winchester illuminators found this Carolingian school so appealing. Franco-Saxon art, however, had no answer to the question of the relationship between ornament and figures; in fact, it had usually preferred to duck the question altogether by omitting figures. Of all the Carolingian schools, Metz was the one that had met this fundamental issue most squarely. In both historiated initials and rectangular frames this Carolingian workshop did strive for an integral decorative relationship between Mediterranean ornament and figures, and herein lay the cause of its profound influence on Winchester miniaturists. Yet the Metz style of the latter half of the ninth century— the period of the Metz manuscript that so influenced Winchester—was devoid of the nervous expressiveness that had energized the figures of Charlemagne's court school and the Reims school. Both the decorative interpretation of Mediterranean figural style and the decorative integration of figure and ornament occurred in Carolingian art, but they did not occur there together. The Benedictional merged these two separate aspects of Carolingian art in a spirit reminiscent of pre-Carolingian Insular art.

We can take the measure of the Benedictional's achievement if we compare one final time the

---

[126] T. D. Kendrick, *Late Saxon and Viking Art* (1949; rpt. London, 1974), p. 2.

representations of the Nativity in the manuscript and on the Brunswick casket (pl. 12, fig. 7). Of the two, the Anglo-Saxon depiction is by far the more decorative and abstract. The superimposition of the scene on the heavy geometric framework with its enormous swirling rosettes gives ornament a prominence in the miniature that is lacking in the ivory, notwithstanding its double border. Nor does the casket's scene exhibit the abstract chiastic and paneled organization that fuses the painting's picture field and borders into a single composition. The surface textures of the ivory's scene and borders remain quite distinct from each other, despite some attempt to unify them with similar forms and rhythms. In the miniature this distinction has disappeared: both the scene and the ornament consist of the same decorative mix of intensely animated and rigidly geometric forms.

Nervous, expressive drapery patterns cause the Anglo-Saxon figures to appear far more ornamental and abstract than their heavy, stolid Carolingian counterparts. Yet closer examination discloses that the Benedictional's figures are much more naturalistic and organic. The anatomy of the Virgin's flexed legs remains clear and correct amid the decoratively flickering lines and highlights of the drapery, while on the casket her right thigh is severely deformed and her lower left leg is entirely omitted. Her stunted right arm and pawlike hand on the ivory contrast with her naturalistically proportioned and articulated limb in the Benedictional. The difference in the rendering of the bed is another indicator of the Anglo-Saxon painters' superior grasp of and concern for naturalism. Compared with the Carolingian work, the Benedictional simultaneously increased both the naturalistic and the decorative values of the representation.

If one considers the ornament apart from the figures, the Benedictional stands in a similar relation to Carolingian art. On the one hand, the conscious replacement of "barbaric" interlace and zoomorphic motifs with three-dimensional acanthus and the substitution of undecorated initials for ornamented ones endow the Benedictional's ornament with a naturalism surpassing that of Franco-Saxon manuscripts. On the other hand, the acanthus in the Anglo-Saxon rosettes interlace in patterns that are more complex and abstract than the Franco-Saxon examples that inspired them. In the Benedictional the forms are more Mediterranean, but the spirit is more Northern.

Whether it is a matter of the figures, the ornament, or the relation between the figures and the ornament, the Benedictional achieved a deliberate, delicate balance between the antithetic values of naturalism and abstraction. In few if any other medieval works of art is there such a profound reconciliation and synthesis of the Mediterranean and Northern traditions. Even within Anglo-Saxon art the Benedictional's achievement remained unique. This is evident in the reprise of the Benedictional's scene of the Nativity in the early-eleventh-century Missal of Robert of Jumièges (fig. 204). The latter work eschewed the Benedictional's rigorous abstraction and reverted to a more customary relationship between the picture and the frame. The composition is no longer geometrically structured and has been brought back within the confines of the borders. The ground line under the Virgin's bed reintroduced a nominal notion of depth. The drapery is simpler and less contorted, and the highlights softer. Nonetheless, the figures as well as the foliage of the Benedictional remain more substantial and organically formed. The later manuscript reduced the high levels of both abstraction and naturalism that the Benedictional had attained.

To regard the genesis of the Winchester style in purely formal terms is probably to view it with modern rather than medieval eyes. Certainly Winchester painters must have been moved by the desire to rise to the challenge of perhaps the most fundamental aesthetic problem of Western medieval art, but they must also have been motivated by ideological concerns. One clear indication of this is that the wave of Continental influence swept over not only figural style and ornament but also script, an aspect of manuscripts which has no bearing on the aesthetic issue of naturalism and abstraction. It is of some significance that the earliest example of the new figural style, the Dunstan drawing (fig. 139), is also one of the earliest instances of English Caroline minuscule, a new style of handwriting from the Continent.[127]

---

[127] Bishop, *Minuscule*, p. 1, no. 1; Dumville, *English Caroline Script*.

The Carolingian ruler Charlemagne had been instrumental in disseminating this uniform, legible script throughout his realm as an essential part of his *renovatio*, which sought to impose more order and higher standards on religious culture.[128] His reform also affected book illumination, which returned to more naturalistic figural styles. In both their minuscule script and their comparatively naturalistic miniatures, the manuscripts of Charlemagne's court school evinced the Carolingian spirit of *renovatio*.

That this Carolingian script and figural style were simultaneously introduced into England, seemingly in a manuscript personally associated with Dunstan, the founder of the monastic reform, suggests that for the Anglo-Saxons, too, they carried ideological associations of the renewal of religious culture.[129] The subsequent history of the Anglo-Saxon script and artistic style tends to confirm this. To judge from the extant books, the early homes of the script and/or the style were Canterbury (and possibly Glastonbury), Worcester, and Winchester—all early major centers of monastic reform ruled by the movement's leaders, Dunstan, Oswald, and Æthelwold.[130] It is scarcely coincidental that one of the earliest examples of English Caroline script, the New Minster Charter (fig. 135), is also in its text and miniature a manifesto of Æthelwold's reform credo. He and the other reformers need not have known of the connection between court school manuscripts and Charlemagne—though this possibility should not be dismissed out of hand—but they certainly must have recognized in more general terms that the Carolingian *renovatio* had fostered the Caroline script and more naturalistic forms of figures and ornament.

The Anglo-Saxons quite consciously modeled their national monastic reform on the earlier Carolingian one, and their adoption of Carolingian styles of writing and illumination, no less than their copying of Carolingian monastic and liturgical texts written in the Caroline minuscule, manifested their acceptance of the Continental ideology of religious reform.

Under Æthelwold's guidance Winchester applied this program of reform to the decoration of books more rigorously than any other center. Eventually ornament as well as figural style and script were purged of overt Insular features such as interlaced and zoomorphic initials. In Æthelwold's mind these must have carried unwelcome connotations of the degenerate state of Anglo-Saxon monasticism before the reform. Other Anglo-Saxon scriptoria seem to have taken a more lenient attitude. A Psalter in Salisbury (Cathedral Lib., MS 150), illuminated between 969 and 987 at some provincial center, perhaps Shaftesbury, contains a frame with the Winchester blend of Franco-Saxon and Metz ornament but also the older kind of Anglo-Saxon zoomorphic forms and initials,[131] and Canterbury manuscripts —even those owned by Dunstan— continued to use the traditional Anglo-Saxon zoomorphic initial types during the second half of the tenth century.[132] A decade or so after the completion of the Benedictional, Winchester itself relented, at least to the extent that it once again allowed the relatively classicizing Franco-Saxon type of zoomorphic interlace initials in its manuscripts.[133]

Despite its strict adherence to the vocabulary of Carolingian style and ornament, the Benedictional remains a quintessentially Anglo-Saxon

---

[128] B. Bischoff, *Latin Palaeography* (Cambridge, 1990), pp. 112ff.; idem, "Die karolingische Minuskel," *Mittelalterliche Studien*, 3 (Stuttgart, 1981), pp. 1–4; also D. Ganz, "The Preconditions for Carolingian Minuscule," *Viator* 18 (1987): 23–44.

[129] Dumville, *English Caroline Script*, pp. 16f., 156, has also independently arrived at the conclusion that the adoption of Caroline script was ideologically motivated.

[130] Bishop, *Minuscule*, pp. xxi–xxii.

[131] Wormald, "Decorated Initials," p. 121, pl. 5d; rpt. Wormald, *Writings*, pp. 59f., fig. 59; Temple, *Manuscripts*, no. 18, figs. 57–61; D. I. Stroud, "The Provenance of the Salisbury Psalter," *The Library*, ser. 6, 1 (1979), pp. 25–35. See also below, Appendix One, n. 14.

[132] Rosenthal, "Pontifical of St. Dunstan," pp. 151ff., figs. 17–24; Gameson, "Manuscript Art at Christ Church," pp. 187ff., figs. 41b–44; Wormald, "Decorated Initials,"

pp. 119ff.; rpt. Wormald, *Writings*, pp. 58ff.; Temple, *Manuscripts*, pp. 46f., nos. 19–22, figs. 65–81, 83. While Winchester and other Æthelwoldian houses used "style I" English Caroline minuscule, which rigorously excluded all English forms, Canterbury practiced "style II," which retained some Anglo-Saxon features; see Dumville, *English Caroline Script*.

[133] See the so-called Ramsey Psalter; Temple, *Manuscripts*, no. 41, figs. 140, 141. Recently, however, the Winchester origin of this manuscript, which was based primarily on certain textual peculiarities, has been rejected by Dumville, *English Caroline Script*, pp. 58–65; M. Lapidge, "Abbot Germanus, Winchcombe, Ramsey and the Cambridge Psalter," *Words, Text and Manuscripts*, ed. M. Korhammer (Woodbridge, 1992), pp. 110–116, argues persuasively that it was made for Ramsey but cautiously refrains from the conclusion that it was made there. That it was written at Winchester for Ramsey use remains a possibility; so *Golden Age*, p. 60, n. 41.

work of art, an heir to the old Insular tradition of decoratively synthesizing ornament and image. Once again ideology as well as aesthetics might have fostered this blend of new and old, of Carolingian and Insular. For Æthelwold the importation of Carolingian monastic practices was a means to restore Anglo-Saxon monasticism to the glorious heights it had attained in the pre-Carolingian age.[134] Insular missionaries from this period had introduced their forms of monasticism and art to northern Europe. Exactly how much the tenth-century Anglo-Saxon reformers knew about this earlier Insular influence on Continental monasticism is unclear, but they probably had at least some knowledge of it, if only from Bede's *Ecclesiastical History*.[135] Did Æthelwold see in Carolingian monasticism the living spirit of the older Insular monasticism that he wished to revive in England? If so, it would have been entirely appropriate for his illuminators to draw inspiration from Carolingian artistic schools that in their own way continued Hiberno-Saxon traditions.

We should not neglect symbolism in assessing what are perhaps the most salient features of the Benedictional's aesthetic, the elaborate frames and the integration of these with the pictures. There can be no doubt that the manuscript's status as a solemn service book and the traditional Anglo-Saxon taste for ornament were important factors motivating its lavish decoration. The makers of early medieval books, however, sometimes attributed deep religious symbolism to script and decoration. Carolingian colophons liken the golden letters of a Psalter to the "golden" heavenly kingdom and the manifold coloration of the words to the "flowers" in fields of scrip-

ture.[136] The Benedictional's own dedication poem explicitly says that Æthelwold ordered that there "be made in this book many frames well adorned and filled with various figures decorated with numerous beautiful colors and with gold."[137] We have seen that this poem was carefully designed to highlight the significant iconographic themes of the picture cycle, and its reference to the frames and figures is no exception to this practice. One of the most pervasive symbolic themes of the manuscript, the equation of the believers with the spiritual edifice of the Church, was often realized by the fusion of the figural composition with a frame representing the Church (pls. 1–3, 12, 20, 32). Nowhere is the symbolic value of the frames more apparent than in the final miniature where the architecture of the church literally replaces the usual foliated borders (pl. 35). Very likely all the frames in the manuscript were intended as symbols of Ecclesia and their integration with the pictures was meant to visualize the believers' edification into a *domus Dei*.[138] The dedication poem affirms that Æthelwold himself was the guiding force behind this symbolic style.

Many later Anglo-Saxon illuminators might have regarded the Winchester style as nothing more than an attractive decorative format, but for some it seems to have retained its symbolic value. The saints inhabiting the rectangular frames of the Grimbald Gospels (figs. 92, 93), for instance, are a variation on the edification of the heavenly choirs into the frames of the Benedictional.[139] The symbolism as well as the aesthetic appeal of the style must have stimulated its widespread diffusion from Winchester in the late tenth and eleventh centuries.

---

[134] See above, pp. 171f.

[135] *Bede's Ecclesiastical History*, 5, 9 and 10, ed. and tr. B. Colgrave and R. A. B. Mynors (Oxford, 1969), pp. 475ff.

[136] Ganz, "Preconditions for Caroline Minuscule," pp. 30f., with references to the colophons.

[137] See above, chap. 3, n. 240.

[138] The language of the Douay translation of Ephesians 2:21 is suggestive: "In whom [Christ the cornerstone] all the building, being *framed* together (in quo omnis aedificatio

constructa), groweth up into a holy temple in the Lord" (emphasis added). But a connotation of "framing" is absent from the Vulgate Latin.

[139] Gameson, "Manuscript Art at Christ Church," pp. 261ff., has noted the unusual historiation of the Gospel book's frames. The evangelist portraits of the Arenberg Gospels were also influenced by the Benedictional's symbolic frames; see above, chap. 3, n. 268.

Chapter Eight

CONCLUSIONS

WITH OUR MANUSCRIPT a new type of illuminated liturgical book came into being—a benedictional illustrated with a cycle of full-page feast pictures. The Benedictional was a synthesis of features taken from several other, more common kinds of illuminated liturgical manuscripts: a Metz sacramentary, and a Franco-Saxon and a Byzantine Gospel lectionary. As in the latter, the subject matter of the pictures systematically focussed on the primary event or saint celebrated in a feast rather than on narrative. Although the Benedictional's prayers did not narrate the incidents portrayed, there was a conscious effort to make the miniatures illustrate and not merely accompany their abstruse liturgical texts.

Even when derived from earlier models, the iconography was often subtly modified to express the prayers' linkage of the liturgical present to the historical past and the eschatological future. Many of the images visualized the relevance of the object of the day's liturgical commemoration to ecclesiastic rites, particularly episcopal benediction, and to the salvation of the congregation. The blessings frequently alluded to the symbolism or typology that integrated individual feasts into the overall scheme of Christian salvation, and the miniatures illustrated these relationships through cyclic symbolism, the repetition of symbolic motifs and themes throughout the cycle.

The iconography was also designed to express the essential nature and function of a benedictional. In conjunction with the dedication poem, the introductory miniatures depicting the heavenly Church emphasized that the manuscript's purpose was to sanctify the members of the earthly Church so that they might join Christ and the saints in heavenly life. The very first feast picture and initial page established the incarnational Christological origin of the blessings in "this book of the advent of the Son," while the typologically related final miniature of the Bishop Blessing the Church represented the liturgical rite that continued to instill God in men.

The germs of some of these ideas were contained in the Benedictional's iconographic sources. Like the Drogo Sacramentary, which used such pictorial leitmotifs as the servant and the Virgin and child, or the Brunswick casket, which juxtaposed such motifs as the chrismatory and the wreath, the Metz model appears to have interrelated symbolically at least some individual images. In the Drogo codex the cyclic symbolism is confined primarily to the infancy scenes; hence this symbolic technique does not seem to unify the entire cycle—which includes depictions of later Christological events as well as hagiographic and liturgical scenes—into a comprehensive program. Other manuscripts, however, had moved in this direction. Some ninth-century Turonian pandects had complex pictorial programs stressing the unity of the two Testaments, a theme that underlined the theological essence of a full Bible,[1] and the iconographic program of the Galba Psalter visualized the typological character and devotional function of a book of psalms.[2] The Benedictional, however, surpassed these earlier manuscripts in the intricacy, the scope, and the systematic nature of its program.

[1] H. Kessler, *The Illustrated Bibles from Tours*, Studies in Manuscript Illumination, 7 (Princeton, 1977); also idem, "An Apostle in Armor and the Mission of Carolingian Art," *Arte medievale*, ser. 2, 4 (1990): 17ff.

[2] R. Deshman, *Studies in Anglo-Saxon Manuscript Illumination*, Cambridge Studies in Anglo-Saxon England, chap. 1, in preparation.

To invest the pictures with such exceptional depth and complexity of abstract symbolic content within the conventions of narrative and portrait iconography was an intellectual and artistic achievement of the highest order. This erudite and systematically conceived book must have been the product of highly intelligent, disciplined thought and planning. We have no information about the exact relationship between Æthelwold and his illuminators and scribes. But the Benedictional's dedication poem says that Æthelwold specified that the manuscript should be decorated with frames, gold and beautiful colors, and "various figures." This implies that the bishop indicated in some detail what he wanted and that he was responsible for the symbolism of the integration of figures and frames. Æthelwold himself might have been a metalworker, though the evidence for this is late.[3] Whether or not he was, many aspects of the Benedictional seem to bear the imprint of his interests, ideas, scholarship, and personality.

Æthelwold's particular concern with liturgy is evident in his drafting of the *Regularis Concordia* and several supplementary devotions for the Divine Office, and in the Benedictional's innovative methodical arrangement of blessings and illustrations. No prior benedictional had been the object of such systematic organization or lavish illumination. His special interest in this type of text and his elevation of his personal benedictional to the status of a deluxe illuminated book seem to have been motivated by the symbolic association of benediction and Benedictine monasticism. The iconographic emphasis on the Benedictional as the "book of the advent of the Son" suggested that liturgical benediction and monasticism spiritually reenacted and renewed the original act of blessing on mankind—the coming of the incarnate Christ to earth. That the beholder could vicariously experience the real presence of Christ or a saint in an image was not new;[4] indeed, it had been implicit in Metz servant iconography. The Benedictional's innovation was to focus this concept on monasticism.[5] In this and many other ways the iconography of

Æthelwold's book enshrined the religious and political beliefs that were the ideological foundation of his religious reforms. The images affirmed that the lives of Christ, Mary, and the saints had established the values that were the basis of the monastic movement. Æthelwold's reforms required royal backing, and the Benedictional, which very likely originated about the time of the coronation of Edgar and his queen in 973, also depicted the divinely ordained concord of *regnum* and *sacerdotium* that was the precedent and model for the cooperation between the Anglo-Saxon monarchy and Church during the reform.

It was not only the manuscript's iconography that manifested the spirit of the religious renewal. The forms of figural style, ornament, and script found in Anglo-Saxon manuscripts antedating the reform were deliberately suppressed, apparently because they were associated with the earlier decadence of religious life. Replacing them were the more Mediterranean styles from abroad that seem to have carried ideological connotations of the reformed Continental religious practices that Æthelwold and the other monastic leaders introduced into England. These imported figural and ornamental styles were recast according to old Insular decorative principles, perhaps to evoke the ideal of early Insular monasticism that Æthelwold sought to emulate in his own era.

Æthelwold's Old English translations reveal a precise and systematic mind.[6] They are impeccably accurate and virtually free of error. Moreover, he consistently preferred only one of several possible Anglo-Saxon equivalents for a Latin word, a technique of translation that established a clear, standardized Old English vocabulary which was adopted by Ælfric and other of his pupils at Winchester. Æthelwold was renowned for his scholarship as well as his teaching.[7] Wulfstan[8] said explicitly that Æthelwold was skilled in metrics and grammar and that he had read the better-known patristic authors. Little information about the exact texts he read has come down to us, but it is significant that two books we know he owned or used—the *Prognosticon* by Julian

---

[3] *Chronicon Monasterii de Abingdon*, ed. J. Stevenson, Rolls Series (London, 1858), 1, pp. 344f.; 2, p. 278; see C. R. Dodwell, *Anglo-Saxon Art* (Ithaca, 1982), p. 49.

[4] Deshman, "Servants," pp. 33ff., with further references.

[5] See also Raw, *Crucifixion*, passim; R. Deshman, "Anglo-Saxon Art: So What's New?" forthcoming.

[6] Lapidge, "Æthelwold as Scholar," pp. 101ff., 107ff.

[7] Lapidge, "Æthelwold as Scholar"; idem, "Schools, Learning and Literature in Tenth-Century England," *Settimane di studio del centro italiano di studi sull'alto medioevo* 38 (1990): 976ff.; Wulfstan, *Life*, pp. lxxxvi–xcii.

[8] Wulfstan, *Life*, 9, pp. 14f.

of Toledo and the *Commentary on the Rule* by Smaragdus—influenced the Benedictional's iconography. Lapidge[9] has suggested that the wide range of literary sources evident in Ælfric's writings might reflect to some extent the texts that he had studied under Æthelwold's tutelage at Winchester. This supposition is supported by the Benedictional's iconography, which frequently relates closely to Ælfric's writings and sources, sometimes anticipating his ideas in striking fashion.[10]

Although a concern for precision of expression marks Æthelwold's Old English compositions, some of his Latin writings reveal a very different aspect of his intellectual character. The New Minster charter and the prologue of the *Regularis Concordia* are written in the "hermeneutic" style.[11] This style, which is common in tenth-century Anglo-Latin literature, employs obscure and flamboyant grecizing vocabulary in a consciously ostentatious and challenging display of learning. Godeman's dedication poem in the Benedictional is also written in this grandiloquent style. Lapidge has plausibly argued that Æthelwold was the inspiration behind this poem, perceptively observing that "the ornateness of its grecizing diction matches that of the book as a whole."[12] Indeed, in the sheer quantity of the illumination, in the opulence of the gold and colors, and in the baroque flamboyance of the ornamental and figural style, the Benedictional is an exceptionally extravagant production. Like the hermeneutic literary style, the images make a conspicuous exhibit of arcane and sophisticated learning that intellectually challenges the viewer. The almost complete absence of explanatory tituli to assist the beholder in plumbing the complex, layered symbolism of the iconography seems deliberately perverse.[13] In their own way the pictures issue the same dare as a tenth-century hermeneutic Canterbury poem that concludes a long series of taxing grecizing medical terms with the

taunt "tricocinare!"—"sort it out for yourself."[14] We might consider this kind of playful attitude incongruous in images of sacred themes in a liturgical book, but the Anglo-Saxons would not have found it so. Dunstan wrote an exceptionally difficult hermeneutic poem on the Trinity, the Virgin, and the saints that also manifested his pride in his ability in Latin and his amusement in outwitting his readers.[15] The makers of the late-tenth-century Exeter Book saw nothing inappropriate in ending a collection of Old English religious poems with a series of riddles, including some with secular or even ribald subjects.[16]

In view of Æthelwold's literary accomplishments, it is noteworthy that a keen literary intelligence informs the pictures, even though they lack explanatory texts. It is entirely characteristic that a word play on *benedictus* was a major factor in the creation of this unusually elaborate benedictional. The iconography is acutely responsive to the meaningful nuances and ambiguities of texts and delights in simultaneously illustrating the literal and the metaphorical meanings of words such as nimbus, cornerstone, column, and member. The technique of literal word illustration in the Utrecht Psalter was probably one of the features that influenced the Benedictional. Given Æthelwold's skill in meter, it is probably not coincidental that the pictures often relate closely to Old English poetry. Indeed, the technique of symbolically interlacing a series of pictures through the repetition and variation of iconographic motifs and concepts has analogies to the way in which a sequence of Old English poems such as the Advent lyrics are unified by the recurrence and modulation of stock themes.[17]

The Benedictional's monastic and political themes, its disciplined textual and pictorial organization, its systematic iconographic programs, its opulent and flamboyant appearance, its esoteric and ostentatious learning, and its lit-

---

[9] Lapidge, "Æthelwold as Scholar," pp. 109f.

[10] See above, pp. 172f.

[11] M. Lapidge, "The Hermeneutic Style in Tenth-Century Anglo-Latin Literature," *ASE* 4 (1975): 67ff., esp. 88f.; Lapidge, "Æthelwold as Scholar," pp. 90ff.

[12] Lapidge, "Æthelwold as Scholar," p. 107; also idem, "Hermeneutic Style," pp. 85f.

[13] Contrast the liberal use of explanatory inscriptions in the learned miniatures of the Ottonian Uta Lectionary; J. Rütz, *Text im Bild. Funktion und Bedeutung der Beischriften in den Miniaturen des Uta-Evangelistars* (Frankfurt am Main,

1991).

[14] For the text and a translation, see Lapidge, "Hermeneutic Style," pp. 84f., 104f.

[15] Lapidge, "Hermeneutic Style," pp. 96f., 108–11.

[16] R. W. Chambers, M. Förster, and R. Flowers, *The Exeter Book of Old English Poetry* (London, 1933), pp. 38–43; from the vast literature on the riddles, we may cite R. Gleissner, *Die "zweideutigen" altenglischen Rätsel des* Exeter Book *in ihrem zeitgenossischen Kontext*, Regensburger Arbeiten, 23 (Frankfurt am Main, 1984).

[17] See above, chap. 2, nn. 82, 83, 119.

erary sensitivity all appear to reflect its patron Æthelwold.

The influence of the Benedictional on Anglo-Saxon art was extensive. Its confection of figures and ornament soon became the lingua franca of deluxe Anglo-Saxon service and Gospel books, and many of its iconographic features were widely copied and developed. Yet some of its more notable innovations had little or no future.

A benedictional illustrated with a cycle of full-page miniatures and initial pages remained a rarity. Although there are a number of later Anglo-Saxon benedictionals,[18] most are unilluminated. The only two exceptions were both produced at Winchester in the wake of Æthelwold's manuscript: the Benedictional of Archbishop Robert[19] and the benedictional in Paris (Bibl. Nat., MS lat. 987).[20] Even in the case of these two the scope of the decoration was drastically curtailed. The former illustrated the texts of five rather than twenty-four feasts, and the latter has nine initial pages but no pictures.[21] The grandness of Æthelwold's Benedictional was bound up with the propagation of the ideals of the monastic reform at its apogee. The consolidation of the reform's achievements in the late tenth and eleventh centuries inevitably resulted in a lessening of ideological fervor, and perhaps this removed one of the chief incentives for the production of deluxe benedictionals. The notion of a cycle of feast pictures did have a limited influence on other types of Anglo-Saxon liturgical books in the eleventh century. The Missal (sacramentary) of Robert of Jumièges marked the be-

ginnings of major feasts with framed full-page miniatures and initial pages, but in contrast to the Benedictional the choice of illustrations was no longer strictly controlled by principles of liturgical hierarchy. There was a renewed interest in pictorial narration.[22] In the Cotton troper only three of the eleven feast pictures are full page and initial pages are lacking.[23]

Such later manuscripts as the Benedictional of Archbishop Robert[24] (figs. 211, 212, 213) and the Missal of Robert of Jumièges (fig. 204) also retreated to some extent from the Benedictional's radical redefinition of the relationship between picture and frame, and the Benedictional's delicate balance of the competing demands of naturalism and abstraction was not maintained, as the emphasis shifted decisively toward the latter.

Cloudy backgrounds continued to be used frequently in later Anglo-Saxon art, but apparently without the elaborate symbolism found in the Benedictional.[25] Rather than show the Virgin in a *doxa* of cloud, the next generation of artists reverted to a conventional nimbus or mandorla (figs. 27, 93). The anthropomorphized altar in the Presentation seems to have been too bizarre to be imitated. Though the Assumption miniature was copied once in the Benedictional of Archbishop Robert (pl. 34, fig. 213),[26] it is revealing that in the process the iconography was simplified into a comparatively conventional mourning scene. The illuminator might no longer have understood the subtle relationship to the Transitus text and Mariological devotional thought, or perhaps he felt uneasy about the apocryphal subject

---

[18] See above, chap. 5, n. 137.

[19] See Appendix Three.

[20] Temple, *Manuscripts*, p. 54, no. 25, figs. 92, 93; Homburger, *Anf.*, pp. 58–64, pls. 8, 9. Prescott, "Text," pp. 133–35, has noted that the Æthelwold Benedictional has a more tidy and rationally structured text than the Paris manuscript and has suggested that the latter was the immediate source of the former. However, Homburger's careful analysis of the ornament, technique, and color of the Paris benedictional conclusively demonstrated that it postdates the Æthelwold manuscript. Many features of the Paris book reflect developments that occurred only in the later stages of work on the Benedictional, for example, the use of multiple geometric borders for the rosettes (Paris, fol. 41) and the supplanting of border friezes by foliate extensions of the rosettes (Paris, fol. 31; cf. our pl. 28). The Paris benedictional either reverted to copying a slightly older text or retreated somewhat from the systematic textual organization of Æthelwold's book. D. N. Dumville, *Liturgy and the Ecclesiastical History of Late Anglo-Saxon England*, Studies in Anglo-Saxon History, 5 (Wood-

bridge, 1992), pp. 84f., also questions the earlier date of the Paris manuscript.

[21] Regarding illustrated Continental benedictionals, see above, chap. 4.

[22] See chap. 4. The manuscript fragment of two leaves now in the Getty Museum in Malibu (Temple, *Manuscripts*, pp. 72f., no. 53, figs. 173–76) might be part of a Gospel book marked with lections rather than a Gospel lectionary, but it is worth noting that two of the three extant full-page miniatures do not focus on the single most important event but illustrate a narrative sequence of scenes.

[23] E. C. Teviotdale, "The Cotton Troper (London, British Library, Cotton MS Caligula A.xiv, ff. 1–36): A Study of an Illustrated English Troper of the Eleventh Century," (Ph.D. diss., University of North Carolina, Chapel Hill, 1991), pp. 10, 144ff.; Temple, *Manuscripts*, pp. 113f., no. 97, figs. 293–95.

[24] See Appendix Three.

[25] See Appendix Three for a possible exception (fig. 212).

[26] See Appendix Three.

matter. For all its influence, many aspects of the Benedictional seem to have been too sophisticated or too eccentric to gain widespread acceptance.

The relation between the Benedictional and subsequent Anglo-Saxon art might be compared to the one between Æthelwold and Ælfric. Ælfric repeatedly declared himself Æthelwold's student,[27] but unlike his teacher he deliberately rejected fanciful apocryphal stories about Mary[28] and obscure, ostentatiously learned vocabulary.

Instead he embraced Æthelwold's preference for lucid, unaffected Old English prose.[29] Ælfric seems to have been much more conservative than Æthelwold, reflecting only one side of his mentor's bold and complex intellectual personality.[30] Similarly, few if any later Anglo-Saxon works of art matched Æthelwold's Benedictional in its paradoxical combination of flamboyant, imaginative showmanship with intellectual rigor and depth.

---

[27] E.g., Ælfric, *Hom.*, 1, p. 1. See also the other instances cited by Lapidge, "Æthelwold as Scholar," pp. 107f., n. 116.

[28] Clayton, *Cult*, pp. 260ff.; idem, "Ælfric and the Nativity of the Blessed Virgin Mary," *Anglia* 104 (1986): 286ff.

[29] For the literary relationship between Ælfric and Æthelwold, see Lapidge, "Æthelwold as Scholar," pp. 107ff.

[30] Ælfric was at Winchester when the Benedictional was made and might even have been familiar with it, but there is some evidence that in art as well as language he preferred simplicity to complexity, in marked contrast to his mentor. See R. Gameson, "Ælfric and the Perception of Script and Picture in Anglo-Saxon England," *Anglo-Saxon Studies in Archaeology and History* 5 (1992): 85ff.

DESCRIPTION, RECONSTRUCTION, AND DATE OF THE BENEDICTIONAL OF ÆTHELWOLD

Description and Reconstruction of the Manuscript

IN ITS PRESENT CONDITION the Benedictional consists of 119 leaves of good quality parchment, each approximately 292 mm. high x 225 mm. wide. Heavier parchment was used for many of the decorated pages. The writing area is 210 x 140 mm., usually with 19 lines ruled with a stylus and rack. The collation is as follows:

1. fols. 1–6 (fols. 1 and 6 are conjoint half-sheets).
2. fols. 7–16 (fols. 7 and 8 are singletons).
3. fols. 17–23, with one leaf missing after fol. 20.
4. fols. 24–35 (fols. 31 and 32 are singletons).
5. fols. 36–43.
6. fols. 44–53.
7. fols. 54–63.
8. fols. 64–67.
9. fols. 68–77.
10. fols. 78–85.
11. fols. 86–89.
12. fols. 90–95.
13. fols. 96–103.
14. fols. 104–110, with two leaves missing after fol. 105 and one after fol. 107:

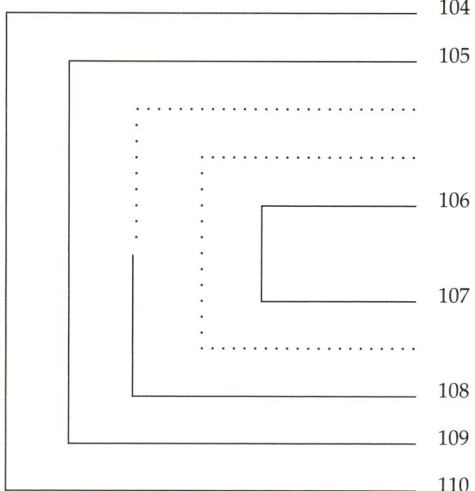

A textual gap and a stub indicate that the conjugate of fol. 108 is missing after fol. 105. No miniature faces the framed initial page on fol. 108 recto (fig. 200); thus a bifolium has also been removed from this quire.

15. fols. 111–118 (fols. 111 and 118 are conjoint half-sheets), plus a singleton (fol. 119).[1]

Dry-point notes, evidently made for the purpose of compiling the manuscript, have recently been detected in the upper margins of thirteen leaves. On folio 6v there is a dry-point sketch of an inverted arch which seems to be a discarded trial for a frame. The folio was then turned upside down and reused for text.[2]

The main script is a large and stately English Caroline minuscule, with uncials, square capitals, and rustic capitals used for display.[3] The binding is modern.

The text consists of a two-page dedication poem (fols. 4v–5) written in gold rustic capitals by Godeman, Æthelwold's chaplain, and episcopal benedictions (fols. 6–119v), arranged in the order of the feasts of the liturgical year.

In its present condition the manuscript is decorated with twenty-eight full-page miniatures and nineteen initial pages in rectangular or arched frames. One of these framed text pages has an historiated initial, and there is also another figured initial on an unframed text page. The manuscript opens with a continuous sequence of seven full-page miniatures of the choirs of the saints and the apostles. The remaining miniatures all occupy the verso of a leaf, facing a recto with an initial page beginning the text of a feast. Usually a miniature and its initial page have matching rectangular or arched frames, but both the final picture and text opposite (the Dedication of the Church) are unframed. One feast (Epiphany) is prefaced by two rather than the usual one full-page miniature.

The following is a list of the extant decoration:

fol. 1
  Choir of Confessors (pl. 1)

fols. 1v–2
  Choir of Virgins (pls. 2, 3)
fols. 2v–4
  Twelve Apostles (pls. 4–7)
fols. 5v–6
  Annunciation (pl. 8) and initial page (pl. 9) (first Sunday in Advent)
fols. 9v–10
  Second Coming (pl. 10) and initial page (pl. 11) (third Sunday in Advent)
fols. 15v–16
  Nativity (pl. 12) and initial page (pl. 13) (Christmas, 25 December)
fols. 17v–18
  Martyrdom of Saint Stephen (pl. 14) and initial page (Birth of Saint Stephen, 26 December)
fols. 19v–20
  John the evangelist (pl. 15) and initial page (Birth of John the evangelist, 27 December)
fol. 21
  Initial page (fig. 181) (Holy Innocents, 28 December)
fols. 22v–23
  Naming of Christ (pl. 16) and initial page (pl. 17) (Octave of the Nativity, 1 January)
fols. 24v–25
  Adoration of the Magi (pl. 18) and Baptism of Christ (pl. 19) (Epiphany, 6 January)
fols. 34v–35
  Presentation in the Temple (pl. 20) and initial page (Purification of the Virgin, 2 February)
fols. 45v–46
  Entry into Jerusalem (pl. 21) and initial page (Palm Sunday)
fols. 51v–52
  Holy Women at the Tomb (pl. 22) and initial page (pl. 23) (Easter)
fols. 56v–57
  Doubting of Thomas (pl. 24) and initial page (first Sunday after Easter)
fols. 64v–65
  Ascension (pl. 25) and initial page (Ascension)
fols. 67v–68
  Pentecost (pl. 26) and initial page (Pentecost)

[1] My thanks to Andrew Prescott, who double-checked the collation for me, and to Professor William Schipper, who kindly allowed me to see an advance copy of his article ("Dry-point Compilation Notes in the Benedictional of Æthelwold," *British Museum Journal* 20 (1994): 17–34). Schipper's collation of the manuscript differs in several points from my own; the tight binding of the manuscript hinders certainty in some instances.

[2] There are also trial drawings of drapery in red on several fols. See Schipper, "Dry-point Compilation Notes," p. 33, n. 14.

[3] Bishop, *Minuscule*, p. 10, no. 12; for the display scripts, see Warner and Wilson, *Ben.*, pp. xi–xii.

fol. 70

The Deity in an initial O (pl. 27) (Octave of Pentecost or Trinity Sunday)

fols. 90v–91

Saint Æthelthryth (pl. 28) and initial page with Christ in an initial O (pl. 29) (Saint Æthelthryth, 23 June)

fols. 92v–93

Birth and Naming of John the Baptist (pl. 30) and initial page (Nativity of John the Baptist, 24 June)

fols. 95v–96

Martyrdoms of Peter and Paul (pl. 31) and initial page (Peter and Paul, 29 June)

fols. 97v–98

Saint Swithun (pl. 32) and initial page (Saint Swithun, 2 July)

fols. 99v–100

Saint Benedict (pl. 33) and initial page (Saint Benedict, 11 July)

fols. 102v–103

Death and Coronation of the Virgin (pl. 34) and initial page (Assumption of the Virgin, 15 August)

fol. 108

Initial page (fig. 200) (Saint Michael, 29 September)

fol. 118v

Bishop Blessing the Congregation (pl. 35) (Dedication of the Church)

Isolated framed initial pages on folios 21 and 108 (figs. 181, 200) show that full-page feast miniatures of the Massacre of the Innocents and the Archangel Michael have been lost, and the collation and a textual gap between folios 105v and 106 indicate that a full-page miniature, presumably depicting the Nativity of the Virgin, and a facing initial page for the feast of the Birth of the Virgin have been removed.

Some pictures have also been lost from the beginning of the manuscript. The incomplete inscription "confessorum" on folio 1 (pl. 1) suggests that there must have been a matching miniature of the confessors inscribed "chorus" on a missing verso, in the manner of the two-page composition of the choir of virgins on folios 1v–2 (pls. 2, 3). The confessors, however, were unlikely to have begun the series, for usually the choirs of the saints were ordered in the fixed sequence of angels, patriarchs, prophets, apostles, martyrs, confessors, and virgins.

This was the order adopted in two miniatures depicting the Last Judgment and the litany of the saints that Anglo-Saxon artists added to the Carolingian Galba Psalter (London, British Lib., MS Cotton Galba A. XVIII) in the early tenth century.[4] The first picture on folio 2v represents Christ enthroned with the choirs of angels, patriarchs, prophets, and apostles (fig. 11), and the second one on folio 21 depicts Christ again with the remaining choirs, the martyrs, confessors, and virgins (fig. 12). These Anglo-Saxon additions were in all probability done at Winchester where the Psalter was certainly located during the early Middle Ages, and there is abundant evidence that its miniatures directly influenced many aspects of the Benedictional's iconography.[5]

With the aid of the Psalter, we can reconstruct the Benedictional's introductory cycle as follows:

fol. I

Christ[6]

fols. Iv–II

Choir of Angels

fols. IIv–III

Choir of Patriarchs

fols. IIIv–IV

Choir of Prophets

fols. IVv–V

Choir of Apostles

fols. Vv–VI

Choir of Martyrs

fols. VIv–1

Choir of Confessors

fols. 1v–2

Choir of Virgins

fols. 2v–4

Twelve Apostles.[7]

---

[4] See chap. 1, nn. 69, 70.

[5] So Warner and Wilson, *Ben.*, p. xv; also Wormald, *Ben.*, p. 12. Regarding the Psalter's influence, see the discussion of the Nativity and Presentation in chap. 1, the Second Coming and Entry into Jerusalem in chap. 2, and the choirs in chap. 3.

[6] There were probably also other figures; see chap. 3.

[7] Wormald's reconstruction (*Ben.*, pp. 12f.) reversed the order of the prophets and patriarchs, while Warner and Wilson, *Ben.*, p. xv, reconstructed only choirs of martyrs, angels, and prophets. These alternate reconstructions were influenced by the Psalter's first miniature (fig. 11), where the patriarchs in the second register were mistakenly labeled as prophets, but it is unlikely that the Benedictional's highly intelligent illuminators would have mindlessly repeated this error.

One problematic feature of this reconstruction is the inclusion of a pair of miniatures of the apostles between the prophets and the martyrs, despite the existence of a set of apostles on the four pages after the virgins. In the usual sequence of choirs, which was followed in the Galba Psalter, the apostles follow in chronological order after the prophets rather than after the virgins; thus the extant group of apostles in the Benedictional seems to be out of order. This cannot be a binding error since the present order of pictures is certainly the original one.[8] If there was a mistake, it could only have been in the initial layout of the cycle. This is conceivable, but certain features of the miniatures of the apostles set them apart from the preceding ones of the choirs of the saints. The disciples are alloted two pairs of facing miniatures rather than the single pair presumably allocated to each of the other choirs, and they lack the expected inscription *chorus apostolorum*. Hence it seems that originally there were two sets of apostles, one within the choirs and another after them, although the reason for the repetition remains obscure. According to this reconstruction, six leaves have been lost and with them no less than twelve of the nineteen full-page miniatures from what originally must have been an extraordinarily opulent pictorial introduction to the book.

Date, Origin, and History of the Manuscript

Since the dedication poem[9] states that Bishop Æthelwold ordered the manuscript for his own personal use, it must have been made between 29 November 963 and 1 August 984, when he was bishop of the Old Minster in Winchester. The *scriptor* Godeman who signed the poem and probably wrote the entire manuscript has been plausibly identified as the Old Minster monk of that name who was Æthelwold's chaplain. Later Godeman became abbot of Thorney, which Æthelwold refounded sometime between 971 and 973.[10] Exactly when Godeman left Winchester to assume his new post is uncertain; hence Godeman's work on the Benedictional does not help to date it more precisely.

Other evidence, however, does permit us to narrow the dates. Saint Æthelthryth, the foundress and abbess of Ely, is one of only two Anglo-Saxon saints honored with a feast picture and initial page (pls. 28, 29), and she is also one of two virgins singled out by name in the minia-tures of the Choir of Virgins (pl. 3). Her prominence no doubt reflects Æthelwold's pride in his refoundation of Ely in 970,[11] and the Benedictional likely postdates this event. The other Anglo-Saxon saint distinguished with a feast picture is the Winchester bishop Swithun (pl. 32). The text for his feast refers to many miracles, which are known to have begun only after Æthelwold translated his remains into the Old Minster on 15 July 971.[12] The columnar symbolism of his portrait also presupposes the translation.[13] If the translation provides a *terminus post quem* of 971, the influence of the Benedictional or a very similar Winchester book on illuminated manuscripts from other scriptoria might suggest a date in the 970s rather than the 980s. The Salisbury Psalter with its Winchester mixture of Franco-Saxon and Metz ornament includes Easter tables for 969–987 and 988–1007 and was probably but not certainly written in the 970s.[14] The Winchester-influenced drawings

---

[8] On the recto of the first picture of the apostles (fol. 2v) is a miniature of the virgins, and on the verso of the last miniature of the apostles (fol. 4) is the first page of the dedication poem. See Warner and Wilson, *Ben.*, fols. 2–5.

[9] Warner and Wilson, *Ben.*, pp. xii–xiii, 1; Wormald, *Ben.*, pp. 7f.; M. Lapidge, "The Hermeneutic Style in Tenth-Century Anglo-Latin Literature," *ASE* 4 (1975): 105–106.

[10] For Godeman and his tenure at Thorney, see Warner and Wilson, *Ben.*, pp. xiiif., lvf.; Wulfstan, *Life*, 24, pp. 40f., n. 41. For the foundation charter of Thorney, see C. R. Hart, *The Early*

Charters of Eastern England (Leicester, 1966), pp. 165–86, no. 7.

[11] This and other factors (see chaps. 6 and 7) are sufficient to explain her importance in the decoration without recourse to the unlikely hypothesis of J. B. Tolhurst, "An Examination of Two Anglo-Saxon Manuscripts of the Winchester School," *Archaeologia* 83 (1933): 44ff., that the Benedictional originated at Ely.

[12] Warner and Wilson, *Ben.*, pp. lvif., 39.

[13] See chaps. 3 and 5.

[14] See above, chap. 7, n. 131. Also N. R. Ker, *Catalogue of*

in the Leofric Missal (Oxford, Bodleian Lib., MS Bodley 579) can be dated in or soon after 979.[15] Finally, the Benedictional's iconography can be associated with the coronation of King Edgar on 11 May 973.[16] The Benedictional was completed between 971 and 984, most likely ca. 973.

The presence of Godeman among the brethren of the Old Minster and the emphasis on Saint Swithun, together with the absence of texts for special New Minster saints such as Grimbald and Judoc, argue that the manuscript was made at the Old Minster.

The subsequent history of the manuscript is dim. It seems to have remained either in Winchester cathedral or Hyde abbey (the later name of the New Minster) until the fifteenth century

and perhaps until the dissolution in 1539, since parchment from a fifteenth-century inventory of Hyde shrines was used to reinforce its binding.[17] The Benedictional reappeared in the estate of Henry Compton, bishop of Oxford (1674–1675) and London (1675–1713).[18] The manuscript then passed to General Hatton Compton, his nephew and the executor of his estate, probably when probate was granted on 8 August 1713. William Cavendish, the second duke of Devonshire, acquired the book from Compton sometime before 18 January 1720, when Wanley tried unsuccessfully to obtain it for Robert Harley, the earl of Oxford. The Benedictional remained in the ducal collection at Chatsworth until 1957, when the British Library acquired it as MS Add. 49598.

Manuscripts Containing Anglo-Saxon (Oxford, 1957), pp. 449ff., no. 379. D. N. Dumville, *English Caroline Script and Monastic History*, Studies in Anglo-Saxon History, 6 (Woodbridge, 1992), p. 153, n. 71, suggests that the book was "perhaps written in or soon after 969," but it certainly does not predate the Benedictional.

[15] Deshman, "Leofric," pp. 145–73; D. N. Dumville, *Liturgy and the Ecclesiastical History of Late Anglo-Saxon England*, Studies in Anglo-Saxon History, 5 (1992), pp. 43f. The outer dating limits are 979–87, based on the manuscript's computistic tables for 969–87 and 979–1011, but presumably the

scribe would not have bothered to copy the former table had it only a few remaining useful years.

[16] See chap. 6. Concerning the theory that the Benedictional's miniature of the Bishop Blessing the Congregation (pl. 35) is associated with the consecration of the remodeled Winchester cathedral in 980, see the discussion of this picture in chap. 3.

[17] Warner and Wilson, *Ben.*, pp. xliii; Wormald, *Ben.*, p. 9.

[18] C. E. Wright, "The Benedictional of St. Ethelwold and Bishop Henry Compton," *The British Museum Quarterly* 27 (1963): 3–5.

THE COPY RELATIONSHIP
TO
THE BRUNSWICK CASKET

SINCE OTTO HOMBURGER discovered the striking iconographic correspondences between the scenes of the Annunciation, Nativity, and Baptism in the Benedictional and on the later Metz ivory casket in Brunswick (ca. 870),[1] opinion has been divided about whether the miniatures copied the ivory or a common model.[2] As nothing is known about the casket's medieval whereabouts,[3] its provenance cannot tell us whether it was ever in Winchester. To resolve the problem we shall have to rely on an iconographic comparison of the two works. This should reveal whether the differences between them were changes the Anglo-Saxon illuminators introduced when copying the casket or modifications the makers of the manuscript and casket interpolated when copying a common model.

THE BAPTISM

Despite the substantial similarity of the two representations of the Baptism (pl. 19, figs. 34, 35), there are some significant differences in the portrayals of the personification of the Jordan, the river water, and John the Baptist that help to establish the relationship of the scenes to one another.

The river god is horned in the miniature but has two snake heads on his head on the casket.[4] Horns were a traditional attribute of river gods in ancient literature and art,[5] and horned personifications of the Jordan occur in Baptism scenes in Byzantine marginal psalters.[6] Snake heads, however, were not a correct attribute, even though they also appear in some other early medieval representations of aquatic per-

[1] Homburger, *Anf.*, pp. 8–13. For the casket, see Goldschmidt, *Elf.*, 1, pp. 52f., no. 96, pls. 44, 45; V. H. Elbern, "Vier karolingische Elfenbeinkästen," *Zeitschrift des deutschen Vereins für Kunstwissenschaft* 20 (1966): 11–16. See also R. Melzak, "The Carolingian Ivory Carvings of the Later Metz Group," Ph.D. diss., Columbia University, 1983.

[2] Opting for a common model are: Homburger, *Anf.*, pp. 41ff.; idem, "L'Art carolingien de Metz et 'l'école de Winchester,'" *Gazette des Beaux-Arts*, ser. 6, 62 (1963): 36, 42; Alexander, "Ben.," p. 177. Favoring a direct copy relationship are: A. M. Friend, Jr., "Carolingian Art in the Abbey of St. Denis," *Art Studies* 1 (1923): 74; H. Swarzenski, *Monuments of Romanesque Art*, 2nd ed. (London, 1974), p. 24; R. H. Randall, Jr., "An Eleventh Century Ivory Pectoral Cross," *Journal of the Warburg and Courtauld Institutes* 25 (1962): 164f.; M.

Wood, "The Making of Æthelstan's Empire: An English Charlemagne?" *Ideal and Reality in Frankish and Anglo-Saxon Society: Studies Presented to J.M. Wallace-Hadrill*, ed. P. Wormald, D. Bullough, and R. Collins (Oxford, 1983), p. 260.

[3] Goldschmidt, *Elf.*, 1, p. 52, no. 96.

[4] Homburger, *Anf.*, p. 9. Cf. the similar eye and mouth of the snake in the casket's scene of the Crucifixion (fig. 36).

[5] Waser, "Flüssgötter," *Paulys Realencyclopädie der classischen Altertumswissenschaft*, 6, 2, cols. 2780–82. G. A. Lester, "A Possible Early Occurrence of Moses with Horns in the Benedictional of St. Aethelwold," *Scriptorium* 27 (1973): 30–33, was unaware of the tradition for the attribute.

[6] See S. Der Nersessian, *L'Illustration des psautiers grecs du moyen âge*, 2, Bibliothèque des Cahiers Archéologiques, 5 (Paris, 1970), fig. 248.

sonifications.[7] The snake heads seem to have been a fairly common medieval misunderstanding of the horns or crab claws in ancient models. Probably the personification was already horned in a common model that was accurately copied in the Benedictional but misunderstood on the casket.

John the Baptist on the ivory wears a tunic and a mantle and holds a scroll in his left hand, but in the manuscript he is clad in a girded exomis of skins and raises the open palm of his left hand in surprise at the theophanic appearance of the dove. The Baptist makes a similar gesture in the Baptism scene on the mid-ninth-century ivory cover of the Drogo Sacramentary in Paris (fig. 40).[8] Since the Sacramentary and its covers were made in Metz, we can be certain that the casket's workshop sometimes used this motif. While no Metz work depicts the Baptist in an exomis of skins, a ninth-century Fulda ivory plaque in Antwerp[9] (fig. 39) does offer a Carolingian precedent for this type of costume. Because these features of the Baptist conform to Carolingian iconography, the probability is that the Benedictional did not copy the casket itself but rather another, closely related Carolingian model.

The river in the two scenes defies gravity to rise to Christ's waist. This illustrates a widely diffused legend that the Jordan had welled up about Christ to be sanctified and blessed by contact with his body.[10] The Benedictional depicts this miracle more clearly since it shows the water rising more abruptly about Christ alone. This is not likely an Anglo-Saxon "correction" of the casket's adulterated iconography, for on the cover of the Drogo Sacramentary the Jordan rises similarly. Like the Baptist's gesture, the swelling river must have been present in a Metz common model that the Benedictional faithfully copied.

The casket's carver probably modified the flow of the river when he adjusted his model's composition to the unusually wide format of the casket.[11] To broaden the composition he stretched out the heaped water, inadvertently obscuring its special relation to Christ. The low height of the panel also required the model's composition to be split horizontally, relegating the dove and flying angels to the lid panel. This impaired one of the main features of the narrative, the descent of the dove upon Christ's head. The Benedictional depicts this much more lucidly, since it retains the dove in its original position directly above Christ.

The Benedictional's painters had to cope with a compositional problem that was just the opposite of the dilemma that the casket's carver had faced: the model's composition was too wide to fit without adjustment into the comparatively narrow and tall format of the page.[12] To solve the problem the illuminators crowded the three left figures together and extended the scene over the lateral borders, and they added thick layers of cloud and earth to the top and bottom of the composition to heighten it. These adjustments were less a handicap than a creative challenge. The clouds not only filled empty space, they also functioned iconographically to represent the heavens from which the dove and the angels descend. The clouds and the similarly formed zone of earth below balance each other and help to organize the composition into a decorative geometric scheme. Only the figures on the left side were compressed, so that the composition mirrored and balanced the weighted composition of the Adoration of the Magi on the facing verso (pl. 18). The illuminators even found an imaginative way to rationalize the crowding of Christ and the angel. Usually such angels stand at some distance from their Lord, waiting upon him with their hands reverently covered with his garments (figs. 34, 40), but the angel in the Benedictional supports Christ's mandorla, a new task which cleverly justified his unaccustomed proximity to Christ. The idea came from the Benedictional's scene of the Stoning of Stephen (pl. 14) or one of the other themes

[7] Goldschmidt, *Elf.*, 1, p. 26, no. 41, pl. 20; 2, p. 29, no. 57, pl. 18.

[8] Goldschmidt, *Elf.*, 1, pp. 41f., no. 74, pl. 30a.

[9] Goldschmidt, *Elf.*, 1, p. 35, no. 66, pl. 27.

[10] A. Jacoby, *Ein bisher unbeachteter apokrypher Bericht über Taufe Jesu* (Strassburg, 1902), pp. 44, 57ff., 76ff.; F. Ohrt, *Die ältesten Segen über Christi Taufe und Christi Tod in religionsgeschichtlichem Lichte* (Copenhagen, 1938), pp. 101ff. See also J. Squilbeck, "Le Jourdain dans l'iconographie médiévale du baptême du Christ," *Bulletin des Musées Royaux d'Art et d'Histoire*, ser. 4, 38–39 (1966–67): 74–77.

[11] H. Schnitzler, "Eine Metzer Emmaustafel," *Wallraf-Richartz Jahrbuch* 20 (1958): 51ff.

[12] O. Pächt, *Buchmalerei des Mittelalters: Eine Einführung* (Munich, 1984), pp. 181f.

in which angels traditionally carried Christ's mandorla.[13]

THE NATIVITY

In the Nativity scenes (pl. 12, figs. 7, 8) there are revealing differences in Mary's bed and pose. Despite its tilt, the bed in the miniature is correctly formed, in contrast to the misshapen one on the ivory. Although the Anglo-Saxon illuminators would have been capable of rectifying this defect had they copied the casket, the simpler assumption is that they accurately copied a correctly formed bed from a common prototype, which the casket's craftsman misunderstood. The Virgin in our manuscript presses her left hand to her left knee and her right hand to her right thigh, while on the ivory she supports her head with her left hand and rests her right one in her lap. The former figural type is conventional in representations of the Nativity. It was certainly known to the Metz atelier since it appears on a later Metz ivory casket in the Louvre (fig. 205),[14] contemporary with the one in Brunswick. The same kind of Virgin is also depicted in the Nativity on a Carolingian Fulda ivory in Munich (fig. 206).[15] The telltale presence of the midwife behind the Virgin indicates that this plaque's iconography ultimately derived from the same archetype as that of the Benedictional and the Brunswick casket. Since the Benedictional faithfully preserves this type of Virgin, one can only conclude it did not copy the casket where the pose was altered.

THE ANNUNCIATION

In the Annunciations in the manuscript and on the casket (pl. 8, figs. 1, 2) there are differences in the archangel Gabriel, the baldachin, and the Virgin's lectern that illuminate the copy relationship. Gabriel holds a short cross-staff in his bare left hand on the casket, while in the miniature he grasps a foliate scepter in his covered left hand and extends his right arm. On the

ivory only the front of the baldachin is visible and its columns are illogically supported on the throne's cushion; but both the front and a side of the baldachin, which adjoins a foreshortened building, appear in the painting, and the columns rise from a substantial plinth. Finally, in the Benedictional Mary reads from a book which she holds open on a lectern, but on the ivory the book is merged with the lectern, which faces Gabriel, and the purpose of her gesture is less clear.

The motif of the Virgin with a book illustrates a legend that at the Annunciation she was reading the prophecy of the Incarnation in Isaiah 14:7.[16] The Benedictional clearly shows her reading, but the various misunderstandings on the casket give the erroneous impression that Gabriel rather than Mary is reading. No doubt the Anglo-Saxon painter would have been capable of correcting the casket's garbled iconography. At the same time, however, we can reasonably suppose that in the archetype of these scenes this motif would have been understood and intelligibly depicted; it is simpler to assume that the Benedictional is an accurate copy of a common prototype rather than a "corrected" derivative of the casket itself.

The other differences between the two scenes must be evaluated in the light of a third representation of the Annunciation on the previously mentioned later Metz casket in the Louvre (fig. 207). The angels of the Louvre casket and the Benedictional are virtual twins, resembling each other even in such minor details as the position of the feet and the manner in which the veiled left hand holds a foliate scepter. The baldachins in the two works are also nearly identical, except that the one in the Benedictional adjoins a building, but even this detail is paralleled elsewhere in Carolingian art.[17] The baldachin on the Brunswick casket is slightly lopsided due to a fifth course of tiles on the right side of the dome. This structural inconsistency resulted from the abbreviation of a foreshortened baldachin with two arches, like the ones in the Benedictional and on the Louvre casket. The Louvre casket demonstrates that many of the features

[13] E.g., Goldschmidt, *Elf.*, 1, nos. 28, 71a, 80b, 87, 90, pls. 15, 28, 33, 37, 38; also our figs. 53, 54, 70, etc.

[14] Goldschmidt, *Elf.*, 1, p. 52, no. 95, pls. 41–43; Elbern, "Elfenbeinkästen," pp. 7f.

[15] Goldschmidt, *Elf.*, 1, p. 35, no. 67a, pl. 27; K.

Weitzmann, "Eine Fuldaer Elfenbeingruppe," *Adolph Goldschmidt zu seinem siebenzigsten Geburtstag* (Berlin, 1935), pp. 14ff., pl. 4, 1.

[16] See chap. 1, n. 6.

[17] E.g., *Utrecht*, fol. 76, also 72v, 75, 75v.

in the Benedictional that differ from those of the Brunswick casket were not Anglo-Saxon inventions but were current in the Metz workshop of the ivories.

The miniature's model must have had a horizontal format similar to the scenes on the two caskets, for once again compositional adjustments to the manuscript's narrower picture field can be detected. The archangel was shifted to the right, bringing it uncomfortably close to the Virgin's lectern. The proportions of the figures and architecture were lengthened, and the baldachin was further heightened by the addition of a cityscape on its dome. A diagonally sloping cloud was added to fill the area above Gabriel and also to counterbalance the baldachin and building. Finally, the empty upper area of the picture field was filled with a two-line titulus.

Each of the three miniatures discussed has features that are absent from the Brunswick casket but present in other Metz works. Since it strains credulity to believe that the Winchester scriptorium had a second Metz model as well as the casket, the Benedictional and the casket must have independently derived from a common Metz archetype. A full assessment of their copy relationship, however, requires the consideration of another monument, the lower Rhenish ivory situla (ca. 1000) from Cranenburg in the Metropolitan Museum in New York.[18]

THE CRANENBURG SITULA

The infancy and Baptism scenes in the lower register of the situla are iconographically affiliated with those on the Brunswick casket. The poses and attributes of the figures in the two depictions of the Annunciation (figs. 1, 208) correspond even in such details as the distorted lectern, though on the situla Mary's baldachin has been reduced to an arch. Lack of space on the situla caused the Nativity to be spread across three adjacent compartments (fig. 209). In the central panel the Virgin's pose, her misshapen bed, and the strangely formed crib floating before an arcade all agree closely with the casket (fig. 7). In the compartments to the left and right respectively are the figures of the midwife and Joseph, who also match their counterparts on the Carolingian casket. The situla's scene of the Baptism (fig. 210) portrays Christ and John in one compartment with a single angelic attendant standing in the left adjacent compartment. Once more the figures correspond to those of the casket (figs. 34, 35), although the situla's limited space necessitated the drastic omission of other important features: the river god, the angel behind the Baptist, the hovering angels, and even the dove.

So strong are the similarities that we might suppose the casket itself was the immediate model for the situla,[19] but several details of the latter cast doubt on this hypothesis. In the Annunciation scene the right column of the baldachin is correctly supported, unlike the one on the casket. The situla's depiction of the Jordan swelling about Christ is somewhat clearer than the casket's, and the angel to the left on the situla is in proper scale and the lower part of his body is not omitted, as on the Metz ivory. In these features the situla betrays its dependence on a common model rather than on the casket itself.

These latter details of the situla's scenes conform to the iconography of the Benedictional and must already have been present in the archetype. In many other respects, however, the situla differs from our manuscript in much the same ways as does the Brunswick casket. The misunderstood form of Mary's lectern, the abbreviated form of her baldachin, the pose and the cross-staff of Gabriel, the tunic and bookroll of the Baptist are all present in the two ivories but absent in the Benedictional. These features, which we have found to be modifications of the archetype, cannot have been the invention of the carver of the Brunswick casket but must already have been in the common model of the casket and the situla. Yet the common model of these two ivories cannot have been the same work that the Benedictional copied, since many of the divergent features of the Anglo-Saxon manuscript faithfully reflect the original, unmodified iconography of the archetype. Hence the relationship between the Benedictional and the Brunswick casket is more indirect than has hitherto been suspected: manuscript and ivory

---

[18] Goldschmidt, *Elf.*, 2, p. 33, no. 71, pl. 23.

[19] Goldschmidt, *Elf.*, 2, p. 33, observed a resemblance between inlaid metal ornament on the situla and later Metz ivories.

derive from a common archetype rather than from the same immediate model. The Benedictional has a more direct iconographic relation to this archetype, which may be designated "X", than the casket and the situla which both derived from an intermediary "Y". The following stemma sums up the copy relationship:

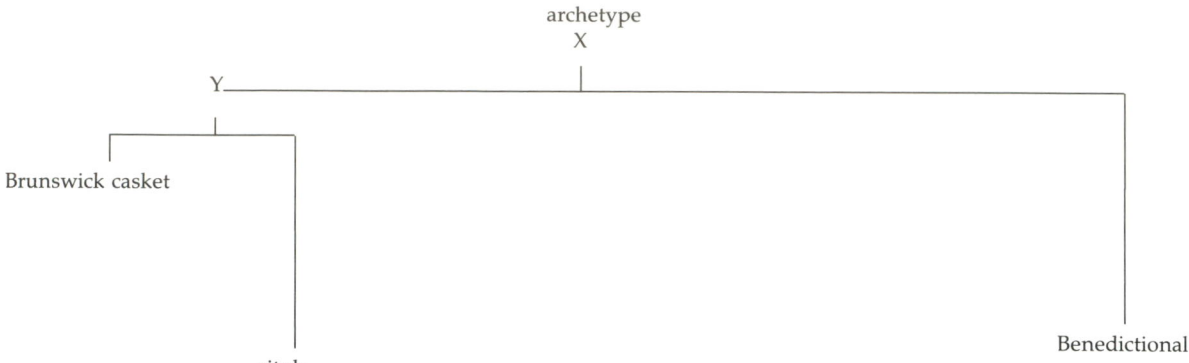

The close resemblances between the Benedictional and the Brunswick casket are evidence that the lost models of the two works cannot have been very far removed from each other in origin and date. Both prototypes must have been made by the Metz workshop of the Brunswick casket. The iconographic connection between the Benedictional and the Louvre casket confirms this. Other surviving Metz ivories testify that this atelier created numerous, slightly differing versions of the same New Testament themes,[20] a practice consistent with the conclusion that the Benedictional and the Brunswick casket independently derived from two very similar yet distinct Metz works. An analysis of the Benedictional's other miniatures[21] suggests that many of them also derived from the same Metz prototype, probably a sacramentary with a more extensive picture cycle than the Brunswick casket.

[20] Goldschmidt, *Elf.*, 1, pp. 38f., mentions that the Crucifixion was represented with minor variations almost a dozen times.

[21] See above, chaps. 1, 2, 4.

Appendix Three

THE COPY RELATIONSHIP TO THE BENEDICTIONAL OF ARCHBISHOP ROBERT

INTIMATELY RELATED to Æthelwold's book is the later Winchester book known as the Benedictional of Archbishop Robert (Rouen, Bibl. Mun., MS Y. 7), which has recently been redated to the second quarter of the eleventh century.[1] Its benedictions are an abbreviated derivative of those in Æthelwold's Benedictional,[2] and like the earlier manuscript it decorated the beginnings of the blessings for important feasts with ensembles of a full-page miniature and an initial page in matching frames. The three extant pictures—the Women at the Tomb (Easter), Pentecost (Whitsun), and the Dormition of the Virgin (Assumption)— closely resemble the corresponding pictures in our manuscript (figs. 211, 212, 213; pls. 22, 26, 34).[3] Homburger[4] believed that the miniatures in the two books derived independently from a common model. If this is correct, then we should be forced to conclude that the decorative layout and at least part of the picture cycle in Æthelwold's manuscript were likely copied more or less intact from an earlier book. Thus the ques-

tion of the copy relationship between the two benedictionals is of some weight and deserves to be reexamined.

In the Benedictional of Æthelwold the scene of the Women at the Tomb retains the horizontal arrangement inherited from its Metz model (cf. figs. 45, 46), but in the Rouen manuscript the composition has been shuffled to adapt it to the narrower format of the full page and to avoid bold overlapping of the frame.[5] The grouping of the women has been changed from isocephalic to triangular. The tomb, compressed at the expense of its architectural coherency, became little more than a frame for the angel, who has been shifted upward to accommodate the guards. These are now below the tomb and the women and are reduced in number. The proximity of the angel and women necessitated the omission of the guards' spears from their clenched hands. Other details of the Metz iconography that were preserved in Æthelwold's Benedictional were adulterated or omitted in

[1] *Ben. Rob.*; Homburger, *Anf.*, pp. 49–57; Temple, *Manuscripts*, pp. 53f., no. 24, color frontispiece, figs. 87, 89. The traditional late-tenth-century date for the manuscript has been revised on the evidence of script by D. N. Dumville, *Liturgy and the Ecclesiastical History of Late Anglo-Saxon England*, Studies in Anglo-Saxon History, 5 (Woodbridge, 1992), pp. 87f. Its figural style and ornament would be extremely conservative for the period of 1025–1050, but perhaps this is due to the strong influence of its tenth-century model.

[2] A. Prescott, "The Structure of English Pre-Conquest Benedictionals," *British Library Journal* 13 (1987): 124ff. The Benedictional of Archbishop Robert is actually a pontifical, since it contains other texts besides pontifical mass blessings.

[3] The illustrations for Christmas and Ascension, presumably pictures of the Nativity and the Ascension, have been cut from the Rouen codex.

[4] Homburger, *Anf.*, pp. 50ff.

[5] O. Pächt, *Buchmalerei des Mittelalters* (Munich, 1984), p. 183, figs. 188, 189.

the Rouen book. The roof tiles of the tomb were transformed into ornamental striations, and the third woman no longer raises her hand in bewilderment to her chin (cf. figs. 44, 45).

The Pentecost miniatures differ in the grouping of the apostles, the treatment of the heavenly zone above them, and the construction of the frame. In each case Homburger concluded the Rouen miniature more faithfully reflected a common source, which he mistakenly believed was early Christian. As we have seen, the primary model must have been a middle Byzantine scene like those in the homilies of Gregory Nazianzus and the St. Petersburg lectionary (figs. 83, 84). Which Anglo-Saxon miniature is closer to the Byzantine iconography?

Peter sits in the center right in Æthelwold's Benedictional but in the center left in the Rouen manuscript. Homburger proposed that the latter position reflected a common model, but in Byzantine scenes Peter can occupy either position.[6] Thus we cannot determine which Anglo-Saxon miniature changed the arrangement of the Eastern model. In another respect, however, Æthelwold's manuscript is manifestly a more accurate copy. Its intricate, overlapping seating arrangement of apostles resembles the one in the Gregory manuscript, while the later benedictional carelessly omits the third apostle from the left and barely manages to squeeze in the head of the corresponding disciple on the right.

The hand of God rather than ornament fills the roundel in the arch of the frame in the Rouen miniature. Homburger thought the hand was in a common prototype, but this was never a feature of Eastern Pentecost iconography. More likely it was interpolated by the illuminator of the Rouen manuscript, who was probably influenced by an earlier Western scene with the motif (figs. 85, 86). Æthelwold's manuscript is truer to the original decorative state of such frames in Franco-Saxon manuscripts. In any event it is improbable that the hand of God would have been replaced with ornament.

Instead of hovering angels, the scene in the Benedictional of Archbishop Robert shows two interior arches supported by a central column, and the empty background has given way to colored atmospheric striations. This type of background is foreign to Byzantine Pentecosts and need not reflect a classicizing common model, as Homburger thought.[7] Both the atmosphere and the central column could have been borrowed from other miniatures in Æthelwold's Benedictional (pls. 1–3, 20, 24, 32). As there, these motifs might not be just ornamental: since the clouds and the column could symbolize respectively preaching and the apostolic "columns" of the Church, they would be appropriate in a scene of Pentecost, when the disciples received the gift of tongues and founded the Church. The angels might have been dropped because the typologically related scene of the Baptism (pl. 19) was not included in the reduced picture cycle.

There were some similar changes in the rendering of the Death and Coronation of the Virgin in the Rouen benedictional. Once again the hand of God was placed in the roundel of the frame. The angels and the lower register illustrating the Transitus account of the Miraculous Reunion of the Apostles were omitted. There are now four servants instead of the three specified in the Transitus, and the lack of a dialogue with the Virgin further weakens the connection to this apocryphal text. Since the maid behind Mary does not adjust her pillows but weeps like her companions, the symbolic contrast between the faithful and sceptical maids is lost. These modifications resulted in a much simpler image focusing more directly on the Virgin's Death and Coronation and her attendants' grief, but in the process the connections to the Transitus and such events as the Nativity and the Ascension were sacrificed. Possibly the painter found the earlier version too complex and subtle, or perhaps he failed to understand its sophisticated symbolism.

All three of the miniatures in the Benedictional of Æthelwold have proven to be much more faithful to their various sources than the ones in the Rouen codex. Nothing in the latter reveals an independent knowledge of a common model, and its divergent features can all be explained as modifications introduced by its illuminator. The pictures in the later benedictional are best understood as simplified, direct copies of the miniatures in Æthelwold's book.

---

[6] For Peter on the right, see figs. 83, 84; for him on the left, see Goldschmidt and Weitzmann, *Byz. Elf.*, 2, no. 221b, pl. 71.

[7] His argument that the basilicas on the arch of the frame must go back to an ancient perspectival model is also fallacious. Such basilicas were common in Anglo-Saxon art; cf. fig. 10; Temple, *Manuscripts*, figs. 93, 201–203, 279–80.

Selected Bibliography

Original Sources

An Account of King Edgar's Establishment of Monasteries. In *Councils & Synods with other Documents relating to the English Church*, 1, 1, ed. and tr. D. Whitelock, M. Brett, and C. N. L. Brooke, pp. 147–49. Oxford, 1981.

The Anglo-Saxon Chronicle. Tr. D. Whitelock. London, 1962.

Acta Apostolorum Apocrypha. Ed. R. A. Lipsius and M. Bonnet. 2 vols. in 3. Hildesheim, 1959.

Ælfric. *Homilies.* In *Homilies of the Anglo-Saxon Church*, ed. and tr. B. Thorpe. 2 vols. London, 1844–46.

———. *Sermo ad Populum in Octauis Pentecosten [Dicendus].* In *Homilies of Ælfric. A Supplementary Collection*, 1, ed. J. C. Pope, pp. 415–52. Early English Text Society, 259. London, 1967.

Ælfric's First Old English Pastoral Letter for Wulfstan, Archbishop of York (Past. L. II). In *Councils & Synods with other Documents relating to the English Church*, 1, 1, ed. and tr. D. Whitelock, M. Brett, and C. N. L. Brooke, pp. 255–302. Oxford, 1981.

Ælfric's Lives of Saints. Ed. W. W. Skeat. Early English Text Society, 76. Oxford, 1881.

Ælfwine's Prayerbook. Ed. B. Günzel. Henry Bradshaw Society, 108. London, 1993.

Alcuin. *Commentaria in S. Joannis Evangelium.* PL, 100, cols. 733–1088. Paris, 1863.

———. *Commentaria super Ecclesiasten.* PL, 100, cols. 665–722. Paris, 1863.

———. *Epistola 134.* In *Epistolae Karolini Aevi*, 4, ed. E. Düemmler, pp. 202–203. MGH. Berlin, 1895.

Aldhelm. *De Virginitate.* In *Aldhelm: The Prose Works*, tr. M. Lapidge and M. Herren, pp. 59–132. Ipswich, 1979.

Das altenglische Martyrologium. Ed. G. Kotzor. Bayerische Akademie der Wissenschaften, Philosophisch-historische Klasse, Abhandlungen, n. s., 88. 2 vols. Munich, 1981.

Amalarius. *Liber de Ordine Antiphonarii.* In *Amalarii Episcopi Opera Liturgica Omnia*, 3, ed. J. M. Hanssens, pp. 9–109. Vatican City, 1950.

———. *Liber Officialis.* In *Amalarii Episcopi Opera Liturgica Omnia*, 2, ed. J. M. Hanssens, pp. 9–543. Vatican City, 1948.

Ambrose. *Expositio Evangelii secundum Lucam.* Ed. M. Adriaen. CC, 14, pp. 1–400. Turnhout, 1957.

———. *Expositio Psalmi 118.* Ed. M. Petschenig. CSEL, 62. Vienna, 1912.

Ambrosius Autpertus. *Expositionis in Apocalypsin Libri 1–4.* Ed. R. Weber. CCCM, 27. Turnhout, 1975.

———. *Sermo de Adsumptione Sanctae Mariae.* Ed. R. Weber. CCCM, 27B, pp. 1027–36. Turnhout, 1979.

———. *Sermo in Purificatione Sanctae Mariae.* Ed. R. Weber. CCCM, 27B, pp. 985–1002. Turnhout, 1979.

Augustine. *De Civitate Dei.* Ed. and tr. D. S. Wiesen. Loeb Classical Library. Vol. 3. Cambridge, Mass., 1968.

———. *De Consensu Evangelistarum.* Ed. F. Weihrich. CSEL, 43. Vienna, 1904.

———. *De Trinitate.* PL, 42. Paris, 1886.

———. *Enarrationes in Psalmos.* Ed. E. Dekkers and J. Fraipont. CC, 38–40. 3 vols. Turnhout, 1956.

———. *In Iohannis Euangelium Tractus 124.* Ed. R. Willems. CC, 36. Turnhout, 1954.

———. *Sermones.* PL, 38. Paris, 1844.

B. *Vita S. Dunstani.* Ed. and tr. M. Lapidge and M. Winterbottom. Forthcoming.

Bede the Venerable. *De Tabernaculo.* Ed. D. Hurst. CC, 119A, pp. 5–139. Turnhout, 1969.

———. *De Templo.* Ed. D. Hurst. CC, 119A, pp. 143–234. Turnhout, 1969.

———. *De Temporum Ratione.* Ed. C. W. Jones. CC, 123B. Turnhout, 1977.

———. *Explanatio Apocalypsis.* PL, 93, cols. 129–206. Paris, 1862.

———. *Homilies on the Gospels.* Tr. L. T. Martin and D. Hurst. Cistercian Studies, 110–111. 2 vols. Kalamazoo, 1991.

———. *In Lucae Evangelium Expositio.* Ed. D. Hurst. CC, 120, pp. 1–425. Turnhout, 1960.

———. *In Marci Evangelium Expositio.* Ed. D. Hurst. CC, 120, pp. 431–648. Turnhout, 1960.

Bede's Ecclesiastical History of the English People. Ed. and tr. B. Colgrave and R. A. B. Mynors. Oxford, 1969.

Benedict of Aniane. *Concordia Regularum.* PL, 103, cols. 701–1380. Paris, 1864.

Benedicti Regula. Ed. R. Hanslik. 2nd ed. CSEL, 75. Vienna, 1977.

The Benedictional of Archbishop Robert. Ed. H. A. Wilson. Henry Bradshaw Society, 24. London, 1903.

The Blickling Homilies of the Tenth Century. Ed. and tr. R. Morris. Early English Text Society, o. s., 58, 63, 73. London, 1880.

Byrhtferth. *Vita Sancti Oswaldi.* In *Byrhtferth of Ramsey: The Lives of Oswald and Ecgwine*, ed. and tr. M. Lapidge. Forthcoming.

Caesarius of Arles. *Sermo 228, De Templo vel Consecratione Altaris.* Ed. G. Morin. CC, 104, pp. 901–904. Turnhout, 1953.

The Canterbury Benedictional. Ed. R. M. Wooley. Henry Bradshaw Society, 51. London, 1917.

Cartularium Saxonicum. Ed. W. de G. Birch. 3 vols. London, 1888–93.

Chronicon Monasterii de Abingdon. Ed. J. Stevenson. Rolls Series. 2 vols. London, 1858.

The Claudius Pontificals. Ed. D. H. Turner. Henry Bradshaw Society, 97. Chichester, 1964.

Cook, A. S., ed. *The Christ of Cynewulf.* Boston, 1900.

The "Constitutions" of Archbishop Oda. In *Councils & Synods with other Documents relating to the English Church*, 1, 1, ed. D. Whitelock, M. Brett, and C. N. L. Brooke, no. 20, pp. 67–74. Oxford, 1981.

Corpus Antiphonalium Officii. Ed. R.-J. Hesbert. 6 vols. Rome, 1963–79.

Corpus Benedictionum Pontificalium. Ed. E. Moeller. CC, 162, 162A-C. 4 vols. Turnhout, 1961–69.

Corpus Christianorum, Continuatio Mediaevalis. Turnhout, 1966–.

Corpus Christianorum, Series Latina. Turnhout, 1953–.

Corpus Consuetudinum Monasticarum. Siegburg, 1963–.

Corpus Scriptorum Ecclesiasticorum Latinorum. Vienna, 1866–.

Dungal. *Liber Adversus Claudium Taurinensem*. PL, 105, cols. 457–530. Paris, 1864.

Epistola Adelardi ad Elfegum Archiepiscopum de Vita Sancti Dunstani. In *Memorials of Saint Dunstan*, ed. W. Stubbs, pp. 53–68. Rolls Series, 63. London, 1874.

The Exeter Book. Part I. Ed. and tr. I. Gollanz. Early English Text Society, o. s., 104. London, 1895.

Faral, E., ed. and tr. *Poème sur Louis le Pieux*. Paris, 1932.

Gregory. *40 Homiliarum in Evangelia*. PL, 76, cols. 1075–1342. Paris, 1878.

———. *Homiliarium in Ezechielem Prophetam Libri Duo*. PL, 76, cols. 785–1072. Paris, 1878.

———. *Moralia in Job*. PL, 75, cols. 510–1162. Paris, 1902; 76, cols. 10–782. Paris, 1878.

Haymo of Auxerre, *Expositio in Apocalypsin*. PL, 117, cols. 937–1220. Paris, 1881.

———. *Homiliae de Sanctis*. PL, 118, cols. 747–804. Paris, 1880.

———. *Homiliae de Tempore*. PL, 118, cols. 11–746. Paris, 1880.

Hrabanus Maurus. *Commentaria in Ecclesiasticum*. PL, 109, cols. 763–1126. Paris, 1864.

———. *Commentaria in Exodum*. PL, 108, cols. 1–246. Paris, 1864.

———. *Commentaria in Ezechielem*. PL, 110, cols. 493–1084. Paris, 1864.

———. *Commentaria in Matthaeum*. PL, 107, cols. 727–1156. Paris, 1864.

———. *De Universo*. PL, 111, cols. 9–614. Paris, 1864.

———. *Enarrationes in Librum Numerorum*. PL, 108, cols. 587–858. Paris, 1864.

———. *Homiliae*. PL, 110, cols. 9–468. Paris, 1864.

———. *Liber de Oblatione Puerorum*. PL, 107, cols. 419–40. Paris, 1864.

Huyghebaert, N.-N., ed. *Une Translation de reliques à Gand en 944*. Brussels, 1978.

Ildefonse of Toledo. *De Virginitate Beatae Mariae*. Ed. V. B. García. Textos latinos de la edad medina española. Madrid, 1937.

Isidore of Seville. *De Natura Rerum*. In *Isidore de Seville: Traité de la nature*, ed. J. Fontaine. Bordeaux, 1960.

———. *Etymologiae*. Ed. M. W. Lindsay. 2 vols. Oxford, 1911.

———. *Mysticorum Expositiones Sacramentorum*. PL, 83, cols. 207–414. Paris, 1862.

James, M. R., tr. *The Apocryphal New Testament*. 2nd ed. Oxford, 1966.

———. *Latin Infancy Gospels*. Cambridge, 1927.

Jerome. *Commentaria in Esaiam*. Ed. M. Adriaen. CC, 73–73A. Turnhout, 1963.

———. *Commentariorum in Matheum Libri 4*. Ed. D. Hurst and M. Adriaen. CC, 77. Turnhout, 1959.

———. *Homilia in Lucam Euangelistam [16, 19–31]*. In *Anecdota Maredsolana*, 3, pt. 2, ed. G. Morin, pp. 376–86. Maredsoli, 1897.

———. *Liber de Viris Inlustribus*. Ed. E. C. Richardson. Leipzig, 1896.

———. *Tractus de Psalmo 77*. Ed. G. Morin. CC, 78, pp. 64–73. Turnhout, 1958.

Jesse of Amiens. *Epistola de Baptismo*. PL, 105, cols. 781–96. Paris, 1864.

John of Salerno. *Vita S. Odonis*. PL, 133, cols. 43–86. Paris, 1881.

John the Scot. *Homilia in Prologum S. Evangelii secundum Joannem*. PL, 122, cols. 283–96. Paris, 1865.

Julian of Toledo. *Prognosticum Futuri Saeculi*. Ed. J. N. Hillgarth. CC, 115, pp. 11–126. Turnhout, 1976.

King Edgar's Privilege for New Minster, Winchester. In *Councils & Synods with other Documents relating to the English Church*, 1, 1, ed. and tr. D. Whitelock, M. Brett, and C. N. L. Brooke, pp. 121–24. Oxford, 1981.

Lantfred. *Translatio et Miracula S. Swithuni*. Ed. and tr. M. Lapidge. In *The Cult of Saint Swithun*, ed. Lapidge. Winchester Studies 4, 2. Oxford, forthcoming.

Lapidge, M., ed. and tr. "Three Latin Poems from Æthelwold's School at Winchester." *ASE*, 1 (1972): 85–137.

Legatine Council. In *Epistolae Karolini Aevi*, 2, ed. E. Dümmler, pp. 19–29. MGH. Berlin, 1895.

Legg, L. G. W., ed. and tr. *English Coronation Records*. Whitehall, 1901.

Libellus Æthelwoldi. In *Anglo-Saxon Ely*, ed. and tr. A. Kennedy and S. Keynes. Forthcoming.

Liber Eliensis. Ed. E. O. Blake. Camden Third Series, 92. London, 1962.

Liber Vitae: Register and Martyrology of New Minster and Hyde Abbey. Ed. W. de G. Birch. London, 1892.

Magnus of Sens. *Libellus de Mysterio Baptismatis*. PL, 102, cols. 981–84. Paris, 1865.

Memoriale Qualiter. Ed. C. Morgand. CCM, 1, pp. 177–282. Siegburg, 1963.

The Missal of Robert of Jumièges. Ed. H. A. Wilson. Henry Bradshaw Society, 11. London, 1896.

The Missal of the New Minster. Ed. D. H. Turner. Henry Bradshaw Society, 93. Leighton Buzzard, Bedfordshire, 1962.

Old English Homilies of the Twelfth Century. Ed. and tr. R. Morris. Early English Text Society, 53. London, 1873.

Origen. *Homilia in Lucam*. In *Origenes Werke*, 9, ed. M. Rauer. 2nd ed. Berlin, 1959.

Paschasius Radbertus (Pseudo-Jerome). *Cogitis me*. PL, 30, cols. 122–42. Paris, 1846.

———. *Expositio in Euangelium Matthaei*. PL, 120, cols. 31–994. Paris, 1879.

——— (Pseudo-Ildefonse). *Sermones 1–3*. PL, 96, cols. 235–58. Paris, 1862.

Patrologia Latina Cursus Completus. Ed. J.-P. Migne. 221 vols. Paris, 1844–64.

Paulinus of Nola. *The Poems of St. Paulinus*. Tr. P. G. Walsh. Ancient Christian Writers, 40. New York, 1975.

Planchart, A. E., ed. *The Repertory of Tropes at Winchester*. 2 vols. Princeton, 1977.

The Portiforium of Saint Wulstan. Ed. A. Hughes. Henry Bradshaw Society, 89 and 90. 2 vols. Leighton Buzzard, Bedfordshire, 1958–60.

Primasius. *Commentarius in Apocalypsin*. Ed. A. W. Adams. CC, 92. Turnhout, 1985.

The Protevangelium of James. Tr. A. J. B. Higgins. In *New Testament Apocrypha*, 1, ed. E. Hennecke, W. Schneemelcher, and R. McL. Wilson, pp. 377–88. Philadelphia, 1963.

Pseudo-Alcuin. *Commentariorum in Apocalypsin Libri Quinque*. PL, 100, cols. 1085–1156. Paris, 1863.

Pseudo-Augustine. *Sermo 155.* PL, 39, cols. 2047–53. Paris, 1865.

Pseudo-Bede. *In Matthaei Evangelium Expositio.* PL, 92, cols. 9–152. Paris, 1862.

Pseudo-Chrysostom. *Homilia in Crucem et in Latronem.* Ed. J.-P. Migne. Patrologia Graeca, 49, cols. 399–418. Paris, 1862.

Pseudo-Jerome. *Breviarium in Psalmos.* PL, 26, cols. 871–1378. Paris, 1884.

———. *Expositio in Quatuor Evangelia.* PL, 30, cols. 531–644. Paris, 1846.

Regularis Concordia Anglicae Nationis. Ed. T. Symons, S. Spath, M. Wegener, and K. Hallinger. CCM, 7, 3, pp. 61–147. Siegburg, 1984.

Remi of Auxerre. *Commentariorum in Isaiam Libri Tres.* PL, 116, cols. 713–1086. Paris, 1879.

———. *De Celebratione Missae* (= Pseudo-Alcuin. *De Divinis Officiis*, 40). PL, 101, cols. 1246–71. Paris, 1863.

———. *Enarrationes in Psalmos.* PL, 131, cols. 133–844. Paris, 1864.

Robertson, A. J., ed. and tr. *Anglo-Saxon Charters.* Cambridge, 1939.

Rudborne, T. *Historia Major de Fundatione et Successione Ecclesiae Wintoniensis.* In *Anglia Sacra*, 1, ed. H. Wharton, pp. 177–286. 1691. Rpt. Farnborough, Hampshire, 1969.

Rufinus. *Commentary on the Apostles' Creed.* Tr. J. N. D. Kelly. Ancient Christian Writers, 20. London, 1955.

Sacramentarium Fuldense Saeculi 10. Ed. G. Richter and A. Schönfelder. 1912. Rpt. Henry Bradshaw Society, 101. Farnborough, Hampshire, 1977.

Smaragdi Abbatis Expositio in Regulam S. Benedicti. Ed. A. Spannagel and P. Engelbert. CCM, 8. Siegburg, 1974.

Smaragdus. *Collectiones in Epistolas et Evangelia.* PL, 102, cols. 15–552. Paris, 1865.

———. *Diadema Monachorum.* PL, 102, cols. 591–690. Paris, 1865.

———. *Via Regia.* PL, 102, cols. 931–70. Paris, 1865.

Theodulf of Orléans. *Liber de Ordine Baptismi ad Magnum Senonensem.* PL, 105, cols. 223–40. Paris, 1864.

Thierry (Theoderich) of Fleury. *Illatio Sancti Benedicti.* In *Acta Sanctorum Ordinis S. Benedicti*, 4, 2, ed. J. Mabillion, pp. 362–67. 2nd ed. Venice, 1738.

The Vercelli Book Homilies. Ed. L. E. Nicholson. Lanham, Maryland, 1991.

The Vercelli Homilies 9–23. Ed. P. E. Szarmach. Toronto Old English Series, 5. Toronto, 1981.

Die Vercelli-Homilien, I. Hälfte. Ed. M. Förster. Bibliothek der angelsächsischen Prosa, 12. Hamburg, 1932.

Walafrid Strabo. *Expositio in Quatuor Evangelia.* PL, 114, cols. 861–916. Paris, 1879.

———. *Homilia in Initium Evangelii S. Matthaei.* PL, 114, cols. 849–62. Paris, 1879.

Wulfstan. *The Homilies of Wulfstan.* Ed. D. Bethurum. Oxford, 1957.

Wulfstan of Winchester. *The Life of St. Æthelwold.* Ed. and tr. M. Lapidge and M. Winterbottom. Oxford, 1991.

———. *Narratio Metrica de S. Swithuno.* In *The Cult of Saint Swithun*, ed. and tr. M. Lapidge. Winchester Studies, 4, 2. Oxford, forthcoming.

———. "Le *Breuiloquium de omnibus sanctis:* un poème inconnu de Wulfstan, chantre de Winchester." Ed. F. Dolbeau. *Analecta Bollandiana* 106 (1988): 35–98.

The Age of Migrating Ideas. Ed. R. M. Spearman and J. Higgitt. Edinburgh, 1993.

Alexander, J. J. G. "The Benedictional of St. Aethelwold and Anglo-Saxon Art of the Reform Period." In *Tenth-Century Studies. Essays in Commemoration of the Millennium of the Council of Winchester and* Regularis Concordia, ed. D. Parsons, pp. 169–83, 241–45. London, 1975.

———. *Insular Manuscripts: 6th to the 9th Century.* A Survey of Manuscripts Illuminated in the British Isles, 1. London, 1978.

———. *Norman Illumination at Mont St. Michel, 966–1100.* Oxford, 1970.

———. "Some Aesthetic Principles in the Use of Colour in Anglo-Saxon Art." *ASE* 4 (1975): 145–54.

Alexander, J. J. G., and E. Temple. *Illuminated Manuscripts in Oxford College Libraries, the University Archives, and the Taylor Institution.* Oxford, 1985.

Andaloro, M. "I mosaici dell'Oratorio di Giovanni VII." In *Fragmenta picta*, pp. 169–77. Rome, 1989.

Angenendt, A. "Das geistliche Bündnis der Päpste mit den Karolingern (754–796)." *Historisches Jahrbuch* 100 (1980): 70–90.

———. *Kaiserherrschaft und Königstaufe.* Arbeiten zur Frühmittelalterforschung, 15. Berlin, 1984.

———. *Monachi Peregrini. Studien zu Pirmin und den monastischen Vorstellungen des frühen Mittelalters.* Münstersche Mittelalter-Schriften, 6. Munich, 1972.

———. "Rex et Sacerdos. Zur Genese der Königssalbung." In *Tradition als historische Kraft*, ed. N. Kamp and J. Wollasch, pp. 100–118. Berlin, 1982.

Anton, H. H. *Fürstenspiegel und Herrscherethos in der Karolingerzeit.* Bonner historische Forschungen, 32. Bonn, 1968.

Avril, F., and P. D. Stirnemann. *Manuscrits enluminés d'origine insulaire VIIe-XXe siècle.* Paris, 1987.

Banton, N. "Monastic Reform and the Unification of Tenth-Century England." In *Religion and National Identity*, ed. S. Mews, pp. 71–85. Oxford, 1982.

Barré, H. "La Royauté de Marie pendant les neuf premiers siècles." *Recherches de Science Religieuse* 29 (1939): 129–62, 303–34.

Baudot, J. "Bénédictionnaire." *Dictionnaire d'Archéologie Chrétienne et de Liturgie*, 2, 1, cols. 727–41. Paris, 1925.

Baumstark, A. "Ein illustriertes griechisches Menaion des Komnenenzeitalters." *Oriens Christianus*, ser. 3, 1 (1926): 67–97.

Beckwith, J. *Ivory Carvings in Early Medieval England.* London, 1972.

Beissel, S. *Des hl. Bernward Evangelienbuch im Dom zu Hildesheim.* Hildesheim, 1891.

———. "Miniaturen aus Prüm." *Zeitschift für christliche Kunst* 19 (1906): 11–22.

Bernards, M. *Speculum Virginum. Geistigkeit und Seelenleben der Frau im Hochmittelalter.* Forschungen zur Volkskunde, 36/38. Cologne, 1955.

Bernward von Hildesheim und das Zeitalter der Ottonen. Ed. M. Brandt and A. Eggebrecht. 2 vols. Hildesheim, 1993.

Bertelli, C. *La Madonna di Santa Maria in Trastevere.* Rome, 1961.

Biddle, M. "Archaeology, Architecture, and the Cult of Saints in Anglo-Saxon England." In *The Anglo-Saxon*

Church, ed. L. A. S. Butler and R. K. Morris, pp. 1–31. Council for British Archaeology, Research Report, 60. London, 1986.

———. "Excavations at Winchester, 1969: Eighth Interim Report." *Antiquaries Journal* 50 (1970): 277–326.

———. "*Felix Urbs Winthonia*: Winchester in the Age of Monastic Reform." In *Tenth-Century Studies. Essays in Commemoration of the Millennium of the Council of Winchester and Regularis Concordia*, ed. D. Parsons, pp. 123–40, 233–37. London, 1975.

———. "Winchester: The Development of an Early Capital," *Vor- und Frühformen der europäischen Stadt im Mittelalter*, 1, pp. 229–61. Abhandlungen der Akademie der Wissenschaften in Göttingen, phil.-hist. Kl., ser. 3, 83. Göttingen, 1973.

Bischoff, B. "Die karolingische Minuskel." In *Mittelalterliche Studien*, 3, pp. 1–4. Stuttgart, 1981.

———. *Latin Palaeography.* Tr. D. Ganz and D. Ó. Cróinín. Cambridge, 1990.

Bishop, T. A. M. *English Caroline Minuscule.* Oxford, 1971.

Bloch, P. *Reichenauer Evangelistar.* Codices Selecti, 31. Graz, 1972.

Boeckler, A. *Abendländische Miniaturen.* Tabulae in Usum Scholarum, 10. Berlin, 1930.

Boinet, A. *La Miniature carolingienne.* Paris, 1913.

Bouman, C. A. *Sacring and Crowning.* Groningen, 1957.

Boutemy, A. "L'Enluminure anglaise de l'époque saxonne (Xᵉ et XIᵉ siècles) et la Flandre française." *Bulletin de la Société Nationale des Antiquaires de France* (1956): 42–50.

———. "Le Style franco-saxon, style de Saint-Amand." *Scriptorium* 3 (1949): 260–64.

Bowen, L. "The Tropology of Mediaeval Dedication Rites." *Speculum* 16 (1941): 469–79.

Braun, J. *Der christliche Altar.* 2 vols. Munich, 1924.

Braunfels, W. *Die Heilige Dreifaltigkeit.* Düsseldorf, 1954.

Brendel, O. "Origin and Meaning of the Mandorla." *Gazette des Beaux-Arts*, 6th ser., 25 (1944): 5–24.

Brenk, B. *Tradition und Neuerung in der christlichen Kunst des ersten Jahrtausends.* Wiener byzantinistische Studien, 3. Vienna, 1966.

Broderick, H. R. "Some Attitudes toward the Frame in Anglo-Saxon Manuscripts of the Tenth and Eleventh Centuries." *Artibus et Historiae* 5 (1982): 31–42.

Bruce-Mitford, R. L. S., et al. *Evangeliorum Quattuor Codex Lindisfarnensis.* 2 vols. Olten, 1956–60.

Brückmann, J. "Latin Manuscript Pontificals and Benedictionals in England and Wales." *Traditio* 29 (1973): 391–458.

Budny, M. "'St. Dunstan's Classbook' and its Frontispiece: Dunstan's Portrait and Autograph." In *St. Dunstan: His Life, Times and Cult*, ed. N. Ramsay, M. Sparks, and T. Tatton-Brown, pp. 103–42. Woodbridge, 1992.

Bullough, D. A. "The Continental Background of the Reform." In *Carolingian Renewal: Sources and Heritage*, pp. 272–96. Manchester, 1991.

Bünger, F. *Geschichte der Neujahrsfeier in der Kirche.* Göttingen, 1911.

Burlin, R. E. *The Old English Advent.* Yale Studies in English, 168. New Haven, 1968.

Byrne, M. *The Tradition of the Nun in Medieval England.* Washington, 1932.

Cahn, W. "Heresy and the Interpretation of Romanesque Art." In *Romanesque and Gothic Art: Essays for George Zarnecki*, 1, pp. 27–33. Woodbridge, 1987.

Campbell, J. J. "To Hell and Back: Latin Tradition and Literary Use of the 'Descensus ad Inferos' in Old English." *Viator* 13 (1982): 107–58.

Carlsson, F. *The Iconology of Tectonics in Romanesque Art.* Hässleholm, 1976.

Cascante Dávila, J. M. "La devoción y el culto a María en los escritos de S. Ildefonso de Toledo (s. VII)." In *De Cultu Mariano Saeculis VI-XI*, 3, pp. 223–48. Acta Congressus Mariologici-Mariana Internationalis in Croatia Anno 1971 Celebrati. Rome, 1972.

Casel, O. "Die Kirche als Braut Christi nach Schrift, Väterlehre und Liturgie." In *Mysterium der Ekklesia*, pp. 59–86. Mainz, 1961.

———. "Die Mönchweihe." *Jahrbuch für Liturgiewissenschaft* 5 (1925): 1–47.

———. "Die Taufe als Brautbad der Kirche." *Jahrbuch für Liturgiewissenschaft* 5 (1925): 144–47.

La Cattedra lignea di S. Pietro in Vaticano. Atti della Pontificia Accademia Romana di Archeologia, ser. 3, Memorie, 10. Vatican City, 1971.

Chambers, R. W., M. Förster and R. Flowers. *The Exeter Book of Old English Poetry.* London, 1933.

Chase, C. "God's Presence through Grace as the Theme of Cynewulf's *Christ II* and the Relationship of this Theme to *Christ I* and *Christ III*." *ASE* 3 (1974): 87–101.

Christe, Y. *La Vision de Matthieu (Matth. 24–25).* Bibliothèque des Cahiers Archéologiques, 10. Paris, 1973.

Clayton, M. "Ælfric and the Nativity of the Blessed Virgin Mary." *Anglia* 104 (1986): 286–315.

———. *The Cult of the Virgin in Anglo-Saxon England.* Cambridge Studies in Anglo-Saxon England, 2. Cambridge, 1990.

———. "Delivering the Damned: A Motif in Old English Homiletic Prose." *Medium Ævum* 55 (1986): 92–102.

———. "Feasts of the Virgin in the Liturgy of the Anglo-Saxon Church." *ASE* 13 (1984): 209–33.

Clemoes, P. "Cynewulf's Image of the Ascension." In *England before the Conquest. Studies in Primary Sources Presented to Dorothy Whitelock*, ed. P. Clemoes and K. Hughes, pp. 293–304. Cambridge, 1971.

Clemoes, P., and C. R. Dodwell. *The Old English Illustrated Hexateuch.* Early English Manuscripts in Facsimile, 18. Copenhagen, 1974.

Coathalem, H. *Le Parallelisme entre la Sainte Vierge et l'église dans la tradition latine jusqu'à la fin du XIIᵉ siècle.* Analecta Gregoriana, 74. Rome, 1954.

Cole, W. "Theology in Paschasius Radbertus' Liturgy-Oriented Marian Works." In *De Cultu Mariano Saeculis VI-XI*, 3, pp. 395–431. Acta Congressus Mariologici-Mariana Internationalis in Croatia Anno 1971 Celebrati. Rome, 1972.

Comoretto, A. *Le miniature del sacramentario fuldense di Udine.* Udine, 1988.

Constable, G. "The Ceremonies and Symbolism of Entering Religious Life and Taking the Monastic Habit, from the Fourth to the Twelfth Century." *Settimane di studio del centro italiano di studi sull'alto medioevo* 33 (1985): 771–834.

———. "Monachisme et pèlerinage au Moyen Âge." *Revue Historique* 258 (1977): 3–27.

Cook, W. W. S. "The Earliest Painted Panels of Catalonia (II)." *AB* 6 (1923–24): 31–60.

Cowdrey, H. E. J. "The Anglo-Norman Laudes Regiae." *Viator* 12 (1981): 37–78.

Cramp, R. *Corpus of Anglo-Saxon Stone Sculpture in England.* Vol. 1. Oxford, 1984.

Cross, J. E. *Cambridge Pembroke College MS 25: A Carolingian Sermonary Used by Anglo-Saxon Preachers.* King's College London Medieval Studies, 1. London, 1987.

———. "Mary Magdalen in the *Old English Martyrology*: The Earliest Extant 'Narrat Josephus' Variant of her Legend." *Speculum* 53 (1978): 16–25.

Dabin, P. *Le Sacerdoce royal des fidèles dans la tradition ancienne et moderne.* Paris, 1950.

Dale, W. "Ivory and Miniature: A Matter of Comparison." *British Museum Yearbook* 1 (1976): 228–36.

Daniélou, J. *Bible and the Liturgy.* London, 1956.

———. *From Shadows to Reality.* London, 1960.

Davril, A. "Un Moine de Fleury aux environs de l'an mil: Thierry, dit d'Amorbach." In *Études ligériennes d'histoire et d'archéologie médiévales,* ed. R. Louis, pp. 97–104. Auxerre, 1975.

Dekkers, E. *Clavis Patrum Latinorum.* Steenbrugis, 1961.

Dell'Ordo, F. "Le benedictiones episcopales del codice warmondiano (Ivrea, bibl. capit., cod. 10 [XX])." *Archiv für Liturgiewissenschaft* 12 (1970): 148–251.

Demus, O. *Romanesque Mural Painting.* London, 1970.

Deshman, R. "Anglo-Saxon Art after Alfred." *AB* 56 (1974): 176–200.

———. "Anglo-Saxon Art: So What's New?" Forthcoming.

———. "Antiquity and Empire in the Throne of Charles the Bald." In *Byzantine East, Latin West: Art Historical Studies in Honor of Kurt Weitzmann.* Princeton, forthcoming.

———. "*Benedictus Monarcha et Monachus*: Early Medieval Ruler Theology and the Anglo-Saxon Reform." *Frühmittelalterliche Studien* 22 (1988): 204–40.

———. "*Christus Rex et Magi Reges*: Kingship and Christology in Ottonian and Anglo-Saxon Art." *Frühmittelalterliche Studien* 10 (1976): 367–405.

———. "The Exalted Servant: The Ruler Theology of the Prayerbook of Charles the Bald." *Viator* 11 (1980): 385–417.

———. "The Imagery of the Living Ecclesia and the English Monastic Reform." In *Sources of Anglo-Saxon Culture,* ed. P. E. Szarmach, pp. 261–82. Studies in Medieval Culture, 20. Kalamazoo, 1986.

———. "The Leofric Missal and Tenth-Century English Art." *ASE* 6 (1977): pp. 145–73.

———. "Otto III and the Warmund Sacramentary." *Zeitschrift für Kunstgeschichte* 34 (1971): 1–20.

———. "Servants of the Mother of God in Byzantine and Medieval Art." *Word and Image* 5 (1989): 33–70.

DeWald, E. T. *The Illustrations of the Utrecht Psalter.* Princeton, 1932.

Dodwell, C. R. *Anglo-Saxon Painting: A New Perspective.* Ithaca, 1982.

———. "Techniques of Manuscript Painting in Anglo-Saxon Manuscripts." *Settimane di studio del centro italiano di studi sull'alto medioevo* 18 (1971): 643–62, 675–83.

Donnat, L. "Recherches sur l'influence de Fleury au Xe siècle." In *Études ligériennes d'histoire et d'archéologie médiévales,* ed. R. Louis, pp. 165–74. Auxerre, 1975.

Dubler, E. *Das Bild des heiligen Benedikt.* Munich, 1966.

Dufrenne, S. *Les Illustrations du Psautier d'Utrecht.* Association des Publications près les Universités de Strasbourg, 161. Paris, n. d.

Dumville, D. N. *English Caroline Script and Monastic History.* Studies in Anglo-Saxon History, 6. Woodbridge, 1993.

———. "English Square Minuscule Script: The Background and Earliest Phases." *ASE* 16 (1987): 147–79.

———. *Liturgy and the Ecclesiastical History of Late Anglo-Saxon England.* Studies in Anglo-Saxon History, 5. Woodbridge, 1992.

Eberhardt, O. *Via Regia. Der Fürstenspiegel Smaragds von St. Mihiel und seine literarische Gattung.* Münstersche Mittelalter-Schriften, 28. Munich, 1977.

Eisenhofer, L. *Handbuch der katholischen Liturgik.* 2 vols. Freiburg im Breisgau, 1932.

Elbern, V. H. "Das Essener Evangelistarfragment aus dem Umkreis des Utrechtpsalter." In *Das erste Jahrtausend,* 2, pp. 992–1006. Düsseldorf, 1964.

———. "Vier karolingische Elfenbeinkästen." *Zeitschrift des deutschen Vereins für Kunstwissenschaft* 20 (1966): 1–16.

Elderkin, G. W. "Shield and Mandorla." *American Journal of Archaeology* 42 (1938): 227–36.

English Romanesque Art 1066–1200. Ed. G. Zarnecki, J. Holt, and T. Holland. London, 1984.

Erdmann, C. *Forschungen zur politischen Ideenwelt des Frühmittelalters.* Berlin, 1951.

Euw, A. von. *Das Buch der vier Evangelien: Kölns karolingische Evangelienbüchen.* Cologne, 1989.

Fisher, J. D. C. *Christian Initiation: Baptism in the Medieval West.* London, 1965.

Frank, H. "Hodie Caelesti Sponso Iuncta est Ecclesia." In *Vom christlichen Mysterium. Gesammelte Arbeiten zum Gedächtnis von Odo Casel OSB,* ed. A. Mayer, J. Quasten, and B. Neunheuser, pp. 192–226. Düsseldorf, 1951.

Franz, A. *Die kirchlichen Benediktionen im Mittelalter.* 2 vols. Freiburg im Breisgau, 1909.

Freyhan, R. "The Stole and Maniples: (c) The Place of the Stole and Maniples in Anglo-Saxon Art of the Tenth Century." In *The Relics of St. Cuthbert,* ed. C. F. Battiscombe, pp. 409–32. Oxford, 1956.

Gage, J. "The Anglo-Saxon Ceremonial of the Dedication and Consecration of Churches." *Archaeologia* 35 (1834): 235–74.

———. "A Dissertation on St. Aethelwold's Benedictional." *Archaeologia* 24 (1832): 1–117.

Galley, E. "Das karolingische Evangelistarfragment aus der Landes- und Stadtbibliothek Düsseldorf." *Düsseldorfer Jahrbuch* 52 (1966): 120–27.

Gamber, K. *Codices Liturgici Latini Antiquiores.* 2nd ed. 2 vols. Freiburg, 1968.

Gameson, R. "Manuscript Art at Christ Church, Canterbury, in the Generation after St. Dunstan." In *St. Dunstan: His Life, Times and Cult,* ed. N. Ramsay, M. Sparks, and T. Tatton-Brown, pp. 187–220. Woodbridge, 1992.

Ganz, D. "The Preconditions for Carolingian Minuscule." *Viator* 18 (1987): 23–44.

Gatch, M. McC. *Preaching and Theology in Anglo-Saxon England.* Toronto, 1977.

Gem, R. "Towards an Iconography of Anglo-Saxon Architecture." *Journal of the Warburg and Courtauld Institutes* 46 (1983): 1–18.

Gerchow, J. *Die Gedenküberlieferung der Angelsachsen.* Berlin, 1988.

Gillen, O. "Christus und die Sponsa." *Die christliche Kunst* 33 (1936–37): 202–24.

Gneuss, H. "Dunstan und Hrabanus Maurus. Zur HS. Bodleian Auctarium F. 4. 32." *Anglia* 96 (1978): 136–48.

———. *Hymnar und Hymnen im englischen Mittelalter.* Tübingen, 1968.

———. "Liturgical Books in Anglo-Saxon England and their Old English Terminology." In *Learning and Literature in Anglo-Saxon England*, ed. H. Gneuss and M. Lapidge, pp. 91–141. Cambridge, 1985.

———. "The Origin of Standard Old English and Æthelwold's School at Winchester." *ASE* 1 (1972): 63–83.

———. "A Preliminary List of Manuscripts Written or Owned in England up to 1100." *ASE* 9 (1981): 1–60.

The Golden Age of Anglo-Saxon Art: 966–1066. Ed. J. Backhouse, D. H. Turner, and L. Webster. London, 1984.

Goldschmidt, A. *Die Elfenbeinskulturen.* 4 vols. 1918–26. Rpt. Berlin, 1969–70.

———. *German Illumination.* 2 vols. 1928. Rpt. 2 vols. in 1. New York, 1970.

Goldschmidt, A., and K. Weitzmann. *Die byzantinischen Elfenbeinskulpturen.* 2nd ed. 2 vols. Berlin, 1979.

Gössmann, M. E. *Die Verkündigung an Maria im dogmatischen Verständnis des Mittelalters.* Munich, 1957.

Grabar, A. "The Virgin in a Mandorla of Light." In *Late Classical and Mediaeval Studies in Honor of Albert Mathias Friend, Jr.*, ed. K. Weitzmann, pp. 305–11. Princeton, 1955.

Gransden, A. "Traditionalism and Continuity during the Last Century of Anglo-Saxon Monasticism." *Journal of Ecclesiastical History* 40 (1989): 159–207.

Green, R., et al. *Hortus Deliciarum.* Studies of the Warburg Institute, 36. 2 vols. London, 1979.

Grégoire, R. "La tradizione manoscritta del 'diadema monachorum' di Smaragdo." *Inter Fratres* 34 (1984): 1–20.

Gretsch, M. "Æthelwold's Translation of the *Regula Sancti Benedicti* and its Latin Exemplar." *ASE* 3 (1974): 125–51.

———. *Die Regula Sancti Benedicti in England und ihre altenglische Übersetzung.* Texte und Untersuchungen zur englischen Philologie, 2. Munich, 1973.

Grierson, P. "Grimbald of St. Bertin's." *English Historical Review* 55 (1940): 529–61.

Grisar, H. *Die Römische Kapelle Sancta Sanctorum und ihr Schatz.* Freiburg im Breisgau, 1908.

Gussone, N. "Adventus-Zeremoniell und Translation von Reliquien. Victrinus von Rouen, De Laude Sanctorum." *Frühmittelalterliche Studien* 10 (1976): 124–33.

Gutberlet, H. *Die Himmelfahrt Christi in der bildenden Kunst.* 2nd ed. Strassburg, 1935.

Hallinger, K. "The Spiritual Life of Cluny in the Early Days." In *Cluniac Monasticism in the Central Middle Ages*, ed. N. Hunt, pp. 29–55. London, 1971.

Haney, K. E. *The Winchester Psalter.* Leicester, 1986.

Hart, C. "Two Queens of England." *The Ampleforth Journal* 82 (1977): 10–15, 54.

Hecht, J. "Die frühesten Darstellungen der Himmelfahrt Mariens." *Das Münster* 4 (1951): 1–12.

Heimann, A. "Three Illustrations from the Bury St. Edmunds Psalter and their Prototypes." *Journal of the Warburg and Courtauld Institutes* 29 (1966): 39–59.

Heinzelmann, M. *Translationsberichte und andere Quellen des Reliquienkultes.* Typologie des Sources du Moyen Âge Occidental, 33. Turnhout, 1979.

Herwegen, I. "Der Gemäldezyklus in der Oberkirche zu Schwarzrheindorf." In *Das Buch Ezechiel in Theologie und*

Kunst bis zum Ende des XII. Jahrhunderts, ed. W. Neuss, pp. 308–25. Münster in Westfalen, 1912.

Higgitt, J. "Glastonbury, Dunstan, Monasticism and Manuscripts." *Art History* 2 (1979): 275–90.

Hill, T. D. " 'Byrht Word' and 'Haelendes Heafod': Christological Allusion in the Old English *Christ and Satan.*" *English Language Notes* 8 (1970): 5–8.

———. "Vision and Judgement in the Old English *Christ III.*" *Studies in Philology* 70 (1973): 233–42.

Hirn, Y. *The Sacred Shrine.* 2nd ed. London, 1958.

Hoffmann, H. *Buchkunst und Königtum im ottonischen und frühsalischen Reich.* 2 vols. Stuttgart, 1986.

Hoffmann, K. "Die Evangelistenbilder des Münchener Otto-Evangeliars (CLM 4453)." *Zeitschrift des deutschen Vereins für Kunstwissenschaft* 20 (1966): 17–46.

———. *Taufsymbolik im mittelalterlichen Herrscherbild.* Bonner Beiträge zur Kunstwissenschaft, 9. Düsseldorf, 1968.

Hofstetter, W. "Winchester and the Standardization of Old English Vocabulary." *ASE* 17 (1988): 139–61.

———. *Winchester und der spätaltenglische Sprachgebrauch.* Texte und Untersuchungen zur englischen Philologie, 14. Munich, 1987.

Hollis, S. *Anglo-Saxon Women and the Church.* Woodbridge, 1992.

Holter, K. *Hrabanus Maurus, Liber de Laudibus Sanctae Crucis.* Codices Selecti, 33. Graz, 1973.

Homburger, O. *Die Anfänge der Malschule von Winchester im X. Jahrhundert.* Studien über christliche Denkmäler, n. s., 13. Leipzig, 1912.

Homburger, O. "L'Art carolingien de Metz et l'école de Winchester.' " *Gazette des Beaux-Arts*, 6th ser., 62 (1963): 35–46.

Iogna-Prat, D. "Le Culte de la Vierge sous le règne de Charles le Chauve," *Les Cahiers de Saint-Michel de Cuxa* 23 (1992): 97–116.

John, E. *Orbis Britanniae.* Studies in Early English History, 4. Leicester, 1966.

Jones, A. "The Significance of the Regal Consecration of Edgar in 973." *Journal of Ecclesiastical History* 33 (1982): 375–90.

Josi, E., V. Federici, and E. Ercadi. *La porta bizantina di San Paolo.* Rome, 1967.

Josten, H. H. *Neue Studien zur Evangelienhandschrift Nr. 18.* Strassburg, 1909.

Jugie, M. *La Mort et l'assomption de la Sainte Vierge.* Studi e Testi, 114. Vatican City, 1944.

Jungmann, J. A. *The Mass of the Roman Rite: Its Origins and Development.* 2 vols. New York, 1951–55.

Kahsnitz, R. "Koimesis—Dormitio—Assumptio." In *Florilegium in Honorem Carl Nordenfalk Octogenarii Contextum*, pp. 92–122. Stockholm, 1987.

Kahsnitz, R., U. Mende, and E. Rücker. *Das Goldene Evangelienbuch von Echternach.* Frankfurt am Main, 1982.

Kantorowicz, E. H. "Ivories and Litanies." *Journal of the Warburg and Courtauld Institutes* 5 (1942): 56–81.

———. "Kaiser Friederich II. und das Königsbild des Hellenismus." In *Selected Studies*, pp. 264–83. Locust Valley, N. Y., 1965.

———. "The 'King's Advent' and the Enigmatic Panels in the Doors of Santa Sabina." In *Selected Studies*, pp. 37–75. Locust Valley, N. Y., 1965.

———. *The King's Two Bodies.* Princeton, 1957.

———. *Laudes Regiae. A Study in Liturgical Acclamations and Mediaeval Ruler Worship.* Berkeley, 1946.

———. "The Quinity of Winchester." *AB* 29 (1947): 73–85. Rpt. in *Selected Studies*, pp. 100–20. Locust Valley, N. Y., 1965 (citations are to the reprint).

Karl der Grosse. Werk und Wirkung. Aachen, 1965.

Kartsonis, A. D. *Anastasis: The Making of an Image.* Princeton, 1986.

Katzenellenbogen, A. *The Sculptural Programs of Chartres Cathedral.* New York, 1959.

Kelly, J. N. D. *Early Christian Creeds.* London, 1952.

Kendrick, T. D. *Late Saxon and Viking Art.* 1949. Rpt. London, 1974.

Ker, N. R. *Catalogue of Manuscripts Containing Anglo-Saxon.* Oxford, 1957.

Kessler, H. L. "'Caput et Speculum Omnium Ecclesiarum': Old St. Peter's and Church Decoration in Medieval Latium." In *Italian Church Decoration of the Middle Ages and Early Renaissance*, ed. W. Tronzo, pp. 119–46. Villa Spelman Colloquia, 1. Bologna, 1989.

———. *The Illustrated Bibles from Tours.* Studies in Manuscript Illumination, 7. Princeton, 1977.

Keynes, S. *Anglo-Saxon Manuscripts in Trinity College.* Binghamton, N. Y., 1992.

———. "King Athelstan's Books." In *Learning and Literature in Anglo-Saxon England*, ed. S. Keynes and H. Gneuss, pp. 143–201. Cambridge, 1985.

Keyssner, K. "Nimbus." *Paulys Realencyclopädie der classischen Altertumswissenschaft*, 17, 1, cols. 591–624. Stuttgart, 1936.

King, E. S. "The Carolingian Frescoes of the Abbey of Saint Germain d'Auxerre." *AB* 11 (1929): 359–75.

Kitzinger, E. "The Mosaics of the Cappella Palatina in Palermo." *AB* 31 (1948): 269–92. Rpt. idem. In *The Art of Byzantium and the Medieval West: Selected Studies*, ed. W. E. Kleinbauer, pp. 290–313. Bloomington, 1976.

———. "Reflections on the Feast Cycle in Byzantine Art." *Cahiers Archéologique* 36 (1988): 51–73.

Klauser, T. "Aurum coronarium." *Mitteilungen des deutschen archäologischen Instituts*, Röm. Abt. 59 (1944): 129–53.

———. *Das Römische Capitulare Evangeliorum.* Liturgiegeschichtliche Quellen und Forschungen, 28. Münster in Westfalen, 1935.

Kleinschmidt, H. "Die Titulaturen englischer Könige im 10. und 11. Jahrhundert." In *Intitulatio*, ed. H. Wolfram and A. Scharer, 3, pp. 75–129. Vienna, 1988.

———. *Untersuchungen über das englische Königtum im 10. Jahrhundert.* Göttinger Bausteine zur Geschichtswissenschaft, 49. Göttingen, 1979.

Klinkenberg, H. M. "Über karolingische Fürstenspiegel." *Geschichte in Wissenschaft und Unterricht* 7 (1956): 82–92.

Knowles, D. *The Monastic Order in England.* 2nd ed. Cambridge, 1966.

Koehler, W. "An Illustrated Evangelistary of the Ada School and its Model." *Journal of the Warburg and Courtauld Institutes* 15 (1952): 48–66.

———. *Die karolingischen Miniaturen.* 4 vols. Berlin, 1930–71.

Koehler, W., and F. Mütherich. *Drogo-Sakramentar.* Codices Selecti, 49. Graz, 1974.

———. *Die karolingischen Miniaturen.* Vol. 5. Berlin, 1982.

Köster, H. M. "Ildefons von Toledo als Theologe der Marienverehrung." In *De Cultu Mariano Saeculis VI–XI*, 3, pp. 197–

222. Acta Congressus Mariologici-Mariani Internationalis in Croatia Anno 1971 Celebrati. Rome, 1972.

Krücke, A. *Der Nimbus und verwandte Attribute in der frühchristliche Kunst.* Strassburg, 1905.

———. "Zwei Beiträge zur Ikonographie des frühen Mittelalters." *Marburger Jahrbuch für Kunstwissenschaft* 10 (1937): 5–36.

Kurth, B. "The Iconography of the Wirksworth Slab." *Burlington Magazine* 86 (1945): 114–21.

Ladner, G. B. "The so-called Square Nimbus." *Mediaeval Studies* 3 (1941): 15–45.

———. "The Symbolism of the Biblical Corner Stone in the Mediaeval West." *Mediaeval Studies* 4 (1942): 43–60.

Lafontaine, J. *Peintures médiévales dans le temple dit la Fortune Virile à Rome.* Brussels, 1959.

Lafontaine-Dosogne, J. *Iconographie de l'enfance de la Vierge dans l'empire byzantin et en occident.* 2 vols. Brussels, 1964–65.

Lanoë, G. "Approche de quelques évêques moines en Angleterre au Xe siècle." *Cahiers de Civilisation Médiévale* 19 (1976): 135–50.

Lapidge, M. "Æthelwold as Scholar and Teacher." In *Bishop Æthelwold: His Career and Influence*, ed. B. Yorke, pp. 89–117. Woodbridge, 1988.

———. *Anglo-Saxon Litanies of the Saints.* Henry Bradshaw Society, 106. London, 1991.

———. "The Hermeneutic Style in Tenth-Century Anglo-Latin Literature." *ASE* 4 (1975): 67–111.

———. "Schools, Learning and Literature in Tenth-Century England." *Settimane di studio del centro italiano de studi sull'alto medioevo* 38 (1990): 951–1005.

———. "Surviving Booklists from Anglo-Saxon England." In *Learning and Literature in Anglo-Saxon England*, ed. M. Lapidge and H. Gneuss, pp. 33–89. Cambridge, 1985.

———, ed. *The Cult of Saint Swithun.* Winchester Studies, 4, 2. Oxford, forthcoming.

Lass, R. "Poem as Sacrament: Transcendence of Time in the *Advent Sequence* from the Exeter Book." *Annuale Mediaevale* 7 (1966): 3–15.

Lauer, P. *L'Évangéliaire carolingien de Lyon.* Documents, paléographiques, typographiques, iconographiques, 7. Lyon, 1928.

Lawrence, M. "Maria Regina." *AB* 7 (1924–25): 150–61.

Leclercq, J. "La Réforme bénédictine anglaise du Xe siècle vue du continent." *Studia Monastica* 24 (1982): 105–25.

———. *La Vie parfaite.* Tradition Monastique, 1. Paris, 1948.

Leesti, E. "The Pentecost Illustration in the Drogo Sacramentary." *Gesta* 28 (1989): 205–16.

Lester, G. A. "A Possible Early Occurrence of Moses with Horns in the Benedictional of St. Aethelwold." *Scriptorium* 27 (1973): 30–33.

Lexikon der christlichen Ikonographie. 8 vols. Rome, 1968–76.

Leyser, K. "Die Ottonen und Wessex." *Frühmittelalterliche Studien* 17 (1983): 73–97.

Little, C. T. "A New Ivory of the Court School of Charlemagne." In *Studien zur mittelalterlichen Kunst 800–1250: Festschrift für Florentine Mütherich zum 70. Geburtstag*, ed. K. Bierbrauer, P. K. Klein, and W. Sauerländer, pp. 11–28. Munich, 1985.

Loerke, W. C. "Observations on the Representation of *Doxa* in the Mosaics of S. Maria Maggiore, Rome, and St. Catherine's, Sinai." *Gesta* 20 (1981): 15–22.

Lopez, R. S. "Le Problème des relations anglo-byzantines du septième au dixième siècle." *Byzantion* 18 (1948): 139–62.

Lowden, J. *Illuminated Prophet Books*, University Park, Penn., 1988.

Magnani, L. *Le miniature del sacramentario d'Ivrea*. Vatican City, 1934.

Maguire, H. *Art and Eloquence in Byzantium*. Princeton, 1981.

Maiburg, U. "Christus der Eckstein." In *Vivarium. Festschrift Theodor Klauser zum 90. Geburtstag*, pp. 247–56. Münster, 1984.

Malone, E. E. "Martyrdom and Monastic Profession as a Second Baptism." In *Vom christlichen Mysterium. Gesammelte Arbeiten zum Gedächtnis von Odo Casel OSB*, ed. A. Mayer et al., pp. 115–34. Düsseldorf, 1951.

Les Manuscrits à peintures en France du VIIe au XIIe siècle. 2nd ed. Paris, 1954.

Mašín, J. *Codex Vyšehradensis*. Edito Cimelia Bohemica, 13. Prague, 1970.

McGurk, P. "The Metrical Calendar of Hampson. A New Edition." *Analecta Bollandiana* 104 (1986): 79–125.

McNally, R. E. "The Evangelists in the Hiberno-Latin Tradition." In *Festschrift Bernhard Bischoff*, pp. 111–22. Stuttgart, 1971.

Metz, R. *La Consécration des vierges dans l'église romaine*. Strasbourg, 1954.

Meyer, H. B. "Zur Symbolik frühmittelalterlicher Majestasbilder." *Das Münster* 14 (1961): 73–88.

Meyer, M. A. "Patronage of the West Saxon Royal Nunneries in Late Anglo-Saxon England." *Revue Bénédictine* 91 (1981): 332–58.

———. "Women and the Tenth Century English Monastic Reform." *Revue Bénédictine* 87 (1977): 34–61.

Micheli, G. *L'Enluminure du moyen âge et les influences irlandaises*. Brussels, 1939.

Millinger, S. P. "Liturgical Devotion in the Vita Oswaldi." In *Saints, Scholars, and Heroes: Studies in Medieval Culture in Honour of Charles W. Jones*, ed. M. H. King and W. M. Stevens, 2, pp. 240–64. Collegeville, Minn., 1979.

Morey, C. R. *The Gold-Glass Collection of the Vatican Library*. Catalogo del Museo Sacro, 4. Vatican City, 1959.

Morrison, S. "The Figure of *Christus Sponsus* in Old English Prose." In *Liebe—Ehe—Ehebruch in der Literatur des Mittelalters*, ed. X. von Ertzdorff and M. Wynn, pp. 5–15. Beiträge zur deutschen Philologie, 58. Giessen, 1984.

Müller, A. *Ecclesia-Maria*. 2nd ed. Paradosis, 5. Freiburg, 1955.

Mütherich, F. *Das Sakramentar von Metz*. Codices Selecti, 28. Graz, 1972.

Nelson, J. L. "Inauguration Rituals." In *Early Medieval Kingship*, ed. P. H. Sawyer and I. N. Wood, pp. 50–71. Leeds, 1977.

———. "The Second English *Ordo*." In *Politics and Ritual in Early Medieval Europe*, pp. 361–74. London, 1986.

Nilgen, U. "Maria Regina—ein politischer Kultbildtypus?" *Römisches Jahrbuch für Kunstgeschichte* 19 (1981): 1–33.

Niver, C. M. "A Study of the More Important Manuscripts of the Franco-Saxon School." Ph.D. diss., Harvard University, 1941.

Noble, T. F. X. "Louis the Pious and his Piety Reconsidered." *Revue Belge de Philologie et d'Histoire* 58 (1980): 297–316.

———. "The Monastic Ideal as a Model for Empire: The Case of Louis the Pious." *Revue Bénédictine* 86 (1976): 235–50.

Nordenfalk, C. *Celtic and Anglo-Saxon Painting*. New York, 1977.

———. "The Draped Lectern." In *Intuition und Kunstwissenschaft. Festschrift für Hanns Swarzenski zum 70. Geburtstag am 30. August 1973*, ed. P. Bloch et al., pp. 81–100. Berlin, 1973.

Nordhagen, P. J. "The Earliest Decorations in Santa Maria Antiqua and their Date." *Acta ad Archaeologiam et Artium Historiam Pertinentia* 1 (1962): 53–71.

———. "The Mosaics of John VII (705–707 A.D.)." *Acta ad Archaeologiam et Artium Historiam Pertinentia* 2 (1965): 121–66.

O'Reilly, J. "Early Medieval Text and Image: The Wounded and Exalted Christ." *Peritia* 6–7 (1987–88): 72–118.

———. "St. John as a Figure of the Contemplative Life: Text and Image in the Art of the Anglo-Saxon Benedictine Reform." In *St. Dunstan: His Life, Times and Cult*, ed. N. Ramsay, M. Sparks, and T. Tatton-Brown, pp. 165–85. Woodbridge, 1992.

Ohlgren, T. *Anglo-Saxon Textual Illustration*. Kalamazoo, 1992.

———. *Insular and Anglo-Saxon Illuminated Manuscripts. An Iconographic Catalogue c. A. D. 625–1100*. New York, 1986.

Okasha, E. *Handlist of Anglo-Saxon Non-Runic Inscriptions*. Cambridge, 1971.

Okasha, E., and J. O'Reilly. "An Anglo-Saxon Portable Altar: Inscription and Iconography." *Journal of the Warburg and Courtauld Institutes* 47 (1984): 32–51.

Omont, H. *Évangiles avec peintures byzantines du XIe siècle*. 2 vols. Paris, n. d.

———. *Miniatures des plus anciens manuscrits grecs de la Bibliothèque Nationale du VIe au XIVe siècle*. Paris, 1929.

———. *Peintures et initiales de la seconde bible de Charles le Chauve*. Paris, n. d.

Oppenheim, P. *Das Mönchskleid im christlichen Altertum*. Freiburg im Breisgau, 1931.

———. *Symbolik und religiöse Wertung des Mönchskleides im christlichen Altertum*. Theologie des christlichen Ostens, 2. Münster in Westfalen, 1932.

Ornamenta Ecclesiae. 3 vols. Cologne, 1985.

Ortenberg, V. "Archbishop Sigeric's Journey to Rome in 990." *ASE* 19 (1990): 197–246.

———. *The English Church and the Continent in the Tenth and Eleventh Centuries*. Oxford, 1992.

Pächt, O. *Buchmalerei des Mittelalters: Eine Einführung*. Munich, 1984.

Pächt, O., and J. J. G. Alexander. *Illuminated Manuscripts in the Bodleian Library, Oxford*. Vol. 3. Oxford, 1973.

Pächt, O., F. Wormald, and C. R. Dodwell. *The St. Albans Psalter (Albani Psalter)*. Studies of the Warburg Institute, 25. London, 1960.

Panofsky, E. "Once More 'the Friedsam Annunciation and the Problem of the Ghent Altarpiece.'" *AB* 20 (1938): 419–42.

Parker McLachlan, E. "The Athelstan Psalter and the Gallican Connection." In *Transactions of the Third Canadian Conference of Medieval Art Historians*, ed. W. Dale, pp. 21–27. London, Ont., 1985.

Pelekanidis, S. M., et al. *The Treasures of Mt. Athos*. Vols. 1 and 2. Athens, 1973–74.

Plotzek, M. *Das Perikopenbuch Heinrichs III. in Bremen und seine Stellung innerhalb der Echternacher Buchmalerei.* Cologne, 1970.

Prescott, A. "The Structure of English Pre-Conquest Benedictionals." *British Library Journal* 13 (1987): 118–58.

———. "The Text of the Benedictional of St. Æthelwold." In *Bishop Æthelwold: His Career and Influence,* ed. B. Yorke, pp. 119–47. Woodbridge, 1988.

Quirk, R. N. "Winchester Cathedral in the Tenth Century." *The Archaeological Journal* 114 (1957): 28–68.

Rädel, F. *Studien zu Smaragd von Saint-Mihiel.* Medium Aevum, Philologische Studien, 29. Munich, 1974.

Rahner, H. "Die Lehre der Kirchenväter von der Geburt Christi aus dem Herzen der Kirche und der Gläubigen." In *Symbole der Kirche,* pp. 13–80. Salzburg, 1964.

Raw, B. *Anglo-Saxon Crucifixion Iconography and the Art of the Monastic Revival.* Cambridge Studies in Anglo-Saxon England, 1. Cambridge, 1990.

———. "What Do We Mean by the Source of a Picture?" In *England in the Eleventh Century,* ed. C. Hickes, pp. 285–300. Harlaxton Medieval Studies, 2. Stamford, 1992.

Reallexikon für Antike und Christentum. 1–. Stuttgart, 1950–.

Reallexikon zur byzantinischen Kunst. 1–. Stuttgart, 1966–.

Regensburger Buchmalerei. Ed. F. Mütherich and K. Dachs. Munich, 1987.

Reudenbach, B. "Säule und Apostel. Überlegungen zum Verhältnis von Architektur und architekturexegetischer Literatur im Mittelalter." *Frühmittelalterliche Studien* 14 (1980): 310–51.

Ridyard, S. J. *The Royal Saints of Anglo-Saxon England.* Cambridge, 1988.

Rollason, D. W. "Relic-Cults as an Instrument of Royal Policy *c.* 900–*c.* 1050." *ASE* 15 (1986): 91–103.

———. *Saints and Relics in Anglo-Saxon England.* Oxford, 1989.

Roosen-Runge, H. *Farbgebung und Technik frühmittelalterlicher Buchmalerei.* Kunstwissenschaftliche Studien, 38. 2 vols. Munich, 1967.

Rosenthal, J. E. "The Historiated Canon Tables of the Arenberg Gospels." Ph. D.diss., Columbia University, 1974.

———. "The Pontifical of St. Dunstan." In *St. Dunstan: His Life, Times and Cult,* ed. N. Ramsay, M. Sparks, and T. Tatton-Brown, pp. 143–63. Woodbridge, 1992.

———. "Three Drawings in an Anglo-Saxon Pontifical: Anthropomorphic Trinity or Threefold Christ?" *AB* 63 (1981): 547–62.

———. "The Unique Architectural Settings of the Arenberg Evangelists." In *Studien zur mittelalterlichen Kunst 800–1250: Festschrift für Florentine Mütherich zum 70. Geburtstag,* ed. K. Bierbrauer, P. K. Klein, and W. Sauerländer, pp. 145–56. Munich, 1985.

Sacopoulo, M. *La Theotokos à la mandorle de Lythrankomi.* Paris, 1973.

St. Cuthbert, his Cult and his Community to AD 1200. Ed. G. Bonner, D. W. Rollason, and C. Stancliffe. Woodbridge, 1989.

Sauer, J. *Symbolik des Kirchengebäudes und seiner Ausstattung in der Auffassung des Mittelalters.* 2nd ed. Freiburg im Breisgau, 1924.

Sawyer, P. H. *Anglo-Saxon Charters.* London, 1968.

Schade, H. "Studien zu der karolingischen Bilderbibel aus St. Paul vor den Mauern in Rom, 2. Teil." *Wallraf-Richartz-Jahrbuch* 22 (1960): 13–48.

Schaffer, C. *Koimesis. Der Heimgang Mariens.* Studia Patristica et Liturgica, 15. Regensburg, 1985.

Schapiro, M. "The Image of the Disappearing Christ: The Ascension in English Art around the Year 1000." *Gazette des Beaux-Arts,* ser. 6, 23 (1943): 135–52. Rpt. idem. *Late Antique, Early Christian, and Mediaeval Art, Selected Papers,* 3, pp. 267–87. New York, 1979 (citations are to the reprint).

———. "On Some Problems in the Semiotics of Visual Art: Field and Vehicle in Image-Signs." *Semiotica* 1 (1969): 223–42.

———. "The Religious Meaning of the Ruthwell Cross." *AB* 26 (1944): 232–45.

———. "Two Romanesque Drawings in Auxerre and Some Iconographic Problems." In *Studies in Art and Literature for Belle da Costa Greene,* ed. D. Miner, pp. 331–49. Princeton, 1954. Rpt. idem. *Romanesque Art. Selected Papers,* 1, pp. 306–27. New York, 1977.

Scheffczyk, L. *Das Mariengeheimnis in Frömmigkeit und Lehre der Karolingerzeit.* Erfurter theologische Studien, 5. Leipzig, 1959.

Schiel, H. *Codex Egberti.* Basel, 1960.

Schiller, G. *Iconography of Christian Art.* Tr. J. Seligman. 2 vols. Greenwich, Conn., 1971–72.

———. *Ikonographie der christlichen Kunst.* 5 vols. Gütersloh, 1969–90.

Schipper, W. "Dry-point Compilation Notes in the Benedictional of Æthelwold." *British Museum Journal* 20 (1994): 17–34.

Schnitzler, H. "Eine Metzer Emmaustafel." *Wallraf-Richartz-Jahrbuch* 20 (1958): 41–54.

Schramm, P. E. *Die deutschen Kaiser und Könige in Bildern ihrer Zeit 751–1190.* 2nd ed. Ed. F. Mütherich. Munich, 1983.

———. *Kaiser, Könige und Päpste.* 4 vols. Stuttgart, 1968–71.

Sears, E. "Louis the Pious as *Miles Christi*: The Dedicatory Image in Hrabanus Maurus's *De Laudibus Sanctae Crucis.*" In *Charlemagne's Heir: New Perspectives on the Reign of Louis the Pious,* ed. P. Godman and R. Collins, pp. 605–28. Oxford, 1990.

Semmler, J. "Das Erbe der karolingischen Klosterreform im 9. und 10. Jahrhundert." In *Monastische Reformen im 9. und 10. Jahrhundert,* pp. 29–77. Vorträge und Forschungen, 38. Sigmaringen, 1989.

———. "Le Souverain occidental et les communautés religieuses du IXe au début du XIe siècle." *Byzantion* 61 (1991): 44–70.

Sheerin, D. J. "The Dedication of the Old Minster, Winchester, in 980." *Revue Bénédictine* 88 (1978): 261–73.

Sinding, O. *Mariae Tod und Himmelfahrt.* Christiania, 1903.

Smetana, C. L. "Ælfric and the Early Medieval Homiliary." *Traditio* 15 (1959): 163–204.

———. "Ælfric and the Homiliary of Halberstadt." *Traditio* 17 (1961): 457–69.

———. "Paul the Deacon's Patristic Anthology." In *The Old English Homily and its Backgrounds,* ed. P. E. Szarmach and B. E. Huppé, pp. 75–97. Albany, 1978.

Sources of Anglo-Saxon Literary Culture: A Trial Version. Ed. F. M. Biggs, T. D. Hill, and P. E. Szarmach. Medieval and Renaissance Texts and Studies, 74. Binghamton, 1990.

Staedel, E. *Ikonographie der Himmelfahrt Mariens.* Strassburg, 1935.

Stafford, P. "Charles the Bald, Judith and England." In *Charles the Bald: Court and Kingdom*, ed. M. Gibson and J. Nelson, pp. 139–53. 2nd ed. Aldershot, 1981.

———. "The King's Wife in Wessex 800–1066." *Past and Present* 91 (1981): 3–27.

———. *Queens, Concubines and Dowagers. The King's Wife in the Early Middle Ages*. London, 1983.

Steigerwald, G. "Das Königtum Mariens in der Literatur der ersten sechs Jahrhunderte." *Marianum* 37 (1975): 1–52.

Stenton, F. *Anglo-Saxon England*. 3rd ed. Oxford History of England, 2. Oxford, 1971.

Stiefenhofer, D. *Die Geschichte der Kirchweihe vom 1.-7. Jahrhundert*. Veröffentlichungen aus dem kirchenhistorischen Seminar München, ser. 3, 8. Munich, 1909.

Stornajolo, C. *Miniature delle omilie di Giacomo monaco e dell'evangeliario greco urbinate*. Rome, 1910.

———. *Le miniature della topografia cristiana di Cosma Indicopleuste*. Milan, 1908.

Stroud, D. I. "The Provenance of the Salisbury Psalter." *The Library*, ser. 6, 1 (1979): 25–35.

Der Stuttgarter Bilderpsalter. 2 vols. Stuttgart, 1968.

Swarzenski, G. *Die Regensburger Buchmalerei*. Leipzig, 1901.

Symons, T. "*Regularis Concordia*: History and Derivation." In *Tenth-Century Studies. Essays in Commemoration of the Millennium of the Council of Winchester and* Regularis Concordia, ed. D. Parsons, pp. 37–59, 214–17. London, 1975.

———. "Sources of the *Regularis Concordia*." *Downside Review* 54 (1941): 14–36, 143–70, 264–89.

Temple, E. *Anglo-Saxon Manuscripts, 900–1066. A Survey of Manuscripts Illuminated in the British Isles*, 2. London, 1976.

Teviotdale, E. C. "The Cotton Troper (London, British Library, Cotton MS Caligula A.XIV, ff. 1–36): A Study of an Illustrated English Troper of the Eleventh Century." Ph.D. diss., University of North Carolina, Chapel Hill, 1991.

Thacker, A. "Æthelwold and Abingdon." In *Bishop Æthelwold: His Career and Influence*, ed. B. Yorke, pp. 43–64. Woodbridge, 1988.

———. "Cults at Canterbury: Relics and Reform under Dunstan and his Successors." In *St. Dunstan: His Life, Times and Cult*, ed. N. Ramsay, M. Sparks, and T. Tatton-Brown, pp. 221–45. Woodbridge, 1992.

Thérel, M.-L. *A l'origine du décor du portail occidental de Notre-Dame de Senlis: le triomphe de la Vierge-Église*. Paris, 1984.

Tolhurst, J. B. "An Examination of Two Anglo-Saxon Manuscripts of the Winchester School: The Missal of Robert of Jumièges and the Benedictional of Aethelwold." *Archaeologia*, ser. 2, 83 (1933): 27–44.

Töpfer, B. "Reliquienkult und Pilgerbewegung zur Zeit der Klosterreform im burgundisch-aquitanischen Gebiet." In *Vom Mittelalter zur Neuzeit. Zum 65. Geburtstag von Heinrich Sproemberg*, ed. H. Kretzschmar, pp. 420–39. Berlin, 1956.

Tschan, F. J. *Saint Bernward of Hildesheim*. 3 vols. Notre Dame, Ind., 1942–52.

Tselos, D. "English Manuscript Illustration and the Utrecht Psalter." *AB* 40 (1959): 137–49.

Turner, D. H., et al. *The Benedictines in Britain*. British Library Series, 3. London, 1980.

Underwood, P. A. "The Fountain of Life in Manuscripts of the Gospels." *DOP* 5 (1950): 43–137.

Unterkircher, F. *Zur Ikonographie und Liturgie des Drogo-Sakramentars*. Interpretationes ad Codices, 1. Graz, 1977.

Van der Horst, K., and J. H. A. Engelbrecht. *Utrecht Psalter*. Codices Selecti, 75. Graz, 1982–84.

Velmans, T. *Le Tétraévangile de la Laurentienne*. Bibliothèque des Cahiers Archéologiques, 6. Paris, 1971.

Verdier, P. *Le Couronnement de la Vierge*. Conférence Albert-le-Grand, 1972. Paris, 1980.

———. "Plaques d'un *antependium* ottonien et iconographie mariale du Baptême." In *Mélanges offerts à René Crozet*, ed. P. Gallais and Y.-J. Riou, 1, pp. 185–95. Poitiers, 1966.

Vidier, A. *L'Historiographie à Saint-Benoît-sur-Loire et les miracles de Saint Benoît*. Paris, 1965.

Vogelsang, T. *Die Frau als Herrscherin im hohen Mittelalter*. Göttingen, 1954.

Volbach, W. F. *Elfenbeinarbeiten der Spätantike und des frühen Mittelalters*. 3rd ed. Mainz am Rhein, 1976.

Vollrath, H. "König Edgar und die Klosterreform in England: die 'Ostersynode' der 'Vita s. Oswaldi auctore anonymo.'" *Annuarium Historiae Conciliorum* 10 (1978): 67–81.

Walter, C. "Marriage Crowns in Byzantine Iconography." *Zographe* 10 (1979): 83–91.

Warner, G. F., and H. A. Wilson. *The Benedictional of St. Aethelwold*. Oxford, 1910.

Weigand, E. "Zum Denkmälerkreis des Christogrammnimbus." *Byzantinische Zeitschrift* 32 (1932): 63–81.

Weisbach, W. "Die Darstellung der Inspiration auf mittelalterlichen Evangelistenbildern." *Rivista di archeologia cristiana* 16 (1939): 101–27.

———. "Les Images des évangélistes dans 'l'évangéliaire d'Othon III.'" *Gazette des Beaux-Arts*, ser. 6, 21 (1939): 131–52.

Weitzmann, K. "Byzantine Miniature and Icon Painting in the Eleventh Century." In *Proceedings of the XIIIth International Congress of Byzantine Studies. Oxford. 5–10 September 1966*, ed. J. M. Hussey et al., pp. 207–24. London, 1967. Rpt. K. Weitzmann. In *Studies in Classical and Byzantine Manuscript Illumination*, ed. H. L. Kessler, pp. 271–313. Chicago, 1971.

———. *Die byzantinische Buchmalerei des 9. und 10. Jahrhunderts*. Berlin, 1935.

———. "The Classical in Byzantine Art as a Mode of Individual Expression." In idem. *Studies in Classical and Byzantine Manuscript Illumination*, ed. H. L. Kessler, pp. 151–75. Chicago, 1971.

———. "Das Evangelion im Skevophylakion zu Lawra." *Seminarium Kondakovianum* 8 (1936): 83–98. Rpt. K. Weitzmann. In *Byzantine Liturgical Psalters and Gospels*, no. 11. London, 1980.

———. "Eine Fuldaer Elfenbeingruppe." In *Adolph Goldschmidt zu seinem siebenzigsten Geburtstag*, pp. 14–18. Berlin, 1935.

———. *Illustrations in Roll and Codex*. Studies in Manuscript Illumination, 2. 1947. Rpt. with addenda Princeton, 1970.

———. "*Loca Sancta* and the Representational Arts of Palestine." *DOP* 28 (1974): 35–55. Rpt. K. Weitzmann. In *Studies in the Arts at Sinai*, pp. 19–62. Princeton, 1982.

———. *The Miniatures of the Sacra Parallela: Parisinus Graecus 923*. Studies in Manuscript Illumination, 8. Princeton, 1979.

———. *The Monastery of Saint Catherine at Mount Sinai, the Icons*, 1. Princeton, 1976.

———. "The Narrative and Liturgical Gospel Illustrations."

In *New Testament Studies*, ed. M. M. Parvis and A. P. Wikgren, pp. 151–74, 215–19. Chicago, 1950. Rpt. K. Weitzmann. In *Studies in Classical and Byzantine Manuscript Illumination*, ed. H. L. Kessler, pp. 247–70. Chicago, 1971.

———. "The Selection of Texts for Cyclic Illustration in Byzantine Manuscripts." In *Byzantine Books and Bookmen*, pp. 69–109. Washington, 1975.

———. "A 10th Century Lectionary. A Lost Masterpiece of the Macedonian Renaissance." *Revue d'Études Sud-est Européennes* 9 (1971): 617–40. Rpt. K. Weitzmann. In *Byzantine Liturgical Psalters and Gospels*, no. 20. London, 1980.

———. "Various Aspects of Byzantine Influence on the Latin Countries from the Sixth to the Twelfth Century." *DOP* 20 (1966): 1–24. Rpt. K. Weitzmann. In *Art in the Medieval West and its Contacts with Byzantium*, no. 1. London, 1982.

Wenger, A. *L'Assomption de la T.S. Vierge dans la tradition byzantine du VIᵉ au Xᵉ siècle*. Archives de l'Orient Chrétien, 5. Paris, 1955.

Westwood, J. O. *Facsimiles of the Miniatures and Ornaments of Anglo-Saxon and Irish Manuscripts*. London, 1868.

Whitelock, D. "The Authorship of the Account of King Edgar's Establishment of the Monasteries." In *Philological Essays: Studies in Old and Middle English Language and Literature in Honour of Herbert Dean Meritt*, ed. J. L. Rosier, pp. 125–36. The Hague, 1970.

Wilhelm, P. *Die Marienkrönung am Westportal der Kathedrale von Senlis*. Hamburg, 1941.

Willmes, P. *Der Herrscher-"Adventus" im Kloster des Frühmittelalters*. Münstersche Mittelalter-Schriften, 22. Munich, 1976.

Witters, W. "Smaragde au moyen âge. La Diffusion de ses écrits d'après la tradition manuscrite." In *Études ligériennes d'histoire et d'archéologie médiévales*, ed. R. Louis, pp. 361–67. Auxerre, 1975.

Wollasch, J. "Das Mönchsgelübde als Opfer." *Frühmittelalterliche Studien* 18 (1984): 529–45. (citations are to the reprint)

Wormald, F. *The Benedictional of St. Ethelwold*. London, 1959.

———. "Continental Influence on English Medieval Illumination." In *Transactions of the Fourth International Congress of Bibliophiles, 1965*, pp. 4–16. London, 1967.

———. "Decorated Initials in English MSS. from A.D. 900 to 1100." *Archaeologia* 91 (1945): 107–35.

———. *English Drawings of the Tenth and Eleventh Centuries*. London, 1952.

———. "An English Eleventh-Century Psalter with Pictures, British Library, Cotton MS Tiberius C. VI." *Walpole Society* 38 (1962): 1–13. Rpt. F. Wormald. In *Collected Writings*, 1, pp. 123–37. London, 1984 (citations are to the reprint).

———. "A Fragment of a Tenth-Century Gospel Lectionary." In *Calligraphy and Paleography. Essays Presented to Alfred Fairbank on his 70th Birthday*, ed. A. S. Osley, pp. 43–46. London, 1965. Rpt. F. Wormald. In *Collected Writings*, 1, pp. 101–104. London, 1984.

———. "Late Anglo-Saxon Art: Some Questions and Suggestions." In *Studies in Western Art*, 1: Romanesque and Gothic Art, pp. 19–26. Acts of the Twentieth International Congress of the History of Art, 1. Princeton, 1963. Rpt. F. Wormald. In *Collected Writings*, 1, pp. 105–110. London, 1984 (citations are to the reprint).

———. "The 'Winchester School' before St. Æthelwold." In *England before the Conquest: Studies in Primary Sources Presented to Dorothy Whitelock*, ed. P. Clemoes and K. Hughes, pp. 305–12. Cambridge, 1971. Rpt. F. Wormald. In *Collected Writings*, 1, pp. 76–84. London, 1984 (citations are to the reprint).

Wormald, P. "Æthelwold and his Continental Counterparts: Contact, Comparison, Contrast." In *Bishop Æthelwold: His Career and Influence*, ed. B. Yorke, pp. 13–42. Woodbridge, 1988.

Wratislaw-Mitrovic, W., and N. Okunev. "La Dormition de la Sainte Vierge dans la peinture médiévale orthodoxe." *Byzantinoslavica* 3 (1931): 134–80.

Wright, C. E. "The Benedictional of St. Ethelwold and Bishop Henry Compton." *The British Museum Quarterly* 27 (1963): 3–5.

Yorke, B. A. E. "Æthelwold and the Politics of the Tenth Century." In *Bishop Æthelwold: His Career and Influence*, ed. idem, pp. 65–88. Woodbridge, 1988.

———. "The Bishops of Winchester, the Kings of Wessex and the Development of Winchester in the Ninth and Early Tenth Centuries." *Proceedings of the Hampshire Field Club and Archaeological Society* 40 (1984): 61–70.

———. "'Sisters under the Skin?' Anglo-Saxon Nuns and Nunneries in Southern England." *Reading Medieval Studies* 15 (1989): 95–117.

Zarnecki, G. "The Coronation of the Virgin on a Capital from Reading Abbey." *Journal of the Warburg and Courtauld Institutes* 13 (1950): 1–12.

Index

Aachen; capitulary of 818–819, 210; cathedral treasury, ivory plaque, 70, 73, fig. 63; royal chapel, 192

Abel, 84

Abingdon, 170, 175, 186, 192

Adam, 65

Adelard, *Epistola ad Elfegum Archiepiscopum de Vita Sancti Dunstani*, 171, 174–175, 177, 183, 187

Advent, 9, 11, 15, 25, 29, 67–69, 185; Office, 13, 64, 68,

Ælfheah, bishop, 140

Ælfric, 4, 252–253, 255; *Hom.*, 7, 11, 23, 29, 33, 62, 67, 73, 82–84, 97, 101, 144–145, 155; *Lives of the Saints*, 123–124; pastoral letters, 172–173; *Sermo ad Populum*, 98

Ælfthryth, queen, 204–207, 213–214

Ælfwine, fig. 87

Æthelflaed, abbess of Romsey, 206

Æthelgifu, abbess of Shaftesbury, 206

Æthelthryth, abbess of Nunnaminster, 172, 173

Æthelthryth, saint, 175, 206–207; in choir of Virgins, 146, 150, 151, 171–172, pl. 3; portrait of, 80, 121–124, 137–138, 151, 163, 164, 172, 173, 184, 207, 216, 218, 219, 223, 225, 229, 230, 260, pl. 28, fig. 154

Æthelwold, pl. 35, fig. 138; as compiler and author of benedictions, 6, 87–88, 122, 166; and cult of Saint Æthelthryth, 173, 260; and cult of Saint Swithun, 138, 182, 187; and devotion to saints, 148, 156; and devotion to Virgin Mary, 133, 156, 163; iconographic influence of, 58, 64, 117, 163, 252–254; and monarchy, 168, 170, 192–193, 206, 252; and monastic chant, 175; and monastic reform, 168, 170, 171, 174, 178–179, 182–184, 187–188, 192–193, 198, 250, 252; as scholar and teacher, 6, 97, 252–253. *See also* London, British Library, MS Cotton Vespasian A. VIII (New Minster charter); Old English translation of Benedictine *Rule*; *Regularis Concordia*

Æthelwulf, king, 167

Alcuin, *Commentaria in S. Joannis Evangelium*, 114

Aldhelm, *De Virginitate*, 111, 175–176, 177, 185

Alexander, Jonathan J. G., 5, 126

Alexios, saint, 229, fig. 155

Alfred, king, 206

All saints, 80, 104, 113, 148, 151, 156, fig. 122

altar; in Bishop Blessing the Congregation, 142, 144, 145, 154, 181; consecration of, 142, 181; as crib of Christ, 20–21, 23, 25, 53, 55; in Nativity 20–21, 23, 25, 53, 55; in Presentation in Temple, 39–43, 55, 144, 181, 242, 254; as symbol of Christ, 42, 55; as symbol of the Church, 25, 142; as symbol of heart of the believer, 42–43, 144, 180; as symbol of Virgin Mary, 17, 17 n. 52, 25, 43, 145. *See also* cornerstone.

Amalarius of Metz, 11–12; *Lib. Off.*, 15

Ambrose, 10, 11; *Secundam Lucam*, 55, 79

Ambrosius Autpertus, 38; *Expositionis in Apocalypsin*, 66; *Sermo in Purificatione Sanctae Mariae*, 40, 41

Amesbury, 206

angels; choir of, 85–86; in choirs of saints and the apostles, 155–156; at Pentecost, 91–92; at the Second Coming, 63, 64; at the Ascension, 60–62

Anglo-Saxon chronicle, 213

Anna, king of East Anglia, 122

Anna, prophetess at Presentation in Temple, 35

Anthony, abbot, 183

Antwerp, Museum Mayer van der Bergh, ivory plaque, 46, 263, fig. 39

apostles, 146–158, 170, 225, 260, pls. 4–7, 24–26, figs. 120, 121, 158, 162; Miraculous Reunion of, 125, 127, 135, 268, pl. 34; as monastic precursors, 171–172

Arius, 113, fig. 105

Arnulf, saint, 245, fig. 203

Arras, Bibliothèque Municipale, MS 1045 (Franco-Saxon lectionary), 165, 234, 236–239, figs. 130, 131, 175, 176, 179, 180, 186, 191, 193, 199

Athelstan, king, 167, 168, 192, 226

Athelstan (Galba) Psalter. *See* London, British Library, MS Cotton Galba A. XVIII

Augustine of Hippo, saint, 66, 177; *De Civitate Dei*, 42; *De Trinitate*, 98; *Enarrationes in Psalmos*, 13–14, 29, 33, 68

aurum coronarium, 201; and Adoration of Magi, 27, 194

Autun, Bibliothèque Municipale; MS 4 (Gospels), 139; MS 19 bis (Raganaldus Sacramentary), 20, 160, fig. 119

Auxerre, cathedral, crypt, fresco, 115, fig. 111

B., *Life of Saint Dunstan*, 176

baldachin, symbolism of, 17, 25, 152, 155, 181

Baltimore, Walters Art Gallery; copper gilt plaque, 51, fig. 43; MS W 530C, 147, fig. 120

baptism, 46, 47, 49, 51, 53, 54, 94, 141–142, 149, 157; and Annunciation, 15; and coronation, 212; and monasticism, 179–180, 213; and Octave of Pentecost, 95–96, 103–105, 108, 213; and Pentecost, 91–92, 213

Barking, 175

Bede, 11, 12, 33; *De Tabernaculo*, 53; *De Temporum Ratione*, 134; *Ecclesiastical History*, 123, 137, 173, 184, 250; *Explanatio Apocalypsis*, 67; *Homilies*, 7, 34, 43, 48–49, 52, 59, 61, 62, 71, 73, 85, 87; *In Lucam*, 25–26, 54

Benedict of Aniane, 120, 210; *Concordia Regularum*, 210

Benedict, saint, 175–176; and Æthelwold, 180, fig. 136; and monks, 140, 209, figs. 136, 137; as bishop, 172–173; in choir of confessors, 150, 151, 171, 172–173, pl. 1; portrait of, 117–121, 123, 150, 155, 170, 173, 175, 177, 202–204, 213, pl. 33; *Rule* of, 119–121, 171–174, 178, 179, 182, 198, 203, 206, 210; translation of relics of, 185–186. *See also* Old English transaltion of Benedictin *Rule*

benediction; for Advent, 15, 16, 25, 27, 29, 68, 69, 101, 145, 191; for All Saints, 79, 80, 123; for Ascension, 65–66, 75; for Assumption, 133; and Benedictine monasticism, 190–191, 252, 253; for Candlemas, 87, 153; for *Cathedra Sancti Petri*, 74; for Christmas, 21, 153; for dedication of church, 139, 141–142; for Easter, 74; for Epiphany, 47, 50, 51, 54; for John the Baptist, 49; for John the evangelist, 178; for Nativity of John the Baptist, 29, 30; for Octave of Easter, 149; for Octave of Pentecost, 95, 96, 97, 103, 113; for Palm Sunday, 80, 84; for Pentecost, 91, 104; for Purification of the Virgin, 37, 38, 144;

benediction; for Advent, (*cont.*)
  for St. Æthelthryth, 122, 123, 151; for St. Benedict, 119, 150; for St. Cecilia, 149; for St. Stephen, 115; for St. Swithun, 152, 182, 260; for Saturday after Easter, 79–80; for several virgins, 143; for Sunday after Ascension day, 75; for translation of St. Benedict, 117–118; for vigil of Christmas, 23; for vigil of Pentecost, 108; for Wednesday after Easter, 75. *See also* Æthelwold as compiler and author of benedictions

benedictional, illuminated, 3, 191, 251, 254; as possible model for Benedictional, 159–161

Benedictus, 86, 175, 188, 190

Benna, Trier artist, 194

Berlin, Staatliche Museen Preussische Kulturbesitz; ivory plaque depicting Entry into Jerusalem, 78, fig. 75; ivory plaque with acanthus frieze, 236, fig. 183; Kupferstichkabinett, MS 78 A 2 (Reichenau lectionary), 28, fig. 17

Bethlehem, 21–22, 25, 40, 52, 56, 85, 86

Boeckler, Albert, 5

Bishop Blessing the Congregation, 39, 139–146, 152, 154–155, 158, 159, 160–161, 180–181, 183, 251, pl. 35

Blickling homilies, 30, 62, 88, 108, 131, 135

Boethius; *De Consolatione Philosophiae*, 227; *De Trinitate*, 99; with Philosophy and the Muses, 227, 230, text fig. 4, figs. 145, 146; and the Trinity, 99, fig. 95

Boulogne-sur-mer, Bibliothèque Mun.; MS 11 (Gospels), 96–97, fig. 91; MS 12 (Gospels), 238, fig. 182

Bremen, Staatsbibliothek, MS b. 21 (lectionary of Henry III), 38, fig. 32

Bristol, cathedral, stone slab, 64, fig. 60

Brunswick, Herzog Anton Ulrich-Museum, ivory casket (Brunswick Casket), figs. 1, 2, 7, 8, 34, 35, 36, 37; influence of, 9–10, 18, 19, 20, 28, 45, 51, 55, 126, 127, 159, 161, 228, 236–237, 246, 248, 251, 262–266; program of, 47–48, 55

Byrhtferth; *Life of St. Ecgwine*, 199; *Life of St. Oswald*, 121, 177, 182, 183, 184, 185, 186, 191, 195, 202, 203–205, 208, 209, 213

byzantine art, 5, 251; iconographic influence of, 58–59, 63–64, 65, 70, 78–79, 89–90, 93, 100, 105, 107, 114, 115, 116, 125, 131–132, 147, 149, 156, 157, 161–164, 166–169, 268; ornamental influence of, 242; stylistic influence of, 224, 229–232, 242, 246–247

Caesarius of Arles, 144; *De Templo vel Consecratione Altaris*, 181

Cain, 84

Cambridge, Corpus Christi College; MS 183 (Life of St. Cuthbert), 226–227, 233, 244, fig. 142; MS 198 (Old English homilies), 147, fig. 121; MS 286 (St. Augustine Gospels), 166

Cambridge, Trinity College, MS B. 15. 34 (homiliary), 96, 119, fig. 90

Cambridge, University Museum of Archaeology and Anthropology, ivory plaque, 72, 156, 196, fig. 68

canon tables, 36, 52, 139, fig. 198

Canterbury, 36, 98, 113, 117, 119, 167–168, 225, 249

Cavendish, William, 261

Charlemagne, 201, 249

Charles the Bald, 106, 167, 168; *Codex Aureus* of, 106, 194, 201, figs. 133, 134; Sacramentary of, 86, 147, 201, figs. 81, 82; throne of, 161, 167

Charles the Simple, 167

Chatsworth, 261

Chester-le-Street, shrine of St. Cuthbert, 168

Chludov Psalter, 36

choirs of the saints, 86, 98, 104, 146–158, 161, 162, 170–173, 175–176, 189, 200–202, 207–208, 225, 229, 259–260, pls. 1–3, figs. 11, 12, 69, 80, 81, 92, 93, 122–124, 126. *See also* litany of the saints

Christ, figs. 26, 82, 90, 140, 163; Adored by Magi, 9, 26–27, 32–33, 34, 44, 45, 50, 51, 55, 89, 118, 136, 155, 163, 193, 218, 219, 246, 263, pl. 18, figs. 13, 14; at Anastasis, 63–66, 162, figs. 58–60; Appearing to the Apostles, fig. 63; Arrest of, fig. 202; Ascension of, 10, 44, 58–62, 63, 64–67, 70–71, 72, 75, 77, 91, 92, 103, 107, 108, 126, 127, 135–136, 152, 159, 161–162, 166, 197, 199, 218, 221, 223, 268, pl. 25, text fig. 2, figs. 48–51, 53–57, 144, 162; Baptism of, 9, 38, 39, 45–54, 70, 91–93, 95, 96, 103, 108, 118, 127, 136–138, 159, 163, 179, 193–194, 209, 212–213, 246, 262–265, 268, pl. 19, figs. 34, 38–40, 42, 43, 210; at Cana, 50; and choir of angels, 85–86, 146, fig. 11; and choirs of saints, 85–86, 146, figs. 11, 12, 69, 81–82, 123, 126; Circumcision of, 31, 34, 35, 37, 45, fig. 19; crowning of, 47, 50, 92, 127; Crucifixion of, 47, 48, 50, 51, 92, 126, 127, 163, 179, 180, figs. 36, 41, 210; "disappearing," 62, fig. 57; and Dunstan, 231–232, 248, fig. 139; Emmanuel, 10, 52, 55, fig. 3; Entering Jerusalem, 77–89, 90, 108, 153, 155, 159, 161–162, 175–176, 184, 185–190, 212, 219, 239, pl. 21, figs. 71–77; gilded hair of, 60, 61, 63, 65, 70, 73, 97; Giving the Law, fig. 70; Harrowing of Hell, 65–66, 68, 69, 70, 75, 81, 88, 197, figs. 60, 61; Healing the Leper, 164; in initial O, 121–124, 137, pl. 29; as judge, 72, 96, 97, 99, 106, 119–121, 149, 156, 189, 200; as king and priest, 46–48, 53, 56, 95, 193–194, 209, 212–213; as King of kings, 27, 72, 88, 96, 102, 194–195, 198, 199; at Last Judgement, 63, 64, 65, 68, 69, 71, 72, 74–76, 80, 88, 94, 95, 96, 97, 98, 103, 105, 107, 119, 120, 121, 130, 138, 147–150, 152, 153, 156, 157, 162, 177, 189–190, 195–197, 202, 206, 259, figs. 68, 69, 123; as Lord of lords, 72, 88, 102; in Majesty, 93, 112, 136, figs. 88, 91; marrying the Church, 51; Miracles of, fig. 77; Naming of, 9, 30–35, 44, 55, pl. 16, fig. 20; Nativity of, 9, 18–26, 31–33, 34, 35, 40, 43, 44, 45, 51, 52, 53, 54, 55, 61–62, 67–68, 69, 86, 108, 116, 126, 127, 130, 131–135, 136, 144, 152, 153, 155, 159, 161, 175–176, 180, 219–220, 223, 236, 237, 238, 244, 246, 248, 262, 264–265, pl. 12, text fig. 1, figs. 7, 9, 10, 18, 127, 204–206, 209; Presented in the Temple, 9, 35–45, 53, 54, 55, 86–88, 89, 100, 144, 152, 153, 154, 175–176, 180–181, 218, 228, 229, 242, pl. 20, figs. 13, 23–25, 32, 132; relatives of, 31; Resurrection of, 58, 71, 72, 136, 179, 199; as royal judge, 195–197, 202, 209; as ruler, 119–121; at Second Coming of, 10, 60, 62–69, 70–72, 75, 80–81, 83–86, 88, 89, 90, 96, 97, 103, 108, 119, 120, 128–130, 135, 161–162, 166, 184, 189, 194, 206, 217, 236, 239, 244, pl. 10; Transfiguration of, 10–11, 70; Women at the Tomb of, 57–58, 159, 161, 219, 227, 229, 243, 267–268, pl. 22, figs. 44–47, 147, 211. *See also* cornerstone; matrimonial symbolism

Christe, Y., 64

Christmas, 9, 34, 68, 69, 165; blessing for, 25; Octave of, 9, 30–35, 45, 159; Office, 22, 25, 53; Office for vigil of, 25; vigil of, 165

Clayton, M., 124 n.99

cloud, 55, 216–217, 224, 242; at the Annunciation, 10–17,

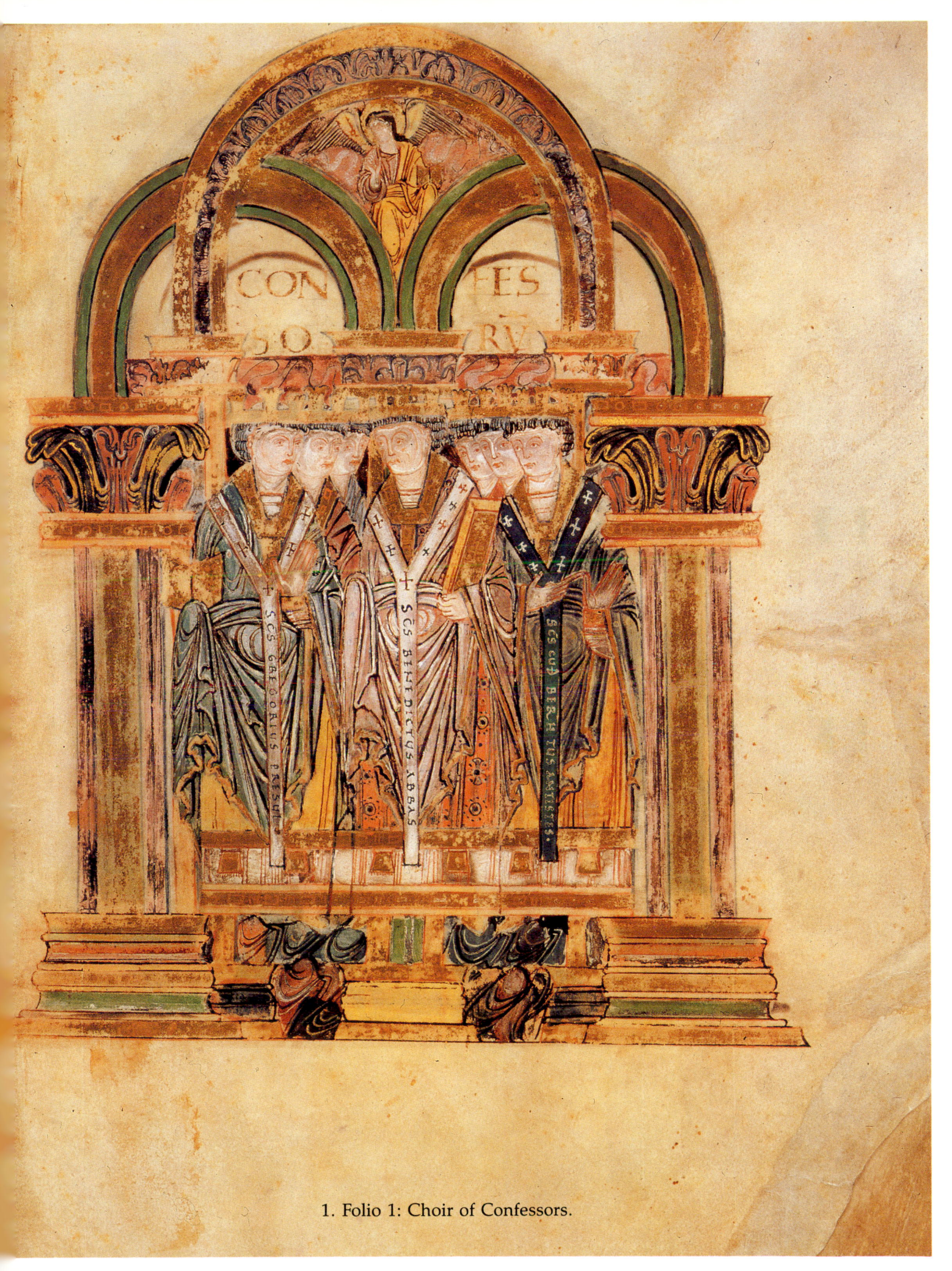

1. Folio 1: Choir of Confessors.

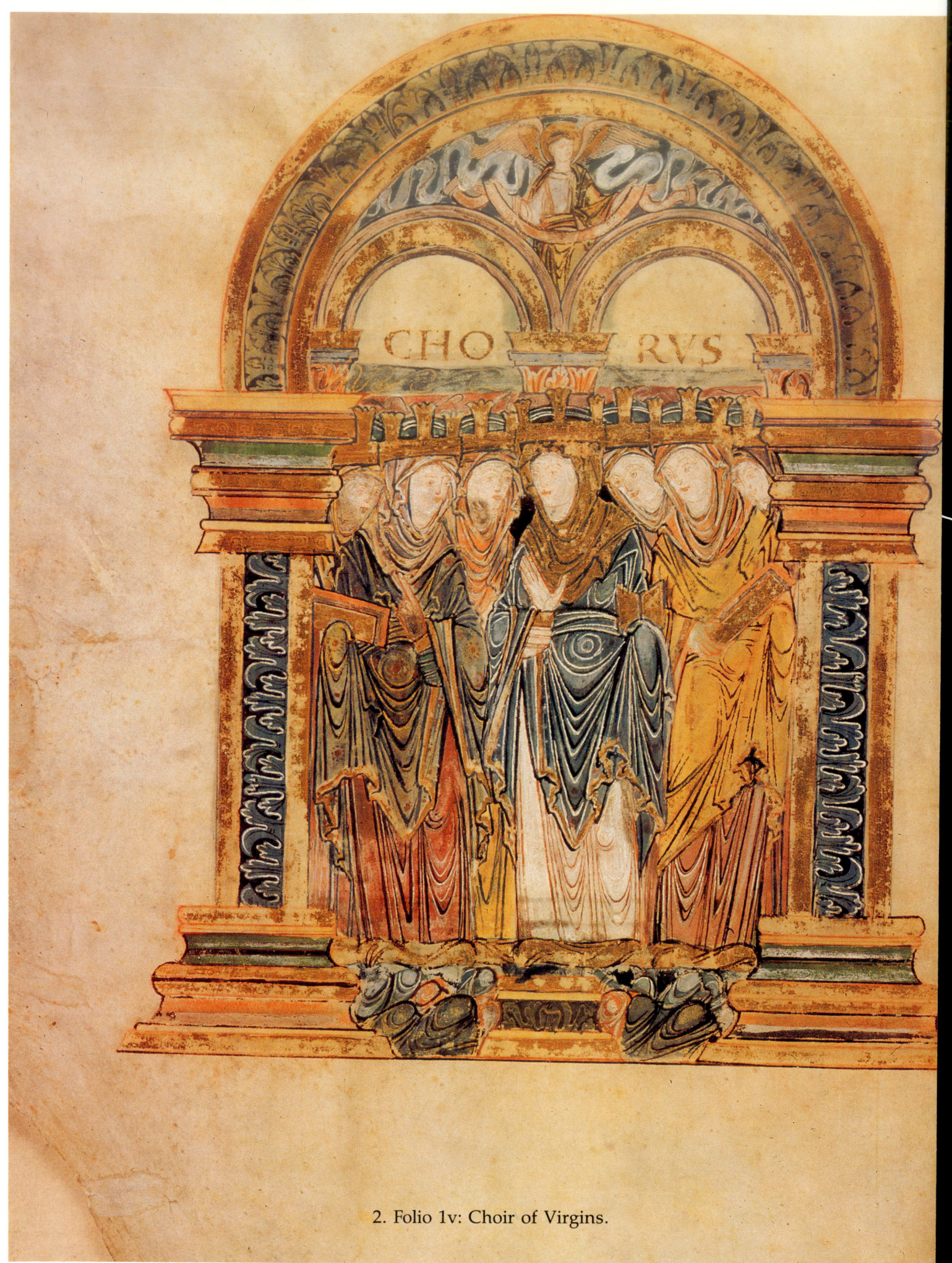

2. Folio 1v: Choir of Virgins.

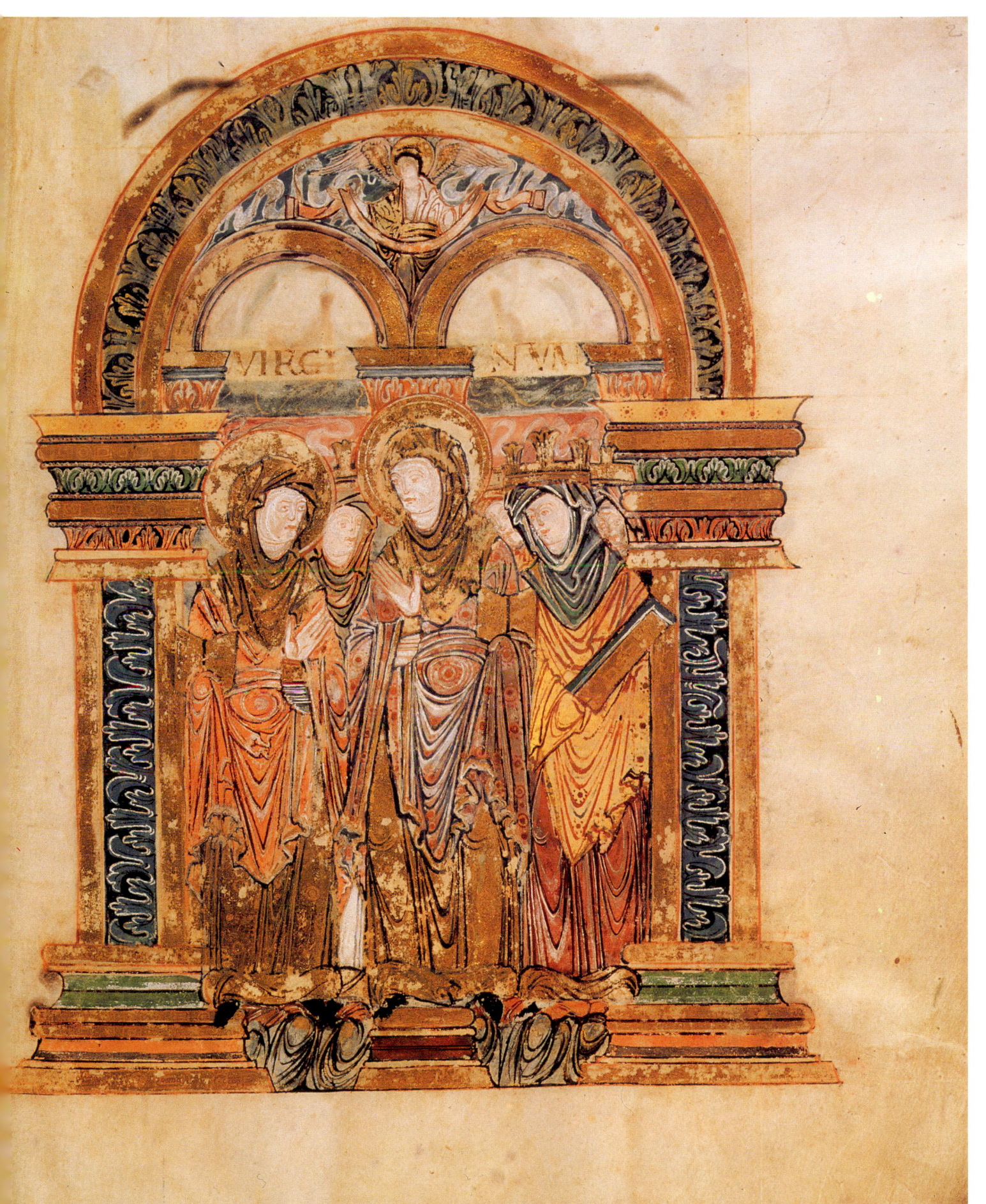

3. Folio 2: Choir of Virgins.

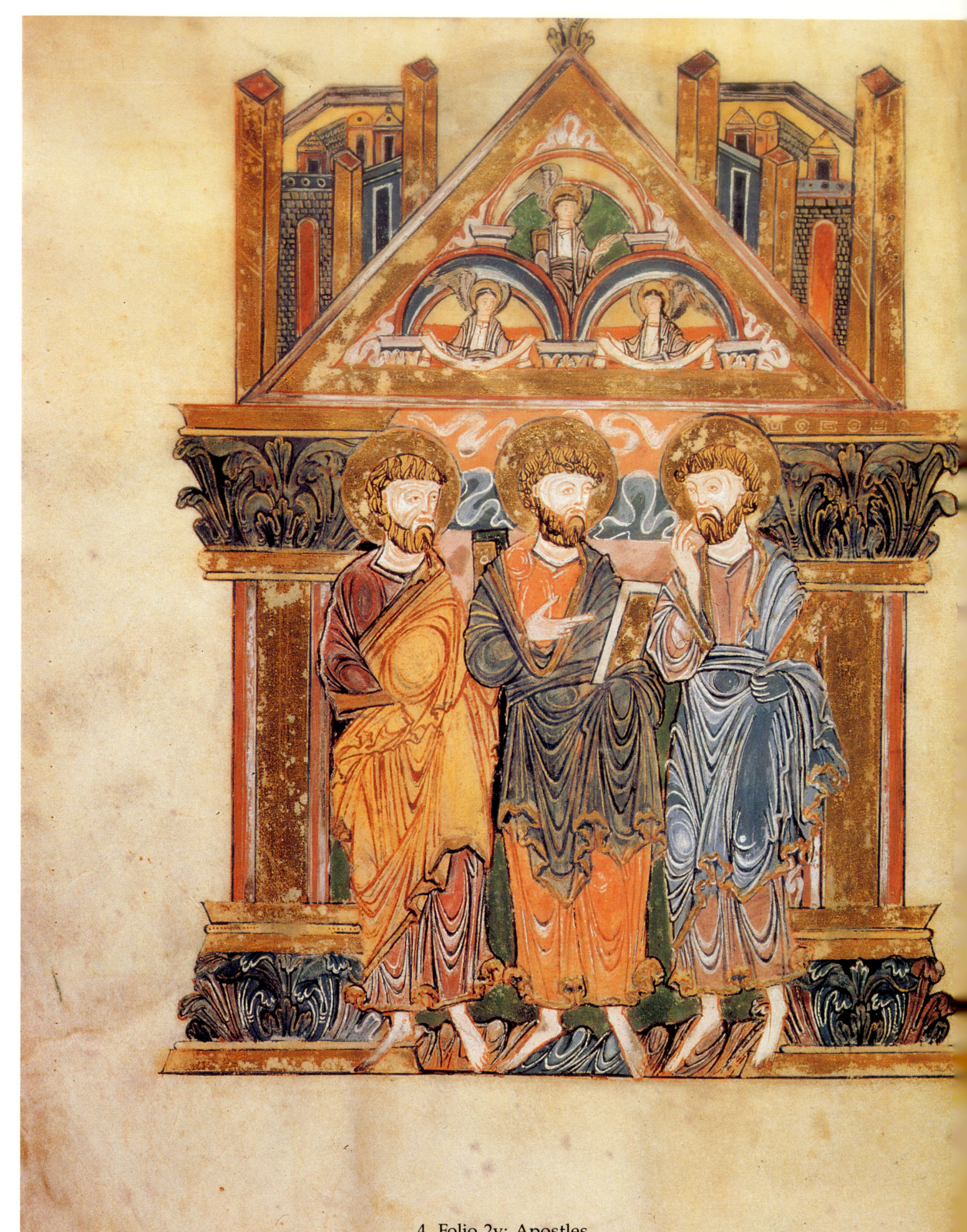

4. Folio 2v: Apostles.

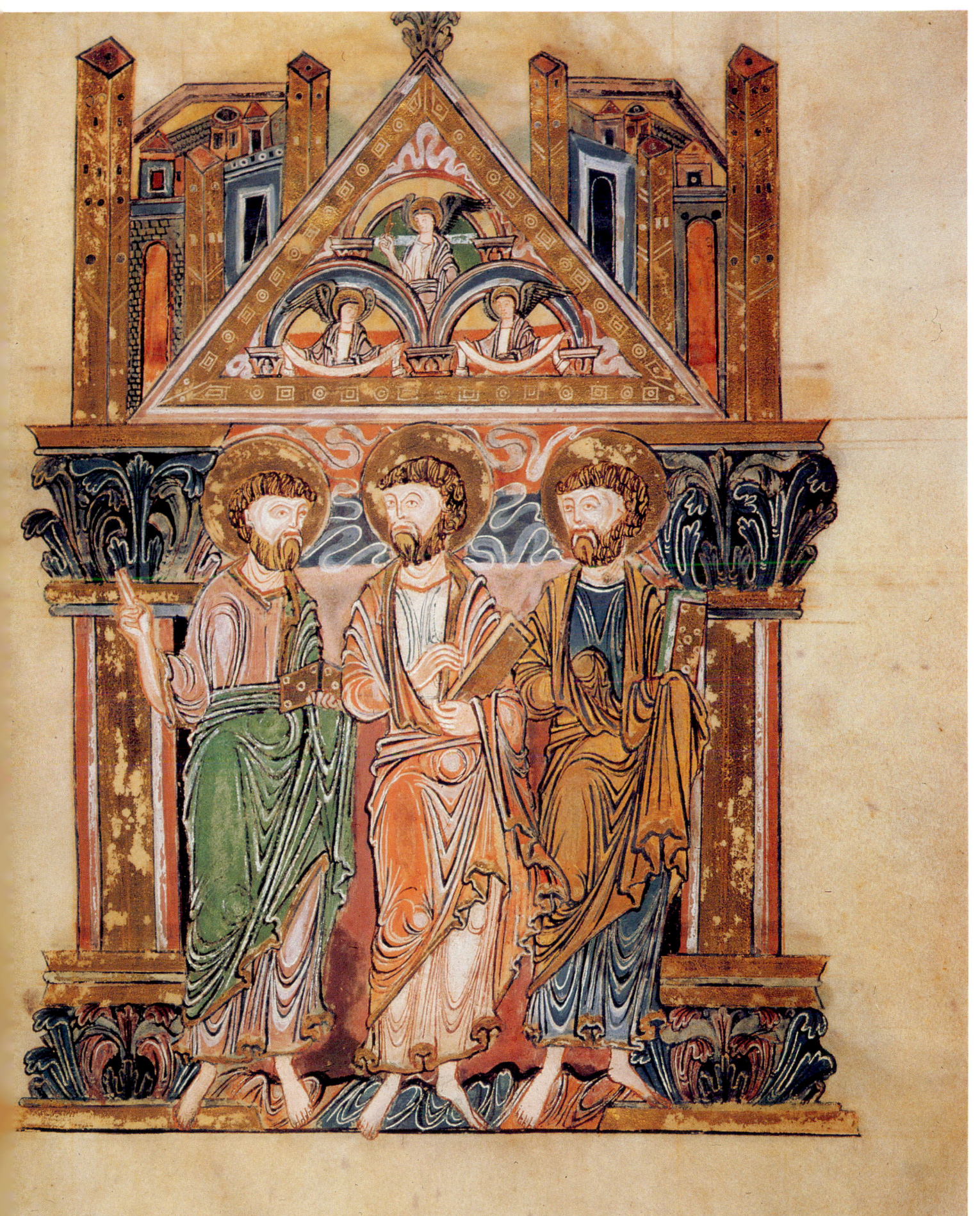

5. Folio 3: Apostles.

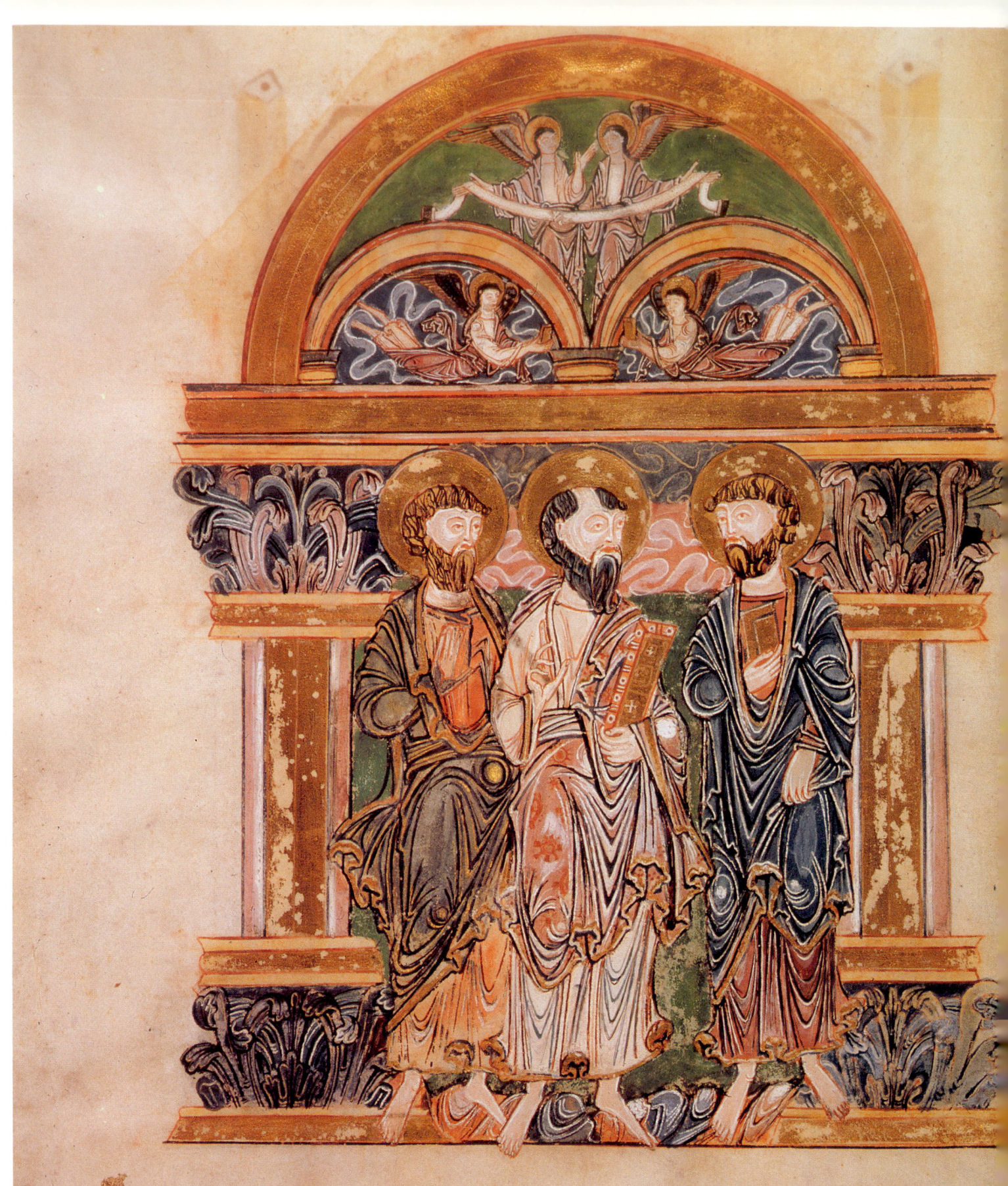

6. Folio 3v: Apostles.

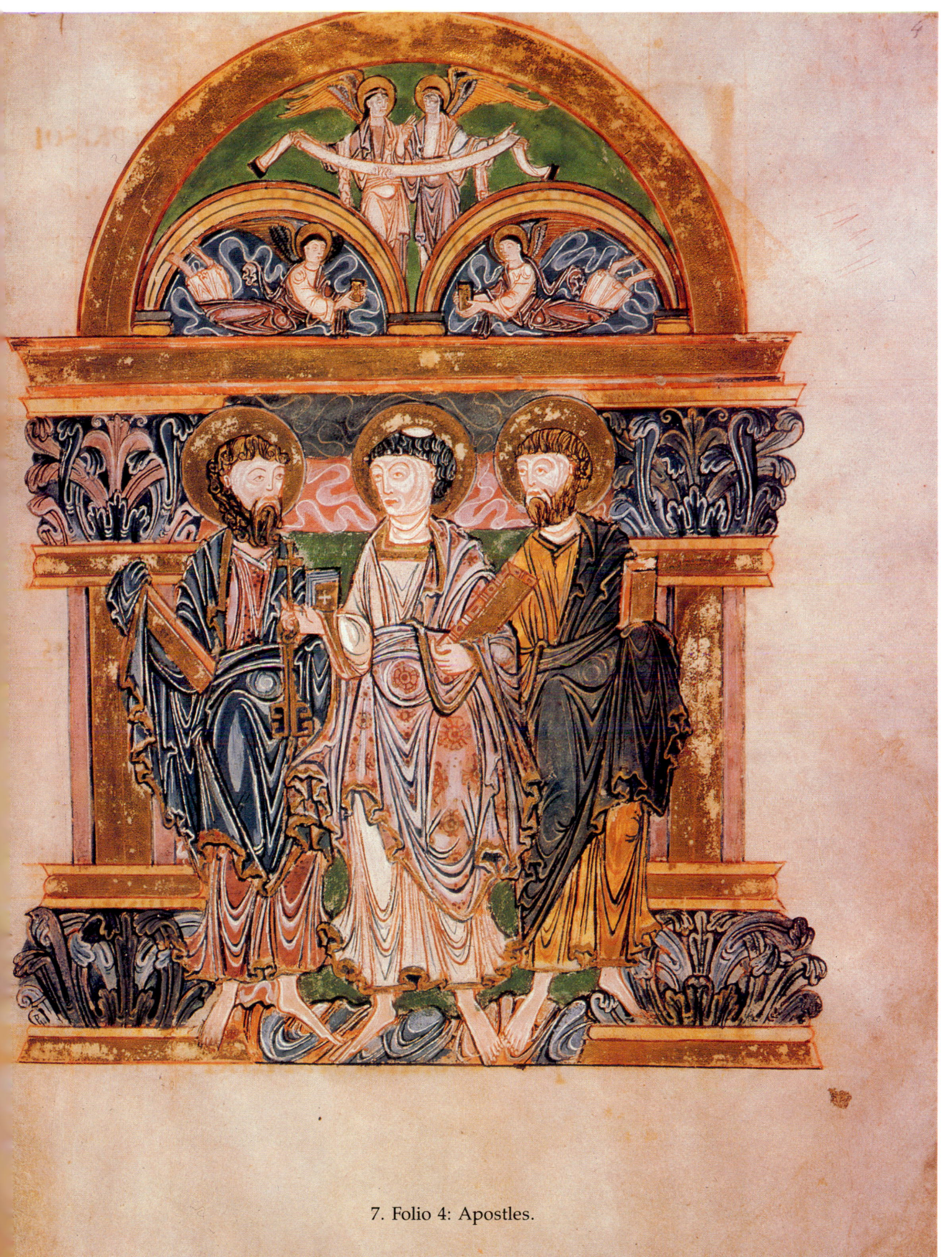

7. Folio 4: Apostles.

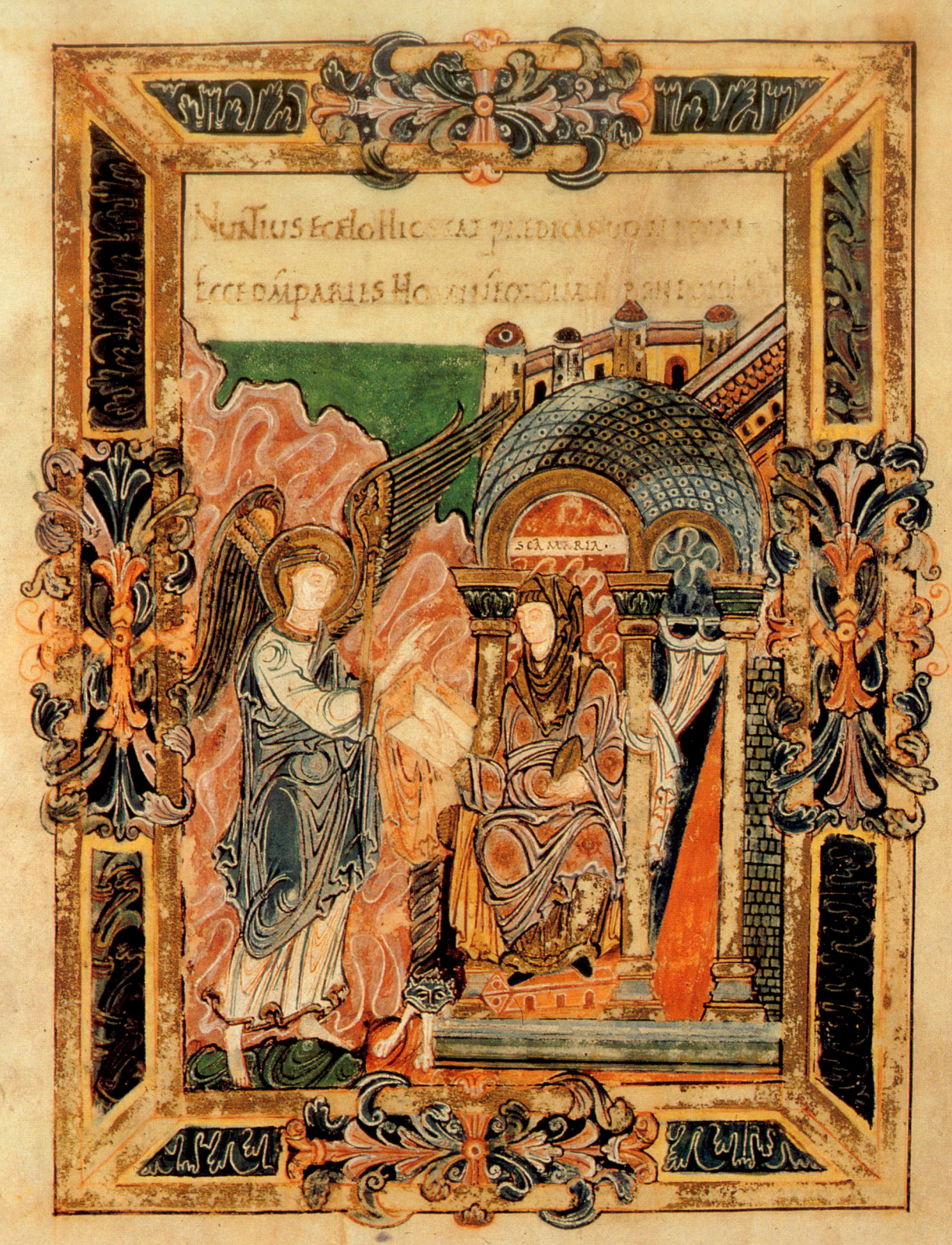

8. Folio 5v: Annunciation.

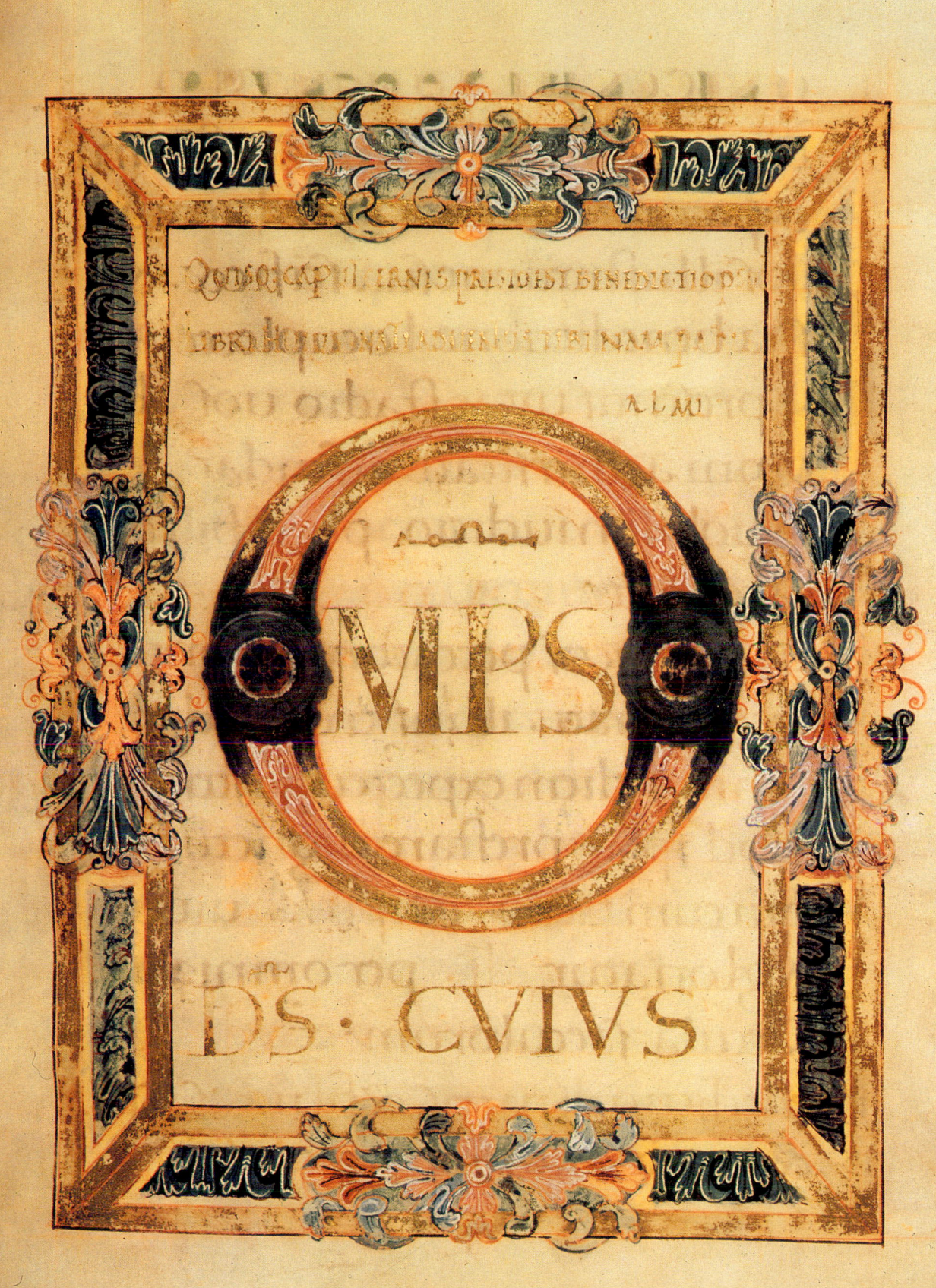

9. Folio 6: initial page.

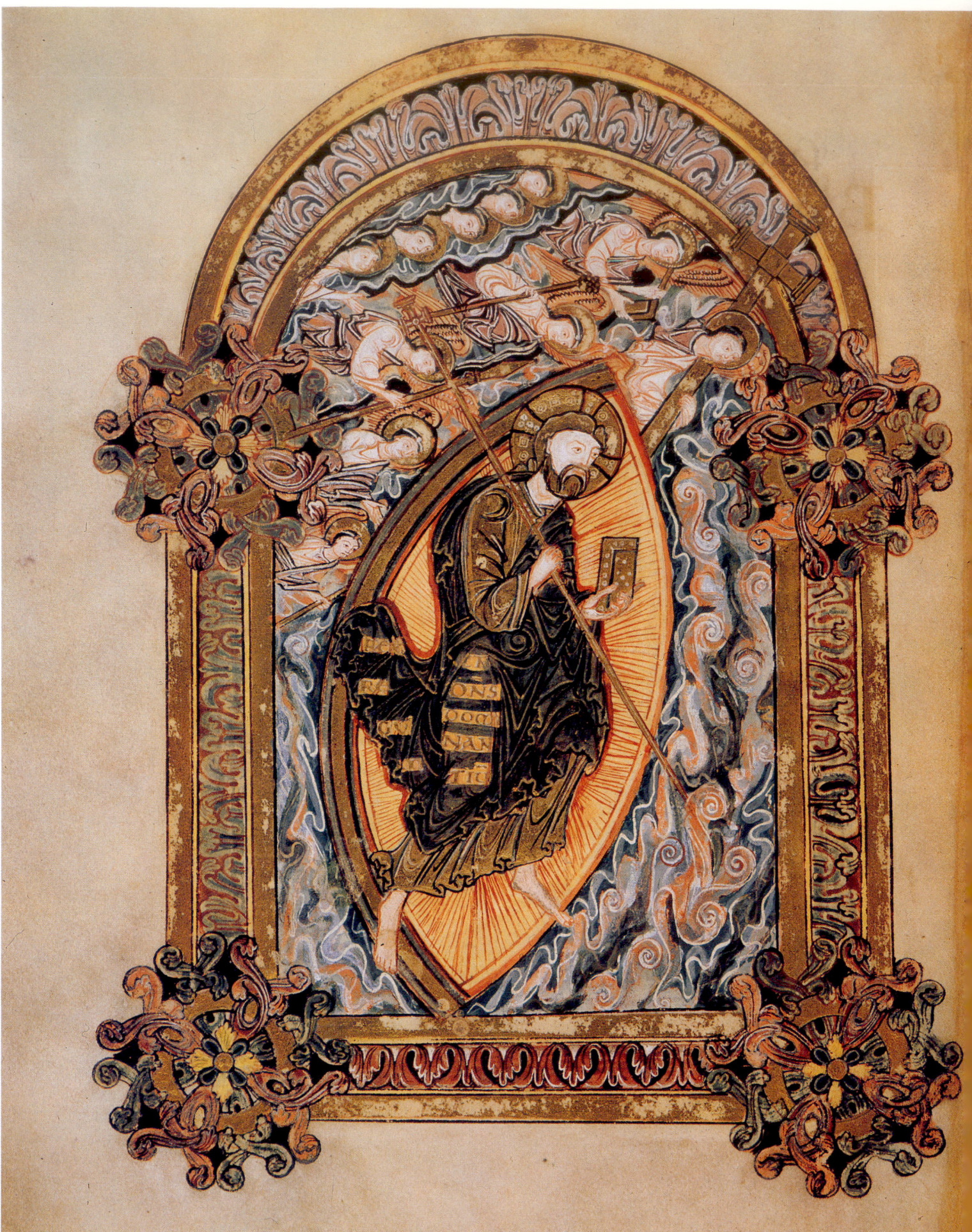

10. Folio 9v: Second Coming.

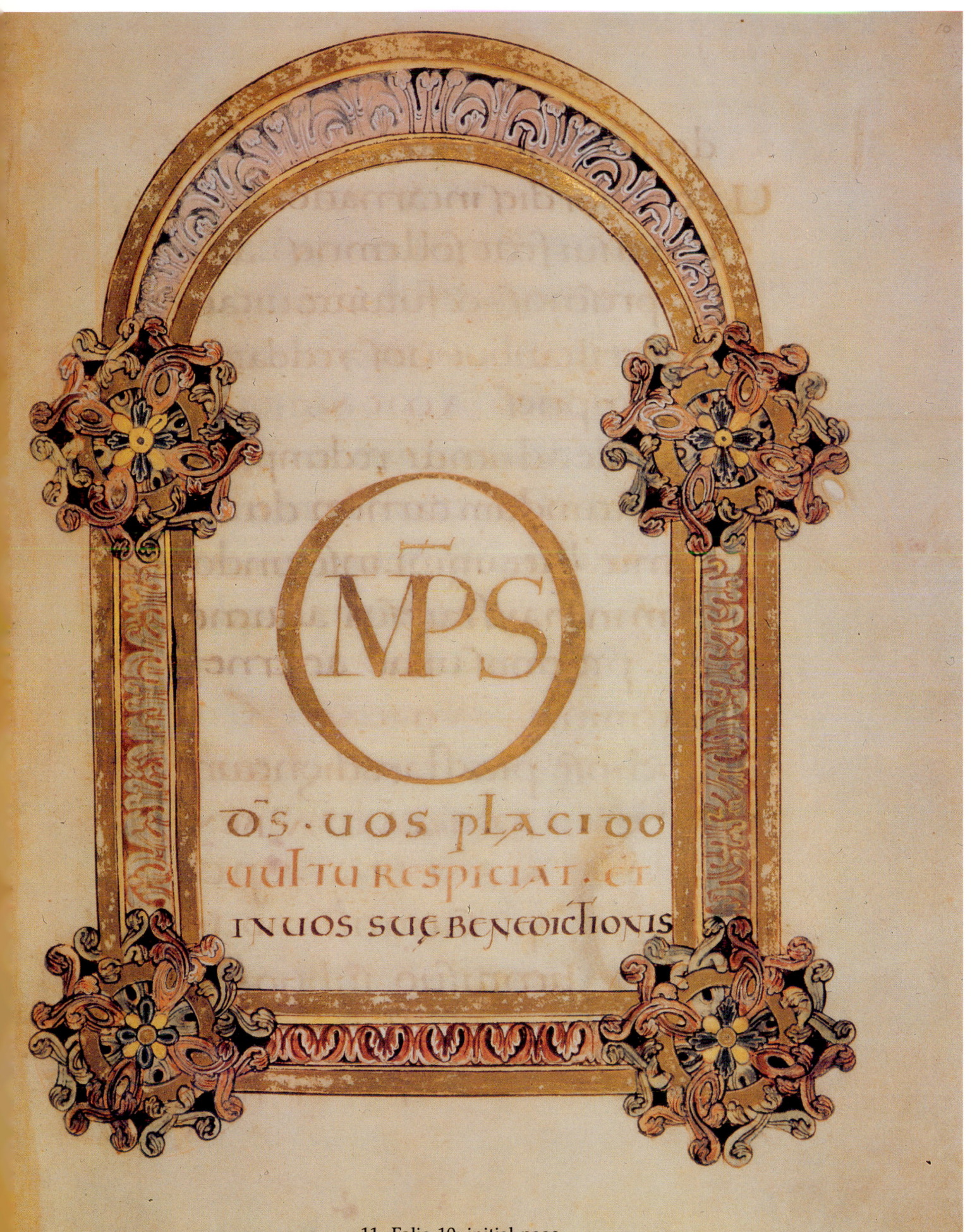

11. Folio 10: initial page.

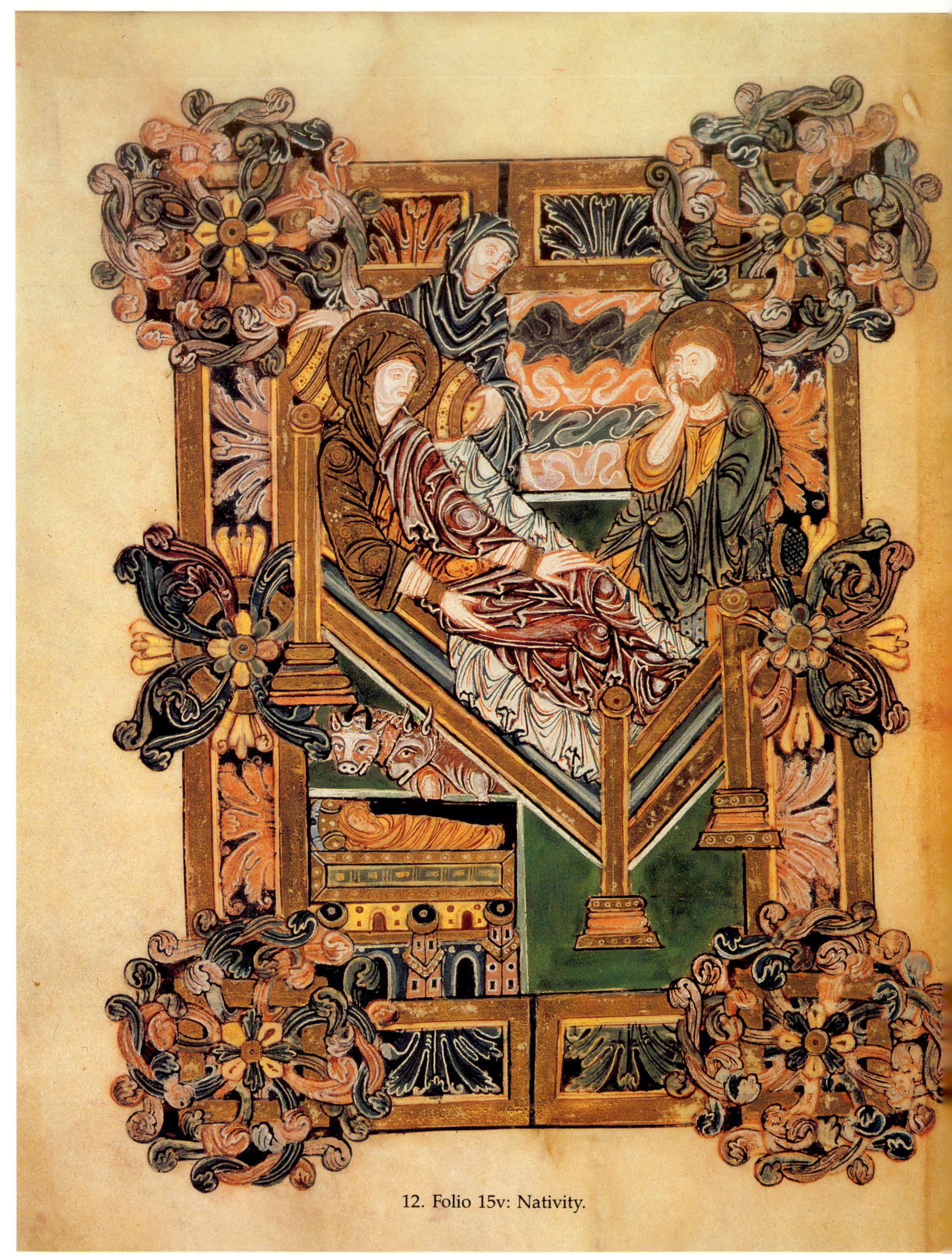

12. Folio 15v: Nativity.

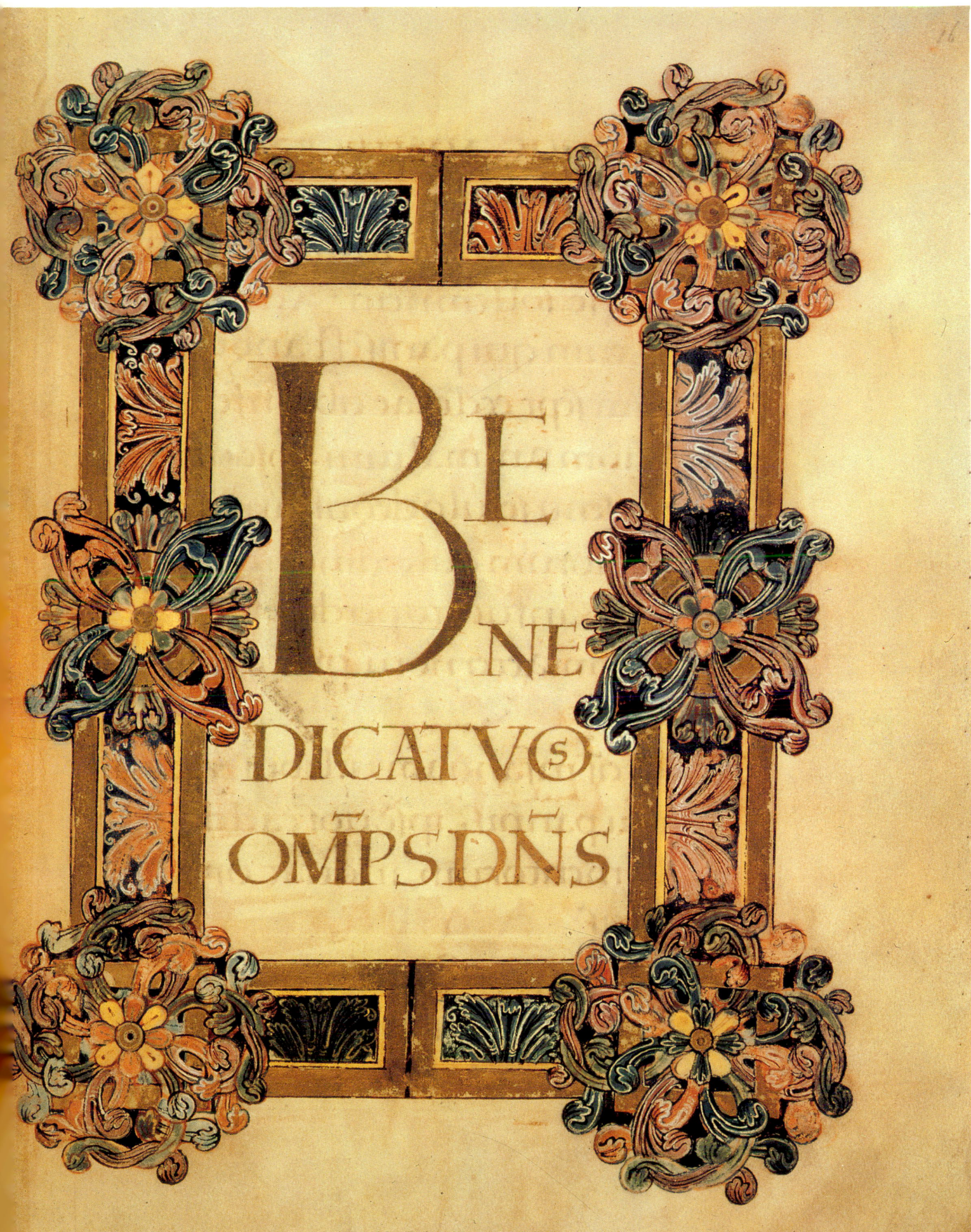

13. Folio 16: initial page.

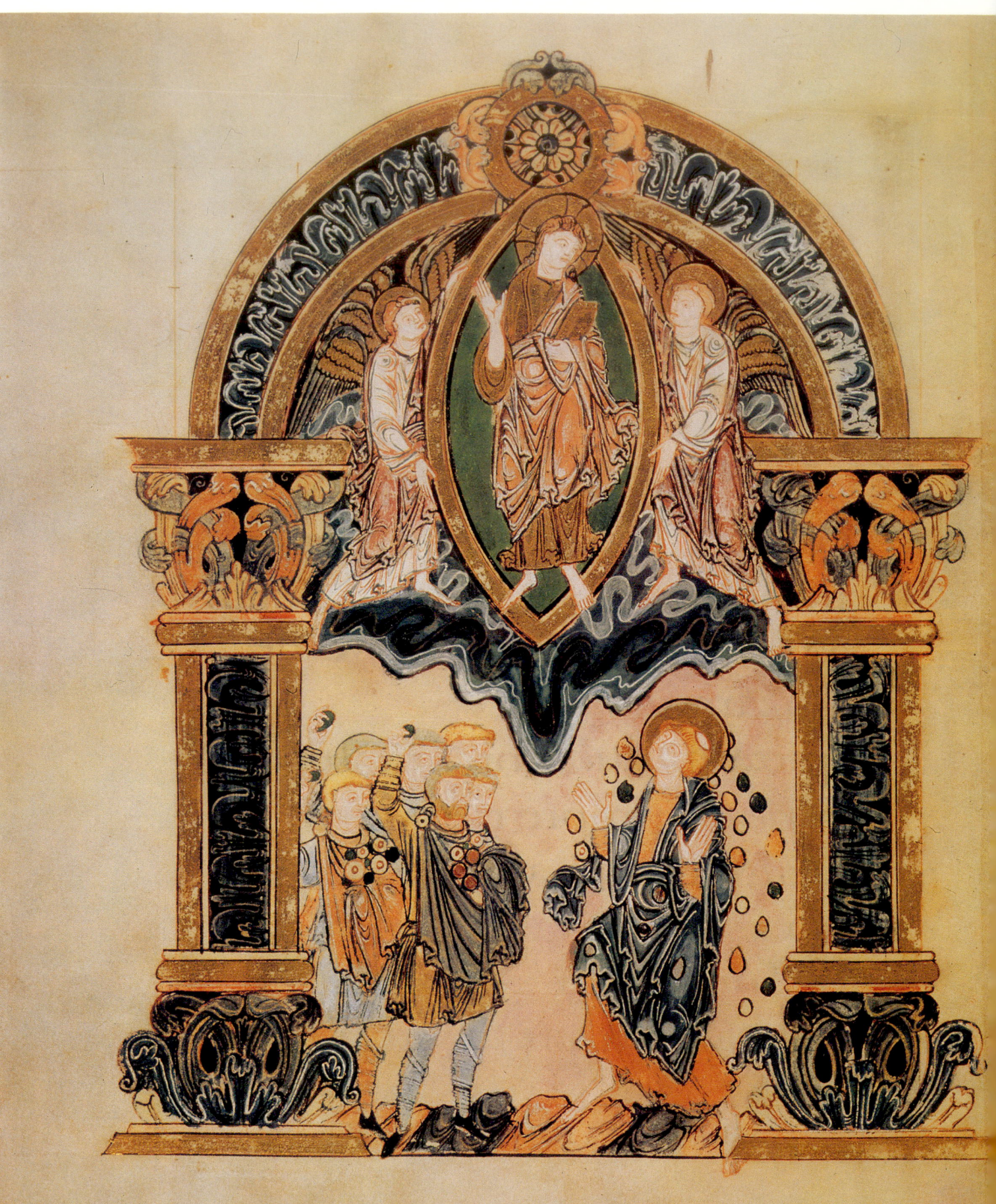

14. Folio 17v: Martyrdom of St. Stephen.

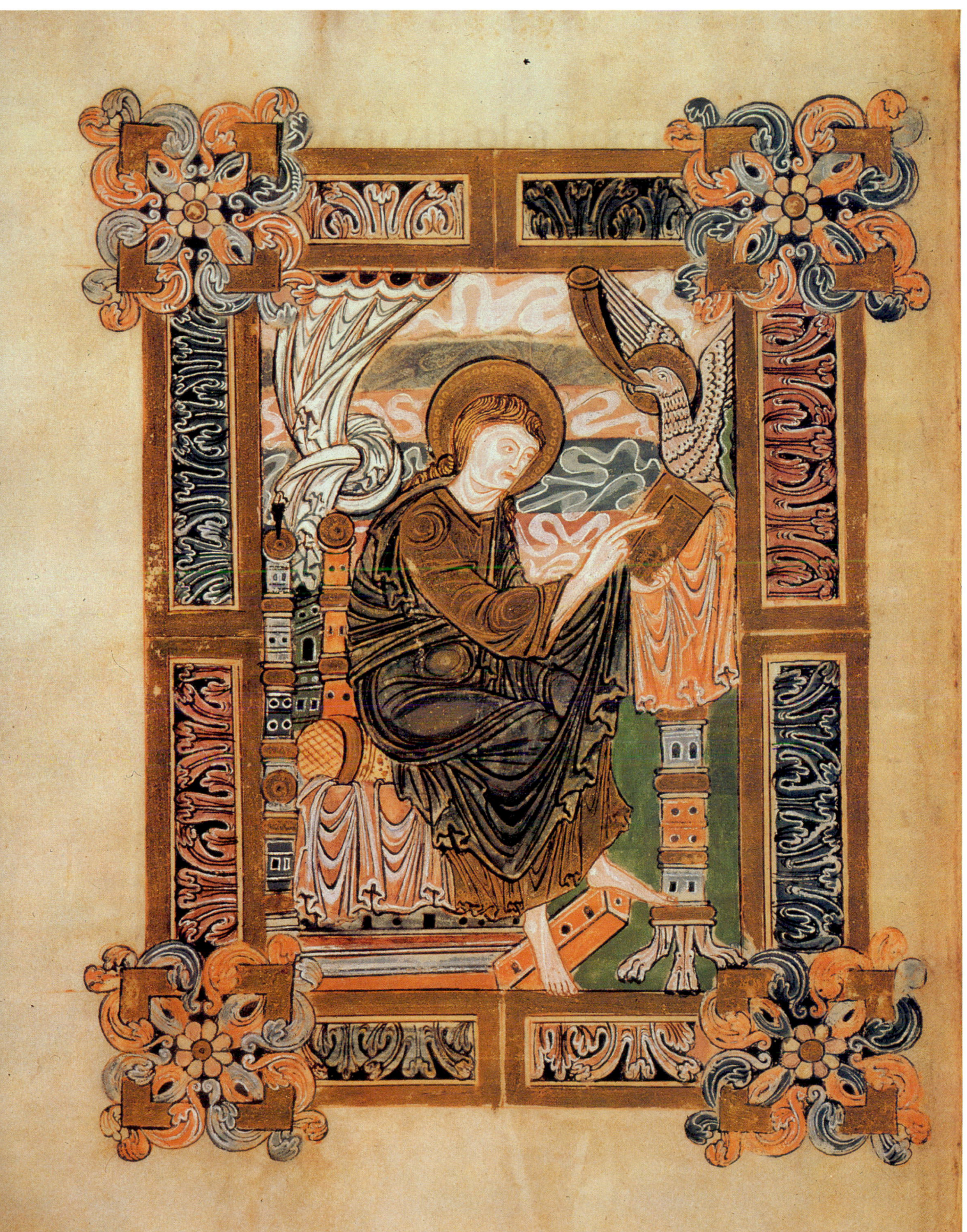

15. Folio 19v: John the evangelist.

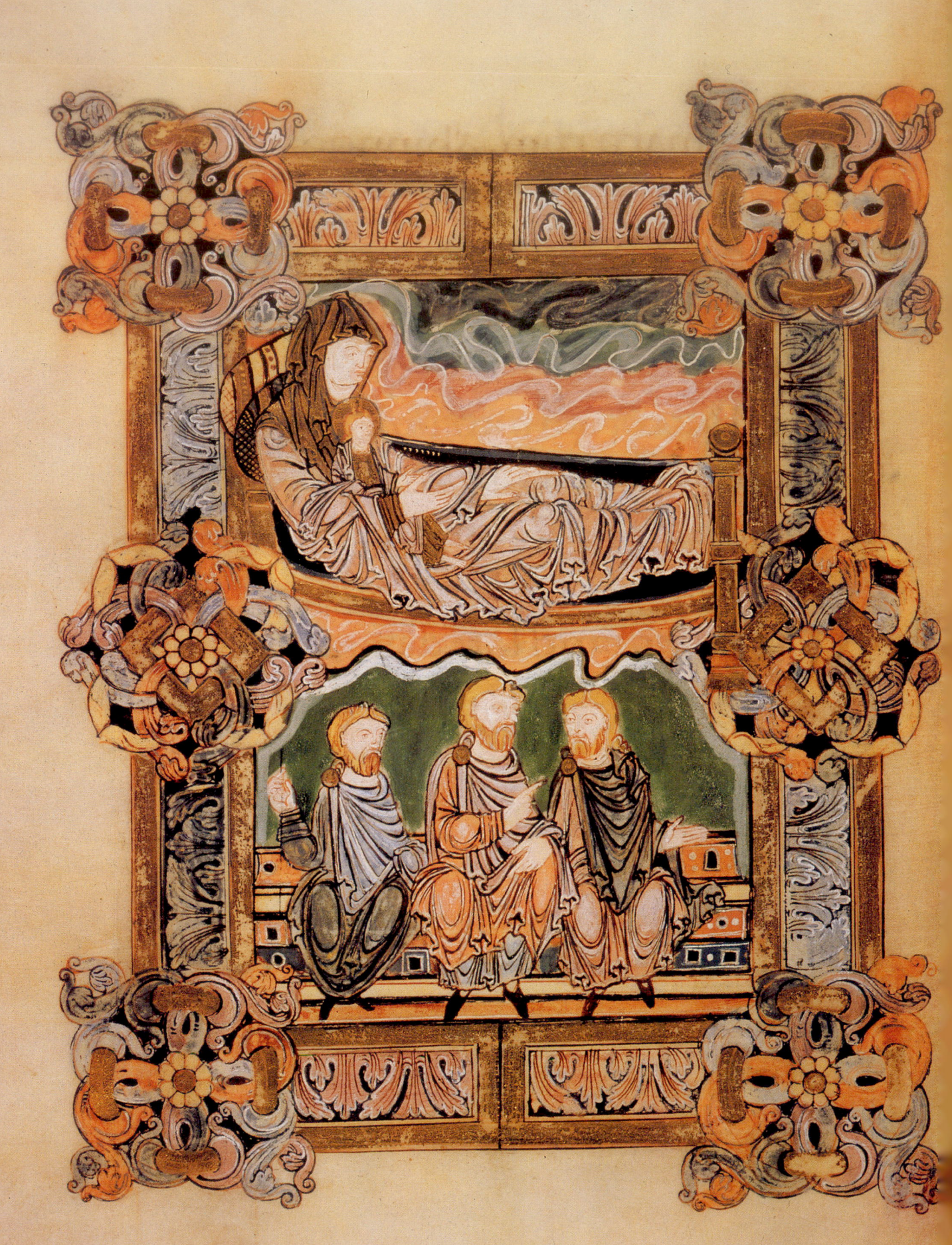

16. Folio 22v: Naming of Christ.

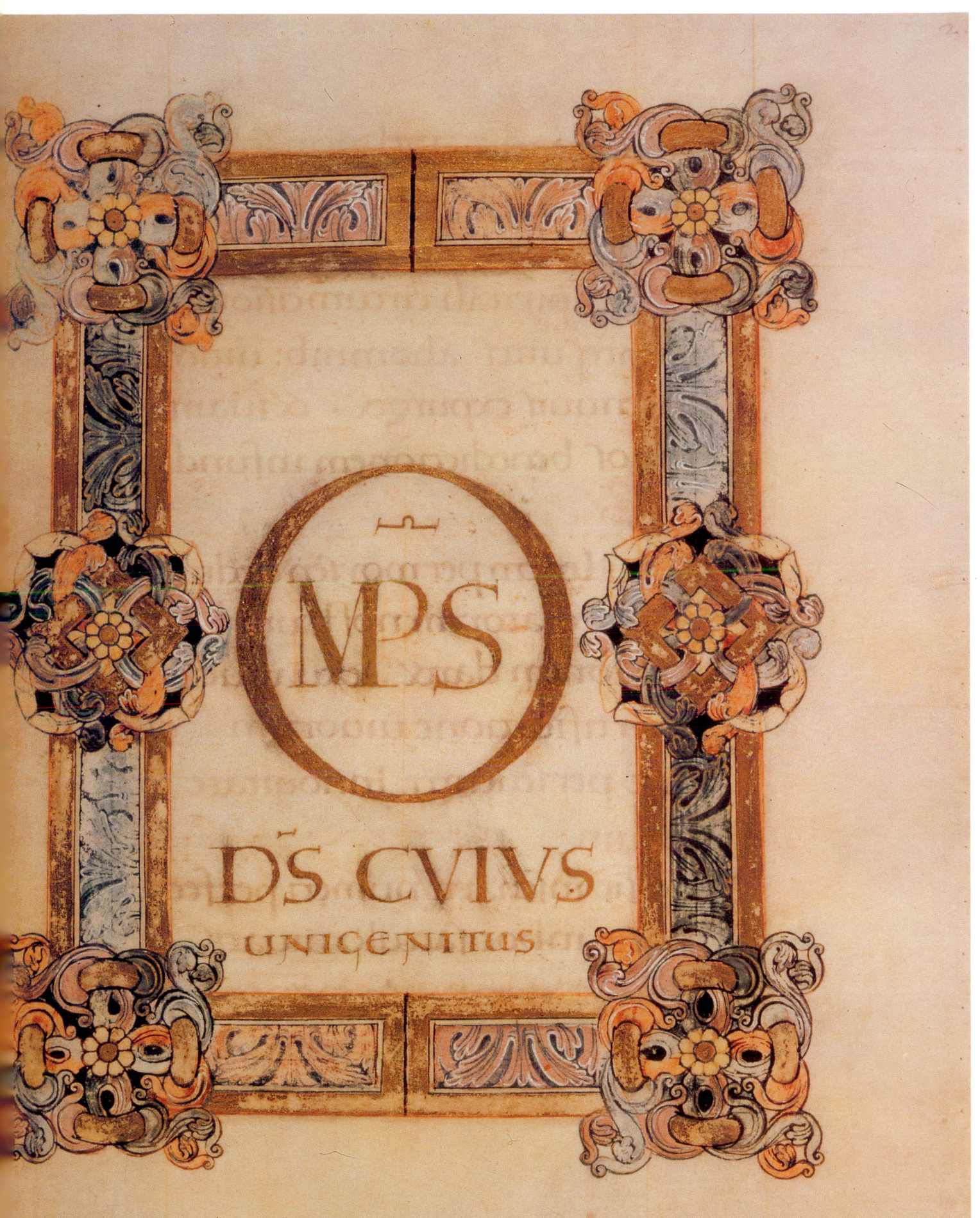

17. Folio 23: initial page.

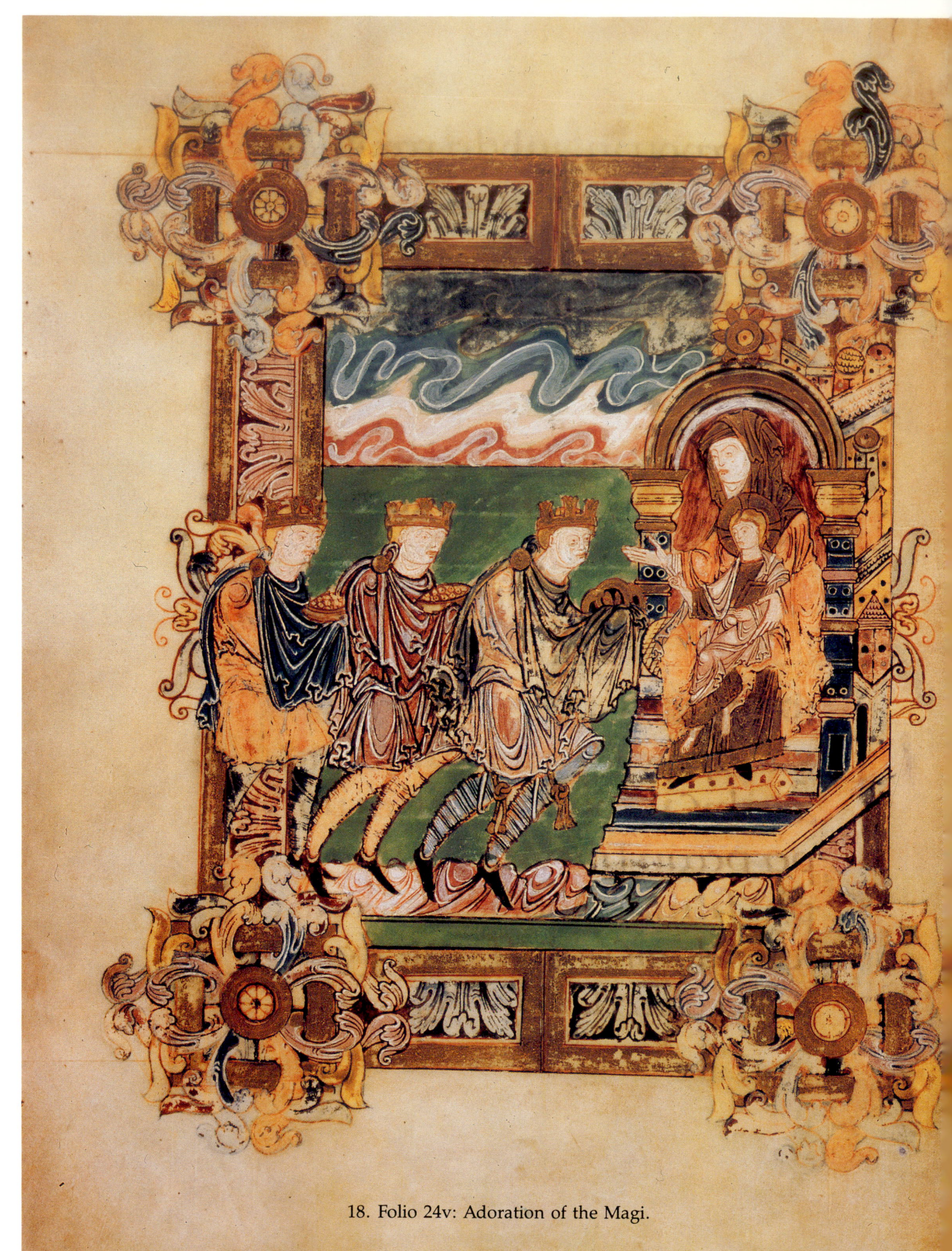

18. Folio 24v: Adoration of the Magi.

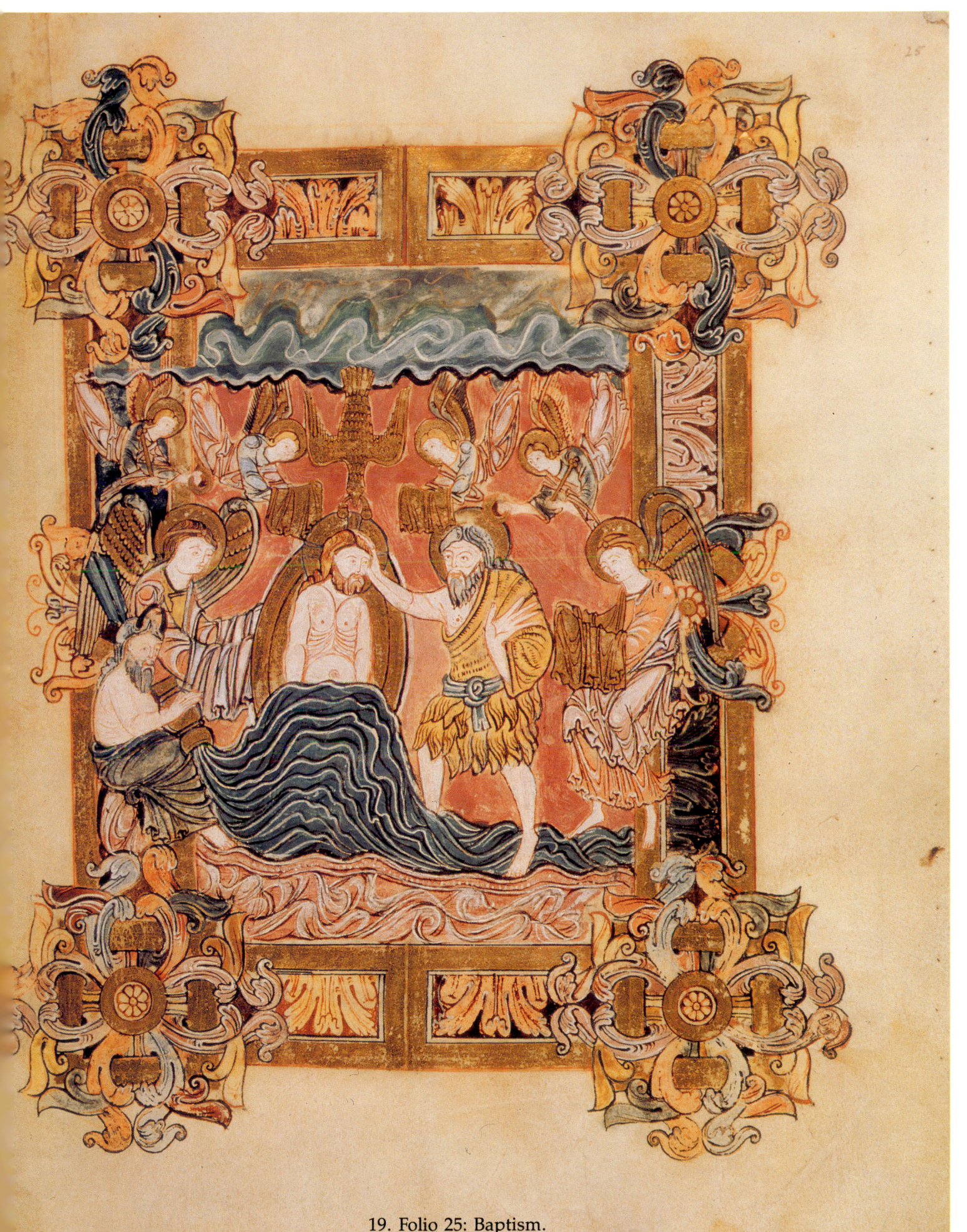

19. Folio 25: Baptism.

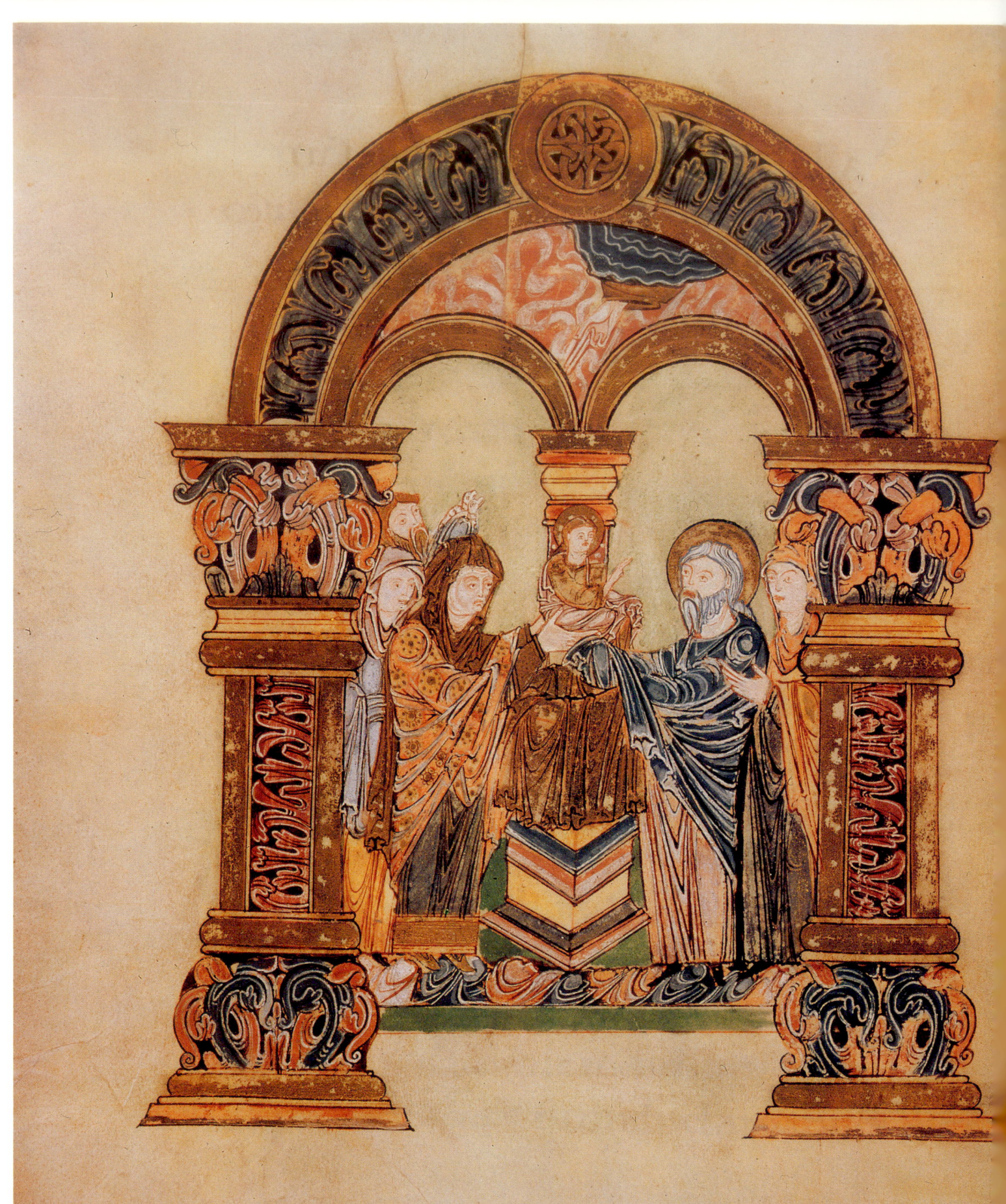

20. Folio 34v: Presentation in the Temple.

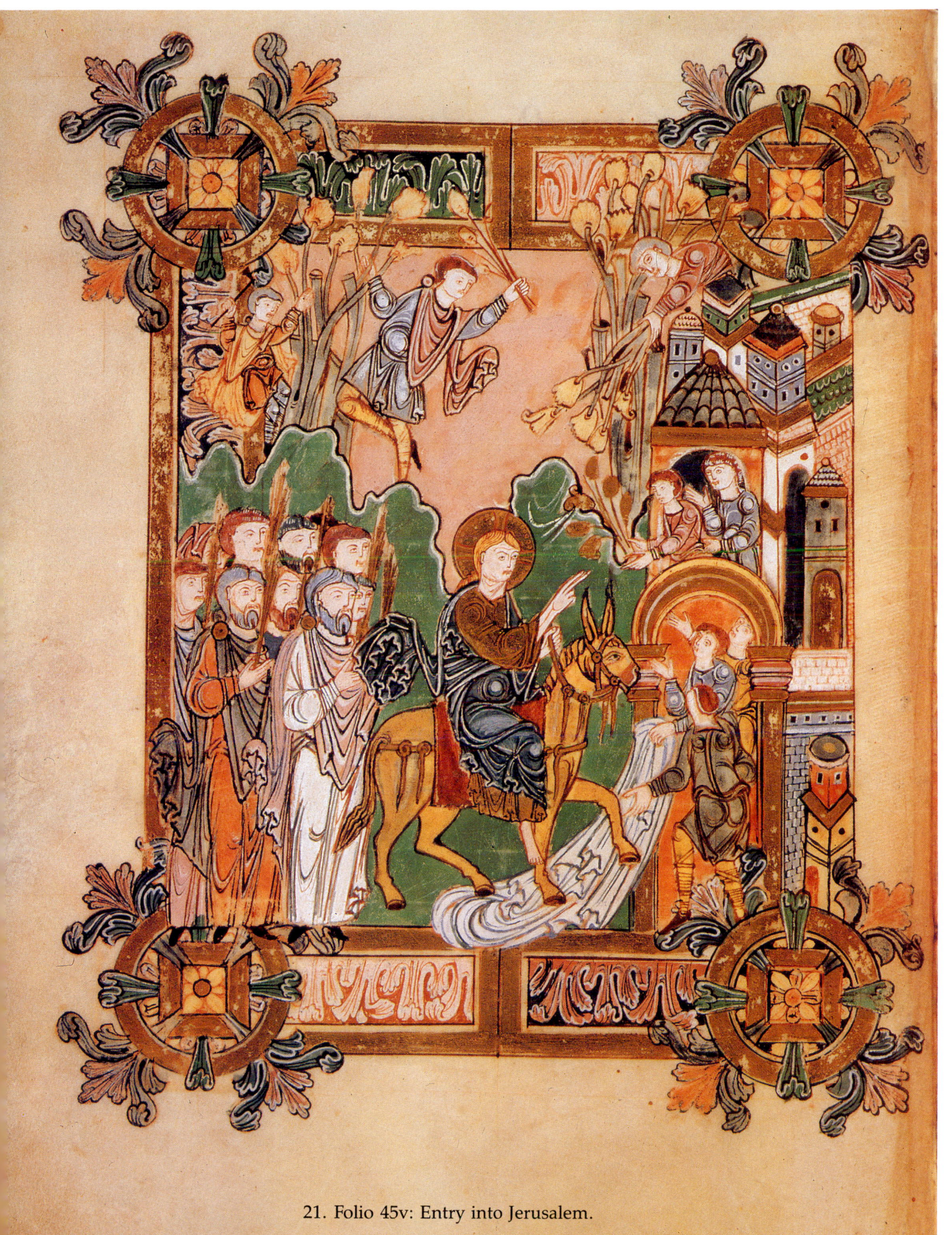

21. Folio 45v: Entry into Jerusalem.

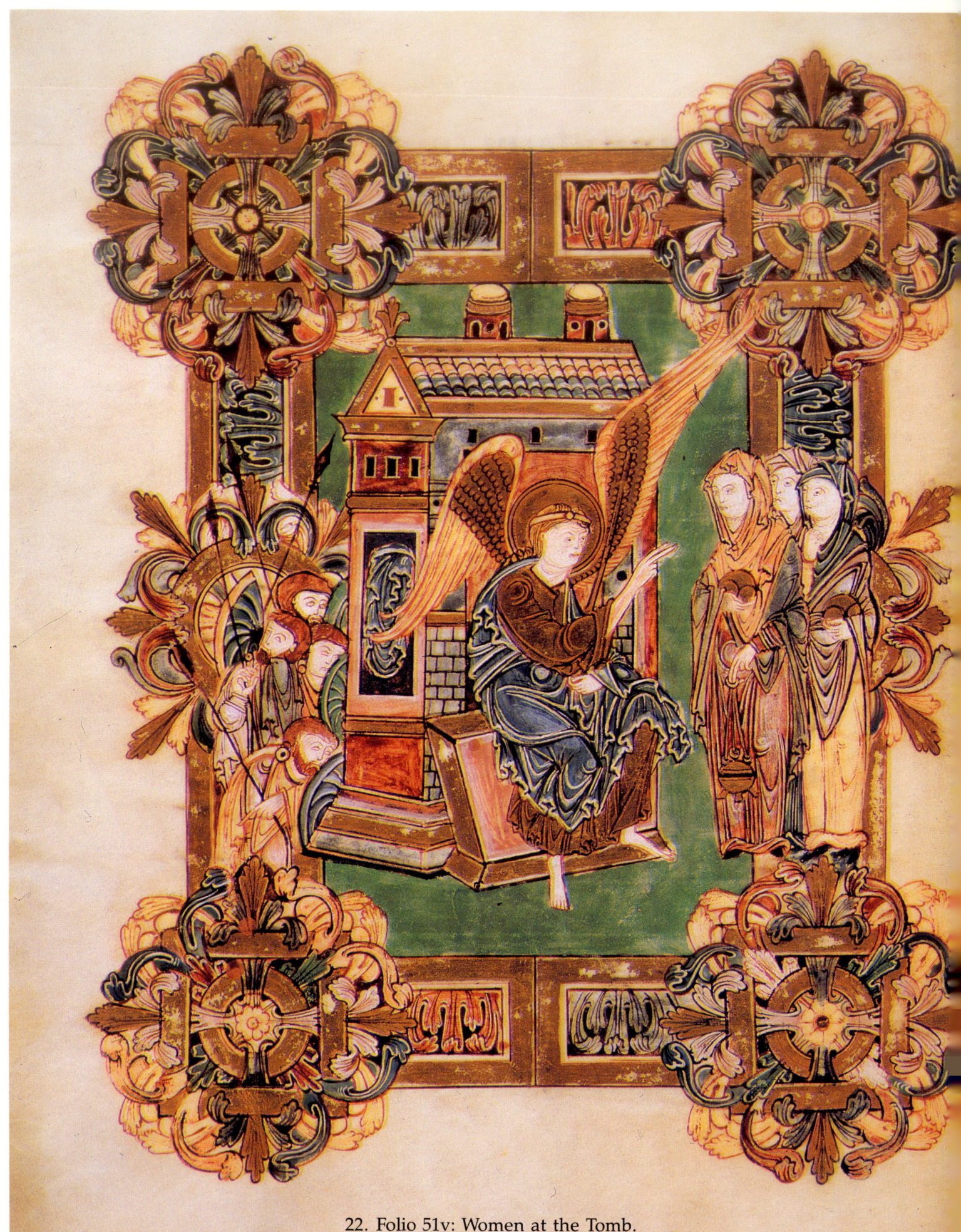

22. Folio 51v: Women at the Tomb.

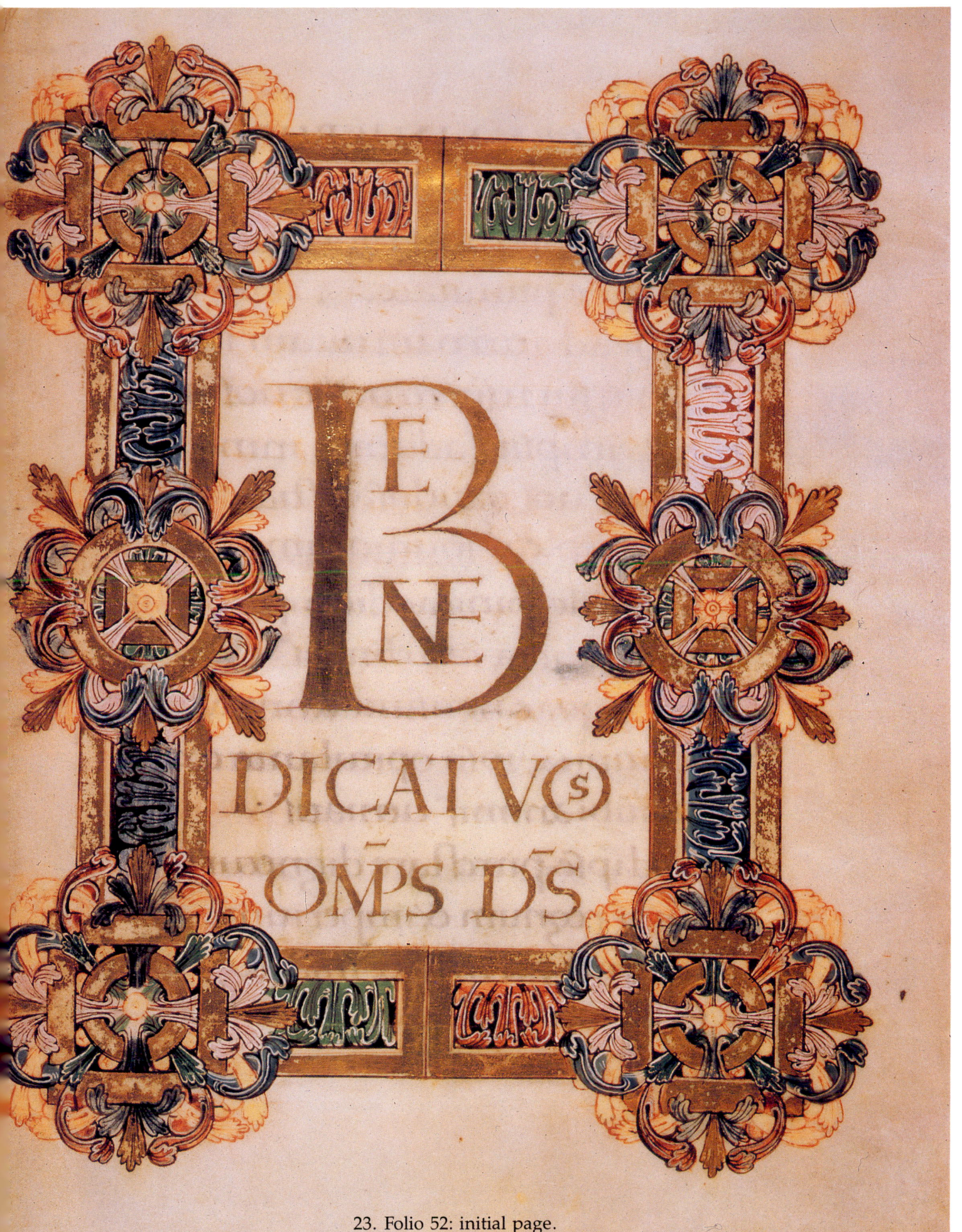

23. Folio 52: initial page.

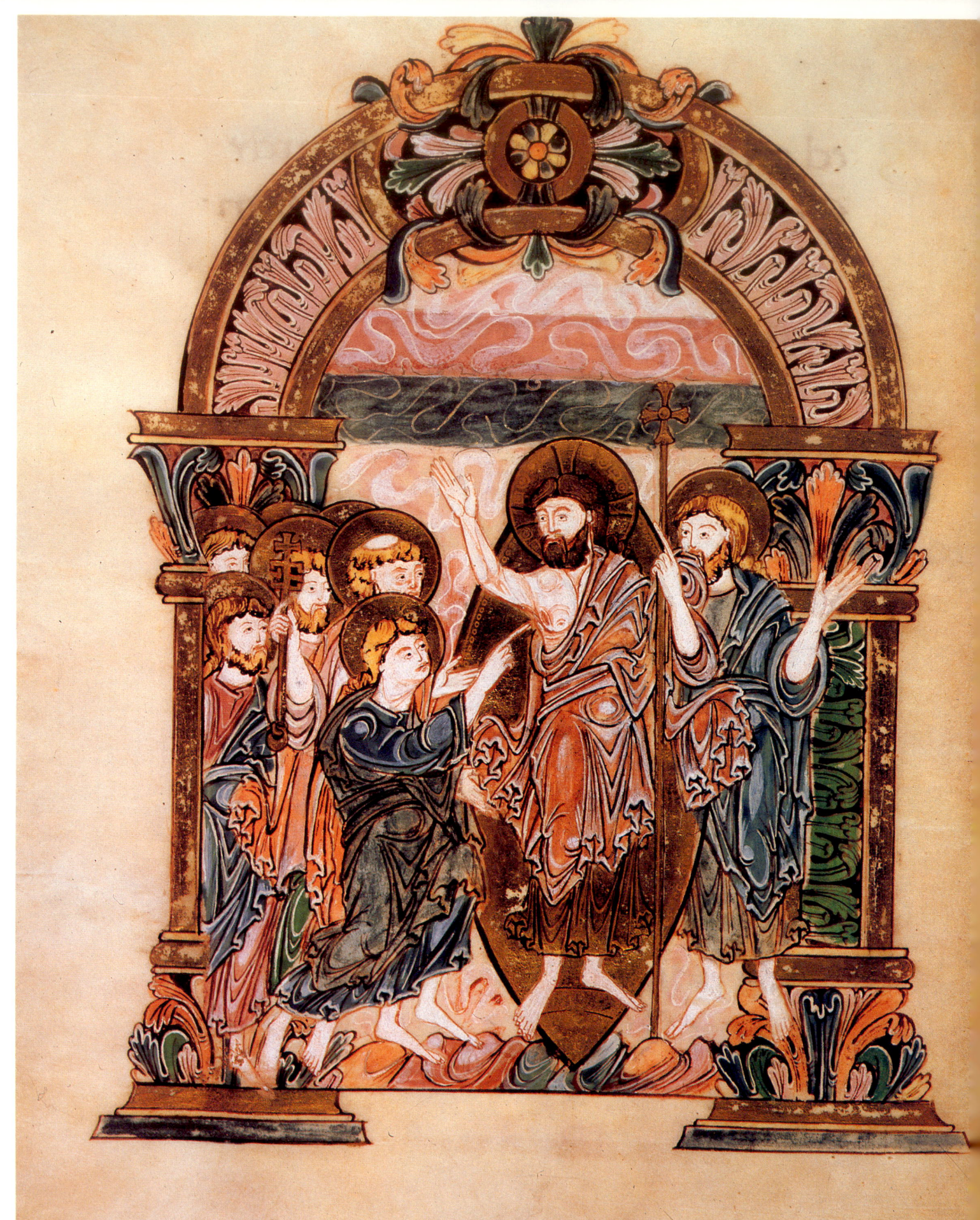

24. Folio 56v: Doubting of Thomas.

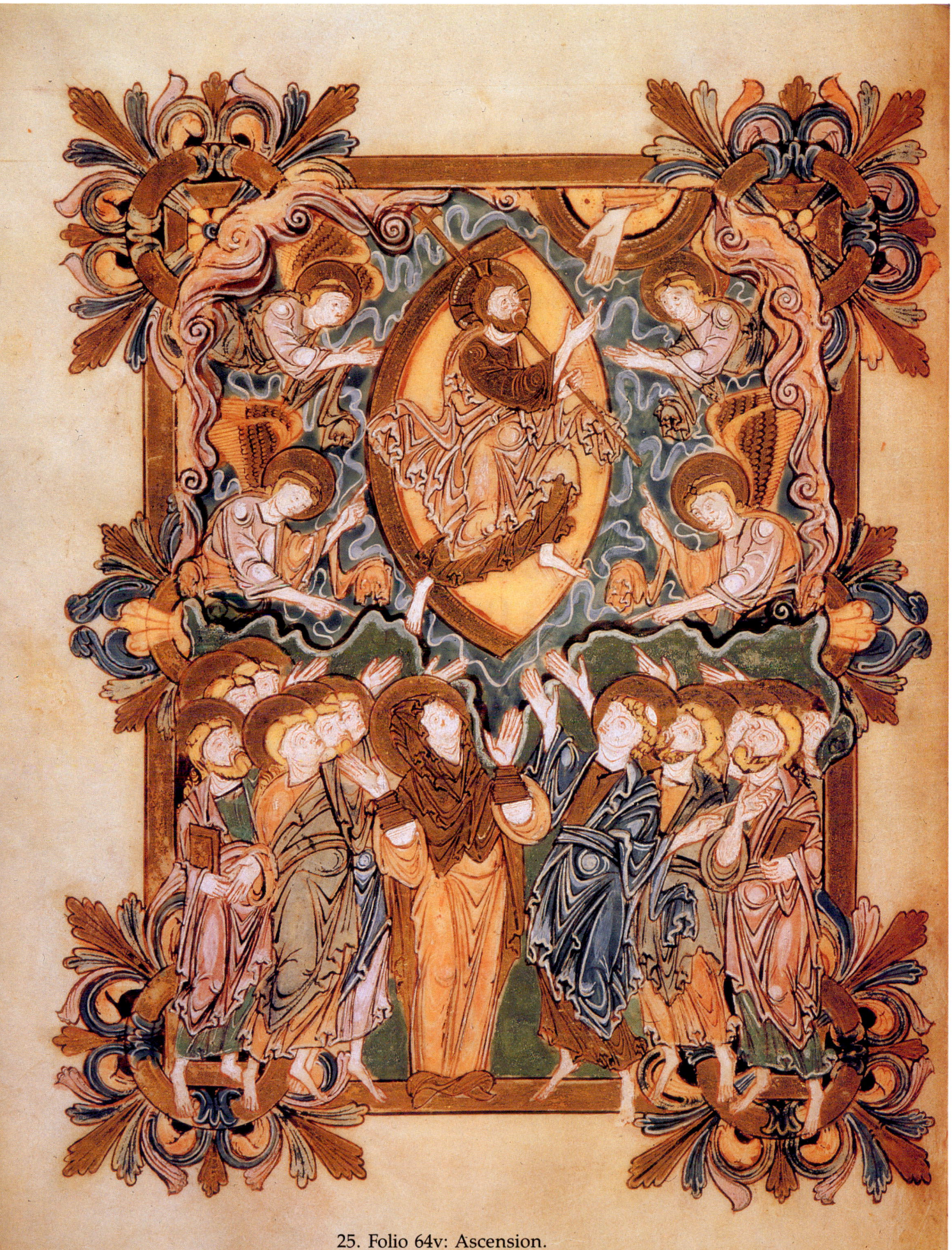

25. Folio 64v: Ascension.

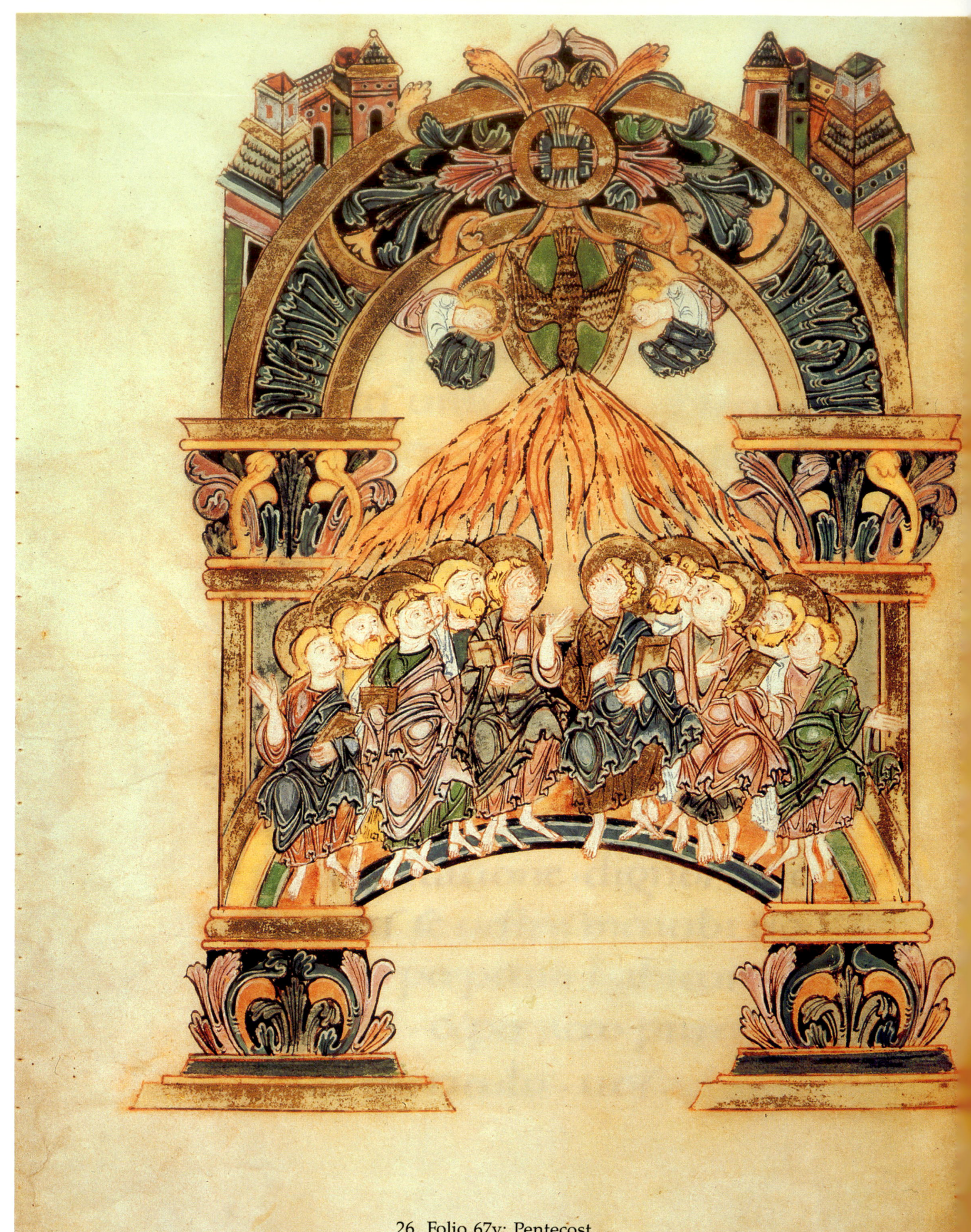

26. Folio 67v: Pentecost.

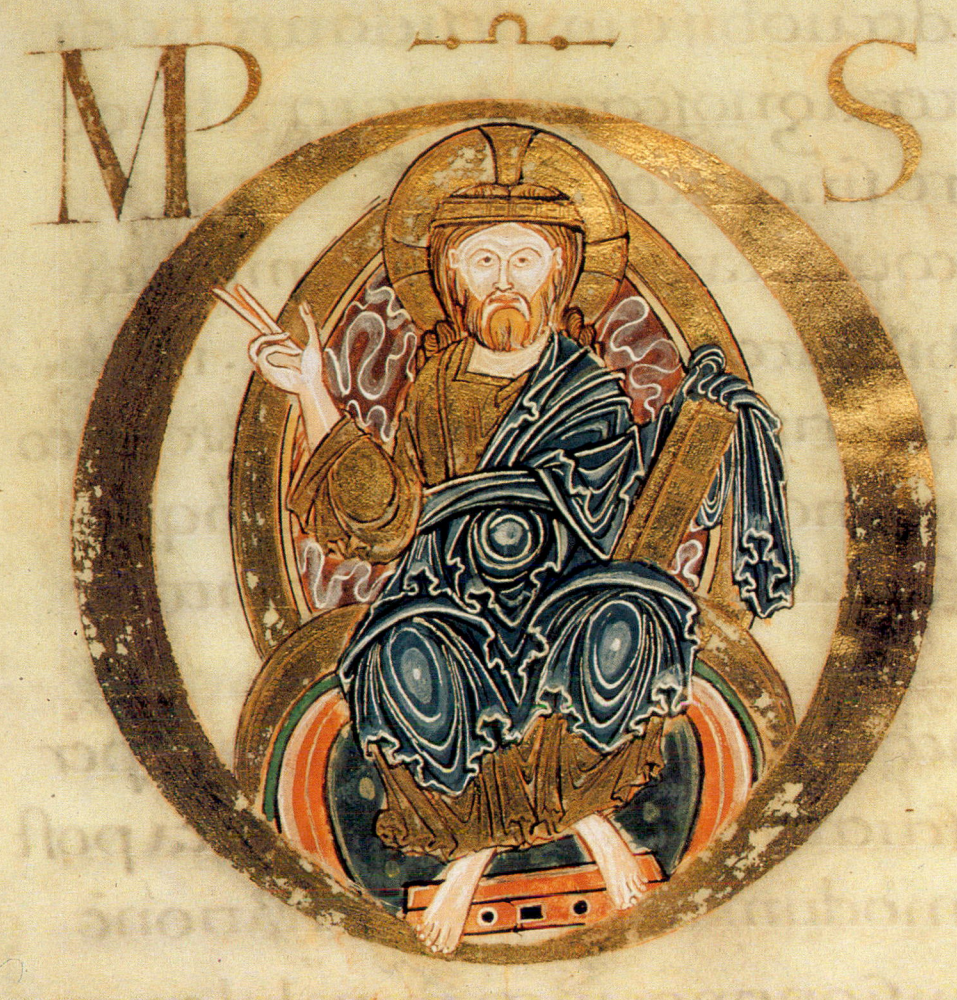

MP · n · S

TRINITAS
VNVS ET VERVS
DS · PATER ET FILIVS ET SSC ·

27. Folio 70: the Deity.

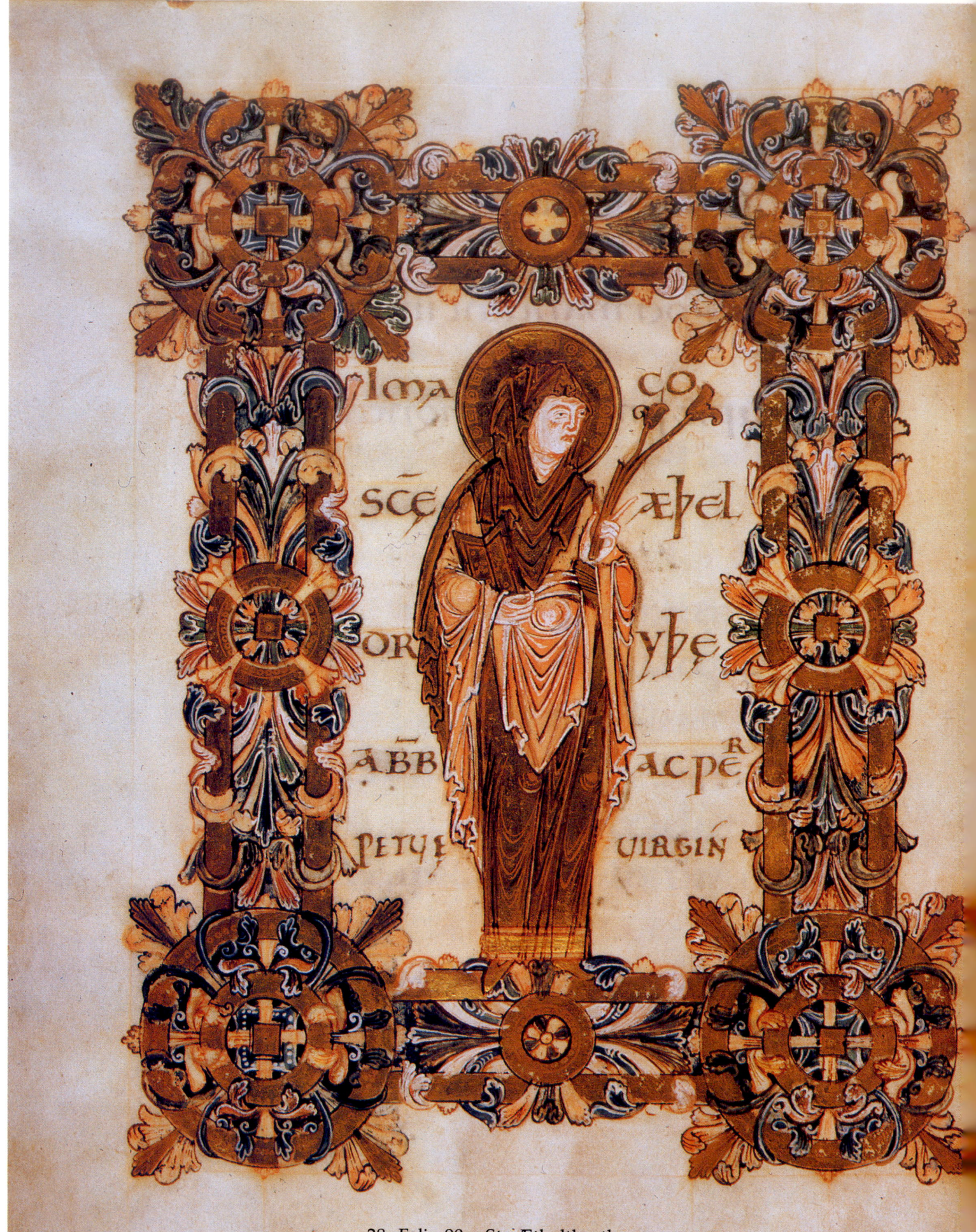

28. Folio 90v: St. Æthelthryth.

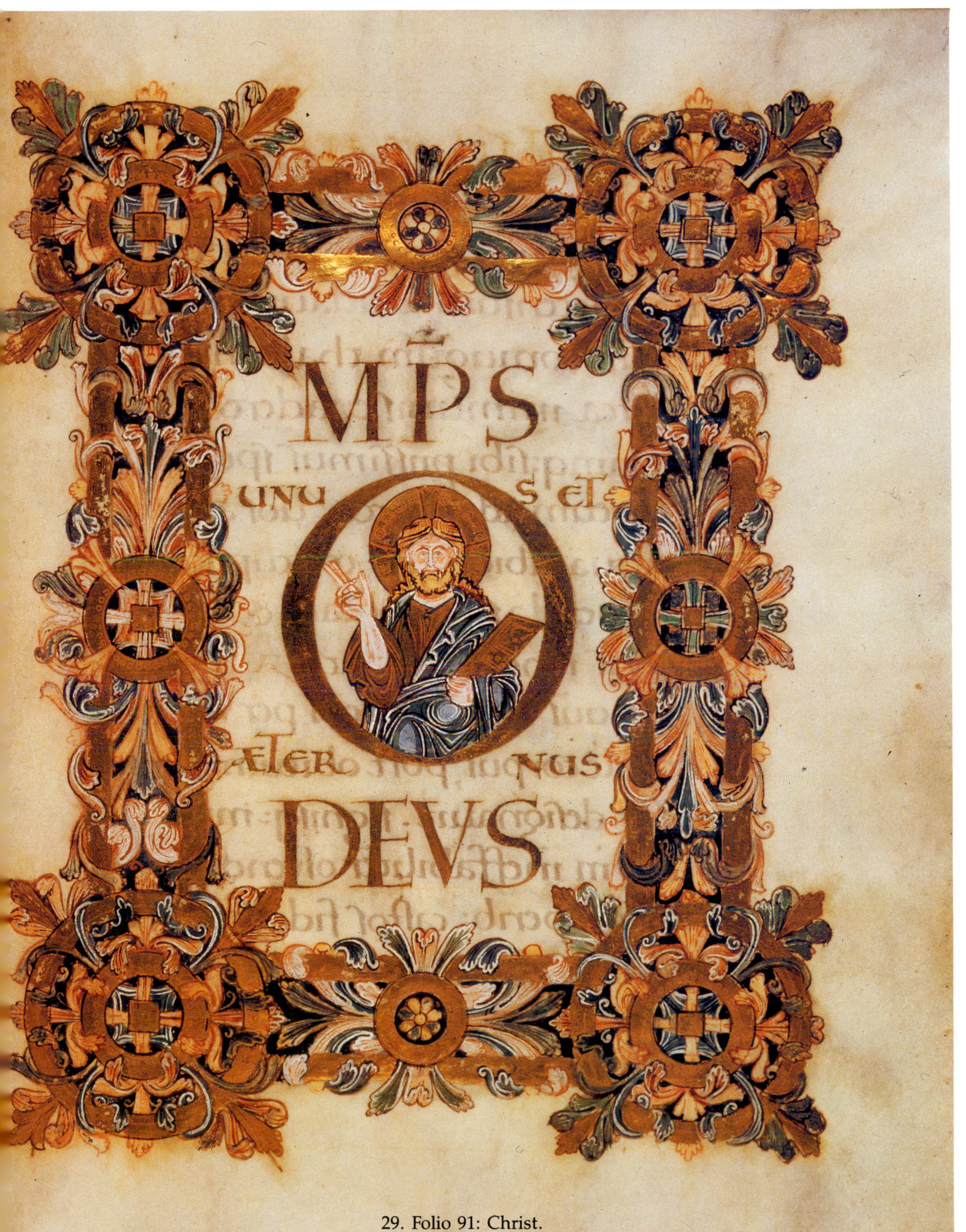

29. Folio 91: Christ.

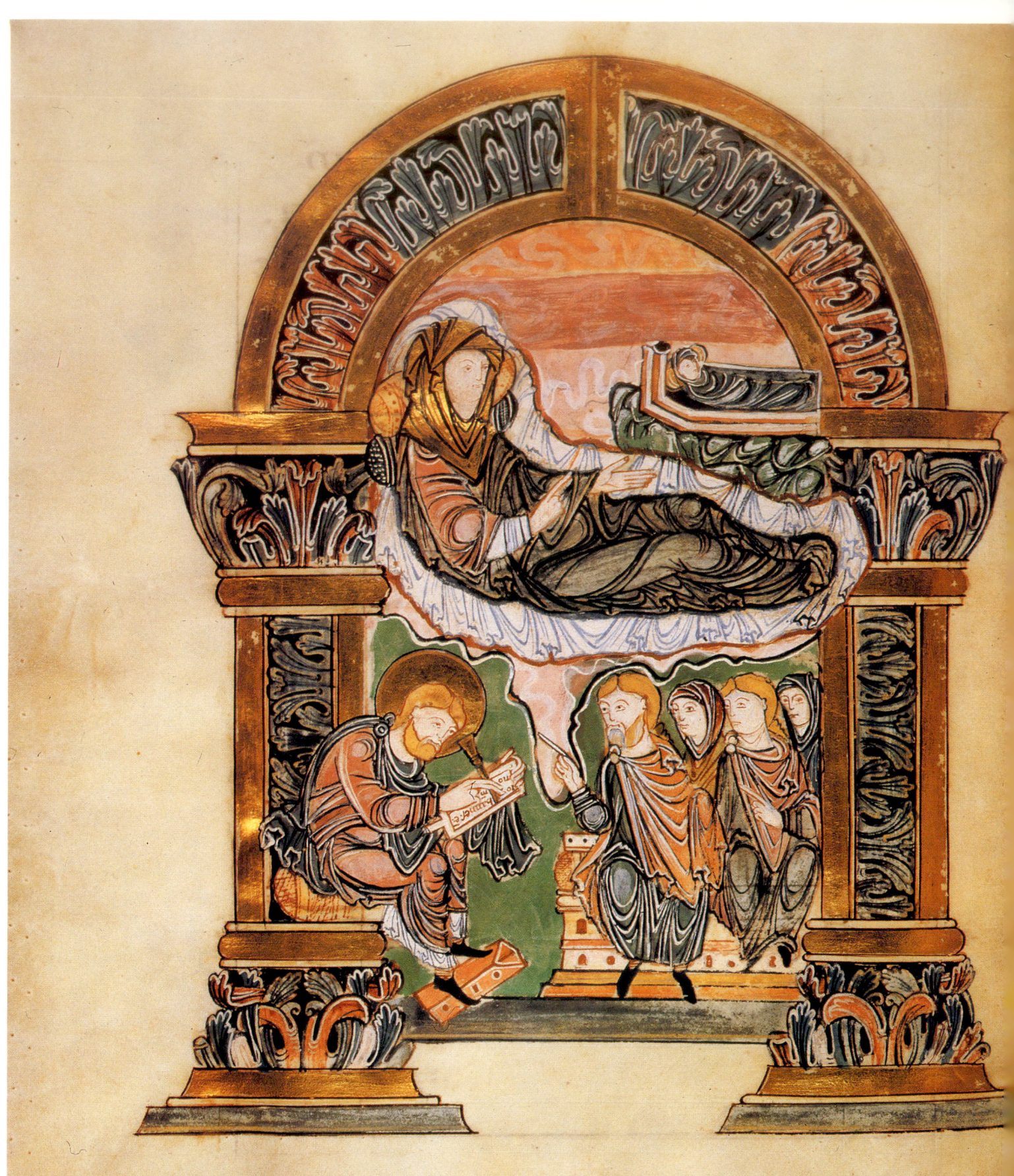

30. Folio 92v: Birth and Naming of John the Baptist.

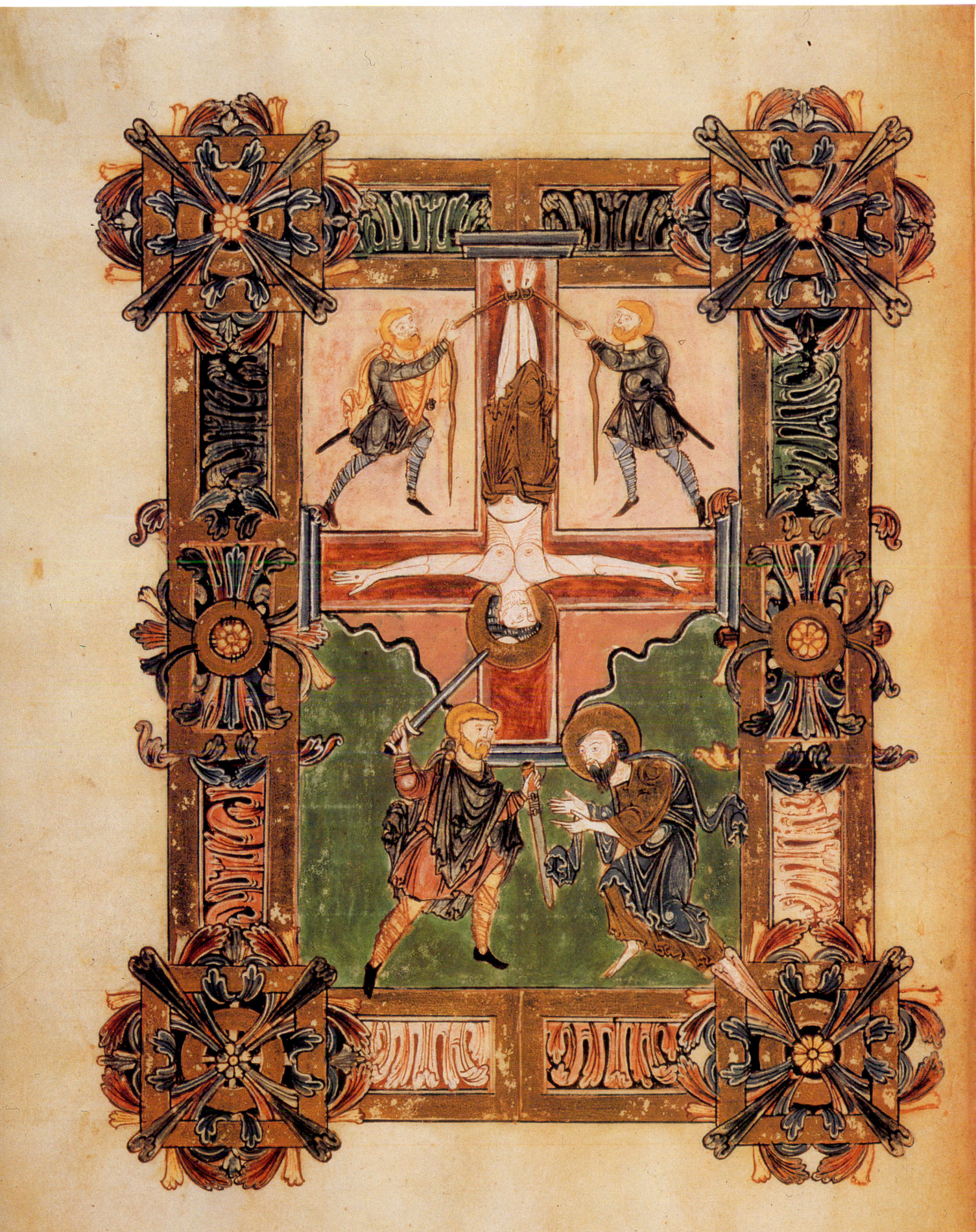

31. Folio 95v: Martyrdoms of Peter and Paul.

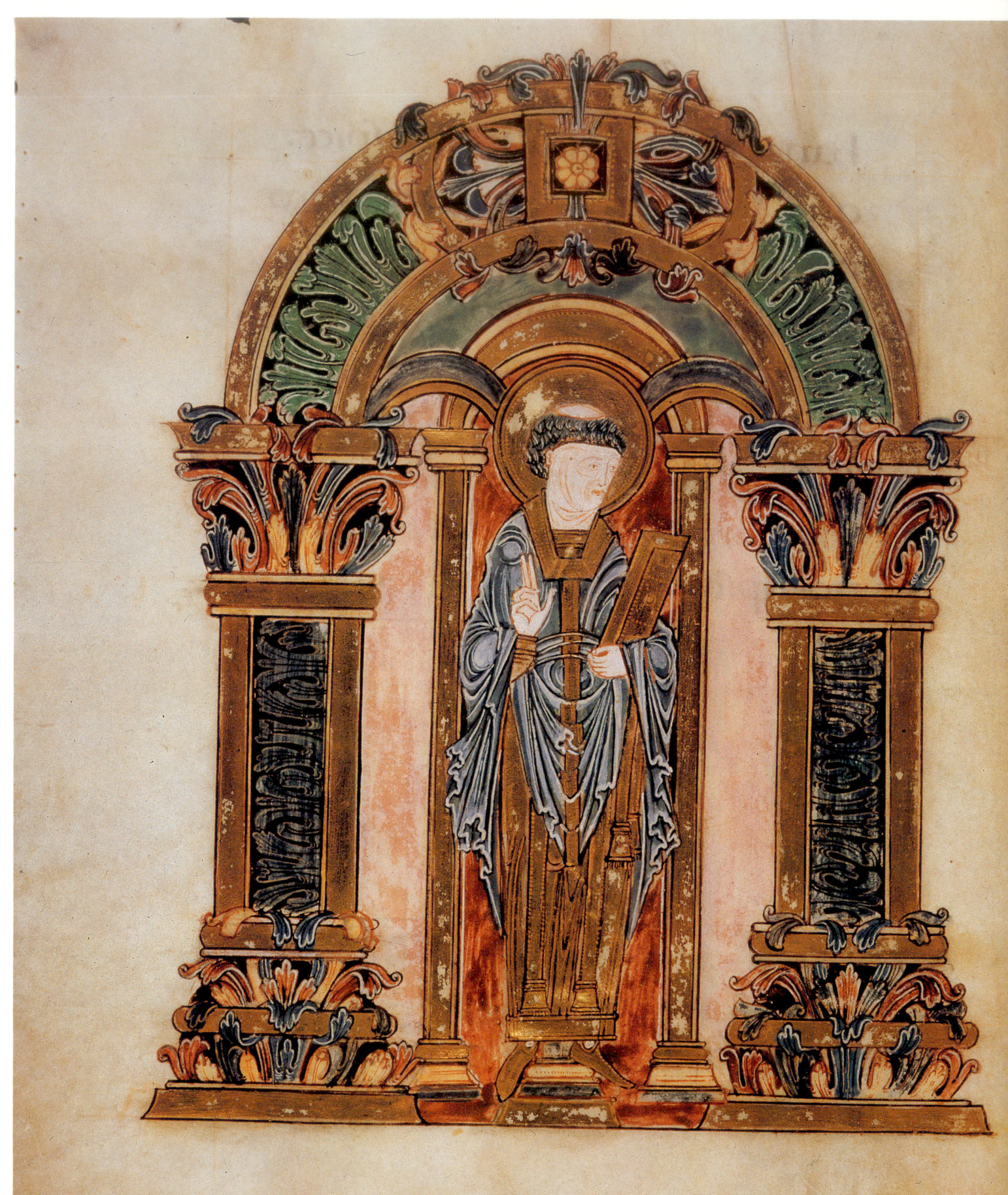

32. Folio 97v: St. Swithun.

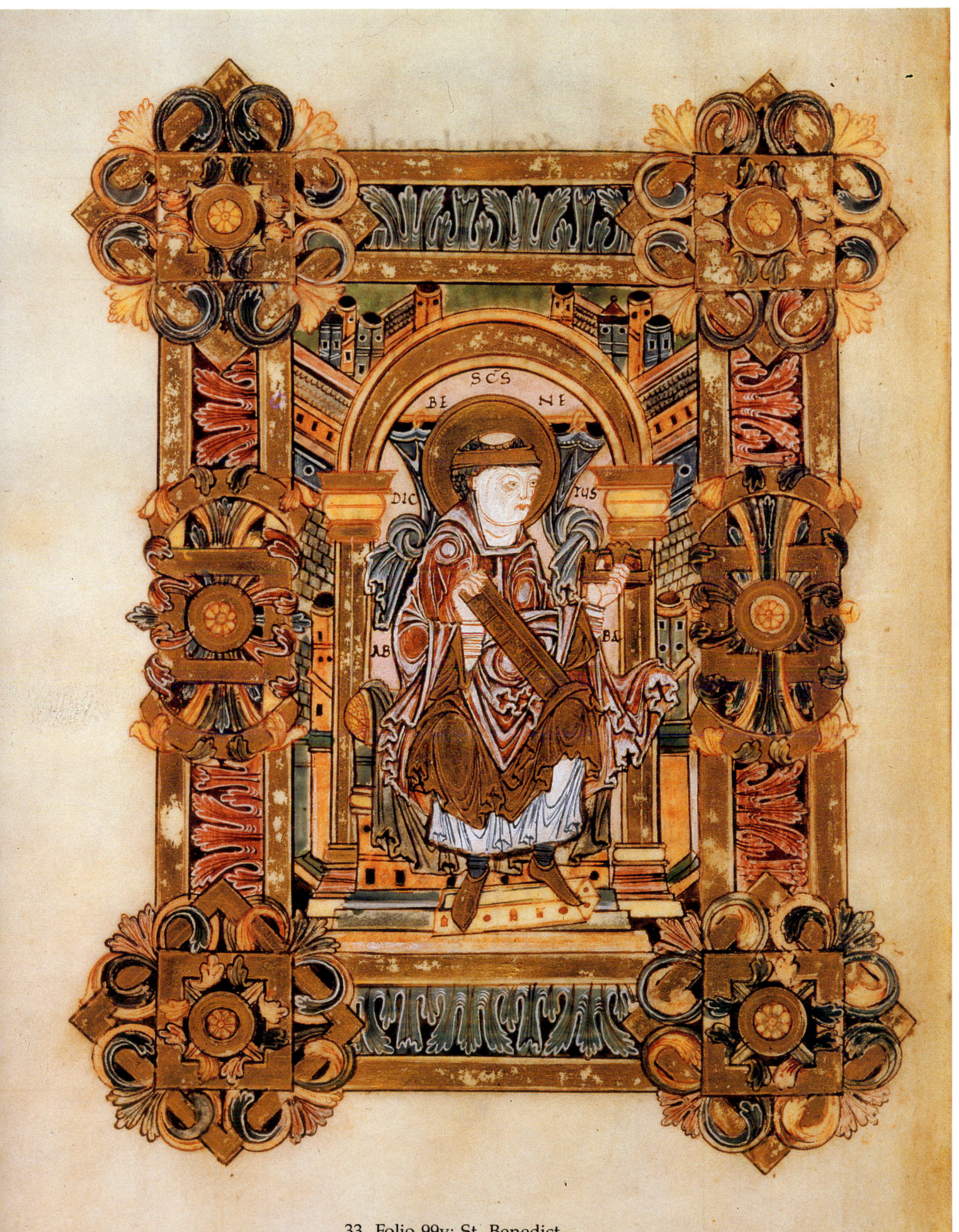

33. Folio 99v: St. Benedict.

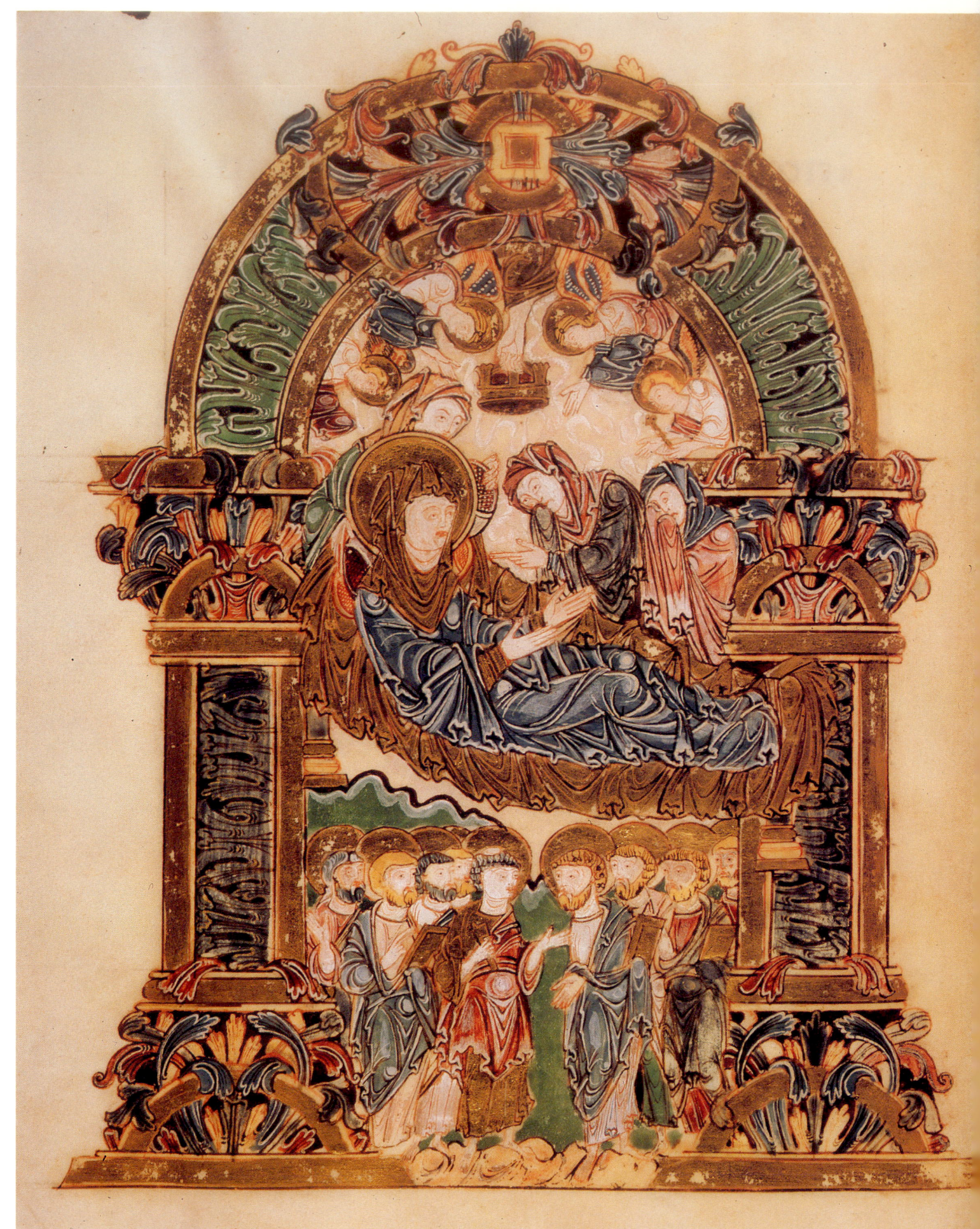

34. Folio 102v: Death and Coronation of the Virgin.

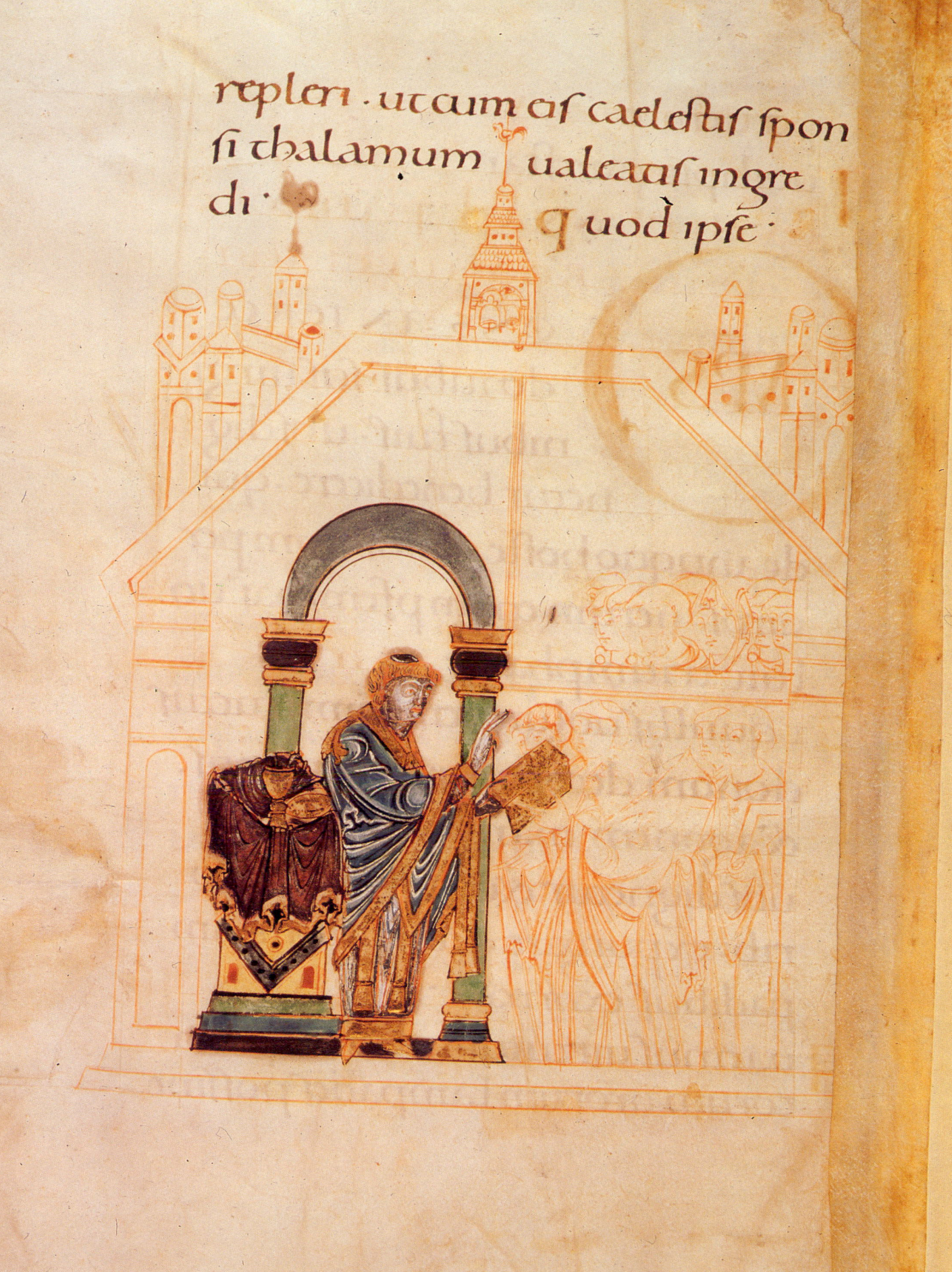

repleri · ut cum eis caelestis spon
si thalamum ualeatis ingre
di · quod ipse ·

35. Folio 118v: Bishop Blessing the Congregation.

NOTE: All Plates are from MS Add. 49598 in the British Library, London.

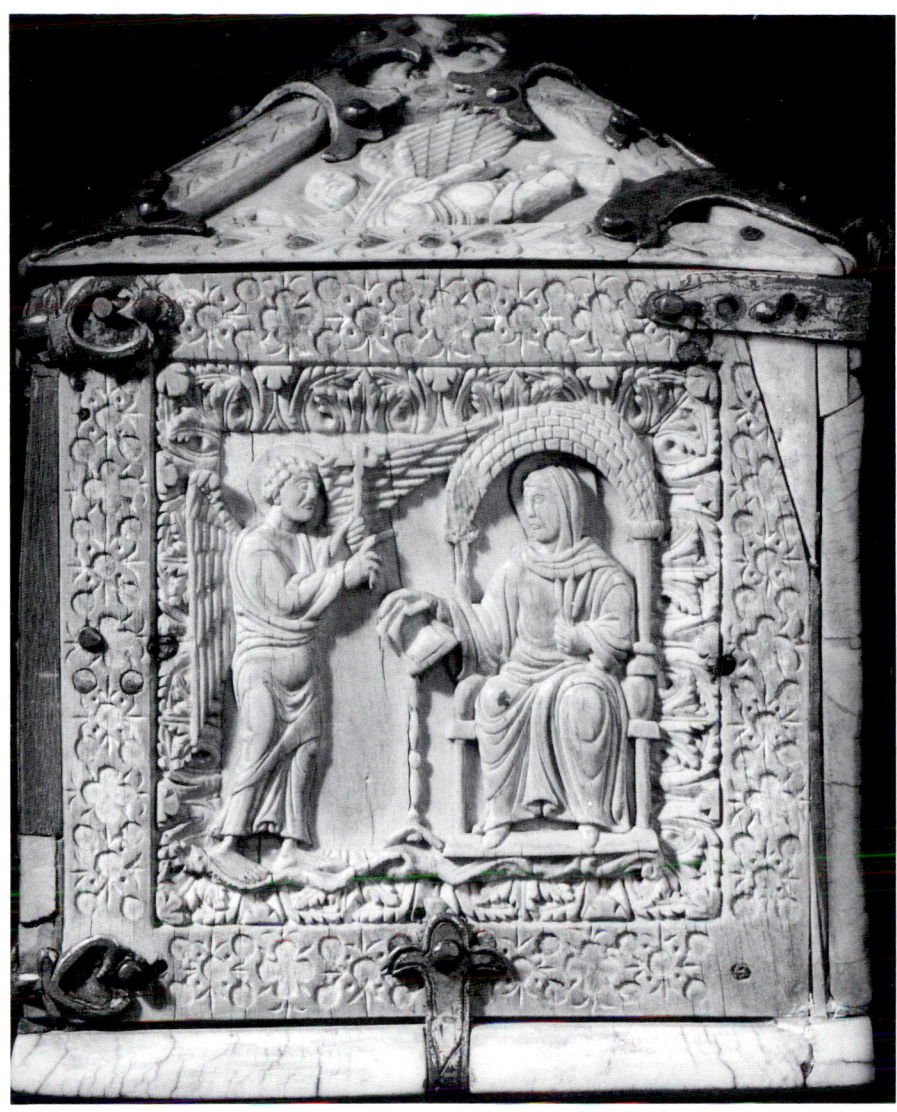

1. Brunswick, Herzog Anton Ulrich-Museum, ivory casket: Annunciation.

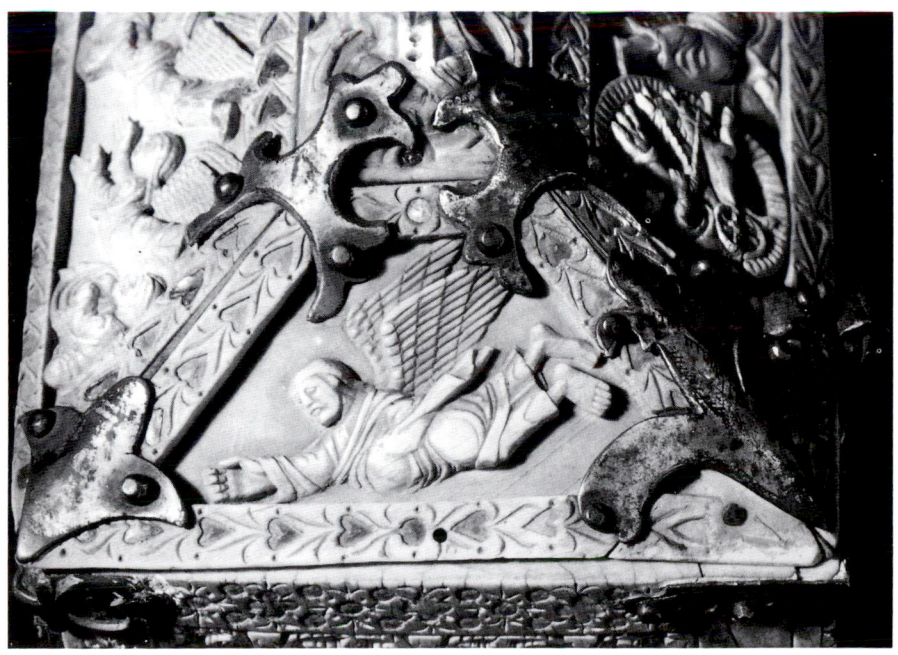

2. Brunswick, Herzog Anton Ulrich-Museum, ivory casket: lid

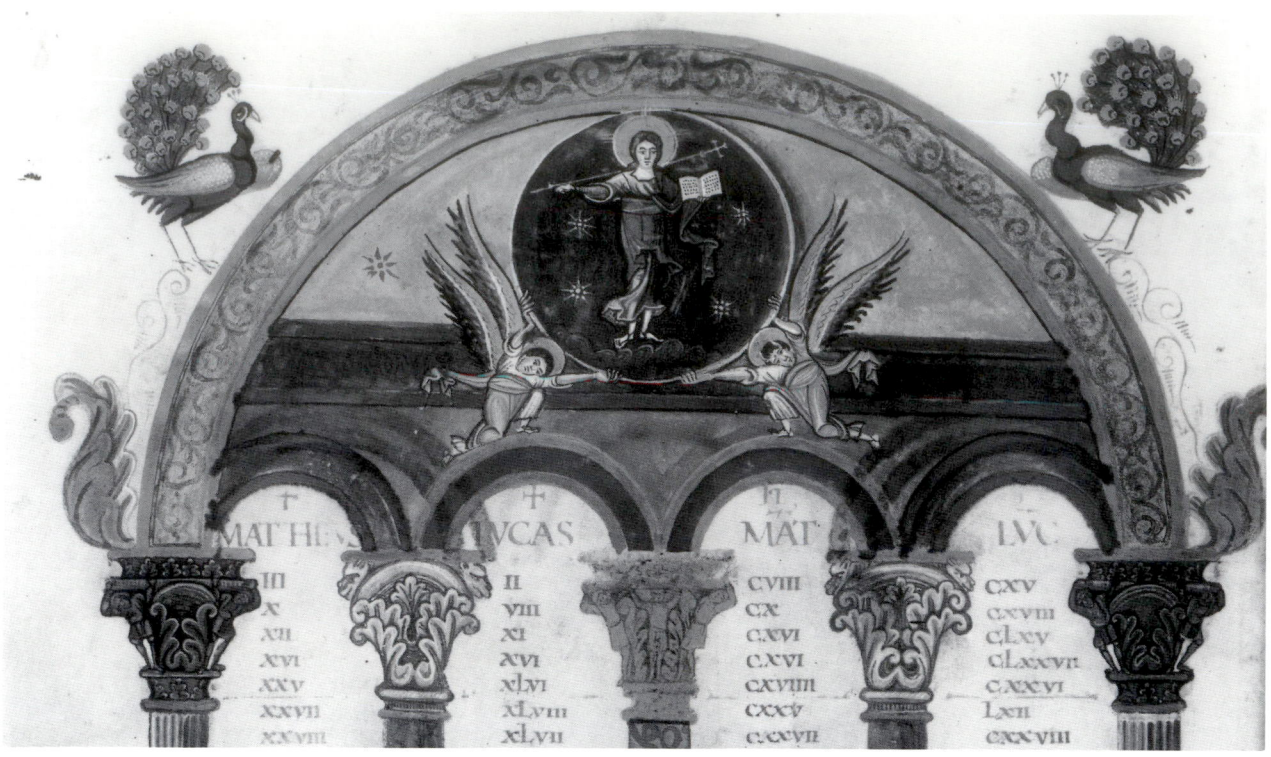

3. Paris, Bibliothèque Nationale, MS lat. 8850, fol. 10v: Christ Emmanuel.

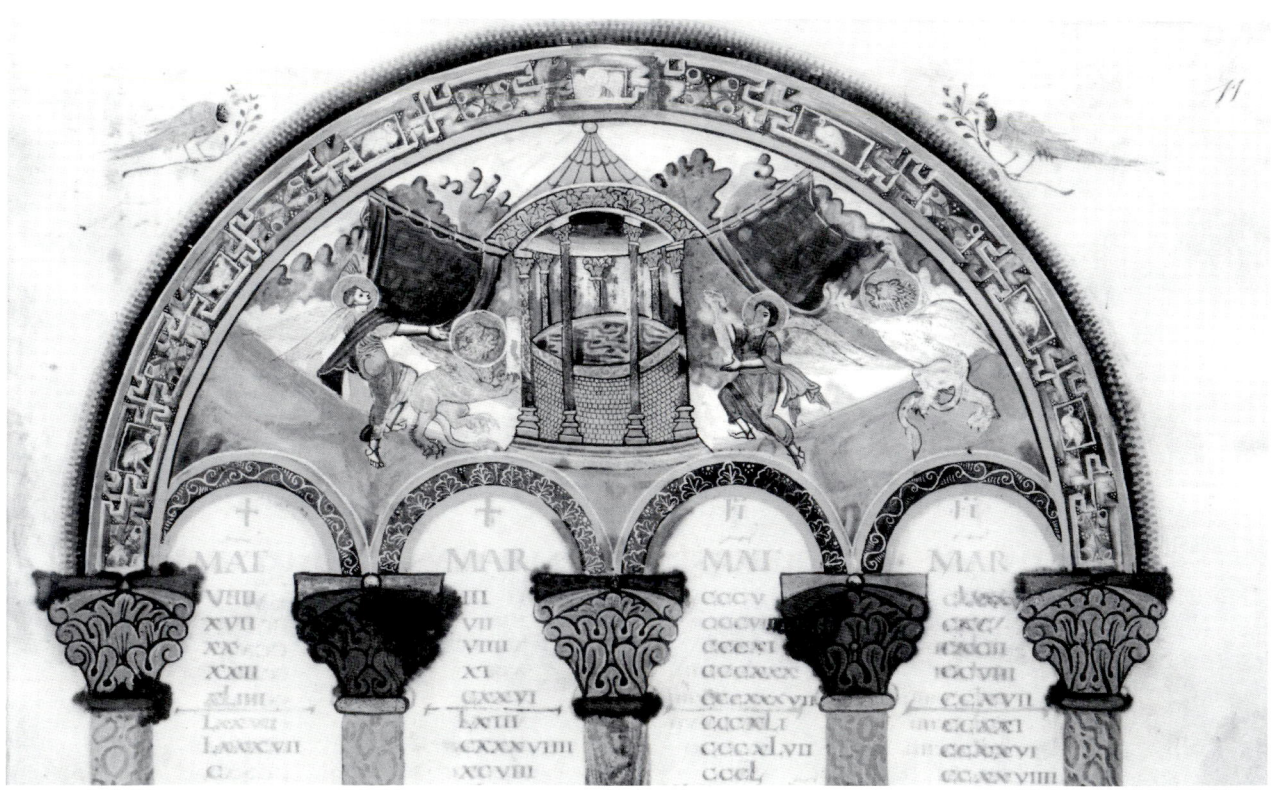

4. Paris, Bibliothèque Nationale, MS lat. 8850, fol. 11: Fons vitae.

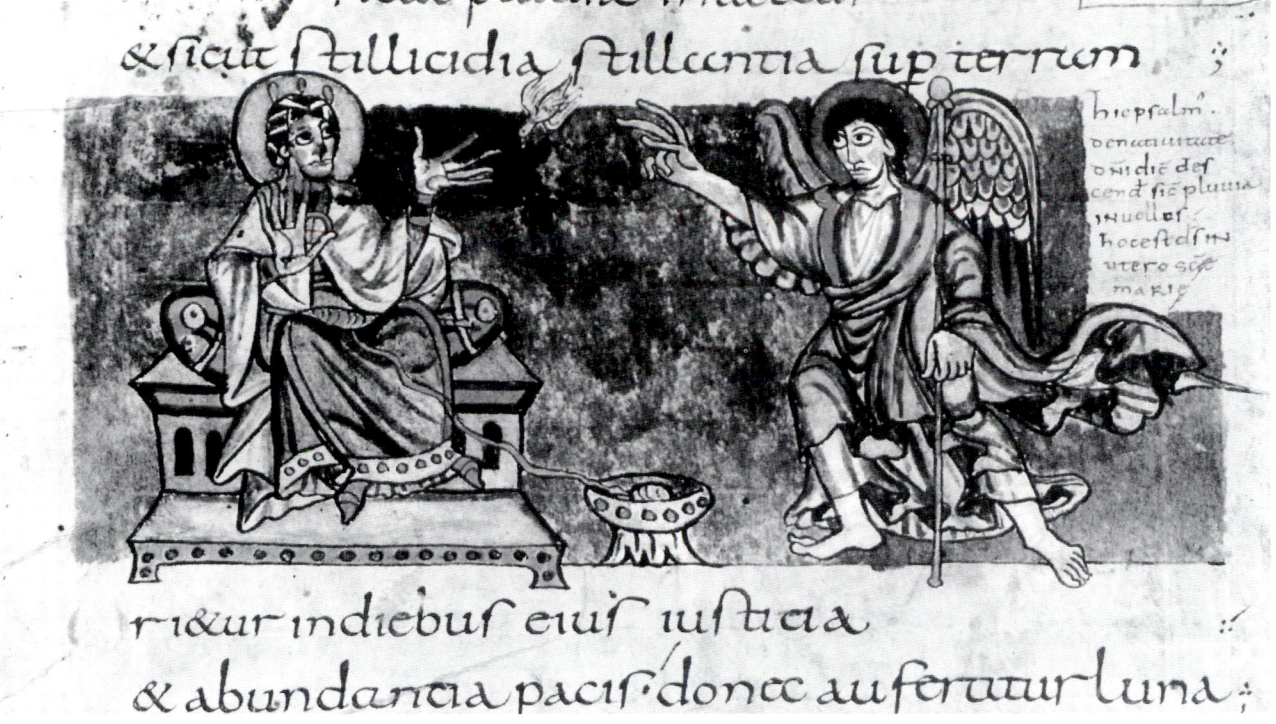

5. Stuttgart, Württembergische Landesbibliothek, MS Bibl. Fol. 23, fol. 83v: Annunciation (Marburg/Art Resource).

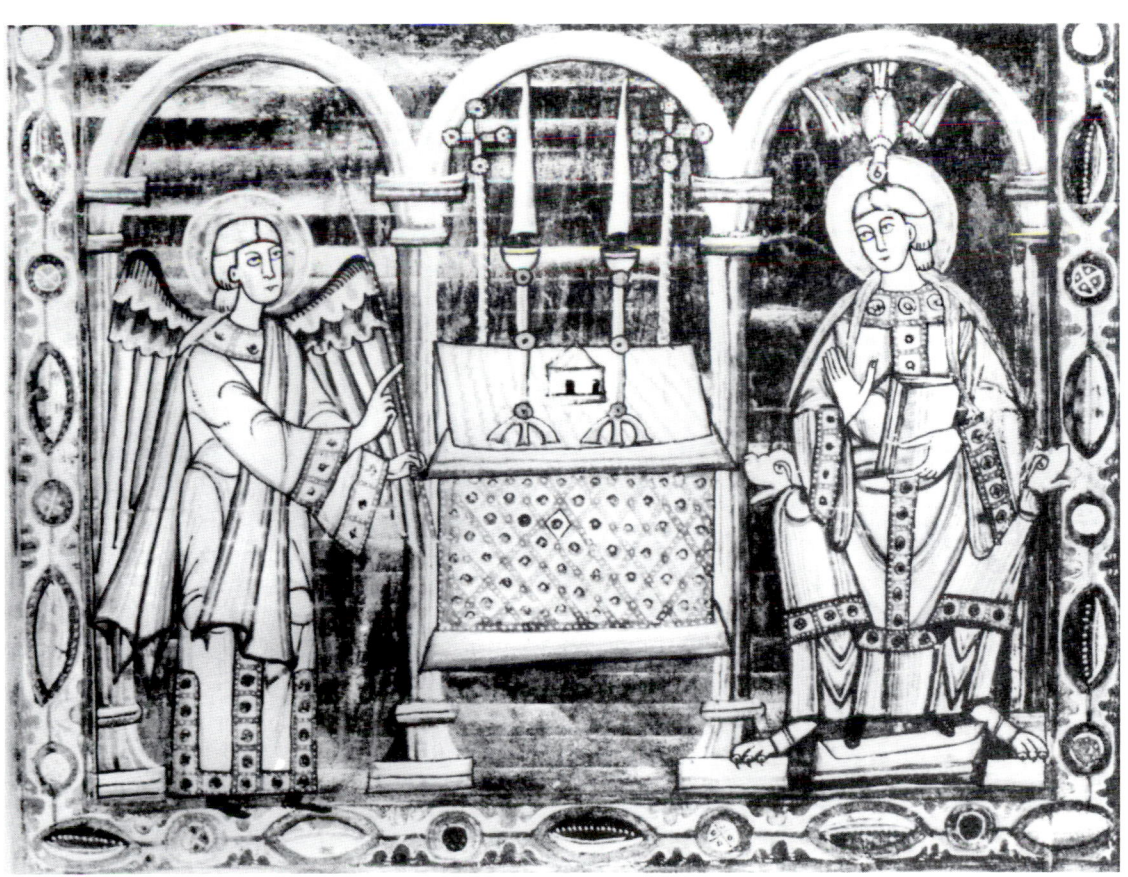

6. Prague, University Lib., MS XIV. A 13, fol. 20v: Annunciation.

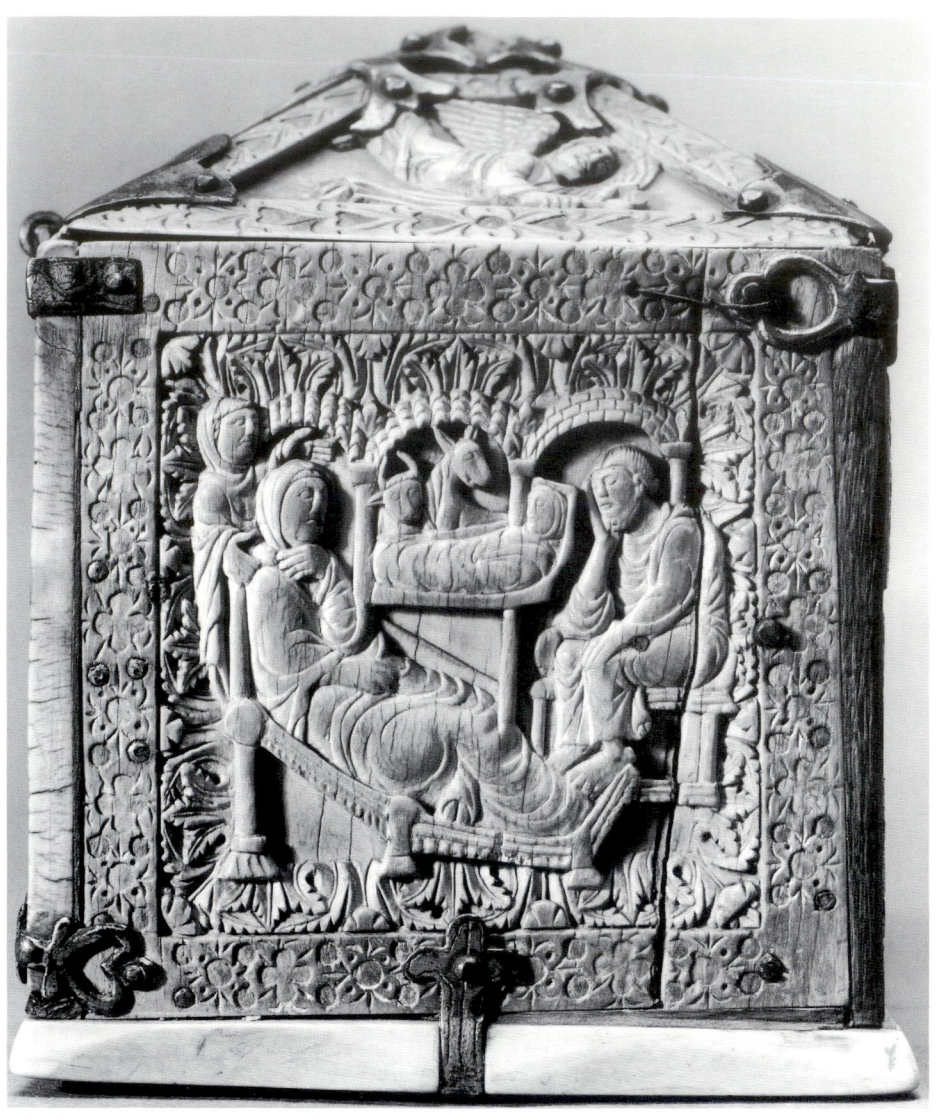

7. Brunswick, Herzog Anton Ulrich-Museum, ivory casket: Nativity.

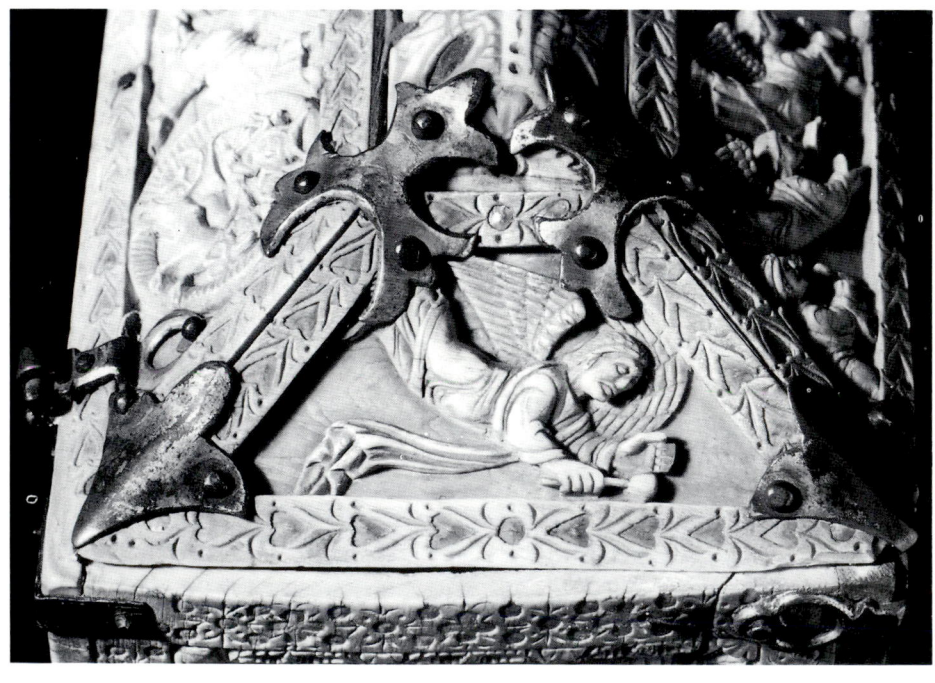

8. Brunswick, Herzog Anton Ulrich-Museum, ivory casket: lid

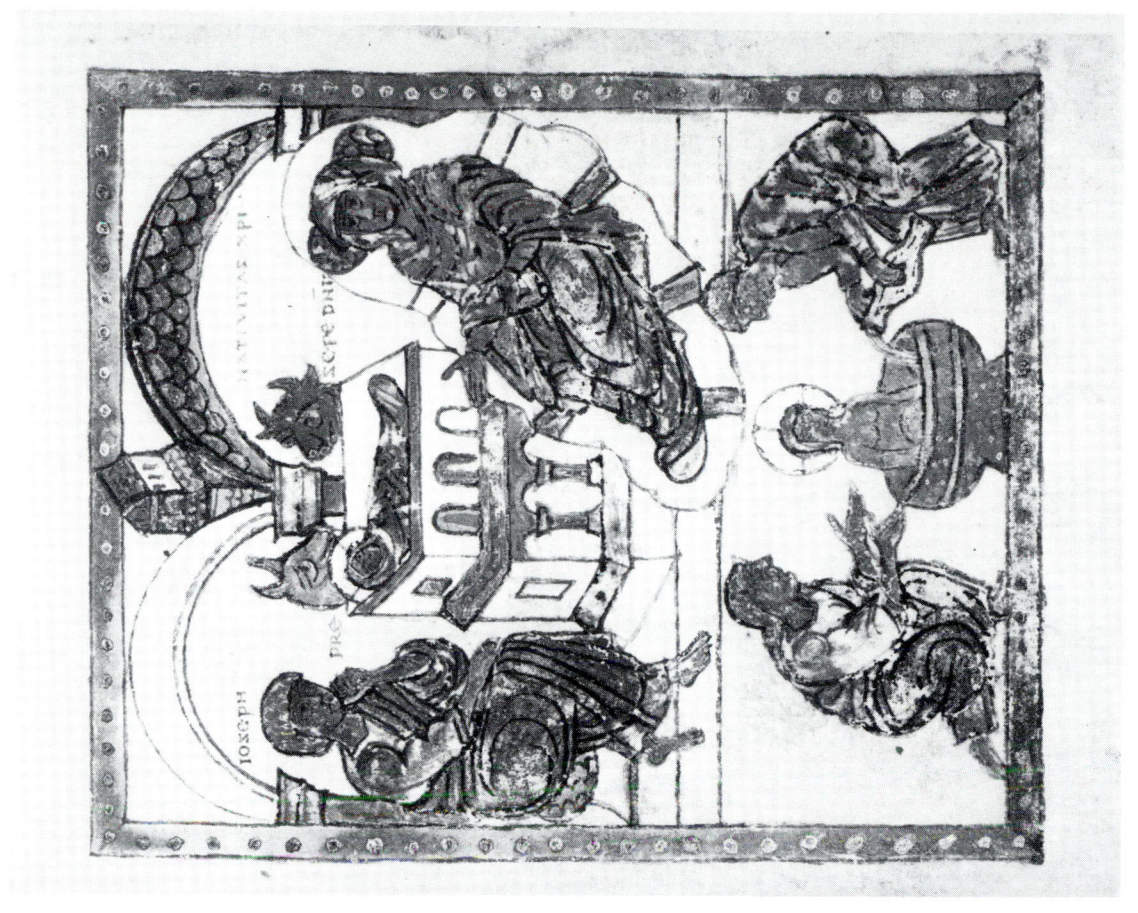

9. London, British Library, MS Cotton Nero C. IV, fol. 10: Nativity (Courtauld Institute).

10. Oxford, Bodleian Library, MS Rawl. B. 484, fol. 85: Nativity.

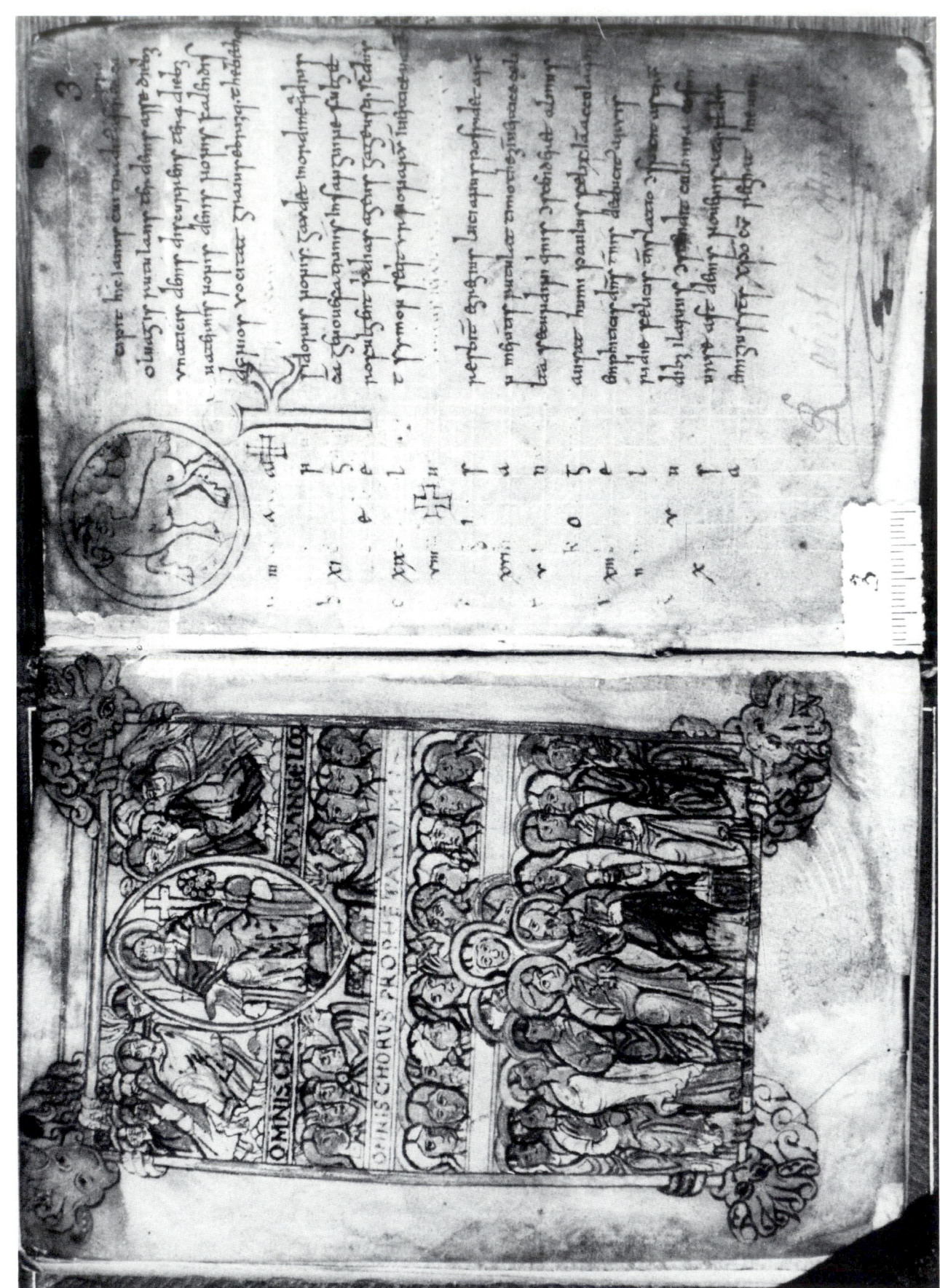

11. London, British Lib., MS Cotton Galba A. XVIII, fols. 2v–3: Christ and saints (Courtauld Institute).

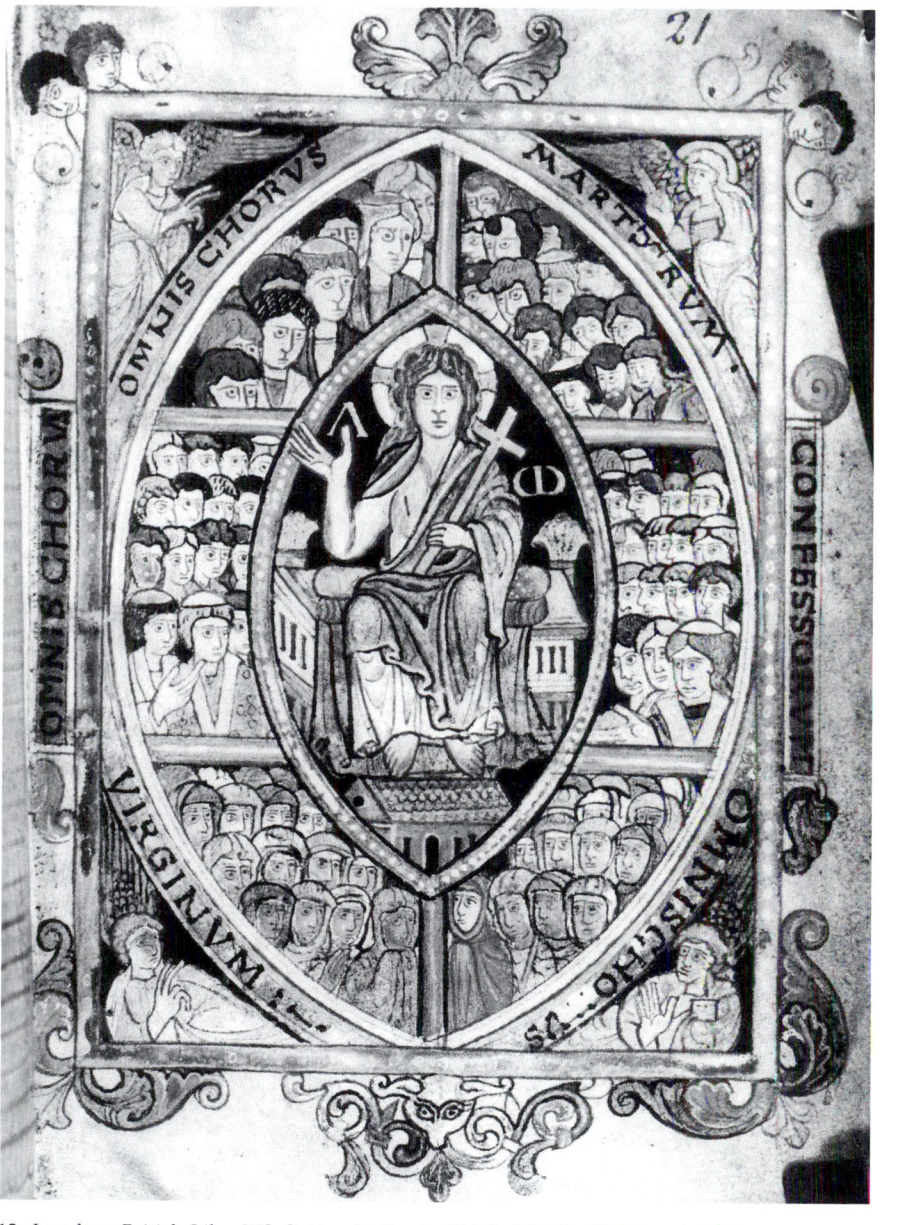

12. London, British Lib., MS Cotton Galba A. XVIII, fol. 21: Christ and saints.

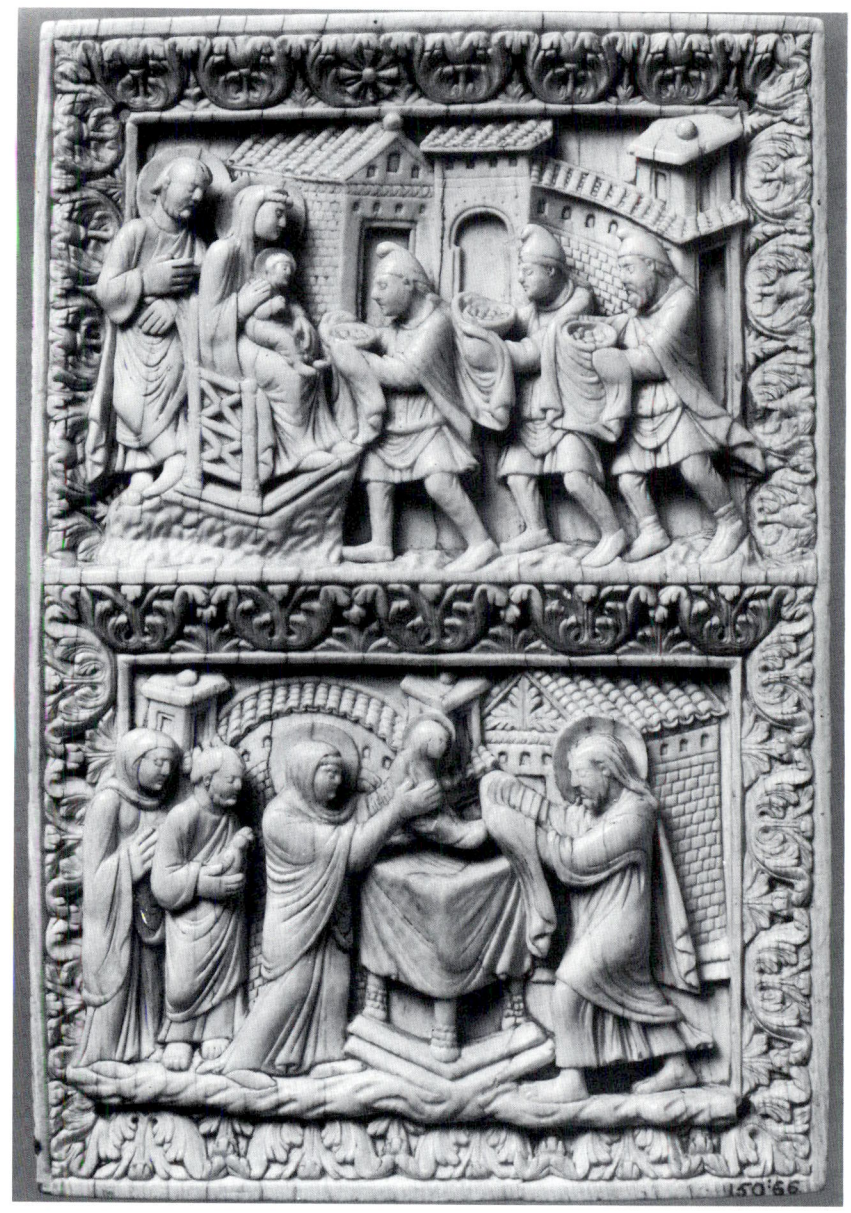

13. London, Victoria and Albert Museum, ivory: Adoration and Presentation.

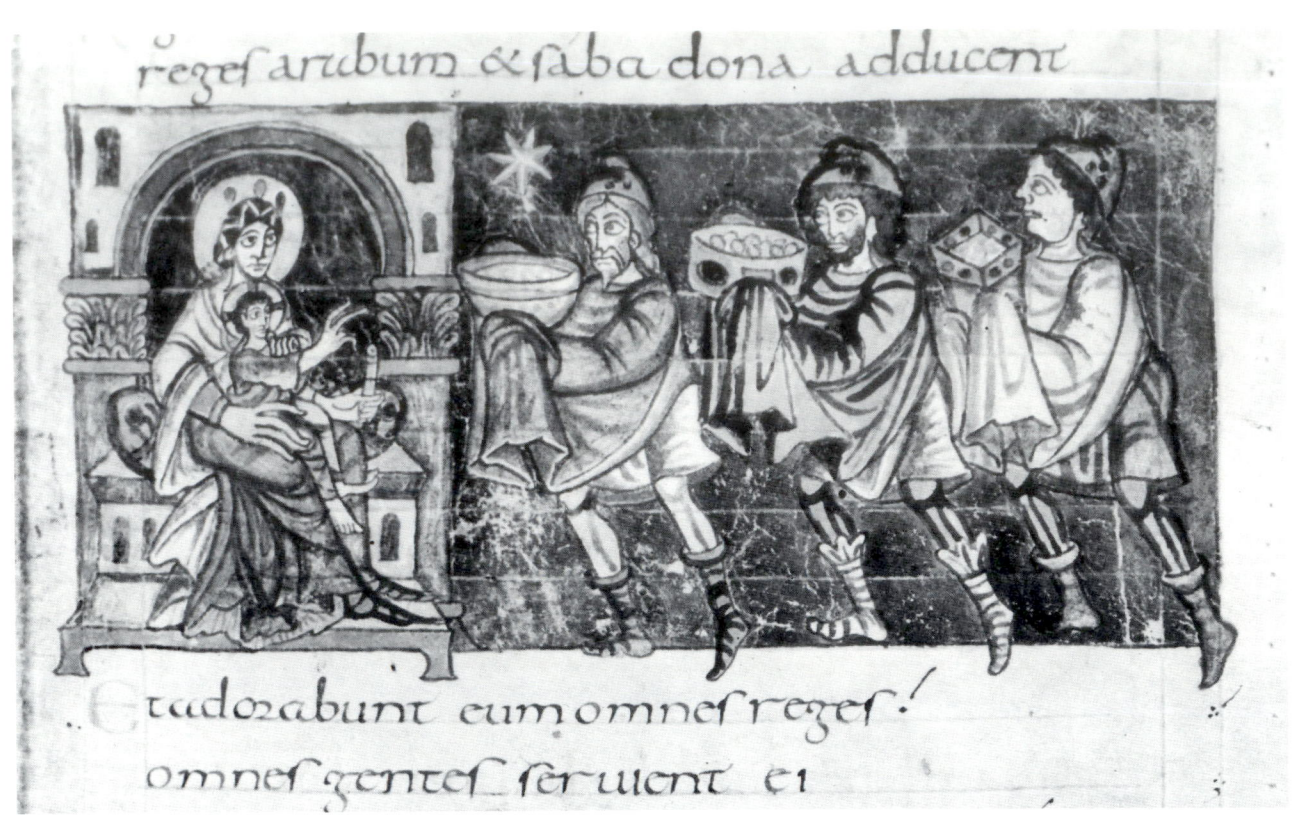

14. Stuttgart, Württembergische Landesbibliothek, MS Bibl. Fol. 23, fol. 84: Adoration of the Magi (Marburg/Art Resource).

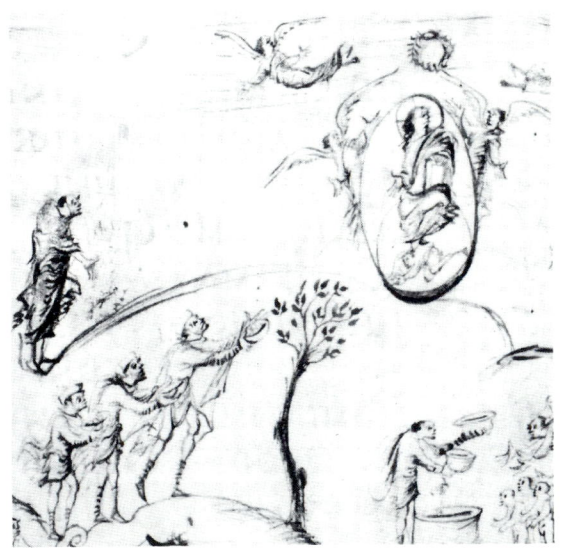

15. Utrecht, University Library, MS 32, fol. 40v (detail): Ps. 71.

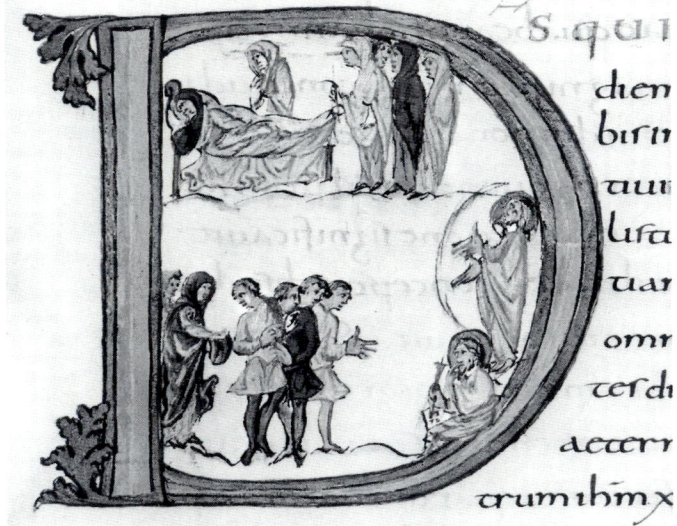

16. Paris, Bibl. Nat., MS lat 9428, fol. 84: Birth and Naming of John the Baptist.

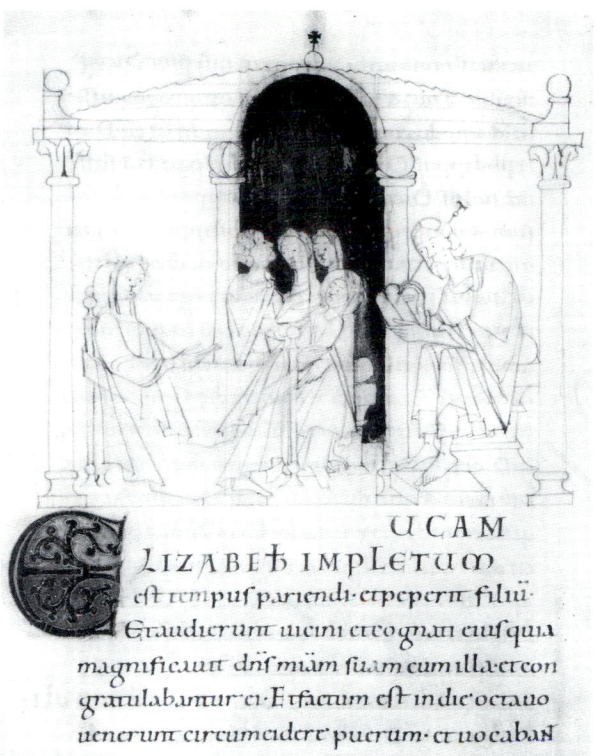

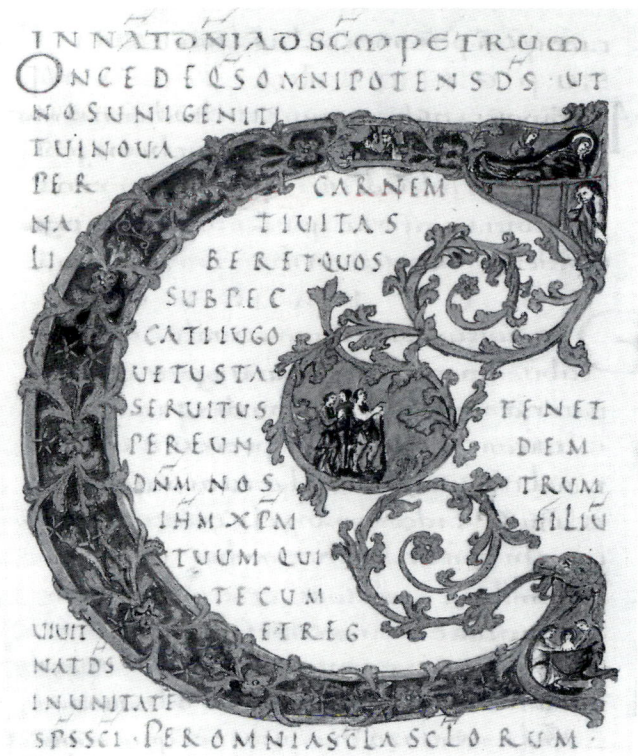

17. Berlin, Staatliche Museen Preussische Kulturbesitz, Kupferstichkabinett, MS 78 A 2, fol. 67v: Birth and Naming of John the Baptist.

18. Paris, Bibliothèque Nationale, MS 9428, fol. 24v: Nativity.

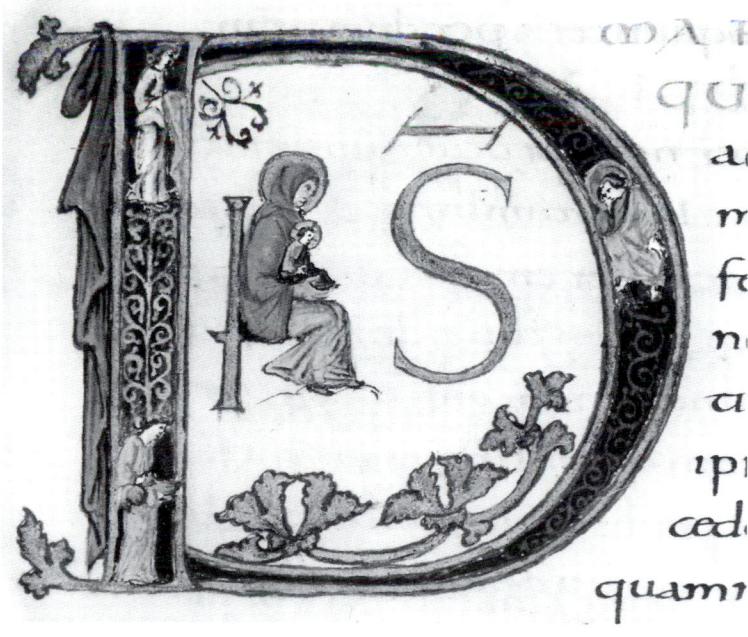

19. Paris, Bibliothèque Nationale, MS lat. 9428, fol. 32v: Circumcision.

Adiuua nos dne qs eorum depca
aone scoru. qui fili tui necdu
humana uoce pficentes. celesa
sunt peius natiuitate gratia
coronati. peunde AL
Ipsi nobis dne qs pos tui lentuina
um puritate. quoru innocen
tui hodie sollemniter celebra
mus. per dnm nrm ihm xpm
II. KL. IAN. NAT SCI
SILUESTRI PAPE

salutem nobis prouenire depos
cat. p AOCOPL
Prs qs omnps ds ut de perceptis
muneribus gratias exhibentes.
beneficia potiora sumamus. p

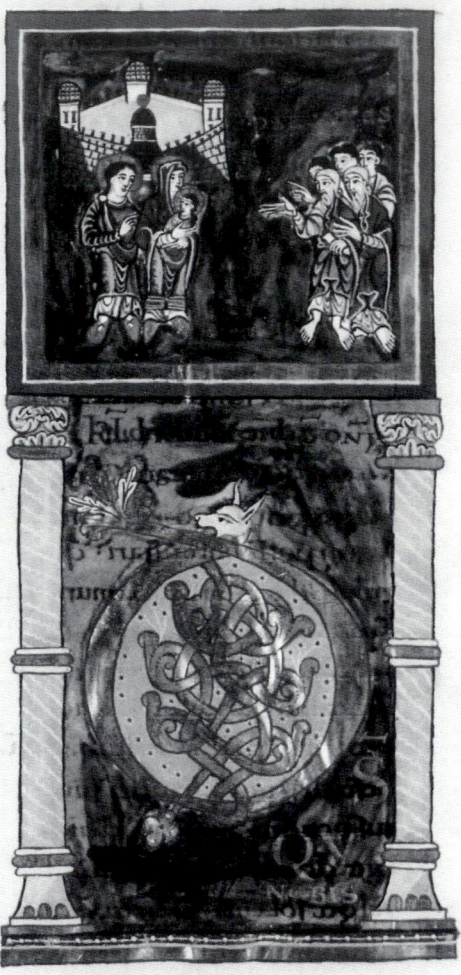

D
quesumus om
mpotens ds. ut beata siluestri
confessoris tui atq; pontificis
ueneranda sollemnitas. & de
uoaone nobis augeat & sa
lutem. p SUPEROBL
Sacris altaribus dne hostias
suppositas. scs siluester qs in

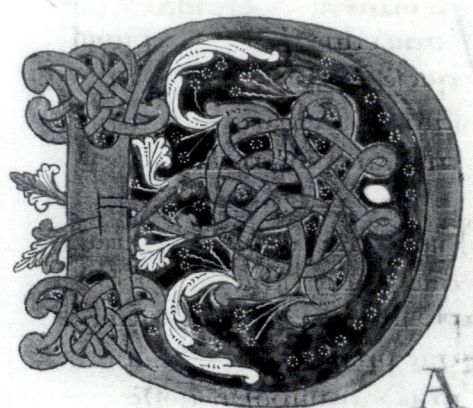

20. Göttingen, Niedersächsische Staats- und Universitätsbibliothek, MS theol. fol. 231, fol. 17v: Naming of Christ (Marburg/Art Resource).

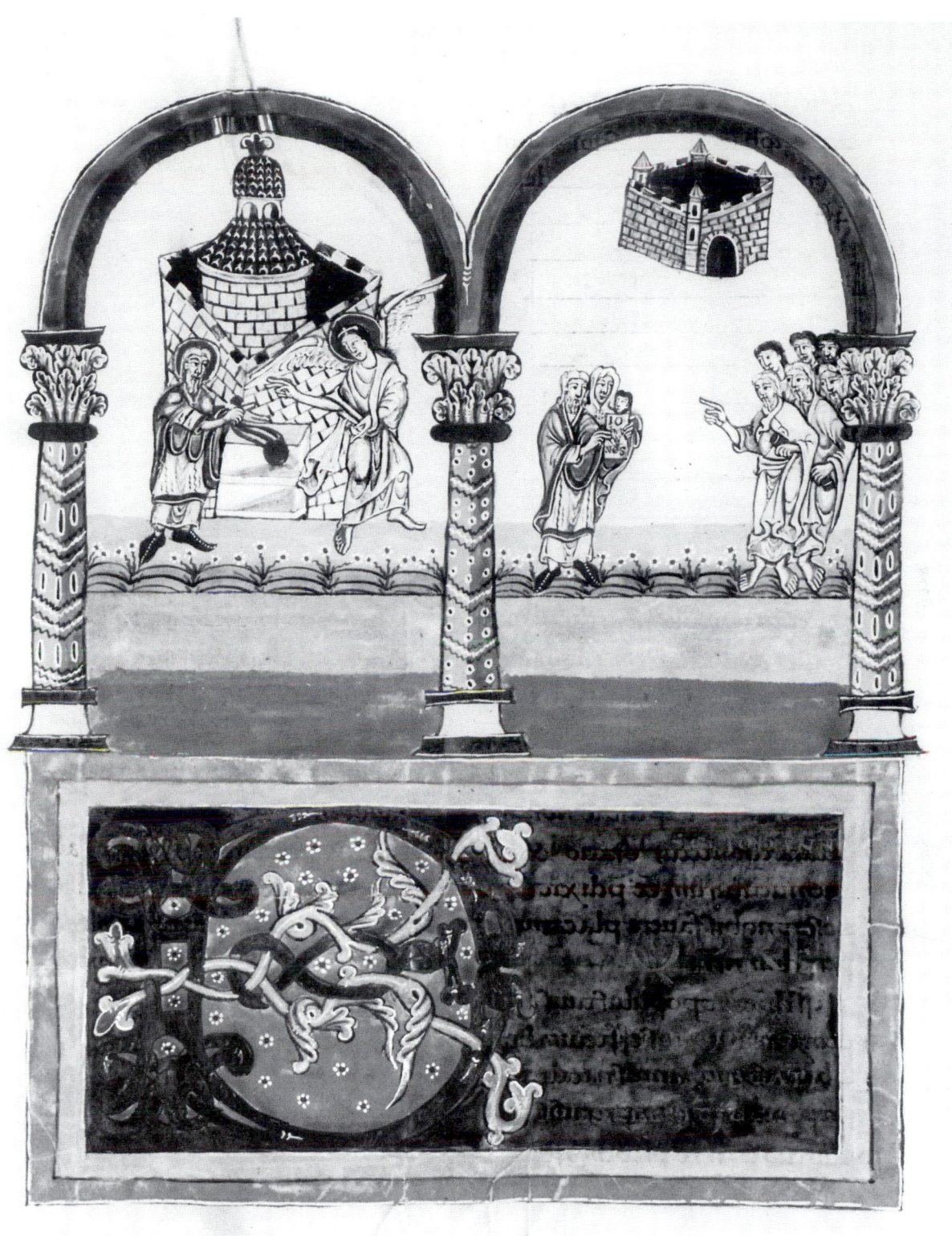

21. Göttingen, Niedersächsische Staats- und Universitätsbibliothek, MS theol. fol. 231, fol. 90v: Annunciation to Zacharias and Naming of John the Baptist (Rheinisches Bildarchiv).

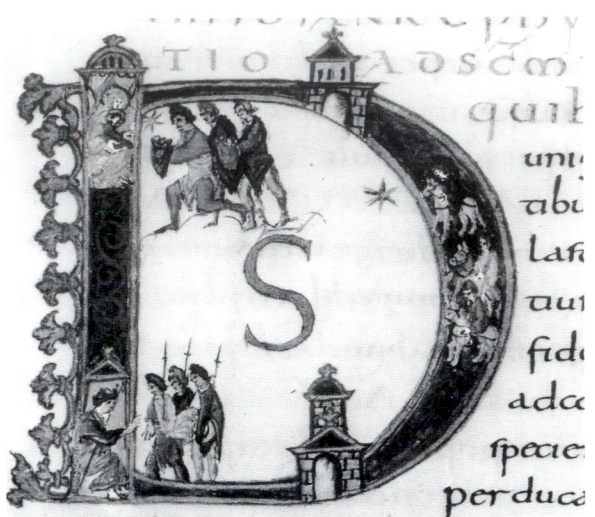

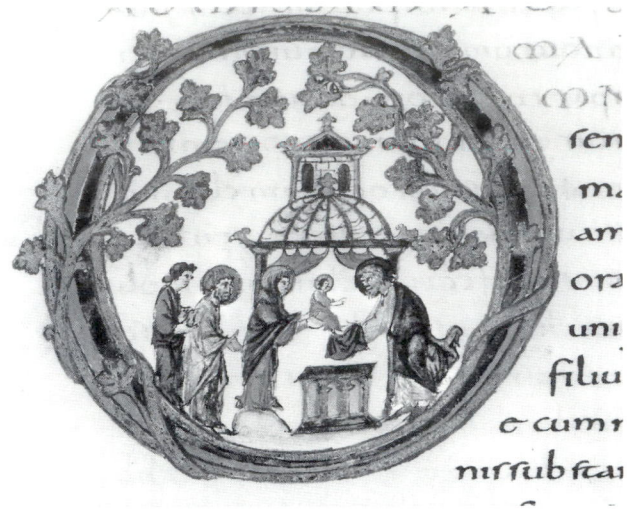

22. Paris, Bibliothèque Nationale, MS lat. 9428, fol. 34v: Magi scenes.

23. Paris, Bibliothèque Nationale, MS lat. 9428, fol. 38: Presentation.

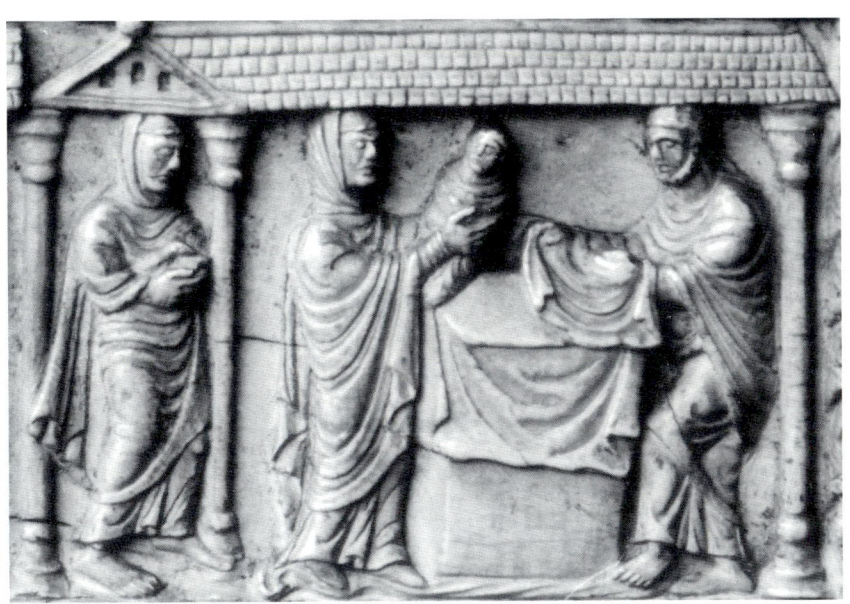

24. Paris, Louvre Museum, ivory casket: Presentation (ARS, New York/SPADEM, Paris).

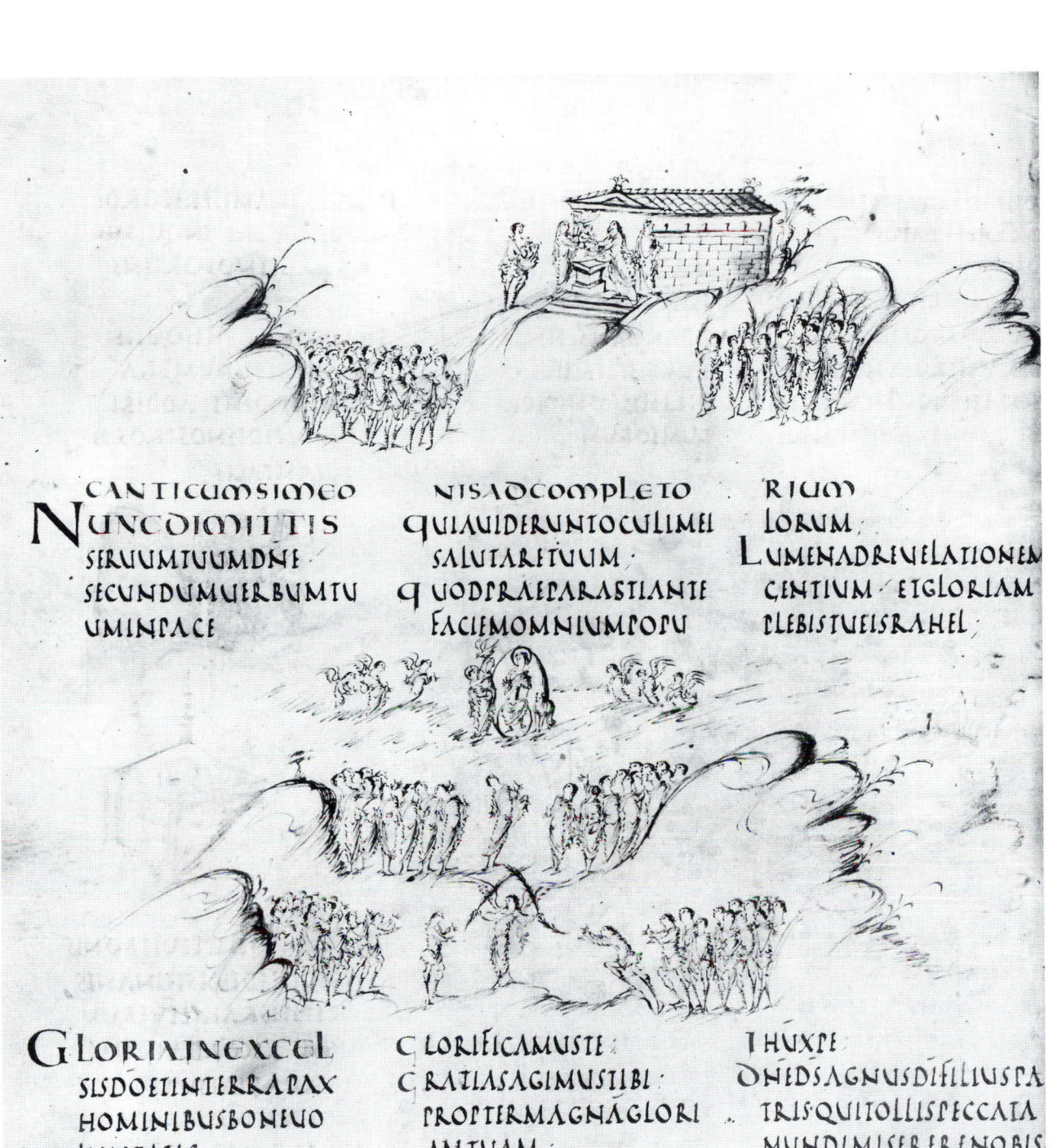

CANTICUMSIMEO NISADCOMPLETO RIUM
NUNCDIMITTIS QUIAUIDERUNTOCULIMEI LORUM
SERUUMTUUMDNE SALUTARETUUM LUMENADREUELATIONEM
SECUNDUMUERBUMTU QUODPRAEPARASTIANTE CENTIUM ETGLORIAM
UMINPACE FACIEMOMNIUMPOPU PLEBISTUEISRAHEL

GLORIAINEXCEL GLORIFICAMUSTE IHUXPE
SISDOETINTERRAPAX GRATIASAGIMUSTIBI DNEDSAGNUSDIFILIUSPA
HOMINIBUSBONEUO PROPTERMAGNAGLORI TRISQUITOLLISPECCATA
LUNTATIS AMTUAM MUNDIMISERERENOBIS
LAUDAMUSTE DNEDSREXCAELESTIS QUITOLLISPECCATAMUND
BENEDICIMUSTE DSPATEROMNIPOTENS SUSCIPEDEPRECATIONEM
ADORAMUSTE DNEFILIUNIGENITAE NOSTRAM

25. Utrecht, University Lib., MS 32, fol. 89v: Presentation and Gloria.

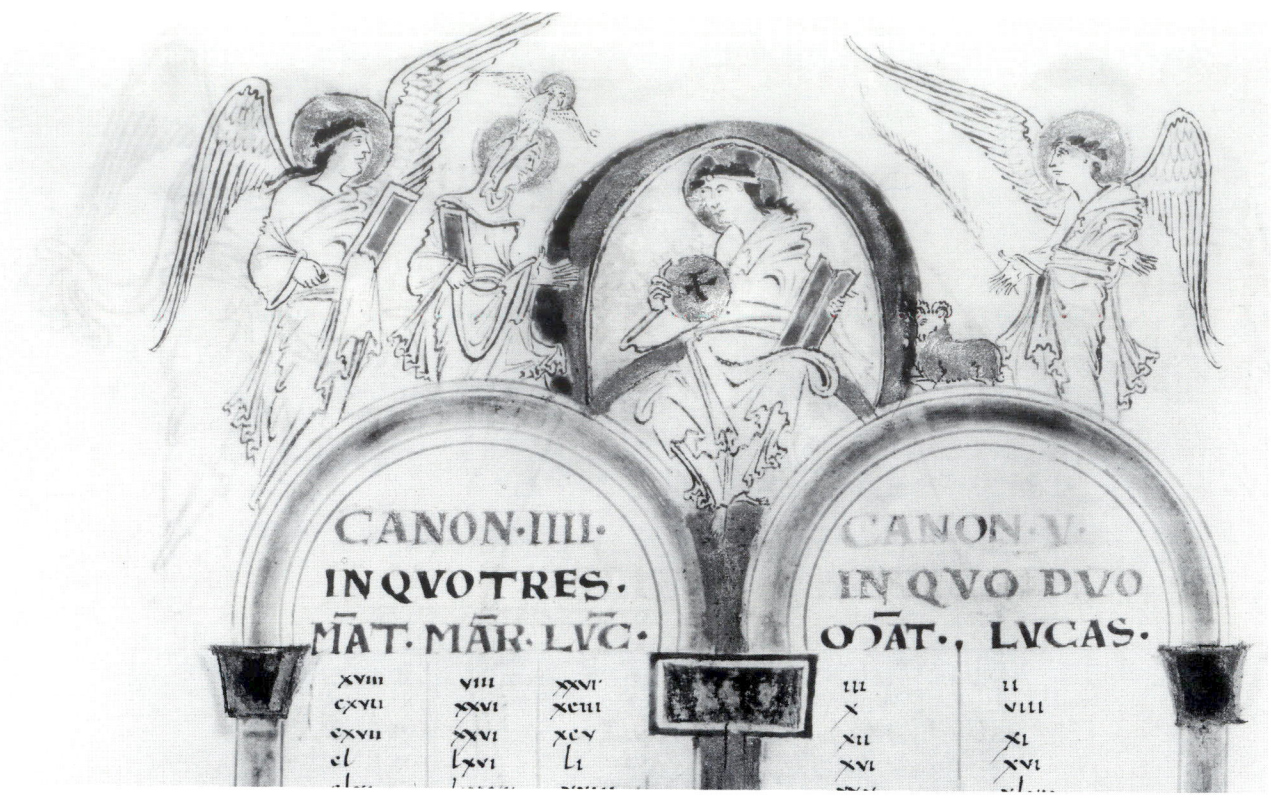

26. New York, Pierpont Morgan Library., MS M. 869, fol. 11v: Virgin, Christ, Lamb, and Holy Spirit.

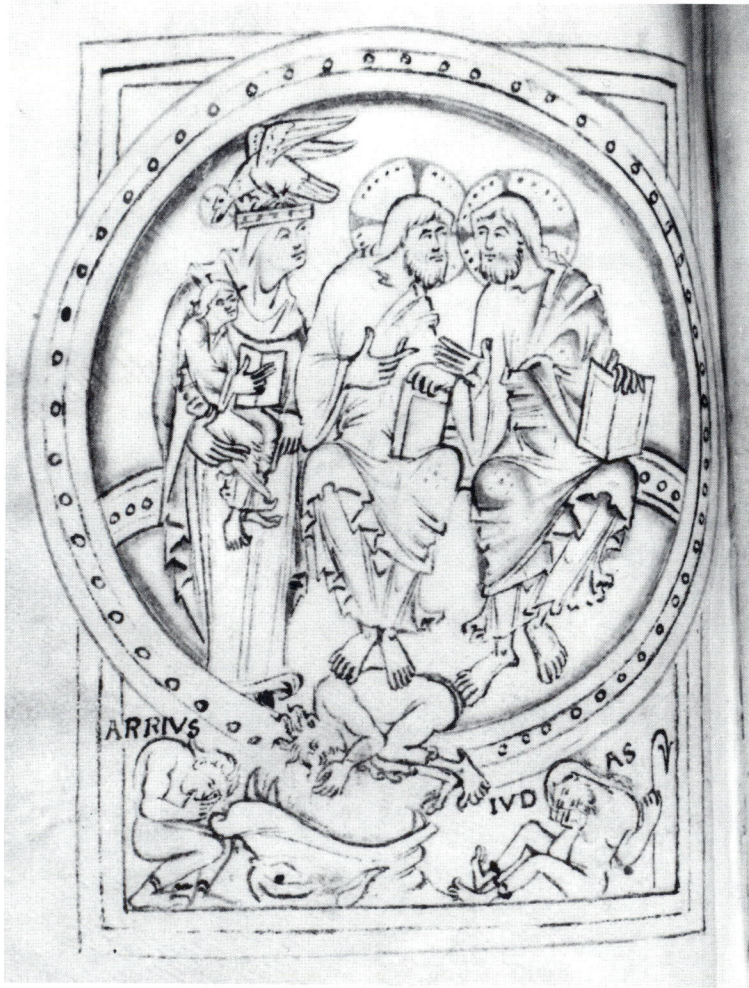

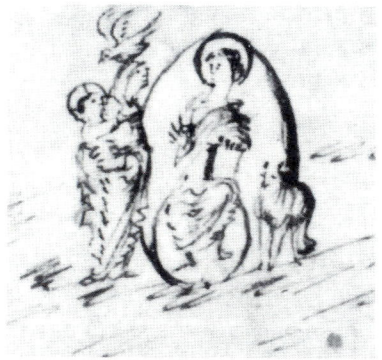

28. Utrecht, University Library, MS 32, fol. 89v (detail of fig. 25): Gloria.

27. London, British Library., MS Cotton Titus D. XXVII, fol. 75v: "Quinity" (Courtauld Institute).

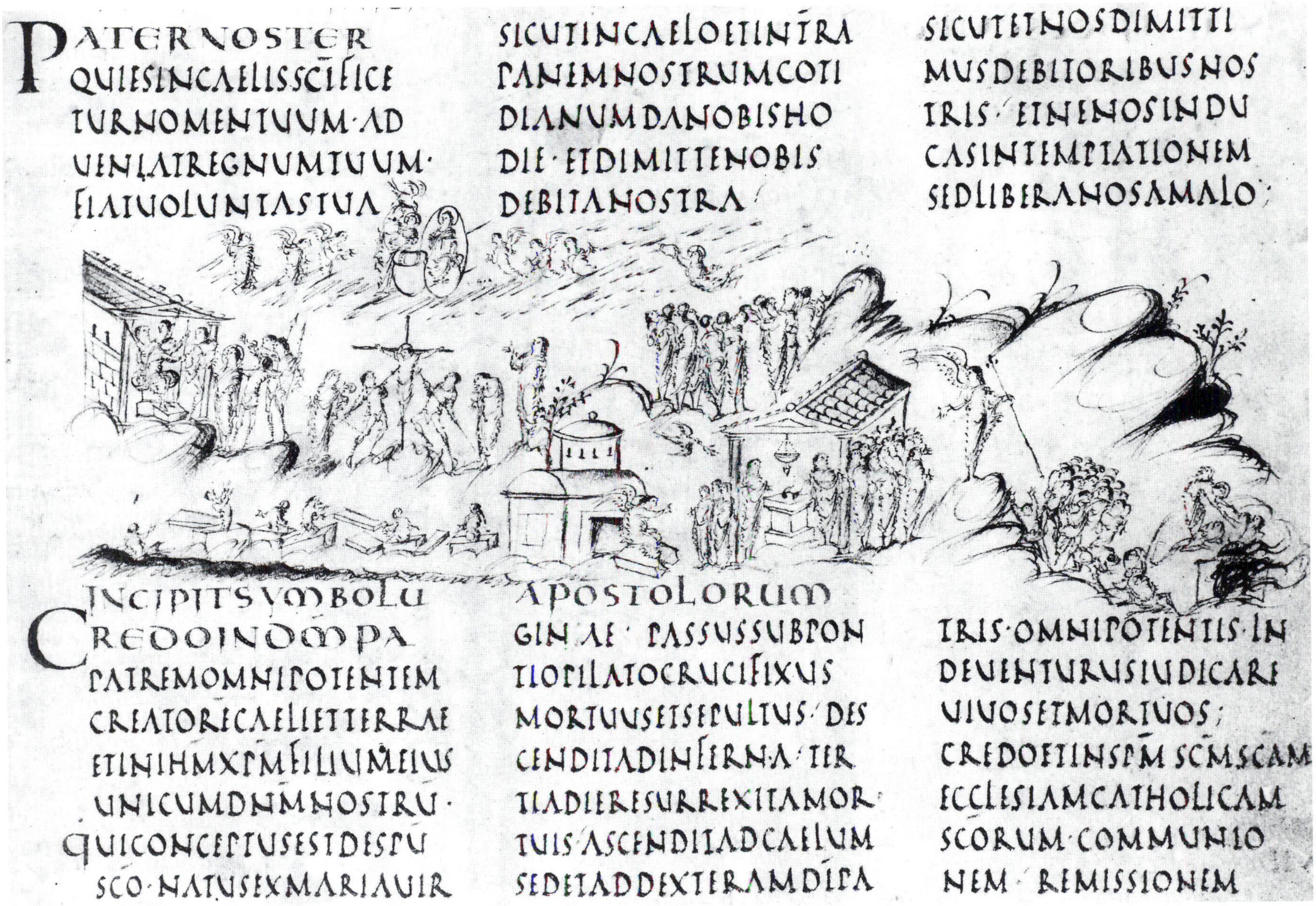

PATER NOSTER
QUI ES IN CAELIS SCILICE
TUR NOMEN TUUM · AD
UENIAT REGNUM TUUM ·
FIAT UOLUNTAS TUA

SICUT IN CAELO ET IN TRA
PANEM NOSTRUM COTI
DIANUM DA NOBIS HO
DIE · ET DIMITTE NOBIS
DEBITA NOSTRA ·

SICUT ET NOS DIMITTI
MUS DEBITORIBUS NOS
TRIS · ET NE NOS INDU
CAS IN TEMPTATIONEM
SED LIBERA NOS A MALO ·

INCIPIT SYMBOLU
CREDO IN DM PA
PATREM OMNIPOTENTEM
CREATORE CAELI ET TERRAE
ET IN IHM XPM FILIUM EIUS
UNICUM DNM NOSTRU ·
QUI CONCEPTUS EST DE SPU
SCO · NATUS EX MARIA UIR

APOSTOLORUM
GIN AE · PASSUS SUB PON
TIO PILATO CRUCIFIXUS
MORTUUS ET SEPULTUS · DES
CENDIT AD INFERNA · TER
TIA DIE RESURREXIT A MOR
TUIS ASCENDIT AD CAELUM
SEDET AD DEXTERAM DI PA

TRIS · OMNIPOTENTIS · IN
DE UENTURUS IUDICARE
UIUOS ET MORTUOS ;
CREDO ET IN SPM SCM SCAM
ECCLESIAM CATHOLICAM
SCORUM · COMMUNIO
NEM · REMISSIONEM

29. Utrecht, University Library, fol. 90: Creed.

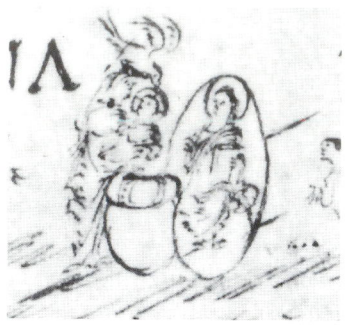

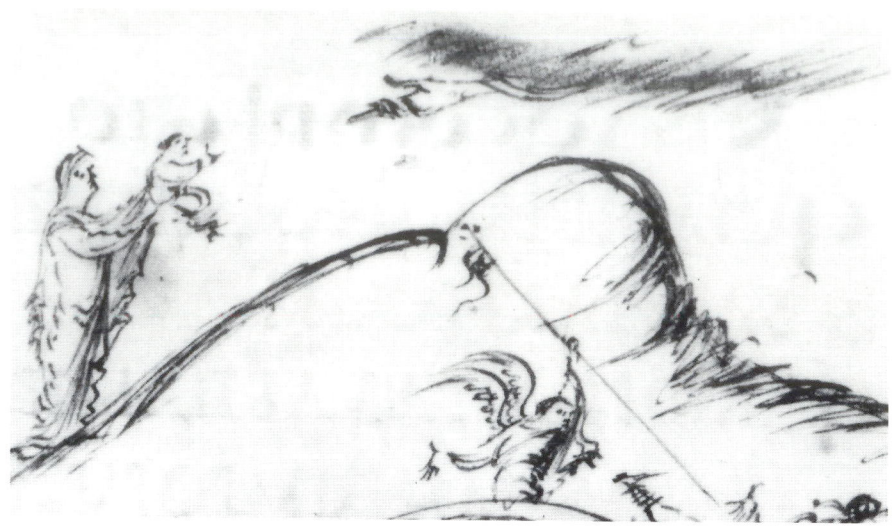

30. Utrecht, University Library, MS 32, fol. 90 (detail) of fig. 29: Creed.

31. Utrecht, University Library, MS 32, fol. 89 (detail): Magnificat.

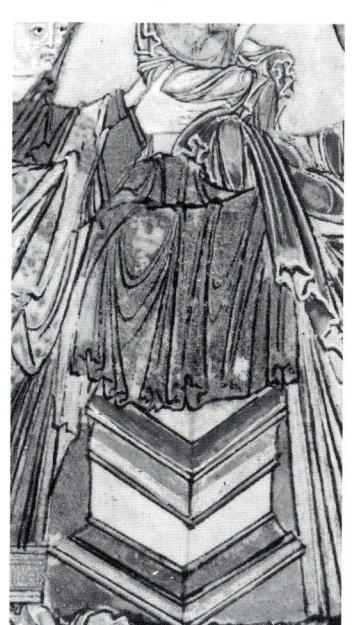

33. London, British Library, MS Add. 49598, fol. 34v (detail): altar.

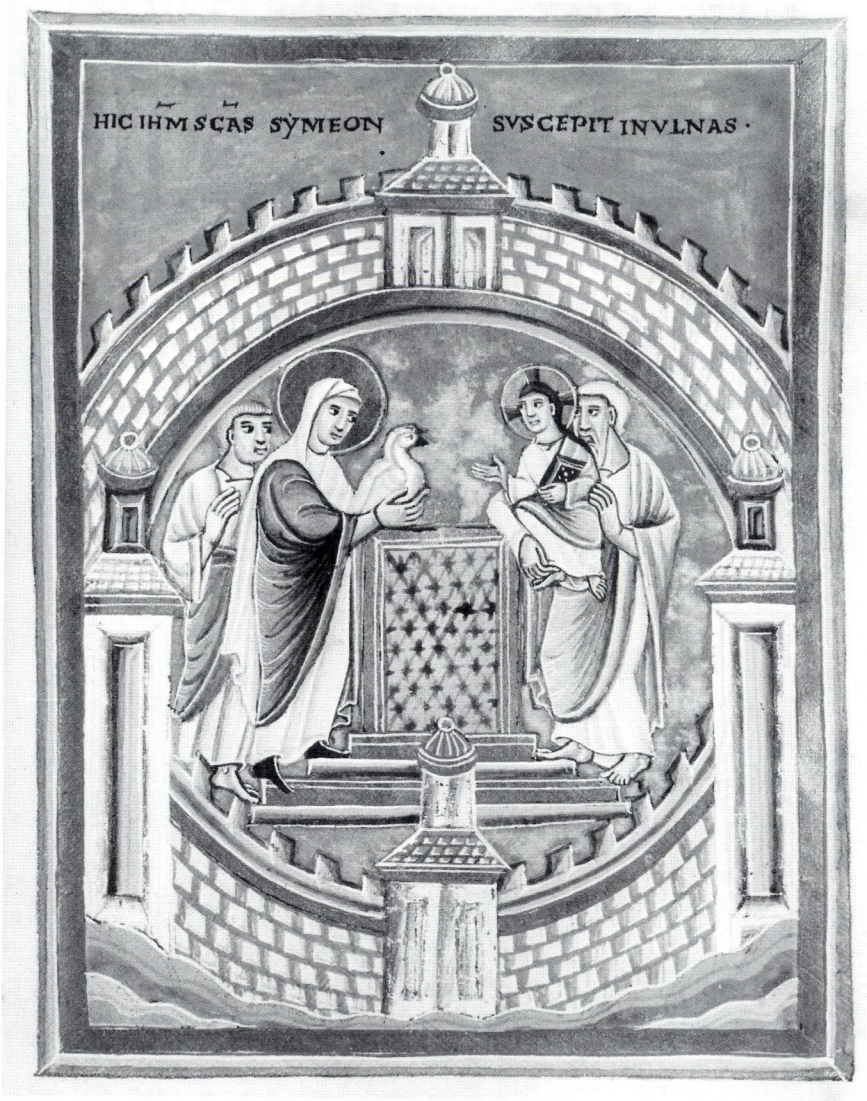

32. Bremen, Staatsbibliothek, MS b. 21, fol. 104: Presentation (Rheinisches Bildarchiv).

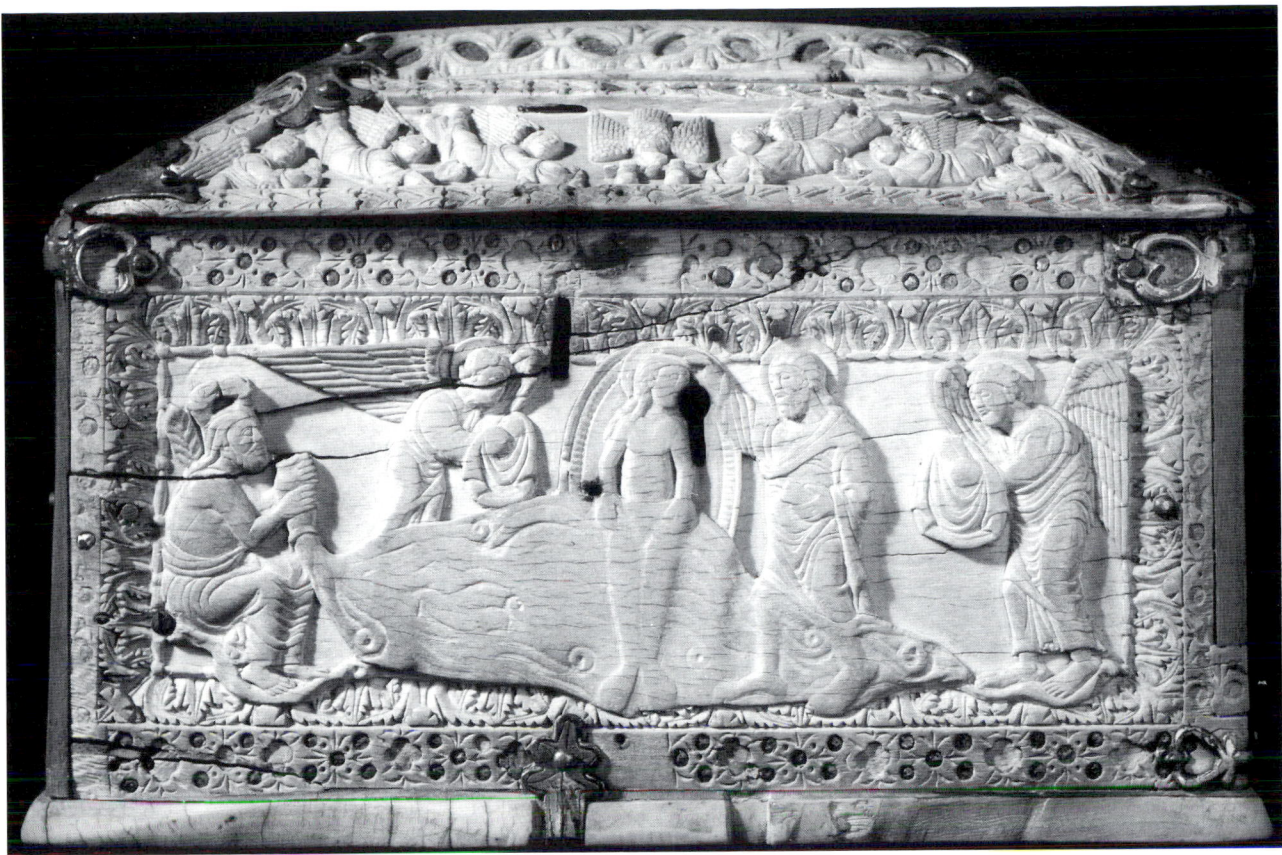

34. Brunswick, Herzog Anton Ulrich-Museum, ivory casket: Baptism.

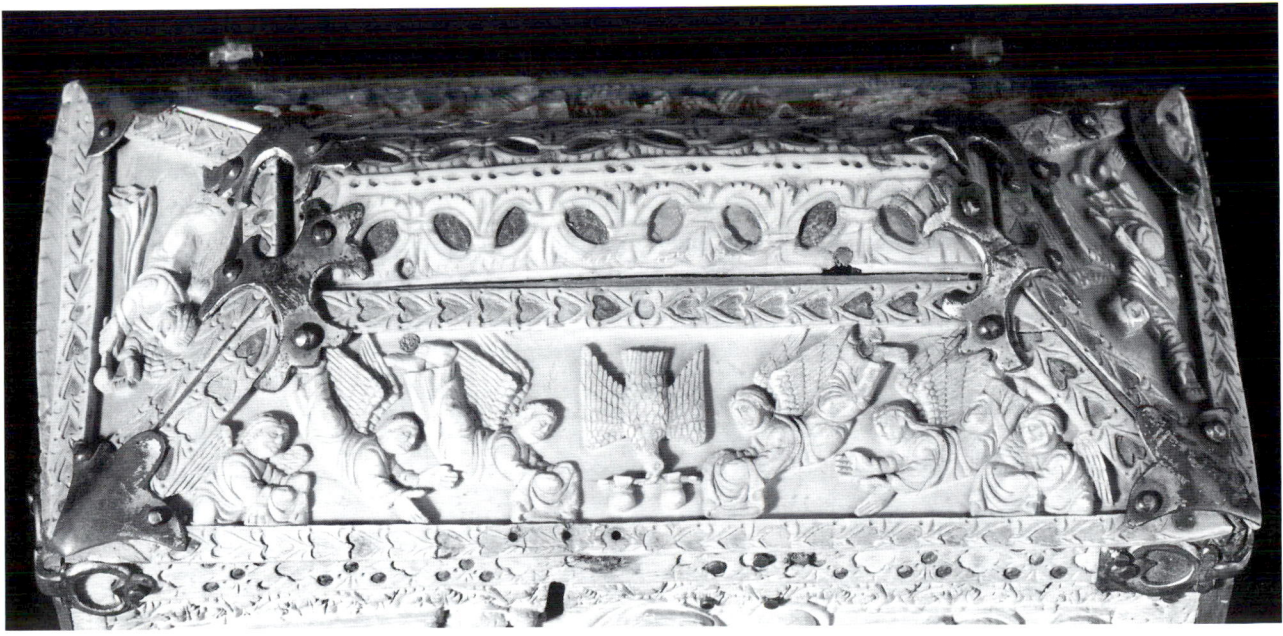

35. Brunswick, Herzog Anton Ulrich-Museum, ivory casket: lid.

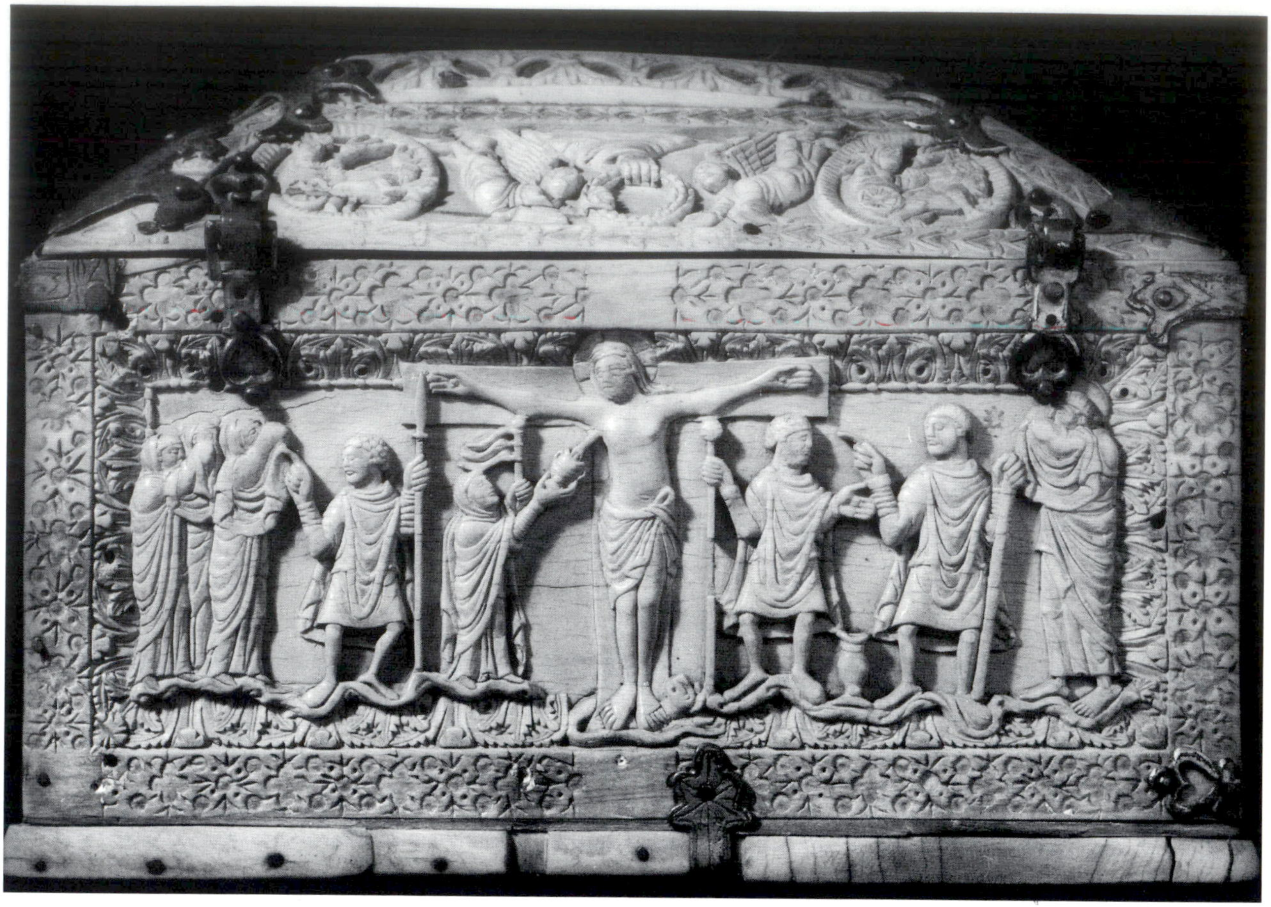

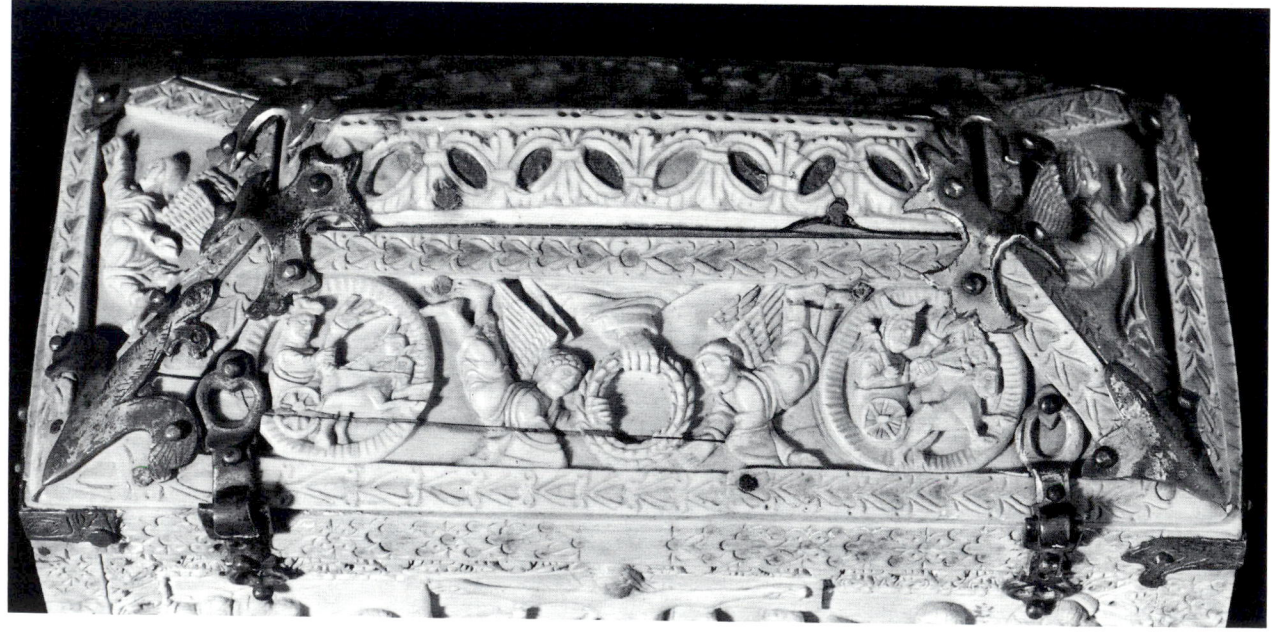

36. Brunswick, Herzog Anton Ulrich-Museum, ivory casket: Crucifixion.

37. Brunswick, Herzog Anton Ulrich-Museum, ivory casket: lid.

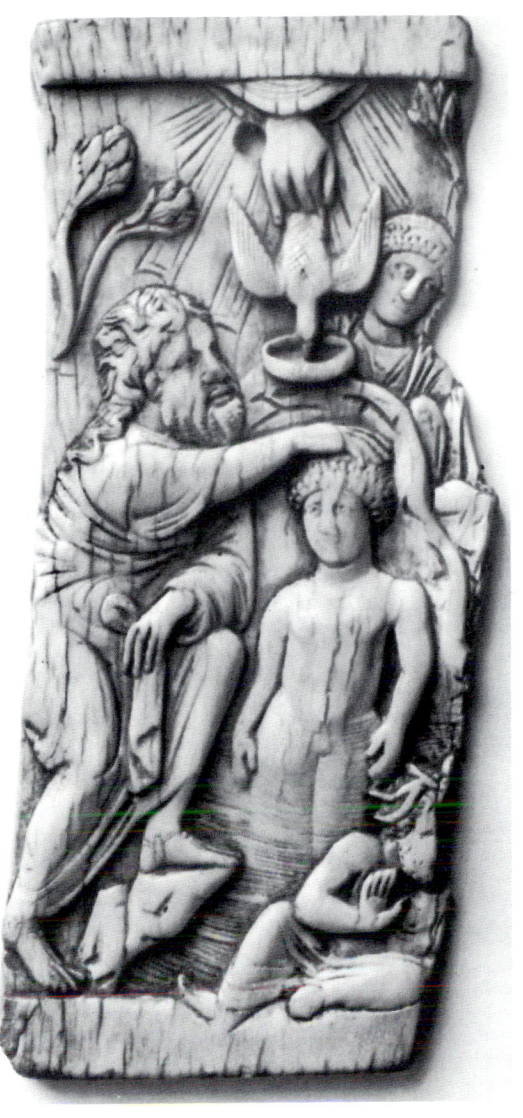

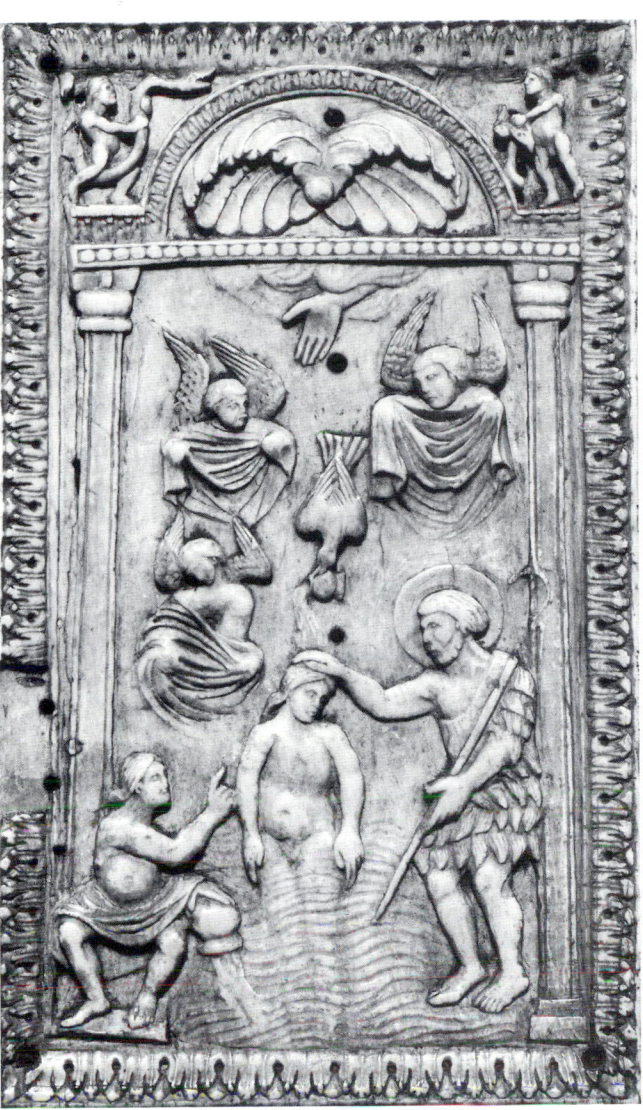

38. London, British Museum, ivory plaque: Baptism.

39. Antwerp, Museum Mayer van der Bergh, ivory: Baptism (ACL, Brussels).

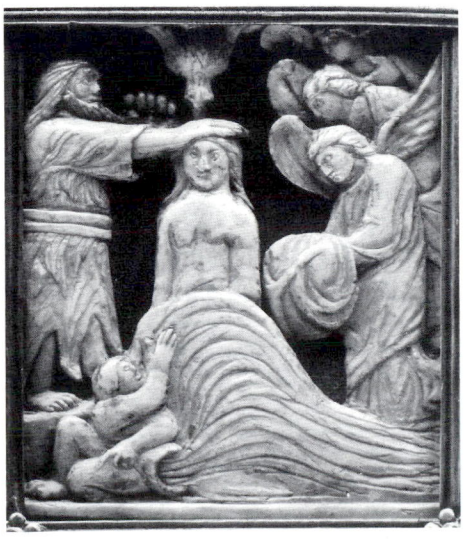

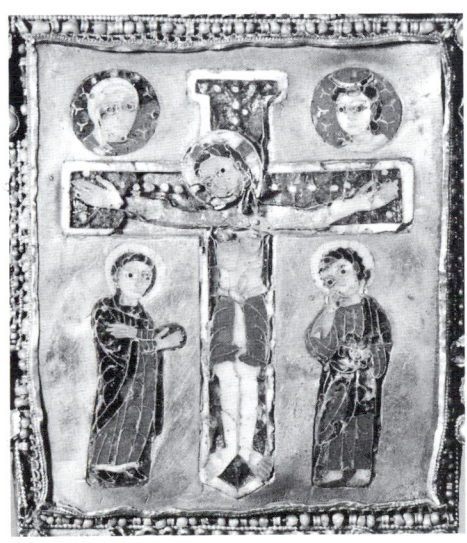

40. Paris, Bibliothèque Nationale, MS lat. 9428, ivory cover (detail): Baptism.

41. Essen, Münsterschatz, processional cross (detail): Crucifixion (Marburg/Art Resource).

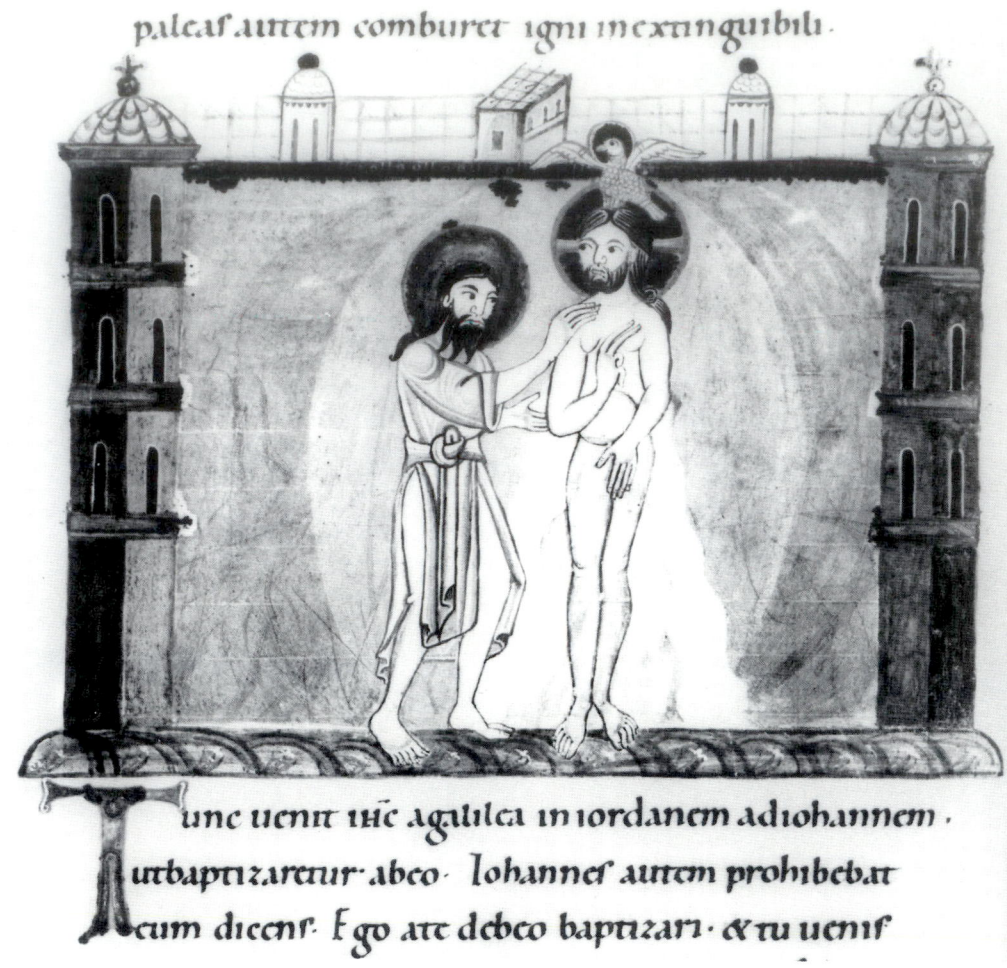

palcaſ auttem comburet igni inextinguibili·

Tunc uenit ihc agalilea iniordanem adiohannem·

utbaptizaretur abeo· Iohanneſ auttem prohibebat

cum diceuſ· Ego ate debeo baptizari· & tu ueniſ

42. New York, Pierpont Morgan Library, MS 781, fol. 40v: Baptism (Courtauld Institute).

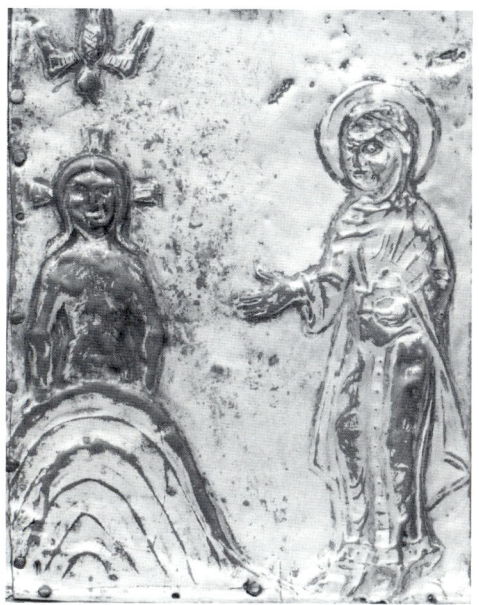

43. Baltimore, Walters Art Gallery, copper gilt plaque: Baptism.

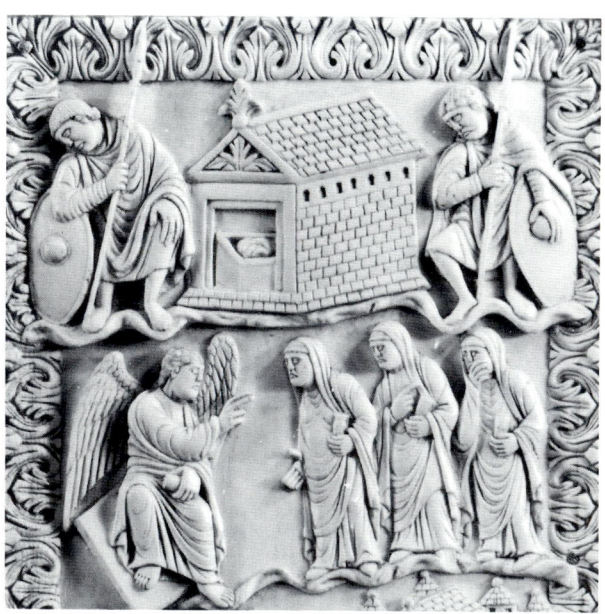

44. Paris, Bibliothèque Nationale, MS lat. 9390, ivory cover (detail): Women at the Tomb.

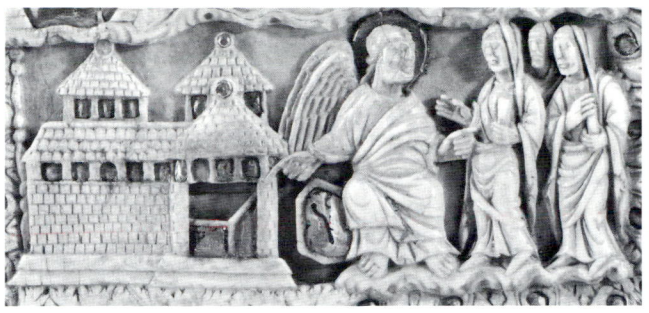

45. Paris, Bibliothèque Nationale, MS lat. 9453, ivory cover (detail): Women at the Tomb.

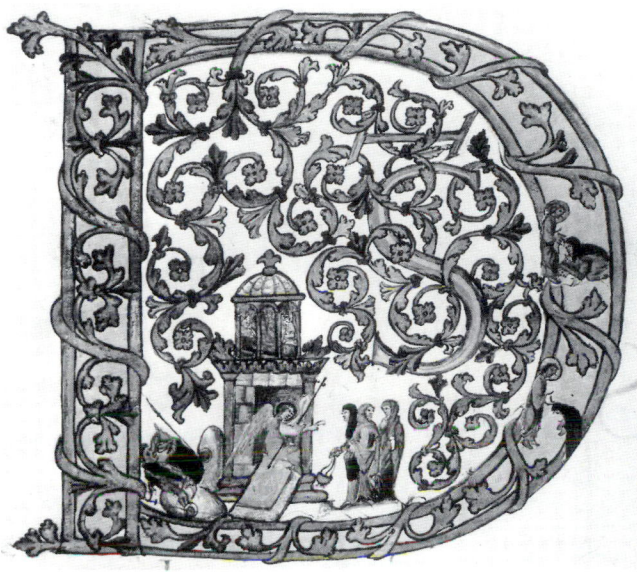

46. Paris, Bibliothèque Nationale, MS lat. 9428, fol. 58: Women at the Tomb.

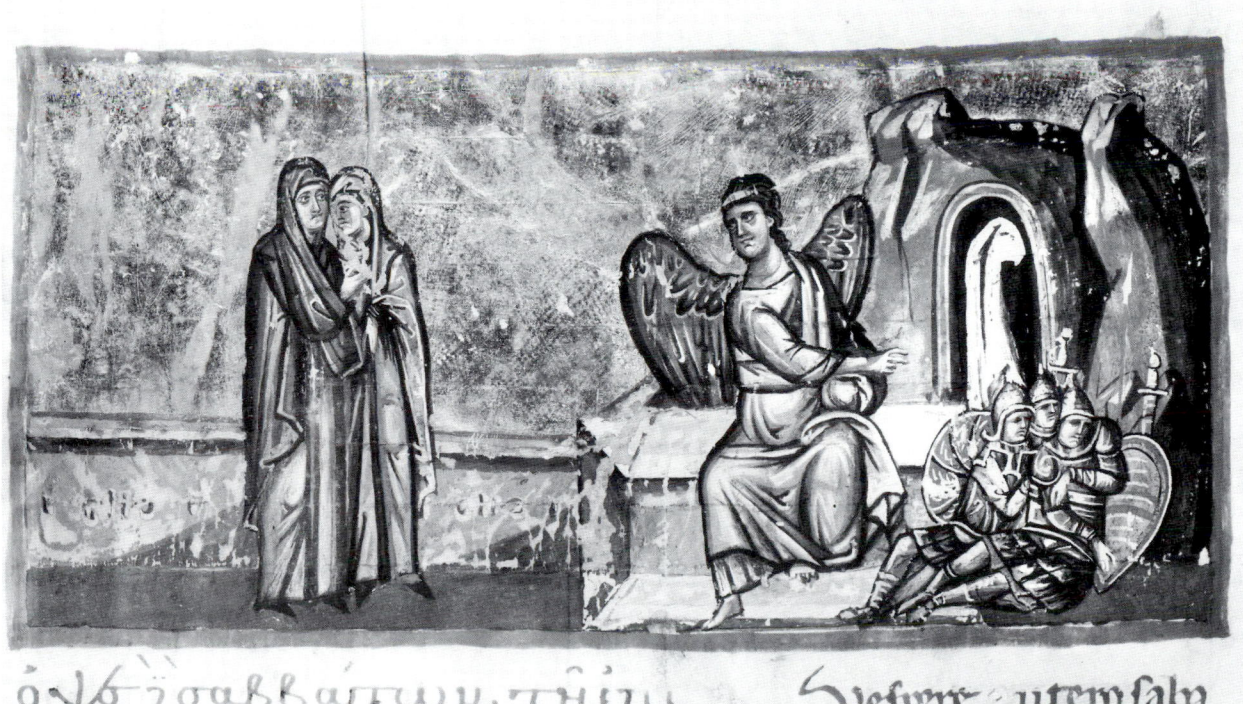

47. Paris, Bibliothèque Nationale, MS gr. 54, fol. 108: Women at the Tomb.

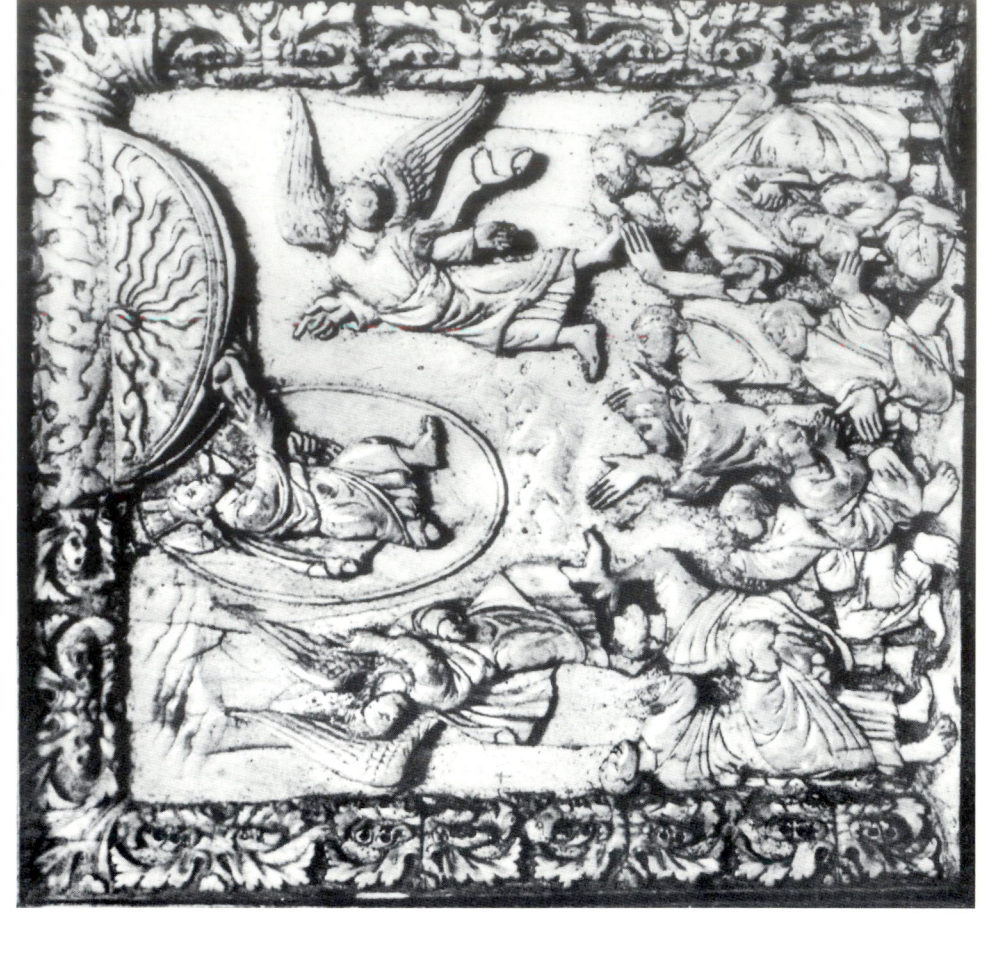

49. Minden, Domschatz, ivory plaque: Ascension (Marburg/Art Resource).

48. Paris, Bibliotheque Nationale, MS lat. 9428, fol. 71v: Ascension.

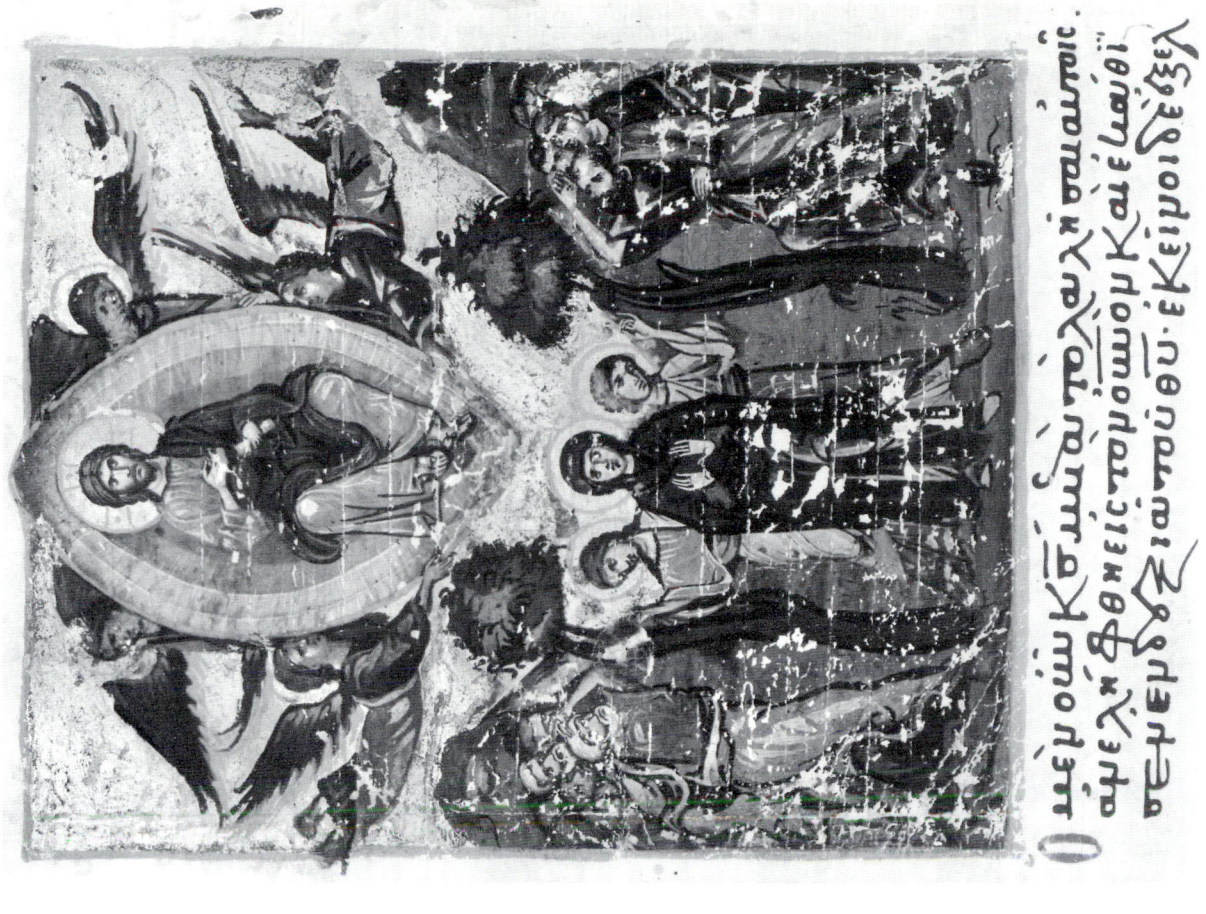

51. London, British Library, MS Harley 1810, fol. 135v: Ascension.

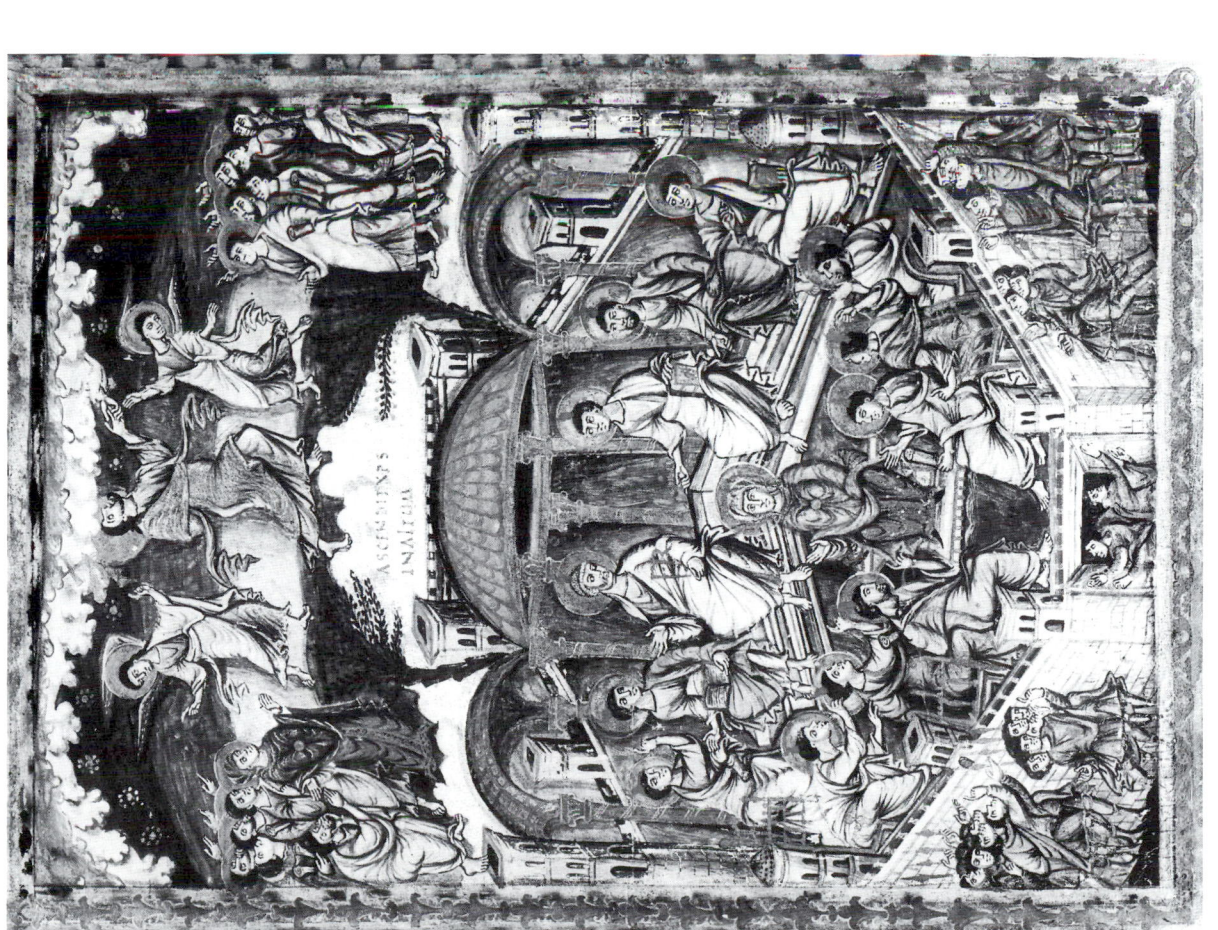

50. Rome, San Paolo f.l.m, Bible, fol. 292v: Ascension and Pentecost.

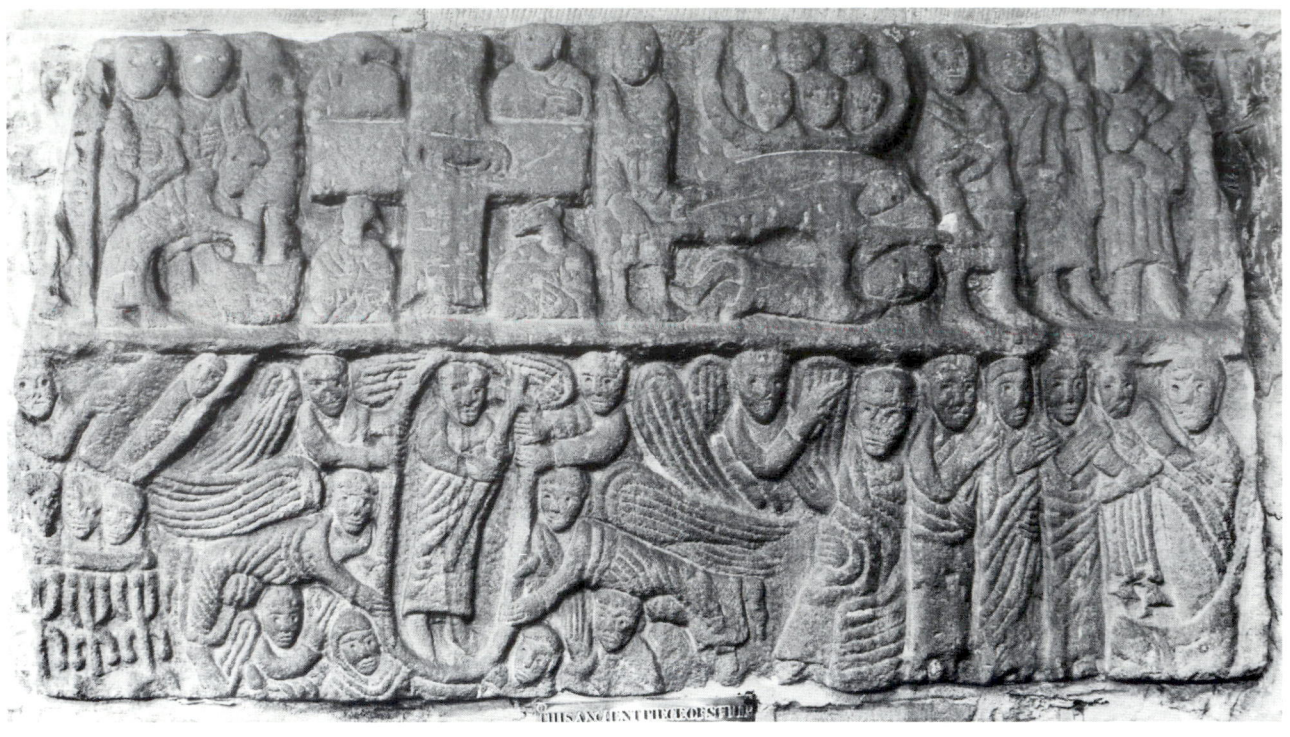

52. Wirksworth, church, stone slab (Courtauld Institute).

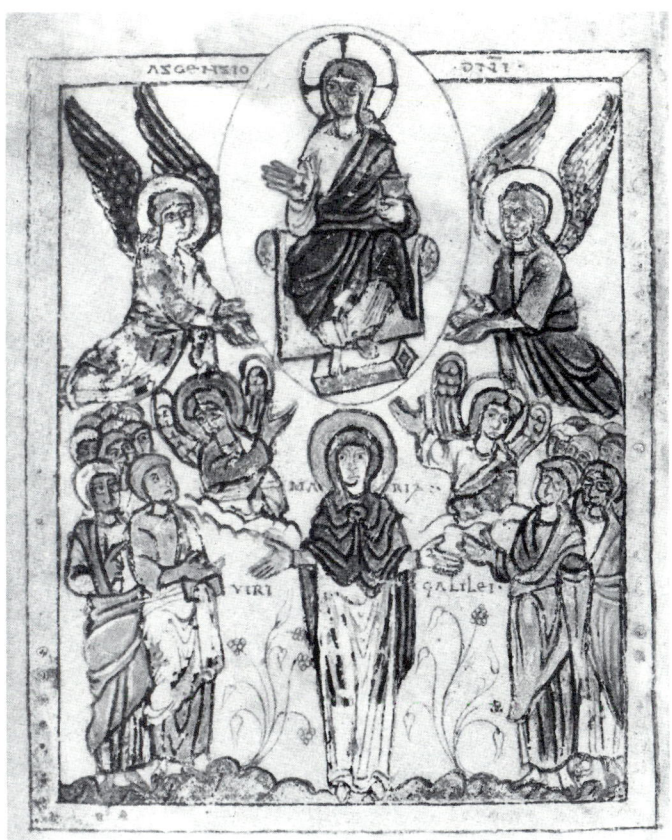

53. London, British Library, MS Cotton Galba A. XVIII, fol. 120v: Ascension.

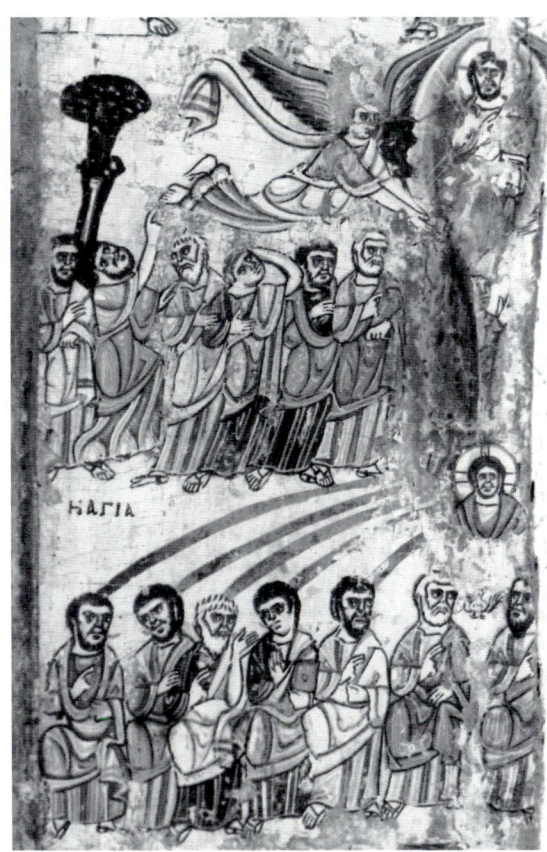

54. Mt. Sinai, St. Catherine's monastery, icon B.45 (detail): Ascension and Pentecost (Princeton-Michigan-Alexandria Expedition to Mt. Sinai).

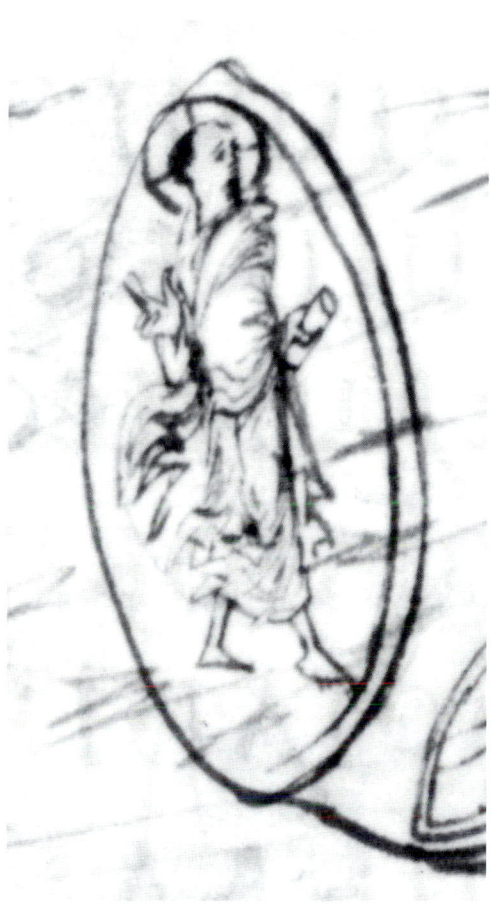

55. Utrecht, University Library, MS 32, fol. 76 (detail): Psalm 76.

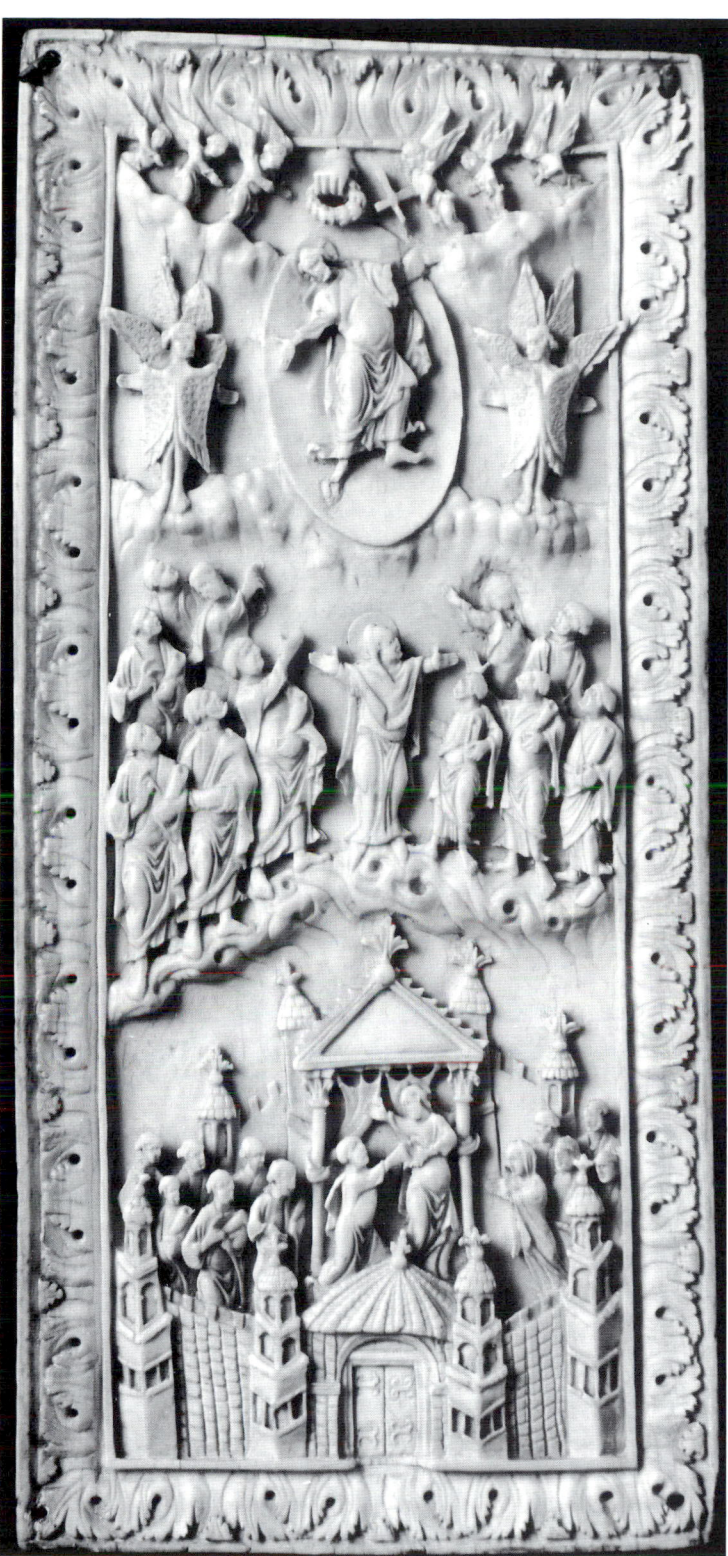

56. Weimar, Kunstgewerbemuseum, ivory plaque: Ascension and Doubting of Thomas.

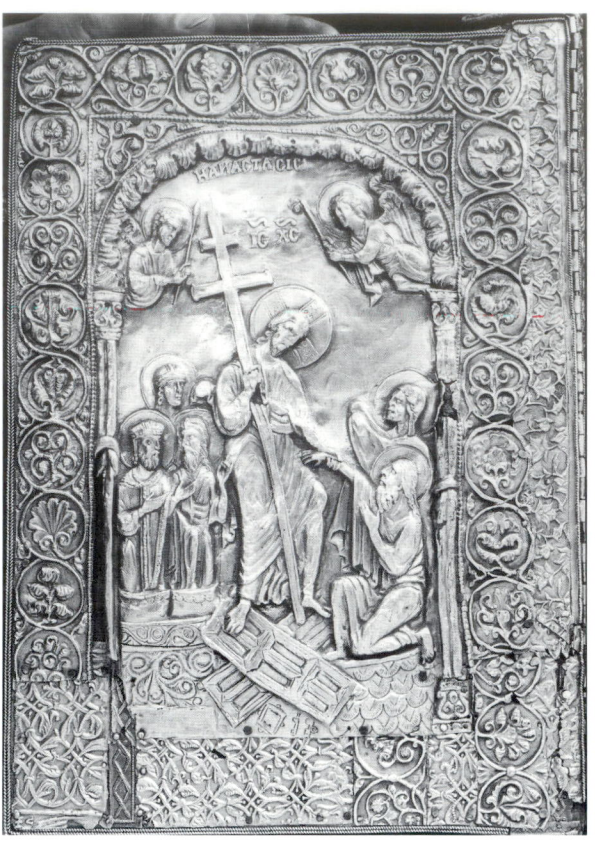

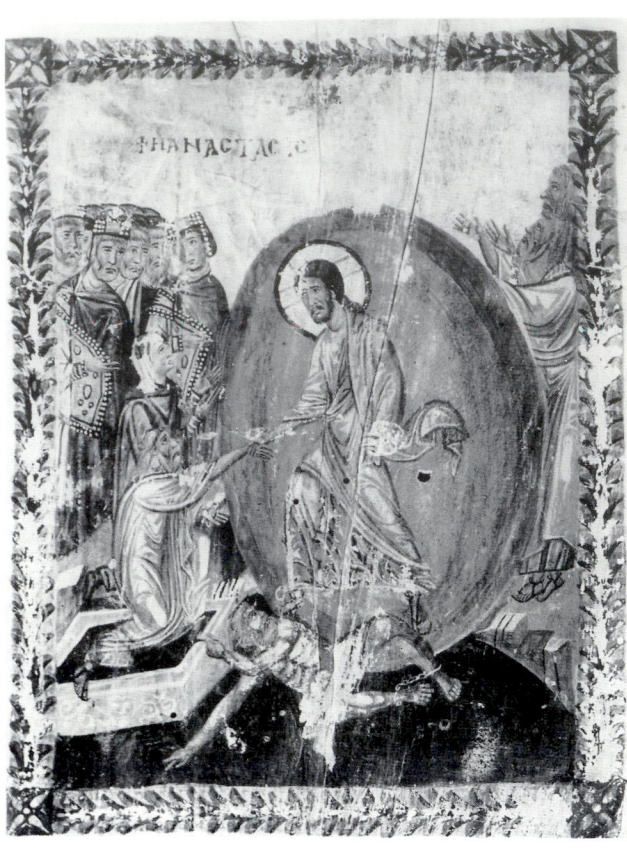

58. Mt. Athos, Lavra, gold bookcover: Anastasis (Kurt Weitzmann).

59. St. Petersburg, Public Library, MS gr. 21, fol. 1v: Anastasis (Marburg/Art Resource).

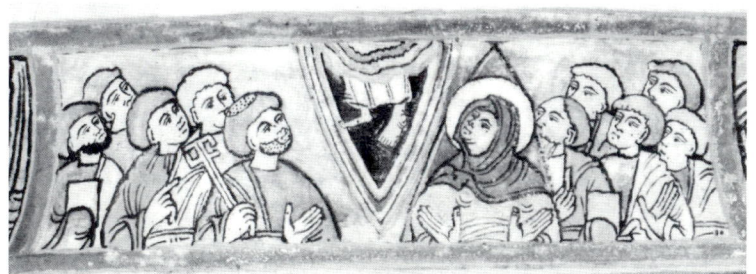

57. New York, Pierpont Morgan Library, MS 333, fol. 85: detail, Ascension.

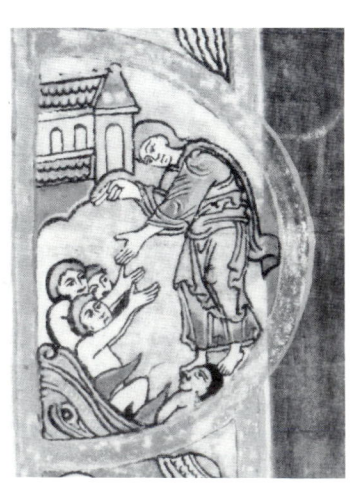

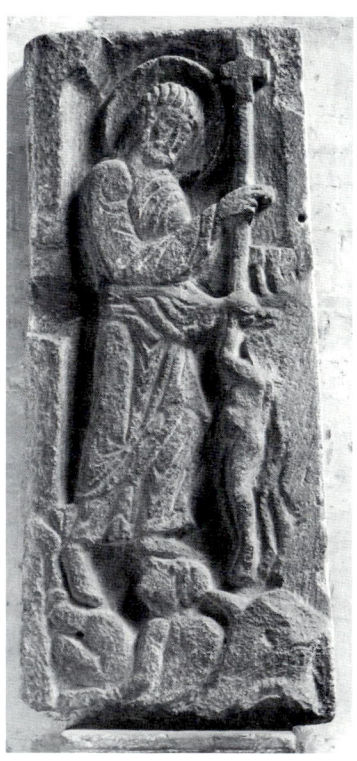

61. New York, Pierpont Morgan Lib., MS 333, fol. 85 (detail of fig. 57): Harrowing of Hell.

60. Bristol, cathedral, stone slab: Harrowing of Hell (National Monuments Record).

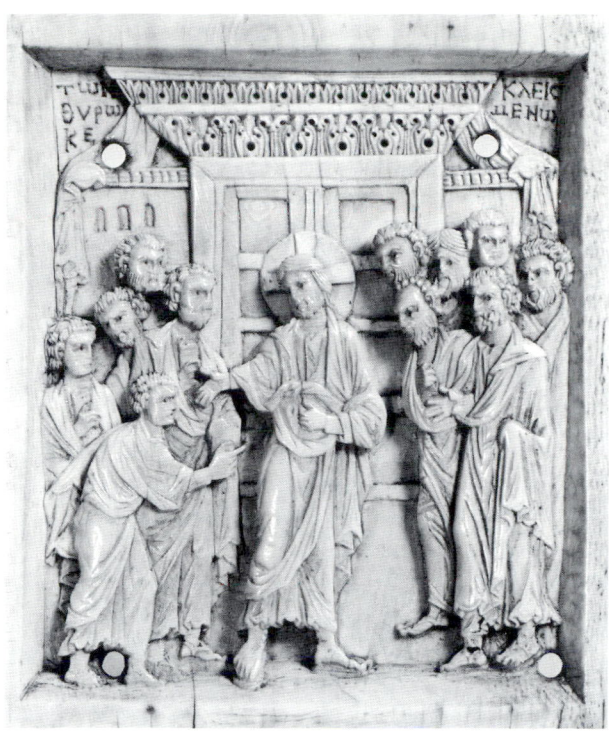

62. Washington, Dumbarton Oaks Collection, ivory plaque: Doubting of Thomas.

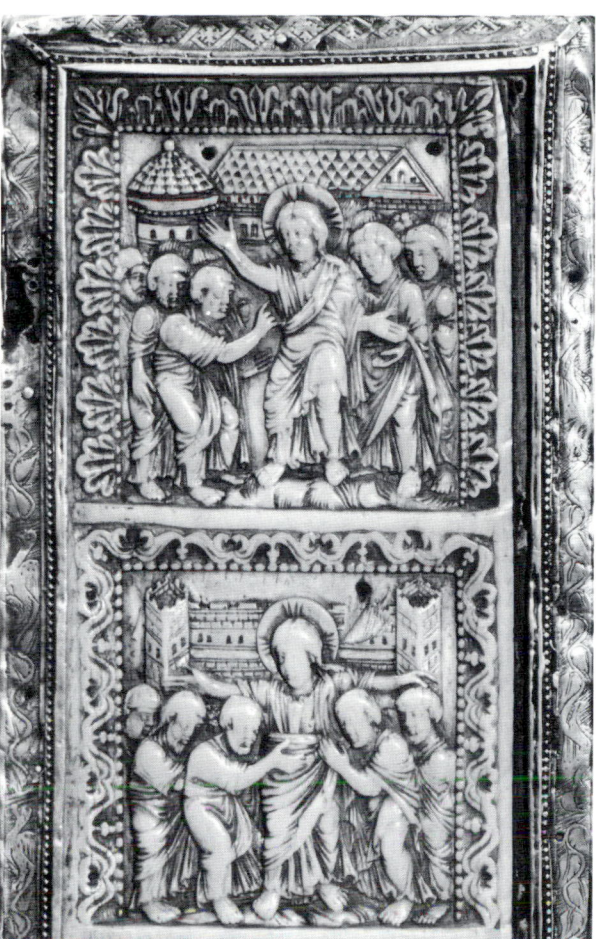

63. Aachen, cathedral treasury, ivory plaque: Doubting of Thomas and Christ Appearing to the Apostles (Foto Ann Münchow).

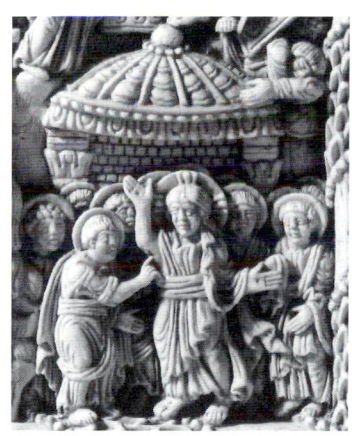

64. Narbonne, St. Just, ivory (detail): Doubting of Thomas.

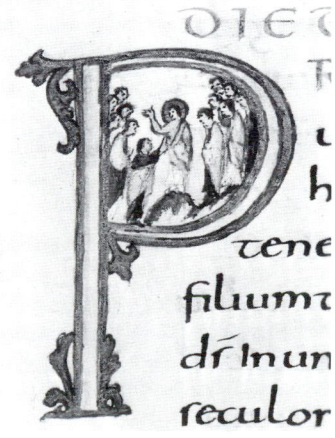

66. Paris, Bibliothèque Nationale, MS lat. 9428, fol. 66: Doubting of Thomas.

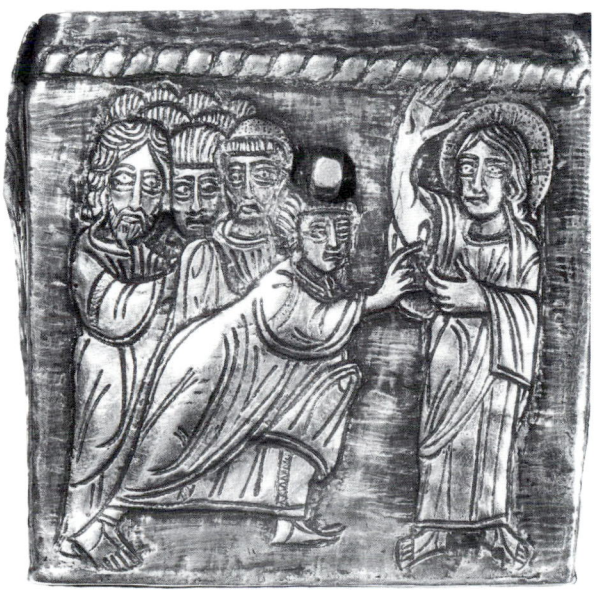

65. Vatican, Museo Sacro, silver reliquary of Paschal I: Doubting of Thomas.

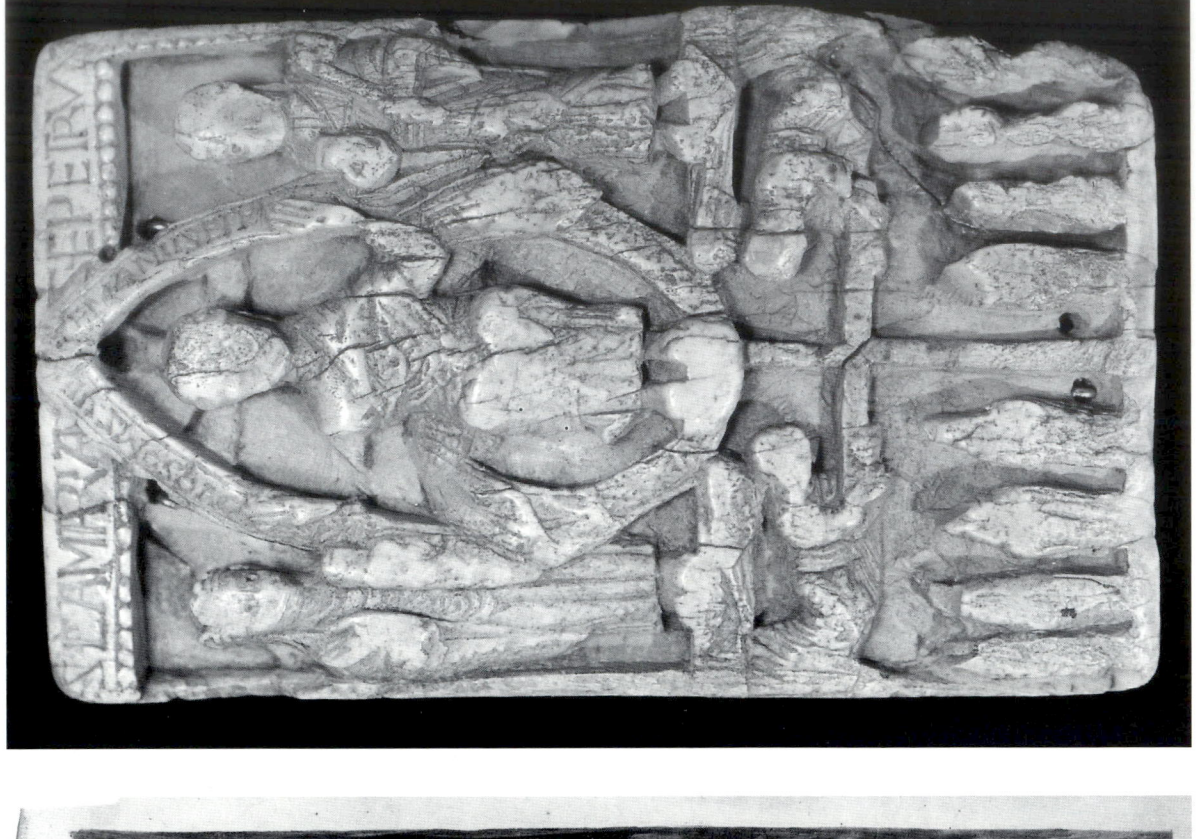

68. Cambridge, University Museum of Archaeology and Ethnology, ivory plaque: Last Judgement.

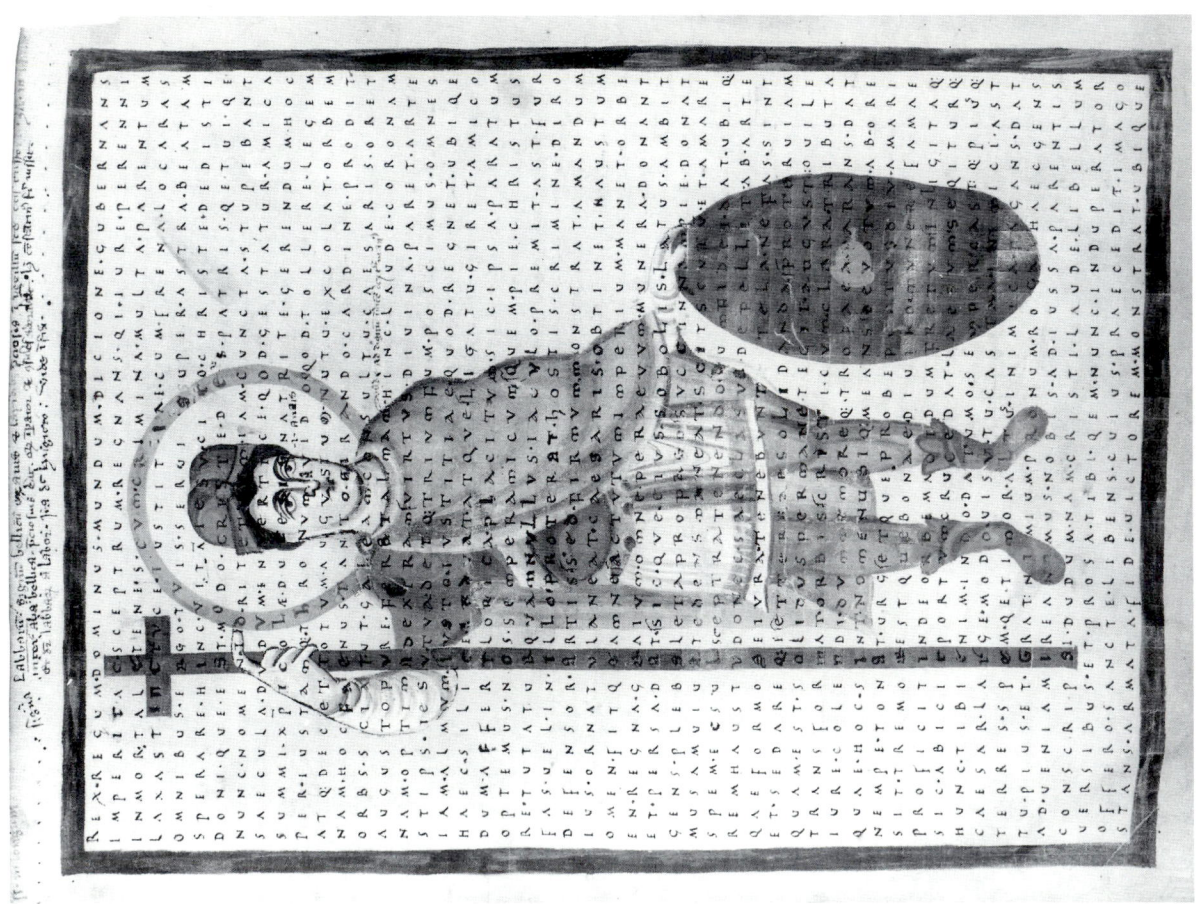

67. Vienna, Österreichische Nationalbibliothek, MS 652, fol. 3v: Louis the Pious.

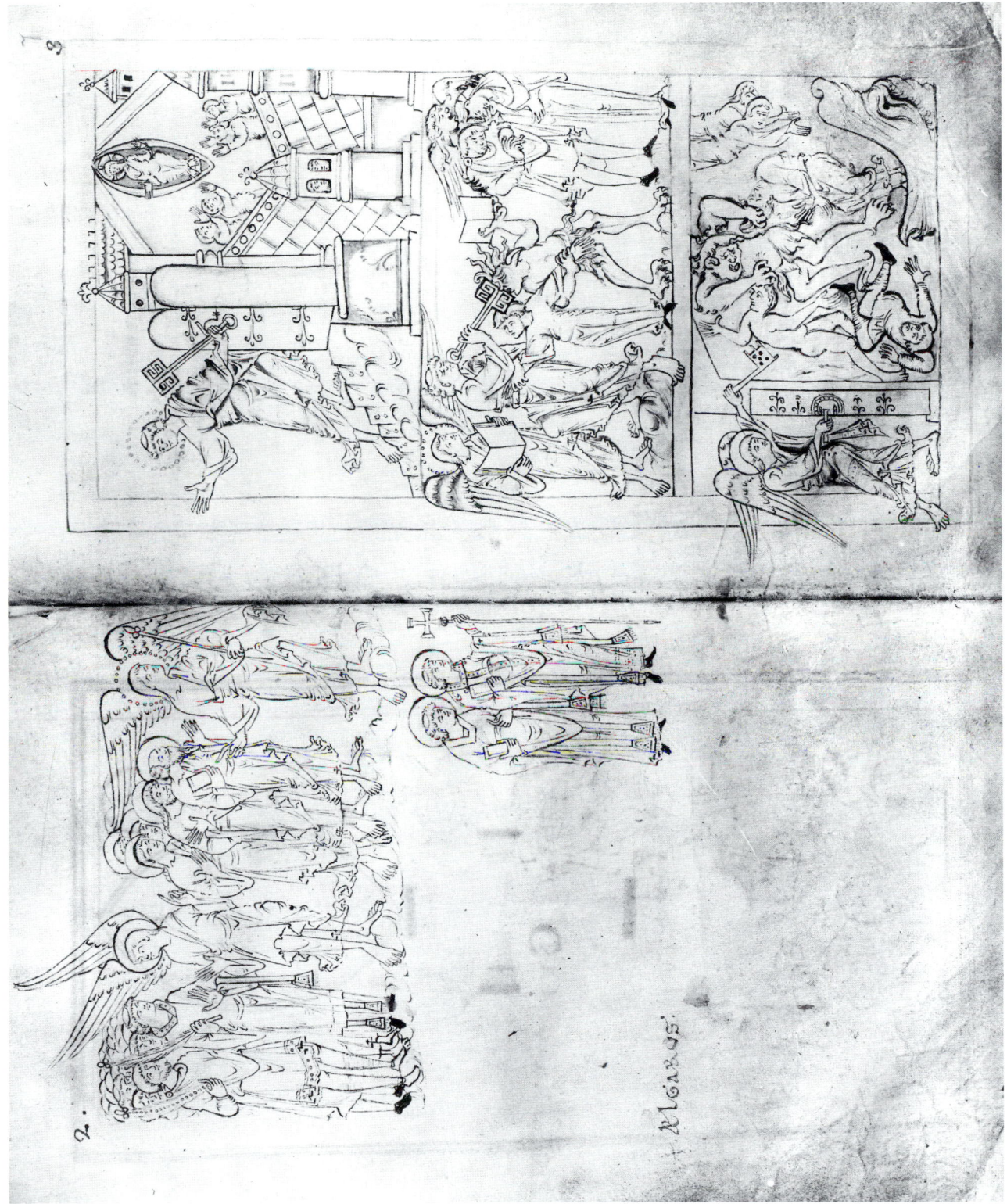

69. London, British Library, MS Stowe 944, fols. 6v–7: Last Judgment.

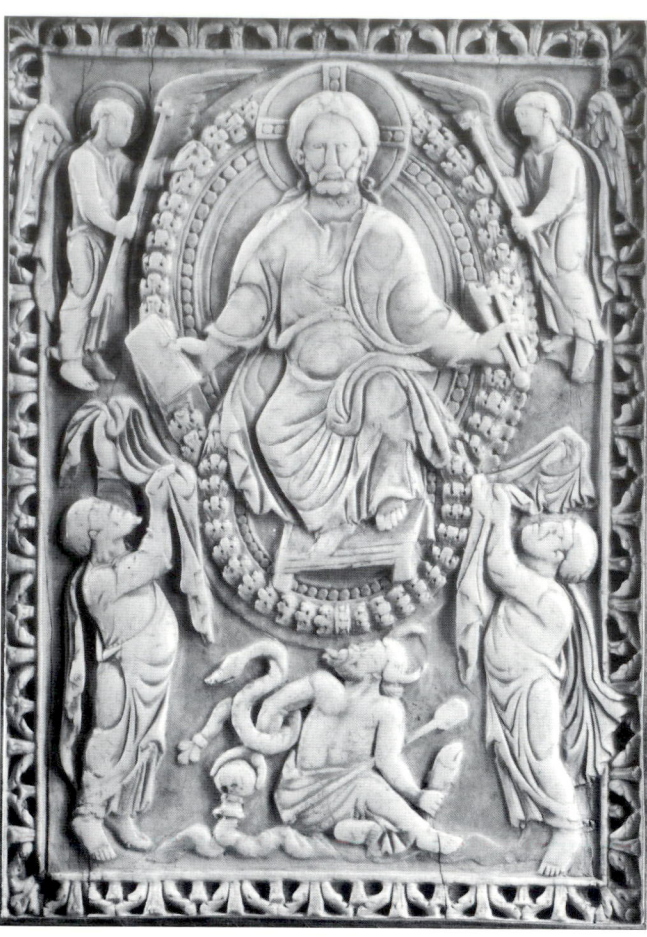

70. Paris, Bibliothèque Nationale, MS lat. 323, ivory cover (detail): Dominus legem dat.

71. London, Victoria and Albert Museum, ivory plaque (detail): Entry into Jerusalem.

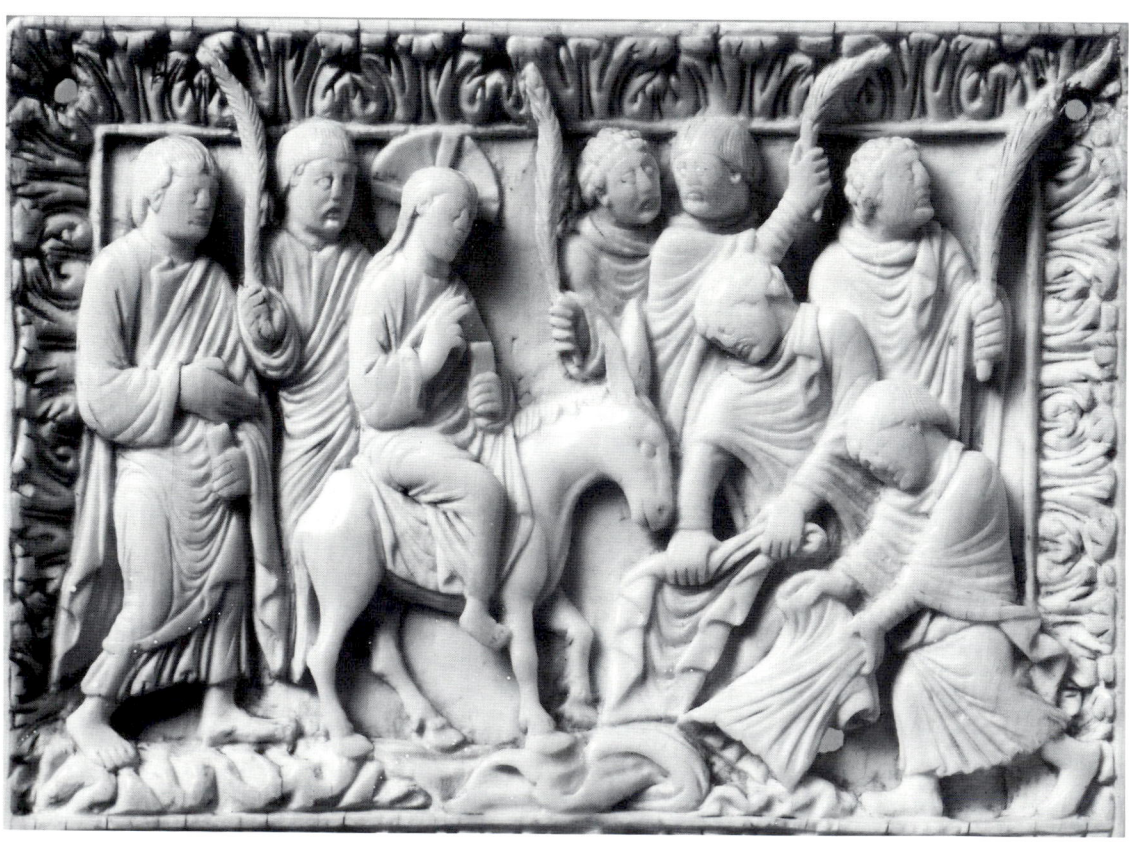

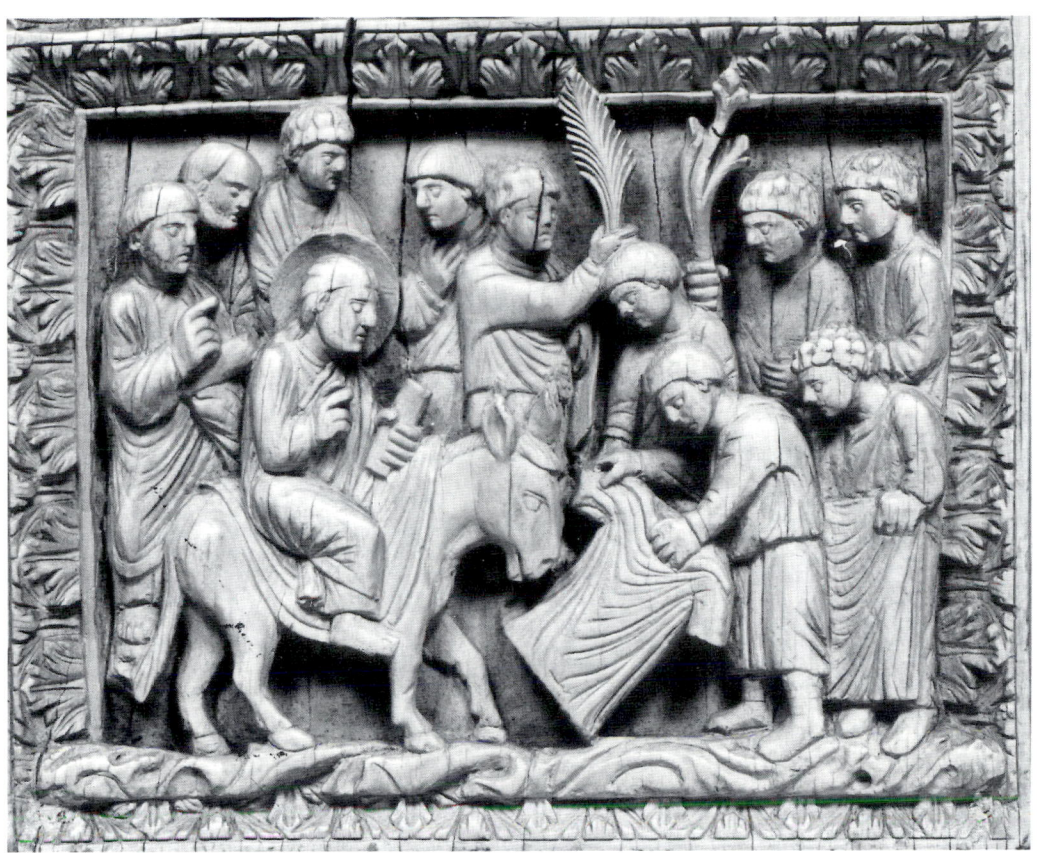

72. London, British Museum, ivory plaque (detail): Entry into Jerusalem.

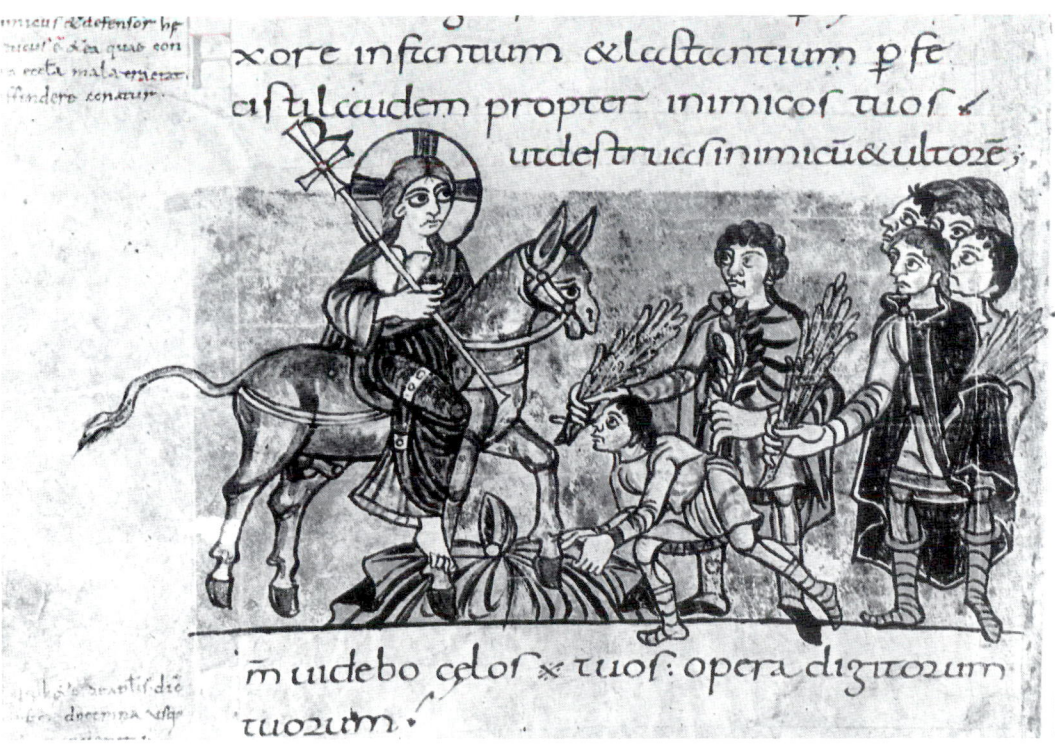

73. Stuttgart, Württembergische Landesbibliothek, MS Bibl. Fol. 23, fol. 8v: Entry into Jerusalem
(Marburg/Art Resource).

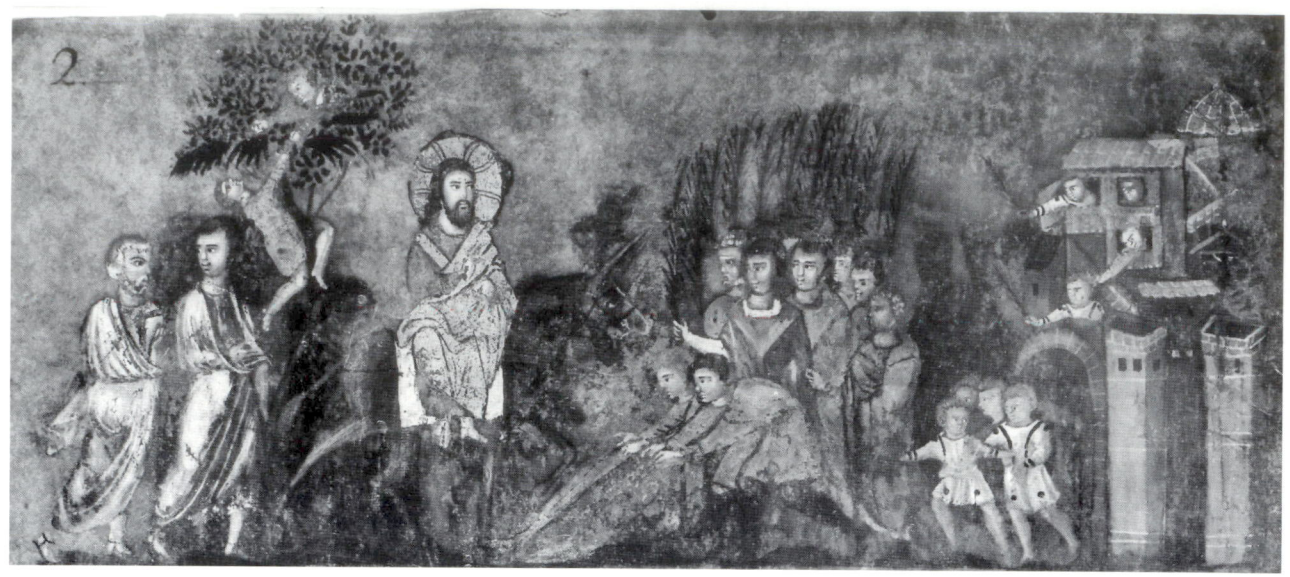

74. Rossano, cathedral, Gospels, fol. 1v: Entry into Jerusalem (Courtauld Institute).

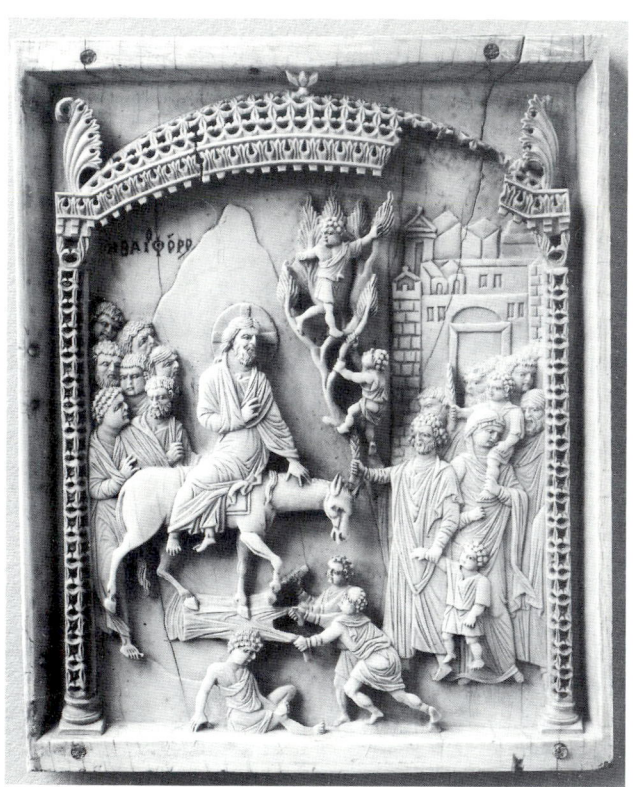

75. Berlin, Staatliche Museen Preussischer Kulturbesitz, ivory plaque: Entry into Jerusalem.

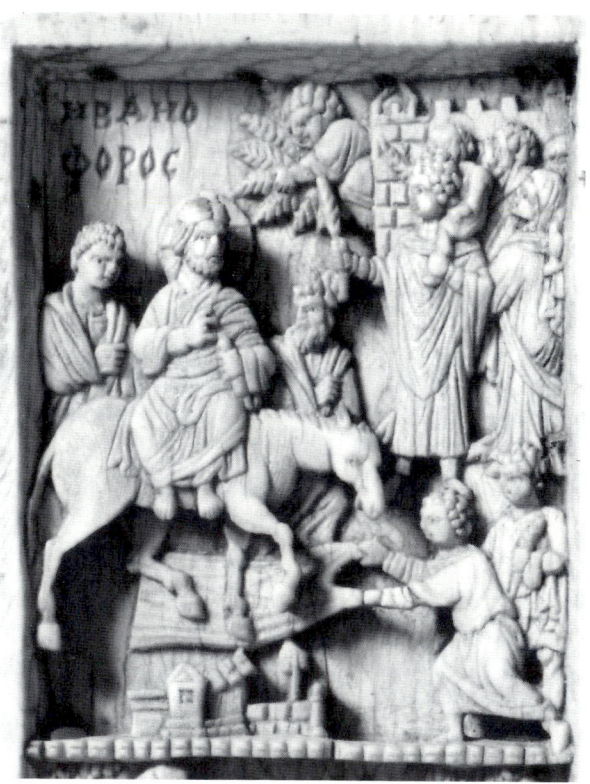

76. Paris, Louvre Museum, ivory triptych (detail): Entry into Jerusalem (ARS, New York/SPADEM, Paris).

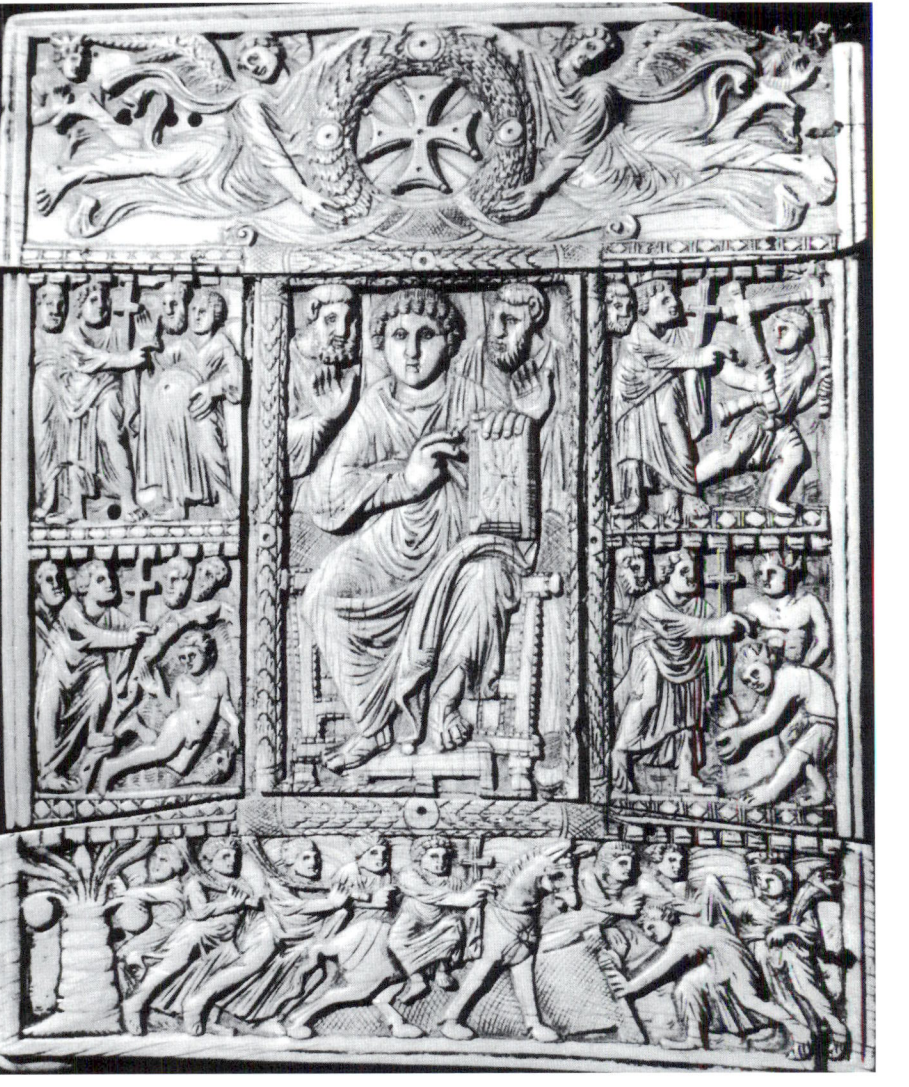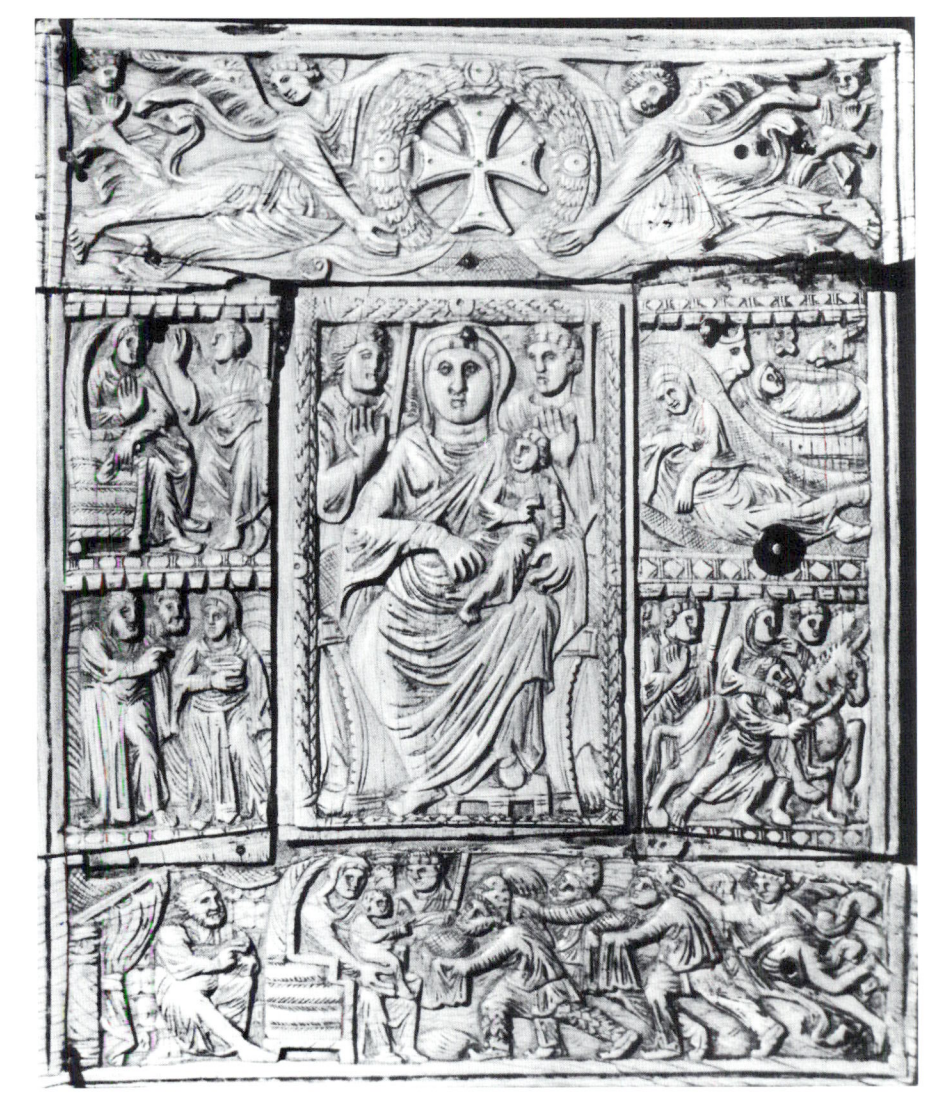

77. Yerevan, Armenia, the Matenadaran, ivory diptych: Christ and Virgin with New Testament scenes.

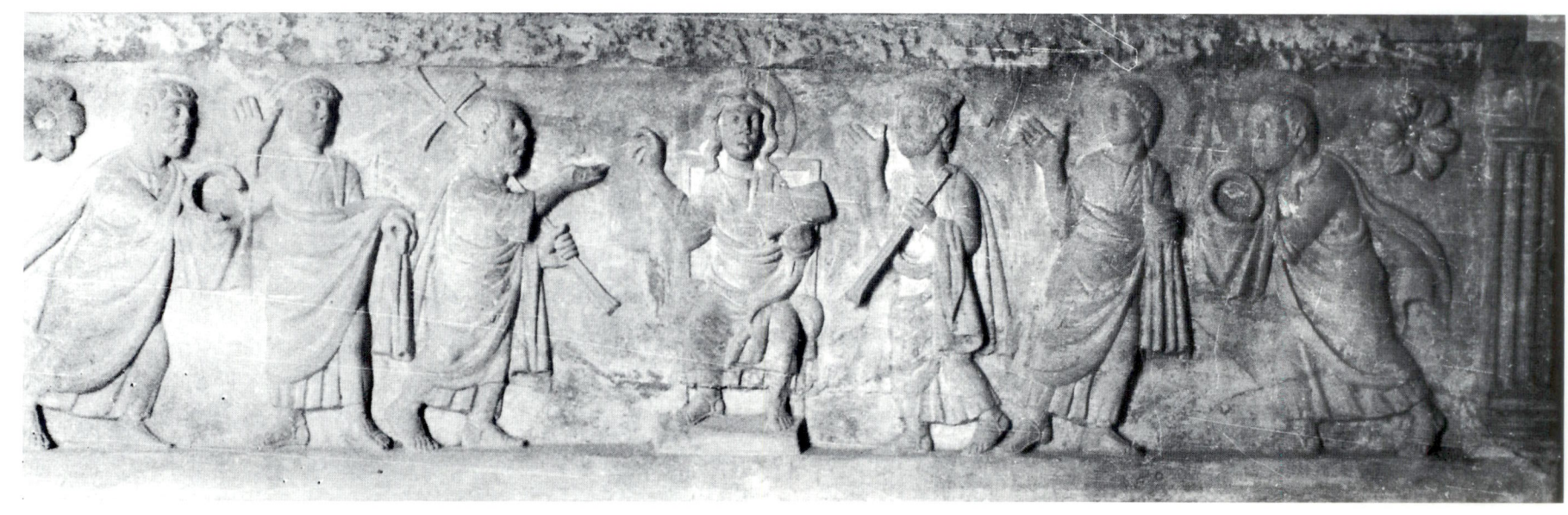

78. Ferrara, cathedral, sarcophagus: Christ and apostles (DAI, Rome).

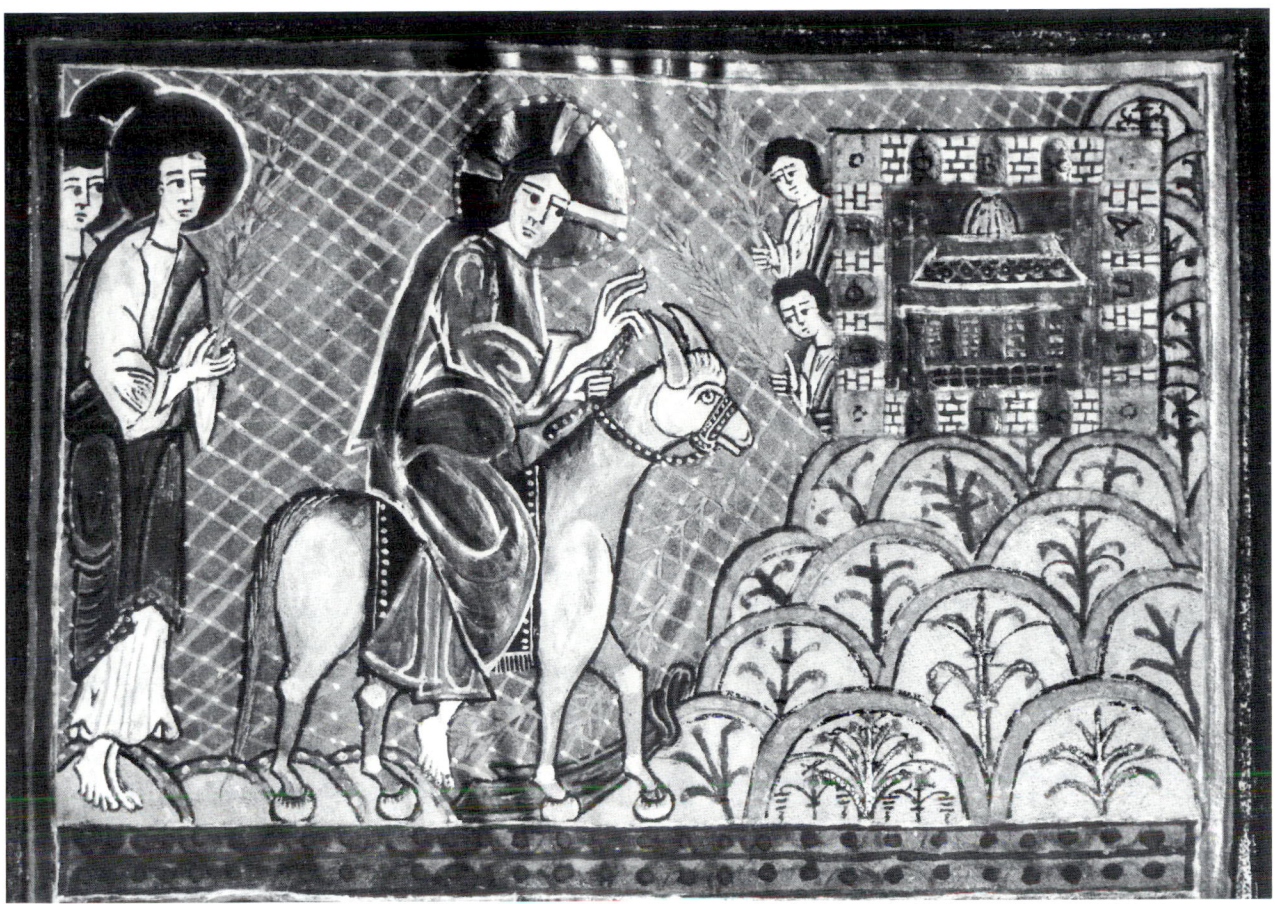

79. Hildesheim, Domschatz, MS 18, fol. 175 (detail): Entry into Jerusalem.

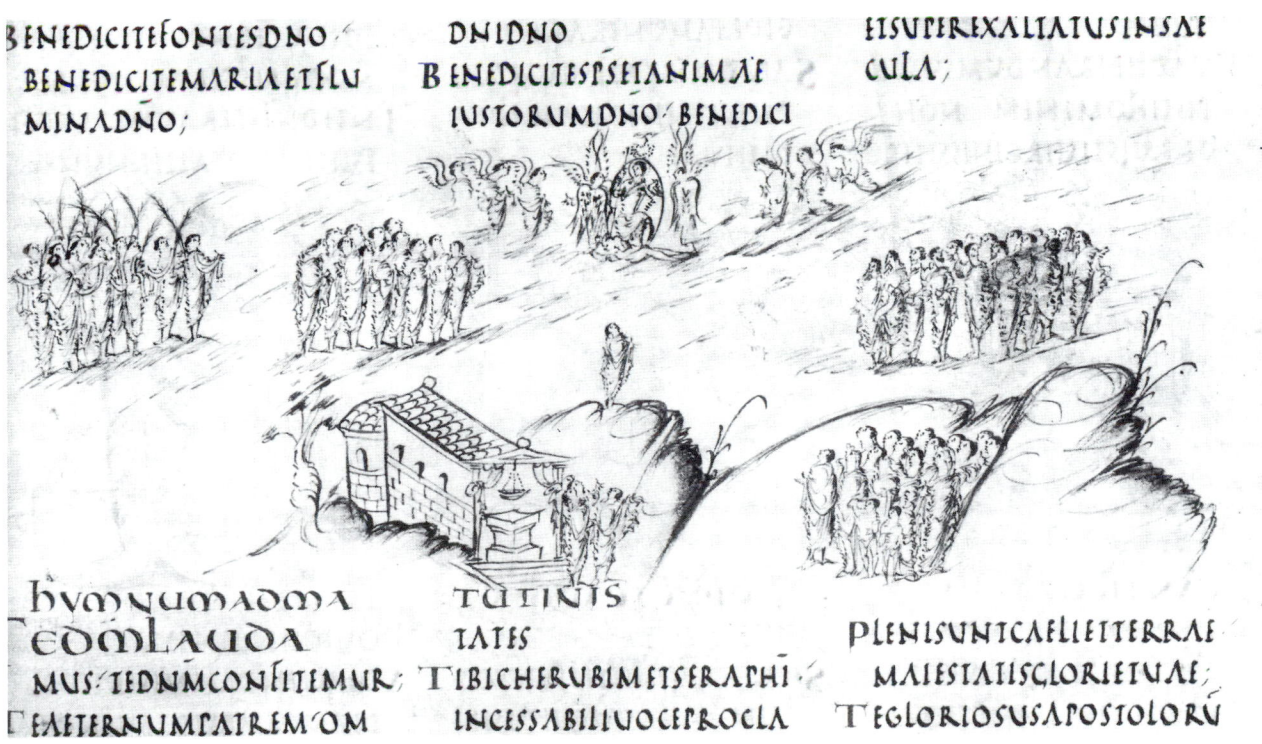

80. Utrecht, University Lib., MS 32, fol. 88: Te Deum.

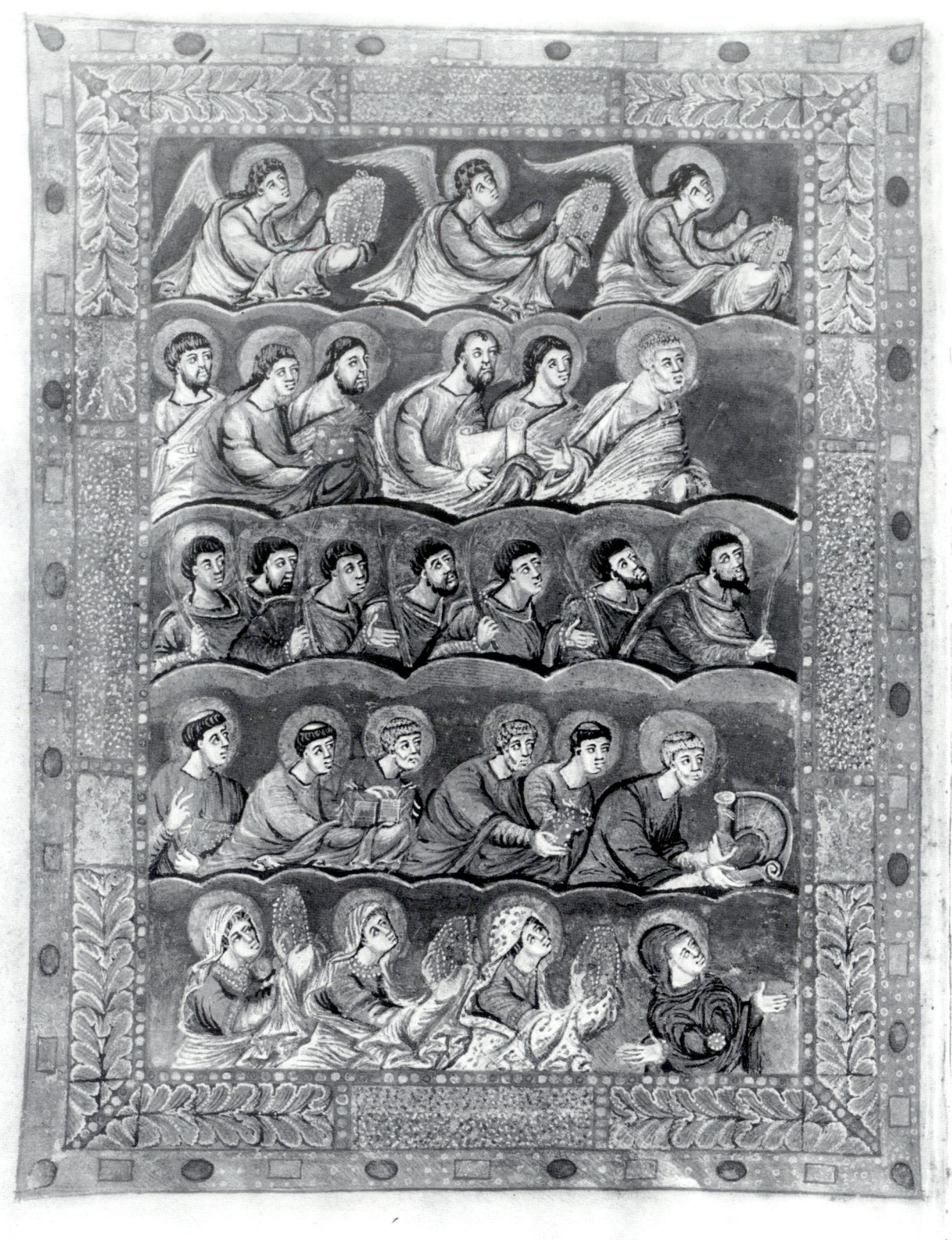

81. Paris, Bibliothèque Nationale, MS lat. 1141, fol. 5v: choirs of the saints.

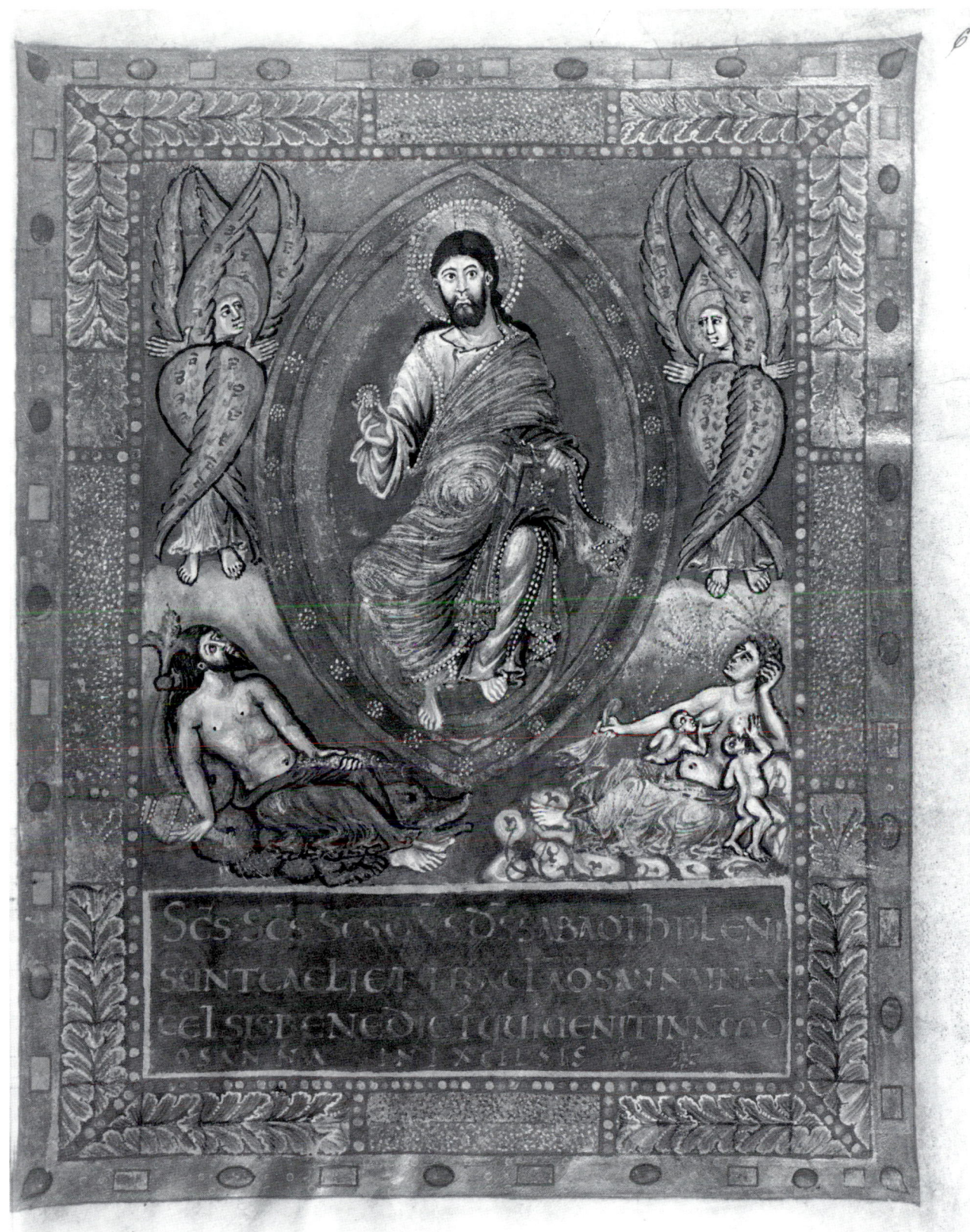

82. Paris, Bibliothèque Nationale, MS lat. 1141, fol. 6: Christ.

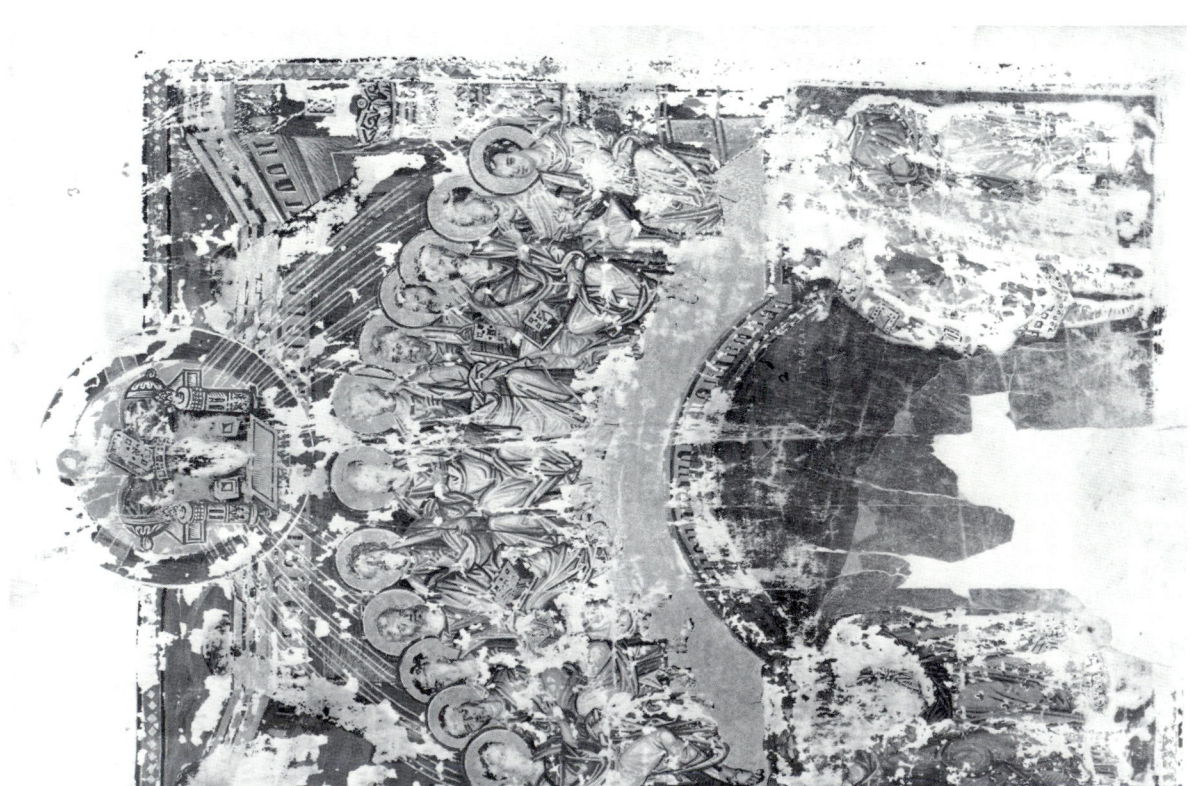

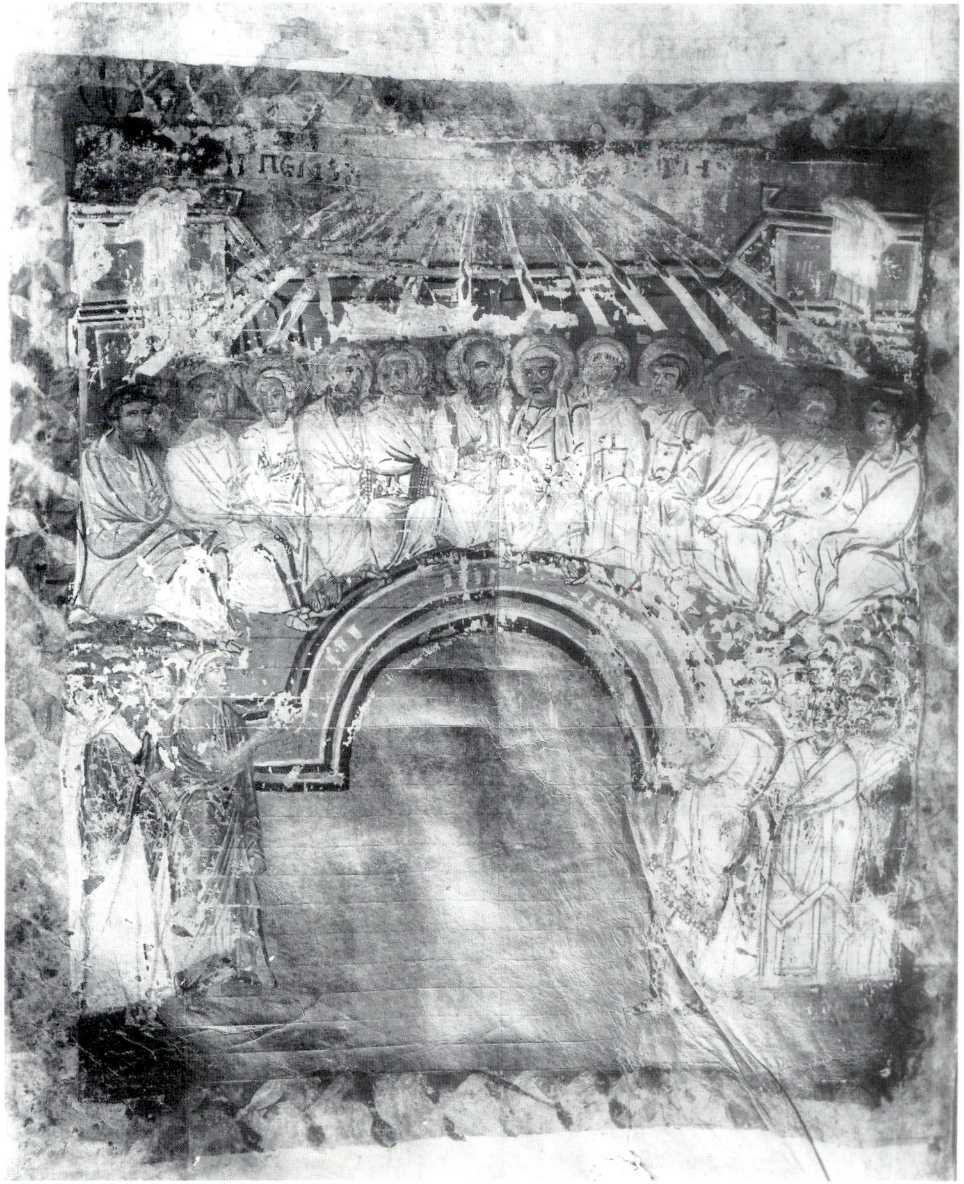

84. St. Petersburg, Public Library, MS gr. 21, fol. 14v: Pentecost (Kurt Weitzmann).

83. Paris, Bibliothèque Nationale, MS gr. 510, fol. 301: Pentecost (Courtauld Institute).

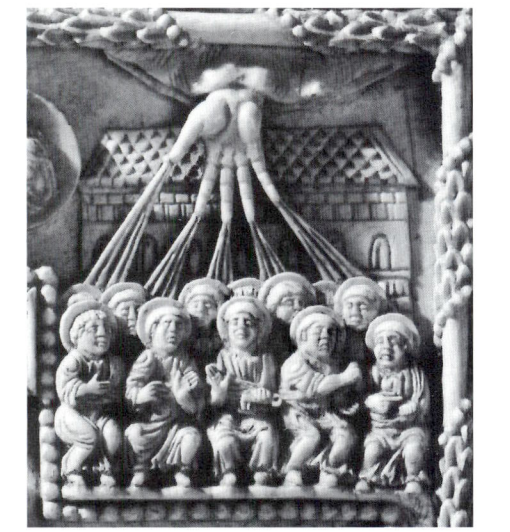

85. Narbonne, St. Just, ivory plaque
(detail of fig. 64): Pentecost.

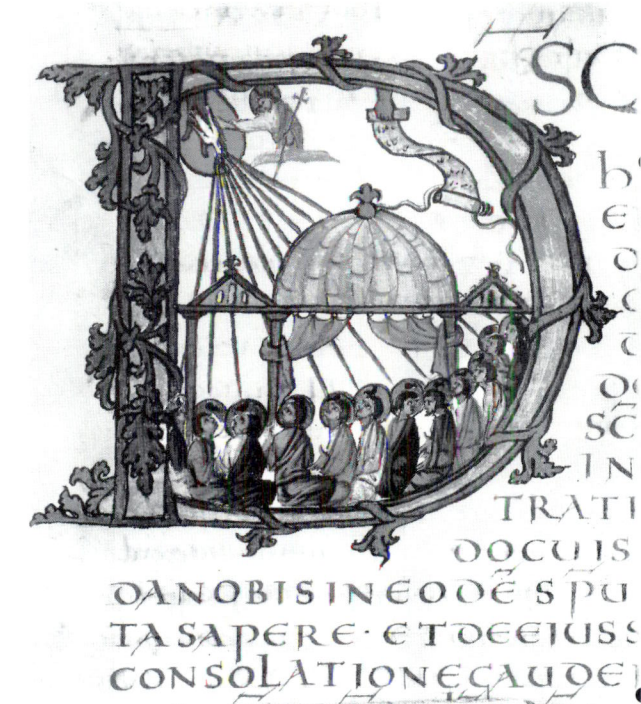

86. Paris, Bibliothèque Nationale, MS 9428, fol. 78: Pentecost.

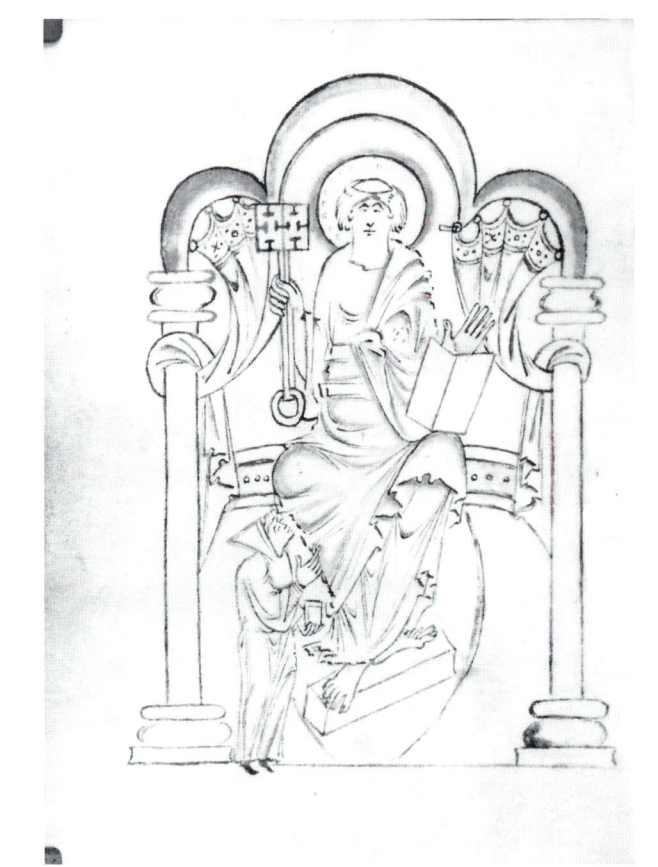

87. London, British Library, MS Cotton Titus D. XXVI, fol.
19v: Peter and Ælfwine.

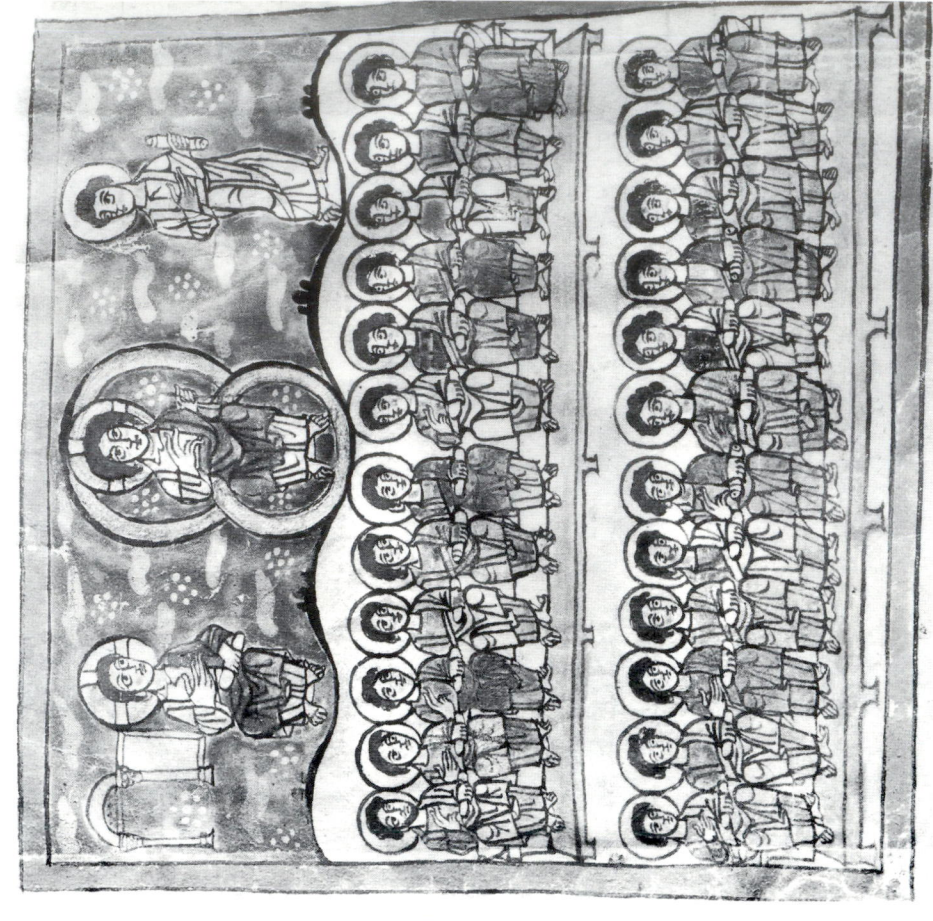

89. Trier, Stadtbibliothek, MS 31, fol. 14v: Adoration of the Elders (Marburg/Art Resource).

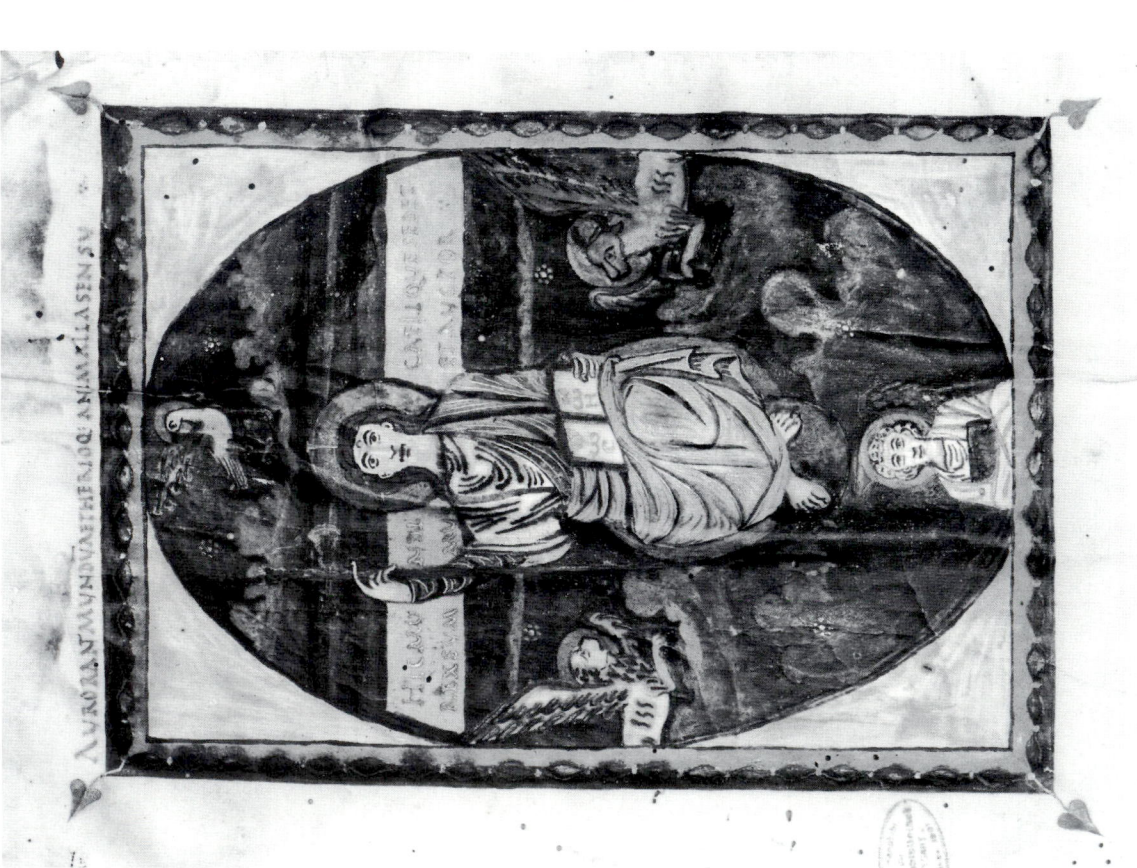

88. Stuttgart, Württembergische Landesbibliothek, MS H. B. II 40, fol. 1v: Christ in Majesty (Marburg/Art Resource).

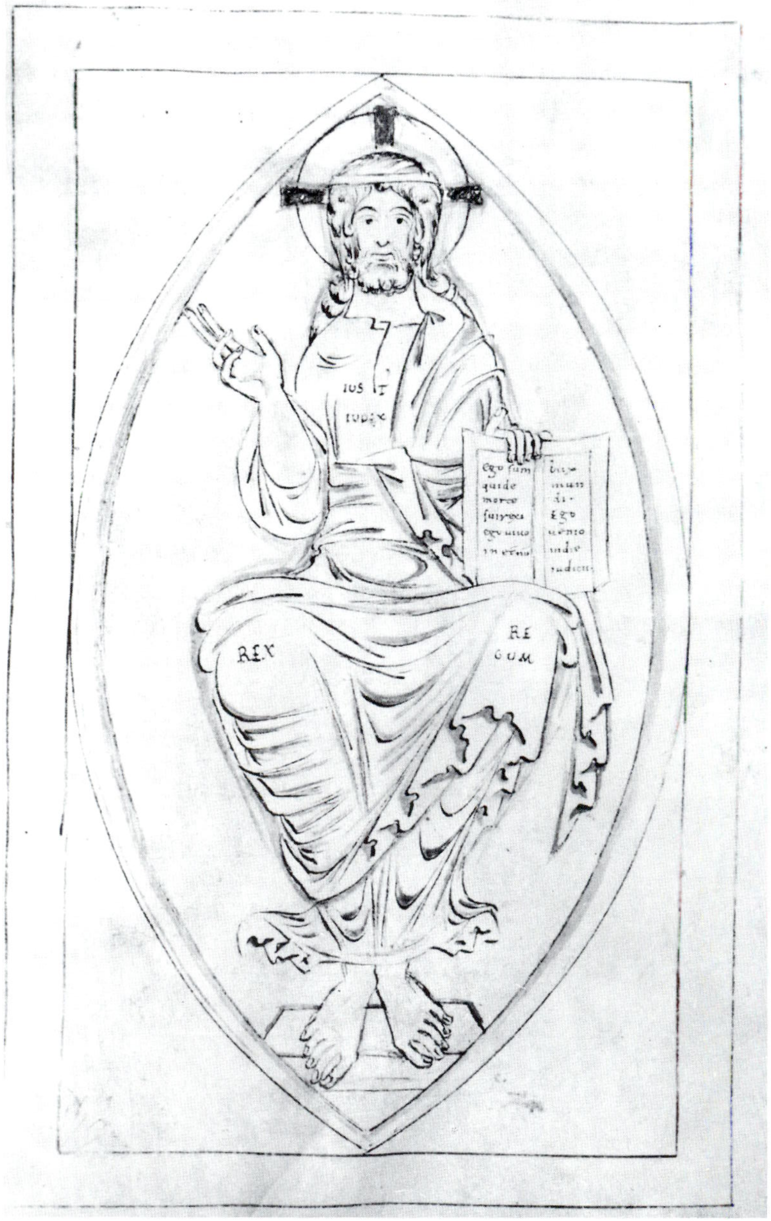

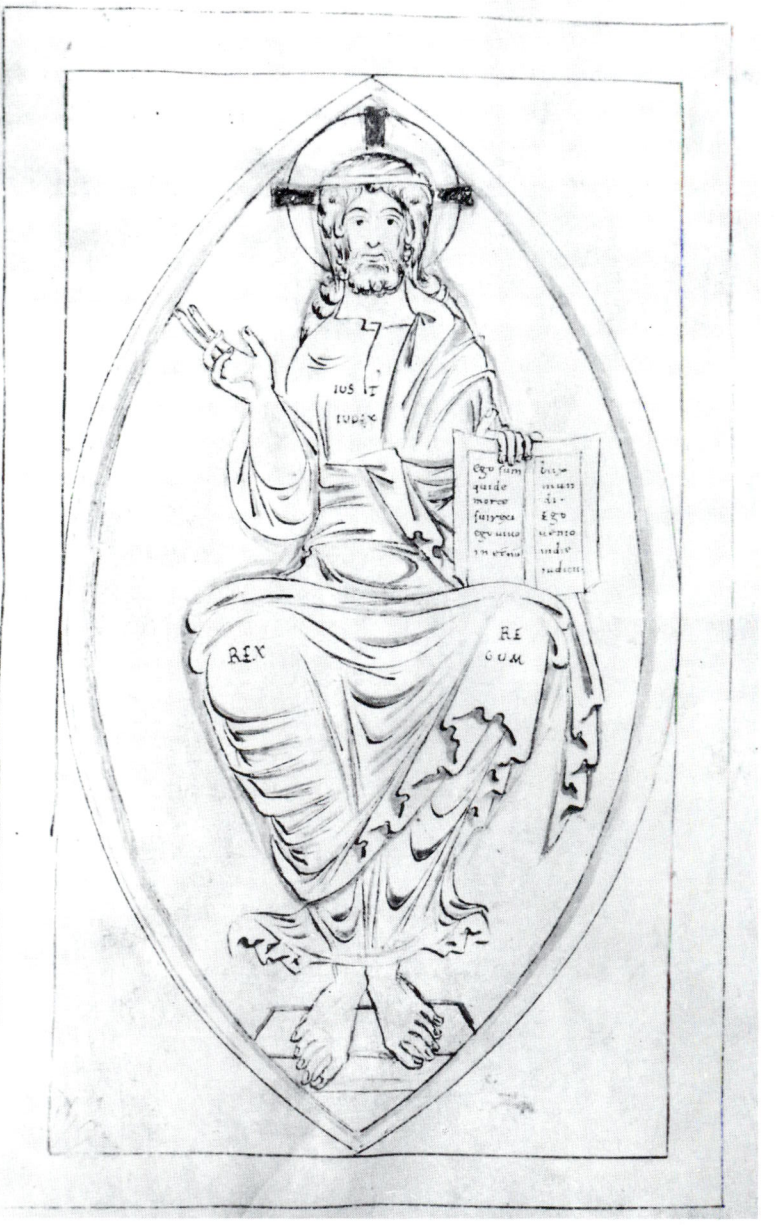

90. Cambridge, Trinity College, MS B. 15. 34, fol. 1: Christ.

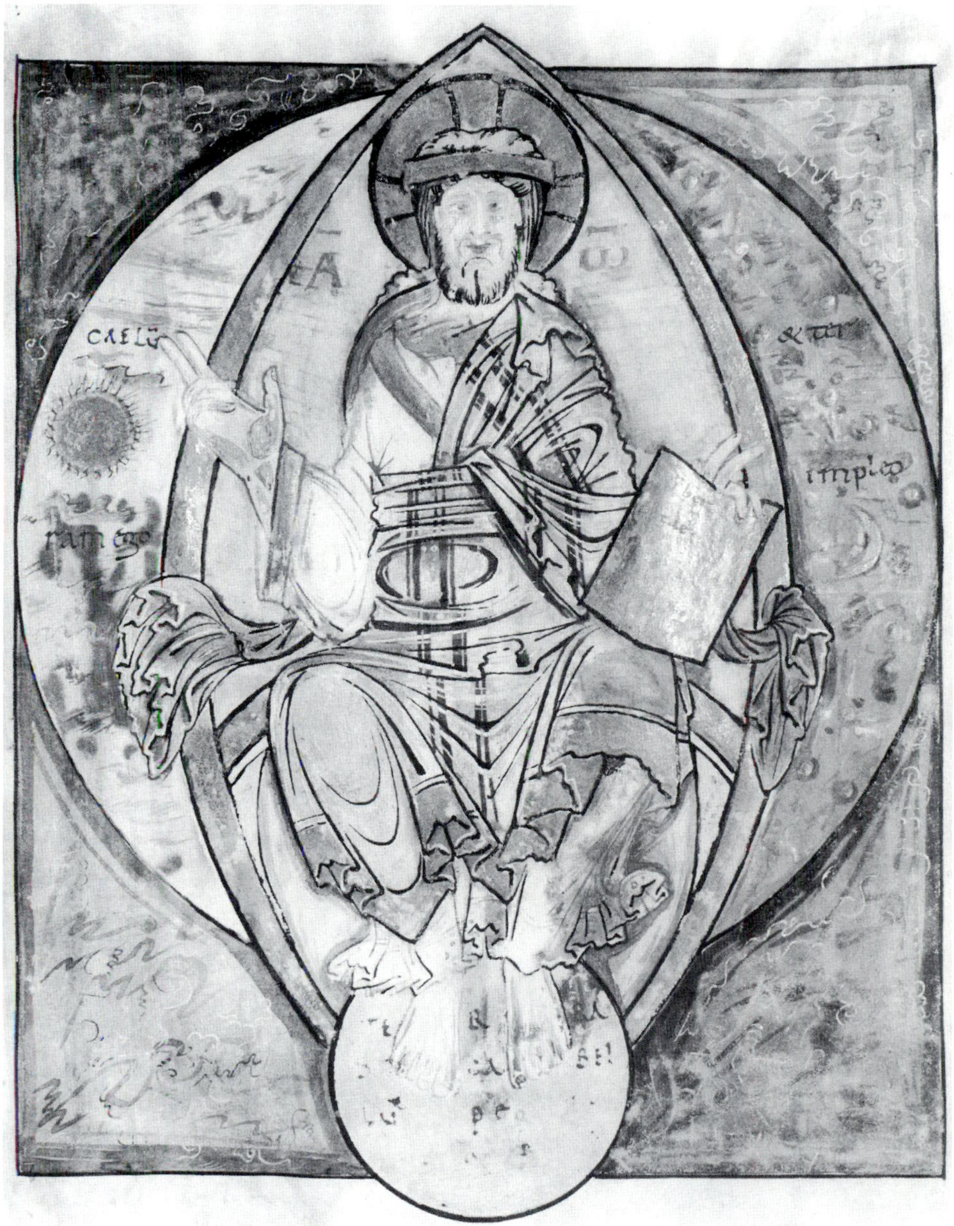

91. Boulogne-sur-mer, Bibliothèque Mun., MS 11, fol. 10: Christ in Majesty.

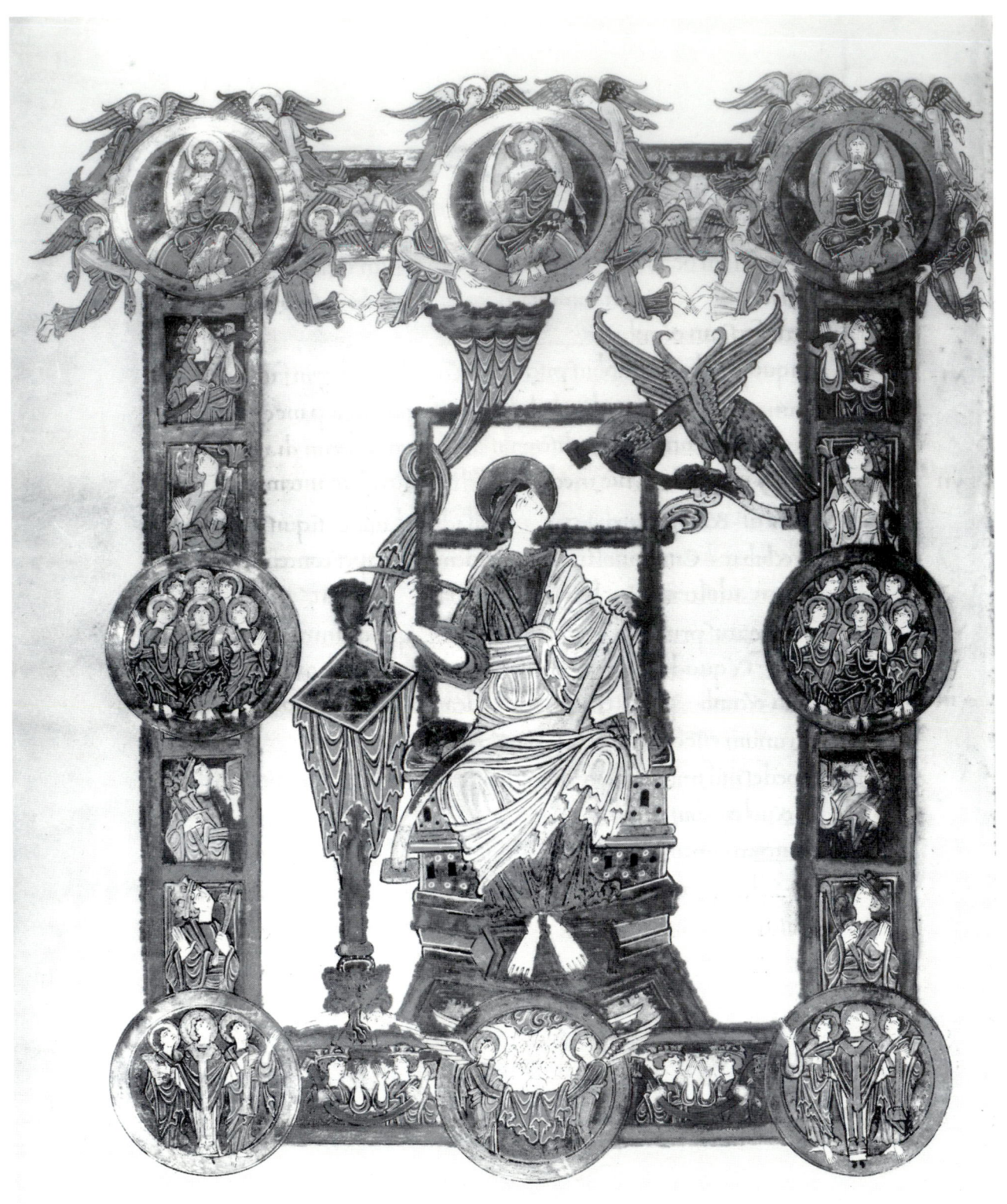

92. London, British Library, MS Add. 34890, fol. 114v: John the evangelist.

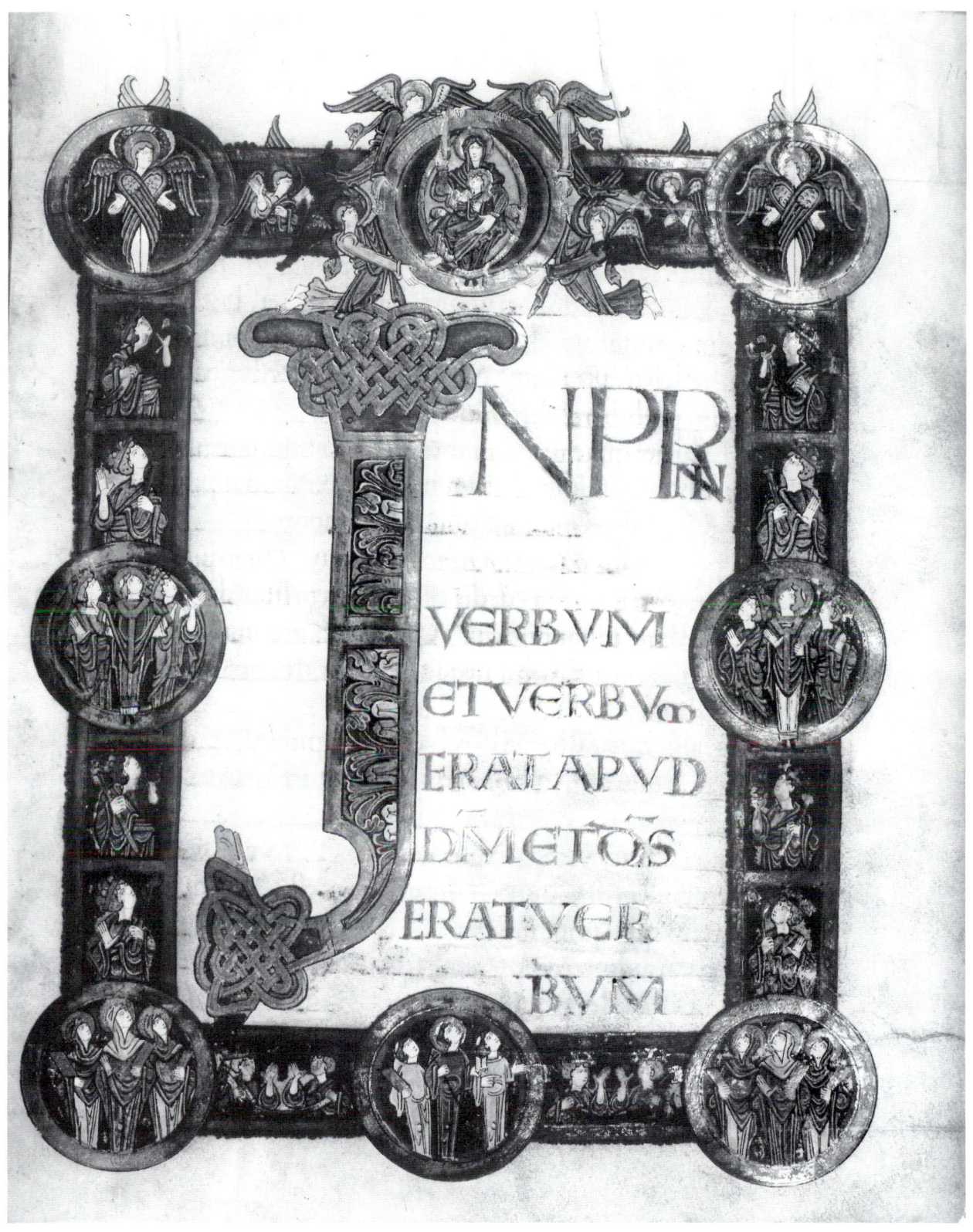

93. London, British Library, MS Add. 34890, fol. 115: initial page.

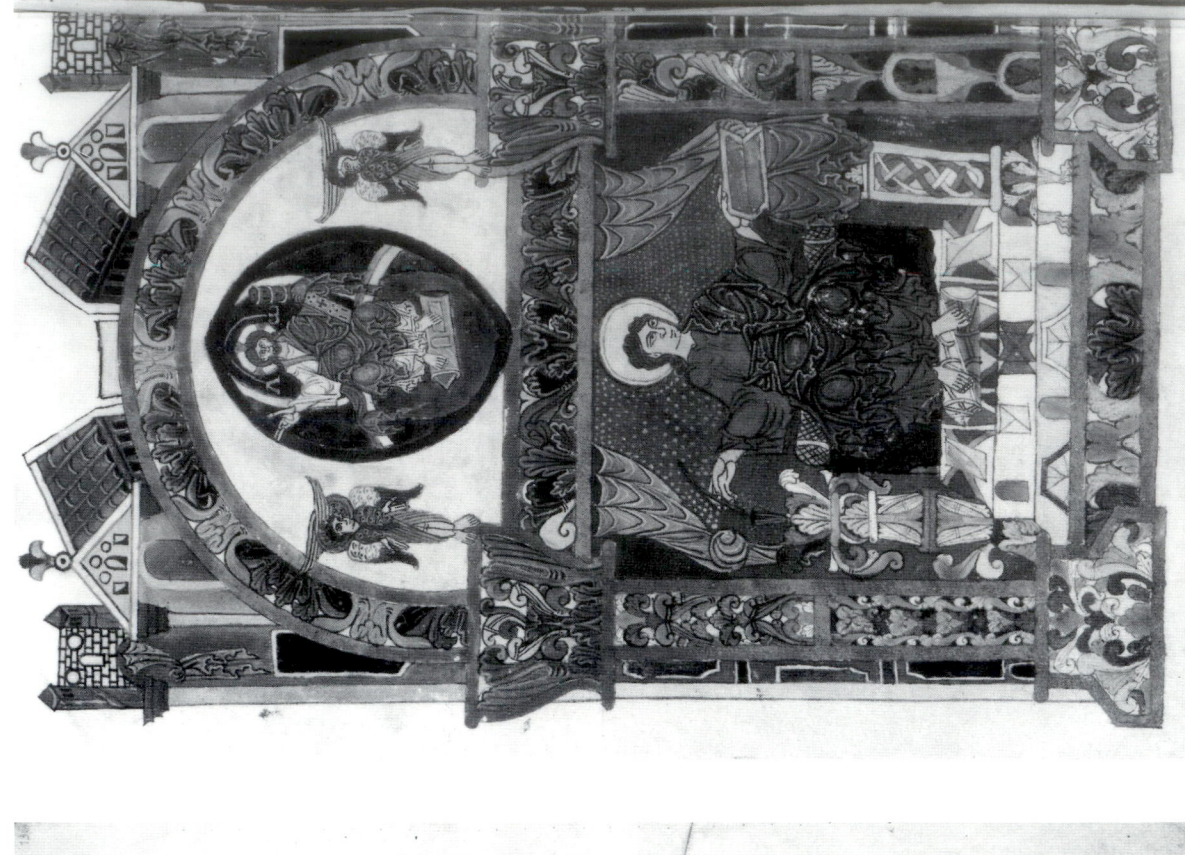

95. Paris, Bibliothèque Nationale, MS lat. 6401, fol. 158v: Boethius and the Trinity.

94. Göttingen, Niedersächsische Staats- und Universitätsbibliothek, MS theol. fol. 231, fol. 136: Trinity (Rheinisches Bildarchiv).

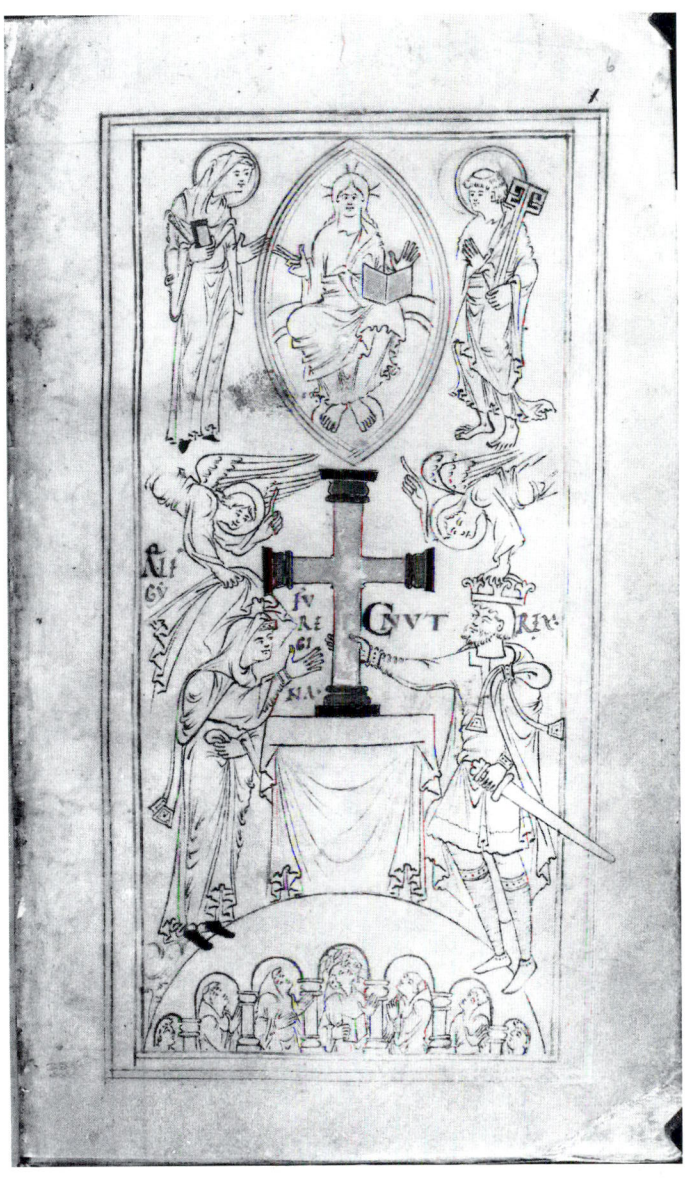

96. Utrecht, University Library,
MS 32, fol. 10v (detail): Psalm 18.

97. London, British Library, MS Stowe 944, fol. 6: donor portrait.

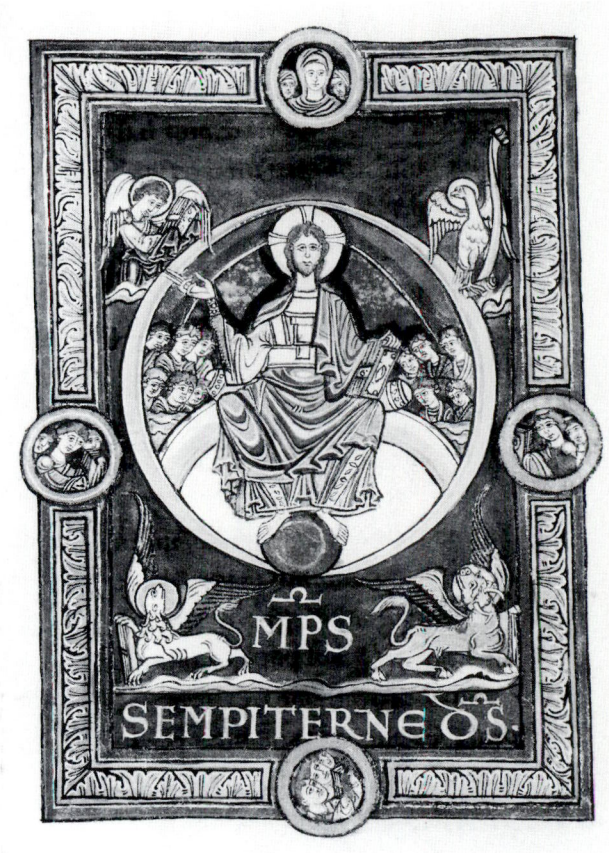

98. New York, Pierpont Morgan Library, MS M. 641, fol. 170:
Christ and saints.

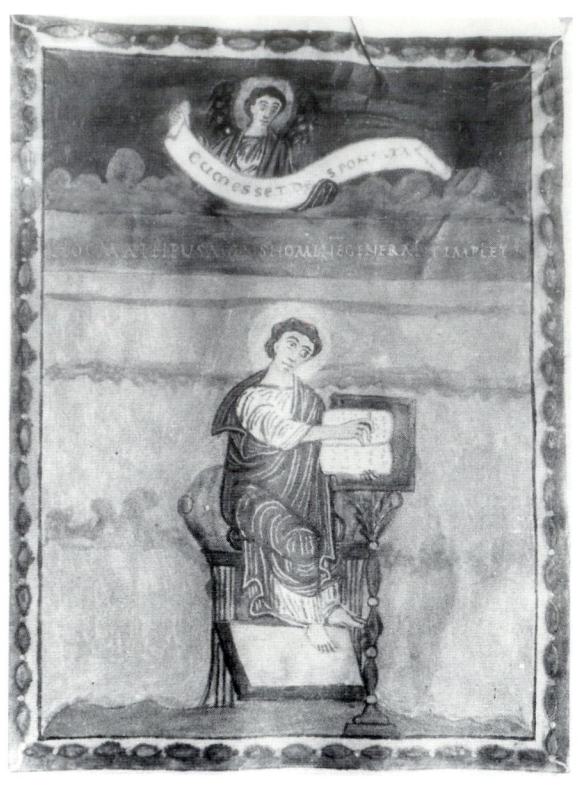

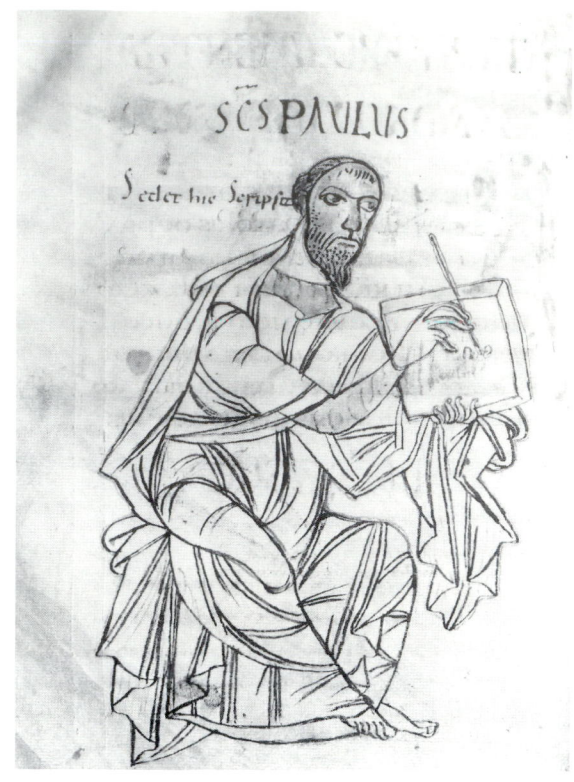

99. Stuttgart, Württembergische Landesbibliothek, MS H. B. II 40, fol. 16v: Matthew (Bildarchiv Foto Marburg).

100. Stuttgart, Württembergische Landesbibliothek, MS H. B. II 54, fol. 25v: Paul.

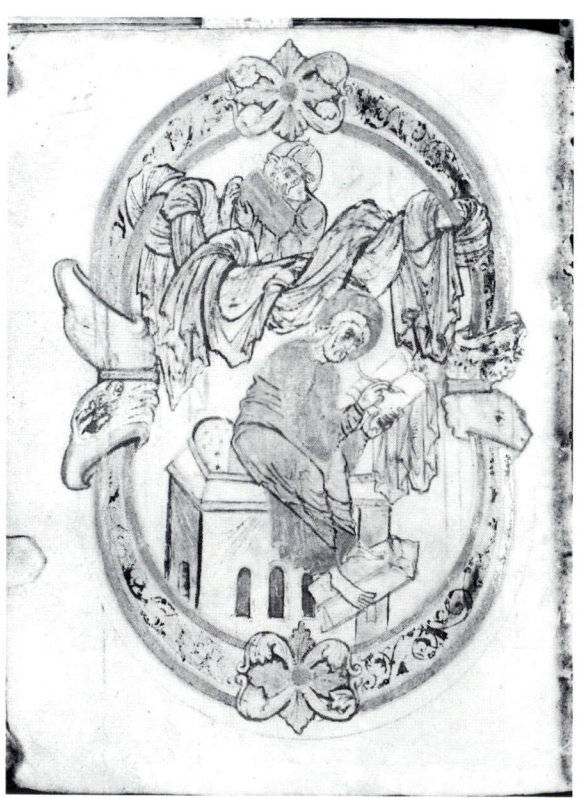

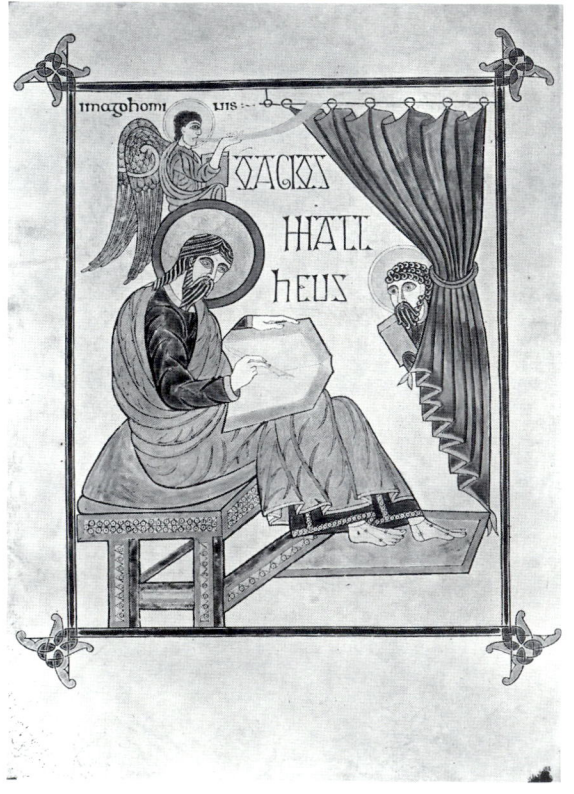

101. London, British Library, MS Add. 40618, fol. 22v: Luke.

102. London, British Library, MS Cotton Nero D. IV, fol. 25v: Matthew.

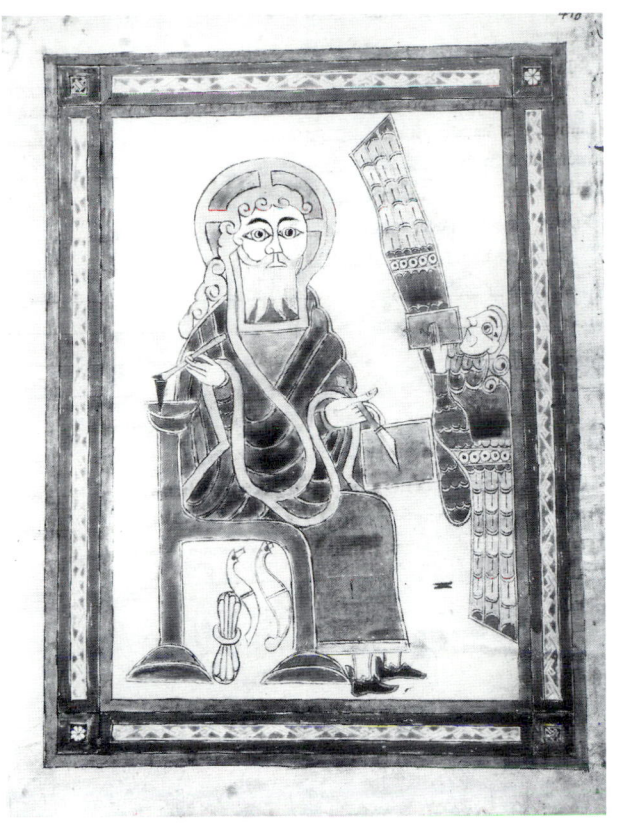

103. St. Gall, Stiftsbibliothek, MS 1395, p. 418: Matthew.

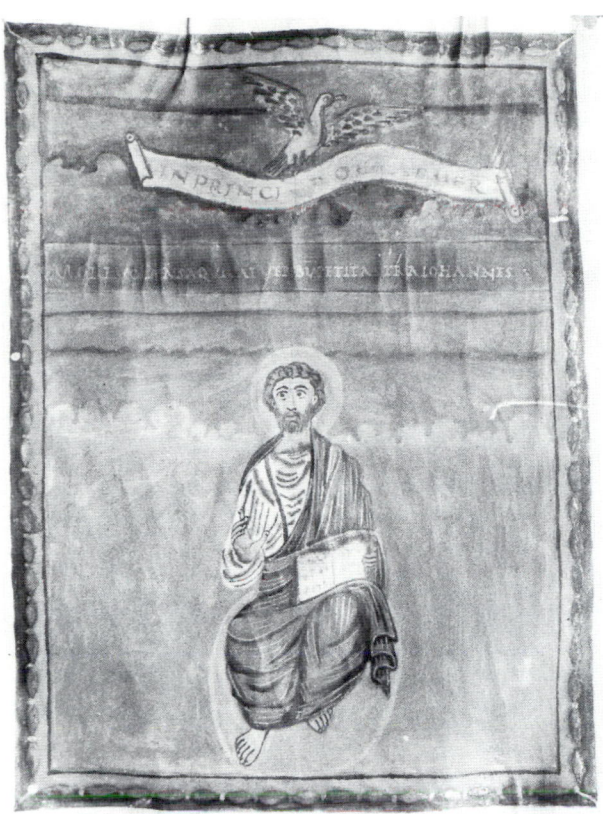

104. Stuttgart, Württembergische Landesbibliothek, MS H. B. II 40, fol. 164v: John (Bildarchiv Foto Marburg).

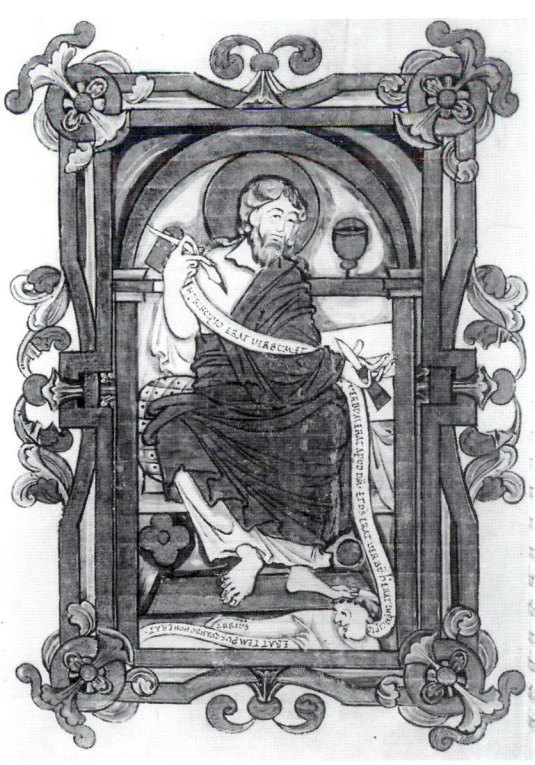

105. Hanover, Kestner-Museum, MS W.M. XXIᵃ, 36, fol. 147v: John.

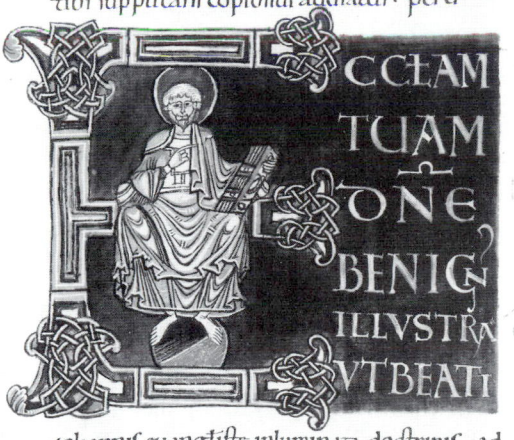

106. New York, Pierpont Morgan Library, MS M. 641, fol. 5: John.

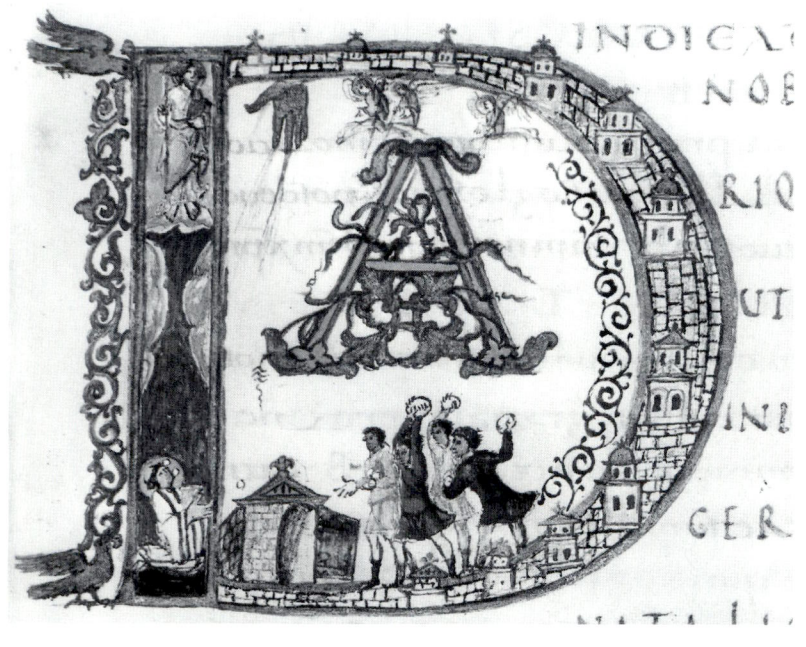

107. Paris, Bibliothèque Nationale, MS lat. 9428, fol. 27: Stoning of Stephen.

retur. huius qf fida famulis   mum ipso quoq; gubernan
auferibue firmitate. utulq;   te peruenunt · quiteum
ad pmiſſum gloriae pre   uuute &regnat ds inunitate

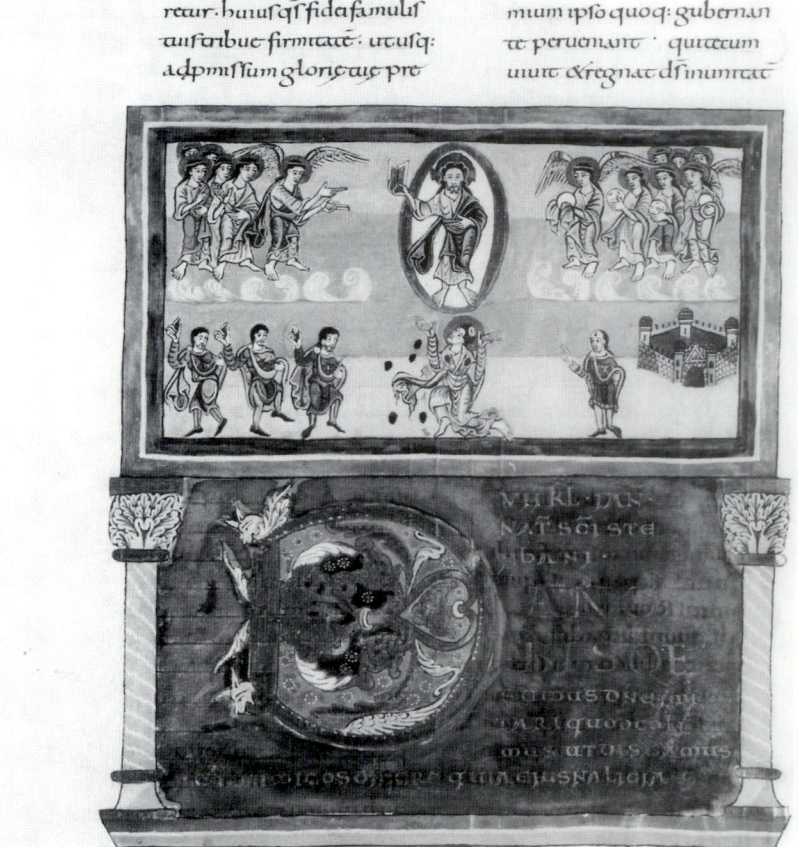

108. Göttingen, Niedersächsiche und Staats- und Universitätsbibliothek, MS theol. fol. 231, fol. 14v: Stoning of Stephen (Rheinisches Bildarchiv).

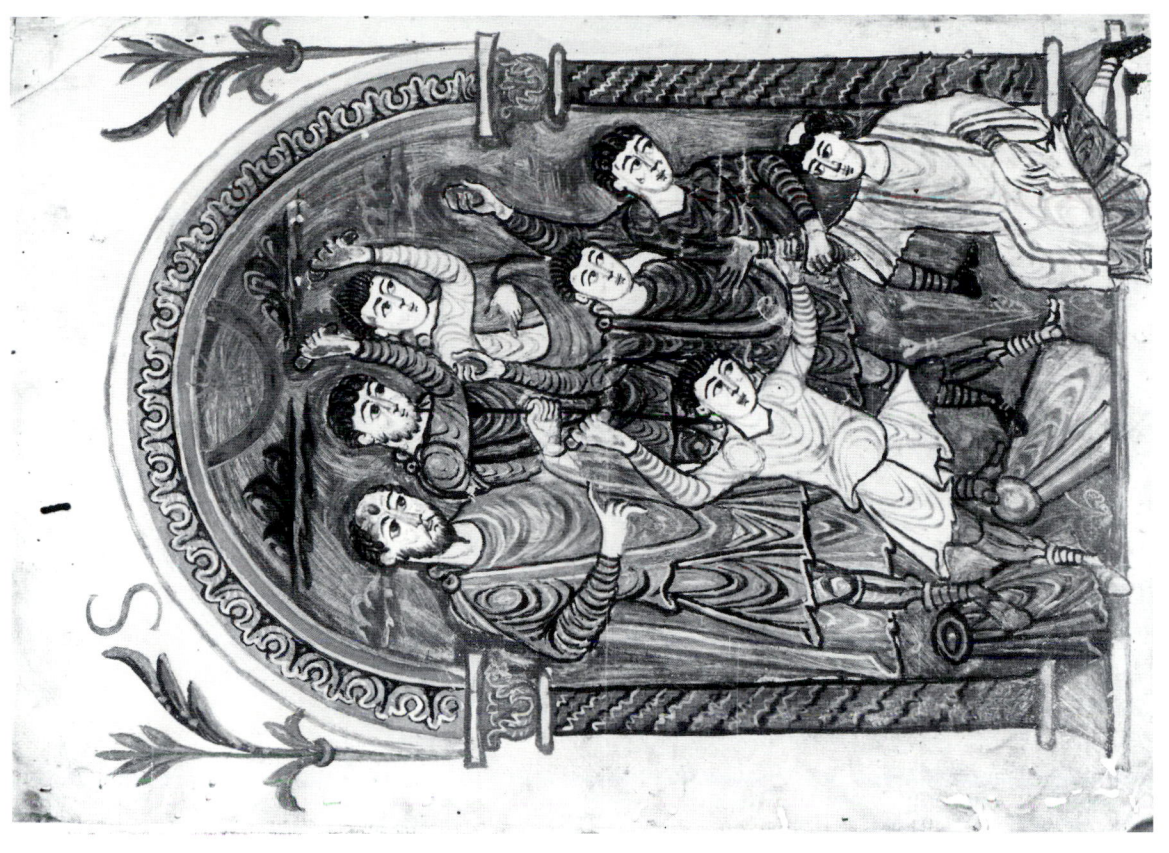

110. Munich, Bayerische Staatsbibliothek., Clm. 14345, fol. 1v: Stoning of Stephen.

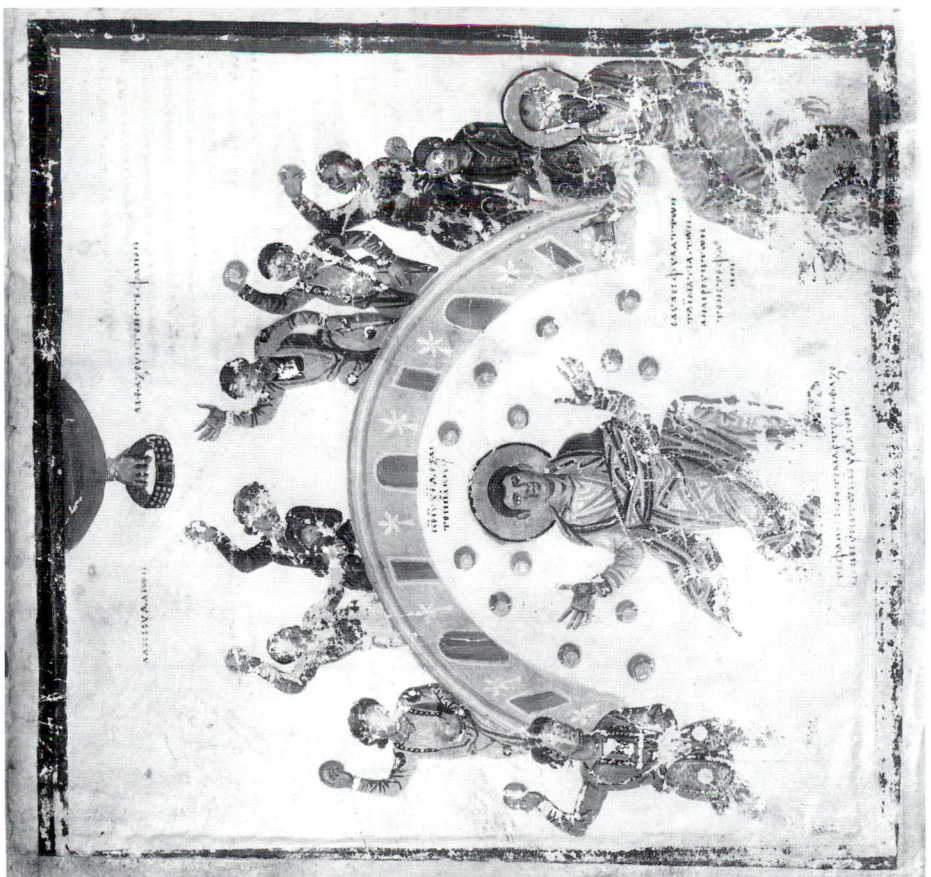

109. Vatican, Biblioteca Apostolica, MS gr. 699, fol. 82v: Stoning of Stephen.

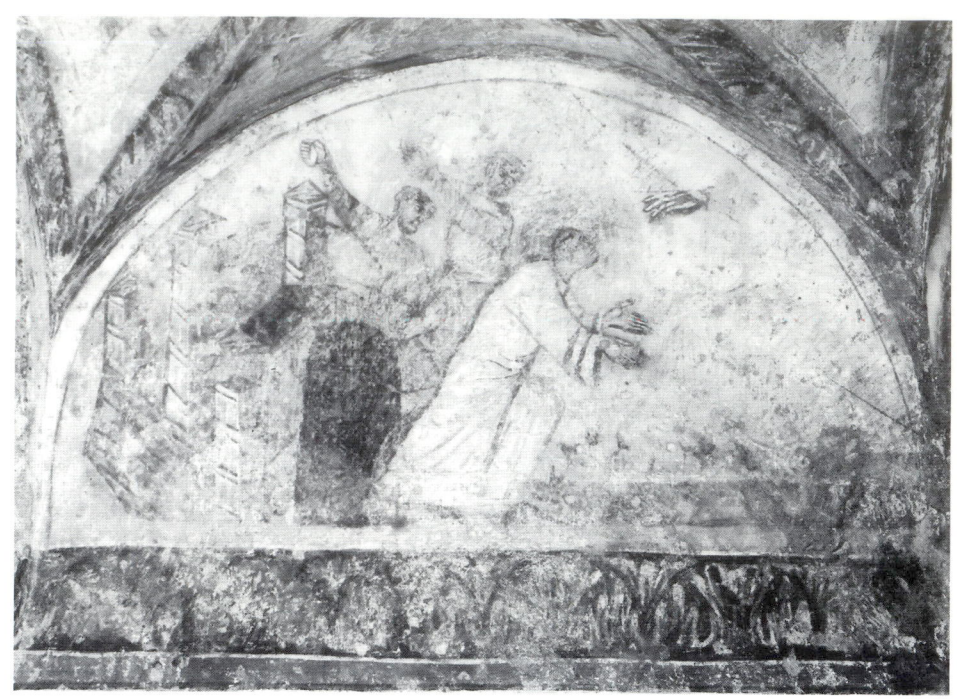

111. Auxerre, cathedral, crypt, fresco: Stoning of Stephen (Archives photographiques).

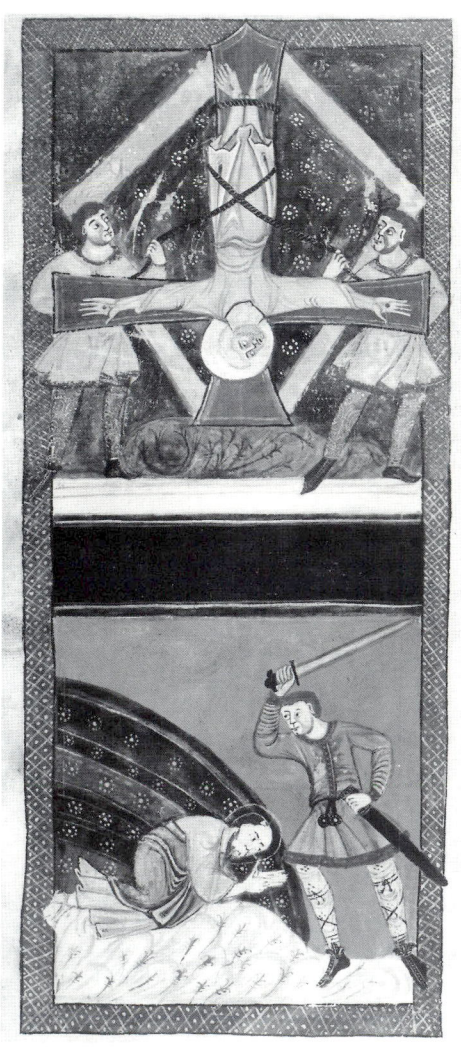

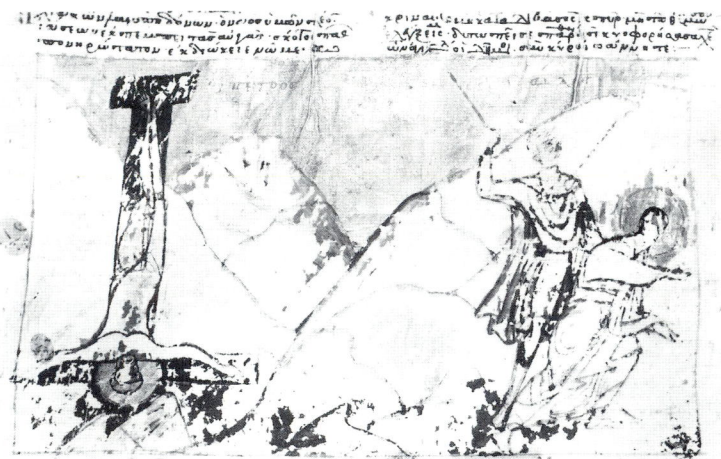

113. Jerusalem, Greek Patriarchal Library, MS Saba 208, fol. 87v: Martyrdoms of Peter and Paul (Kurt Weitzmann).

112. Paris, Bibliothèque Nationale, MS lat. 9448, fol. 55: Martyrdoms of Peter and Paul.

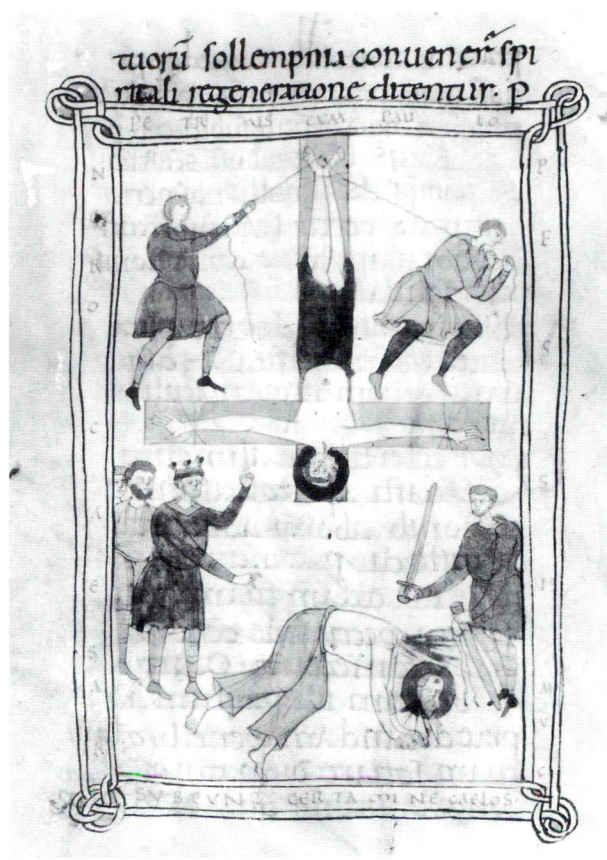

114. Ivrea, Biblioteca Capitolare, MS 86, fol. 90v (detail): Martyrdom of Peter (Lavarino Foto).

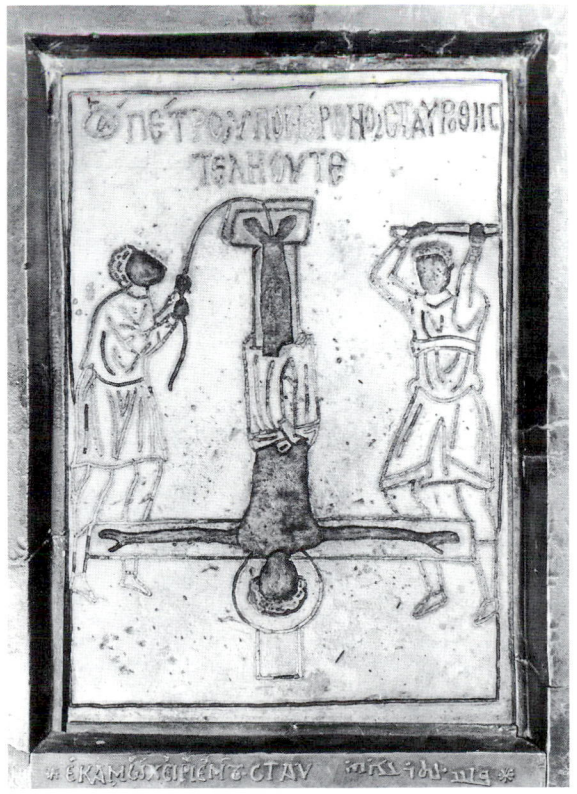

116. Rome, S. Paolo f.l.m., bronze door (detail): Martyrdom of Peter.

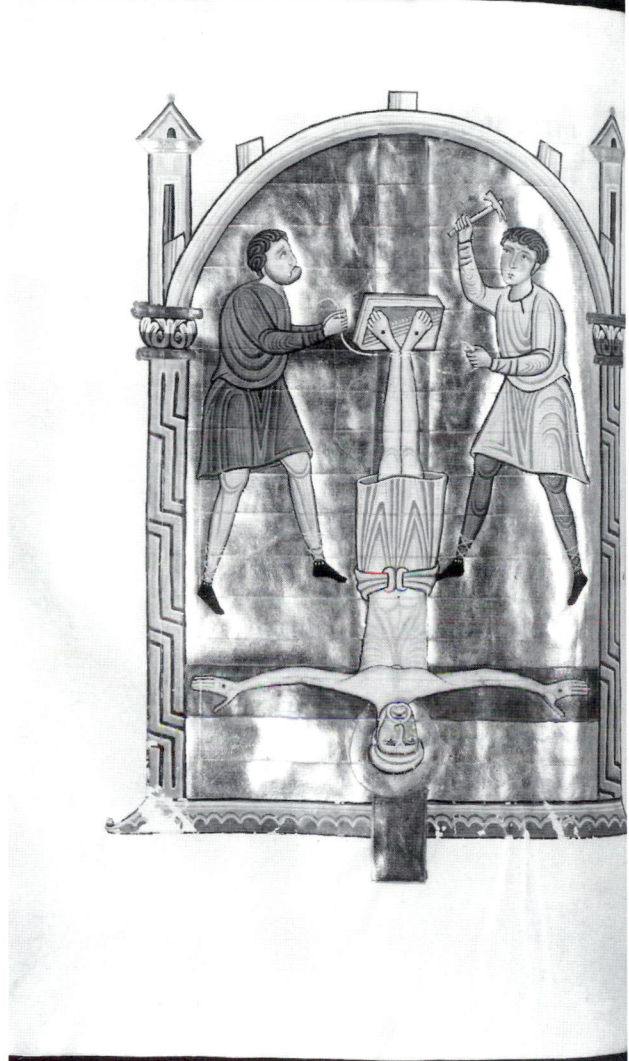

115. New York, Pierpont Morgan Library, MS M. 780, fol. 60v: Martyrdoms of Peter and Paul.

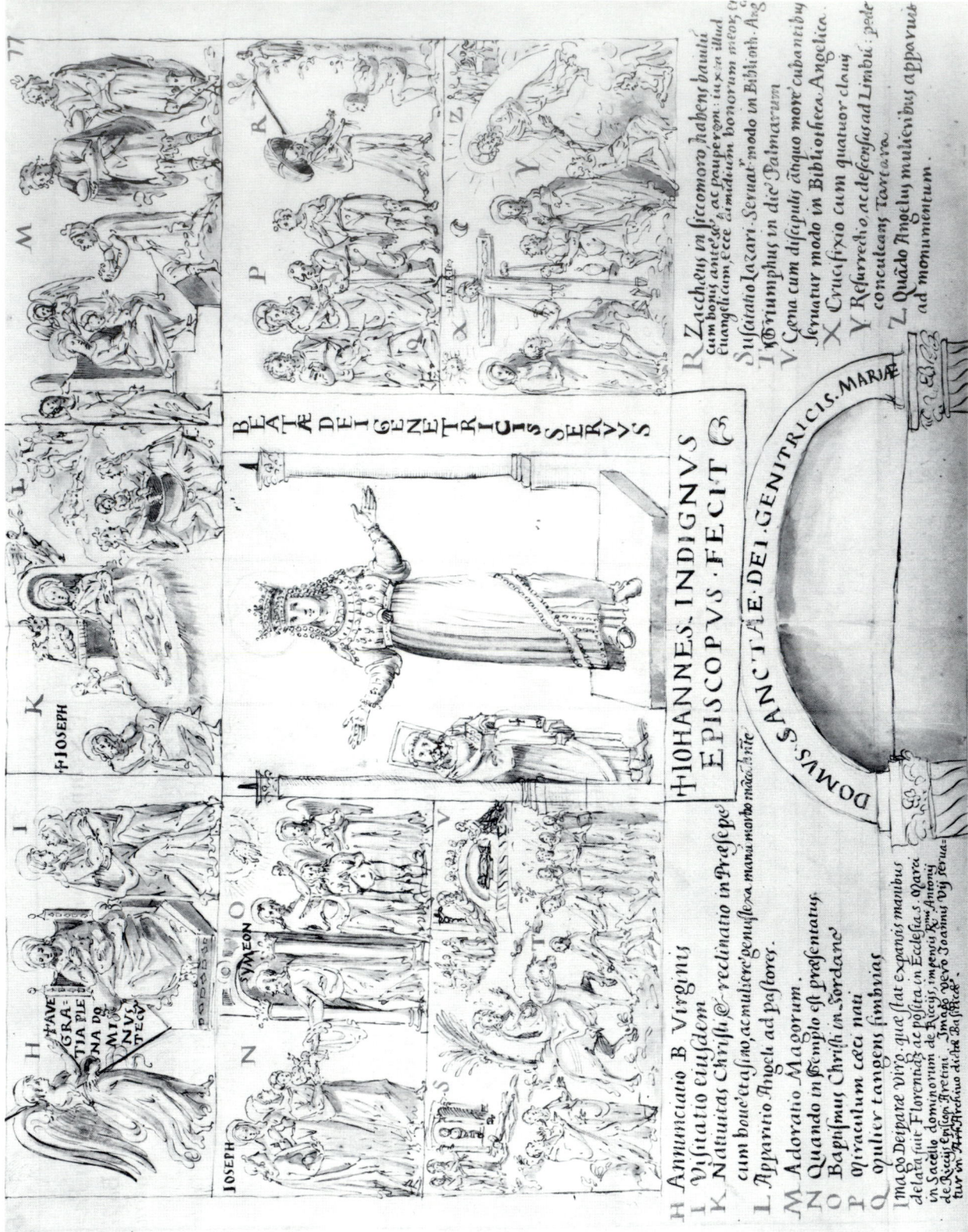

117. Vatican, Biblioteca Apostolica, MS Barb. lat. 2732, fols. 76v–77: Rome, St. Peter's, mosaics from the Oratory of John VII.

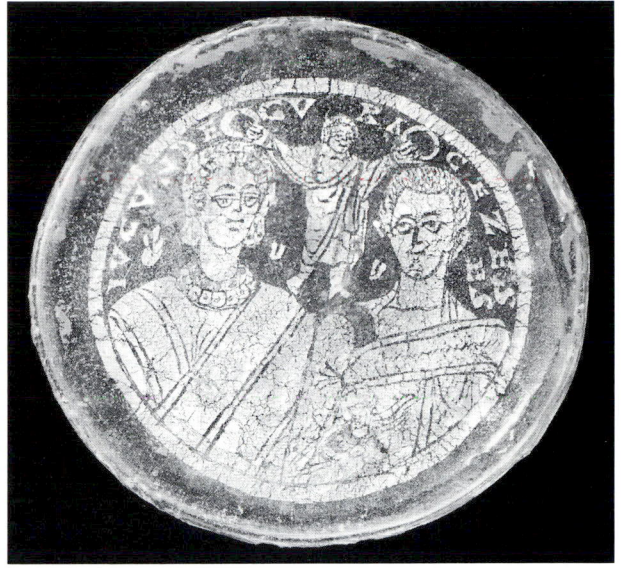

118. Paris, Bibliothèque Nationale, Cabinet de Médailles, gold glass: bridal coronation.

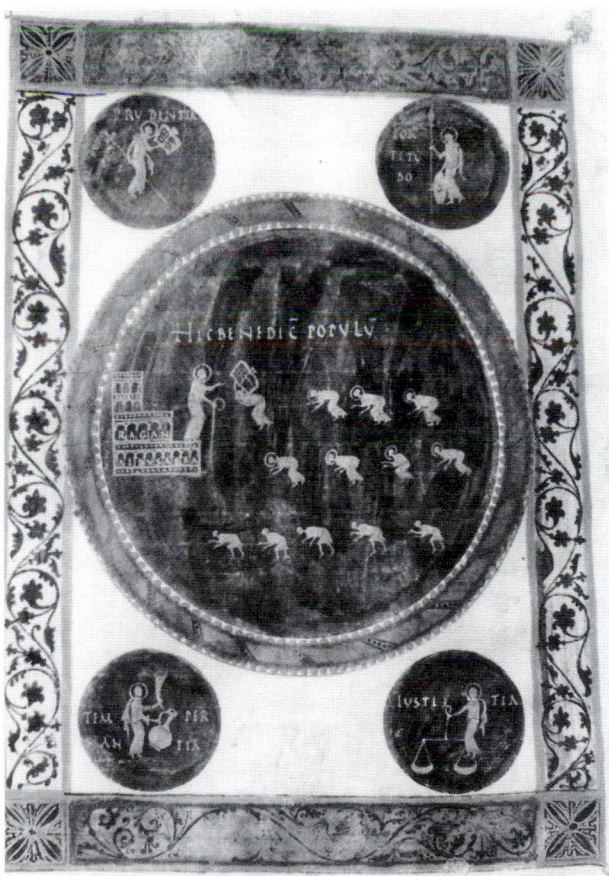

119. Autun, Bibliothèque Mun., MS 19 bis, fol. 173v: Raganaldus Blessing (Lawrence Nees).

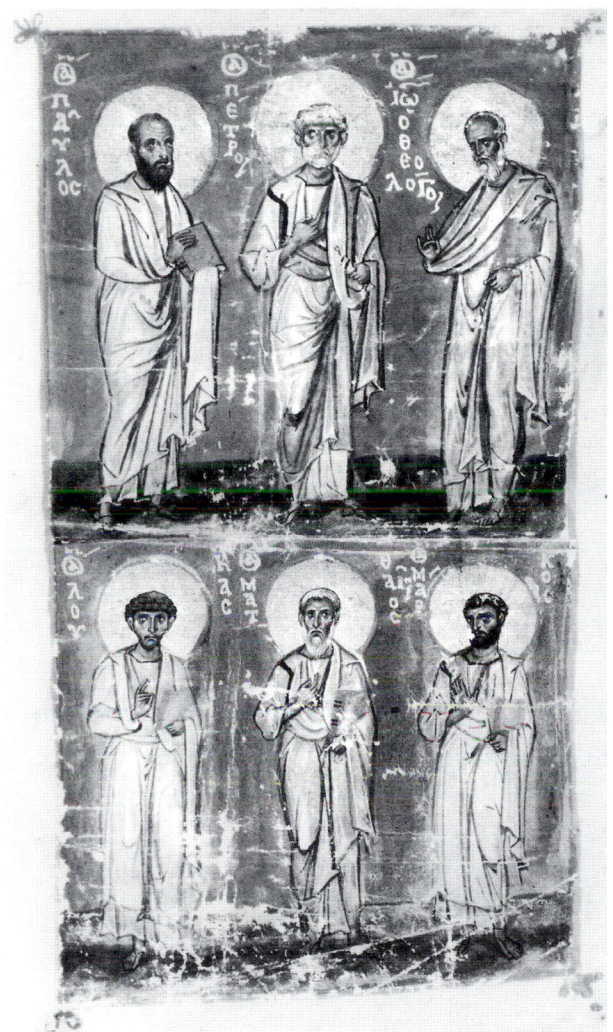

120. Baltimore, Walters Art Gallery, MS W 530C: apostles.

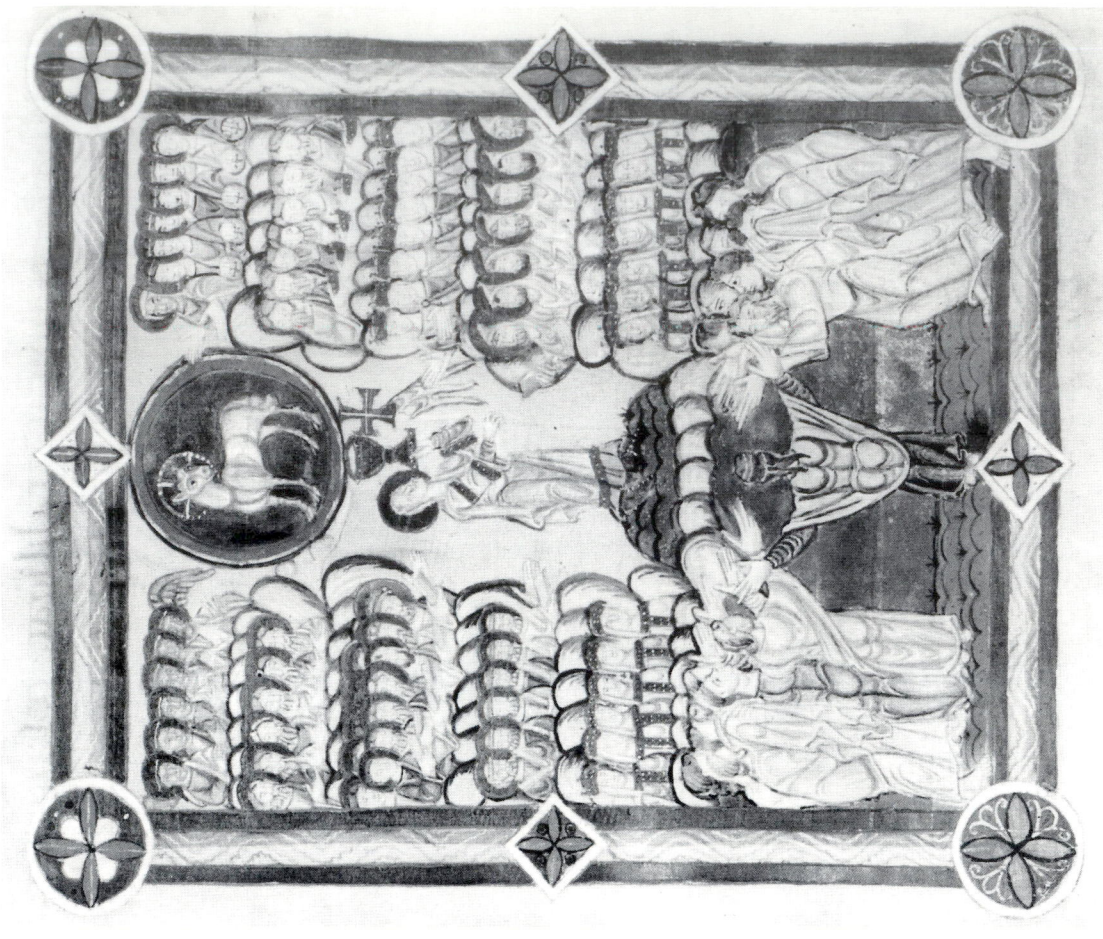

122. Udine, Archivio Capitolare, MS 1, fol. 66v: All Saints.

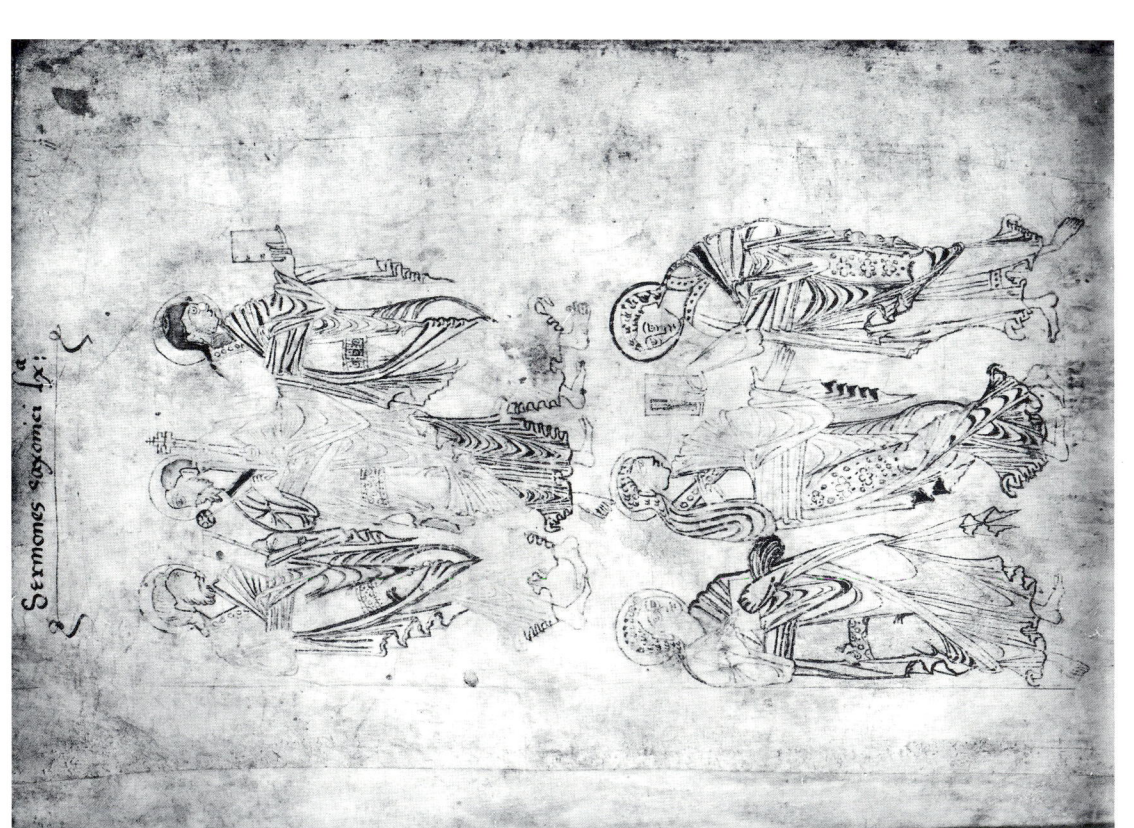

121. Cambridge, Corpus Christi College, MS 198, p. 1: apostles.

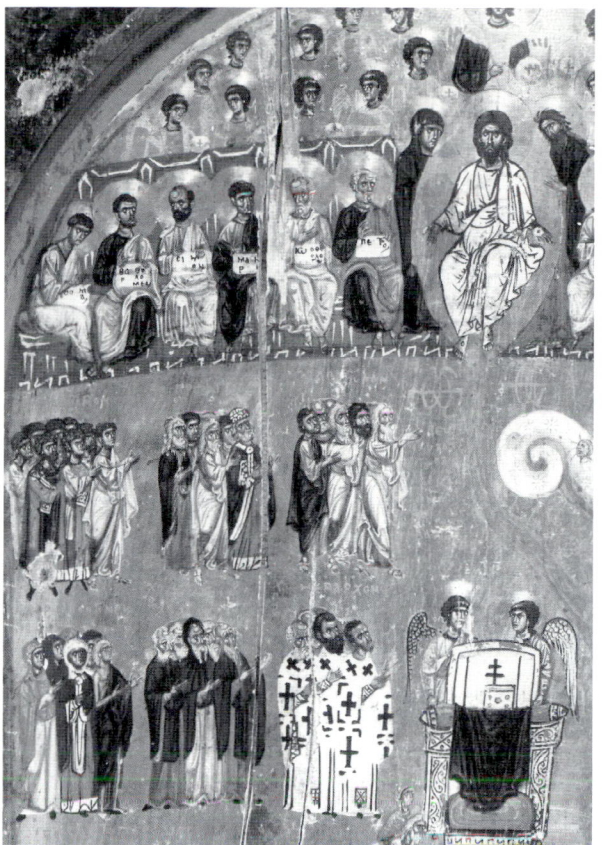

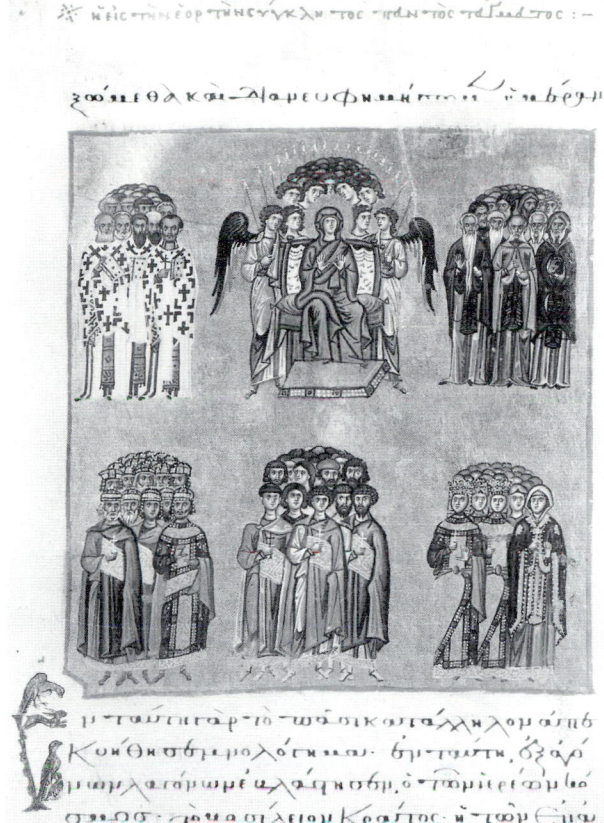

123. Mt. Sinai, St. Catherine's monastery, icon (detail): Last Judgment (Michigan-Princeton-Alexandria Expedition to Mt. Sinai).

124. Vatican, Biblioteca Apostolica, MS gr. 1162, fol. 5: Virgin and saints.

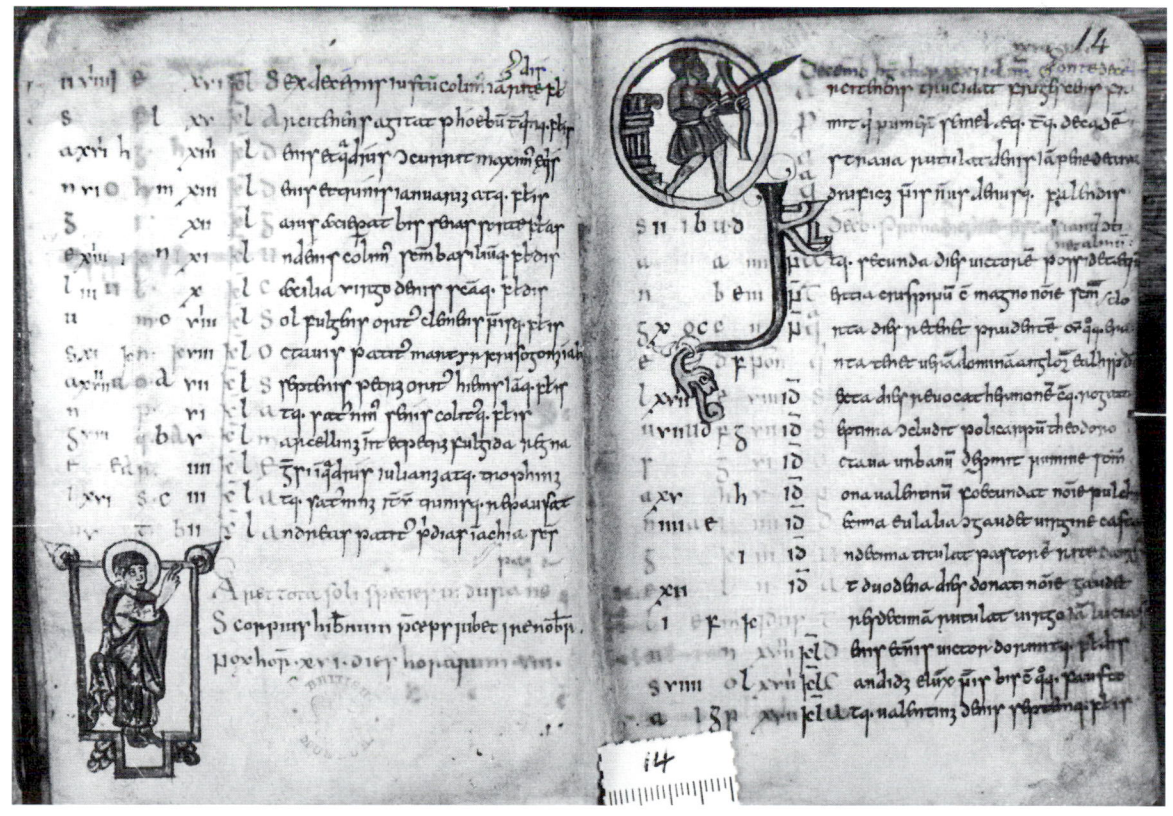

125. London, British Library, MS Cotton Galba A. XVIII, fols. 13v–14: calendar (Courtauld Institute).

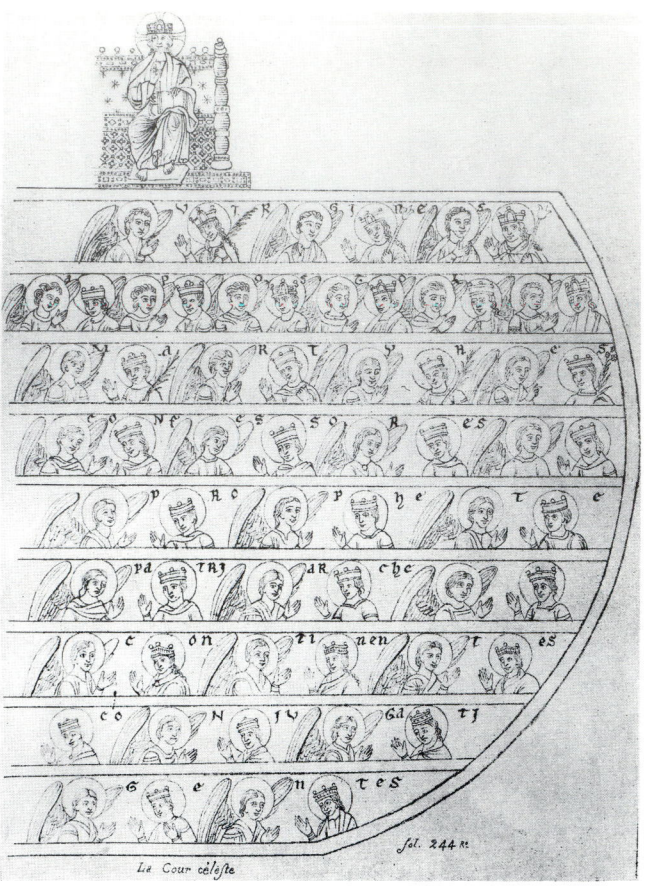

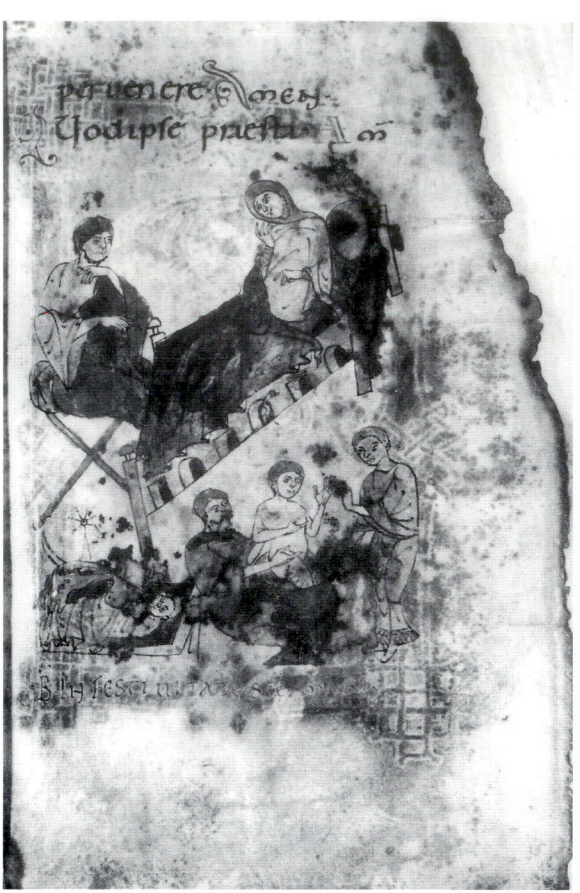

126. *Hortus Deliciarum*, fol. 244: Christ and choirs of the saints (after book 955, Strasbourg, Bibliothèque et Archives).

127. Ivrea, Biblioteca Capitolare, MS XVIII [8], fol. 35: Nativity.

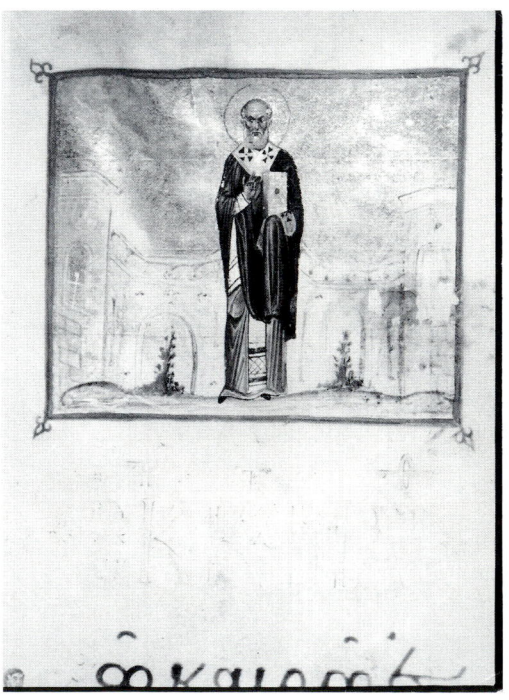

128. Mt. Athos, Dionysiu, MS 587, fol. 143: Gregory the theologian (Kurt Weitzmann).

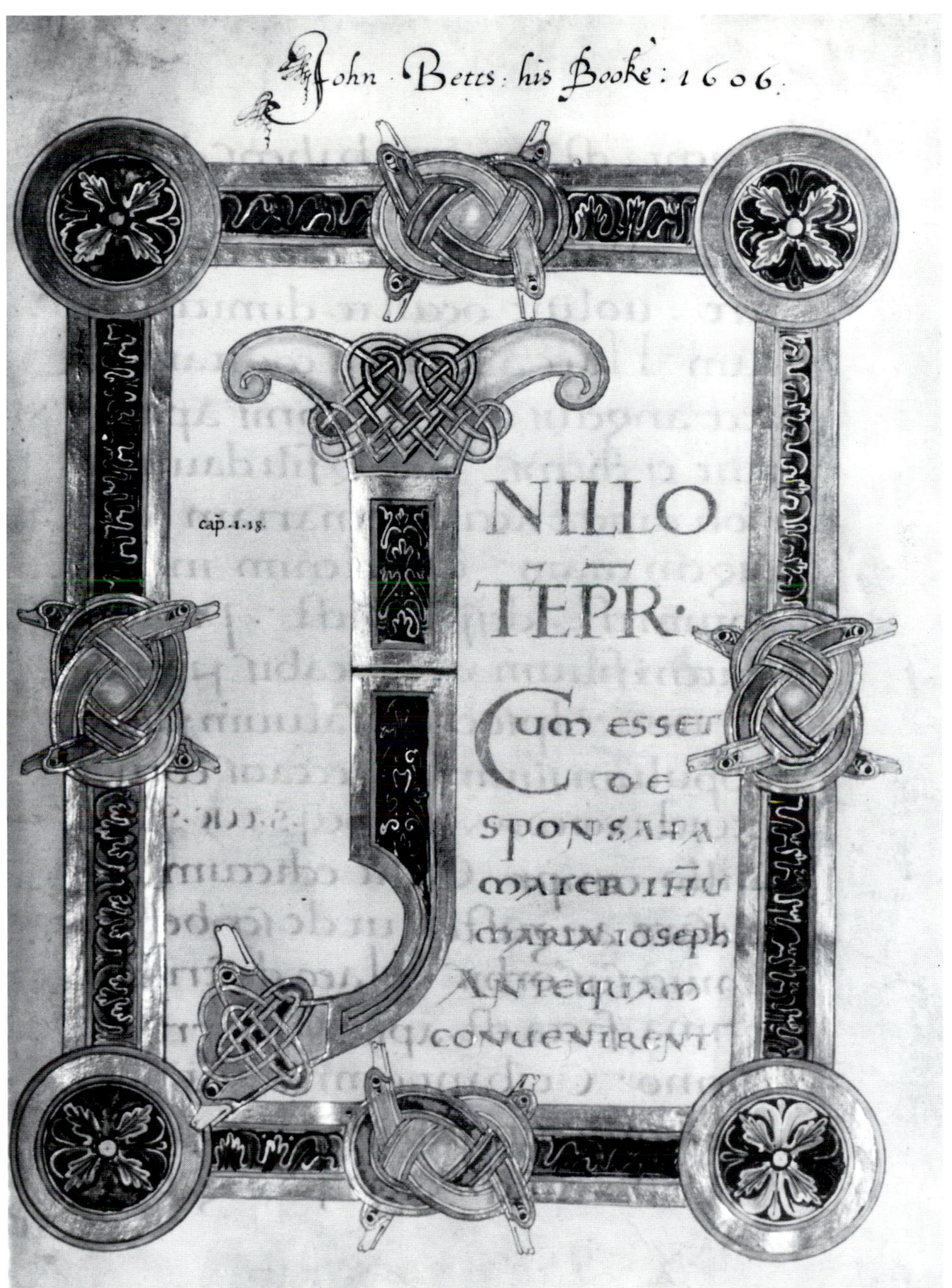

129. London, College of Arms, MS Arundel 22, fol. 84: initial page.

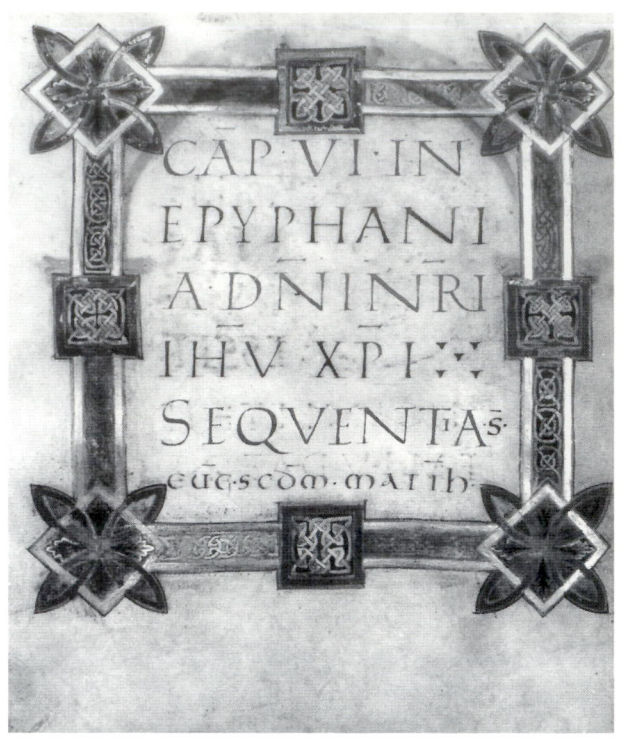

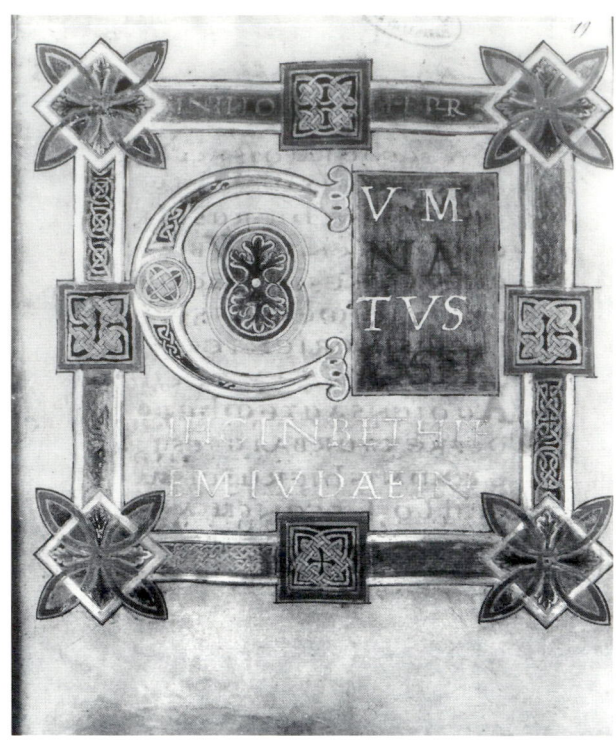

130. Arras, Bibliothèque Mun., MS 1045, fol. 18v: title page (author).

131. Arras, Bibliothèque Mun., MS 1045, fol. 19: initial page (author).

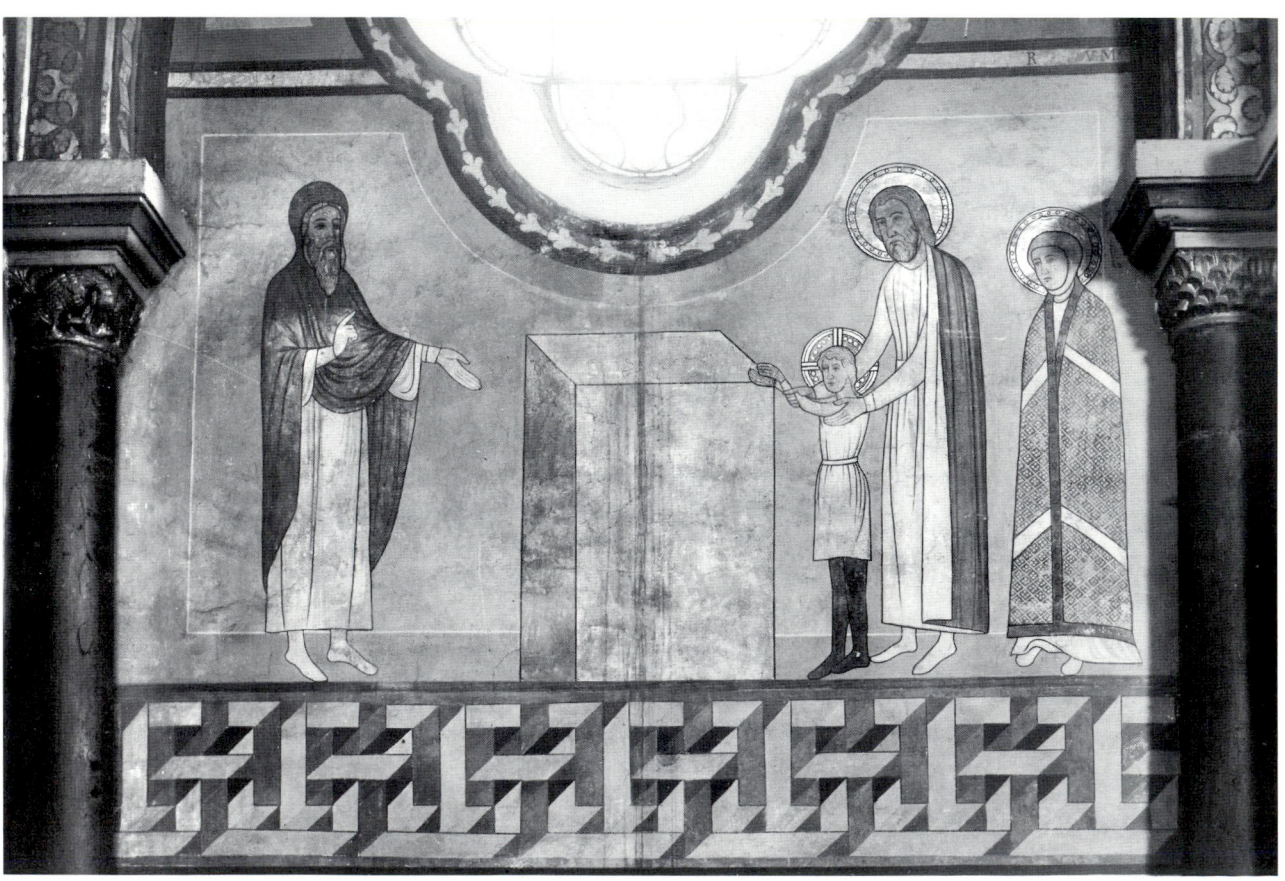

132. Schwartzrheinidorf, St. Clemens, fresco: Presentation (Rheinisches Bildarchiv).

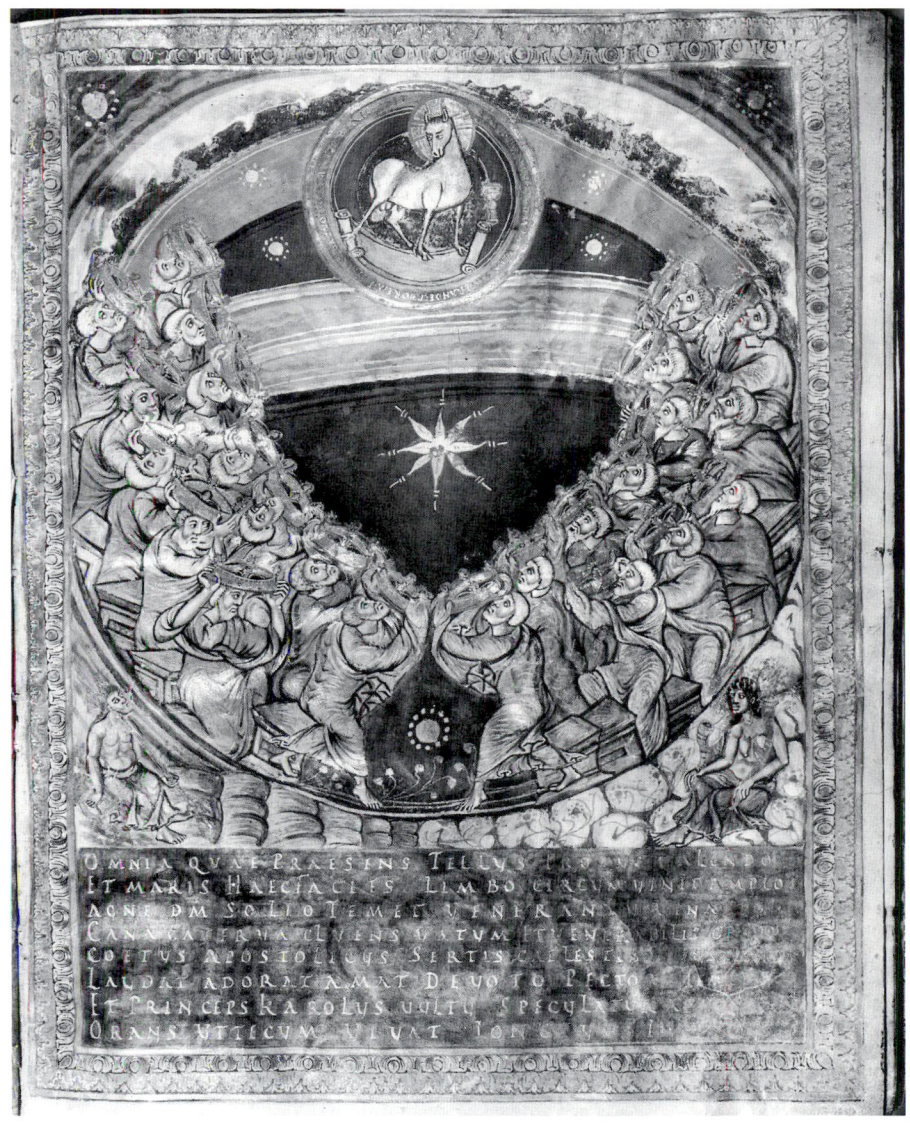

133. Munich, Bayerische Staatsbibliothek, Clm 14000, fol. 5v: Charles the Bald (Bildarchiv Foto Marburg).

134. Munich, Bayerische Staatsbibliothek, Clm 14000, fol. 6: Adoration of the Elders (Bildarchiv Foto Marburg).

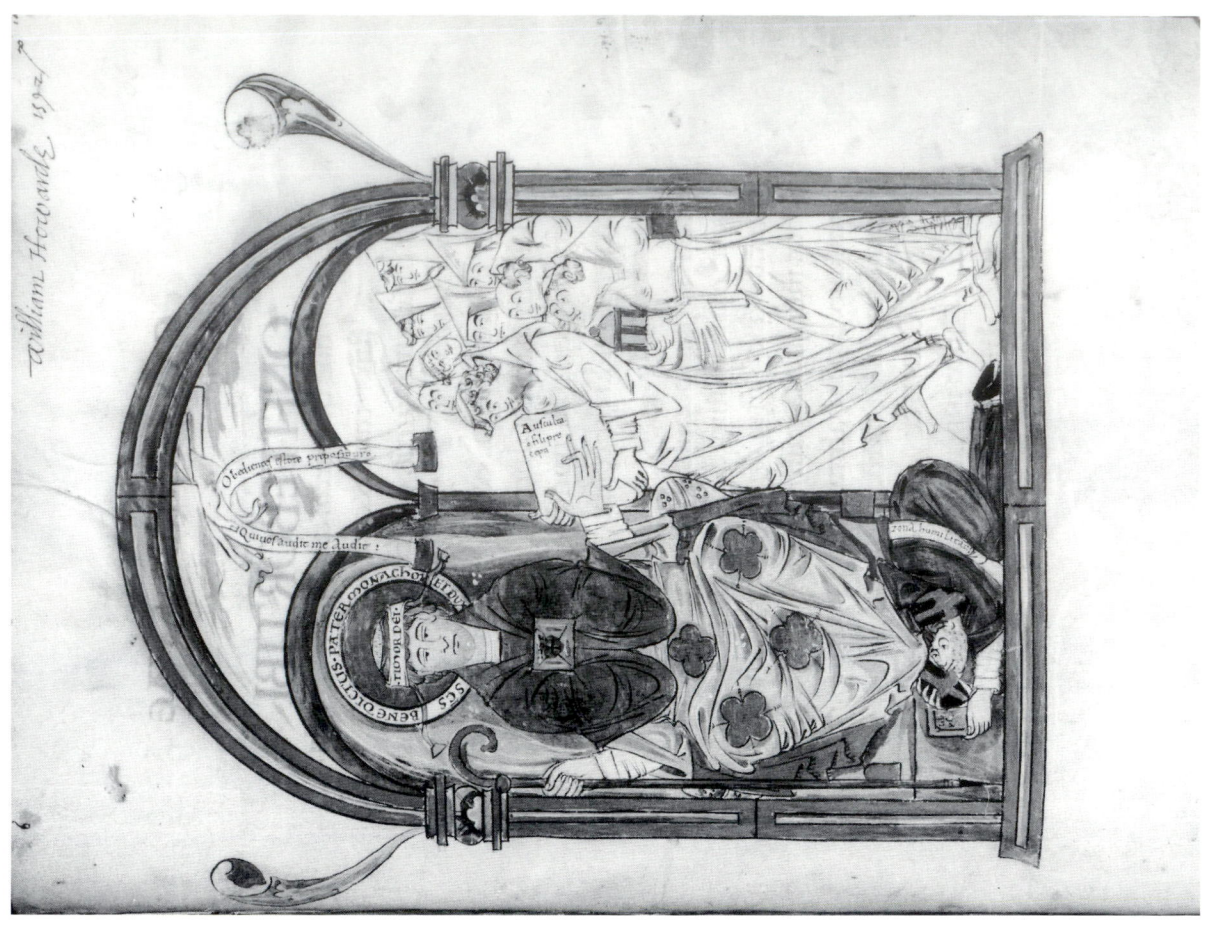

136. London, British Library, MS Arundel 155, fol. fol. 133: Benedict and monks.

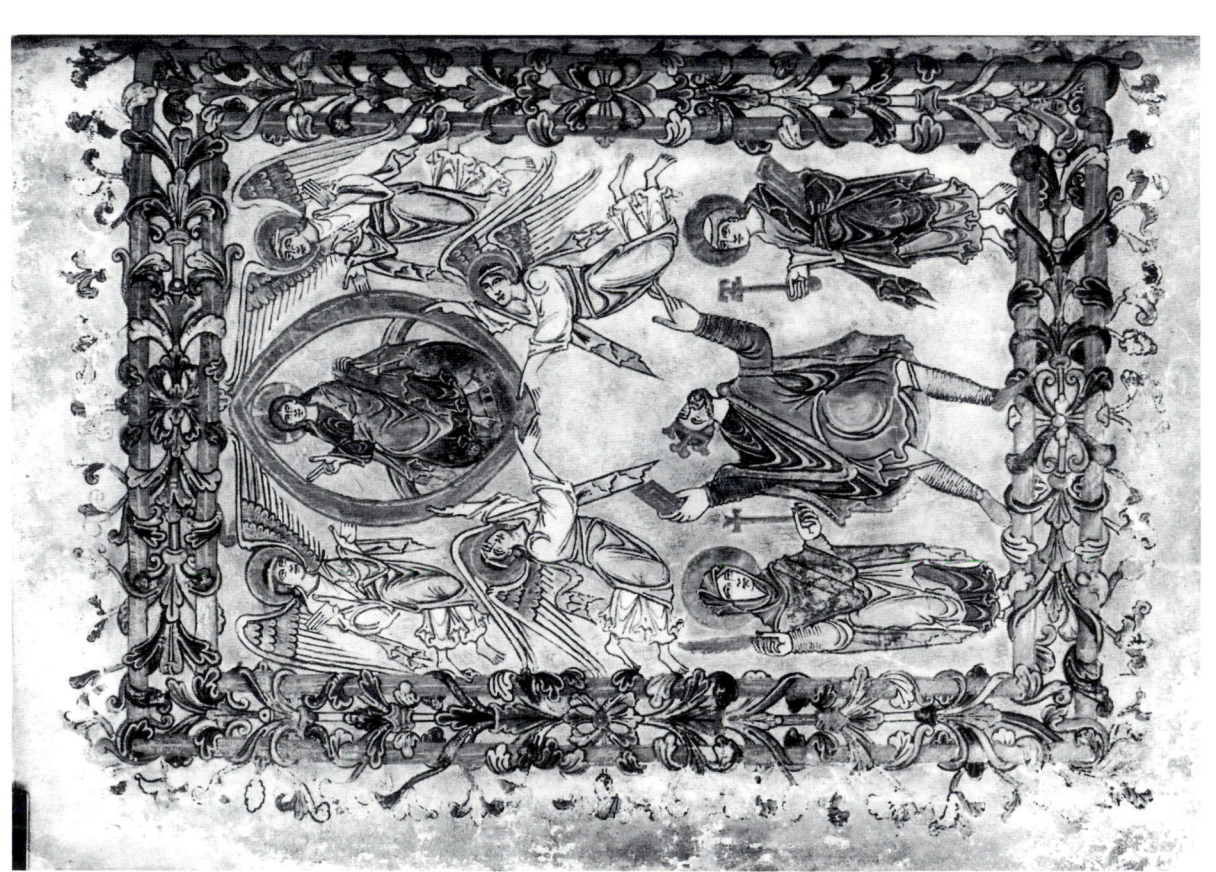

135. London, British Library, MS Cotton Vespasian A. VIII, fol. 2v: donor portrait.

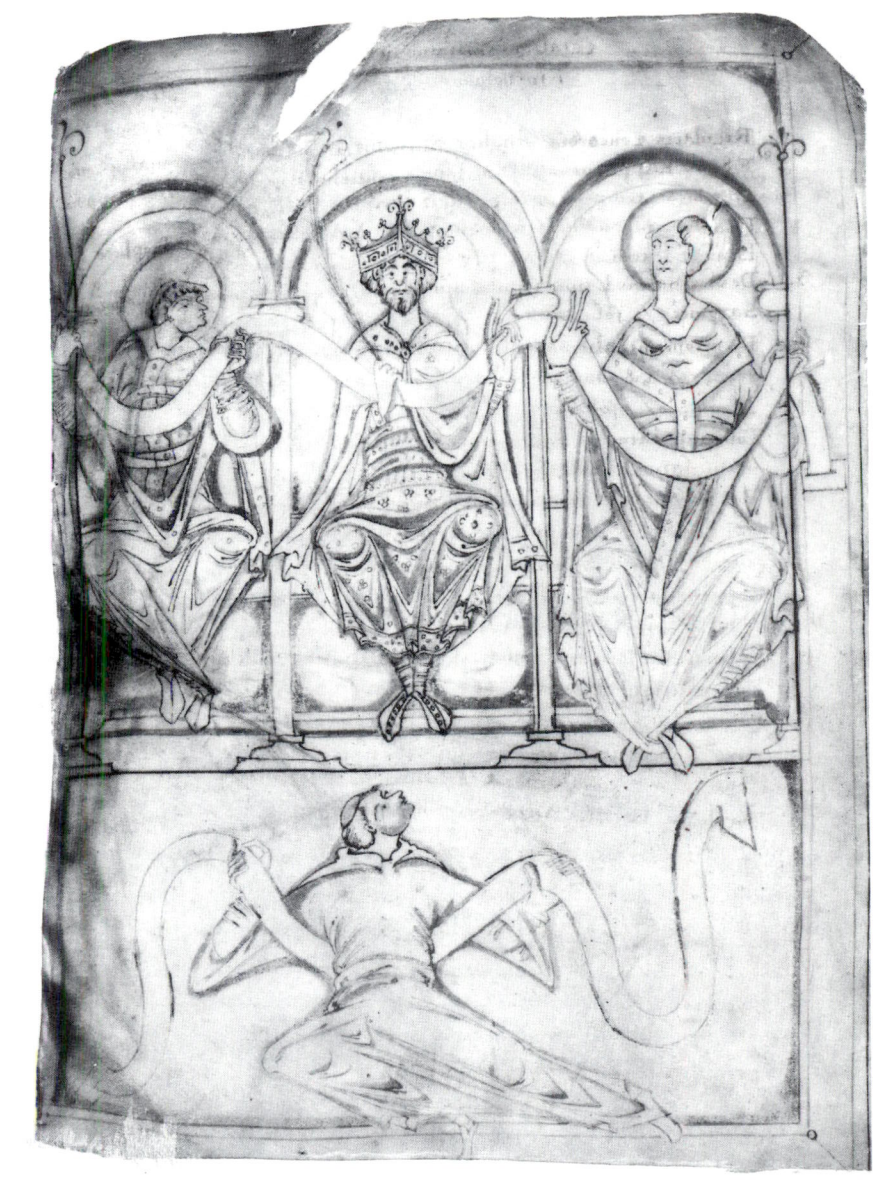

137. London, British Library, MS Cotton Tiberius A. III, fol. 117v: Benedict and monks.

138. London, British Library, MS Cotton Tiberius A. III, fol. 2v.

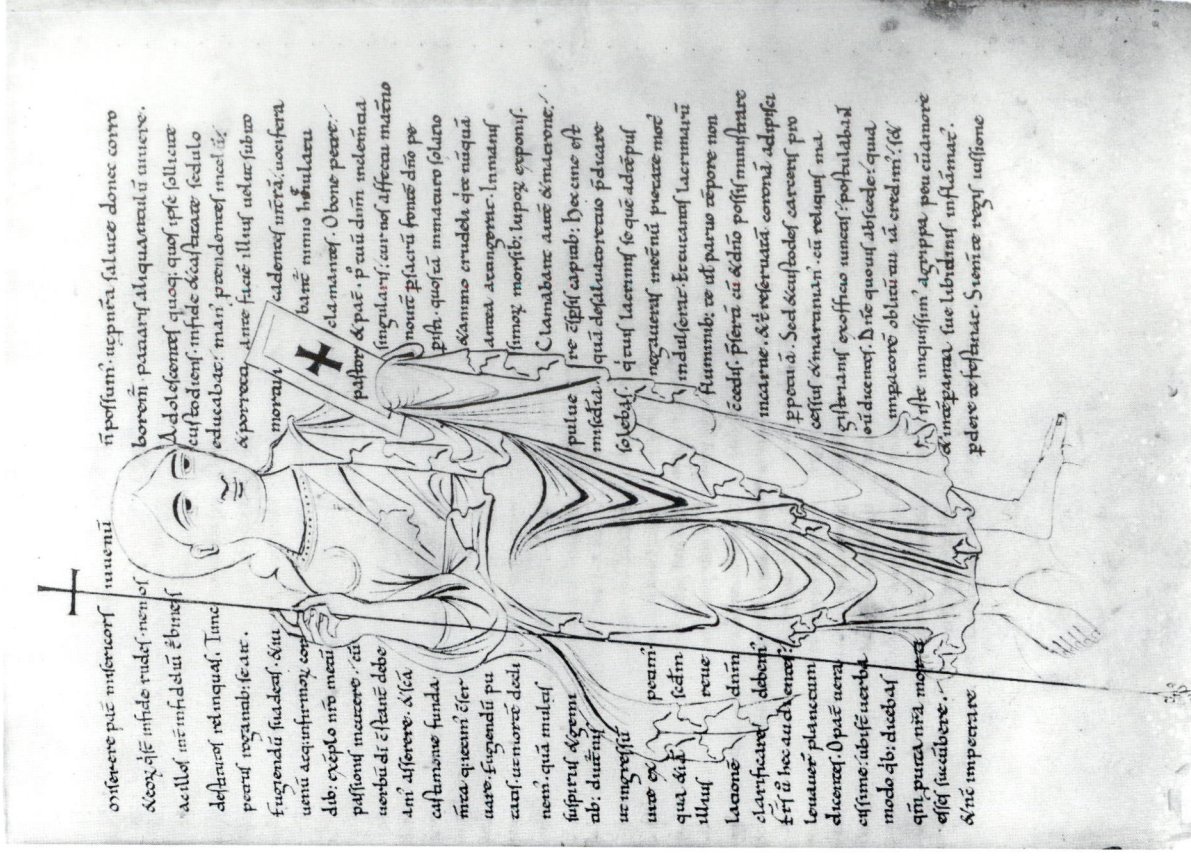

140. Oxford, St. John's College, MS 28, fol. 2: Christ.

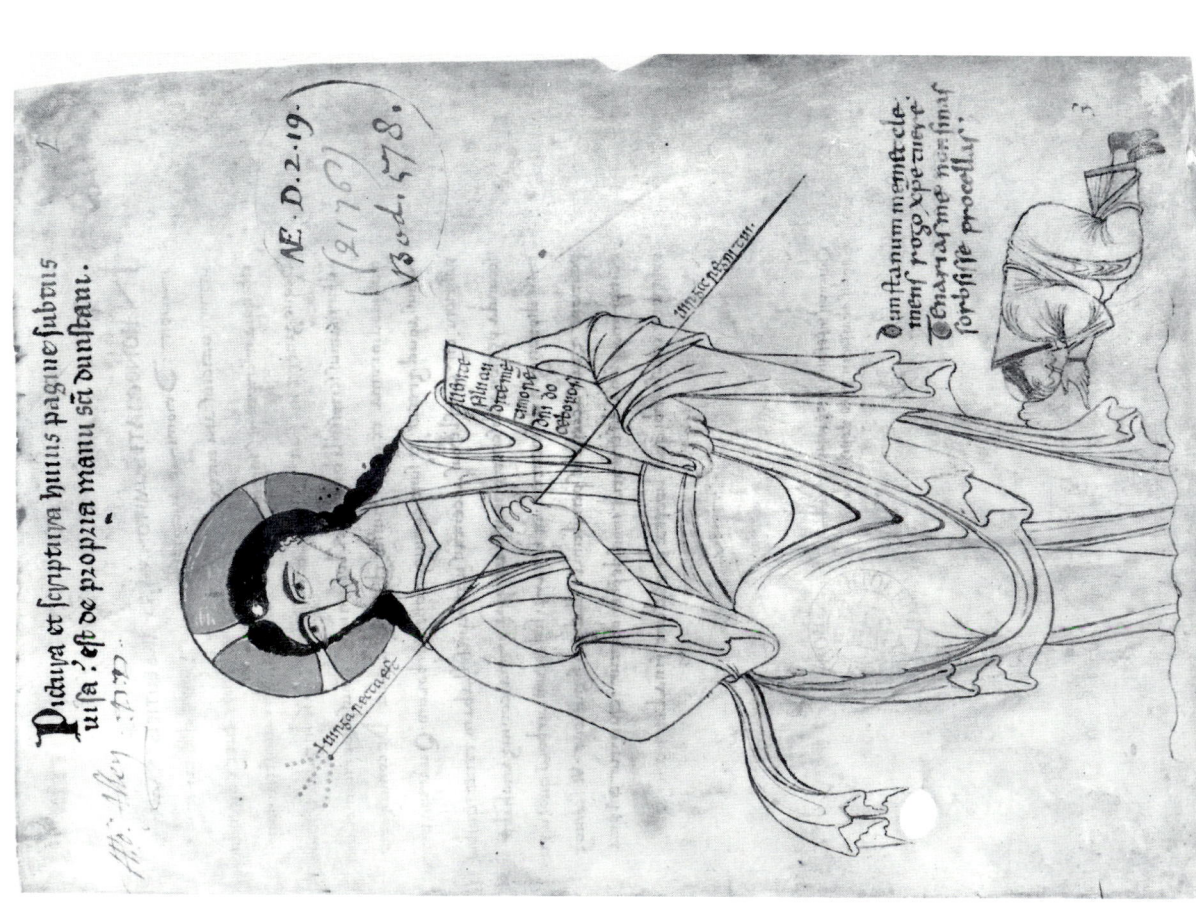

139. Oxford, Bodleian Library, MS Auct. F. 4. 32, fol. 1: Christ and Dunstan.

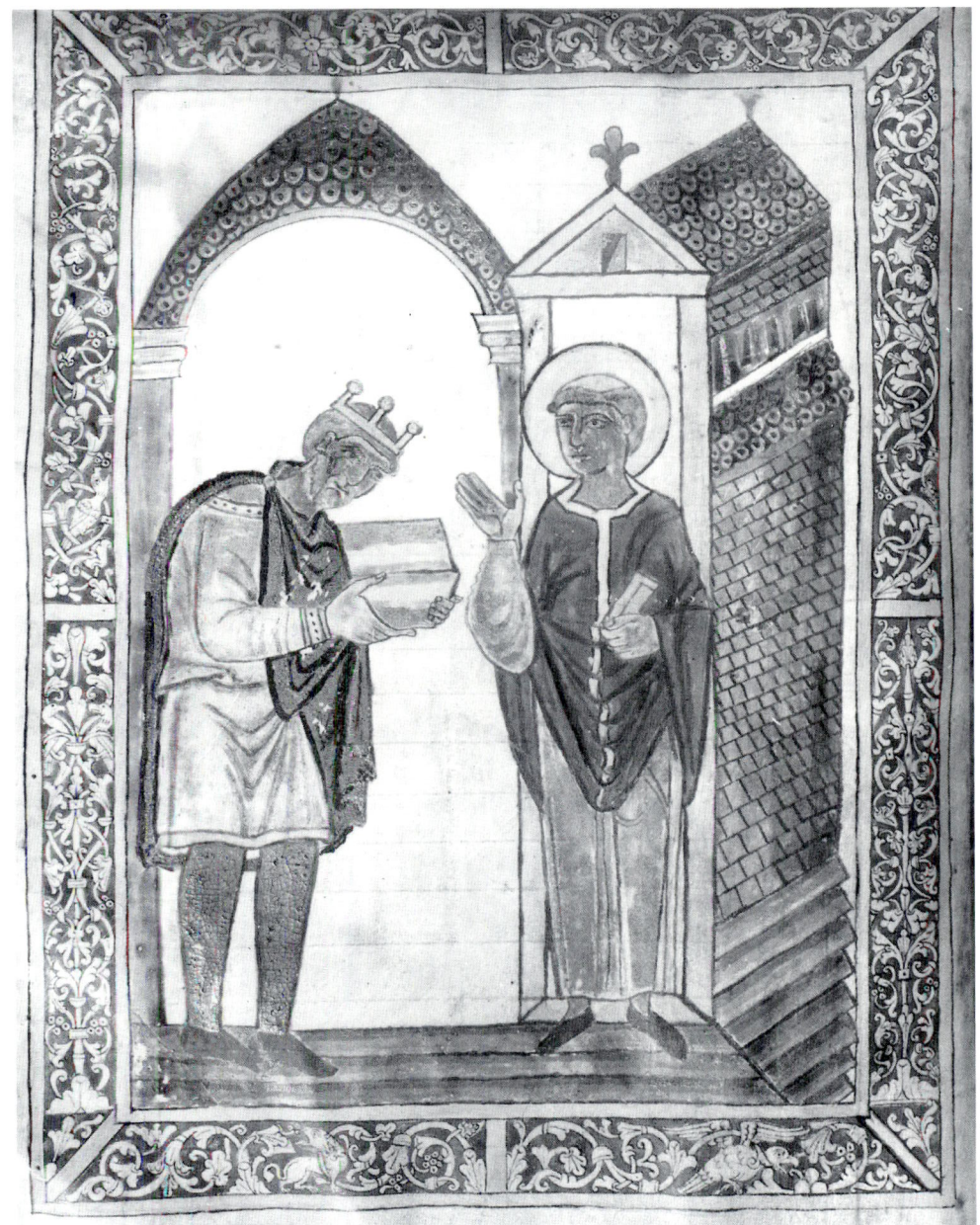

141. London, British Library, MS Cotton Vespasian A. VIII, fol. 2v (detail).

142. Cambridge, Corpus Christi College, MS 183, fol. 1v: donor portrait.

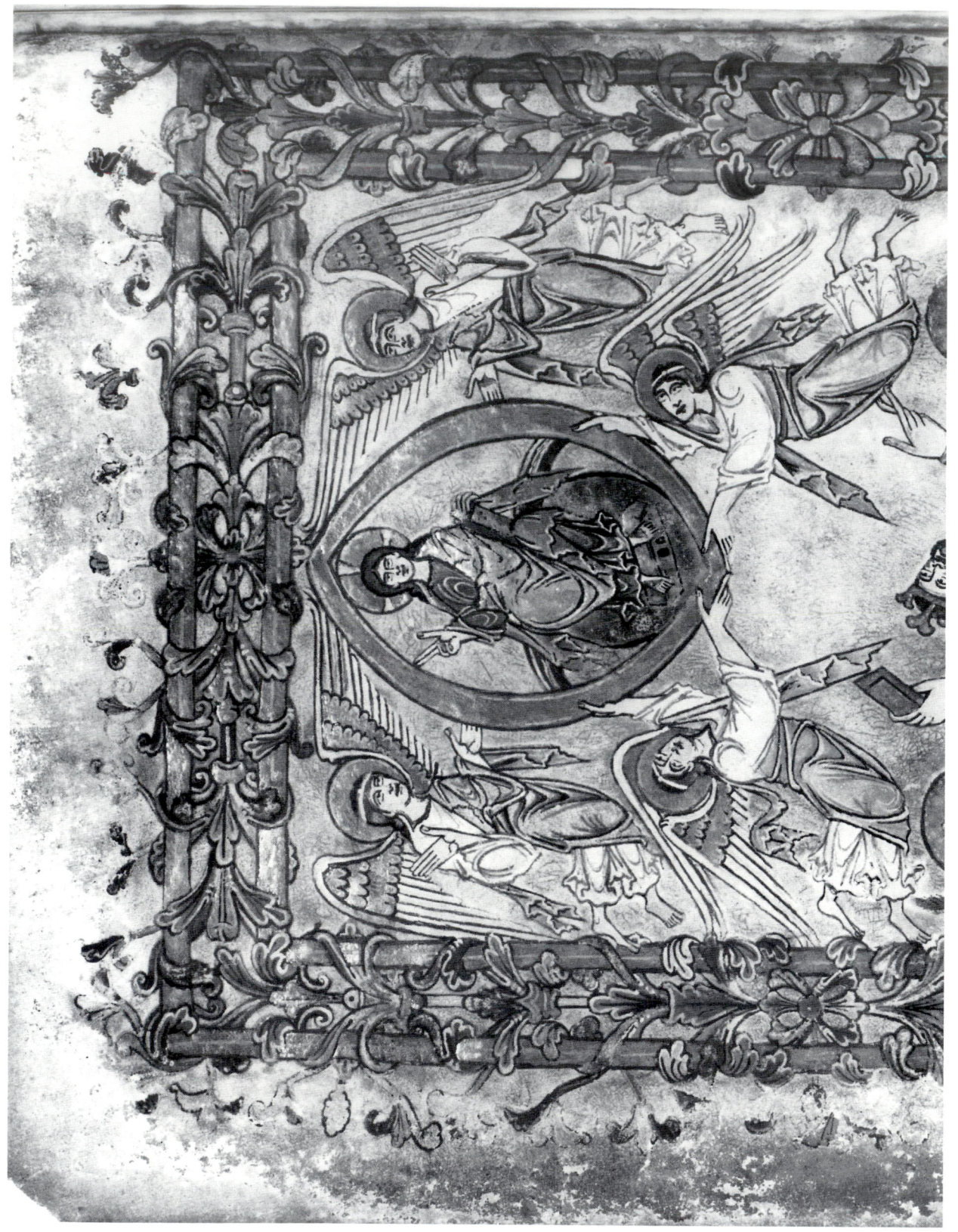

143. London, British Library, MS Cotton Vespasian A. VIII, fol. 2v (detail).

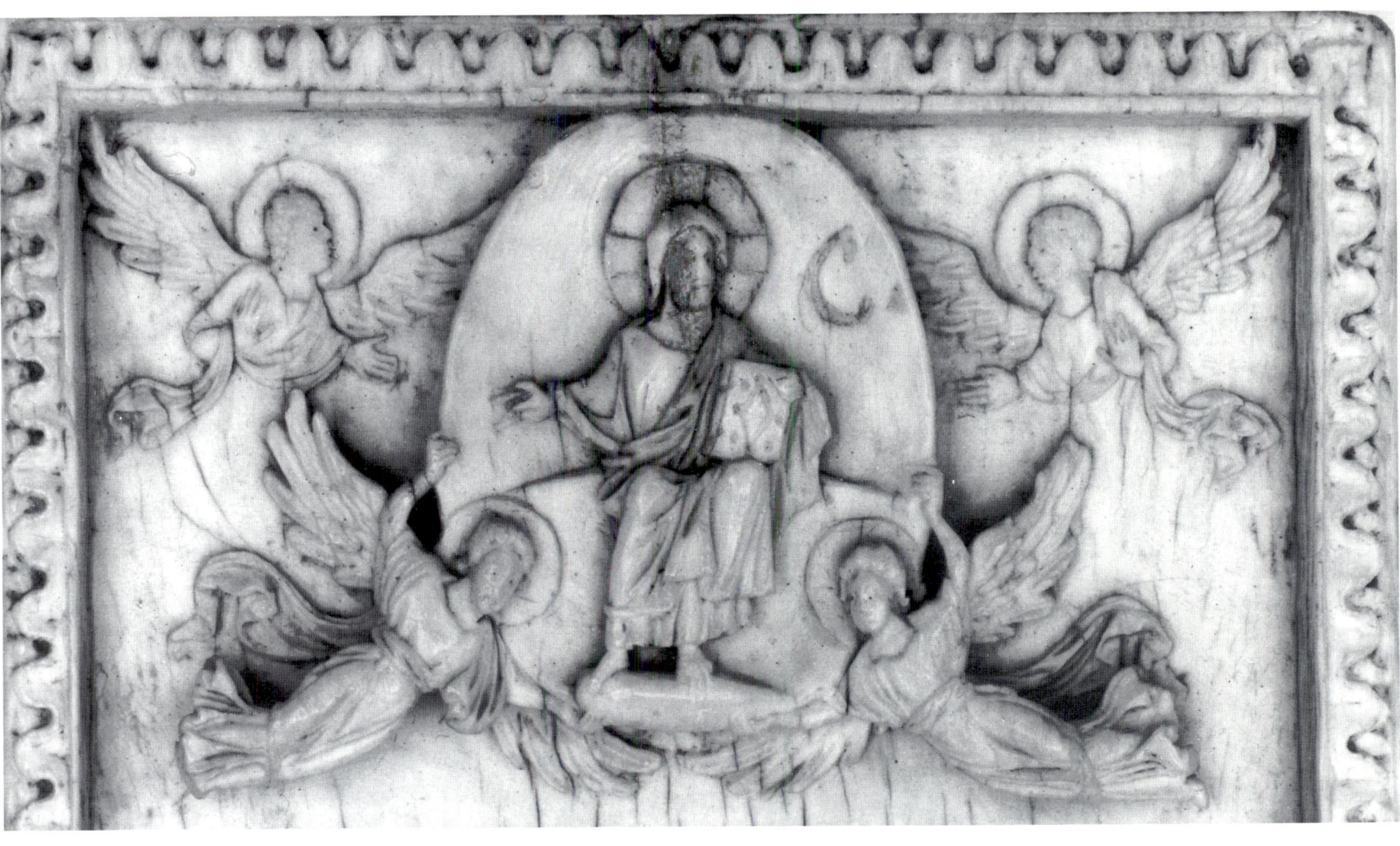

144. Stuttgart, Württembergische Landesbibliothek, ivory casket (detail): Ascension.

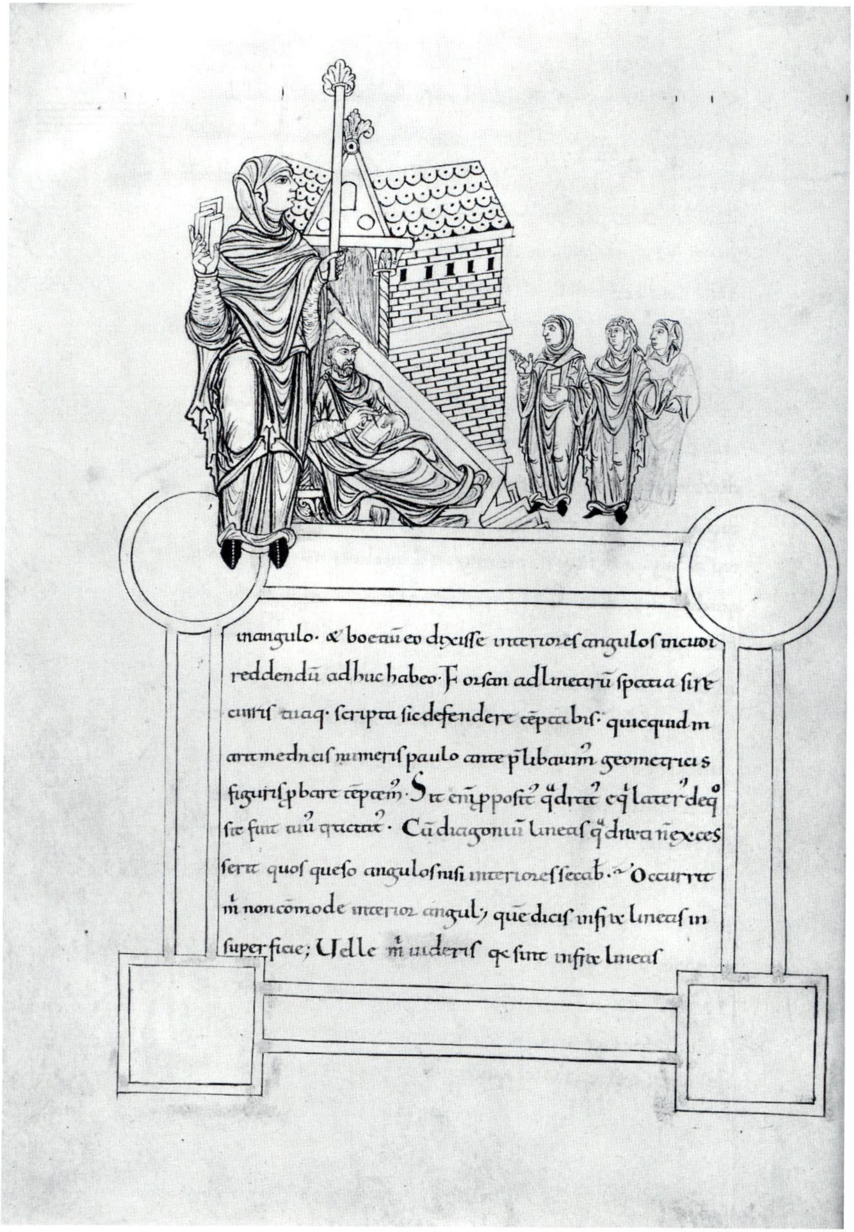

inangulo. & boetiu eo dixisse interiores angulos includi
reddendu adhuc habeo. Forsan ad linearu spatia sir
curris tuaq. scripta sic defendere ceperis. quicquid in
arte medit eis numeris paulo ante plibauim geometrias
figuris sp bare ceperim. Sit eni pposite qdrate eq later deq
sic sunt uiu quciai. Cu diagonui lineas qd dura ii exces
serit quos queso angulos nisi interiores secab. Occurrit
in non comode interior angul, que dicis infix lineas in
superficie; Uelle in uideris qe sint infix lineas

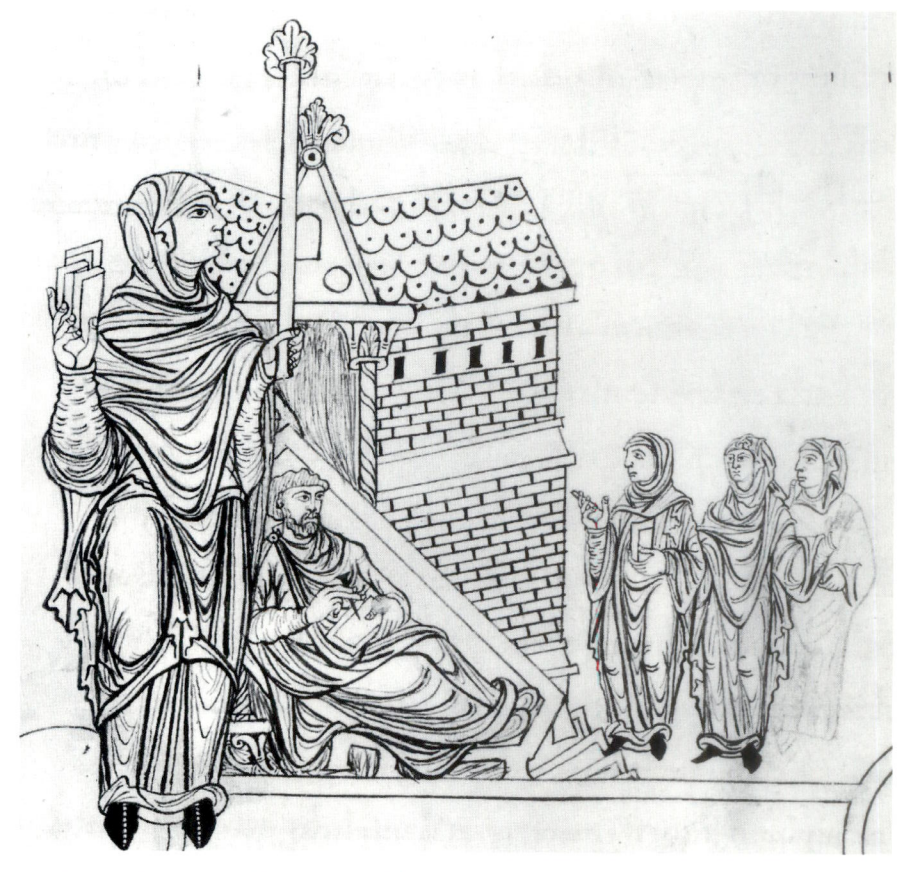

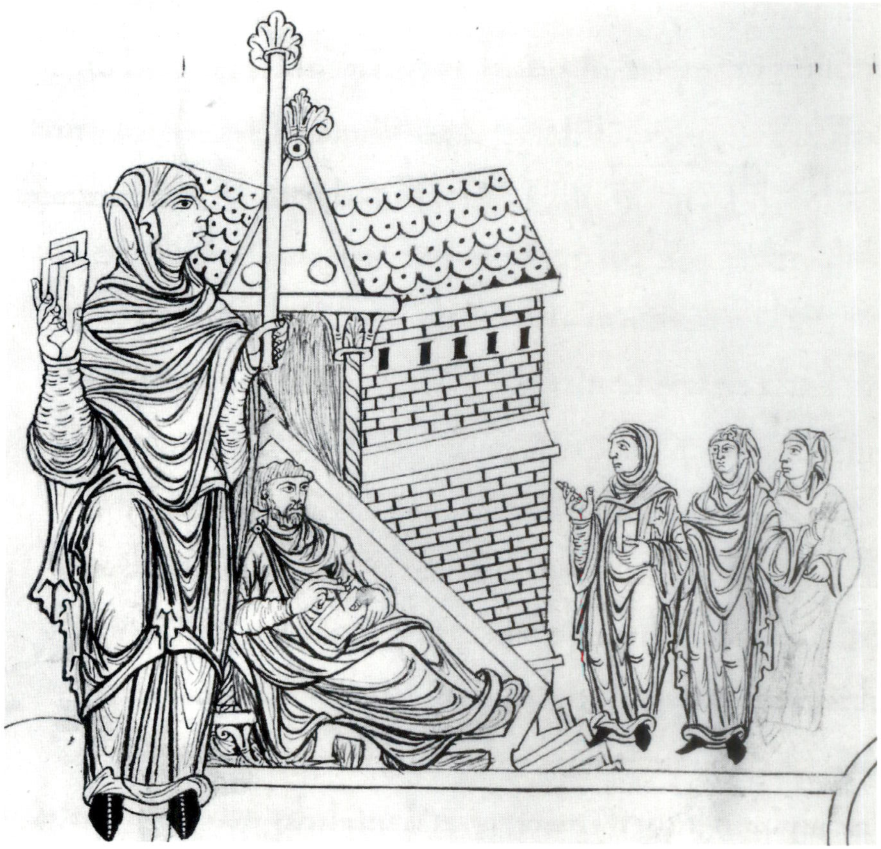

146. Paris, Bibliothèque Nationale, MS lat. 6401, fol. 5v (detail of fig. 145).

145. Paris, Bibliothèque Nationale, MS lat. 6401, fol. 5v: Boethius, Philosophy, and
the Muses.

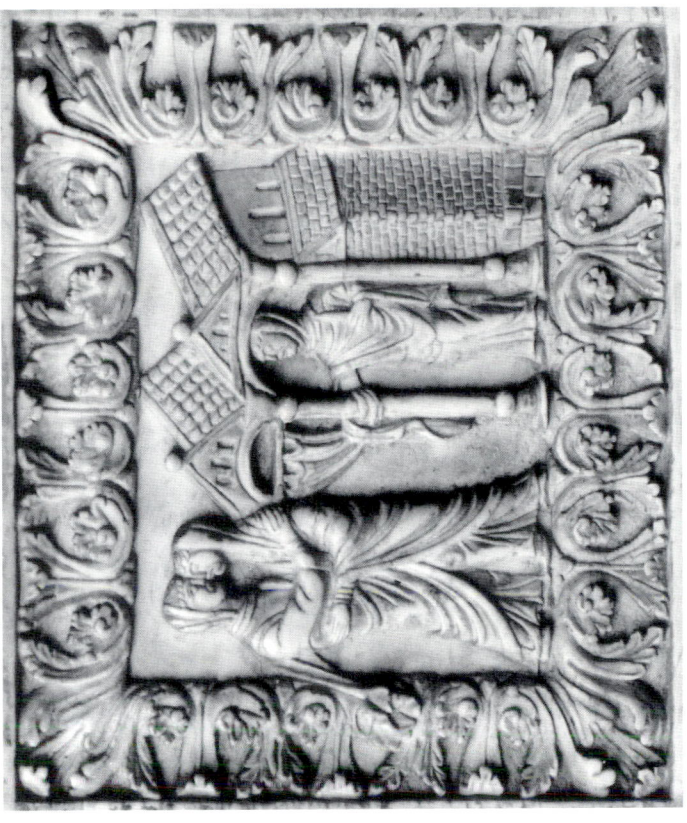

148. Paris, Louvre Museum, ivory casket: Visitation (ARS, New York/SPADEM, Paris).

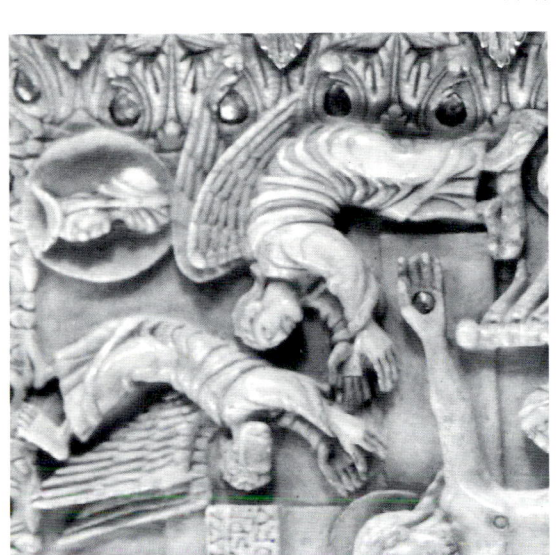

149. Paris, Bibliothèque Nationale, MS lat. 9453, ivory cover (detail): angels.

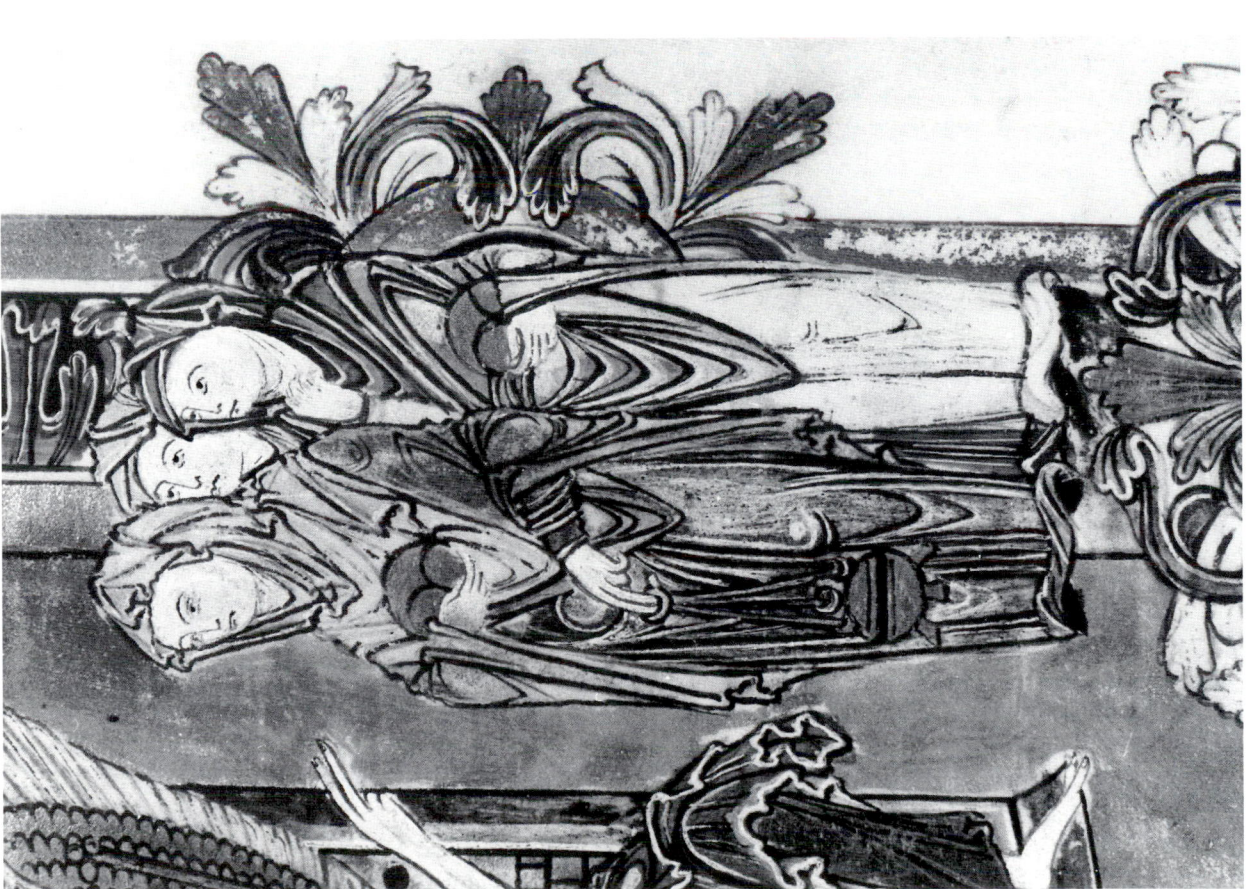

147. London, British Library, MS Add. 49598, fol. 51v (detail): Holy Women (Warburg Institute).

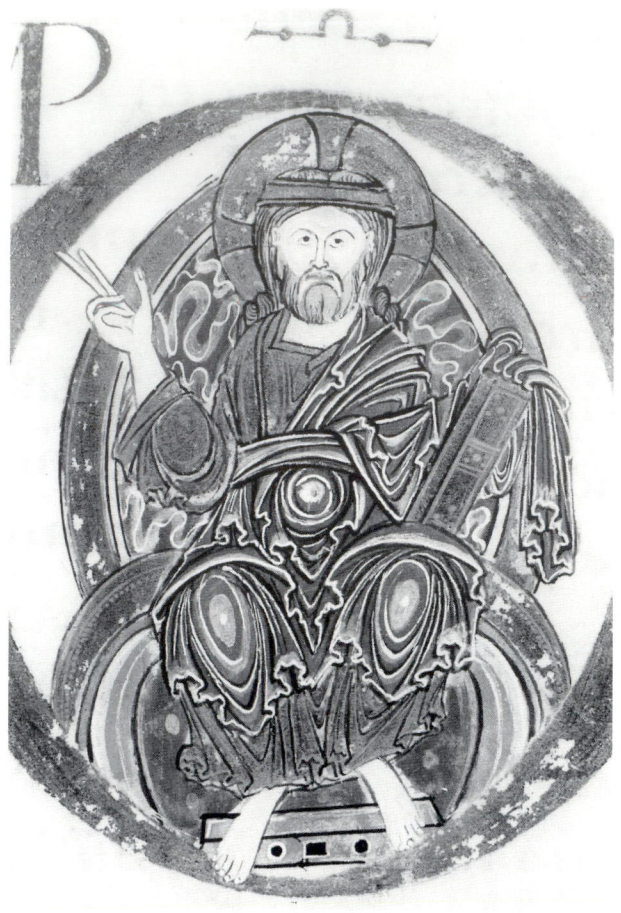

150. London, British Library, MS Add. 49598, fol. 70 (detail): the Deity (Warburg Institute).

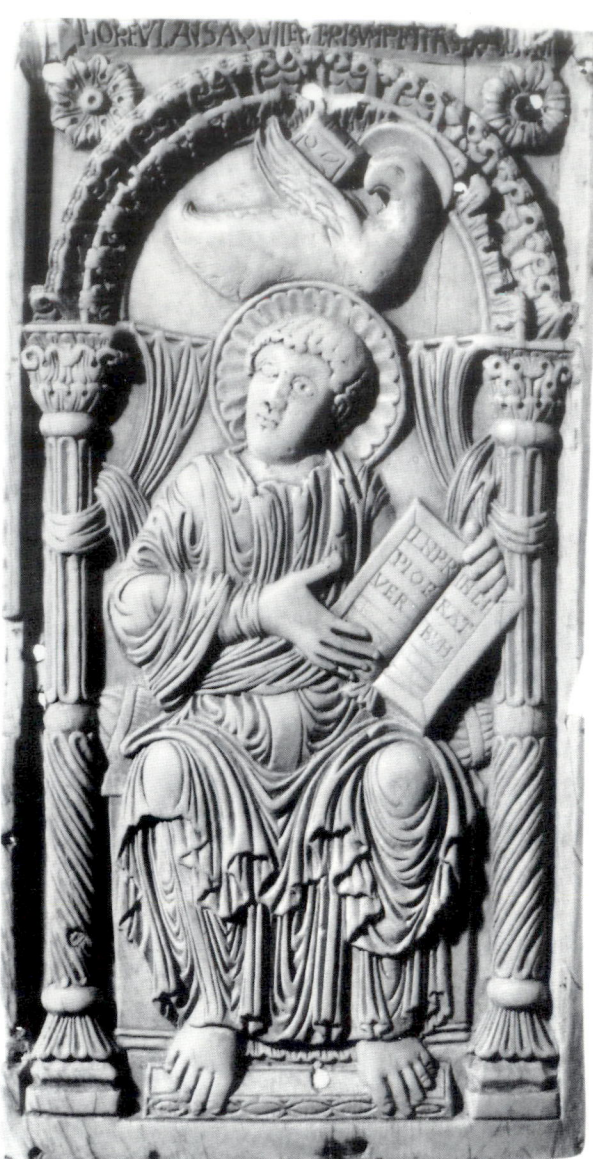

151. New York, Metropolitan Museum of Art, The Cloisters Collection, ivory plaque: John the evangelist (author).

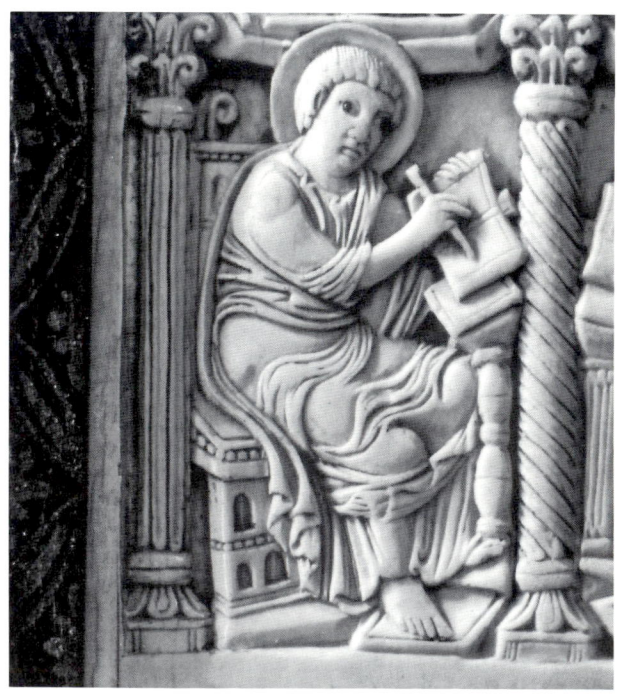

152. Cologne, Schnütgen Museum, ivory diptych (detail): Matthew.

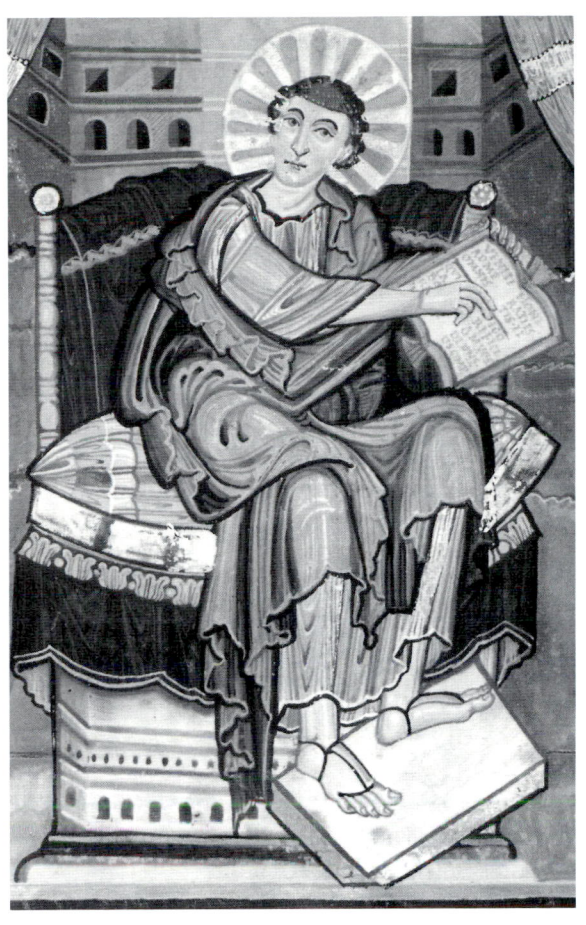

153. London, British Library, MS Harley 2788, fol. 13v: Matthew.

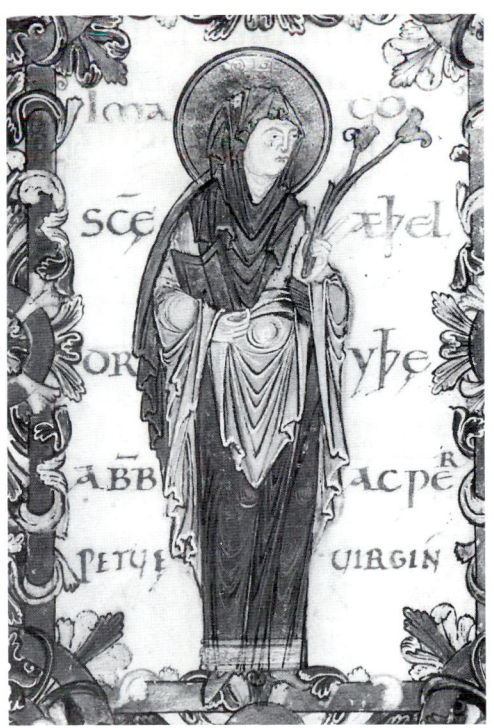

154. London, British Library, MS Add. 49598, fol. 90v (detail): St. Æthelthryth (Warburg Institute).

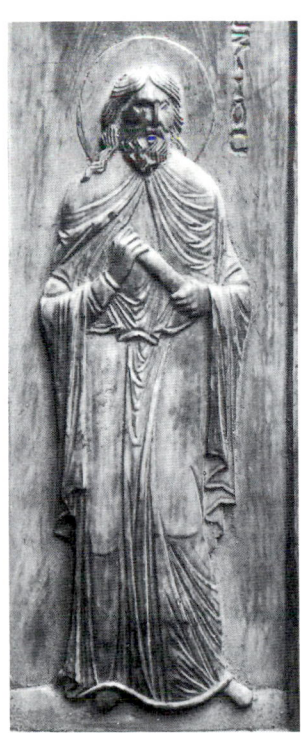

155. Verona Museo Castelvecchio, ivory plaque: St. Alexios (Kurt Weitzmann).

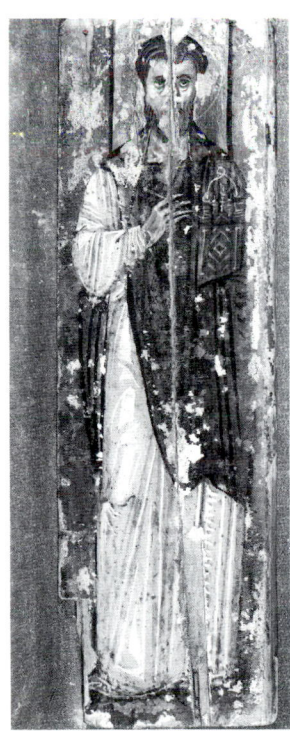

156. Mt. Sinai, St. Catherine's monastery, icon B.55: St. Damian (?) (Princeton-Michigan-Alexandria Expedition to Mt. Sinai).

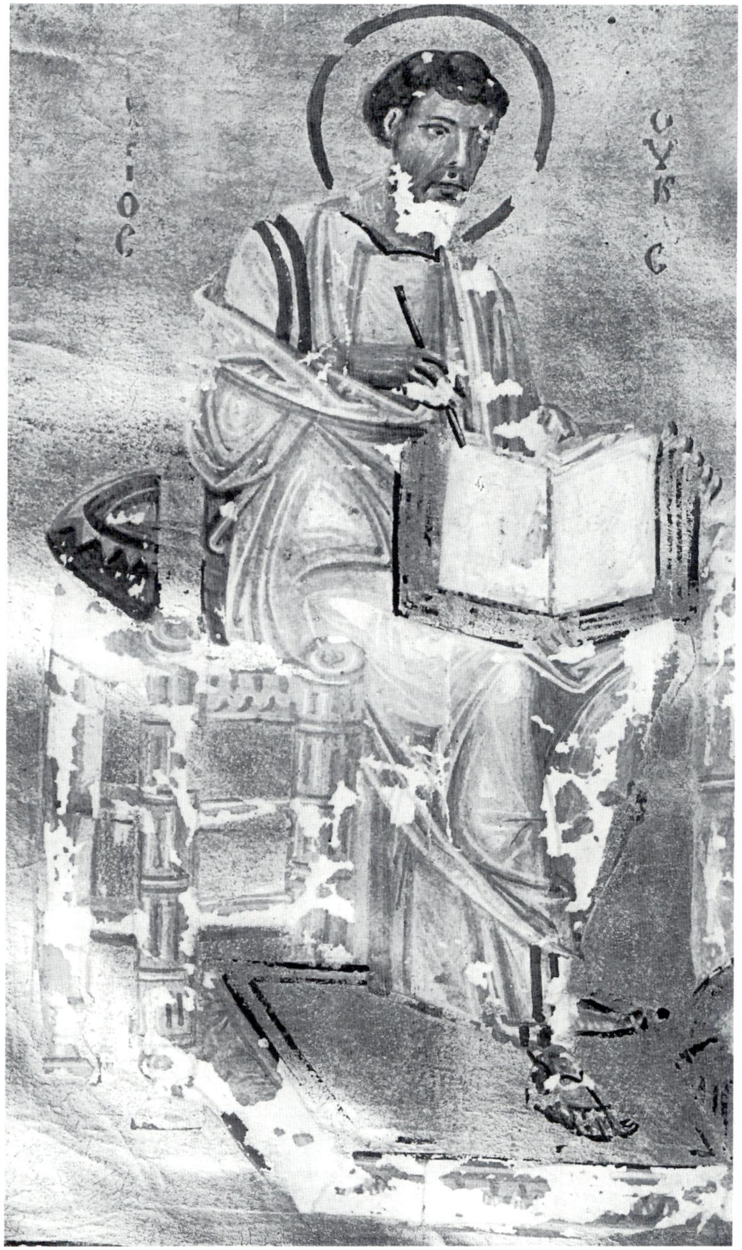

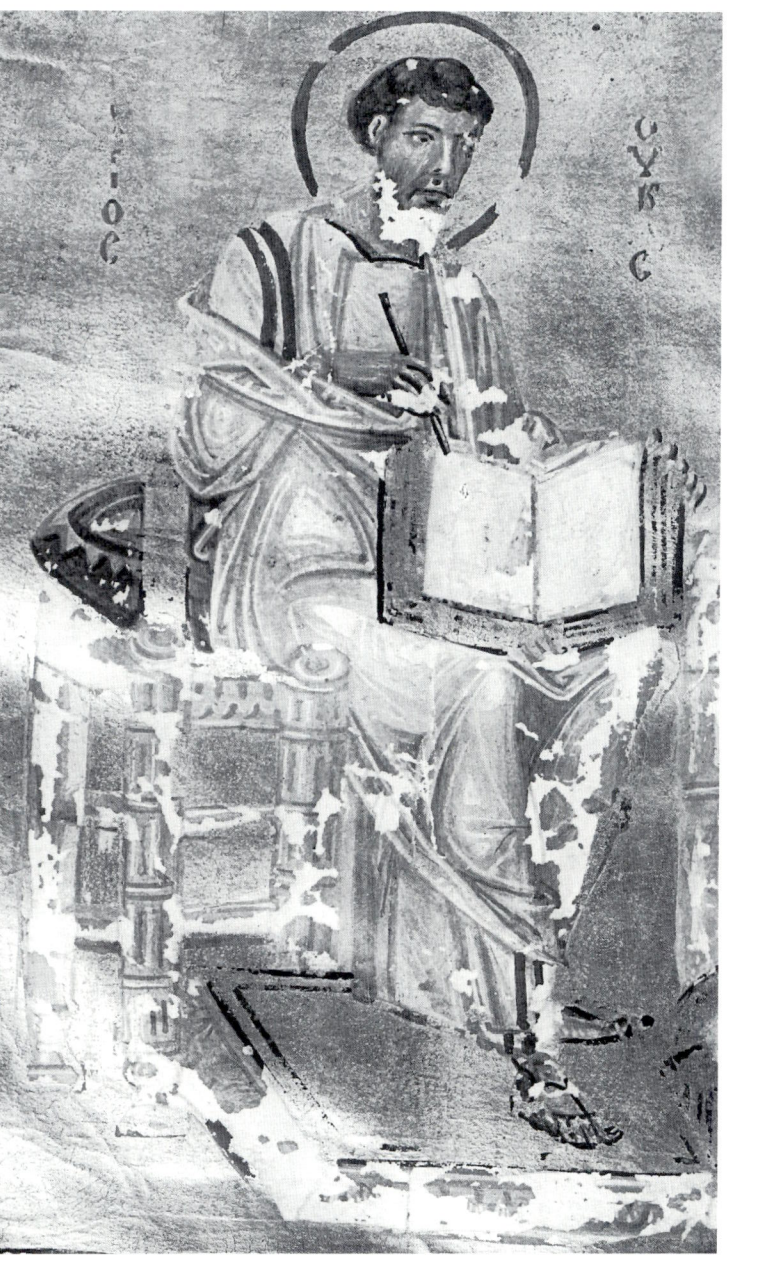

157. Vatican, Biblioteca Apostlica, MS gr. 1522, fol. 93v: Luke.

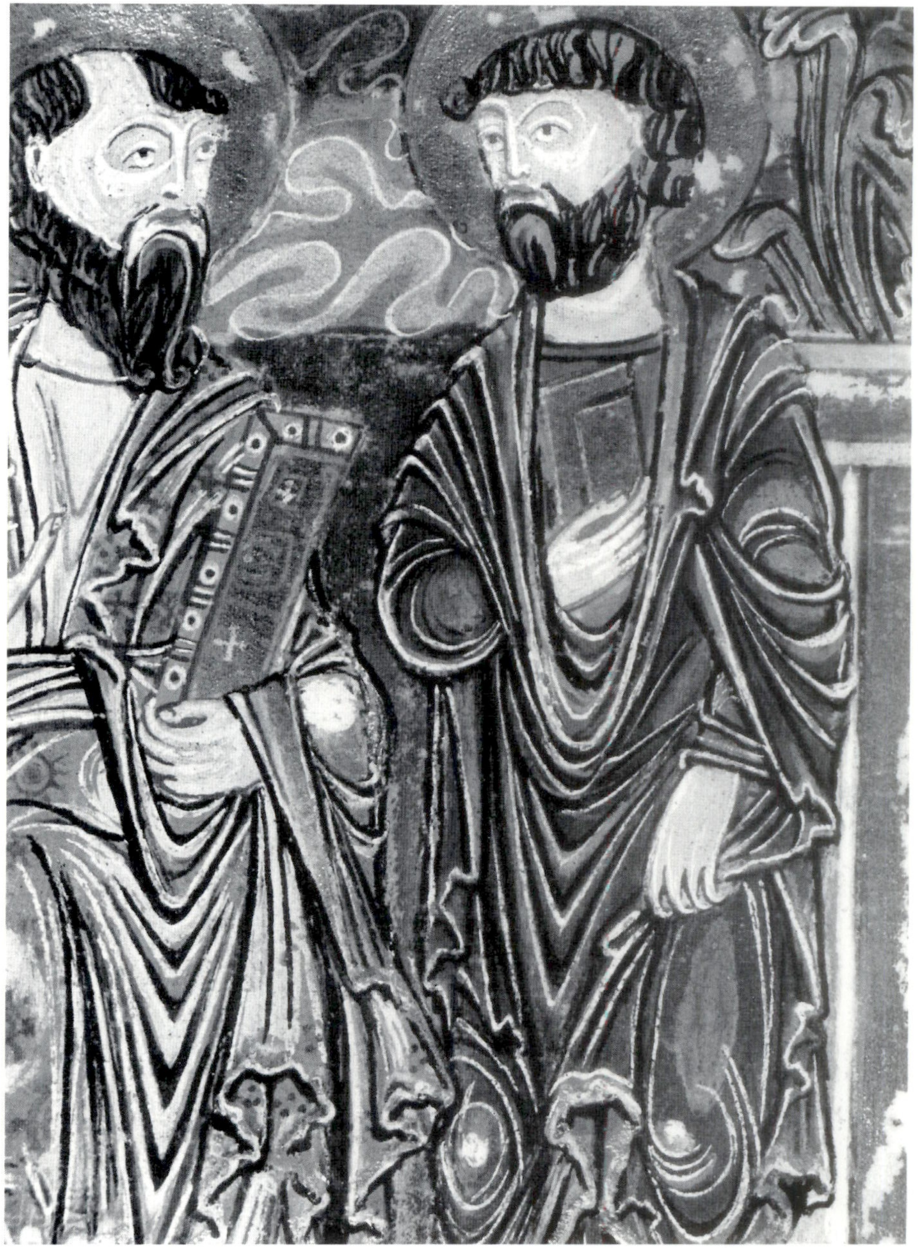

158. London, British Library, MS Add. 49598, fol. 3v (detail): apostles (Warburg Institute).

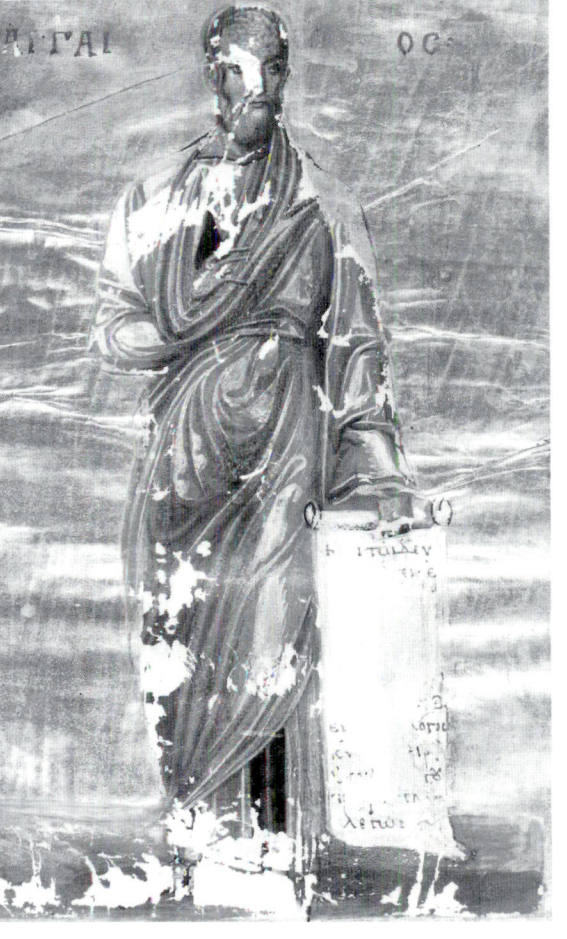

159. Vatican, Biblioteca Apostolica, MS Chisianus R. VIII. 54, fol. 91v: Isaiah.

160. Vatican, Biblioteca Apostolica, MS Chisianus R. VIII. 54, fol. 61v: Haggai.

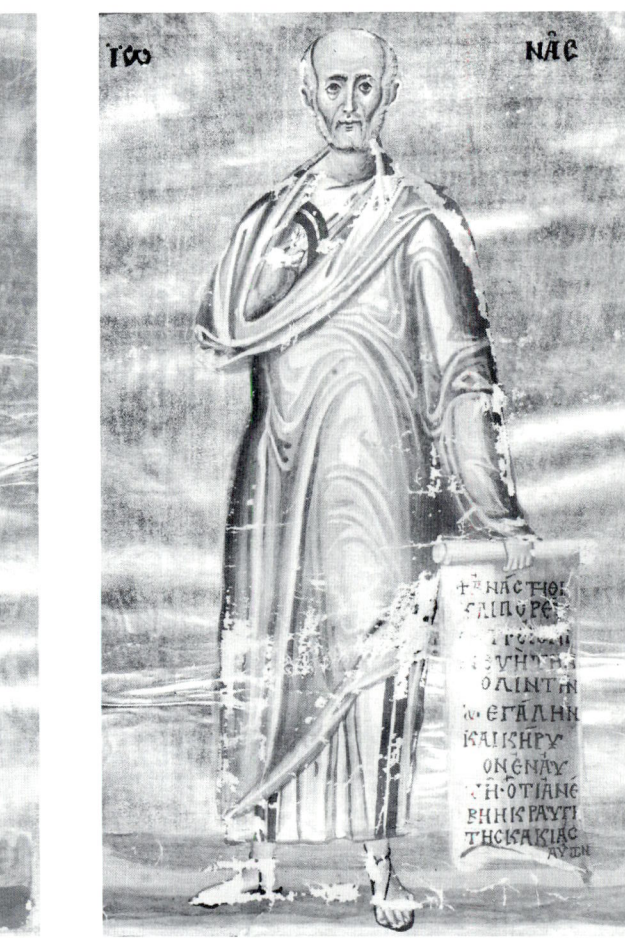

161. Vatican, Biblioteca Apostolica, MS Chisianus R. VIII. 54, fol. 36v: Jonah.

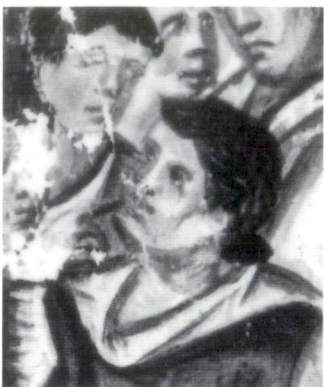

162. Vatican, Biblioteca Apostolica, MS Regina gr. 1 B, fol. 155v (detail).

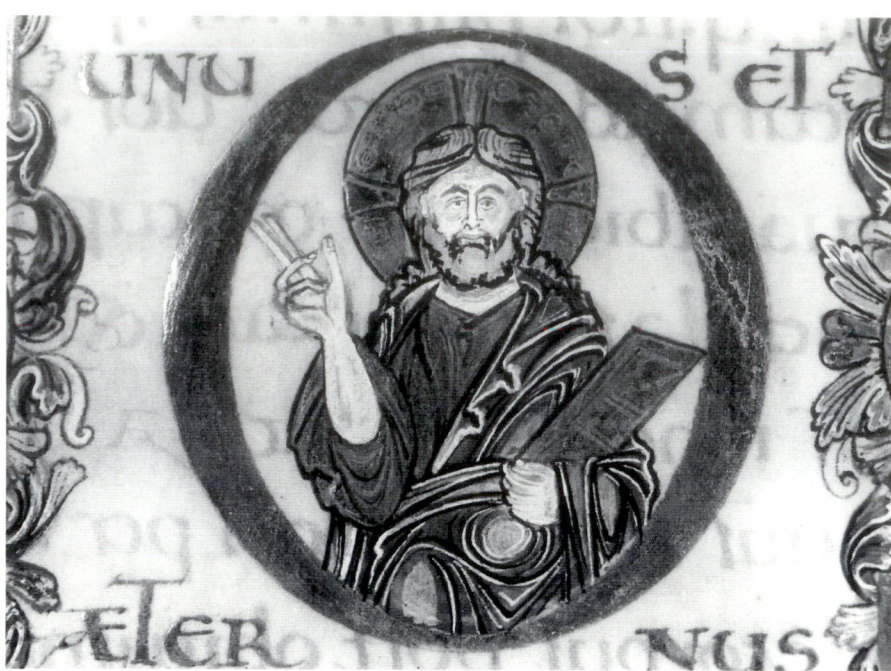

163. London, British Library., MS Add. 49598, fol. 91 (detail): Christ (Warburg Institute).

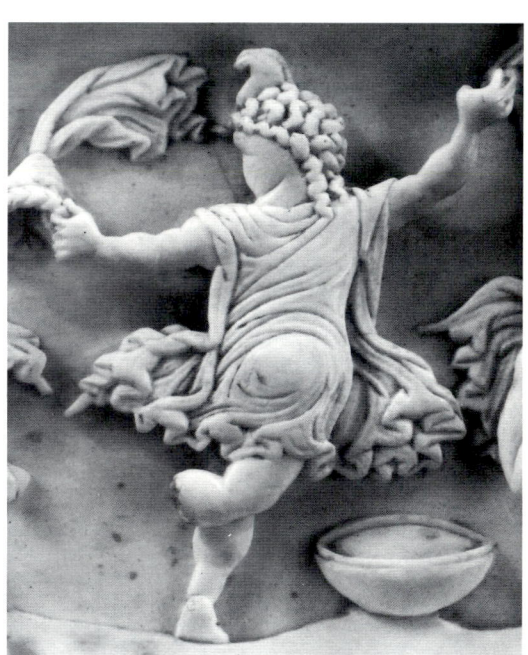

164. London, Victoria and Albert Museum, ivory casket (detail).

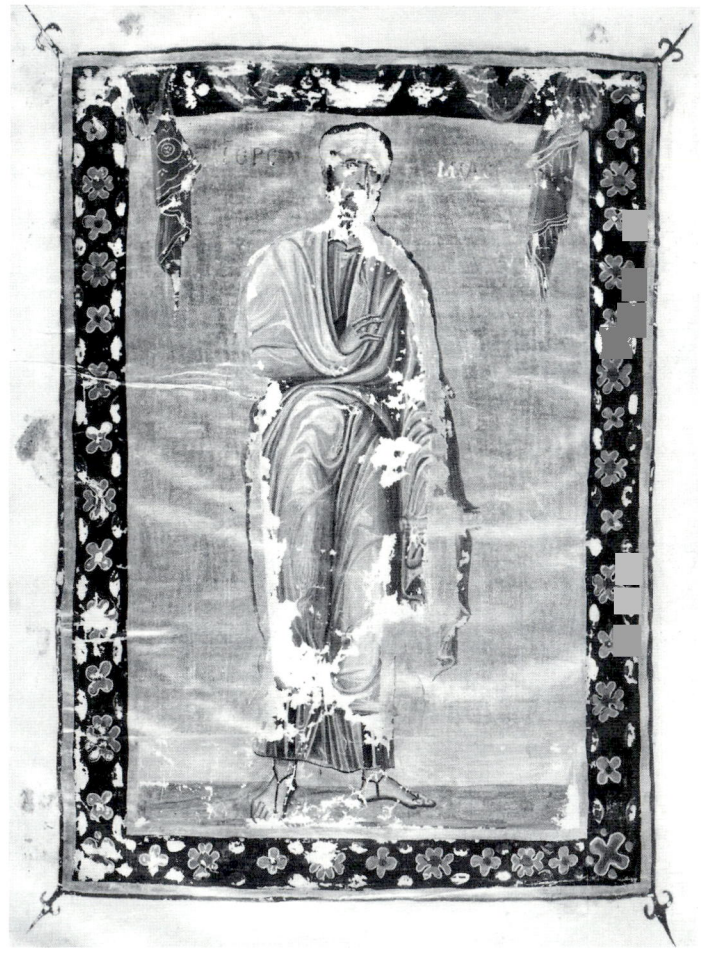

165. Vatican, Biblioteca Apostolica, MS Chisianus R. VIII. 54, fol. 246v: Jeremiah.

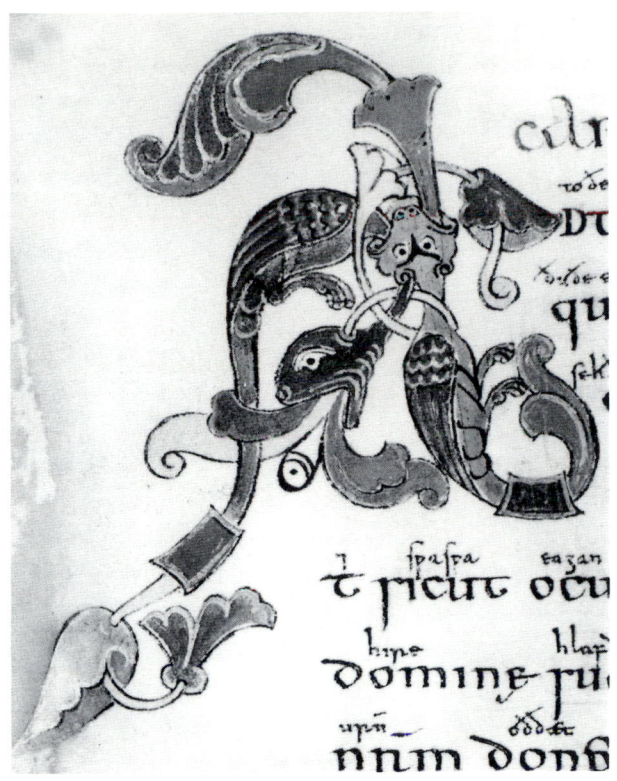

166. Oxford, Bodleian Library, MS Junius 27, fol. 135v (detail): initial.

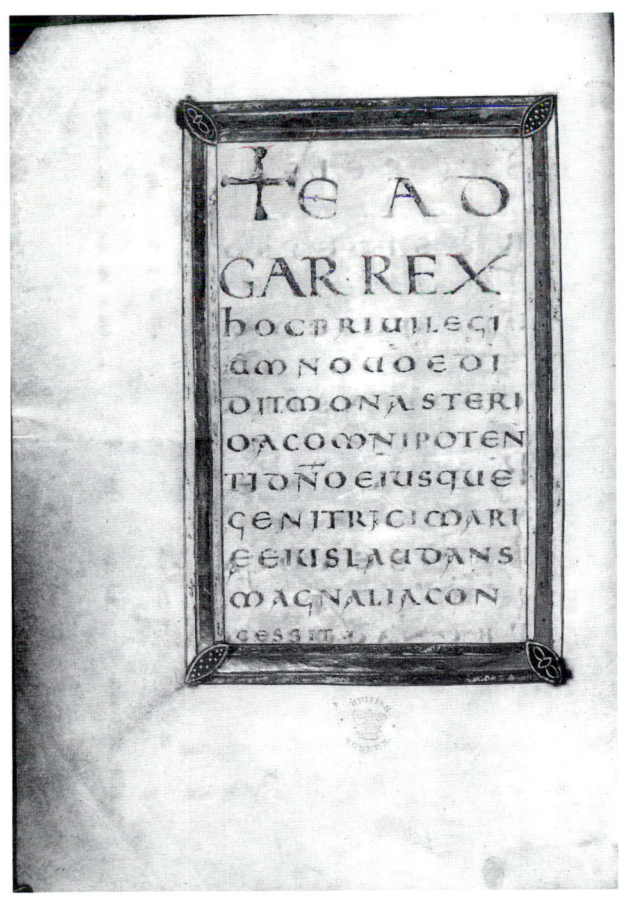

167. London, British Library, MS Cotton Vespasian A. VIII, fol. 3v.

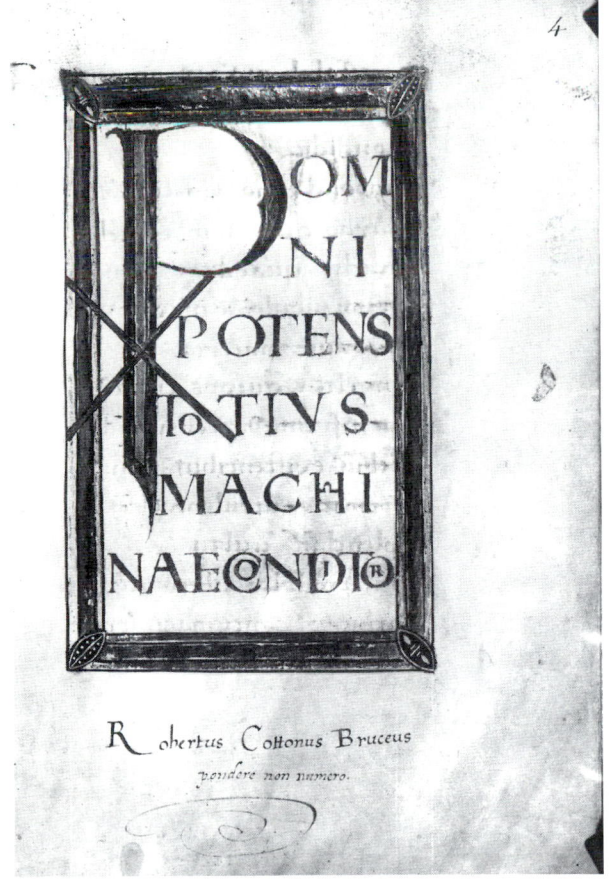

168. London, British Library, MS Cotton Vespasian A. VIII, fol. 4.

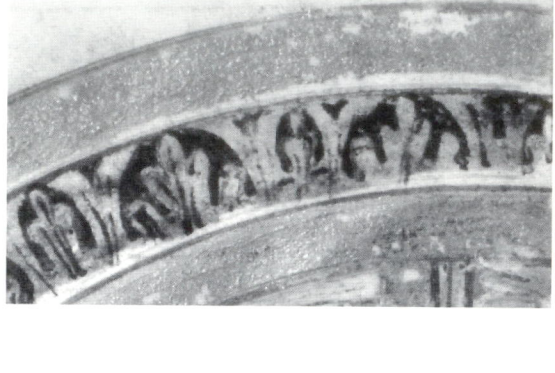

172. London, British Library, MS Add. 49598, fol. 2 (detail).

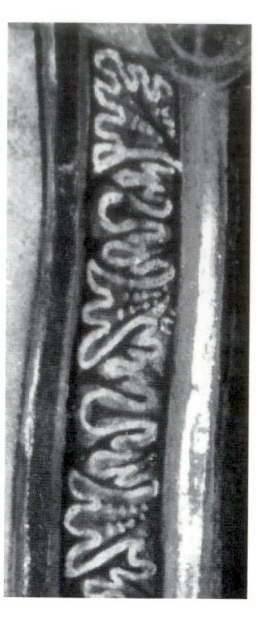

176. Arras, Bibliothèque Mun., MS 1045, fol. 32 (detail) (author).

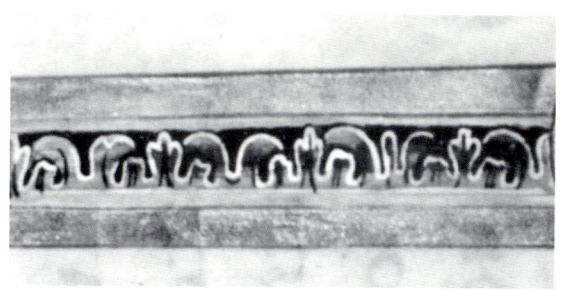

171. London, College of Arms, MS Arundel 22, fol. 84 (detail of fig. 129).

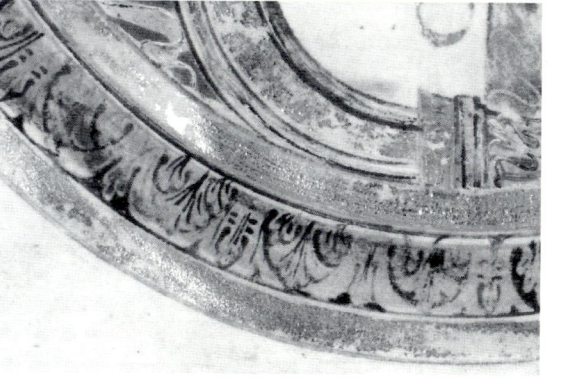

170. London, British Library, MS Add. 49598, fol. 1v (detail).

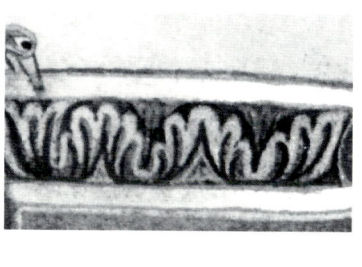

175. Arras, Bibliothèque Mun., MS 1045, fol. 16 (detail) (author).

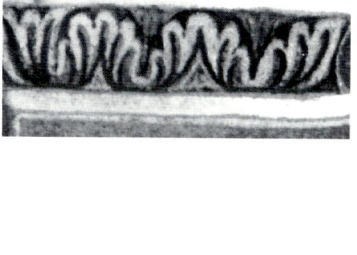

174. London, British Library, MS Add. 49598, fol. 5v (detail).

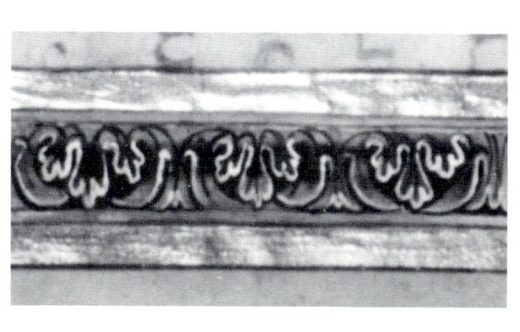

169. London, College of Arms, MS Arundel 22, fol. 84 (detail of fig. 129).

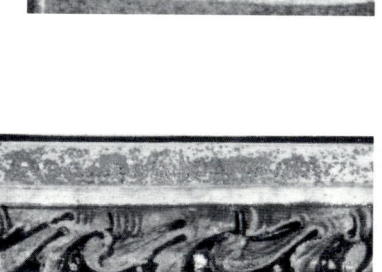

173. London, College of Arms, MS Arundel 22, fol. 84 (detail of fig. 129).

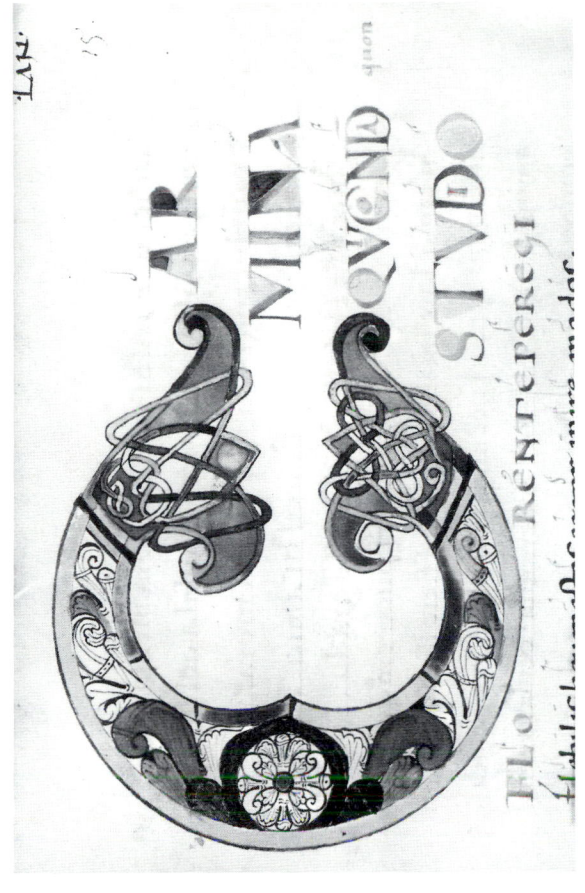

178. Paris, Bibliothèque Nationale, MS lat. 6401, fol. 15: initial.

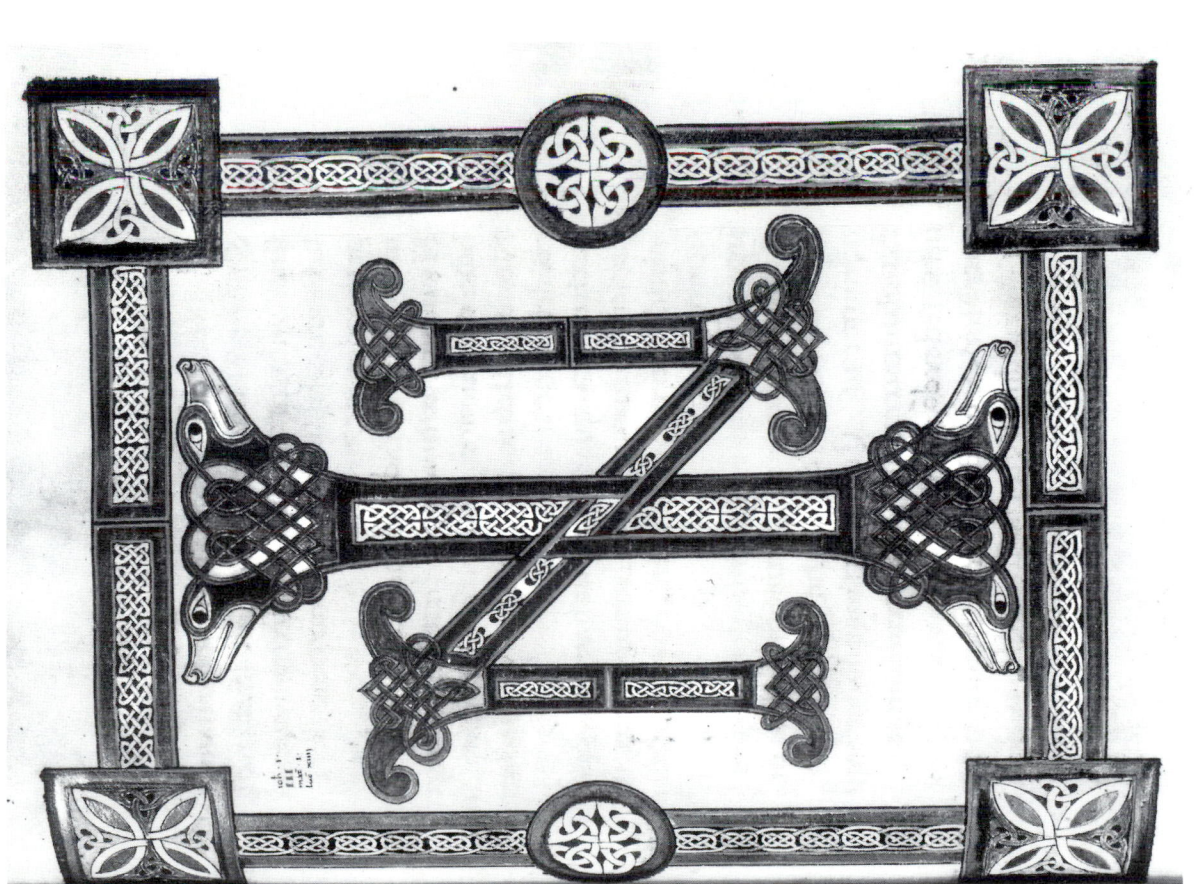

177. Paris, Bibliothèque Nationale, MS lat. 257, fol 149: initial page.

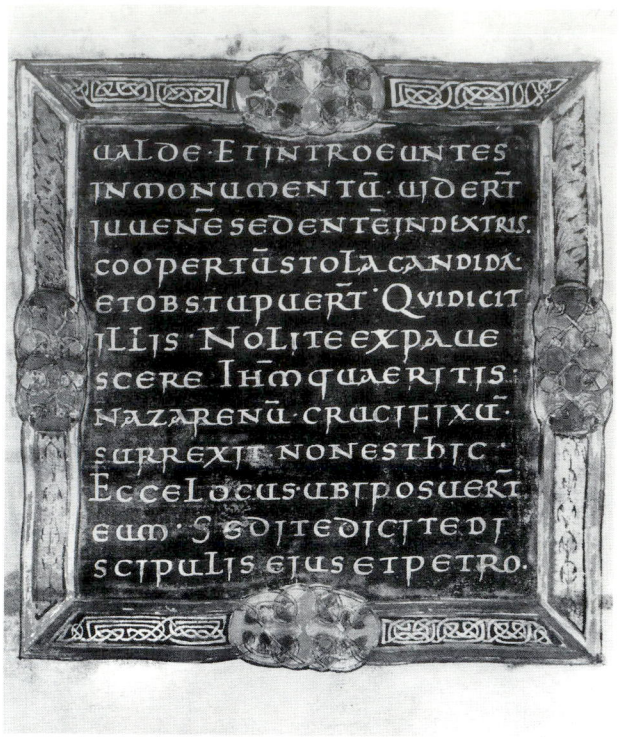

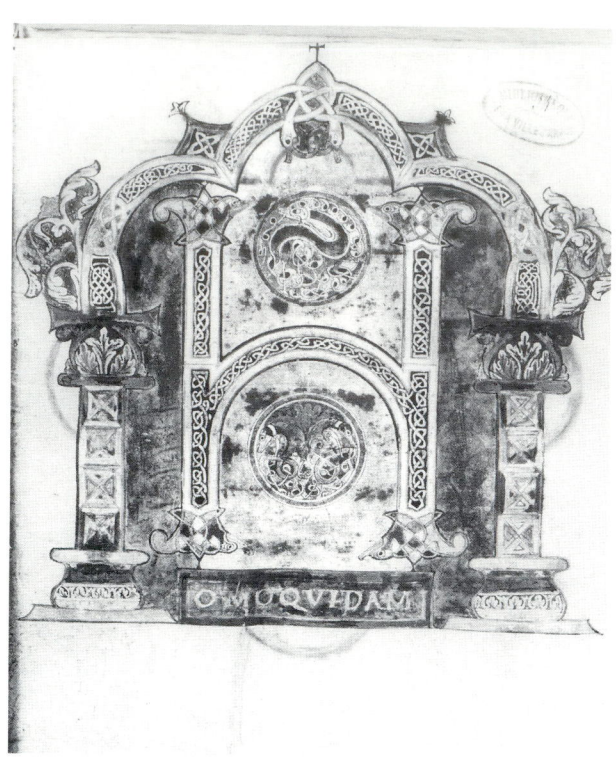

179. Arras, Bibliothèque Mun., MS 1045, fol. 44 (author).

180. Arras, Bibliothèque Mun., MS 1045, fol. 34: initial page (author).

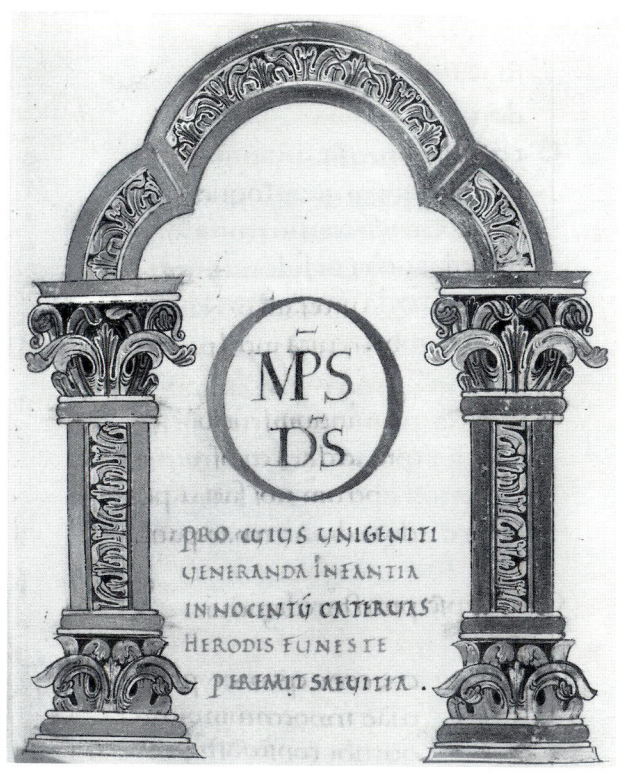

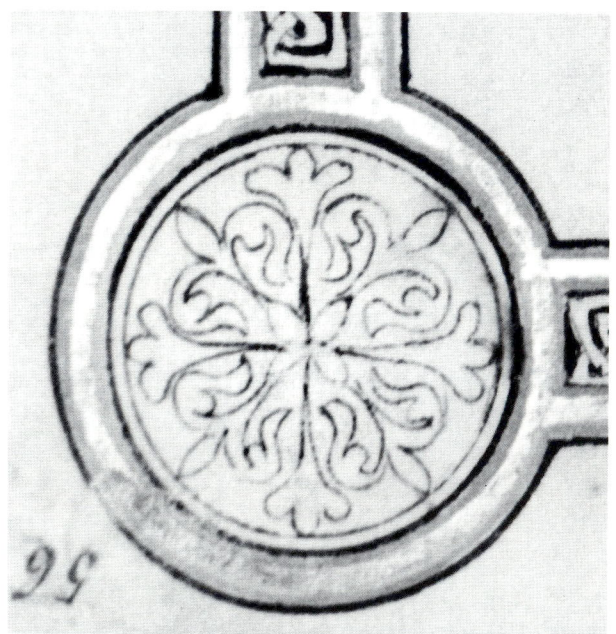

181. London, British Lib., MS Add. 49598, fol. 21: initial page (Warburg Institute).

182. Boulogne-sur-mer, Bibliothèque Mun., MS 12, fol. 56 (detail).

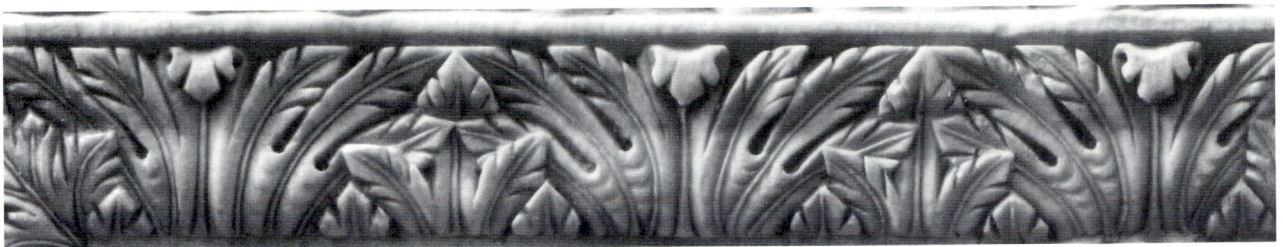

183. Berlin, Staatliche Museen Preussischer Kulturbesitz, ivory plaque (detail).

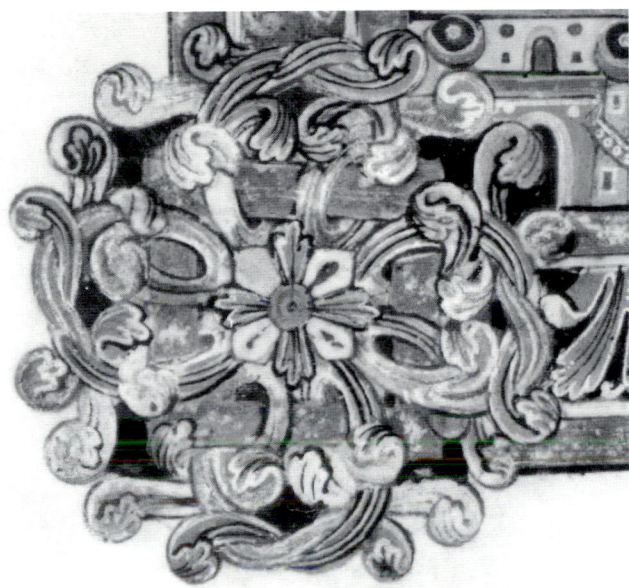

184. London, British Library, MS Add 49598, fol. 15v (detail).

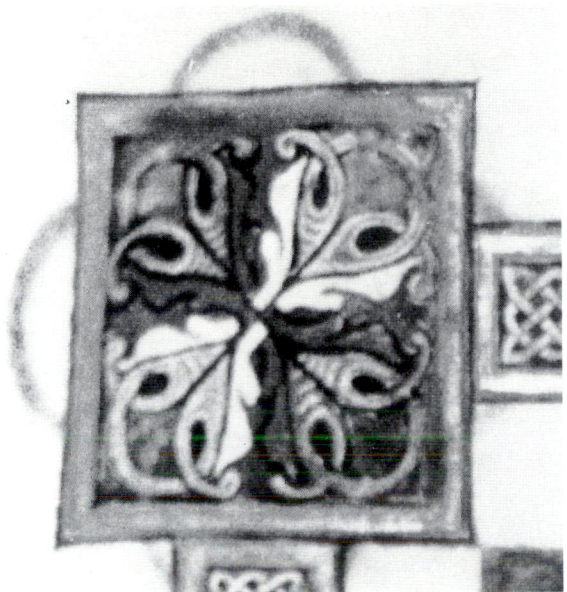

185. Reims, Bibliothèque Mun., MS 213, fol. 11 (detail) (author).

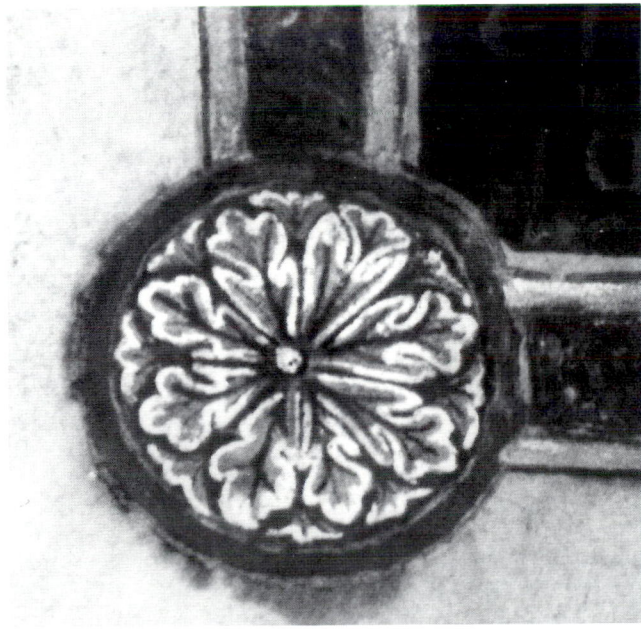

186. Arras, Bibliothèque Mun., MS 1045, fol. 37v (detail) (author).

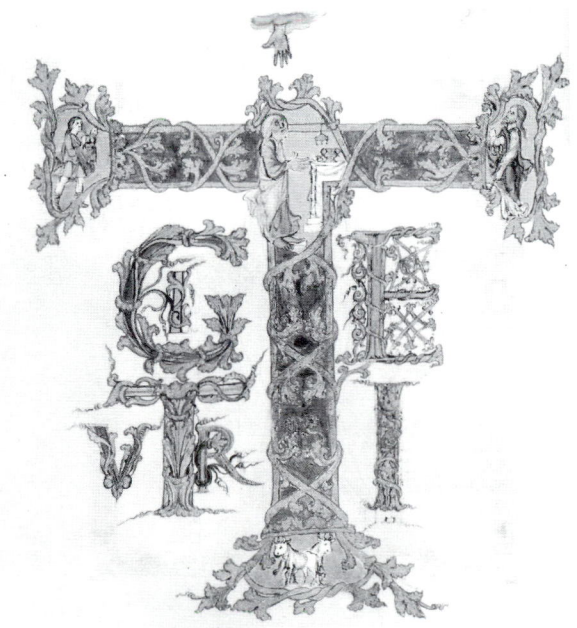

187. Paris, Bibliothèque Nationale, MS lat. 9428, fol. 15v: *Te Igitur* initial.

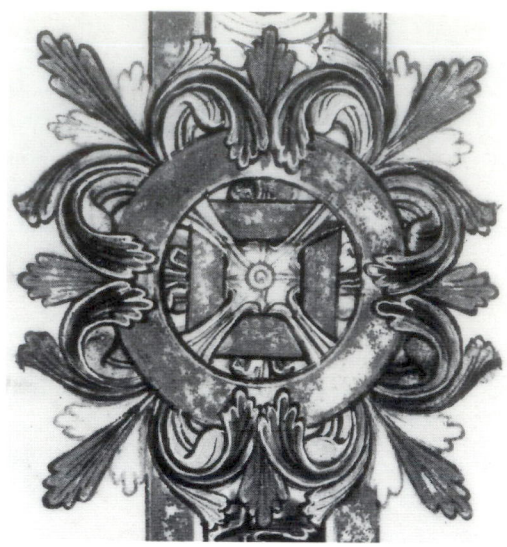

188. London, British Library, MS Add. 49598, fol. 52 (detail) (Warburg Institute).

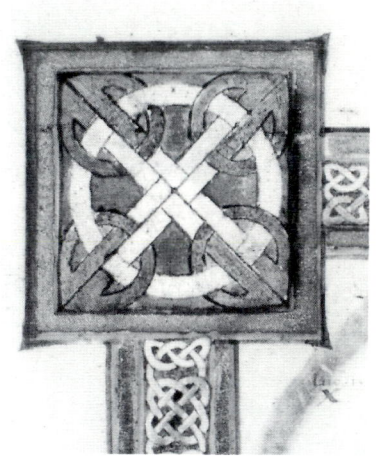

189. New York, Pierpont Morgan Library, MS 862, fol. 92v (detail).

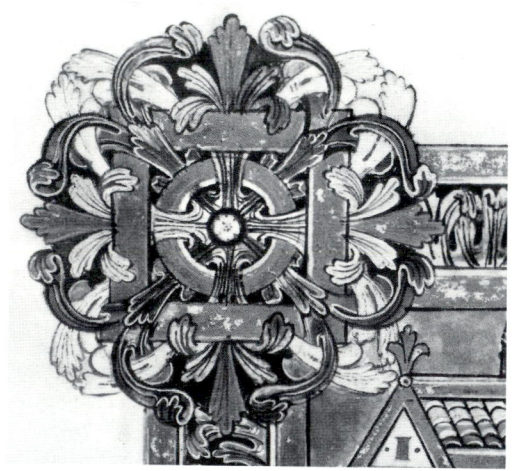

190. London, British Library, MS 49598, fol. 51v (detail).

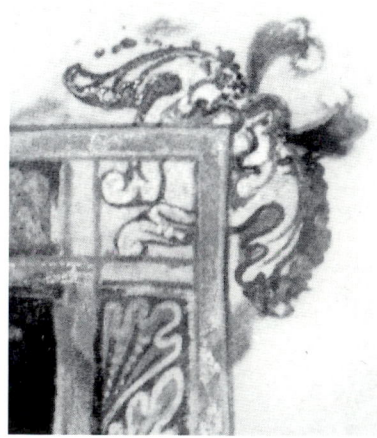

191. Arras, Bibliothèque Mun., MS 1045, fol. 35 (detail) (author).

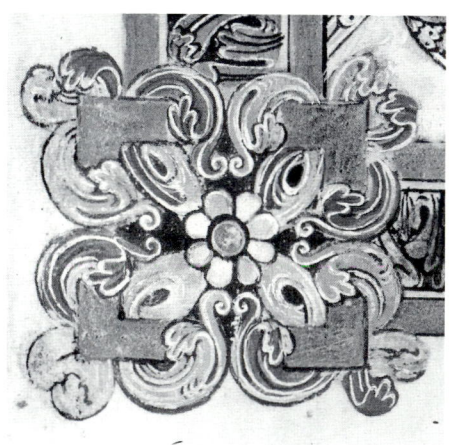

192. London, British Library, MS Add. 49598, fol. 19v (detail).

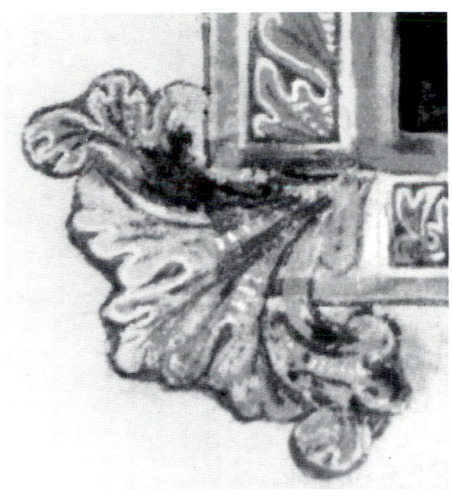

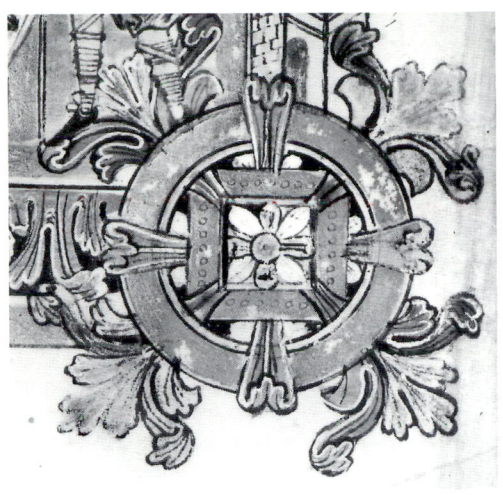

193. Arras, Bibliothèque Mun., MS 1045, fol. 34v (detail) (author).

194. London, British Library, MS Add. 49598, fol. 45v (detail).

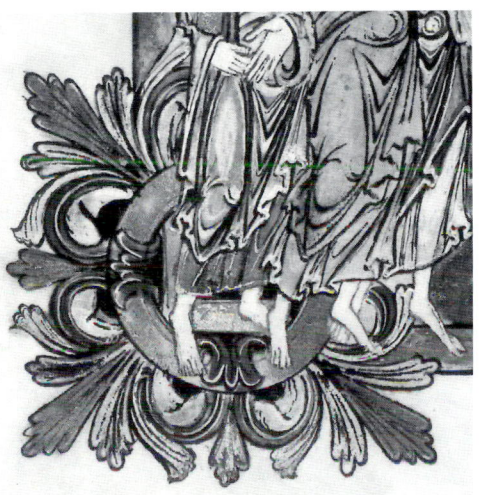

195. London, British Library, MS Add. 49598, fol. 64v (detail).

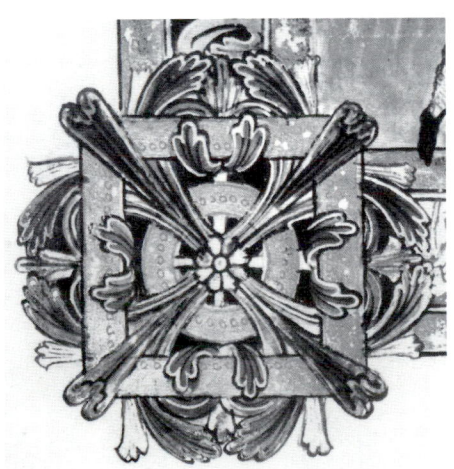

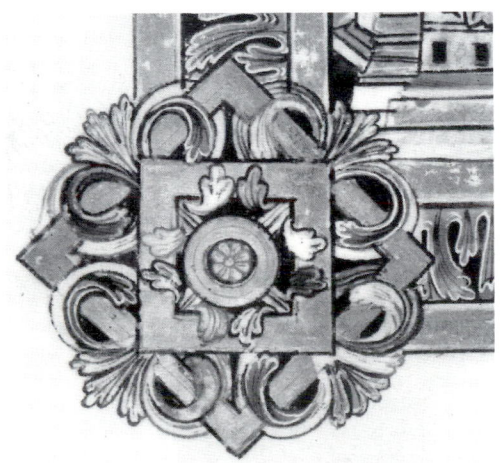

196. London, British Library, MS Add. 49598, fol. 95v (detail).

197. London, British Library, MS Add. 49598, fol. 99v (detail).

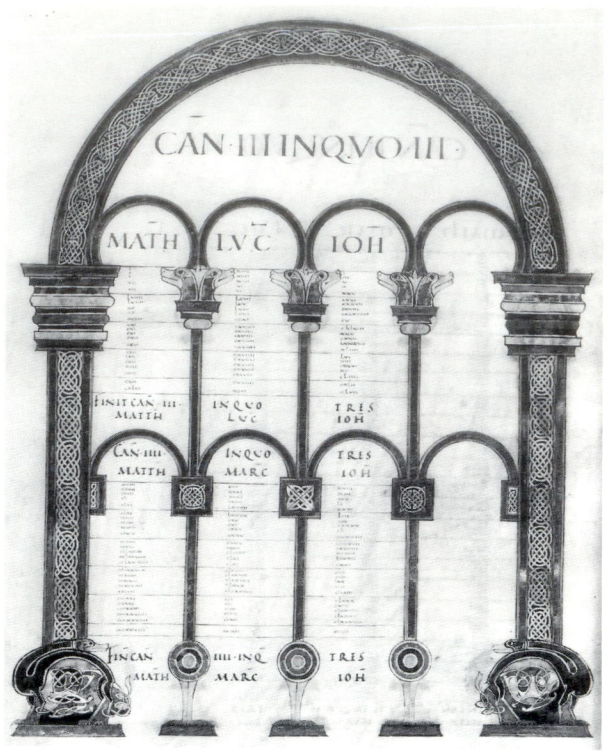

198. Paris, Bibliothèque Nationale, MS lat. 2, fol. 352: canon table.

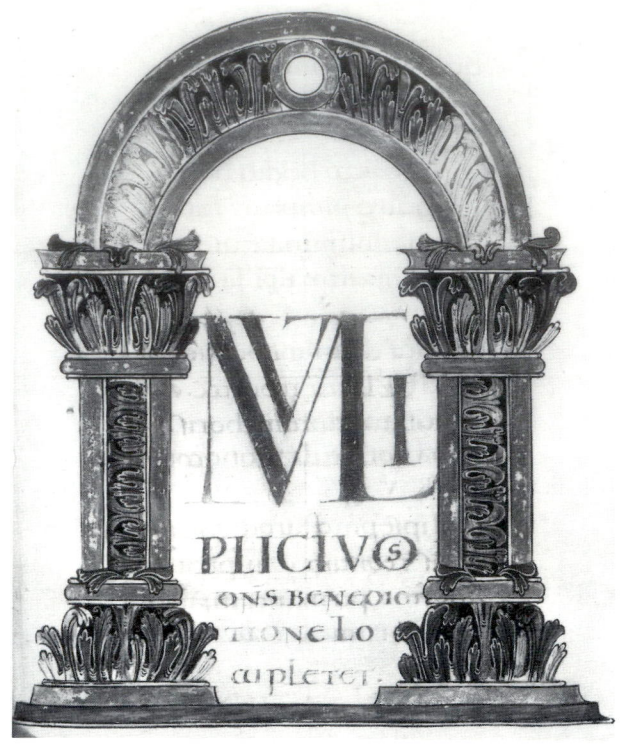

200. London, British Lib., MS Add. 49598, fol. 108: initial page, St. Michael (Warburg Institute).

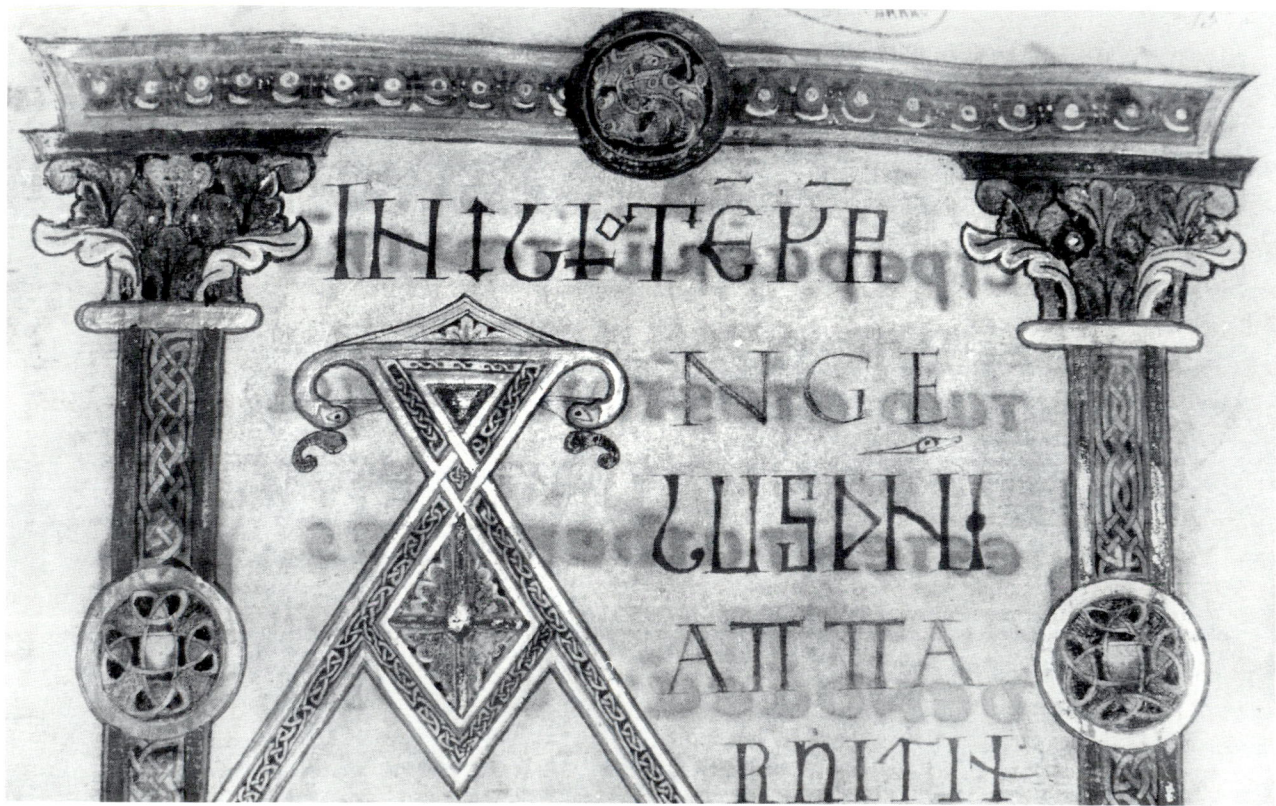

199. Arras, Bibliothèque Mun., MS lat. 1045, fol. 15 (detail) (author).

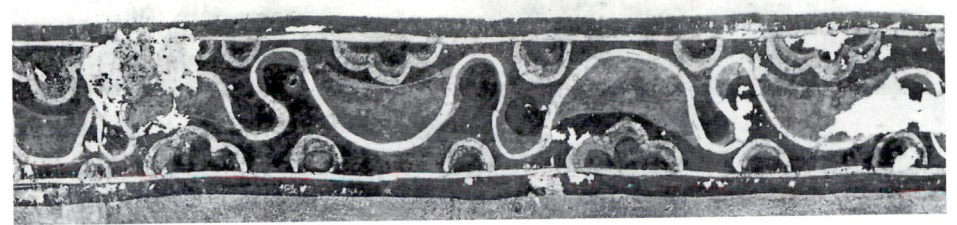

201. Vatican, Biblioteca Apostolica, MS gr. 1522, fol. 127v (detail).

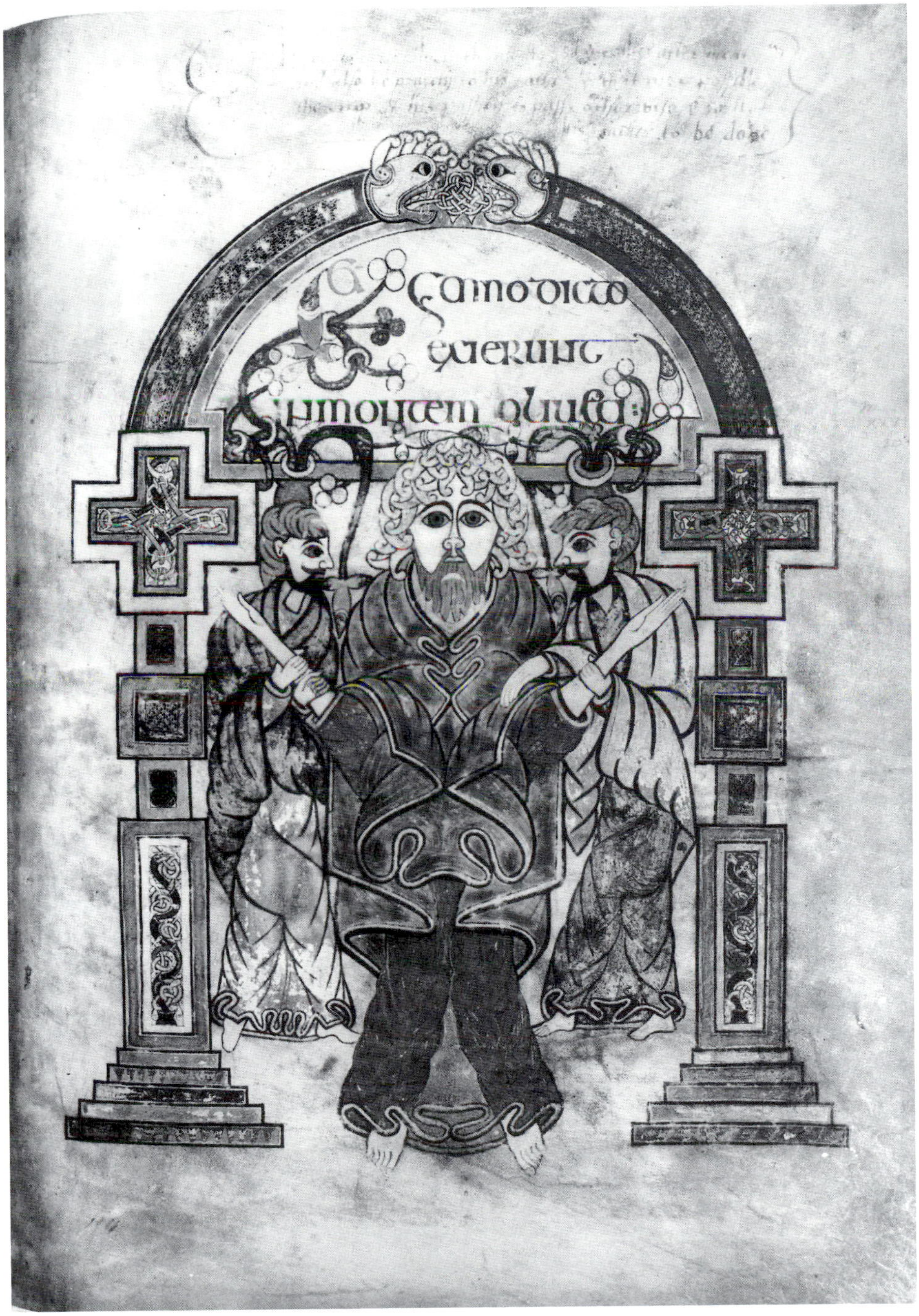

202. Dublin, Trinity College Library, MS 58, fol. 114: Arrest of Christ.

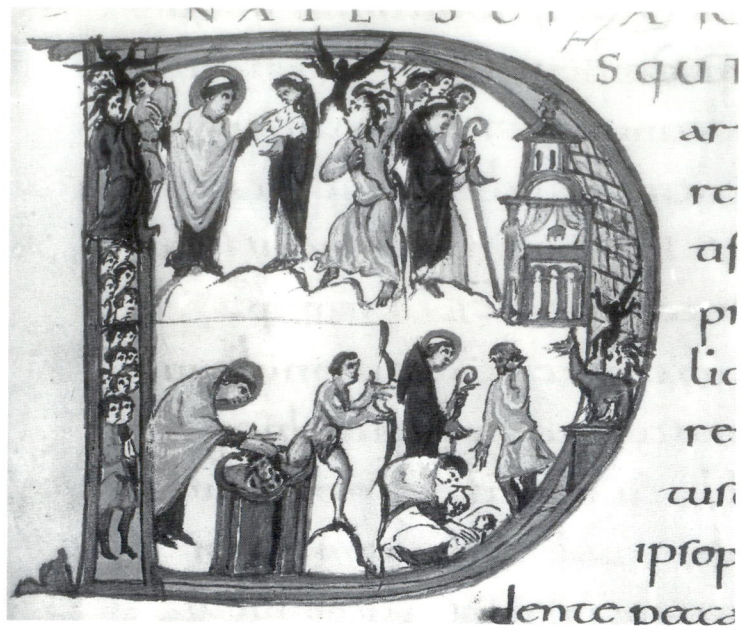

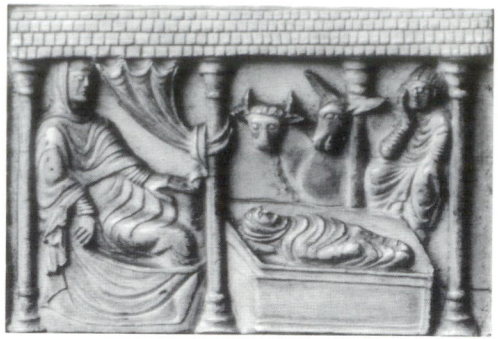

205. Paris, Louvre Museum, ivory casket: Nativity (ARS, New York/SPADEM, Paris).

203. Paris, Bibliothèque Nationale, MS lat. 9428, fol. 91: Life of St. Arnulf.

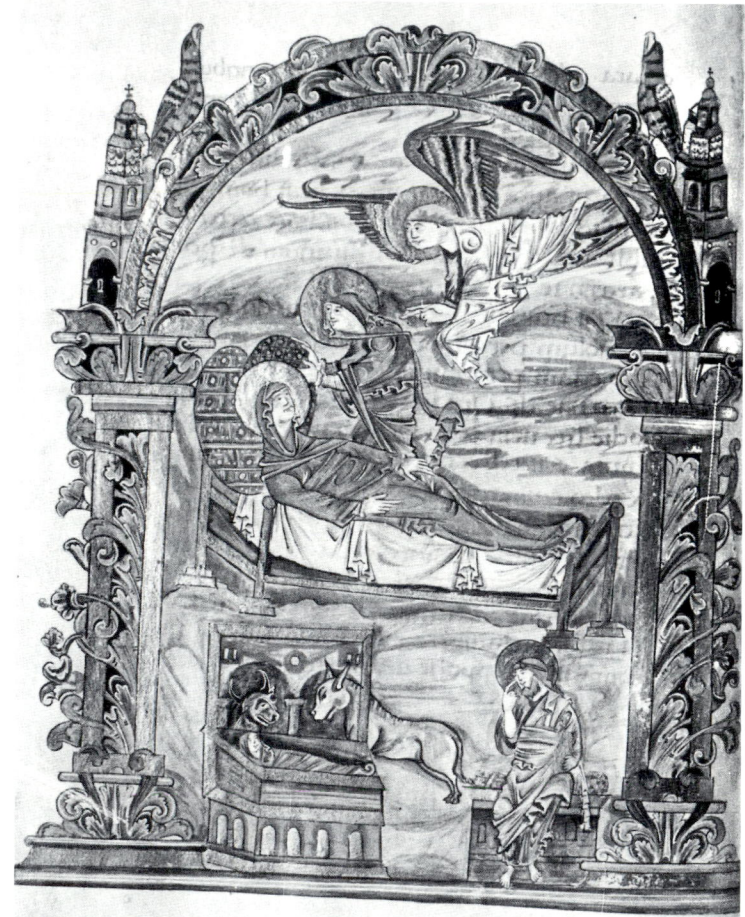

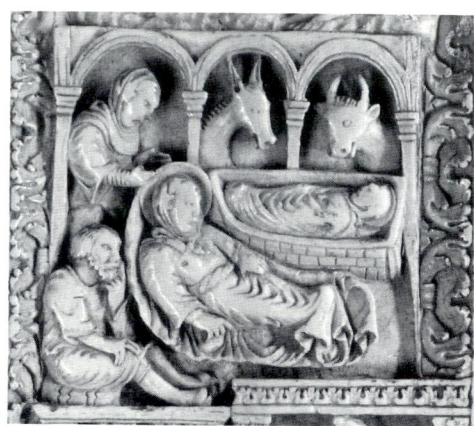

206. Munich, Staatsbibliothek, Clm. 10077, ivory cover (detail): Nativity.

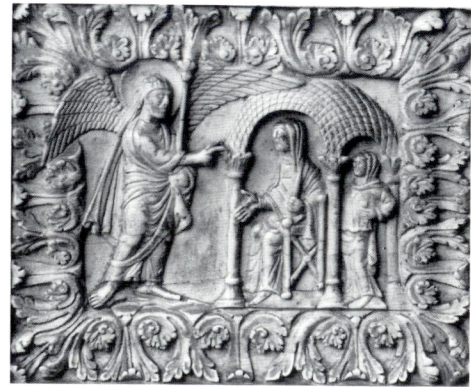

204. Rouen, Bibliothèque Mun., MS Y. 6 (274), fol. 32v: Nativity (C. R. Dodwell).

207. Paris, Louvre Museum, ivory casket: Annunciation (ARS, New York/SPADEM, Paris).

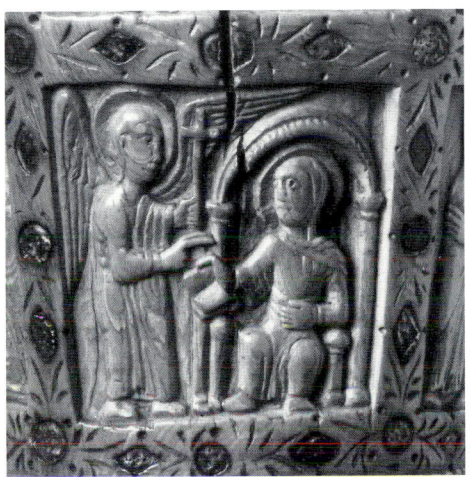

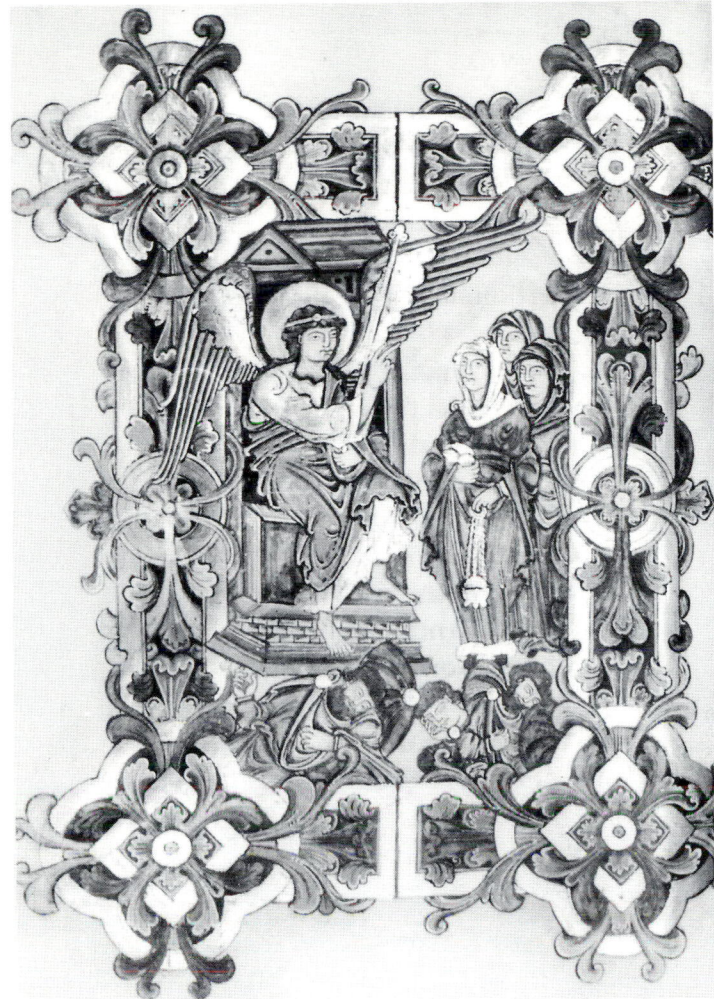

208. New York, Metropolitan Museum of Art, ivory situla, detail: Annunciation.

211. Rouen, Bibliothèque Mun., MS Y. 7 (369), fol. 21v: Women at the Tomb (Kathleen Openshaw).

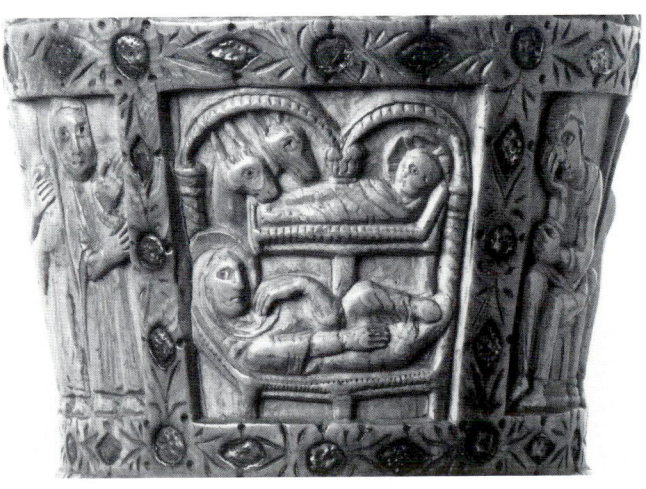

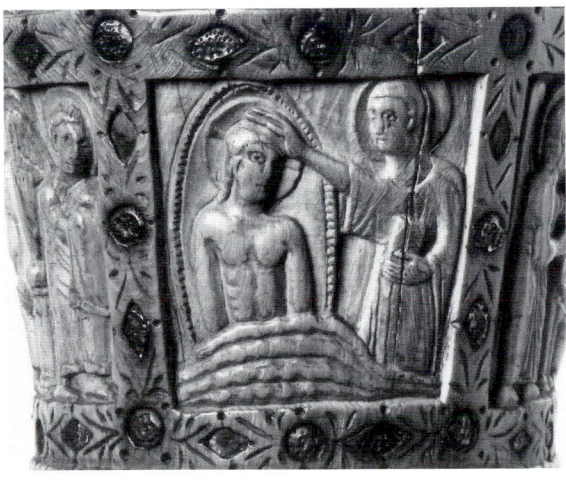

209. New York, Metropolitan Museum, ivory situla, detail: Nativity.

210. New York, Metropolitan Museum, ivory situla: Baptism.

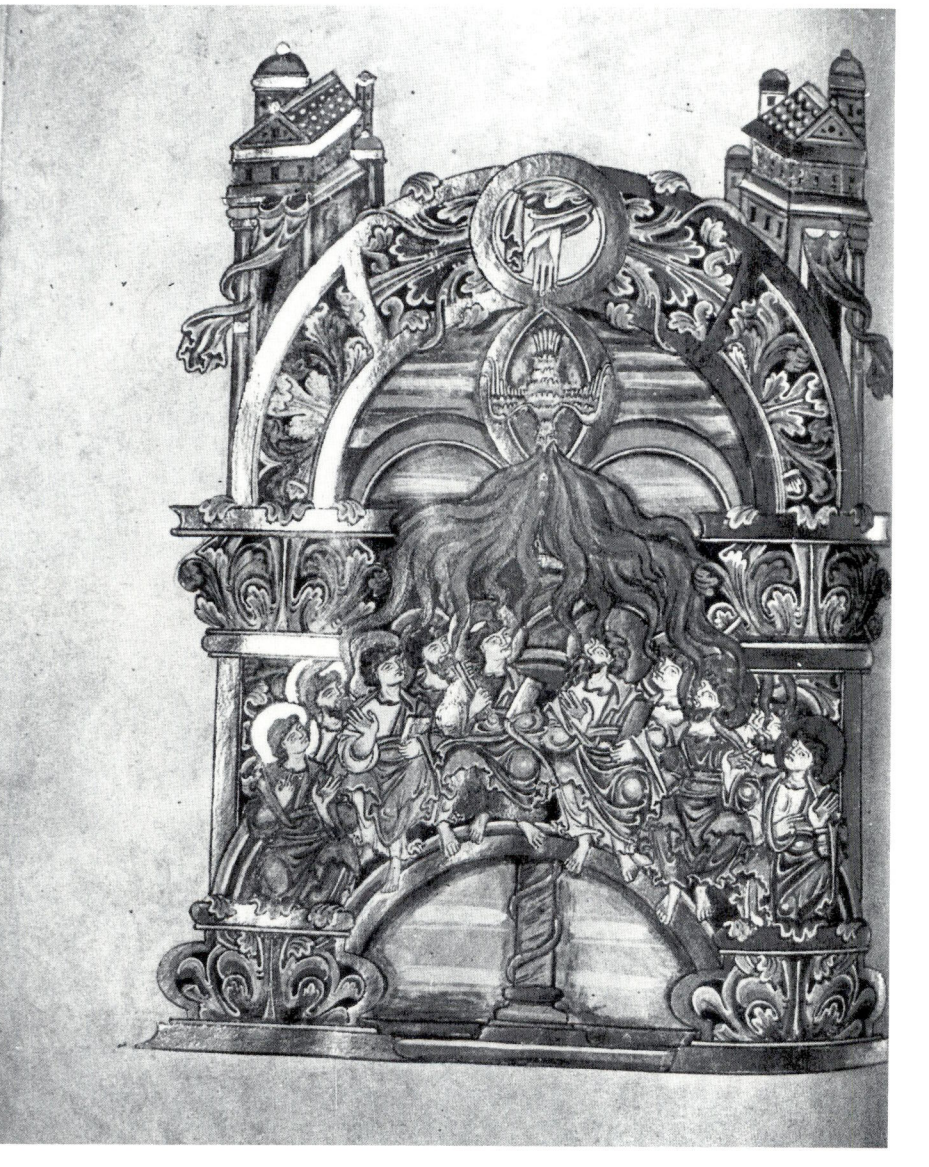

212. Rouen, Bibliothèque Mun., MS Y 7 (369), fol. 29v: Pentecost (C. R. Dodwell).

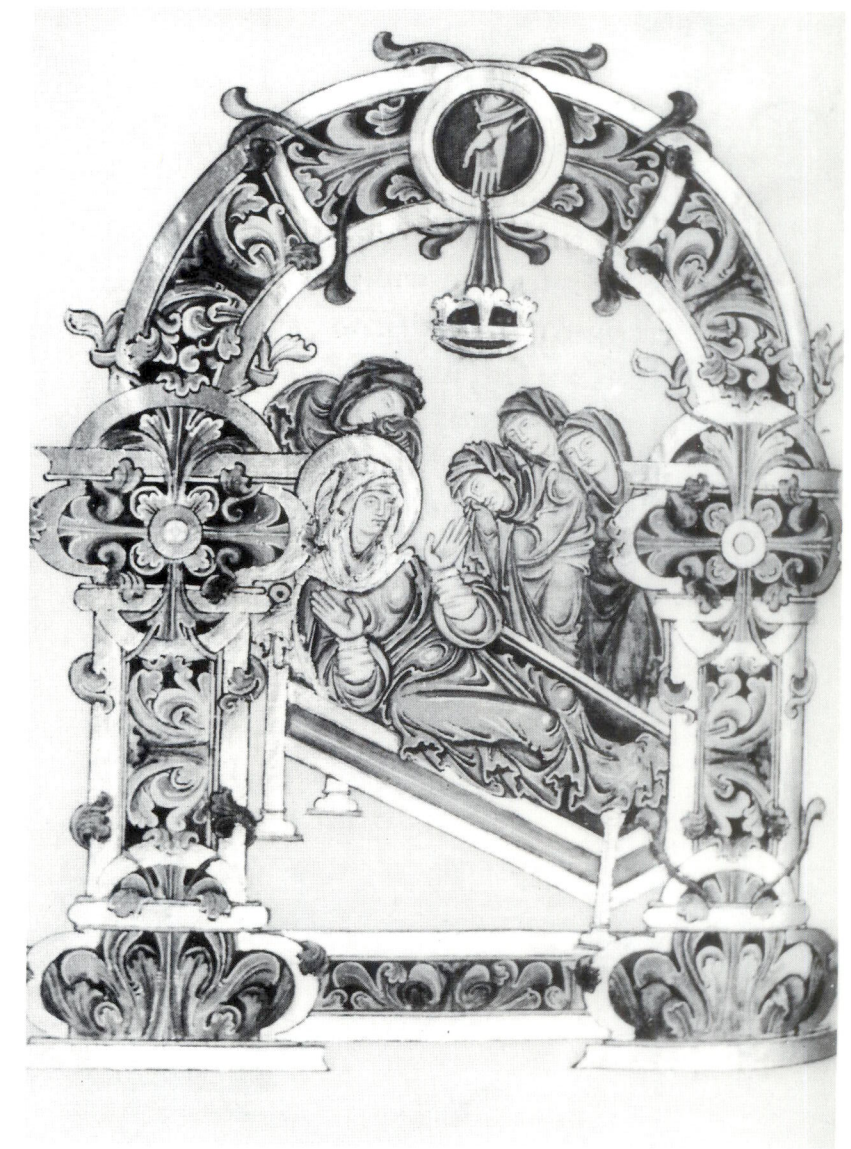

213. Rouen, Bibliothèque Mun., MS Y 7 (369), fol. 54v: Death and Cornoation of the Virgin (Kathleen Openshaw).